Readings in Philosophy of Religion

READINGS IN PHILOSOPHY OF RELIGION

ANCIENT TO CONTEMPORARY

Edited by

Linda Zagzebski

and

Timothy D. Miller

A John Wiley & Sons, Ltd., Publication

This edition first published 2009

Blackwell Publishing was acquired by John Wiley & Sons in February 2007. Blackwell's publishing program has been merged with Wiley's global Scientific, Technical, and Medical business to form Wiley-Blackwell.

Registered Office
John Wiley & Sons Ltd, The Atrium, Southern Gate, Chichester, West Sussex, PO19 8SQ, United Kingdom

Editorial Offices
350 Main Street, Malden, MA 02148-5020, USA
9600 Garsington Road, Oxford, OX4 2DQ, UK
The Atrium, Southern Gate, Chichester, West Sussex, PO19 8SQ, UK

For details of our global editorial offices, for customer services, and for information about how to apply for permission to reuse the copyright material in this book please see our website at www.wiley.com/wiley-blackwell.

Library of Congress Cataloging-in-Publication Data

Readings in philosophy of religion : ancient to contemporary / edited by Linda Zagzebski and Timothy D. Miller.
p. cm.
Includes bibliographical references.
ISBN 978-1-4051-8092-4 (hardcover : alk. paper) – ISBN 978-1-4051-8091-7 (pbk. : alk. paper)
1. Religion–Philosophy. I. Zagzebski, Linda Trinkaus, 1946– II. Miller, Timothy, 1944–
BL51.R3235 2009
210–dc22

2008032198

A catalogue record for this book is available from the British Library.

Set in 9.5/11.5pt Minion by Graphicraft Limited, Hong Kong

01 2009

Contents

Acknowledgments

The editors and publisher gratefully acknowledge the permission granted to reproduce the copyright material in this book:

Cicero, "Book 1" from *The Nature of the Gods*, trans. P. G. Walsh (Oxford: Oxford University Press, 1998), extracts from pp. 3–46 plus notes. © 1997, 1998 by P. G. Walsh. Reprinted by permission of Oxford University Press.

Cicero, "Book 2" from *The Nature of the Gods*, trans. P. G. Walsh (Oxford: Oxford University Press, 1998), pp. 81–2 plus notes. © 1997, 1998 by P. G. Walsh. Reprinted by permission of Oxford University Press.

Thomas Aquinas, *Summa Theologica*, trans. Fathers of the English Dominican Province (Benziger Bros, 1947).

William Paley, "Natural Theology", chs 1–3 from William Paley, *Natural Theology* (C. Knight, 1836).

David Hume, from *Dialogues Concerning Natural Religion*, ed. Norman Kemp Smith (Indianapolis, IN: Bobbs-Merrill, 1947), pp. 143–151, 165–169.

Robin Collins, "The Teleological Argument"; © 2008 by Robin Collins. Reprinted with permission from the author.

J. J. C. Smart, "The Argument from the Appearance of Design" from *Atheism and Theism*, second edition, ed. J. J. C. Smart and J. J. Haldane (Oxford: Blackwell Publishing, 1996, 2003), pp. 21–6. © 1996, 2003 by J. J. C. Smart and J. J. Haldane. Reprinted with permission from Blackwell Publishing.

Plato, "Laws X" and "Timaeus", trans. A. E. Taylor, *The Collected Dialogues of Plato: Including the Letters*, ed. Edith Hamilton and Huntington Cairns (Princeton, NJ: Princeton University Press, 1961), pp. 1448–51, 1161–3, 1167–8. © 1961 by Princeton University Press. Copyright renewed © 1989 by Princeton University Press. Reprinted with permission from Princeton University Press.

Aristotle, Book VIII from "Physics" from *The Oxford Aristotle*, ed. D. W. Ross (Oxford: The Clarendon Press, 1941). © 1941 by The Clarendon Press. Reprinted by permission of Oxford University Press.

Al-Ghazāli, "The Jerusalem Tract" trans. A. L. Tibawi, *The Islamic Quarterly* 9 (1965): 98–9. © 1965 by A. L. Tibawi. Reprinted with permission from *The Islamic Quarterly*.

Moses Maimonides, From Part II, Chapter 1: "On the Existence and Oneness of God" in *Classics of Philosophy*, vol. 1: *Ancient and Medieval*, ed. Louis P. Pojman (Oxford and New York: Oxford University Press, 1998), pp. 438–9. © 1998. Reprinted by permission of Oxford University Press.

Thomas Aquinas, *Summa Theologica*, trans. Fathers of the English Dominican Province (Benziger Bros, 1947).

Samuel Clarke, *A Demonstration of the Being and Attributes of God and Other Writings*, ed. Ezio Vailati (Cambridge: Cambridge University Press, 1998), pp. 8, 10–12. © 1998 by Cambridge University Press. Reprinted with permission from Cambridge University Press.

David Hume, Part IX from *Dialogues Concerning Natural Religion*, ed. Norman Kemp Smith (Indianapolis, IN: Bobbs-Merrill, 1947), pp. 188–92.

St Anselm, Chapters II, III, IV, XV from *Proslogium, Monologium; An Appendix in Behalf of the Fool By Gaunilon; and Cur Deus Homo*, trans. Sidney Norton Deane (La Salle, IL: Open Court, 1951), pp. 7–10, 22. © 1951 by Open Court Publishing. Reprinted with permission from Open Court Publishing Company, a division of Carus Publishing Company, Peru, IL.

René Descartes, "Meditation V, Objections I, Reply to Objections I" from *The Philosophical Works of Descartes*, trans. Elizabeth S. Haldane and G. R. T. Ross, vol. 1 (Cambridge: Cambridge University Press, 1968), pp. 180–3, vol. 2 (Cambridge: Cambridge University Press, 1967), pp. 6–8, 18–22. © 1967, 1968 by Cambridge University Press. Reprinted with permission from Cambridge University Press.

Immanuel Kant, Chapter III, Sections 4 and 6 from *Critique of Pure Reason*, trans. Norman Kemp Smith (New York: St Martin's, 1965), pp. 500–7, 518–24. Translation © The estate of Norman Kemp Smith 1929, 1933, 2003. Reprinted with permission of Palgrave Macmillan.

Alvin Plantinga, "The Ontological Argument" from *God, Freedom and Evil* (Grand Rapids, MI: William B. Eerdmans, 1977), pp. 85–112. © 1974 by Wm. B. Eerdmans Publishing Company, Grand Rapids, Michigan. Reprinted by permission of the publisher; all rights reserved.

Rudolf Otto, Chapter II: "Numen and the Numinous" and Chapter III: "The Elements in the Numinous" from *The Idea of the Holy*, trans. John W. Harvey (Oxford: Oxford University Press, 2nd edn., 1950), pp. 5–11. © 1968. Reprinted by permission of Oxford University Press.

William J. Wainwright, "Mysticism and Religious Experience" from *Philosophy of Religion*, 2nd edn. (Belmont, CA: Wadsworth, 1999), pp. 121–40. © 1999 by Wadsworth, a part of Cengage Learning, Inc. Reproduced by permission. www.cengage.com/permissions

Sandra Menssen and Thomas D. Sullivan, "The Existence of God and the Existence of Homer: Rethinking Theism and Revelatory Claims". *Faith and Philosophy* 19:3 (2002): 331–47. © 2002 by The Society of Christian Philosophers. Reprinted with permission from *Faith and Philosophy*.

Søren Kierkegaard, "Truth Is Subjectivity" from *Kierkegaard's Concluding Unscientific Postscript*, trans. David F. Swenson and Walter Lowrie (Princeton, NJ: Princeton University Press, 1944), pp. 178–83. © 1941 by Princeton University Press, 1969 renewed. Reprinted with permission from Princeton University Press.

Robert M. Adams, "Kierkegaard's Arguments against Objective Reasoning in Religion". *The Monist* 60:2 (1977): 228–43. © 1977, THE MONIST: An International Quarterly Journal of General Philosophical Inquiry. Peru, Illinois, U.S.A. 61354. Reprinted by permission.

Ludwig Wittgenstein, "Lectures on Religious Belief" from *Lectures and Conversations on Aesthetics, Psychology and Religious Belief*, ed. Cyril Barrett (Berkeley, CA: University of California Press, 1972), pp. 53–64. © 1972 by Blackwell Publishing. Reprinted with permission from Blackwell Publishing.

David Hume, "The Natural History of Religion" from *Essays, Moral, Political, and Literary*, ed. T. H. Green and T. H. Grose, vol. 2 (London: Longmans, 1912), pp. 313–19, 328–32.

Ludwig Feuerbach, "Introduction" from *The Fiery Brook*, trans. Zawar Hanfi (Garden City, NY: Anchor Books, 1972).

Sigmund Freud, Chapters V and VI from *The Future of an Illusion*, ed. and trans. James Strachey (New York: W.W. Norton & Co., 1961), pp. 33–4, 36–7, 38–42. © 1961 by James Strachey, renewed 1989 by Alix Strachey. Used by permission of W. W. Norton & Company, Inc and The Random House Group Ltd.

Melissus of Samos, *Ancilla to the Pre-Socratic Philosophers*, trans. Kathleen Freeman (Cambridge, MA: Harvard University Press, 1966), pp. 48–50. © 1966 by Blackwell Publishing. Reprinted with permission from Blackwell Publishing.

Aristotle, Book XII, Chapter 6 from "Metaphysics" from *The Oxford Aristotle*, ed. D. W. Ross (Oxford: The Clarendon Press, 1941). © 1941 by The Clarendon Press. Reprinted by permission of Oxford University Press.

Pseudo-Dionysius the Areopagite, excerpts from *Pseudo-Dionysius: The Complete Works*, trans. Colm Luibheid (New York/Mahwah, NJ: Paulist Press, Inc., 1987). © 1987 by Colm Luibheid. Reprinted by permission of Paulist Press, Inc. www.paulistpress.com

St Anselm, Chapters V, VI, VII, VIII, XII, XIII, XVIII from *Proslogium, Monologium; An Appendix in Behalf of the Fool By Gaunilon; and Cur Deus Homo*, trans. Sidney Norton Deane (La Salle, IL: Open Court, 1951), pp. 10–14, 19–20, 23–5. © 1951 by Open Court Publishing. Reprinted with permission from Open Court Publishing Company, a division of Carus Publishing Company, Peru, IL.

Richard of St Victor, selections from Book Three of *On the Trinity*, translated by Allan B. Wolter. From *Medieval Philosophy: From St. Augustine to Nicholas of Cusa*, edited by John F. Wippel and Allan B. Wolter (New York: The Free Press, 1969), pp. 223–5. Copyright © 1969 by The Free Press. Reprinted with the permission of The Free Press, A Division of Simon & Schuster, Inc. All rights reserved.

P. T. Geach, "Omnipotence". *Philosophy* 48:183 (1973): 7–20. © 1973 by Cambridge University Press. Reprinted with permission from Cambridge University Press.

Norman Kretzmann, "Omniscience and Immutability". *The Journal of Philosophy* 63:14 (1966): 409–21. © 1966. Reprinted with permission from *The Journal of Philosophy*.

William L. Craig, "The Impossibility of Atemporal Personhood" from *Time and Eternity* (Wheaton, IL: Crossway Books, 2001), pp. 77–86. © 2001 by William Lane Craig. Used by permission of Crossway Books, a publishing ministry of Good News Publishers, Wheaton, IL 60187, USA, www.crossway.com

Aristotle, Chapter 9 from *Aristotle's Categories and De Interpretatione*, trans. J. L. Ackrill (Oxford: Clarendon Press, 1963), pp. 50–3. © 1963 by Oxford University Press. Reprinted by permission of Oxford University Press.

Cicero, from *Treatises of M. T. Cicero*, ed. and trans. C. D. Yonge (London and New York: Bell, 1892), pp. 271–2, 207–8.

Boethius, Book V: III, Book V: VI, from *The Consolation of Philosophy*, trans. Victor Watts, revised edition (London: Penguin, 1999), pp. 119–22, 132–7. © 1969, 1999 by V. E. Watts. Reproduced by permission of Penguin Books Ltd.

Marilyn Adams, "Analysis of The Treatise". Introduction to *William of Ockham, Predestination, God's Foreknowledge, and Future Contingents* 2e, trans. Marilyn McCord Adams and Norman Kretzmann (Indianapolis, IN: Hackett, 1983), pp. 2–12, 16–20. © 1983 by Marilyn McCord Adams and Norman Kretzmann. Reprinted with permission from Hackett Publishing Company, Inc. All rights reserved.

William Hasker, "The Classical Theory" from *God, Time, and Knowledge* (Ithaca, NY: Cornell University Press, 1989), pp. 20–5. © 1989 by Cornell University. Used by permission of the publisher, Cornell University Press.

Plato, "Laws IV" trans. A. E. Taylor, *The Collected Dialogues of Plato: Including the Letters*, ed. Edith Hamilton and Huntington Cairns (Princeton, NJ: Princeton University Press, 1961), pp. 1307–8. © 1961 by Princeton University Press. Copyright renewed © 1989 by Princeton University Press. Reprinted with permission from Princeton University Press.

Immanuel Kant, *Critique of Practical Reason*, trans. and ed. Mary Gregor (Cambridge: Cambridge University Press, 1997), pp. 104–9. © 1997 by Cambridge University Press. Reprinted with permission from Cambridge University Press.

Plato, "Euthyphro" trans. Lane Cooper from *The Collected Dialogues of Plato: Including the Letters*, ed. Edith Hamilton and Huntington Cairns (Princeton, NJ: Princeton University Press, 1961), pp. 174–9. © 1961 by Princeton University Press. Copyright renewed © 1989 by Princeton University Press. Reprinted with permission from Princeton University Press.

Pierre d'Ailly, *Questions on the Books of the Sentences* in *Divine Command Morality: Historical and Contemporary Readings*, ed. Janine Marie Idziak (New York: The Edward Mellen Press, 1979), trans. from reprint of original (Frankfurt: Minerva, 1968), pp. 58–63. © 1979 by The Edward Mellen Press. Reprinted with permission from The Edward Mellen Press.

Martin Luther, "Lectures on Romans" from *Luther's Works*, vol. 25, ed. Karl H. Hertz. © 1972 by Concordia Publishing House. Used with permission.

Robert Merrihew Adams, "Divine Commands" from *Finite and Infinite Goods: A Framework for Ethics* (New York: Oxford University Press, 1999), pp. 249–62. © 1999 by Robert Merrihew Adams. Reprinted by permission of Oxford University Press.

Linda Zagzebski, "The Virtues of God and the Foundations of Ethics". *Faith and Philosophy* 15:4 (1998): 538–53. © 1998 by The Society of Christian Philosophers. Reprinted with permission from *Faith and Philosophy*.

Thomas Aquinas, *Treatise on Law* from *Summa Theologica*, trans. Fathers of the English Dominican Province (Benziger Bros, 1947), pp. 12–22.

Plato, "Republic II" from *The Collected Dialogues of Plato: Including the Letters*, ed. Edith Hamilton and Huntington Cairns (Princeton, NJ: Princeton University Press, 1961), pp. 625–7. © 1961 by Princeton University Press. Copyright renewed © 1989 by Princeton University Press. Reprinted with permission from Princeton University Press.

Lactantius, *On the Anger of God* from *Works of Lactantius*, vol. 2, ed. Alexander Roberts and James Donaldson. Ante-Nicene Christian Library 22 (Edinburgh: T. & T. Clark, 1871), pp. 26–8.

Augustine, Book VII: Chapters 11, 12, 16 from *The Confessions of St Augustine*, trans. Rex Warner (New York: New American Library, 1963), extracts from pp. 150–1, 153. © 1963 by Rex Warner, renewed © 1991 by F. C. Warner. Used by permission of Dutton Signet, a division of Penguin Group (USA) Inc.

Augustine, Books II and III from *Augustine: Earlier Writings*, LCC vol. VI, ed. John H. S. Burleigh (John Knox Press, 1953; SCM Press, 1958), pp. 396–9. © 1953. Used by permission of SCM-Canterbury Press and Westminster John Knox Press.

G. W. Leibniz, "Essays on the Justice of God and Freedom of Man in the Origin of Evil" and "Summary of the Controversy Reduced to Formal Arguments" from *Theodicy: Essays on the Goodness of God, the Freedom of Man and the Origin of Evil*, ed. Austin Farrer (La Salle, IL: Open Court, 1985), pp. 377–88, 369–73. © 1985. Reprinted with permission from Taylor & Francis Books UK.

J. L. Mackie, "Evil and Omnipotence". *Mind* 64 (1955): 200–12. © 2006 by the Mind Association. Reprinted with permission from Oxford University Press.

Alvin Plantinga, "The Free Will Defense" from *God, Freedom, and Evil* (Grand Rapids, MI: William B. Eerdmans, 1977), pp. 12–49. © 1974 by Wm. B. Eerdmans Publishing Company, Grand Rapids, Michigan. Reprinted by permission of the publisher; all rights reserved.

John Hick, "Soul-Making Theodicy" in *Encountering Evil: Live Opinions in Theodicy*, ed. Stephen T. Davis (Atlanta, GA: Westminster, John Knox, 1981), pp. 39–52. Used by permission of Westminster John Knox Press.

William L. Rowe, "Friendly Atheism, Skeptical Theism, and the Problem of Evil". *International Journal for Philosophy of Religion* 59 (2006): 79–92. © 2006 by Springer. Reprinted with permission from the author and Springer Science and Business Media.

Marilyn Adams, "Horrendous Evils and the Goodness of God", *Proceedings of the Aristotelian Society*, supp. vol. 63 (1989): 297–310. © 1989 by The Aristotelian Society. Reprinted by courtesy of the Editor of the Aristotelian Society. (Revised version in Marilyn McCord Adams and Robert Merrihew Adams (eds.) *The Problem of Evil*. Oxford: Oxford University Press, 1990, pp. 209–21.)

Epicurus, "Letter to Menoeceus" trans. Robert Drew Hicks. http://classics.mit.edu/Epicurus/menoec.html

Thomas Nagel, "Death" from *Mortal Questions* (Cambridge: Cambridge University Press, 1979), pp. 1–10. © 1979 by Cambridge University Press. Reprinted with permission from the author and publisher.

Plato, "Phaedo" trans. Hugh Tredennick from *The Collected Dialogues of Plato: Including the Letters*, ed. Edith Hamilton and Huntington Cairns (Princeton, NJ: Princeton University Press, 1961), pp. 49–50. © 1961 by Princeton University Press. Copyright renewed © 1989 by Princeton University Press. Reprinted with permission from Princeton University Press.

Averroes (Ibn Rushd), "The Future Life" from *Averroes on the Harmony of Religion and Philosophy*, trans. George F. Hourani (London: Luzac, 1961), pp. 76–8. © 1961. Reprinted by permission of the E. J. W. Gibb Memorial Trust.

René Descartes, "The Possibility of Immortality" from *The Philosophical Works of Descartes*, trans. Elizabeth S. Haldane and G. R. T. Ross, vol. 1 (Cambridge: Cambridge University Press, 1968), p. 190; vol. 2 (Cambridge: Cambridge University Press, 1967), pp. 29, 47. © 1967, 1968 by Cambridge University Press. Reprinted with permission from Cambridge University Press.

John Locke, *An Essay Concerning Human Understanding*, ed. Alexander Campbell Fraser, vol. 1 (New York: Dover, 1959), pp. 445–6, 448–52, 454–64. © 1959 by Dover Publications. Reprinted with permission from Dover Publications.

Bertrand Russell, "Do We Survive Death?" from *Why I am Not a Christian*, ed. Paul Edwards (Simon & Schuster, 1957), pp. 88–93. © 1957, 1995 by George Allen & Unwin Ltd. Reprinted with the permission of Simon & Schuster Adult Publishing Group, Taylor & Francis Books UK, and The Bertrand Russell Peace Foundation.

Paul Badham, "Religious and Near-death Experience in Relation to Belief in a Future Life". *Mortality* 2:1 (1997): 7–21. © 1997 by Routledge. Reprinted by permission of the author and publisher (Taylor & Francis Ltd, http://www.tandf.co.uk/journals).

John Hick, "Religious Pluralism and Salvation". *Faith and Philosophy* 5:4 (1988): 365–77. © 1988 by The Society of Christian Philosophers. Reprinted with permission from *Faith and Philosophy*.

The Dalai Lama, excerpts from "The 1981 Interview" from *The Bodhgaya Interviews: His Holiness the Dalai Lama*, edited by José I. Cabezón (Ithaca, NY: Snow Lion Publications, 1988), extracts from pp. 11–14, 21–4. © 1988 by José Cabezón. Used with the permission of Snow Lion Publications, www.snowlionpub.com

Karl Rahner, "Christianity and the Non-Christian Religions" in *Christianity and Other Religions*, ed. John Hick and Brian Hebblethwaite (London: Fortress Press, 1981), extracts from pp. 52–79. © 1980 by John Hick and Brian Hebblethwaite. Reprinted with permission from Oneworld Publications.

Linda Zagzebski, "Self-trust and the Diversity of Religions" in *Philosophic Exchange*, 36 (2005–6): 63–76. © 2006 by the Center for Philosophic Exchange, State University of New York, College at Brockpoint, New York.

St Justin Martyr, Chapters 2–8, "How Justin Found Philosophy" from *Selections from the Fathers of the Church*, vol. 3; *St Justin Martyr Dialogue with Trypho*, trans. Thomas B. Falls, rev. Thomas P. Halton, ed. Michael Slusser (Washington, DC: The Catholic University of America Press, 2003), extracts from pp. 5–15. © 2003 by The Catholic University of American Press, Washington, DC, USA. Used with permission.

Tertullian, *The Prescriptions against the Heretics* in S. L. Greenslade (ed.), *Early Latin Theology*, Library of Christian Classics vol. V (London: SCM Press, 1956), extracts from pp. 34–5. © 1956. Original text adapted by permission of SCM-Canterbury Press and Westminster John Knox Press.

Clement, "In What Respect Philosophy Contributes to the Comprehension of Divine Truth" from Ante-Nicene Christian Library: *Translations of the Writings of the Fathers*, ed. Rev. Alexander Roberts and James Donaldson, vol. 4, *Clement of Alexandria*, vol. 1 (Edinburgh: T. and T. Clark, 1867), chapter XX, pp. 418–20.

Averroes (Ibn Rushd), *The Decisive Treatise, Determining the Nature of the Connection between Religion and Philosophy* from *Averroes on the Harmony of Religion and Philosophy*, trans. of Ibn Rushd's *Kitab fasl al-maqal*, with its app. (Damima) and an extract from *Kitab al-kashf 'an manahiju al-adilla*, by George F. Hourani (London: Luzac & Co., 1961), extracts from pp. 44–5, 50–3. © 1961. Reprinted by permission of the E. J. W. Gibb Memorial Trust.

St Thomas Aquinas, Chapters 4–7 from *On the Truth of the Catholic Faith: Summa Contra Gentiles*, Book One: *God*, trans., with intro. and notes, by Anton C. Pegis (Garden City, NY: Image Books, 1955), pp. 66–75. © 1955 by Doubleday, a division of Random House, Inc. Used by permission of Doubleday, a division of Random House, Inc.

John Calvin, *Institutes of the Christian Religion*, Library of Christian Classics vol. XX, I.iii. 1–3, trans. Ford Lewis Battles, ed. John T. McNeill (London: SCM Press, 1961), pp. 43–5. © 1960 by W. L. Jenkins. Reprinted with permission from SCM-Canterbury Press and Westminster John Knox Press. This reading taken from Paul Helm (ed.), *Faith and Reason*. Oxford and New York: Oxford University Press, 1999, pp. 142–5.

John Locke, "Faith, Reason, and Enthusiasm" from *An Essay Concerning Human Understanding*, ed. Alexander Campbell Fraser, vol. 2 (New York: Dover, 1959), pp. 383–4, 412–41. © 1959 by Dover Publications. Reprinted with permission from Dover Publications.

Kelly James Clark, "Return to Reason: The Irrationality of Evidentialism" from *Return to Reason: A Critique of Enlightenment Evidentialism and a Defense of Reason and Belief in God* (Grand Rapids, MI: William B. Eerdmans Pub. Co., 1990), pp. 125–58. © 1990 by Wm. B. Eerdmans Publishing Company, Grand Rapids, Michigan. Reprinted by permission of the publisher; all rights reserved.

Blaise Pascal, *Pascal's Pensées*, trans. and intro. by Martin Turnell (New York: Harper & Brothers, 1962), extracts from pp. 200–5, 206–7. © 1962. Reprinted by permission of HarperCollins Publishers.

Thomas V. Morris, "Pascalian Wagering" from *Anselmian Explorations: Essays in Philosophical Theology* (Notre Dame, IN: University of Notre Dame Press, 1987), pp. 194–202, 210–12. © 1987 by University of Notre Dame Press. Reprinted with permission from University of Notre Dame Press.

W. K. Clifford, "The Ethics of Belief" from *Lectures and Essays*, ed. Leslie Stephen and Sir Frederick Pollock, vol. 2 (London: Macmillan and Co., 1901), pp. 163–76.

William James, "The Will to Believe" in *Philosophy in the Twentieth Century: An Anthology*, vol. 1, ed. and with intros by William Barrett and Henry D. Aiken (New York: Random House, 1962), extracts from pp. 241–7, 250–8. Originally published in *Essays in Pragmatism*, William James, edited by Alburey Castell, pp. 88–109. Hafner Publishing Company, Inc., New York, 1948.

St Thomas Aquinas, *Of God and His Creatures*, trans. of the *Summa Contra Gentiles of Saint Thomas Aquinas* by Joseph Rickaby (London: Burns and Oates, 1905), chs 100–2.

John Locke, "A Discourse of Miracles" from *The Reasonableness of Christianity*, ed. I. T. Ramsey (Stanford, CA: Stanford University Press, 1958), pp. 79–87.

David Hume, "Of Miracles" from *Essays: Moral, Political, and Literary*, ed. T. H. Green and T. H. Grose, vol. 2 (London: Longmans, Green, and Co., 1912), pp. 88–108.

George I. Mavrodes, "David Hume and the Probability of Miracles" in *International Journal for Philosophy of Religion*, 43(3) (1998): 167–82. © 2004 by Springer. Reprinted with permission from Springer Science and Business Media.

Galileo Galilei, "Galileo's Letter to Castelli" from Richard J. Blackwell, *Galileo, Bellarmine, and the Bible* (Notre Dame, IN: University of Notre Dame Press, 1991), pp. 195–201. © 1991 by University of Notre Dame Press. Reprinted with permission from University of Notre Dame Press.

William A. Dembski, "Signs of Intelligence: A Primer on the Discernment of Intelligent Design" from *Signs of Intelligence: Understanding Intelligent Design*, eds. William A. Dembski and James M. Kushiner (Grand Rapids, MI: Brazos Press, 2001), pp. 171–92. © 2001 by The Fellowship of St. James. Reprinted with permission of Brazos Press, a division of Baker Publishing Group.

Daniel C. Dennett, "Atheism and Evolution" from *The Cambridge Companion to Atheism*, ed. Michael Martin (Cambridge: Cambridge University Press, 2007), ch. 8, pp. 135–48. © 2007 by Cambridge University Press. Reprinted with permission from the editor and publisher.

John F. Haught, "Darwin, Design, and Divine Providence" from *Debating Design: From Darwin to DNA*, ed. William A. Dembski and Michael Ruse (New York: Cambridge University Press, 2004), pp. 229–45. © 2004 by Cambridge University Press. Reprinted with permission from the author and Cambridge University Press.

Alvin Plantinga, "How Naturalism Implies Skepticism" from *Analytic Philosophy without Naturalism*, ed. Antonella Corradini, Sergio Galvan, and E. Jonathan Lowe (London: Routledge, 2006), ch. 2, pp. 29–44. © 2006 by Alvin Plantinga. Reprinted with permission from the author.

Timothy O'Connor, "A House Divided Against Itself Cannot Stand: Plantinga on the Self-defeat of Evolutionary Naturalism" from *Naturalism Defeated? Essays on Plantinga's Evolutionary Argument against Naturalism*, ed. James Beilby (Ithaca, NY: Cornell University Press, 2002), pp. 129–34. © 2002 by Cornell University. Used by permission of the publisher, Cornell University Press.

William A. Dembski, chart from *Mere Creation*, ed. William A. Dembski (Downers Grove, IL: InterVarsity Press, 1998), p. 99. © 1998 by Christian Leadership Ministries. Used with permission of InterVarsity Press, PO Box 1400, Downers Grove, IL 60515. ivpress.com

Every effort has been made to trace copyright holders and to obtain their permission for the use of copyright material. The publisher apologizes for any errors or omissions in the above list and would be grateful if notified of any corrections that should be incorporated in future reprints or editions of this book.

General Introduction

Philosophy of religion is a vibrant field with a long history. Most of the major issues were treated by the ancient Greeks, and continued uninterrupted until some time in the nineteenth century, followed by a period of religious skepticism and consequent neglect of philosophical problems arising from the theory and practice of religion. During the last third of the twentieth century there was an important revival of the field in English-speaking countries. Much of this work adopted a new style to address the basic issues in religious philosophy, and it can be tempting to emphasize this period because it is our own. In this collection we have included enough contemporary selections to give students a sense of the kind of work that is currently getting attention, but we think that readers acquire a better appreciation for the range of the field and the enduring importance of its questions if they study works from its entire twenty-five hundred year history. Consequently, about two-thirds of the selections we have chosen were written prior to the contemporary revival of philosophy of religion.

The collection follows the convention of arranging the readings around topics, but the readings on each topic are presented chronologically, encouraging readers to imagine continuing a conversation with important figures in our collective past on questions we still care about. Most sections begin with readings from antiquity, and selections from subsequent periods are chosen from philosophy that derives from the ancient Greeks, so we have included work by medieval Islamic philosophers who kept the works of Plato and Aristotle alive for centuries while they were lost in the Latin West. When the works of ancient Greek philosophers were reintroduced into the West through Moorish Spain in the twelfth century, the Latin philosophers were influenced by the writings of the Muslims, and so medieval Islamic philosophy is an important part of a continuous philosophical conversation that began with the Greeks. We think it will become apparent why ancient Greek philosophy enjoys primacy in Western philosophy. Most of the questions we ask, the methods we use to answer them, and even some of the answers began with the Greeks. Western philosophy of religion also began with the Greeks. Contemporary philosophers of religion are part of that dialogue, whether or not they are also part of a faith tradition.

There are ninety-three readings in the anthology, divided into eleven major sections: (I) the philosophical treatment of religion; (II) the classical arguments for the existence of God, including the teleological, cosmological, and ontological arguments; (III) other approaches to religious belief, including experience and revelation, fideism, and naturalistic reinterpretations of religion; (IV) the nature of God; (V) fate, freedom, and foreknowledge; (VI) religion and morality, (VII) the problem of evil; (VIII) death and immortality; (IX) the diversity of religions;

(X) faith, reason, and the ethics of belief; and (XI) science, religion, and naturalism. Each section has an introduction and each entry begins with a brief abstract.

Since the works in this collection are philosophical rather than theological, they do not generally presuppose any religious beliefs on the part of the reader. They are aimed at an audience of intelligent, reflective persons who care about these issues, and who believe that their own understanding of these problems can be clarified, critically examined, and deepened by studying the work of some of the best philosophers of the past and present. The book can be used alone or as a companion to an introductory text. It is well suited to accompany Zagzebski's *Philosophy of Religion: An Historical Introduction* (Wiley-Blackwell, 2007).

I

THE PHILOSOPHICAL TREATMENT OF RELIGION

Introduction

Philosophy of religion is part of philosophy, not religion, and it would not exist were it not for the fact that philosophy is distinct from religion and has assumed the role of critic of all major human practices, including the practice of religion. These conditions never existed in the East, where philosophies and religions are not separated as they are in the Western world. Philosophy and religion are divided in Western culture because of the Greeks. Unlike the great Asian religions, the Greek religion did not attempt to answer ultimate questions about the nature of the universe. Its function was primarily that of giving people traditions and rituals that enabled them to propitiate the gods and to have continuity with their past and future. Whatever was ultimately responsible for the existence of the world and its ultimate fate, it was not the gods, and Greek religion was silent on the ultimate issues. It was the philosophers who explored such questions as these: Where did the universe come from and how is it put together? Is there any other world besides the world of our experience? What is the relation between human beings and nature? What happens to us after we die? Can we control our fate? What is the origin of good and evil?

It is customary to say that the method used by the Greek philosophers was reason, but that cannot be quite right because everybody reasons, whether or not they are philosophers. What was different about the Greek philosophers was that they used reason in a disciplined and focused manner, eschewing convention when necessary, and treating reason as subservient to no authority but its own. Actually, that is probably not entirely true either, but it is close enough. So our first point about the history of the development of philosophy of religion is that philosophy of religion only makes sense if philosophy and religion are distinct, and they are distinct in Western culture because of the Greeks. Philosophy of religion is part of philosophy. It is not part of religion, not even the intellectual component of the practice of a religion.

The next question is how philosophy of religion became distinguished from other branches of philosophy, the way it is today. For much of the history of Western philosophy, philosophy of religion was just philosophy; it was not a subfield. All of the major philosophers until the nineteenth century discussed some of the topics in this anthology, and some discussed all of them. If asked what they were doing, they would not say they were doing philosophy of religion. For example, Plato did not take himself to be writing philosophy of religion in the *Phaedo* where we get the first extended set of arguments in Western philosophy for life after death. Aristotle did not think he was doing philosophy of religion in his argument for an Unmoved Mover or in his argument that the universe did not have a beginning. Medieval philosophers did not distinguish philosophy of religion from other parts of philosophy either. The distinction they thought important was something else – the difference between revealed theology and what they called natural theology, which was philosophy. So they were not concerned with distinguishing philosophy of religion from other parts of philosophy, but rather to distinguish philosophy from theology, which presupposes revelation.

So when was philosophy of religion invented? Probably not until after the Enlightenment, when skepticism about the truth of religious beliefs became prevalent among philosophers who no longer gave theistic answers to questions in metaphysics or ethics. It was commonly thought that David Hume and Immanuel Kant had demolished the traditional arguments for the existence of God in the eighteenth century, and by the nineteenth century many philosophical theists abandoned the rationalist approach to religion and attempted pragmatic or anti-rationalist defenses of religion instead. The work of philosophers who continued to ask questions that pertained to theism and to explore theistic responses to ordinary philosophical questions was put into a sub-field called philosophy of religion.

If this historical hypothesis is accurate, many of the philosophers included in this anthology would not recognize the title of the book as applying to their own work. Nonetheless, they would all recognize the questions and most of the methods used to answer them. To illustrate the philosophical method of addressing these issues, we are beginning the book with a selection from Cicero's *The Nature of the Gods*. This book is rarely anthologized, but it is a gem. Cicero's dialogue raises a number of issues that will be discussed in the readings in this anthology, and it illustrates the dialectical clash so prized by philosophers. The dialogue covers a range of views on the nature of the gods and whether and how they relate to human beings, particularly the issue of whether there is a providential god (Stoic view), or whether the gods ignore human affairs (Epicurean view). It includes arguments for the existence of the gods (*consensus gentium* and teleological arguments), fatalism, and the connection between religion and morality, and it mentions the modern argument that diversity of religions tends to lead to skepticism. The excerpt we have included here therefore illustrates both the antiquity of the range of questions included in this anthology and some of the methodological constraints practiced in Western philosophy.

1

The Nature of the Gods, Book 1

Cicero

Marcus Tullius Cicero (106–43 BC) was an important Roman philosopher, statesman, and orator. In the *The Nature of the Gods* Cicero narrates a dialogue between an Academic Skeptic named Gaius Cotta, an Epicurean named Gaius Vellius, and a Stoic named Quintus Lucilius Balbus. In addition to its wit and entertaining style, the dialogue provides insight into the theological views of many of the prominent philosophers and philosophical schools in the ancient world. It also illustrates the fact that most of the philosophical questions examined in this anthology have a long history with roots in the ancient world.

1 There are many issues in philosophy which to this day have by no means been adequately resolved. But there is one enquiry, Brutus,[1] which is particularly difficult and obscure, as you are well aware. This concerns the nature of the gods, the noblest of studies for the human mind to grasp, and one vital for the regulation of religious observance. On this question, the pronouncements of highly learned men are so varied and so much at odds with each other that inevitably they strongly suggest that the explanation is human ignorance, and that the Academics have been wise to withhold assent on matters of such uncertainty; for what can be more degrading than rash judgement, and what can be so rash and unworthy of the serious and sustained attention of a philosopher, as either to hold a false opinion or to defend without hesitation propositions inadequately examined and grasped?

Take our subject as an example. Most philosophers have stated that gods exist, the most likely 2
view to which almost all of us are led by nature's guidance. But Protagoras[2] expressed his doubts about it, and Diagoras of Melos and Theodorus[3] of Cyrene believed that gods do not exist at all. As for those who have claimed that they do exist, their views are so varied and at loggerheads with each other that to list their opinions would be an

Cicero, "Book 1" from *The Nature of the Gods*, trans. P. G. Walsh (Oxford: Oxford University Press, 1998), extracts from pp. 3–46 plus notes.

endless task. Many views are presented about the forms that gods take, where they are to be found and reside, and their manner of life; and there is total disagreement and conflict among philosophers concerning them. There is particularly wide disagreement on the most important element in the case: are the gods inactive and idle, absenting themselves totally from the supervision and government of the universe, or is the opposite true, that they created and established all things from the beginning, and that they continue to control the world and keep it in motion eternally? Unless a judgement is made between these views, we must inevitably labour under grievous misapprehension,
3 in ignorance of the supreme issues. For there are and have been philosophers[4] who maintain that the gods exercise absolutely no supervision over human affairs. If their opinion is true, how can we show devotion to the gods, or have a sense of the holy or of religious obligation? All such chaste and scrupulous acknowledgement of the divine power is pointless unless the gods take notice of it, and unless the immortal gods make some acknowledgement to the human race. But if the gods have neither the power nor the desire to help us, if they have no interest whatever and they pay no attention to our activities, if there is nothing which can percolate from them to affect our human lives, what reason have we for addressing any acts of worship or honours or prayers to the immortal gods? If such activities are a mere façade of feigned pretence, they can contain no true devotion, nor indeed any other virtue, and without devotion to the gods all sense of the holy and of religious obligation is also lost. Once these disappear, our lives become fraught with dis-
4 turbance and great chaos. It is conceivable that, if reverence for the gods is removed, trust and the social bond between men and the uniquely pre-eminent virtue of justice will disappear.

But there are other philosophers of high and notable stature who hold that the entire universe is ordered and governed by the intelligence and reason of the gods. They go further, and claim that the gods take counsel and forethought for our lives as men. They believe that harvests and all that the earth bears, the atmospheric changes, the alternation of the seasons, the variations in weather, by which all the produce of the earth ripens and matures, are bestowed by the gods on the human race. They adduce many features (and these will be mentioned in the present work) such as seem to have been fashioned, so to speak, by the immortal gods for human use. In opposition to these thinkers, Carneades[5] mounted so many arguments against them as to stimulate even the lowest intelligence with a desire to probe the
truth. Indeed, there is no topic on which not 5
merely the unlearned but even educated people disagree so much, and since their beliefs range so widely and are so much at odds with each other, two possibilities exist: it may be that none of them is true, or at any rate no more than one of them can be.

In my discussion of this question, I can both appease my well-disposed critics and refute malicious backbiters,[6] forcing the second group to regret their censure, and the first to have the pleasure of being instructed; for those who offer friendly admonition need to be enlightened, while those who make hostile attacks need to be refuted.

[. . .]

My request instead is that all should attend, inves- 14
tigate, and pass judgement on the views we are to hold on religion, divine observance, holiness, and religious ceremonial; on good faith and oath-taking; on temples and shrines and solemn sacrifices, as well as on the very auspices over which I myself preside.[7] For each and every one of these things relates to the issue of the immortal gods, and certainly the widespread disagreement on this important matter amongst highly learned men must occasion doubts in the minds of those who believe that they have attained a measure of certainty concerning it.

My thoughts have often turned to this con- 15
troversy, but never more so than when we held a most rigorous and careful discussion[8] on the immortal gods at the home of my friend Gaius Cotta. At his request and invitation we gathered there during the Latin festival. When I arrived, I found him sitting in an alcove arguing with the senator Gaius Velleius, whom Epicureans regarded as their leading light among Romans at that time. Also present was Quintus Lucilius Balbus, whose studies among the Stoics were so advanced that he bore comparison with the outstanding Greeks of the school.

When Cotta caught sight of me, he said: 'Your arrival is timely, for I am just getting involved in an argument with Velleius on an important topic. In view of your interests, you will not be reluctant to join us.'

[. . .]

17 We were discussing the nature of the gods, a question which as always I find extremely opaque; so I was sounding out Velleius on the views of Epicurus. 'So, Velleius, if it is not too much trouble, recapitulate your initial remarks.'

'I'll do that', he replied. 'Mind you, his arrival is a reinforcement for you rather than for me, since both of you' (this he added with a grin) 'have been taught by the same teacher Philo to know nothing.'[9]

18 Then I interposed. 'That teaching I leave to Cotta to explain; please don't think that I'm here as his second; I shall listen impartially and without prejudice. No compulsion binds me to defend any particular view willy-nilly.'

Then Velleius, with the breezy confidence[10] customary with Epicureans, and fearing nothing so much as to give the impression of doubt about anything, spoke as if he had just come down from attending the gods' assembly up in the Epicurean *intermundia*.[11]

'What you are going to hear are no airy-fairy, fanciful opinions, like the craftsman-god in Plato's *Timaeus*[12] who constructs the world, or the prophetic old lady whom the Stoics call Pronoia, and whom in Latin we can term Providentia. I am not going to speak of the universe itself as a round, blazing, revolving deity endowed with mind and feelings. These are the prodigies and wonders of philosophers who prefer dreaming to reasoning.
19 I ask you, what sort of mental vision enabled your teacher Plato to envisage the construction of so massive a work, the assembling and building of the universe by the god in the way which he describes? What was his technique of building? What were his tools and levers and scaffolding?[13] Who were his helpers in so vast an enterprise? How could the elements of air and fire, water and earth knuckle under and obey the will of the architect? How did those solids of five shapes[14] from which all other things were fashioned originate, and conveniently station themselves to strike the mind and to produce sensations?[15] It would be a tedious business to recount all the particulars which appear as castles in the air
rather than as genuine discoveries; what takes 20
the palm is that though he represented the world as not merely born but virtually manufactured, he claimed that it would be eternal.

[. . .]

'The question I put to both of you is this: why 21
did these world-builders suddenly emerge after lying asleep for countless generations? For the non-existence of the universe does not necessarily imply absence of periods of time; by "periods of time" I do not mean those fixed by the yearly courses of the stars numbered in days and nights, for I grant that such eras would not have come into being without the circular movement of the universe. What I do mean is eternity, so to say, from the boundless past; one cannot measure it by any definite period of time, but one can understand what it must have been in extent,[16] for one cannot even envisage that there may have been a time when no time existed.

'So what I am asking, Balbus, is this: why did 22
your Pronoia remain idle throughout that boundless length of time? Was she avoiding hard work? But hard work does not impinge upon a god, and in any case there was no such labour, for all the elements of sky, stars, lands, and seas obeyed the divine will. Why should the god have sought, like some aedile, to adorn the world with decorative figures and illuminations? If his motive was to improve his own living-quarters, then presumably he had earlier been dwelling for an infinite time in darkness, enclosed, so to say, in a windowless hovel. And what happened next? Do we assume that he took pleasure in the varied adornment which we behold in the heavens and on earth? What pleasure can a god take in such things? And if he did derive such pleasure, he could not have foregone it for so long.

[. . .]

'As for those who have maintained that the world itself possesses life and wisdom, they have totally failed to see into what shape the nature of
intelligent mind could be installed.[17] I shall treat 24
this matter myself in a moment; for the present I shall merely express surprise at the slow-wittedness of those who would have it that a living creature endowed with both immortality and

blessedness is spherical in shape, merely because Plato maintains that no shape is more beautiful than the sphere. In my view, the cylinder, the cube, the cone, the pyramid are more beautiful. And what sort of life is assigned to this rotund god? Why, to be spun round at speed the like of which cannot even be imagined; I cannot envisage mental stability or a life of happiness resident in that! If an experience were to manifest itself as troublesome even in the slightest degree in our own bodies, it should surely be regarded as troublesome also in the god; now clearly the earth as a constituent part of the universe is also a part of your god, yet we observe that massive tracts of the earth cannot be populated and cultivated, because some of them are scorched by the impact of the sun, and others are in the hard grip of snow and frost owing to the sun's prolonged departure. So if the universe is god, since these lands are a part of the universe, we are to posit that some of god's limbs are ablaze, while others are frozen stiff!

[. . .]

43 'If anyone were to contemplate the thoughtless and random nature of all these claims, he would be bound to revere Epicurus, and to consign him to the company of those very gods who are the focus of our enquiry. He was the only person to realize first, that gods exist because nature herself has imprinted the conception of them in the minds of all – for what nation or category of men does not have some anticipation of gods, without being indoctrinated? Epicurus terms this *prolepsis*,[18] in other words the conception of an object previously grasped by the mind, without which nothing can be understood, investigated, or discussed. We have come to appreciate the force and usefulness of this reasoning as a result of the divine treatise of Epicurus[19] entitled *Rule and Judgement*.

44 'So you see that the foundations of this enquiry have been impressively laid: this belief of ours is not based on any prescription, custom, or law, but it abides as the strong, unanimous conviction of the whole world. We must therefore come to the realization that gods must exist because we have an implanted, or rather an innate, awareness of them. Now when all people naturally agree on something, that belief must be true; so we are to acknowledge that gods exist. Since this is agreed by virtually everyone – not just philosophers, but also the unlearned – we further acknowledge that we possess what I earlier called an "anticipation" or prior notion of gods (we must use neologisms for new concepts, just as Epicurus himself adopted *prolepsis* in a sense which no previous philosopher had employed).

'As I was saying, then, we have this prior 45
notion causing us to believe that the gods are blessed and immortal; for just as nature has bestowed on us the concept of the gods themselves, so also she has etched the notion on our minds to make us believe that they are eternal and blessed. If this is the case, the dictum expounded by Epicurus is true: "What is blessed and immortal neither is troubled itself, nor causes trouble to its neighbour; thus it is gripped by neither anger nor partiality, for all such attitudes are a mark of weakness."

'If our aim was merely to worship the gods devotedly and to free ourselves from superstition, we would need to say nothing more; the preeminent nature of the gods would be venerated by the devotion of mankind because it is both eternal and truly blessed, for reverence is rightly accorded to all that is supreme. Moreover, all fear of the gods would have been excised, through our awareness that anger and partiality are remote from the gods' blessed and immortal nature. Once these misapprehensions are banished, no fears of the gods loom over us.

'But our minds seek to strengthen these convictions by investigating the shape, the manner of life, the mental activity, and the mode of operation of the god.

'So far as the divine appearance is concerned, 46
we are prompted partly by nature, and instructed partly by reason. Each one of us from every nation has a natural conviction that the gods have no other than human shape, for what other appearance do they present to us at any of our waking or sleeping hours? But we need not base our entire judgement on such primary concepts,[20] for reason itself pronounces the same judgement. It seems fitting that the most outstanding 47
nature, in virtue of its blessedness and its immortality, should also be the most beautiful; and what arrangement of limbs, what fashioning of features, what shape or appearance can be more beautiful than the human form? You Stoics, Lucilius (I call you to witness rather than my friend Cotta here,

whose views differ according to the moment),[21]
when depicting the divine skill and workmanship, frequently point out how everything in the
human form is designed not merely with utility
48 in mind, but also for beauty. So if the human shape
is superior to the beauty of all living creatures, and
god is a living creature, he certainly possesses that
shape which is the most beautiful of all. Since
it is certain that the gods are the most blessed of
creatures, and no one can be blessed without
possessing virtue, and virtue cannot exist without reason, and reason can subsist only in the
human form, we must accordingly acknowledge
49 that the gods have human shape. Yet this form
of theirs is not corporeal but quasi-corporeal,[22]
containing not blood, but quasi-blood.

'Epicurus' researches were too penetrating, and his explanations too subtle, to be grasped by any Tom, Dick, or Harry, but I rely on the intelligence of my audience here in offering this explanation, which is more succinct than the theme demands. By virtue of his mental outlook and practical handling of things hidden and deeply buried, Epicurus teaches that the vital nature of the gods is such that it is first perceptible not to the senses, but to the mind;[23] and not in substance or in measurable identity, like the things which he calls solid bodies because they are substantial. Rather, an infinite appearance of very similar images formed out of innumerable atoms arises, and flows towards the gods. Our minds focus and latch on to these images with the greatest sensations of pleasure; thus they obtain an understanding of what a blessed and eternal being is.

50 'The significance of the infinity just mentioned is supremely important, and repays close and careful scrutiny. We must grasp that its nature is such that there is an exact balance in all creation – what Epicurus calls *isonomia*[24] or equal distribution. What follows from this principle is that if there is a specific quantity of mortal creatures, the tally of immortals is no fewer; and again, if the destructive elements in the world are countless, the forces of conservation must likewise be infinite.

'Another enquiry, Balbus, which you Stoics
often make, concerns the nature of the gods' life,
51 how they spend their days.[25] Well, their life is such
that nothing imaginable is more blessed, more
abounding in all good things. The god is wholly
inactive; he has no round of tasks to perform, and
no structures to set up. He takes pleasure in his
own wisdom and virtue,[26] utterly certain that he
will be perennially surrounded by the greatest and
most abiding pleasures.'

[. . .]

Cotta at once responded with his customary 57
bonhomie.[27] 'But if you had not had something to say, Velleius, you could certainly not have heard anything from me, for usually my mind more readily apprehends the reasons for the falsehood of a statement rather than its truth. This has often struck me before, as it did just now as I was listening to you. If you were to ask me my view of the nature of the gods, I should perhaps have nothing to reply; but if you were to enquire whether I think their nature is such as you have just outlined, I would say that nothing seems to me less likely.

[. . .]

During my time in Athens, I often attended 59
Zeno's lectures. [. . .] Yet in listening to you just now, I experienced the same reaction as I often had when listening to him; I felt irritated that so talented an individual, if you will forgive my saying so, had become associated with such trivial, not to say stupid, doctrines.

[. . .]

'In this investigation of the nature of the gods, 61
the primary issue is whether they exist or not. You say that it is difficult to deny it. I agree, if the question is posed in public, but it is quite easy in this type of conversation conducted between friends. So though I am a *pontifex* myself,[28] and though I believe that our ritual and our state-observances should be most religiously maintained, I should certainly like to be persuaded of the fundamental issue that gods exist, not merely as an expression of opinion but as a statement of truth; for many troubling considerations occur to me which sometimes lead me to think that they do not exist at all.

'But note how generously I intend to deal 62
with you. Beliefs like this one, which you share with other philosophers, I shall not tackle, for virtually all philosophers – and I include myself

particularly – like the idea that gods exist. So I do not dispute the fact, but the argument you adduce I do not consider to be sufficiently strong. You advanced, as a sufficiently compelling proof for us to acknowledge the existence of gods, that persons of all communities and nations believe it to be so.[29] But this argument is not merely unsubstantial in itself, but also untrue. To begin with, what is the source of your knowledge of the beliefs of nations? My own opinion is that many races are so monstrously barbarous that they entertain no suspicion that gods exist.

[. . .]

65 'I grant you that gods exist; so now inform me of their provenance, location, and the nature of their bodies, minds, and lives. These are the answers I am keen to have. To explain all of them, you exploit the dominion and the free movement of atoms. From them you fashion and create everything on earth, as the saying goes. But in the first place, atoms do not exist; for there is nothing [so small that it cannot be divided; moreover, assuming that atoms exist, they cannot be impelled through the void, assuming that you mean by void that][30] which contains no body; so there can be no void, and nothing which is indivisible.

66 'These arguments with which I make free are the cryptic utterances of the natural philosophers. Whether they are true or not I do not know, but they seem more probable than yours.[31] The reprehensible theories which you mouth emanate from Democritus – perhaps also from his predecessor Leucippus: that there are tiny bodies, some smooth, some rough, some round, some oblong, some curved and hook-shaped, and that heaven and earth have been formed from these not under the compulsion of any natural law, but by some sort of accidental collision.[32] You, Velleius, have carried this theory through to our own day; one could dislodge you from your whole life's course sooner than from the authority which you cite, for you decided on becoming an Epicurean before you acquainted yourself with these tenets, and so you had either to take aboard these outrageous doctrines, or to abandon your claim to the philosophy which you had embraced.

67 'For what would induce you to stop being an Epicurean? "Absolutely nothing", you reply "would make me forsake the rationale of the happy life and the truth." So is this creed of yours the truth? I do not challenge you on your claim to the happy life, for in your eyes even a god does not attain it unless he lives a life of torpid idleness. But where is this truth you claim? I suppose it lies in all those countless worlds of yours, which come into being and fade away at the drop of a hat! Or does it lie in the indivisible particles which without the direction of nature or reason[33] can fashion such notable structures? But I am forgetting the forbearing attitude which I had begun to show to you a moment ago, and I am challenging too many of your tenets. So I shall let pass your claim that all things are composed of atoms. But what relevance has this when the subject of our investigation is the nature of the gods?

'Granted, then, that the gods are composed of 68 atoms, it follows that they are not eternal,[34] for what is formed from atoms came into being at some time. Now if an atomic compound comes into being, gods did not exist earlier, and if gods have a beginning, they must also die – as you argued a moment ago yourself in the case of Plato's universe. So where are this much-vaunted blessedness and this eternity of yours, the two criteria which you demand for divinity, to be found? In trying to establish them, you take refuge in a thicket of philosophical jargon, in your statement that a god does not have a body but a quasi-body, and does not have blood but quasi-blood.

'This is a frequent practice of your school. 69 When you try to avoid censure for proposing an unlikely theory, you advance a thesis so utterly impossible that you would have been better to concede the matter in dispute than to offer such shameless resistance. For example,[35] Epicurus realized that if atoms were borne downwards by their own weight, free will would be out of the question, because the movement of the atoms would be fixed and inevitable. So he devised a means of avoiding such determinism (this idea had doubtless not occurred to Democritus); he stated that when the atom was borne directly downward by the force of gravity, it swerved[36] ever so slightly.
This explanation is tawdrier than his inability to 70
defend his thesis[37] would have been.

'He does the same thing in confronting the logicians.[38] Their traditional teaching is that in all disjunctive propositions of the "either true or not" type, one or other of the two standpoints is true. But Epicurus was afraid that if he granted the validity of the statement "Epicurus will be alive tomorrow, or he will not", one or other conclusion would be necessary; so he denied that the entire category of "either true or not" was necessary; what can possibly be more asinine than that? Arcesilaus used to hammer away at Zeno,[39] for while he himself labelled all sense-impressions fallacious, Zeno claimed that some were false, but not all. But Epicurus feared that if one single sensation appeared false, none of them would be true, so he stated that all sense-impressions registered the truth. In none of these doctrines was he too clever; while seeking to ward off the lighter punch, he ran into one heavier.

71 'He does the same thing in discussing the nature of the gods; in seeking to avoid the charge that they are an accretion of atoms, with the inevitable consequence of their destruction and dispersal, he claims that they do not have bodies, but "quasi-bodies", and not blood, but "quasi-blood". It seems remarkable that one augur can look another in the eye without grinning,[40] but it is more remarkable still how you Epicureans can restrain your laughter when in each other's company. "Not bodies, but quasi-bodies"; I could grasp the meaning of this if they were made of wax or earthenware, but what a "quasi-body" or "quasi-blood" is in the case of a god, I cannot imagine. Nor can you, Velleius, but you are unwilling to admit it.

72 'You Epicureans repeat these doctrines like parrots, as though they have been dictated to you. Epicurus dreamt them up when half-asleep, for as we note from his writings, he boasted that he never had a teacher. Even if he had not proclaimed this, I myself could readily have believed it of him. He reminds me of the owner of a badly constructed house who boasts of not having employed an architect.

[...]

76 Explain to me, please, the outline and shape of these shadowy gods of yours. You have a number of arguments to advance here, in the attempt of your school to demonstrate that gods have human shape. First, you claim that we have an inbuilt, preconceived notion in our minds, so that when we think of "god", the human form is what presents itself to us. Second, since the gods' nature excels all things, its shape must likewise be the most beautiful, and no shape is more beautiful than the human. Third, you adduce the argument that in no other shape can a mind have a home.[41]

'So first you must analyse the nature of each of these claims. It seems to me that you Epicureans arrogate as your rightful possession an assumption which is wholly improbable. 77

'To begin with, was anyone ever so blind in his survey of realities as not to see that these human shapes have been ascribed to the gods for one of two possible reasons? Either some strategy of philosophers[42] sought to divert more easily the minds of the unsophisticated from debased living towards observance of the gods; or superstition ensured that statues were furnished for men to worship in the belief that they were addressing the gods themselves. Poets, painters, sculptors have nurtured these attitudes, because it was not easy to preserve the impression that gods were active and creative if they were represented by non-human shapes.

'There was also a belief of yours perhaps reinforcing this, that to a human person nothing seems more beautiful than another human being. But you as a natural philosopher must see how nature plays the role of a seductive brothel-madam, a procuress recommending her wares. You surely cannot imagine that there is a single beast on land or sea which does not take delight above all in one of its own species? If this were not the case, why should a bull not seek to couple with a mare, or a horse with a cow? Do you perhaps suppose that an eagle or lion or dolphin prefers any other shape to its own? So it is hardly surprising that nature has similarly prevailed on humans to believe that nothing is more beautiful than a human being. [It is likely that this is why the gods have been thought to resemble men.]

[...]

'And tell me this: are we also to assume that the gods bear the names which we allot to them? 84
Yet they have as many names as there are human languages. Wherever you go, your name remains Velleius, but unlike you, Vulcan does not bear the same name in Italy, France, and Spain. Then again, even our pontifical registers do not contain

numerous names, whereas the number of gods is beyond counting. So are there anonymous gods? You are forced to make such an admission, for since they are look-alikes, what point is there in a plurality of names? How splendid it would be, Velleius, if you were to admit ignorance of what you do not know, rather than puking and feeling disgust with yourself for uttering such balderdash! You cannot genuinely believe that a god is in my likeness or yours: of course not.

[. . .]

88 'Let us assume, then, the non-existence of the courses of the sun, moon, and planets,[43] since nothing can exist except what we have touched or seen. But you have not had sight of God himself, have you, so why believe in his existence? On this basis we must dispense with everything brought to our notice by history or science; it leads to the conclusion that folks in the hinterland do not believe in the existence of the sea. What downright narrow-mindedness this is! It is like imagining that you were born on Seriphus[44] and had never left the island, where you were used to seeing small creatures like hares and foxes – and refusing to believe in lions and panthers when they were described to you. As for the elephant, if anyone told you about it, you would believe that you were the butt of a joke!

'To press this argument still further, can any statement be more childish than the claim that the types of beasts found in the Indian Ocean or in India[45] do not exist? Yet even the most diligent of researchers cannot gather information about all the many animals which dwell on land and sea, in marshes and rivers. So are we to claim that they do not exist because we have never set eyes on them?

[. . .]

94 'As for this Epicurean account of yours, it is utter eyewash, hardly worthy of the old women who spin yarns by candlelight. You simply do not realize how much you let yourselves in for if you extract from us the admission that men and gods are identical in shape. You will have to allot to a god all the physical cares and concerns that we ascribe to a man – walking and running, reclining and bending, sitting down and grasping things, and to crown all, even chatting and declaiming.
As for your thesis that deities are both male and 95
female, you realize the significance of that! I for my part never cease to wonder how your famous founder came to hold those beliefs.

'But your interminable cry is that we must cleave fast to the doctrine of the divine blessedness and immortality. But what prevents a god being happy even if he is not endowed with two legs? Why cannot this blessedness, however you like to term it – whether we are to use the word *beatitas* or alternatively *beatitudo*,[46] both quite hard on the ears, but we have to soften words by use – be applied to the sun up yonder, or to this world of ours, or to some eternal Mind
possessed of no bodily shape or limbs? Your only 96
response is: "I never saw a happy sun or a happy world." So have you ever set eyes on a world other than this? You will say you have not. Why, then, had you the temerity to maintain the existence not merely of thousand upon thousand, but of worlds beyond counting? You reply: "Reason has taught us this." So in your search for the nature that is truly outstanding, blessed, and eternal, which alone possesses the attributes of divinity, will reason not also instruct you that just as divine nature surpasses us in immortality, so too it surpasses us in mental excellence – and not only in mental but also in physical excellence? So why are we peers of the gods physically, when we fall behind them in all other respects? One would have thought that human beings attained closer likeness to the gods in virtue than in appearance.[47]

[. . .]

'"God", says Epicurus, "has no concerns." Like 102
boy-favourites, he clearly likes nothing better than the idle life. But even those boys in their idleness seek enjoyment by playing some physical sport; do we want God to be so idle and sluggish as to make us fear that he cannot he happy if he bestirs himself? That maxim of his not merely deprives the gods of the movements and action appropriate to divinity, but also makes humans lazy, the assumption being that even God cannot be happy if he is doing something.

[. . .]

'So my first question is: where does that God 104
of yours dwell? Second, what makes him move

from his position, if he ever does? Next, since living creatures have a native tendency to seek what is suited to their nature, what is it that God seeks? For what purpose does he exercise the thrust of his mind and reason? Finally, what form do his blessedness and eternity take? Touching on any of these issues probes a sensitive spot, for reasoning without a solid premiss cannot attain a proper conclusion.

[. . .]

121 'But Epicurus, in refusing to allow the gods to accord help and favour to men, has wholly uprooted religion from human hearts; for though he states that the divine nature is best and most outstanding of all, he further says that God manifests no favour, and thus he removes what is chiefly characteristic of the best and most outstanding nature. For what better or more outstanding quality is there than the kindness which confers benefits? When your school envisages a God lacking this quality, the message you preach is that no one, divine or human, is dear to God, that no one is held in love and affection by him. The conclusion is that not only is the human race of no concern to the gods, but the gods themselves are of no concern to each other.

'How much better is the attitude of the Stoics,[48] whom you censure! They maintain that the friendship of the wise extends even to the wise men with whom they are not acquainted; for nothing is more lovable than virtue, and the person who has acquired it will be held in our affection
122 no matter where he lives. But what harm you Epicureans do by regarding kindness and goodwill as weaknesses! Leaving aside the gods' impact and nature, do you suggest even that humans would not have shown beneficence and affability if it had not been for their weakness? Does no natural affection exist between persons who are good? The very word *amor* (love), from which the word *amicitia* (friendship) derives, carries an affectionate sound. But if we exploit that friendship for our own advantage, and not in the interests of the person we love, it will cease to be friendship,[49] and become a kind of trafficking in the benefits it offers. We show regard for meadows and fields and herds of cattle, because profits are derived from them, but affection and friendship between human beings are spontaneous; how much more, then, is the friendship shown by the gods, for they lack nothing, and they both show mutual affection and have the interests of mankind at heart. If this were not so, what point would there be in our revering and imploring the gods, or in priests presiding over sacrifices, and augurs over the auspices, or in petitioning and making vows to the immortal gods?

'You object that Epicurus too wrote a book on 123
reverence. The man makes sport with us, though he is not so much a wit as one undisciplined with the pen. How can there be reverence if the gods take no thought for human affairs? How can a nature be invested with life, yet remain wholly insensitive?

'So undoubtedly closer to the truth is the claim made in the fifth book of his *Nature of the Gods* by Posidonius,[50] whose friendship we all share: that Epicurus does not believe in any gods, and that the statements which he made affirming the immortal gods were made to avert popular odium. He could not have been such an idiot as to fashion God on the lines of a poor human, even if merely in broad outline and not in substantial appearance, yet endowed with all the human limbs but without the slightest use of them, an emaciated, transparent being conferring no gifts or kindness on anyone, and in short discharging no duties and performing no actions.

'First, such a nature cannot exist. In his awareness of this, Epicurus in actuality discards the gods, while paying lip-service to them. Second, should such a god actually exist, prompted by no favour or affection for mankind, I bid him farewell. There is no point in my urging him "Be gracious", for he can be gracious to no one, since all favour and affection, as you Epicureans state, is a mark of weakness.'

Notes

1 *Brutus*: this is the Marcus Iunius Brutus who planned the assassination of Julius Caesar in March 44. He was a considerable intellectual; as a former pupil of Antiochus, he claimed allegiance, like Cicero himself, to the Academic school. Cicero's close friendship with him is attested by their voluminous correspondence, only a fraction of which has survived, and by Cicero's dedication to him of *De finibus* and *Tusculans.*

2 *Protagoras*: our knowledge of him comes chiefly from the dialogue of Plato bearing his name. Two of his statements have gained him immortality. Eusebius (*Praep. Evang.* 14.3.7) has preserved one sentence of his from his treatise *On the gods*: 'So far as gods are concerned, I cannot know whether they exist or not, nor what they are like in appearance; for many factors impede our knowledge – obscurity and the shortness of life.' Plato, *Theaetetus* 151e, attributes to him the statement that 'Man is the measure of all things, of things that are that they are, and of things that are not that they are not' – a statement which excludes any appeal to divine revelation about the gods' existence.

3 *Diagoras . . . Theodorus*: Diagoras, a lyric poet of the late fifth century, was said to have lost his faith in the existence of gods when a man who broke his oath remained unpunished by them. See further 3.84, and L. Woodbury, *Phoenix* (1965), 178 ff. Theodorus of Cyrene was an adherent of the Cyrenaic school in the late fourth and early third centuries, and a pupil of Aristippus (on whom, see 3.77 nn.). For Theodorus, see Diogenes Laertius 2.98 ff.

4 *there are and have been philosophers*, etc.: Cicero now briefly visualizes the difficulties which the Epicurean theology raises for Roman religious practice, and indirectly for the coherence of Roman society. This observation is a challenge to contemporary Epicureans, who include Cicero's friend Atticus and other acquaintances mentioned in his correspondence (*Fam.* 15.19).

5 *Carneades*: the President of the New or Third Academy from a date before 155 to 137–136 is the philosopher who exercises greatest influence on Cicero, as is clear from *De finibus, Tusculans*, and above all *Academica*. See Introduction, p. xxxvi.

6 *well-disposed critics . . . malicious backbiters*: when he settled to compose this treatise, Cicero had already published *Hortensius, Academica, De finibus*, and *Tusculans*. He here reflects on the reactions aroused by them.

7 *auspices over which I myself preside*: Cicero had held the office of augur since 53 BC.

8 *a most rigorous and careful discussion*: the dialogue is imaginary. In a letter to Varro (*Fam.* 9.8), Cicero warns his friend that he will find himself involved in the *Academica* in a conversation which never took place! The dramatic date of this dialogue is 76 BC, when Cicero was still a relatively unknown figure, during the *Feriae Latinae*, a movable feast, which the consuls arranged between April and July. The depiction of time and place is in imitation of Plato's practice in his dialogues.

9 *taught . . . to know nothing*: a humorous allusion to the scepticism of the Academics.

10 *with the breezy confidence*, etc.: this scathing presentation of Velleius is an index to Cicero's aversion from the pontificating tendencies of the Epicureans, and more fundamentally from their ethical tenets.

11 *the Epicurean intermundia*: the Epicurean doctrine that the gods inhabit the *intermundia*, or empty spaces between the worlds.

12 *the craftsman-god in Plato's* Timaeus: Cicero himself translated this dialogue; the celebrated myth in it (89d–92e) recounts how the *demiourgos* created an orderly universe out of existing matter.

13 *tools and levers and scaffolding*: Cicero makes Velleius take Plato's creation-myth literally, ignoring the preliminary comment at *Timaeus* 28c: 'To find the maker and father of the universe is a hard task, and when you have found him, it is impossible to speak of him before all the people.' Such poetic myths make an easy target when interpreted literally; hence these knockabout jokes from Velleius. For Plato's discussion of the four elements, see *Timaeus* 32c and following.

14 *those solids of five shapes*: according to Pythagorean theory adopted by Plato, the four elements are represented by geometrical shapes; earth by particles in the shape of a cube, fire by a triangular pyramid, air by an octahedron, and water by an ikosahedron (twenty-sided). These are selected as the only possible regular rectilinear solids (all the faces being identical in size and shape) which can be enclosed in a sphere with all their corners touching the surface; see I. M. Crombie, *An Explanation of Plato's Doctrines* (London, 1962), ii.197 ff.

15 *to strike the mind and to produce sensations*: the theory of perception outlined in the *Timaeus* posits a cone of light formed between the object seen and the eye. Particles from the object impinge on the eye, which transmits the shock to the mind.

16 *what it must have been in extent*: Velleius argues that we can comprehend the notion of eternity before creation by thinking of it as spatial extension back from the moment of creation.

17 *they . . . failed to see into what shape . . . intelligent mind could be installed*: both Plato and the Stoics posit a sentient world endowed with mind. The Timaeus myth describes how the world obtains its soul, and for the Stoics the soul of the universe is identical with Pronoia. Epicureans argue that since reason is embraced within the human form alone, intelligent mind can pass only into that form, which the gods share with men.

18 *Epicurus terms this* prolepsis: in § 44 Cicero claimed to have coined the Latin word *anticipatio*

to render this Greek concept. Thereby he distorts (whether intentionally or not is disputed) the true sense of *prolepsis*. Epicureans argue that following the repeated impact of images on the senses or the mind, we grasp a general conception of an object (as in this case of the gods); this is what *prolepsis* implies. Cicero's rendering appears to interpret it as previous knowledge of objects before their images have impacted on the senses, in other words a knowledge which predates sense-experience.

19 *the divine treatise of Epicurus*: this work, *Rule and Judgement*, which discussed the Epicurean theory of knowledge, has not survived. We are dependent upon Epicurus' *Principal Doctrines* and his *Letter to Herodotus* for reconstruction of the theory.

20 *primary concepts*: the evidences afforded by nature before reviewed by the reason.

21 *whose views differ according to the moment*: a jocular criticism of the Academics' doctrine of probability, by which judgements may vary according to circumstances.

22 *not corporeal, but quasi-corporeal*, etc.: the Epicureans believed that the gods, like everything else, are atomic compounds, but they are composed of atoms so fine that they differ in kind from the atoms which constitute the human frame.

23 *perceptible not to the senses, but to the mind*: unlike mundane objects which give off images composed of atoms which strike the senses, the images of gods are so fine that they bypass the senses and impinge directly on the mind.

24 *an exact balance . . .* isonomia: no attempt is made by Velleius to defend this doctrine, perhaps because it was such a familiar feature in Presocratics like Heraclitus and Empedocles. For the views expressed here, see Rist, *Epicurus*, 144 ff. Cicero introduces the doctrine here to indicate that in Epicureanism the gods are infinite in number.

25 It is surprising that in this account of the life of the Epicurean gods, no mention is made of their locale. It is strange, too, that Velleius refers to 'god' in the singular, perhaps to contrast the leisurely existence of the individual Epicurean deity with the ceaseless activity of the Stoic god next described.

26 *He takes pleasure in his own wisdom and virtue*: this is the Aristotelian view of god absorbed in his own excellence.

27 *with his customary bonhomie*: Cicero contrasts Velleius' bellicose demeanour (§ 18) with Cotta's greater urbanity. Cotta then takes the characteristic Academic stance by promising a Socratic scrutiny of Epicurean falsehood rather than a positive exposition of his own.

28 *though I am a* pontifex, etc.: of the four main colleges of priests at Rome, the sixteen *pontifices* took precedence over the augurs, the *decemviri sacrorum* (the college was increased to fifteen by 51 BC) who supervised the Sibylline books, and the *epulones*, who organized religious feasts. Cotta was elected *pontifex* soon after his return to Rome in 82 BC; tenure of this priesthood reflected his high stature in the state.

29 *persons of all communities . . . believe it to be so*: see § 43. The argument for the existence of gods *ex consensu gentium* was widely maintained in antiquity; where atheism is noted, it is usually ascribed to uneducated barbarians as here, or to ignoramuses; Plato, *Laws* 886a, remarks that there are many young atheists, but no old ones.

30 The supplement in brackets, or similar formulation, is added by editors. But possibly the addition is unnecessary, and Cotta, imitating Velleius, is arguing by syllogism: 'There is nothing which lacks a body; everywhere is occupied by bodies; therefore there can be no void.'

31 *the cryptic utterances of the natural philosophers . . . seem more probable*: like a true Academic, Cotta claims only probability and not truth. By 'natural philosophers' he means Aristotle, who in *Physics* 4.6 ff. argues that void does not exist, and in *Physics* 6.1 that matter is infinitely divisible.

32 *by some sort of accidental collision*: Cotta is wrong to attribute this view to the Greek atomists; in fact in § 69 he absolves Democritus of this doctrine. The notion of accidental swerve (*clinamen*) was introduced by Epicurus to support his ethical teaching; it allowed him to combat the Stoic doctrine of necessity.

33 *without the direction of nature or reason*: Cotta here exploits Stoic cosmological theory, for these terms are often used for the Stoic *pneuma*.

34 *it follows that they are not eternal*: this argument, that only simple and not composite substances can be eternal, is a familiar feature in earlier philosophy. The Epicureans argued that in the purer region of the *intermundia*, the finer atoms of which the gods are allegedly composed are not liable to separate; but the argument is frail.

35 Cotta now presents three alleged instances of absurd Epicurean tenets; the swerve of the atoms, the denial of the disjunctive proposition, and the infallibility of the senses.

36 *it swerved*: the theory of the swerve (*clinamen*) of the atoms is Epicurus' attempt to correct the thesis of Democritus that the heavier atoms overtake the lighter in their downward path, resulting in an impact which initiates movement in all directions. Since all atoms of whatever weight descend at the same rate (see Cicero, *Fin.* 1.19, Diogenes Laertius 10.61), a different explanation is necessary to defend the doctrine of free will against Stoic determinism.

37 *inability to defend his thesis*: that is, the thesis that the atoms latch on to each other to create material objects.

38 *confronting the logicians*: ancient philosophers combined logic and dialectic as the first branch of philosophy, the science of reasoning, which embraces also epistemology. In the science of logic, the disjunctive proposition is what is often nowadays called 'the law of the excluded middle'; given two conflicting propositions, one or other must be true. The Epicureans adopted Aristotle's solution (*De interpretatione* 9), that necessity is present only if the two prepositions are combined; if taken separately, the statements 'Epicurus will be alive tomorrow/Epicurus will not be alive tomorrow' are not necessary. Again Epicurus is concerned here to combat the notion of Stoic necessity.

39 *Arcesilaus used to hammer away at Zeno*: Arcesilaus, founder of the Second Academy, here attacks not the Epicurean Zeno but the founder of the Stoics of the same name, who argued that sense-perceptions give us certain knowledge in some things, but that in others we must suspend judgement. Epicurus claimed that all sense-perceptions are reliable, but that our judgement of them may be distorted, a view inherited from Aristotle (*De anima* 3.3).

40 *one augur can look another in the eye without grinning*: the author of this *mot* was the elder Cato (Cicero, *Div.* 2.51). Augurs were able to suspend public business when it suited them, by claiming unpropitious signs from heaven, while simultaneously regarding these religious practices, inherited from the Etruscans, with some contempt. Cicero recounts the *mot* with relish as an augur himself.

41 The arguments here are a resumé of Velleius' statements in §§43, 47f.

42 *some strategy of philosophers*: the allusion may be to Aristotle, *Metaphysics* 1074b.

43 *the non-existence of the courses of sun, moon, and planets*: (the Latin does not have 'the courses of', but such an addition is demanded by the sense.) The argument is directed at the Epicurean epistemology, by which certain knowledge is attainable only through the senses.

44 *imagining that you were born on Seriphus*: this tiny island in the Cyclades was proverbial for its backwardness. See the famous story of Themistocles and the Seriphian at Plato, *Rep.* 329e–330a, repeated by Cato in Cicero's *De senectute* 8.

45 *beasts found in the Indian Ocean or in India*: literally 'in the Red Sea and in India'. Both Greeks and Romans apply the term Red Sea to the Indian Ocean and to the Persian Gulf, as well as to the Red Sea. The additional mention of India here suggests that the Indian Ocean is in Cotta's mind; the 'beasts' are presumably whales, monsters of the deep comparable in size with elephants on land.

46 *beatitas or . . . beatitudo*: Roman pioneers in philosophy had sometimes to coin neologisms to express Greek concepts. Cicero here wonders how to render Greek *eudaimonia*, for which earlier he used *beata vita*. Of the two neologisms launched here, *beatitudo* catches on, but *beatitas* fades out.

47 *in virtue than in appearance*: Cotta uses Stoic arguments to rebut the Epicurean claims, whereas at 3.38 he roundly rejects the Stoic notion, that God has need of the cardinal virtues.

48 *the attitude of the Stoics*: this praise of Stoicism for its superior doctrine of friendship is disingenuous, for Epicureans laid great store by friendship at the human level (cf. *Principal Doctrines* 27: 'Of the things which wisdom acquires for the blessedness of life as a whole, by far the greatest is the possession of friendship'). At the level of divine benevolence, Cotta could have argued that the Stoic divinity was more helpful to the human race, but not in any personal sense.

49 *it will cease to be friendship*: Aristotle (*NE* 1155b) recognizes three levels of friendship: utility, pleasure, and goodness; Cotta here rejects the first, and espouses the Stoics' belief that 'friendship exists only between the virtuous' (Diogenes Laertius 7.124). Cicero develops the theme of friendship at greater length in his *De amicitia*.

50 *Posidonius*: The Stoic philosopher and historian (*c.*135–*c.*50 BC) had studied under Panaetius at Athens, and later settled at Rhodes, where Cicero encountered him in 78. When Cotta claims acquaintance with him for himself and for Velleius and Balbus, he perhaps recalls the occasion of the visit of Posidonius to Rome in 87. (Cicero may have forgotten that Cotta was in exile at that time.) The work of Posidonius on the gods mentioned here must have been an important source for Cicero's discussion in the two following books, but surprisingly it is cited only once (2.88).

II

CLASSICAL ARGUMENTS FOR THEISM

Introduction

The three classical "arguments" for the existence of God are actually three groups of arguments. "The Teleological Argument" is the group of arguments that attempt to show that the existence of God is the best explanation of the orderliness of the universe or the purposiveness of nature. "The Cosmological Argument" is the class of arguments that conclude that if God does not exist, there is no sensible answer to the question, "Where did the universe come from?" "The Ontological Argument" is the class of arguments that claim that an analysis of a certain concept requires the actual existence of a being that falls under the concept – that than which nothing greater can be conceived, or the greatest possible being, or that which cannot not exist. All three types of argument have a long history.

The classical theistic arguments have been offered in response to a number of different questions, sometimes posed to oneself, and sometimes posed to another person. Unless we know what question the argument is attempting to answer and who is asking the question, it is impossible to assess the argument's success. One type of questioner is the agnostic inquirer who is asking herself whether or not there is a God. Another is the atheist attacker who challenges the theist to defend his belief in God. A third is the theist who wants to know whether his belief is defensible by the use of reason. The task of bolstering a pre-existent belief is obviously quite different from answering an attack from a skeptic, and both of those projects differ from the task of finding out the answer to a question with no prior inclination to believe one way or the other.

The issue of who is asking the question, "Does God exist?" is closely related to another issue that is important in formulating and criticizing the traditional arguments – the issue of what can be presupposed. The classical arguments do not refer to religious experience, special insight, revelation, or anything else inaccessible to the atheist or the agnostic inquirer. Does this mean they are meant to be convincing to the agnostic and the atheist? Probably none of them was addressed to the agnostic or atheist before the modern era, and rarely has any of them convinced an agnostic or changed the mind of an atheist, although there are some interesting exceptions. In any case, some theists think that the arguments are useful for people who are already theists.

In the modern era philosophers have often thought that the theistic arguments are crucial because the practice of religion stands or falls with the arguments. That is because they accept two forms of foundationalism: (i) the practice of religion depends upon the reasonableness of particular religious beliefs, the beliefs that undergird the religion. So belief is the foundation for the other aspects of religious practice such as religious ritual, religious emotions, and commitment to a faith community; (ii) all religious beliefs depend upon belief in God, so if belief in God is not reasonable, no other religious belief is reasonable either. It follows from (i) and (ii) that religious practice itself depends upon the success of at least one argument for the existence of God.

One can criticize either or both of these assumptions, yet many philosophers think that some of the traditional arguments are as successful as arguments in philosophy ever are. That is to say, they do not convince everybody, but they are convincing enough for many people to have a reasonable belief on their basis. At a minimum the arguments are intriguing. This section includes a series of forms of these arguments and critiques. The popularity of any given argument waxes and wanes, but all of them have contemporary defenders and detractors. Currently, forms of the Teleological Argument seem to be getting the most attention.

The earliest Teleological Argument we have included is from the second book of Cicero's *The Nature of the Gods* (first century BC), which anticipates both Aquinas' Fifth Way (thirteenth century) and the famous analogical version of the eighteenth-century philosopher William Paley, in which the universe is compared to an intricate machine, such as a watch. We have also included a contemporary version by Robin Collins. Versions of the argument since Darwin tend to focus on physics rather than biology, and Collins supports an argument from the "fine-tuning" of the physical universe.

The earliest Cosmological Argument we have included is from Plato's last dialogue, *Laws*, in which Plato addresses the existence of God as part of a discussion about the laws pertaining to religion. Plato argues that only a Self-moved Mover can be the primary element in change. We have also included Aristotle's argument for an Unmoved Mover from his *Physics*, as well as Aristotle's argument that time had no beginning, and a passage from Plato's *Timaeus*, in which he arguably implies that time had a beginning. Sometimes the Cosmological Argument is connected with the position that the universe (and time) had a beginning, as in the Kalam version of the eleventh-century Islamic philosopher al-Ghazāli, but sometimes it is distinguished from a commitment to the finitude of time, as in Aquinas' Third Way. In the modern period, the version of Samuel Clarke has nothing to do with time at all, arguing from the principle that every contingent fact needs an explanation for its truth.

As far as we know, there was no ancient version of the Ontological Argument, which originated with St Anselm in the eleventh century. Anselm argued that since we cannot conceive that that than which nothing greater can be conceived does not exist, such a being must exist. Aquinas rejected the argument and there was skepticism about it in the medieval period, but it was defended by Descartes in the seventeenth century and in an amended form by Leibniz, then famously criticized by Kant in the eighteenth century, and brought back again in the twentieth century by philosophers such as Alvin Plantinga, Charles Hartshorne, and Norman Malcolm.

One other historically important traditional argument for theism is Kant's Moral argument, which we have included in section VI. That argument can be studied in conjunction with the arguments of this section, or in conjunction with readings on the relation between religion and morality.

Debates over the usefulness of the classical arguments for theism include attacks on the two forms of foundationalism mentioned above, as well as concerns about the connection between accepting the conclusion of any of these arguments and believing in the God of religious practice. Of course, we cannot expect any one argument to prove everything, but many philosophers believe that these arguments are only a piece of a much larger case for theism, and an even larger case for a theistic religion. In addition to evaluating the arguments on their merits, readers will want to consider how we should respond if they succeed, and how we should respond if they fail.

A

Teleological Arguments

1

The Design Argument

Cicero

For more background on Cicero's *The Nature of the Gods* see section I. In the following passage, the Stoic philosopher Quintus Lucilius Balbus criticizes the Epicurean view that the universe is the result of chance collisions of atoms and argues that reason must be behind the order within the universe.

Part II

[. . .]

'Now our Epicurean friends maintain that the universe has been formed from atoms endowed with no colour or quality (the Greek term for quality is *poiotes*) or feeling[1] – or rather, that countless worlds at every moment of time come into being or perish. But if a collision of atoms can form the universe, why not a colonnade, a temple, a house, a city – all of them less laborious tasks – or many things even easier to create?

'In fact these people talk such nonsense about the universe that it seems to me that they have never gazed upwards at the remarkable embellishment of the heavens lying before their very eyes. As Aristotle sagely comments:[2]

Imagine that there were people who had always dwelt below the earth in decent and well-lit accommodation embellished with statues and pictures, and endowed with all the possessions which those reputed to be wealthy have in abundance. These people had never set foot on the earth, but through rumour and hear-say they had heard of the existence of some divine power wielded by gods. A moment came when the jaws of the earth parted, and they were able to emerge from their hidden abodes, and to set foot in this world of ours. They were confronted by the sudden sight of earth, seas, and sky; they beheld towering clouds, and felt the force of winds; they gazed on the sun, and became aware of its power and beauty, and its ability to create daylight by shedding its beams over the whole sky. Then, when night overshadowed the earth, they saw the entire sky dotted and

Cicero, "Book 2" from *The Nature of the Gods*, trans. P. G. Walsh (Oxford: Oxford University Press, 1998), pp. 81–2 plus notes.

adorned with stars, and the phases of the moon's light as it waxed and waned; they beheld the risings and settings of all those heavenly bodies, and their prescribed, unchangeable courses through all eternity. When they observed all this, they would certainly believe that gods existed, and that these great manifestations were the works of gods.

'This is as far as Aristotle takes it; but let us further envisage a darkness as dense as that which, when the volcano erupted at Aetna,[3] is said to have blotted out the neighbouring districts. For two days no one could recognize his neighbour, and when on the third day the sun broke through, people felt that they had come to life again. Now supposing after an eternity of darkness we suddenly and similarly beheld the light of day, how would the heavens appear to us? But as things stand, because we routinely see them every day and they are a familiar sight, our minds grow inured to them, so we do not experience wonder, or seek to explain what lies always before our eyes. It is as if novelty rather than the majesty of creation is what must rouse us to investigate the causes of the universe. Who would regard a human being as worthy of the name, if upon observing the fixed movements of heaven, the prescribed dispositions of the stars, and the conjunction and interrelation of all of creation he denied the existence of rationality in all these, and claimed that chance was responsible for works created with a degree of wisdom such as our own wisdom fails totally to comprehend? When we observe that some object – an orrery, say, or a clock,[4] or lots of other such things – is moved by some mechanism, we have no doubt that reason lies behind such devices; so when we note the thrust and remarkable speed with which the heavens revolve, completing with absolute regularity their yearly changes, and preserving the whole of creation in perfect safety, do we hesitate to acknowledge that this is achieved not merely by reason, but by reason which is preeminent and divine?

'At this point we can abandon the refinements of argument, and concentrate our gaze, so to say, on the beauty of the things which we declare have been established by divine providence.'

Notes

1 *colour or quality . . . or feeling*: 'quality' (*qualitas* means 'suchness') is one of the many words which we owe to Cicero's coining. It seems likely that he here remembers the long discussion in Lucretius 2.730 ff., where arguments are presented for atoms being without colour; these are followed (842 ff.) by the claim that they do not possess qualities of heat, sound, taste, smell, and that they lack sensation (865 ff.).

2 This long extract is from Aristotle's *De philosophia*, from which Cicero has already quoted at 1.33, 2.42 and 44; the treatise has not survived.

3 *when the volcano erupted at Aetna*: the volcanic mountain overlooking Catana in Sicily had most recently erupted shortly before Caesar's death in 44 BC; Servius (on Vergil, *Georgics* 1.472) reports that the disturbance was felt as far away as Rhegium.

4 *a clock*: Balbus thinks here of a water-clock rather than a sun-dial.

2

The Fifth Way

Thomas Aquinas

Thomas Aquinas (1225–74) was a Dominican friar and arguably the most influential Christian philosopher and theologian of all time. The following brief selection is from a famous passage in his *Summa Theologica* commonly referred to as "The Five Ways" because Aquinas offers five ways of proving God's existence. The fifth of these is a succinct statement of a teleological argument.

The fifth way is taken from the governance of the world. We see that things which lack intelligence, such as natural bodies, act for an end, and this is evident from their acting always, or nearly always, in the same way, so as to obtain the best result. Hence it is plain that not fortuitously, but designedly, do they achieve their end. Now whatever lacks intelligence cannot move towards an end, unless it be directed by some being endowed with knowledge and intelligence; as the arrow is shot to its mark by the archer. Therefore some intelligent being exists by whom all natural things are directed to their end; and this being we call God.

Thomas Aquinas, *Summa Theologica*, trans. Fathers of the English Dominican Province (Benziger Bros, 1947).

3

The Watch and the Watchmaker

William Paley

William Paley (1743–1805) was a prominent English theologian and philosopher. The following passage from his *Natural Theology* contains history's most famous and widely read statement of the teleological argument. Paley compares the evidence of design found in the universe to the evidence of design found in a watch, arguing that in both cases the evidence supports the inference to an intelligent designer.

State of the Argument

In crossing a heath, suppose I pitched my foot against a *stone*, and were asked how the stone came to be there, I might possibly answer, that, for anything I knew to the contrary, it had lain there for ever; nor would it, perhaps, be very easy to show the absurdity of this answer. But suppose I had found a *watch* upon the ground, and it should be inquired how the watch happened to be in that place, I should hardly think of the answer which I had before given – that, for anything I knew, the watch might have always been there. Yet why should not this answer serve for the watch as well as for the stone? Why is it not as admissible in the second case as in the first? For this reason, and for no other, viz., that, when we come to inspect the watch, we perceive (what we could not discover in the stone) that its several parts are framed and put together for a purpose, e.g. that they are so formed and adjusted as to produce motion, and that motion so regulated as to point out the hour of the day; that, if the different parts had been differently shaped from what they are, of a different size from what they are, or placed after any other manner, or in any other order than that in which they are placed, either no motion at all would have been carried on in the machine, or none which would have answered the use that is now served by it. To reckon up a few of the plainest of these parts, and of their offices, all tending to one result: – We see a cylindrical box containing a coiled elastic spring, which, by its endeavour to relax itself, turns round the box. We next observe a flexible chain (artificially wrought for the sake of

William Paley, "Natural Theology", chs 1–3 from William Paley, *Natural Theology* (C. Knight, 1836).

flexure) communicating the action of the spring from the box to the fusee. We then find a series of wheels, the teeth of which catch in, and apply to, each other, conducting the motion from the fusee to the balance, and from the balance to the pointer, and, at the same time, by the size and shape of those wheels, so regulating that motion as to terminate in causing an index, by an equable and measured progression, to pass over a given space in a given time. We take notice that the wheels are made of brass, in order to keep them from rust; the springs of steel, no other metal being so elastic; that over the face the watch there is placed a glass, a material employed in no other part of the work, but in the room of which, if there had been any other than a transparent substance, the hour could not be seen without opening the case. This mechanism being observed, (it requires indeed an examination of the instrument, and perhaps some previous knowledge of the subject, to perceive and understand it; but being once, as we have said, observed and understood,) the inference, we think, is inevitable, that the watch must have had a maker: that there must have existed, at some time, and at some place or other, an artificer or artificers who formed it for the purpose which we find it actually to answer; who comprehended its construction, and designed its use.

I. Nor would it, I apprehend, weaken the conclusion, that we had never seen a watch made; that we had never known an artist capable of making one; that we were altogether incapable of executing such a piece of workmanship ourselves, or of understanding in what manner it was performed; all this being no more than what is true of some exquisite remains of ancient art, of some lost arts, and, to the generality of mankind, of the more curious productions of modern manufacture. Does one man in a million know how oval frames are turned? Ignorance of this kind exalts our opinion of the unseen and unknown artist's skill, if he be unseen and unknown, but raises no doubt in our minds of the existence and agency of such an artist, at some former time, and in some place or other. Nor can I perceive that it varies at all the inference, whether the question arise concerning a human agent, or concerning an agent of a different species, or an agent possessing, in some respect, a different nature.

II. Neither, secondly, would it invalidate our conclusion, that the watch sometimes went wrong, or that it seldom went exactly right. The purpose of the machinery, the design, and the designer, might be evident, and, in the case supposed, would be evident, in whatever way we accounted for the irregularity of the movement, or whether we could account for it or not. It is not necessary that a machine be perfect, in order to show with what design it was made: still less necessary, where the only question is, whether it were made with any design at all.

III. Nor, thirdly, would it bring any uncertainty into the argument, if there were a few parts of the watch, concerning which we could not discover, or had not yet discovered, in what manner they conduced to the general effect; or even some parts, concerning which we could not ascertain whether they conduced to that effect in any manner whatever. For, as to the first branch of the case, if by the loss, or disorder, or decay of the parts in question, the movement of the watch were found in fact to be stopped, or disturbed, or retarded, no doubt would remain in our minds as to the utility or intention of these parts, although we should be unable to investigate the manner according to which, or the connexion by which, the ultimate effect depended upon their action or assistance; and the more complex is the machine, the more likely is this obscurity to arise. Then, as to the second thing supposed, namely, that there were parts which might be spared without prejudice to the movement of the watch, and that he had proved this by experiment, these superfluous parts, even if we were completely assured that they were such, would not vacate the reasoning which we had instituted concerning other parts. The indication of contrivance remained, with respect to them, nearly as it was before.

IV. Nor, fourthly, would any man in his senses think the existence of the watch, with its various machinery, accounted for, by being told that it was one out of possible combinations of material forms; that whatever he had found in the place where he found the watch, must have contained some internal configuration or other; and that this configuration might be the structure now exhibited, viz., of the works of a watch, as well as a different structure.

V. Nor, fifthly, would it yield his inquiry more satisfaction, to be answered, that there existed in things a principle of order, which had disposed the parts of the watch into their present form and situation. He never knew a watch made by the principle of order; nor can he even form to himself an idea of what is meant by a principle of order, distinct from the intelligence of the watchmaker.

VI. Sixthly, he would be surprised to hear that the mechanism of the watch was no proof of contrivance, only a motive to induce the mind to think so:

VII. And not less surprised to be informed, that the watch in his hand was nothing more than the result of the laws of *metallic* nature. It is a perversion of language to assign any law as the efficient, operative cause of anything. A law presupposes an agent; for it is only the mode according to which an agent proceeds: it implies a power; for it is the order according to which that power acts. Without this agent, without this power, which are both distinct from itself, the *law* does nothing, is nothing. The expression, 'the law of metallic nature,' may sound strange and harsh to a philosophic ear; but it seems quite as justifiable as some others which are more familiar to him, such as 'the law of vegetable nature,' 'the law of animal nature,' or, indeed, as 'the law of nature' in general, when assigned as the cause of phenomena, in exclusion of agency and power, or when it is substituted into the place of these.

VIII. Neither, lastly, would our observer be driven out of his conclusion, or from his confidence in its truth, by being told that he knew nothing at all about the matter. He knows enough for his argument: he knows the utility of the end: he knows the subserviency and adaptation of the means to the end. These points being known, his ignorance of other points, his doubts concerning other points, affect not the certainty of his reasoning. The consciousness of knowing little need not beget a distrust of that which he does know.

4

Critique of the Design Argument

David Hume

The skeptical Scottish empiricist, David Hume (1711–76), is widely regarded as the greatest philosopher of the English language. Although his *Dialogues Concerning Natural Religion* was published over twenty years prior to Paley's *Natural Theology*, it contains influential criticisms of the kind of argument Paley offered. The selection begins with Cleanthes, a natural theologian, presenting a version of the teleological argument. Next to speak is Demea, a more orthodox theist who finds Cleanthes' argument an inadequate defense of traditional theism. Finally, the skeptic Philo joins the discussion, raising several classic objections to the teleological argument.

Part II

[. . .]

Look round the world: Contemplate the whole and every part of it: You will find it to be nothing but one great machine, subdivided into an infinite number of lesser machines, which again admit of subdivisions, to a degree beyond what human senses and faculties can trace and explain. All these various machines, and even their most minute parts, are adjusted to each other with an accuracy, which ravishes into admiration all men, who have ever contemplated them. The curious adapting of means to ends, throughout all nature, resembles exactly, though it much exceeds, the productions of human contrivance; of human design, thought, wisdom, and intelligence. Since therefore the effects resemble each other, we are led to infer, by all the rules of analogy, that the causes also resemble; and that the Author of nature is somewhat similar to the mind of man; though possessed of much larger faculties, proportioned to the grandeur of the work, which he has executed. By this argument *a posteriori*, and by this argument alone, we do prove at once the existence of a Deity, and his similarity to human mind and intelligence.

David Hume, from *Dialogues Concerning Natural Religion*, ed. Norman Kemp Smith (Indianapolis, IN: Bobbs-Merrill, 1947), pp. 143–51, 165–9.

I shall be so free, Cleanthes, said Demea, as to tell you, that from the beginning, I could not approve of your conclusion concerning the similarity of the Deity to men; still less can I approve of the mediums, by which you endeavour to establish it. What! No demonstration of the being of a God! No abstract arguments! No proofs *a priori*! Are these, which have hitherto been so much insisted on by philosophers, all fallacy, all sophism? Can we reach no farther in this subject than experience[1] and probability? I will not say, that this is betraying the cause of a Deity: But surely, by this affected candour, you give advantage to atheists, which they never could obtain, by the mere dint of argument and reasoning.

What I chiefly scruple in this subject, said Philo, is not so much, that all religious arguments are by Cleanthes reduced to experience, as that they appear not to be even the most certain and irrefragable of that inferior kind. That a stone will fall, that fire will burn, that the earth has solidity, we have observed a thousand and a thousand times; and when any new instance of this nature is presented, we draw without hesitation the accustomed inference. The exact similarity of the cases gives us a perfect assurance of a similar event; and a stronger evidence is never desired nor sought after. But wherever you depart, in the least, from the similarity of the cases, you diminish proportionably the evidence; and may at last bring it to a very weak *analogy*, which is confessedly liable to error and uncertainty. After having experienced the circulation of the blood in human creatures, we make no doubt that it takes place in Titius and Mævius: But from its circulation in frogs and fishes, it is only a presumption, though a strong one, from analogy, that it takes place in men and other animals. The analogical reasoning is much weaker, when we infer the circulation of the sap in vegetables from our experience that the blood circulates in animals; and those, who hastily followed that imperfect analogy, are found, by more accurate experiments, to have been mistaken.

If we see a house, Cleanthes, we conclude, with the greatest certainty, that it had an architect or builder; because this is precisely that species of effect, which we have experienced to proceed from that species of cause. But surely you will not affirm, that the universe bears such a resemblance to a house, that we can with the same certainty infer a similar cause, or that the analogy is here entire and perfect. The dissimilitude is so striking, that the utmost you can here pretend to is a guess, a conjecture, a presumption concerning a similar cause; and how that pretension will be received in the world, I leave you to consider.

It would surely be very ill received, replied Cleanthes; and I should be deservedly blamed and detested, did I allow that the proofs of a Deity amounted to no more than a guess or conjecture. But is the whole adjustment of means to ends in a house and in the universe so slight a resemblance? The œconomy of final causes? The order, proportion, and arrangement of every part? Steps of a stair are plainly contrived, that human legs may use them in mounting; and this inference is certain and infallible. Human legs are also contrived for walking and mounting; and this inference, I allow, is not altogether so certain, because of the dissimilarity which you remark; but does it, therefore, deserve the name only of presumption or conjecture?

Good God! cried Demea, interrupting him, where are we? Zealous defenders of religion allow, that the proofs of a Deity fall short of perfect evidence! And you, Philo, on whose assistance I depended, in proving the adorable mysteriousness of the divine nature, do you assent to all these extravagant opinions of Cleanthes? For what other name can I give them? Or why spare my censure, when such principles are advanced, supported by such an authority, before so young a man as Pamphilus?

You seem not to apprehend, replied Philo, that I argue with Cleanthes in his own way; and by showing him the dangerous consequences of his tenets, hope at last to reduce him to our opinion. But what sticks most with you, I observe, is the representation which Cleanthes has made of the argument *a posteriori*; and finding that that argument is likely to escape your hold and vanish into air, you think it so disguised that you can scarcely believe it to be set in its true light. Now, however much I may dissent, in other respects, from the dangerous principles of Cleanthes, I must allow, that he has fairly represented that argument; and I shall endeavour so to state the matter to you, that you will entertain no farther scruples with regard to it.

Were a man to abstract from every thing which he knows or has seen, he would be altogether incapable, merely from his own ideas, to determine what kind of scene the universe must be, or to give the preference to one state or situation of things above another. For as nothing, which he clearly conceives, could be esteemed impossible or implying a contradiction, every chimera of his fancy would be upon an equal footing; nor could he assign any just reason, why he adheres to one idea or system, and rejects the others, which are equally possible.

Again; after he opens his eyes, and contemplates the world, as it really is, it would be impossible for him, at first, to assign the cause of any one event; much less, of the whole of things or of the universe. He might set his fancy a rambling; and she might bring him in an infinite variety of reports and representations. These would all be possible; but being all equally possible, he would never, of himself, give a satisfactory account for his preferring one of them to the rest. Experience alone can point out to him the true cause of any phenomenon.

Now according to this method of reasoning, DEMEA, it follows (and is, indeed, tacitly allowed by CLEANTHES himself) that order, arrangement, or the adjustment of final causes is not, of itself, any proof of design; but only so far as it has been experienced to proceed from that principle. For aught we can know *a priori*, matter may contain the source or spring of order originally, within itself, as well as mind does; and there is no more difficulty in conceiving, that the several elements, from an internal unknown cause, may fall into the most exquisite arrangement, than to conceive that their ideas, in the great, universal mind, from a like internal, unknown cause, fall into that arrangement. The equal possibility of both these suppositions is allowed. By experience we find (according to CLEANTHES), that there is a difference between them. Throw several pieces of steel together, without shape or form; they will never arrange themselves so as to compose a watch: Stone, and mortar, and wood, without an architect, never erect a house. But the ideas in a human mind, we see, by an unknown, inexplicable œconomy, arrange themselves so as to form the plan of a watch or house. Experience, therefore, proves, that there is an original principle of order in mind, not in matter. From similar effects we infer similar causes. The adjustment of means to ends[2] is alike in the universe, as in a machine of human contrivance. The causes, therefore, must be resembling.

I was from the beginning scandalised, I must own, with this resemblance, which is asserted, between the Deity and human creatures; and must conceive it to imply such a degradation of the supreme Being as no sound theist could endure. With your assistance, therefore, DEMEA, I shall endeavour to defend what you justly call the adorable mysteriousness of the divine nature, and shall refute this reasoning of CLEANTHES; provided he allows, that I have made a fair representation of it.

When CLEANTHES had assented, PHILO, after a short pause, proceeded in the following manner.

That all inferences, CLEANTHES, concerning fact, are founded on experience, and that all experimental reasonings are founded on the supposition, that similar causes prove similar effects, and similar effects similar causes; I shall not, at present, much dispute with you. But observe, I entreat you, with what extreme caution all just reasoners proceed in the transferring of experiments to similar cases. Unless the cases be exactly similar, they repose no perfect confidence in applying their past observation to any particular phenomenon. Every alteration of circumstances occasions a doubt concerning the event; and it requires new experiments to prove certainly, that the new circumstances are of no moment or importance. A change in bulk, situation, arrangement, age, disposition of the air, or surrounding bodies; any of these particulars may be attended with the most unexpected consequences: And unless the objects be quite familiar to us, it is the highest temerity to expect with assurance, after any of these changes, an event similar to that which before fell under our observation. The slow and deliberate steps of philosophers, here, if any where, are distinguished from the precipitate march of the vulgar, who, hurried on by the smallest similitude, are incapable of all discernment or consideration.

But can you think, CLEANTHES, that your usual phlegm and philosophy have been preserved in so wide a step as you have taken, when you compared to the universe houses, ships, furniture, machines; and from their similarity in some circumstances inferred a similarity in their causes? Thought, design, intelligence, such as we discover in men and other animals, is no more than one of the springs and principles of the universe, as well as heat or cold, attraction or repulsion, and a hundred others, which fall under daily observation. It is an active cause, by which some particular parts of nature, we find, produce alterations on other parts. But can a conclusion, with any propriety, be transferred from parts to the whole? Does not the great disproportion bar all comparison and inference? From observing the growth of a hair, can we learn any thing concerning the generation of a man? Would the manner of a leaf's blowing, even though perfectly known, afford us any instruction concerning the vegetation of a tree?

But allowing that we were to take the *operations* of one part of nature upon another for the foundation of our judgment concerning the *origin* of the whole (which never can be admitted) yet why select so minute, so weak, so bounded a principle as the reason and design of animals is found to be upon this planet? What peculiar privilege has this little agitation of the rain which we call thought, that we must thus make it the model of the whole universe? Our partiality in our own favour does indeed present it on all occasions: But sound philosophy ought carefully to guard against so natural an illusion.

So far from admitting, continued PHILO, that the operations of a part can afford us any just conclusion concerning the origin of the whole, I will not allow any one part to form a rule for another part, if the latter be very remote from the former. Is there any reasonable ground to conclude, that the inhabitants of other planets possess thought, intelligence, reason, or any thing similar to these faculties in men? When nature has so extremely diversified her manner of operation in this small globe; can we imagine, that she incessantly copies herself throughout so immense a universe? And if thought, as we may well suppose, be confined merely to this narrow corner, and has even there so limited a sphere of action; with what propriety can we assign it for the original cause of all things? The narrow views of a peasant, who makes his domestic œconomy the rule for the government of kingdoms, is in comparison a pardonable sophism.

But were we ever so much assured, that a thought and reason, resembling the human, were to be found throughout the whole universe, and were its activity elsewhere vastly greater and more commanding than it appears in this globe: Yet I cannot see, why the operations of a world, constituted, arranged, adjusted, can with any propriety be extended to a world, which is in its embryo-state, and is advancing towards that constitution and arrangement. By observation, we know somewhat of the œconomy, action, and nourishment of a finished animal; but we must transfer with great caution that observation to the growth of a fœtus in the womb, and still more, to the formation of an animalcule in the loins of its male parent. Nature, we find, even from our limited experience, possesses an infinite number of springs and principles, which incessantly discover themselves on every change of her position and situation. And what new and unknown principles would actuate her in so new and unknown a situation as that of the formation of a universe, we cannot, without the utmost temerity, pretend to determine.

[A very small part of this great system, during a very short time, is very imperfectly discovered to us: And do we thence pronounce decisively concerning the origin of the whole?]

Admirable conclusion! Stone, wood, brick, iron, brass have not, at this time, in this minute globe of earth, an order or arrangement without human art and contrivance: Therefore the universe could not originally attain its order and arrangement, without something similar to human art. But is a part of nature a rule for another part very wide of the former? Is it a rule for the whole?[3] Is a very small part a rule for the universe? Is nature in one situation, a certain rule for[4] nature in another situation, vastly different from the former?

And can you blame me, CLEANTHES, if I here imitate the prudent reserve of SIMONIDES, who, according to the noted story,[5] being asked by HIERO, *What God was?* desired a day to think of it, and then two days more; and after that manner continually prolonged the term, without ever bringing in his definition or description? Could you even blame me, if I had answered at first, *that I did not know*, and was sensible that this subject lay vastly beyond the reach of my faculties? You might cry out sceptic and raillier as much as you pleased: But having found, in so many other subjects, much more familiar, the imperfections and even contradictions of human reason, I never should expect any success from its feeble conjectures, in a subject, so sublime, and so remote from the sphere of our observation. When two *species* of objects have always been observed to be conjoined together, I can *infer*, by custom, the existence of one wherever I *see* the existence of the other: And this I call an argument from experience. But how this argument can have place, where the objects, as in the present case,[6] are single, individual, without parallel, or specific resemblance, may be difficult to explain. And will any man tell me with a serious countenance, that an orderly universe must arise from some thought and art, like the human; because we have experience of it? To ascertain this reasoning, it were requisite, that we had experience of the origin of worlds; and it is not sufficient surely, that we have seen ships and cities arise from human art and contrivance. . . .

PHILO was proceeding in this vehement manner, somewhat between jest and earnest, as it appeared to me; when he observed some signs of impatience in CLEANTHES, and then immediately stopped short. What I had to suggest, said CLEANTHES, is only that you would not abuse terms, or make use of popular expressions to subvert philosophical reasonings. You know, that the vulgar often distinguish reason from experience, even where the question relates only to matter of fact and existence; though it is found, where that *reason* is properly analysed, that it is nothing but a species of experience. To prove by experience the origin of the universe from mind is not more contrary to common speech than to prove the motion of the earth from the same principle. And a caviller might raise all the same objections to the COPERNICAN system, which you have urged against my reasonings. Have you other earths, might he say, which you have seen to move? Have. . . .

Yes! cried PHILO, interrupting him, we have other earths. Is not the moon another earth, which we see to turn round its centre? Is not Venus another earth, where we observe the same phenomenon? Are not the revolutions of the sun also a confirmation, from analogy, of the same theory? All the planets, are they not earths, which revolve about the sun? Are not the satellites moons, which move round Jupiter and Saturn, and along with these primary planets, round the sun? These analogies and resemblances, with others, which I have not mentioned, are the sole proofs of the COPERNICAN system: And to you it belongs to consider, whether you have any analogies of the same kind to support your theory.

In reality, CLEANTHES, continued he, the modern system of astronomy is now so much received by all enquirers, and has become so essential a part even of our earliest education, that we are not commonly very scrupulous in examining the reasons upon which it is founded. It is now become a matter of mere curiosity to study the first writers on that subject, who had the full force of prejudice to encounter, and were obliged to turn their arguments on every side, in order to render them popular and convincing. But if we peruse GALILÆO's famous Dialogues concerning the system of the world, we shall find, that that great genius, one of the sublimest that ever existed, first bent all his endeavours to prove, that there was no foundation for the distinction commonly made between elementary and celestial substances. The schools, proceeding from the illusions of sense, had carried this distinction very far; and had established the latter substances to be ingenerable, incorruptible, unalterable, impassible; and had assigned all the opposite qualities to the former. But GALILÆO, beginning with the moon, proved its similarity in every particular to the earth; its convex figure, its natural darkness when not illuminated, its density, its distinction into solid and liquid, the variations of its phases, the mutual illuminations of the earth and moon, their mutual eclipses, the inequalities of the lunar surface, &c. After many instances of this kind, with regard to all the planets, men plainly saw, that these bodies became proper objects of experience; and that the similarity of their nature enabled us to extend the same arguments and phenomena from one to the other.

In this cautious proceeding of the astronomers, you may read your own condemnation, CLEANTHES; or rather may see, that the subject in which you are engaged exceeds all human reason and enquiry. Can you pretend to show any such similarity between the fabric of a house, and the generation of a universe? Have you ever seen nature in any such situation as resembles the first arrangement of the elements? Have worlds ever been formed under your eye? and have you had leisure to observe the whole progress of the phenomenon, from the first appearance of order to its final consummation? If you have, then cite your experience, and deliver your theory.

[...]

Part V

But to show you still more inconveniences, continued PHILO, in your anthropomorphism; please to take a new survey of your principles. *Like effects prove like causes.* This is the experimental argument; and this, you say too, is the sole theological[7] argument. Now it is certain, that the liker the effects are, which are seen, and the liker the causes, which are inferred, the stronger is the argument. Every departure on either side diminishes the probability, and renders the experiment less conclusive. You cannot doubt of[8] this principle: Neither ought you to reject its consequences.

All the new discoveries in astronomy, which prove the immense grandeur and magnificence of the works of nature, are so many additional arguments for a Deity, according to the true system of theism: But according to your hypothesis of experimental theism,[9] they become so many objections, by removing the effect still farther from all resemblance to the effects of human art and contrivance. For if Lucretius,[10] even following the old system of the world, could exclaim,

> Quis regere immensi summam, quis habere profundi
> Indu manu validas potis est moderanter habenas?
> Quis pariter cœlos omnes convertere? et omnes
> Ignibus ætheriis terras suffire feraces?
> Omnibus inve locis esse omni tempore præsto?

If *Tully*[11] esteemed this reasoning so natural, as to put it into the mouth of his EPICUREAN. *Quibus enim oculis animi intueri potuit vester Plato fabricam illam tanti operis, qua construi a Deo atque œdificari mundum facit? quœ molitio? quœ ferramenta? qui vectes? quœ machinœ? qui ministri tanti muneris fuerunt? quemadmodum autem obedire et arere voluntati architecti aer, ignis, aqua, terra potuerunt?* If this argument, I say, had any force in former ages; how much greater must it have at present; when the bounds of nature are so infinitely enlarged, and such a magnificent scene is opened to us? It is still more unreasonable to form our idea of so unlimited a cause from our experience of the narrow productions of human design and invention.

The discoveries by microscopes, as they open a new universe in miniature, are still objections, according to you; arguments, according to me. The farther we push our researches of this kind, we are still led to infer the universal cause of All to be vastly different from mankind, or from any object of human experience and observation.

And what say you to the discoveries in anatomy, chemistry, botany?.... These surely are no objections, replied CLEANTHES: They only discover new instances of art and contrivance. It is still the image of mind reflected on us from unnumerable objects. Add, a mind *like the human*, said PHILO. I know of no other, replied CLEANTHES. And the liker the better, insisted PHILO. To be sure, said CLEANTHES.

Now, CLEANTHES, said PHILO, with an air of alacrity and triumph, mark the consequences. *First*, By this method of reasoning, you renounce all claim to infinity in any of the attributes of the Deity. For as the cause ought only to be proportioned to the effect, and the effect, so far as it falls under our cognisance, is not infinite; what pretensions have we, upon your suppositions,[12] to ascribe that attribute to the divine Being? You will still insist, that, by removing him so much from all similarity to human creatures, we give into the most arbitrary hypothesis, and at the same time weaken all proofs of his existence.

Secondly, You have no reason, on your theory, for ascribing perfection to the Deity, even in his finite capacity; or for supposing him free from every error, mistake, or incoherence in his undertakings. There are many inexplicable difficulties in the works of nature, which, if we allow a perfect Author to be proved *a priori*, are easily solved, and become only seeming difficulties, from the narrow capacity of man, who cannot trace infinite relations. But according to your method of reasoning, these difficulties become all real; and perhaps will be insisted on, as new instances of likeness to human art and contrivance. At least, you must acknowledge, that it is impossible for us to tell, from our limited views, whether this system contains any great faults, or deserves any considerable praise, if compared to other possible, and even real systems. Could a peasant, if the ÆNEID were read to him, pronounce that poem to be absolutely faultless, or even assign to it its proper rank among the productions of human wit; he, who had never seen any other production?

[But were this world ever so perfect a production, it must still remain uncertain, whether all the excellencies of the work can justly be ascribed to the workman. If we survey a ship, what an exalted idea must we form of the ingenuity of the carpenter, who framed so complicated, useful, and beautiful a machine? And what surprise must we entertain, when we find him a stupid mechanic, who imitated others, and copied an art, which, through a long succession of ages, after multiplied trials, mistakes, corrections, deliberations, and controversies, had been gradually improving? Many worlds might have been botched and bungled, throughout an eternity, ere this system was struck out: Much labour lost: Many fruitless trials made: And a slow, but continued improvement carried on during infinite ages in the art of world-making. In such subjects, who can determine, where the truth; nay, who can conjecture where the probability, lies; amidst a great number of hypotheses which may be proposed, and a still greater number which may be imagined?][13]

And what shadow of an argument, continued PHILO, can you produce, from your hypothesis, to prove the unity of the Deity? A great number of men join in building a house or ship, in rearing a city, in framing a commonwealth: Why may not several Deities combine in contriving and framing a world? This is only so much greater similarity to human affairs. By sharing the work among several, we may so much farther limit the attributes of each, and get rid of that extensive power and knowledge, which must be supposed in one Deity, and which, according to you, can only serve to weaken the proof of his existence. And if such foolish, such vicious creatures as man can yet often unite in framing and executing one plan; how much more those Deities or Dæmons, whom we may suppose several degrees more perfect?

[To multiply causes, without necessity, is indeed contrary to true philosophy: But this principle applies not to the present case. Were one Deity antecedently proved by your theory, who were possessed of every attribute requisite to the production of the universe; it would be needless, I own (though not absurd) to suppose any other Deity existent. But while it is still a question, whether all these attributes are united in one subject, or dispersed among several independent Beings: By what phenomena in nature can we pretend to decide the controversy? Where we see a body raised in a scale, we are sure that there is in the opposite scale, however concealed from sight, some counterpoising weight equal to it: But it is still allowed to doubt, whether that weight be an aggregate of several distinct bodies, or one uniform united mass. And if the weight requisite very much exceeds any thing which we have ever seen conjoined in any single body, the former supposition becomes still more probable and natural. An intelligent Being of such vast power and capacity, as is necessary to produce the universe, or, to speak in the language of ancient philosophy, so prodigious an animal, exceeds all analogy, and even comprehension.]

But farther, CLEANTHES; men are mortal, and renew their species by generation; and this is common to all living creatures. The two great sexes of male and female, says MILTON, animate the world. Why must this circumstance, so universal, so essential, be excluded from those numerous and limited Deities? Behold then the theogony of ancient times brought back upon us.

And why not become a perfect anthropomorphite? Why not assert the Deity or Deities to be corporeal, and to have eyes, a nose, mouth, ears, &c.? EPICURUS maintained, that no man had ever seen reason but in a human figure; therefore the gods must have a human figure. And this argument, which is deservedly so much ridiculed by Cicero,[14] becomes, according to you, solid and philosophical.

In a word, CLEANTHES, a man, who follows your hypothesis, is able, perhaps, to assert, or conjecture, that the universe, sometime, arose from something like[15] design: But beyond that position he cannot ascertain one single circumstance, and is left afterwards to fix every point of his theology, by the utmost licence of fancy and hypothesis. This world, for aught he knows, is very faulty and imperfect, compared to a superior standard; and was only the first rude essay of some infant Deity, who afterwards abandoned it, ashamed of his lame performance; it is the work only of some dependent, inferior Deity; and is the object of derision to his superiors: it is the production of old age and dotage in some superannuated Deity; and ever since his death, has run on at adventures, from the first impulse and active force, which it received from him. . . . You justly give signs of horror, DEMEA, at these strange suppositions: But these, and a thousand more of the same kind, are CLEANTHES's suppositions, not mine. From the moment the attributes of the Deity are supposed finite, all these have place. And I cannot, for my part, think, that so wild and unsettled a system of theology is, in any respect, preferable to none at all.

These suppositions I absolutely disown, cried CLEANTHES: They strike me, however, with no horror; especially, when proposed in that rambling way in which they drop from you. On the contrary, they give me pleasure, when I see, that, by the utmost indulgence of your imagination, you never get rid of the hypothesis of design in the universe; but are obliged, at every turn, to have recourse to it. To this concession I adhere steadily; and this I regard as a sufficient foundation for religion.

Notes

[Notes in square brackets were added by the editor of the 1947 edition.]

1 [moral evidence *substituted for* experience, and *then* experience *restored*]

2 [means to ends *for* final causes]

3 [whole *for* world]

4 [a certain rule for *for* precisely similar to]

5 [*Cf.* Cicero, *De Natura Deorum,* Bk. 1, 22]

6 [concerning the origin of the world *omitted*]

7 [theological *for* religious]

8 [doubt of *for* deny]

9 [of experimental theism *added*]

10 Lib. II, 1095 ["Who can rule the sum, who hold in his hand with controlling force the strong reins, of the immeasurable deep? who can at once make all the different heavens to roll and warm with ethereal fires all the fruitful earths, or be present in all places at all times" (Munro's translation).]

11 *De Nat*[*ura*] *Deor*[*um*], Lib. I [8. "For with what eyes of the mind could your Plato have beheld that workshop of such stupendous toil, in which he represents the world as having been put together and built by God? How was so vast an undertaking set about? What tools, what levers, what machines, what servants, were employed in so great a work? How came air, fire, water, and earth to obey and submit to the architect's will?"]

12 [upon your suppositions *added*]

13 [This paragraph, and the paragraph in square brackets [below], [were] added on the last page of Part V, with marks to indicate points of insertion.]

14 [Cicero *for* Divines]

15 [something like *for* some kind of]

5

The Teleological Argumen

Robin Collins

Robin Collins (b. 1961) is Professor of Philosophy at Messiah College in Pennsylvania and one of the foremost contemporary defenders of the design argument. Collins acknowledges that many classic statements of the design argument have become unpersuasive due to Hume's criticisms and, more importantly, Darwin's theory of evolution; however, he goes on to argue that recent developments in physics and cosmology provide strong support for another version of the argument commonly referred to as "the argument from fine-tuning."

Introduction and Historical Background

My contention in this essay will be that discoveries in physics and cosmology, along with developments in philosophy, particularly in the logic of inference, have significantly bolstered the traditional teleological argument, or argument from design. Today, I contend, the evidence from physics and cosmology offers us significant, well-formulated reasons for believing in theism.

The design argument has a long history, probably being the most commonly cited argument for believing in a deity. Before the eighteenth century, design arguments typically appealed to the idea that the universe is orderly, or appears to be ordered toward some end. In ancient India, for instance, the argument from design was advanced by the so-called Ny~ya (or logical-atomist) school (100–1000 CE), which argued for the existence of a deity based on the order of the world, which they compared both to human artifacts and to the human body.[2] In the West, the design argument goes back at least to Heraclitus, who attempted to account for the order in the universe by hypothesizing that the universe was directed by a principle of intelligence or reason. Related arguments were offered by Plato, Aristotle, and the Stoics. This sort of argument was further elaborated upon by Thomas Aquinas, in his famous Fifth Way. According to Aquinas, nature appears to be directed toward an end, yet it lacks owledge to direct itself. Thus, Aquinas claimed, "some intelligent being exists by whom all natural things are directed to their end; and this being we call God." From the perspective of our modern scientific understanding of the world, one outstanding problem with Aquinas's argument is that it is unclear in what sense nature is "directed toward an end," other than that it simply appears to be orderly.

More generally, since the rise of the scientific revolution, these versions of the teleological argument that simply appealed to the orderliness of the universe lost much of their force as philosophers and scientists became increasingly contented with appealing to the laws of nature as a sufficient explanation of the regular operation of the universe, although God was still appealed to by some as the explanation of the existence of these laws. The version of the design argument that began to take its place was one based on the *intricate* ordering of various natural systems for some end, not the mere regularity of some aspect of the world. In William Paley's famous presentation of the design argument, the intricate organization of the organs of the body – such as an eye – is compared to the intricate ordering of the parts of a watch for the apparent purpose of telling of time. Since, Paley argues, upon finding such an object on a heath (or somewhere else), one would attribute it to some intelligence, the same should be done for the intricate structure of plants and animals. As skeptical philosophers such as David Hume pointed out, however, there is an important disanalogy between the universe or plants and animals and the case of watches that seems to undercut the argument: we know from experience that the watches are produced by minds, but we have no experience of animal life or universes being created by minds.

In the view of many, however, the real blow to Paley's argument came from a different quarter: Darwin's theory of evolution. Before Darwin, the problem facing atheists was to offer some alternative explanation for the extraordinarily complex and well-ordered biological systems in animal and plant life. One could raise philosophical doubts about the validity of the inference to design, as Hume did, but without an alternative explanation the impression of design remained overwhelming. After Darwin, however, one no longer needed to appeal to some transcendent intelligence as responsible for the apparent design of plants and animals, but could appeal to the "blind watchmaker" (to use one of Richard Dawkins's phrases) of evolution by chance plus natural selection. In his *Natural Theology*,[3] however, Paley presented another design argument that was not subject to the "evolution objection." This was the argument that in order for life to exist, the laws of nature and the physical environment of the earth must also be well designed. Partly because of the lack of detailed physical and astrophysical knowledge at the time, this version of Paley's argument was never considered particularly strong.

In recent decades, however, this version of the argument has become much more convincing. Scientists have increasingly come to realize how the initial conditions of the universe and the basic constants of physics must be balanced on a razor's edge for intelligent life to evolve – something known in the literature as the "fine-tuning" of the cosmos for (intelligent) life. Calculations show that if the constants of physics – such as the physical constant governing the strength of gravity – were slightly different, the evolution of complex, embodied life-forms of comparable intelligence to ourselves would be seriously inhibited, if not rendered impossible. These calculations added an important quantitative element to the argument from design: instead of simply appealing to a qualitative impression of the intricate ordering of nature for some end, as in Aquinas's Fifth Way, one could now give "hard" numerical content to these qualitative impressions. Because of this new quantitative data, along with developments in the logic of inference during the twentieth century, the design argument can be cast into a much more rigorous form than in the past, as I will now elaborate. We will begin by looking at the evidence for the fine-tuning of the cosmos for intelligent life.

The Evidence of Fine-tuning

Many examples of the fine-tuning for intelligent life can be given, a few of which we will briefly recount here.[4] One particularly important category of fine-tuning is that of the *constants* of physics. The constants of physics are a set of fundamental numbers that, when plugged into the laws of physics, determine the basic structure of the universe. An example of such a constant is the gravitational constant G that is part of Newton's law of gravity, $F = GM_1M_2/r^2$. G determines the strength of gravity between two masses. If one were to double the value of G, for instance, then the force of gravity between any two masses would double.

So far, physicists have discovered four forces in nature: gravity, the weak force, electromagnetism, and the strong nuclear force that binds protons and neutrons together in an atom. As measured in a certain set of standard dimensionless units,[5] gravity is the weakest of the forces, and the strong nuclear force is the strongest, being a factor of 10^{40} – or ten thousand billion, billion, billion, billion – times stronger than gravity.

Various calculations show that the strength of at least two of the forces of nature must fall into a relatively small life-permitting region for highly complex life to exist. As just one example, consider gravity. Compared with the total range of forces, the strength of gravity must fall in a relatively narrow range in order for complex life to exist. If we increased the strength of gravity a billionfold, for instance, the force of gravity on a planet with the mass and size of the earth would be so great that organisms anywhere near the size of human beings, whether land-based or aquatic, would be crushed. (The strength of materials depends on the electromagnetic force via the fine-structure constant, which would not be affected by a change in the strength of gravity.) Even a much smaller planet of only 40 feet in diameter – which is not large enough to sustain organisms of our size – would have a gravitational pull of 1000 times that of earth, still too strong for organisms of our brain size, and hence level of intelligence, to exist. As astrophysicist Martin Rees notes, "In an imaginary strong gravity world, even insects would need thick legs to support them, and no animals could get much larger."[6] Other calculations show that if the gravitational force were increased by more than a factor of 3000, the maximum life-time of a star would be a billion years, thus severely inhibiting the probability of intelligent life evolving.[7] Of course, a 3000-fold increase in the strength of gravity is a lot, but compared with the total range of the strengths of the forces in nature (which span a range of 10^{40}, as we saw above), it is very small, being one part in a billion, billion, billion, billion.

There are other cases of the fine-tuning of the constants of physics besides the strength of the forces, however. Probably the most widely discussed among physicists and cosmologists – and esoteric – is the fine-tuning of what is known as the *cosmological constant*. The cosmological constant is a term that Einstein included in his central equation of his theory of gravity – that is, general relativity – that today is thought to correspond to the energy density of empty space. A positive cosmological constant acts as a sort of anti-gravity, a repulsive force causing space itself to expand. If the cosmological constant had a significant positive value, space would expand so rapidly that all matter would quickly disperse, and thus galaxies, stars, and even small aggregates of matter could never form. If significantly negative, the universe would almost immediately collapse back in on itself. The conclusion is that it must fall exceedingly close to zero, relative to its natural range of values, for complex life to be possible in our universe.

Now, the fundamental theories of particle physics set a natural range of values for the cosmological constant. This natural range of values, however, is at least 10^{53} – that is, one followed by fifty three zeros – times the range of life-permitting values. That is, if 0 to L represent the range of life-permitting values, the physically natural range of values is at least 0 to 10^{53}L. To intuitively see what this means, consider a dart-board analogy: suppose that we had a dart-board that extended across the entire visible galaxy, with a target on the dart-board of less than an inch in diameter. The amount of fine-tuning of the cosmological constant could be compared to randomly throwing a dart at the board and landing exactly in the target![8]

Further examples of the fine-tuning of the fundamental constants of physics can also be given, such as that of mass difference between the neutron and the proton. If, for example, the mass of the neutron were slightly increased by about one part in seven hundred, stable hydrogen burning stars would cease to exist.[9]

Besides the constants of physics, however, there is also the "fine-tuning" of the laws. If the laws of nature were not just right, life would probably be impossible. For example, consider again the four forces of nature. If gravity did not exist, masses would not clump together to form stars or planets; if the electromagnetic force did not exist, there would be no chemistry; if the strong force did not exist, protons and neutrons could not bind together and hence no atoms with atomic number greater than hydrogen would exist; and if the strong force were a long-range force (like gravity and electromagnetism) instead of a short range force that only acts between protons and neutrons in the nucleus, all matter would either almost instantaneously undergo nuclear fusion and explode or be sucked together forming a black hole. Each of these consequences would seriously inhibit, if not render impossible, the existence of complex intelligent life.

Similarly, other laws and principles are necessary for complex life: as prominent Princeton physicist Freeman Dyson points out,[10] if the Pauli-exclusion principle did not exist, which dictates that no two fermions can occupy the same quantum state, all electrons would occupy the lowest atomic orbit, eliminating complex chemistry; and if there were no quantization principle, which dictates that particles can only occupy certain discrete quantum states, there would be no atomic orbits and hence no chemistry, since all electrons would be sucked into the nucleus.

Finally, in his book *Nature's Destiny*, biochemist Michael Denton extensively discusses various higher-level features of the natural world, such as the many unique properties of carbon, oxygen, water, and the electromagnetic spectrum, that are conducive to the existence of complex biochemical systems. As one of many examples that Denton presents, both the atmosphere and water are transparent to electromagnetic radiation in a thin band in the visible region, but nowhere else except in radio waves. If, instead, either of them absorbed electromagnetic radiation in the visible region, the existence of terrestrial life would be seriously inhibited, if not rendered impossible.[11] These higher-level coincidences indicate a deeper-level fine-tuning of the fundamental laws and constants of physics.

As the above examples indicate, the evidence for fine-tuning is extensive, even if one has doubts about some individual cases. As philosopher John Leslie has pointed out, "clues heaped upon clues can constitute weighty evidence despite doubts about each element in the pile."[12] At the very least, these cases of fine-tuning show the truth of Freeman Dyson's observation that there are many "lucky accidents in physics,"[13] without which our existence as intelligent embodied beings would be impossible.

The Argument Formulated

Now it is time to consider the way in which the fine-tuning supports theism. In this section, I will argue that the evidence of fine-tuning primarily gives us a reason for preferring theism over what could be called the atheistic single-universe hypothesis – that is, the hypothesis that there is only one universe, and it exists as a brute fact. We will examine the typical alternative explanation of the fine-tuning offered by many atheists – what I call the "many-universes hypothesis" – in the section 'The many-worlds hypothesis' below.

Although the fine-tuning argument against the atheistic single-universe hypothesis can be cast in several different forms – such as inference to the best explanation – I believe that the most rigorous way of formulating the argument is in terms of what I will call the *prime principle of confirmation* (PPC), and which Rudolph Carnap has called the "*increase in firmness*" principle, and others have simply called the *likelihood principle*.[14] The PPC is a general principle of reasoning that tells us when some observation counts as evidence in favor of one hypothesis over another. *Simply put, the principle says that whenever we are considering two competing hypotheses, an observation counts as evidence in favor of the hypothesis under which the observation has the highest probability (or is the least improbable).* (Or, put slightly differently, the principle says that whenever we are considering two competing hypotheses, H_1 and H_2, an observation, O, counts as evidence in favor of H_1 over H_2 if O is more probable under H_1 than it is under H_2.) Moreover, the degree to which the evidence counts in favor of one hypothesis over another is proportional to the degree to which the observation is more probable under the one hypothesis than the other.[15] To illustrate, consider a case of finding a defendant's fingerprints on the murder weapon. Normally, we would take such a finding as strong evidence that the defendant was guilty. Why? Because we judge that it would be *unlikely* for these fingerprints to be on the murder weapon if the defendant was innocent, but *not unlikely* if the defendant was guilty. Then by the prime principle of confirmation, we would conclude that the fingerprints offered significant evidence that the defendant was guilty.

Using this principle, we can develop the fine-tuning argument in a two-step form as follows:

1 The existence of the fine-tuning is not highly improbable under theism.
2 The existence of the fine-tuning is very improbable under the atheistic single-universe hypothesis.[16]

We can conclude from premises 1 and 2 and the prime principle of confirmation that the fine-tuning data provide significant evidence in favor of the design hypothesis over the atheistic single-universe hypothesis.

At this point, we should pause to note two features of this argument. First, the argument does not say that the fine-tuning evidence proves that the universe was designed, or even that it is likely that the universe was designed. Indeed, of itself it does not even show that we are epistemically warranted in believing in theism over the atheistic single-universe hypothesis. In order to justify these sorts of claims, we would have to look at the full range of evidence both for and against the theistic hypothesis – something I am not doing in this essay (but note the range of essays in this volume). Rather, the argument merely concludes that the fine-tuning significantly *supports* theism *over* the atheistic single-universe hypothesis. (I say significantly supports, because presumably the ratio of probabilities for the fine-tuning under theism versus the atheistic single-universe hypothesis is quite large. See note 15.)

In this way, the evidence of the fine-tuning argument is much like fingerprints found on a gun: although they can provide strong evidence that the defendant committed the murder, one could not conclude merely from them alone that the defendant is guilty; one would also have to look at all the other evidence offered. Perhaps, for instance, ten reliable witnesses claimed to see the defendant at a party at the time of the shooting. In this case, the fingerprints would still count as significant evidence of guilt, but this evidence would be counterbalanced by the testimony of the witnesses. Similarly the evidence of fine-tuning significantly supports theism over the atheistic single-universe hypothesis, but it does not itself show that, everything considered, theism is the most plausible explanation of the fine-tuning or the world.

The second feature of the argument we should note is that, given the truth of *the prime principle of confirmation*, the conclusion of the argument follows from the premises. Specifically, if the premises of the argument are true, then we are guaranteed that the conclusion is true: that is, the argument is what philosophers call *valid*. Thus, insofar as we can show that the premises of the argument are true, we will have shown that the conclusion is true. Our next task, therefore, is to attempt to show that the premises are true, or at least that we have good reasons to believe them.

Support for the premises

Support for premise 1

Premise 1 is easy to support and somewhat less controversial than premise 2. The argument in support of it can be simply stated as follows: *since God is an all good being, and it is good for embodied moral agents to exist, it not highly surprising or highly improbable that God would create a reality that could support such agents – that is, a reality in which there is a universe that can sustain complex, embodied, intelligent life.* Thus, the fine-tuning is not highly improbable under theism.[17]

Support for premise 2

Upon looking at the data, many people find it very obvious that the fine-tuning is highly improbable under the atheistic single-universe hypothesis. And it is easy to see why when we think of the fine-tuning in terms of various analogies. In the "dart-board analogy," for example, the theoretically possible values for fundamental constants of physics can be represented as a dart-board that fills the whole galaxy, and the conditions necessary for life to exist as a small inch-wide target. Accordingly, from this analogy it seems obvious that it would be highly improbable for the fine-tuning to occur under the atheistic single-universe hypothesis – that is, for the dart to hit the target by chance.

Now some philosophers object to the claim that the fine-tuning is highly improbable under the atheistic single-universe hypothesis by arguing that since there is only one universe, the notion of the fine-tuning of the universe being probable or improbable is meaningless. Ian Hacking, for instance, claims that a probability could only be meaningfully assigned to the fine-tuning if we had some model of universe generation which implied that a certain percentage of universes would turn out to be fine-tuned.[18] Given such a model, and given that a single-universe is generated, we could then assign the universe a certain probability of being fine-tuned. Keith Parsons raises similar objections.[19]

Although I do not have space to provide a full-scale response to this objection, I will briefly sketch an answer. The first is to note that the relevant notion of probability occurring in the fine-tuning argument is a widely recognized type of probability called *epistemic probability*.[20] Roughly, the epistemic probability of a proposition can be thought of as the degree of confidence or belief that we rationally should have in the proposition. Further, the conditional epistemic probability of a proposition R on another proposition S – written as P(R/S) – can be defined as the degree to which the proposition S *of itself* should rationally lead us to expect that R is true. Under the epistemic conception of probability, therefore, the statement that *the fine-tuning of the cosmos is very improbable under the atheistic single-universe hypothesis* is to be understood as making a statement about the degree to which the atheistic single-universe hypothesis would or should, *of itself*, rationally lead us to expect cosmic fine-tuning.

The phrase "*of itself*" is important here. The rational degree of expectation should not be confused with the degree to which one should expect the constants of physics to fall within the life-permitting range if one believed the atheistic single-universe hypothesis. For even those who believe in this atheistic hypothesis should expect the values of the constants of physics to be life-permitting since this follows from the fact that we are alive. Rather, the conditional epistemic probability in this case is the degree to which the atheistic single-universe hypothesis *of itself* should lead us to expect the values of the constants of physics to be life-permitting. This means that in assessing the conditional epistemic probability in this and other similar cases, one must exclude contributions to our expectations arising from other information that we have, such as that we are alive. In the case at hand, one way of doing this is by means of the following sort of thought experiment. Imagine a disembodied being with mental capacities and a knowledge of physics similar to that of the most intelligent physicists alive today, except that the being does not know whether the values of the constants of physics allow for embodied, intelligent life to arise. Further, suppose that this disembodied being believed in the atheistic single-universe hypothesis. Then, the degree that being should rationally expect the values of the constants of physics to be life-permitting would be equal to our conditional epistemic probability, since its expectation is solely a result of its belief in the atheistic single-universe hypothesis, not other factors such as its awareness of its own existence.

Given this understanding of the notion of conditional epistemic probability, it is not difficult to see that the conditional epistemic probability of a constant of physics having a life-permitting value under the atheistic single-universe hypothesis will be much smaller than under theism. The reason is simple when we think about our imaginary disembodied being. If such a being were a theist, it would have some reason to believe that the values of the constants would fall into the intelligent life-permitting region. (See the argument in support of premise 1 above.) On the other hand, if the being were a subscriber to the atheistic single-universe hypothesis, it would have no reason to think that the values would be in the intelligent life-permitting range instead of any other part of an appropriately chosen comparison range.[21] Thus, the being has more reason to believe that the constants would fall into the life-permitting region under theism than the atheistic single-universe hypothesis – that is, the epistemic probability under theism is larger than under this atheistic hypothesis. How much larger? That depends on the degree of fine-tuning. Here, I will simply note that it seems obvious that in general the higher the degree of fine-tuning – that is, the smaller the width of the life-permitting range is to the "comparison" range – the greater the surprise under the atheistic single-universe hypothesis, and hence the greater the ratio of the two probabilities. To go beyond these statements and to assign actual probabilities under the atheistic single-universe hypothesis – or to further justify these claims of improbability – would require appealing to the probabilistic principle of indifference, which is beyond the scope of this essay to defend.

Objections to the Argument

As powerful as the fine-tuning argument against the atheistic single-universe hypothesis is, several major objections have been raised to it by both atheists and theists. In this section, we will consider these objections in turn.

Objection 1: more fundamental law objection

One criticism of the fine-tuning argument is that, as far as we know, there could be a more fundamental law under which the constants of physics *must* have the values they do. Thus, given such a law, it is not improbable that the known constants of physics fall within the life-permitting range.

Besides being entirely speculative, the problem with postulating such a law is that it simply moves the improbability of the fine-tuning up one level, to that of the postulated physical law itself. As astrophysicists Bernard Carr and Martin Rees note, "even if all apparently anthropic coincidences could be explained [in terms of some grand unified theory], it would still be remarkable that the relationships dictated by physical theory happened also to be those propitious for life."[22] A similar sort of response can be given to the claim that the fine-tuning is not improbable because it might be *logically necessary* for the constants of physics to have life-permitting values. That is, according to this claim, the constants of physics must have life-permitting values in the same way that 2 + 2 must equal 4, or the interior angles of a triangle must add up to 180 degrees in Euclidian geometry. Like the "more fundamental law" proposal above, however, this postulate simply transfers the improbability up one level: of all the laws and constants of physics that conceivably could have been logically necessary, it seems highly improbable that it would be those that are life-permitting.[23]

Objection 2: other forms of life objection

Another objection people commonly raise against the fine-tuning argument is that, as far as we know, other forms of life could exist even if the constants of physics were different. So, it is claimed, the fine-tuning argument ends up presupposing that all forms of intelligent life must be like us. One answer to this objection is that many cases of fine-tuning do not make this presupposition. If, for example, the cosmological constant were much larger than it is, matter would disperse so rapidly that no planets, and indeed no stars could exist. Without stars, however, there would exist no stable energy sources for complex material systems of any sort to evolve. So, all the fine-tuning argument presupposes in this case is that the evolution of intelligent life requires some stable energy source. This is certainly a very reasonable assumption.

Of course, if the laws and constants of nature were changed enough, other forms of embodied intelligent life might be able to exist of which we cannot even conceive. But this is irrelevant to the fine-tuning argument since the judgment of improbability of fine-tuning under the atheistic single-universe hypothesis only requires that, given our current laws of nature, the life-permitting range for the values of the constants of physics (such as gravity) is small compared with the *surrounding* range of non-life-permitting values.

Objection 3: anthropic principle objection

According to the weak version of the so-called *anthropic principle*, if the laws of nature were not fine-tuned, we would not be here to comment on the fact. Some have argued, therefore, that the fine-tuning is not really *improbable or surprising* at all under atheism, but simply follows from the fact that we exist. The response to this objection is simply to restate the argument in terms of our existence: our existence as embodied, intelligent beings is extremely unlikely under the atheistic single-universe hypothesis (since our existence requires fine-tuning), but not improbable under theism. Then, we simply apply the prime principle of confirmation to draw the conclusion that *our existence* significantly confirms theism over the atheistic single-universe hypothesis.

To further illustrate this response, consider the following "firing-squad" analogy. As John Leslie points out, if fifty sharp shooters all miss me, the response "if they had not missed me I wouldn't be here to consider the fact" is not adequate. Instead, I would naturally conclude that there was some reason why they all missed, such as that they never really intended to kill me. Why would I conclude this? Because my continued existence would be very improbable under the hypothesis that they missed me by chance, but not improbable under the hypothesis that there was some reason why they missed me.[24] Thus, by the prime principle of confirmation, my continued existence, strongly confirms the latter hypothesis.

Objection 4: the "Who designed God?" objection

Perhaps the most common objection that atheists raise to the argument from design, of which the fine-tuning argument is one instance, is that postulating the existence of God does not solve the problem of design, but merely transfers it up one level, to the question of who designed God. In fact, philosopher J. J. C. Smart claims that hypothesizing God as an explanation for the order and complexity of the universe makes us explanatorily worse off:

> If we postulate God in addition to the created universe we increase the complexity of our hypothesis. We have all the complexity of the universe itself, and we have in addition the at least equal complexity of God. (The designer of an artifact must be at least as complex as the designed artifact). . . . If the theist can show the atheist that postulating God actually reduces the complexity of one's total world view, then the atheist should be a theist.[25]

In response, we can first note that even if Smart is correct in claiming that God exhibits enormous internal complexity, it still would be the case that the fine-tuning provides evidence in favor of theism over the atheistic single-universe hypothesis. The reason is that the above argument only relies on comparison of probabilities of fine-tuning under the two different hypotheses, not on whether the new hypothesis reduces the overall complexity of one's worldview. As an analogy, if complex, intricate structures (such as aqueducts and buildings) existed on Mars, one could conclude that they would support the hypothesis that intelligent, extraterrestrial beings existed on Mars in the past, even if such beings are much more complex than the structures to be explained. Second, however, for reasons entirely independent of the argument from design, God has been thought to have little, if any, internal complexity. Indeed, medieval philosophers and theologians often went as far as advocating the doctrine of divine simplicity, according to which God is claimed to be absolutely simple, without any internal complexity. So, atheists who push this objection have a lot of arguing to do to make it stick.

The Many-worlds Hypothesis

In response to the theistic explanation of the fine-tuning, many atheists have offered an alternative explanation, what I will call the *many-universes hypothesis*, but which in the literature goes under a variety of names, such as many-worlds hypothesis, the many-domains hypothesis, the world-ensemble hypothesis, the multi-universe hypothesis, etc. According to this hypothesis, there are a very large – perhaps infinite – number of universes, with the constants of physics varying from universe to universe.[26] Of course, in the vast majority of these universes, the constants of physics would *not* have life-permitting values. Nonetheless, in a small proportion of universes they would, and consequently it is no longer improbable that universes such as ours exist that have life-permitting values for their constants.

Further, usually these universes are thought to be produced by some sort of physical mechanism, which I call a many-universe generator. The universe generator can be thought of as analogous to a lottery ticket generator: just as it would be no surprise that a winning number is eventually produced if enough tickets are generated, it would be no surprise that a universe fine-tuned for life would occur if enough universes are generated.[27]

Most many-universes models are entirely speculative, having little basis in current physics. However, many physicists, such as Steven Weinberg, have proposed a model that does have a reasonable basis in current physics – namely, inflationary cosmology. Inflationary cosmology is a currently widely discussed cosmological theory that attempts to explain the origin of the universe, and which has recently passed some preliminary observational tests. Essentially, it claims that our universe was formed by a small area of pre-space being massively blown up by a hypothesized *inflation* field, in much the same way as a soup bubble would form in an ocean full of soap. In chaotic inflation models – widely considered the most plausible – various points of the pre-space are randomly blown up, forming an enormous number of bubble universes.[28]

In order to get the initial conditions and constants of physics to vary from universe to universe, as they must do if this scenario is going to explain the fine-tuning, there must be a further physical mechanism to cause the variation. Such a mechanism *might* be given by superstring theory, one of the most hotly discussed hypotheses about the fundamental structure of matter, but it is too early to tell. Other leading alternatives to string theory being explored by physicists, such as the currently proposed models for Grand Unified Theories (GUTs), do not appear to allow for enough variation (e.g. they only give a dozen or so different values for the constants, not the enormous number needed to account for the fine-tuning).[29]

Although at present these theories are highly speculative (for example, superstring theory has no experimental evidence in its favor),[30] I do not believe that simply rejecting the many-universe generator hypothesis is an adequate response. Not only does the inflationary/superstring scenario have some plausibility, but God could have created our universe via some many-universe generator, just as God created our planet by the Big Bang – a sort of many-planets generator. A better response is to note that the "many-universe generator" itself, whether that given by chaotic inflationary models or some other type, seems to need to be "well-designed" in order to produce life-sustaining universes. After all, even a mundane item like a bread machine, which only produces loaves of bread instead of universes, must be well designed to produce decent loaves of bread. If this is right, then, to some extent, invoking some sort of many-universe generator as an explanation of the fine-tuning only kicks the issue of design up one level, to the question of who designed the many-universe generator.

For example, the inflationary scenario discussed above only works to produce universes because of the prior existence of the inflation field, and the peculiar nature of the central equation of general relativity, that is Einstein's equation.[31] Without either factor, there would neither be regions of space that inflate nor would those regions have the mass–energy necessary for a universe to exist. If, for example, the universe obeyed Newton's theory of gravity instead of Einstein's, the inflation field would at best simply create a gravitational attraction causing space to contract, not to expand. Moreover, as mentioned above, one needs a special underlying physical theory – such as perhaps superstring theory – that allows for enough variation in the constants of physics among universes.

Further, the inflationary many-universe generator can only produce life-sustaining universes if the right background laws are in place. For example, without the Pauli-exclusion principle, electrons would occupy the lowest atomic orbit and hence complex and varied atoms would be impossible; or, without a universally attractive force between all masses, such as gravity, matter would not be able to form sufficiently large material bodies (such as planets) for life to develop or for long-lived stable energy sources such as stars to exist. The universe generator hypothesis, however, does not explain these background laws.

Finally, I would argue, the many-universes generator hypothesis cannot explain other features of the universe that seem to exhibit apparent design whereas theism can. For example, many physicists, such as Albert Einstein, have observed that the basic laws of physics exhibit an extraordinary degree of beauty, elegance, harmony, and ingenuity. Nobel Prize winning physicist Steven Weinberg, for instance, devotes a whole chapter of his book *Dreams of a Final Theory* to explaining how the criteria of beauty and elegance are commonly used to guide physicists in formulating the right laws.[32] Indeed, one of the most prominent theoretical physicists of this century, Paul Dirac, went so far as to claim that "it is more important to have beauty in one's equations than to have them fit experiment."[33] Now such beauty, elegance, and ingenuity make sense if the universe was designed by God; I would contend, however, that apart from some sort of design hypothesis, there is no reason to expect the fundamental laws to be elegant or beautiful. Thus theism makes more sense of this aspect of the world than atheism, whether that atheism is of the single-universe or many-universe variety.[34]

Conclusion

In this chapter, I argued that the fine-tuning of the cosmos for life provides strong evidence for preferring theism over the atheistic single-universe hypothesis. I then argued that although one can partially explain the fine-tuning of the constants of physics by invoking some sort of many-universes generator, we have good reasons to believe that the many-universe generator itself would need to be well designed, and hence that hypothesizing some sort of many-universes generator only pushes the case for design up one level. The arguments I have offered do not prove the truth of theism, or even show that theism is epistemically warranted or the most plausible position to adopt. To show this would require examining all the evidence both for and against theism, along with looking at all the alternatives to theism. Rather, the arguments in this essay were only intended to show that the fine-tuning of the cosmos offers us significant reasons for preferring theism over atheism (where atheism is understood as not simply the denial of theism but as also including the denial of any sort of intelligence behind the existence or structure of the universe). As with the design argument in general, by itself the fine-tuning argument cannot get one all the way to theism. Other arguments or considerations must be brought into play to do that. Thus, although quite significant, it only constitutes one part of the case for theism, other parts of which are explored in this book.

Notes

1 A full-scale treatment of the fine-tuning argument, and related design arguments, will be presented in a book I am currently working on tentatively entitled *The Well-tempered Universe: God, Fine-tuning, and the Laws of Nature*; [see also my "The Fine-Tuning Argument," in *The Blackwell Companion to Natural Theology*, edited by William Lane Craig and J. P. Moreland (Oxford: Wiley-Blackwell, 2009)]. Some parts of this paper were adapted from previous articles and book chapters: "The Fine-tuning Design Argument" in *Reason for the Hope Within*, ed. Michael Murray (Grand Rapids, MI: Eerdmans, 1999); "The Argument from Design and the Many-worlds Hypothesis," in *Philosophy of Religion: A Reader and Guide*, ed. William Lane Craig (New Brunswick, NJ: Rutgers University Press, 2002); "God, Design, and Fine-tuning" in *God Matters: Readings in the Philosophy of Religion*, eds. Raymond Martin and Christopher Bernard (New York: Longman Press, 2002); "The Evidence for Fine-tuning," in *God and Design*, ed. Neil Manson (London: Routledge, 2003). Work on this topic was made possible by a year-long fellowship from the Pew Foundation, several grants from the Discovery Institute, and a grant from Messiah College.

2 Ninian Smart, *Doctrine and Argument in Indian Philosophy* (London: George Allen and Unwin, 1964), 153–4.

3 William Paley, *Natural Theology* (Boston: Gould and Lincoln, 1852 [1802]).

4 For an up-to-date analysis of the evidence for fine-tuning, with a careful physical analysis of what I consider the six strongest cases, see my "The Evidence for Fine-Tuning," in Manson, *God and Design*.

More detailed treatments of the cases of fine-tuning cited below are presented in that paper, along with more detailed references to the literature. Other useful references are: John Barrow and Frank Tipler, *The Anthropic Cosmological Principle* (Oxford: Oxford University Press, 1986); Paul Davies, *The Accidental Universe* (Cambridge: Cambridge University Press, 1982); John Leslie, *Universes* (London: Routledge, 1989); B. J. Carr and M. J. Rees, "The Anthropic Cosmological Principle and the Structure of the Physical World," *Nature* 278 (12 April 1979), 605–12; Martin Rees, *Just Six Numbers: The Deep Forces that Shape the Universe* (New York: Basic Books, 2000).

5 Barrow and Tipler, *Anthropic Cosmological Principle*, 292–5.

6 Rees, *Just Six Numbers*, 30.

7 For the actual calculations, see Collins, "The Evidence for Fine-tuning."

8 The fine-tuning of the cosmological constant is widely discussed in the literature. See Davies, *The Accidental Universe*, 105–9; Rees, *Just Six Numbers*, 95–102, 154–5. For an accessible, current discussion, see Collins, "The Evidence for Fine-tuning."

9 Leslie, *Universes*, 39–40; Collins, "The Evidence for Fine-tuning."

10 *Disturbing the Universe* (New York: Harper and Row, 1979), 251.

11 Michael Denton, *Nature's Destiny: How the Laws of Biology Reveal Purpose in the Universe* (New York: The Free Press, 1998), 56–7.

12 John Leslie, "How to Draw Conclusions from a Fine-tuned Cosmos," in *Physics, Philosophy and Theology: A Common Quest for Understanding*, ed. Robert Russell *et al.* (Vatican City State: Vatican Observatory Press, 1988), 300.

13 *Disturbing the Universe*, 251.

14 See Rudolph Carnap, *The Logical Foundations of Probability* (Chicago: University of Chicago Press, 1962). For a basic, but somewhat dated, introduction to confirmation theory and the prime principle of confirmation, see Richard Swinburne, *An Introduction to Confirmation Theory* (London: Methuen and Co. Ltd., 1973). For literature specifically casting design arguments as likelihood comparisons, see A. W. F. Edwards, *Likelihood* (Baltimore, MD: Johns Hopkins University Press, 1992).

15 For those familiar with the probability calculus, a precise statement of the degree to which evidence counts in favor of one hypothesis over another can be given in terms of the odds form of Bayes's Theorem: that is, $P(H_1/E)/P(H_2/E) = [P(H_1)/P(H_2)] \times [P(E/H_1)/P(E/H_2)]$. The general version of the principle stated here, however, does not require the applicability or truth of Bayes's theorem. Further, to deal with potential counterexamples arising from our intuitions about when a body of data counts as evidence, it is best to restrict the principle to those cases in which the hypothesis being confirmed is not ad hoc in the sense that there are motivations for believing the hypothesis apart from the evidence in question. This is certainly the case with theism.

16 To be precise, the fine-tuning refers to the joint fact that the life-permitting values of the constants of physics is small compared to some suitably chosen comparison range for each constant *and* the fact that a universe exists that has these values for the constants. It is only this latter fact that we are arguing is highly improbable under the atheistic single-universe hypothesis. Collins, "The Evidence for Fine-tuning," provides some physically natural candidates for a comparison range for each fine-tuned constant. A more philosophically rigorous approach, however, would take the comparison range to be what I call the "epistemically illuminated" region: that is, the region over which we can determine whether a constant is life-permitting. Because all current models of physics have a built in limitation of their domains of validity (specifically with regard to energy scale), in most cases this range turns out very large but finite. See Robin Collins, "The Argument from Fine-tuning," in *The Blackwell Companion to Natural Theology*, ed. William Lane Craig and J. P. Moreland, Oxford: Wiley-Blackwell, 2009, and "How to Rigorously Define Fine-tuning," at www.fine-tuning.org.

17 One might question whether the existence of embodied moral agents is overall a good thing. To respond to this objection, one must address the problem of evil. Elsewhere, I argue that, when both the existence of evil and the fine-tuning data are considered, the balance of evidence significantly favors theism. (See Collins, "Clarifying the Case for Cosmic Design," in *God or Blind Nature? Philosophers Debate the Evidence (2007–2008)*, edited by Paul Draper, at www.infidels.org/library/modern/debates/great-debate.html). Because the existence of embodied moral agents is what is claimed to add to the overall value of reality (not the mere existence of life, such as bacteria), it is the existence of a universe that allows for the existence of such agents that is claimed to be evidence for theism, not merely the existence of life.

18 "Coincidences: Mundane and Cosmological," in *Origin and Evolution of the Universe: Evidence for Design*, ed. John M. Robson (Montreal: McGill-Queen's University Press, 1987), 128–30.

19 "Is There a Case for Christian Theism?" In *Does God Exist? The Great Debate*, ed. J. P. Moreland and Kai Nielsen (Nashville, TN: Thomas Nelson, 1990), 182.

20 For an in-depth discussion of epistemic probability, see Swinburne, *An Introduction to Confirmation Theory*; Ian Hacking, *The Emergence of Probability: A Philosophical Study of Early Ideas About Probability, Induction and Statistical Inference* (Cambridge: Cambridge University Press, 1975); and Alvin Plantinga, *Warrant and Proper Function* (Oxford: Oxford University Press, 1993), chapters 8 and 9.

21 See note 16 for how to determine the comparison range.

22 Carr and Rees, "The Anthropic Cosmological Principle and the Structure of the Physical World," 612.

23 Those with some training in probability theory will want to note that the kind of probability invoked here is what philosophers call *epistemic probability*, which, as we discussed above, is a measure of the rational degree of belief we should have in a proposition. Since our rational degree of belief in a necessary truth can be less than 1, we can sensibly speak of it being improbable for a given law of nature to exist necessarily. For example, we

can speak of an unproven mathematical hypothesis – such as Goldbach's conjecture that every even number greater than 6 is the sum of two odd primes – as being probably true or probably false given our current evidence, even though all mathematical hypotheses are either necessarily true or necessarily false.

24 Leslie, "How To Draw Conclusions from a Fine-Tuned Cosmos," 304.

25 J. J. C. Smart, "Laws of Nature and Cosmic Coincidence," *The Philosophical Quarterly* 35 (1981), 275–6.

26 I define a "universe" as any region of space–time that is disconnected from other regions in such a way that the constants of physics in that region could differ significantly from the other regions. A more thorough discussion of the many-universes hypothesis is presented in my essay, "The Argument from Design and the Many-worlds Hypothesis," in *Philosophy of Religion: A Reader and Guide*, ed. William Lane Craig (Edinburgh: Edinburgh University Press, 2001).

27 Some have proposed what could be called a *metaphysical* many-universe hypothesis, according to which universes are thought to exist on their own without being generated by any physical process. Typically, advocates of this view – such as the late Princeton University philosopher David Lewis (*On the Plurality of Worlds* [New York: Basil Blackwell, 1986]) and University of Pennsylvania astrophysicist Max Tegmark ("Is 'The Theory of Everything' Merely the Ultimate Ensemble Theory?" *Annals of Physics* 270 [1998]: 1–51) – claim that every possible world exists. According to Lewis, for instance, there exists a reality parallel to our own in which I am president of the United States and a reality in which objects can travel faster than the speed of light. Dream up a possible scenario, and it exists in some parallel reality, according to Lewis. Besides being completely speculative (and in many people's mind, outlandish), a major problem with this scenario is that the vast majority of possible universes are ones which are chaotic, just as the vast majority of possible arrangement of letters of a thousand characters would not spell a meaningful pattern. So, the only way that these metaphysical hypotheses can explain the regularity and predictability of our universe, and the fact that it seems to be describable by a few simple laws, is to invoke an "observer selection" effect. That is, Lewis and Tegmark must claim that only universes like ours in this respect could support intelligent life, and hence be observed. The problem with this explanation is that it is much more likely for there to exist local islands of the sort of order necessary for intelligent life than for the entire universe to have such an ordered arrangement. Thus, their hypothesis cannot explain the highly ordered character of the universe as a whole.

Among others, George Schlesinger has raised this objection against Lewis's hypothesis ("Possible Worlds and the Mystery of Existence," *Ratio* 26 [1984], 1–18). This sort of objection was raised against a similar explanation of the high degree of order in our universe offered by the famous physicist Ludwig Boltzman, and has generally been considered fatal to Boltzman's explanation (Paul Davies, *The Physics of Time Asymmetry* [Berkeley, CA: University of California Press, 1974], 103).

28 For an accessible introduction to superstring theory, see Alan Guth, *The Inflationary Universe: The Quest for a New Theory of Cosmic Origins* (New York: Helix Books, 1997).

29 Andrei Linde, *Particle Physics and Inflationary Cosmology*, trans. Marc Damashek (Longhorne, PA: Harwood Academic Publishers, 1990), 3; *Inflation and Quantum Cosmology* (New York: Academic Press, 1990), 6.

30 Michio Kaku, *Introduction to Superstrings and M-Theory*, 2nd ed. (New York: Springer-Verlag, 1999), 17.

31 John Peacock, *Cosmological Physic* (Cambridge: Cambridge University Press, 1999), 24–6.

32 Steven Weinberg, *Dreams of a Final Theory* (New York: Vintage Books, 1992), ch. 6 ("Beautiful Theories").

33 P. A. M. Dirac, "The Evolution of the Physicist's Picture of Nature," *Scientific American* (May 1963), 47.

34 For a further development of this argument for design from the simplicity and beauty of the laws of nature, see part II of my "Argument from Design and the Many-worlds Hypothesis," in Craig, *Philosophy of Religion*.

6

The Argument from the Appearance of Design

J. J. C. Smart

J. J. C. Smart (b. 1920) is Emeritus Professor of Philosophy at Australian National University. In this selection, Smart offers a critical assessment of the design argument, particularly in its more recent forms. He objects that a designer's mind would have to be at least as complex as the universe it designs, and hence if the complexity of the universe requires a designer, then the complexity of the designer's mind should require a designer as well. He also argues that it is ad hoc to suggest that God designed the vast universe primarily to produce consciousness.

6 The Argument from the Appearance of Design

Contemplating the beautiful laws of nature, many physicists have quite understandably taken them as evidence of design, and, as has been noted above, the apparent 'fine tuning' of the fundamental constants of nature has lent additional weight to this way of looking at things. It should be clear of course that this talk of 'fine tuning' is not to be taken as by itself implying a fine tuner: if so the argument would become both quick and circular. This argument from ostensible fine tuning is the currently fashionable form of the traditional 'teleological argument' for the existence of God. Sometimes this is called 'the argument from design' but this, like a too literal construal of 'fine tuning', would be question begging. Years ago Norman Kemp Smith suggested that the argument should be called 'the argument to design'.[1] Equally we could call it 'the argument from apparent design', or for brevity 'the design argument'.

Unlike some other traditional arguments for the existence of God the design argument was never meant to be apodeictic. In contrast the ontological argument was meant to be quite *a priori* and the cosmological argument almost so, requiring only the assertion that something contingently

J. J. C. Smart, "The Argument from the Appearance of Design" from *Atheism and Theism*, second edition, ed. J. J. C. Smart and J. J. Haldane (Oxford: Blackwell Publishing, 1996, 2003), pp. 21–6.

exists. The design argument is best thought of as an argument to the best explanation, such as we use in science and everyday life. The best explanation for the appearance of design in the world is said to be a designer.

David Hume in his great posthumously published book, *Dialogues Concerning Natural Religion*,[2] obviously thought that there were alternative explanations which are as plausible as that of design. However, he retained a sceptical position, rather than a dogmatically atheist one. Philo, who was probably Hume's representative mouthpiece in the *Dialogues*, said that the universe might as well be compared to an organism as to an artefact, and organisms, *prima facie*, are not designed. They 'just grow'. (Antony Flew has commended the childlike acumen and common sense of Topsy in Harriet Beecher Stowe's *Uncle Tom's Cabin*.)[3] Of course we know from the modern synthesis of the theory of evolution by natural selection together with neo-Mendelian genetics that organisms do not need to have been designed. If we appreciate the huge time-scale of evolutionary processes and the opportunistic way in which they work, our minds need not be intellectually overwhelmed, even though perhaps imaginatively at a loss. However, I am here considering the argument from design in a post-Darwinian context, the new teleology not the old, in relation to the great appearance of design in the laws of physics.

As was just remarked, Hume held that the analogy between the universe and an organism was as good as that between the universe and an artefact. There are possibly many other analogies, equally good or bad. Indeed Hume's *Dialogues* concludes with Philo's concession to his main interlocutor Cleanthes that there is *some* analogy between the cause of the universe and a human mind. This is perhaps in one way a very small concession since with enough ingenuity one can find *some* analogy between almost any two things. However, in another way it is a big concession, namely that the universe does have a cause external to itself.

One trouble with the design argument is that there would have to be a 'cosmic blueprint'[4] in the mind of God. This conflicts with the supposition that God could be a perfectly simple being. At first sight, as Hume seems to have thought, the designer of a universe would need to be at least as complex as the universe itself. It is not clear that this need be so. Complex forms of life evolve as a result of physical law together with the randomness characteristic of mutation and natural selection. Even repeated application of a fairly simple set of rules will allow for very complex but in the large regular patterns, as with the Mandelbrot set which is discussed in chaos theory. Does this mean that the designer of the universe could be *less* complex than the universe that is designed? Such a designer need not be the infinite creator God of the great theisms, at least. Nevertheless the designer's mind would have to have within it a structure at least as complex as the conjunction of fundamental laws and initial conditions. So the question surely arises: what designed the designer? The design hypothesis thus seems to raise more questions (and so is less explanatory) than the atheist one. (I shall reconsider this when I come to discuss John Leslie's conception of God as an ethical principle.)[5] Stephen Hawking has famously, or notoriously, looked forward to a simple 'theory of everything', which would give us knowledge of 'the mind of God'.[6] Of course if God's internal structure were that of the fundamental laws and initial conditions this would make Hawking's metaphor of 'the mind of God' appropriate. Nevertheless, the hypothesis of God, at least as designer, would be redundant, and belief in this sort of mind of God would collapse ontologically into atheism.

If the universe needed a designer which was not identical with the structure of the universe (i.e. laws and initial conditions) we would get into a regress, the designer needing a designer, and so on *ad infinitum*. One may be reminded of Fred Hoyle's fictional interstellar 'Black Cloud'.[7] Hoyle believed in an infinite steady state universe. If one asked where the (highly intelligent) black cloud came from the answer was supposed to be that it was designed by another black cloud, and this by yet another black cloud, and so on *ad infinitum*. Whether or not the cosmology was good (the steady state theory is in fact not generally accepted) the biology was unsatisfying. One expects a complex organism, even a 'black cloud', to have evolved from simpler organisms and ultimately from inorganic life.

Artefacts do not evolve in this way, though it is possible that one day self-replicating robots with occasional random variations in their programming may mimic biological evolution. An engineer designing an apparatus may produce a blueprint. Any complexity in the apparatus will then appear in the blueprint. (If we neglect complexity antecedently inherent in the components, such as transistors, which are the original materials for the engineer's design.) Here I am taking 'apparatus' in the sense of 'hardware'. One may be reminded of Descartes' rather obscure dictum that there must be as much reality in the cause as there is in the effect.[8] (Descartes used the principle in an attempted proof of the existence of God, but my reference to it has a different motivation.) There can be a simple recipe for creating complexity, so long as one does not want to predict the particular *type* of complexity. Illuminate a planet rather like the Earth which is about a hundred million miles from a star rather like the Sun for so many hundreds of millions of years and (with luck) complex organisms, perhaps like elephants or mermaids, will eventually evolve. Still, this is not like the case of designing the universe itself – designing the fundamental laws and boundary conditions. For this there would have to be something like a blueprint in the mind of the designer, and it would have to have a complexity equal to that of a complete specification of laws and boundary conditions. Or can a regional order arise spontaneously out of a universal chaos, the chilling thought of a few pages back? But if we accepted this last idea there would be no need to suppose a designer, or anything else for that matter.

Thus, even if it were supposed that the designer determines only the laws of nature (with non-arbitrary constants in them) and a suitable set of initial conditions, then considerations of simplicity and of Ockham's razor suggest that the supposition was an unnecessary one which should be rejected. Any complexity in the laws and initial conditions would be duplicated in the mind of the designer. (Otherwise I could get no purchase on the notion of design that is involved.)

The matter may take on a different complexion if we look at the apparent arbitrariness of the fundamental constants of nature, as we at present understand them, and the way in which the relations between them are peculiarly fitted for the evolution of a universe which contains life, consciousness and intelligence. There is an appearance of a cosmic purpose which may appeal to someone who concedes the points made in the previous paragraph. It is tempting to think that the arbitrary constants must have been chosen by some purposive agent so as to make the universe conducive to the evolution of galaxies, stars, planets and eventually conscious and intelligent life.

At any rate this purposive explanation of the happy values of the constants of nature and of the forms of the fundamental laws could strengthen belief in a deity whose existence was made probable by some other argument. Of course the view that God designed the universe because he wanted conscious beings in it who would be the objects of his love is a not unfamiliar theological one. I have wondered whether this view could have a touch in it of psychocentric hubris. (I say 'psychocentric' not 'anthropocentric' in view of the possibility that conscious and intelligent life is scattered throughout the universe.) Certainly the Judaeo-Christian tradition sets a high value on humans in the scheme of things, and this value should also be ascribed to minds on other worlds, some of which may indeed be far superior to our human ones. Perhaps there is a bit of human vanity involved in the idea that the universe was created in order for there to be consciousness and intelligence. Bertrand Russell held that vanity is a prime motive for religious belief. Even the horrible view that there is a hell to which the infinite God will consign us for our sins may give us an admittedly miserable sense of importance. Belief in highly superior beings on distant planets may be a blow to our hubris. Of course religious belief in the existence of angels may have had a similar effect,[9] even though in the nineteenth century angels came to be thought of as rather pale creatures, whose main talent was playing the harp. (There did not seem to be reports of super-Einsteins among them.)

Still we should not put too high a value on intelligence. Nor should we forget the sufferings of the non-human animals on earth. As Jeremy Bentham said, 'The question is not "Can they reason?" or "Can they talk?" but "Can they suffer?"'.[10] To see suffering is a corrective to disparagement of a possible 'psychocentrism'. It would be inconsistent of me to object to psychocentrism while at the same time taking seriously – as surely one must – the importance of human and animal suffering when I come to discuss the problem of evil.

Even so, the hypothesis that God designed this huge material universe so as to produce consciousness seems to be *ad hoc*. What a long-winded and chancy way of creating conscious beings. Surely an omnipotent being could have created happy spirits directly, rather than a universe which might produce entities like us, or higher than us, as a result of long and chancy evolutionary processes.

The possibility that the universe contains vast numbers of (and if the universe is infinite, which is of course questionable, infinitely many) stars like our sun, with planets suitable for evolution of life and ultimately intelligent beings, raises interesting theological problems, which have, with some exceptions, been neglected by theologians. Christianity appears to be anthropocentric in its doctrine of the incarnation, that God became man. To avoid this anthropocentrism we should envisage the possibility of incarnations on other worlds throughout the universe, a question to which, with a few exceptions, theologians seem to me to have given insufficient attention.

The new teleology, as I have said, is quite different from that associated with such as Paley. It concentrates on the awe and wonder at the beauties of the laws of physics and the starry heavens above. In its most recent form it focuses on the apparent 'fine tuning', the happy coincidences of the value of the fundamental constants. The ontological extravagance of postulating 'a Designer' could be outweighed by its value in explaining these coincidences. However, in assessing the plausibility of such a hypothesis we might also consider the possibility of there being an as yet unknown physical or cosmological hypothesis which might have as its consequence these arbitrary looking values. This would also provide an alternative to the 'many universes' hypothesis.

As a possibly misleading analogy consider the way in which three at first sight unrelated numbers, i the square root of minus one, π the ratio of a Euclidean circle to its diameter and the Euler number e should be related by the simple formula $e^{i\pi} = -1$. Once one knows the proof it becomes almost obvious, though still beautiful. Could the fine tuning one day be deduced from some simple laws, the constants in which do not have an arbitrary appearance? The trouble is that the ratios of the fundamental constants do not look mathematically significant, as do i, e and π. This consideration of a possible theory to explain the fine tuning is more parsimonious than the design hypothesis and than the many universes hypotheses. It partakes, however, of an appearance of wishful thinking, 'something may turn up', to which a theist could rightly object. Furthermore, since i, e and π are all mathematically significant (π can indeed be defined analytically, without geometry) they could be expected, antecedently of the proof, to be related somehow, even if not so beautifully. One trouble with the fine tuning is that the constants involved do not have importance in pure mathematics, and this does support the design hypothesis. There are pros and cons in this part of the debate.

Notes

1 Norman Kemp Smith, 'Is Divine Existence Credible?', *Proceedings of the British Academy*, 17 (1931), 209–34.

2 Norman Kemp Smith (ed.), *Dialogues Concerning Natural Religion* (Edinburgh: Nelson, 1947).

3 Antony Flew, 'Arguments to Design', *Cogito*, 6 (1992), 93–6.

4 Cf. title of book by Paul Davies, *The Cosmic Blueprint* (London: Heinemann, 1987).

5 John Leslie, *Value and Existence* (Oxford: Basil Blackwell, 1979) and John Leslie, *Universes* (London: Routledge, 1989).

6 Stephen W. Hawking, *A Brief History of Time* (London and New York: Bantam, 1988).

7 F. Hoyle, *The Black Cloud* (London: Heinemann, 1957).

8 René Descartes, *Meditation* III.

9 On changes in our beliefs about angels, see Enid Gauldie, 'Flights of Angels', *History Today*, 42, December 1992, 13–20.

10 Jeremy Bentham, *Introduction to the Principles of Morals and Legislation*, ch. 17, section 1, subsection 2, footnote. In Wilfrid Harrison (ed.), *A Fragment on Government and an Introduction to the Principles of Morals and Legislation* (Oxford: Basil Blackwell, 1948).

B

Cosmological Arguments

1

Plato's Cosmological Argument

Plato

Plato (429–347 BC) and his student, Aristotle, are probably the most influential philosophers who ever lived. Plato was a follower of Socrates and later founded a philosophical school in Athens known as the Academy. The following two selections are taken from his late dialogues *Laws* and *Timaeus*. In the first, an unnamed character, referred to simply as the Athenian, argues for the existence of a self-moved mover. In the second, Timaeus argues that the universe was fashioned out of chaos by a divine creator who imitated an eternal unchanging pattern. Although the Platonic position is open to some interpretation, these passages suggest that time had a beginning.

[Laws]

[. . .]

ATHENIAN: Let us take it as understood that the gods have, of course, been invoked in all earnest to assist our proof of their own being, and plunge into the waters of the argument before us with the prayer as a sure guiding rope for our support. If put to the proof, then, on such a subject, the safest course, I take it, is to meet the following questions with the following answers.

Sir – so someone may say – are all things at rest, and nothing in motion? Or is the truth the very reverse? Or are some things in motion, others at rest?

Of course, I shall reply, some are moving and others at rest.

And those which move are moving, just as those which are at rest are resting, in a space of some kind?

Of course.

And some of them, you will grant, do this in a single situation, others in more than one?

Plato, "Laws X" and "Timaeus", trans. A. E. Taylor, *The Collected Dialogues of Plato: Including the Letters*, ed. Edith Hamilton and Huntington Cairns (Princeton, NJ: Princeton University Press, 1961), pp. 1448–51, 1161–3, 1167–8.

When you speak of moving in a single situation, I shall reply, you refer to things characterized by the immobility of their centers, as is the case with the revolution of so-called 'sleeping' circles.

Yes.

And we observe, in the case of this revolution, that such a motion carries round the greatest and the smallest circle together, dividing itself proportionately to lesser and greater, and being itself proportionately less and greater. This, in fact, is what makes it a source of all sorts of marvels, since it supplies greater and smaller circles at once with velocities high or low answering to their sizes – an effect one might have imagined impossible.

Just so.

And by things which move in several situations I suppose you mean those which have a motion of translation and shift at every moment to a fresh place, sometimes having a single point of support, sometimes, in the case of rolling, more than one. In their various encounters one with another, collision with a stationary object disintegrates, while impact upon other moving objects coming from an opposite quarter integrates them into new combinations which are betwixt and between the original components?

Yes, I grant the facts are as you state them.

And further, with integration goes augmentation in bulk, and reduction of bulk with disintegration – provided, that is, the preestablished constitution of the object persists. If it does not, both processes give rise to dissolution.

But the condition under which coming-to-be universally takes place – what is it?

Manifestly 'tis effected whenever its starting point has received increment and so come to its second stage, and from this to the next, and so by three steps acquired perceptibility to percipients. 'Tis ever by such change and transformation of motion that a thing comes to be; it is in veritable being so long as it persists. When it has changed to a different constitution, it is utterly destroyed. Perhaps, my friends, we have now classed and numbered all the types of motion – except, indeed, two.

CLINIAS: And what are those two?

ATHENIAN: Why, the very pair, my good sir, with an eye to which our whole discussion is now in progress.

CLINIAS: I must ask you to be plainer.

ATHENIAN: The discussion began with a view to soul, did it not?

CLINIAS: To be sure, it did.

ATHENIAN: Then let us take for one of our pair the motion which can regularly set other things in movement but not itself. As a second single type in the scheme of motions in general we will take that which can regularly set itself going as well as other things, alike in processes of integration and disintegration, by way of augmentation and its opposite, or by coming into and perishing out of being.

CLINIAS: And so we will.

ATHENIAN: We may proceed, then, to place the type which regularly moves some object other than itself, and is itself induced by such an object, ninth on our list. That which moves itself as well as other things – it finds its place in all doing and all being-done-to, and is veritably called transformation and motion of all that is – this we will reckon as tenth.

CLINIAS: Yes, certainly.

ATHENIAN: Now of these ten motions which should we be most right to pronounce most powerful of all, and most superlatively effective?

CLINIAS: Why, of course, we are bound to say that that which can move itself is infinitely most effective, and all the rest posterior to it.

ATHENIAN: Excellent. Then we should perhaps find one or two mistakes in what has just been said?

CLINIAS: And what mistakes are they?

ATHENIAN: We were wrong, I think, in using that word *tenth*.

CLINIAS: But why wrong?

ATHENIAN: It is demonstrably *first* in procedure, as in power, and the next in order is, as we hold, *second*, though we have just called it – oddly enough – ninth.

CLINIAS: How am I to understand you?

ATHENIAN: Why, thus. When we have one thing making a change in a second, the second, in turn, in a third, and so on – will there ever, in such a series, be a first source of change? Why, how can what is set moving by something other than itself ever be the first of the causes of alteration? The thing is an impossibility. But when something which has set itself moving alters a second thing, this second thing still a third, and the motion is thus passed on in course to thousands and tens of thousands of things, will there be any starting point for the whole movement of all, other than the change in the movement which initiated itself?

CLINIAS: Admirably put, and the position must be conceded.

ATHENIAN: Besides, let us put the point over again in this way, once more answering our own question. Suppose all things were to come together and stand still – as most of the party have the hardihood to affirm. Which of the movements we have specified must be the first to arise in things? Why, of course, that which can move itself; there can be no possible previous origination of change by anything else, since, by hypothesis, change was not previously existent in the system. Consequently, as the source of all motions whatsoever, the first to occur among bodies at rest and the first in rank in moving bodies, the motion which initiates itself we shall pronounce to be necessarily the earliest and mightiest of all changes, while that which is altered by something else and sets something else moving is secondary.

CLINIAS: Unquestionably.

ATHENIAN: Then, now that the discussion has reached this point, we may answer a further question.

CLINIAS: And what question is it?

ATHENIAN: When we see that this motion has shown itself in a thing composed of earth, water, or fire – separately or in combination – how should we describe the character resident in such a thing?

CLINIAS: Am I right in supposing you to ask whether, when the thing moves itself, we speak of it as *alive*?

ATHENIAN: Certainly.

CLINIAS: Alive? Of course it is alive.

[Timaeus]

TIMAEUS: All men, Socrates, who have any degree of right feeling, at the beginning of every enterprise, whether small or great, always call upon God. And we, too, who are going to discourse of the nature of the universe, how created or how existing without creation, if we be not altogether out of our wits, must invoke the aid of gods and goddesses and pray that our words may be above all acceptable to them and in consequence to ourselves. Let this, then, be our invocation of the gods, to which I add an exhortation of myself to speak in such manner as will be most intelligible to you, and will most accord with my own intent.

First then, in my judgment, we must make a distinction and ask, What is that which always is and has no becoming, and what is that which is always becoming and never is? That which is apprehended by intelligence and reason is always in the same state, but that which is conceived by opinion with the help of sensation and without reason is always in a process of becoming and perishing and never really is. Now everything that becomes or is created must of necessity be created by some cause, for without a cause nothing can be created. The work of the creator, whenever he looks to the unchangeable and fashions the form and nature of his work after an unchangeable pattern, must necessarily be made fair and perfect, but when he looks to the created only and uses a created pattern, it is not fair or perfect. Was the heaven then or the world, whether called by this or by any other more appropriate name – assuming the name, I am asking a question which has to be asked at the beginning of an inquiry about anything – was the world, I say, always in existence and without beginning, or created, and had it a beginning? Created, I reply, being visible and tangible and having a body, and therefore sensible, and all sensible things are apprehended by opinion and sense, and are in a process of creation and created. Now that which is created must, as we affirm, of necessity be created by a cause. But the father and maker of all this universe is past finding out, and even if we found him, to tell of him to all men would be impossible. This question, however, we must ask about the world. Which of the patterns had the artificer in view when he made it – the pattern of the unchangeable or of that which is created? If the world be indeed fair and the artificer good, it is manifest that he must have looked to that which is eternal, but if what cannot be said without blasphemy is true, then to the created pattern. Everyone will see that he must have looked to the eternal, for the world is the fairest of creations and he is the best of causes. And having been created in this way, the world has been framed in the likeness of that which is apprehended by reason and mind and is unchangeable, and must therefore of necessity, if this is admitted, be a copy of something. Now it is all-important that the beginning of everything should be according to nature. And in speaking of the copy and the original we may assume that words are akin to the matter which they describe; when they relate to the lasting and permanent and intelligible, they ought to be lasting and unalterable, and, as far as their nature allows, irrefutable and invincible – nothing less. But when they express only the copy or likeness and not the eternal things themselves, they need only be likely and analogous to the former words. As being is to becoming, so is truth to belief. If then, Socrates, amidst the many opinions about the gods and the generation of the universe, we are not able to give notions which are altogether and in every respect exact and consistent with one another, do not be surprised. Enough if we adduce probabilities as likely as any others, for we must remember that I who am the speaker and you who are the judges are only mortal men, and we ought to accept the tale which is probable and inquire no further.

SOCRATES: Excellent, Timaeus, and we will do precisely as you bid us. The prelude is charming and is already accepted by us – may we beg of you to proceed to the strain?

TIMAEUS: Let me tell you then why the creator made this world of generation. He was good, and the good can never have any jealousy of anything. And being free from jealousy, he desired that all things should be as like himself as they could be. This is in the truest sense the origin of creation and of the world, as we shall do well in believing on the testimony of wise men. God desired that all things should be good and nothing bad, so far as this was attainable. Wherefore also finding the whole visible sphere not at rest, but moving in an irregular and disorderly fashion, out of disorder he brought order, considering that this was in every way better than the other. Now the deeds of the best could never be or have been other than the fairest, and the creator, reflecting on the things which are by nature visible, found that no unintelligent creature taken as a whole could ever be fairer than the intelligent taken as a whole, and again that intelligence could not be present in anything which was devoid of soul. For which reason, when he was framing the universe, he put intelligence in soul, and soul in body, that he might be the creator of a work which was by nature fairest and best. On this wise, using the language of probability, we may say that the world came into being – a living creature truly endowed with soul and intelligence by the providence of God.

[. . .]

When the father and creator saw the creature which he had made moving and living, the created image of the eternal gods, he rejoiced, and in his joy determined to make the copy still more like the original, and as this was an eternal living being, he sought to make the universe eternal, so far as might be. Now the nature of the ideal being was everlasting, but to bestow this attribute in its fullness upon a creature was impossible. Wherefore he resolved to have a moving image of eternity, and when he set in order the heaven, he made this image eternal but moving according to number, while eternity itself rests in unity, and this image we call time. For there were no days and nights and months and years before the heaven was created, but when he constructed the heaven he created them also. They are all parts of time, and the past and future are created species of time, which we unconsciously but wrongly transfer to eternal being, for we say that it 'was,' or 'is,' or 'will be,' but the truth is that 'is' alone is properly attributed to it, and that 'was' and 'will be' are only to be spoken of becoming in time, for they are motions, but that which is immovably the same forever cannot become older or younger by time, nor can it be said that it came into being in the past, or has come into being now, or will come into being in the future, nor is it subject at all to any of those states which affect moving and sensible things and of which generation is the cause. These are the forms of time, which imitates eternity and revolves according to a law of number. Moreover, when we say that what has become *is* become and what becomes *is* becoming, and that what will become *is* about to become and that the nonexistent *is* nonexistent – all these are inaccurate modes of expression. But perhaps this whole subject will be more suitably discussed on some other occasion.

Time, then, and the heaven came into being at the same instant in order that, having been created together, if ever there was to be a dissolution of them, they might be dissolved together. It was framed after the pattern of the eternal nature – that it might resemble this as far as was possible, for the pattern exists from eternity, and the created heaven has been and is and will be in all time. Such was the mind and thought of God in the creation of time. The sun and moon and five other stars, which are called the planets, were created by him in order to distinguish and preserve the numbers of time, and when he had made their several bodies, he placed them in the orbits in which the circle of the other was revolving – in seven orbits seven stars. First, there was the moon in the orbit nearest the earth, and the next the sun, in the second orbit above the earth; then came the morning star and the star said to be sacred to Hermes, moving in orbits which have an equal swiftness with the sun, but in an opposite direction, and this is the reason why the sun and Hermes and Lucifer regularly overtake and are overtaken by each other. To enumerate the places which he assigned to the other stars and to give all the reasons why he assigned them, although a secondary matter, would give more trouble than the primary. These things at some future time, when we are at leisure, may have the consideration which they deserve, but not at present.

2

The Eternality of Motion and the Unmoved Mover

Aristotle

Aristotle (384–322 BC) was born in the Greek colony of Stagirus. As a teenager he was sent to Athens to complete his education and for many years he was a student of Plato at the Academy. Leaving Athens, he served in several royal courts and tutored Alexander the Great when the latter was still a young teenager. When he later returned to Athens, he founded his own competing philosophical school known as the Lyceum. In the following selection from his *Physics* Aristotle argues that motion (and hence, time) is without beginning or end and that it must be caused by a mover that is itself unmoved.

Book VIII

1 It remains to consider the following question. Was there ever a becoming of motion before which it had no being, and is it perishing again so as to leave nothing in motion? Or are we to say that it never had any becoming and is not perishing, but always was and always will be? Is it in fact an immortal never-failing property of things that are, a sort of life as it were to all naturally constituted things?

Now the *existence* of motion is asserted by all who have anything to say about nature, because they all concern themselves with the construction of the world and study the question of becoming and perishing, which processes could not come about without the existence of motion. But those who say that there is an infinite number of worlds, some of which are in process of becoming while others are in process of perishing, assert that there is always motion (for these processes of becoming and perishing of the worlds necessarily involve motion), whereas those who hold that there is only one world, whether everlasting or not, make corresponding assumptions in regard to motion. If then it is possible that at any time nothing should be in motion, this must come about in one of two ways: either in the manner described by Anaxagoras, who says that all things were together and at rest for an infinite period of

Aristotle, Book VIII from "Physics" from *The Oxford Aristotle*, ed. D. W. Ross (Oxford: The Clarendon Press, 1941).

time, and that then Mind introduced motion and separated them; or in the manner described by Empedocles, according to whom the universe is alternately in motion and at rest – in motion, when Love is making the one out of many, or Strife is making many out of one, and at rest in the intermediate periods of time – his account being as follows:

> 'Since One hath learned to spring from Manifold,
> And One disjoined makes Manifold arise,
> Thus they Become, nor stable is their life:
> But since their motion must alternate be,
> Thus have they ever Rest upon their round':

for we must suppose that he means by this that they alternate from the one motion to the other. We must consider, then, how this matter stands, for the discovery of the truth about it is of importance, not only for the study of nature, but also for the investigation of the First Principle.

Let us take our start from what we have already[1] laid down in our course on Physics. Motion, we say, is the fulfilment of the movable in so far as it is movable. Each kind of motion, therefore, necessarily involves the presence of the things that are capable of that motion. In fact, even apart from the definition of motion, every one would admit that in each kind of motion it is that which is capable of that motion that is in motion: thus it is that which is capable of alteration that is altered, and that which is capable of local change that is in locomotion: and so there must be something capable of being burned before there can be a process of being burned, and something capable of burning before there can be a process of burning. Moreover, these things also must either have a beginning before which they had no being, or they must be eternal. Now if there was a becoming of every movable thing, it follows that before the motion in question another change or motion must have taken place in which that which was capable of being moved or of causing motion had its becoming. To suppose, on the other hand, that these things were in being throughout all previous time without there being any motion appears unreasonable on a moment's thought, and still more unreasonable, we shall find, on further consideration. For if we are to say that, while there are on the one hand things that are movable, and on the other hand things that are motive, there is a time when there is a first movent and a first moved, and another time when there is no such thing but only something that is at rest, then this thing that is at rest must previously have been in process of change: for there must have been some cause of its rest, rest being the privation of motion. Therefore, before this first change there will be a previous change. For some things cause motion in only one way, while others can produce either of two contrary motions: thus fire causes heating but not cooling, whereas it would seem that knowledge may be directed to two contrary ends while remaining one and the same. Even in the former class, however, there seems to be something similar, for a cold thing in a sense causes heating by turning away and retiring, just as one possessed of knowledge voluntarily makes an error when he uses his knowledge in the reverse way.[2] But at any rate all things that are capable respectively of affecting and being affected, or of causing motion and being moved, are capable of it not under all conditions, but only when they are in a particular condition and approach one another: so it is on the approach of one thing to another that the one causes motion and the other is moved, and when they are present under such conditions as rendered the one motive and the other movable. So if the motion was not always in process, it is clear that they must have been in a condition not such as to render them capable respectively of being moved and of causing motion, and one or other of them must have been in process of change: for in what is relative this is a necessary consequence: e.g. if one thing is double another when before it was not so, one or other of them, if not both, must have been in process of change. It follows, then, that there will be a process of change previous to the first.

(Further, how can there be any 'before' and 'after' without the existence of time? Or how can there be any time without the existence of motion? If, then, time is the number of motion or itself a kind of motion, it follows that, if there is always time, motion must also be eternal. But so far as time is concerned we see that all with one exception are in agreement in saying that it is uncreated: in fact, it is just this that enables Democritus to show that all things cannot have had a becoming: for time, he says, is uncreated.

Plato alone asserts the creation of time, saying[3] that it had a becoming together with the universe, the universe according to him having had a becoming. Now since time cannot exist and is unthinkable apart from the moment, and the moment is a kind of middle-point, uniting as it does in itself both a beginning and an end, a beginning of future time and an end of past time, it follows that there must always be time: for the extremity of the last period of time that we take must be found in some moment, since time contains no point of contact for us except the moment. Therefore, since the moment is both a beginning and an end, there must always be time on both sides of it. But if this is true of time, it is evident that it must also be true of motion, time being a kind of affection of motion.)

The same reasoning will also serve to show the imperishability of motion: just as a becoming of motion would involve, as we saw, the existence of a process of change previous to the first, in the same way a perishing of motion would involve the existence of a process of change subsequent to the last: for when a thing ceases to be moved, it does not therefore at the same time cease to be movable – e.g. the cessation of the process of being burned does not involve the cessation of the capacity of being burned, since a thing may be capable of being burned without being in process of being burned – nor, when a thing ceases to be movent, does it therefore at the same time cease to be motive. Again, the destructive agent will have to be destroyed, after what it destroys has been destroyed, and then that which has the capacity of destroying *it* will have to be destroyed afterwards, (so that there will be a process of change subsequent to the last,) for being destroyed also is a kind of change. If, then, the view which we are criticizing involves these impossible consequences, it is clear that motion is eternal and cannot have existed at one time and not at another: in fact, such a view can hardly be described as anything else than fantastic.

[. . .]

6 Since there must always be motion without intermission, there must necessarily be something, one thing or it may be a plurality, that first imparts motion, and this first movent must be unmoved. Now the question whether each of the things that are unmoved but impart motion[4] is eternal is irrelevant to our present argument: but the following considerations will make it clear that there must necessarily be some such thing, which, while it has the capacity of moving something else, is itself unmoved and exempt from all change, which can affect it neither in an unqualified nor in an accidental sense. Let us suppose, if any one likes, that in the case of certain things it is possible for them at different times to be and not to be, without any process of becoming and perishing (in fact it would seem to be necessary, if a thing that has not parts at one time is and at another time is not, that any such thing should without undergoing any process of change at one time be and at another time not be). And let us further suppose it possible that some principles that are unmoved but capable of imparting motion at one time are and at another time are not. Even so, this cannot be true of *all* such principles, since there must clearly be something that *causes* things that move themselves at one time to be and at another not to be. For, since nothing that has not parts can be in motion, that which moves itself must as a whole have magnitude, though nothing that we have said makes this necessarily true of every movent. So the fact that some things become and others perish, and that this is so continuously, cannot be caused by any one of those things that, though they are unmoved, do not always exist: nor again can it be caused by any of those which move certain particular things, while others move other things. The eternity and continuity of the process cannot be caused either by any one of them singly or by the sum of them because this causal relation must be eternal and necessary, whereas the sum of these movents is infinite and they do not all exist together. It is clear, then, that though there may be countless instances of the perishing of some principles that are unmoved but impart motion, and though many things that move themselves perish and are succeeded by others that come into being, and though one thing that is unmoved moves one thing while another moves another, nevertheless there is something that comprehends them all, and that as something apart from each one of them, and this it is that is the cause of the fact that some things are and others are not and of the continuous process of change: and this causes the

motion of other movents, while they are the causes of the motion of other things. Motion, then, being eternal, the first movent, if there is but one, will be eternal also: if there are more than one, there will be a plurality of such eternal movents. We ought, however, to suppose that there is one rather than many, and a finite rather than an infinite number. When the consequences of either assumption are the same, we should always assume that things are finite rather than infinite in number, since in things constituted by nature that which is finite and that which is better ought, if possible, to be present rather than the reverse: and here it is sufficient to assume only one movent, the first of unmoved things, which being eternal will be the principle of motion to everything else.

[. . .] the first movent must be something that is one and eternal. We have shown[5] that there must always be motion. That being so, motion must also be continuous, because what is always is continuous, whereas what is merely in succession is not continuous. But further, if motion is continuous, it is one: and it is one only if the movent and the moved that constitute it are each of them one, since in the event of a thing's being moved now by one thing and now by another the whole motion will not be continuous but successive.

Notes

1 iii. 1.
2 i.e. by means of his knowledge he can be sure of giving a wrong opinion and thus deceiving some one.
3 Aristotle is thinking of a passage in the *Timaeus* (38 B).
4 e.g. individual souls.
5 Chapter 1.

3

The Kalām Cosmological Argument

Al-Ghazāli

Al-Ghazāli (1055–1111) was an influential philosopher and theologian in the tradition of Sunni Islam. His most famous work, *The Incoherence of the Philosophers*, was a sophisticated critique of certain aspects of Aristotelian philosophy. One Aristotelian doctrine that he rejected was the past eternity of the world. In the following selection from his "Jerusalem Tract" al-Ghazāli argues that an infinite past is impossible. The universe must have begun to exist, and since anything that begins to exist must have a cause, the universe must depend upon a creator. This argument is now known as the Kalām Cosmological Argument.

There is then in the nature of man and in the testimony of the Qur'ān enough evidence to make the necessity of [logical] proof (*burhān*) superfluous. However, we wish to produce such supporting proofs in emulation of the well known among the learned, as follows: It is self-evident to human reason that there must be a cause (*sabab*) for the origination (*ḥudūth*) of anything originated (*ḥādith*). Since the universe is originated it follows that there was a cause for its origination.

Our statement that there must be a cause for the origination of anything originated is clear, since everything originated is related to time which human reason can assume to be early or late. The assignment of the originated to a particular time, which is neither before nor after its own, is necessarily dependent upon the one who so assigns it. Then the proof of our statement that the universe is originated is that material objects in the universe are either at rest or in motion, and since both rest and motion are originated, it follows that what is subject to the originated (*ḥawādith*) is itself originated (*ḥādith*).

There are thus three propositions in this proof. The first is our statement that material

Al-Ghazāli, "The Jerusalem Tract" trans. A. L. Tibawi, *The Islamic Quarterly* 9 (1965): 98–9.

objects are either at rest or in motion. This statement is self-evident and requires no mental reflection for its comprehension. For he who can conceive a material object which is neither at rest nor in motion is both obstinately ignorant and unwilling to follow the path of reason.

The second proposition is our statement that rest and motion are originated. This is proved by their alternate occurrence, as is observable in all material objects, those that can be seen as well as those that cannot. For there can be nothing at rest which human reason does not decide that it is capable of moving, and there can be nothing in motion which human reason does not decide that it is capable of coming to a standstill. Of the two states of rest and motion that which happens to occur at a time (*ṭārī'*) is originated, because it did occur. The previous state [of an object whether at rest or in motion] is also originated, for were its eternity (*qidam*) proved, its non-existence (*'adam*) would be impossible (as we shall show in proving that the Creator, most high and hallowed, is pre-existent and everlasting).

The third proposition is our statement that what is subject to the originated is itself originated. The proof is that were it not so, it would be necessary to assume the existence before everything originated of another so originated, and so on *ad infinitum*, so that unless all these originated things did come and pass, the turn of the one in question would never come. But this is impossible because there is no end to infinity.

Another proof is the revolutions of the celestial spheres. Were these revolutions infinite, their number would be either odd or even, or both odd and even, or neither odd nor even. But it is impossible that the number could be both odd and even, or neither odd nor even, for this would combine the positive with the negative, so that affirmation of the one would involve the negation of the other, and vice versa. Further, it is impossible for the number of revolutions to be even [only], since even becomes odd by the addition of one to it – and [behold] how the infinite stands in need of one! It is also impossible to be odd [only] since odd becomes even by the addition of one – and [behold] how the infinite stands in need of one! Finally, it is impossible for that number to be neither odd nor even, for this would mean that it is finite.

The sum of all this is that the universe is subject to origination (*ḥawādith*), that it is therefore originated (*ḥādith*), that its actual origination (*ḥudūth*) is proved, and that its dependence upon the Creator (*al-muḥdith*) is *ipso facto* (*biḍ-ḍarūrah*) comprehensible.

4

The Existence and Oneness of God

Moses Maimonides

Moses Maimonides (1138–1204) was a medieval Jewish philosopher whose writings had a great influence on many later thinkers including Aquinas and Leibniz. Written in the form of a letter to a student, his *Guide for the Perplexed* is an extensive philosophical attempt to reconcile the deliverances of reason with the Jewish scriptures. In the following selection Maimonides offers two arguments for God's existence. His first argument, which reasons from the existence of temporary beings to the existence of an eternal being, is very similar to the third of Aquinas' famous "five ways." Maimonides' second argument in this selection, which reasons from the constant transitions from potentiality to actuality to the existence of a being that has no potentiality, is similar to Aquinas' first way. (See the following reading selection for Aquinas' arguments.)

From Part II, Chapter 1: On the Existence and Oneness of God

This ([. . .] argument) is taken from the words of Aristotle, though he gives it in a different form. It runs as follows: There is no doubt that many things actually exist, as, e.g., things perceived with the senses. Now there are only three cases conceivable, viz., either all these things are without beginning and without end, or all of them have beginning and end, or some are with and some without beginning and end. The first of these three cases is altogether inadmissible, since we clearly perceive objects which come into existence and are subsequently destroyed. The second case is likewise inadmissible, for if everything had but a temporary existence all things might be destroyed, and that which is enunciated of a whole class of things as possible is necessarily actual. All things must therefore come to an end, and then

Moses Maimonides, From Part II, Chapter 1: "On the Existence and Oneness of God" in *Classics of Philosophy*, vol. 1: *Ancient and Medieval*, ed. Louis P. Pojman (Oxford and New York: Oxford University Press, 1998), pp. 438–9.

nothing would ever be in existence, for there would not exist any being to produce anything. Consequently nothing whatever would exist [if all things were transient]; but as we see things existing, and find ourselves in existence we conclude as follows: – Since there are undoubtedly beings of a temporary existence, there must also be an eternal being that is not subject to destruction, and whose existence is real, not merely possible.

It has been further argued that the existence of this being is necessary, either on account of itself alone or on account of some external force. In the latter case its existence and non-existence would be equally possible, because of its own properties, but its existence would be necessary on account of the external force. That force would then be the being that possesses absolute existence. It is therefore certain that there must be a being which has absolutely independent existence, and is the source of the existence of all things, whether transient or permanent, if, as Aristotle assumes, there is in existence such a thing, which is the effect of an eternal cause, and must therefore itself be eternal. This is a proof the correctness of which is not doubted, disputed, or rejected, except by those who have no knowledge of the method of proof. We further say that the existence of anything that has independent existence is not due to any cause, and that such a being does not include any plurality whatever; consequently it cannot be a body, nor a force residing in a body. It is now clear that there must be a being with absolutely independent existence, a being whose existence cannot be attributed to any external cause, and which does not include different elements; it cannot therefore be corporeal, or a force residing in a corporal object; this being is God.

It can easily be proved that absolutely independent existence cannot be attributed to two beings. For, if that were the case, absolutely independent existence would be a property added to the substance of both; neither of them would be absolutely independent on account of their essence, but only through a certain property, viz., that of this independent existence, which is common to both. It can besides be shown in many ways that independent existence cannot be reconciled with the principle of dualism by any means. It would make no difference, whether we imagine two beings of similar or of different properties. The reason for all this is to be sought in the absolute simplicity and in the utmost perfection of the essence of this being, which is the only member of its species, and does not depend on any cause whatever; this being has therefore nothing in common with other beings.

This ([. . .] argument) is likewise a well-known philosophical argument. We constantly see things passing from a state of potentiality to that of actuality, but in every such case there is for that transition of a thing an agent separate from it. It is likewise clear that the agent has also passed from potentiality to actuality. It has at first been potential, because it could not be actual, owing to some obstacle contained in itself, or on account of the absence of a certain relation between itself and the object of its action; it became an actual agent as soon as that relation was present. Whichever cause be assumed, an agent is again necessary to remove the obstacle or to create the relation. The same can be argued respecting this last-mentioned agent that creates the relation or removes the obstacle. This series of causes cannot go on *ad infinitum*; we must at last arrive at a cause of the transition of an object from the state of potentiality to that of actuality, which is constant, and admits of no potentiality whatever. In the essence of this cause nothing exists potentially, for if its essence included any possibility of existence it would not exist at all; it cannot be corporeal, but it must be spiritual; and the immaterial being that includes no possibility whatever, but exists actually by its own essence, is God. Since He is incorporeal, as has been demonstrated, it follows that He is One.

Even if we were to admit the Eternity of the Universe, we could by any of these methods prove the existence of God; that He is One and incorporeal and that He does not reside as a force in a corporeal object.

The following is likewise a correct method to prove the Incorporeality and the Unity of God: If there were two Gods, they would necessarily have one element in common by virtue of which they were Gods, and another element by which they were distinguished from each other and existed as two Gods, the distinguishing element would either be in both different from the property common to both – in that case both of them would consist of different elements, and neither of them would be the First Cause, or have absolutely independent existence; but their existence would depend on certain causes – or the distinguishing element would only in one of them be different from the element common to both: then that being could not have absolute independence.

The principle laid down in the foregoing must be well understood; it is a high rampart erected round the Law, and able to resist all missiles directed against it. Aristotle, or rather his followers, may perhaps ask us how we know that the Universe has been created; and that other forces than those it has at present were acting in its Creation, since we hold that the properties of the Universe, as it exists at present, prove nothing as regards its creation? We reply, there is no necessity for this according to our plan; for we do not desire to prove the Creation, but only its possibility; and this possibility is not refuted by arguments based on the nature of the present Universe, which we do not dispute. When we have established the admissibility of our theory, we shall then show its superiority. In attempting to prove the inadmissibility of *creation from nothing*, the Aristotelians can therefore not derive any support from the nature of the Universe; they must resort to the notion our mind has formed of God. Their proofs include the three methods which I have mentioned above, and which are based on the notion conceived of God.

5

The First Three Ways

Thomas Aquinas

A brief introduction to Aquinas and his "Five Ways" is given in section II.A.2. The following selection includes the first three of Aquinas' arguments for God's existence, each of them variations of the cosmological argument. The first is an argument from the existence of motion to the existence of an unmoved first mover. The second is an argument from the nature of causes to the existence of a first cause. Finally, the third is an argument from contingent beings (i.e. beings that exist, but might not have existed) to the existence of a necessary being.

The existence of God can be proved in five ways.

The first and more manifest way is the argument from motion. It is certain, and evident to our senses, that in the world some things are in motion. Now whatever is in motion is put in motion by another, for nothing can be in motion except it is in potentiality to that towards which it is in motion; whereas a thing moves inasmuch as it is in act. For motion is nothing else than the reduction of something from potentiality to actuality. But nothing can be reduced from potentiality to actuality, except by something in a state of actuality. Thus that which is actually hot, as fire, makes wood, which is potentially hot, to be actually hot, and thereby moves and changes it. Now it is not possible that the same thing should be at once in actuality and potentiality in the same respect, but only in different respects. For what is actually hot cannot simultaneously be potentially hot; but it is simultaneously potentially cold. It is therefore impossible that in the same respect and in the same way a thing should be both mover and moved, i.e. that it should move itself. Therefore, whatever is in motion must be put in motion by another. If that by which it is put in motion be itself put in motion, then this also must needs be put in motion by another, and that by another again. But this cannot go on to infinity, because then there would be no first mover, and, consequently, no other mover; seeing that

Thomas Aquinas, *Summa Theologica*, trans. Fathers of the English Dominican Province (Benziger Bros, 1947).

subsequent movers move only inasmuch as they are put in motion by the first mover; as the staff moves only because it is put in motion by the hand. Therefore it is necessary to arrive at a first mover, put in motion by no other; and this everyone understands to be God.

The second way is from the nature of the efficient cause. In the world of sense we find there is an order of efficient causes. There is no case known (neither is it, indeed, possible) in which a thing is found to be the efficient cause of itself; for so it would be prior to itself, which is impossible. Now in efficient causes it is not possible to go on to infinity, because in all efficient causes following in order, the first is the cause of the intermediate cause, and the intermediate is the cause of the ultimate cause, whether the intermediate cause be several, or only one. Now to take away the cause is to take away the effect. Therefore, if there be no first cause among efficient causes, there will be no ultimate, nor any intermediate cause. But if in efficient causes it is possible to go on to infinity, there will be no first efficient cause, neither will there be an ultimate effect, nor any intermediate efficient causes; all of which is plainly false. Therefore it is necessary to admit a first efficient cause, to which everyone gives the name of God.

The third way is taken from possibility and necessity, and runs thus. We find in nature things that are possible to be and not to be, since they are found to be generated, and to corrupt, and consequently, they are possible to be and not to be. But it is impossible for these always to exist, for that which is possible not to be at some time is not. Therefore, if everything is possible not to be, then at one time there could have been nothing in existence. Now if this were true, even now there would be nothing in existence, because that which does not exist only begins to exist by something already existing. Therefore, if at one time nothing was in existence, it would have been impossible for anything to have begun to exist; and thus even now nothing would be in existence – which is absurd. Therefore, not all beings are merely possible, but there must exist something the existence of which is necessary. But every necessary thing either has its necessity caused by another, or not. Now it is impossible to go on to infinity in necessary things which have their necessity caused by another, as has been already proved in regard to efficient causes. Therefore we cannot but postulate the existence of some being having of itself its own necessity, and not receiving it from another, but rather causing in others their necessity. This all men speak of as God.

6

The Argument from Dependent Beings

Samuel Clarke

Samuel Clarke (1675–1729) was an important English philosopher and a close associate of Isaac Newton. His *A Demonstration of the Being and Attributes of God*, originally presented in 1704 for the prestigious Boyle Lecture, contains a powerful defense of the cosmological argument. Clarke's argument is based upon the distinction between dependent beings – those that depend upon something else for their existence – and independent beings. He argues that there must be an independent being by reducing to an absurdity the opposing view that all beings are dependent.

I

First, then, it is absolutely and undeniably certain that *something has existed from all eternity*. This is so evident and undeniable a proposition, that no atheist in any age has ever presumed to assert the contrary, and therefore there is little need of being particular in the proof of it. For, since something now is, it is evident that something always was, otherwise the things that now are must have been produced out of nothing, absolutely and without a cause, which is a plain contradiction in terms. For, to say a thing is produced and yet that there is no cause at all for that production, is to say that something is effected when it is effected by nothing, that is, at the same time when it is not effected at all. Whatever exists has a cause, a reason, a ground of its existence, a foundation on which its existence relies, a ground or reason why it does exist rather than not exist, either in the necessity of its own nature (and then it must have been of itself eternal), or in the will of some other being (and then that other being must, at least in the order of nature and causality, have existed before it).

That something, therefore, has really existed from eternity, is one of the most certain and evident truths in the world, acknowledged by all

Samuel Clarke, *A Demonstration of the Being and Attributes of God and Other Writings*, ed. Ezio Vailati (Cambridge: Cambridge University Press, 1998), pp. 8, 10–12.

men and disputed by no one. Yet, as to the manner how it can be, there is nothing in nature more difficult for the mind of men to conceive than this very first plain and self-evident truth. For how anything can have existed eternally, that is, how an eternal duration can be now actually past, is a thing utterly as impossible for our narrow understandings to comprehend, as anything that is not an express contradiction can be imagined to be. And yet, to deny the truth of the proposition, that an eternal duration is now actually past, would be to assert something still far more unintelligible, even a real and express contradiction.

[. . .]

II

There has existed from eternity some one unchangeable and independent being.[1] For, since something must needs have been from eternity, as has been already proved and is granted on all hands, either there has always existed some one unchangeable and independent being from which all other beings that are or ever were in the universe have received their original, or else there has been an infinite succession of changeable and dependent beings produced one from another in an endless progression without any original cause at all. Now this latter supposition is so very absurd that, though all atheism must in its accounts of most things (as shall be shown hereafter) terminate in it, yet I think very few atheists ever were so weak as openly and directly to defend it. For it is plainly impossible and contradictory to itself. I shall not argue against it from the supposed impossibility of infinite succession, barely and absolutely considered in itself, for a reason which shall be mentioned hereafter. But, if we consider such an infinite progression as one entire endless series of dependent beings, it is plain this whole series of beings can have no cause from without of its existence because in it are supposed to be included all things that are, or ever were, in the universe. And it is plain it can have no reason within itself for its existence because no one being in this infinite succession is supposed to be self-existent or necessary (which is the only ground or reason of existence of anything that can be imagined within the thing itself, as will presently more fully appear), but every one dependent on the foregoing. And, where no part is necessary, it is manifest the whole cannot be necessary – absolute necessity of existence not being an extrinsic, relative, and accidental denomination but an inward and essential property of the nature of the thing which so exists.

An infinite succession, therefore, of merely dependent beings without any original independent cause is a series of beings that has neither necessity, nor cause, nor any reason or ground at all of its existence either within itself or from without. That is, it is an express contradiction and impossibility. It is a supposing something to be caused (because it is granted in every one of its stages of succession not to be necessarily and of itself), and yet that, in the whole, it is caused absolutely by nothing, which every man knows is a contradiction to imagine done in time; and because duration in this case makes no difference, it is equally a contradiction to suppose it done from eternity. And consequently there must, on the contrary, of necessity have existed from eternity some one immutable and independent being.

To suppose an infinite succession of changeable and dependent beings produced one from another in an endless progression without any original cause at all is only a driving back from one step to another and, as it were, removing out of sight the question concerning the ground or reason of the existence of things.[2] It is, in reality and in point of argument, the very same supposition as it would be to suppose one continued being of beginningless and endless duration neither self-existent and necessary in itself, nor having its existence founded in any self-existent cause, which is directly absurd and contradictory.

Otherwise, thus: either there has always existed some unchangeable and independent being from which all other beings have received their original, or else there has been an infinite succession of changeable and dependent beings, produced one from another in an endless progression without any original cause at all. According to this latter supposition, there is nothing in the universe self-existent or necessarily existing. And if so, then it was originally equally possible that from eternity there should never have existed anything at all, as that there should from eternity have existed a succession of changeable and dependent beings.

Which being supposed, then, what is it that has from eternity determined such a succession of beings to exist, rather than that from eternity there should never have existed anything at all? Necessity it was not because it was equally possible, in this supposition, that they should not have existed at all. Chance is nothing but a mere word, without any signification. And other being it is supposed there was none, to determine the existence of these. Their existence, therefore, was determined by nothing; neither by any necessity in the nature of the things themselves, because it is supposed that none of them are self-existent, nor by any other being, because no other is supposed to exist. That is to say, of two equally possible things, viz., whether anything or nothing should from eternity have existed, the one is determined rather than the other absolutely by nothing, which is an express contradiction. And consequently, as before, there must on the contrary of necessity have existed from eternity some one immutable and independent being. Which, what it is, remains in the next place to be inquired.

III

That unchangeable and independent being which has existed from eternity, without any external cause of its existence, must be self-existent, that is, necessarily existing. For whatever exists must either have come into being out of nothing, absolutely without cause, or it must have been produced by some external cause, or it must be self-existent. Now to arise out of nothing absolutely without any cause has been already shown to be a plain contradiction. To have been produced by some external cause cannot possibly be true of every thing, but something must have existed eternally and independently, as has likewise been shown already. Which remains, therefore, [is] that that being which has existed independently from eternity must of necessity be self-existent. Now to be self-existent is not to be produced by itself, for that is an express contradiction, but it is (which is the only idea we can frame of self-existence, and without which the word seems to have no signification at all) – it is, I say, to exist by an absolute necessity originally in the nature of the thing itself.

Notes

1 The meaning of this proposition, and all [that] the argument here requires, is that there must needs have always been some independent being, some one at least. To show that there can be no more than one is not the design of this proposition but of the seventh.

2 This matter has been well illustrated by a late able writer: "Suppose a chain hung down out of the heavens from an unknown height, and though every link of it gravitated toward the Earth and what it hung upon was not visible, yet it did not descend but kept its situation; and [suppose] upon this a question should arise, what supported or kept up this chain? Would it be a sufficient answer to say that the first or lowest link hung upon the second, or that next above it, [and] the first, or rather the first and the second together, upon the third, and so on *in infinitum*? For what holds up the *whole*? A chain of ten links would fall down unless something able to bear it hindered. One of twenty, if not staid by something of a yet greater strength, [would fall] in proportion to the increase of weight, and therefore one of infinite links, certainly, if not sustained by something infinitely strong and capable to bear up an infinite weight. And thus it is in a chain of causes and effects tending or, as it were, gravitating towards some end. The last or lowest depends or, as one may say, is suspended upon the cause above it. This again, if it be not the first cause, is suspended as an effect upon something above it, etc. And if they should be infinite, unless agreeably to what has been said there is some cause upon which all hang or depend, they would be but an infinite effect without an efficient. And so to assert there is any such thing would be as great an absurdity as to say that a finite or little weight wants something to sustain it, but an infinite one, or the greatest, does not." W. Wollaston, *The Religion of Nature Delineated* (London, Samuel Palmer, 1724; reprint New York, Garland Publishing Co., 1978), p. 67.

7

Critique of the Cosmological Argument

David Hume

The skeptical Scottish empiricist, David Hume (1711–76), is widely regarded as the greatest philosopher of the English language. The following selection from his *Dialogues Concerning Natural Religion* begins with the orthodox theist, Demea, stating a cosmological argument similar to that defended by Samuel Clarke. In the remainder of the passage, the natural theologian, Cleanthes, and the skeptic, Philo, present several important and influential objections to the argument.

Part IX

But if so many difficulties attend the argument *a posteriori*, said DEMEA; had we not better adhere to that simple and sublime argument *a priori*, which, by offering to us infallible demonstration, cuts off at once all doubt and difficulty? By this argument, too, we may prove the INFINITY of the divine attributes, which, I am afraid, can never be ascertained with certainty from any other topic. For how can an effect, which either is finite, or, for aught we know, may be so; how can such an effect, I say, prove an infinite cause? The unity too of the divine nature, it is very difficult, if not absolutely impossible, to deduce merely from contemplating the works of nature; nor will the uniformity alone of the plan, even were it allowed, give us any assurance of that attribute. Whereas the argument *a priori*. . . .

You seem to reason, DEMEA, interposed CLEANTHES, as if those advantages and conveniences in the abstract argument were full proofs of its solidity. But it is first proper, in my opinion, to determine what argument of this nature you choose to insist on; and we shall afterwards, from itself, better than from its *useful* consequences, endeavour to determine what value we ought to put upon it.

The argument, replied DEMEA, which I would insist on is the common one. Whatever exists must

David Hume, Part IX from *Dialogues Concerning Natural Religion*, ed. Norman Kemp Smith (Indianapolis, IN: Bobbs-Merrill, 1947), pp. 188–92.

have a cause or reason of its existence; it being absolutely impossible for any thing to produce itself, or be the cause of its own existence. In mounting up, therefore, from effects to causes, we must either go on in tracing an infinite succession, without any ultimate cause at all, or must at last have recourse to some ultimate cause, that is *necessarily* existent: Now that the first supposition is absurd may be thus proved. In the infinite chain or succession of causes and effects, each single effect is determined to exist by the power and efficacy of that cause which immediately preceded; but the whole eternal chain or succession, taken together, is not determined or caused by any thing: And yet it is evident that it requires a cause or reason, as much as any particular object, which begins to exist in time. The question is still reasonable, why this particular succession of causes existed from eternity, and not any other succession, or no succession at all. If there be no necessarily existent Being, any supposition, which can be formed, is equally possible; nor is there any more absurdity in nothing's having existed from eternity, than there is in that succession of causes, which constitutes the universe. What was it, then, which determined something to exist rather than nothing, and bestowed being on a particular possibility, exclusive of the rest? *External causes*, there are supposed to be none. *Chance* is a word without a meaning. Was it *nothing*? But that can never produce any thing. We must, therefore, have recourse to a necessarily existent Being, who carries the REASON of his existence in himself; and who cannot be supposed not to exist without an express contradiction. There is consequently such a Being, that is, there is a Deity.

I shall not leave it to PHILO, said CLEANTHES (though I know that starting objections is his chief delight), to point out the weakness of this metaphysical reasoning. It seems to me so obviously ill-grounded, and at the same time of so little consequence to the cause of true piety and religion, that I shall myself venture to show the fallacy of it.

I shall begin with observing, that there is an evident absurdity in pretending to demonstrate a matter of fact, or to prove it by any arguments *a priori*. Nothing is demonstrable, unless the contrary implies a contradiction. Nothing, that is distinctly conceivable, implies a contradiction. Whatever we conceive as existent, we can also conceive as non-existent. There is no Being, therefore, whose non-existence implies a contradiction. Consequently there is no Being, whose existence is demonstrable. I propose this argument as entirely decisive, and am willing to rest the whole controversy upon it.

It is pretended that the Deity is a necessarily existent Being; and this necessity of his existence is attempted to be explained by asserting, that, if we knew his whole essence or nature, we should perceive it to be as impossible for him not to exist as for twice two not to be four. But it is evident, that this can never happen, while our faculties remain the same as at present. It will still be possible for us, at any time, to conceive the non-existence of what we formerly conceived to exist; nor can the mind ever lie under a necessity of supposing any object to remain always in being; in the same manner as we lie under a necessity of always conceiving twice two to be four. The words, therefore, *necessary existence*, have no meaning; or, which is the same thing, none that is consistent.

But farther; why may not the material universe be the necessarily existent Being, according to this pretended explication of necessity? We dare not affirm that we know all the qualities of matter; and for aught we can determine, it may contain some qualities, which, were they known, would make its non-existence appear as great a contradiction as that twice two is five. I find only one argument employed to prove, that the material world is not the necessarily existent Being; and this argument is derived from the contingency both of the matter and the form of the world. "Any particle of matter," it is said,[1] "may be *conceived* to be annihilated; and any form may be *conceived* to be altered. Such an annihilation or alteration, therefore, is not impossible." But it seems a great partiality not to perceive, that the same argument extends equally to the Deity, so far as we have any conception of him; and that the mind can at least imagine[2] him to be non-existent, or his attributes to be altered. It must be some unknown, inconceivable qualities, which can make his non-existence appear impossible, or his attributes unalterable: And no reason can be assigned, why these qualities may not belong to matter. As they are altogether unknown and inconceivable, they can never be proved incompatible with it.

Add to this, that in tracing an eternal succession of objects, it seems absurd to inquire for a general cause or first Author. How can any thing, that exists from eternity, have a cause, since that relation implies a priority in time and a beginning of existence?

In such a chain too, or succession of objects, each part is caused by that which preceded it, and causes that which succeeds it. Where then is the difficulty? But the WHOLE, you say, wants a cause. I answer, that the uniting of these parts into a whole, like the uniting of several distinct counties into one kingdom, or several distinct members into one body, is performed merely by an arbitrary act of the mind, and has no influence on the nature of things. Did I show you the particular causes of each individual in a collection of twenty particles of matter, I should think it very unreasonable, should you afterwards ask me, what was the cause of the whole twenty. This is sufficiently explained in explaining the cause of the parts.

[Though the reasonings, which you have urged, CLEANTHES, may well excuse me, said PHILO, from starting any farther difficulties; yet I cannot forbear insisting still upon another topic.[3] It is observed by arithmeticians, that the products of 9 compose always either 9 or some lesser product of 9; if you add together all the characters, of which any of the former products is composed. Thus, of 18, 27, 36, which are products of 9, you make 9 by adding 1 to 8, 2 to 7, 3 to 6. Thus 369 is a product also of 9; and if you add 3, 6, and 9, you make 18, a lesser product of 9.[4] To a superficial observer, so wonderful a regularity may be admired as the effect either of chance or design; but a skilful algebraist immediately concludes it to be the work of necessity, and demonstrates, that it must for ever result from the nature of these numbers. Is it not probable, I ask, that the whole œconomy of the universe is conducted by a like necessity, though no human algebra can furnish a key which solves the difficulty? And instead of admiring the order of natural beings, may it not happen, that, could we penetrate into the intimate nature of bodies, we should clearly see why it was absolutely impossible, they could ever admit of any other disposition? So dangerous is it to introduce this idea of necessity into the present question! And so naturally does it afford an inference directly opposite to the religious hypothesis!

But dropping all these abstractions, continued PHILO; and confining ourselves to more familiar topics; I shall venture to add an observation,][5] that the argument *a priori* has seldom been found very convincing, except to people of a metaphysical head, who have accustomed themselves to abstract reasoning, and who finding from mathematics, that the understanding frequently leads to truth, through obscurity, and contrary to first appearances, have transferred the same habit of thinking to subjects where it ought not to have place. Other people, even of good sense and the best inclined to religion, feel always some deficiency in such arguments, though they are not perhaps able to explain distinctly where it lies. A certain proof, that men ever did, and ever will, derive their religion from other sources than from this species of reasoning.

Notes

[Notes in square brackets were added by the editor of the 1947 edition.]

1 Dr Clarke.

2 [imagine *for* conceive]

3 [Passage in brackets is written on the reverse side of the last sheet of Part IX with marks to indicate point of insertion. The whole passage is scored out by Hume and then the instruction added, also by Hume, on the margin: "Print this passage."]

4 *République des Lettres*, Août, 1685.

5 [*The original opening of this concluding paragraph runs*: I shall venture, said PHILO, to add to these reasonings of CLEANTHES an observation.]

C

Ontological Arguments

1

Anselm's Ontological Argument

Anselm

St Anselm (1033–1109) was for many years the abbot of the Benedictine abbey at Bec, Normandy and in 1093 was made the Archbishop of Canterbury. Although he wrote on a broad range of theological and philosophical topics, he is most famous for the ontological argument contained in his *Proslogium*. Anselm argues that if one reflects on the idea of God – that is, the idea of "a being than which nothing greater can be conceived" – one can see that this being must exist. An important objection to Anselm's argument was offered by one of his contemporaries, a monk named Gaunilo. Although Gaunilo's criticisms are frequently reprinted with Anselm's argument, we have omitted them here because they are quoted and discussed in selection II.C.4 below.

Chapter II

Truly there is a God, although the fool hath said in his heart, There is no God.

And so, Lord, do thou, who dost give understanding to faith, give me, so far as thou knowest it to be profitable, to understand that thou art as we believe; and that thou art that which we believe. And, indeed, we believe that thou art a being than which nothing greater can be conceived. Or is there no such nature, since the fool hath said in his heart, there is no God? (Psalms xiv. 1). But, at any rate, this very fool, when he hears of this being of which I speak – a being than which nothing greater can be conceived – understands what he hears, and what he understands is in his understanding; although he does not understand it to exist.

St Anselm, Chapters II, III, IV, XV from *Proslogium; Monologium; An Appendix in Behalf of the Fool By Gaunilon; and Cur Deus Homo*, trans. Sidney Norton Deane (La Salle, IL: Open Court, 1951), pp. 7–10, 22.

For, it is one thing for an object to be in the understanding, and another to understand that the object exists. When a painter first conceives of what he will afterwards perform, he has it in his understanding, but he does not yet understand it to be, because he has not yet performed it. But after he has made the painting, he both has it in his understanding, and he understands that it exists, because he has made it.

Hence, even the fool is convinced that something exists in the understanding, at least, than which nothing greater can be conceived. For, when he hears of this, he understands it. And whatever is understood, exists in the understanding. And assuredly that, than which nothing greater can be conceived, cannot exist in the understanding alone. For, suppose it exists in the understanding alone: then it can be conceived to exist in reality; which is greater.

Therefore, if that, than which nothing greater can be conceived, exists in the understanding alone, the very being, than which nothing greater can be conceived, is one, than which a greater can be conceived. But obviously this is impossible. Hence, there is no doubt that there exists a being, than which nothing greater can be conceived, and it exists both in the understanding and in reality.

Chapter III

God cannot be conceived not to exist. – God is that, than which nothing greater can be conceived. – That which can be conceived not to exist is not God.

And it assuredly exists so truly, that it cannot be conceived not to exist. For, it is possible to conceive of a being which cannot be conceived not to exist; and this is greater than one which can be conceived not to exist. Hence, if that, than which nothing greater can be conceived, can be conceived not to exist, it is not that, than which nothing greater can be conceived. But this is an irreconcilable contradiction. There is, then, so truly a being than which nothing greater can be conceived to exist, that it cannot even be conceived not to exist; and this being thou art, O Lord, our God.

So truly, therefore, dost thou exist, O Lord, my God, that thou canst not be conceived not to exist; and rightly. For, if a mind could conceive of a being better than thee, the creature would rise above the Creator; and this is most absurd. And, indeed, whatever else there is, except thee alone, can be conceived not to exist. To thee alone, therefore, it belongs to exist more truly than all other beings, and hence in a higher degree than all others. For, whatever else exists does not exist so truly, and hence in a less degree it belongs to it to exist. Why, then, has the fool said in his heart, there is no God (Psalms xiv. 1), since it is so evident, to a rational mind, that thou dost exist in the highest degree of all? Why, except that he is dull and a fool?

Chapter IV

How the fool has said in his heart what cannot be conceived. – A thing may be conceived in two ways: (1) when the word signifying it is conceived; (2) when the thing itself is understood. As far as the word goes, God can be conceived not to exist; in reality he cannot.

But how has the fool said in his heart what he could not conceive; or how is it that he could not conceive what he said in his heart? since it is the same to say in the heart, and to conceive.

But, if really, nay, since really, he both conceived, because he said in his heart; and did not say in his heart, because he could not conceive; there is more than one way in which a thing is said in the heart or conceived. For, in one sense, an object is conceived, when the word signifying it is conceived; and in another, when the very entity, which the object is, is understood.

In the former sense, then, God can be conceived not to exist; but in the latter, not at all. For no one who understands what fire and water are can conceive fire to be water, in accordance with the nature of the facts themselves, although this is possible according to the words. So, then, no one who understands what God is can conceive that God does not exist; although he says these words in his heart, either without any, or with some foreign, signification. For, God is that than which a greater cannot be conceived. And he who thoroughly understands this, assuredly understands that this being so truly exists, that not even in concept can it be non-existent. Therefore, he who understands that God so exists, cannot conceive that he does not exist.

I thank thee, gracious Lord, I thank thee; because what I formerly believed by thy bounty, I now so understand by thine illumination, that if I were unwilling to believe that thou dost exist, I should not be able not to understand this to be true.

[...]

Chapter XV

He is greater than can be conceived.

Therefore, O Lord, thou art not only that than which a greater cannot be conceived, but thou art a being greater than can be conceived. For, since it can be conceived that there is such a being, if thou art not this very being, a greater than thou can be conceived. But this is impossible.

2

Descartes's Ontological Argument

René Descartes

A prolific scientist, mathematician, and philosopher, René Descartes (1596–1650) is often credited as the father of modern philosophy. Prior to publishing his most important work, *Meditations on First Philosophy*, Descartes sent copies to other scholars seeking their comments and criticisms. Their objections, along with Descartes's answers, were appended to the text under the title "Objections and Replies." The following selection includes Descartes's version of the ontological argument from "Meditation V" along with objections by a Dutch theologian named Johannes Caterus and Descartes's response.

But now, if just because I can draw the idea of something from my thought, it follows that all which I know clearly and distinctly as pertaining to this object does really belong to it, may I not derive from this an argument demonstrating the existence of God? It is certain that I no less find the idea of God, that is to say, the idea of a supremely perfect Being, in me, than that of any figure or number whatever it is; and I do not know any less clearly and distinctly that an [actual and] eternal existence pertains to this nature than I know that all that which I am able to demonstrate of some figure or number truly pertains to the nature of this figure or number, and therefore, although all that I concluded in the preceding Meditations were found to be false, the existence of God would pass with me as at least as certain as I have ever held the truths of mathematics (which concern only numbers and figures) to be.

This indeed is not at first manifest, since it would seem to present some appearance of being a sophism. For being accustomed in all other things to make a distinction between existence and essence, I easily persuade myself that the existence can be separated from the essence of God, and that we can thus conceive God as not actually

René Descartes, "Meditation V, Objections I, Reply to Objections I" from *The Philosophical Works of Descartes*, trans. Elizabeth S. Haldane and G. R. T. Ross, vol. 1 (Cambridge: Cambridge University Press, 1968), pp. 180–3, vol. 2 (Cambridge: Cambridge University Press, 1967), pp. 6–8, 18–22.

existing. But, nevertheless, when I think of it with more attention, I clearly see that existence can no more be separated from the essence of God than can its having its three angles equal to two right angles be separated from the essence of a [rectilinear] triangle, or the idea of a mountain from the idea of a valley; and so there is not any less repugnance to our conceiving a God (that is, a Being supremely perfect) to whom existence is lacking (that is to say, to whom a certain perfection is lacking), than to conceive of a mountain which has no valley.

But although I cannot really conceive of a God without existence any more than a mountain without a valley, still from the fact that I conceive of a mountain with a valley, it does not follow that there is such a mountain in the world; similarly although I conceive of God as possessing existence, it would seem that it does not follow that there is a God which exists; for my thought does not impose any necessity upon things, and just as I may imagine a winged horse, although no horse with wings exists, so I could perhaps attribute existence to God, although no God existed.

But a sophism is concealed in this objection; for from the fact that I cannot conceive a mountain without a valley, it does not follow that there is any mountain or any valley in existence, but only that the mountain and the valley, whether they exist or do not exist, cannot in any way be separated one from the other. While from the fact that I cannot conceive God without existence, it follows that existence is inseparable from Him, and hence that He really exists; not that my thought can bring this to pass, or impose any necessity on things, but, on the contrary, because the necessity which lies in the thing itself, i.e. the necessity of the existence of God determines me to think in this way. For it is not within my power to think of God without existence (that is of a supremely perfect Being devoid of a supreme perfection) though it is in my power to imagine a horse either with wings or without wings.

And we must not here object that it is in truth necessary for me to assert that God exists after having presupposed that He possesses every sort of perfection, since existence is one of these, but that as a matter of fact my original supposition was not necessary, just as it is not necessary to consider that all quadrilateral figures can be inscribed in the circle; for supposing I thought this, I should be constrained to admit that the rhombus might be inscribed in the circle since it is a quadrilateral figure, which, however, is manifestly false. [We must not, I say, make any such allegations because] although it is not necessary that I should at any time entertain the notion of God, nevertheless whenever it happens that I think of a first and a sovereign Being, and, so to speak, derive the idea of Him from the storehouse of my mind, it is necessary that I should attribute to Him every sort of perfection, although I do not get so far as to enumerate them all, or to apply my mind to each one in particular. And this necessity suffices to make me conclude (after having recognised that existence is a perfection) that this first and sovereign Being really exists; just as though it is not necessary for me ever to imagine any triangle, yet, whenever I wish to consider a rectilinear figure composed only of three angles, it is absolutely essential that I should attribute to it all those properties which serve to bring about the conclusion that its three angles are not greater than two right angles, even although I may not then be considering this point in particular. But when I consider which figures are capable of being inscribed in the circle, it is in no wise necessary that I should think that all quadrilateral figures are of this number; on the contrary, I cannot even pretend that this is the case, so long as I do not desire to accept anything which I cannot conceive clearly and distinctly. And in consequence there is a great difference between the false suppositions such as this, and the true ideas born within me, the first and principal of which is that of God. For really I discern in many ways that this idea is not something factitious, and depending solely on my thought, but that it is the image of a true and immutable nature; first of all, because I cannot conceive anything but God himself to whose essence existence [necessarily] pertains; in the second place because it is not possible for me to conceive two or more Gods in this same position; and, granted that there is one such God who now exists, I see clearly that it is necessary that He should have existed from all eternity, and that He must exist eternally; and finally, because I know an infinitude of other properties in God, none of which I can either diminish or change.

For the rest, whatever proof or argument I avail myself of, we must always return to the point that it is only those things which we conceive clearly and distinctly that have the power of persuading me entirely. And although amongst the matters which I conceive of in this way, some indeed are manifestly obvious to all, while others only manifest themselves to those who consider them closely and examine them attentively; still, after they have once been discovered, the latter are not esteemed as any less certain than the former. For example, in the case of every right-angled triangle, although it does not so manifestly appear that the square of the base is equal to the squares of the two other sides as that this base is opposite to the greatest angle; still, when this has once been apprehended, we are just as certain of its truth as of the truth of the other. And as regards God, if my mind were not pre-occupied with prejudices, and if my thought did not find itself on all hands diverted by the continual pressure of sensible things, there would be nothing which I could know more immediately and more easily than Him. For is there anything more manifest than that there is a God, that is to say, a Supreme Being, to whose essence alone existence pertains?[1]

[. . .]

Caterus's Critique

Let us then concede that someone has a clear and distinct idea of a highest and most perfect being; what further conclusion do you draw? That this infinite being exists, and that so certainly that the existence of God should have certitude, at least for my mind, as great as that which mathematical truths have hitherto enjoyed. Hence there is no less[2] contradiction in thinking of a God (that is of a being of the highest perfection) who lacks existence (a particular perfection) than in thinking of a hill which is not relative to a valley. *The whole dispute hinges on this; he who gives way here must admit defeat. Since my opponent is the stronger combatant I should like for a little to avoid engaging him at close quarters in order that, fated as I am to lose, I may yet postpone what I cannot avoid.*

Firstly then, though reason only and not authority is the arbiter in our discussion, yet, lest I be judged impertinent in gainsaying the contentions of such an illustrious philosopher, let me quote you what St Thomas says; it is an objection he urges against his own doctrine: – As soon as the intellect grasps the signification of the name God, it knows that God exists; for the meaning of His name is an object nothing greater than which can be conceived.[3] Now that which exists in fact as well as in the mind is greater than what exists in the mind alone. Hence, since the name 'God' being understood, God consequently exists in the mind, it follows that He really exists. *This argument formally expressed becomes – God is a being, a greater than which cannot be conceived; but that, a greater than which cannot be conceived, includes its existence; hence God by His very name or notion includes His existence, and as a direct consequence can neither be conceived as being, nor can be, devoid of existence. But now, kindly tell me is not this M. Descartes' own proof? St Thomas defines God thus:* – A being than which nothing greater can be conceived. *M. Descartes calls Him a being of extreme perfection; certainly nothing greater than this can be conceived. St Thomas goes on to argue* – That than which nothing greater can be conceived includes its existence; *otherwise a greater than it could be conceived, namely that which is conceived to contain its existence. Now does not M. Descartes bring up the same proposition as minor premise? 'God is the most perfect being, the most perfect being comprises within itself its existence, for otherwise it would not have the highest perfection.' St Thomas's conclusion is:* – Therefore since *God*, His name being understood, exists in the understanding, He exists in reality. *That is to say, owing to the very fact that in the very concept of the essence of an entity, nothing greater than which can be conceived, existence is involved, it follows that that very entity exists. M. Descartes draws the same inference:* – Yet, *says he*, owing to the fact that we cannot think of God as not existing, it follows that His existence is inseparable from Him, and hence that He in truth exists.[4] *But now let St Thomas reply both to himself and to M. Descartes.* Granted that everyone and anyone knows that by the name God is understood that which has been asserted, to wit, a being than which nothing greater can be thought, yet it does not follow that he understands that the thing signified by the name exists in reality, but only that it exists in the apprehension of the understanding. Nor can it be proved that it really exists, unless it be conceded that something really exists than which nothing greater can be thought – a proposition not granted by those who deny the existence of God. *This furnishes me with my reply, which will be brief – Though it be conceded that an entity of the highest perfection implies its existence by its very name, yet it does not follow that that very existence is anything actual in the real world, but merely that the concept of existence is inseparably united with the concept of highest being. Hence you cannot infer that the existence of God is anything actual, unless you assume that that highest being actually exists; for then it will actually contain all its perfections, together with this perfection of real existence.*

Pardon me, gentlemen, if now I plead fatigue; but here is something in a lighter vein. This complex existent Lion *includes both lion and the mode existence; and includes them essentially, for if you take away either it will not be the same complex. But now, has not God from all eternity had clear and distinct knowledge of this composite object? Does not also the idea of this composite, in so far as it is composite, involve both its elements essentially? That is to say, does not its existence flow from the essence of this composite,* existent Lion? *Yet, I affirm, the distinct cognition of it which God possesses, that which he has from all eternity does not constrain either part of the complex to exist, unless you assume that the complex does exist; for then, indeed, it will imply all its essential perfections and hence also that of actual existence. Therefore, also, even though you have a distinct knowledge of a highest being, and granted that a being of supreme perfection includes existence in the concept of its essence, yet it does not follow that its existence is anything actual, unless on the hypothesis that that highest being does exist; for then indeed along with its other perfections it will in actuality include this, its existence, also. Hence the proof of the existence of this highest being must be drawn from some other source.*

[...]

Descartes's Reply

My opponent here compares one of my arguments with another of St Thomas's, so, as it were to force me to show which of the two has the more force. This I seem to be able to do with a good enough grace, because neither did St Thomas use that argument as his own, nor does he draw the same conclusion from it; consequently there is nothing here in which I am at variance with the Angelic Doctor. He himself asked whether the existence of God is in itself[5] known to man, i.e. whether it is obvious to each single individual; he denies this, and I along with him.[6] Now the argument to which he puts himself in opposition can be thus propounded. *When we understand what it is the word God signifies, we understand that it is that, than which nothing greater can be conceived; but to exist in reality as well as in the mind is greater than to exist in the mind alone; hence, when the meaning of the word God is understood, it is understood that God exists in fact as well as in the understanding.* Here there is a manifest error in the form of the argument; for the only conclusion to be drawn is – *hence, when we understand what the word God means, we understand that it means that God exists in fact as well as in the mind*: but because a word implies something, that is no reason for this being true. My argument, however, was of the following kind – That which we clearly and distinctly understand to belong to the true and immutable nature of anything, its essence, or form, can be truly affirmed of that thing; but, after we have with sufficient accuracy investigated the nature of God, we clearly and distinctly understand that to exist belongs to His true and immutable nature; therefore we can with truth affirm of God that He exists. This is at least a legitimate conclusion. But besides this the major premise cannot be denied, because it was previously[7] conceded that *whatever we clearly and distinctly perceive is true.* The minor alone remains, and in it there is, I confess, no little difficulty. This is firstly because we are so much accustomed to distinguish existence from essence in the case of other things, that we do not with sufficient readiness notice how existence belongs to the essence of God in a greater degree than in the case of other things. Further, because we do not distinguish that which belongs to the true and immutable nature of a thing from that which we by a mental fiction assign to it, even if we do fairly clearly perceive that existence belongs to God's essence, we nevertheless do not conclude that God exists, because we do not know whether His essence is true and immutable or only a fiction we invent.

But, in order to remove the first part of this difficulty we must distinguish between possible and necessary existence, and note that in the concept or idea of everything that is clearly and distinctly conceived, possible existence is contained, but necessary existence never, except in the idea of God alone. For I am sure that all who diligently attend to this diversity between the idea of God and that of all other things, will perceive that, even though other things are indeed conceived[8] only as existing, yet it does not thence follow that they do exist, but only that they may exist, because we do not conceive that there is any necessity for actual existence being conjoined with their other properties; but, because we understand that actual existence is necessarily and at all times linked to God's other attributes, it follows certainly that God exists.

Further, to clear away the rest of the difficulty, we must observe that those ideas which do not contain a true and immutable nature, but only a fictitious one due to a mental synthesis, can be by that same mind analysed, not merely by abstraction (or restriction of the thought)[9] but by a clear and distinct mental operation; hence it will be clear that those things which the understanding cannot so analyse have not been put together by it. For example, when I think of a winged horse, or of a lion actually existing, or of a triangle inscribed in a square, I easily understand that I can on the contrary think of a horse without wings, of a lion as not existing and of a triangle apart from a square, and so forth, and that hence these things have no true and immutable nature. But if I think of the triangle or the square (I pass by for the present the lion and the horse, because their natures are not wholly intelligible to us), then certainly whatever I recognise as being contained in the idea of the triangle, as that its angles are equal to right, etc., I shall truly affirm of the triangle; and similarly I shall affirm of the square whatsoever I find in the idea of it. For though I can think of the triangle, though stripping from it the equality of its angles to two right, yet I cannot deny that attribute of it by any clear and distinct mental operation, i.e. when I myself rightly understand what I say. Besides, if I think of a triangle inscribed in a square, not meaning to ascribe to the square that which belongs to the triangle alone, or to assign to the triangle the properties of the square, but for the purpose only of examining that which arises from the conjunction of the two, the nature of that composite will be not less true and immutable than that of the square or triangle alone; and hence it will be right to affirm that the square cannot be less than double the inscribed triangle, together with the similar properties which belong to the nature of this composite figure.

But if I think that existence is contained in the idea of a body of the highest perfection, because it is a greater perfection to exist in reality as well as in the mind than to exist in the intellect alone, I cannot then conclude that this utterly perfect body exists, but merely that it may exist; for I can well enough recognize that that idea has been put together by my mind uniting together all corporeal perfections, and that existence does not arise out of its other corporeal perfections, because it (existence) can be equally well affirmed and denied of them. Nay, because when I examine this idea of body I see in it no force by means of which it may produce or preserve itself, I rightly conclude that necessary existence, which alone is here in question, does not belong to the nature of a body, howsoever perfect it may be, any more than it belongs to the nature of a mountain not to have a valley, or any more than it pertains to the nature of a triangle to have its angles greater than two right angles. But now, if we ask not about a body but about a thing (of whatever sort this thing may turn out to be) which has all those perfections which can exist together, whether existence must be included in the number of these perfections we shall at first be in doubt, because our mind, being finite, and not accustomed to consider them unless separately, will perchance not at first see how necessary is the bond between them. But yet if we attentively consider whether existence is congruous with a being of the highest perfection, and what sort of existence is so, we shall be able clearly and distinctly to perceive in the first place that possible existence is at least predicable of it, as it is of all other things of which we have a distinct idea, even of those things which are composed by a fiction of the mind. Further, because we cannot think of God's existence as being possible, without at the same time, and by taking heed of His immeasurable power, acknowledging that He can exist by His own might, we hence conclude that He really exists and has existed from all eternity; for the light of nature makes it most plain that what can exist by its own power always exists. And thus we shall understand that necessary existence is comprised in the idea of a being of the highest power, not by any intellectual fiction, but because it belongs to the true and immutable nature of that being to exist. We shall at the same time easily perceive that that all-powerful being must comprise in himself all the other perfections that are contained in the idea of God, and hence these by their own nature and without any mental fiction are conjoined together and exist in God.

Notes

1 'In the idea of whom alone necessary or eternal existence is comprised.' French version.
2 'More,' Latin version.
3 Significari.
4 Cf. Med. v. Vol. 1. p. 181 sub fin.
5 So as not to need proof, F. V.
6 F. V. merito, L. V.
7 Significari, L. V.
8 intelligamus.
9 This phrase occurs only in the French version.

3

Kant's Critique of the Three Traditional Proofs

Immanuel Kant

Immanuel Kant (1724–1804) spent his entire life in Königsberg, Germany, lecturing in his later years at the same university he once attended as a student. Although Kant was raised in Lutheran Pietism and remained a deeply religious man throughout his life, his criticisms of the traditional theistic arguments are among the most influential ever written. In the following selection from his *Critique of Pure Reason* Kant argues that the teleological argument (which he refers to as the "physico-theological proof") depends upon the cosmological argument, and that the cosmological argument depends upon the ontological argument. He then argues that the ontological argument (and hence, natural theology in general) fails to demonstrate God's existence.

Chapter III, Section 4

The Impossibility of an Ontological Proof of the Existence of God

It is evident, from what has been said, that the concept of an absolutely necessary being is a concept of pure reason, that is, a mere idea the objective reality of which is very far from being proved by the fact that reason requires it. For the idea instructs us only in regard to a certain unattainable completeness, and so serves rather to limit the understanding than to extend it to new objects. But we are here faced by what is indeed strange and perplexing, namely, that while the inference from a given existence in general to some absolutely necessary being seems to be both imperative and legitimate, all those conditions under which alone the understanding can form a concept of such a necessity are so many obstacles in the way of our doing so.

Immanuel Kant, Chapter III, Sections 4 and 6 from *Critique of Pure Reason*, trans. Norman Kemp Smith (New York: St Martin's, 1965), pp. 500–7, 518–24.

In all ages men have spoken of an *absolutely necessary* being, and in so doing have endeavoured, not so much to understand whether and how a thing of this kind allows even of being thought, but rather to prove its existence. There is, of course, no difficulty in giving a verbal definition of the concept, namely, that it is something the non-existence of which is impossible. But this yields no insight into the conditions which make it necessary[1] to regard the non-existence of a thing as absolutely unthinkable. It is precisely these conditions that we desire to know, in order that we may determine whether or not, in resorting to this concept, we are thinking anything at all. The expedient of removing all those conditions which the understanding indispensably requires in order to regard something as necessary, simply through the introduction of the word *unconditioned*, is very far from sufficing to show whether I am still thinking anything in the concept of the unconditionally necessary, or perhaps rather nothing at all.

Nay more, this concept, at first ventured upon blindly, and now become so completely familiar, has been supposed to have its meaning exhibited in a number of examples; and on this account all further enquiry into its intelligibility has seemed to be quite needless. Thus the fact that every geometrical proposition, as, for instance, that a triangle has three angles, is absolutely necessary, has been taken as justifying us in speaking of an object which lies entirely outside the sphere of our understanding as if we understood perfectly what it is that we intend to convey by the concept of that object.

All the alleged examples are, without exception, taken from *judgments*, not from *things* and their existence. But the unconditioned necessity of judgments is not the same as an absolute necessity of things. The absolute necessity of the judgment is only a conditioned necessity of the thing, or of the predicate in the judgment. The above proposition does not declare that three angles are absolutely necessary, but that, under the condition that there is a triangle (that is, that a triangle is given), three angles will necessarily be found in it. So great, indeed, is the deluding influence exercised by this logical necessity that, by the simple device of forming an *a priori* concept of a thing in such a manner as to include existence within the scope of its meaning, we have supposed ourselves to have justified the conclusion that because existence necessarily belongs to the object of this concept – always under the condition that we posit the thing as given (as existing) – we are also of necessity, in accordance with the law of identity, required to posit the existence of its object, and that this being is therefore itself absolutely necessary – and this, to repeat, for the reason that the existence of this being has already been thought in a concept which is assumed arbitrarily and on condition that we posit its object.

If, in an identical proposition, I reject the predicate while retaining the subject, contradiction results; and I therefore say that the former belongs necessarily to the latter. But if we reject subject and predicate alike, there is no contradiction; for nothing is then left that can be contradicted. To posit a triangle, and yet to reject its three angles, is self-contradictory; but there is no contradiction in rejecting the triangle together with its three angles. The same holds true of the concept of an absolutely necessary being. If its existence is rejected, we reject the thing itself with all its predicates; and no question of contradiction can then arise. There is nothing outside it that would then be contradicted, since the necessity of the thing is not supposed to be derived from anything external; nor is there anything internal that would be contradicted, since in rejecting the thing itself we have at the same time rejected all its internal properties. 'God is omnipotent' is a necessary judgment. The omnipotence cannot be rejected if we posit a Deity, that is, an infinite being; for the two concepts are identical. But if we say, 'There is no God', neither the omnipotence nor any other of its predicates is given; they are one and all rejected together with the subject, and there is therefore not the least contradiction in such a judgment.

We have thus seen that if the predicate of a judgment is rejected together with the subject, no internal contradiction can result, and that this holds no matter what the predicate may be. The only way of evading this conclusion is to argue that there are subjects which cannot be removed, and must always remain. That, however, would only be another way of saying that there are absolutely necessary subjects; and that is the very assumption which I have called in question, and the possibility of which the above argument professes to establish. For I cannot form the least concept of a thing which, should it be rejected with all its predicates, leaves behind a contradiction; and in the absence of contradiction I have, through pure *a priori* concepts alone, no criterion of impossibility.

Notwithstanding all these general considerations, in which every one must concur, we may be challenged with a case which is brought forward as proof that in actual fact the contrary holds, namely, that there is one concept, and indeed only one, in reference to which the not-being or rejection of its object is in itself contradictory, namely, the concept of the *ens realissimum*. It is declared that it possesses all reality, and that we are justified in assuming that such a being is possible (the fact that a concept does not contradict itself by no means proves the possibility of its object: but the contrary assertion I am for the moment willing to allow).[2] Now [the argument proceeds] 'all reality' includes existence; existence is therefore contained in the concept of a thing that is possible. If, then, this thing is rejected, the internal possibility of the thing is rejected – which is self-contradictory.

My answer is as follows. There is already a contradiction in introducing the concept of existence – no matter under what title it may be disguised – into the concept of a thing which we profess to be thinking solely in reference to its possibility. If that be allowed as legitimate, a seeming victory has been won; but in actual fact nothing at all is said: the assertion is a mere tautology. We must ask: Is the proposition that *this or that thing* (which, whatever it may be, is allowed as possible) *exists*, an analytic or a synthetic proposition? If it is analytic, the assertion of the existence of the thing adds nothing to the thought of the thing; but in that case either the thought, which is in us, is the thing itself, or we have pre-supposed an existence as belonging to the realm of the possible, and have then, on that pretext, inferred its existence from its internal possibility – which is nothing but a miserable tautology. The word 'reality', which in the concept of the thing sounds other than the word 'existence' in the concept of the predicate, is of no avail in meeting this objection. For if all positing (no matter what it may be that is posited) is entitled reality, the thing with all its predicates is already posited in the concept of the subject, and is assumed as actual; and in the predicate this is merely repeated. But if, on the other hand, we admit, as every reasonable person must, that all existential propositions are synthetic, how can we profess to maintain that the predicate of existence cannot be rejected without contradiction? This is a feature which is found only in analytic propositions, and is indeed precisely what constitutes their analytic character.

I should have hoped to put an end to these idle and fruitless disputations in a direct manner, by an accurate determination of the concept of existence, had I not found that the illusion which is caused by the confusion of a logical with a real predicate (that is, with a predicate which determines a thing) is almost beyond correction. Anything we please can be made to serve as a logical predicate; the subject can even be predicated of itself; for logic abstracts from all content. But a *determining* predicate is a predicate which is added to the concept of the subject and enlarges it. Consequently, it must not be already contained in the concept.

'*Being*' is obviously not a real predicate; that is, it is not a concept of something which could[3] be added to the concept of a thing. It is merely the positing of a thing, or of certain determinations, as existing in themselves. Logically, it is merely the copula of a judgment. The proposition, 'God is omnipotent', contains two concepts, each of which has its object – God and omnipotence. The small word 'is' adds no new predicate, but only serves to posit the predicate *in its relation* to the subject. If, now, we take the subject (God) with all its predicates (among which is omnipotence), and say 'God is', or 'There is a God', we attach no new predicate to the concept of God, but only posit the subject in itself with all its predicates, and indeed posit it as being an *object* that stands in relation to my *concept*. The content of both must be one and the same; nothing can have been added to the concept, which expresses merely what is possible, by my thinking its object (through the expression 'it is') as given absolutely. Otherwise stated, the real contains no more than the merely possible. A hundred real thalers do not contain the least coin more than a hundred possible thalers. For as the latter signify the concept, and the former the object and the positing of the object, should the former contain more than the latter, my concept would not, in that case, express the whole object, and would not therefore be an adequate concept of it. My financial position is, however, affected very differently by a hundred real thalers than it is by the mere concept of them (that is, of their possibility). For the object, as it actually exists, is not analytically contained in my concept, but is added to my concept (which is a determination of my state) synthetically; and yet the conceived hundred thalers are not themselves in the least increased through thus acquiring existence outside my concept.

By whatever and by however many predicates we may think a thing – even if we completely determine it – we do not make the least addition to the thing when we further declare that this thing *is*. Otherwise, it would not be exactly the same thing that exists, but something more than we had thought in the concept; and we could not, therefore, say that the exact object of my concept exists. If we think in a thing every feature of reality except one,[4] the missing reality is not added by my saying that this defective thing exists. On the contrary, it exists with the same defect with which I have thought it, since otherwise what exists would be something different from what I thought. When, therefore, I think a being as the supreme reality, without any defect, the question still remains whether it exists or not. For though, in my concept, nothing may be lacking of the possible real content of a thing in general, something is still lacking in its relation to my whole state of thought, namely, [in so far as I am unable to assert] that knowledge of this object is also possible *a posteriori*. And here we find the source of our present difficulty. Were we dealing with an object of the senses, we could not confound the existence of the thing with the mere concept of it. For through the concept the object is thought only as conforming to the *universal conditions* of possible empirical knowledge in general, whereas through its existence it is thought as belonging to the context of experience as a whole. In being thus connected with the *content* of experience as a whole, the concept of the object is not, however, in the least enlarged; all that has happened is that our thought has thereby obtained an additional possible perception. It is not, therefore, surprising that, if we attempt to think existence through the pure category alone, we cannot specify a single mark distinguishing it from mere possibility.

Whatever, therefore, and however much, our concept of an object may contain, we must go outside it, if we are to ascribe existence to the object. In the case of objects of the senses, this takes place through their connection with some one of our perceptions, in accordance with empirical laws. But in dealing with objects of pure thought, we have no means whatsoever of knowing their existence, since it would have to be known in a completely *a priori* manner. Our consciousness of all existence (whether immediately through perception, or mediately through inferences which connect something with perception) belongs exclusively to the unity of experience; any [alleged] existence outside this field, while not indeed such as we can declare to be absolutely impossible, is of the nature of an assumption which we can never be in a position to justify.

The concept of a supreme being is in many respects a very useful idea; but just because it is a mere idea, it is altogether incapable, by itself alone, of enlarging our knowledge in regard to what exists. It is not even competent to enlighten us as to the *possibility* of any existence beyond that which is known in and through experience.[5] The analytic criterion of possibility, as consisting in the principle that bare positives (realities) give rise to no contradiction, cannot be denied to it. But since the realities are not given to us in their specific characters; since even if they were, we should still[6] not be in a position to pass judgment; since the criterion of the possibility of synthetic knowledge is never to be looked for save in experience, to which the object of an idea cannot belong,[7] the connection of all real properties in a thing is a synthesis, the possibility of which we are unable to determine *a priori*. And thus the celebrated Leibniz is far from having succeeded in what he plumed himself on achieving – the comprehension *a priori* of the possibility of this sublime ideal being.

The attempt to establish the existence of a supreme being by means of the famous ontological argument of Descartes is therefore merely so much labour and effort lost; we can no more extend our stock of [theoretical] insight by mere ideas, than a merchant can better his position by adding a few noughts to his cash account.

[...]

Chapter III, Section 6

The Impossibility of the Physico-theological Proof

If, then, neither the concept of things in general nor the experience of any *existence in general* can supply what is required, it remains only to try whether a *determinate experience*, the experience of the things of the present world, and the constitution and order of these, does not provide the basis of a proof which may help us to attain to an assured conviction of a supreme being. Such proof we propose to entitle the *physico-theological*. Should this attempt also fail, it must follow that no satisfactory proof of the existence of a being corresponding to our transcendental idea can be possible by pure speculative reason.

In view of what has already been said, it is evident that we can count upon a quite easy and conclusive answer to this enquiry. For how can any experience ever be adequate to an idea? The peculiar nature of the latter consists just in the fact that no experience can ever be equal to it. The transcendental idea of a necessary and all-sufficient original being is so overwhelmingly great, so high above everything empirical, the latter being always conditioned, that it leaves us at a loss, partly because we can never find in experience material sufficient to satisfy such a concept, and partly because it is always in the sphere of the conditioned that we carry out our search, seeking there ever vainly for the unconditioned – no law of any empirical synthesis giving us an example of any such unconditioned or providing the least guidance in its pursuit.

If the supreme being should itself stand in this chain of conditions, it would be a member of the series, and like the lower members which it precedes, would call for further enquiry as to the still higher ground from which it follows. If, on the other hand, we propose to separate it from the chain, and to conceive it as a purely intelligible being, existing apart from the series of natural causes, by what bridge can reason contrive to pass over to it? For all laws governing the transition from effects to causes, all synthesis and extension of our knowledge, refer to nothing but possible experience, and therefore solely to objects of the sensible world, and apart from them can have no meaning whatsoever.

This world presents to us so immeasurable a stage of variety, order, purposiveness, and beauty, as displayed alike in its infinite extent and in the unlimited divisibility of its parts, that even with such knowledge as our weak understanding can acquire of it, we are brought face to face with so many marvels immeasurably great, that all speech loses its force, all numbers their power to measure, our thoughts themselves all definiteness, and that our judgment of the whole resolves itself into an amazement which is speechless, and only the more eloquent on that account. Everywhere we see a chain of effects and causes, of ends and means, a regularity in origination and dissolution. Nothing has of itself come into the condition in which we find it to exist, but always points to something else as its cause, while this in turn commits us to repetition of the same enquiry. The whole universe must thus sink into the abyss of nothingness, unless, over and above this infinite chain of contingencies, we assume something to support it – something which is original and independently self-subsistent, and which as the cause of the origin of the universe secures also at the same time its continuance. What magnitude are we to ascribe to this supreme cause – admitting that it is supreme in respect of all things in the world? We are not acquainted with the whole content of the world, still less do we know how to estimate its magnitude by comparison with all that is possible. But since we cannot, as regards causality, dispense with an ultimate and supreme being,[8] what is there to prevent us ascribing to it a degree of perfection that sets it *above everything else that is possible*? This we can easily do – though only through the slender outline of an abstract concept – by representing this being to ourselves as combining in itself all possible perfection, as in a single substance. This concept is in conformity with the demand of our reason for parsimony of principles; it is free from self-contradiction, and is never decisively contradicted by any experience; and it is likewise of such a character that it contributes to the extension of the employment of reason within experience, through the guidance which it yields in the discovery of order and purposiveness.

This proof always deserves to be mentioned with respect. It is the oldest, the clearest, and the most accordant with the common reason of mankind. It enlivens the study of nature, just as it itself derives its existence and gains ever new vigour from that source. It suggests ends and purposes, where our observation would not have detected them by itself, and extends our knowledge of nature by means of the guiding-concept of a special unity, the principle of which is outside nature. This knowledge again reacts on its cause, namely, upon the idea which has led to it, and so strengthens the belief in a supreme Author [of nature] that the belief acquires the force of an irresistible conviction.

It would therefore not only be uncomforting but utterly vain to attempt to diminish in any way the authority of this argument. Reason, constantly upheld by this ever-increasing evidence, which, though empirical, is yet so powerful, cannot be so depressed through doubts suggested by subtle and abstruse speculation, that it is not at once aroused from the indecision of all melancholy reflection, as from a dream, by one glance at the wonders of nature and the majesty of the universe – ascending from height to height up to the all-highest, from the conditioned to its conditions, up to the supreme and unconditioned Author [of all conditioned being].

But although we have nothing to bring against the rationality and utility of this procedure, but have rather to commend and to further it, we still cannot approve the claims, which this mode of argument would fain advance, to apodeictic certainty and to an assent founded on no special favour or support from other quarters. It cannot hurt the good cause, if the dogmatic language of the overweening sophist be toned down to the more moderate and humble requirements of a belief adequate to quieten our doubts, though not to command unconditional submission. I therefore maintain that the physico-theological proof can never by itself establish the existence of a supreme being, but must always fall back upon the ontological argument to make good its deficiency. It only serves as an introduction to the ontological argument; and the latter therefore contains (in so far as a speculative proof is possible at all) *the one possible ground of proof* with which human reason can never dispense.[9]

The chief points of the physico-theological proof are as follows: (1) In the world we everywhere find clear signs of an order in accordance with a determinate purpose, carried out with great wisdom; and this in a universe which is indescribably varied in content and unlimited in extent. (2) This purposive order is quite alien to the things of the world, and only belongs to them contingently; that is to say, the diverse things could not of themselves have co-operated, by so great a combination of diverse means, to the fulfilment of determinate final purposes, had they not been chosen and designed for these purposes by an ordering rational principle in conformity with underlying ideas. (3) There exists, therefore, a sublime and wise cause (or more than one), which must be the cause of the world not merely as a blindly working all-powerful nature, by *fecundity*, but as intelligence, through *freedom*. (4) The unity of this cause may be inferred from the unity of the reciprocal relations existing between the parts of the world, as members of an artfully arranged structure – inferred with certainty in so far as our observation suffices for its verification, and beyond these limits with probability, in accordance with the principles of analogy.

We need not here criticise natural reason too strictly in regard to its conclusion from the analogy between certain natural products and what our human art produces when we do violence to nature, and constrain it to proceed not according to its own ends but in conformity with ours – appealing to the similarity of these particular natural products with houses, ships, watches. Nor need we here question its conclusion that there lies at the basis of nature a causality similar to that responsible for artificial products, namely, an understanding and a will; and that the inner possibility of a self-acting[10] nature (which is what makes all art, and even, it may be, reason itself, possible) is therefore derived from another, though superhuman, art – a mode of reasoning which could not perhaps withstand a searching transcendental criticism. But at any rate we must admit that, if we are to specify a cause at all, we cannot here proceed more securely than by analogy with those purposive productions of which alone the cause and mode of action are fully known to us. Reason could never be justified in abandoning the causality which it knows for grounds of explanation which are obscure, of which it does not have any knowledge, and which are incapable of proof.

On this method of argument, the purposiveness and harmonious adaptation of so much in nature can suffice to prove the contingency of the form merely, not of the matter, that is, not of the substance in the world. To prove the latter we should have to demonstrate that the things in the world would not of themselves be capable of such order and harmony, in accordance with universal laws, if they were not *in their substance* the product of supreme wisdom. But to prove this we should require quite other grounds of proof than those which are derived from the analogy with human art. The utmost, therefore, that the argument can prove is an *architect* of the world who is always very much hampered by the adaptability of the material in which he works, not a *creator* of the world to whose idea everything is subject. This, however, is altogether inadequate to the lofty purpose which we have before our eyes, namely, the proof of an all-sufficient primordial being. To prove the contingency of matter itself, we should have to resort to a transcendental argument, and this is precisely what we have here set out to avoid.

The inference, therefore, is that the order and purposiveness everywhere observable throughout the world may be regarded as a completely contingent arrangement, and that we may argue to the existence of a cause *proportioned* to it. But the concept of this cause must enable us to know something quite *determinate* about it, and can therefore be no other than the concept of a being who possesses all might, wisdom, etc., in a word, all the perfection which is proper to an all-sufficient being. For the predicates – 'very great', 'astounding', 'immeasurable' in power and excellence – give no determinate concept at all, and do not really tell us what the thing is in itself. They are only relative representations of the magnitude of the object, which the observer, in contemplating the world, compares with himself and with his capacity of comprehension, and which are equally terms of eulogy whether we be magnifying the object or be depreciating the observing subject in relation to that object. Where we are concerned with the magnitude (of the perfection) of a thing, there is no determinate concept except that which comprehends all possible perfection; and in that concept only the allness (*omnitudo*) of the reality is completely determined.

Now no one, I trust, will be so bold as to profess that he comprehends the relation of the magnitude of the world as he has observed it (alike as regards both extent and content) to omnipotence, of the world order to supreme wisdom, of the world unity to the absolute unity of its Author, etc. Physico-theology is therefore unable to give any determinate concept of the supreme cause of the world, and cannot therefore serve as the foundation of a theology which is itself in turn to form the basis of religion.

To advance to absolute totality by the empirical road is utterly impossible. None the less this is what is attempted in the physico-theological proof. What, then, are the means which have been adopted to bridge this wide abyss?

The physico-theological argument can indeed lead us to the point of admiring the greatness, wisdom, power, etc., of the Author of the world, but can take us no further. Accordingly, we then abandon the argument from empirical grounds of proof, and fall back upon the contingency which, in the first steps of the argument, we had inferred from the order and purposiveness of the world. With this contingency as our sole premiss, we then advance, by means of transcendental concepts alone, to the existence of an absolutely necessary being, and [as a final step] from the concept of the absolute necessity of the first cause to the completely determinate or determinable concept of that necessary being, namely, to the concept of an all-embracing reality. Thus the physico-theological proof, failing in its undertaking, has in face of this difficulty suddenly fallen back upon the cosmological proof; and since the latter is only a disguised ontological proof, it has really achieved its purpose by pure reason alone – although at the start it disclaimed all kinship with pure reason and professed to establish its conclusions on convincing evidence derived from experience.

Those who propound the physico-theological argument have therefore no ground for being so contemptuous in their attitude to the transcendental mode of proof, posing as clear-sighted students of nature, and complacently looking down upon that proof as the artificial product of obscure speculative refinements. For were they willing to scrutinise their own procedure, they would find that, after advancing some considerable way on the solid ground of nature and experience, and finding themselves just as far distant as ever from the object which discloses itself to their reason, they suddenly leave this ground, and pass over into the realm of mere possibilities, where they hope upon the wings of ideas to draw near to the object – the object that has refused itself to all their *empirical* enquiries. For after this tremendous leap, when they have, as they think, found firm ground, they extend their concept – the *determinate* concept, into the possession of which they have now come, they know not how – over the whole sphere of creation. And the ideal, [which this reasoning thus involves, and] which is entirely a product of pure reason, they then elucidate by reference to experience, though inadequately enough, and in a manner far below the dignity of its object; and throughout they persist in refusing to admit that they have arrived at this knowledge or hypothesis by a road quite other than that of experience.

Thus the physico-theological proof of the existence of an original or supreme being rests upon the cosmological proof, and the cosmological upon the ontological. And since, besides these three, there is no other path open to speculative reason, the ontological proof from pure concepts of reason is the only possible one, if indeed any proof of a proposition so far exalted above all empirical employment of the understanding is possible at all.

Notes

[Notes in square brackets were added by the editor of the *Critique*]

1 [Reading, with Noiré, *notwendig* for *unmöglich.*]
2 A concept is always possible if it is not self-contradictory. This is the logical criterion of possibility, and by it the object of the concept is distinguishable from the *nihil negativum.* But it may none the less be an empty concept, unless the objective reality of the synthesis through which the concept is generated has been specifically proved; and such proof, as we have shown above, rests on principles of possible experience, and not on the principle of analysis (the law of contradiction). This is a warning against arguing directly from the logical possibility of concepts to the real possibility of things.
3 [Reading, with Erdmann, *könnte* for *könne.*]
4 [*alle Realität ausser einer.*]
5 [*in Ansehung der Möglichkeit eines Mehreren.*]
6 [Reading, with B, *da aber* for *weil aber.*]
7 [Reading, with Wille, *stattfände* for *stattfinde.*]
8 [*ein äusserstes und oberstes Wesen.*]
9 [*vorbeigehen.*]
10 [*freiwirkenden.*]

4

The Ontological Argument

Alvin Plantinga

Alvin Plantinga (b. 1932) is John A. O'Brien Professor of Philosophy at the University of Notre Dame and one of the leading contributors to the contemporary philosophy of religion. In the following selection from *God, Freedom, and Evil* (1974) Plantinga discusses several important versions of the ontological argument (including Anselm's) as well as some of the most important criticisms of the argument (including Gaunilo's and Kant's). In the end, Plantinga argues that there is a sound version of the argument, although he is doubtful that its premises will be accepted by anyone who does not already accept theism.

The third theistic argument I wish to discuss is the famous "ontological argument" first formulated by Anselm of Canterbury in the eleventh century. This argument for the existence of God has fascinated philosophers ever since Anselm first stated it. Few people, I should think, have been brought to belief in God by means of this argument; nor has it played much of a role in strengthening and confirming religious faith. At first sight Anselm's argument is remarkably unconvincing if not downright irritating; it looks too much like a parlor puzzle or word magic. And yet nearly every major philosopher from the time of Anselm to the present has had something to say about it; this argument has a long and illustrious line of defenders extending to the present. Indeed, the last few years have seen a remarkable flurry of interest in it among philosophers. What accounts for its fascination? Not, I think, its religious significance, although that can be underrated. Perhaps there are two reasons for it. First, many of the most knotty and difficult problems in philosophy meet in this argument. Is existence a property? Are existential propositions

Alvin Plantinga, "The Ontological Argument" from *God, Freedom and Evil* (Grand Rapids, MI: William B. Eerdmans, 1977), pp. 85–112.

– propositions of the form *x exists* – ever necessarily true? Are existential propositions about what they seem to be about? Are there, in any respectable sense of "are," some objects that do not exist? If so, do they have any properties? Can they be compared with things that do exist? These issues and a hundred others arise in connection with Anselm's argument. And second, although the argument certainly looks at first sight as if it ought to be unsound, it is profoundly difficult to say what, exactly, is wrong with it. Indeed, I do not believe that any philosopher has ever given a cogent and conclusive refutation of the ontological argument in its various forms.

Anselm states his argument as follows:

> And so, Lord, do thou, who dost give understanding to faith, give me, so far as thou knowest it to be profitable, to understand that thou art as we believe; and that thou art that which we believe. And indeed, we believe that thou art a being than which nothing greater can be conceived. Or is there no such nature, since the fool hath said in his heart, there is no God? . . . But, at any rate, this very fool when he hears of this being of which I speak – a being than which nothing greater can be conceived – understands what he hears, and what he understands is in his understanding, although he does not understand it to exist.
>
> For, it is one thing for any object to be in the understanding, and another to understand that the object exists. When a painter first conceives of what he will afterwards perform, he has it in his understanding, but he does not yet understand it to be, because he has not yet performed it. But after he has made the painting, he both has it in his understanding, and he understands that it exists, because he has made it.
>
> Hence, even the fool is convinced that something exists in the understanding, at least, than which nothing greater can be conceived. For when he hears of this, he understands it. And whatever is understood, exists in the understanding. And assuredly that, than which nothing greater can be conceived, cannot exist in the understanding alone. For, suppose it exists in the understanding alone; then it can be conceived to exist in reality; which is greater.
>
> Therefore, if that, than which nothing greater can be conceived, exists in the understanding alone, the very being, than which nothing greater can be conceived, is one, than which a greater can be conceived. But obviously this is impossible. Hence, there is no doubt that there exists a being, than which nothing greater can be conceived, and it exists both in the understanding and in reality.[1]

At first sight, this argument smacks of trumpery and deceit; but suppose we look at it a bit more closely. Its essentials are contained in these words:

> And assuredly that, than which nothing greater can be conceived, cannot exist in the understanding alone. For suppose it exists in the understanding alone; then it can be conceived to exist in reality; which is greater.
>
> Therefore, if that, than which nothing greater can be conceived, exists in the understanding alone, the very being, than which nothing greater can be conceived, is one, than which a greater can be conceived. But obviously this is impossible. Hence there is no doubt that there exists a being, than which nothing greater can be conceived, and it exists both in the understanding and in reality.[2]

How can we outline this argument? It is best construed, I think, as a *reductio ad absurdum* argument. In a *reductio* you prove a given proposition *p* by showing that its denial, *not-p*, leads to (or more strictly, entails) a contradiction or some other kind of absurdity. Anselm's argument can be seen as an attempt to deduce an absurdity from the proposition that there is no God. If we use the term "God" as an abbreviation for Anselm's phrase "the being than which nothing greater can be conceived," then the argument seems to go approximately as follows: Suppose

(1) God exists in the understanding but not in reality.
(2) Existence in reality is greater than existence in the understanding alone. (premise)
(3) God's existence in reality is conceivable. (premise)
(4) If God did exist in reality, then He would be greater than He is. [from (1) and (2)]

(5) It is conceivable that there is a being greater than God is. [(3) and (4)]
(6) It is conceivable that there be a being greater than the being than which nothing greater can be conceived. [(5) by the definition of "God"]

But surely (6) is absurd and self-contradictory; how could we conceive of a being greater than the being than which none greater can be conceived? So we may conclude that

(7) It is false that God exists in the understanding but not in reality

It follows that if God exists in the understanding, He also exists in reality; but clearly enough He *does* exist in the understanding, as even the fool will testify; therefore, He exists in reality as well.

Now when Anselm says that a being *exists in the understanding*, we may take him, I think, as saying that someone has *thought of* or thought about that being. When he says that something *exists in reality*, on the other hand, he means to say simply that the thing in question really does exist. And when he says that a certain state of affairs is *conceivable*, he means to say, I believe, that this state of affairs is possible in our broadly logical sense; there is a possible world in which it obtains. This means that step (3) above may be put more perspicuously as

(3′) It is possible that God exists

and step (6) as

(6′) It is possible that there be a being greater than the being than which it is not possible that there be a greater.

An interesting feature of this argument is that all of its premises are *necessarily* true if true at all. (1) is the assumption from which Anselm means to deduce a contradiction. (2) is a premise, and presumably necessarily true in Anselm's view; and (3) is the only remaining premise (the other items are consequences of preceding steps); it says of some *other* proposition (*God exists*) that it is possible. Propositions which thus ascribe a modality – possibility, necessity, contingency – to another proposition are themselves either necessarily true or necessarily false. So all the premises of the argument are, if true at all, necessarily true. And hence if the premises of this argument are true, then [provided that (6) is really inconsistent] a contradiction can be deduced from (1) together with necessary propositions; this means that (1) entails a contradiction and is, therefore, necessarily false.

1. *Gaunilo's objection*

Gaunilo, a contemporary of Anselm's, wrote a reply which he entitled *On Behalf of the Fool.* Here is the essence of his objection.

> For example: it is said that somewhere in the ocean is an island, which, because of the difficulty, or rather the impossibility, of discovering what does not exist, is called the lost island. And they say that this island has an inestimable wealth of all manner of riches and delicacies in greater abundance than is told of the Islands of the Blest; and that having no owner or inhabitant, it is more excellent than all other countries, which are inhabited by mankind, in the abundance with which it is stored.
>
> Now if some one should tell me that there is such an island, I should easily understand his words, in which there is no difficulty. But suppose that he went on to say, as if by a logical inference: "You can no longer doubt that this island which is more excellent than all lands exists somewhere, since you have no doubt that it is in your understanding. And since it is more excellent not to be in the understanding alone, but to exist both in the understanding and in reality, for this reason it must exist. For if it does not exist, any land which really exists will be more excellent than it; and so the island already understood by you to be more excellent will not be more excellent."
>
> If a man should try to prove to me by such reasoning that this island truly exists, and that its existence should no longer be doubted, either I should believe that he was jesting, or I know not which I ought to regard as the greater fool: myself, supposing that I should allow this proof; or him, if he should suppose that he had established with any certainty the existence of this island.[3]

Gaunilo was the first of many to try to discredit the ontological argument by showing that one can find similar arguments to prove the existence of all sorts of absurd things – a greatest possible island, a highest possible mountain, a greatest possible middle linebacker, a meanest possible man, and the like. But Anselm was not without a reply.[4]

He points out, first, that Gaunilo misquotes him. What is under consideration is not a being that is *in fact* greater than any other, but one such that a greater *cannot be conceived*; a being than which it's *not possible* that there be a greater. Gaunilo seems to overlook this. And thus his famous lost island argument isn't strictly parallel to Anselm's argument; his conclusion should be only that there is an island such that no other island is greater than it – which, if there are any islands at all, is a fairly innocuous conclusion.

But obviously Gaunilo's argument can be revised. Instead of speaking, as he did, of an island that is more excellent than all others, let's speak instead of an island than which a greater or more excellent cannot be conceived – an island, that is, than which it's not possible that there be a greater. Couldn't we use an argument like Anselm's to "establish" the existence of such an island, and if we could, wouldn't that show that Anselm's argument is fallacious?

2. *Anselm's reply*

Not obviously. Anselm's proper reply, it seems to me, is that it's impossible that there be such an island. The idea of an island than which it's not possible that there be a greater is like the idea of a natural number than which it's not possible that there be a greater, or the idea of a line than which none more crooked is possible. There neither is nor could be a greatest possible natural number; indeed, there isn't a greatest *actual* number, let alone a greatest possible. And the same goes for islands. No matter how great an island is, no matter how many Nubian maidens and dancing girls adorn it, there could always be a greater – one with twice as many, for example. The qualities that make for greatness in islands – number of palm trees, amount and quality of coconuts, for example – most of these qualities have no *intrinsic maximum*. That is, there is no degree of productivity or number of palm trees (or of dancing girls) such that it is impossible that an island display more of that quality. So the idea of a greatest possible island is an inconsistent or incoherent idea; it's not possible that there be such a thing. And hence the analogue of step (3) of Anselm's argument (it is possible that God exists) is not true for the perfect island argument; so that argument fails.

But doesn't Anselm's argument itself founder upon the same rock? If the idea of a greatest possible island is inconsistent, won't the same hold for the idea of a greatest possible being? Perhaps not. For what are the properties in virtue of which one being is greater, just as a being, than another? Anselm clearly has in mind such properties as wisdom, knowledge, power, and moral excellence or moral perfection. And certainly knowledge, for example, does have an intrinsic maximum: if for every proposition p, a being B knows whether or not p is true, then B has a degree of knowledge that is utterly unsurpassable. So a greatest possible being would have to have this kind of knowledge: it would have to be *omniscient*. Similarly for *power*; omnipotence is a degree of power that can't possibly be excelled. Moral perfection or moral excellence is perhaps not quite so clear; still a being could perhaps always do what is morally right, so that it would not be possible for it to be exceeded along those lines. But what about a quality like *love*? Wouldn't that be a property that makes for greatness? God, according to Christian theism, loves His children and demonstrated His love in the redemptive events of the life and death of Jesus Christ. And what about the relevant qualities here – love, or acting out of love: do they have intrinsic maxima? The answer isn't very clear either way. Rather than pause to discuss this question, let's note simply that there may be a weak point here in Anselm's argument and move on.

3. *Kant's objection*

The most famous and important objection to the ontological argument is contained in Immanuel Kant's *Critique of Pure Reason*.[5] Kant begins his criticism as follows:

> If, in an identical proposition, I reject the predicate while retaining the subject, contradiction results; and I therefore say that the former belongs necessarily to the latter. But if we reject the subject and predicate alike, there is no

> contradiction; for nothing is then left that can be contradicted. To posit a triangle, and yet to reject its three angles, is self-contradictory; but there is no contradiction in rejecting the triangle together with its three angles. The same holds true of the concept of an absolutely necessary being. If its existence is rejected, we reject the thing itself with all its predicates; and no question of contradiction can then arise. There is nothing outside it that would then be contradicted, since the necessity of the thing is not supposed to be derived from anything external; nor is there anything internal that would be contradicted, since in rejecting the thing itself we have at the same time rejected all its internal properties. "God is omnipotent" is a necessary judgment. The omnipotence cannot be rejected if we posit a Deity, that is, an infinite being; for the two concepts are identical. But if we say "There is no God," neither the omnipotence nor any other of its predicates is given; they are one and all rejected together with the subject, and there is therefore not the least contradiction in such a judgment. . . .
>
> For I cannot form the least concept of a thing which, should it be rejected with all its predicates, leaves behind a contradiction.[6]

One characteristic feature of Anselm's argument, as we have seen, is that if successful, it establishes that *God exists* is a *necessary* proposition. Here Kant is apparently arguing that no *existential* proposition – one that asserts the existence of something or other – is necessarily true; the reason, he says, is that no *contra-existential* (the denial of an existential) is contradictory or inconsistent. But in which of our several senses of inconsistent? What he means to say, I believe, is that no existential proposition is necessary in the broadly logical sense. And this claim has been popular with philosophers ever since. But why, exactly, does Kant think it's true? What is the argument? When we take a careful look at the purported reasoning, it looks pretty unimpressive; it's hard to make out an argument at all. The conclusion would apparently be this: if we deny the existence of something or other, we can't be contradicting ourselves; no existential proposition is necessary and no contra-existential is impossible. Why not? Well, if we say, for example, that God does not exist, then says Kant, "There is nothing outside it (i.e., God) that would then be contradicted, since the necessity of the thing is not supposed to be derived from anything external; nor is there anything internal that would be contradicted, since in rejecting the thing itself we have at the same time rejected all its internal properties."

But how is this even *relevant*? The claim is that *God does not exist* can't be necessarily false. What could be meant, in this context, by saying that there's nothing "outside of" God that would be contradicted if we denied His existence? What would contradict a proposition like *God does not exist* is some other proposition – *God does exist*, for example. Kant seems to think that if the proposition in question *were* necessarily false, it would have to contradict, not a proposition, but some *object* external to God – or else contradict some internal part or aspect or property of God. But this certainly looks like confusion; it is *propositions* that contradict each other; they aren't contradicted by objects or parts, aspects or properties of objects. Does he mean instead to be speaking of *propositions* about things external to God, or about his aspects or parts or properties? But clearly many such propositions do contradict *God does not exist*; an example would be *the world was created by God*. Does he mean to say that no *true* proposition contradicts *God does not exist*? No, for that would be to affirm the *nonexistence* of God, an affirmation Kant is by no means prepared to make.

So this passage is an enigma. Either Kant was confused or else he expressed himself very badly indeed. And either way we don't have any argument for the claim that contra-existential propositions can't be inconsistent. This passage seems to be no more than an elaborate and confused way of *asserting* this claim.

The heart of Kant's objection to the ontological argument, however, is contained in the following passage:

> "Being" is obviously not a real predicate; that is, it is not a concept of something which could be added to the concept of a thing. It is merely the positing of a thing, or of certain determinations, as existing in themselves. Logically, it is merely the copula of a judgment. The proposition "God is omnipotent" contains two concepts, each of which has its object – God and omnipotence. The small word "is" adds no new predicate, but only serves to posit the predicate in its relation to the

subject. If, now, we take the subject (God) with all its predicates (among which is omnipotence), and say "God is," or "There is a God," we attach no new predicate to the concept of God, but only posit it as an object that stands in relation to my concept. The content of both must be one and the same; nothing can have been added to the concept, which expresses merely what is possible, by my thinkings its object (through the expression "it is") as given absolutely. Otherwise stated, the real contains no more than the merely possible. A hundred real thalers not contain the least coin more than a hundred possible thalers. For as the latter signify the concept and the former the object and the positing of the concept, should the former contain more than the latter, my concept would not, in that case, express the whole object, and would not therefore be an adequate concept of it. My financial position, however, is affected very differently by a hundred real thalers than it is by the mere concept of them (that is, of the possibility). For the object, as it actually exists, is not analytically contained in my concept, but is added to my concept (which is a determination of my state) synthetically; and yet the conceived hundred thalers are not themselves in the least increased through thus acquiring existence outside my concept.

By whatever and by however many predicates we may think a thing – even if we completely determine it – we do not make the least addition to the thing when we further declare that this thing is. Otherwise it would not be exactly the same thing that exists, but something more than we had thought in the concept: and we could not, therefore, say that the object of my concept exists. If we think in a thing every feature of reality except one, the missing reality is not added by my saying that this defective thing exists.[7]

Now how, exactly is all this relevant to Anselm's argument? Perhaps Kant means to make a point that we could put by saying that it's not possible to *define things into existence*. (People sometimes suggest that the ontological argument is just such an attempt to define *God* into existence.) And this claim is somehow connected with Kant's famous but perplexing *dictum* that *being* (or existence) is not a real predicate or property. But how shall we understand Kant here? What does it mean to say that existence isn't (or is) a real property?

Apparently Kant thinks this is equivalent to or follows from what he puts variously as "the real *contains* no more than the merely possible"; "the *content* of both (i.e., concept and object) must be one and the same"; "being is not the concept of something that could be *added to* the concept of a thing," and so on. But what does all this mean? And how does it bear on the ontological argument? Perhaps Kant is thinking along the following lines. In defining a concept – *bachelor*, let's say, or *prime number* – one lists a number of properties that are *severally necessary* and *jointly sufficient* for the concept's applying to something. That is, the concept applies to a given thing only if that thing has each of the listed properties, and if a thing does have them all, then the concept in question applies to it. So, for example, to define the concept *bachelor* we list such properties as *being unmarried, being male, being over the age of twenty-five*, and the like. Take any one of these properties: a thing is a bachelor only if it has it, and if a thing has all of them, then it follows that it is a bachelor.

Now suppose you have a concept C that has application *contingently* if at all. That is to say, it is not necessarily true that there are things to which this concept applies. The concept *bachelor* would be an example; the proposition *there are bachelors*, while *true*, is obviously not necessarily true. And suppose $P_1, P_2, \ldots, P_n$ are the properties jointly sufficient and severally necessary for something's falling under C. Then C can be defined as follows:

> A thing x is an instance of C (i.e., C applies to x) if and only if x has $P_1, P_2, \ldots, P_n$.

Perhaps Kant's point is this. There is a certain kind of mistake here we may be tempted to make. Suppose $P_1, \ldots, P_n$ are the defining properties for the concept *bachelor*. We might try to define a new concept *superbachelor* by adding *existence* to $P_1, \ldots, P_n$. That is, we might say

> x is a superbachelor if and only if x has $P_1, P_2, \ldots, P_n$, and x exists.

Then (as we might mistakenly suppose) just as it is a necessary truth that bachelors are unmarried, so it is a necessary truth that superbachelors exist. And in this way it looks as if we've defined superbachelors into existence.

But of course this is a mistake, and perhaps that is Kant's point. For while indeed it is a necessary truth that bachelors are unmarried, what this means is that the proposition

(8) Everything that is a bachelor is unmarried

is necessarily true. Similarly, then,

(9) Everything that is a superbachelor exists

will be necessarily true. But obviously it doesn't follow that there *are* any superbachelors. All that follows is that

(10) All the superbachelors there are *exist*

which is not really very startling. If it is a contingent truth, furthermore, that there are bachelors, it will be equally contingent that there are superbachelors. We can see this by noting that the defining properties of the concept *bachelor* are included among those of *superbachelor*; it is a necessary truth, therefore, that every superbachelor is a bachelor. This means that

(11) There are some superbachelors

entails

(12) There are some bachelors.

But then if (12) is contingent, so is (11). Indeed, the concepts *bachelor* and *superbachelor* are equivalent in the following sense: it is impossible that there exists an object to which one but not the other of these two concepts applies. We've just seen that every superbachelor must be a bachelor. Conversely, however, every bachelor is a superbachelor: for every bachelor exists and every existent bachelor is a superbachelor. Now perhaps we can put Kant's point more exactly. Suppose we say that a property or predicate P is *real* only if there is some list of properties P_1 to P_n such that the result of adding P to the list does not define a concept equivalent (in the above sense) to that defined by the list. It then follows, of course, that existence is not a real property or predicate. Kant's point, then, is that one cannot *define things into existence* because *existence* is not a real property or predicate in the explained sense.[8]

4. *The irrelevance of Kant's objection*

If this is what he means, he's certainly right. But is it relevant to the ontological argument? Couldn't Anselm thank Kant for this interesting point and proceed merrily on his way? Where did he try to define God into being by adding existence to a list of properties that defined some concept? According to the great German philosopher and pessimist Arthur Schopenhauer, the ontological argument arises when "someone excogitates a conception, composed out of all sorts of predicates, among which, however, he takes care to include the predicate actuality or existence, either openly or wrapped up for decency's sake in some other predicate, such as perfection, immensity, or something of the kind." If this were Anselm's procedure – if he had simply added existence to a concept that has application contingently if at all – then indeed his argument would be subject to the Kantian criticism. But he didn't, and it isn't.

The usual criticisms of Anselm's argument, then, leave much to be desired. Of course, this doesn't mean that the argument is successful, but it does mean that we shall have to take an independent look at it. What about Anselm's argument? Is it a good one? The first thing to recognize is that the ontological argument comes in an enormous variety of versions, some of which may be much more promising than others. Instead of speaking of *the* ontological argument, we must recognize that what we have here is a whole family of related arguments. (Having said this I shall violate my own directive and continue to speak of *the* ontological argument.)

5. *The argument restated*

Let's look once again at our initial schematization of the argument. I think perhaps it is step (2)

(2) Existence in reality is greater than existence in the understanding alone

that is most puzzling here. Earlier we spoke of the properties in virtue of which one being is greater, just as a being, than another. Suppose we call them *great-making properties*. Apparently Anselm means to suggest that *existence* is a great-making property. He seems to suggest that a nonexistent being would be greater than in fact it is, if it did exist. But how can we make sense of that? How could there be a nonexistent being anyway? Does that so much as make sense?

Perhaps we can put this perspicuously in terms of possible worlds. You recall that an object may exist in some possible worlds and not others. There are possible worlds in which you and I do not exist; these worlds are impoverished, no doubt, but are not on that account impossible. Furthermore, you recall that an object can have different properties in different worlds. In the actual world Paul J. Zwier is not a good tennis player; but surely there are worlds in which he wins the Wimbledon Open. Now if a person can have different properties in different worlds, then he can have different degrees of greatness in different worlds. In the actual world Raquel Welch has impressive assets; but there is a world RW_f in which she is fifty pounds overweight and mousy. Indeed, there are worlds in which she does not so much as exist. What Anselm means to be suggesting, I think, is that Raquel Welch enjoys very little greatness in those worlds in which she does not exist. But of course this condition is not restricted to Miss Welch. What Anselm means to say, more generally, is that for any being *x* and worlds *W* and *W′*, if *x* exists in *W* but not in *W′*, then *x*'s greatness in *W* exceeds *x*'s greatness in *W′*. Or, more modestly, perhaps he means to say that if a being *x* does not exist in a world *W* (and there is a world in which *x* does exist), then *there is at least one world* in which the greatness of *x* exceeds the greatness of *x* in *W*. Suppose Raquel Welch does not exist in some world *W*. Anselm means to say that there is at least one possible world in which she has a degree of greatness that exceeds the degree of greatness she has in that world *W*. (It is plausible, indeed, to go much further and hold that she has *no greatness at all* in worlds in which she does not exist.)

But now perhaps we can restate the whole argument in a way that gives us more insight into its real structure. Once more, use the term "God" to abbreviate the phrase "the being than which it is not possible that there be a greater." Now suppose

(13) God does not exist in the actual world

Add the new version of premise (2):

(14) For any being *x* and world *W*, if *x* does not exist in *W*, then there is a world *W′* such that the greatness of *x* in *W′* exceeds the greatness of *x* in *W*.

Restate premise (3) in terms of possible worlds:

(15) There is a possible world in which God exists.

And continue on:

(16) If God does not exist in the actual world, then there is a world *W′* such that the greatness of God in *W′* exceeds the greatness of God in the actual world. [from (14)]

(17) So there is a world *W′* such that the greatness of God in *W′* exceeds the greatness of God in the actual world. [(13) and (16)]

(18) So there is a possible being *x* and a world *W′* such that the greatness of *x* in *W′* exceeds the greatness of God in actuality. [(17)]

(19) Hence it's possible that there be a being greater than God is. [(18)]

(20) So it's possible that there be a being greater than the being than which it's not possible that there be a greater. (19), replacing "God" by what it abbreviates.

But surely

(21) It's not possible that there be a being greater than the being than which it's not possible that there be a greater.

So (13) [with the help of premises (14) and (15)] appears to imply (20), which, according to (21), is necessarily false. Accordingly, (13) is false. So the actual world contains a being than which it's not possible that there be a greater – that is, God exists.

Now where, if anywhere, can we fault this argument? Step (13) is the hypothesis for *reductio*, the assumption to be reduced to absurdity, and is thus entirely above reproach. Steps (16) through (20) certainly look as if they follow from the items they are said to follow from. So that leaves only (14), (15), and (20). Step (14) says only that it is possible that God exists. Step (15) also certainly seems plausible: if a being doesn't even *exist* in a given world, it can't have much by way of greatness in that world. At the very least it can't have its *maximum* degree of greatness – a degree of greatness that it does not excel in any other world – in a world where it doesn't exist. And consider (20): surely it has the ring of truth. How could there be a being greater than the being than which it's not possible that there be a greater? Initially, the argument seems pretty formidable.

6. *Its fatal flaw*

But there is something puzzling about it. We can see this if we ask what sorts of things (14) is supposed to be *about*. It starts off boldly: "For any being *x* and world *W*, . . ." So (14) is talking about worlds and beings. It says something about each world-being pair. And (16) follows from it, because (16) asserts of *God* and *the actual world* something that according to (14) holds of every being and world. But then if (16) follows from (14), God must be a *being*. That is, (16) follows from (14) only with the help of the additional premise that God is a being. And doesn't this statement – that God is a being – imply that *there is* or *exists* a being than which it's not possible that there be a greater? But if so, the argument flagrantly begs the question; for then we can accept the inference from (14) to (16) only if we already know that the conclusion is true.

We can approach this same matter by a slightly different route. I asked earlier what sorts of things (14) was *about*; the answer was: beings and worlds. We can ask the same or nearly the same question by asking about the *range* of the *quantifiers* – "for any being," "for any world" – in (14). What do these quantifiers range over? If we reply that they range over possible worlds and beings – *actually existing* beings – then the inference to (16) requires the additional premise that God is an actually existing being, that there *really is* a being than which it is not possible that there be a greater. Since this is supposed to be our conclusion, we can't very gracefully add it as a *premise*. So perhaps the quantifiers don't range just over actually existing beings. But what else is there? Step (18) speaks of a *possible being* – a thing that may not in fact exist, but *could* exist. Or we could put it like this. A possible being is a thing that exists in some possible world or other; a thing *x* for which there is a world *W*, such that if *W* had been actual, *x* would have existed. So (18) is really about worlds and *possible beings*. And what it says is this: take any possible being *x* and any possible world *W*. If *x* does not exist in *W*, then there is a possible world *W′* where *x* has a degree of greatness that surpasses the greatness that it has in *W*. And hence to make the argument complete perhaps we should add the affirmation that God is a *possible being*.

But *are* there any possible beings – that is, *merely* possible beings, beings that don't in fact exist? If so, what sorts of things are they? Do they have properties? How are we to think of them? What is their status? And what reasons are there for supposing that there are any such peculiar items at all?

These are knotty problems. Must we settle them in order even to consider this argument? No. For instead of speaking of *possible beings* and the worlds in which they do or don't exist, we can speak of *properties* and the worlds in which they do or don't *have instances*, are or are not *instantiated* or *exemplified*. Instead of speaking of a possible being named by the phrase, "the being than which it's not possible that there be a greater," we may speak of the property *having an unsurpassable degree of greatness* – that is, *having a degree of greatness such that it's not possible that there exist a being having more.* And then we can ask whether this property is instantiated in this or other possible worlds. Later on I shall show how to restate the argument this way. For the moment please take my word for the fact that we can speak as freely as we wish about possible objects; for we can always translate ostensible talk about such things into talk about properties and the worlds in which they are or are not instantiated.

The argument speaks, therefore, of an unsurpassably great being – of a being whose greatness is not excelled by any being in any world. This being has a degree of greatness so impressive that no other being in any world has more. But here we hit the question crucial for this version of the argument. *Where* does this being have that degree of greatness? I said above that the same being may have different degrees of greatness in different worlds; in which world does the possible being in question have the degree of greatness in question? All we are really told, in being told that God is a possible being, is this: among the possible beings there is one that in some world or other has a degree of greatness that is nowhere excelled.

And this fact is fatal to this version of the argument. I said earlier that (21) has the ring of truth; a closer look (listen?) reveals that it's more of a dull thud. For it is ambiguous as between

(21′) It's not possible that there be a being whose greatness surpasses that enjoyed by the unsurpassably great being *in the worlds where its greatness is at a maximum*

and

(21″) It's not possible that there be a being whose greatness surpasses that enjoyed by the unsurpassably great being *in the actual world.*

There is an important difference between these two. The greatest possible being may have different degrees of greatness in different worlds. Step (21′) points to the worlds in which this being has its maximal greatness; and it says, quite properly, that the degree of greatness this being has in those worlds is nowhere excelled. Clearly this is so. The greatest possible being is a possible being who in some world or other has unsurpassable greatness. Unfortunately for the argument, however, (21′) does not contradict (20). Or to put it another way, what follows from (13) [together with (14) and (15)] is not the denial of (21′). If that *did* follow, then the *reductio* would be complete and the argument successful. But what (20) says is not that there is a possible being whose greatness exceeds that enjoyed by the greatest possible being *in a world where the latter's greatness is at a maximum*; it says only that there is a possible being whose greatness exceeds that enjoyed by the greatest possible being *in the actual world* – where, for all we know, its greatness is *not* at a maximum. So if we read (21) as (21′), the *reductio* argument falls apart.

Suppose instead we read it as (21″). Then what it says is that there couldn't be a being whose greatness surpasses that enjoyed by the greatest possible being in Kronos, the actual world. So read, (21) does contradict (20). Unfortunately, however, we have no reason, so far, for thinking that (21″) is true at all, let alone necessarily true. If, among the possible beings, there is one whose greatness *in some world or other* is absolutely maximal – such that no being in any world has a degree of greatness surpassing it – then indeed there couldn't be a being that was greater than *that.* But it doesn't follow that this being has that degree of greatness in the *actual* world. It has it *in some world or other* but not necessarily in Kronos, the actual world. And so the argument fails. If we take (21) as (21′), then it follows from the assertion that God is a possible being; but it is of no use to the argument. If we take it as (21″), on the other hand, then indeed it is useful in the argument, but we have no reason whatever to think it true. So this version of the argument fails.[9]

7. *A modal version of the argument*

But of course there are many other versions; one of the argument's chief features is its many-sided diversity. The fact that *this* version is unsatisfactory does not show that *every* version is or must be. Professors Charles Hartshorne[10] and Norman Malcolm[11] claim to detect two quite different versions of the argument in Anselm's work. In the first of these versions *existence* is held to be a perfection or a great-making property; in the second it is *necessary existence.* But what could *that* amount to? Perhaps something like this. Consider a pair of beings *A* and *B* that both do in fact exist. And suppose that *A* exists in every other possible world as well – that is, if any other possible world has been actual, *A* would have existed. On the other hand, *B* exists in only some possible worlds; there are worlds *W* such that had any of *them* been actual, *B* would not have existed. Now according to the doctrine under consideration, *A* is so far greater than *B*. Of course, *on balance* it may be that *A* is not greater than *B*; I believe that the number seven, unlike Spiro Agnew, exists in every possible world; yet I should be hesitant to affirm on that account that the number seven is greater than Agnew. Necessary existence is just one of several great-making properties, and no doubt Agnew has more of some of these others than does the number seven. Still, all this is compatible with saying that necessary existence is a great-making property. And given this notion, we can restate the argument as follows:

(22) It is possible that there is a greatest possible being.

(23) Therefore, there is a possible being that in some world *W′* or other has a maximum degree of greatness – a degree of greatness that is nowhere exceeded.

(24) A being *B* has the maximum degree of greatness in a given possible world *W* only if *B exists in every possible world.*

(22) and (24) are the premises of this argument; and what follows is that if *W′* had been actual, *B* would have existed in every possible world. That is, if *W′* had been actual, *b*'s nonexistence would have been impossible. But logical possibilities and impossibilities do not vary from world to world. That is to say, if a given proposition or state of affairs is impossible in at least one possible world, then it is impossible in every possible world. There are no propositions that in fact are possible but could have been impossible; there are none that are in fact impossible but could have been possible.[12] Accordingly, *B*'s nonexistence is impossible in every possible world; hence it is impossible in *this* world; hence *B* exists and exists necessarily.

8. *A flaw in the ointment*

This is an interesting argument, but it suffers from at least one annoying defect. What it shows is that if it is possible that there be a greatest possible being (if the idea of a greatest possible being is coherent) and if that idea includes necessary existence, then in fact there is a being that exists in every world and in *some* world has a degree of greatness that is nowhere excelled. Unfortunately it doesn't follow that the being in question has the degree of greatness in question in Kronos, the actual world. For all the argument shows, this being might *exist* in the actual world but be pretty insignificant here. In some world or other it has maximal greatness; how does this show that it has such greatness in Kronos?

But perhaps we can repair the argument. J. N. Findlay once offered what can only be called an ontological *disproof* of the existence of God.[13] Findlay begins by pointing out that God, if He exists, is an "adequate object of religious worship." But such a being, he says, would have to be a *necessary* being; and, he adds, this idea is incredible "for all who share a contemporary outlook." "Those who believe in necessary truths which aren't merely tautological think that such truths merely connect the *possible* instances of various characteristics with each other; they don't expect such truths to tell them whether there *will* be instances of any characteristics. This is the outcome of the whole medieval and Kantian criticism of the ontological proof."[14] I've argued above that "the whole medieval and Kantian criticism" of Anselm's argument may be taken with a grain or two of salt. And certainly most philosophers who believe that there are necessary truths, believe that *some* of them *do* tell us whether there will be instances of certain characteristics; the proposition *there are no married bachelors* is necessarily true, and it tells us that there will be no instances whatever of the characteristic *married bachelor*. Be that as it may what is presently relevant in Findlay's piece is this passage:

> Not only is it contrary to the demands and claims inherent in religious attitudes that their object should *exist* "accidentally"; it is also contrary to these demands that it should *possess its various excellences* in some merely adventitious manner. It would be quite unsatisfactory from the religious stand point, if an object merely *happened* to be wise, good, powerful, and so forth, even to a superlative degree. . . . And so we are led on irresistibly, by the demands inherent in religious reverence, to hold that an adequate object of our worship must possess its various excellences *in some necessary manner.*[15]

I think there is truth in these remarks. We could put the point as follows. In determining the greatness of a being *B* in a world *W*, what counts is not merely the qualities and properties possessed by *B in W*; what *B* is like in *other* worlds is also relevant. Most of us who believe in God think of Him as a being than whom it's not possible that there be a greater. But we don't think of Him as a being who, had things been different, would have been powerless or uninformed or of dubious moral character. God doesn't *just happen* to be a greatest possible being; He couldn't have been otherwise.

Perhaps we should make a distinction here between *greatness* and *excellence*. A being's excellence in a given world *W*, let us say, depends only upon the properties it has in *W*; its *greatness* in *W* depends upon these properties but also upon what it is like in other worlds. Those who are fond of the calculus might put it by saying that there is a function assigning to each being in each world a degree of excellence; and a being's *greatness* is to be computed (by someone unusually well informed) by integrating its excellence over all possible worlds. Then it is plausible to suppose that the maximal degree of greatness entails *maximal excellence in every world*. A being, then, has the maximal degree of *greatness* in a given world *W* only if it has *maximal excellence in every possible world*. But *maximal excellence* entails *omniscience, omnipotence*, and *moral perfection*. That is to say, a being *B* has maximal excellence in a world *W* only if *B* has omniscience, omnipotence, and moral perfection in *W* – only if *B* would have been omniscient, omnipotent, and morally perfect if *W* had been actual.

9. *The argument restated*

Given these ideas, we can restate the present version of the argument in the following more explicit way.

(25) It is possible that there be a being that has maximal greatness.
(26) So there is a possible being that in some world *W* has maximal greatness.
(27) A Being has maximal greatness in a given world only if it has maximal excellence in every world.
(28) A being has maximal excellence in a given world only if it has omniscience, omnipotence, and moral perfection in that world.

And now we no longer need the supposition that necessary existence is a perfection; for obviously a being can't be omnipotent (or for that matter omniscient or morally perfect) in a given world unless it *exists* in that world. From (25), (27), and (28) it follows that there actually exists a being that is omnipotent, omniscient, and morally perfect; this being, furthermore, exists and has these qualities in every other world as well. For (26), which follows from (25), tells us that there is a possible world *W′*, let's say, in which there exists a being with maximal greatness. That is, had *W′* been actual, there would have been a being with maximal greatness. But then according to (27) this being has maximal excellence in every world. What this means, according to (28), is that in *W′* this being has omniscience, omnipotence, and moral perfection *in every world*. That is to say, if *W′* had been actual, there would have existed a being who was omniscient and omnipotent and morally perfect and who would have had these properties in every possible world. So if *W′* had been actual, it would have been *impossible* that there be no omnipotent, omniscient, and morally perfect being. But while *contingent* truths vary from world to world, what is logically impossible does not. Therefore, in every possible world *W* it is impossible that there be no such being; each possible world *W* is such that if it had been actual, it would have been impossible that there be no such being. And hence it is impossible in the *actual* world (which is one of the possible worlds) that there be no omniscient, omnipotent, and morally perfect being. Hence there really does exist a being who is omniscient, omnipotent, and morally perfect and who exists and has these properties in every possible world. Accordingly these premises, (25), (27), and (28), entail that God, so thought of, exists. Indeed, if we regard (27) and (28) as consequences of a *definition* – a definition of maximal greatness – then the only premise of the argument is (25).

But now for a last objection suggested earlier. What about (26)? It says that there is a *possible being* having such and such characteristics. But what *are* possible beings? We know what *actual* beings are – the Taj Mahal, Socrates, you and I, the Grand Teton – these are among the more impressive examples of actually existing beings. But what is a *possible* being? Is there a possible mountain just like Mt. Rainier two miles directly south of the Grand Teton? If so, it is located at the same place as the Middle Teton. Does that matter? Is there another such possible mountain three miles east of the Grand Teton, where Jenny Lake is? Are there possible mountains like this all over the world? Are there also possible oceans at all the places where there are possible mountains? For any place you mention, of course, it is *possible* that there be a mountain there; does it follow that in fact *there is* a possible mountain there?

These are some questions that arise when we ask ourselves whether there are merely possible beings that don't in fact exist. And the version of the ontological argument we've been considering seems to make sense only on the assumption that there are such things. The earlier versions also depended on that assumption; consider for example, this step of the first version we considered:

(18) So there is a possible being x and a world W' such that the greatness of x in W' exceeds the greatness of God in actuality.

This possible being, you recall, was God Himself, supposed not to exist in the actual world. We can make sense of (18), therefore, only if we are prepared to grant that there are possible beings who don't in fact exist. Such beings exist in other worlds, of course; had things been appropriately different, they would have existed. But in fact they don't exist, although nonetheless there *are* such things.

I am inclined to think the supposition that there are such things – things that are possible but don't in fact exist – is either unintelligible or necessarily false. But this doesn't mean that the present version of the ontological argument must be rejected. For we can restate the argument in a way that does not commit us to this questionable idea. Instead of speaking of *possible beings* that do or do not exist in various possible worlds, we may speak of *properties* and the worlds in which they are or are not *instantiated*. Instead of speaking of the possible fat man in the corner, noting that he doesn't exist, we may speak of the property *being a fat man in the corner*, noting that it isn't instantiated (although it could have been). Of course, the *property* in question, like the property *being a unicorn*, exists. It is a perfectly good property which exists with as much equanimity as the property of equininity, the property of being a horse. But it doesn't happen to apply to anything. That is, in *this* world it doesn't apply to anything; in other possible worlds it does.

10. The argument triumphant

Using this idea we can restate this last version of the ontological argument in such a way that it no longer matters whether there are any merely possible beings that do not exist. Instead of speaking of the possible being that has, in some world or other, a maximal degree of greatness, we may speak of *the property of being maximally great* or *maximal greatness*. The premise corresponding to (25) then says simply that maximal greatness is possibly instantiated, i.e., that

(29) There is a possible world in which maximal greatness is instantiated.

And the analogues of (27) and (28) spell out what is involved in maximal greatness:

(30) Necessarily, a being is maximally great only if it has maximal excellence in every world

and

(31) Necessarily, a being has maximal excellence in every world only if it has omniscience, omnipotence, and moral perfection in every world.

Notice that (30) and (31) do not imply that there are possible but nonexistent beings – any more than does, for example,

(32) Necessarily, a thing is a unicorn only if it has one horn.

But if (29) is true, then there is a possible world W such that if it had been actual, then there would have existed a being that was omnipotent, omniscient, and morally perfect; this being, furthermore, would have had these qualities in every possible world. So it follows that if W had been actual, it would have been *impossible* that there be no such being. That is, if W had been actual,

(33) There is no omnipotent, omniscient, and morally perfect being

would have been an impossible proposition. But if a proposition is impossible in at least one possible world, then it is impossible in every possible world; what is impossible does not vary from world to world. Accordingly (33) is impossible in the *actual* world, i.e., impossible *simpliciter*. But if it is impossible that there be no such being, then there actually exists a being that is omnipotent, omniscient, and morally perfect; this being, furthermore, has these qualities essentially and exists in every possible world.

What shall we say of this argument? It is certainly valid; given its premise, the conclusion follows. The only question of interest, it seems to me, is whether its main premise – that maximal greatness *is* possibly instantiated – is *true*. I think it *is* true; hence I think this version of the ontological argument is sound.

But here we must be careful; we must ask whether this argument is a successful piece of natural theology, whether it *proves* the existence of God. And the answer must be, I think, that it does not. An argument for God's existence may be *sound*, after all, without in any useful sense proving God's existence.[16] Since I believe in God, I think the following argument is sound:

> Either God exists or 7 + 5 = 14
> It is false that 7 + 5 = 14
> Therefore God exists.

But obviously this isn't a *proof*; no one who didn't already accept the conclusion, would accept the first premise. The ontological argument we've been examining isn't just like this one, of course, but it must be conceded that not everyone who understands and reflects on its central premise – that the existence of a maximally great being is *possible* – will accept it. Still, it is evident, I think, that there is nothing *contrary to reason* or *irrational* in accepting this premise.[17] What I claim for this argument, therefore, is that it establishes, not the *truth* of theism, but its rational acceptability. And hence it accomplishes at least one of the aims of the tradition of natural theology.

Notes

1 St. Anselm, *Proslogium*, chap. 2, in *The Ontological Argument*, ed. A. Plantinga (New York: Doubleday Anchor, 1965), pp. 3–4.

2 Ibid., p. 4.

3 Plantinga, *The Ontological Argument*, p. 11.

4 Ibid., pp. 13–27.

5 Immanuel Kant, *Critique of Pure Reason*, ed. Norman Kemp Smith (New York: Macmillan Co., 1929). Some relevant passages are reprinted in Plantinga, *The Ontological Argument*, pp. 57–64.

6 Plantinga, *The Ontological Argument*, p. 59.

7 Ibid., pp. 61–2.

8 For a more detailed and extensive discussion of this argument, see Plantinga, *God and Other Minds*, pp. 29–38 and A. Plantinga, "Kant's Objection to the Ontological Argument," *Journal of Philosophy* 63 (1966): 537.

9 This criticism of this version of the argument essentially follows David Lewis, "Anselm and Actuality," *Nous* 4 (1970): 175–88. See also Plantinga, *The Nature of Necessity*, pp. 202–5.

10 Charles Hartshorne, *Man's Vision of God* (New York: Harper and Row, 1941). Portions reprinted in Plantinga, *The Ontological Argument*, pp. 123–35.

11 Norman Malcolm, "Anselm's Ontological Arguments," *Philosophical Review* 69 (1960); reprinted in Plantinga, *The Ontological Argument*, pp. 136–59.

12 See Plantinga, "World and Essence," *Philosophical Review* 79 (October 1970): 475; and Plantinga, *The Nature of Necessity*, chap. 4, sec. 6.

13 J. N. Findlay, "Can God's Existence Be Disproved?" *Mind* 57 (1948): 176–83. Reprinted in ed., Plantinga, *The Ontological Argument*, pp. 111–22.

14 P. 119. Mr. Findlay no longer endorses this sentiment. See the preface to his *Ascent to the Absolute* (1970).

15 J. N. Findlay, "Can God's Existence Be Disproved?" p. 117.

16 See George Mavrodes, *Belief in God* (New York: Macmillan Co., 1970), pp. 22ff.

17 For more on this see Plantinga, *The Nature of Necessity*, chap. 10, sec. 8.

III

OTHER APPROACHES TO RELIGIOUS BELIEF

Introduction

In section II we looked at the classical arguments for the existence of God. For hundreds of years these arguments were used to show intellectual theists that belief in God could be supported by reason, so they were used primarily by the believer seeking understanding. However, by the seventeenth century they were used by theologians to answer attacks by atheists or to aid the agnostic inquirer. By that time all sides accepted the idea that the justification of religious beliefs rests upon the justification of theism, and the justification of theism requires demonstration by argument whose premises are accessible to any normal intelligent person. They assumed that no special experience or privileged access to knowledge may be presupposed in a successful argument for theism. This was also an era dominated by skeptical worries, and in such a context it is not surprising that by the eighteenth century many influential philosophers judged the classical arguments to be failures. This section is devoted to responses to the perceived failure of the rationalist defense of religion. The responses are from both theists and atheists. The theistic selections include anti-rationalist defenses of religion, and defenses that reject the assumption that arguments for theism must make no appeal to special experience or privileged access to knowledge. Another sort of response came from atheists or skeptics who offered naturalistic reinterpretations of the existence of religion.

The first subsection contains three selections on experience or revelation as grounds for religious belief. The first is the important proposal by Rudolf Otto (early twentieth century) that the core of religion is a certain emotion he calls "the numinous," which combines elements of awe, dread, fascination, the feeling of being overpowered, and an experience of the wholly other. The second is a contemporary treatment of religious experience by William Wainwright, who gives reasons for and against the view that such experiences justify belief that there is a divine reality outside the mind, concluding that religious experience can constitute grounds for rational religious belief.

In the third reading in the first subsection, Sandra Menssen and Thomas Sullivan argue for the possibility that divine revelation directly supports belief in God without relying upon a previous defense of theism. Menssen and Sullivan do not assume the failure of the classical arguments for theism, but they bypass those arguments by arguing that we often learn that a person exists (e.g. Homer) through that person's communications. We accept the communication as a communication from an intelligent person without first establishing the person's existence. This is a model in which revelation can support both divine existence and some of the contents of revelation without resting upon the classical arguments.

Another kind of defense of theism is the pragmatic arguments for religious belief, which we have included in section X.B. Some teachers may want to assign readings from that section along with the readings in this section because pragmatic arguments, such as Pascal's Wager, are arguments that religious practice can be rationally justified even though the justification does not derive from the epistemic justification of religious beliefs. Pascal (seventeenth century) cannot be interpreted as directly responding to the perceived failure of arguments for theism at least a century later, but he anticipates it, and his style of defense of religion was well suited to addressing the concerns of those who hoped for alternate defenses of theism.

The second subsection includes more radically anti-rationalist defenses of religion: Kierkegaard's famous attack on objective reasoning in religion, and Wittgenstein's contrast between empirical claims and judgments that express symbolically a commitment to a way of life. It would no doubt be inaccurate to say that Wittgenstein intended to defend religion or religious belief, but his radical interpretation of what religious belief amounts to was embraced by many theists.

The third subsection is devoted to some famous naturalistic interpretations of religion under the assumption that the truth claims of religion have failed. Hume's natural history of religion does not assume that *others* have demonstrated the failure of the classical arguments for theism since it was partly his own work that led to the perception of failure. Feuerbach and Freud proposed that religion is a projection of human psychological needs, from which Freud concluded that religion is an illusion. A more recent naturalistic attack on religion by Daniel Dennett is included in section XI's treatment of science and religion. Some readers may prefer to read that section together with the naturalistic interpretations of religion presented here.

A

Experience and Revelation as Grounds for Religious Belief

1

The Numinous

Rudolf Otto

Rudolph Otto (1869–1937) was a German theologian best known for his work *The Idea of the Holy*, from which the following selection is taken. Otto argues that at the core of all religions is a certain sort of emotional response to something he calls the *numinous*. The numinous is felt in terms of an emotion Otto calls the *mysterium tremendum*, which includes aspects of mystery, awe, fascination, dread, over-poweringness, and wholly-otherness.

Chapter II

'Numen' and the 'Numinous'

'Holiness' – 'the holy' – is a category of interpretation and valuation peculiar to the sphere of religion. It is, indeed, applied by transference to another sphere – that of ethics – but it is not itself derived from this. While it is complex, it contains a quite specific element or 'moment', which sets it apart from 'the rational' in the meaning we gave to that word above, and which remains inexpressible – an ἄρρητον or *ineffable* – in the sense that it completely eludes apprehension in terms of concepts. The same thing is true (to take a quite different region of experience) of the category of the beautiful.

Now these statements would be untrue from the outset if 'the holy' were merely what is meant by the word, not only in common parlance, but in philosophical, and generally even in theological usage. The fact is we have come to use the words 'holy', 'sacred' (*heilig*) in an entirely derivative sense, quite different from that which they originally bore. We generally take 'holy' as meaning 'completely good'; it is the absolute moral attribute, denoting the consummation of moral goodness. In this sense Kant calls the will which remains unwaveringly obedient to the moral law from the motive of duty a 'holy' will; here clearly we have simply the *perfectly moral* will. In the same way we may speak of the holiness or sanctity of duty or law, meaning merely that

Rudolf Otto, Chapter II: "Numen and the Numinous" and Chapter III: "The Elements in the Numinous" from *The Idea of the Holy*, trans. John W. Harvey (Oxford: Oxford University Press, 2nd edn., 1950), pp. 5–11.

they are imperative upon conduct and universally obligatory.

But this common usage of the term is inaccurate. It is true that all this moral significance is contained in the word 'holy', but it includes in addition – as even we cannot but feel – a clear overplus of meaning, and this it is now our task to isolate. Nor is this merely a later or acquired meaning; rather, 'holy', or at least the equivalent words in Latin and Greek, in Semitic and other ancient languages, denoted first and foremost *only* this overplus: if the ethical element was present at all, at any rate it was not original and never constituted the whole meaning of the word. Any one who uses it to-day does undoubtedly always feel 'the morally good' to be implied in 'holy'; and accordingly in our inquiry into that element which is separate and peculiar to the idea of the holy it will be useful, at least for the temporary purpose of the investigation, to invent a special term to stand for 'the holy' *minus* its moral factor or 'moment', and, as we can now add, minus its 'rational' aspect altogether.

It will be our endeavour to suggest this unnamed Something to the reader as far as we may, so that he may himself feel it. There is no religion in which it does not live as the real innermost core, and without it no religion would be worthy of the name. It is pre-eminently a living force in the Semitic religions, and of these again in none has it such vigour as in that of the Bible. Here, too, it has a name of its own, viz. the Hebrew *qādôsh*, to which the Greek ἅγιος and the Latin *sanctus*, and, more accurately still, *sacer*, are the corresponding terms. It is not, of course, disputed that these terms in all three languages connote, as part of their meaning, *good*, *absolute goodness*, when, that is, the notion has ripened and reached the highest stage in its development. And we then use the word 'holy' to translate them. But this 'holy' then represents the gradual shaping and filling in with ethical meaning, or what we shall call the 'schematization', of what was a unique original feeling-response, which can be in itself ethically neutral and claims consideration in its own right. And when this moment or element first emerges and begins its long development, all those expressions (*qādôsh*, ἅγιος, *sacer*, &c.) mean beyond all question something quite other than 'the good'. This is universally agreed by contemporary criticism, which rightly explains the rendering of *qādôsh* by 'good' as a mistranslation and unwarranted 'rationalization' or 'moralization' of the term.

Accordingly, it is worth while, as we have said, to find a word to stand for this element in isolation, this 'extra' in the meaning of 'holy' above and beyond the meaning of goodness. By means of a special term we shall the better be able, first, to keep the meaning clearly apart and distinct, and second, to apprehend and classify connectedly whatever subordinate forms or stages of development it may show. For this purpose I adopt a word coined from the Latin *numen*. *Omen* has given us 'ominous', and there is no reason why from *numen* we should not similarly form a word 'numinous'. I shall speak, then, of a unique 'numinous' category of value and of a definitely 'numinous' state of mind, which is always found wherever the category is applied. This mental state is perfectly *sui generis* and irreducible to any other; and therefore, like every absolutely primary and elementary datum, while it admits of being discussed, it cannot be strictly defined. There is only one way to help another to an understanding of it. He must be guided and led on by consideration and discussion of the matter through the ways of his own mind, until he reach the point at which 'the numinous' in him perforce begins to stir, to start into life and into consciousness. We can co-operate in this process by bringing before his notice all that can be found in other regions of the mind, already known and familiar, to resemble, or again to afford some special contrast to, the particular experience we wish to elucidate. Then we must add: 'This X of ours is not precisely *this* experience, but akin to this one and the opposite of that other. Cannot you now realize for yourself what it is?' In other words our X cannot, strictly speaking, be taught, it can only be evoked, awakened in the mind; as everything that comes 'of the spirit' must be awakened.

Chapter III
The Elements in the 'Numinous'

Creature-feeling

The reader is invited to direct his mind to a moment of deeply-felt religious experience, as little as possible qualified by other forms of consciousness. Whoever cannot do this, whoever knows no such moments in his experience, is requested to read no farther; for it is not easy to discuss questions of religious psychology with one who can recollect the emotions of his adolescence, the discomforts of indigestion, or, say, social feelings, but cannot recall any intrinsically religious feelings. We do not blame such an one, when he tries for himself to advance as far as he can with the help of such principles of explanation as he knows, interpreting 'aesthetics' in terms of sensuous pleasure, and 'religion' as a function of the gregarious instinct and social standards, or as something more primitive still. But the artist, who for his part has an intimate personal knowledge of the distinctive element in the aesthetic experience, will decline his theories with thanks, and the religious man will reject them even more uncompromisingly.

Next, in the probing and analysis of such states of the soul as that of solemn worship, it will be well if regard be paid to what is unique in them rather than to what they have in common with other similar states. To be *rapt* in worship is one thing; to be morally *uplifted* by the contemplation of a good deed is another; and it is not to their common features, but to those elements of emotional content peculiar to the first that we would have attention directed as precisely as possible. As Christians we undoubtedly here first meet with feelings familiar enough in a weaker form in other departments of experience, such as feelings of gratitude, trust, love, reliance, humble submission, and dedication. But this does not by any means exhaust the content of religious worship. Not in any of these have we got the special features of the quite unique and incomparable experience of solemn worship. In what does this consist?

Schleiermacher has the credit of isolating a very important element in such an experience. This is the 'feeling of dependence'. But this important discovery of Schleiermacher is open to criticism in more than one respect.

In the first place, the feeling or emotion which he really has in mind in this phrase is in its specific quality not a 'feeling of dependence' in the 'natural' sense of the word. As such, other domains of life and other regions of experience than the religious occasion the feeling, as a sense of personal insufficiency and impotence, a consciousness of being determined by circumstances and environment. The feeling of which Schleiermacher wrote has an undeniable analogy with these states of mind: they serve as an indication to it, and its nature may be elucidated by them, so that, by following the direction in which they point, the feeling itself may be spontaneously felt. But the feeling is at the same time also qualitatively different from such analogous states of mind. Schleiermacher himself, in a way, recognizes this by distinguishing the feeling of pious or religious dependence from all other feelings of dependence. His mistake is in making the distinction merely that between 'absolute' and 'relative' dependence, and therefore a difference of degree and not of intrinsic quality. What he overlooks is that, in giving the feeling the name 'feeling of dependence' at all, we are really employing what is no more than a very close analogy. Anyone who compares and contrasts the two states of mind introspectively will find out, I think, what I mean. It cannot be expressed by means of anything else, just because it is so primary and elementary a datum in our psychical life, and therefore only definable through itself. It may perhaps help him if I cite a well-known example, in which the precise 'moment' or element of religious feeling of which we are speaking is most actively present. When Abraham ventures to plead with God for the men of Sodom, he says (Gen. xviii.27): 'Behold now, I have taken upon me to speak unto the Lord, which am but dust and ashes.' There you have a self-confessed 'feeling of dependence', which is yet at the same time far more than, and something other than, *merely* a feeling of dependence. Desiring to give it a name of its own, I propose to call it 'creature-consciousness' or creature-feeling. It is the emotion of a creature, submerged and overwhelmed by its own nothingness in contrast to that which is supreme above all creatures.

It is easily seen that, once again, this phrase, whatever it is, is not a *conceptual* explanation of the matter. All that this new term, 'creature-feeling', can express, is the note of submergence into nothingness before an overpowering, absolute might of some kind; whereas everything turns upon the *character* of this overpowering might, a character which cannot be expressed verbally, and can only be suggested indirectly through the tone and content of a man's feeling-response to it. And this response must be directly experienced in oneself to be understood.

We have now to note a second defect in the formulation of Schleiermacher's principle. The religious category discovered by him, by whose means he professes to determine the real content of the religious emotion, is merely a category of *self*-valuation, in the sense of self-depreciation. According to him the religious emotion would be directly and primarily a sort of *self*-consciousness, a feeling concerning oneself in a special, determined relation, viz. one's dependence. Thus, according to Schleiermacher, I can only come upon the very fact of God as the result of an inference, that is, by reasoning to a cause beyond myself to account for my 'feeling of dependence'. But this is entirely opposed to the psychological facts of the case. Rather, the 'creature-feeling' is itself a first subjective concomitant and effect of another feeling-element, which casts it like a shadow, but which in itself indubitably has immediate and primary reference to an object outside the self.[1]

Now this object is just what we have already spoken of as 'the numinous'. For the 'creature-feeling' and the sense of dependence to arise in the mind the 'numen' must be experienced as present, a *numen praesens*, as is in the case of Abraham. There must be felt a something 'numinous', something bearing the character of a 'numen', to which the mind turns spontaneously; or (which is the same thing in other words) these feelings can only arise in the mind as accompanying emotions when the category of 'the numinous' is called into play.

The numinous is thus felt as objective and outside the self. We have now to inquire more closely into its nature and the modes of its manifestation.

Note

1 This is so manifestly borne out by experience that it must be about the first thing to force itself upon the notice of psychologists analysing the facts of religion. There is a certain naïveté in the following passage from William James's *Varieties of Religious Experience* (p. 58), where, alluding to the origin of the Grecian representations of the gods, he says: 'As regards the origin of the Greek gods, we need not at present seek an opinion. But the whole array of our instances leads to a conclusion something like this: It is as if there were in the human consciousness *a sense of reality, a feeling of objective presence,* a *perception* of what we may call "*something there*", more deep and more general than any of the special and particular "senses" by which the current psychology supposes existent realities to be originally revealed.' (The italics are James's own.) James is debarred by his empiricist and pragmatist standpoint from coming to a recognition of faculties of knowledge and potentialities of thought in the spirit itself, and he is therefore obliged to have recourse to somewhat singular and mysterious hypotheses to explain this fact. But he grasps the fact itself clearly enough and is sufficient of a realist not to explain it away. But this 'feeling of reality', the feeling of a 'numinous' *object* objectively given, must be posited as a primary immediate datum of consciousness, and the 'feeling of dependence' is then a consequence, following very closely upon it, viz. a depreciation of the *subject* in his own eyes. The latter presupposes the former.

2

Mysticism and Religious Experience

William J. Wainwright

William Wainwright (b. 1935) is Distinguished Professor Emeritus of Philosophy at the University of Wisconsin, Milwaukee. In the following selection Wainwright identifies several different types of religious experience, argues that religious experiences can lend support to religious beliefs, and responds to several of the most common objections to basing religious beliefs on religious experience.

The Nature of Religious Experience

There are many types of religious experience. Devout theists, for example, experience gratitude, love, fear, awe, and trust, and sometimes enjoy a sense of God's reality and presence.

Visionary experiences play an important role in some religious traditions and in the lives of some religious people. For example, Jewish Merkabah mysticism sought visions of God's throne chariot and "the mysteries of the celestial throne-world."[1] "Visions of the Bodhisattvas and of the Buddhas and their paradises" are cultivated in some forms of Mahāyāna Buddhism.[2] Visions of the Virgin or Jesus are common in Christianity.

"Numinous experiences" play an especially important role in theistic traditions. Their object is experienced as overwhelmingly vital and active, a power so great that one is reduced to insignificance in its presence. The unfathomable mystery one encounters is both "dreadful" and "fascinating." It is eerie, uncanny, and potentially dangerous (though not bad or evil) but, at the same time, so splendid and wonderful that other values seem worthless in comparison.

Rudolf Otto (1869–1937) describes these experiences in this way. The soul " 'shudders,' " is "held speechless, trembles inwardly to the farthest fibre of its being," as it faces something "'uncanny' and 'aweful,'" which can only be expressed by terms suggesting "vitality, passion, emotional temper, will, force, movement, excitement, activity, impetus." The soul responds to this mystery with "blank wonder, an astonishment that

William J. Wainwright, "Mysticism and Religious Experience" from *Philosophy of Religion*, 2nd edn. (Belmont, CA: Wadsworth, 1999), pp. 121–40.

strikes us dumb, amazement absolute." Completely overwhelmed, it feels that it is "impotence and general nothingness as against overpowering might, dust and ashes as against majesty." But the mystery also "allures with a potent charm." It "is experienced . . . as something that bestows upon man a beatitude beyond compare." The numinous experience is not only "fear and trembling" but also "wonderfulness and rapture."[3]

Numinous experiences are sometimes focused on a human being, a sacred place, a tree, a mountain, or some other natural object – Jesus or the Buddha, for example, Mount Sinai or the Kaaba Stone in Mecca. But their object can't always be identified with ordinary things. In many cases, a person seems to encounter a power or will that transcends nature and actively thrusts itself into his or her own life and consciousness.

Other religious experiences are "mystical." Returning home one evening, Richard Bucke (1837–1902) suddenly found himself "wrapped around as it were by a flame-colored cloud. For an instant," he said,

> he thought of fire, some sudden conflagration in the great city; the next, he knew that the light was within himself. Directly afterwards came upon him a sense of exultation, of immense joyousness accompanied or immediately followed by an intellectual illumination quite impossible to describe . . . he saw and knew that the Cosmos is not dead matter but a living Presence, that the soul of man is immortal, that . . . all things work together for the good of each and all. . . . The illumination itself continued not more than a few moments, but its effect proved ineffaceable . . . neither did he, or could he, ever doubt the truth of what was then presented to his mind.[4]

Another speaks of an experience in which, as he lay on the seashore, "distance and nearness become blurred into one; without and within glide into each other . . . the world exhales in the soul and the soul dissolves in the world."[5]

The "disciple" in Śaṅkara's *Crest Jewel of Discrimination* offers the following description of absorption in Brahman.

> The ego has disappeared. I have realized my identity with Brahman and so all my desires have melted away. I have arisen above my ignorance and my knowledge of this seeming universe. What is this joy I feel? Who shall measure it? I know nothing but joy, limitless, unbounded! . . . The treasure I have found there cannot be described in words. The mind cannot conceive of it. My mind fell like a hailstone into that vast expanse of Brahman's ocean. Touching one drop of it, I melted away and became one with Brahman. . . . Where is this universe? Who took it away? Has it merged into something else? A while ago, I beheld it – now it exists no longer. . . . Is there anything apart or distinct from Brahman? Now, finally and clearly, I know that I am the Atman [which, in this context, can be identified with Brahman], whose nature is eternal joy. I see nothing, I hear nothing, I know nothing that is separate from me.[6]

The Christian mystic Teresa of Avila (1515–82) reports that the soul is sometimes

> conscious of having been most delectably wounded. . . . It complains to its Spouse with words of love, and even cries aloud, being unable to help itself, for it realizes that He is present but will not manifest Himself in such a way as to allow it to enjoy Him, and this is a great grief, though a sweet and delectable one. . . . So powerful is the effect of this upon the soul that it becomes consumed with desire, yet cannot think what to ask, so clearly conscious is it of the presence of its God.[7]

Teresa's contemporary, John of the Cross (1542–91), speaks of a state in which "the soul lives the life of God." In this state, its understanding

> is now moved and informed by . . . the supernatural light of God, and has been changed into the Divine, for its understanding and that of God are now both one. And the will . . . has now been changed into the life of Divine love; for it loves after a lofty manner with Divine affection and is moved by the Holy Spirit in Whom it now lives, since its will and His will are now only one. . . . And finally, all the movements and operations which the soul had aforetime . . . are now in this union changed into movements of God.[8]

As these quotations indicate, mysticism takes different forms. Sometimes the space-time world is seen in a new way. For example, natural objects are perceived as somehow identical with each other and the mystic. The boundaries between things collapse, and the mystic finds that he or she includes, or is included in, nature as a whole. Or, as in Bucke's case, nature is experienced as a living presence, imbued with life or soul. (The first two experiences are sometimes called "nature mysticism.") Buddhism cultivates a different experience in which spatio-temporal reality is perceived as "empty" – a conceptually unstructured flow of "dharmas" (momentary events or states that resist further analysis). The object of the Buddhist's experience isn't some permanent substance or force underlying things. It is simply the process of becoming itself. But the Buddhist doesn't experience nature as we ordinarily do. He or she views it without attempting to conceptualize it and without attachment to it.

Another common experience is "monistic mystical consciousness." The mind progressively empties itself of percepts, sensations, images, and concepts until nothing remains but consciousness itself – joyous and without any object. The experience that Śaṅkara described may be an example.

In "theistic mystical experiences," the mind also empties itself of percepts, images, and all but the most general and abstract concepts such as "being," "presence," or "love." But unlike monistic experiences, these have an object or content. Their object isn't identical with any part of the space-time world, however, or the space-time world as a whole. The character or tone of the experiences is indicated by the fact that when mystics express them, they usually employ "erotic" imagery, comparing their relation to the object of their experience with that between human lovers. Teresa's and John of the Cross's experiences provide examples.

While all these experiences may have some evidential value, philosophers should be especially interested in numinous and mystical experience.

Visionary, numinous, and mystical experiences are "noetic." They involve an intuitive perceptionlike sense of objective reality or presence. For example, someone who has a vision of Krishna usually thinks that he or she is in Krishna's presence. Many numinous experiences seem to involve confrontations with an overwhelming transcendent will. The nature mystic is convinced that he or she is seeing the space-time world as it really is. Taken at face value, these experiences provide direct information about aspects or dimensions of reality that are normally hidden from us.

Visions are more problematic than numinous or mystical experiences, however, because their contents seem culturally conditioned. Buddhists don't have visions of the Virgin Mary or hear the voice of Jesus. Devout Christians don't have visions of Bodhisattvas or celestial Buddhas. Some of these experiences may be veridical, but caution is called for.

Numinous and mystical experiences, on the other hand, occur cross-culturally. For example, Christian mystics and theistic Hindu mystics have similar experiences. Monistic mystical consciousness is important in Advaita Vedānta, Yoga, and some forms of Buddhism. Numinous experiences aren't restricted to a particular time, place, or culture. It is therefore less obvious that these experiences are culturally conditioned. Are they genuine perceptions of a transcendent dimension or order? We will address this question by focusing on mystical experience.

What must be the case for mystical experiences to be veridical? A comparison with sense experience is helpful.

Suppose I see a hat on the table. We can distinguish (1) the "given" – visual sensations caused by the stimulation of the optic nerve, (2) the experience's "presentational object" – that which appears to be directly presented to my vision, namely, a hatlike surface perceived from a particular point of view, and (3) the experience's "apparent object" – what the object presented to my vision *appears* to be, namely, a hat. Since the experience has two objects, it is a basis for two perceptual claims – a claim to perceive the experience's presentational object ("I see a hatlike surface"), and a claim to perceive its apparent object ("I see a hat"). These perceptual claims should be distinguished from (4) perceptual claims that are partly based on beliefs which are indirectly connected with the experience and may not be shared by other observers. For example, thinking that the hat belongs to John, I might say "I see John's hat."

While all three perceptual claims may be correct, only the first ("I see a hatlike surface") is *immediately* warranted by the experience. That is, the first is the only one that *must* be true for my experience to be veridical. I might be mistaken in thinking that the hat is John's or even that it *is* a hat. (Perhaps it is only a papier-mâché facsimile.) Nevertheless, if I really see a hatlike surface, my perceptual experience is veridical.

When we ask whether an ordinary perceptual experience is veridical, we are thus asking whether its presentational object is really perceived. It is therefore important to distinguish its presentational object from its apparent object or its object as described by perceptual claims like "I see John's hat." It is equally important to distinguish mysticism's presentational object from its apparent object or its object as described by doctrinal systems like Buddhism or Christianity. Can this be done?

Mystics from different traditions frequently describe their experiences in similar ways. For example, theistic mystical experiences occur in Christianity, Vaiṣnavism, Śaiva Siddhānta, and Islam. Monistic mystical consciousness plays an important role in Buddhism, Advaita Vedānta, Yoga, and other traditions. Apparent perceptions of nature's unity, or its "life" or "soul," also occur cross-culturally. Furthermore, men and women who are comparatively untouched by *any* religious tradition sometimes have experiences like these (usually some form of nature mysticism or monistic mystical consciousness). These facts suggest that (1) mystical experiences aren't simply reflections of the mystic's tradition and that (2) their presentational object can be distinguished from their apparent object or their object as described by a particular tradition.

For example, the presentational object of theistic mystical consciousness appears to be an overwhelming loving presence that transcends nature and draws the mystic to itself. Its apparent object is an unembodied person or mind that various traditions then identify as Vishnu, Allah, or the triune God of Christianity. The presentational object of monistic mystical consciousness seems to be one's own empty consciousness. Different traditions identify this as the true self, the Brahman, and so on. (In this case, there doesn't seem to be an apparent object distinct from the experience's presentational object, on the one hand, and its object as described by one's tradition, on the other.)

We can now answer the question "What must be the case for mystical experiences to be veridical?" They are veridical if their presentational objects are really perceived. If empty consciousness is real and the mystic apprehends it, monistic consciousness is veridical. If the mystic is united with an overwhelming loving presence and is aware of the union, so are theistic experiences. A monistic mystic may also claim to perceive his or her identity with Brahman, and a theistic mystic may claim to apprehend an infinite mind or the triune God of Christianity. These perceptual claims too may be correct. Nevertheless, they can be mistaken without its following that the mystic's experiences are delusive. Even if they didn't perceive Brahman or apprehend the triune God, the mystics *may* have perceived their own empty consciousness or an overwhelming loving presence.

The question, then, is whether these experiences *are* veridical – that is, whether their presentational object really is perceived. We will investigate this question next.

Do Religious Experiences have Cognitive Value?

Ordinary perceptual experiences are "noetic" in the sense that (1) they are experiences *of* something (they have a presentational object) and (2) they incorporate the conviction that the presentational object exists and one is directly perceiving it. Perceptual experiences differ in this respect from feelings, emotions, and moods.

Mystical experiences are noetic. Monistic mystical experiences don't have an object distinct from consciousness but do seem to incorporate an implicit awareness of consciousness itself. Theistic mystical experiences and nature mysticism have objects and incorporate the conviction that the objects are real and one is directly perceiving them. Mystical experiences *seem*, then, to be perceptions of reality or some aspect of it. Should these apparent perceptions be accepted at face value?

There are two ways of addressing this question. The first focuses on the perceptual experiences themselves. Advaita Vedānta maintains that all apparent perceptions or cognitions are "intrinsically valid": ideas, judgments, and experiences should be accepted as valid unless they are called into question by other ideas, judgments, or experiences. Richard Swinburne makes a similar point when he appeals to the "principle of credulity": in the absence of good reasons for thinking otherwise, "if it seems (epistemically) to a subject that x is present, then probably x is present."[9]

The idea is that apparent cognitions or perceptions are *presumptively* valid – that is, they should be accepted at face value if there are no special reasons for discounting them. Thus, if it seems to me that I see a table or remember having an apple for lunch, then "I see a table" or "I remember having an apple for lunch" should be accepted in the absence of good reasons for not doing so. (Examples of such reasons are discovering that I was drugged, that there aren't any tables in my immediate vicinity, or that my memory is unreliable.)

Some principle of this kind is needed to avoid an infinite regress or circle. Why is this the case? Suppose that no apparent cognitions are presumptively valid. Each apparent cognition would then have to be justified by another apparent cognition. This cognition must in turn be justified, and so on. Either the chain of justifications goes on forever, or it eventually doubles back on itself. Both alternatives are unsatisfactory. A finite mind can't embrace an infinite chain of apparent cognitions, and a cognition can't contribute to its own support. Thus, if no apparent cognitions are presumptively valid, no cognition is ultimately justified.

So if knowledge is possible, some apparent cognitions are presumptively valid. But if some are, then all are – including mystical experiences. Restricting the principle of credulity to only some apparent cognitions is arbitrary.

The second way of addressing the question of mysticism's cognitive validity focuses on perceptual *practices*. William Alston (1921–) takes this approach.[10] A doxastic practice is a practice of forming certain kinds of beliefs under certain sorts of conditions where the content of the beliefs is a function of those conditions. For example, we form beliefs about what we did or experienced in the past when we are strongly inclined to believe that we did them or experienced them and have certain past-tinged experiences. Variations in the conditions under which our beliefs about the past are formed are correlated with variations in the beliefs themselves. Thus, the past-tinged experience associated with my belief that I had breakfast this morning is different from the past-tinged experience associated with my belief that I left my car in the parking lot. Doxastic practices also include procedures for epistemically evaluating beliefs formed under the appropriate conditions. For example, sense perceptual practice includes the procedures we use to sort out veridical sense perceptual beliefs from nonveridical ones.

Doxastic practices are basic when they provide our primary access to their subject matter. For example, memory is basic because it provides our primary access to the past. Sense perception is basic because it provides our primary access to physical objects. The reliability of basic practices can't be established without circularity. Sense perceptual practices, for instance, can't be justified by appealing to scientific theories because those theories are acceptable only if the observational data on which they are based are correct. Nor can we appeal to the fact that sense perception enables us to successfully find our way about in our physical environment because our belief that it does so is based on sense perception.

But if a basic doxastic practice like sense perception or memory can't be justified without circularity, why should we trust it? For four reasons: (1) The practice is internally consistent. Its outputs are, on the whole, mutually compatible. Most of our perceptual beliefs, for instance, are consistent with each other. (2) Its outputs are consistent with the outputs of other well-established doxastic practices. For example, our memory beliefs are generally consistent with our sense perceptual beliefs and with the beliefs we have based on inference. (3) The practice is socially established – widely accepted and deeply entrenched in the lives of those who employ it. Finally, (4) the practice is self-supporting in the sense that its outputs support its claim to reliability. Thus, sense perceptual practice displays the features it *would* have if it *were* reliable and therefore effectively controlled by the sort of objects it seems to reveal (namely, physical objects). If sense perceptual practice were reliable, for instance, we could use sense experiences to make accurate predictions about the course of future experience. (For the behavior of the physical objects that cause them is law like and hence predictable.) In addition, perceptual claims would be intersubjectively testable. (Physical objects are publicly accessible and their behavior regular. Hence, if I observe an accident on Route 66, other suitably situated observers should do so as well.) People would also conceptualize their experiences in roughly the same way. (For their experiences are controlled by the same sorts of objects.) So even though we can't show that our sense perceptual practice *is* reliable without falling into circularity, it displays the features it would have if it *were* reliable. In the absence of strong philosophical reasons for doubting its reliability, it is therefore reasonable to trust it.

The practice of forming beliefs about God on the basis of a sense of empowerment, guidance, or forgiveness, classical mystical experiences, and other apparent perceptions of God ("Christian mystical practice") displays similar features. (1) As a basic practice, it provides our primary access to its subject matter (God and His relations to us). As such, its reliability can't be established without circularity. Attempts to do so will appeal to beliefs about God that ultimately rest on the practice itself. (2) The outputs of Christian mystical practice are mutually consistent and (3) consistent with the outputs of other well-established practices. (Alston believes that philosophical and scientific objections to Christian beliefs can be met.) (4) The practice is socially established. It is deeply entrenched in the lives of countless men and women. (5) Christian mystical practice doesn't display the features exhibited by sense perceptual practice. It doesn't lead to a significant number of accurate predictions. Nor are its outputs intersubjectively testable. (At least not in the same way or to the same extent. As we shall see in the next section, a Christian mystic's claim to perceive God *is* subject to the tests the Christian community uses to distinguish perceptions of God from their counterfeits. But that that mystic perceived God while praying doesn't imply that other suitably situated observers would have done so if they had been praying in the same location.) Christian theists also conceptualize their experience in different ways. (There are significant differences, for example, in the ways in which Eastern Orthodox ascetics, Anglicans from south India, and fundamentalist British Baptists conceptualize the object of their religious experiences.) But these disanalogies with sense perceptual practice are irrelevant. The signs of the reliability of a practice are determined by the nature of the practice's subject matter. And God is very different from physical objects. Christian mystical practice has the features it would have if it were reliable. If the practice were reliable, it would provide access to a God who is good but "too 'wholly other' for us to grasp any regularities in His behavior," or to adequately understand what He is like.[11] We would therefore expect to find that we couldn't predict God's behavior with much accuracy. Nor would the practice's outputs be intersubjectively testable in the way that ordinary perceptual claims are since that depends on the publicity and regularity of physical objects. And because our grasp of God is partial and inadequate, we should expect people to conceptualize Him differently. Finally, if the practice were to promise spiritual insight, sanctification, and other ethical and spiritual fruits to those who engage in it, those who do so should be (as they are) more likely to experience them.

Alston concludes that Christian mystical practice is epistemically on a par with sense perceptual practice. It is therefore arbitrary to countenance one while rejecting the other. If it is reasonable to engage in a socially established doxastic practice like sense perceptual practice, it is also reasonable to engage in Christian mystical practice.

The rationality at issue, however, isn't epistemic. Neither practice can be shown to be epistemically rational since it is impossible to establish their reliability without circularity. But it *is* practically or pragmatically rational to engage in them.[12] (The distinction between epistemic and practical rationality is roughly this. A doxastic practice is epistemically rational if we have good reasons to believe that it is reliable. It is practically rational if the benefits of engaging in it outweigh the costs.)

To sum up. The first approach to the question of mysticism's cognitive validity focuses on mystical *experiences*. Since mystical experiences are apparent cognitions, they should be accepted at face value unless there are good reasons for discounting them. The second approach focuses on mystical *practices*. Mystical practices and sense perceptual practices display similar epistemic features. It is therefore unreasonable to engage in the latter and discount the former unless one has special reasons for believing that mystical practices are unreliable.

The following sections examine the most important reasons for discounting mystical perceptions and practices. Although we will focus on theistic mystical experiences and practices, most of the points made also apply to other forms of mysticism.

Dissimilarities with sense perception

Critics sometimes dismiss mysticism because it isn't like sense perception. C. B. Martin (1924–) is an example. Perceptual claims like "I see a table" should be distinguished from first-person psychological reports like "I seem to see a table" or "I am in pain." The former are "corrigible" – a person who sincerely makes them can be mistaken. Furthermore, there are "tests and checkup procedures" for determining whether the person is mistaken or not. (These include his or her own future observations and the observations of others.) First-person psychological reports are "incorrigible." I may mistakenly think I *see* a table, but I can't be mistaken in thinking that I *seem* to see one. Perceptual claims and first-person psychological reports also differ in another way. Perceptual claims are public claims about objective reality. First-person psychological reports are private claims about the contents of our own mind, how things seem to us, and so on. Martin believes that the mystics' claims are incorrigible because they allow nothing to count against them. They are thus more like first-person psychological reports than perceptual claims. He concludes that mystical experience tells us nothing about objective reality.[13]

Martin bases his argument on a factual mistake. Mystics are often certain of the validity of their experience, but neither they nor their communities believe that the experiences are incorrigible.

A comparison with ordinary perceptual experience may be helpful. Suppose I am certain that I see a hat. There are two ways of showing I am mistaken. One could show that no hat is there. (Suppose other suitably situated observers don't see it.) Alternatively, one could show that, whether or not the hat is there, I don't *see* it. (Perhaps I am looking in the wrong direction or suffer from a neurological disorder that makes me susceptible to hat illusions.)

There are also two ways in which mystics' claims can be shown to be mistaken. Their claims are false if the reality they allegedly perceive doesn't exist. Their claims should also be withdrawn if it can be shown that, whether or not a divine reality exists, they aren't perceiving it. Mystics and their communities believe this can sometimes be done. For example, the Christian tradition employs a variety of tests to determine whether a mystic really is perceiving God. These include the consequences of the experience for the mystic and others. (Does it promote charity and humility? Is its effect peace and psychological integration or, on the contrary, psychic disintegration? Do the mystic's experiences build up the community?) The tests also include the depth, profundity, and spiritual "sweetness" of what the mystic says on the basis of his or her experiences, its agreement or disagreement with known truths, and a comparison of the mystic's experiences with others generally acknowledged to be genuine. (In a traditional community, "known truths" include orthodox religious teaching, and the experiences with which the mystic's states of consciousness are compared are those regarded as paradigmatic by his or her community.) In some cases, the judgments of authority are decisive (authority being the mystic's spiritual director, for example, or an official representative of the mystic's community).

Martin is thus mistaken in thinking that the mystics' claims are incorrigible. Nevertheless, there *is* a significant difference between the tests used by mystics and their communities and the tests used to assess ordinary perceptual claims. Suppose a woman in Brooklyn claims she saw a bear rummaging in her garbage can. Her claim is strengthened if other suitably situated observers also thought they saw the bear. If they denied seeing it, her claim would probably be dismissed. Or suppose a man claims he sighted a new star. When others check his observations, their results are inconclusive. His claim will be strengthened if he can derive novel predictions from his observations and if these predictions are subsequently confirmed. These tests (appeals to agreement and successful predictions) play a major role in the evaluation of ordinary perceptual experience. They play only a minor role in the assessment of mystical experience.

Agreement *is* a criterion. Veridical sense experiences can be confirmed by any normal person who is placed in the appropriate circumstances. Our sense experiences are thus massively confirmed by the agreement of others. Mystical experiences aren't. Nevertheless, the mystic's experiences are often compared with other experiences that the community regards as paradigmatic. For example, a Christian's experiences may be compared with those of John of the Cross or Teresa of Avila. Because of their sanctity, these figures are regarded as "suitably situated observers." If a mystic's experience agrees with theirs, the case for its validity is strengthened. If it doesn't, the case is weakened. Agreement isn't as important, however, as the consequences of the mystic's experience for the mystic and others, and the mystic's sanity, sanctity, and orthodoxy. Successful predictions are even less important. Mystics seldom base predictions on their experiences. The accuracy of their predictions thus isn't an issue.

Does the lack of analogy between the tests used to assess mystical experience and those used to assess ordinary perceptual experience cast doubt on the cognitive validity of mystical states of consciousness? It isn't clear that it does.

As we noted in the previous section, the tests for an apparent cognition should be determined by the nature of its alleged object. Ordinary perceptual experiences provide our primary access to physical objects. Physical objects are publicly accessible, comparatively easy to discern, relatively permanent, and behave in lawlike and predictable ways. It is thus reasonable to think that veridical experiences of physical objects can be confirmed by others having similar experiences under similar conditions and by successful predictions.

The objects allegedly revealed by mystical experience are different. For example, if theistic mystics are right, the object of their experiences is God. But God is eternal and nonspatial – a self-existent, omnipotent will whose inner nature is ultimately incomprehensible. Classical theists also believe that God discloses Himself when and as He pleases and that His plans and purposes aren't fully understood. If this is correct, God's actions won't be completely predictable, and there is little reason to think that veridical experiences of Him will be confirmed by similar disclosures to most people. It is therefore unlikely that a veridical experience of God would be confirmed by massive agreement or successful predictions. Hence, these tests shouldn't be imposed on theistic mystical experiences.

Successful predictions and (massive) agreement are inappropriate tests for assessing theistic mystical experience. The tests used, however, *are* appropriate. A veridical experience of a maximally perfect being would presumably have beneficial consequences, and an encounter with it would produce profound insights rather than nonsense. Since a maximally perfect being isn't a deceiver, its disclosures would be compatible with known truths. Because it is holy, holiness is likely to be a necessary condition for being a "suitably situated observer." A comparison of one's experiences with those of the saints is therefore reasonable. Appeals to authority are also reasonable if there are grounds for thinking that their authority comes from God. In short, the tests used in evaluating theistic mystical experiences are appropriate to their alleged object. They specify conditions one would expect experiences to meet if they were perceptions of God.

Let us summarize our results. Our standard examples of perceptual experience are ordinary sense experiences. Critics think that mystical experiences aren't genuine perceptions because they aren't like them. Martin, for example, believes that mystical experiences aren't corrigible and that there are no "tests and checkup procedures" for evaluating them. They are private claims about our own thoughts and feelings rather than public claims about objective reality.

Martin is mistaken. The mystics' claims are corrigible, and there are tests for evaluating them. These tests differ from those used to evaluate ordinary perceptual claims. But differences can be explained by differences in the alleged objects of mystical experience and those of sense experience. The dissimilarity with sense perception thus isn't a good reason for discounting mystical experience.

The absence of independent justification

Another common objection is that there isn't any way to check the mystics' claims. They might be acceptable if there were independent reasons for believing that the mystics' experiences provide reliable information about reality. But there aren't.

Why should one think that an independent justification is necessary? Consider the following example. I have a toothache and therefore conclude I have a cavity. Judgments of this kind are warranted because we have independent access to teeth (we can see and touch them) and know that toothaches and cavities are often connected. What is true of toothaches is true of other sensations and feelings. A person is entitled to move from first-person psychological reports about his or her private experiences to facts about the public world only if we have independent access to those facts and know that the experiences are reliable signs of them. We don't have independent access to the objects of mystical experience. Hence mystical experiences can't be independently checked. Therefore, we shouldn't rely on them.[14]

Several things are wrong with this argument. For example, we may *have* independent access to the object of the mystics' experiences. If the existence of a divine reality can be proved or the claims made for the Bible, Qurān, or some other holy book are credible, then reason or revelation provides access to the experience's object. It is also misleading to describe the subjective side of mystical experience as "having certain feelings or sensations." This description neglects mysticism's noetic quality. Mystical experiences are apparent *perceptions*. Having a mystical experience isn't like feeling pain or being depressed.

The most important point, however, is this. While toothaches provide reliable indications of cavities, the *primary* mode of access to teeth and other physical objects is sense experience. It is therefore reasonable to demand independent certification when a person claims that a toothache or other sensation provides reliable information about them. An acceptable certification will appeal to facts established by employing the primary mode of access to the kind of object that the disputed claim is about (namely, teeth).

Mystical experiences, however, aren't like toothaches. Religious experiences and impressions seem to be a basic mode of cognitive experience. That is, if these experiences and impressions are valid, they provide our primary cognitive access to the objects that the mystic's reports are about.

Now, as we saw earlier, it is doubtful whether we can independently justify *any* basic mode of cognitive experience – that is, any mode of experience which, if reliable, provides our primary access to a domain of reality. Sense perception is a case in point. We have no independent way of establishing the reality of physical objects or showing that sense experiences are systematically correlated with their presence.

Every test for establishing the existence or presence of physical objects or correlations between physical objects and human experiences directly or indirectly appeals to sense experience.

Nor can sense experience be certified "pragmatically" – by the fact that relying on it enables us to successfully deal with the external world. For this appeal is circular. That relying on sense experience leads to successful adaptation can be established only by statements about human beings and their environment that are themselves based on sense experience.

The implication is clear. If a mode of experience provides primary access to a domain of reality, it can't be independently justified. Any justification begs the question by implicitly appealing to facts established *by* that mode of experience. Hence, if *religious* experience provides our primary access to *divine* reality, a lack of independent justification casts no more doubt on its reliability than on the reliability of sense perception.

Basic modes of cognitive experience, then, needn't be independently justified; proofs of their reliability are unnecessary. Still, certain things would show that they are *un*reliable. We should distrust a basic mode of cognitive experience if (1) there are reasons for thinking that the objects to which it allegedly provides access don't exist, if (2) conclusions based on it conflict with conclusions based on other equally well-entrenched bases for beliefs, if (3) the experiences are produced by causes which suggest that they are unreliable, or if (4) claims based on the mode of experience in question are inconsistent with each other.

If the arguments for naturalism were rationally compelling, one could dismiss mysticism and other types of religious experience on the ground that their object doesn't exist and on the ground that the supernaturalistic conclusions drawn from them conflict with truths established by such deeply entrenched methods as reasoning and sense experience. Since the anti-supernaturalist's arguments aren't clearly compelling, however, this line of attack isn't promising. The third and fourth possibilities must be taken more seriously and will be discussed next.

Natural explanations of religious experience

Many believe that a scientific explanation of mystical experience would discredit it. The discovery of natural mechanisms underlying these experiences would show they aren't veridical.

But why would it? There are two possibilities to consider. We know that some mechanisms are unreliable; that is, they systematically produce delusive experiences and false beliefs. Psychosis and wish-fulfillment are examples. If religious experiences and beliefs are caused by *this* sort of mechanism, we should discount them.

If this line of attack is to be effective, however, one must not only show that the unreliable mechanism is *operating*, but one must also show that it *produces* the experiences and beliefs.[15] For example, some psychotics are nature mystics. Nevertheless, psychosis may not *cause* their religious experiences. Psychotics have many experiences that can't be ascribed to their illness. (Most of their sense experiences are perfectly normal.) Furthermore, most nature mystics aren't psychotic. It thus isn't clear that the psychotic's mystical experiences should be *attributed* to a psychological disorder.

The other possibility is that the psychological, neurological, and social mechanisms underlying religious experiences *aren't* known to be unreliable. That is, they aren't known to produce delusive experiences and false beliefs. Would a discovery of mechanisms of *this* kind show that mystical experiences were untrustworthy? It isn't clear that it would.

Many philosophers think that an experience of x is veridical only if x is one of its causes. Thus, a visual experience of my desk is a perception of my desk only if the desk causes my experience. Suppose, then, that a scientifically adequate natural explanation of religious experience is discovered. Would it follow that (1) God or some other supernatural entity isn't its cause or, at least, that (2) there is no reason for *thinking* that a supernatural entity is its cause? It would not.

Classical theists believe that scientifically adequate explanations can be provided for most natural phenomena. But they also believe these phenomena are immediately grounded in God's causal activity. Hence, an adequate scientific explanation of religious experience wouldn't show that God isn't its cause. Nor would it show that God's causal activity isn't *necessary* for its occurrence.

Why is this the case? There are two senses of "x is a causally sufficient condition of y." In a broad sense, x is a causally sufficient condition of y if and only if x, together with certain background conditions, produces y. In this sense, the temperature's dropping below 32 degrees Fahrenheit is a causally sufficient condition of water's freezing. But in a stronger sense, x is a causally sufficient condition of y if and only if x *alone* (in the absence of other conditions) produces y. The temperature's dropping below 32 degrees isn't a causally sufficient condition of water's freezing in this sense, for many other conditions are necessary. (The water can't be salty, atmospheric pressure must be normal, and so on.) In short, "x is a causally sufficient condition of y in the strong sense" entails that nothing else is necessary for its occurrence. However, "x is a causally sufficient condition of y in the broad sense" does not.

If this is correct, scientifically adequate explanations of religious experience won't imply that God's causal activity isn't necessary for their occurrence unless the mechanisms involved in the explanation are causally sufficient in the *strong* sense – that is, unless they are capable of producing the experience even if God doesn't exist or is causally inactive. But how could one show that a natural cause is sufficient in this sense? Only by showing that the mechanisms produce the experience in situations in which God doesn't exist or is causally inactive. It is difficult to see how one could do this without establishing God's nonexistence.

Thus, the discovery of an adequate scientific explanation of religious experience wouldn't show that God wasn't its cause. Would it show that there is no justification for *thinking* that God is its cause or that the experiences are veridical? There are two reasons one might think so.

If we have an adequate scientific explanation of religious experiences, we can explain them without appealing to the causal activity of their alleged object. An inference to the latter is thus unwarranted. But if so, we have no reason for thinking that a transcendent reality is their cause and thus no reason to believe they are veridical.

This argument is unsound. In the first place, we might have *independent* reasons for thinking that God or some other supernatural reality causes mystical states of consciousness and other religious experiences. But suppose we don't. Are the mystic's claims therefore baseless? It isn't clear that they are. If the mystic's perceptual judgments and the scientific account were rival *explanations* of the experience, then the mystic's contentions might be superfluous. If natural mechanisms are sufficient for the occurrence of the experience, no other explanation seems necessary. But the mystic *isn't* offering a rival explanation. Perceptual judgments ("I see a hat" or "I perceive God") aren't *inferences* to the presence of the objects of the experiences on which they are based, and they aren't causal explanations of the experiences. We aren't, then, dealing with rival explanations or inferences but with a causal explanation and a *perceptual judgment*. Since natural causes don't preclude God's causal activity and since apparent perceptions are presumptively valid (the principle of credulity), why shouldn't the mystic's claim be accepted at face value? The discovery of an adequate scientific explanation of mystical experiences might justify concluding that there are no grounds for thinking that a transcendent reality is their cause *if* there are no other reasons for doing so. But there are – the fact that the experiences are apparent perceptions and the principle of credulity.

The second reason for thinking that the discovery of an adequate scientific explanation of religious experiences would show that they aren't veridical is this. For my visual experience of my desk to be veridical, it isn't sufficient that the desk be included among the experience's causes. Suppose I am blindfolded. A researcher notices the desk in front of me and manipulates my brain to produce impressions of it. The desk is a cause of my experience. But I don't *see* it. For the desk hasn't caused my experience in the right way. Similarly, if an apparent experience of God is to be veridical, it isn't enough that God cause it. If it were, all apparent experiences of God would be veridical. For God is a cause of everything and hence of all experiences – including the most bizarre. To be veridical God must cause them in the right way.[16] Jeff Jordan (1959–) argues that the discovery of an adequate scientific explanation of religious experience would show that it wasn't caused by God in the right way.

But why would it? An experience of God has been caused in the right way if the spiritual faculties of the person having the experience are operating as they should[17] and God's intention to reveal Himself by means of that experience is among its causes. The discovery of an adequate scientific explanation of the experience wouldn't show that these conditions aren't met.

Let us summarize. If one could show that religious experiences are produced by unreliable mechanisms, one could discount them. But the discovery of natural causes of religious experience won't discredit it if the causes aren't known to systematically produce delusive experiences and false beliefs. God or other supernatural entities can work through natural causes. The fact that religious experiences are apparent cognitions and the principle of credulity provide a reason for trusting them even if an adequate scientific explanation is available. Not only is the existence of an adequate scientific explanation compatible with God's causing religious experiences, it is compatible with His causing them in the right way.

Conflicting claims

Critics sometimes argue that religious experience can't be reliable because it supports incompatible claims. On the basis of their experiences, men and women make claims about Brahman, Allah, Yahweh, Thor, the Tao, Nirvāna, and many other things. These claims conflict. For example, if Nirvāna is real, God isn't, and vice versa. Religious experience isn't reliable because the information it allegedly provides is inconsistent.

How strong is this objection? We must distinguish claims that are directly based on an experience from claims that aren't and claims that are incompatible from claims that are merely different.

Claims that are indirectly based upon veridical experiences can be infected with error from other sources. If I claim that the hat on the table is John's, I may be mistaken. But the mistake needn't be due to a faulty visual experience. I may just be wrong in thinking the hat belongs to John. If my wife (who is looking at the hat) says she sees Tom's hat, her claim conflicts with mine. Nevertheless, while each of our claims is (partly) based on our visual experiences, the conflict doesn't show that either of our experiences is delusive. One or both of us may simply be mistaken about the hat's owner.

The point is this. The only claim immediately warranted by a veridical noetic experience is the claim to perceive its presentational object. Other perceptual claims may also be based on the experience (for example, "I see John's hat"). But showing that these claims are mistaken doesn't cast doubt on the cognitive validity of the experience itself. Now God, or the Brahman, or Nirvāna don't appear to be presentational objects of mystical experience. If they aren't, the fact that they can't all exist is beside the point. "I perceive *Brahman*" or "I perceive *God*" could be false even though the experiences on which they are based are veridical.

Different experiences do support *different* claims – that nature is one and holy (nature mysticism), that the flow of becoming escapes our inherently abstract and static concepts (the emptiness experience), that pure empty consciousness is a reality (monistic mysticism), and that an unembodied and overwhelming loving consciousness exists (theistic mysticism). These claims are obviously different. It isn't clear they are incompatible.

The claims that are *immediately* based on *mystical* experience may therefore be consistent. Some noetic religious experiences, however, do conflict. If visions of celestial Buddhas are veridical, visions of Krishna or Jesus probably aren't.[18] Visionary experiences *are* a source of inconsistent claims and hence seem unreliable. Is religious experience in general therefore unreliable?

It probably isn't. When we spoke of religious experience as a basic mode of perceptual consciousness, we were speaking loosely. There are several kinds of religious experience and important differences between them. John of the Cross, Jonathan Edwards, and many nontheistic mystics believe that mystical, numinous, and other nonvisionary experiences provide the primary, or best, or deepest access to the transcendent. These experiences are only loosely connected with visions. (The same people often have both. Nevertheless, if people stopped having visions or believing that visions were real perceptions, there is little reason to think they would stop having or trusting numinous and mystical experiences.) If this is correct, the unreliability of visionary experience doesn't imply that more basic types of religious experience lack cognitive value.[19]

But don't claims immediately based on the more *fundamental* religious experiences conflict? It isn't clear that they do. For example, a transcendent and powerful will that thrusts itself into our life and consciousness (numinous experience), an overwhelming loving presence that draws us to itself (theistic mystical consciousness), and empty consciousness (monistic mysticism) could *all* be real. The first two might be the same reality (namely, God), and the third might be our true selves.

Let us summarize. No reliable source of information produces inconsistent results. A basic mode of perceptual experience that leads to incompatible claims should therefore be discounted. The only relevant perceptual judgments, however, are claims to perceive the experience's presentational object. Conflicts between other kinds of perceptual judgment are beside the point.

Visionary experiences do lead to incompatible claims and are consequently unreliable. But many traditions believe that visions are a relatively shallow form of religious consciousness. The deepest access to ultimate reality is provided by mystical, numinous, and other nonvisionary experiences. Perhaps, then, these deeper experiences (and not religious experience in general) are the basic mode of religious perceptual experience. If they are, the objection we are discussing loses most of its force. The perceptual claims that are *immediately* based on these experiences differ, but they aren't obviously inconsistent.

The apparent inconsistency of the claims mystics make is only part of the problem, however. Claims to perceive ultimate reality are the outputs of doxastic practices that are embedded in religious traditions such as Buddhism or Christianity. These traditions are clearly incompatible.

Doxastic practices include ways of forming beliefs. But they also include procedures for epistemically evaluating them. These involve systems of "background beliefs." Suppose I think I see a tiger in my backyard. My claim would be "rebutted" if it were determined that no tigers were in the neighborhood. For in that case my claim would be false. It would be "undermined" if it were determined that I was feverish and my mind was wandering. For under those conditions perceptual reports aren't reliable. In both cases my perceptual report would be "overridden" by other things we know. In the case of sense perceptions, our background beliefs not only include beliefs about the likelihood of tigers being in the vicinity. They also include our convictions about the nature of physical objects, the conditions under which they can be accurately perceived, and so on. In the case of Christian mystical practice, background beliefs include beliefs about the nature of God and about the circumstances under which God is likely to reveal Himself. Similarly, Buddhists epistemically evaluate mystical claims by appealing to beliefs about Nirvāna, the self's relation to it, and so on. But Christian metaphysics and Buddhist metaphysics are incompatible. Hence, Christian mystical practice and Buddhist mystical practice are also incompatible.

Alston admits that the diversity of mystical practices counts against the reliability of each of them. How strongly does it do so? The answer depends partly on whether we are already engaged in a mystical practice or not.

Suppose we are not. Christian mystical practice and Buddhist mystical practice are both socially established and are both significantly self-supporting. (Both yield the moral and spiritual fruits they promise.) Neither has been shown to be unreliable. (Their outputs appear to be consistent with each other and with the outputs of such noncontroversial practices as science and sense perceptual practice.) So I have as good a reason for engaging in one as in the other. But I can't engage in both. (The practices are incompatible.) If there are no independent metaphysical or empirical reasons for preferring one mystical practice to another, it seems that I should engage in neither.[20]

What about people who *are* engaged in Christian or some other mystical practice? It seems unreasonable for them to abandon a socially established doxastic practice that they find deeply satisfying in the absence of good reasons for thinking it unreliable. But of course there *are* reasons for doubting its reliability – the existence of incompatible mystical practices that initially at least, seem equally well supported. Whether this reason is sufficiently strong to warrant *abandoning* their mystical practice is unclear, however. Alston thinks it is not, although he admits that the diversity of mystical practices should *weaken* their confidence in their practice.[21]

Ultimately, metaphysical and empirical argumentation of a familiar sort[22] may be needed to show that commitment to a mystical practice is fully rational. Alston's case for Christian mystical practice is impressive. To be fully successful it must form part of a persuasive cumulative case argument for the Christian worldview. Similarly, commitment to Buddhist or Hindu mystical practice is fully rational only if one has good reasons for thinking that the Buddhist or Hindu worldview is superior to its rivals. Can one construct an argument for the superiority of a Christian or Buddhist or some other religious worldview?

Conclusion

If the principle of credulity is sound, apparent cognitions should be accepted in the absence of good reasons for not doing so. Mystical consciousness and some other forms of religious experience are noetic; people who have these experiences make perceptual claims. We should therefore accept their claims unless there are good reasons for discounting them.

The only conclusive grounds for rejecting mystical or numinous experience would be (1) proofs of the nonexistence of God or other supernatural entities, (2) evidence that the experiences are produced by natural mechanisms which are known to systematically cause false beliefs and delusive experiences, or (3) good reasons for thinking that the perceptual claims immediately based on those experiences are inconsistent. So far, critics haven't provided these grounds.

The cognitive claims of mysticism and some other forms of religious experience must therefore be taken seriously. If there is independent (of religious experience) evidence for claims about God or other supernatural realities, the argument for religious experience's cognitive validity is even stronger. Religious experience seems to provide some support for religious beliefs and thus strengthens the case for them.

Whether the support provided by religious beliefs, or by religious experience in conjunction with other evidence, is sufficiently strong to *justify* religious beliefs is another question. Philosophers as well as other men and women are divided on the matter.

Nor is it clear that most people's religious beliefs rest on either arguments *or* special experiences like mysticism. While religious belief may derive its strength from feeling, few have had the *noetic* experiences that would *support* them. Are these people's beliefs somehow improper? Or is it instead possible that their beliefs *are* justified even though they aren't grounded in noetic experiences or any other kind of evidence?

Notes

1 Gershom Scholem, *Major Trends in Jewish Mysticism* (New York: Schocken Books, 1961), 44.

2 Edward Conze, *Buddhist Meditation* (New York: Harper & Row, 1969), 59f.

3 Rudolf Otto, *The Idea of the Holy* (London: Oxford University Press, 1936), 17–26, 31–3.

4 Richard Bucke, *Cosmic Consciousness* (New York: Dutton, 1956), 9–10.

5 Carl Jung, *Psychology of the Unconscious* (New York: Dodd, Mead, 1947), 360–1.

6 *Shankara's Crest Jewel of Discrimination*, trans. Swami Prabhavananda (New York: Mentor Books, 1970), 103–4.

7 Teresa of Avila, *Interior Castle*, trans. and ed. E. Allison Peers (Garden City, NY: Doubleday Image, 1961), 135–6.

8 John of the Cross, *Living Flame of Love*, trans. and ed. E. Allison Peers (Garden City, NY: Doubleday Image, 1962), 78–9.

9 Richard Swinburne, *The Existence of God* (Oxford: Clarendon Press, 1979), 254.

10 William P. Alston, *Perceiving God: The Epistemology of Religious Experience* (Ithaca, NY: Cornell University Press, 1991).

11 William P. Alston, "Christian Experience and Christian Belief," in *Faith and Rationality*, ed. Alvin Plantinga and Nicholas Wolterstorff (Notre Dame, IN: University of Notre Dame Press, 1983), 129.

12 It should be noted, however, that engaging in a doxastic practice involves accepting its outputs as *true* and therefore *believing* (justifiably or not) that it is reliable.

13 C. B. Martin, *Religious Belief* (Ithaca, NY: Cornell University Press, 1959), chapter 5.

14 Paul Schmidt, *Religious Knowledge* (Glencoe, IL: Free Press, 1961), chapter 8.

15 As Gary Gutting has pointed out in *Religious Beliefs and Religious Skepticism* (Notre Dame, IN: University of Notre Dame Press, 1982), chapter 5.

16 This point has been made by Michael Levine ("If there is a God, any Experience which Seems to be of God will be Genuine," *Religious Studies* 26 [1990]: 207–17) and Jeff Jordan ("Religious Experiences and Naturalistic Explanations," *Sophia* 33 [1994]: 60–73).

17 She isn't insane or vicious. She sincerely loves God or seeks Him. And so on.

18 All these entities could coexist in some sense. Nevertheless, the import of visions of Christ in majesty is incompatible with the import of visions of celestial Buddhas.

19 This doesn't imply that a vision might not be caused by its alleged object or that there couldn't be independent reasons for trusting a particular vision. It does imply that visions shouldn't be trusted in the absence of independent certification. Visions are like toothaches. A person may be justified in claiming to have a cavity on the basis of his or her toothache. But pains and aches aren't reliable indicators of facts about physical objects in the absence of independent reasons for thinking the two are correlated.

20 Why not engage in (for example) Buddhist mystical practice? Since the reasons for engaging in Buddhist mystical practice are no stronger than those for engaging in Christian mystical practice, it seems arbitrary to do so. Furthermore, Christian mystical practice and Buddhist mystical practice are incompatible. Hence, any reasons for the first reasons against the second, and vice versa.

21 Alston defends this claim in chapter VII of *Perceiving God*. For a critical evaluation of Alston's arguments, see section II of William Wainwright's "Religious Language, Religious Experience, and Religious Pluralism," in *The Rationality of Belief and the Plurality of Faith*, ed. Thomas D. Senor (Ithaca, NY: Cornell University Press, 1995).

22 Arguments for God's or Nirvāna's existence, evidence of Christ's or the Buddha's authority, and so on.

3

The Existence of God and the Existence of Homer: Rethinking Theism and Revelatory Claims

Sandra Menssen and Thomas D. Sullivan

Sandra Menssen (b. 1953) and Thomas Sullivan (b. 1938) are professors of philosophy at the University of St Thomas in St Paul, Minnesota. In the following essay, they develop a novel evidentialist approach to defending theistic belief. Philosophers have typically assumed that one must first establish the existence of a good God before one can seriously consider claims that God has communicated something. On the contrary, Menssen and Sullivan argue that purported communications from God might themselves provide evidence of God's existence.

Can a convincing case be made for the claim that a good God has revealed something to us? We are not asking whether religious belief is rational, or might be properly basic. We are rather asking the question the unconvinced demand be confronted. The standard way of arguing the affirmative creates a huge, unnecessary problem by tacitly presupposing that a sound case for a revelatory claim requires first working up a highly plausible argument for the existence of a good God. Once it is seen that this presupposition is false, the way is open to following a nonstandard philosophical path. For if facts about the universe yield enough evidence to show that the existence of a creator of some ilk is not highly implausible, it is possible that the content of a putative revelation might serve to close the evidential gap. And, we contend, our knowledge of the universe does yield the required modicum of evidence. It turns out, then, that *a negative conclusion about the existence of God is unwarranted unless the content of revelatory claims has been considered.*

Sandra Menssen and Thomas D. Sullivan, "The Existence of God and the Existence of Homer: Rethinking Theism and Revelatory Claims". *Faith and Philosophy* 19:3 (2002): 331–47.

I. The Standard way of Building a Case for Theism and Revelatory Claims: Its Rationale and its Troubles

Has a good God given us a revelation?[1] Many philosophically-inclined nonbelievers wonder. They are not particularly interested in the rationality of the claim that God has revealed. A belief can be rational, but false. They want to know whether the claim is *true*. Nor are they engaged by the question of whether belief in God or some particular revelatory claim might be properly basic. They judge that they have no belief at all in God, and certainly not properly basic belief. Hopeful, often, of becoming believers, but wary of religious enthusiasms and determined to follow reason, such agnostics seek a *philosophical case* that there is a God who has communicated to us.

Can they find a convincing case? The long tradition of natural theology provides an intricate tangle of arguments, elaborated over the years. The paths typically cut for an agnostic inquirer facing this thicket of arguments share an important feature. These paths tacitly presuppose:

(P) One cannot obtain a convincing philosophical case for a revelatory claim without first obtaining a highly plausible case for a good God.

On the view marked by presupposition (P), which we will call the *standard*[2] view, an inquirer begins by trying to establish a highly plausible case for the existence of a good God, a case sufficiently plausible that when the best argument available for the truth of some putative revelation is tacked on, the outcome is a case for the revelatory claim that is at least equiprobable, and ideally more probable than not.

Presupposition (P) carries some intuitive appeal. And logical considerations about complex questions may well appear to support (P). In general, it may seem, if one is trying to answer a complex question, one must first answer any embedded simpler questions. And it is, indeed, easy to find cases where it is eminently sensible to answer at least some of the subquestions before tackling the complex question. It is, for instance, preposterous for a physician to try to decide whether a certain cancer therapy will benefit a patient without first getting a fairly good fix on whether the patient has cancer.

Logical though it may seem, the standard approach to building a case for a revelatory claim routinely stymies inquirers. It is exceedingly difficult for many agnostics (and many theists as well) to believe that a good God could have created this world, with all its evils, *unless* there is an afterlife in which wrongs are righted. And in the minds of many, agnostics and theists alike, arguments available through philosophy, through unaided natural reason, are insufficient to establish the existence of an afterlife of the right sort. Theists who accept a revelatory claim that includes a good God's promise of eternal salvation have resources to handle the problem of evil. But it looks like an agnostic cannot build a case that a revelatory claim is plausible without first assenting to the claim that there is a good God; and it looks to many agnostics like the existence of evil makes this impossible.[3] And even if an agnostic can assign a fairly high probability to the claim that there is a good God, that is a long way from endorsing a particular revelatory claim. (Alvin Plantinga argues that even if an *extremely* generous estimate concerning the probability of theism is made, it will be virtually impossible to move on in the standard way and push the probability of Christianity up above .5.)[4]

It is thus easy to despair of the standard approach. Dissatisfaction with it may drive theistic philosophers to seek an alternative to natural theology, an alternative to building a reasoned case for theism and revelatory claims. Philosophical believers certainly do offer alternatives. Plantinga, for instance, defends a "testimonial" model of belief, which portrays Christian belief as warranted (if true); Paul Moser articulates a "filial" approach to knowledge of God, which he contrasts with an approach reliant on natural theology.[5] However, such alternatives have extremely limited appeal to philosophically-inclined nonbelievers interested in exploring religion, but resolved to accept Christianity, or any revealed religion, *only* if there is a good case to be had for it.

Is there an alternative to the standard approach that can engage inquiring agnostics? Recall that the standard way of building a case presupposes (P), and that (P) enjoys an initial plausibility, backed by reflection on the problem of handling complex questions. It turns out, however, that the philosophical rationale supporting (P) is defective. Examples show it is a mistake to think that if the truth of a complex proposition is at issue, and that proposition embeds sub-propositions, then each embedded sub-proposition must first be established.

Here is a particularly pertinent example: it is sometimes clearly reasonable to ask whether an intelligent but nonhuman being has sent a message, rather than *first* asking whether there are any intelligent beings who are not human, and *then* asking whether such a being has sent a message. The SETI research program (Search for Extra-Terrestrial Intelligence) involves monitoring millions of radio signals from outer space. Many natural objects emit these signals, but SETI researchers look for signals that almost certainly would have to be sent by intelligent agents. Imagine that researchers discover a 1126 bit sequence corresponding to the prime numbers from 2 to 101. The statement "Some highly intelligent life form in outer space has sent this signal" embeds "There is (or was) some highly intelligent life in outer space," but it is eminently reasonable to try to confirm the embedding statement in order to confirm the embedded statement.

Perhaps it will be objected that the investigative procedures just described *cannot* be proper, not in the way we described them, because the procedures commit "the fallacy of the complex question." In fact, however, there is no relevant fallacy here to worry about. Yes, Aristotle talked about the fallacy of the complex question. And one finds it in most logic texts that deal with informal fallacies. But Aristotle's account is less than luminously clear.[6] The text-book discussions of the so-called fallacy are typically defective.[7] And a bit of reflection shows that for *any* complex question there is always at least one sub-question that cannot be answered before the complex question is answered, because there is no such thing as presuppositionless inquiry. Questions are always about propositions, and every proposition presupposes (at the very least) a domain of discourse. "Do unicorns exist?" will be answered in one way if the domain of discourse includes mental or fictional objects, in another way if these things are excluded from discussion.

Since the philosophical rationale supporting (P) does not survive scrutiny, an agnostic inquirer might well wonder whether a nonbeliever could find a philosophical case for accepting *at once* both the claim that God exists and the claim that God has revealed. In subsequent sections we will argue that an outsider could, indeed, discover such a case. In fact, we will argue for the stronger thesis that *a negative conclusion about the existence of God is unwarranted unless the content of revelatory claims has been considered.*

Before getting into details of our argument, an analogy may be useful. (Readers with a taste for mathematics might find the analogy helpful; others may prefer to skip to Section II.)

Over 2,000 years ago the Greeks worked with early forms of integral calculus. Archimedes developed a method for approximately measuring the area of a given region by inscribing within it regions whose areas can be easily computed, and summing the areas of these regions. The more regions that are inscribed, the closer one gets to exhausting the original region, and the more accurate the total area measurement. Newton and Leibniz, taking a cue from this "method of exhaustion," developed general, systematic treatments of both integral and differential calculus. Notoriously, though their systems were powerful in application, they had defective foundations. Both men (most regularly Leibniz) spoke of infinitely small quantities, "infinitesimals" or "differentials." The notion had intuitive appeal, but as Berkeley and others showed, the formal accounts of infinitesimals were internally inconsistent. It was not until the 19th century that mathematicians such as Cauchy and Weierstrass developed the "epsilon-delta" concept of moving toward a limit in a way sufficiently clear and rigorous to ground calculus. Reference to infinitesimals became thoroughly disreputable. There was a cost, however, to the epsilon-delta approach to calculus: though precise, its proofs and manipulations are awkward, and it is something of a disaster pedagogically.

In the 1960s the mathematician Abraham Robinson proposed an approach to calculus that he called "nonstandard analysis." Returning to the intuitively appealing notion of an infinitesimal, an idea that appears in ordinary language when, for instance, we refer to "instants" of time, Robinson showed it is possible to set up a rigorous, consistent framework of analysis which includes infinitesimals. Drawing on work in mathematical logic, Robinson showed how to extend the real number system to include "hyperreals" (in something like the way rational numbers were extended to include "reals" in order to allow 2 to have a square root). The hyperreals include infinitesimals.

Nonstandard analysis is intuitively appealing to many, and further, much easier to learn and teach once modern mathematical logic is mastered. The delta-epsilon approach perfected by Weierstrass is certainly not wrong; it gives the right results – but for many students nonstandard analysis will be the pedagogically superior approach. The consensus among mathematicians today is that Robinson has rehabilitated the concept of an infinitesimal.

We will soon propose a nonstandard approach to building a philosophical case for revelatory claims, an approach that has certain advantages, just as in mathematics it is possible to develop a nonstandard approach to analysis that has its advantages. The awkward standard approach in analysis abandons infinitesimals (hyperreals) and pays a big price in the complications of its proofs. The nonstandard approach in analysis, which is in fact far more natural and easier to grasp, gains its advantages by allowing the use of hyperreals. Nonstandard analysis is in no way less rigorous. So too, the standard paths through natural theology, which ignore some elements inquirers are naturally inclined to bring into the discussion early on, unnecessarily complicate matters. There is no good reason for inquiring agnostics not to proceed in a way that many find natural, taking into account early the content of revelatory claims. By proceeding in this nonstandard but natural way, progress can be made at least equally well.

II. Investigating the Existence of Homer: First Premise of an Argument for an Alternative Approach

We here defend a claim that will serve as the first premise in our argument that a negative conclusion about the existence of God is unwarranted unless the content of revelatory claims has been considered. The claim at issue is this:

(1) If the existence of some being x is problematic, but not exceedingly improbable, then the question of whether x exists has not adequately been considered unless communications widely alleged to have come from x have been considered.

The example introduced above concerning the SETI research program provides some implicit support for this contention. But because of the claim's importance, we wish to offer more explicit support by developing a parallel between the investigation of the existence of God and investigation of the existence of Homer.[8]

Despite the fact that even the ancient Athenians knew almost nothing about the life of Homer, they seem not to have doubted that the *Iliad* and the *Odyssey* were both composed by a single individual. In the 6th century BC stories began to arise about the heritage and personality of the man believed to have authored the epics, but contemporary scholars find little in those traditions that is plausible except for the claim that Homer was an Ionian associated with Smurne and Khios.[9] Much later, Cicero and Josephus both suggested that the *Iliad* had been composed without the aid of writing, but neither seems to have doubted that the composition was the work of a single individual.[10]

The first widespread debate about whether there actually was a single person responsible at least for the *Iliad* surfaced in the 18th century. In 1715 a work by the Abbe d'Aubignac was published that argued that Homer never lived,[11] and by the end of the century the powerful and influential work of the German scholar F. A. Wolf had persuaded a large number of scholars that there never was a Homer, a single person who composed the *Iliad*. In developing his case Wolf relied on a newly discovered tenth-century "Homer" manuscript with commentary going back to the Alexandrians, and on the sophisticated tools of Biblical scholarship being developed by German theologians.

Wolf appears to argue in his grand (but unfinished) *Prolegomena to Homer*[12] that there could not have been a single individual who composed the *Iliad*, because if the *Iliad* had been composed by one individual that person would have needed to rely on writing, and writing was not known in the time and place of composition of the *Iliad*. Now if one is convinced that without writing it is impossible for a poem the length of the *Iliad* to be retained in the human mind, then it is not going to matter much what the poem itself contains, what the internal or intrinsic evidence for a single author is. Bitter debate between the "analysts" (who took up the Wolfian argument) and the "unitarians," who disputed it on grounds of internal textual evidence, raged on up through the first part of the 20th century.

But in the 1930s the field work of Milman Parry showed that there is no doubt that epics the length of the *Iliad* can be composed orally when writing is absent from a culture. Parry transcribed an epic poem of the proper length from a bard in southern Serbia unable to read or write. Subsequently, other field workers documented similar feats of memory (e.g. by Uzbek and Kara-kirgiz bards).[13] As the *Oxford Classical Dictionary* tells us:

> The early arguments [against the existence of Homer] . . . based on the belief that no man could have composed poems of such a length before writing was known, have now been dispelled by our knowledge of what memory can do when writing is not familiar.[14]

Given that it is not impossible, perhaps even not wildly implausible for a single poet to have had primary responsibility for the *Iliad*, scholars can ask: was there in fact one author? In answering this question, of course, the content of the poem is carefully considered. The cohesiveness of each poem as a whole is examined. The consistency and strength of the characters in the poem, and the development, power, and resolution of the main plot and of sub-themes within it is examined. The consistency and richness of the language is analyzed, and the regular appearance of certain features of vocabulary (including particular abstract nouns, Aeolic forms, and patronymics) studied. Types and number of similes and types of transitions used between major scenes are evaluated. The current consensus of opinion among the classicists seems to be that it is more likely than not that Homer did actually exist:

> Most scholars now accept that the Homeric epics are the result of a developing oral epic tradition on the one hand, the unifying and creative work of an exceptional monumental composer on the other.[15]

How does all this bear on investigating theism and revelatory claims? It yields a central principle. The classicist begins reflection on the question of authorship of the *Iliad* conscious of a serious problem for anyone who says there was a single or principal author: absent writing, it is not clear the human mind is capable of the task of composition. Learning the feats of memory illiterate peoples accomplish clarifies things. It may not *fully* establish that a principal author could have composed the great poem: perhaps, for instance, the poem contains what seem to be eye-witness accounts of landmarks no single individual could have visited at the time (dealing with this problem would require arguing that the accounts are not eye-witness accounts, or that they were initially, but could have been woven into the *Iliad* by a principal author, or something of the sort). But fully establishing that a principal author could have composed the great poem is not necessary in order for a classicist to be motivated to undertake further inquiry about Homer, motivated to study the contents of the *Iliad* with the question of authorship in mind. Now it may seem that the most we can get out of reflection on the case of Homer is merely an analogy that allows us to gesture towards an approach for the investigation of the existence of God and the truth of revelatory claims. But it would be a mistake to see the case of Homer in this way, because we can get a generalization out of this case, and (eventually) deduce from the generalization. The general principle the Homer example establishes is this: *If the existence of some being x is problematic, but not exceedingly improbable, then the question of whether x exists has not adequately been considered unless communications widely alleged to have come from x have been considered.*

III. Reflecting on the Likelihood of an Originator: Second Premise of an Argument for an Alternative Approach

This brings us to the second premise:

(2) While the existence of an originator is problematic, it is not exceedingly improbable.

We understand an *originator* to be a cause of the universe – more specifically, a certain sort of necessary condition of the existence of the universe. As we use the term, "originator" does not even imply intellect. Nevertheless, to show that the existence of an originator is not highly implausible, not exceedingly unlikely or improbable, may *in one sense* be to show that God's existence is not highly implausible. For if in fact God – the traditional God, the God not only of the philosophers but of Abraham, Isaac, and Jacob – does exist, a proof of an originator may be a proof of God in the sense that a proof of the existence of an electron is the proof of the existence of something with a charge of 1.6021^{-19} C. One might establish that the existence of an originator is not highly unlikely without claiming that the hypothesis that there is an originator is explanatory in some rich sense. One might establish that an originator is not highly unlikely without saying a word about *how* the originator originates, without giving any details about how the universe is caused. And one might establish that an originator is not highly unlikely without saying a word about other attributes the originator may have.

It can, in fact, be shown – with surprisingly little effort – that the existence of an originator is not highly unlikely. All we need do is show that the conjunction of three quite appealing propositions is not highly improbable. The three, which we will list in a moment, are familiar small fragments of certain versions of the Kalam argument. But the use we make of them is unusual. Kalam arguments aim to establish that there is a creator. In keeping with our over-all strategy, we aim only to establish that the existence of a creator or originator is not highly unlikely. Therefore, we need not insist that each of the three propositions is true, or even highly probable; we need only show that the conjunction is not highly improbable. Here are the propositions:

(A) The physical universe came to be (that is, had a beginning).[16]

(B) Whatever comes to be has a cause (a certain sort of necessary condition).

(C) Nothing causes itself to come to be.

If on some sensible reading of each proposition the conjunction of the three is not highly implausible, then it is not highly implausible that the universe has a cause distinct from itself, an originator. For all the argument tells us, there may be more than one cause of the universe, more than one originator: to say that there is *a* being causally responsible for the existence of the universe is not to say there is only one such being.[17] But if the argument is correct, it cannot be claimed that it is known or all but known that there is no creator.

Why think that the world came to be? Even many nontheists these days have been persuaded that the claim is true, given the theory that the world began from an initial singularity. The preponderance of opinion among contemporary cosmologists seems to be that the world did not always exist, that there was an initial singularity out of which the world developed. On this basis alone it looks like we can assign the claim that "the world came to be" a probability of at least .5. How are we to assess the probability of (B), that whatever comes to be has a cause (a certain sort of necessary condition)? There was a time when this universal causal principle seemed obvious to virtually everyone. Since Hume, the claim no longer strikes philosophers as obviously true. On the other hand, it does not strike them as obviously false, either. Though we think the principle is highly likely, let us cautiously assign it a probability (roughly) of merely .5. What about (C)? Quentin Smith offers three arguments intended to open up the possibility that the universe created itself.[18] But we can put them to one side here, because they have no impact on the position we are taking. Even if for the sake of discussion every point in all three of Smith's arguments is conceded, all that follows is that it is *possible* that the world caused itself. Smith insists that the atheist's position cannot be dismissed out of hand. But neither can the theist's. We have good reason to think the existence of a creator, an originator, is more than a remote possibility.

We want to emphasize how conservative our estimates concerning the likelihood of an originator are. We have said that each of the three premises just discussed is *at least* equiprobable with its contradictory. But at least two of the propositions would be assigned a higher probability by most people: proposition (B) is often taken to be self-evident, and (C) is scarcely ever denied, even by atheists. The conjunction of the three propositions may have a probability considerably higher than .125.

IV. Drawing Conclusions: The Alternative Approach

So we now have at our disposal the general principle established by the Homer example, and we have a key claim concerning an originator. We are equipped to mount the following argument:

(1) If the existence of some being x is problematic, but not exceedingly improbable, then the question of whether x exists has not adequately been considered unless communications widely alleged to have come from x have been considered.

(2) While the existence of an originator is problematic, it is not exceedingly improbable.

(3) If the question of whether an originator exists has not adequately been considered unless communications widely alleged to have come from the originator have been considered, then the question of whether God exists has not adequately been considered unless the content of some major revelatory claims has been considered.

(4) So the question of whether God exists has not adequately been considered unless the content of some major revelatory claims has been considered.

The first two premises of this argument, of course, have been established in the preceding two sections.

It should not take much work to see that premise (3) is true. The requirement that one must take into account the content of putative communications in order to investigate the existence of a mere originator is, indeed, surprising. But once that point is recognized, (3) should be easy to accept. If one must look at the content of putative communications even to establish the existence of a bare originator, apart from the originator's properties, then *a fortiori* it is important to look at putative communications if one is interested in whether the originator might have a property such as goodness.

The point may be illustrated by recalling our example involving SETI, the Search for Extra-Terrestrial Intelligence. Examining potential communications from possibly-existing alien beings helps us judge whether aliens do actually exist. If we decide that there is a good chance alien minds are out there, we will want to know something about the characteristics of those intelligences – how smart they are, how good they are, and so on. And to acquire information about these matters we surely will look very closely indeed at messages purporting to come from them.

Obviously, too, anyone interested in determining something about the character of Homer will consult the contents of works he is alleged to have produced. If the question of whether a single author of the *Iliad* existed has not adequately been considered unless communications alleged to have come from the author have been examined, then *a fortiori* the question of whether a single virtuous and praiseworthy author of the *Iliad* existed has not adequately been considered unless the content of the author's putative communications have been studied.

V. An Objection to the Alternative Approach: Handling the Problem of Evil

In setting out the inadequacies of the standard philosophical approach to investigating revelatory claims we emphasized the seriousness of the problem of evil. Yet our defense of an alternative, nonstandard approach has said little about how the agnostic is to handle that problem. It may be objected that the nonstandard approach fails to present a solution to the problem of evil.

Notice, however, that the agnostic need not judge that there is a solution to the problem of evil to proceed with inquiry into the content of revelatory claims; what is needed is recognition that there may be revelatory claims that, *if true*, provide a satisfactory account of evil. A satisfactory account (we have maintained) will include reference to other-worldly goods. What else will it include? It is hard to say at the outset. It is easy enough to imagine accounts that clearly would *not* be satisfactory. It will not do, for instance, to be told that the creator plays with human beings as a small, malicious child plays with animals, at whim subjecting them to cruel tortures. This tale, even *if true*, is wholly unsatisfactory for an agnostic seeking evidence of a good God.

An account of evil might be both acceptable *and* incomplete. If a good friend misses an appointment with you, and says that he could not make the appointment because an important but confidential matter came up, you presumably will accept your friend's remarks as a satisfactory explanation of the missed meeting, though it is obviously incomplete. Christianity purports to give an acceptable, though incomplete, account of evil. One who investigates a Christian revelatory claim should not expect the veil to lift completely – at least not in this lifetime. Some obscurity in explanation may be necessary because depth is necessary, and obscurity attends depth. What the agnostic investigator needs to ask is not whether the Christian account of evil is in all details complete, but rather whether the account, *if true*, would be acceptable.

One sort of evil that a revelatory claim fitting for the human condition might not address in any detail is animal suffering (or at least the suffering of nonhuman animals). A revelation that tells us what we need to know and do to be saved may in all sorts of ways fall short of being an exhaustive account of evil: highly technical accounts of natural laws involving animal suffering may easily be omitted. That is consistent with the revelation meeting our deepest needs, and giving a satisfactory account of evil. Explanations in the sciences, after all, almost always butt up against some fact that cannot be accounted for: there were objections to Galileo's theory that could not be answered (in Galileo's day, anyway), but that did not show Galileo's explanatory account was incorrect or unsatisfactory.

Interestingly, many theists and atheists agree that if there is a perfectly good God it is not unreasonable for us to expect some kind of communication from that God. Richard Swinburne, for instance, develops the argument that "if there is a God there is good a priori reason for expecting a propositional revelation."[19] And J. L. Schellenberg presents an argument pointing towards atheism for the claim that if there *were* a God, his existence would be obvious, and reasonable nonbelief would not be an option (in fact, Schellenberg suggests, nonbelief *is* a reasonable option).[20] But the arguments Swinburne and Schellenberg set forth actually do not depend on there being a *perfectly* good God: a "basically" good god, a minimally decent god, would do. No human parents are perfectly good parents, but virtually all human parents are good enough that they would seek to establish communication with their children if the children were separated from them and the children could not by themselves close the gap.

It may be pointed out that standard treatments of the problem of evil – treatments belonging to the mainstream approach to natural theology, and included in the paths typically recommended to agnostic inquirers – often appeal to an afterlife as a possible justifying reason for God's permitting evil. Is the approach we are recommending really all that different from the standard approach? We think that it is. Standardly, the possibility of life after death is regarded as a mere logical possibility. *Particular* revelatory claims that there is life after death are not considered in any detail. Thus one obtains nothing like the whole picture. The standard paths ignore (until very late in the game) enigmatic but arresting assertions such as St Paul's claim that by his suffering he makes up what is lacking in the sufferings of Christ. Furthermore, the pronouncements of some religious groups that the doctrine of life after death has been *revealed* is not engaged in the standard treatments. But it is only by examining the claim that the doctrine has been revealed that one can assess evidence concerning the development of doctrine over time, within a particular community.

VI. An Objection to the Alternative Approach: The Alleged Difficulty of Investigating Revelatory Claims

A critic may at this point object that evaluating the contents of revelatory claims is impossibly difficult, at least for an agnostic inquirer. Many questions arise. What is the criterion for individuating revelatory claims? How should an inquirer choose one or more claims for investigation? What guidelines should be used in assessing the various claims?

These are serious questions. But several considerations blunt the objection. First, if the intricacy or multitude of revelatory claims completely prevented investigation, then the claims could not sensibly be *dismissed* out of hand, as some critics are inclined to do. Second, an agnostic interested in revelatory claims at some point will end up exploring them if the standard ordering protocol for investigation is pursued, the protocol that accepts presupposition (P), *assuming the inquiry is not abandoned* (that is rather a large assumption, we have suggested). The question is not *whether*, but *when*, the claims will be investigated. Third, an agnostic investigator who is interested in the truth of a revelatory claim will, in the end, have to make an "all things considered" judgment. And the things to be considered include *not only* the difficulty in investigating revelatory claims, but plenty of difficulties on the other side (such as problems in making sense of a thoroughly materialistic world-view). Fourth, it is, in fact, manifestly possible for nonbelievers to evaluate (fairly early in the game) the truth of at least some revelatory claims without expert application of the tools of historians and scripture scholars.

That fourth point needs some explanation. How is an inquirer untrained in scripture scholarship, an agnostic, supposed to evaluate the contents of a revelatory claim?

What agnostics typically will reflect on when investigating revelatory claims are *reports* concerning revelatory claims. Such reports contain dual intermediaries: an individual (one intermediary) makes a report; the report states that God has revealed to an intermediary (who may or may not be identical with the reporter). It may be natural for Christian believers to skip over both sorts of intermediaries, but it is not at all natural for an agnostic to do so: what agnostics actually encounter are claims *human beings* make, and it is impossible for an agnostic to forget that fact. Revelatory claims are asserted by fallible, limited, all-too-human beings with their share of vices and psychological difficulties.

We understand a *report* of a *revelatory claim* to have the form:

> S asserts that R revealed that p to T.

S will be an individual or a group of individuals. R will be a super-natural (extra-cosmic) revealer. p will be a proposition. And T will be an individual or a group of individuals. A *revelatory claim* (rather than a report of such a claim) takes the form:

> R revealed that p to T.

The following are examples of reports of revelatory claims. Embedded in the reports are revelatory claims themselves.

> *The Ayatollahs* assert that God revealed that *the Quran contains God's will for all the world* to *Muhammad*.
>
> *The authors of the Catholic Catechism* assert that God revealed that *the Roman Catholic Church is the oracle of God* to *the Roman Catholic Church*.
>
> *My great-aunt* asserts that God revealed that *only Caucasians will have a place in heaven* to *her next-door neighbor*.

The notion of a report of a revelatory claim can be sharpened in various ways. One might, for instance, require that a specific revelatory claim give some indication of the *means* of the revelation – maybe it came through a dream, or a vision, or a voice. One might require that the time of S's assertion, or of R's alleged communication, be indexed. But it is a mistake to think we are not entitled to use a concept for the purposes of inference until we can offer a full definition. In order to explain that a spoon is moving across the table because someone is pulling it with a nearly invisible thread, one need not first define motion – in fact, motion is taken as an undefined primitive concept by physicists. Similarly, we do not need a completely precise account of a revelatory claim in order to make use of the concept. If the project at hand requires it, the account can be detailed.

How is an agnostic to evaluate the contents of a revelatory claim? One may begin by asking, in Newman's words, whether the contents are "what divine goodness would vouchsafe, did it vouchsafe anything." Does the alleged revelation provide moral guidance? Is it noble and elevated and illuminating? Does it satisfy spiritual hunger and heal the deepest of human wounds? Does it offer a satisfactory (though possibly incomplete) account of evil? The questions are not easy to answer. But that is no reason for leaving them out of the picture altogether. One cannot ignore data about whether a revelatory claim is fitting for the human condition and say that one has looked at the total evidential base.

Questions beyond those concerning fittingness can and should be raised in evaluating the content of a revelatory claim. Is the content original? Is the content of the revelatory claim consistent with what we know about history and science – is it free from error on these matters (at least in those instances where it promises to be free from error)? What are the metaphysical presuppositions of the revelation at issue – is the content of the revelatory claim consistent with philosophical knowledge? Is the claim self-consistent? Is the doctrinal content of the putative revelation strikingly developed over time, developed in a way that suggests providential guidance through the ages?

Questions concerning the fittingness of a revelatory claim or its originality or development may seem very subjective. But subjective judgments occur in every field. Consider the physicist's judgment that there is a "serious lack of agreement" between a body of data on certain spin variables, P and Q, and the values a particular theory predicts:

> Theoretical values of the desired parameters, in this case P and Q, are calculated using one or more standard models. The data points are plotted on the same graph with "error bars" representing the expected statistical variation in the data.

But there is no exactitude about handling the data:

> One then *visually compares* the theoretical curves with the data points and judges whether the fit is "extraordinarily good," "very good," "good," "reasonably good," "lacking in agreement," "seriously lacking in agreement," and so on. . . .[21]

The judgment about fit is not formed by applying any sort of algorithm; the judgment is subjective. Now we do not pretend that investigating a revelatory claim for fit with the human condition, or judging whether the development of some revelatory claim displays Newman's "chronic vigor," is just like doing nuclear physics. But when one asks whether the content of some claim is "what divine goodness would vouchsafe," or whether it has displayed a striking staying power over the years, one is posing questions recognizably similar to ones asked by physicists and other scientists.

It is worth noting that the path standardly recommended for those who want philosophically to assess the truth of a revelatory claim – particularly the Christian claim – requires judging the legitimacy of putative miracles prior to investigating the contents of putative revelations. Locke and Swinburne are paradigmatic representatives of the standard attitude towards assessing putative miracles. Both argue that in order to accept Christianity we need to discover a validating miracle (such as the resurrection).[22] Most agnostics, however, will be hard pressed to follow the strategy of *first* deciding that it is probable Christ was resurrected, and *then* going on to examine other details of Christian revelatory claims.

Since Locke and Swinburne have already argued that it is at least probable there is a good God by the time they get to evaluation of revelatory claims, it is surprising that they both require a validating miracle for believing Christian claims. Suppose you have no doubts that your college has a dean. Someone says "there is a shocking e-mail out from the dean." Your natural response is to believe that the dean did in fact send an e-mail, and probably, further, that it is at least mildly surprising. You certainly do not think you first must investigate whether your college still has a dean before you judge how likely it is that the dean sent out an e-mail. If there is a creator, it is not bizarre to think it would communicate to creatures. One can imagine all sorts of non-miraculous evidences of a divine communication *given that the existence of a divine being is not highly unlikely*.

In any event, the standard approach to building a philosophical case for revelatory claims requires difficult judgments relatively early about the plausibility of miracle claims. Though investigation of the content of revelatory claims will not be trouble-free, it may be easier for the inquiring agnostic and more appealing than evaluation of miracle-claims.

It is worth noting, finally, that even if an agnostic thought it unlikely that examining the contents of revelatory claims would yield a positive pay-off, the examination might be worthwhile. Imagine you are in an abandoned mine, a mine nobody knows you have entered, and are suddenly shut off from the entrance by the collapse of the ceilings both in front of and behind you. It seems pretty clear to you that the oxygen left will last only a short time. As you search in the dark for a way out, you see – or think you see – the faintest line of light passing through what may be a thin passage leading up and out. And you hear – or think you hear – a voice above calling down to you. The climb will be difficult, and you have no proof that it will get you into the open air. But it is hardly foolish to begin climbing.

Notes

1 For a more detailed presentation of the argument in this paper, see Sandra Menssen and Thomas D. Sullivan, *The Agnostic Inquirer: Revelation from a Philosophical Standpoint* (Grand Rapids, MI: Eerdmans, 2007).

2 The presupposition marking the standard approach is very common. To begin to get a sense of the breadth and depth of the presupposition consider (a) the order of topics typically addressed in philosophy of religion anthologies; (b) Scott McDonald's account of the order of topics in his entry on "natural theology" in the *Routledge Encyclopedia of Philosophy*; (c) the sequencing of Richard Swinburne's cumulative-case argument for Christianity; and (d) Alvin Plantinga's account of sequence in the "Enlightenment model" for investigating religious belief (*Warranted Christian Belief*, Oxford: Oxford University Press, 2000), pp. 266–80.

This is not to say presupposition (P) is highlighted in accounts of the standard approach. It is not. Nor is the presupposition challenged, so far as we can see, by any of the people we have just mentioned. What some *do* question is the very need for an argument.

Though presupposition (P) is frequently found in works in natural theology, we do not suggest that natural theology cannot be done without adhering to (P). Indeed, we take our own work in this essay, work consisting in part of an attack on (P), to be work *in natural theology*. That is to say, we build *philosophical* arguments, arguments whose premises do not appeal to the authority of putative revelations.

3 Theists accustomed to the skillful defenses made by Plantinga, Swinburne, and others may think that agnostics are over-anxious about the problem of evil. But they surely are not. It is interesting to note the shift in Swinburne's own position on the need to refer to an afterlife to handle the problem of evil. In *The Existence of God* he presented a theodicy that made no reference to the possibility of an afterlife. An inquirer might, Swinburne noted, try to bring in the possibility by appealing to Christian doctrine in the early stages of investigation. But Swinburne rejected this move on the grounds that if the hypothesis of an afterlife is added into the theistic hypothesis, the hypothesis becomes more complicated, and hence has a lower prior probability (pp. 221–2). Once an inquirer has worked through Christian doctrine, Swinburne said, the inquirer can go back over the equations, and come to a fuller understanding of divine goodness. But lots of people – lots of agnostics – will have been stopped short long before reaching the point at which Swinburne urges investigation of Christian doctrine, stopped by the order of inquiry Swinburne used and apparently recommended.

In a more recent work, *Providence and the Problem of Evil* (Oxford: Clarendon Press; New York: Oxford University Press, 1998), Swinburne says that he is not certain the order of inquiry he earlier recommended will be satisfactory for an agnostic inquirer (he doesn't explicitly refer to agnostics, but one may draw the inference). He writes (pp. x–xi):

> But, while continuing to endorse the general approach of that book [*The Existence of God*], I have come to believe subsequently that theodicy is a considerably more difficult enterprise than I represented it there. . . . I assumed in that book that theodicy does not need to bring in doctrines peculiar to different religions (such as reincarnation in Eastern religions; or life after death in a new world etc. in Christianity), in order to show that the occurrence of evil does not count against the existence of God. I am not fully convinced about that any more.

The theodicy Swinburne goes on to set out explicitly appeals to "the whole Christian doctrinal package taken together." Missing is any account of how the skeptical agnostic inquirer can be motivated to examine that doctrinal package, given the lack of an argument establishing a probable case for the existence of God. (Swinburne's argument in *The Existence of God* that there is a probable case for God's existence depended on the theodicy he expresses doubts about in *Providence and the Problem of Evil.*)

4 Plantinga, *Warranted Christian Belief*, p. 280. We cannot entirely concur with Plantinga on this point. In the course of the present essay we argue that even if a low probability is initially assigned to the likelihood that a creator exists, it may well be possible to bring the probability up above .5 through philosophical investigation of the content of revelatory claims.

5 Plantinga, *Warranted Christian Belief*; Paul Moser, "Divine Hiding" and "A God Who Hides and Seeks," *Philosophia Christi* 3:1 (2001), pp. 91–107, 119–25.

6 See Ch. 5 of *On Sophistical Refutations*. Aristotle's main idea seems to be that we fall victim to the fallacy if we fail to detect that a question seemingly *one* really involves *several* questions, and either proceed to answer with a "yes" or a "no" in a way bound to be misleading, or freeze and fail to answer at all. A familiar example (though not Aristotle's) is presented by the question "Have you stopped beating your spouse?" No fallacy is committed, however, if one simply distinguishes the questions at issue, and explains one's answer. There is a truthful answer a nonabusive spouse can give to the question "Have you stopped beating your spouse?" The answer is: "No – I have not stopped beating my spouse, because to stop something you must have been doing it at some point, and I never have beaten my spouse."

7 The definitions of "the fallacy of the complex question" provided by most logic texts are vague and ill-formed. Irving Copi and Carl Cohen define the fallacy as:

> asking a question in such a way as to presuppose the truth of some conclusion buried in that question (*Introduction to Logic*, 10th ed. (New York: Macmillan), p. 183).

But this formulation has us mark innumerable perfectly reasonable questions as fallacious. "Will you pick Sarah up after her classes end today?" presupposes that you exist, and Sarah exists, and Sarah is female, and she has more than one class, and she has more than one class today, and the classes will end today rather than extend past midnight.

8 We thank Professor Jeremiah Reedy of the Classics Department at Macalester College for helpful comments about the history of scholarship on Homer.

9 G. S. Kirk, *The Iliad: A Commentary* (Cambridge: Cambridge University Press, 1985), p. 1.

10 F. A. Wolf, *Prolegomena to Homer*, orig. publ. 1795, trans., intro., notes by Anthony Grafton, Glenn W. Most, James E. G. Zetzel (Princeton, NJ: Princeton University Press, 1985), p. 5.

11 See Joachim Latacz, *Homer: His Art and His World*, trans. James P. Holoka (Ann Arbor: The University of Michigan Press, 1996), pp. 7–8.

12 Wolf, *Prolegomena to Homer*.

13 "Heroic Poetry," *Britannica Online*, accessed 05 August 1998. <www.eb.com:180/cgi-bin/g?DocF=micro/268/58.html>

14 *Oxford Classical Dictionary*, 2nd ed. (Oxford: Clarendon Press, 1970), p. 524.

15 Kirk, p. xv. Some classical scholars (at this point in time apparently a minority) are now arguing there is decent reason to think Homer did have access to writing after all: as the so-called Dark Ages of ancient Greece are illuminated by modern archeology and history and philology some classicists have become convinced that significant aspects of the old Mycenaean aristocratic culture survived the "catastrophic event" (whatever it was) of about 1,200 BC that was once thought to have extinguished Mycenaean civilization. But whether Homer did or did not read and write does not affect the legitimacy of the reasoning of the novice classicist.

16 By "universe" we mean *this* universe, a space that includes all matter and energy, and nothing beyond that space. (Some theorists have proposed that this universe is not alone, that there are alternate universes to the one we inhabit, entirely unconnected to ours.) The universe is commonly thought to proceed from a singularity, and the singularity commonly thought to be a physical reality such as gravity, mass, or charge, that has an apparent value of infinity. The concept of a singularity as applied to the entity appearing before the big bang is controversial within science, but these controversies can be ignored here. Details concerning alternative understandings of the universe's beginnings do not affect our argument, so long as it is understood that we are not claiming the world came to be in the course of an already-existing time.

17 Thus when we speak of "the originator" we will *not* mean "the one and only originator or cause." Rather, we mean "either the one and only originator, *or* one of the originators."

18 See Quentin Smith, "The Reason the Universe Exists is that it Caused Itself to Exist," *Philosophy* 74 (1999), pp. 579–86.

19 Richard Swinburne, *Revelation: From Metaphor to Analogy* (Oxford: Clarendon Press, 1992), p. 83; the argument stretches through chapter five of the book.

20 J. L. Schellenberg, *Divine Hiddenness and Human Reason* (Ithaca, NY: Cornell University Press, 1993).

21 Ronald N. Giere, *Explaining Science: A Cognitive Approach* (Chicago: The University of Chicago Press, 1988), p. 190.

22 In one way, the requirement of a miracle might be seen as an incidental feature of Swinburne's approach to revelation; at times he seems to allow the theoretical possibility that the *content* of a revelatory claim might suffice. But in fact, he asserts, none of the major revelatory traditions contains a content that suffices for credibility.

The problem faced by the inquirer following Swinburne's approach is exacerbated by his views on how one identifies the repository of true revelation. Swinburne wants to rely exclusively on evidence about early church history in judging whether there was a resurrection, because he wants to pin down a validating miracle and identify the "original" revelation before identifying the church or tradition that is today the oracle of God. Once the original revelation is identified, he thinks, one is positioned to ask which among the later institutions or churches is the "closest continuer" of the group receiving the original revelation. But one needs maybe a .4 or .5 or .6 probability that the resurrection occurred *given the evidence about early history* if one is going to get what counts as a substantiating miracle. Few agnostics are able to accept such an estimate. With an enhanced base that includes a long tradition of developing doctrine, it might be reasonable for one to believe Jesus was resurrected *because* one believes that a particular community has received the fullness of divine revelation, and this community proclaims the resurrection.

B

Fideism

1

Truth is Subjectivity

Søren Kierkegaard

Søren Kierkegaard's (1813–55) writings are fascinating and profound, but also difficult and challenging. Credited with being the father of existentialism, Kierkegaard was determined in his writings to undermine his own authority as author (e.g. by using a variety of pseudonyms) and force his readers to think for themselves and make their own choices. It is often difficult to determine precisely what Kierkegaard thinks, which was almost certainly his intention. In the following selection from his *Concluding Unscientific Postscript* Kierkegaard criticizes an objective, rational approach to religious belief and defends a subjective approach that pits faith against reason. Having faith, argues Kierkegaard, is holding fast with infinite passion to that which is objectively uncertain.

When the question of truth is raised in an objective manner, reflection is directed objectively to the truth, as an object to which the knower is related. Reflection is not focussed upon the relationship, however, but upon the question of whether it is the truth to which the knower is related. If only the object to which he is related is the truth, the subject is accounted to be in the truth. When the question of the truth is raised subjectively, reflection is directed subjectively to the nature of the individual's relationship; if only the mode of this relationship is in the truth, the individual is in the truth even if he should happen to be thus related to what is not true.[1] Let us take as an example the knowledge of God. Objectively, reflection is directed to the problem of whether this object is the true God; subjectively, reflection is directed to the question whether the individual is related to a something *in such a manner* that his relationship is in truth a God-relationship. On which side is the truth now

Søren Kierkegaard, "Truth Is Subjectivity" from *Kierkegaard's Concluding Unscientific Postscript*, trans. David F. Swenson and Walter Lowrie (Princeton, NJ: Princeton University Press, 1944), pp. 178–83.

to be found? Ah, may we not here resort to a mediation, and say: It is on neither side, but in the mediation of both? Excellently well said, provided we might have it explained how an existing individual manages to be in a state of mediation. For to be in a state of mediation is to be finished, while to exist is to become. Nor can an existing individual be in two places at the same time – he cannot be an identity of subject and object. When he is nearest to being in two places at the same time he is in passion; but passion is momentary, and passion is also the highest expression of subjectivity.

The existing individual who chooses to pursue the objective way enters upon the entire approximation-process by which it is proposed to bring God to light objectively. But this is in all eternity impossible, because God is a subject, and therefore exists only for subjectivity in inwardness. The existing individual who chooses the subjective way apprehends instantly the entire dialectical difficulty involved in having to use some time, perhaps a long time, in finding God objectively; and he feels this dialectical difficulty in all its painfulness, because every moment is wasted in which he does not have God.[2] That very instant he has God, not by virtue of any objective deliberation, but by virtue of the infinite passion of inwardness. The objective inquirer, on the other hand, is not embarrassed by such dialectical difficulties as are involved in devoting an entire period of investigation to finding God – since it is possible that the inquirer may die tomorrow; and if he lives he can scarcely regard God as something to be taken along if convenient, since God is precisely that which one takes *a tout prix*, which in the understanding of passion constitutes the true inward relationship to God.

It is at this point, so difficult dialectically, that the way swings off for everyone who knows what it means to think, and to think existentially; which is something very different from sitting at a desk and writing about what one has never done, something very different from writing *de omnibus dubitandum* and at the same time being as credulous existentially as the most sensuous of men. Here is where the way swings off, and the change is marked by the fact that while objective knowledge rambles comfortably on by way of the long road of approximation without being impelled by the urge of passion, subjective knowledge counts every delay a deadly peril, and the decision so infinitely important and so instantly pressing that it is as if the opportunity had already passed.

Now when the problem is to reckon up on which side there is most truth, whether on the side of one who seeks the true God objectively, and pursues the approximate truth of the God-idea; or on the side of one who, driven by the infinite passion of his need of God, feels an infinite concern for his own relationship to God in truth (and to be at one and the same time on both sides equally, is as we have noted not possible for an existing individual, but is merely the happy delusion of an imaginary I-am-I): the answer cannot be in doubt for anyone who has not been demoralized with the aid of science. If one who lives in the midst of Christendom goes up to the house of God, the house of the true God, with the true conception of God in his knowledge, and prays, but prays in a false spirit; and one who lives in an idolatrous community prays with the entire passion of the infinite, although his eyes rest upon the image of an idol: where is there most truth? The one prays in truth to God though he worships an idol; the other prays falsely to the true God, and hence worships in fact an idol.

When one man investigates objectively the problem of immortality, and another embraces an uncertainty with the passion of the infinite: where is there most truth, and who has the greater certainty? The one has entered upon a never-ending approximation, for the certainty of immortality lies precisely in the subjectivity of the individual; the other is immortal, and fights for his immortality by struggling with the uncertainty. Let us consider Socrates. Nowadays everyone dabbles in a few proofs; some have several such proofs, others fewer. But Socrates! He puts the question objectively in a problematic manner: *if* there is an immortality. He must therefore be accounted a doubter in comparison with one of our modern thinkers with the three proofs? By no means. On this "if" he risks his entire life, he has the courage to meet death, and he has with the passion of the infinite so determined the pattern of his life that it must be found acceptable – *if* there is an immortality. Is any better proof capable of being given for the immortality of the soul? But those who have the three proofs do not at all determine their lives in conformity therewith; if there is an immortality it must feel disgust over their manner of life: can any better refutation be given of the three proofs? The bit of uncertainty that Socrates had, helped him because he himself contributed the passion of the infinite; the three proofs that the others have do not profit them at all, because they are dead to spirit and enthusiasm, and their three proofs, in lieu of proving anything else, prove just this. A young girl may enjoy all the sweetness of love on the basis of what is merely a weak hope that she is beloved, because she rests everything on this weak hope; but many a wedded matron more than once subjected to the strongest expressions of love, has in so far indeed had proofs, but strangely enough has not enjoyed *quod erat demonstrandum*. The Socratic ignorance, which Socrates held fast with the entire passion of his inwardness, was thus an expression for the principle that the eternal truth is related to an existing individual, and that this truth must therefore be a paradox for him as long as he exists; and yet it is possible that there was more truth in the Socratic ignorance as it was in him, than in the entire objective truth of the System, which flirts with what the times demand and accommodates itself to *Privatdocents*.

The objective accent falls on WHAT is said, the subjective accent on HOW it is said. This distinction holds even in the aesthetic realm, and receives definite expression in the principle that what is in itself true may in the mouth of such and such a person become untrue. In these times this distinction is particularly worthy of notice, for if we wish to express in a single sentence the difference between ancient times and our own, we should doubtless have to say: "In ancient times only an individual here and there knew the truth; now all know it, except that the inwardness of its appropriation stands in an inverse relationship to the extent of its dissemination.[3] Aesthetically the contradiction that truth becomes untruth in this or that person's mouth, is best construed comically: In the ethico-religious sphere, accent is again on the "how." But this is not to be understood as referring to demeanor, expression, or the like; rather it refers to the relationship sustained by the existing individual, in his own existence, to the content of his utterance. Objectively the interest is focussed merely on the thought-content, subjectively on the inwardness. At its maximum this inward "how" is the passion of the infinite, and the passion of the infinite is the truth. But the passion of the infinite is precisely subjectivity, and thus subjectivity becomes the truth. Objectively there is no infinite decisiveness, and hence it is objectively in order to annul the difference between good and evil, together with the principle of contradiction, and therewith also the infinite difference between the true and the false. Only in subjectivity is there decisiveness, to seek objectivity is to be in error. It is the passion of the infinite that is the decisive factor and not its content, for its content is precisely itself. In this manner subjectivity and the subjective "how" constitute the truth.

But the "how" which is thus subjectively accentuated precisely because the subject is an existing individual, is also subject to a dialectic with respect to time. In the passionate moment of decision, where the road swings away from objective knowledge, it seems as if the infinite decision were thereby realized. But in the same moment the existing individual finds himself in the temporal order, and the subjective "how" is transformed into a striving, a striving which receives indeed its impulse and a repeated renewal from the decisive passion of the infinite, but is nevertheless a striving.

When subjectivity is the truth, the conceptual determination of the truth must include an expression for the antithesis to objectivity, a memento of the fork in the road where the way swings off; this expression will at the same time serve as an indication of the tension of the subjective inwardness. Here is such a definition of truth: *An objective uncertainty held fast in an appropriation-process of the most passionate inwardness is the truth*, the highest truth attainable for an *existing* individual. At the point where the way swings off (and where this is cannot be specified objectively, since it is a matter of subjectivity), there objective knowledge is placed in abeyance. Thus the subject merely has, objectively, the uncertainty; but it is this which precisely increases the tension of that infinite passion which constitutes his inwardness. The truth is precisely the venture which chooses an objective uncertainty with the passion of the infinite. I contemplate the order of nature in the hope of finding God, and I see omnipotence and wisdom; but I also see much else that disturbs my mind and excites anxiety. The sum of all this is an objective uncertainty. But it is for this very reason that the inwardness becomes as intense as it is, for it embraces this objective uncertainty with the entire passion of the infinite. In the case of a mathematical proposition the objectivity is given, but for this reason the truth of such a proposition is also an indifferent truth.

But the above definition of truth is an equivalent expression for faith. Without risk there is no faith. Faith is precisely the contradiction between the infinite passion of the individual's inwardness and the objective uncertainty. If I am capable of grasping God objectively, I do not believe, but precisely because I cannot do this I must believe. If I wish to preserve myself in faith I must constantly be intent upon holding fast the objective uncertainty, so as to remain out upon the deep, over seventy thousand fathoms of water, still preserving my faith.

In the principle that subjectivity, inwardness, is the truth, there is comprehended the Socratic wisdom, whose everlasting merit it was to have become aware of the essential significance of existence, of the fact that the knower is an existing individual. For this reason Socrates was in the truth by virtue of his ignorance, in the highest sense in which this was possible within paganism. To attain to an understanding of this, to comprehend that the misfortune of speculative philosophy is again and again to have forgotten that the knower is an existing individual, is in our objective age difficult enough. "But to have made an advance upon Socrates without even having understood what he understood, is at any rate not "Socratic."

Notes

1 The reader will observe that the question here is about essential truth, or about the truth which is essentially related to existence, and that it is precisely for the sake of clarifying it as inwardness or as subjectivity that this contrast is drawn.

2 In this manner God certainly becomes a postulate, but not in the otiose manner in which this word is commonly understood. It becomes clear rather that the only way in which an existing individual comes into relation with God, is when the dialectical contradiction brings his passion to the point of despair, and helps him to embrace God with the "category of despair" (faith). Then the postulate is so far from being arbitrary that it is precisely a life-necessity. It is then not so much that God is a postulate, as that the existing individual's postulation of God is a necessity.

3 [. . .] Though ordinarily not wishing an expression of opinion on the part of reviewers, I might at this point almost desire it, provided such opinions, so far from flattering me, amounted to an assertion of the daring truth that what I say is something that everybody knows, even every child, and that the cultured know infinitely much better. If it only stands fast that everyone knows it, my standpoint is in order, and I shall doubtless make shift to manage with the unity of the comic and the tragic. If there were anyone who did not know it I might perhaps be in danger of being dislodged from my position of equilibrium by the thought that I might be in a position to communicate to someone the needful preliminary knowledge. It is just this which engages my interest so much, this that the cultured are accustomed to say: that everyone knows what the highest is. This was not the case in paganism, nor in Judaism, nor in the seventeen centuries of Christianity. Hail to the nineteenth century! Everyone knows it. What progress has been made since the time when only a few knew it. To make up for this, perhaps, we must assume that no one nowadays does it.

2

Kierkegaard's Arguments against Objective Reasoning in Religion

Robert M. Adams

In the following essay Robert M. Adams (b. 1937), Professor Emeritus of Philosophy at Yale University, attempts to clarify Kierkegaard's criticisms of the objective approach to religious belief. Adams identifies three different arguments in Kierkegaard's writings and argues that while one of them is clearly a failure, the other two are not easily resisted.

It is sometimes held that there is something in the nature of religious faith itself that renders it useless or undesirable to reason objectively in support of such faith, even if the reasoning should happen to have considerable plausibility. Søren Kierkegaard's *Concluding Unscientific Postscript* is probably the document most commonly cited as representative of this view. In the present essay I shall discuss three arguments for the view. I call them the Approximation Argument, the Postponement Argument, and the Passion Argument; and I suggest they can all be found in the *Postscript*. I shall try to show that the Approximation Argument is a bad argument. The other two will not be so easily disposed of, however. I believe they show that Kierkegaard's conclusion, or something like it, does indeed follow from a certain conception of religiousness – a conception which has some appeal, although for reasons which I shall briefly suggest, I am not prepared to accept it.

Kierkegaard uses the word "objective" and its cognates in several senses, most of which need not concern us here. We are interested in the sense in which he uses it when he says, "it is precisely a misunderstanding to seek an objective assurance," and when he speaks of "an objective uncertainty held fast in the appropriation-process of the most passionate inwardness" (pp. 41, 182).[1] Let us say that a piece of reasoning, *R*, is *objective reasoning* just in case every (or almost every) intelligent, fair-minded, and sufficiently informed person would regard *R* as showing or tending to show (in the circumstances in which

Robert M. Adams, "Kierkegaard's Arguments against Objective Reasoning in Religion". *The Monist* 60:2 (1977): 228–43.

R is used, and to the extent claimed in *R*) that *R*'s conclusion is true or probably true. Uses of "objective" and "objectively" in other contexts can be understood from their relation to this one; for example, an objective uncertainty is a proposition which cannot be shown by objective reasoning to be certainly true.

1. The Approximation Argument

"Is it possible to base an eternal happiness upon historical knowledge?" is one of the central questions in the *Postscript*, and in the *Philosophical Fragments* to which it is a "postscript." Part of Kierkegaard's answer to the question is that it is not possible to base an eternal happiness on objective reasoning about historical facts.

> For nothing is more readily evident than that the greatest attainable certainty with respect to anything historical is merely an *approximation*. And an approximation, when viewed as a basis for an eternal happiness, is wholly inadequate, since the incommensurability makes a result impossible. [p. 25]

Kierkegaard maintains that it is possible, however, to base an eternal happiness on a belief in historical facts that is independent of objective evidence for them, and that that is what one must do in order to be a Christian. This is the Approximation Argument for the proposition that Christian faith cannot be based on objective reasoning.[2] (It is assumed that some belief about historical facts is an essential part of Christian faith, so that if religious faith cannot be based on objective historical reasoning, then Christian faith cannot be based on objective reasoning at all.) Let us examine the argument in detail.

Its first premise is Kierkegaard's claim that "the greatest attainable certainty with respect to anything historical is merely an approximation." I take him to mean that historical evidence, objectively considered, never completely excludes the possibility of error. "It goes without saying," he claims, "that it is impossible in the case of historical problems to reach an objective decision so certain that no doubt could disturb it" (p. 41). For Kierkegaard's purposes it does not matter how small the possibility of error is, so long as it is finitely small (that is, so long as it is not literally infinitesimal). He insists (p. 31) that his Approximation Argument makes no appeal to the supposition that the objective evidence for Christian historical beliefs is weaker than the objective evidence for any other historical belief. The argument turns on a claim about *all* historical evidence. The probability of error in our belief that there was an American Civil War in the nineteenth century, for instance, might be as small as $\frac{1}{10^{2,000,000}}$; that would be a large enough chance of error for Kierkegaard's argument.

It might be disputed, but let us assume for the sake of argument that there is some such finitely small probability of error in the objective grounds for all historical beliefs, as Kierkegaard held. This need not keep us from saying that we "know," and it is "certain," that there was an American Civil War. For such an absurdly small possibility of error is as good as no possibility of error at all, "for all practical intents and purposes," as we might say. Such a possibility of error is too small to be worth worrying about.

But would it be too small to be worth worrying about if we had an *infinite* passionate interest in the question about the Civil War? If we have an infinite passionate interest in something, there is no limit to how important it is to us. (The nature of such an interest will be discussed more fully in section 3 below.) Kierkegaard maintains that in relation to an infinite passionate interest *no* possibility of error is too small to be worth worrying about. "In relation to an eternal happiness, and an infinite passionate interest in its behalf (in which latter alone the former can exist), an iota is of importance, of infinite importance . . ." (p. 28). This is the basis for the second premise of the Approximation Argument, which is Kierkegaard's claim that "an approximation, when viewed as a basis for an eternal happiness, is wholly inadequate" (p. 25). "An approximation is essentially incommensurable with an infinite personal interest in an eternal happiness" (p. 26).

At this point in the argument it is important to have some understanding of Kierkegaard's conception of faith, and the way in which he thinks faith excludes doubt. Faith must be decisive; in fact it seems to consist in a sort of decision-making. "The conclusion of belief is not so much a conclusion as a resolution, and it is for this reason that belief excludes doubt."[3] The decision of faith is a decision to disregard the possibility of error – to act on what is believed, without hedging one's bets to take account of any possibility of error.

To disregard the possibility of error is not to be unaware of it, or fail to consider it, or lack anxiety about it. Kierkegaard insists that the believer must be keenly *aware* of the risk of error. "If I wish to preserve myself in faith I must constantly be intent upon holding fast the objective uncertainty, so as to remain out upon the deep, over seventy thousand fathoms of water, still preserving my faith" (p. 182).

For Kierkegaard, then, to ask whether faith in a historical fact can be based on objective reasoning is to ask whether objective reasoning can justify one in disregarding the possibility of error which (he thinks) historical evidence always leaves. Here another aspect of Kierkegaard's conception of faith plays its part in the argument. He thinks that in all genuine religious faith the believer is *infinitely* interested in the object of his faith. And he thinks it follows that objective reasoning cannot justify him in disregarding *any* possibility of error about the object of faith, and therefore cannot lead him all the way to religious faith where a historical fact is concerned. The farthest it could lead him is to the conclusion that *if* he had only a certain finite (though very great) interest in the matter, the possibility of error would be too small to be worth worrying about and he would be justified in disregarding it. But faith disregards a possibility of error that *is* worth worrying about, since an infinite interest is involved. Thus faith requires a "leap" beyond the evidence, a leap that cannot be justified by objective reasoning (cf. p. 90).

There is something right in what Kierkegaard is saying here, but his Approximation Argument is a bad argument. He is right in holding that grounds of doubt which may be insignificant for most practical purposes can be extremely troubling for the intensity of a religious concern, and that it may require great decisiveness, or something like courage, to overcome them religiously. But he is mistaken in holding that objective reasoning could not justify one in disregarding any possibility of error about something in which one is infinitely interested.

The mistake, I believe, lies in his overlooking the fact that there are at least two different reasons one might have for disregarding a possibility of error. The first is that the possibility is too small to be worth worrying about. The second is that the risk of not disregarding the possibility of error would be greater than the risk of disregarding it. Of these two reasons only the first is ruled out by the infinite passionate interest.

I will illustrate this point with two examples, one secular and one religious. A certain woman has a very great (though not infinite) interest in her husband's love for her. She rightly judges that the objective evidence available to her renders it 99.9% probable that he loves her truly. The intensity of her interest is sufficient to cause her some *anxiety* over the remaining 1/1,000 chance that he loves her not; for her this chance is not too small to be worth worrying about. (Kierkegaard uses a similar example to support his Approximation Argument; see p. 511.) But she (very reasonably) wants to *disregard* the risk of error, in the sense of not hedging her bets, if he does love her. This desire is at least as strong as her desire not to be deceived if he does not love her. Objective reasoning should therefore suffice to bring her to the conclusion that she ought to disregard the risk of error, since by not disregarding it she would run 999 times as great a risk of frustrating one of these desires.

Or suppose you are trying to base your eternal happiness on your relation to Jesus, and therefore have an infinite passionate interest in the question whether he declared Peter and his episcopal successors to be infallible in matters of religious doctrine. You want to be committed to whichever is the true belief on this question, disregarding any possibility of error in it. And suppose, just for the sake of argument, that objective historical evidence renders it 99% probable that Jesus did declare Peter and his successors to be infallible – or 99% probable that he did not – for our present discussion it does not matter which. The one per cent chance of error is enough to make you *anxious*, in view of your infinite interest. But objective reasoning leads to the conclusion that you ought to commit yourself to the more probable opinion, *disregarding* the risk of error, if your strongest desire in the matter is to be so committed to be true opinion.

For the only other way to satisfy this desire would be to commit yourself to the less probable opinion, disregarding the risk of error in it. The first way will be successful if and only if the more probable opinion is true, and the second way if and only if the less probable opinion is true. Surely it is prudent to do what gives you a 99% chance of satisfying your strong desire, in preference to what gives you only a one per cent chance of satisfying it.

In this argument your strong desire to be committed to the true opinion is presupposed. The reasonableness of this desire may depend on a belief for which no probability can be established by purely historical reasoning, such as the belief that Jesus is God. But any difficulties arising from this point are distinct from those urged in the Approximation Argument, which itself presupposes the infinite passionate interest in the historical question.

There is some resemblance between my arguments in these examples and Pascal's famous Wager argument. But whereas Pascal's argument turns on weighing an infinite interest against a finite one, mine turn on weighing a large chance of success against a small one. An argument closer to Pascal's will be discussed in section 4 below.

The reader may well have noticed in the foregoing discussion some unclarity about what sort of justification is being demanded and given for religious beliefs about historical facts. There are at least two different types of question about a proposition which I might try to settle by objective reasoning: (1) Is it probable that the proposition is true? (2) In view of the evidence which I have for and against the proposition, and my interest in the matter, is it prudent for me to have faith in the truth of the proposition, disregarding the possibility of error? Correspondingly, we may distinguish two ways in which a belief can be *based on* objective reasoning. The proposition believed may be the conclusion of a piece of objective reasoning, and accepted because it is that. We may say that such a belief is *objectively probable*. Or one might hold a belief or maintain a religious faith because of a piece of objective reasoning whose conclusion is that it would be prudent, morally right, or otherwise desirable for one to hold that belief or faith. In this latter case let us say that the belief is *objectively advantageous*. It is clear that historical beliefs can be objectively probable; and in the Approximation Argument, Kierkegaard does not deny Christian historical beliefs can be objectively probable. His thesis is, in effect, that in view of an infinite passionate interest in their subject matter, they cannot be objectively advantageous, and therefore cannot be fully justified objectively, even if they are objectively probable. It is this thesis that I have attempted to refute. I have not been discussing the question whether Christian historical beliefs are objectively probable.

2. The Postponement Argument

The trouble with objective historical reasoning, according to the Approximation Argument, is that it cannot yield complete certainty. But that is not Kierkegaard's only complaint against it as a basis for religious faith. He also objects that objective historical inquiry is never completely finished, so that one who seeks to base his faith on it postpones his religious commitment forever. In the process of historical research "new difficulties arise and are overcome, and new difficulties again arise. Each generation inherits from its predecessor the illusion that the method is quite impeccable, but the learned scholars have not yet succeeded . . . and so forth. . . . The infinite personal passionate interest of the subject . . . vanishes more and more, because the decision is postponed, and postponed as following directly upon the result of the learned inquiry" (p. 28). As soon as we take "an historical document" as "our standard for the determination of Christian truth," we are "involved in a parenthesis whose conclusion is everlastingly prospective" (p. 28) – that is, we are involved in a religious digression which keeps religious commitment forever in the future.[4]

Kierkegaard has such fears about allowing religious faith to rest on *any* empirical reasoning. The danger of postponement of commitment arises not only from the uncertainties of historical scholarship, but also in connection with the design argument for God's existence. In the *Philosophical Fragments* Kierkegaard notes some objections to the attempt to prove God's existence from evidence of "the wisdom in nature, the goodness, the wisdom in the governance of the world," and then says, "even if I began I would never finish, and would in addition have to live constantly in suspense, lest something so terrible should suddenly happen that my bit of proof would be demolished."[5] What we have before us is a quite general sort of objection to the treatment of religious beliefs as empirically testable. On this point many analytical philosophers seem to agree with Kierkegaard. Much discussion in recent analytical philosophy of religion has proceeded from the supposition that religious beliefs are not empirically testable. I think it is far from obvious that that supposition is correct; and it is interesting to consider arguments that may be advanced to support it.

Kierkegaard's statements suggest an argument that I call the Postponement Argument. Its first premise is that one cannot have an authentic religious faith without being totally committed to it. In order to be totally committed to a belief, in the relevant sense, one must be determined not to abandon the belief under any circumstances that one recognizes as epistemically possible.

The second premise is that one cannot yet be totally committed to any belief which one bases on an inquiry in which one recognizes any possibility of a future need to revise the results. Total commitment to any belief so based will necessarily be postponed. I believe that this premise, suitably interpreted, is true. Consider the position of someone who regards himself as committed to a belief on the basis of objective evidence, but who recognizes some possibility that future discoveries will destroy the objective justification of the belief. We must ask how he is disposed to react in the event, however unlikely, that the objective basis of his belief is overthrown. Is he prepared to abandon the belief in that event? If so, he is not totally committed to the belief in the relevant sense. But if he is determined to cling to his belief even if its objective justification is taken away, then he is not basing the belief on the objective justification – or at least he is not basing it solely on the justification.[6]

The conclusion to be drawn from these two premises is that authentic religious faith cannot be based on an inquiry in which one recognizes any possibility of a future need to revise the results. We ought to note that this conclusion embodies two important restrictions on the scope of the argument.

In the first place, we are not given an argument that authentic religious faith cannot *have* an objective justification that is subject to possible future revision. What we are given is an argument that the authentic believer's holding of his religious belief cannot *depend* entirely on such a justification.

In the second place, this conclusion applies only to those who *recognize* some epistemic possibility that the objective results which appear to support their belief may be overturned. I think it would be unreasonable to require, as part of total commitment, a determination with regard to one's response to circumstances that one does not recognize as possible at all. It may be, however, that one does not recognize such a possibility when one ought to.

Kierkegaard needs one further premise in order to arrive at the conclusion that authentic religious faith cannot without error be based on any objective empirical reasoning. This third premise is that in every objective empirical inquiry there is always, objectively considered, some epistemic possibility that the results of the inquiry will need to be revised in view of new evidence or new reasoning. I believe Kierkegaard makes this assumption; he certainly makes it with regard to historical inquiry. From this premise it follows that one is in error if in any objective empirical inquiry one does not recognize any possibility of a future need to revise the results. But if one does recognize such a possibility, then according to the conclusion already reached in the Postponement Argument, one cannot base an authentic religious faith on the inquiry.

Some philosophers might attack the third premise of this argument; and certainly it is controversial. But I am more inclined to criticize the first premise. There is undoubtedly something plausible about the claim that authentic religious faith must involve a commitment so complete that the believer is resolved not to abandon his belief under any circumstances that he regards as epistemically possible. If you are willing to abandon your ostensibly religious beliefs for the sake of objective inquiry, mightn't we justly say that objective inquiry is your real religion, the thing to which you are most deeply committed?

There is also something plausible to be said on the other side, however. It has commonly been thought to be an important part of religious ethics that one ought to be humble, teachable, open to correction, new inspiration, and growth of insight, even (and perhaps especially) in important religious beliefs. That view would have to be discarded if we were to concede to Kierkegaard that the heart of commitment in religion is an unconditional determination not to change in one's important religious beliefs. In fact I think there is something radically wrong with this conception of religious commitment. Faith ought not to be thought of as unconditional devotion to a belief. For in the first place the object of religious devotion is not a belief or attitude of one's own, but God. And in the second place it may be doubted that religious devotion to God can or should be completely unconditional. God's love for sinners is sometimes said to be completely unconditional, not being based on any excellence or merit of theirs. But religious devotion to God is generally thought to be based on His goodness and love. It is the part of the strong, not the weak, to love unconditionally. And in relation to God we are weak.

3. The Passion Argument

In Kierkegaard's statements of the Approximation Argument and the Postponement Argument it is assumed that a system of religious beliefs might be objectively probable. It is only for the sake of argument, however, that Kierkegaard allows this assumption. He really holds that religious faith, by its very nature, needs objective *im*probability. "Anything that is almost probable, or probable, or extremely and emphatically probable, is something [one] can almost know, or as good as know, or extremely and emphatically almost *know* – but it is impossible to *believe*" (p. 189). Nor will Kierkegaard countenance the suggestion that religion ought to go beyond belief to some almost-knowledge based on probability. "Faith is the highest passion in a man. There are perhaps many in every generation who do not even reach it, but no one gets further."[7] It would be a betrayal of religion to try to go beyond faith. The suggestion that faith might be replaced by "probabilities and guarantees" is for the believer "a temptation to be resisted with all his strength" (p. 15). The attempt to establish religious beliefs on a foundation of objective probability is therefore no service to religion, but inimical to religion's true interests. The approximation to certainty which might be afforded by objective probability is rejected, not only for the reasons given in the Approximation Argument and Postponement Argument, but also from a deeper motive, "since on the contrary it behooves us to get rid of introductory guarantees of security, proofs from consequences, and the whole mob of public pawnbrokers and guarantors, so as to permit the absurd to stand out in all its clarity – in order that the individual may believe if he wills it; I merely say that it must be strenuous in the highest degree so to believe" (p. 190).

As this last quotation indicates, Kierkegaard thinks that religious belief ought to be based on a strenuous exertion of the will – a passionate striving. His reasons for thinking that objective probability is religiously undesirable have to do with the place of passion in religion, and constitute what I call the Passion Argument. The first premise of the argument is that the most essential and the most valuable feature of religiousness is passion, indeed an infinite passion, a passion of the greatest possible intensity. The second premise is that an infinite passion requires objective improbability. And the conclusion therefore is that that which is most essential and most valuable in religiousness requires objective improbability.

My discussion of this argument will have three parts. (a) First I will try to clarify, very briefly, what it is that is supposed to be objectively improbable. (b) Then we will consider Kierkegaard's reasons for holding that infinite passion requires objective improbability. In so doing we will also gain a clearer understanding of what a Kierkegaardian infinite passion is. (c) Finally I will discuss the first premise of the argument – although issues will arise at that point which I do not pretend to be able to settle by argument.

(a) What are the beliefs whose improbability is needed by religious passion? Kierkegaard will hardly be satisfied with the improbability of just any one belief; it must surely be at least an important belief. On the other hand it would clearly be preposterous to suppose that every belief involved in Christianity must be objectively improbable. (Consider, for example, the belief that the man Jesus did indeed live.) I think that what is demanded in the Passion Argument is the objective improbability of at least one belief which must be true if the goal sought by the religious passion is to be attained.

(b) We can find in the *Postscript* suggestions of several reasons for thinking that an infinite passion needs objective improbability. The two that seem to me most interesting have to do with (i) the risks accepted and (ii) the costs paid in pursuance of a passionate interest.

(i) One reason that Kierkegaard has for valuing objective improbability is that it increases the *risk* attaching to the religious life, and risk is so essential for the expression of religious passion that "without risk there is no faith" (p. 182). About the nature of an eternal happiness, the goal of religious striving, Kierkegaard says "there is nothing to be said . . . except that it is the good which is attained by venturing everything absolutely" (p. 382).

> But what then does it mean to venture? A venture is the precise correlative of an uncertainty; when the certainty is there the venture becomes impossible. . . . If what I hope to gain by venturing is itself certain, I do not risk or venture, but make an exchange. . . . No, if I am in truth resolved to venture, in truth resolved to strive for the attainment of the highest good, the uncertainty must be there, and I must have room to move, so to speak. But the largest space I can obtain, where there is room for the most vehement gesture of the passion that embraces the infinite, is uncertainty of knowledge with respect to an eternal happiness, or the certain knowledge that the choice is in the finite sense a piece of madness: now there is room, now you can venture! [pp. 380–2]

How is it that objective improbability provides the largest space for the most vehement gesture of infinite passion? Consider two cases. (A) You plunge into a raging torrent to rescue from drowning someone you love, who is crying for help. (B) You plunge into a raging torrent in a desperate attempt to rescue someone you love, who appears to be unconscious and *may* already have drowned. In both cases you manifest a passionate interest in saving the person, risking your own life in order to do so. But I think Kierkegaard would say there is more passion in the second case than in the first. For in the second case you risk your life in what is, objectively considered, a smaller chance that you will be able to save your loved one. A greater passion is required for a more desperate attempt.

A similar assessment may be made of the following pair of cases. (A′) You stake everything on your faith in the truth of Christianity, knowing that it is objectively 99% probable that Christianity is true. (B′) You stake everything on your faith in the truth of Christianity, knowing that the truth of Christianity is, objectively, possible but so improbable that its probability is, say, as small as $\frac{1}{10^{2,000,000}}$. There is passion in both cases, but Kierkegaard will say that there is more passion in the second case than in the first. For to venture the same stake (namely, everything) on a much smaller chance of success shows greater passion.

Acceptance of risk can thus be seen as a *measure* of the intensity of passion. I believe this provides us with one way of understanding what Kierkegaard means when he calls religious passion "infinite." An *infinite* passionate interest in x is an interest so strong that it leads one to make the greatest possible sacrifices in order to obtain x, on the smallest possible chance of success. The infinity of the passion is shown in that there is no sacrifice so great one will not make it, and no chance of success so small one will not act on it. A passion which is infinite in this sense requires, by its very nature, a situation of maximum risk for its expression.

It will doubtless be objected that this argument involves a misunderstanding of what a passionate interest is. Such an interest is a disposition. In order to have a great passionate interest it is not necessary actually to make a great sacrifice with a small chance of success; all that is necessary is to have such an intense interest that one *would* do so if an appropriate occasion should arise. It is therefore a mistake to say that there *is* more passion in case (B) than in case (A), or in (B′) than in (A′). More passion is *shown* in (B) than in (A), and in (B′) than in (A′); but an equal passion may exist in cases in which there is no occasion to show it.

This objection may well be correct as regards what we normally mean by "passionate interest." But that is not decisive for the argument. The crucial question is what part dispositions, possibly unactualized, ought to play in religious devotion. And here we must have a digression about the position of the *Postcript* on this question – a position that is complex at best and is not obviously consistent.

In the first place I do not think that Kierkegaard would be prepared to think of passion, or a passionate interest, as primarily a disposition that might remain unactualized. He seems to conceive of passion chiefly as an intensity in what one actually does and feels. "Passion is momentary" (p. 178), although capable of continual repetition. And what is momentary in such a way that it must be repeated rather than protracted is presumably an occurrence rather than a disposition. It agrees with this conception of passion that Kierkegaard idealizes a life of "persistent striving," and says that the religious task is to "exercise" the God-relationship and to give "existential expression" to the religious choice (pp. 110, 364, 367).

All of this supports the view that what Kierkegaard means by "an infinite passionate interest" is a pattern of actual decision-making, in which one continually exercises and expresses one's religiousness by making the greatest possible sacrifices on the smallest possible chance of success. In order to actualize such a pattern of life one needs chances of success that are as small as possible. That is the room that is required for "the most vehement gesture" of infinite passion.

But on the other hand Kierkegaard does allow a dispositional element in the religious life, and even precisely in the making of the greatest possible sacrifices. We might suppose that if we are to make the greatest possible sacrifices in our religious devotion, we must do so by abandoning all worldly interests and devoting all our time and attention to religion. That is what monasticism attempts to do, as Kierkegaard sees it; and (in the *Postscript*, at any rate) he rejects the attempt, contrary to what our argument to this point would have led us to expect of him. He holds that "resignation" (pp. 353, 367) or "renunciation" (pp. 362, 386) of *all* finite ends is precisely the first thing that religiousness requires; but he means a renunciation that is compatible with pursuing and enjoying finite ends (pp. 362–71). This renunciation is the practice of a sort of detachment; Kierkegaard uses the image of a dentist loosening the soft tissues around a tooth, while it is still in place, in preparation for pulling it (p. 367). It is partly a matter of not treating finite things with a desperate seriousness, but with a certain coolness or humor, even while one pursues them (pp. 368, 370).

This coolness is not just a disposition. But the renunciation also has a dispositional aspect. "Now if for any individual an eternal happiness is his highest good, this will mean that all finite satisfactions are volitionally relegated to the status of what may have to be renounced in favor of an eternal happiness" (p. 350). The volitional relegation is not a disposition but an act of choice. The object of this choice, however, appears to be a dispositional state – the state of being such that one *would* forgo any finite satisfaction *if* it *were* religiously necessary or advantageous to do so.

It seems clear that Kierkegaard, in the *Postscript*, is willing to admit a dispositional element at one point in the religious venture, but not at another. It is enough in most cases, he thinks, if one is *prepared* to cease for the sake of religion from pursuing some finite end; but it is not enough that one *would* hold to one's belief in the face of objective improbability. The belief must actually be improbable, although the pursuit of the finite need not actually cease. What is not clear is a reason for this disparity. The following hypothesis, admittedly somewhat speculative as interpretation of the text, is the best explanation I can offer.

The admission of a dispositional element in the religious renunciation of the finite is something to which Kierkegaard seems to be driven by the view that there is no alternative to it except idolatry. For suppose one actually ceases from all worldly pursuits and enters a monastery. In the monastery one would pursue a number of particular ends (such as getting up in the middle of the night to say the offices) which, although religious in a way ("churchy," one might say), are still finite. The absolute *telos* or end of religion is no more to be identified with them than with the ends pursued by an alderman (pp. 362–71).

To pretend otherwise would be to make an idolatrous identification of the absolute end with some finite end. An existing person cannot have sacrificed everything by actually having ceased from pursuing *all* finite ends. For as long as he lives and acts he is pursuing some finite end. Therefore his renouncing *everything* finite must be at least partly dispositional.

Kierkegaard does not seem happy with this position. He regards it as of the utmost importance that the religious passion should come to expression. The problem of finding an adequate expression for a passion for an infinite end, in the face of the fact that in every concrete action one will be pursuing some finite end, is treated in the *Postscript* as the central problem of religion (see especially pp. 386–468). If the sacrifice of everything finite must remain largely dispositional, then perhaps it is all the more important to Kierkegaard that the smallness of the chance for which it is sacrificed should be fully actual, so that the infinity of the religious passion may be measured by an actuality in at least one aspect of the religious venture.

(ii) According to Kierkegaard, as I have argued, the intensity of a passion is measured in part by the smallness of the chances of success that one acts on. It can also be measured in part by its *costliness* – that is, by how much one gives up or suffers in acting on those chances. This second measure can also be made the basis of an argument for the claim that an infinite passion requires objective improbability. For the objective improbability of a religious belief, if recognized, increases the costliness of holding it. The risk involved in staking everything on an objectively improbable belief gives rise to an anxiety and mental suffering whose acceptance is itself a sacrifice. It seems to follow that if one is not staking everything on a belief one sees to be objectively improbable, one's passion is not infinite in Kierkegaard's sense, since one's sacrifice could be greater if one did adhere to an improbable belief.

Kierkegaard uses an argument similar to this. For God to give us objective knowledge of Himself, eliminating paradox from it, would be "to lower the price of the God-relationship."

> And even if God could be imagined willing, no man with passion in his heart could desire it. To a maiden genuinely in love it could never occur that she had bought her happiness too dear, but rather that she had not bought it dear enough. And just as the passion of the infinite was itself the truth, so in the case of the highest value it holds true that the price is the value, that a low price means a poor value. . . . [p. 207]

Kierkegaard here appears to hold, first, that an increase in the objective probability of religious belief would reduce its costliness, and second, that the value of a religious life is measured by its cost. I take it his reason for the second of these claims is that passion is the most valuable thing in a religious life and passion is measured by its cost. If we grant Kierkegaard the requisite conception of an infinite passion, we seem once again to have a plausible argument for the view that objective improbability is required for such a passion.

(c) We must therefore consider whether infinite passion, as Kierkegaard conceives of it, ought to be part of the religious ideal of life. Such a passion is a striving, or pattern of decision-making, in which, with the greatest possible intensity of feeling, one continually makes the greatest possible sacrifices on the smallest possible chance of success. This seems to me an impossible ideal. I doubt that any human being could have a passion of this sort, because I doubt that one could make a sacrifice so great that a greater could not be made, or have a (nonzero) chance of success so small that a smaller could not be had.

But even if Kierkegaard's ideal is impossible, one might want to try to approximate it. Intensity of passion might still be measured by the greatness of sacrifices made and the smallness of chances of success acted on, even if we cannot hope for a greatest possible or a smallest possible here. And it could be claimed that the most essential and valuable thing in religiousness is a passion that is very intense (though it cannot be infinite) by this standard – the more intense the better. This claim will not support an argument that objective improbability is absolutely required for religious passion. For a passion could presumably be very intense, involving great sacrifices and risks of some other sort, without an objectively improbable belief. But it could still be argued that objectively improbable religious beliefs enhance the value of the religious life by increasing its sacrifices and diminishing its chances of success, whereas objective probability detracts from the value of religious passion by diminishing its intensity.

The most crucial question about the Passion Argument, then, is whether maximization of sacrifice and risk are so valuable in religion as to make objective improbability a desirable characteristic of religious beliefs. Certainly much religious thought and feeling places a very high value on sacrifice and on passionate intensity. But the doctrine that it is desirable to increase without limit, or to the highest possible degree (if there is one) the cost and risk of a religious life is less plausible (to say the least) than the view that *some* degree of cost and risk may add to the value of a religious life. The former doctrine would set the religious interest at enmity with all other interests, or at least with the best of them. Kierkegaard is surely right in thinking that it would be impossible to live without pursuing some finite ends. But even so it would be possible to exchange the pursuit of better finite ends for the pursuit of worse ones – for example, by exchanging the pursuit of truth, beauty, and satisfying personal relationships for the self-flagellating pursuit of pain. And a way of life would be the costlier for requiring such an exchange. Kierkegaard does not, in the *Postscript*, demand it. But the presuppositions of his Passion Argument seem to imply that such a sacrifice would be religiously desirable. Such a conception of religion is demonic. In a tolerable religious ethics some way must be found to conceive of the religious interest as inclusive rather than exclusive of the best of other interests – including, I think, the interest in having well-grounded beliefs.

4. Pascal's Wager and Kierkegaard's Leap

Ironically, Kierkegaard's views about religious passion suggest a way in which his religious beliefs could be based on objective reasoning – not on reasoning which would show them to be objectively probable, but on reasoning which shows them to be objectively advantageous. Consider the situation of a person whom Kierkegaard would regard as a genuine Christian believer. What would such a person want most of all? He would want above all else to attain the truth through Christianity. That is, he would desire both that Christianity be true and that he himself be related to it as a genuine believer. He would desire that state of affairs (which we may call *S*) so ardently that he would be willing to sacrifice everything else to obtain it, given only the smallest possible chance of success.

We can therefore construct the following argument, which has an obvious analogy to Pascal's Wager. Let us assume that there is, objectively, some chance, however small, that Christianity is true. This is an assumption which Kierkegaard accepts (p. 31), and I think it is plausible. There are two possibilities, then: either Christianity is true, or it is false. (Others might object to so stark a disjunction, but Kierkegaard will not.) If Christianity is false it is impossible for anyone to obtain *S*, since *S* includes the truth of Christianity. It is only if Christianity is true that anything one does will help one or hinder one in obtaining *S*. And if Christianity is true, one will obtain *S* just in case one becomes a genuine Christian believer. It seems obvious that one would increase one's chances of becoming a genuine Christian believer by becoming one now (if one can), even if the truth of Christian beliefs is now objectively uncertain or improbable. Hence it would seem to be advantageous for anyone who can to become a genuine Christian believer now, if he wants *S* so much that he would be willing to sacrifice everything else for the smallest possible chance of obtaining *S*. Indeed I believe that the argument I have given for this conclusion is a piece of objective reasoning, and that Christian belief is therefore *objectively* advantageous for anyone who wants *S* as much as a Kierkegaardian genuine Christian must want it.

Of course this argument does not tend at all to show that it is objectively probable that Christianity is true. It only gives a practical, prudential reason for believing, to someone who has a certain desire. Nor does the argument do anything to prove that such an absolutely overriding desire for *S* is reasonable.[8] It does show, however, that just as Kierkegaard's position has more logical structure than one might at first think, it is more difficult than he probably realized for him to get away entirely from objective justification.[9]

Notes

1 Søren Kierkegaard, *Concluding Unscientific Postscript*, translated by David F. Swenson; introduction, notes, and completion of translation by Walter Lowrie (Princeton, NJ: Princeton University Press, 1941). Page references in parentheses in the body of the present paper are to this work.

2 The argument is not original with Kierkegaard. It can be found in works of G. E. Lessing and D. F. Strauss that Kierkegaard had read. See especially Thulstrup's quotation and discussion of a passage from Strauss in the commentary portion of Søren Kierkegaard, *Philosophical Fragments*, translated by David F. Swenson, second edition, translation revised by Howard V. Hong, with introduction and commentary by Niels Thulstrup (Princeton, NJ: Princeton University Press, 1962), pp. 149–51.

3 Kierkegaard, *Philosophical Fragments*, p. 104; cf. pp. 102–3.

4 Essentially the same argument can be found in a plea, which has had great influence among more recent theologians, for making Christian faith independent of the results of critical historical study of the Bible: Martin Kähler's famous lecture, first delivered in 1892, *Der sogenannte historische Jesus und der geschichtliche biblische Christus* (München: Christus Kaiser Verlag, 1961), p. 50f.

5 Kierkegaard, *Philosophical Fragments*, p. 52.

6 Kierkegaard notes the possibility that in believing in God's existence "I make so bold as to defy all objections, even those that have not yet been made." But in that case he thinks the belief is not really based on the evidence of God's work in the world; "it is not from the works that I make my proof" (*Philosophical Fragments*, p. 52).

7 Søren Kierkegaard, *Fear and Trembling*, trans. Walter Lowrie, 2nd ed. (Princeton, NJ: Princeton University Press, 1970; published in one volume with *The Sickness unto Death*), p. 131. Cf. *Postscript*, p. 31f.

8 It is worth noting, though, that a similar argument might still provide some less overriding justification of belief to someone who had a strong, but less overriding, desire for *S*.

9 Versions of this paper have been read to philosophical colloquia at Occidental College and California State University, Fullerton. I am indebted to participants in those discussions, to students in many of my classes, and particularly to Marilyn McCord Adams, Van Harvey, Thomas Kselman, William Laserow, and James Muyskens, for helpful comment on the ideas which are contained in this paper (or which would have been, had it not been for their criticisms).

3

Lectures on Religious Belief

Ludwig Wittgenstein

Ludwig Wittgenstein (1889–1951) is considered by many to be the greatest philosopher of the twentieth century. One of the ideas for which he is best known is the notion that there are many different "language games" and that the meaning of a word is the way it is used in a language game. Wittgenstein contends that it is a mistake to think of religious beliefs on the model of scientific or fact-stating beliefs, and he criticizes someone named Father O'Hara for thinking of them this way. Moreover, Wittgenstein argues that religious beliefs can only be fully understood by those who participate in the religious language game.

I

An Austrian general said to someone: "I shall think of you after my death, if that should be possible." We can imagine one group who would find this ludicrous, another who wouldn't.

(During the war, Wittgenstein saw consecrated bread being carried in chromium steel. This struck him as ludicrous.)

Suppose that someone believed in the Last Judgement, and I don't, does this mean that I believe the opposite to him, just that there won't be such a thing? I would say: "not at all, or not always."

Suppose I say that the body will rot, and another says "No. Particles will rejoin in a thousand years, and there will be a Resurrection of you."

If some said: "Wittgenstein, do you believe in this?" I'd say: "No." "Do you contradict the man?" I'd say: "No."

If you say this, the contradiction already lies in this.

Would you say: "I believe the opposite", or "There is no reason to suppose such a thing"? I'd say neither.

Suppose someone were a believer and said: "I believe in a Last Judgement," and I said: "Well,

Ludwig Wittgenstein, "Lectures on Religious Belief" from *Lectures and Conversations on Aesthetics, Psychology and Religious Belief*, ed. Cyril Barrett (Berkeley, CA: University of California Press, 1972), pp. 53–64.

I'm not so sure. Possibly." You would say that there is an enormous gulf between us. If he said "There is a German aeroplane overhead," and I said "Possibly I'm not so sure," you'd say we were fairly near.

It isn't a question of my being anywhere near him, but on an entirely different plane, which you could express by saying: "You mean something altogether different, Wittgenstein."

The difference might not show up at all in any explanation of the meaning.

Why is it that in this case I seem to be missing the entire point?

Suppose somebody made this guidance for this life: believing in the Last Judgement. Whenever he does anything, this is before his mind. In a way, how are we to know whether to say he believes this will happen or not?

Asking him is not enough. He will probably say he has proof. But he has what you might call an unshakeable belief. It will show, not by reasoning or by appeal to ordinary grounds for belief, but rather by regulating for in all his life.

This is a very much stronger fact – foregoing pleasures, always appealing to this picture. This is one sense must be called the firmest of all beliefs, because the man risks things on account of it which he would not do on things which are by far better established for him. Although he distinguishes between things well-established and not well-established.

Lewy: Surely, he would say it is extremely well-established.

First, he may use "well-established" or not use it at all. He will treat this belief as extremely well-established, and in another way as not well-established at all.

If we have a belief, in certain cases we appeal again and again to certain grounds, and at the same time we risk pretty little – if it came to risking our lives on the ground of this belief.

There are instances where you have a faith – where you say "I believe" – and on the other hand this belief does not rest on the fact on which our ordinary everyday beliefs normally do rest.

How should we compare beliefs with each other? What would it mean to compare them?

You might say: "We compare the states of mind."

How do we compare states of mind? This obviously won't do for all occasions. First, what you say won't be taken as the measure for the firmness of a belief? But, for instance, what risks you would take?

The strength of a belief is not comparable with the intensity of a pain.

An entirely different way of comparing beliefs is seeing what sorts of grounds he will give.

A belief isn't like a momentary state of mind. "At 5 o'clock he had very bad toothache."

Suppose you had two people, and one of them, when he had to decide which course to take, thought of retribution, and the other did not. One person might, for instance, be inclined to take everything that happened to him as a reward or punishment, and another person doesn't think of this at all.

If he is ill, he may think: "What have I done to deserve this?" This is one way of thinking of retribution. Another way is, he thinks in a general way whenever he is ashamed of himself: "This will be punished."

Take two people, one of whom talks of his behaviour and of what happens to him in terms of retribution, the other one does not. These people think entirely differently. Yet, so far, you can't say they believe different things.

Suppose someone is ill and he says: "This is a punishment," and I say: "If I'm ill, I don't think of punishment at all." If you say: "Do you believe the opposite?" – you can call it believing the opposite, but it is entirely different from what we would normally call believing the opposite.

I think differently, in a different way. I say different things to myself. I have different pictures.

It is this way: if someone said: "Wittgenstein, you don't take illness as punishment, so what do you believe?" – I'd say: "I don't have any thoughts of punishment."

There are, for instance, these entirely different ways of thinking first of all – which needn't be expressed by one person saying one thing, another person another thing.

What we call believing in a Judgement Day or not believing in a Judgement Day – The expression of belief may play an absolutely minor role.

If you ask me whether or not I believe in a Judgement Day, in the sense in which religious people have belief in it, I wouldn't say: "No. I don't believe there will be such a thing." It would seem to me utterly crazy to say this.

And then I give an explanation: "I don't believe in . . .", but then the religious person never believes what I describe.

I can't say. I can't contradict that person.

In one sense, I understand all he says – the English words "God", "separate", etc. I understand. I could say: "I don't believe in this," and this would be true, meaning I haven't got these thoughts or anything that hangs together with them. But not that I could contradict the thing.

You might say: "Well, if you can't contradict him, that means you don't understand him. If you did understand him, then you might." That again is Greek to me. My normal technique of language leaves me. I don't know whether to say they understand one another or not.

These controversies look quite different from any normal controversies. Reasons look entirely different from normal reasons.

They are, in a way, quite inconclusive.

The point is that if there were evidence, this would in fact destroy the whole business.

Anything that I normally call evidence wouldn't in the slightest influence me.

Suppose, for instance, we knew people who foresaw the future; make forecasts for years and years ahead; and they described some sort of a Judgement Day. Queerly enough, even if there were such a thing, and even if it were more convincing than I have described but, belief in this happening wouldn't be at all a religious belief.

Suppose that I would have to forego all pleasures because of such a forecast. If I do so and so, someone will put me in fires in a thousand years, etc. I wouldn't budge. The best scientific evidence is just nothing.

A religious belief might in fact fly in the face of such a forecast, and say "No. There it will break down."

As it were, the belief as formulated on the evidence can only be the last result – in which a number of ways of thinking and acting crystallize and come together.

A man would fight for his life not to be dragged into the fire. No induction. Terror. That is, as it were, part of the substance of the belief.

That is partly why you don't get in religious controversies, the form of controversy where one person is *sure* of the thing, and the other says: "Well, possibly."

You might be surprised that there hasn't been opposed to those who believe in Resurrection those who say "Well, possibly."

Here believing obviously plays much more this role: suppose we said that a certain picture might play the role of constantly admonishing me, or I always think of it. Here, an enormous difference would be between those people for whom the picture is constantly in the foreground, and the others who just didn't use it at all.

Those who said: "Well, possibly it may happen and possibly not" would be on an entirely different plane.

This is partly why one would be reluctant to say: "These people rigorously hold the opinion (or view) that there is a Last Judgement." "Opinion" sounds queer.

It is for this reason that different words are used: "dogma", "faith".

We don't talk about hypothesis, or about high probability. Nor about knowing.

In a religious discourse we use such expressions as: "I believe that so and so will happen," and use them differently to the way in which we use them in science.

Although, there is a great temptation to think we do. Because we do talk of evidence, and do talk of evidence by experience.

We could even talk of historic events.

It has been said that Christianity rests on an historic basis.

It has been said a thousand times by intelligent people that indubitability is not enough in this case. Even if there is as much evidence as for Napoleon. Because the indubitability wouldn't be enough to make me change my whole life.

It doesn't rest on an historic basis in the sense that the ordinary belief in historic facts could serve as a foundation.

Here we have a belief in historic facts different from a belief in ordinary historic facts. Even, they are not treated as historical, empirical, propositions.

Those people who had faith didn't apply the doubt which would ordinarily apply to *any* historical propositions. Especially propositions of a time long past, etc.

What is the criterion of reliability, dependability? Suppose you give a general description as to when you say a proposition has a reasonable weight of probability. When you call it reasonable, is this *only* to say that for it you have such and such evidence, and for others you haven't?

For instance, we don't trust the account given of an event by a drunk man.

Father O'Hara[1] is one of those people who make it a question of science.

Here we have people who treat this evidence in a different way. They base things on evidence which taken in one way would seem exceedingly flimsy. They base enormous things on this evidence. Am I to say they are unreasonable? I wouldn't call them unreasonable.

I would say, they are certainly not *reasonable*, that's obvious.

"Unreasonable" implies, with everyone, rebuke.

I want to say: they don't treat this as a matter of reasonability.

Anyone who reads the Epistles will find it said: not only that it is not reasonable, but that it is folly.

Not only is it not reasonable, but it doesn't pretend to be.

What seems to me ludicrous about O'Hara is his making it appear to be *reasonable*.

Why shouldn't one form of life culminate in an utterance of belief in a Last Judgement? But I couldn't either say "Yes" or "No" to the statement that there will be such a thing. Nor "Perhaps," nor "I'm not sure."

It is a statement which may not allow of any such answer.

If Mr Lewy is religious and says he believes in a Judgement Day, I won't even know whether to say I understand him or not. I've read the same things as he's read. In a most important sense, I know what he means.

If an atheist says: "There won't be a Judgement Day, and another person says there will," do they mean the same? – Not clear what criterion of meaning the same is. They might describe the same things. You might say, this already shows that they mean the same.

We come to an island and we find beliefs there, and certain beliefs we are inclined to call religious. What I'm driving at is, that religious beliefs will not . . . They have sentences, and there are also religious statements.

These statements would not just differ in respect to what they are about. Entirely different connections would make them into religious beliefs, and there can easily be imagined transitions where we wouldn't know for our life whether to call them religious beliefs or scientific beliefs.

You may say they reason wrongly.

In certain cases you would say they reason wrongly, meaning they contradict us. In other cases you would say they don't reason at all, or "It is an entirely different kind of reasoning." The first, you would say in the case in which they reason in a similar way to us, and make something corresponding to our blunders.

Whether a thing is a blunder or not – it is a blunder in a particular system. Just as something is a blunder in a particular game and not in another.

You could also say that where we are reasonable, they are not reasonable – meaning they don't use *reason* here.

If they do something very like one of our blunders, I would say, I don't know. It depends on further surroundings of it.

It is difficult to see, in cases in which it has all the appearances of trying to be reasonable.

I would definitely call O'Hara unreasonable. I would say, if this is religious belief, then it's all superstition.

But I would ridicule it, not by saying it is based on insufficient evidence. I would say: here is a man who is cheating himself. You can say: this man is ridiculous because he believes, and bases it on weak reasons.

II

The word "God" is amongst the earliest learnt – pictures and catechisms, etc. But not the same consequences as with pictures of aunts. I wasn't shown [that which the picture pictured].

The word is used like a word representing a person. God sees, rewards, etc.

"Being shown all these things, did you understand what this word meant?" I'd say: "Yes and no. I did learn what it didn't mean. I made myself understand. I could answer questions, understand questions when they were put in different ways – and in that sense could be said to understand."

If the question arises as to the existence of a god or God, it plays an entirely different role to that of the existence of any person or object I ever heard of. One said, had to say, that one *believed* in the existence, and if one did not believe, this was regarded as something bad. Normally if I did not believe in the existence of something no one would think there was anything wrong in this.

Also, there is this extraordinary use of the word "believe". One talks of believing and at the same time one doesn't use "believe" as one does ordinarily. You might say (in the normal use): "You only believe – oh well. . . ." Here it is used entirely differently; on the other hand it is not used as we generally use the word "know".

If I even vaguely remember what I was taught about God, I might say: "Whatever believing in God may be, it can't be believing in something we can test, or find means of testing." You might say: "This is nonsense, because people say they believe on *evidence* or say they believe on religious experiences." I would say: "The mere fact that someone says they believe on evidence doesn't tell me enough for me to be able to say now whether I can say of a sentence 'God exists' that your evidence is unsatisfactory or insufficient."

Suppose I know someone, Smith. I've heard that he has been killed in a battle in this war. One day you come to me and say: "Smith is in Cambridge." I inquire, and find you stood at Guildhall and saw at the other end a man and said: "That was Smith." I'd say: "Listen. This isn't sufficient evidence." If we had a fair amount of evidence he was killed I would try to make you say that you're being credulous. Suppose he was never heard of again. Needless to say, it is quite impossible to make inquiries: "Who at 12.05 passed Market Place into Rose Crescent?" Suppose you say: "He was there." I would be extremely puzzled.

Suppose there is a feast on Mid-Summer Common. A lot of people stand in a ring. Suppose this is done every year and then everyone says he has seen one of his dead relatives on the other side of the ring. In this case, we could ask everyone in the ring. "Who did you hold by the hand?" Nevertheless, we'd all say that on that day we see our dead relatives. You could in this case say: "I had an extraordinary experience. I had the experience I can express by saying: 'I saw my dead cousin'." Would we say you are saying this on insufficient evidence? Under certain circumstances I would say this, under other circumstances I wouldn't. Where what is said sounds a bit absurd I would say: "Yes, in this case insufficient evidence." If altogether absurd, then I wouldn't.

Suppose I went to somewhere like Lourdes in France. Suppose I went with a very credulous person. There we see blood coming out of something. He says: "There you are, Wittgenstein, how can you doubt?" I'd say: "Can it only be explained one way? Can't it be this or that?" I'd try to convince him that he'd seen nothing of any consequence. I wonder whether I would do that under all circumstances. I certainly know that I would under normal circumstances.

"Oughtn't one after all to consider this?" I'd say: "Come on. Come on." I would treat the phenomenon in this case just as I would treat an experiment in a laboratory which I thought badly executed.

"The balance moves when I will it to move." I point out it is not covered up, a draught can move it, etc.

I could imagine that someone showed an extremely passionate belief in such a phenomenon, and I couldn't approach his belief at all by saying: "This could just as well have been brought about by so and so" because he could think this blasphemy on my side. Or he might say: "It is possible that these priests cheat, but nevertheless in a different sense a miraculous phenomenon takes place there."

I have a statue which bleeds on such and such a day in the year. I have red ink, etc. "You are a cheat, but nevertheless the Deity uses you. Red ink in a sense, but not red ink in a sense."

Cf. Flowers at seance with label. People said: "Yes, flowers are materialized with label." What kind of circumstances must there be to make this kind of story not ridiculous?

I have a moderate education, as all of you have, and therefore know what is meant by insufficient evidence for a forecast. Suppose someone dreamt of the Last Judgement, and said he now knew what it would be like. Suppose someone said: "This is poor evidence." I would say: "If you want to compare it with the evidence for it's raining to-morrow it is no evidence at all." He may make it sound as if by stretching the point you may call it evidence. But it may be more than ridiculous as evidence. But now, would I be prepared to say: "You are basing your belief on extremely slender evidence, to put it mildly." Why should I regard this dream as evidence – measuring its validity as though I were measuring the validity of the evidence for meteorological events?

If you compare it with anything in Science which we call evidence, you can't credit that anyone could soberly argue: "Well, I had this dream . . . therefore . . . Last Judgement". You might say: "For a blunder, that's too big." If you suddenly wrote numbers down on the blackboard, and then said: "Now, I'm going to add," and then said: "2 and 21 is 13," etc. I'd say: "This is no blunder."

There are cases where I'd say he's mad, or he's making fun. Then there might be cases where I look for an entirely different interpretation altogether. In order to see what the explanation is I should have to see the sum, to see in what way it is done, what he makes follow from it, what are the different circumstances under which he does it, etc.

I mean, if a man said to me after a dream that he believed in the Last Judgement, I'd try to find what sort of impression it gave him. One attitude: "It will be in about 2,000 years. It will be bad for so and so and so, etc." Or it may be one of terror. In the case where there is hope, terror, etc., would I say there is insufficient evidence if he says: "I believe . . ."? I can't treat these words as I normally treat "I believe so and so". It would be entirely beside the point, and also if he said his friend so and so and his grandfather had had the dream and believed, it would be entirely beside the point.

I would not say: "If a man said he dreamt it would happen to-morrow," would he take his coat?, etc.

Case where Lewy has visions of his dead friend. Cases where you don't try to locate him. And case where you try to locate him in a business-like way. Another case where I'd say: "We can pre-suppose we have a broad basis on which we agree."

In general, if you say: "He is dead" and I say: "He is not dead" no-one would say: "Do they mean the same thing by 'dead'?" In the case where a man has visions I wouldn't offhand say: "He means something different."

Cf. A person having persecution mania.

What is the criterion for meaning something different? Not only what he takes as evidence for it, but also how he reacts, that he is in terror, etc.

How am I to find out whether this proposition is to be regarded as an empirical proposition – "You'll see your dead friend again?" Would I say: "He is a bit superstitious?" Not a bit.

He might have been apologetic. (The man who stated it categorically was more intelligent than the man who was apologetic about it).

"Seeing a dead friend," again means nothing much to me at all. I don't think in these terms. I don't say to myself: "I shall see so and so again" ever.

He always says it, but he doesn't make any search. He puts on a queer smile. "His story had that dreamlike quality." My answer would be in this case "Yes," and a particular explanation.

Take "God created man". Pictures of Michelangelo showing the creation of the world. In general, there is nothing which explains the meanings of words as well as a picture, and I take it that Michelangelo was as good as anyone can be and did his best, and here is the picture of the Deity creating Adam.

If we ever saw this, we certainly wouldn't think this the Deity. The picture has to be used in an entirely different way if we are to call the man in that queer blanket "God", and so on. You could imagine that religion was taught by means of these pictures. "Of course, we can only express ourselves by means of picture." This is rather queer . . . I could show Moore the pictures of a tropical plant. There is a technique of comparison between picture and plant. If I showed him the picture of Michelangelo and said: "Of course, I can't show you the real thing, only the picture". . . . The absurdity is, I've never taught him the technique of using this picture.

It is quite clear that the role of pictures of Biblical subjects and role of the picture of God creating Adam are totally different ones. You might ask this question: "Did Michelangelo think that Noah in the ark looked like this, and that God creating Adam looked like this?" He wouldn't have said that God or Adam looked as they look in this picture.

It might seem as though, if we asked such a question as: "Does Lewy *really* mean what so and so means when he says so and so is alive?" – it might seem as though there were two sharply divided cases, one in which he would say he didn't mean it literally. I want to say this is not so. There will be cases where we will differ, and where it won't be a question at all of more or less knowledge, so that we can come together. Sometimes it will be a question of experience, so you can say: "Wait another 10 years." And I would say: "I would disencourage this kind of reasoning" and Moore would say: "I wouldn't disencourage it." That is, one would *do* something. We would take sides, and that goes so far that there would really be great differences between us, which might come out in Mr Lewy saying: "Wittgenstein is trying to undermine reason", and this wouldn't be false. This is actually where such questions rise.

Note

1 Contribution to a Symposium on *Science and Religion* (London: Gerald Howe, 1931, pp. 107–16).

C

Naturalistic Re-interpretations of Religious Belief

1

Origin of Religion

David Hume

The following selection is taken from David Hume's *The Natural History of Religion* (1757). Although Hume seems to endorse the teleological argument at the beginning of this selection and affirms the divine origin and consistency of the Christian religion at the end, these remarks are probably intended to be understood ironically. (For a brief introduction to Hume and his criticisms of the teleological argument see section II.A.4.) Hume's goal in the *Natural History* is to offer a non-*super*natural explanation of the origin of religious belief. Contrary to natural theologians, Hume contends that religious belief arises not from reason but from emotions such as fear and ignorance. These emotions first give rise to polytheistic religion and monotheism is a later development.

Sect. II. *Origin of Polytheism*

If we would, therefore, indulge our curiosity, in enquiring concerning the origin of religion, we must turn our thoughts towards[1] polytheism, the primitive religion of uninstructed mankind.

Were men led into the apprehension of invisible, intelligent power by a contemplation of the works of nature, they could never possibly entertain any conception but of one single being, who bestowed existence and order on this vast machine, and adjusted all its parts, according to one regular plan or connected system. For though, to persons of a certain turn of mind, it may not appear altogether absurd, that several independent beings, endowed with superior wisdom, might conspire in the contrivance and execution of one regular plan; yet is this a merely arbitrary supposition, which, even if allowed possible, must be confessed neither to be supported by probability nor necessity. All things in the universe are evidently of a piece. Every thing is adjusted to every thing. One design prevails throughout the whole. And this uniformity leads

David Hume, "The Natural History of Religion" from *Essays, Moral, Political, and Literary*, ed. T. H. Green and T. H. Grose, vol. 2 (London: Longmans, 1912), pp. 313–19, 328–32.

the mind to acknowledge one author; because the conception of different authors, without any distinction of attributes or operations, serves only to give perplexity to the imagination, without bestowing any satisfaction on the understanding.[2] The statue of LAOCOON, as we learn from PLINY, was the work of three artists: But it is certain, that, were we not told so, we should never have imagined, that a groupe of figures, cut from one stone, and united in one plan, was not the work and contrivance of one statuary. To ascribe any single effect to the combination of several causes, is not surely a natural and obvious supposition.

On the other hand, if, leaving the works of nature, we trace the footsteps of invisible power in the various and contrary events of human life, we are necessarily led into polytheism and to the acknowledgment of several limited and imperfect deities. Storms and tempests ruin what is nourished by the sun. The sun destroys what is fostered by the moisture of dews and rains. War may be favourable to a nation, whom the inclemency of the seasons afflicts with famine. Sickness and pestilence may depopulate a kingdom, amidst the most profuse plenty. The same nation is not, at the same time, equally successful by sea and by land. And a nation, which now triumphs over its enemies, may anon submit to their more prosperous arms. In short, the conduct of events, or what we call the plan of a particular providence, is so full of variety and uncertainty, that, if we suppose it immediately ordered by any intelligent beings, we must acknowledge a contrariety in their designs and intentions, a constant combat of opposite powers, and a repentance or change of intention in the same power, from impotence or levity. Each nation has its tutelar deity. Each element is subjected to its invisible power or agent. The province of each god is separate from that of another. Nor are the operations of the same god always certain and invariable. To-day he protects: To-morrow he abandons us. Prayers and sacrifices, rites and ceremonies, well or ill performed, are the sources of his favour or enmity, and produce all the good or ill fortune, which are to be found amongst mankind.

We may conclude, therefore, that, in all nations, which have embraced polytheism,[3] the first ideas of religion arose not from a contemplation of the works of nature, but from a concern with regard to the events of life, and from the incessant hopes and fears, which actuate the human mind. Accordingly, we find, that all idolaters, having separated the provinces of their deities, have recourse to that invisible agent, to whose authority they are immediately subjected, and whose province it is to superintend that course of actions, in which they are, at any time, engaged. JUNO is invoked at marriages; LUCINA at births. NEPTUNE receives the prayers of seamen; and MARS of warriors. The husbandman cultivates his field under the protection of CERES; and the merchant acknowledges the authority of MERCURY. Each natural event is supposed to be governed by some intelligent agent; and nothing prosperous or adverse can happen in life, which may not be the subject of peculiar prayers or thanksgivings.[4]

It must necessarily, indeed, be allowed, that, in order to carry men's intention beyond the present course of things, or lead them into any inference concerning invisible intelligent power, they must be actuated by some passion, which prompts their thought and reflection; some motive, which urges their first enquiry. But what passion shall we here have recourse to, for explaining an effect of such mighty consequence? Not speculative curiosity surely, or the pure love of truth. That motive is too refined for such gross apprehensions; and would lead men into enquiries concerning the frame of nature, a subject too large and comprehensive for their narrow capacities. No passions, therefore, can be supposed to work upon such barbarians, but the ordinary affections of human life; the anxious concern for happiness, the dread of future misery, the terror of death, the thirst of revenge, the appetite for food and other necessaries. Agitated by hopes and fears of this nature, especially the latter, men scrutinize, with a trembling curiosity, the course of future causes, and examine the various and contrary events of human life. And in this disordered scene, with eyes still more disordered and astonished, they see the first obscure traces of divinity.

Sect. III. *The Same Subject Continued*

We are placed in this world, as in a great theatre, where the true springs and causes of every event are entirely concealed from us; nor have we either sufficient wisdom to foresee, or power to prevent those ills, with which we are continually threatened. We hang in perpetual suspence between life and death, health and sickness, plenty and want; which are distributed amongst the human species by secret and unknown causes, whose operation is oft unexpected, and always unaccountable. These *unknown causes*, then, become the constant object of our hope and fear; and while the passions are kept in perpetual alarm by an anxious expectation of the events, the imagination is equally employed in forming ideas of those powers, on which we have so entire a dependance. Could men anatomize nature, according to the most probable, at least the most intelligible philosophy, they would find, that these causes are nothing but the particular fabric and structure of the minute parts of their own bodies and of external objects; and that, by a regular and constant machinery, all the events are produced, about which they are so much concerned. But this philosophy exceeds the comprehension of the ignorant multitude, who can only conceive the *unknown causes* in a general and confused manner; though their imagination, perpetually employed on the same subject, must labour to form some particular and distinct idea of them. The more they consider these causes themselves, and the uncertainty of their operation, the less satisfaction do they meet with in their researches; and, however unwilling, they must at last have abandoned so arduous an attempt, were it not for a propensity in human nature, which leads into a system, that gives them some satisfaction.

There is an universal tendency among mankind to conceive all beings like themselves, and to transfer to every object, those qualities, with which they are familiarly acquainted, and of which they are intimately conscious. We find human faces in the moon, armies in the clouds; and by a natural propensity, if not corrected by experience and reflection, ascribe malice or good-will to every thing, that hurts or pleases us. Hence the frequency and beauty of the *prosopopœia* in poetry; where trees, mountains and streams are personified, and the inanimate parts of nature acquire sentiment and passion. And though these poetical figures and expressions gain not on the belief, they may serve, at least, to prove a certain tendency in the imagination, without which they could neither be beautiful nor natural. Nor is a river-god or hamadryad always taken for a mere poetical or imaginary personage; but may sometimes enter into the real creed of the ignorant vulgar; while each grove or field is represented as possessed of a particular *genius* or invisible power, which inhabits and protects it. Nay, philosophers cannot entirely exempt themselves from this natural frailty; but have oft ascribed to inanimate matter the horror of a *vacuum*, sympathies, antipathies, and other affections of human nature. The absurdity is not less, while we cast our eyes upwards; and transferring, as is too usual, human passions and infirmities to the deity, represent him as jealous and revengeful, capricious and partial, and, in short, a wicked and foolish man, in every respect but his superior power and authority. No wonder, then, that mankind, being placed in such an absolute ignorance of causes, and being at the same time so anxious concerning their future fortune, should immediately acknowledge a dependence on invisible powers, possessed of sentiment and intelligence. The *unknown causes*, which continually employ their thought, appearing always in the same aspect, are all apprehended to be of the same kind or species. Nor is it long before we ascribe to them thought and reason and passion, and sometimes even the limbs and figures of men, in order to bring them nearer to a resemblance with ourselves.

In proportion as any man's course of life is governed by accident, we always find, that he encreases in superstition; as may particularly be observed of gamesters and sailors, who, though, of all mankind, the least capable of serious reflection, abound most in frivolous and superstitious apprehensions. The gods, says Coriolanus in Dionysius,[5] have an influence in every affair; but above all, in war; where the event is so uncertain. All human life, especially before the institution of order and good government, being subject to fortuitous accidents; it is natural, that superstition should prevail every where in barbarous ages, and put men on the most earnest enquiry concerning those invisible powers, who dispose of their happiness or misery. Ignorant of astronomy and the anatomy of plants and animals, and too little curious to observe the admirable adjustment of final causes; they remain still unacquainted with a first and supreme creator, and with that infinitely perfect spirit, who alone, by his almighty will, bestowed order on the whole frame of nature. Such a magnificent idea is too big for their narrow conceptions, which can neither observe the beauty of the work, nor comprehend the grandeur of its author. They suppose their deities, however potent and invisible, to be nothing but a species of human creatures, perhaps raised from among mankind, and retaining all human passions and appetites, together with corporeal limbs and organs. Such limited beings, though masters of human fate, being, each of them, incapable of extending his influence every where, must be vastly multiplied, in order to answer that variety of events, which happen over the whole face of nature. Thus every place is stored with a crowd of local deities; and thus polytheism has prevailed, and still prevails, among the greatest part of uninstructed mankind.[6]

Any of the human affections may lead us into the notion of invisible, intelligent power; hope as well as fear, gratitude as well as affliction: But if we examine our own hearts, or observe what passes around us, we shall find, that men are much oftener thrown on their knees by the melancholy than by the agreeable passions. Prosperity is easily received as our due, and few questions are asked concerning its cause or author. It begets cheerfulness and activity and alacrity and a lively enjoyment of every social and sensual pleasure: And during this state of mind, men have little leisure or inclination to think of the unknown invisible regions. On the other hand, every disastrous accident alarms us, and sets us on enquiries concerning the principles whence it arose: Apprehensions spring up with regard to futurity: And the mind, sunk into diffidence, terror, and melancholy, has recourse to every method of appeasing those secret intelligent powers, on whom our fortune is supposed entirely to depend.

[. . .]

Sect. VI. *Origin of Theism from Polytheism*

The doctrine of one supreme deity, the author of nature, is very ancient, has spread itself over great and populous nations, and among them has been embraced by all ranks and conditions of men: But whoever thinks that it has owed its success to the prevalent force of those invincible reasons, on which it is undoubtedly founded, would show himself little acquainted with the ignorance and stupidity of the people, and their incurable prejudices in favour of their particular superstitions. Even at this day, and in EUROPE, ask any of the vulgar, why he believes in an omnipotent creator of the world; he will never mention the beauty of final causes, of which he is wholly ignorant: He will not hold out his hand, and bid you contemplate the suppleness and variety of joints in his fingers, their bending all one way, the counterpoise which they receive from the thumb, the softness and fleshy parts of the inside of his hand, with all the other circumstances, which render that member fit for the use, to which it was destined. To these he has been long accustomed; and he beholds them with listlessness and unconcern. He will tell you of the sudden and unexpected death of such a one: The fall and bruise of such another: The excessive drought of this season: The cold and rains of another. These he ascribes to the immediate operation of providence: And such events, as, with good reasoners, are the chief difficulties in admitting a supreme intelligence, are with him the sole arguments for it.

Many theists, even the most zealous and refined, have denied a *particular* providence, and have asserted, that the Sovereign mind or first principle of all things, having fixed general laws, by which nature is governed, gives free and uninterrupted course to these laws, and disturbs not, at every turn, the settled order of events by particular volitions. From the beautiful connexion, say they, and rigid observance of established rules, we draw the chief argument for theism; and from the same principles are enabled to answer the principal objections against it. But so little is this understood by the generality of mankind, that, wherever they observe any one to ascribe all events to natural causes, and to remove the particular interposition of a deity, they are apt to suspect him of the grossest infidelity. *A little philosophy*, says lord BACON, *makes men atheists: A great deal reconciles them to religion*. For men, being taught, by superstitious prejudices, to lay the stress on a wrong place; when that fails them, and they discover, by a little reflection, that the course of nature is regular and uniform, their whole faith totters, and falls to ruin. But being taught, by more reflection, that this very regularity and uniformity is the strongest proof of design and of a supreme intelligence, they return to that belief, which they had deserted; and they are now able to establish it on a firmer and more durable foundation.

Convulsions in nature, disorders, prodigies, miracles, though the most opposite to the plan of a wise superintendent, impress mankind with the strongest sentiments of religion; the causes of events seeming then the most unknown and unaccountable. Madness, fury, rage, and an inflamed imagination, though they sink men nearest to the level of beasts, are, for a like reason, often supposed to be the only dispositions, in which we can have any immediate communication with the Deity.

We may conclude, therefore, upon the whole, that, since the vulgar, in nations, which have embraced the doctrine of theism, still build it upon irrational and superstitious principles, they are never led into that opinion by any process of argument, but by a certain train of thinking, more suitable to their genius and capacity.

It may readily happen, in an idolatrous nation, that though men admit the existence of several limited deities, yet is there some one God, whom, in a particular manner, they make the object of their worship and adoration. They may either suppose, that, in the distribution of power and territory among the gods, their nation was subjected to the jurisdiction of that particular deity; or reducing heavenly objects to the model of things below, they may represent one god as the prince or supreme magistrate of the rest, who, though of the same nature, rules them with an authority, like that which an earthly sovereign exercises over his subjects and vassals. Whether this god, therefore, be considered as their peculiar patron, or as the general sovereign of heaven, his votaries will endeavour, by every art, to insinuate themselves into his favour; and supposing him to be pleased, like themselves, with praise and flattery, there is no eulogy or exaggeration, which will be spared in their addresses to him. In proportion as men's fears or distresses become more urgent, they still invent new strains of adulation; and even he who outdoes his predecessor in swelling up the titles of his divinity, is sure to be outdone by his successor in newer and more pompous epithets of praise. Thus they proceed; till at last they arrive at infinity itself, beyond which there is no farther progress: And it is well, if, in striving to get farther, and to represent a magnificent simplicity, they run not into inexplicable mystery, and destroy the intelligent nature of their deity, on which alone any rational worship or adoration can be founded. While they confine themselves to the notion of a perfect being, the creator of the world, they coincide, by chance, with the principles of reason and true philosophy; though they are guided to that notion, not by reason, of which they are in a great measure incapable, but by the adulation and fears of the most vulgar superstition.

We often find, amongst barbarous nations, and even sometimes amongst civilized, that, when every strain of flattery has been exhausted towards arbitrary princes, when every human quality has been applauded to the utmost; their servile courtiers represent them, at last, as real divinities, and point them out to the people as objects of adoration. How much more natural, therefore, is it, that a limited deity, who at first is supposed only the immediate author of the particular goods and ills in life, should in the end be represented as sovereign maker and modifier of the universe?

Even where this notion of a supreme deity is already established; though it ought naturally to lessen every other worship, and abase every object of reverence, yet if a nation has entertained the opinion of a subordinate tutelar divinity, saint, or angel; their addresses to that being gradually rise upon them, and encroach on the adoration due to their supreme deity. The Virgin Mary, ere checked by the reformation, had proceeded, from being merely a good woman, to usurp many attributes of the Almighty: God and St NICHOLAS go hand in hand, in all the prayers and petitions of the MUSCOVITES.

Thus the deity, who, from love, converted himself into a bull, in order to carry off EUROPA; and who, from ambition, dethroned his father, SATURN, became the OPTIMUS MAXIMUS of the heathens. Thus, the God of ABRAHAM, ISAAC, and JACOB, became the supreme deity or JEHOVAH of the JEWS.[7]

[. . .]

Rather than relinquish this propensity to adulation, religionists, in all ages, have involved themselves in the greatest absurdities and contradictions.

HOMER, in one passage, calls OCEANUS and TETHYS the original parents of all things, conformably to the established mythology and tradition of the GREEKS: Yet, in other passages, he could not forbear complimenting JUPITER, the reigning deity, with that magnificent appellation; and accordingly denominates him the father of gods and men. He forgets, that every temple, every street was full of the ancestors, uncles, brothers, and sisters of this JUPITER; who was in reality nothing but an upstart parricide and usurper. A like contradiction is observable in HESIOD; and is so much the less excusable, as his professed intention was to deliver a true genealogy of the gods.

Were there a religion (and we may suspect Mahometanism of this inconsistence) which sometimes painted the Deity in the most sublime colours, as the creator of heaven and earth; sometimes degraded him nearly to a level with human creatures in his powers and faculties;[8] while at the same time it ascribed to him suitable infirmities, passions, and partialities, of the moral kind: That religion, after it was extinct, would also be cited as an instance of those contradictions, which arise from the gross, vulgar, natural conceptions of mankind, opposed to their continual propensity towards flattery and exaggeration. Nothing indeed would prove more strongly the divine origin of any religion, than to find (and happily this is the case with Christianity) that it is free from a contradiction, so incident to human nature.

Notes

[Notes in square brackets were added by the editors of the *Essays*]

1 [Idolatry or polytheism: Editions L to Q.]

2 [The remainder of the paragraph was given as a note in Editions L to P.]

3 [Polytheism or idolatry: Editions L to Q.]

4 'Fragilis & laboriosa mortalitas in partes ista digessit, infirmitatis suæ memor, ut portionibus coleret quisque, quo maxime indigeret.' PLIN. lib. ii. cap. 5. So early as HESIOD's time there were 30,000 deities. *Oper. & Dier.* lib.i. ver. 250 But the task to be performed by these seems still too great for their number. The provinces of the deities were so subdivided, that there was even a God of *Sneezing*. See ARIST. *Probl.* sect. 33. cap. 7. The province of copulation, suitably to the importance and dignity of it, was divided among several deities.

5 Lib. viii. 33.

6 The following lines of EURIPIDES are so much to the present purpose, that I cannot forbear quoting them:

Οὐκ ἔστιν οὐδὲν πιστὸν, οὔτ' εὐδοξία,
Οὔτ' αὖ καλῶς πράσσοντα μὴ πράξειν κακῶς.
Φύρουσι δ' αὔθ' οἱ θεοὶ πάλιν τε καὶ πρόσω,
Ταραγμὸν ἐντιθέντες, ὡς ἀγνωσίᾳ
Σέβωμεν αὐτούς.

HECUBA, 956.

There is nothing secure in the world; no glory, no prosperity. The gods toss all life into confusion; mix every thing with its reverse; that all of us, from our ignorance and uncertainty, may pay them the more worship and reverence.

7 [For this sentence the Proof reads: Thus the deity, whom the vulgar Jews conceived only as the God of *Abraham, Isaac,* and *Jacob*, became their *Jehovah* and Creator of the world.

Editions L to N read: Thus, notwithstanding the sublime idea suggested by *Moses* and the inspired writers, many vulgar *Jews* seem still to have conceived the supreme Being as a mere topical deity or national protector.]

8 [The Proof reads: 'Sometimes degraded him so far to a level with human creatures as to represent him wrestling with a man, walking in the cool of the evening, showing his back parts, and descending from heaven to inform himself of what passes on earth: while, &c.' The pen is drawn through all from 'as' to 'earth:' and for 'so far' the margin gives 'nearly.']

2

The Essence of Religion in General

Ludwig Feuerbach

Ludwig Feuerbach (1804–72) was very religious in his youth and studied theology in his university years. After being introduced to Hegelianism, his interests turned from theology to philosophy and he went to Berlin to study under Hegel. Feuerbach eventually became known for his criticisms of both Hegelianism and Christianity. In the following selection from *The Essence of Christianity* (1841) he argues that God is simply a projection of human nature.

What we have so far maintained concerning the general relationship between man and his object, and between man and sensuous objects, is particularly true of man's relationship to the religious object.

In view of its relation to the objects of the senses, the consciousness of the object can be distinguished from self-consciousness; but, in the case of the religious object, consciousness and self-consciousness directly coincide. A sensuous object exists apart from man, but the religious object exists within him – it is itself an inner, intimate object, indeed, the closest object, and hence an object which forsakes him as little as his self-consciousness or conscience. "God," says. Augustine, for example, "is nearer, more closely related to us and therefore more easily known by us than sensuous and physical things." Strictly speaking, the object of the senses is in itself indifferent, having no relevance to our disposition and judgment. But the object of religion is a distinguished object – the most excellent, the first, the highest being. It essentially presupposes a critical judgment – the discrimination between the divine and the non-divine, between that which is worthy of adoration and that which is not. It is in this context, therefore, that the following statement is unconditionally true: The object of man is nothing else than his objective being itself. As man thinks, as is his understanding of things, so is his God; so much worth as a man has, so much and no more has his God. The consciousness of God is the self-consciousness of man; the knowledge of God is the self-knowledge

Ludwig Feuerbach, "Introduction" from *The Fiery Brook*, trans. Zawar Hanfi (Garden City, NY: Anchor Books, 1972).

of man. Man's notion of himself is his notion of God, just as his notion of God is his notion of himself – the two are identical. What is God to man, that is man's own spirit, man's own soul; what is man's spirit, soul, and heart – that is his God. God is the manifestation of man's inner nature, his expressed self; religion is the solemn unveiling of man's hidden treasures, the avowal of his innermost thoughts, the open confession of the secrets of his love.

But if religion, i.e., the consciousness of God, is characterised as the self-consciousness of man, this does not mean that the religious man is directly aware that his consciousness of God is his self-consciousness, for it is precisely the absence of such an awareness that is responsible for the peculiar nature of religion. Hence, in order to eliminate this misunderstanding, it would be better to say that religion is the first, but indirect, self-consciousness of man. That is why religion precedes philosophy everywhere, in the history of mankind as well as in the history of the individual. Man transposes his essential being outside himself before he finds it within himself. His own being becomes the object of his thought first as another being. Religion is the essential being of man in his infancy; but the child sees his essential being, namely, man outside himself, as a child; a man is object to himself as another man. Hence, the historical development occurring within religions takes the following course: What an earlier religion regarded as objective, is now recognised as subjective; i.e., what was regarded and worshiped as God, is now recognised as something human. From the standpoint of a later religion, the earlier religion turns out to be idolatry: Man is seen to have worshiped his own essence. Man has objectified himself, but he has not yet recognised the object as his own essential being – a step taken by later religion. Every progress in religion means therefore, a deepening of man's knowledge of himself. But every religion, while designating older religions as idolatrous, looks upon itself as exempted from their fate. It does so necessarily, for otherwise it would no longer be religion; it sees only in other religions what is the fault – if a fault it can be called – of religion as such. Because its object, its content, is a different one, because it has superseded the content of earlier religions, it presumes to be exalted above the necessary and eternal laws that constitute the essence of religion; it gives itself to the illusion that its object, its content, is superhuman. However, the hidden nature of religion, which remains opaque to religion itself, is transparent to the thinker who makes it the object of his thought. And our task consists precisely in showing that the antithesis of the divine and human is illusory; that is, that it is nothing other than the antithesis between the essential being of man and his individual being, and that consequently the object and the content of the Christian religion are altogether human.

Religion, at least the Christian religion, is the expression of how man relates to himself, or more correctly, to his essential being; but he relates to his essential being as to another being. The Divine Being is nothing other than the being of man himself, or rather, the being of man abstracted from the limits of the individual man or the real, corporeal man, and objectified, i.e., contemplated and worshiped as another being, as a being distinguished from his own. All determinations of the Divine Being are, therefore, determinations of the being of man.

In relation to the predicates – attributes or determinations – of God, this is admitted without hesitation, but by no means admitted in relation to the subject of these predicates, in relation to the being in which they are grounded. The negation of the subject is taken to mean the negation of religion, atheism, but not the negation of the predicates. That which has no determinations, also has no effect upon me; that which has no effect upon me, also does not exist for me. To eliminate all determinations of a being is the same as to eliminate that being itself. A being without determinations is a being that cannot be an object of thought; it is a nonentity. Where man removes all determinations from God, God is reduced to a negative being, to a being that is not a being. To a truly religious man, however, God is not a being without determinations, because he is a definite, real being to him. Hence, the view that God is without determinations, that he cannot be known, is a product of the modern era, of modern unbelief.

Just as reason can be, and is, determined as finite only where man regards sensual enjoyment, religious feeling, aesthetic contemplation, or moral sentiment as the absolute, the true, so the view as to the unknowability or indeterminateness of God can be fixed as a dogma only where this object commands no interest for cognition, where reality alone claims the interest of man or where the real alone has for him the significance of being an essential, absolute, divine object, but where at the same time this purely worldly tendency is contradicted by a still-existing remnant of old religiosity. By positing God as unknowable, man excuses himself to what is still left of his religious conscience for his oblivion of God, his surrender to the world. He negates God in practice – his mind and his senses have been absorbed by the world – but he does not negate him in theory. He does not attack his existence; he leaves it intact. But this existence neither affects nor incommodes him, for it is only a negative existence, an existence without existence; it is an existence that contradicts itself – a being that, in view of its effects, is indistinguishable from non-being. The negation of determinate, positive predicates of the Divine Being is nothing else than the negation of religion, but one which still has an appearance of religion, so that it is not recognised as a negation – it is nothing but a subtle, sly atheism. The alleged religious horror of limiting God by determinate predicates is only the irreligious wish to forget all about God, to banish him from the mind. He who is afraid to be finite is afraid to exist. All real existence, that is, all existence that really is existence, is qualitative, determinate existence. He who seriously, truly believes in the existence of God is not disturbed even by grossly sensuous qualities attributed to God. He who regards the fact of his existence as an insult, he who recoils from that which is gross, may just as well give up existing. A God to whom his determinateness is an insult lacks the courage and strength to exist. Determinateness is the fire, the oxygen, the salt of existence. An existence in general, an existence without qualities, is an insipid and preposterous existence. But there is nothing more, and nothing less, in God than what religion puts in him. Only when man loses his taste for religion, that is, when religion itself becomes insipid, does God become an insipid existence.

Moreover, there is yet a milder way of denying the divine predicates than the direct one just described. One admits that the predicates of the Divine Being are finite and, more particularly, human determinations, but one rejects the idea of rejecting them. One even defends them on the ground that they are necessary for man; that being man, he cannot conceive God in any way other than human. One argues that although these determinations have no meaning in relation to God, the fact is that God, if he is to exist for man, can appear to man in no other way than he does, namely, as a being with human attributes. However, this distinction between what God is in himself and what he is for man destroys the peace of religion as well as being an unfeasible and unfounded distinction. It is not at all possible for me to know whether God as he is in and for himself is something different from what he is for me. The manner in which he exists for me is also the totality of his existence for me. The determinations in terms of which he exists for me contain also the "in-itself-ness" of his being, his essential nature itself; he exists for me in a way in which he can exist for me alone. The religious man is completely satisfied with how he sees God in relation to himself – and he knows nothing of any other relation – for God is to him what he can be to man at all. In the distinction made above, man transgresses the boundaries of himself, his being and its absolute measure, but this transcending is only an illusion. For I can make the distinction between the object as it is in itself and the object as it is for me only where an object can really appear different from what it actually appears to me. I cannot make such a distinction where the object appears to me as it does according to my absolute measure; that is, as it must appear to me. It is true that my conception can be subjective; that is, one which is not bound by the essential constitution of my species. However, if my conception corresponds to the measure of my species, the distinction between what something is in itself and what it is for me ceases; for in that case this conception is itself an absolute one. The measure of the species is the absolute measure, law, and criterion of man. Yet religion has the conviction that its conceptions and determinations of God are such as every man ought to have if he is to have true conceptions, that these are conceptions necessitated by human nature, that they are indeed objective, conforming to the nature of God. To every religion, the gods of other religions are only conceptions of God; but its own conception of God is itself its God – God as it conceives him to be, God genuinely and truly so, God as he is in himself. Religion is satisfied only with a complete and total God – it will not have merely an appearance of God, it can be, satisfied with nothing less than God himself, God in person. Religion abandons itself if it abandons God in his essential being; it is no longer true if it renounces its possession of the true God. Scepticism is the archenemy of religion. But the distinction between object and concept, between God as he is in himself and as he is for me, is a sceptical, that is, irreligious distinction.

That which is subsumed by man under the concept of "being-in-itself," that which he regards as the most supreme being or as the being of which he can conceive none higher, that is the Divine Being. How can he therefore still ask, what this being is in itself? If God were an object to the bird, he would be an object to it only as a winged being – the bird knows nothing higher, nothing more blissful than the state of being winged. How ludicrous would it be if this bird commented: "God appears to me as a bird, but I do not know what he is in himself." The highest being to the bird is the "bird-being." Take from it its conception of "bird-being," and you take from it its conception of the highest being. How, therefore, could the bird ask whether God in himself were winged? To ask whether God is in himself what he is for me, is to ask whether God is God; it is to raise oneself above God and to rebel against him.

Given, therefore, the situation in which man is seized by the awareness that religious predicates are mere anthropomorphisms, his faith has also come under the sway of doubt and unbelief. And if this awareness does not lead him to the formal negation of the predicates and thence to the negation of the being in which they are grounded, it is only due to an inconsistency for which his faint-heartedness and irresolute intellect are responsible. If you doubt the objective truth of the predicates, you must also doubt the objective truth of the subject to which they belong. If your predicates are anthropomorphisms, their subject, too, is an anthropomorphism. If love, goodness, and personality are human determinations, the being which constitutes their source and, according to you, their presupposition is also an anthropomorphism; so is the existence of God; so is the belief that there is a God – in short, all presuppositions that are purely human. What tells you that the belief in a God at all is not an indication of the limitedness of man's mode of conception? Higher beings – and you assume that such beings exist – are perhaps so blissful in themselves, so at unity with themselves that they are not exposed to a tension between themselves and a higher being. To know God and not to be God, to know blissfulness and not to enjoy it, is to be in conflict with oneself, is to be delivered up to unhappiness.

3

The Future of an Illusion

Sigmund Freud

An Austrian psychologist, Sigmund Freud (1856–1939) was one of the twentieth century's most influential thinkers. In the following selection from *The Future of an Illusion* he argues that religious ideas are illusions. As Freud defines it, an illusion can be either true or false; what defines a belief as an illusion is simply that wish fulfillment is one of its primary motives. Freud explicitly acknowledges that he does not directly address the question of the truth of religious beliefs; nevertheless, he clearly takes the thesis that they are illusions to undermine their support. He suggests at the end of the reading that it would be quite odd if things should turn out to be precisely the way we would wish them to be.

V

[...]

When we ask on what [religious dogmas'] claim to be believed is founded, we are met with three answers, which harmonize remarkably badly with one another. Firstly, these teachings deserve to be believed because they were already believed by our primal ancestors; secondly, we possess proofs which have been handed down to us from those same primaeval times; and thirdly, it is forbidden to raise the question of their authentication at all. In former days anything so presumptuous was visited with the severest penalties, and even to-day society looks askance at any attempt to raise the question again.

This third point is bound to rouse our strongest suspicions. After all, a prohibition like this can only be for one reason – that society is very well aware of the insecurity of the claim it makes on behalf of its religious doctrines. Otherwise it would certainly be very ready to put the necessary data at the disposal of anyone

Sigmund Freud, Chapters V and VI from *The Future of an Illusion*, ed. and trans. James Strachey (New York: WW Norton & Co., 1961), pp. 33–4, 36–7, 38–42.

who wanted to arrive at conviction. This being so, it is with a feeling of mistrust which it is hard to allay that we pass on to an examination of the other two grounds of proof. We ought to believe because our forefathers believed. But these ancestors of ours were far more ignorant than we are. They believed in things we could not possibly accept to-day; and the possibility occurs to us that the doctrines of religion may belong to that class too. The proofs they have left us are set down in writings which themselves bear every mark of untrustworthiness. They are full of contradictions, revisions and falsifications, and where they speak of factual confirmations they are themselves unconfirmed. It does not help much to have it asserted that their wording, or even their content only, originates from divine revelation; for this assertion is itself one of the doctrines whose authenticity is under examination, and no proposition can be a proof of itself.

Thus we arrive at the singular conclusion that of all the information provided by our cultural assets it is precisely the elements which might be of the greatest importance to us and which have the task of solving the riddles of the universe and of reconciling us to the sufferings of life – it is precisely those elements that are the least well authenticated of any. We should not be able to bring ourselves to accept anything of so little concern to us as the fact that whales bear young instead of laying eggs, if it were not capable of better proof than this.

This state of affairs is in itself a very remarkable psychological problem. And let no one suppose that what I have said about the impossibility of proving the truth of religious doctrines contains anything new. It has been felt at all times – undoubtedly, too, by the ancestors who bequeathed us this legacy. Many of them probably nourished the same doubts as ours, but the pressure imposed on them was too strong for them to have dared to utter them. And since then countless people have been tormented by similar doubts, and have striven to suppress them, because they thought it was their duty to believe; many brilliant intellects have broken down over this conflict, and many characters have been impaired by the compromises with which they have tried to find a way out of it.

[. . .]

I am reminded of one of my children who was distinguished at an early age by a peculiarly marked matter-of-factness. When the children were being told a fairy story and were listening to it with rapt attention, he would come up and ask: 'Is that a true story?' When he was told it was not, he would turn away with a look of disdain. We may expect that people will soon behave in the same way towards the fairy tales of religion [. . .]

But at present they still behave quite differently; and in past times religious ideas, in spite of their incontrovertible lack of authentication, have exercised the strongest possible influence on mankind. This is a fresh psychological problem. We must ask where the inner force of those doctrines lies and to what it is that they owe their efficacy, independent as it is of recognition by reason.

VI

I think we have prepared the way sufficiently for an answer to both these questions. It will be found if we turn our attention to the psychical origin of religious ideas. These, which are given out as teachings, are not precipitates of experience or end-results of thinking: they are illusions, fulfilments of the oldest, strongest and most urgent wishes of mankind. The secret of their strength lies in the strength of those wishes. As we already know, the terrifying impression of helplessness in childhood aroused the need for protection – for protection through love – which was provided by the father; and the recognition that this helplessness lasts throughout life made it necessary to cling to the existence of a father, but this time a more powerful one. Thus the benevolent rule of a divine Providence allays our fear of the dangers of life; the establishment of a moral world-order ensures the fulfilment of the demands of justice, which have so often remained unfulfilled in human civilization; and the prolongation of earthly existence in a future life provides the local and temporal framework in which these wish-fulfilments shall take place. Answers to the riddles that tempt the curiosity of man, such as how the universe began or what the relation is between body and mind, are developed in conformity with the underlying assumptions of this system. It is an enormous relief to the individual psyche if the conflicts of its childhood arising from the father-complex – conflicts which it has never wholly overcome – are removed from it and brought to a solution which is universally accepted.

When I say that these things are all illusions, I must define the meaning of the word. An illusion is not the same thing as an error; nor is it necessarily an error. Aristotle's belief that vermin are developed out of dung (a belief to which ignorant people still cling) was an error; so was the belief of a former generation of doctors that *tabes dorsalis* is the result of sexual excess. It would be incorrect to call these errors illusions. On the other hand, it was an illusion of Columbus's that he had discovered a new sea-route to the Indies. The part played by his wish in this error is very clear. One may describe as an illusion the assertion made by certain nationalists that the Indo-Germanic race is the only one capable of civilization; or the belief, which was only destroyed by psychoanalysis, that children are creatures without sexuality. What is characteristic of illusions is that they are derived from human wishes. In this respect they come near to psychiatric delusions. But they differ from them, too, apart from the more complicated structure of delusions. In the case of delusions, we emphasize as essential their being in contradiction with reality. Illusions need not necessarily be false – that is to say, unrealizable or in contradiction to reality. For instance, a middle-class girl may have the illusion that a prince will come and marry her. This is possible; and a few such cases have occurred. That the Messiah will come and found a golden age is much less likely. Whether one classifies this belief as an illusion or as something analogous to a delusion will depend on one's personal attitude. Examples of illusions which have proved true are not easy to find, but the illusion of the alchemists that all metals can be turned into gold might be one of them. The wish to have a great deal of gold, as much gold as possible, has, it is true, been a good deal damped by our present-day knowledge of the determinants of wealth, but chemistry no longer regards the transmutation of metals into gold as impossible. Thus we call a belief an illusion when a wish-fulfilment is a prominent factor in its motivation, and in doing so we disregard its relations to reality, just as the illusion itself sets no store by verification.

Having thus taken our bearings, let us return once more to the question of religious doctrines. We can now repeat that all of them are illusions and insusceptible of proof. No one can be compelled to think them true, to believe in them. Some of them are so improbable, so incompatible with everything we have laboriously discovered about the reality of the world, that we may compare them – if we pay proper regard to the psychological differences – to delusions. Of the reality value of most of them we cannot judge; just as they cannot be proved, so they cannot be refuted. We still know too little to make a critical approach to them. The riddles of the universe reveal themselves only slowly to our investigation; there are many questions to which science to-day can give no answer. But scientific work is the only road which can lead us to a knowledge of reality outside ourselves. It is once again merely an illusion to expect anything from intuition and introspection; they can give us nothing but particulars about our own life, which are hard to interpret, never any information about the questions which religious doctrine finds it so easy to answer. It would be insolent to let one's own arbitrary will step into the breach and, according to one's personal estimate, declare this or that part of the religious system to be less or more acceptable. Such questions are too momentous for that; they might be called too sacred.

At this point one must expect to meet with an objection. 'Well then, if even obdurate sceptics admit that the assertions of religion cannot be refuted by reason, why should I not believe in them, since they have so much on their side – tradition, the agreement of mankind, and all the consolation they offer?' Why not, indeed? Just as no one can be forced to believe, so no one can be forced to disbelieve. But do not let us be satisfied with deceiving ourselves that arguments like these take us along the road of correct thinking. If ever there was a case of a lame excuse we have it here. Ignorance is ignorance; no right to believe anything can be derived from it. In other matters no sensible person will behave so irresponsibly or rest content with such feeble grounds for his opinions and for the line he takes. It is only in the highest and most sacred things that he allows himself to do so. In reality these are only attempts at pretending to oneself or to other people that one is still firmly attached to religion, when one has long since cut oneself loose from it. Where questions of religion are concerned, people are guilty of every possible sort of dishonesty and intellectual misdemeanour. Philosophers stretch the meaning of words until they retain scarcely anything of their original sense. They give the name of 'God' to some vague abstraction which they have created for themselves; having done so they can pose before all the world as deists, as believers in God, and they can even boast that they have recognized a higher, purer concept of God, notwithstanding that their God is now nothing more than an insubstantial shadow and no longer the mighty personality of religious doctrines. Critics persist in describing as 'deeply religious' anyone who admits to a sense of man's insignificance or impotence in the face of the universe, although what constitutes the essence of the religious attitude is not this feeling but only the next step after it, the reaction to it which seeks a remedy for it. The man who goes no further, but humbly acquiesces in the small part which human beings play in the great world – such a man is, on the contrary, irreligious in the truest sense of the word.

To assess the truth-value of religious doctrines does not lie within the scope of the present enquiry. It is enough for us that we have recognized them as being, in their psychological nature, illusions. But we do not have to conceal the fact that this discovery also strongly influences our attitude to the question which must appear to many to be the most important of all. We know approximately at what periods and by what kind of men religious doctrines were created. If in addition we discover the motives which led to this, our attitude to the problem of religion will undergo a marked displacement. We shall tell ourselves that it would be very nice if there were a God who created the world and was a benevolent. Providence, and if there were a moral order in the universe and an after-life; but it is a very striking fact that all this is exactly as we are bound to wish it to be. And it would be more remarkable still if our wretched, ignorant and downtrodden ancestors had succeeded in solving all these difficult riddles of the universe.

IV

WHO OR WHAT IS GOD?

Introduction

The classical arguments for the existence of God conclude that a being of a certain description exists. In the Teleological Argument it is a designer of the universe. In the Cosmological Argument it is a first cause or a necessary being. In the Ontological Argument it is that than which nothing greater can be conceived. These arguments are usually interpreted as aiming to establish the existence of the same being, but what reason do we have for thinking that? Furthermore, what reason do we have to think that such a being is the God of the monotheistic religions? More arguments are needed to connect the conclusion of the theistic arguments with the attributes that are considered essential to religious practice. The readings in this section are a sampling of the attempt by philosophers to unpack the nature of deity and to resolve some puzzles that arise from the idea of a perfect being.

The influence of ancient Greek philosophy on traditional Christian and Islamic theology will be obvious in this section. In the fifth century BC, Parmenides argued that Being is One, eternal, simple, unchangeable, perfect, and immaterial. This view is defended in our first reading by one of Parmenides' followers, Melissus of Samos, who has been dated to around the middle of the fifth century BC. Aristotle's discussion of the Unmoved Mover in the selection from his *Metaphysics* is more theological than the selection from the *Physics* in section II. In the entry in this section, Aristotle proposes that the Unmoved Mover attracts everything in the universe towards itself like a giant magnet. It is a being that thinks about the only thing worth thinking about – itself. It is not clear that it is a person, but it is capable of pleasure. Both Parmenidean and Aristotelian views influenced the development of Christian theology, as we can see from the selection from Anselm. An alternative strain of thought in Christian religious thought was the view of Pseudo-Dionysius the Areopagite in the sixth century, who argued that the divine nature is incomprehensible, and we can understand God more by what we can say God is not rather than by what we can say God is. Pseudo-Dionysius influenced Eastern and Western mysticism as well as an important strain of Christian theology.

Christian philosophers combined elements of the Greek notion of divinity with the Jewish notion of a personal deity. In the early centuries of the Christian era the idea of a personal God was elaborated into the doctrines of the Trinity (three persons in one God) and the Incarnation (one person with both a divine and a human nature). There is a broad consensus in the Christian tradition that the latter doctrines exceed the reach of philosophical reasoning, and in any case, it seems unlikely that reason alone can demonstrate that something is or is not a person. Discussions of divine personhood are therefore at the place where philosophy meets theology.

There are a number of puzzles about the coherence of the traditional divine attributes and the consistency of some of those attributes with divine personhood. For instance, the idea that God is timeless and unchangeable has been attacked as incompatible with personhood (see the Craig entry), and it has been argued that these attributes are incompatible with omniscience (see the Kretzmann entry). There are also numerous disputes about perfect goodness and its compatibility with attributes such as omnipotence and divine freedom. That is because perfect goodness was traditionally interpreted as implying that God cannot do evil. But if God cannot do evil, then God seems to lack omnipotence, since there is something God cannot do, and God seems to lack freedom for the same reason. There are other problems in defining omnipotence in a way that preserves the intuition that an omnipotent being is "almighty" without running into contradictions such as the famous Paradox of the Stone (Can God create a stone too heavy for him to lift?) In this volume the paper by Peter Geach critiques a number of contemporary accounts of omnipotence and argues that the doctrine is not essential to Christian theism.

Problems with the coherence of the divine attributes are not limited to problems with the consistency between one attribute and another. Two of the most serious problems in understanding the relation between the deity and human beings involve an apparent inconsistency between divine attributes and deep-seated beliefs about the world humans live in. The first problem is the apparent inconsistency between the existence of an omniscient being (where omniscience includes infallible foreknowledge) and human free will. The second problem is the apparent inconsistency between the existence of an omnipotent and perfectly good being and the existence of evil. These problems are important enough to get their own sections. Readings on the dilemma of freedom and foreknowledge are collected in section V. Readings on the problem of evil are included in section VII.

1

On Being

Melissus of Samos

Melissus of Samos (fifth century BC) was a member of the Eleatic school of pre-Socratic philosophers and a follower of Parmenides. In the following reading he argues that Being is one, eternal, infinite, and unchanging. These attributes later appear in many Islamic and Christian views of the deity.

1. That which was, was always and always will be. For if it had come into being, it necessarily follows that before it came into being, Nothing existed. If however Nothing existed, in no way could anything come into being out of nothing.
2. Since therefore it did not come into being, it Is and always was and always will be, and has no beginning or end, but it is eternal. For if it had come into being, it would have a beginning (for it would have come into being at some time, and so begun), and an end (for since it had come into being, it would have ended). But since it has neither begun nor ended, it always was and always will be and has no beginning nor end. For it is impossible for anything to Be, unless it Is completely.
3. But as it Is always, so also its size must always be infinite.
4. Nothing that has a beginning and an end is either everlasting or infinite.
5. If it were not One, it will form a boundary in relation to something else.
6. If it were infinite, it would be One; for if it were two, (*these*) could not be (*spatially*) infinite, but each would have boundaries in relation to each other.
7. (1) Thus therefore it is everlasting and unlimited and one and like throughout (*homogeneous*).

   (2) And neither could it perish or become larger or change its (*inner*) arrangement, nor does it feel pain or grief. For if it suffered any of these things, it would no longer be

Melissus of Samos, *Ancilla to the Pre-Socratic Philosophers*, trans. Kathleen Freeman (Cambridge, MA: Harvard University Press, 1966), pp. 48–50.

One. For if Being alters, it follows that it is not the same, but that that which previously Was is destroyed, and that Not-Being has come into being. Hence if it were to become different by a single hair in ten thousand years, so it must be utterly destroyed in the whole of time.

(3) But it is not possible for it to be rearranged either, for the previous arrangement is not destroyed, nor does a non-existent arrangement come into being. And since it is neither increased by any addition, nor destroyed, nor changed, how could it have undergone a rearrangement of what exists? For if it were different in any respect, then there would at once be a rearrangement.

(4) Nor does it feel pain; for it could not Be completely if it were in pain; for a thing which is in pain could not always Be. Nor has it equal power with what is healthy. Nor would it be the same if it were in pain; for it would feel pain through the subtraction or addition of something, and could no longer be the same.

(5) Nor could that which is healthy feel pain, for the Healthy – That which Is – would perish, and That which Is Not would come into being.

(6) And with regard to grief, the same reasoning applies as to pain.

(7) Nor is there any Emptiness; for the Empty is Nothing; and so that which is Nothing cannot Be. Nor does it move; for it cannot withdraw in any direction, but (*all*) is full. For if there were any Empty, it would have withdrawn into the Empty; but as the Empty does not exist, there is nowhere for it (*Being*) to withdraw.

(8) And there can be no Dense and Rare. For the Rare cannot possibly be as full as the Dense, but the Rare must at once become more empty than the Dense.

(9) The following distinction must be made between the Full and the Not-Full: if a thing has room for or admits something, it is not full; if it neither has room for nor admits anything, it is full.

(10) It (*Being*) must necessarily be full, therefore, if there is no Empty. If therefore it is full, it does not move.

8\. (1) This argument is the greatest proof that it (*Being*) is One only; but there are also the following proofs:

(2) If Things were Many, they would have to be of the same kind as I say the One is. For if there is earth and water and air and fire and iron and gold, and that which is living and that which is dead, and black and white and all the rest of the things which men say are real: if these things exist, and we see and hear correctly, each thing must be of such a kind as it seemed to us to be in the first place, and it cannot change or become different, but each thing must always be what it is. But now, we say we see and hear and understand correctly,

(3) and it seems to us that the hot becomes cold and the cold hot, and the hard soft and the soft hard, and that the living thing dies and comes into being from what is not living, and that all things change, and that what was and what now is are not at all the same, but iron which is hard is worn away by contact[1] with the finger, and gold and stone and whatever seems to be entirely strong (*is worn away*); and that from water, earth and stone come into being. So that it comes about that we neither see nor know existing things.

(4) So these statements are not consistent with one another. For although we say that there are many things, everlasting (?), having forms and strength, it seems to us that they all alter and change from what is seen on each occasion.

(5) It is clear therefore that we have not been seeing correctly, and that those things do not correctly seem to us to

be Many; for they would not change if they were real, but each would Be as it seemed to be. For nothing is stronger than that which is real.

(6) And if it changed, Being would have been destroyed, and Not-Being would have come into being. Thus, therefore, if Things are Many, they must be such as the One is.

9. If therefore Being Is, it must be One; and if it is One, it is bound not to have body. But if it had Bulk, it would have parts, and would no longer Be.

10. If Being is divided, it moves; and if it moved, it could not Be.

Spurious

11. What came into being Is now and always will be.

Note

1 *ὁμουρέων*; also *ὁμοῦ ῥέων* ('changing with the finger').

2

The Final Cause

Aristotle

Aristotle famously distinguished four kinds of cause, or explanation, for a state of affairs – material, formal, efficient, and final. Consider, for example, the existence of a knife. Its *material* cause is simply the material, say steel and bone, of which it is made. Its *formal* cause is, roughly, its essential design – the size, shape, and so on of its parts. An *efficient* cause is what we most commonly think of when we hear the word *cause*; simply put, it is that which produces the effect. Thus, the knife-maker, who imposes a certain form upon the steel and bone, is the efficient cause of the knife. Lastly, a *final* cause is the end for which something is done; thus, cutting may be the final cause of a knife. Earlier, in section II.B.2, we saw Aristotle's argument that motion requires an Unmoved Mover as its efficient cause. In the following passage from his *Metaphysics* Aristotle argues that the Unmoved Mover, or God, is also the final cause; that is, God is the most good being toward which all action is aimed.

7 Since (1) this is a possible account of the matter, and (2) if it were not true, the world would have proceeded out of night and 'all things together' and out of non-being, these difficulties may be taken as solved. There is, then, something which is always moved with an unceasing motion, which is motion in a circle; and this is plain not in theory only but in fact. Therefore the first heaven[1] must be eternal. There is therefore also something which moves it. And since that which is moved and moves is intermediate, there is something which moves without being moved, being eternal, substance, and actuality. And the object of desire and the object of thought move in this way; they move without being moved. The primary objects of desire and

of thought are the same. For the apparent good is the object of appetite, and the real good is the primary object of rational wish. But desire is consequent on opinion rather than opinion on desire; for the thinking is the starting-point. And thought is moved by the object of thought, and one of the two columns of opposites is in itself the object of thought; and in this, substance is first, and in substance, that which is simple and exists actually. (The one and the simple are not the same; for 'one' means a measure, but 'simple' means that the thing itself has a certain nature.) But the beautiful, also, and that which is in itself desirable are in the same column; and the first in any class is always best, or analogous to the best.

That a final cause may exist among unchangeable entities is shown by the distinction of its meanings. For the final cause is (*a*) some being for whose good an action is done, and (*b*) something at which the action aims; and of these the latter exists among unchangeable entities though the former does not. The final cause, then, produces motion as being loved, but all other things move by being moved.

Now if something is moved it is capable of being otherwise than as it is. Therefore if its actuality is the primary form of spatial motion, then in so far as it is subject to change, in *this* respect it is capable of being otherwise – in place, even if not in substance. But since there is something which moves while itself unmoved, existing actually, this can in no way be otherwise than as it is. For motion in space is the first of the kinds of change, and motion in a circle the first kind of spatial motion; and this the first mover *produces*.[2] The first mover, then, exists of necessity; and in so far as it exists by necessity, its mode of being is good, and it is in this sense a first principle. For the necessary has all these senses – that which is necessary perforce because it is contrary to the natural impulse, that without which the good is impossible, and that which cannot be otherwise but can exist only in a single way.

On such a principle, then, depend the heavens and the world of nature. And it is a life such as the best which we enjoy, and enjoy for but a short time (for it is ever in this state, which we cannot be), since its actuality is also pleasure. (And for this reason[3] are waking, perception, and thinking most pleasant, and hopes and memories are so on account of these.) And thinking in itself deals with that which is best in itself, and that which is thinking in the fullest sense with that which is best in the fullest sense. And thought thinks on itself because it shares the nature of the object of thought; for it becomes an object of thought in coming into contact with and thinking its objects, so that thought and object of thought are the same. For that which is *capable* of receiving the object of thought, i.e. the essence, is thought. But it is *active* when it *possesses* this object. Therefore the possession rather than the receptivity is the divine element which thought seems to contain, and the act of contemplation is what is most pleasant and best. If, then, God is always in that good state in which we sometimes are, this compels our wonder; and if in a better this compels it yet more. And God *is* in a better state. And life also belongs to God; for the actuality of thought is life, and God is that actuality; and God's self-dependent actuality is life most good and eternal. We say therefore that God is a living being, eternal, most good, so that life and duration continuous and eternal belong to God; for this *is* God.

Those who suppose, as the Pythagoreans[4] and Speusippus[5] do, that supreme beauty and goodness are not present in the beginning, because the beginnings both of plants and of animals are *causes*, but beauty and completeness are in the *effects* of these,[6] are wrong in their opinion. For the seed comes from other individuals which are prior and complete, and the first thing is not seed but the complete being; e.g. we must say that before the seed there is a man – not the man produced from the seed, but another from whom the seed comes.

It is clear then from what has been said that there is a substance which is eternal and unmovable and separate from sensible things. It has been shown also that this substance cannot have any magnitude, but is without parts and indivisible (for it produces movement through infinite time, but nothing finite has infinite power; and, while every magnitude is either infinite or finite, it cannot, for the above reason, have finite magnitude, and it cannot have infinite magnitude because there is no infinite magnitude at all). But it has also been shown that it is impassive and unalterable; for all the other changes are posterior to[7] change of place.

Notes

1 i.e. the outer sphere of the universe, that in which the fixed stars are set.
2 If it had any movement, it would have the first. But it produces this and therefore cannot share in it; for if it did, we should have to look for something that is prior to the first mover and imparts this motion to it.
3 *sc.* because they are activities or actualities.
4 Cf. 1075^a 36.
5 Cf. vii. 1028^b 21, xiv. 1091^a 34, 1092^a 11.
6 i.e. the animal or plant is more beautiful and perfect than the seed.
7 i.e. impossible without.

3

The Divine Darkness

Pseudo-Dionysius the Areopagite

In the late fifth or early sixth century an unknown Syrian author posing as Dionysius the Areopagite (a prominent first-century Athenian converted by St Paul) adapted the ideas of neoplatonism to a Christian context. Although the use of pseudonyms was common at the time, his writings were especially influential in part because many mistook them to be genuine works of the Pauline convert. As the following selections illustrate, his writings are filled with difficult and paradoxical statements because he believes God to be beyond human conceptions.

IX.2.1. The Transcendent Good (from *The Divine Names*, ch. 5)

4. . . .

But now let me speak about the Good, about that which truly is and which gives being to everything else. The God who is transcends everything by virtue of his power. He is the substantive Cause and maker of being, of subsistence, of existence, of substance, and of nature. He is the Source and the measure of the ages. He is the reality beneath time and the eternity behind being. He is the time within which things happen. He is being for whatever is. He is coming-to-be amid whatever happens. From him who is come eternity, essence and being, come time, genesis, and becoming. He is the being immanent in and underlying the things which are, however they are. For God is not some kind of being. No. But in a way that is simple and indefinable he gathers himself and anticipates every existence. So he is called "King of the ages,"[1] for in him and around him all being is and subsists. He was not. He will not be. He did not come to be. He is not in the midst of becoming. He will not come to be. No. He is not. Rather, he is the essence of being for the things which have being. Not only things that are but also the essence of what they are come from him who precedes the ages. For he is the age of ages, the "predecessor of the ages."[2]

[. . .]

IX.2.2. How God can be called Wisdom (*The Divine names*, ch. 7)

[. . .]

1. Now, if you will, let us give praise to the good and eternal Life for being wise, for being the principle of wisdom, the subsistence of all wisdom, for transcending all wisdom and all understanding. It is not simply the case that God is so overflowing with wisdom that "his understanding is beyond all measure"[3] but, rather, he actually transcends all reason, all intelligence, and all wisdom. This is something which was marvelously grasped by that truly divine man, my teacher[4] and yours[5] and the light of our common instructor. For this is what he said: "The foolishness of God is wiser than men."[6] Those words are true not only because all human thinking is a sort of error when compared with the solid permanence of the perfect divine thoughts but also because it is customary for theologians to apply negative terms to God, but contrary to the usual sense of a deprivation. Scripture, for example, calls the all-apparent light "invisible."[7] It says of the One who is present in all things and who may be discovered from all things that he is ungraspable and "inscrutable."[8] And here the divine apostle is said to be praising God for his "foolishness," which in itself seems absurd and strange, but uplifts [us] to the ineffable truth which is there before all reasoning. But, as I have often said elsewhere, we have a habit of seizing upon what is actually beyond us, clinging to the familiar categories of our sense perceptions, and then we measure the divine by our human standards and, of course, are led astray by the apparent meaning we give to divine and unspeakable reason. What we should really consider is this: The human mind has a capacity to think, through which it looks on conceptual things, and a unity which transcends the nature of the mind, through which it is joined to things beyond itself. And this transcending characteristic must be given to the words we use about God. They must not be given the human sense. We should be taken wholly out of ourselves and become wholly of God, since it is better to belong to God rather than to ourselves. Only when we are with God will the divine gifts be poured out onto us, therefore let us supremely praise this foolish "Wisdom," which has neither reason nor intelligence and let us describe it as the Cause of all intelligence and reason, of all wisdom and understanding. All counsel belongs to it, from it come all knowledge and understanding, and "in it are hid all the treasures of wisdom and knowledge."[9] From all that has been said above, it follows that the transcendently wise Cause is indeed the subsistence of absolute wisdom and of the sum total and individual manifestations of wisdom.

[. . .]

I have said already that the divine Wisdom is the source, the cause, the substance, the perfection, the protector, and the goal of Wisdom itself, of mind, of reason, and of all sense perception. How, then, is it that God who is more-than-wise, is praised as wisdom, mind, word, and a knower? If he does not have intellectual activities, how can he possess understanding of conceptual things? How does he have knowledge of sense data when he himself transcends the domain of sense, while scripture, on the other hand, proclaims that he knows everything[10] and that nothing escapes the divine knowledge? But, as I have often said previously, we must interpret the things of God in a way that befits God, and when we talk of God as being without mind and without perception, this is to be taken in the sense of what he has in superabundance and not as a defect. Hence we attribute absence of reason to him because he is above reason; we attribute lack of perfection to him because he is above and before perfection, and we posit intangible and invisible darkness of that Light which is unapproachable[11] because it so far exceeds the visible light. The divine Mind, therefore, takes in all things in a total knowledge which is transcendent. Because it is the Cause of all things it has a foreknowledge of everything. Before there are angels he has knowledge of angels and he brings them into being. He knows everything else and, if I may put it so, he knows them from the very beginning and therefore brings them into being. This, I think, is what scripture means with the declaration, "He knows all things before their birth."[12] The divine mind does not acquire the knowledge of things from things. Rather, of itself and in itself it precontains and comprehends the awareness and understanding and being of everything in terms of their cause. This is not a knowledge of each specific class. What is here is a single embracing causality which knows and contains all things. Take the example of light. In itself it has a prior and causal knowledge of darkness. What it knows about darkness it knows not from another, but from the fact of being light. So too the divine Wisdom knows all things by knowing itself. Uniquely it knows and produces all things by its oneness: material things immaterially, divisible things indivisibly, plurality in a single act. If with one causal gesture God bestows being on everything, in that one same act of causation he will know everything through derivation from him and through their preexistence in him, and, therefore, his knowledge of things will not be owed to the things themselves. He will be a leader, giving to each the knowledge it has of itself and of others. Consequently, God does not possess a private knowledge of himself and a separate knowledge of all the creatures in common. The universal Cause, by knowing itself, can hardly be ignorant of the things which proceed from it and of which it is the source. This, then, is how God knows all things, not by understanding things, but by understanding himself.

Scripture also says that the angels know the things of earth not because these latter may be perceived by the senses but because of the proper capacity and nature inherent in a God-like intelligence.

3. If God cannot be grasped by mind or sense-perception, if he is not a particular being, how do we know him? This is something we must inquire into.

It might be more accurate to say that we cannot know God in his nature, since this is unknowable and is beyond the reach of mind or of reason. But we know him from the arrangement of everything, because everything is, in a sense, projected out from him, and this order possesses certain images and semblances of his divine paradigms. We therefore approach that which is beyond all as far as our capacities allow us and we pass by way of the denial and the transcendence of all things and by way of the cause of all things. God is therefore known in all things and as distinct from all things. He is known through knowledge and through unknowing. Of him there is conception, reason, understanding, touch, perception, opinion, imagination, name, and many other things. On the other hand he cannot be understood, words cannot contain him, and no name can lay hold of him. He is not one of the things that are and he cannot be known in any of them. He is all things in all things and he is no thing among things. He is known to all from all things and he is known to no one from anything.

This is the sort of language we must use about God, for he is praised from all things according to their proportion to him as their Cause. But again, the most divine knowledge of God, that which comes through unknowing, is achieved in a union far beyond mind, when mind turns away from all things, even from itself, and when it is made one with the dazzling rays, being then and there enlightened by the inscrutable depth of Wisdom.

Still, as I have said already, we must learn about Wisdom from all things. As scripture says, Wisdom has made and continues always to adapt everything.[13] It is the cause of the unbreakable accommodation and order of all things and it is forever linking the goals of one set of things with the sources of another and in this fashion it makes a thing of beauty of the unity and the harmony of the whole.

4. God is praised as "Logos" [word] by the sacred scriptures not only as the leader of word, mind, and wisdom, but because he also initially carries within his own unity the causes of all things and because he penetrates all things, reaching, as scripture says, to the very end of all things.[14] But the title is used especially because the divine Logos is simpler than any simplicity and, in its utter transcendence, is independent of everything. This Word is simple total truth. Divine faith revolves around it because it is pure and unwavering knowledge of all. It is

the one sure foundation for those who believe, binding them to the truth, building the truth in them as something unshakably firm so that they have an uncomplicated knowledge of the truth of what they believe. If knowledge unites knower and known, while ignorance is always the cause of change and of the inconsistency of the ignorant, then, as scripture tells us,[15] nothing shall separate the one who believes in truth from the ground of true faith and it is there that he will come into the possession of enduring, unchanging identity. The man in union with truth knows clearly that all is well with him, even if everyone else thinks that he has gone out of his mind. What they fail to see, naturally, is that he has gone out of the path of error and has in his real faith arrived at truth. He knows that far from being mad,[16] as they imagine him to be, he has been rescued from the instability of error and that he has been set free by simple and immutable stable truth. That is why the principle leaders of our divine wisdom die each day for the truth. They bear witness in every word and deed to the single knowledge of the truth possessed by Christians. They prove that truth to be more simple and more divine than every other. Or, rather, what they show is that here is the only true, single, and simple knowledge of God.

[. . .]

IX.2.4. The Divine Darkness (from the *Letters of Dionysius*)

Letter One

To the monk Gaius

Darkness disappears in the light, the more so as there is more light. Knowledge makes unknowing disappear, the more so as there is more knowledge.

However, think of this not in terms of deprivation but rather in terms of transcendence and then you will be able to say something truer than all truth, namely, that the unknowing regarding God escapes anyone possessing physical light and knowledge of beings:

His transcendent darkness remains hidden from all light and concealed from all knowledge. Someone beholding God and understanding what he saw has not actually seen God himself but rather something of his which has being and which is knowable. For he himself solidly transcends mind and being. He is completely unknown and non-existent. He exists beyond being and he is known beyond the mind. And this quite positively complete unknowing is knowledge of him who is above everything that is known.

Letter Five

To Dorotheus, the deacon

The divine darkness is that "unapproachable light"[17] where God is said to live. And if it is invisible because of a superabundant clarity, if it cannot be approached because of the outpouring of its transcendent gift of light, yet it is here that is found everyone worthy to know God and to look upon him. And such a one, precisely because he neither sees him nor knows him, truly arrives at that which is beyond all seeing and all knowledge. Knowing exactly this, that he is beyond everything perceived and conceived, he cries out with the prophet, "Knowledge of you is too wonderful for me; it is high, I cannot attain it."[18]

It is in this sense that one says of the divine Paul that he knew God, for he knew that God is beyond every act of mind and every way of knowing. He says too that "inscrutable are his ways and unsearchable his judgments,"[19] that "his gifts are inexpressible,"[20] and that "his peace passes all understanding,"[21] for he found him who is beyond all things and he knew, in a way surpassing any conception, that the cause of all surpasses all.

Notes

1 *Timothy* 1:17.
2 *Psalm* 55:19.
3 *Psalm* 147:5.
4 The author here pretends to have been instructed by St Paul.
5 The whole treatise pretends to be addressed to the Timothy to whom St Paul wrote the letters found in Scripture.
6 1 *Corinthians* 1:25.
7 *Colossians* 1:15; 1 *Timothy* 1:17, 6:16; *Hebrews* 11:27.

8 *Romans* 11:33.
9 *Colossians* 2:3.
10 *John* 21:17.
11 1 *Timothy* 6:16.
12 *Daniel* 13:42 *(Susanna* 42).
13 *Psalm* 104:24; *Proverbs* 8:30.
14 *Hebrews* 4:12; *Wisdom* 7:24.
15 *Romans* 8:29, 11:20.
16 *Acts* 26:24.
17 *Timothy* 6:16.
18 *Psalm* 139:6.
19 *Romans* 11:33.
20 2 *Corinthians* 9:15.
21 *Philippians* 4:7.

4

Perfect Being

Anselm

The following selection from Anselm's *Proslogium* is the immediate sequel to his ontological argument (see section II.C.1). After arguing that the definition of God – "a being than which nothing greater can be conceived" – implies God's existence, Anselm goes on to argue that it also implies many divine attributes. Anselm reasons that God must possess whatever qualities it is greater to possess than not to possess; this approach to the divine nature is often referred to as Perfect Being Theology.

Chapter V

God is whatever it is better to be than not to be; and he, as the only self-existent being, creates all things from nothing.

What art thou, then, Lord God than whom nothing greater can be conceived? But what art thou, except that which, as the highest of all beings, alone exists through itself, and creates all other things from nothing? For, whatever is not this is less than a thing which can be conceived of. But this cannot be conceived of thee. What good, therefore, does the supreme Good lack, through which every good is? Therefore, thou art just, truthful, blessed, and whatever it is better to be than not to be. For it is better to be just than not just; better to be blessed than not blessed.

Chapter VI

*How God is sensible (*sensibilis*) although he is not a body. – God is sensible, omnipotent, compassionate, passionless; for it is better to be these than not be. He who in any way knows, is not improperly said in some sort to feel.*

St Anselm, Chapters V, VI, VII, VIII, XII, XIII, XVIII from *Proslogium; Monologium; An Appendix in Behalf of the Fool By Gaunilon; and Cur Deus Homo*, trans. Sidney Norton Deane (La Salle, IL: Open Court, 1951), pp. 10–14, 19–20, 23–5.

But, although it is better for thee to be sensible, omnipotent, compassionate, passionless, than not to be these things; how art thou sensible, if thou art not a body; or omnipotent, if thou hast not all powers; or at once compassionate and passionless? For, if only corporeal things are sensible, since the senses encompass a body and are in a body, how art thou sensible, although thou art not a body, but a supreme Spirit, who is superior to body? But, if feeling is only cognition, or for the sake of cognition, – for he who feels obtains knowledge in accordance with the proper functions of his senses; as through sight, of colors; through taste, of flavors, – whatever in any way cognises is not inappropriately said, in some sort, to feel.

Therefore, O Lord, although thou art not a body, yet thou art truly sensible in the highest degree in respect of this, that thou dost cognise all things in the highest degree; and not as an animal cognises, through a corporeal sense.

Chapter VII

How he is omnipotent, although there are many things of which he is not capable. – To be capable of being corrupted, or of lying, is not power, but impotence. God can do nothing by virtue of impotence, and nothing has power against him.

But how art thou omnipotent, if thou art not capable of all things? Or, if thou canst not be corrupted, and canst not lie, nor make what is true, false – as, for example, if thou shouldst make what has been done not to have been done, and the like – how art thou capable of all things? Or else to be capable of these things is not power, but impotence. For, he who is capable of these things is capable of what is not for his good, and of what he ought not to do; and the more capable of them he is, the more power have adversity and perversity against him; and the less has he himself against these.

He, then, who is thus capable is so not by power, but by impotence. For, he is not said to be able because he is able of himself, but because his impotence gives something else power over him. Or, by a figure of speech, just as many words are improperly applied, as when we use "to be" for "not to be," and "to do" for what is really "not to do," or "to do nothing." For, often we say to a man who denies the existence of something: "It is as you say it to be," though it might seem more proper to say, "It is not, as you say it is not." In the same way, we say: "This man sits just as that man does," or, "This man rests just as that man does"; although to sit is not to do anything, and to rest is to do nothing.

So, then, when one is said to have the power of doing or experiencing what is not for his good, or what he ought not to do, impotence is understood in the word power. For, the more he possesses this power, the more powerful are adversity and perversity against him, and the more powerless is he against them.

Therefore, O Lord, our God, the more truly art thou omnipotent, since thou art capable of nothing through impotence, and nothing has power against thee.

Chapter VIII

How he is compassionate and passionless. God is compassionate, in terms of our experience, because we experience the effect of Compassion. God is not compassionate, in terms of his own being, because he does not experience the feeling (affectus) *of compassion.*

But how art thou compassionate, and, at the same time, passionless? For, if thou art passionless, thou dost not feel sympathy; and if thou dost not feel sympathy, thy heart is not wretched from sympathy for the wretched; but this it is to be compassionate. But if thou art not compassionate, whence cometh so great consolation to the wretched? How, then, art thou compassionate and not compassionate, O Lord, unless because thou art compassionate in terms of our experience, and not compassionate in terms of thy being.

Truly, thou art so in terms of our experience, but thou art not so in terms of thine own. For, when thou beholdest us in our wretchedness, we experience the effect of compassion, but thou dost not experience the feeling. Therefore, thou art both compassionate, because thou dost save the wretched, and spare those who sin against thee; and not compassionate, because thou art affected by no sympathy for wretchedness.

[...]

Chapter XII

God is the very life whereby he lives; and so of other like attributes.

But undoubtedly, whatever thou art, thou art through nothing else than thyself. Therefore, thou art the very life whereby thou livest; and the wisdom wherewith thou art wise; and the very goodness whereby thou art good to the righteous and the wicked; and so of other like attributes.

Chapter XIII

How he alone is uncircumscribed and eternal, although other spirits are uncircumscribed and eternal. – No place and time contain God. But he is himself everywhere and always. He alone not only does not cease to be, but also does not begin to be.

But everything that is in any way bounded by place or time is less than that which no law of place or time limits. Since, then, nothing is greater than thou, no place or time contains thee; but thou art everywhere and always. And since this can be said of thee alone, thou alone art uncircumscribed and eternal. How is it, then, that other spirits also are said to be uncircumscribed and eternal?

Assuredly thou art alone eternal; for thou alone among all beings not only dost not cease to be, but also dost not begin to be.

But how art thou alone uncircumscribed? Is it that a created spirit, when compared with thee, is circumscribed, but when compared with matter, uncircumscribed? For altogether circumscribed is that which, when it is wholly in one place, cannot at the same time be in another. And this is seen to be true of corporeal things alone. But uncircumscribed is that which is, as a whole, at the same time everywhere. And this is understood to be true of thee alone. But circumscribed, and, at the same time, uncircumscribed is that which, when it is anywhere as a whole, can at the same time be somewhere else as a whole, and yet not everywhere. And this is recognised as true of created spirits. For, if the soul were not as a whole in the separate members of the body, it would not feel as a whole in the separate members.

Therefore, thou, Lord, art peculiarly uncircumscribed and eternal; and yet other spirits also are uncircumscribed and eternal.

[...]

Chapter XVIII

God is life, wisdom, eternity, and every true good. – Whatever is composed of parts is not wholly one; it is capable, either in fact or in concept, of dissolution. In God wisdom, eternity, etc., are not parts, but one, and the very whole which God is, or unity itself, not even in concept divisible.

And lo, again confusion; lo, again grief and mourning meet him who seeks for joy and gladness. My soul now hoped for satisfaction; and lo, again it is overwhelmed with need. I desired now to feast, and lo, I hunger more. I tried to rise to the light of God, and I have fallen back into my darkness. Nay, not only have I fallen into it, but I feel that I am enveloped in it. I fell before my mother conceived me. Truly, in darkness I was conceived, and in the cover of darkness I was born. Truly, in him we all fell, in whom we all sinned. In him we all lost, who kept easily, and wickedly lost to himself and to us that which when we wish to seek it, we do not know; when we seek it, we do not find; when we find, it is not that which we seek.

Do thou help me for thy goodness' sake! Lord, I sought thy face; thy face, Lord, will I seek; hide not thy face far from me (Psalms xxvii. 8). Free me from myself toward thee. Cleanse, heal, sharpen, enlighten the eye of my mind, that it may behold thee. Let my soul recover its strength, and with all its understanding let it strive toward thee, O Lord. What art thou, Lord, what art thou? What shall my heart conceive thee to be?

Assuredly thou art life, thou art wisdom, thou art truth, thou art goodness, thou art blessedness, thou art eternity, and thou art every true good. Many are these attributes: my straitened understanding cannot see so many at one view, that it may be gladdened by all at once. How, then, O Lord, art thou all these things? Are they parts of thee, or is each one of these rather the whole, which thou art? For, whatever is composed of parts is not altogether one, but is in some sort plural, and diverse from itself; and either in fact or in concept is capable of dissolution.

But these things are alien to thee, than whom nothing better can be conceived of. Hence, there are no parts in thee, Lord, nor art thou more than one. But thou art so truly a unitary being, and so identical with thyself, that in no respect art thou unlike thyself; rather thou art unity itself, indivisible by any conception. Therefore, life and wisdom and the rest are not parts of thee, but all are one; and each of these is the whole, which thou art, and which all the rest are.

In this way, then, it appears that thou hast no parts, and that thy eternity, which thou art, is nowhere and never a part of thee or of thy eternity. But everywhere thou art as a whole, and thy eternity exists as a whole forever.

5

On the Trinity

Richard of St Victor

Rather little is known about the life of Richard of St Victor. He was born in Scotland, although the year is unknown, and he spent much of his life at St Victor's Abbey in Paris where he was prior for the last eleven years of his life (d. 1173). Although many theologians have regarded the Christian doctrine of the Trinity as a mystery that could only be known or comprehended by means of revelation, in his work *On the Trinity* Richard offers a purely speculative argument for the doctrine. In short, he argues that God's perfect goodness requires supreme charity and that supreme charity cannot exist apart from a trinity of divine persons.

Up to now we have discussed as best we could the unity and proper attributes of the divine substance. In what follows however we propose to examine what we ought to think about the plurality of persons and their properties.

The first question it seems we should discuss is whether in that true and simple divinity there is a plurality of persons and whether they are three in number as we believe. . . .

We have learned from what was said earlier [in Book Two] that in the highest and universally perfect good there is the plenitude and perfection of all goodness. Where the fullness of goodness exists, however, true and supreme charity or love cannot be absent, for nothing is better or more perfect than charity. Now no one is said to have charity by virtue of the private love he has for himself, since to be charity, love must tend towards another; and where there are not several persons, charity simply cannot exist.

But perhaps you will say: Even if there were but a single person in that true divinity, he still

Richard of St Victor, selections from Book Three of *On the Trinity*, translated by Allan B. Wolter. From *Medieval Philosophy: From St. Augustine to Nicholas of Cusa*, edited by John F. Wippel and Allan B. Wolter (New York: The Free Press, 1969), pp. 223–5.

could, and indeed would have charity towards his creatures. But surely he could not have the supreme degree of charity for a person who was created. For if he loved supremely one unworthy of supreme love, his charity would be inordinate. But it is impossible that inordinate charity should exist in goodness that is also supremely wise. A divine person then could not have the highest charity towards a person unworthy of supreme love. For charity to be supreme and all-perfect then, it must be so great that it could not be greater and of such quality that it could not be better. But as long as one loves only himself, this private love he bears himself shows he has yet to reach the highest degree of charity. A divine person would have no one he could fittingly love as himself had he no deserving person as his peer. But no person who was not God would be a worthy peer of a divine person. In order to have the plenitude of charity in that true divinity, therefore, what any divine person must have is the companionship of a person who is his peer in dignity and who is therefore divine.

See how easily then reason proves a plurality of persons must be present in true divinity. Certainly God alone is supremely good; God alone then is to be loved supremely. A divine person consequently could not display the highest love towards a person who lacked divinity. But the fullness of divinity could not be present if complete goodness was missing; and complete goodness could not be present without the fullness of charity, nor the complete charity without a plurality of divine persons . . . .

It is clear that there is a plurality of divine persons, but it is not yet evident that they constitute a trinity. For there can be plurality without a trinity. Duality itself is a plurality. Let us ask the same witnesses about trinity that attested to the presence of a plurality. And, if you will, let us see first what sovereign charity has to say on the subject.

Sovereign charity must be perfect on all counts. To be supremely perfect, however, charity must be such that it can be neither greater nor better. No degree or kind of excellence could be missing. Now to wish that another be loved as we are loved seems to be the sort of thing that should be present in true charity. Where love is ardent and mutual, nothing is rarer, nothing more admirable than the desire that another be loved to the same degree as you by the one whom you love supremely and by whom you are supremely loved. The proof of consummate charity then is this desire to share the love shown to oneself. Surely one who loves supremely and desires to be loved supremely would be wont to find perfect joy in the fulfillment of that desire, in obtaining the love desired. Never to have the satisfaction of sharing such perfect joy, therefore, is proof that perfect charity is not present. To be unable to enjoy this companionship of love is a sign of weakness. But if it is great to be *able* to do so, it is still greater to do so *in fact*, and greatest of all if one *must* do so. The first is a great good, the second a greater good, the third the greatest good. Such excellence we owe to the Supreme Being; to the best we owe the best.

Our earlier discussion revealed the presence of two persons united in mutual love. The perfection of each, however, if it is to be consummate, requires that each for the same reason have someone to share the love shown to himself. For if either did not want what perfect goodness requires, where would the plenitude of power be? Hence reason clearly reveals that where some defect of power or will precludes such sharing in love, such participation of perfect joy, there the supreme degree of charity and plenitude of goodness cannot exist. Each of these persons who is and should be supremely loved must needs require by common desire a third person to be loved and must needs possess such a one in perfect harmony as they desire.

See then how the consummation of charity demands a trinity of persons without which it could not subsist whole and entire! Where something universally perfect is present in its entirety, neither integral charity nor true trinity can be absent. Hence there is not only plurality but also true trinity in true unity, and true unity in true trinity. . . .

Note indeed in these divine persons that the perfection of one demands it be joined to another and consequently the perfection of the pair requires their union with a third. For, as we said above, if each of the pair deserves the supreme love of the other, each must be supremely perfect. As the pair must be one in wisdom and power, so too in supreme generosity. But the hallmark of the highest and most perfect generosity is that it share with another the full measure of its richness. But if each of the two has the same generosity, they must share the same desire for the same reasons; both require a third partner to share their supreme joy. For where a loving pair are seized by supreme desire and each delighted by the supreme love of the other, then the supreme joy of the one comes from his intimate love of the other, and conversely, the supreme joy of the second stems from his intimate love of the first. But so long as one is loved only by the other, he seems to be the sole possessor of his supremely sweet delight; similarly with the other, so long as he has no partner in the love shown him, he misses sharing this supreme joy. But that both can share their own delight, they need another loved one. Where such colovers are so generous, then, that they want to share whatever perfection they possess, both, by common desire and for equal reasons, need to have another who is loved even as they and, by virtue of the plenitude of their power, to possess what they desire.

6

Omnipotence

Peter Geach

Peter Geach (b. 1916) taught for many years at the University of Leeds. He is one of the preeminent Catholic philosophers of the twentieth century and in 1999 he was awarded the order of *Pro Ecclesia et Pontifice* by the Holy See. In this essay Geach distinguishes between God's being *almighty* (having power over all things) and God's being *omnipotent* (being able to do anything). He argues that almightiness is essential to the traditional Christian view of God, but that omnipotence is not. Moreover, Geach examines four specific theories of omnipotence and argues that they all lead to logical tangles and must be rejected.

It is fortunate for my purposes that English has the two words 'almighty' and 'omnipotent', and that apart from any stipulation by me the words have rather different associations and suggestions. 'Almighty' is the familiar word that comes in the creeds of the Church; 'omnipotent' is at home rather in formal theological discussions and controversies, e.g. about miracles and about the problem of evil. 'Almighty' derives by way of Latin 'omnipotens' from the Greek word '*pantokratōr*'; and both this Greek word, like the more classical '*pankratēs*', and 'almighty' itself suggest God's having power *over* all things. On the other hand the English word 'omnipotent' would ordinarily be taken to imply ability to *do* everything; the Latin word 'omnipotens' also predominantly has this meaning in Scholastic writers, even though in origin it is a Latinization of '*pantokratōr*'. So there already is a tendency to distinguish the two words; and in this paper I shall make the distinction a strict one. I shall use the word 'almighty' to express God's power over all things, and I shall take 'omnipotence' to mean ability to do everything.

I think we can in a measure understand what God's almightiness implies, and I shall argue that almightiness so understood must be ascribed to God if we are to retain anything

P. T. Geach, "Omnipotence". *Philosophy* 48:183 (1973): 7–20.

like traditional Christian belief in God. The position as regards omnipotence, or as regards the statement 'God can do everything', seems to me to be very different. Of course even 'God can do everything' may be understood simply as a way of magnifying God by contrast with the impotence of man. McTaggart described it as 'a piece of theological etiquette' to call God omnipotent: Thomas Hobbes, out of reverence for his Maker, would rather say that 'omnipotent' is an attribute of honour. But McTaggart and Hobbes would agree that 'God is omnipotent' or 'God can do everything' is not to be treated as a proposition that can figure as premise or conclusion in a serious theological argument. And I too wish to say this. I have no objection to such ways of speaking if they merely express a desire to give the best honour we can to God our Maker, whose Name only is excellent and whose praise is above heaven and earth. But theologians have tried *to prove* that God can do everything, or to derive conclusions from this thesis as a premise. I think such attempts have been wholly unsuccessful. When people have tried to read into 'God can do everything' a signification not of Pious Intention but of Philosophical Truth, they have only landed themselves in intractable problems and hopeless confusions; no graspable sense has ever been given to this sentence that did not lead to self-contradiction or at least to conclusions manifestly untenable from a Christian point of view.

I shall return to this; but I must first develop what I have to say about God's almightiness, or power over all things. God is not just more powerful than any creature; no creature can compete with God in power, even unsuccessfully. For God is also the source of all power; any power a creature has comes from God and is maintained only for such time as God wills. Nebuchadnezzar submitted to praise and adore the God of heaven because he was forced by experience to realize that only by God's favour did his wits hold together from one end of a blasphemous sentence to the other end. Nobody can deceive God or circumvent him or frustrate him; and there is no question of God's trying to do anything and failing. In Heaven and on Earth, God does whatever he will. We shall see that some propositions of the form 'God cannot do so-and-so' have to be accepted as true; but what God cannot be said to be able to do he likewise cannot will to do; we cannot drive a logical wedge between his power and his will, which are, as the Scholastics said, really identical, and there is no application to God of the concept of trying but failing.

I shall not spend time on citations of Scripture and tradition to show that this doctrine of God's almightiness is authentically Christian; nor shall I here develop rational grounds for believing it is a true doctrine. But it is quite easy to show that this doctrine is indispensable for Christianity, not a bit of old metaphysical luggage that can be abandoned with relief. For Christianity requires an absolute faith in the promises of God: specifically, faith in the promise that some day the whole human race will be delivered and blessed by the establishment of the Kingdom of God. If God were not almighty, he might will and not do; sincerely promise, but find fulfilment beyond his power. Men might prove untamable and incorrigible, and might kill themselves through war or pollution before God's salvific plan for them could come into force. It is useless to say that after the end of this earthly life men would live again; for as I have argued elsewhere, only the promise of God can give us any confidence that there will be an after-life for men, and if God were not almighty, this promise too might fail. If God is true and just and unchangeable and almighty, we can have absolute confidence in his promises: otherwise we cannot – and there would be an end of Christianity.

A Christian must therefore believe that God is almighty; but he need not believe that God can do everything. Indeed, the very argument I have just used shows that a Christian must not believe that God can do everything: for he may not believe that God could possibly break his own word. Nor can a Christian even believe that God can do everything that is logically possible; for breaking one's word is certainly a logically possible feat.

It seems to me, therefore, that the tangles in which people have enmeshed themselves when trying to give the expression 'God can do everything' an intelligible and acceptable content are tangles that a Christian believer has no need to enmesh himself in; the spectacle of others enmeshed may sadden him, but need not cause him to stumble in the way of faith. The denial that

God is omnipotent, or able to do everything, may seem dishonouring to God; but when we see where the contrary affirmation, in its various forms, has led, we may well cry out with Hobbes: 'Can any man think God is served with such absurdities?. . . As if it were an acknowledgment of the Divine Power, to say, that which is, is not; or that which has been, has not been.'

I shall consider four main theories of omnipotence. The first holds that God can do everything absolutely; everything that can be expressed in a string of words that makes sense; even if that sense can be shown to be self-contradictory, God is not bound in action, as we are in thought, by the laws of logic. I shall speak of this as the doctrine that God is *absolutely* omnipotent.

The second doctrine is that a proposition 'God can do so-and-so' is true when and only when 'so-and-so' represents a logically consistent description.

The third doctrine is that 'God *can* do so-and-so' is true just if 'God does so-and-so' is logically consistent. This is a weaker doctrine than the second; for 'God is doing so-and-so' is logically consistent only when 'so-and-so' represents a logically consistent description, but on the other hand there may be consistently describable feats which it would involve contradiction to suppose done *by God.*

The last and weakest view is that the realm of what can be done or brought about includes all future possibilities, and that whenever 'God *will* bring so-and-so about' is logically possible, 'God *can* bring so-and-so about' is true.

The first sense of 'omnipotent' in which people have believed God to be omnipotent implies precisely: ability to do absolutely everything, everything describable. You mention it, and God can do it. McTaggart insisted on using 'omnipotent' in this sense only; from an historical point of view we may of course say that he imposed on the word a sense which it, and the corresponding Latin word, have not always borne. But Broad seems to me clearly unjust to McTaggart when he implies that in demolishing this doctrine of omnipotence McTaggart was just knocking down a man of straw. As Broad must surely have known, at least one great philosopher, Descartes, deliberately adopted and defended this doctrine of omnipotence: what I shall call the doctrine of absolute omnipotence.

As Descartes himself remarked, nothing is too absurd for some philosopher to have said it some time; I once read an article about an Indian school of philosophers who were alleged to maintain that it is only a delusion, which the wise can overcome, that anything exists at all – so perhaps it would not matter all that much that a philosopher is found to defend absolute omnipotence. Perhaps it would not matter all that much that the philosopher in question was a very great one; for very great philosophers have maintained the most preposterous theses. What does make the denial of absolute omnipotence important is not that we are thereby denying what a philosopher, a very great philosopher, thought he must assert, but that this doctrine has a live influence on people's religious thought – I should of course say, a pernicious influence. Some naive Christians would explicitly assert the doctrine; and moreover, I think McTaggart was right in believing that in popular religious thought a covert appeal to the doctrine is sometimes made even by people who would deny it if it were explicitly stated to them and its manifest consequences pointed out.

McTaggart may well have come into contact with naive Protestant defenders of absolute omnipotence when he was defending his atheist faith at his public school. The opinion is certainly not dead, as I can testify from personal experience. For many years I used to teach the philosophy of Descartes in a special course for undergraduates reading French; year by year, there were always two or three of them who embraced Descartes' defence of absolute omnipotence *con amore* and protested indignantly when I described the doctrine as incoherent. It would of course have been no good to say I was following Doctors of the Church in rejecting the doctrine; I did in the end find a way of producing silence, though not, I fear, conviction, and going on to other topics of discussion; I cited the passages of the Epistle to the Hebrews which say explicitly that God cannot swear by anything greater than himself (vi. 13) or break his word (vi. 18). Fortunately none of them ever thought of resorting to the ultimate weapon which, as I believe George Mavrodes remarked, is available to the defender of absolute omnipotence; namely, he can always say: 'Well, you've stated a difficulty, but of course being omnipotent God can overcome that difficulty, though I don't see how.' But what I may call, borrowing from C. S. Lewis's story, victory by the Deplorable Word is a barren one; as barren as a victory by an incessant demand that your adversary should prove his premises or define his terms.

Let us leave these naive defenders in their entrenched position and return for a moment to Descartes. Descartes held that the truths of logic and arithmetic are freely made to be true by God's will. To be sure we clearly and distinctly see that these truths are necessary; they are necessary in our world, and in giving us our mental endowments God gave us the right sort of clear and distinct ideas to see the necessity. But though they are necessary, they are not necessarily necessary; God could have freely chosen to make a different sort of world, in which other things would have been necessary truths. The possibility of such another world is something we cannot *comprehend*, but only dimly *apprehend*; Descartes uses the simile that we may girdle a tree-trunk with our arms but not a mountain – but we can *touch* the mountain. Proper understanding of the possibility would be possessed by God, or, no doubt, by creatures in the alternative world, who would be endowed by God with clear and distinct ideas corresponding to the necessities of their world.

In recent years, unsound philosophies have been defended by what I may call shyster logicians: some of the more dubious recent developments of modal logic could certainly be used to defend Descartes. A system in which 'possibly p' were a theorem – in which everything is possible – has indeed never been taken seriously; but modal logicians have taken seriously systems in which 'possibly possibly p', or again 'it is not necessary that necessarily p', would be a theorem for arbitrary interpretation of 'p'. What is more, some modern modal logicians notoriously take possible worlds very seriously indeed; some of them even go to the length of saying that what you and I vulgarly call the actual world is simply the world we happen to live in. People who take *both* things seriously – the axiom 'possibly possibly p' and the ontology of possible worlds – would say: You mention any impossibility, and there's a possible world in which that isn't impossible but possible. And this is even further away out than Descartes would wish to go; for he would certainly not wish to say that 'It is possible that God should not exist' is even *possibly* true. So *a fortiori* a shyster logician could fadge up a case for Descartes. But to my mind all that this shows is that modal logic is currently a rather disreputable discipline: not that I think modal notions are inadmissible – on the contrary, I think they are indispensable – but that current professional standards in the discipline are low, and technical ingenuity is mistaken for rigour. On that showing, astrology would be rigorous.

Descartes' motive for believing in absolute omnipotence was not contemptible: it seemed to him that otherwise God would be *subject to* the inexorable laws of logic as Jove was to the decrees of the Fates. The nature of logical truth is a very difficult problem, which I cannot discuss here. The easy conventionalist line, that it is our arbitrary way of using words that makes logical truth, seems to me untenable, for reasons that Quine among others has clearly spelled out. If I could follow Quine further in regarding logical laws as natural laws of very great generality – revisable in principle, though most unlikely to be revised, in a major theoretical reconstruction – then perhaps after all some rehabilitation of Descartes on this topic might be possible. But in the end I have to say that as we cannot say how a non-logical world would look, we cannot say how a supra-logical God would act or how he could communicate anything to us by way of revelation. So I end as I began: a Christian need not and cannot believe in absolute omnipotence.

It is important that Christians should clearly realize this, because otherwise a half-belief in absolute omnipotence may work in their minds subterraneously. As I said, I think McTaggart was absolutely right in drawing attention to this danger. One and the same man may deny the doctrine of absolute omnipotence when the doctrine is clearly put to him, and yet reassure himself that God can certainly do so-and-so by using *merely* the premise of God's omnipotence. And McTaggart is saying this is indefensible. At the very least this 'so-and-so' must represent a logically consistent description of a feat; and proofs of logical consistency are notoriously not always easy. Nor, as we shall see, are our troubles at an end if we assume that God *can* do anything whose description is logically consistent.

Logical consistency in the description of the feat is certainly a *necessary* condition for the truth of 'God can do so-and-so': if 'so-and-so' represents an inconsistent description of a feat, then 'God can do so-and-so' is certainly a false and impossible proposition, since it entails 'It could be the case that so-and-so came about'; so, by contraposition, if 'God can do so-and-so' is to be true, or even logically possible, then 'so-and-so' must represent a logically consistent description of a feat. And whereas only a minority of Christians have explicitly believed in absolute omnipotence, many have believed that a proposition of the form 'God can do so-and-so' is true whenever 'so-and-so' represents a description of a logically possible feat. This is our second doctrine of omnipotence. One classic statement of this comes in the *Summa Theologica* Ia q. xxv art. 3. Aquinas rightly says that we cannot explain 'God can do everything' in terms of what is within the power of some agent; for 'God can do everything any created agent can do', though true, is not a comprehensive enough account of God's power, which exceeds that of any created agent; and 'God can do everything God can do' runs uselessly in a circle. So he puts forward the view that if the description 'so-and-so' is in itself possible through the relation of the terms involved – if it does not involve contradictories' being true together – then 'God can do so-and-so' is true. Many Christian writers have followed Aquinas in saying this; but it is not a position consistently maintainable. As we shall see, Aquinas did not manage to stick to the position himself.

Before I raise the difficulties against this thesis, I wish to expose a common confusion that often leads people to accept it: the confusion between self-contradiction and gibberish. C. S. Lewis in *The Problem of Pain* says that meaningless combinations of words do not suddenly acquire meaning simply because we prefix to them the two other words 'God can', and Antony Flew has quoted this with just approval. But if we take Lewis's words strictly, his point is utterly trivial, and nothing to our purpose. For gibberish, syntactically incoherent combination of words, is quite different from self-contradictory sentences or descriptions; the latter certainly have an intelligible place in our language.

It is a common move in logic to argue that a set of premises A, B, C together yield a contradiction, and that therefore A and B as premises yield as conclusion the contradictory of C; some logicians have puritanical objections to this manoeuvre, but I cannot stop to consider them; I am confident, too, that neither Aquinas nor Lewis would share these objections to *reductio ad absurdum*. If, however, a contradictory formula were gibberish, *reductio ad absurdum* certainly would be an illegitimate procedure – indeed it would be a nonsensical one. So we have to say that when 'so-and-so' represents a self-contradictory description of a feat, 'God can do so-and-so' is likewise self-contradictory, but that being self-contradictory it is *not* gibberish, but merely false.

I am afraid the view of omnipotence presently under consideration owes part of its attractiveness to the idea that then 'God can do so-and-so' would never turn out *false*, so that there would be no genuine counterexamples to 'God can do everything'. Aquinas says, in the passage I just now cited: 'What implies contradiction cannot be a word, for no understanding can conceive it.' Aquinas, writing seven centuries ago, is excusable for not being clear about the difference between self-contradiction and gibberish; we are not excusable if we are not. It is not gibberish to say 'a God can bring it about that in Alcalá there lives a barber who shaves all those and only those living in Alcalá who do not shave themselves'; this is a perfectly well-formed sentence, and not on the face of it self-contradictory; all the same, the supposed feat notoriously is self-contradictory, so this statement of what God can do is not nonsense but false.

One instance of a description of a feat that is really but not overtly self-contradictory has some slight importance in the history of conceptions of omnipotence. It appeared obvious to Spinoza that *God can bring about everything that God can bring about*, and that to deny this would be flatly incompatible with God's omnipotence (*Ethics* I.17, scholium). Well, the italicized sentence is syntactically ambiguous. 'Everything that God can bring about God can bring about' is one possible reading of the sentence, and this is an obvious, indeed trivial predication about God, which must be true if there is a God at all. But the other way of taking the sentence relates to a supposed feat of *bringing about everything that God can bring about* – *all* of these bringable-about things *together* – and it says that God is capable of *this* feat. This is clearly the way Spinoza wishes us to take the sentence. But taken this way, it is not obvious at all; quite the contrary, it's obviously false. For among the things that are severally possible for God to bring about, there are going to be some pairs that are not *com*possible, pairs which it is logically impossible should both come about; and then it is beyond God's power to bring about such a pair together – let alone, to bring about all the things together which he can bring about severally.

This does not give us a description of a *logically possible* feat which God cannot accomplish. However, there is nothing easier than to mention feats which are logically possible but which God cannot do, if Christianity is true. Lying and promise-breaking are logically possible feats: but Christian faith, as I have said, collapses unless we are assured that God cannot lie and cannot break his promises.

This argument is an *ad hominem* argument addressed to Christians; but there are well-known logical arguments to show that on any view there must be some logically possible feats that are beyond God's power. One good example suffices: making a thing which its maker cannot afterwards destroy. This is certainly a possible feat, a feat that some human beings have performed. Can God perform the feat or not? If he cannot there is already some logically possible feat which God cannot perform. If God can perform the feat, then let us suppose that he does: *ponatur in esse*, as medieval logicians say. Then we are supposing God to have brought about a situation in which he *has* made something he cannot destroy; and in that situation destroying this thing is a *logically* possible feat that God cannot accomplish, for we surely cannot admit the idea of a creature whose destruction is logically *im*possible.

There have been various attempts to meet this argument. The most interesting one is that the proposition 'God cannot make a thing that he cannot destroy' can be turned round to 'Any thing that God can make he can destroy' – which does not even look like an objection to God's being able to do everything logically possible. But this reply involves the very same bracketing fallacy that I exposed a moment ago in Spinoza. There, you will remember, we had to distinguish two ways of taking 'God can bring about everything that God can bring about':

A. Everything that God can bring about, God can bring about.
B. God can bring about the following feat: to bring about everything that God can bring about.

And we saw that A is trivially true, given that there *is* a God, and B certainly false. Here, similarly, we have to distinguish two senses of 'God cannot make a thing that its maker cannot destroy':

A. Anything that its maker cannot destroy, God cannot make.
B. God cannot bring about the following feat: to make something that its maker cannot destroy.

And here A does contrapose, as the objectors would have it, to 'Anything that God can make, its maker can destroy', which on the face of it says nothing against God's power to do anything logically possible. But just as in the Spinoza example, the B reading purports to describe a single feat, *bringing about everything that God can bring about* (this feat, I argued, is impossible for God, because logically impossible): so in our present case, the B reading purports to describe a single feat, *making something that its maker cannot destroy*. This, as I said, is a logically possible feat, a feat that men sometimes do perform; so we may press the question whether this is a feat God can accomplish or not; and either way there will be some *logically possible* feat God cannot accomplish. So this notion of omnipotence, like the Cartesian idea of absolute omnipotence, turns out to be obviously incompatible with Christian faith, and moreover logically untenable.

Let us see, then, if we fare any better with the third theory: the theory that the only condition for the truth of 'God can do so-and-so' is that 'God does so-and-so' or 'God is doing so-and-so' must be logically possible. As I said, this imposes a more restrictive condition than the second theory: for there are many feats that we can consistently suppose to be performed but cannot consistently suppose to be performed by God. This theory might thus get us out of the logical trouble that arose with the second theory about the feat: *making a thing that its maker cannot destroy*. For though this is a logically possible feat, a feat some creatures do perform, it might well be argued that '*God* has made a thing that its maker cannot destroy' is a proposition with a buried inconsistency in it; and if so, then on the present account of omnipotence we need not say 'God *can* make a thing that its maker cannot destroy'.

This suggestion also, however, can easily be refuted by an example of great philosophical importance that I borrow from Aquinas. 'It comes about that Miss X never loses her virginity' is plainly a logically possible proposition: and so also is 'God brings it about that Miss X never loses her virginity'. All the same, if it so happens that Miss X already has lost her virginity, 'God *can* bring it about that Miss X never loses her virginity' is false (Ia q. xxv art. 4 ad 3 um). Before Miss X had lost her virginity, it would have been true to say this very thing; so what we can truly say about what God can do will be different at different times. This appears to imply a change in God, but Aquinas would certainly say, and I think rightly, that it doesn't really do so. It is just like the case of Socrates coming to be shorter than Theaetetus because Theaetetus grows up; here, the change is on the side of Theaetetus not of Socrates. So in our case, the change is really in Miss X not in God; something about her passes from the realm of possibility to the realm of *fait accompli*, and thus *no longer* comes under the concept of the accomplishable – *deficit a rations possibilium* (Aquinas, *loc. cit.*, ad 2 um). I think Aquinas's position here is strongly defensible; but if he does defend it, he has abandoned the position that God can do everything that it is not *a priori* impossible *for God to do*, let alone the position that God can bring about everything describable in a logically consistent way.

Is it *a priori* impossible for God to do something wicked? And if not, *could* God do something wicked? There have been expressed serious doubts about this: I came across them in that favourite of modern moral philosophers, Richard Price. We must distinguish, he argues, between God's natural and his moral attributes: if God is a free moral being, even as we are, it must not be absolutely impossible for God to do something wicked. There must be just a chance that God should do something wicked: no doubt it will be a really infinitesimal chance – after all, God has persevered in ways of virtue on a vast scale for inconceivably long – but the chance must be there, or God isn't free and isn't therefore laudable for his goodness. The way this reverend gentleman commends his Maker's morals is so startling that you may suspect me of misrepresentation; I can only ask any sceptic to check in Daiches Raphael's edition of Price's work! Further comment on my part is I hope needless.

A much more restrained version of the same sort of thing is to be found in the Scholastic distinction between God's *potentia absoluta* and *potentia ordinata*. The former is God's power considered in abstraction from his wisdom and goodness, the latter is God's power considered as controlled in its exercise by his wisdom and goodness. Well, as regards a man it makes good sense to say: 'He has the bodily and mental power to do so-and-so, but he certainly will not, it would be pointlessly silly and wicked.' But does anything remotely like this make sense to say about Almighty God? If not, the Scholastic distinction I have cited is wholly frivolous.

Let us then consider our fourth try. Could it be said that the 'everything' in 'God can do everything' refers precisely to things that are not in the realm of *fait accompli* but of futurity? This will not do either. If God can promulgate promises to men, then as regards any promises that are not yet fulfilled we know that they certainly will be fulfilled: and in that case God clearly has not *a potentia ad utrumque* – a two-way power of either actualizing the event that will fulfil the promise or not actualizing it. God can then only do what will fulfil his promise. And if we try to evade this by denying that God can make promises known to men, then we have once more denied something essential to Christian faith, and we are still left with something that God cannot do.

I must here remove the appearance of a fallacy. God cannot but fulfil his promises, I argued; so he has not a two-way power, *potentia ad utrumque*, as regards these particular future events. This argument may have seemed to involve the fallacy made notorious in medieval logical treatises, of confusing the necessity by which something follows – *necessitas consequentiae* – with the necessity of that very thing which follows – *necessitas consequentis*. If it is impossible for God to promise and not perform, then if we know God has promised something we may infer with certainty that he will perform it. Surely, it may be urged, this is enough for Christian faith and hope; we need not go on to say that God *cannot not* bring about the future event in question. If we do that, are we not precisely committing the hoary modal fallacy I have just described?

I answer that there are various senses of 'necessary'. The future occurrence of such-and-such, when God has promised that such-and-such shall be, is of course not logically necessary; but it may be necessary in the sense of being, as Arthur Prior puts it, now unpreventable. If God *has* promised that Israel shall be saved, then there is nothing that anybody, even God, can do about that; this past state of affairs is now unpreventable. But it is also necessary in the same way that if God has promised then he will perform; God cannot do anything about that either – cannot make himself liable to break his word. So we have as premises 'Necessarily p' and 'Necessarily if p then q' in the same sense of 'necessarily'; and from these premises it not merely necessarily follows that q – the conclusion in the necessitated form, 'Necessarily q' with the same sense of 'necessarily', follows from the premises. So if God has promised that Israel shall be saved, the future salvation of Israel is not only certain but inevitable; God must save Israel, because he cannot not save Israel without breaking his word given in the past and he can neither alter the past nor break his word.

Again, in regard to this and other arguments, some people may have felt discomfort at my not drawing in relation to God the sort of distinction between various applications of 'can' that are made in human affairs: the 'can' of knowing how to, the 'can' of physical power to, the 'can' of opportunity, the 'can' of what fits in with one's plans. But of course the way we make these distinct applications of 'he can' to a human agent will not be open if we are talking about God. There is no question of God's knowing how but lacking the strength, or being physically able to but not knowing how; moreover (to make a distinction that comes in a logical example of Aristotle's) though there is a right time when God may bring something about, it is inept to speak of his then having the opportunity to do it. (To develop this distinction: if 'x' stands for a finite agent and 'so-and-so' for an act directly in x's power, there is little difference between 'At time t it is suitable for x to bring so-and-so about' and 'It is suitable for x to bring so-and-so about at time t'; but if 'x' means God, the temporal qualification 'at time t' can attach only to what is brought about; God does not live through successive times and find one more suitable than another.)

These distinct applications of 'can' are distinct only for finite and changeable agents, not for a God whose action is universal and whose mind and character and design are unchangeable. There is thus no ground for fear that in talking about God we may illicitly slip from one sort of 'can' to another. What we say God can do is always in respect of his changeless supreme power.

All the same, we have to assert different propositions at different times in order to say truly what God can do. What is past, as I said, ceases to be alterable even by God; and thus the truth-value of a proposition like 'God can bring it about that Miss X never loses her virginity' alters once she has lost it. Similarly, God's promise makes a difference to what we can thereafter truly say God can do; it is less obvious in this case that the real change involved is a change in creatures, not in God, than it was as regards Miss X's virginity, but a little thought should show that the promulgation or making known of God's intention, which is involved in a promise, is precisely a change in the creatures to whom the promise is made.

Thus all the four theories of omnipotence that I have considered break down. Only the first overtly flouts logic; but the other three all involve logical contradictions, or so it seems; and moreover, all these theories have consequences fatal to the truth of Christian faith. The last point really ought not to surprise us; for the absolute confidence a Christian must have in God's revelation and promises involves, as I said at the outset, both a belief that God is almighty, in the sense I explained, and a belief that there are certain describable things that God cannot do and therefore will not do.

If I were to end the discussion at this point, I should leave an impression of Aquinas's thought that would be seriously unfair to him; for although in the passage I cited Aquinas appears verbally committed to our second theory of omnipotence, it seems clear that this does not adequately represent his mind. Indeed, it was from Aquinas himself and from the *Summa Theologica* that I borrowed an example which refutes even the weaker third theory, let alone the second one. Moreover, in the other Summa (Book II, c. xxv) there is an instructive list of things that *Deus omnipotens* is rightly said not to be able to do. But the mere occurrence of this list makes me doubt whether Aquinas can be said to believe, in any reasonable interpretation, the thesis that God can do everything. That God is almighty in my sense Aquinas obviously did believe; I am suggesting that here his 'omnipotens' means 'almighty' rather than 'omnipotent'. Aquinas does not say or even imply that he has given an *exhaustive* list of kinds of case in which 'God can do so-and-so' or 'God can make so-and-so' turns out false; so what he says here does not commit him to 'God can do everything' even in the highly unnatural sense 'God can do everything that is not excluded under one or other of the following heads'.

I shall not explore Aquinas's list item by item, because I have made open or tacit use of his considerations at several points in the foregoing and do not wish to repeat myself. But one batch of items raises a specially serious problem. My attention was drawn to the problem by a contribution that the late Mr Michael Foster made orally during a discussion at the Socratic Club in Oxford. Aquinas tells us that if 'doing so-and-so' implies what he calls passive potentiality, then 'God can do so-and-so' is false. On this ground he excluded all of the following:

> God can be a body or something of the sort.
> God can be tired or oblivious.
> God can be angry or sorrowful.
> God can suffer violence or be overcome.
> God can undergo corruption.

Foster pointed out that as a Christian Aquinas was committed to asserting the contradictory of all these theses. *Contra factum non valet ratio*; it's no good arguing that God cannot do what God has done, and in the Incarnation God did do all these things Aquinas said God cannot do. The Word that was God *was* made flesh (and the literal meaning of the Polish for this is: The Word became a body!); God the Son *was* tired and did sink into the oblivion of sleep; he *was* angry and sorrowful; he was bound like a thief, beaten, and crucified; and though we believe his Body did not decay, it suffered corruption in the sense of becoming a corpse instead of a living body – Christ in the Apocalypse uses of himself the startling words 'I became a corpse', '*egenomēn nekros*', and the Church has always held that the dead Body of Christ during the *triduum mortis* was adorable with Divine worship for its union to the Divine Nature.

Foster's objection to Aquinas is the opposite kind of objection to the ones I have been raising against the various theories of omnipotence I have discussed. I have been saying that these theories say by implication that God *can* do certain things which Christian belief requires one to say God *cannot* do; Foster is objecting that Aquinas's account says God *cannot* do some things which according to Christian faith God *can* do and has in fact done.

It would take me too far to consider how Aquinas might have answered this objection. It would not of course be outside his intellectual milieu; it is the very sort of objection that a Jew or Moor might have used, accepting Aquinas's account of what God cannot do, in order to argue against the Incarnation. I shall simply mention one feature that Aquinas's reply would have had: it would have to make essential use of the particle 'as', or in Latin '*secundum quod*'. God did become man, so God can become man and have a human body; but God *as* God cannot be man or have a body.

The logic of these propositions with 'as' in them, reduplicative propositions as they are traditionally called, is a still unsolved problem, although as a matter of history it was a problem raised by Aristotle in the *Prior Analytics*. We must not forget that such propositions occur frequently in ordinary discourse; we use them there with an ill-founded confidence that we know our way around. Jones, we say, is Director of the Gnome Works and Mayor of Middletown; he gets a salary *as* Director and an expense allowance *as* Mayor; he signs one letter *as* Director, another *as* Mayor. We say all this, but how far do we understand the logical relations of what we say? Very little, I fear. One might have expected some light and leading from medieval logicians; the theological importance of reduplicative propositions did in fact lead to their figuring as a topic in medieval logical treatises. But I have not found much that is helpful in such treatments as I have read.

I hope to return to this topic later. Meanwhile, even though it has nothing directly to do with almightiness or omnipotence, I shall mention one important logical point that is already to be found in Aristotle. A superficial grammatical illusion may make us think that 'A as P is Q' attaches the predicate 'Q' to a complex subject 'A as P'. But Aristotle insists, to my mind rightly, on the analysis: 'A' subject, 'is, as P, Q' predicate – so that we have not a complex subject-term, but a complex predicate-term; clearly, this predicate entails the simple conjunctive predicate 'is both P and Q' but not conversely. This niggling point of logic has in fact some theological importance. When theologians are talking about Christ as God and Christ as Man, they may take the two phrases to be two logical subjects of predication, if they have failed to see the Aristotelian point; and then they are likely to think or half think that Christ as God is one entity or *Gegenstand* and Christ as Man is another. I am sure some theologians have yielded to this temptation, which puts them on a straight road to the Nestorian heresy.

What Aquinas would have done, I repeat, to meet Foster's objection in the mouth of a Jew or Moor is to distinguish between what we say God can do, *simpliciter*, and what we say God *as God* can do, using the reduplicative form of proposition. Now if we do make such a distinction, we are faced with considerable logical complications, particularly if we accept the Aristotelian point about the reduplicative construction. Let us go back to our friend Jones: there is a logical difference between:

1. Jones as Mayor can attend this committee meeting.
2. Jones can as Mayor attend this committee meeting

as we may see if we spell the two out a little:

1. Jones as Mayor has the opportunity of attending this committee meeting
2. Jones has the opportunity of (attending this committee meeting as Mayor).

We can easily see now that 1 and 2 are logically distinct: for one thing, if Jones is not yet Mayor but has an opportunity of becoming Mayor and *then* attending the committee meeting, 2 would be true and 1 false. And if we want to talk about what Jones as Mayor *cannot* do, the complexities pile up; for then we have to consider how the negation can be inserted at one or other position in a proposition of one of these forms, and how all the results are logically related.

All this is logical work to be done if we are to be clear about the implications of saying that God can or cannot do so-and-so, or again that God *as God* can or cannot do so-and-so. It is obvious, without my developing the matter further, that the logic of all this will not be simple. It's a far cry from the simple method of bringing our question 'Can God do so-and-so?' under a reassuring principle 'God can do *everything*'. But I hope I have made it clear that any reassurance we get that way is entirely spurious.

7

Omniscience and Immutability

Norman Kretzmann

Norman Kretzmann (1928–98) was Susan Linn Sage Professor of Philosophy at Cornell University and made important contributions to the history of medieval philosophy and the philosophy of religion. In the following essay, Kretzmann argues that no absolutely perfect being exists. He does so by attempting to demonstrate that two requirements of absolute perfection, omniscience and immutability, are incompatible with one another.

It is generally recognized that omniscience and immutability are necessary characteristics of an absolutely perfect being. The fact that they are also incompatible characteristics seems to have gone unnoticed.

In the main body of this paper I will present first an argument that turns on the incompatibility of omniscience and immutability and, secondly, several objections to that argument with my replies to the objections.

(1) A perfect being is not subject to change.[1]
(2) A perfect being knows everything.[2]
(3) A being that knows everything always knows what time it is.[3]
(4) A being that always knows what time it is is subject to change.[4]
∴(5) A perfect being is subject to change.
∴(6) A perfect being is not a perfect being.

Finally, therefore,

(7) There is no perfect being.[5]

In discussing this argument with others[6] I have come across various objections against one or another of its premises. Considering such objections here helps to clarify the line taken in the argument and provides an opportunity to

Norman Kretzmann, "Omniscience and Immutability". *The Journal of Philosophy* 63:14 (1966): 409–21. © 1966. Reprinted with permission from *The Journal of Philosophy*.

anticipate and turn aside several natural criticisms of that line.

Because premises (1) and (2) present the widely accepted principles of immutability and omniscience, objections against them are not so much criticisms of the line taken in the argument as they are attempts to modify the concept of a perfect being in the light of the argument. And since premise (3) gives every impression of being an instance of a logical truth, premise (4) is apparently the one most vulnerable to attacks that are genuinely attacks on the argument. The first four of the following seven objections are all directed against premise (4), although Objection D raises a question relevant to premise (3) as well.

Objection A. It must be granted that a being that always knows what time it is knows something that is changing – say, the state of the universe. But change in the object of knowledge does not entail change in the knower.

The denial that a change in the object necessitates a change in the knower depends on imprecise characterizations of the object. For example, I know that the Chrysler Building in Manhattan is 1,046 feet tall. If it is said that the Chrysler Building is the object of my knowledge, then of course many changes in it – in its tenants or in its heating system, for example – do not necessitate changes in the state of my knowledge. If, however, it is more precisely said that the object of my knowledge is the *height* of the Chrysler Building, then of course a change in the object of my knowledge does necessitate a change in me. If a 40-foot television antenna is extended from the present tip of the tower, either I will cease to know the height of the Chrysler Building or I will give up believing that its height is 1,046 feet and begin believing that its height is 1,086 feet. In the case of always knowing what time it is, if we are to speak of an object of knowledge at all it must be characterized not as the state of the universe (which might also be said to be the object of, for example, a cosmologist's knowledge), but as the *changing* of that state. To know the changing of anything is to know first that *p* and then that not-*p* (for some particular instance of *p*), and a knower that knows first one proposition and then another is a knower that changes.

Objection B. The beliefs of a being that always knows what time it is are subject to change, but a change in a being's beliefs need not constitute a change in the being itself. If last year Jones believed the Platonic epistles to be genuine and this year he believes them to be spurious, then Jones has changed his mind; and that sort of change in beliefs may be considered a change in Jones. But if last year Jones believed that it was 1965 and this year he believes that it is 1966, he has not changed his mind, he has merely taken account of a calendar change; and that sort of change in beliefs should not be considered a change in Jones. The change in beliefs entailed by always knowing what time it is is that taking-account sort of change rather than a change of mind, the sort of change in beliefs that might reasonably be said to have been at least in part initiated by the believer and that might therefore be reasonably attributed to him.

It seems clear, first of all, that the sort of change in beliefs entailed by knowing the changing of anything is the taking-account sort of change rather than a change of mind. But once that much has been allowed, Objection B seems to consist in no more than an expression of disappointment in the *magnitude* of the change necessitated by always knowing what time it is. The entailed change in beliefs is not, it is true, sufficiently radical to qualify as a change of character or of attitude, but it is no less incompatible with immutability for all that. If Jones had been immutable from December 1965 through January 1966 he could no more have taken account of the calendar change than he could have changed his mind.

It may be worth noting that just such small-scale, taking-account changes in beliefs have sometimes been recognized by adherents of the principle of immutability as incompatible with immutability. Ockham, for example, argues at length against the possibility of a change in the state of God's foreknowledge just because God's changelessness could not be preserved through such a change. In Question Five of his *Tractatus de praedestinatione et de praescientia Dei et de futuris contingentibus* Ockham maintains that "if 'God knows that *A*' (where *A* is a future contingent proposition) and 'God does not know that *A*' *could* be true successively, it *would* follow that God was changeable," and the principle on which Ockham bases that claim is in no way restricted to future contingents. (As an adherent of the principle of immutability Ockham of course proceeds to deny that God could first know that *A* and then not know that *A*, but his reasons for doing so involve considerations peculiar to future contingent propositions and need not concern us here.)[7]

Objection C. For an omniscient being always to know what time it is is to know the state of the universe at every instant, but it is possible for an omniscient being to know the state of the universe at every instant all at once rather than successively. Consequently it is possible for an omniscient being always to know what time it is without being subject to change.

The superficial flaw in this objection is the ambiguity of the phrase 'to know the state of the universe at every instant', but the ambiguity is likely to be overlooked because the phrase is evidently an allusion to a familiar, widely accepted account of omniscience, according to which omniscience regarding contingent events is nothing more nor less than knowledge of the entire scheme of contingent events from beginning to end at once. I see no reason for quarreling here with the ascription of such knowledge to an omniscient being; but the underlying flaw in Objection C is the drastic *incompleteness* of this account of omniscience regarding contingent events.

The kind of knowledge ascribed to an omniscient being in this account is sometimes characterized as "seeing all time at a glance," which suggests that if one sees the entire scheme of contingent events from beginning to end at once one sees all there is to see of time. The totality of contingent events, we are to suppose, may be known either simultaneously or successively, and an omniscient being will of course know it not successively but simultaneously. In his *Summa contra gentiles* (Book I, Ch. 55, sects. [6]–[9]) Aquinas presents a concise version of what seems to be the standard exposition of this claim.

> . . . the intellect of one considering *successively* many things cannot have only one operation. For since operations differ according to their objects, the operation by which the first is considered must be different from the operation by which the second is considered. But the divine intellect has only one operation, namely, the divine essence, as we have proved. Therefore God considers all that he knows not successively, but *together*. Moreover, succession cannot be understood without time nor time without motion . . . But there can be no motion in God, as may be inferred from what we have said. There is, therefore, no succession in the divine consideration. . . . Every intellect, furthermore, that understands one thing after another is at one time *potentially* understanding and at another time *actually* understanding. For while it understands the first thing actually it understands the second thing potentially. But the divine intellect is never potentially but always actually understanding. Therefore it does not understand things successively but rather understands them together.

On this view an omniscient being's knowledge of contingent events is the knowledge that event *e* occurs at time *t* (for every true instance of that form). Thus an omniscient being knows that my birth occurs at t_n, that my writing these words occurs at t_{n+x}, that my death occurs at t_{n+x+y}. This omniscient being also knows what events occur simultaneously with each of those events – knows, for example, that while I am writing these words my desk calendar lies open at the page bearing the date "Friday, March 4, 1966," and the watch on my wrist shows 10:15. Moreover, since an omniscient being by any account knows all necessary truths, including the truths of arithmetic, this omniscient being knows how much time elapses between my birth and my writing these words and between my writing these words and my death. But I *am* writing these words just *now*, and on this view of omniscience an omniscient being is incapable of knowing that that is what I am now doing, and for all this omniscient being knows I might just as well be dead or as yet unborn. That is what knowing everything amounts to if knowing "everything" does not include always knowing what time it is. Alternatively, that is what knowing the state of the universe at every instant comes to if that phrase is interpreted in the way required by the claim that it is possible to have that sort of knowledge all at once.

According to this familiar account of omniscience, the knowledge an omniscient being has of the entire scheme of contingent events is in many relevant respects exactly like the knowledge you might have of a movie you had written, directed, produced, starred in, and seen a thousand times. You would know its every scene in flawless detail, and you would have the length of each scene and the sequence of scenes perfectly in mind. You would know, too, that a clock pictured in the first scene shows the time to be 3:45, and that a clock pictured in the fourth scene shows 4:30, and so on. Suppose, however, that your movie is being shown in a distant theater today. You know the movie immeasurably better than do the people in the theater who are now seeing it for the first time, but they know one big thing about it you don't know, namely, what is now going on on the screen.

Thus the familiar account of omniscience regarding contingent events is drastically incomplete. An omniscient being must know not only the entire scheme of contingent events from beginning to end at once, but also *at what stage of realization that scheme now is*. It is in this sense of knowing what time it is that it is essential to claim in premise (3) that a being that knows everything always knows what time it is, and it is in this sense that always knowing what time it is entails incessant change in the knower, as is claimed in premise (4).

In orthodox Christianity the prevalence of the incomplete account of omniscience regarding contingent events effectively obscures the incompatibility of omniscience and immutability. Aquinas, for example, is not content with proving merely that "it is impossible for God to change in any way." He goes on in the *Summa theologica* (Book I, Q. 14, art. 15) to argue that "since God's knowledge is his substance, as is clear from the foregoing, just as his substance is altogether immutable, as was shown above, so *his knowledge likewise must be altogether invariable*." What Aquinas, Ockham, and others *have* recognized is that God's knowledge cannot be variable if God is to remain immutable. What has *not* been seen is that God's knowledge cannot be altogether invariable if it is to be perfect, if it is to be genuine omniscience.

Objection D. A perfect being transcends space and time. Such a being is therefore not subject to change, whether as a consequence of knowing what time it is or for any other reason.

The importance of this objection lies in its introduction of the pervasive, mysterious doctrine of the transcendence of space and time, a doctrine often cited by orthodox Christians as if it were both consistent with their theology and explanatory of the notion that God sees all time at a glance. It seems to me to be neither.

In *Proslogium* Chapters XIX and XX Anselm apostrophizes the being transcendent of space and time as follows:

> Thou wast not, then, yesterday, nor wilt thou be tomorrow; but yesterday and today and tomorrow thou art; or, rather, neither yesterday nor today nor tomorrow thou art, but simply *thou art, outside all time*. For yesterday and today and tomorrow have no existence except in time, but thou, although nothing exists without thee, nevertheless dost not exist in space or time, but all things exist in thee. For nothing contains thee, but thou containest all.

For present purposes the spatial aspect of this doctrine may be ignored. What is meant by the claim that an entity transcends time? The number 2 might, I suppose, be said to transcend time in the sense that it does not age, that it is no older now than it was a hundred years ago. I see no reason to quarrel with the doctrine that a perfect being transcends time in *that* sense, since under that interpretation the doctrine is no more than a gloss on the principle of immutability. But under that interpretation the doctrine begs the question of premise (4) rather than providing a basis for objecting to it.

Only one other interpretation of the doctrine of the transcendence of time suggests itself, and that is that from a God's-eye point of view there is no time, that the passage of time is a universal human illusion. (Whatever else may be said of this interpretation, it surely cannot be considered compatible with such essential theses of Christian doctrine as the Incarnation and the Resurrection.) Under this interpretation the doctrine of the transcendence of time does have a devastating effect on the argument, since it implies either that there are no true propositions of the form 'it is now t_n' or that there is exactly one (eternally) true proposition of that form. Thus under this interpretation premise (3) either is vacuous or has a single trivializing instance, and premise (4) is false. But this interpretation preserves the immutability of a perfect being by imposing immutability on everything else, and that is surely an inconceivably high price to pay, in the view of Christians and non-Christians alike.

The remaining three objections are directed against premises (1) or (2) and may, therefore, be considered not so much criticisms of the argument as attempts to revise the principle of immutability or the principle of omniscience in the light of the argument. Objections E and F have to do with premise (2), Objection G with premise (1).

Objection E. Since a perfect being transcends time it is logically impossible that a perfect being know what time it is and hence logically impossible that such a being know everything. But it is no limitation on a perfect being that it cannot do what is logically impossible. Therefore, its not knowing absolutely everything (in virtue of not knowing what time it is) does not impair its perfection.

Objections E and F are attempts to hedge on omniscience as philosophers and theologians have long since learned to hedge on omnipotence. In Objection E this attempt depends on directly invoking one of the standard limitations on omnipotence, but the attempt does not succeed. Perhaps the easiest way of pointing up its failure is to produce analogous inferences of the same form, such as this: since I am a human being and a human being is a mortal rational animal, it is logically impossible that I should live forever; therefore it is no limitation on me that I must die – or this: since I am a creature of limited power, it is logically impossible that I be capable of doing whatever is logically possible; therefore it is no limitation on me that I cannot do whatever is logically possible. What is wrong with all these inferences is that the crucial limitation is introduced in the initial description of the being in question, after which it does of course make sense to deny that mere consequences of the limiting description are to be introduced as if they constituted additional limitations. It is not an *additional* limitation on a legless man that he cannot walk, or on a mortal being that it must die, or on a creature of limited power that it cannot do whatever it might choose to do. No more is it an *additional* limitation on a being that is *incapable* of knowing what time it is that it *does not* know what time it is. But any claim to perfection that might have been made on behalf of such a being has already been vitiated in the admission that its transcendence of time renders it incapable of omniscience.

Objection F. Just as in explicating the concept of omnipotence we have been forced to abandon the naive formula 'a perfect being can do anything' and replace it with 'a perfect being can do anything the doing of which does not impair its perfection', so the argument suggests that the naive formula 'a perfect being knows everything' must be revised to read 'a perfect being knows everything the knowing of which does not impair its perfection'. Thus, since the argument does show that knowing what time it is impairs the perfection of the knower, it cannot be a part of the newly explicated omniscience to know what time it is.

Even if Objection F could be sustained, this particular grasping of the nettle would surely impress many as just too painful to bear, for in deciding whether or not to try to evade the conclusion of the argument in this way it is important to remember that in the context of the argument 'knowing what time it is' means knowing *what is going on*. Objection F at best thus provides an exceptionally costly defense of absolute perfection, emptying it of much of its content in order to preserve it; for under the newly explicated notion of omniscience Objection F commits one to the view that it is impossible for a *perfect, omniscient* being to know what is going on.

Objection F attempts to draw an analogy between an explication of omnipotence and a proposed explication of omniscience, borrowing strength from the fact that in the ease of omnipotence such an explication has long since been recognized as a necessary condition of the coherence of the notion. In evaluating this attempt it is helpful to note that there are at least three types of provisos that may be inserted into formulas of omnipotence for that purpose. The first is relevant to omnipotence generally, the second specifically to eternal omnipotence, and the third specifically to eternal omnipotence as one perfect characteristic of a being possessed of certain other perfect characteristics. (For present purposes it is convenient to say simply that the third is relevant specifically to eternal omnipotence as one aspect of an absolutely perfect being.) These three types of provisos may be exemplified in the following three formulas of omnipotence:

I. A being that is omnipotent (regardless of its other characteristics) can do anything provided that (a) the description of what is to be done does not involve a logical inconsistency.
II. A being that is eternally omnipotent (regardless of its other characteristics) can do anything provided that (a) . . . and (b) the doing of it does not constitute or produce a limitation on its power.
III. A being that is absolutely perfect (and hence eternally omnipotent) can do anything provided that (a) . . . and (b) . . . and (c) the doing of it does not constitute a violation of some aspect of its perfection other than its power.

Provisos of type (c) only are at issue in Objection F, no doubt because provisos of types (a) and (b) have no effective role to play in the explication of omniscience. No being knows anything that is *not* the case; *a fortiori* no omniscient being knows anything that *cannot be* the case. So much for type (a). As for type (b), since certain things the description of which involves no logical inconsistency would if done incapacitate the doer – committing suicide, for example, or creating another omnipotent being – there is good reason for such a proviso in the explication of eternal omnipotence. It might likewise be claimed that an omniscient being knows everything except things that would if known limit the being's *capacity for knowledge*, the formal justification for this claim being just the same as that for the corresponding omnipotence-claim. The significant difference between these two claims is that the omniscience-claim is evidently vacuous. There is no reason to suspect that there *are* things that would if known limit the knower's capacity for knowledge. More directly to the point at issue in the argument, there is no reason whatever to think that knowing what is going on is a kind of knowing that limits the knower's capacity for knowledge. Thus although a type (b) proviso is needed in the explication of eternal omnipotence in order to preserve the coherence of the notion of eternal omnipotence, no such proviso need be inserted into the formula of omniscience in order to preserve the coherence of that notion.

The putative analogy in Objection F presupposes that a proviso of type (c) will preserve omniscience as it preserves omnipotence in such a (Cartesian) argument as the following. It is impossible for an absolutely perfect being to lie, for although such a being, as omnipotent, has the power to lie, the exercise of that power would violate the perfect goodness of the being. To say that it is impossible for an absolutely perfect being to lie is not to say that it lacks the power to lie but rather that its absolute perfection in another aspect – perfect goodness – necessitates its refraining from the exercise of that power. Whether or not this line of argument succeeds in doing what it is designed to do, it seems clear that there is no genuine analogue for it in the case of omniscience. Consider the following candidate. It is impossible for an absolutely perfect being to know what is going on, for although such a being, as omniscient, has the power to know what is going on, the exercise of that power would violate the immutability of the being. To say that it is impossible for an absolutely perfect being to know what is going on is not to say that it lacks the power to know what is going on but rather that its absolute perfection in another aspect – immutability – necessitates its refraining from the exercise of that power. A being that has the power to do something that it refrains from doing may not thereby even jeopardize its omnipotence. All the same, a being that has the power to know something that it refrains from knowing does thereby forfeit its omniscience. Omniscience is not the *power to know* everything; it is the *condition of knowing* everything, and that condition cannot be preserved through even a single instance of omitting to exercise the power to know everything.

Therefore, whatever strength Objection F seems to derive from its appeal to the putative analogy between omnipotence and omniscience in this respect is illusory, and this attempted evasion of the argument's conclusion reduces to an arbitrary decision to sacrifice omniscience to immutability.

Objection G. The traditional view of philosophers and theologians that absolute perfection entails absolute immutability is mistaken, founded on the misconception that in a perfect being any change would have to be for the worse. In particular the kind of change entailed by always knowing what time it is is a kind of change that surely cannot be construed as deterioration, even when it is ascribed to an absolutely perfect being. No doubt an absolutely perfect being must be immutable in most and perhaps in all other respects, but the argument shows that absolute perfection *entails* mutability in at least this one respect.

Objection G proceeds on the assumption that immutability is ascribed to a perfect being for only one reason – namely, that all change in such a being must constitute deterioration. There is, however, a second reason, as has been indicated at several points in the discussion so far – namely, that any change in a "perfect" being must indicate that the being was in some respect not in the requisite state of completion, actualization, fixity. The aspect of absolute completion is no less essential an ingredient in the concept of absolute perfection than is the aspect of absolute excellence. Moreover, those such as Aquinas and Ockham who argue against the mutability of a perfect being's *knowledge* would surely agree that the change they are intent on ruling out would not constitute *deterioration*, since they regularly base their arguments on the inadmissibility of *process* in an absolutely perfect being.

An absolutely perfect being may be described as a being possessing all logically compossible perfections. Thus if the argument had shown that omniscience and immutability were logically incompossible, it would have called for no more than an adjustment in the concept of absolute perfection, an adjustment of the sort proposed in Objection G. The proposition 'things change' is, however, not necessarily but only contingently true. If as a matter of fact nothing else ever did change, an omniscient being could of course remain immutable. In Objection G, however, an absolutely perfect being has been confused with a being possessing all *really* compossible perfections, the best of all *really* possible beings. Perhaps, as the objection implies, the most *nearly* absolutely perfect being in the circumstances that happen to prevail *would* be mutable in the respect necessitated by always knowing what time it is. But that is of no consequence to the argument, which may be taken as showing that the prevailing circumstances do not admit of the existence of an absolutely perfect being.

This concluding section of the paper is in the nature of an appendix. It might be subtitled "Omniscience and Theism"; for it may be shown that the doctrine that God knows everything is incompatible also with theism, the doctrine of a personal God distinct from other persons.[8]

Consider these two statements.

S_1. Jones knows that he is in a hospital.
S_2. Jones knows that Jones is in a hospital.

S_1 and S_2 are logically independent. It may be that Jones is an amnesia case. He knows perfectly well that he is in a hospital, and after reading the morning papers he knows that Jones is in a hospital. An omniscient being surely must know all that Jones knows. Anyone can know what S_2 describes Jones as knowing, but no one other than Jones can know what S_1 describes Jones as knowing. (A case in point: Anyone could have proved that Descartes existed, but that is not what Descartes proved in the Cogito, and what he proved in the Cogito could not have been proved by anyone else.) The kind of knowledge S_1 ascribes to Jones is, moreover, the kind of knowledge characteristic of every self-conscious entity, of every person. Every person knows certain propositions that no *other* person *can* know. Therefore, if God is omniscient, theism is false; and if theism is true, God is not omniscient.

It may fairly be said of God, as it once was said of William Whewell, that "omniscience [is] his foible."

Notes

1 This principle of immutability is regularly supported by one of two arguments. (I) *From Supreme Excellence*: A perfect being is a supremely excellent being; thus any change in such a being would constitute corruption, deterioration, loss of perfection. (See Plato, *Republic*, II, 381B.) (II) *From Complete Actualization*: A perfect being is a being whose capacities for development are all fully realised. A being subject to change, however, is in that respect and to that extent a being with an unrealized capacity for development, a being merely potential and not fully actualized, a being in a state of process and not complete; hence not perfect. (See Aristotle, *Metaphysics*, XII, 9; 1074b26.) The principle of immutability is a thesis of orthodox Christian theology, drawn from Greek philosophy and having among its credentials such biblical passages as Malachi 3.6 and James 1.17. (See Aquinas, *Summa theologica*, I, Q. 9, art. 1.)

2 Being incapable of knowing all there is to know or being capable of knowing all there is to know and knowing less than that are conditions evidently incompatible with absolute perfection. Hence (2), which seems even more familiar and less problematic than (1).

3 Part of what is meant by premise (3) is, of course, that a being that knows everything always knows what time it is in every time zone on every planet in every galaxy; but it is not quite in that horological sense that its knowledge of what time it is is most plainly relevant to considerations of omniscience and immutability. The relevant sense can be brought out more easily in the consideration of objections against the argument.

4 Adopting 'it is now t_n' as a convenient standard form for propositions as to what time it is, we may say of a being that always knows what time it is that the state of its knowledge changes incessantly with respect to propositions of the form 'it is now t_n'. First such a being knows that it is now t_1 (and that it is not now t_2), and then it knows that it is now t_2, (and that it is not now t_1). To say of any being that it knows something different from what it used to know is to say that it has changed; hence (4).

5 [1f] $(x)(Px \supset \sim Cx)$; [2f] $(x)(Px \supset (p)(p \equiv Kxp))$ [K: . . . knows that . . .]; [3f] $(x)((p)(p \equiv Kxp) \supset (p)(Tp \supset (p \equiv Kxp)))$ [T: . . . is of the form 'it is now t_n']; [4f] $(x)((p)(Tp \supset (p \equiv Kxp)) \supset Cx)$; [5f] $(x)(Px \supset Cx)$ [entailed by 2f, 3f, 4f]; [6f] $(x)(Px \supset \sim Px)$ [entailed by 1f, 5f]; [7f] $(x) \sim Px$ [equivalent to 6f]. The formalization [3f] is an instance of a logical truth; nevertheless, premise (3) is not one of the established principles in philosophical or theological discussions of the nature of a perfect being. Not only is it not explicitly affirmed, but it seems often to be implicitly denied. This circumstance may arouse a suspicion that the formalization [3f] is inaccurate or question-begging. Any such suspicion will, I think, be dissipated in the course of considering the objections to the argument, but it may be helpful in the meantime to point out that the validity of the argument does not depend on this formalization. It is of course possible to adopt less detailed formalizations that would not disclose the special logical status of premise (3) and would nevertheless exhibit the validity of the argument. For example, [2f′] $(x)(Px \supset Ox)$; [3f′] $(x)(Ox \supset Nx)$ together with a similarly imprecise formalization of premise (4) would serve that purpose.

6 I am indebted especially to Miss Marilyn McCord and to Professors H. N. Castañeda, H. G. Frankfurt, C. Ginet, G. B. Matthews, G. Nakhnikian, W. L. Rowe, S. Shoemaker, and W. Wainwright.

7 The most interesting historical example of this sort that I have seen was called to my attention by Professor Hugh Chandler after I had submitted this paper for publication. It is Problem XIII in the *Tahāfut al-Falāsifah* of al-Ghazali (d. ca. 1111): "REFUTATION OF THEIR [i.e., the philosophers', but principally Avicenna's] DOCTRINE THAT GOD (MAY HE BE EXALTED ABOVE WHAT THEY SAY) DOES NOT KNOW THE PARTICULARS WHICH ARE DIVISIBLE IN ACCORDANCE WITH THE DIVISION OF TIME INTO 'WILL BE', 'WAS', AND 'IS'" (tr. S. A. Kamali (Lahore, Pakistan Philosophical Congress, 1963), pp. 153–62). This work was not known to medieval Christian philosophers. [See Etienne Gilson, *History of Christian Philosophy in the Middle Ages* (New York: Random House, 1955), p. 216.]

8 The following argument was suggested to me by certain observations made by Professor Hector Castañeda in a paper entitled "He," presented at the Wayne State University philosophy colloquium in the fall of 1964.

8

Atemporal Personhood

William L. Craig

William Lane Craig (b. 1949) is Research Professor of Philosophy at Talbot School of Theology in California and the author of numerous books and articles on the recent debates over the nature of God's relationship to time. One of the central issues in these debates concerns whether God should be conceived as existing timelessly (i.e. entirely transcending the temporal realm) or as having an everlasting temporal existence. Those who endorse the temporal conception of divine existence sometimes criticize divine timelessness by arguing that timelessness is incompatible with divine personhood. Although Craig rejects timelessness himself for other reasons, in the following selection from *Time and Eternity* (2001) he argues that there is no conflict between timelessness and personhood.

We have seen that Isaac Newton founded his belief in the existence of absolute time on God's infinite temporal duration. But so far as I can tell, Newton never offered any argument for thinking God to be temporal – he just asserted it. He regarded temporality and spatiality as inherent dispositions of being; that is to say, anything that exists must exist in time and space. But this assumption is far from obvious. Indeed, quite the contrary, it seems easy to conceive of God as transcending space, since He is incorporeal. Moreover, philosophers often regard abstract entities such as numbers or sets as existing in neither time nor space. So why could God not exist timelessly? Is there no logically conceivable world in which God exists and time does not?

According to the Christian doctrine of creation, God's decision to create a universe was a freely willed decision from which God could have refrained. We can conceive, then, of a possible world in which God does refrain from creation, a world which is empty except for God. Would time exist in such a world? Certainly it would

William L. Craig, "The Impossibility of Atemporal Personhood" from *Time and Eternity* (Wheaton, IL: Crossway Books, 2001), pp. 77–86.

if God were changing, experiencing a stream of consciousness. As we have seen, even a succession in the contents of consciousness is sufficient to generate a temporal series.

But suppose God were altogether changeless. Suppose that He did not experience a succession of thoughts but grasped all truth in a single, changeless intuition. Would time exist? A relationalist like Leibniz would say no, for there are no events to generate a relation of *earlier than* or *later than*. There is just a single, timeless state.

It is true that in recent years there has been a good deal written about the possibility of time without change, and most contemporary relationalists espouse a view which allows there to be changeless periods of time sandwiched in between periods of change.[1] But I know of no relationalist account that would allow a totally changeless world such as we are envisioning to be temporal. Such a world would, indeed, seem to be just a single, timeless state.

Newton would have disagreed, of course. For him timeless existence was a logical impossibility. But my point is that no reason has been offered why we should side with Newton on this score rather than with Leibniz, whose view seems extremely plausible.

If timeless existence as such is not demonstrably impossible, then, why should we think that God could not exist timelessly? Let us stick with our envisioned empty world in which God alone exists. Why could God not exist timelessly in such a world?

"Because God is personal!" is the answer given by certain advocates of divine temporality. They contend that the idea of a timeless person is incoherent and therefore God must be temporal. They argue that in order to be a person, one must possess certain properties which inherently involve time. Since God is essentially personal, He therefore cannot be timeless.

We can formulate this argument as follows (using *x*, *y*, *z* to represent certain properties to be specified later):

1. Necessarily, if God is timeless, He does not have the properties *x*, *y*, *z*.
2. Necessarily, if God does not have the properties *x*, *y*, *z*, then God is not personal.
3. Necessarily, God is personal.
4. Therefore, necessarily, God is not timeless.

The argument, if successful, shows that timelessness and personhood are incompatible and, since God is essentially personal, it is timelessness which must be jettisoned.

Critique

The defender of divine timelessness may attempt to turn back this argument either by challenging the claim that the properties in question are necessary conditions of personhood or by showing that a timeless God could possess the relevant properties after all. So what are the properties *x*, *y*, *z* that the advocate of divine temporality is talking about?

In his article "Conditions of Personhood,"[2] Daniel Dennett, a philosopher who specializes in the philosophy of mind, delineates six different conceptions of personhood, each of which lays down a necessary condition of any individual *P*'s being a person:

P is a person only if:

i. *P* is a rational being.
ii. *P* is a being to which states of consciousness can be attributed.
iii. Others regard (or can regard) *P* as a being to which states of consciousness can be attributed.
iv. *P* is capable of regarding others as beings to which states of consciousness can be attributed.
v. *P* is capable of verbal communication.
vi. *P* is self-conscious; that is, *P* is capable of regarding him/her/itself as a subject of states of consciousness.

All of these criteria depend in some way on *P*'s having or being said to have consciousness. So, as an initial step in assessing the present argument, we may ask whether the concept of a conscious, timeless being is possible.

John Lucas is one of those philosophers who maintains that this is not possible. He writes,

> Time is not a thing that God might or might not create, but a category, a necessary concomitant of the existence of a personal being, though not of a mathematical entity. This is not to say that time is an independent category, existing

> independently of God. It exists because of God: not because of some act of will on His part, but because of His nature: if ultimate reality is personal, then it follows that time must exist. God did not make time, but time stems from God.[3]

On Lucas's view, even in an otherwise empty world, time would exist if a personal God exists. Unfortunately, Lucas never explains why personal consciousness could not be unchanging and therefore, plausibly, atemporal. Why could not the contents of God's consciousness in such a world be comprised exclusively of such changelessly true beliefs as "No human beings exist," "7 + 5 = 12," "Anything that has a shape has a size," "If I were to create a world of free creatures, they would fall into sin," and so forth? If God never acquires any new beliefs and never loses any beliefs, why could not such a changeless consciousness of truth be plausibly regarded as timeless? Why think that such a changeless, timeless consciousness is impossible? Here Lucas has nothing to say. He confesses, "My claim . . . that time is a concomitant of consciousness, is of course only a claim, and I have been unable to argue for it, except by citing poetry. . . . arguments would be better."[4]

Indeed, they would! So what arguments are there against the possibility of an atemporal consciousness? Richard Gale, a well-known philosopher of time, would make short work of the question: "the quickest and most direct way of showing the absurdity of a timeless mind is as follows: A mind is conscious, and consciousness is a temporally elongated process."[5] The difficulty with Gale's reasoning, however, is that he fails to show that being temporally extended is an *essential* property of consciousness, rather than just a *common* property of consciousness. Defenders of divine timelessness have frequently pointed out that the act of knowing something need not take any time at all.[6] It makes sense, for example, to say that a timeless being knows the multiplication table. So why is an atemporal, conscious knowledge of unchanging truth impossible?

Gale responds that anyone who knows some particular truth must have a disposition to engage in certain temporal activities. But Gale's assertion is clearly false. There is no reason to think that God cannot know 2 + 2 = 4 without having a disposition to engage in temporal activities. And remember, on the Christian view, God is free to refrain from creation altogether, in which case I see no reason to think He must be disposed to engage in temporal activities at all.

I am not aware of any other arguments in the literature aimed at showing that an atemporal consciousness is impossible. Accordingly, we may conclude that no good reason has been given for thinking that God could not satisfy condition (ii) above. Similarly, condition (iii) is satisfied, since on the basis of our investigation thus far, I (and, I trust, the reader) can regard God, existing timelessly, as a being to whom a state of consciousness can be attributed. Again, even in our envisioned empty, timeless world, God is at least *capable* of regarding others as conscious – even if, were He to create such beings, He would not then be timeless. (We may leave that hypothesis an open question at this point.) Thus, God could satisfy condition (iv). What about condition (v)? God in the empty world is once more at least *capable* of verbal communication, for He could create language users like us and communicate to them by inspiring prophets or even causing sound waves in the thin air. Thus, (v) is met.

Could a timeless God be self-conscious, as (vi) stipulates? In order to be self-conscious a being must hold beliefs about himself not only from the third-person perspective, such as, in God's case, "God is omnipotent" or "God believes that 2 + 2 = 4," but also from the first-person perspective, such as "I am omnipotent" or "I believe that 2 + 2 = 4."[7] But it takes no more time to believe truly that "I have no human company," for example, than it does to believe that "No human beings exist." For any truth God knows from a third-person viewpoint, we can formulate a corresponding belief from the first-person perspective. Hence, if God can be timelessly conscious, there is no reason He cannot be timelessly self-conscious. Hence, criterion (vi) is also met.

That leaves criterion (i), that God must be rational in order to be personal. Without going into the debate over what it means to be rational, we may say rather confidently that God's being timeless impairs neither God's noetic structure (His system of beliefs) nor His ability to discharge any intellectual duties He might be thought to have. Since He is omniscient, it is pretty silly to think that God could be indicted for irrationality! Nor, as we have seen, would timelessness inhibit His knowing all truth in a timeless world such as we are contemplating.

Thus, a timeless God could fulfill all the various necessary conditions laid down for being personal. More than that, I should say that being self-conscious is not merely a *necessary* but also a *sufficient* condition for personhood. Our thought experiment of God's existing timelessly alone suggests that it is quite possible for God to be both timeless and self-conscious in such a state and, hence, personal.

Now some philosophers have denied that a timeless God can be a self-conscious, rational being, because He could not exhibit certain forms of consciousness which we normally associate with personal beings (namely, ourselves). The metaphysician Robert Coburn has written,

> Surely it is a necessary condition of anything's being a person that it should be capable (logically) of, among other things, doing at least some of the following: remembering, anticipating, reflecting, deliberating, deciding, intending, and acting intentionally. To see that this is so one need but ask oneself whether anything which necessarily lacked all of the capacities noted would, under any conceivable circumstances, count as a person. But now an eternal being would necessarily lack all of these capacities in as much as their exercise by a being clearly requires that the being exist in time. After all, reflection and deliberation take time, deciding typically occurs at some time – and in any case it always makes sense to ask, "When did you (he, they, etc.) decide?"; remembering is impossible unless the being doing the remembering has a past; and so on. Hence, no eternal being, it would seem, could be a person.[8]

Now even if Coburn were correct that a personal being must be capable of exhibiting the forms of consciousness he lists, it does not follow that a timeless God cannot be personal. For God could be *capable* of exhibiting such forms of consciousness but be timeless just in case (that is, "if and only if") He does not *in fact* exhibit any of them. In other words, the hidden assumption behind Coburn's reasoning is that God's being timeless or temporal is an essential property of God, that either God is necessarily timeless or He is necessarily temporal. But that assumption seems to me dubious. Suppose, for the sake of argument, that God is in fact temporal. Is it logically impossible that God could have been timeless instead? Since God's decision to create is free, we can conceive of possible worlds in which God alone exists. If He is unchanging in such a world, then on any relational view of time God would be timeless, as we have seen. In such an atemporal world God would lack certain properties which we have supposed Him to have in the actual world – for example, the property of *knowing what time it is* or the property of *co-existing with temporal creatures* – and He would have other properties which He lacks in the actual world – for example, the property of *being alone* or of *knowing that He is alone* – but none of these differences seems significant enough to deny that God could be either timeless or temporal and still be the same being. Just as my height is a contingent rather than essential property of mine, so God's temporal status is plausibly a contingent rather than essential property of His. So apart from highly controversial claims on behalf of divine simplicity or immutability, I see no reason to think that God is either *essentially* temporal or *essentially* timeless.

So if timelessness is a merely contingent property of God, He could be entirely capable of remembering, anticipating, reflecting, and so on; only were He to do so, then He would not be timeless. So long as He freely refrains from such activities He is timeless, even though He has the *capacity* to engage in those activities. Thus, by Coburn's own lights God must be regarded as personal.

At a more fundamental level, it is in any case pretty widely recognized that most of the forms of consciousness mentioned by Coburn are not essential to personhood – indeed, not even the capacity for them is essential to personhood. Take remembering, for example. Any temporal individual who lacked memory would be mentally ill or a mere animal. But if an individual exists timelessly, then he has no past to remember. He thus never forgets anything! Given God's omniscience, there is just no reason to think that His personhood requires memory. Similarly with regard to anticipation: Since a timeless God has no future, there just is nothing to anticipate.

Only a temporal person needs to have beliefs about the past or future.

As for reflecting and deliberating, these are ruled out not so much by God's timelessness as by His omniscience. An omniscient being cannot reflect and deliberate because He already knows the conclusions to be arrived at! Even if God is in time, He does not engage in reflection and deliberation. But He is surely not impersonal as a result.

What about deciding, intending, and acting intentionally? I should say that all of these forms of consciousness are exhibited by a timeless God. With respect to deciding, again, omniscience alone precludes God's deciding in the sense of making up His mind after a period of indecision. Even a temporal God does not decide in that sense. But God does decide in the sense that His will intends toward one alternative rather than another and does so freely. It is up to God what He does; He could have willed otherwise. This is the strongest sense of libertarian freedom of the will. In God's case, because He is omniscient, His free decisions are either everlasting or timeless rather than preceded by a period of ignorance and indecision.

As for intending or acting intentionally, there is no reason to think that intentions are necessarily future-directed. One can direct one's intentions at one's present state. God, as the Good, can timelessly desire and will His own infinite goodness. Such a changeless intention can be as timeless as God's knowing His own essence. Moreover, in the empty world we have envisioned, God may timelessly will and intend to refrain from creating a universe. God's willing to refrain from creation should not be confused with the mere absence of the intention to create. A stone is characterized by the absence of any will to create but cannot be said to will to refrain from creating. In a world in which God freely refrains from creation, His abstaining from creating is a result of a free act of the will on His part. Hence, it seems to me that God can timelessly intend, will, and choose what He does.

Now some theologians have objected to the picture I have painted of a timeless, solitary deity, for such a being lacks all interpersonal relationships, and such relationships, they believe, are essential to personhood. If God is to be personal, He must be engaged in relationships with other persons. But the give-and-take of personal relationships inherently involves temporality.

In response to this objection, I think it would be extraordinarily difficult to prove that engaging in personal relationships, as opposed to the *capacity* to engage in personal relationships, is essential to personhood. A timeless God could have the capacity for such relationships even if, were He to engage in them, He would in that case be temporal. But let that pass. The more important assumption underlying this objection is the assumption that the persons to whom God is related must be *human* persons. For on the Christian conception of God, that assumption is false. Within the fullness of the Godhead itself, the persons of the Father, the Son, and the Holy Spirit enjoy the interpersonal relations afforded by the Trinity which God is. As a Trinity, God is eternally complete with no need of fellowship with finite persons. It is a marvel of God's grace and love that He would freely create finite persons and invite them to share in the love and joy of the inner Trinitarian life of God.

But would the existence of these Trinitarian interrelationships necessitate that God be temporal? I see no reason to think that the persons of the Trinity could not be affected, prompted, or responsive to one another in an unchanging and, hence, timeless way. To use a mundane example, think of iron filings clinging to a magnet. The magnet and the filings need not change their positions in any way in order for it to be the case that the filings are stuck to the magnet because the magnet is affecting them and they are responding to the magnet's force. Of course, on a deeper level change is going on constantly in this case because the magnet's causal influence is mediated by finite velocity electromagnetic radiation. Nonetheless, the example is instructive because it illustrates how on a macroscopic level action and response can be simultaneous and, hence, involve neither change nor temporal separation. How much more is this so when we consider the love relationship between the members of the Trinity! Since intra-Trinitarian relations are not based on physical influences or rooted in any material substratum but are purely mental, the response of the Son to the Father's love implies neither change nor temporal separation. Just as we speak metaphorically of two lovers who sit, not speaking a word, gazing into each other's eyes as "lost in that timeless moment," so we may speak literally of the timeless mutual love of the Father, Son, and Spirit for one another.

The ancient doctrine of *perichoreisis*, championed by the Greek Church Fathers, expresses the timeless interaction of the persons of the Godhead.[9] According to that doctrine, there is a complete interpenetration of the persons of the Trinity, such that each is intimately bound up in the activities of the other. Thus, what the Father wills, the Son and Spirit also will; what the Son loves, the Father and Spirit also love, and so forth. Each person is completely transparent to the others. There is nothing new that the Son, for example, might communicate to the Spirit, since that has already been communicated. There exists a full and perfect exchange of the divine love and knowledge, so that nothing is left undone which needs to be completed. In this perfect interpenetration of divine love and life, no change need occur, so that God existing alone in the self-sufficiency of His being would, on a relational view of time, be timeless.

Thus, I think it is evident that God can enjoy interpersonal relations and yet be timeless. So even if we conceded that God is essentially timeless and that interpersonal relations are essential to personhood, it is still not true that if God is timeless, He cannot stand in interpersonal relations.

In conclusion, then, the argument for divine temporality based on God's personhood cannot be deemed a success. Advocates of a temporal God have not been able to show that God cannot possess timelessly the properties essential to personhood. On the contrary, we have seen that a timeless God can be plausibly said to fulfill the necessary and sufficient conditions of being a person. A timeless, divine person can be a self-conscious, rational individual endowed with freedom of the will and engaged in interpersonal relations.

All this has been said, however, in abstraction from the reality of a temporal universe. Given that such a universe exists, it remains to be seen whether God can remain untouched by its temporality.

Notes

1 See the seminal paper by Sidney Shoemaker, "Time without Change," *Journal of Philosophy* 66 (1969): 363–81.

2 Daniel Dennett, "Conditions of Personhood," in *The Identities of Persons*, ed. Amelie Oksenberg Rorty (Berkeley: University of California Press, 1976), 175–96. Dennett's criteria were first used in defense of divine, timeless personhood by William E. Mann, "Simplicity and Immutability in God," *International Philosophical Quarterly* 23 (1983): 267–76.

3 J. R. Lucas, *The Future: An Essay on God, Temporality, and Truth* (Oxford: Basil Blackwell, 1989), 213; cf. 212.

4 Ibid., 175.

5 Richard M. Gale, *On the Nature and Existence of God* (Cambridge: Cambridge University Press, 1991), 52.

6 Nelson Pike, *God and Timelessness*, Studies in Ethics and the Philosophy of Religion (New York: Schocken, 1970), 124; Mann, "Simplicity and Immutability," 270; Paul Helm, *Eternal God* (Oxford: Clarendon, 1988), 64–5; John C. Yates, *The Timelessness of God* (Lanham, MD.: University Press of America, 1990), 173–4; Brian Leftow, *Time and Eternity*, Cornell Studies in the Philosophy of Religion (Ithaca, NY: Cornell University Press, 1991), 285–90.

7 Philosophers distinguish between knowledge *de re*, which is non-perspectival knowledge of a thing, and knowledge *de se*, which is self-knowledge.

8 Robert C. Coburn, "Professor Malcolm on God," *Australasian Journal of Philosophy* 41 (1963), 155.

9 See St John Damascene, *An Exact Exposition of the Orthodox Faith* 2.1 (St John of Damascus, *Writings* [New York: Fathers of the Church, 1958], 204).

V

FATE, FREEDOM, AND FOREKNOWLEDGE

Introduction

If there is a God who knows the entire future in a way that cannot be mistaken, it appears that nothing can happen differently than it does. If so, human beings cannot act differently than they do. But if human freedom requires the ability to do otherwise, humans are not free. This is the dilemma of freedom and foreknowledge. Cicero mentions the problem in *On Fate* (first century BC), included in this collection, and Augustine discusses it in *On the Free Choice of the Will* (fourth–fifth centuries). Throughout most of the Christian era, philosophers have attempted to reconcile divine foreknowledge and human freedom, and the readings in this section include the three most historically important ways out of the dilemma – those by Boethius (sixth century), William of Ockham (thirteenth century), and Luis de Molina (sixteenth century).

Past infallible knowledge of the future makes it appear that the future is necessary because of the combination of two facts about past infallible knowledge: (i) it is too late to do anything about the fact that a past event happened, and (ii) a past infallible belief can't be false. If God is omniscient and essentially so, God had a belief at every moment in the past about every event that will occur in the future. It is too late to prevent God from having those beliefs because the events already occurred, and since God is infallible, those beliefs cannot be false. So it looks like everything that will happen, will happen by necessity.

Some philosophers think that propositions about the future have no truth value, so there is nothing to know about what will happen in the future. Even an omniscient being cannot know the unknowable, so even an omniscient being cannot have foreknowledge. Aristotle seems to have defended the view that future contingent propositions have no truth value in his famous Sea Battle Argument of *De Interpretatione* 9, included in this section. There are some contemporary philosophers who accept this position.

Boethius' way out was to deny that God is in time. If God is timeless, then although he is infallible, he did not know anything *yesterday*, he does not know anything *today*, and he will not know anything *tomorrow*. We need not worry about the fact that we can't do anything about the past (there is no use crying over spilt milk), because God's infallible beliefs are not in the past. Aquinas adopted this solution as well.

The solution of Ockham is more subtle. Ockham argued that the distinction between propositions about the past and propositions about the future is not cut and dried. Some propositions that appear to be about the past are partly about the future, for instance, the proposition *It was true yesterday that I would go skating tomorrow*. That proposition does not have the necessity of the past, the kind of necessity that applies to spilled milk. Similarly, Ockham argued, the proposition *God believed yesterday that I would go skating tomorrow* is partly about the future, and it also does not have the necessity of the past. It might seem odd to say that it is *not* too late to do something about the fact that God believed yesterday that I would go skating tomorrow, but Ockham seems to have thought something close to that. We have not included a primary reading from Ockham, but have added part of Marilyn Adams' introduction to Ockham on predestination and foreknowledge. Adams explains Ockham's quite complicated view on the distinction between the truth and the necessity of propositions, and compares his view to that of Aristotle.

The third traditional way of reconciling divine foreknowledge and human free will is the Molinist solution, summarized in the selection by William Hasker. Molina did not directly address the fatalist argument, but proposed a theory about the structure of divine knowledge that aimed at explaining how God knows the entire contingent future in a way that does not take away human free will. Molina argued that God has "Middle Knowledge," or knowledge of what every free creature would freely choose in every possible circumstance. By combining his knowledge of his own creative will with his Middle Knowledge, God knows all actual circumstances, past, present, and future.

Other solutions to the foreknowledge dilemma concentrate on the analysis of free will – in particular, the assumption that free will includes the ability to do otherwise. In addition, there are approaches that focus on the other side of the dilemma – whether it is religiously and philosophically important that God has infallible foreknowledge. Some argue that it is not. The issues brought out in this section therefore touch on a number of important issues in philosophy – the nature of time and the causal relation, the relation between truth and necessity, the nature of free will, and the part played by divine foreknowledge in religious practice.

1

The Sea Battle Argument

Aristotle

The following reading from chapter nine of Aristotle's *De Interpretatione* is a classic discussion of the problem of logical fatalism. Although Aristotle's position is not entirely clear, he seems to deny that propositions about the contingent future have a truth value.

Chapter 9

18^a28. With regard to what is and what has been it is necessary for the affirmation or the negation to be true or false. And with universals taken universally it is always necessary for one to be true and the other false, and with particulars too, as we have said; but with universals not spoken of universally it is not necessary. But with particulars that are going to be it is different.

18^a34. For if every affirmation or negation is true or false it is necessary for everything either to be the case or not to be the case. For if one person says that something will be and another denies this same thing, it is clearly necessary for one of them to be saying what is true – if every affirmation is true or false; for both will not be the case together under such circumstances. For if it is true to say that it is white or is not white, it is necessary for it to be white or not white; and if it is white or is not white, then it was true to say or deny this. If it is not the case it is false, if it is false it is not the case. So it is necessary for the affirmation or the negation to be true. It follows that nothing either is or is happening, or will be or will not be, by chance or as chance has it, but everything of necessity and not as chance has it (since either he who says or he who denies is saying what is true). For otherwise it might equally well happen or not happen, since what is as chance has it is no more thus than not thus, nor will it be.

Aristotle, Chapter 9 from *Aristotle's Categories and De Interpretatione*, trans. J. L. Ackrill (Oxford: Clarendon Press, 1963), pp. 50–3.

18^b9. Again, if it is white now it was true to say earlier that it would be white; so that it was always true to say of anything that has happened that it would be so. But if it was always true to say that it was so, or would be so, it could not not be so, or not be going to be so. But if something cannot not happen it is impossible for it not to happen; and if it is impossible for something not to happen it is necessary for it to happen. Everything that will be, therefore, happens necessarily. So nothing will come about as chance has it or by chance; for if by chance, not of necessity.

18^b17. Nor, however, can we say that neither is true – that it neither will be nor will not be so. For, firstly, though the affirmation is false the negation is not true, and though the negation is false the affirmation, on this view, is not true. Moreover, if it is true to say that something is white and large,[1] both have to hold of it, and if true that they will hold tomorrow, they will have to hold tomorrow;[2] and if it neither will be nor will not be the case tomorrow, then there is no 'as chance has it'. Take a sea-battle: it would *have* neither to happen nor not to happen.

18^b26. These and others like them are the absurdities that follow if it is necessary, for every affirmation and negation either about universals spoken of universally or about particulars, that one of the opposites be true and the other false, and that nothing of what happens is as chance has it, but everything is and happens of necessity. So there would be no need to deliberate or to take trouble (thinking that if we do this, this will happen, but if we do not, it will not). For there is nothing to prevent someone's having said ten thousand years beforehand that this would be the case, and another's having denied it; so that whichever of the two was true to say then, will be the case of necessity. Nor, of course, does it make any difference whether any people made the contradictory statements or not. For clearly this is how the actual things are even if someone did not affirm it and another deny it. For it is not because of the affirming or denying that it will be or will not be the case, nor is it a question of ten thousand years beforehand rather than any other time. Hence, if in the whole of time the state of things was such that one or the other was true, it was necessary for this to happen, and for the state of things always to be such that everything that happens happens of necessity. For what anyone has truly said would be the case cannot not happen; and of what happens it was always true to say that it would be the case.

19^a7. But what if this is impossible? For we see that what will be has an origin both in deliberation and in action, and that, in general, in things that are not always actual there is the possibility of being and of not being; here both possibilities are open, both being and not being, and, consequently, both coming to be and not coming to be. Many things are obviously like this. For example, it is possible for this cloak to be cut up, and yet it will not be cut up but will wear out first. But equally, its not being cut up is also possible, for it would not be the case that it wore out first unless its not being cut up were possible. So it is the same with all other events that are spoken of in terms of this kind of possibility. Clearly, therefore, not everything is or happens of necessity: some things happen as chance has it, and of the affirmation and the negation neither is true rather than the other; with other things it is one rather than the other and as a rule, but still it is possible for the other to happen instead.

19^a23. What is, necessarily is, when it is; and what is not, necessarily is not, when it is not. But not everything that is, necessarily is; and not everything that is not, necessarily is not. For to say that everything that is, is of necessity, when it is, is not the same as saying unconditionally that it is of necessity. Similarly with what is not. And the same account holds for contradictories: everything necessarily is or is not, and will be or will not be; but one cannot divide and say that one or the other is necessary. I mean, for example: it is necessary for there to be or not to be a sea-battle tomorrow; but it is not necessary for a sea-battle to take place tomorrow, nor for one not to take place – though it is necessary for one to take place or not to take place. So, since statements are true according to how the actual things are, it is clear that wherever these are such as to allow of contraries as chance has it, the same necessarily holds for the contradictories also. This happens with things that are not always so or are not always not so. With these it is necessary for one or the other of the contradictories to be true or false – not, however, this one or that one, but as chance has it; or for one to be true *rather* than the other, yet not *already* true or false.

19a39. Clearly, then, it is not necessary that of every affirmation and opposite negation one should be true and the other false. For what holds for things that are does not hold for things that are not but may possibly be or not be; with these it is as we have said.

Notes

1 Read *λευκὸν καὶ μέγα.*

2 Read *εἰ δὲ ὑπάρξει . . . , ὑπάρξειν . . .*

2

On Fate and *On Divination*

Cicero

Marcus Tullius Cicero (106–43 BC) was an important Roman philosopher, statesman, and orator. The following two selections are taken from his works *On Fate* and *On Divination*, respectively. In the first, Cicero discusses Diodorus Cronus' argument for fatalism and criticizes Epicurus' attempt to avoid fatalism by positing that atoms occasionally take random "swerves." In the second, Cicero argues that if fatalism is true, then divination (the practice of foretelling the future) is a useless practice, for fate cannot be avoided, even if it is foreknown.

IX. But let us return to the question concerning *possibility*, so warmly contested by Diodorus, in which the question is examined, What is the signification of the term possible? Diodorus asserts that nothing is possible, except what either is true or is going to be so. This statement comes to this, that nothing happens which is not unavoidable; and that every thing which is possible either exists now, or will exist; and that things future, being certain, can no more be changed from true to false than things past; but that in things already past, the impossibility of change is very apparent; but that in things future, as they do not yet appear, we cannot equally discern that immutability. For instance, we may say with truth, of a person attacked by a mortal disease – This person will die of this malady; and if this same thing were to be said with equal truth of another person in whom the same violence of disease is not apparent, it will certainly happen as well as it will in the case of the other. Hence, we affirm that even in the case of future things, for instance, there cannot possibly be any change from true to false. This proposition, "Scipio will die," has such force, that although we announce a future event, it is still such an one that it cannot be converted into a false one, for it is said of a man, and all men are sure to die.

But if it were said, "Scipio will die in his bed during the night by the hand of his enemy," it might still be said with truth, as it might be about to happen; but it can only be known to have been about to happen from the fact that it has happened. Nor was it more true to say, Scipio

Cicero, from *Treatises of M. T. Cicero*, ed. and trans. C. D. Yonge (London and New York: Bell, 1892), pp. 271–2, 207–8.

will die, than to say, Scipio will die in such and such a manner; and his death itself was not less inevitable than the circumstances which attended it. Nor was it more possible to alter from true to false, the statement of, "Scipio has been slain," than this, "Scipio will be slain." Nor, since this is the case, do I see any reason why Epicurus has such a horror of Fate or Destiny, and why he flies for assistance to his atoms, and leads them out of the way, and why he endeavours to establish two inexplicable principles at the same time: first, that anything is produced without cause, from which it will follow that nothing can produce something; an opinion adopted neither by Epicurus himself nor by any other natural philosopher: secondly, that when two atoms move in empty space, one proceeds in a right line, and the other in an oblique.

For Epicurus, granting as he does that every proposition is either true or false, ought not to have hesitated to admit that everything eventually takes places in consequence of Fate. For there are no natural causes flowing from the necessity of things which determine the truth of this proposition. Carneades came down into the Academy. This fact was not without its causes; but we must distinguish between those antecedent causes which depend on chance, and those efficient causes which contain a physical energy and influence. Thus this proposition was always true and certain, "Epicurus will die at the age of seventy-two, in the Archonship of Pitharatus." And yet there were no fatal causes which determined this event: but since it took place we may be sure that it necessarily happened in the way it did. And those who affirm that things future are immutable, and that things true and certain cannot become false and uncertain, ought not to be regarded as the partisans of strict fatalism, since they are only explaining the meaning of words. But those philosophers who introduce a chain of eternal causes of absolute necessity, despoil the human soul of its free-will, and bind it hand and foot in the necessity of fate.

[...]

To return to the question at issue. If all things happen by fate, what is the use of divination?

VIII. For that which he who divines predicts, will truly come to pass; so that I do not know what character to affix to that circumstance of an eagle making our friend King Deiotaris renounce his journey; when, if he had not turned back, he would have slept in a chamber which fell down in the ensuing night, and have been crushed to death in the ruins. For if his death had been decreed by fate, he could not have avoided it by divination; and if it was not decreed by fate, he could not have experienced it.

What, then, is the use of divination, or what reason is there why I should be moved by lots, or entrails, or any kind of prediction? For if in the first Punic war it had been settled by fate, that one of the Roman fleets, commanded by the consuls Lucius Junius and Publius Clodius, should perish by a tempest, and that the other should be defeated by the Carthaginians, then even if the chickens had eaten ever so greedily, still the fleets must have been lost. But if the fleets would not have perished, if the auspices had been obeyed, then they were not destroyed by fate. But you say that everything is owing to fate; therefore there is no such thing as divination.

If fate had determined, that in the second Punic war the army of the Romans should be defeated near the lake Thrasimenus, then could this event have been avoided, even if Flaminius the consul had been obedient to those signs and those auspices which forbade him to engage in battle? Certainly it might. Either, then, the army did not perish by fate – for the fates cannot be changed, – or if it did perish by fate (as you are bound to assert), then, even if Flaminius had obeyed the auspices, he must still have been defeated.

Where, then, is the divination of the Stoics? which is of no use to us whatever to warn us to be more prudent, if all things happen by destiny. For do what we will, that which is fated to happen, must happen. On the other hand, whatever event may be averted is not fated. There is, therefore, no divination, since this appertains to things which are certain to happen; and nothing is certain to happen, which may by any means be frustrated.

3

God's Timeless Knowing

Boethius

Anicius Severinus Manlius Boethius (*c.* 475–526) was a Roman aristocrat and philosopher who, toward the end of his life, was given a high place in the court of the Ostrogoth king Theodoric. When his political enemies accused him of disloyalty and practicing magic he was put in prison and eventually executed. During this time in prison he produced *The Consolation of Philosophy*, written in the form of a dialogue between himself and the personification of philosophy. The reading begins with Boethius' statement of the problem of freedom and foreknowledge and his critiques of several attempted solutions. Then Philosophy responds, arguing that the solution to the problem lies in a proper understanding of divine eternity.

III

'Look,' I said, 'there is something even more difficult which I find perplexing and confusing.'

'Tell me,' she said, 'though I can guess what is troubling you.'

'Well, the two seem clean contrary and opposite, God's universal foreknowledge and freedom of the will. If God foresees all things and cannot be mistaken in any way, what Providence has foreseen as a future event must happen. So that if from eternity Providence foreknows not only men's actions but also their thoughts and desires, there will be no freedom of will. No action or desire will be able to exist other than that which God's infallible Providence has foreseen. For if they can be changed and made different from how they were foreseen, there will be no sure foreknowledge of the future, only an uncertain opinion; and this I do not think can be believed of God.

'I do not agree with the argument by which some people believe they can cut this Gordian knot. They say that it is not because Providence has foreseen something as a future event that it must happen, but the other way round, that because something is to happen it cannot be

Boethius, Book V: III, Book V: VI, from *The Consolation of Philosophy*, trans. Victor Watts, revised edition (London: Penguin, 1999), pp. 119–22, 132–7.

concealed from divine Providence. In this way the necessity is passed to the other side. It is not necessary, they say, that what is foreseen must happen, but it is necessary that what is destined to happen must be foreseen, as though the point at issue was which is the cause; does foreknowledge of the future cause the necessity of events, or necessity cause the foreknowledge? But what I am trying to show is that, whatever the order of the causes, the coming to pass of things foreknown is necessary even if the foreknowledge of future events does not seem to impose the necessity on them.

'If a man is sitting, it is necessary that the opinion which concludes that he is sitting is true; and on the other hand, if the opinion about the man is true, because he is sitting, it is necessary that he is sitting. There is necessity, therefore, in both statements; in the one that the man is sitting, and in the other that the opinion is true. But it is not because the opinion is true, that the man sits; rather, the opinion is true because it is preceded by the man's act of sitting. So although the cause of the truth proceeds from the one side, there is, nevertheless, a common necessity in either side. Clearly the same reasoning applies to Providence and future events. For even if it is the case that they are foreseen because they are going to happen and not that they happen because they are foreseen, it is nonetheless necessary that either future events be foreseen by God or that things foreseen happen as foreseen, and this alone is enough to remove freedom of the will.

'But how absurd it is to say that the occurrence of temporal events is the cause of eternal prescience! Yet the opinion that God foresees the future because it is destined to happen is the same as believing that events of a single occurrence are the cause of that supreme Providence.

'Moreover, just as when I know something is, it is necessary that it be, so when I know that something is to be, it is necessary that it shall be. It comes about, therefore, that the occurrence of the event foreknown cannot be avoided.

'Finally, if anyone thinks something is different from what it is, not only is it not knowledge, but it is a false opinion very far from the truth of knowledge. So, if something is destined to happen in such a way that its occurrence is not certain and necessary, who could foreknow that it is to happen? For just as knowledge is unalloyed by falseness, so that which is comprehended by knowledge cannot be other than as it is comprehended. Indeed, the reason why there is no deception in knowledge is because it is necessary for things to be exactly as knowledge understands them to be.

'The question is, therefore, how can God foreknow that these things will happen, if they are uncertain? If He thinks that they will inevitably happen while the possibility of their non-occurrence exists, He is deceived, and this is something wicked both to think and to say. But if His knowledge that they will happen as they do is of such a kind that He knows they may as equally not happen as happen, what sort of knowledge is this, which comprehends nothing sure or stable? How does it differ from that ridiculous prophecy of Tiresias in Horace's *Satires*[1]

> Whatever I say either will be or won't?

And how is divine Providence superior to opinion if like men it considers those things uncertain whose occurrence is uncertain? If there can be no uncertainty at that most sure fount of all things, the coming to pass of those things which God firmly foreknows as future events is certain. Therefore, human thoughts and actions have no freedom, because the divine mind in foreseeing all things without being led astray by falseness binds human thoughts and actions to a single manner of occurrence.

'Once this has been admitted, the extent of the disruption of human affairs is obvious. In vain is reward offered to the good and punishment to the bad, because they have not been deserved by any free and willed movement of the mind. That which is now judged most equitable, the punishment of the wicked and the reward of the good, will be seen to be the most unjust of all; for men are driven to good or evil not by their own will but by the fixed necessity of what is to be. Neither vice nor virtue will have had any existence; but all merit will have been mixed up and undifferentiated. Nothing more wicked can be conceived than this, for as the whole order of things is derived from Providence and there is no room for human thoughts, it follows that our wickedness, too, is derived from the Author of all good.

'It is pointless, therefore, to hope for anything or pray to escape anything. What can a man hope for, or pray to escape, when an inflexible bond binds all that can be wished for?

'And so the one and only means of communication between man and God is removed, that is hope and prayer – if indeed we do obtain for the price of due humility the inestimable return of divine grace. And this is the only way by which it seems men can talk with God and join themselves to that inaccessible light before they obtain it, by means of supplication. And if admitting the necessity of future events means believing that hope and prayer have no power, what way will there be left by which we can be joined and united to that supreme Lord of the world? Cut off and separated from its source, the human race, as you were singing just now, will be destined to grow weak and exhausted.'

[. . .]

VI

'Since, therefore, as we have just shown, every object of knowledge is known not as a result of its own nature, but of the nature of those who comprehend it, let us now examine, as far as we may, the nature of the divine substance, so that we may also learn what is its mode of knowledge.

'It is the common judgement, then, of all creatures that live by reason that God is eternal. So let us consider the nature of eternity, for this will make clear to us both the nature of God and his manner of knowing.[2] Eternity, then, is the complete, simultaneous and perfect possession of everlasting life; this will be clear from a comparison with creatures that exist in time. Whatever lives in time exists in the present and progresses from the past to the future, and there is nothing set in time which can embrace simultaneously the whole extent of its life: it is in the position of not yet possessing tomorrow when it has already lost yesterday. In this life of today you do not live more fully than in that fleeting and transitory moment. Whatever, therefore, suffers the condition of being in time, even though it never had any beginning, never has any ending and its life extends into the infinity of time, as Aristotle thought was the case of the world, it is still not such that it may properly be considered eternal.

'Its life may be infinitely long, but it does not embrace and comprehend its whole extent simultaneously. It still lacks the future, while already having lost the past. So that that which embraces and possesses simultaneously the whole fullness of everlasting life, which lacks nothing of the future and has lost nothing of the past, that is what may properly be said to be eternal. Of necessity it will always be present to itself, controlling itself, and have present the infinity of fleeting time.

'Those philosophers are wrong, therefore, who when told that Plato believed the world had had no beginning in time and would have no end, maintain that the created world is co-eternal with the Creator. For it is one thing to progress like the world in Plato's theory through everlasting life, and another thing to have embraced the whole of everlasting life in one simultaneous present. This is clearly a property of the mind of God. God ought not to be considered as older than the created world in extent of time, but rather in the property of the immediacy of His nature. The infinite changing of things in time is an attempt to imitate this state of the presence of unchanging life, but since it cannot portray or equal that state it falls from sameness into change, from the immediacy of presence into the infinite extent of past and future. It cannot possess simultaneously the whole fullness of its life, but by the very fact that it is impossible for its existence ever to come to an end, it does seem in some measure to emulate that which it cannot fulfil or express. It does this by attaching itself to some sort of presence in this small and fleeting moment, and since this presence bears a certain resemblance to that abiding present, it confers on whatever possesses it the appearance of being that which it imitates.

'But since it could not remain, it seized upon the infinite journey through time, and in this way it became possible for it to continue by progression forward that life whose fullness it could not embrace by remaining still. And so, if we want to give things their proper names, let us follow Plato and say that God is eternal, the world perpetual.

'Since, therefore, all judgement comprehends those things that are subject to it according to its own nature, and since the state of God is ever that of eternal presence, His knowledge, too, transcends all temporal change and abides in the immediacy of His presence. It embraces all the infinite recesses of past and future and views them in the immediacy of its knowing as though they are happening in the present. If you wish to consider, then, the foreknowledge or prevision by which He discovers all things, it will be more correct to think of it not as a kind of foreknowledge of the future, but as the knowledge of a never ending presence. So that it is better called providence or "looking forth" than prevision or "seeing beforehand". For it is far removed from matters below and looks forth at all things as though from a lofty peak above them.

'Why, then, do you insist that all that is scanned by the sight of God becomes necessary? Men see things but this certainly doesn't make them necessary. And your seeing them doesn't impose any necessity on the things you see present, does it?'

'No.'

'And if human and divine present may be compared, just as you see certain things in this your present time, so God sees all things in His eternal present. So that this divine foreknowledge does not change the nature and property of things; it simply sees things present to it exactly as they will happen at some time as future events. It makes no confused judgements of things, but with one glance of its mind distinguishes all that is to come to pass whether it is necessitated or not. Similarly you, when you see at the same time a man walking on the earth and the sun rising in the sky, although the two sights coincide yet you distinguish between them and judge the one to be willed and the other necessitated. In the same way the divine gaze looks down on all things without disturbing their nature; to Him they are present things, but under the condition of time they are future things. And so it comes about that when God knows that something is going to occur and knows that no necessity to be is imposed upon it, it is not opinion, but rather knowledge founded upon truth.

'If you say at this point that what God sees as a future event cannot but happen, and what cannot but happen, happens of necessity, and if you bind me to this word necessity, I shall have to admit that it is a matter of the firmest truth, but one which scarcely anyone except a student of divinity has been able to fathom. I shall answer that the same future event is necessary when considered with reference to divine foreknowledge, and yet seems to be completely free and unrestricted when considered in itself. For there are two kinds of necessity;[3] one simple, as for example the fact that it is necessary that all men are mortal; and one conditional, as for example, if you know someone is walking, it is necessary that he is walking. For that which a man knows cannot be other than as it is known; but this conditional necessity does not imply simple necessity, because it does not exist in virtue of its own nature, but in virtue of a condition which is added. No necessity forces the man to walk who is making his way of his own free will, although it is necessary that he walks when he takes a step.

'In the same way, if Providence sees something as present, it is necessary for it to happen, even though it has no necessity in its own nature. God sees those future events which happen of free will as present events; so that these things when considered with reference to God's sight of them do happen necessarily as a result of the condition of divine knowledge; but when considered in themselves they do not lose the absolute freedom of their nature. All things, therefore, whose future occurrence is known to God do without doubt happen, but some of them are the result of free will. In spite of the fact that they do happen, their existence does not deprive them of their true nature, in virtue of which the possibility of their non-occurrence existed before they happened.

'What does it matter, then, if they are not necessary, when because of the condition of divine foreknowledge it will turn out exactly as if they were necessary? The answer is this. It is impossible for the two events I mentioned just now – the rising of the sun and the man walking – not to be happening when they do happen; and yet it was necessary for one of them to happen before it did happen, but not so for the other. And so, those things which are present to God will without doubt happen; but some of them result from the necessity of things, and some of them from the power of those who do them. We are not wrong, therefore, to say that if these things are considered with reference to divine foreknowledge, they are necessary, but if they are considered by themselves, they are free of the bonds of necessity; just as everything that the senses perceive is universal if considered with reference to the reason, but individual if considered in itself.

'But, you will reply, if it lies in my power to change a proposed course of action, I will be able to evade Providence, for I will perhaps have altered things which Providence foreknows. My answer will be that you can alter your plan, but that since this is possible, and since whether you do so or in what way you change it is visible to Providence the ever present and true, you cannot escape divine foreknowledge, just as you cannot escape the sight of an eye that is present to watch, though of your own free will you may turn to a variety of actions.

'Well, you will ask, isn't divine knowledge changed as a result of my rearrangement, so that as I change my wishes it, too, seems to change its knowledge? The answer is no. Each future thing is anticipated by the gaze of God which bends it back and recalls it to the presence of its own manner of knowledge; it does not change, as you think, with alternate knowledge of now this and now that, but with one glance anticipates and embraces your changes in its constancy. God receives this present mode of knowledge and vision of all things not from the issue of future things but from His own immediacy. So that the difficulty you put forward a short time ago,[4] that it was unfitting if our future is said to provide a cause of God's knowledge, is solved. The power of this knowledge which embraces all things in present understanding has itself established the mode of being for all things and owes nothing to anything secondary to itself. And since this is so, man's freedom of will remains inviolate and the law does not impose reward and punishment unfairly, because the will is free from all necessity. God has foreknowledge and rests a spectator from on high of all things; and as the ever present eternity of His vision dispenses reward to the good and punishment to the bad, it adapts itself to the future quality of our actions. Hope is not placed in God in vain and prayers are not made in vain, for if they are the right kind they cannot but be efficacious. Avoid vice, therefore, and cultivate virtue; lift up your mind to the right kind of hope, and put forth humble prayers on high. A great necessity is laid upon you, if you will be honest with yourself, a great necessity to be good, since you live in the sight of a judge who sees all things.'[5]

Notes

1 II, 5, 59.

2 For much of the following section Boethius follows his Neoplatonist sources: but his exultant definition (cf. Helen Waddell, *The Wandering Scholars*, Pelican Books, 1954, p. 27) of eternity is remarkably close to the view of St Augustine. For him the universe was not created in time, but with time. In virtue of His eternity, God transcends time. Created things came into existence only in time. God knew them before their creation and it is in virtue of this eternal act of knowledge that He can foresee and know beforehand even the free acts of men. [. . .]

3 For his distinction between simple and conditional or hypothetical necessity, Boethius relies ultimately on Aristotle. The distinction is parallel to that already used by Boethius and likewise derived from Aristotle – along with the example of the buried gold – between absolute and incidental causes in the explanation of chance in Chapter 1 of book V. For a full and illuminating analysis of the way in which Boethius turns at the end of his work from the Platonic to the Aristotelian tradition for his final solution of the problem of necessity and free will, see H. R. Patch, *Necessity in Boethius and the Neoplatonists*, in *Speculum*, X, 1935, pp. 393–404.

4 V, chapter 3.

5 Note the ironic artistry with which, just having dismissed the arguments for necessity, Boethius reintroduces the very word in his statement of the final moral imperative.

4

Ockham on God's Foreknowledge, and Future Contingents

Marilyn Adams

One of the great medieval English thinkers to work on the problem of freedom and foreknowledge was William of Ockham (*c.* 1287–1347), famous for the methodological principle known as "Ockham's Razor" (*Do not multiply entities beyond necessity*). Ockham argues that some propositions that appear to be about the past are partially about the future, and thus do not have necessity *per accidens* (the necessity of the past). God's past beliefs about the future are in this category. In the following essay, Oxford professor Marilyn McCord Adams (b. 1943) gives a clear statement of the problem of freedom and foreknowledge and then summarizes and explains Ockham's attempted solution.

Analysis of the *Treatise*

Ockham's main business in this *Treatise* is to resolve problems for Christian theology, arising from its acceptance of the philosophical claim that some things are both future and contingent.[1] Briefly, an event, action, or state of affairs is contingent, if and only if it is both possible for it to be and possible for it not to be.[2] Ockham takes it to be part of Christian doctrine (i) that 'Peter will be saved' and the like are future contingent propositions, and (ii) that God has infallible foreknowledge of future contingents. But Aristotle's fatalistic arguments in *De interpretatione*, Chapter 9, seem to imply that (i) and (ii) are incompatible.[3] Ockham responds by developing a view regarding truth and future contingents which he uses to deal with other problems about predestination and God's foreknowledge as well.

Marilyn Adams, "Analysis of The Treatise". Introduction to *William of Ockham, Predestination, God's Foreknowledge, and Future Contingents* 2e, trans. Marilyn McCord Adams and Norman Kretzmann (Indianapolis, IN: Hackett, 1983), pp. 2–12, 16–20.

[. . .]

I. Fatalism, God's foreknowledge, and predestination

Briefly, fatalism is the view that whatever happens must happen of necessity and whatever does not happen of necessity does not happen at all. According to the fatalist, it is never both possible that something will happen and possible that it will not happen. That is, the fatalist denies that any events, actions, or states of affairs are contingent. It is generally taken to be an obvious consequence of fatalism that nothing a man does is ever really up to him. What he has done he had to do; and what he will do he must do.[4]

Many philosophers, including Aristotle, have thought that this highly implausible conclusion could be deduced from apparently impeccable principles of logic. In his *De interpretatione*, Chapter 9, Aristotle argues for this conclusion along the following line. Every singular proposition,[5] whether about the past or about the future, is either true or false. (The generalized form of this principle is sometimes called "the principle of bivalence" because it recognizes only two truth-values, excluding for propositions any middle ground between being true and being false. It is sometimes described as a "law of thought" because it has been commonly taken to be not only unexceptionable but also one of the principles on which all reasoning is founded.) Consider some singular proposition about the future – 'The Empire State Building will be colored white on January 1, 2068'. Either that proposition is true or it is false. But, so the reasoning goes, if it is true now that the Empire State Building will be colored white at that time, then nothing that can occur between now and January 1, 2068, can prevent it from being colored white then. In fact, if it is true now that the Empire State Building will be colored white on January 1, 2068, then it always was true. Consequently, it never was possible for anything or anyone to prevent the Empire State Building from being colored white at that time. On the other hand, if that proposition is now and always has been false, then it never was possible for anything or anyone to bring it about that the building will be colored white then. Thus, if it is now and always has been true that the Empire State Building will be colored white at that time, then the Empire Building will *of necessity* be colored white at that time; and if it is now and always has been false that the building will be colored white at that time, then it is *impossible* that the Empire State Building will be colored white on January 1, 2068. No matter how much anyone deliberates about the color of the building, no matter what steps are taken to give it that color then or to prevent it from having that color, it will make no difference. What will be will be of necessity. Obviously, if these observations hold regarding our example, they hold regarding any and every singular proposition about the future. But every event, action, or state of affairs either is now or was at some time future. The general conclusion, then, is that no events, actions, or states of affairs are contingent.

The crux of this line of reasoning is the inference from the hypothesis that a singular proposition of the form '*x* will be *A* at *tn*' is true (or is false) at every time prior to *tn* to the conclusion that at *tn x* will be *A* (or will not be *A*) necessarily. Many philosophers have challenged this step in the argument. In his commentary on *De interpretatione*, Chapter 9, Ockham understands the inference as depending on special notions of modality, truth, and falsity.[6]

The modalities at issue are not logical, but real: *p* is contingent in the relevant sense, if and only if there is a potency in things (*in rebus*) for *p* and a potency in things for not-*p*; necessary, if and only if there is no potency in things for not-*p*; and impossible, where there is no potency in things for *p*. From one side, such potencies are measured causally: if something is causally sufficient for *p*, there is no potency in things for not-*p* and *p* is necessary; but where nothing is causally sufficient for *p* and nothing for not-*p*, there is a potency for each (*potentia ad utrumlibet*) in things and *p* is contingent. From another side, contingency may be identified with ontological indeterminateness, by appeal to the principle that

(T1) where there is a potency for opposites, the potency for *p* (not-*p*) does not survive the reduction of the potency for not-*p* (*p*) to act.

If in the past there was a potency for opposites – say a potency for Peter's denying Christ and a potency for Peter's not denying Christ – the one has now been actualized to the exclusion of the other – Peter's denial has cancelled whatever potency there was in things for his not denying Christ on that occasion. Thus, Ockham will say that merely past events, actions, or states or affairs, such as Peter's denial, are necessary, not in the sense that their opposites – e.g., Peter's never having denied Christ – are logically impossible, but in the sense that there is no longer any potency in things for their being otherwise. To mark the distinction, some logicians referred to this as "necessity *per accidens*."[7] Where the double potency of contingency remains, neither *p* nor not-*p* has been determinately actualized yet.

Thus, Ockham follows standard medieval interpretation when he ascribes to Aristotle

(T2) *x*'s being *A* at *tm* is determinate at *tn*, if and only if there is no potency in things at *tn* for *x*'s not being (having been, being going to be) *A* at *tm*.

along with the view that propositions are true or false according as they correspond or fail to correspond with reality. Because, by (T2), everything past or present is determinate, propositions solely about the past or present have determinate truth-value. So do propositions about future things necessitated by past or present things. But since singular future contingent propositions represent a double potentiality or "gap" in actuality that has yet to be filled in, there must be a corresponding "gap" in truth-values. That is,

(T3) '*x* is (was, will be) *A* at *tm*' is determinately true at *tn*, if and only if there is no potency in things at *tn* for *x*'s not being (having been, being going to be) *A* at *tm*,

and

(T4) '*x* is (was, will be) A at *tm*' is determinately false at *tn*, if and only if there is no potency in things at *tn* for *x*'s being (having been, being going to be) *A* at *tm*.

Just as, by (T2), things (events, actions, states of affairs) are determinate (or indeterminate) only at a given time, so singular propositions are determinately true or determinately false (if at all), not absolutely, but at a given time. Propositions about future contingents will not, so long as they are future, satisfy either (T3) or (T4) and so will be neither determinately true nor determinately false. This does not mean, Ockham cautions, that the disjunction of a singular future contingent proposition and its denial lacks truth value. Quite the contrary, it is always true, because future contingents will be rendered determinate one way or the other at the future time in question.

Returning to Aristotle's fatalistic arguments, Ockham represents the key inference of the first in these words: "what happens fortuitously is no more determined to one part than to the other – i.e., no more determined to being than to not being. Therefore, if it is determined that this will be, or that it will not be, it happens not fortuitously but of necessity." In view of the allegedly Aristotelian truth-conditions in (T3) and (T4), however, if '*x* will be *A*' is determinately true now (or determinately false now), it is determinate now that *x* will be *A* (or determinate now that *x* will not be *A*). Therefore, if '*x* will be *A*' is determinately true now (or determinately false now), there is now no potency in things for *x* not to be going to be *A* (for *x* being going to be *A*) and *x* will of necessity come to be *A* (or not come to be *A*). And in general, if every singular proposition about the future is either determinately true or determinately false, then nothing occurs (or fails to occur) contingently but all things occur (or fail to occur) of necessity.

Ockham exposes the nerve of Aristotle's second argument in this passage: "This argument is based on the proposition that a singular proposition true about the past is necessary. Therefore if 'this is white' is true now, '"this will be white" was true' is necessary. Consequently, it is necessary that it happen, and it cannot come about otherwise."[8] If '"*x* will be white" was true' is necessary about the past, then something actual in the past necessitated *x*'s being white now, so that there was no potency in the way things were then for *x*'s not being white now. It follows that *x* did not come to be white contingently but necessarily. Thus, if every singular proposition about the future is determinately true or determinately false, everything that happens happens necessarily.

Aristotle draws the further consequence that the efficacy of deliberation would be destroyed. For, on the medieval reading, he held that

(T5) future free actions are among the future contingents.

Ockham goes so far as to say that "... nothing of which the Philosopher speaks here is fortuitously contingent except what is in the power of someone acting freely or depends on such an agent ..."[9] But if every singular proposition were either determinately true or determinately false, "there would be no need to deliberate or to take trouble, since from the fact that it is determined [it follows that] it will occur as it was determined from the outset, whether or not we deliberate."[10] Aristotle's reasoning is remarkably fallacious: if everything came to pass of necessity, our deliberations would come to pass just as necessarily as our actions. Nevertheless, (T3)–(T5) do combine with the original hypothesis – that every singular proposition is either determinately true or determinately false – to yield Aristotle's conclusion. On the medieval interpretation, he takes it to be a *reductio ad absurdum* of the original hypothesis; and, refusing to give up his belief in human freedom, he admits exceptions to the principle of bivalence where singular future contingent propositions are concerned.

As philosophers and logicians, Ockham and other medievals were fascinated with the idea that such a substantive metaphysical position as fatalism might follow from impeccable principles of logic together with plausible assumptions about truth-conditions. But their interest in Aristotle's fatalistic arguments was intensified when they saw how additional theological problems could be derived from them. Two sets of arguments advanced by Ockham's opponents in the *Treatise* do just that.

(a) Arguments (1), (2), and (4) in Question II, Article I of the *Treatise* make use of Aristotle's arguments to challenge

(T6) God has determinate knowledge of future contingents.

Arguments (1) and (4) are substantially alike except that (1) omits the first premiss found in (4); both contend that if there are any future contingents (if anything is indeterminate), then God has no determinate knowledge of them. Replying to argument (1), Ockham acknowledges its Aristotelian underpinnings by citing his Assumption 5, where he has explained in detail how Aristotle's position yields a denial of (T6). The reasoning developed there mirrors the account found in his commentary on Aristotle's *De interpretatione*, Chapter 9, where he explicitly concludes that Aristotle "would say that God does not know one part of such a contradiction more than the other; neither is known by God."[11]

Argument (2) goes the other way around: if God has determinate knowledge of one or the other part of a contradiction involving future contingents, then one or the other part is determinately true – i.e., the doctrine of God's universal foreknowledge entails the principle of bivalence as applied to all singular propositions. But as shown above, it follows from the principle of bivalence together with the Aristotelian truth conditions (T3) and (T4) that deliberation is in vain.

(b) The objector's argument in Question 1, Objection 2 of the *Treatise* begins with an appeal to the principle of the necessity of the past, which is then applied to the proposition 'Peter is predestinate.' The objector and Ockham agree that at least part of what that proposition means is that Peter will be granted supreme blessedness on the day of judgment. Thus, even though 'Peter is predestinate' is a present-tense proposition, consideration of it involves one in the Aristotelian problems regarding singular propositions about the future. The argument is to the effect that if 'Peter is predestinate' is true now, there will never again be any potency in the way things are for Peter's not being granted supreme blessedness in the future. But in that case Peter will be granted supreme blessedness necessarily, and his receiving supreme blessedness or eternal punishment in no way depends on his deliberation hereafter or, indeed, on any subsequent event, created or divine – which is contrary to the faith. The objector assumes in accordance with the faith that we must say that the truth or falsity of some propositions – and in particular of propositions about one's eternal destiny – depends in part on human deliberation and choice. And he intends to show that since it is only with respect to indeterminate things that deliberation and choice can conceivably make a difference, it must be the case that some propositions – such as 'Peter is predestinate' – are about indeterminate things and hence neither determinately true nor determinately false.

The strategy of the objection parallels that of Aristotle's *reductio* arguments. It begins with a specific application of the principle of bivalence to singular propositions about the future and from that principle, together with the Aristotelian truth conditions (T3) and (T4), deduces the conclusion (absurd from a fourteenth-century Christian point of view) that a man's receiving supreme blessedness or eternal punishment has nothing to do with his deliberation or choice. The rejection of that absurd conclusion leads the objector to an Aristotelian denial of the principle of bivalence as applied to singular propositions in the specific case of singular future contingent propositions.

Thus, all three of these objectors' arguments (the first and third considered under (a) and the second considered under (b) above) may be seen to depend more or less explicitly on Ockham's account of Aristotle's stipulations regarding determinate truth and determinate falsity.

The substance of Ockham's replies to these objections is dictated by the need to preserve the doctrine of God's universal foreknowledge in the face of the contention that (T5) future free actions are future contingents. Conceding the validity of these arguments, Ockham seems to regard them as a *reductio ad absurdum* of the Aristotelian truth-conditions on which they rest. He apparently reasons that if the Aristotelian conditions in (T2)–(T4) for being determinate, determinately true, and determinately false, respectively, are accepted, conclusions incompatible with truth and the faith must be granted; hence (T2)–(T4) must be replaced with others that permit an unproblematic application of the principle of bivalence to every singular future contingent proposition.

Ockham's alternatives can be reconstructed from his many remarks (in the *Treatise* and elsewhere) on the way in which singular future contingent propositions are determinately true and determinately known by God. For (T2), he substitutes

(T7) *x*'s being *A* at *tm* is determinate at *tn*, if and only if *at some time or other* there is (was, will be) no potency in things for *x*'s not being (having been, being going to be) *A* at *tm*,

which allows a thing future relative to *tn* to be determinate at *tn*, even if nothing real or actual in the past or present relative to *tn* necessitates its future existence, provided that something that exists *at some time or other* settles its future existence. By contrast with (T2), (T7) makes being determinate only trivially time-relative, because the fact that something – e.g., Peter's denial of Christ – is actual at some time or other suffices – on (T7) – to make it determinate at any and every time.

Assenting to the fundamental thesis of Aristotelian truth-theory – viz., that propositions are determinately true or determinately false as they correspond or fail to correspond with what is determinately actual – Ockham likewise replaces (T3) and (T4) with

(T8) '*x* is (was, will be) *A* at *tm*' is determinately true at *tn*, if and only if at some time or other there is (was, will be) no potency in things for *x*'s not being (having been, being going to be) *A* at *tm*

and

(T9) '*x* is (was, will be) *A* at *tm*' is determinately false at *tn*, if and only if at some time or other there is (was, will be) no potency in things for *x*'s being (having been, being going to be) *A* at *tm*,

which close the truth-value gaps where future contingents are concerned and restore the principle of bivalence. On Ockham's view, every singular future contingent proposition is either determinately true or determinately false, and the doctrine of God's universal foreknowledge is preserved.

Ockham insists that his solution does not compromise the efficacy of human deliberation and choice either. According to (T3) and (T4), the determinate truth (falsity) of a proposition at a time is settled by something real or actual in the past or present relative to that time and so is something past relative to any later time. Hence, if '*p* is true' is true (false) now, '*p* was true' will be necessary (impossible) at any later time; as Ockham's Aristotelian opponents stipulate,

> (T10) Every proposition true (false) about the present relative to one time has corresponding to it a necessary (impossible) proposition about the past relative to a later time.

By contrast, (T8) and (T9) allow that where future contingents are concerned the past or present truth of a proposition may be something yet to be settled by what will become actual in the future. In such cases, Ockham says that the proposition is true in such a way that it can be false and can never have been true, since nothing real or actual excludes the potency for the opposite. Thus, he maintains that (T10) applies only where "propositions are about the present as regards both their wording and their subject matter (*secundum vocem et secundum rem*)" and not otherwise.[12] Apparently, a proposition of whatever tense is about the future as regards its subject matter (*secumdum rem*), if it is exponible by such in the way in which 'God foreknew from eternity "Peter will deny Christ" ' is. And Ockham concludes that "just as this or that future contingent contingently will be, so God knows that it contingently will be, for if He knows it, He can *not* know that it will be."[13] And if neither the past truth nor God's past foreknowledge of future contingents falls under the necessity of the past, the Aristotelian argument that His determinate knowledge of them would destroy the efficacy of human deliberation and choice, fails.

Thus, just as the objectors' arguments in Question I, Objection 2, and in (1), (2), and (4) of Question II, Article I, are based on the Aristotelian truth-theory (in (T3) and (T4)), so Ockham's replies are grounded on his own alternative theory (in (T8) and (T9)). Several of the more important features of Ockham's truth-theory are brought out in Assumptions 2, 3, and 4 of the *Treatise*.

[...]

III. Is God's knowledge of future contingents certain and infallible?

In Assumption 6, Ockham affirms,

> It must be held beyond question that God knows *with certainty* all future contingents – i.e., He knows with certainty which part of the contradiction is true and which false,

but immediately acknowledges,

> It is difficult, however, to see *how* He knows this [with certainty], since one part [of the contradiction] is no more determined to truth than the other.

The question is equally about divine psychology and the logical or metaphysical possibility of such knowledge. Both prove difficult for Ockham.

His predecessor, Duns Scotus, had not found them so. For he had held that God eternally has determinate knowledge of one part of a contradiction regarding future contingents, because He eternally wills one part to be true and the other to be false and His willing eternally settles it that one part rather than the other is determinately true.

Scotus's explanation may seem plausible at first. On the one hand, because God is omnipotent, 'God wills that Socrates will sit down at *tm*' entails 'Socrates will sit down at *tm*'. Thus, it seems that God's willing one part of a contradiction to be true would suffice for His knowing that part to be true. On the other hand, because everything owes its existence and duration to God's creating and conserving it, nothing can come to be or continue to be unless God wills that it comes to be or continues to be. That is, 'Socrates will sit down at *tm*' entails 'God wills that Socrates will sit down at *tm*.' Thus, it might seem that for any pair of contradictories whatever, God wills one part rather than the other to be true. Therefore, God's willing one part rather than the other to be true would suffice to insure the certainty of God's determinate foreknowledge of one part of a contradiction in every case.

Scotus assumes that where propositions about the creation are concerned, God has a potency for willing the truth of *p* and a potency for willing the truth of not-*p* and that His eternally willing the truth of *p* eternally actualizes the former potency to the exclusion of the latter. Relying on his own understanding of the scope of the antecedent and consequent disposing will of God, Ockham contends that Scotus's account cannot "preserve the certainty of God's knowledge in respect of future things that depend absolutely on a created will."[14]

To begin with, Ockham holds, it is the antecedent disposing will of God that is settled by what is actual from eternity. But where future things that depend absolutely on a created will are concerned, God's antecedent disposing will regarding them cannot insure the infallibility of His determinate cognition of them from eternity:

> For I ask whether or not the determination of a created will necessarily follows the determination of the divine will. If it does, then the will necessarily acts [as it does], just as fire does, and so merit and demerit are done away with. If it does not, then the determination of a created will is required for knowing determinately one or the other part of a contradiction regarding those [future things that depend absolutely on a created will]. For the determination of the created will does not suffice, because a created will can oppose the determination [of the uncreated will]. Therefore, since the determination of the [created] will was not from eternity, God did not receive certain cognition of the things that remained [for a created will to determine].[15]

For what the antecedent will eternally determines regarding acts of a created will is only (a) that every person should have certain natural properties – e.g., being a rational animal – and (b) that every person should be provided with precepts and counsels to guide him in his actions. Ockham assumes that the latter do not suffice to make the created will go one way rather than another. Consequently, if God's antecedent will determined a created will to act in a certain manner, this would be because (a) the natural properties thereby endowed determined the will so to choose, just as the nature of fire (or heat) determines fire to heat nearby combustible objects. In that case, the created will would be a natural cause that acted by natural necessity and hence not an appropriate subject of merit or demerit. And this is contrary to the doctrine that Ockham shares with Scotus – viz., that the will is a self-determining power for opposites.

It is only where the *consequent* disposing will of God is at issue that such propositions as 'God wills that Peter will deny Christ at *tm*' and 'Peter will deny Christ at *tm*' are equivalent. But that fact cannot help explain the eternal certainty of God's knowledge regarding future things that depend absolutely on a created will. For it follows from this equivalence that the consequent will of God regarding the truth of a future contingent proposition is just as contingent as is the truth of the proposition. Thus, even if 'God wills that Peter will deny Christ at *tm*' and 'Peter will deny Christ at *tm*' were – by (T8) and (T9) – determinately true from eternity, the exclusion of the potency in things for their determinate falsity had to await Peter's actual choice at *tm*. Ockham makes this very point regarding the (consequent) will of God in the second part of his critique of Scotus.

> Secondly, when something is determined contingently, so that it is still possible that it is not determined and it is possible that it was never determined, then one cannot have certain and infallible cognition based on such a determination. But the determination of the divine will in respect of future contingents is such a determination, both according to him [Scotus] and in truth. Therefore God cannot have certain cognition of future contingents based on such a determination.
>
> [The argument] is supported as follows. All such propositions as 'God from eternity willed this part of the contradiction to be true' and 'God from eternity determined this' are contingent, as is clear from Assumption 2. Consequently they can be true and [they can be] false. Therefore one will have no certain cognition based on such a determination.[16]

If the consequent disposing will of God regarding the truth of a future contingent proposition is just as contingent as is the truth of the proposition, then God's cognition of (or belief about) what His consequent will regarding such a proposition is, is no more and no less certainly correct than is His belief that the proposition is true.

According to Ockham, then, it is not by knowing something eternally actual that God eternally has certain and infallible knowledge of one part of a contradiction regarding future contingents. For he denies that anything that is eternally actual excludes the possibility of falsity (truth) for true (false) future contingent propositions. What alternative explanation can Ockham give of how God knows such propositions with certainty? He admits that 'it is impossible to express clearly the way in which God knows future contingents . . .' Nevertheless, foregoing silence, he suggests that

> . . . the following way [of knowing future contingents] can be ascribed [to God]. Just as the [human] intellect on the basis of one and the same [intuitive] cognition of certain non-complexes can have evident cognition of contradictory contingent propositions such as '*A* exists' and '*A* does not exist', in the same way it can be granted that the divine essence is an intuitive cognition that is so perfect, so clear, that it is an evident cognition of all things past and future, so that it knows which part of a contradiction [involving such things] is true and which part false.[17]

Ockham recalls his own doctrine that in human knowledge, an intuitive cognition of Socrates is a cognition by virtue of which one has evident knowledge that Socrates exists when he exists, or evident knowledge that Socrates does not exist if he does not exist. An evident cognition is a cognition of a true proposition, a sufficient mediate or immediate cognition of which is an apprehension of its terms. If I have an intuitive cognition of Socrates, whether I am caused to judge that Socrates exists or that he does not exist depends on whether Socrates exists, is present, and acts together with the intuitive cognition to cause the former judgment in me. Since all possible particular creatures are objects of God's thought, Ockham is proposing to regard the divine act of understanding as an intuitive cognition of all of them and hence as an act by virtue of which God can have evident knowledge that they exist when they exist and that they do not exist when they do not exist. Unfortunately, the analogy falters at crucial points. Given the medieval doctrine of divine impassibility, no object ever causes anything in God. Further, our perfect intuitive cognitions cause evident judgments about the present only, whereas the puzzle is how God has certain and determinate knowledge regarding future contingents. Ockham does allow that we have imperfect intuitive cognitions which cause evident judgments about the past and even the future (*Reportatio* II, q.16; q.20 E). But the latter shed no light on how God knows future contingents with certainty, since Ockham offers no account of how we know on the basis of such premonitory cognitions either.

If Ockham is forced to plead ignorance of divine psychology, he must also face the charge that divine certainty and infallibility regarding future contingents is not even logically or metaphysically possible. For God could not have known from eternity that Peter would deny Christ at *tm* unless He judged from eternity that Peter would deny Christ at *tm*. Assuming that God's judgments are analogous to ours, for Him to judge that Peter would deny Christ at *tm* is for His act of understanding to be determinately directed in a certain way towards the proposition 'Peter will deny Christ at *tm*' rather than the proposition 'It is not the case that Peter will deny Christ at *tm*'. If so, given Ockham's position that temporal predicates apply non-metaphorically to God, the proposition 'God judged from eternity that Peter would deny Christ at *tm*' was always a necessary proposition about the past. By contrast, 'Peter will deny Christ at *tm*' was a contingent proposition about the future for all times prior to *tm*, so that there was, for all that time, a possibility in things that God's eternal judgment should turn out to be false. Yet, if God were infallible regarding such propositions, it would be logically impossible for Him to be mistaken.

Ockham's response would be to insist on divine infallibility and compromise the analogy between divine and human judgment. For if God's judgments are all infallible, 'God judges that *p* is true' is expounded in part by '*p* is true', just as much as 'God knows that *p* is true' is. Where *p* is a future contingent proposition, 'God judges (judged) that *p* is true' will also be a future contingent proposition, so far as its subject matter is concerned (*secundum rem*). But Ockham can sustain the latter claim only by denying that (T1) applies to divine judgments. Further, he would have to maintain the bizarre thesis that nothing real about the divine act of judgment, considered as it really is in itself, determines whether it is directed towards *p* or towards not-p instead. The latter move had already been made by Robert Grosseteste, but it leaves the intentionality of divine judgment utterly mysterious.

Notes

1 For information on treatises of this sort before Ockham, see J. Groblicki, *De scientia Dei futurorum contingentium secundum S. Thomam eiusque primos sequaces*. Cracow: University Press, 1938; and J. Isaac, *Le Peri Hermeneias en Occident de Boèce á Saint Thomas*, Paris: J. Vrin, 1953.

2 The senses of 'necessary', 'possible', 'contingent', and 'impossible' most relevant to the discussion in the Treatise are explained more precisely below.

3 A translation of the medieval Latin text of this chapter is included as part of Appendix II [see n. 8 below]. Cf. J. L. Ackrill's translation of the original Greek in *Aristotle's Categories and De Interpretatione*, Oxford: Clarendon Press, 1963.

4 On fatalism see Antony Flew's article "Precognition" (*Encyclopedia of Philosophy*, Vol. VI, pp. 436–41, especially, pp. 438–9) and Richard Taylor's article "Determinism" (*Encyclopedia of Philosophy*, Vol. II, pp. 359–73).

5 A singular proposition is a proposition the subject term of which is a proper name or a definite description – e.g., 'Socrates', 'the man to whom you introduced me yesterday', 'her only brother'.

6 Ockham's interpretation of Aristotle's two arguments is substantially the same as that of Boethius and Thomas Aquinas. G. E. M. Anscombe has contested this traditional interpretation in her article "Aristotle and the Sea Battle" (*Mind*, Vol. LXV (1956), pp. 1–15), and much discussion has followed. [. . .]

7 See William of Sherwood, *Introduction to Logic*, translated by Norman Kretzmann, University of Minnesota, 1966, chapter 1, section 23, p. 41.

8 William of Ockham, *Predestination, God's Foreknowledge, and Future Contingents*, trans. Marilyn M. Adams and Norman Kretzmann (Indianapolis, IN: Hackett, 1983, Appendix II, p. 99.

9 Ibid., p. 106.

10 Ibid., p. 101.

11 Ibid., Appendix II, p. 105; cf. *Summa Logicae* III (3), ch. 30 (Appendix III, p. 110.)

12 Ibid., Assumption 3, pp. 46–7. Cf. *Ordinatio* I,d.38,q.1 P; Appendix I, p. 92.

13 Ibid., *Treatise*, q.2,a.4 L, p. 67.

14 Ibid., Assumption 6, p. 49.

15 Ibid.

16 Ibid., Assumption 6, pp. 49–50.

17 Ibid., Assumption 6, p. 50.

5

Middle Knowledge

William Hasker

William Hasker (b. 1935) is Professor Emeritus of Philosophy at Huntington University in Indiana. Among his many books and papers, Hasker has published *Providence, Evil, and the Openness of God* (2004), *The Emergent Self* (1999), and *The Triumph of God Over Evil* (2008). The following reading is taken from *God, Time, and Knowledge* (1989) in which he argues that infallible divine foreknowledge is incompatible with human free will. Hasker believes that God foregoes infallibly knowing the future for the sake of human freedom. One of the traditional ways out of the foreknowledge dilemma that he considers and then rejects is the theory of Middle Knowledge, supported by the sixteenth-century Spanish philosopher, Luis de Molina. According to Molina, God knows the actual future by knowing what contemporary philosophers call "counterfactuals of freedom," propositions that specify what every possible free creature would freely choose in every possible circumstance. In this selection Hasker summarizes the theory and some of the principal objections to it.

The Classical Theory

The theory of middle knowledge holds that, for each possible free creature that might exist, and for each possible situation in which such a creature might make a free choice, there is a truth, known to God prior to and independent of any decision on God's part, concerning what definite choice that creature would freely make if placed in that situation. In effect, middle knowledge extends the doctrine of divine foreknowledge to include knowledge of the outcome of choices that *might have been* made but in fact were not.

On casual consideration, middle knowledge may appear to be simply an obvious implication of divine omniscience: If God knows everything, how could he fail to know *this*? And by the same token, it may seem relatively innocuous. Both impressions, however, are mistaken. Middle knowledge is not a straightforward implication of omniscience, because it is not evident that the truths postulated by this theory exist to be known. In ordinary foreknowledge, it may be argued, what God knows is the agent's *actual decision* to do one thing or another. But with regard to a situation that never in fact arises, no decision is ever made, and none exists for God to know. And if the decision in question is supposed to be *free* decision, then all of the circumstances of the case (including the agent's character and prior inclinations) are consistent with any of the possible choices that might be made. Lacking the agent's *actual* making of the choice, then, there is nothing that disambiguates the situation and makes it true that some one of the options is the one that *would be* selected. This line of argument indicates the single most important objection that the proponent of middle knowledge must seek to answer.

But the very same feature that makes middle knowledge problematic (viz., that God can know the outcome of choices that are never actually made) also makes it extraordinarily useful for theological purposes. Consider the following counterfactual: "If A were in circumstances *C*, she would do *X*." According to middle knowledge, God knows the truth of this *whether or not* A ever actually *is* placed in circumstances *C*; indeed, God knows this whether or not A even exists, so that his knowledge about this is entirely independent of any of *God's own decisions* about creation and providence. But this, of course, makes such knowledge ideal for God to use in *deciding* whether or not to create A, and, if he does create her, whether or not to place her in circumstances *C*. As Molina says:

> God in his eternity knew by natural knowledge all the things that he could do: that he could create this world and infinitely many other worlds ... [and] given his complete comprehension and penetrating insight concerning all things and causes, he saw what would be the case if he chose to produce this order or a different order; how each person, left to his own free will, would make use of his liberty with such-and-such an amount of divine assistance, given such and such opportunities, temptations and other circumstances, and what he would freely do, retaining all the time the ability to do the opposite in the same opportunities temptations and other circumstances.[1]

Another way to look at the matter is this: It is evident that, if God had created a thoroughly deterministic world, his creative plan would have involved no risks whatsoever; all of the causal antecedents of such a world would be set up to produce exactly the results God intended. But it seems extremely plausible that in a world involving libertarian free choice, some risks are inevitable: God in creating such a world makes it possible for us to freely bring about great good, but also great evil – and which we in fact choose is up to us, not to God. Thus, the frequently heard statement that God "limits his power" by choosing to create free creatures. But according to the theory of middle knowledge, this is not quite correct. To be sure, it is still the creatures, not God, who determine their own free responses to various situations. But God, in choosing to create them and place them in those situations, knew exactly what their responses would be; he views the future, not as a risk taker seeking to optimize probable outcomes, but as a planner who knowingly accepts and incorporates into his plan exactly those outcomes that in fact occur – though, to be sure, some of them may not be the outcomes he would most prefer. The element of risk is entirely eliminated.

As we have already seen, the chief difficulty that the proponent of middle knowledge must confront is the contention that the truths God is alleged to know, commonly called "counterfactuals of freedom," do not exist to be known. Most of the arguments *for* counterfactuals of freedom seem to depend on general considerations of philosophical plausibility, but in the medieval controversy there were also arguments based on Scripture. A favorite text for this purpose is found in I Samuel 23, which recounts an incident in the troubled relationship of David with King Saul.[2] David, currently in occupation of the city of Keilah, consults Yahweh by means of the ephod about the rumors that Saul intends to attack the city:

> "Will Saul come down, as thy servant has heard? O LORD, the God of Israel, I beseech thee, tell thy servant." And the LORD said, "He will come down." Then said David, "Will the men of Keilah surrender me and my men into the hand of Saul?" And the LORD said, "They will surrender you." (I Samuel 23:11–12, RSV)

The advocates of middle knowledge took this passage as evidence that God knew the following two propositions to be true:

(1) If David stayed in Keilah, Saul would besiege the city.
(2) If David stayed in Keilah and Saul besieged the city, the men of Keilah would surrender David to Saul.

But (given the assumption that Saul and the men of Keilah would act freely in performing the specified actions), these two propositions are counterfactuals of freedom, and the incident as a whole is a dramatic demonstration of the existence and practical efficacy of middle knowledge.

But this argument is hardly compelling. As Anthony Kenny points out, the ephod seems to have been a yes–no device hardly possessing the subtlety required to distinguish between various possible conditionals that might have been asserted in answer to David's questions. Kenny, indeed, suggests that we may understand material conditionals here,[3] but that seems hardly likely, since on that construal both conditionals would be true simply in virtue of the fact that their antecedents are false. Much more plausible candidates are given by Robert Adams:

(3) If David stayed in Keilah, Saul would *probably* besiege the city.
(4) If David stayed in Keilah and Saul besieged the city, the men of Keilah would *probably* surrender David to Saul.

As Adams points out, "(3) and (4) are enough for David to act on, if he is prudent, but they will not satisfy the partisans of middle knowledge.[4] The prospects for a scriptural proof of middle knowledge, therefore, do not seem promising.

But of course, the argument just given shows only that the responses to David's questions *need not* be taken as asserting counterfactuals of freedom, not that they *cannot* be so understood. And there are not lacking situations in everyday life in which it seems plausible that we are taking counterfactuals of freedom to be true. Plantinga, for example, says he believes that "If Bob Adams were to offer to take me climbing at Tahquitz Rock the next time I come to California, I would gladly (and freely) accept."[5] And Adams notes that "there does not normally seem to be any uncertainty at all about what a butcher, for example, would have done if I had asked him to sell me a pound of ground beef, although we suppose he would have had free will in the matter."[6]

So the discussion of examples seems to end in a stand-off. Still, the proponent of middle knowledge needs to address the question mentioned earlier: How is it possible for counterfactuals of freedom to be *true*? What is the truth maker for these propositions? At this point the advocate of middle knowledge is presented with an attractive opportunity, but one that it is imperative for her to resist. The opportunity is simply to claim that counterfactuals of freedom are true in virtue of the *character and psychological tendencies* of the agents named in them. The attractiveness of this is evident in that in nearly all of the cases where we are disposed to accept such counterfactuals as true, the epistemic grounds for our acceptance would be found precisely in our knowledge of such psychological facts – Saul besieging Keilah, Adams's compliant butcher, and Plantinga climbing Tahquitz Rock are all cases in point. But the weakness of the suggestion becomes apparent when the following question is asked: Are the psychological facts about the agent, together with a description of the situation, plus relevant psychological laws, supposed to *entail* that the agent would respond as indicated? If the answer is yes, then the counterfactual may be *true* but it is not a counterfactual of *freedom*; the agent is not then free in the relevant (libertarian) sense.[7] If on the other hand the answer is no, then how can those psychological facts provide good grounds for the assertion that the agent *definitely would* (as opposed, say, to *very probably would*) respond in that way?

Probably the best line for the proponent of middle knowledge to take here is the one suggested by Suárez: When a counterfactual of freedom is true, it is simply an ultimate fact about the free agent in question that, if placed in the indicated circumstances, she would act as the counterfactual states; this fact requires no analysis or metaphysical grounding in terms of further, noncounterfactual states of affairs. (Or, if the agent in question does not actually exist, it is a fact about a particular *essence* that, if it were instantiated and its instantiation were placed in such circumstances, the instantiation would act as stated.) Adams, commenting on this, says, "I do not think I have any conception . . . of the sort of . . . property that Suárez ascribes to possible agents with respect to their acts under possible conditions. Nor do I think that I have any other primitive understanding of what it would be for the relevant subjunctive conditionals to be true." Nevertheless, he admits that Suárez's view on this is of the "least clearly unsatisfactory type," because "It is very difficult to refute someone who claims to have a primitive understanding which I seem not to have."[8]

Notes

1 L. Molina, "De Scientia Dei," quoted by Anthony Kenny, *The God of the Philosophers* (Oxford: Oxford University Press, 1979), pp. 62–3.

2 For my discussion of this passage I rely chiefly on R. M. Adams, "Middle Knowledge and the Problem of Evil," *American Philosophical Quarterly* 14 (1977): 109–17. See also Kenny, *The God of the Philosophers*, pp. 63–71.

3 Kenny, *The God of the Philosophers*, p. 64.

4 Adams, "*Middle Knowledge*," p. 111.

5 "Reply to Robert M. Adams," in Tomberlin and van Inwagen, eds., *Alvin Plantinga* (Dordrecht and Boston, MA: Reidel, 1985), p. 373.

6 Adams, "Middle Knowledge," p. 115.

7 There are complexities in our use of such expressions as "acting freely" that are not always sufficiently taken note of. For example, it may happen that an action is "psychologically inevitable" for a person, based on that person's character and dispositions, yet we say that the person acts "freely" *if the character and dispositions are thought to be the result of previous freely chosen actions of the person*. Thus, it is said of the redeemed in heaven both that they freely serve and worship God, and that they are not able to sin; this happy inability is the result of their own free choices and is not typically seen as a diminution of freedom. But acts of this sort are *not* free in the very strict sense required by libertarianism. If we are exacting in our *definition* of "free" but lax in *applying* the term, trouble is inevitable.

8 Adams, "*Middle Knowledge*," p. 112.

VI
RELIGION AND MORALITY

Introduction

The practice of religion generally includes moral teaching, and sometimes rituals for obtaining forgiveness and performing penance for wrongdoing. So morality is almost always a component of religion. A harder question is whether religion must be a component of morality. It is common in the modern era to think that morality is autonomous, but there are at least three ways in which morality might need religion to support it: (1) to provide the goal of the moral life, (2) to provide the motive to be moral, and (3) to provide morality with its foundation and justification.

Kant's Moral Argument for the existence of God falls under the first category. According to Kant, morality puts a demand on the agent to seek the highest good. The highest good is a state in which human happiness is proportional to virtue, a state that requires both a divine judge and an afterlife. Kant is not arguing that the practice of religion is necessary to reach the goal of morality, nor is he arguing that religious beliefs are necessary to provide the motive to be moral, so Kant does not argue that morality needs religion for the second reason above. He proposes that the existence of God is a postulate of pure practical reason.

In the short passage from Plato's *Laws* included in this section, Plato says that God is the measure of all things and the good man is one who is like God. The connection between being like God and being a good person can be found in many religions in many parts of the world. Some philosophers have also thought that the foundation of morality is something in God, so morality needs religion for the third reason above. Natural Law theory makes morality rest upon God's nature. Divine Command theory makes morality rest upon God's will. Zagzebski's Divine Motivation theory makes morality rest upon the motives that are the primary constituents of God's virtues.

Divine Command theory has a long and important history in religious ethics. A common form of Divine Command theory is the following: An act is morally required (an obligation) just in case God commands us to do it; an act is morally wrong just in case God forbids us to do it. Since a divine command is the expression of God's will with respect to human and other creaturely acts, the divine will is the fundamental source of the moral properties of acts. There are many variations of this theory. Some claim that the source of the *goodness* of acts is in divine commands, whereas others claim that commands are only the ground of *obligation*. Some require that there be an actual command, whereas others do not. We have included a reading from Martin Luther in which he claims that what is good or meritorious is so because it is pleasing to God.

Plato offered a famous objection to the structure of Divine Command theory in the *Euthyphro*.

Socrates engages the young Euthyphro in a discussion on the nature of holiness, and asks whether an act is holy because the gods disapprove of it, or whether they disapprove because it is holy. If it is the former, it looks like holiness (or morality) is arbitrary. If it is the latter, then the foundation of morality is not in the attitude (or will) of the gods.

Several contemporary philosophers have defended versions of Divine Command theory that they believe avoid the Euthyphro dilemma. One version of the relation between divine commands and human obligation has been proposed by Robert Adams, who argues that obligations arise from something demanded by a person with whom we have a relationship we value. Only God is good enough to make demands that are binding in the moral sense, and only God can provide the objectivity we expect from moral obligation.

In Zagzebski's Divine Motivation theory, the ground of what is morally good and morally right is God's motives rather than God's will. Motives are emotions that are constituents of traits of character, so Divine Motivation theory is a theological virtue theory. The structure of the theory is exemplarist. Moral properties of acts, persons, and outcomes are defined via direct reference to exemplars of virtue, and God is the supreme exemplar.

Aquinas resolves the problem of what grounds morality by giving it a two-tier grounding – one in God, the other in human nature. In his form of Natural Law theory, the basic norms of morality sufficient for civil society have a foundation in human nature, and so morality is common to all human beings and is accessible, in principle, by ordinary human reason. The Natural Law, however, is not ultimate. Everything outside of God comes from God, including the Natural Law, which is an expression in the created order of the Eternal Law of God. So the nature of God is ultimately the ground of morality, as it is in Divine Command Theory and in Divine Motivation Theory.

There is a need for a common morality even in a pluralistic culture, and it is becoming increasingly crucial that in a shrinking world there are basic moral restrictions recognized by people in all parts of the world. Some people fear that this goal is threatened if religion is tied to morality, but the readings in this section do not undermine that goal. People can agree on the content of a large part of morality without agreeing on its metaphysical ground or the ultimate source of its authority.

A

Is Religion Needed for Morality?

1

God is the Measure of All Things

Plato

In the following brief selection from Plato's last dialogue *Laws*, the character referred to as the Athenian argues that God is "the measure of all things" and that man must strive to be like God.

ATHENIAN: What line of conduct, then, is dear to God and a following of him? There is but one, and it is summed up in one ancient rule, the rule that 'like' – when it is a thing of due measure – 'loves its like.' For things that have no measure can be loved neither by one another nor by those that have. Now it is God who is, for you and me, of a truth the 'measure of all things,' much more truly than, as they say, 'man.' So he who would be loved by such a being must himself become such to the utmost of his might, and so, by this argument, he that is temperate among us is loved by God, for he is like God, whereas he that is not temperate is unlike God and at variance with him; so also it is with the unjust, and the same rule holds in all else. Now from this rule, I would have you note, follows another – of all rules, to my mind, the grandest and truest, which is this. For the good man 'tis most glorious and good and profitable to happiness of life, aye, and most excellently fit, to do sacrifice and be ever in communion with heaven through prayer and offerings and all manner of worship, but for the evil, entirely the contrary. For the evil man is impure of soul, where the other is pure, and from the polluted neither good men nor God may ever rightly accept a gift; thus all this toil taken with heaven is but labor thrown away for the impious, though ever seasonable in the pious.

Plato, "Laws IV" trans. A. E. Taylor, *The Collected Dialogues of Plato: Including the Letters*, ed. Edith Hamilton and Huntington Cairns (Princeton, NJ: Princeton University Press, 1961), pp. 1307–8.

2

The Moral Argument for the Existence of God

Immanuel Kant

As we saw in an earlier reading (see section II.C.3), Immanuel Kant (1724–1804) raised influential criticisms of the traditional arguments for God's existence in his *Critique of Pure Reason*. However, in his *Critique of Practical Reason*, from which the following reading is taken, he famously argued that God's existence is a necessary postulate of morality. Kant argues that we are obligated to pursue the highest good and since we can have no obligations that are impossible to fulfill, the highest good must be attainable. The highest good consists of two parts – morality and happiness – and although morality is under our control, happiness is not. Since there is no necessary connection between morality and happiness, the highest good will be attainable only if there is a supreme intelligence that ensures their correspondence.

Happiness is the state of a rational being in the world in the whole of whose existence *everything goes according to his wish and will*, and rests, therefore, on the harmony of nature with his whole end as well as with the essential determining ground of his will. Now, the moral law as a law of freedom commands through determining grounds that are to be quite independent of nature and of its harmony with our faculty of desire (as incentives); the acting rational being in the world is, however, not also the cause of the world and of nature itself. Consequently, there is not the least ground in the moral law for a necessary connection between the morality and the proportionate happiness of a being belonging to the world as part of it and hence dependent upon it, who for that reason cannot by his will be a cause of this nature and, as far as his happiness is concerned, cannot by his own powers make it harmonize thoroughly with his practical

Immanuel Kant, *Critique of Practical Reason*, trans. and ed. Mary Gregor (Cambridge: Cambridge University Press, 1997), pp. 104–9.

principles. Nevertheless, in the practical task of pure reason, that is, in the necessary pursuit of the highest good, such a connection is postulated as necessary: we *ought* to strive to promote the highest good (which must therefore be possible). Accordingly, the existence of a cause of all nature, distinct from nature, which contains the ground of this connection, namely of the exact correspondence of happiness with morality, is also *postulated*. However, this supreme cause is to contain the ground of the correspondence of nature not merely with a law of the will of rational beings but with the representation of this *law*, so far as they make it the *supreme determining ground of the will*, and consequently not merely with morals in their form but also with their morality as their determining ground, that is, with their moral disposition. Therefore, the highest good in the world is possible only insofar as a supreme cause of nature having a causality in keeping with the moral disposition is assumed. Now, a being capable of actions in accordance with the representation of laws is *an intelligence* (a rational being), and the causality of such a being in accordance with this representation of laws is his *will*. Therefore the supreme cause of nature, insofar as it must be presupposed for the highest good, is a being that is the cause of nature by *understanding* and *will* (hence its author), that is, God. Consequently, the postulate of the possibility of the *highest derived good* (the best world) is likewise the postulate of the reality of a *highest original good*, namely of the existence of **God**. Now, it was a duty for us to promote the highest good; hence there is in us not merely the warrant but also the necessity, as a need connected with duty, to presuppose the possibility of this highest good, which, since it is possible only under the condition of the existence of God, connects the presupposition of the existence of God inseparably with duty; that is, it is morally necessary to assume the existence of God.

It is well to note here that this moral necessity *is subjective*, that is, a need, and not *objective*, that is, itself a duty; for, there can be no duty to assume the existence of anything (since this concerns only the theoretical use of reason). Moreover, it is not to be understood by this that it is necessary to assume the existence of God *as a ground of all obligation in general* (for this rests, as has been sufficiently shown, solely on the autonomy of reason itself). What belongs to duty here is only the striving to produce and promote the highest good in the world, the possibility of which can therefore be postulated, while our reason finds this thinkable only on the presupposition of a supreme intelligence; to assume the existence of this supreme intelligence is thus connected with the consciousness of our duty, although this assumption itself belongs to theoretical reason; with respect to theoretical reason alone, as a ground of explanation, it can be called a *hypothesis*; but in relation to the intelligibility of an object given us by the moral law (the highest good), and consequently of a need for practical purposes, it can be called *belief* and, indeed, a pure *rational belief* since pure reason alone (in its theoretical as well as in its practical use) is the source from which it springs.

From this *deduction* it now becomes comprehensible why the *Greek* schools could never solve their problem of the practical possibility of the highest good: it was because they made the rule of the use which the human will makes of its freedom the sole and sufficient ground of this possibility, without, as it seemed to them, needing the existence of God for it. They were indeed correct in establishing the principle of morals by itself, independently of this postulate and solely from the relation of reason to the will, so that they made it the *supreme* practical condition of the highest good; but this principle was not on this account the *whole* condition of its possibility. The Epicureans had indeed assumed an altogether false principle of morals as supreme, namely that of happiness, and had substituted for a law a maxim of each choosing as he pleased according to his inclination; they proceeded, however, *consistently* enough in this by demeaning their highest good in the same way, namely in proportion to the meanness of their principle, and expecting no greater happiness than can be acquired by human prudence (including temperance and moderation of the inclinations), which, as we know, has to be paltry enough and turn out very differently according to circumstances, not to mention the exceptions which their maxims had to constantly admit and which made them unfit for laws. The Stoics, on the contrary, had chosen their supreme practical principle quite correctly, namely virtue, as the condition of the highest good; but inasmuch as they represented the degree of virtue required by its pure law as fully attainable in this life, they not only strained the moral capacity of the *human being*, under the name of a *sage*, far beyond all the limits of his nature and assumed something that contradicts all cognition of the human being, but also and above all they would not let the second *component* of the highest good, namely happiness, hold as a special object of the human faculty of desire but made their *sage*, like a divinity in his consciousness of the excellence of his person, quite independent of nature (with respect to his own contentment), exposing him indeed to the ills of life but not subjecting him to them (at the same time representing him as also free from evil); and thus they really left out the second element of the highest good, namely one's own happiness, placing it solely in acting and in contentment with one's personal worth and so including it in consciousness of one's moral cast of mind – though in this they could have been sufficiently refuted by the voice of their own nature.

The doctrine of Christianity, even if it is not regarded as a religious doctrine, gives on this point a concept of the highest good (of the kingdom of God) which alone satisfies the strictest demand of practical reason. The moral law is holy (inflexible) and demands holiness of morals, although all the moral perfection that a human being can attain is still only virtue, that is, a disposition conformed with law *from respect* for law, and thus consciousness of a continuing propensity to transgression or at least impurity, that is, an admixture of many spurious (not moral) motives to observe the law, hence a self-esteem combined with humility; and so, with respect to the holiness that the Christian law demands, nothing remains for a creature but endless progress, though for that very reason he is justified in hoping for his endless duration. The *worth* of a disposition *completely* conformed with the moral law is infinite, since all possible happiness in the judgment of a wise and all-powerful distributor of it has no restriction other than rational beings' lack of conformity with their duty. But the moral law of itself still does not *promise* any happiness, since this is not necessarily connected with observance of the law according to our concepts of a natural order as such. The Christian doctrine of morals now supplements this lack (of the second indispensable component of the highest good) by representing the world in which rational beings devote themselves with their whole soul to the moral law as a *kingdom of God*, in which nature and morals come into a harmony, foreign to each of them of itself, through a holy author who makes the derived highest good possible. *Holiness* of morals is prescribed to them as a rule even in this life, while the well-being proportioned to it, namely *beatitude*, is represented as attainable only in an eternity; for, the *former* must always be the archetype of their conduct in every state, and progress toward it is already possible and necessary in this life, whereas the *latter*, under the name of happiness, cannot be attained at all in this world (so far as our own capacity is concerned) and is therefore made solely an object of hope. Nevertheless, the Christian principle of *morals* itself is not theological (and so heteronomy); it is instead autonomy of pure practical reason by itself, since it does not make cognition of God and his will the basis of these laws but only of the attainment of the highest good subject to the condition of observing these laws, and since it places even the proper *incentive* to observing them not in the results wished for but in the representation of duty alone, faithful observance of which alone constitutes worthiness to acquire the latter.

In this way the moral law leads through the concept of the highest good, as the object and final end of pure practical reason, *to religion, that is, to the recognition of all duties as divine commands, not as sanctions – that is, chosen and in themselves contingent ordinances of another's will* – but as essential *laws* of every free will in itself, which must nevertheless be regarded as commands of the supreme being because only from a will that is morally perfect (holy and beneficent) and at the same time all-powerful, and so through harmony with this will, can we hope to attain the highest good, which the moral law makes it our duty to take as the object of our endeavors. Here again, then, everything remains disinterested and grounded only on duty, and there is no need to base it on incentives of fear and hope, which if they became principles would destroy the whole moral worth of actions. The moral law commands me to make the highest possible good in a world the final object of all my conduct. But I cannot hope to produce this except by the harmony of my will with that of a holy and beneficent author of the world; and although in the concept of the highest good, as that of a whole in which the greatest happiness is represented as connected in the most exact proportion with the greatest degree of moral perfection (possible in creatures), *my own happiness* is included, this is nevertheless not the determining ground of the will that is directed to promote the highest good; it is instead the moral law (which, on the contrary, limits by strict conditions my unbounded craving for happiness).

For this reason, again, morals is not properly the doctrine of how we are to *make* ourselves happy but of how we are to become *worthy* of happiness. Only if religion is added to it does there also enter the hope of some day participating in happiness to the degree that we have been intent upon not being unworthy of it.

Someone is *worthy* of possessing a thing or a state when it harmonizes; with the highest good that he is in possession of it. It can now be readily seen that all worthiness depends upon moral conduct, since in the concept of the highest good this constitutes the condition of the rest (which belongs to one's state), namely, of one's share of happiness. Now, from this it follows that *morals* in itself must never be treated as a *doctrine of happiness*, that is, as instruction in how to become happy; for morals has to do solely with the rational condition (*conditio sine qua non*) of happiness and not with the means of acquiring it. But when morals (which merely imposes duties and does not provide rules for selfish wishes) has been set forth completely, then – after the moral wish, based on a law, to promote the highest good (to bring the kingdom of God to us) has been awakened, which could not previously have arisen in any selfish soul, and for the sake of this wish the step to religion has been taken – then for the first time can this ethical doctrine also be called a doctrine of happiness, because it is only with religion that the *hope* of happiness first arises.

B

Divine Command Theory and Divine Motivation Theory

1

The Euthyphro Dilemma

Plato

The following reading is taken from Plato's dialogue *Euthyphro*, in which Socrates questions Euthyphro concerning the nature of holiness. Euthyphro attempts to define holiness in terms of what the gods love, which prompts Socrates to pose the famous question: "Is what is holy holy because the gods approve it, or do they approve it because it is holy?" When Euthyphro answers that the gods approve it because it is holy, Socrates objects that Euthyphro still has not explained the nature of holiness.

EUTHYPHRO: Well then, what is pleasing to the gods is holy, and what is not pleasing to them is unholy.

SOCRATES: Perfect, Euthyphro! Now you give me just the answer that I asked for. Meanwhile, whether it is right I do not know, but obviously you will go on to prove your statement true.

EUTHYPHRO: Indeed I will.

SOCRATES: Come now, let us scrutinize what we are saying. What is pleasing to the gods, and the man that pleases them, are holy; what is hateful to the gods, and the man they hate, unholy. But the holy and unholy are not the same; the holy is directly opposite to the unholy. Isn't it so?

EUTHYPHRO: It is.

SOCRATES: And the matter clearly was well stated.

EUTHYPHRO: I accept it, Socrates; that was stated.

SOCRATES: Was it not also stated, Euthyphro, that the gods revolt and differ with each other, and that hatreds come between them?

EUTHYPHRO: That was stated.

SOCRATES: Hatred and wrath, my friend – what kind of disagreement will produce them? Look at the matter thus. If you and I were to differ about numbers, on the question which of two was the greater, would a disagreement about that make

Plato, "Euthyphro" trans. Lane Cooper from *The Collected Dialogues of Plato: Including the Letters*, ed. Edith Hamilton and Huntington Cairns (Princeton, NJ: Princeton University Press, 1961), pp. 174–9.

us angry at each other, and make enemies of us? Should we not settle things by calculation, and so come to an agreement quickly on any point like that?

EUTHYPHRO: Yes, certainly.

SOCRATES: And similarly if we differed on a question of greater length or less, we would take a measurement, and quickly put an end to the dispute?

EUTHYPHRO: Just that.

SOCRATES: And so, I fancy, we should have recourse to scales, and settle any question about a heavier or lighter weight?

EUTHYPHRO: Of course.

SOCRATES: What sort of thing, then, is it about which we differ, till, unable to arrive at a decision, we might get angry and be enemies to one another? Perhaps you have no answer ready, but listen to me. See if it is not the following – right and wrong, the noble and the base, and good and bad. Are not these the things about which we differ, till, unable to arrive at a decision, we grow hostile, when we do grow hostile, to each other, you and I and everybody else?

EUTHYPHRO: Yes, Socrates, that is where we differ, on these subjects.

SOCRATES: What about the gods, then, Euthyphro? If, indeed, they have dissensions, must it not be on these subjects?

EUTHYPHRO: Quite necessarily.

SOCRATES: Accordingly, my noble Euthyphro, by your account some gods take one thing to be right, and others take another, and similarly with the honorable and the base, and good and bad. They would hardly be at variance with each other, if they did not differ on these questions. Would they?

EUTHYPHRO: You are right.

SOCRATES: And what each one of them thinks noble, good, and just, is what he loves, and the opposite is what he hates?

EUTHYPHRO: Yes, certainly.

SOCRATES: But it is the same things, so you say, that some of them think right, and others wrong, and through disputing about these they are at variance, and make war on one another. Isn't it so?

EUTHYPHRO: It is.

SOCRATES: Accordingly, so it would seem, the same things will be hated by the gods and loved by them; the same things would alike displease and please them.

EUTHYPHRO: It would seem so.

SOCRATES: And so, according to this argument, the same things, Euthyphro, will be holy and unholy.

EUTHYPHRO: That may be.

SOCRATES: In that case, admirable friend, you have not answered what I asked you. I did not ask you to tell me what at once is holy and unholy, but it seems that what is pleasing to the gods is also hateful to them. Thus, Euthyphro, it would not be strange at all if what you now are doing in punishing your father were pleasing to Zeus, but hateful to Cronus and Uranus, and welcome to Hephaestus, but odious to Hera, and if any other of the gods disagree about the matter, satisfactory to some of them, and odious to others.

EUTHYPHRO: But, Socrates, my notion is that, on this point, there is no difference of opinion among the gods – not one of them but thinks that if a person kills another wrongfully, he ought to pay for it.

SOCRATES: And what of men? Have you never heard a man contending that someone who has killed a person wrongfully, or done some other unjust deed, ought not to pay the penalty?

EUTHYPHRO: Why! There is never any end to their disputes about these matters; it goes on everywhere, above all in the courts. People do all kinds of wrong, and then there is nothing they will not do or say in order to escape the penalty.

SOCRATES: Do they admit wrongdoing, Euthyphro, and, while admitting it, deny that they ought to pay the penalty?

EUTHYPHRO: No, not that, by any means.

SOCRATES: Then they will not do and say quite everything. Unless I am mistaken, they dare not say or argue that if they do wrong they should not pay the penalty. No, I think that they deny wrongdoing. How about it?

EUTHYPHRO: It is true.

SOCRATES: Therefore they do not dispute that anybody who does wrong should pay the penalty.
No, the thing that they dispute about is likely to be who is the wrongdoer, what he did, and when.

EUTHYPHRO: That is true.

SOCRATES: Well then, isn't that precisely what goes on among the gods, if they really do have quarrels about right and wrong, as you say they do? One set will hold that some others do wrong, and the other set deny it? For that other thing, my friend, I take it no one, whether god or man, will dare to say – that the wrongdoer should not pay the penalty!

EUTHYPHRO: Yes, Socrates, what you say is true – in the main.

SOCRATES: It is the individual act, I fancy, Euthyphro, that the disputants dispute about, both men and gods, if gods ever do dispute. They differ on a certain act; some hold that it was rightly done, the others that it was wrong. Isn't it so?

EUTHYPHRO: Yes, certainly.

SOCRATES: Then come, dear Euthyphro, teach me as well, and let me grow more wise. What proof have you that all the gods think that your servant died unjustly, your hireling, who, when he had killed a man, was shackled by the master of the victim, and perished, dying because of his shackles before the man who shackled him could learn from the seers what ought to be done with him? What proof have you that for a man like him it is right for a son to prosecute his father, and indict him on a charge of murder? Come on. Try to make it clear to me beyond all doubt that under these conditions the gods must all consider this action to be right. If you can adequately prove it to me, I will never cease from praising you for your wisdom.

EUTHYPHRO: But, Socrates, that, very likely, would be no small task, although I could indeed make it very clear to you.

SOCRATES: I understand. You think that I am duller than the judges; obviously you will demonstrate to them that what your father did was wrong, and that the gods all hate such deeds.

EUTHYPHRO: I shall prove it absolutely, Socrates, if they will listen to me.

SOCRATES: They are sure to listen if they think that you speak well. But while you were talking, a notion came into my head, and I asked myself, Suppose that Euthyphro proved to me quite clearly that all the gods consider such a death unjust; would I have come one whit the nearer for him to knowing what the holy is, and what is the unholy? The act in question, seemingly, might be displeasing to the gods, but then we have just seen that you cannot define the holy and unholy in that way, for we have seen that a given thing may be displeasing, and also pleasing, to gods. So on this point, Euthyphro, I will let you off; if you like, the gods shall all consider the act unjust, and they all shall hate it. But suppose that we now correct our definition, and say what the gods all hate is unholy, and what they love is holy, whereas what some of them love, and others hate, is either both or neither. Are you willing that we now define the holy and unholy in this way?

EUTHYPHRO: What is there to prevent us, Socrates?

SOCRATES: Nothing to prevent me, Euthyphro. As for you, see whether when you take this definition you can quite readily instruct me, as you promised.

EUTHYPHRO: Yes, I would indeed affirm that holiness is what the gods all love, and its opposite is what the gods all hate, unholiness.

SOCRATES: Are we to examine this position also, Euthyphro, to see if it is sound? Or shall we let it through, and thus accept our own and others' statement, and agree to an assertion simply when somebody says that a thing is so? Must we not look into what the speaker says?

EUTHYPHRO: We must. And yet, for my part, I regard the present statement as correct.

SOCRATES: We shall soon know better about that, my friend. Now think of this. Is what is holy holy because the gods approve it, or do they approve it because it is holy?

EUTHYPHRO: I do not get your meaning.

SOCRATES: Well, I will try to make it clearer. We speak of what is carried and the carrier, do we not, of led and leader, of the seen and that which sees? And you understand that in all such cases the things are different, and how they differ?

EUTHYPHRO: Yes, I think I understand.

SOCRATES: In the same way what is loved is one thing, and what loves is another?

EUTHYPHRO: Of course.

SOCRATES: Tell me now, is what is carried 'carried' because something carries it, or is it for some other reason?

EUTHYPHRO: No, but for that reason.

SOCRATES: And what is led, because something leads it? And what is seen, because something sees it?

EUTHYPHRO: Yes, certainly.

SOCRATES: Then it is not because a thing is seen that something sees it, but just the opposite – because something sees it, therefore it is seen. Nor because it is led, that something leads it, but because something leads it, therefore it is led. Nor because it is carried, that something carries it, but because something carries it, therefore it is carried. Do you see what I wish to say, Euthyphro? It is this. Whenever an effect occurs, or something is effected, it is not the thing effected that gives rise to the effect; no, there is a cause, and then comes this effect. Nor is it because a thing is acted on that there is this effect; no, there is a cause for what it undergoes, and then comes this effect. Don't you agree?

EUTHYPHRO: I do.

SOCRATES: Well then, when a thing is loved, is it not in process of becoming something, or of undergoing something, by some other thing?

EUTHYPHRO: Yes, certainly.

SOCRATES: Then the same is true here as in the previous cases. It is not because a thing is loved that they who love it love it, but it is loved because they love it.

EUTHYPHRO: Necessarily.

SOCRATES: Then what are we to say about the holy, Euthyphro? According to your argument, is it not loved by all the gods?

EUTHYPHRO: Yes.

SOCRATES: Because it is holy, or for some other reason?

EUTHYPHRO: No, it is for that reason.

SOCRATES: And so it is because it is holy that it is loved; it is not holy because it is loved.

EUTHYPHRO: So it seems.

SOCRATES: On the other hand, it is beloved and pleasing to the gods just because they love it?

EUTHYPHRO: No doubt of that.

SOCRATES: So what is pleasing to the gods is not the same as what is holy, Euthyphro, nor, according to your statement, is the holy the same as what is pleasing to the gods. They are two different things.

EUTHYPHRO: How may that be, Socrates?

SOCRATES: Because we are agreed that the holy is loved because it is holy, and is not holy because it is loved. Isn't it so?

EUTHYPHRO: Yes.

SOCRATES: Whereas what is pleasing to the gods is pleasing to them just because they love it, such being its nature and its cause. Its being loved of the gods is not the reason of its being loved.

EUTHYPHRO: You are right.

SOCRATES: But suppose, dear Euthyphro, that what is pleasing to the gods and what is holy were not two separate things. In that case if holiness were loved because it was holy, then also what was pleasing to the gods would be loved because it pleased them. And, on the other hand, if what was pleasing to them pleased because they loved it, then also the holy would be holy because they loved it. But now you see that it is just the opposite, because the two are absolutely different from each other, for the one [what is pleasing to the gods] is of a sort to be loved because it is loved, whereas the other [what is holy] is loved because it is of a sort to be loved. Consequently, Euthyphro, it looks as if you had not given me my answer – as if when you were asked to tell the nature of the holy, you did not wish to explain the essence of it. You merely tell an attribute of it, namely, that it appertains to holiness to be loved by all the gods. What it *is*, as yet you have not said. So, if you please, do not conceal this from me. No, begin again. Say what the holy is, and never mind if gods do love it, nor if it has some other attribute; on that we shall not split.

2

Questions on the Books of the Sentences

Pierre d'Ailly

Pierre d'Ailly (1350–1420) was a prominent Christian theologian and philosopher who served as chancellor of the University of Paris. The following selection from his commentary on Peter Abelard's *Books of the Sentences* contains a clear statement of the view that all moral obligations are based, ultimately, upon the divine will.

Introductory Commentary on the First Book of the Sentences

D ... Thus the first thesis is this: Just as the divine will is the first efficient cause in the class of efficient cause, so, in the class of obligatory law, it is the first law or rule. Now the first part of this thesis is commonly granted by all philosophers; therefore it is assumed as something evident. But in order to prove the second part, I must first advance some preliminary propositions.

The first proposition is that, among obligatory laws, one is a law absolutely first.

Proof: For just as there is not an infinite regress in efficient causes, as Aristotle proves in *Metaphysics* II. 3; so there is not an infinite regress in obligatory laws. Therefore, just as it is necessary to reach one first efficient cause, so it is necessary to arrive at one first obligatory law; for the principle is entirely the same in both cases. Therefore, etc.

The second proposition is that no created law is absolutely first.

Proof: For just as no created thing has of itself the power of creating, so no created law has of itself the power of binding; for as the Apostle states, *Romans* 13, "Power comes only from God," etc. Therefore, just as no created thing is the first efficient cause, so no created law is the first obligatory law; for just as "first cause" is a

Pierre d'Ailly, *Questions on the Books of the Sentences* in *Divine Command Morality: Historical and Contemporary Readings*, ed. Janine Marie Idziak (New York: The Edward Mellen Press, 1979), trans. from reprint of original (Frankfurt: Minerva, 1968), pp. 58–63.

sign that it is God who is involved in the causal activity, so "first law" is an indication that it is God who is imposing the obligation. Therefore, etc.

The third proposition is that the divine will is the law which is absolutely first.

This is obviously proven by the two preceding propositions. For just as it is ascribed to the divine will to be the first efficient cause, so it must be ascribed to the same thing to be the first obligatory law; for just as the former belongs to perfection, so does the latter. Therefore, etc.

Furthermore, this proposition is demonstrated by Augustine in *Against Faustus*, 22, when he states that the eternal law is the divine intellect or will commanding that the natural order be maintained and forbidding that it be disturbed. Now the eternal law is a law absolutely first; similarly, nothing is superior to the divine will. Therefore, etc.

And thus, the truth of the second part of the thesis is clear.

The fourth proposition is that it is impossible that something be obligatory according to a certain law and not likewise be obligatory according to the divine will.

Proof: For just as it is impossible that a secondary cause act while the first cause does not act, so it is impossible that any law oblige while the first law does not. For just as the first cause contributes more to the effect than does a secondary cause, as states the author of *On Causes*; so the first law binds more than does any other law whatever. Therefore, etc.

The fifth proposition is that it is possible that something be obligatory according to the divine will while it is not obligatory according to any other law.

Proof: For just as the first cause brings something about when a secondary cause cannot do so by itself alone, so the first law or rule makes something obligatory when no other law can bind by itself alone; for the principle is entirely the same in both cases. Therefore, etc.

The sixth proposition is that it is impossible that anything created be a law or rule unless it is in accord with the divine will.

Proof: For just as it is impossible that anything created be a cause except through the first cause, so it is impossible that anything created be a law or rule except through the first law. Therefore, just as it is impossible that any cause be in conflict with the first cause, so it is impossible that any law or rule disagree with the first law. Therefore, etc.

So, therefore, stand proven the six previously stated preliminary propositions, from which the demonstration of the entire first thesis is evident.

E Now from the previously stated thesis and the proof of it, I infer some corollary propositions.

. . . The fifth corollary is that all sin is the performance or the omission of something contrary to a prohibition or precept of law. . . .

The sixth corollary is that nothing is a sin in itself but precisely because forbidden by law. . . .

Introductory Commentary on the Second Book of the Sentences

D . . . Nevertheless, certain reverend Fathers and teachers of mine have maintained the opposite of these propositions, which I advanced and proved in my first introductory commentary. . . .

E Thus Friar Jacob raised objection to the first proposition.[1] And he proved three claims. The first is that the divine will should not properly be called a "law" or "rule" . . .

F . . . Against this reverend Father, I advance four propositions.

The first proposition is that the divine will and the divine intellect or reason are, just as much "formally" as "really," the same in all respects; nor is there a distinction between them in any way. . . .

G The second proposition is that whatever, from the nature of the thing, belongs to the divine will, likewise belongs to the divine intellect. . . .

The third proposition is that, if the divine intellect is an obligatory law or rule, so also is the divine will, and vice versa. . . .

The fourth proposition, not precluded by the previous claims, is this: that, in accordance with the mode of speaking of holy men and scholars, it is more properly assigned to the divine will than to the divine intellect to be an obligatory law. So that this is true per se: "The divine will is an obligatory law"; and not this: "The divine intellect is an obligatory law." And the reasoning is this: for just as the mode of speaking of scholars is that the divine will, and not the divine intellect, is the effective cause of things, on account of this consideration, that whatever the divine will commands, exists or is done, and not whatever the divine intellect has knowledge of; so it is in the proposition, since whatever the divine will commands to be obligatory, is obligatory, while this is not so with respect to the divine intellect. Whence this line of reasoning is good: "The divine will commands that Sortes be obligated to do *X*, therefore Sortes is so obligated." And therefore this is true per se, "The divine will is an obligatory law," and not this, "The divine intellect is an obligatory law," although either one is true. Therefore, etc.

Q But reverend Father Friar Michael raises objection against the fifth and sixth propositions,[2] and advances a thesis contradicting these propositions.

. . . Secondly, . . . this reverend Father proves that there is something which is a sin in itself and not precisely because prohibited by law.

And he argues first in this way: For it would be possible for a man to sin when no precept has been given to him, namely, when he neglects eternal and spiritual goods, directing his attention to temporal goods; for this is what it is to sin according to Augustine, *On Free Choice*, I. For, through this activity, the natural order is disturbed, which the eternal law commands to be maintained and forbids to be disturbed; but no less can a man do this having no precept, as with a precept. Therefore, etc.

Secondly, on this matter we have the opinion of blessed Augustine in the same book, when he says: "It is not, indeed, the case that adultery is therefore evil because it is prohibited by law; on the contrary, it is therefore prohibited by law because it is evil."

Thirdly, on this matter we have the opinion of Aristotle, *Ethics*, II, when he states: "Not every activity, however, nor every passion admits a middle course. For certain ones, as soon as named, are linked with evil, such as rejoicing in evil, envy, adultery, and homicide." These, he states, and all which are of such a kind, are said to be evil in themselves. Therefore, it follows against me, etc.

But briefly I reply that these considerations do not count against me, but make use of equivocation. Whence I may well concede that something is a sin not precisely because it is prohibited by law, understanding this of written or human law; and the previously stated opinions prove nothing other than this. But nevertheless, with this concession it remains true that nothing is a sin except for the reason that it is prohibited by law, that is, except for the reason that it is against the eternal law and the divine will. And consequently, nothing is a sin in itself; for there is nothing which is of a particular nature in itself, that is not of this nature intrinsically but only through an extrinsic denomination. And the previous arguments do not prove the contrary of this . . .

Notes

1 D'Ailly is not here referring to the first proposition of the Introductory Commentary on the First Book of the Sentences, D. Rather, in this section of his work, he speaks of the following claim as the "first proposition": "that the divine will is the obligatory law or rule which is absolutely first in the class of obligatory laws." [editor].

2 D'Ailly is here referring to the fifth and sixth corollaries of the Introductory Commentary on the First Book of the Sentences, E. [editor].

3

Lectures on Romans

Martin Luther

Martin Luther (1483–1546) was a German monk and later a professor of theology at the University of Wittenberg. In 1517 he posted a sheet of *Ninety-Five Theses* on the university's chapel door, inviting scholarly discussion. These theses contained criticisms of the church's sale of indulgences and outlined the essentials of his doctrine of justification by grace alone. This act set in motion a series of events that led ultimately to his excommunication and the initiation of the Protestant Reformation. In the following excerpt from Luther's lectures on Romans, he claims that God's will is the highest good. He explicitly notes one of the radical implications of this when he suggests that one must conform one's will to God's own, even if that means willing one's own damnation.

Scholia

Chapter Nine

6. *For not all who are descended from Israel.* This passage is opposed to the presumptuousness of the Jews and as a commendation of grace, for the destruction of all haughty trust in righteousness and good works. For the Jews want to be considered the children of the Kingdom because they are the children of Abraham. Against them the apostle argues with an invincible argument, first, because they themselves cannot deny its validity. For if their presumption were true, then also Ishmael and the sons of Keturah would all be heirs of Abraham and deserving of the same dignity as Isaac, but the text plainly contains the very opposite of this. Therefore their contention is vain that they are of the same status as Isaac on the grounds that they, too, are the children of Abraham. For this does not follow, as the test

makes clear. But if they should object and say that Ishmael and the others do not deserve to be on the same plane with Isaac, not only because they were evil and deserved to be deprived of their status because of their sin, but also in the second place because they were not born of the same mother Sarah, he meets them with another example, not refuting their arguments and in a sense granting their objections, although we do not read that the other children of Keturah had sinned, and Ishmael had sinned only once. But even if this point is conceded, that they were not of the same mother what about Rebecca? In the first place, in this case there is the same mother; in the second place, the same father; in the third place, two brothers, neither of whom as yet is either good or bad; and yet without any deserving the one is called to be a son and the other to be a servant. Therefore it inexorably follows that flesh does not make sons of God and the heirs of the promise, but only the gracious election of God. Thus and only thus the Spirit and grace of God can arise only when the pride of the flesh has been humbled.

Therefore, why does man take pride in his merits and works, which in no way are pleasing to God? For they are good, or meritorious, works, but only because they have been chosen by God from eternity that they please Him. Therefore we do good works only in giving thanks, for the works do not make us good, but our goodness, rather, the goodness of God, makes us good and our works good. For they would not be good in themselves except for the fact that God regards them as good. And they only are, or are not, what He reputes them to be or not to be. Therefore our reputing or non-reputing is nothing. That is, the man who knows this is always afraid, always trembling at God's reckoning and always awaiting it. Therefore he does not know how to be proud or to argue, as the arrogant self-righteous people do, who are so sure concerning their own good works. . . .

14. *Is there injustice on God's part? By no means!* The apostle gives no other reason as to why there is not injustice with God than to say: "I will have mercy on whom I have mercy" (v. 15), which is the same as saying: "I will have mercy on whom I wish," or to him who is predestined to receive mercy. . . .

For the fact is that there neither is nor can be any other reason for His righteousness than His will. So why should man murmur that God does not act according to the Law, since this is impossible? Or will it be possible for God not to be God? Furthermore, since His will is the highest good, why are we not glad and willing and eager to see it be done, since it cannot possibly be evil? But do I hear you say: "It is evil for me"? Perish the thought! It is evil for no one. But because we cannot affect His will nor cause it to be done, this becomes an evil thing for men. For if they were willing to do what God wills, even if He should will that they be damned and reprobated, they would have no evil. For they would will what God wills, and they would have in themselves the will of God in patience.

4

Divine Commands

Robert M. Adams

The most articulate contemporary proponent of divine command morality has been Robert M. Adams (b. 1937), Professor Emeritus of Philosophy at Yale University. The following reading is taken from chapter 10 of his book *Finite and Infinite Goods* (1999). In the previous chapter, Adams argues that the concept of obligation should be understood in terms of social requirements – i.e. to be obligated to do something is to be required by some person(s) to do it. However, not just any social requirement constitutes a genuine moral obligation; if it did, morality would be too subjective and there would be conflicting moral obligations. In this chapter Adams argues that divine commands provide a more powerful basis for a social requirement theory of obligation.

1. Placing the Theory in Its Context

A divine command theory of the nature of moral obligation can be seen as an idealized version of the social requirement theory. Our relationship with God is in a broad sense an interpersonal and hence a social relationship. And talk about divine commands plainly applies to God an analogy drawn from human institutions. A possible history of the conception of moral obligation begins with social practices of promising and of commanding and obeying, and associated roles of authority. In these practices there is necessarily a place for some sort of conception of obligation, though it is not likely to have been at first a fully moral conception. Initially no need may have been felt to distinguish between what is required by human authorities and what is truly, objectively, or morally required. Experiences of abusive authority and conflicting social demands naturally

Robert Merrihew Adams, "Divine Commands" from *Finite and Infinite Goods: A Framework for Ethics* (New York: Oxford University Press, 1999), pp. 249–62.

give rise, however, to a search for a source and standard of moral obligation that is superior to human authorities. Belief in superior personal powers or gods suggests the obvious hypothesis as to the nature of such a superior standard. This history is an imaginative construction, not based on anthropological research; but I suspect that it approximates the actual history of the conception of moral obligation in more than one society.

More important, I believe that a theory according to which moral obligation is constituted by divine commands remains tenable, and is the best theory on the subject for theists, inheriting most of the advantages, and escaping the salient defects, of a social theory of the nature of moral obligation. In section 2 I will sketch what I take to be the main reasons for thinking that divine commands are (at least for theists) the best candidates for the role of broadly social facts that would constitute moral (and of course religious) obligation. Theories of this general type are sometimes stated in terms of God's "will" rather than God's "commands," and in section 3 I will explain why I prefer the formulation in terms of commands. [...]

We should be clear, first of all, about some things that are *not* claimed in the divine command theory that I espouse. Two restrictions, in particular, will be noted here. One is that when I say that an action's being morally obligatory consists in its being commanded by God, and that an action's being wrong consists in its being contrary to a divine command, I assume that the character and commands of God satisfy certain conditions. More precisely, I assume that they are consistent with the divine nature having properties that make God an ideal candidate, and the salient candidate, for the semantically indicated role of the supreme and definitive Good, [...]. It is only the commands of a definitively good God, who, for example, is not cruel but loving, that are a good candidate for the role of defining moral obligation. This point and its implications will be developed further in section 2 of this chapter [...]

The other restriction to be noted here is adumbrated in chapter 10 [of *Finite and Infinite Goods*, see bibliographical information for this reading]. It is that the divine command theory, as I conceive of it, is a theory of the nature of obligation only, and not of moral properties in general. In particular, it is not a theory of the nature of the good, but presupposes a theory of the good. The first restriction, noted in the previous paragraph, is one of the points at which this is important; for in articulating the necessary conditions on the characteristics of a God whose commands are to constitute the standard of moral obligation, and in developing the related reasons for accepting divine commands as such a standard, I make full use of the account of the nature of the good that I have given in part I [in *Finite and Infinite Goods*].[1]

This restriction of the scope of the divine command theory to the realm of obligation may be contrary to the expectations of some readers. Much of the discussion of divine command theories in analytical philosophy of religion has assumed that they would be intended to explain the nature of all values. On this point, however, my approach is not untraditional; the pattern of a divine command theory of the nature of obligation presupposing an independent conception of the good was familiar in the seventeenth century, during the heyday of divine command metaethics.

A clear example of this is found in John Locke's *Essay Concerning Human Understanding* (1690).[2] He holds that

> Good and Evil . . . are nothing but Pleasure or Pain, or that which occasions, or procures Pleasure or Pain to us. *Morally Good and Evil* then, is only the Conformity or Disagreement of our voluntary Actions to some Law, whereby Good or Evil is drawn on us, from the Will and Power of the Law-maker. (II, xxviii, 5)

The most important such law is the divine law commanded by God.

> This is the only true touchstone of *moral Rectitude*; and by comparing them to this Law, it is, that men judge of the most considerable *Moral Good* or *Evil* of their Actions; that is, whether as *Duties, or Sins*, they are like to procure them happiness, or misery, from the hands of the ALMIGHTY. (II, xxviii, 8)

Here the nature of nonmoral good and evil (as pleasure and pain) is understood independently of God's commands, and is used to explain the nature of the obligation imposed by divine commands.

A similar theoretical structure may be discerned in the writings of Richard Cumberland and Samuel Pufendorf, who define natural good as "that which preserves, or enlarges and perfects, the Faculties of any one thing, or of several"[3] or as consisting "in that aptitude by which a thing is capable of benefitting, preserving, or perfecting another thing,"[4] and then assume facts of good and evil in explaining obligation in terms of divine commands.[5]

To be sure, the good presupposed by moral obligation according to Cumberland, Pufendorf, and Locke is not the excellent, as in my theory, but only what is good *for* someone. I think all three of them rely much too heavily on reward and punishment in explaining the nature of moral obligation, though Cumberland and Pufendorf struggle to reduce this reliance. But their dependence on ideas of reward and punishment serves to underline the point that their divine command theories are theories of obligation only and not of all values; for the idea that something might be made noninstrumentally good or bad by a promise of reward or a threat of punishment has no plausibility, and I doubt that it has been endorsed by any serious philosopher.

2. Divine Commands and the Role of Obligation

Since my theory incorporates these restrictions, I will rely freely on the account of the nature of the good that I have presented in part I, and on assumptions about the character of God, in arguing, in the present section, that a divine command theory agrees very well with the features of the role conceptually assigned to moral obligation [...]. I will develop this argument with regard to several features, beginning with the reason-giving force required by the role. [...]

Writers on divine commands have often stressed hope of reward and especially fear of punishment as a motive or reason for compliance. This was noted in section 1 with regard to major seventeenth-century authors; and there can be no doubt that this motive has been showcased in much theistic ethics. I can hardly claim that this is wholely wrongheaded, inasmuch as my underlying social theory of obligation, developed in chapter 10 [of *Finite and Infinite Goods*], makes the possibility of someone being offended, and the appropriateness of sanctions, in the event of nonfulfillment, a central feature of the nature of obligation. It remains true, however, that the fear of punishment is not the best of motives, either morally or religiously; and emphasis on it can lead to the suspicion that the obligations under discussion do not fully fill the emotional and motivational role that we expect of *moral* obligations. There are better motives for compliance with divine commands, grounded in subtler aspects of a complex structure of requirements and sanctions.

1. I would particularly stress reasons for compliance that arise from a social bond or relationship with God. As in the case of human social bonds, the force of these reasons depends on the value of the relationship, which theistic devotion will rate very high indeed. If God is our creator, if God loves us, if God gives us all the good that we enjoy, those are clearly reasons to prize God's friendship. Further reasons may be found in more particular religious beliefs about covenants God has made with us for our good, or other things God has done to save us or bring us to the greatest good. Such beliefs are obviously subject to test by the problem of evil, but that is too large an additional topic to be adequately discussed here.

Many reasons of the sort I have just suggested can be characterized as reasons of gratitude. Gratitude is instanced by Pufendorf as a source of reasons for regarding the command of another as giving rise to obligation,[6] and I should perhaps indicate here my response to two objections that J. B. Schneewind has recently proposed against this point in Pufendorf's theory.[7] "One is that the appropriateness of repaying benefits with gratitude must itself be ... imposed by God, which raises the question of its justifiability." On my views, the appropriateness of gratitude is an excellence, a form of the excellence of prizing excellent relationships and of acknowledging the good deeds of others; and like excellence in general, it does not depend on God's commands. (I grant that Pufendorf's very austere conception of natural goodness may not allow him this treatment of the appropriateness as an excellence.) Schneewind's other objection is "that gratitude is only an imperfect duty and hence may not be exacted" with the strictness with which Pufendorf would exact obedience to God's commands. In my account, however (whatever may be true of Pufendorf's), gratitude is not what is being exacted but is rather a motive for complying with God's commands. Perhaps gratitude to God is religiously required, but my present argument does not depend on that.

2. I have noted that it contributes importantly to our reasons for complying with demands if the personal characteristics of the demander are excellent or admirable in relevant respects. This desideratum is spectacularly overfulfilled in the case of divine commands. God is supremely knowledgeable and wise – indeed, omniscient. On the view advocated here, indeed, God is the Good itself, supremely beautiful and rich in nonmoral as well as moral perfection.[8]

The motivational relevance of this point did not escape the great sociologist Émile Durkheim in his attempt to parody theistic ethics to get a conception of society as the source of moral obligation. "The good," he wrote, "is society . . . insofar as it is a reality richer than our own, to which we cannot attach ourselves without a resulting enrichment of our nature."[9] The religious root of this idea is obvious. Durkheim is right in thinking that the richness, for us, of the being from which requirements proceed is an important reason for compliance; but I think human society is not good enough for the role in which he casts it. The majesty of moral requirement is much better sustained by a source in a transcendent Good than in any human society.

It might be thought that if God is the constitutive standard of excellence as I have claimed, the ascription of excellence to God will be trivial and without content, merely saying that God is like God. This does not follow, for the claim that God is the standard is not inscribed as the first line on a blank slate of ethical theory. It is made, rather, against the background of many substantive beliefs about what properties are excellences that must be reflected somehow in the character of any being that is the standard of excellence.

One important excellence is justice. It clearly matters to the persuasive power of God's character, as a source of moral requirement, that the divine will is just.[10] Here, if my theory of obligation is not to be circular, I must be using a "thin theory" of justice, so to speak, which does not presuppose moral obligation as such.[11] Without going beyond such a thin theory I can say, for example, that God judges in accordance with the facts, and cares about each person's interests in a way that is good – and that it will be important to resist those inferences from the course of history that have often led to the belief that the rich enjoy more of God's favor than the poor.

Not that it is enough for a divine command theory of obligation to avoid triviality and circularity in characterizing the justice of God. It must also avoid contradiction. The latter threat is vividly presented in Schneewind's account of Leibniz's objection to Pufendorf's divine command theory. Leibniz argues that

> the voluntarist [i.e., the divine command theorist] can make no sense of the fact that God is praised because he is just. Leibniz is not making the point that linguistic philosophers of our century, believing they follow G. E. Moore, would have in mind. He is not simply claiming that voluntarism mistakenly makes the sentence "God is just" vacuous. His point is rather that we can think that God is just even though he has no superior over him. We think, that is, that someone can be just or law-abiding without the existence of a superior imposing law on him and sanctioning him. But the voluntarist thinks justice requires such a superior. Voluntarism is therefore mistaken about the concept of justice.[12]

My response to this objection turns on the relation of justice to obligation or duty. It depends on what I have called a "thin theory" of justice. Leibniz takes Pufendorf to suppose that "duty and acts prescribed by justice coincide."[13] And certainly philosophers sometimes speak of justice in a sense in which it essentially includes discharging one's obligations and doing one's duty. But that is not the sense in which it seems to me important to say that God is just. God is not praised as dutiful or law-abiding. The justice for which God is praised belongs in the first instance to the ethics of excellence or virtue rather than to that of obligation. It chiefly involves responding well to the various claims and interests involved in a situation (and we have, as I have said, a lot of substantive beliefs about what it is to respond well). Responding well is an excellence, and God is praised as the supreme and definitive standard of it, as of excellence in general. It does not essentially involve being under obligation, and can therefore belong to God even if God is not subject to obligation in the same sense as we are. God's justice, so understood, grounds obligation, rather than being grounded in it. God's commands, that is, spring from God's way of relating to creatures and their interests; and it is partly because the latter is taken to be an ideal candidate for the role of definitive exemplar of the relevant sort of excellence, that God's commands can plausibly be taken as constituting moral obligation.

3. The goodness of the command is particularly important to our reason for obeying a divine command. It is crucial (and plausible on the assumption that God is the supreme Good) that God's commands spring from a design and purpose that is good, and that the behavior that God commands is not bad, but good, either intrinsically or by serving a pattern of life that is very good. It matters to the plausibility of a divine command theory, for example, that we do not believe that God demands cruelty.

The goodness that I have thus ascribed to God's commands, to God's personal characteristics, and to God's relationship to us is the goodness whose nature I discussed in previous chapters – a goodness of which God is the standard, but which we can recognize to a significant extent. The order of presentation is significant here; it reflects the restrictions on the force and scope of a divine command theory that I stated in section 1. A theory of the good for which God is the constitutive standard of excellence need not presuppose moral obligation, but my theory of moral obligation does presuppose my theory of the good. It is only a God who is supremely excellent in being, in commanding, and more generally in relating to us, whose commands can plausibly be regarded as constituting moral obligation.

4. Given the importance I have ascribed to goodness, we might wonder if it matters whether commands are really issued by God. It may be suspected that all the work in my theory is being done by the supposed goodness of God and God's commands – that really nothing would be lost if we just said that our overriding, fully moral obligation is constituted by what *would* be commanded by a supremely good God, whether there is one or not.[14] My reasons for thinking that that is not an adequate substitute for actual divine commands parallel my reasons for not being satisfied with an ideal, nonactual human authority as a source of moral obligation.

First of all, I do not believe in the counterfactuals. I do not believe that there is a unique set of commands that would be issued by any supremely good God.[15] Some commands, surely, could not issue from a perfectly good being; but there are some things that such a deity might command and might not command. This is most obvious, perhaps, where religious ceremonies are concerned. Many people believe they are under divine commands to perform certain rituals. Few of them would claim that any supremely good God must have commanded everyone, or someone, to perform those particular rituals. Something similar may be true of more controversial cases. It is not obvious to me, for example, that there is not a diversity of principles regarding euthanasia that could have been commanded by a supremely good God; perhaps different weightings of the importance of preventing suffering as compared with other values at stake would be possible for such a deity. I may still think I have grounds, in my own and other people's moral sensibilities, and in whatever evidence I take myself to have of God's dealings with humanity, to believe that God has in fact issued certain commands on the subject. And since commands must be communicated in order to be commands, those who are subject to the commands would presumably have had different feelings, perceptions, or evidence on the subject if God's commands had been different; but that does not imply that a perfectly good God could not have commanded differently.[16]

In the second place, even aside from any doubts about whether these counterfactuals about good Gods are true, it seems to me that they are motivationally weak. They do not have anything like the motivational or reason-generating power of the belief that something actually is demanded of me by an unsurpassably wonderful being who created me and loves me. The latter belief is therefore one that ethical theory cannot easily afford to exchange for the belief that such and such *would* have been demanded of me by a supremely good God.

Besides their reason-giving force, there are several other ways in which divine commands are well suited to the role of constitutive standard of moral obligation.

1. A main advantage of a divine command theory of the nature of moral obligation is that it satisfies the demand for the *objectivity* of moral requirement. Being commanded and forbidden by God are properties that actions have independently of whether we think they do, or want them to. Divine commands are more unqualifiedly objective than human social requirements, inasmuch as their factuality is independent of socially established as well as individual opinions and preferences.

2. [...] we rightly expect a theory of the nature of right and wrong to yield a large measure of agreement with our *pretheoretical beliefs* about what actions are right and wrong. Divine commands do not have the same connection as human social requirements with pretheoretical moral opinion, and therefore do not have the same guarantee of agreement with it. But there is another way in which divine command theorists can be reasonably assured of sufficient agreement with pretheoretical views. For our existing moral beliefs are bound in practice, and I think ought in principle, to be a constraint on our beliefs about what God commands. We simply will not and should not accept a theological ethics that ascribes to God a set of commands that is *too much* at variance with the ethical outlook that we bring to our theological thinking.

I do not mean to reject the possibility of a conversion in which one's whole ethical outlook is revolutionized, and reorganized around a new center. That should be possible even in a secular approach to ethics, and all the more in a religious one. But if we are to retain our grip on ethics as a subject of discourse, we can hardly hold open the possibility of anything too closely approaching a revolution in which, so to speak, good and evil would trade places. [...]

3. A divine command theory easily satisfies the principle that facts of moral obligation should *play a part in our coming to recognize* actions as right and wrong. For it is part of the notion of a divine command, as of any command, that it is communicated (as we will see more fully in section 3 [...]). A God who issues commands must act in such a way as to make it more likely that those to whom the commands are revealed will come to think right what is divinely commanded and wrong what is divinely forbidden. God may do this in creating our faculties, in providentially governing human history, in inspiring prophets, and perhaps in other ways.

4. In chapter 10 [of *Finite and Infinite Goods*] I stressed the connection of moral obligation with the possibility of *guilt*, and the connection of guilt with rupture or straining of valued relationships. It is obvious that in theistic traditions guilt has been powerfully connected with rupture or straining of our relationship with God. A divine command theory of the nature of obligation facilitates the understanding of moral guilt as involving offense against a person. It also enriches the possibilities for dealing with guilt by helping us to understand guilt as something that can be removed, at least in one significant dimension, by divine forgiveness.

This is a significant advantage of a divine command theory, but it needs to be seen in a more complex context. Concretely, in typical cases, in theistic perspective, the problem of guilt has at least four dimensions. The most important for theists, the transcendent dimension of guilt, is damage to one's relationship with God. It is this that is most obviously and directly repaired by the repentance and forgiveness that constitute reconciliation with God. A second dimension is damage to relationships with human persons one has wronged; if this is to be repaired, it must be by reconciliation with *them*, and this is not always possible, nor always morally advisable to attempt (in "this life," at any rate).

In the third and fourth dimensions, it is the offender personally that is ruined, rather than a social relationship. And here we may distinguish, a bit artificially perhaps, between corruption and defilement. Corruption and defilement are as deeply connected with the good as with the right. By themselves, apart from their relation to an offended person, they do not constitute guilt, in my view, but they are certainly felt to be connected with it in serious cases.

Guilty action typically proceeds from a morally (and perhaps religiously) *corrupt* disposition. This calls for a sort of regeneration or healing, which may in some measure be inseparable from reconciliation with God and other people. It involves repentance, but may also involve much more; and religious traditions have much to say (and to do) about it.

In guilt one may also feel a *defilement*, from which one wishes to be cleansed.[17] This is a problem about the excellence or worth of one's life.[18] It is in principle distinct from the problem of corruption, for the defilement most closely connected with guilt could remain even if the corrupt disposition were healed. Guilt is rooted in the past, but one's past remains a part of one's life. If one has done wrong, there is still that evil in one's life. If it is significant enough, it raises the question how, as a religiously or morally serious person, one can continue to affirm one's own life as a worthwhile project.

Religious language about being "cleansed" from sin, or about the sinner being "justified" by being "counted" as "righteous" by God, serves mainly, in my opinion, to address this problem of defilement. This problem is not primarily social, but the religious solutions on offer have a fundamentally social and relational aspect. God offers renewed love; God offers rituals of expiation; Christ dies for us.[19] In ways such as these God invites us to participate in a larger story, and a relationship, that has, from its divine participant, sufficient value to swallow up the negative value of our sin.

That such a relationship is indeed the source or ground of the greatest value in our lives is a nontrivial assumption of typical religious solutions of the problem of moral defilement. More than any other of the "great dead philosophers" of the modern period, Immanuel Kant took this problem seriously, as a problem about one's moral worthiness. It was difficult for him to accept any solution to the problem, in my opinion, because he was committed to finding the chief value of one's life in the goodness of one's individual will, rather than in a larger, relational whole deriving most of its worth from a much better being to whom one is related.[20]

3. Divine Command and Divine Will

If we are to understand moral obligation in terms of divine commands, we must suppose that God has issued the relevant commands. Commands are speech acts, and this suggests difficult questions about the application of the concept of commanding to God [...] One might be tempted to escape these difficulties right at the outset by replacing the concept of God's commands with that of God's will. The two concepts often seem interchangeable in theistic ethics, and believers may think of their ethical reflection as an attempt to "discern the will of God." And God's will, unlike God's commands, seems to exist and have its content independently of what God does to communicate it. Theories similar to mine have sometimes used the concept of divine will rather than that of divine command in explaining the primary ground of obligation. Mark C. Murphy has recently presented an illuminating and uncommonly well-developed argument for preferring the divine will formulation,[21] which puts additional pressure on me to explain why I still adhere to the divine command formulation.

One reason is that a shift of attention to the concept of divine will can hardly dispense the student of religious ethics from the task of trying to understand a concept that plays such an important role as that of divine commands does in the ethics of most theistic traditions. But that is not yet a very deep explanation, and may not carry very much theoretical weight. Reasons that dig deeper are more complex and require a fuller discussion.

1. The most obvious problem for divine will theories of obligation is that according to most theologies, not everything wrong or forbidden by God is in every way contrary to God's will. It has commonly been taken as following from God's omnipotence and providence that nothing happens that is totally contrary to God's will, though deeds are in fact done that are wrong and contrary to God's commands. Many theologians have distinguished between God's *antecedent will* and God's *consequent will*. God's antecedent will is God's preference regarding a particular issue considered rather narrowly in itself, other things being equal. God's consequent will is God's preference regarding the matter, all things considered. It has commonly been held that nothing happens contrary to God's consequent will, though many things happen contrary to God's antecedent will. On the typical view, to be sure,

God's consequent will is partly permissive; some things are permitted by God that are not fully caused, or even intended, by God.

Clearly, the ground of our obligations is not to be found in God's merely *permissive will*, or more broadly in God's consequent will, inasmuch as all the wrongdoing that actually occurs is not contrary to them. An identification of the ground of obligation with God's antecedent will confronts the difficulty that we are sometimes morally obliged to make the best of a bad situation by doing something that it seems a good God would not have preferred antecedently, other things being equal. With what divine will, then, can we identify the ground of ethical obligation? The usual response has been to say that the divine will by which we are ethically bound is God's *revealed will*. And what is God's revealed will? Either it is substantially the same as God's commands; or, if it includes something else, perhaps advice or "counsels," the commands will be the most stringently binding part of it. Either way it will be God's commands that will ground obligation as such.

Murphy's paper has convinced me, however, that partisans of a divine will theory of obligation may be able to escape this argument. The key point for their escape would be that the concept of antecedent will involves a certain abstraction. God's antecedent will is what God prefers relative to a subset abstracted from the complete actual circumstances of the event. There are degrees of abstraction, and God's antecedent will that determines obligation, on Murphy's view, will be among the least abstract in the circumstances assumed in it. Murphy suggests that it will be one "which takes into account all relevant circumstances other than the actual choice."[22] That may do the trick for him; so I will not lay much weight on this argument.

2. The seriousness of the difference between divine will and divine command formulations of a theory of obligation obviously lies in what we say about the cases (if any are possible) in which there is a divergence between what God wills in the relevant way and what God commands. If God commands something that God does not (in the relevant way) want us to do, are we obliged to do it? If God (in the relevant way) wants us to do something but does not command us to do it, are we obliged to do it?

It is not easy to answer the first question either way, but I think the case it poses should not be taken as a relevant possibility in theistic ethical theory. Some theistic thinkers have thought it might even be actual – that God may, for example, have commanded Abraham to kill his son Isaac as a sacrifice without (in the relevant sense) wanting him to do it.[23] Murphy seems to think that in such a case one's obligation would be to do what God wants rather than what God commands,[24] but I think that is far from obvious for theists. Religiously, after all, obedience to God is in large part a matter of *respect* for God; and interhuman examples suggest that respect would follow commands in preference to unexpressed desires. The wait staff in a restaurant show me benevolence, perhaps, but scant respect, if they bring me what they think I want instead of what I actually ordered.

The issue is further complicated by the consideration that any reason for believing that God does not (in the relevant sense) want us to do something will virtually always be a reason, of approximately equal strength, for believing that God has not commanded us to do it. This is related to the even more fundamental point that, as Murphy puts it, "there is something troubling about the idea of God's commanding us to do something that He wills that we not do."[25] Troubling indeed: the inconsistency seems grounds for doubt that either the volition or the command involved in it could be serious enough to consitute an obligation. I therefore believe that neither a divine command nor a divine will theory of obligation should build on the supposition of such a possibility. Having said this, I may owe an explanation of how I would understand such a story as that of Abraham and Isaac; at this point I will just issue a promissory note, which will be elaborately paid off in chapter 12 [*Finite and Infinite Goods*].

3. The opposite sort of divergence between divine will and divine command, in which God wants us to do something but does not command us to do it, is an important possibility for theistic ethics. It is on this point chiefly that I think the divine command account is to be preferred. The important possibility for theistic ethics here is the possibility of supererogation. It should be possible for God to decide not to require us to do everything that God would prefer that we

do, thus leaving some of the preferred actions supererogatory rather than required. It is controversial within theistic religious traditions whether God in fact has left anything supererogatory; but I think it is no virtue in a theistic metaethics to rule out supererogation as impossible by the very nature of obligation.

This is connected with the distinctiveness of obligation. [. . .] to say that an action is obligatory is to say more than that it is the best thing to do. It is to say that one in some sense *has* to do it, and that various sanctions against not doing it are appropriate. For many reasons, we often do not want people to be *obliged* to do what we want them to *do*. So far as I can see, God can have such reasons too, so that we should not expect God to want God's wanting someone to do something to impose, automatically, an obligation to do it.

Once we are clear that there is a difference in principle between its being best that we should do something and our being obliged to do it, and a related difference between wanting someone to do something and wanting her or him to be obliged to do it, I think it should be clear that if any divine volition is suited to issue directly in an obligation that we should do something, it would be a volition that we should be obliged to do it rather than a volition that we should do it. Otherwise God will have no opportunity to take into account possible reasons for wanting something to be done *without* wanting it to be obligatory. For this reason divine will theorists might prefer the alternative of taking the existence of the obligation, rather than the doing of the deed, as the object of the divine volition that is to ground obligation.[26]

This alternative would share with divine command theories the advantage of leaving it open to God to allow for supererogation. It leaves us faced, however, with the question why God would ever leave the obligatory uncommanded. Given the strong connection, for which I have argued, between obligation and the appropriateness of social pressure, why would God ever want something to be obligatory but not command it? Perhaps, of course, in view of a mix of advantages and disadvantages, God would have an antecedent but not a consequent volition that the action be obligatory, and would not command it; but in that case the action would presumably not be obligatory, since what God wills antecedently but not consequently does not happen – certainly not insofar as it depends on God. So it seems implausible to think of divine volitions regarding obligations as grounding obligations without God issuing the relevant commands.

4. The main benefit that I can see in replacing divine commands with divine will in a theory of obligation would be avoiding the problems that attend the requirement that commands must be revealed or communicated in order to exist as commands. This benefit would depend on the assumption that the relevant divine will can be what it is, and impose obligation, without being revealed. But this yields an unattractive picture of divine-human relations, one in which the wish of God's heart imposes binding obligations without even being communicated, much less issuing in a command. Games in which one party incurs guilt for failing to guess the unexpressed wishes of the other party are not nice games. They are no nicer if God is thought of as a party to them.

It is implausible to suppose that uncommunicated volitions impose obligations. This is not a point about the knowability of moral facts in general, and I do not mean to derive it simply or directly from the principle that 'ought' implies 'can', though that principle may be hovering in the background.[27] It is rather a point about how obligations can be grounded in interpersonal relations, broadly understood. We are considering views on which moral obligation is understood in terms of what God *requires* of us. But requiring is something people *do* in relation to each other. It essentially involves communicative *acts*. The will of a legislator imposes no obligation without being communicated, as Francisco Suárez, for example, acknowledges, although he is one who uses the terminology of divine *will* in explaining the "special" or "preceptive" obligation of divine law.[28]

5. Murphy seems to favor the view that a divine volition can ground obligation without being communicated in a divine command, but he is unwilling to rest his position heavily on the assumption that it is true. Even if "moral obligation . . . must depend on divine command," he holds, "all that would follow is that the expression of God's will is at least a *validating condition* of obligation." The *grounds*, or "cause, or

source," could still be in the divine will, and that is what Murphy mainly wants to affirm.[29] I am more than willing to affirm it too, in an important sense, inasmuch as divine commands, as voluntary acts, must necessarily have their grounds or cause or source in the divine will. More than that, the divine commander will surely be conceived as willing rationally, coherently, harmoniously. We will therefore suppose that the commands of such a deity are grounded in volitions that the commanded acts be obligatory, and that they be done. What I mean to insist on is just that the divine will must be communicated in order to impose obligations. As long as that is true, I don't see why we should not interpret obligation in terms of divine commands; I also don't see why we should not regard the commands as at least *part* of the grounds of the obligations.

Notes

1 Although the divine command theory that I presented in my first essay on the subject differs in important ways from that presented here, it largely agrees on this point, stating that value concepts may be presupposed "in giving reasons for . . . attitudes toward God's commands. . . . Divine command theorists, including the modified divine command theorist, need not maintain that *all* value concepts, or even all moral concepts, must be understood in terms of God's commands" (Robert Merrihew Adams, "A Modified Divine Command Theory of Ethical Wrongness," in Gene Outka and John P. Reeder, eds., *Religion and Morality*. Garden City, NY: Anchor Press, 1973, pp. 318–47. Reprinted as ch. 7 of Adams, *The Virtue of Faith and Other Essays in Philosophical Theology*. New York: Oxford University Press, 1987, p. 109). This restriction of the scope of the divine command theory to the obligation portion of ethics is (in my opinion) not sufficiently observed in Chandler, "Divine Command Theories and the Appeal to Love," which criticizes my earlier theory precisely with regard to the viability of the restriction that I impose in terms of God's character. [John] Chandler ("Divine Command Theories and the Appeal to Love," *American Philosophical Quarterly* 22 (1985), p. 231) states that a divine command theory "asserts that ethical facts consist in facts about the will or commands of God"; and this broad conception of the theory seems to me to be presupposed in his arguments, though 'ethical facts' includes facts about the good that I have never claimed to understand in terms of divine commands.

2 The following two quotations are from the *Essay*. The view of Locke's early *Essays on the Law of Nature* may be different.

3 Richard A. Cumberland, *A Treatise of the Laws of Nature* [*De legibus naturae*]. Trans. John Maxwell. London, 1727. Fascimile reprint, New York: Garland Publishing, 1978, p. 165.

4 Pufendorf, *On the Law of Nature and of Nations*, I, iv, 4, in Samuel Pufendorf, *Political Writings*. Ed. Craig L. Carr; trans. Michael J. Seidler. New York: Oxford University Press, 1994.

5 The presupposition of an independent theory of the good in a divine command account of obligation is also foreshadowed in Francisco Suárez's discussion of natural law, when he declares, "This will, prohibition, or precept of God is not the whole reason for the good or evil involved in the observance or transgression of the law of nature. On the contrary, it necessarily presupposes the existence of a certain honorableness [*honestas*] or shamefulness in the actions themselves, and joins to them a special obligation of divine law (Francisco Suárez, *On Laws and God the Lawgiver* (*De legibus, ac Deo legislatore*). Cited by standard divisions from the portions in Suárez, *Selections from Three Works*. Ed. James Brown Scott. Vol. 1, Latin texts. Vol. 2, English translations by Gwladys L. Williams, Ammi Brown, John Waldron, and Henry Davis. Oxford: Clarendon Press, 1944, II, vi, 11). Suárez, however, is less thoroughly a divine command theorist of the nature of obligation than Cumberland, Pufendorf, and Locke. Regarding all of these thinkers, I have found the discussion of the relation of divine command theories to natural law theories in the seventeenth century in Schneewind, *The Invention of Autonomy*, very illuminating.

6 Pufendorf, *On the Law of Nature and of Nations*, I, vi, 12.

7 J. B. Schneewind, *The Invention of Autonomy: A History of Modern Moral Philosophy*. Cambridge: Cambridge University Press, 1998, p. 136.

8 Cf. Cumberland, *A Treatise of the Laws of Nature*, p. 13: the "*Authority*" of the "*Laws of God*" (which for Cumberland include "the *Conclusions of Reason* in *moral* Matters") arises in part from the "essential *Perfections*" of "their *first Author* or efficient Cause."

9 Émile Durkheim, *L'éducation morale*. Paris: Félix Alcan, 1925, p. 110.

10 The importance of God's justice for the grounding of a divine command theory is rightly emphasized in Alasdair MacIntyre, "Which God Ought We to Obey and Why?" *Faith and*

Philosophy 3 (1986): 359–71. It was wrongly neglected in some of my previous papers on divine command metaethics.

11 The terminology of a "thin theory" comes from John Rawls, *A Theory of Justice*. Cambridge, MA: Harvard University Press, 1971, though I am making a most un-Rawlsian use of it.

12 Schneewind, *The Invention of Autonomy*, p. 252. The argument under discussion is found in Leibniz, *Political Writings*, pp. 70ff. If this were a historical essay, I would want to discuss the primary source; but Schneewind's formulation, while it seems to me faithful to Leibniz's intent, puts more clearly and vividly the point that concerns us here.

13 Gottfried Wilhelm Leibniz, *The Political Writings of Leibniz*, Trans. and ed. Patrick Riley. Cambridge: Cambridge University Press, 1972, p. 70.

14 This type of objection is emphasized in Chandler, "Divine Command Theories and the Appeal to Love."

15 Nor, likewise, do I believe that, apart from an actual divine act of prohibiting, there is a unique set of prohibitions that it would be consonant with the nature of a supremely good God (and thus appropriate) to sanction with the adverse reactions characteristic of moral prohibition.

16 The issues of this paragraph are discussed more fully in Robert Merrihew Adams, "Moral Arguments for Theistic Belief," in C. F. Delaney, ed., *Rationality and Religious Belief*, pp. 116–40. Reprinted as chap. 10 of Adams, *The Virtue of Faith*, p. 148f.

17 Cf. Richard Swinburne, *Responsibility and Atonement*. Oxford: Clarendon Press, 1989, p. 74.

18 Cf. Rudolph Otto, *The Idea of the Holy*. 2nd ed. Trans. John W. Harvey. London: Oxford University Press, 1950, p. 55. Otto's vivid account of the sense of sin as a negative valuation of the self is illuminating and relevant at this point, though I do not mean to endorse it in every detail.

19 If God uses ritual and historic events to enhance the meaning of our lives, the enhancement is typically effected, I suspect, by the *symbolic* value of the events.

20 I have discussed this topic more fully in my introduction to Immanuel Kant, *Religion within the Boundaries of Mere Reason: And Other Writings*. Trans. and ed. Allen W. Wood and George di Giovanni, with introduction by Robert Merrihew Adams. Cambridge: Cambridge University Press, 1998.

21 Mark Murphy, "Divine Command, Divine Will, and Moral Obligation," *Faith and Philosophy* 15 (1998): 3–27. Cf. also P. Quinn, "Divine Command Theory," in Hugh LaFollette (ed.), *The Blackwell Guide to Ethical Theory*. Malden, MA: Blackwell Publishing, 2000, pp. 53–73, which cites Murphy's paper.

22 Murphy, "Divine Command, Divine Will, and Moral Obligation," p. 20. Murphy states his account of obligation in terms of "antecedent intention" instead of "antecedent will." The appeal to intention is part of a commendable effort to avoid allowing mere divine *wishes* to constitute obligations. I am uneasy about the conception of a divine "intention" regarding what *we* should do (which we may frustrate), even if it is an "antecedent" intention; but I pass over this issue here.

23 A recent example of this interpretation of the biblical story is cited in Murphy, "Divine Command, Divine Will, and Moral Obligation," p. 9.

24 A similar opinion on this point may be suggested in Ezekiel 20:25–6.

25 Murphy, "Divine Command, Divine Will, and Moral Obligation," p. 23 n. 17.

26 This alternative is considered and rejected in Murphy, "Divine Command, Divine Will, and Moral Obligation," pp. 10–16. The argument I propose here is not one of those discussed there.

27 Murphy ("Divine Command, Divine Will, and Moral Obligation," p. 8) seems to assume that principle would be the reason for requiring communication for voluntary grounding of an obligation.

28 Suárez, *On Laws and God the Lawgiver*, II, vi, 24.

29 Murphy, "Divine Command, Divine Will, and Moral Obligation," p. 8f.; emphases mine.

5

The Virtues of God and the Foundations of Ethics

Linda Zagzebski

Linda Zagzebski (b. 1946) is George Lynn Cross Research Professor of Philosophy at the University of Oklahoma and one of the editors of this volume. In her book *Divine Motivation Theory* (2004) she develops a form of virtue ethics based upon divine emotions. The following essay offers a brief introduction to Divine Motivation Theory (DM) and compares it to Divine Command Theory (DC). Zagzebski argues that DM has several important advantages over DC and that it avoids the standard objections to DC.

In this paper I give a theological foundation to a radical type of virtue ethics I call motivation-based. In motivation-based virtue theory all moral concepts are derivative from the concept of a good motive, the most basic component of a virtue, where what I mean by a motive is an emotion that initiates and directs action towards an end. Here I give a foundation to motivation-based virtue theory by making the motivations of one person in particular the ultimate foundation of all moral value, and that person is God. The theory is structurally parallel to Divine Command Theory, but has a number of advantages over DC theory without the well-known problems. In particular, DM theory does not face a dilemma parallel to the famous Euthyphro *problem, nor does it have any difficulty answering the question whether God could make cruelty morally right. Unlike DC theory, it explains the importance of Christology in Christian ethics, and it has the advantage of providing a unitary account of all evaluative properties, divine and human. I call the theory Divine Motivation Theory.*

"Nothing will be called good except in so far as it has a certain likeness of the divine goodness." SCG I. 40. 326.

Linda Zagzebski, "The Virtues of God and the Foundations of Ethics". *Faith and Philosophy* 15:4 (1998): 538–53.

I. The Foundations of Virtue Ethics

A moral theory is an abstract structure that aims to simplify, systematize, and justify our moral practices and beliefs. The shape of the structure itself is typically either foundationalist or coherentist, although well-known problems with both of these structures within epistemology may lead some ethicists to seek an alternative. A more radical approach is to give up the very *idea* of a moral theory, and virtue ethicists have been among the most prominent of the anti-theorists.[1] Contemporary virtue ethics, then, is often portrayed as not only an alternative to act-based theories, but as an alternative to theory itself.

Virtue ethicists are particularly skeptical about foundationalist moral theory. Aretaic theories deriving from Aristotle or Aquinas make the foundational moral concept *eudaimonia*, or human flourishing, where *eudaimonia* is derivative from or dependent upon the allegedly non-moral concept of human nature.[2] But many contemporary ethicists have despaired of ever giving a clear and plausible account of *eudaimonia*, much less one that has universal applicability, and the concept of nature has been attacked throughout the modern era on the grounds that it depends upon an outdated biology. Nonetheless, the concept of human nature has survived, if somewhat bruised,[3] and even *eudaimonia* has survived, although typically without the pretense of being foundational in the sense I mean here.[4] So skepticism about the ability of virtue ethics to even get started has kept many a contemporary philosopher away from it. And virtue theorists themselves are prone to this skepticism. So when virtue ethics entered a renaissance in the last two decades, it did so without most of the theoretical trappings of modern theories.

I am convinced that if virtue ethics is ever to be the equal rival of deontological and consequentialist ethics, it should have a form that is purely theoretical, one that addresses such basic issues as whether moral properties are grounded in non-moral properties, whether moral judgments have a truth value, where morality gets its authority, how the moral properties of persons, acts, and states of affairs are related to each other, and many others.[5] I would not deny that it is desirable to have forms of virtue ethics that ignore these theoretical issues, and we probably cannot do both at the same time. But I believe that the human need to theorize is a powerful one. We want to understand the moral world as well as the natural world and, indeed, to understand the relation between the two. For Christians there is also the need to understand the relation between the moral world and the supernatural world. The reliance of the moral world on God puts constraints on the way we answer the deep questions just mentioned, although, as far as I can tell, belief in the Christian God puts no special constraint on whether the theory is deontological, consequentialist, aretaic, or some alternative, nor on whether the structure of the theory is foundationalist, coherentist, or some alternative. But Christian philosophers have traditionally agreed that in some sense God is the foundation of moral value, and that makes the search for a foundationalist structure a natural one even though I see no reason to think that a belief in moral foundationalism is a requirement of Christianity.

In this paper I want to exhibit one way to structure a virtue ethics with a theological foundation; in fact, the theological foundation is an extension of virtue theory to God himself. It is, then, a divine virtue theory. In other work I have outlined a strong form of virtue ethics I call motivation-based.[6] This theory makes all moral concepts derivative from the concept of a good motive, the most basic component of a virtue, where what I mean by a motive is an emotion that initiates and directs action towards an end. In outlining that theory I left unanswered the important question of what makes a motive a good one. In this paper I will give motivation-based virtue theory a theological foundation by making the motivations of one person in particular the ultimate foundation of all moral value, and that person is God. I call the theory Divine Motivation Theory.

Divine Motivation Theory has the following structure: The motivational states of God are ontologically and explanatorily the basis for all moral properties. God's motives are perfectly good and human motives are good in so far as they are similar to the divine motives as those motives would be expressed in finite and embodied beings. Like motivation-based virtue theory, all moral properties, including the moral properties of persons, acts and states of affairs, are grounded in their relation to good motives, but they are more specifically grounded in their relation to the motives of a perfect being whose nature is the metaphysical foundation of all value. The theory is structurally parallel to Divine Command Theory, but it has many advantages over that theory while avoiding the disadvantages.

II. The Theory without the Foundation: Motivation-based Virtue Theory

In any foundationalist moral theory there is something that is good in the most basic way. If the goodness of something is really foundational, it cannot be justified or explained by the goodness of something else, and it is usually claimed that it *needs* no justification or explanation. Theorists almost always hedge this claim, however, and try to think of some way of justifying what the theory says cannot be justified, as Mill does in attempting to justify the goodness of pleasure in chap. 4 of *Utilitarianism*. Even Aristotle (who may not be intending to present a foundationalist structure anyway), appeals to common belief in justifying his claim that *eudaimonia* is the ultimate good in Book I of the *Nicomachean Ethics*. Kant uses a transcendental argument to defend the primacy of the Categorical Imperative. And Sidgwick reaches his allegedly self-evident moral principles from reflection upon moral intuition in *Methods of Ethics*.

What I mean by a pure virtue theory is one in which the concept of a good human trait (a virtue) is logically prior to the concept of a right act, and in the strongest form, the concept of a virtue is also prior to the concept of a good state of affairs. The theory I will outline here is an instance of the strongest form of pure virtue theory, making all evaluative concepts logically dependent upon the concept of a virtue – more specifically, on the most basic component of a virtue, a motivation. In this section I will outline the structure of a motivation-based virtue theory only briefly since my principal interest in this paper is to show how a theological foundation can be given for this theory that should be attractive to the Christian philosopher. That task will be left for sections III–V.

I propose that moral properties presuppose the existence of persons. They are either properties of persons or their acts, or they are derivative from the properties of persons, e.g., the properties of personal creations – social institutions, practices, laws, etc.[7] It is common in ethics to think of the will as the center of the moral self, and for this reason, moral properties are often thought to be most fundamentally properties of the will. The primacy of the will as the bearer of moral value emerged gradually throughout the medieval period, reaching its clearest expression during that period in the work of Duns Scotus, and, of course, reaching its zenith in the modern period in Kant's famous claim that there is nothing good without qualification but a good will. My proposal is to retain the focus of moral evaluation on the person, but to shift it away from the will, both when we are talking about God and when we are talking about human beings, and to focus instead on emotion.

I suggest that moral properties in the primary sense attach to emotions. Emotions are good or bad in themselves; they do not derive their goodness or badness from their relation to anything else that is good or bad. In particular, they are not good or bad in virtue of their relationship to the states of affairs which are their intentional objects or the states of affairs which produce them. For example, it is bad to take delight in the misfortune of others or to enjoy the sight of animals in pain, even when these emotions never motivate the agent to act on them. And the badness of these emotions is not derivative from the badness of the pain of animals or the misfortune of others. I will not give an account of the state of emotion here, but it suffices for the purposes of this paper to say that an emotion has a cognitive component as well as a feeling component. The cognitive component may or may not be as fully formed as a belief or a judgment, although it always involves taking or supposing or imagining some portion of the world to be a certain way[8] – e.g., threatening, exciting, boring, pitiful, contemptible, etc. The feeling component accompanies seeing something as threatening, exciting, contemptible. The agent feels threatened by something seen as threatening, feels excited by something seen as exciting, feels contemptuous of something seen as contemptible, and so on.

The cognitive aspect of emotion suggests that emotions have intentional objects, which is to say, a person is afraid *of* something, is angry *at* someone, is excited *about* something, loves *someone*, and so on, and some writers have taken the intentionality of emotion to be a characteristic distinguishing emotions from similar psychic states such as moods or pure feelings. I am inclined to accept this position, although it is not critical for the thesis of this paper.

A motive is an emotion that initiates, sustains, and directs action towards an end. Not all motives are emotions since some motives are almost purely physiological, such as the motives of hunger, thirst, or fatigue, and for this reason these states are sometimes called "drives". But the motives that have foundational ethical significance are emotions. It is also possible that not all emotions are motivating since some emotions may be purely passive, which is why emotions were formerly called "passions". Examples of passive emotions might include joy, sadness, tranquillity, and the enjoyment of beauty. But even these emotions probably can motivate in certain circumstances. It is usual to *call* an emotion a motive only when it actually operates to motivate on a particular occasion. But when an emotion that sometimes motivates does not operate to motivate at a particular time, it retains its motivational potential. So not all motives are emotions, but the morally significant ones are emotions, and most, if not all, emotions are or can be motives. That is, they have potential motivational force.[9]

Motives tend to be persistent and become dispositions, at which point they become components of enduring traits of character – virtues or vices. Each virtue has a motivational component which is the disposition to have an action-guiding emotion characteristic of the particular virtue. The virtuous person is disposed to perform acts motivated by such an emotion. So a person with the virtue of benevolence is disposed to act in ways motivated by the emotion of benevolence; a person with the virtue of courage is disposed to act in ways motivated by the distinctive emotion underlying the behavior of those who face danger when they judge it to be necessary to obtain a greater good; a person with the virtue of justice is disposed to act in ways expressing an attitude of equal respect for the humanity of others, and so on.[10]

A virtue also has a success component which is a component of reliability in reaching the end of the motivational component of the virtue. Some virtuous motives aim at *producing* a state of affairs of a certain kind. The state of affairs may either be internal to the agent or external to the agent. Other virtuous motives aim to *express* the emotion of the agent. Temperance is an example of a virtue whose motivational component aims at producing a state within the agent, whereas fairness is a virtue whose motivational component aims at producing a state of affairs external to the agent. Empathy and gratitude are examples of virtues whose motivational components aim at expressing the agent's emotional state. Successfully achieving the end of a virtuous motive, then, sometimes amounts to bringing about a state of affairs completely distinct from the motivating emotion, and sometimes success is achieved by merely expressing the emotion itself.

Some human motivations are good and others are bad. Good human motivations are components of virtues; bad human motivations are components of vices. If a human motive is a good one, reliable success in achieving its end is also a good thing. The goodness of the virtuous end is derivative from the goodness of the motive, not the other way around. The combination of a good human motivation with reliable success in reaching its end is a good human trait – a virtue. A vice is the combination of a bad human motivation with reliable success in reaching the end of the bad motivation.

The evaluative properties of acts are derivative from the evaluative properties of persons. Roughly, a right (permissible) act is an act a virtuous person might do. That is, it is not the case that she would not do it.[11] A wrong act is an act a virtuous person characteristically would not do. Vicious persons characteristically perform wrong acts, but so do persons who are neither vicious nor virtuous, and virtuous persons also may perform wrong acts, but uncharacteristically. A moral duty is an act a virtuous person characteristically *would* do. A virtuous act is one that expresses the motivational component of the virtue. For example, a compassionate act is one that expresses the motivation of compassion. It is an act in which the agent is motivated by compassion and acts with the intention of reaching the motivational end of compassion, the alleviation of the suffering of someone else. In the case of certain virtues, most especially justice, acts expressing the virtue are all moral duties. In the case of other virtues (e.g., compassion, kindness, mercy) many acts express the virtue but are not moral duties.[12]

The moral properties of states of affairs can also be defined in terms of good and bad motivations. Roughly, a good state of affairs is one that is the end of a good motive. A bad state of affairs is one that is the end of a bad motive.[13] Goodness and badness of motives are more fundamental than goodness and badness of states of affairs. This is a generalization of the point that all moral value derives from a personal God. (Of course, non-moral value does also, but the subject of this paper is moral value). My conjecture is that the nature of moral value is such that it must derive from persons and more particularly, from the motivational states of persons. This view on the relation between the value of a motive and the value of the state of affairs at which it aims reverses the more usual view that the motive to bring about a bad state of affairs such as pain in others is bad because pain is a bad thing. Instead, my suggestion is that pain is a bad thing in the morally relevant sense because of the badness of the motive to bring it about. That motive is an emotional state that is bad in a sense that does not derive from the badness of anything other than other motives (the motives of God).

In motivation-based virtue theory there is a logical connection between the two senses of good – the admirable and the desirable, with the latter deriving from the former. Similarly, there is a logical connection between two senses of bad – the despicable and the undesirable.[14] Intuitively the distinction between the two senses of good and bad can be important since we think there is a fundamental difference between the sense in which injustice is bad and the sense in which pain is bad, or the sense in which compassion is good and the sense in which tranquillity is good. And this difference is not simply the difference between moral and non-moral good and bad because those things that are good or bad in the sense of desirable/undesirable can have moral significance. If so, it would be very peculiar if the two senses of good and bad just distinguished were unconnected, and I am proposing that they are not. The good in the most fundamental sense of good is the admirable, and the bad in the most fundamental sense of bad is the despicable. The good in the sense of desirable is defined in terms of what is desired by admirable people, while the bad in the sense of undesirable is what admirable people desire to prevent or to eliminate.[15]

In motivation-based virtue theory motives are good or bad in the most fundamental sense of good or bad. But what makes a motive good? One way we might answer this question is to borrow a suggestion from Plato in the *Republic*, where Socrates states that a good (just) person is one whose soul is in harmony. The idea would be that motives (emotions) are good when they integrate into a harmonious whole. This suggestion is worth pursuing, but the answer I want to give here is a theological one. Moral value is constituted by a harmony with the divine, not just a harmony within the soul. Human motives are good in so far as they are like God's motives. Since motives are emotions, this means that God must have emotions, a controversial position in Christian theology, although I will argue that the theory can stand without the claim that the states in God which are the counterparts of human emotions are also emotions. In any case, human virtues are modeled on the virtues of God. In humans virtues are finite representations of the traits of a perfect God. Since the gap between God and ourselves is infinite, it may seem to be hopelessly impractical, even if theologically and metaphysically desirable, to model our moral traits on God in this way. But we have Christ incarnate as our archetype. What I will propose in what follows is a way to give the traditional Christian idea of ethics as the imitation of Christ a theoretical structure.

III. The Virtues of God

There are many accounts of virtue in the history of ethics, but all accounts agree that virtues are excellences; they are good personal traits. If we assume that the goodness of God is the metaphysical ground of all value, it is natural to ask whether God has virtues. It may seem that the answer is no, and in good Thomistic fashion I will start with the objections to the thesis before proceeding to argue that God does have virtues, and that the divine virtues include both a motivational component and a success component as described in section II. More importantly, the divine virtues are not simply pale imitations of the more robust and richly nuanced traits of embodied and encultured beings. The relationship between divine and human virtues is, in fact, the reverse: Human virtues are pale imitations of the divine virtues. Admittedly we cannot really grasp perfection and we tend to find imperfection more interesting, perhaps because it admits of more variety than perfection and we find that thinking about perfection is too demanding a task since our experience is limited to the imperfect. Nonetheless, I believe that God is the only being who is virtuous in a pure and unqualified sense. As Aquinas says, all moral properties are attributed primarily to God and only analogously to humans. I believe that this includes the virtues and the primary component of virtue, a motivation.

In giving the following objections I will work with the high metaphysical view of God's nature that was developed in the medieval period and has its most subtle and penetrating expression in the thought of Aquinas. I will, however, propose a modification of that view since I submit that God has emotions.

Objection 1: God cannot have a virtue if a virtue includes a motivational component and a motive is an emotional state since God has no emotions. God cannot have emotions since (i) emotions involve the sense appetite and require a body, but God has no body or sensory appetite, and (ii) emotions are passions, ways of being acted upon, and that implies imperfection, but God is perfect and, hence, impassible.

Objection 2: Virtues are habits that involve overcoming contrary temptations and take time to develop, so they only make sense when attributed to imperfect beings who undergo change. But God does not *develop* his traits and has no contrary temptations; he is perfect and unchangeable.

Objection 3: Virtues are traditionally explained teleologically by reference to the natural end of a thing of a certain kind, an end that is not already actualized. This means that virtue presupposes potency. The virtues are goods *for* a thing as a member of a natural kind. But God is not lacking anything and has no potency, nor does God belong to a natural kind. Furthermore, it's hard to see how anything could be good for God.

Objection 4: Virtues in their richer and more interesting forms are socially and culturally conditioned. Honesty in parts of Asia is very different from honesty in the US even when we consider only the later twentieth century. Cultural differences are even greater when we look at other historical periods. The practical usefulness of the concept of virtue depends upon our learning these richer, culture-dependent concepts. But it is hard to see how the virtues of God could serve such a practical purpose, even assuming that God does have virtues. We learn virtues by learning social practices, not by learning theology.

Virtues are the good traits of moral agents. The more perfect the moral agent, the more perfect the virtues. God is both a moral agent and a perfect being. Therefore, God has perfectly good moral traits – perfect virtues. Like all moral agents, God has motives, where motives are both explanations of and justifications for an agent's acts. In humans motives become dispositions, but if God has no dispositions, then God's motives are always *in act*, and God is always acting upon them. Since God is the perfect agent, God's motives are the perfect motives. God's love is the perfect motive of love; God's compassion is the perfect motive of compassion; God's mercy is the perfect motive of mercy, and so on. Since compassion, love, mercy, etc. are emotions, God's compassion, love, mercy, etc. are perfect emotions. I am not suggesting that it necessarily follows from the fact that God acts from compassion, and that the state of compassion in humans is an emotion, that God has emotions. I do think that having emotions is part of what makes a being a moral agent. But the minimum I want to insist upon in this paper is that God's virtues, like our virtues, include a component of motivation – a state that is act-directing, as well as reliable success in bringing about the aim of the motive. God's motives are perfect, and his success is perfect as well. God is, therefore, not just reliable, he is perfectly reliable. A divine virtue, then, is the combination of a perfect motive with perfect success in bringing about the end of the motive.[16]

Reply to objection 1: An emotion is a state of consciousness of a certain kind. I have suggested that that state includes a cognitive aspect whereby the emotion's intentional object is understood or construed to be a certain way. But an emotion is also an affective state; it has a certain "feel". Now the fact that God has no body precludes God from having emotions only if the possession of a body is a necessary condition for the states of consciousness in question, and that, of course, is denied by the Cartesian view on the relation between mind and body. Furthermore, even if Aquinas is right that sensory experience necessarily requires a body, it is not obvious that emotions necessarily have a sensory component if we mean by "sensory" a state that is of the same kind as states of consciousness that arise from the five senses or that are localized, such as the sensation of pain. But suppose we grant the objection. Suppose we agree with Aquinas that God has no passions (*passiones*) since these belong to the sensory appetite and the sensory appetite requires a body. Aquinas agrees that God does have *affectiones* since the latter admits of two kinds, sensory and intellective. God has intellective appetites which belong to the will. In this category are included states that we call emotions, states such as love and joy. We see, then, that there are two words that refer to affective states in Aquinas, "*passiones*" and "*affectiones.*" "*Passiones*" may be translated "passion" or "emotion," whereas Norman Kretzmann suggests "attitudes" as the translation for "*affectiones.*"[17] As Kretzmann translates Aquinas, then, God has certain "attitudes" of love and joy, but these states are not emotions since Kretzmann maintains that Aquinas maintains that God has no emotions. But a case could be made for translating "*affectiones*" as "emotions" if it is true that even in us, states of emotion are not necessarily sensory. If some of our emotions are, or could be, intellective *affectiones* this would mean that the sensory aspect of an emotion is not essential to a state's being one of emotion. If so, a state could not be denied the categorization of an emotion on the grounds that it is not a sensory state. Thus, even if God has no sensory states it would not follow that he has no emotions.

Objection 1 gives a second reason for thinking that God cannot have emotions and that is that emotions are passions, ways of being acted upon, and thereby imply lack of perfection. I will not here address the issue of whether emotions are necessarily passive, but I do want to raise the question of whether emotion is an intrinsically defective state, a state that only makes sense when attributed to defective beings. I do not see that there is anything about emotion *per se* that implies imperfection, although there is no doubt that there are particular emotions that do have such an implication – e.g., fear, hope, jealousy, envy, hatred, bitterness. I hesitate to say that sadness implies a defect since sadness need not require any lack in the agent who has the emotion since it is a response to defects outside of the agent. The issue of whether the agent who has a certain emotion is defective does not correspond to the distinction that is sometimes made between positive and negative emotions. Some negative emotions such as sadness may imply no defect, whereas some positive emotions such as hope probably do imply a defect. This means that while God does have emotions, he does not have the range of emotions that human beings have.

I have already said that it is not necessary to accept that God has emotions for the argument of this paper in spite of what I have said in this reply. Even if God does not have emotions, God nonetheless has states that are the counterparts of the states which in us are emotions. God has emotions in at least the same sense that God has beliefs. God's emotions may not be just like ours, but God's cognitive states are not just like ours either. What is of particular importance for Divine Motivation Theory is not so much that God's emotions are similar to ours in the way they feel, but that the divine states which are the counterparts of human emotions are motivations. That much should not be controversial. Since God is a moral agent, God acts from motives, and among those motives are compassion, forgiveness, and love.

Reply to objection 2: As Norman Kretzmann has pointed out to me, while Aquinas says that virtue is a habit, "*habitus*" to Aquinas means fundamentally the same thing as "having." The dispositional aspect of a *habitus* is important in his account of human virtues and vices because of our temporality and imperfection, but the idea of a disposition or habit is not essential to a *habitus* as Aquinas means it and does not prevent God from having qualities that in us would be habits or dispositions. For example, knowledge is a *habitus* and most human knowledge is dispositional. But the fact that God has no dispositions does not prevent God from having knowledge, nor does it prevent God's knowledge from being a *habitus* since God's knowledge is the eternal *having* of all truths. Similarly, even though a virtue such as compassion is a *habitus* which in us requires development over time culminating in a disposition distinctive of the virtue of compassion, that does not prevent God from having compassion, nor does it prevent compassion in God from being a *habitus*. God eternally has the emotion of compassion, not just as a disposition, but as an eternal motive-in-act.

Reply to objection 3: If a natural kind is a species, then God is not a natural kind, although God does have a nature and God *is* a certain kind of thing, namely, Absolutely Perfect Being, or Necessarily Existent Being. Each of the traditional arguments for the existence of God identifies a kind of thing that must be God, a kind of thing which, it must be argued, can have only one member. The divine virtues express the perfections of the kind God. There is no potency in God, but we can see that there is nothing inconsistent in the claim that a being with no potency has virtues since if, *per impossibile*, a human being reached full actualization of her potential with respect to some virtue, say, compassion, we certainly would not on that account deny that she is compassionate. The way in which a virtue is acquired is not essential to the virtue itself, although it may be essential to beings with a human nature to acquire virtue in a certain way. This means that there is nothing good *for* God if that means an extrinsic good that God needs for actualization, but there is still a sense in which God's virtues are good for him since even in the human case we do not cease claiming that what is good for us is good for us once it is attained. It is good for a human to have knowledge even when the knowledge is possessed; it is good for a knife to be sharp even when it *is* sharp. And it is good for God to be perfectly just, merciful, etc.[18]

Reply to objection 4: This is not an objection to the claim that God has virtues, nor even to the theoretical usefulness of understanding human moral properties in terms of God's virtues, but to the practical relevance of the claim for moral education and training. An answer to this objection would require a demonstration of the way the idea of a virtuous God can be integrated into the biblical doctrine of *imitatio Dei*. That issue will be addressed in the next section.

IV. Divine Motivation Theory

Motivation-based virtue theory is a very general form of pure virtue ethics in which motivational states are the most basic bearers of moral value and the moral properties of persons, acts, and states of affairs are defined in terms of the goodness and badness of motives. I outlined the way to give these definitions in section II. Divine Motivation Theory makes the motives of one being in particular the primary bearer of moral value, and that is God. The complete theory can still make the goodness of human motives the primary bearer of moral value in a universe of human persons, human acts, and the states of affairs encountered by human beings. But the goodness of human motives needs to be explained since we humans are quite clearly imperfect in our nature and the goodness of our motives is never pure.

God has such virtues as justice, benevolence, mercy, forgiveness, kindness, love, compassion, loyalty, generosity, trustworthiness, integrity, and wisdom. God does not have courage, temperance, chastity, piety, nor perhaps humility, nor does he have faith or hope. Each of the virtues in the latter group involve handling emotions that are distinctive of limited and embodied creatures like ourselves. Sexual feelings make no sense when applied to a disembodied being, and since God does not have to deal with fear, the awareness of inferiority to a superior being, the sense of powerlessness, nor the need for faith in God, which is to say, himself, it does not make sense to say that God has the virtues in this category. This means that God's virtues correspond to only some of the traits we consider human virtues. Of course, it does not follow that God's virtues are limited to these traits. It would be presumptuous of us to think that all divine virtues are perfections of human traits. If there are angels, God's virtues no doubt include perfections of angelic virtues, and if there are any other moral creatures in existence, God's virtues would include the perfections of the virtues of those beings as well. This position is expressed by Aquinas as follows:

> For just as God's being is universally perfect, in some way or other containing within itself the perfection of all beings, so also must his goodness in some way or other contain within itself

> the goodness of all things. Now a virtue is a goodness belonging to a virtuous person, for "it is in accordance with it that one is called good, and what one does is called good" [NE 1106a22–4]. Therefore, *in its own way* the divine goodness must contain all virtues. (*SCG* I. 92.768).[19]

But how are we to understand what it means for God to "contain" all the virtues, even those I have already agreed God does not have – virtues like chastity, humility, and courage? And how can the virtues God *does* have give us any practical guidance in the moral life? The answer, I suggest, is that we humans ought to think of Divine Motivation Theory in conjunction with the doctrines of the Trinity and the Incarnation. The arguments in natural theology about the nature of God do not pertain to Christ, the Incarnate Son of God. Christ did have the virtues of chastity, humility, and courage, as well as all the other virtues humans ought to develop, so the virtues of Christ are "contained" in the nature of God in the way that Christ is contained in God according to the doctrines of the Trinity and the Incarnation. This means that these important Christian doctrines have a special place in the metaphysics of Christian morals. The Incarnation also helps us to resolve the practical problem of how we learn to be moral since we are called to develop the virtues by the imitation of Christ.

The idea that humans should become as much like God as is humanly possible is the basis of the primary ethical doctrine of the Hebrew Bible, that of *imitatio Dei*.[20] "Ye shall be holy, for I the Lord your God am holy" (Lev. 19:2). To become like God is to follow God's commands: "The Lord will establish you for a holy people unto Himself, as He has sworn unto you; if you shall keep the commandments of the Lord your God, and walk in His ways" (Deut 28:9). The focus of Christian ethics, in contrast, is less on following divine commands than on imitating the virtues of Christ, and the focus of the New Testament is primarily on the motivational component of these virtues. We see Jesus in a variety of human circumstances that produce recognizable human emotions, including temptation, weariness, anxiety, sadness, and anger. Jesus makes very few commands, but when he does, his injunctions generally call us to have motivations (emotion-dispositions) which I claim are the basic components of virtues, as in the Beatitudes and the two great commandments of love. The New Testament does not typically call us to will, but to be motivated in a virtuous way, so St Paul says, "Owe no one anything but to love one another" (Romans 13:8). The Golden Rule appeals to a motive, not to a volition. We imagine how we would want to be treated and imaginatively project our own wants onto others. This leads us to have an emotional response to other persons that motivates our treatment of them. Our motive for loving and forgiving is not that we are to follow God's commands, but that God himself loves and forgives. And we see that there is no limit on the forgiveness of injuries because it corresponds to God's forgiveness of us, not because it will win over the offender or because God wills it (Matt. l8:21ff). The same point applies to the call "Be perfect even as your heavenly father is perfect" (Matt. 5:48).

Many Christian ethicists have worked on basing ethics on the imitation of Christ. Much of this work uses the narrative approach to ethics, and my purpose is not to duplicate it, but to show how this approach can be combined with the theoretical structure I have outlined here to produce a theory that is both theoretically powerful and practically useful. In addition to narrative ethics, many Christian ethicists have produced careful and subtle elucidations of the individual virtues based on Scripture and the Christian tradition of veneration of the saints. Here also I neither intend nor am able to duplicate this work which has, in any case, been done very well by others, but to show how the philosopher's theoretical urge can be formulated in a way that combines naturally with these other approaches to Christian ethics.

V. Advantages of DM Theory over DC Theory

Divine Motivation Theory is structurally parallel to Divine Command Theory in that DM theory makes moral properties derivative from God's motives, whereas DC theory makes moral properties derivative from God's will. In this section I will briefly compare the two theories to show how DM theory avoids the well-known problems of DC theory and has some decided advantages.

Divine Command theory makes the divine will the source of moral value. Roughly, good states of affairs are what God wills to exist; bad states of affairs are what God wills not to exist. The focus of the theory, however, is generally on the rightness and wrongness of human acts. An act is morally required (a duty) just in case God commands us to do it; an act is morally wrong just in case God forbids us to do it. Since a divine command is the expression of God's will with respect to human and other creaturely acts, the divine will is the fundamental source of the moral properties of acts as well as of states of affairs.

The nature of the relation between God's commands and moral requirements is an important issue for DC theorists. To say that "x is morally required" just *means* "x is commanded by God" is too strong since that has the consequence that to say "x is right because God commands it" is a mere tautology; it is just to say "x is commanded by God because x is commanded by God." On the other hand, to say that God's commands and moral requirements are extensionally equivalent is too weak. That is compatible with the lack of any metaphysical connection whatever between the existence of moral properties and God's will. The DC theory, then, aims at something in between identity of meaning and mere extensional equivalence. It should turn out that God's will *makes* what's good to be good and what's right to be right. States of affairs are good/bad and acts are right/wrong *because* of the will of God. God's will is the metaphysical ground of all moral properties. This is also the sense in which God's motives ground moral value in DM theory.

An important objection to Divine Command theory goes back to Plato's *Euthyphro* where Socrates asks, "Is what is holy holy because the gods approve it, or do they approve it because it is holy?" (10a). As applied to DC theory this question produces a famous dilemma: If God wills the good because it is good, then goodness is independent of God's will and the latter does not explain the former. On the other hand, if something is good because God wills it, then it looks as if the divine will is arbitrary. God is not constrained by any moral reason from willing anything whatever, and it is hard to see how any nonmoral reason could be the right sort of reason to determine God's choice of what to make good or bad. The apparent consequence is that good/bad and right/wrong are determined by an arbitrary divine will; God could have commanded cruelty or hatred, and if he had done so, cruel and hateful acts would have been right, even duties. This is not only an unacceptable consequence for our sense of the essentiality of the moral properties of acts of certain kinds, but it also makes it hard to see how it can be true that God himself is good in any important, substantive sense of good.

Robert Adams has attempted to address this problem by modifying DC theory to say that the property of rightness is the property of being commanded by a *loving* God. This permits Adams to allow that God could command cruelty for its own sake, but if God did so he would not love us, says Adams, and if that were the case, he argues, morality would break down. Morality *is* dependent upon divine commands, but they are dependent upon the commands of a deity with a certain nature. If God's nature were not loving, morality would fall apart.[21]

But even if Adams's proposal succeeds at answering the objection it is designed to address, it seems to me that it is unsatisfactory because it is *ad hoc*. There is no intrinsic connection between a command and the property of being loving, so to tie morality to the commands of a loving God is to tie it to two distinct properties of God. In DM theory, however, there is no need to solve the problem of whether God could make it right that we brutalize the innocent by making any such modification to the theory since being loving is one of God's essential motives. The right thing for humans to do is to act on motives that imitate the divine motives. Brutalizing the innocent is not an act that expresses a motive that imitates the divine motives. Hence, it is impossible for brutalizing the innocent to be right as long as (i) it is impossible for such an act to be an expression of a motive that is like the motives of God, and (ii) it is impossible for God to have different motives. (ii) follows from the highly plausible assumption that God's motives are part of his nature.

DC theory also can argue that God's will is part of his nature, and Stump and Kretzmann have used the Thomistic doctrine of divine simplicity, which has the consequence that God's will is identical with his nature, to solve both the arbitrariness problem and the problem that God could command something like cruelty.[22] This solution is not *ad hoc*, but it requires argument to make the needed connection between the divine will and the divine nature. That is because a will is logically separable from its possessor in a way that motives are not. In fact, the feature of a will that led to the theory of the existence of a will in the first place, namely, its freedom, is the very feature that seems to have that consequence. In contrast, God's love, mercy, justice, compassion, etc., make God what he is. There is no need to overcome by argument a prior expectation that God's motives are dissociated from his nature as in the case of God's commands.

The arbitrariness problem may or may not be answerable in a DC theory, but the problem does not even arise in DM theory. That is because a will needs a reason, but a motive *is* a reason. The will, according to Aquinas, always chooses "under the aspect of good," which means that reasons are not inherent in the will itself. In contrast, motives provide not only the impetus to action, but the reason *for* the action. If we know that God acts from a motive of love there is no need to look for a further reason for the act. On the other hand, a divine command requires a reason, and if the reason is or includes fundamental divine motivational states such as love, it follows that even DC theory needs to refer to God's motives to avoid the consequence that moral properties are arbitrary and God himself is not good. This move makes divine motives more basic than the divine will even in DC theory.

Aside from DC's difficulty with these objections, Divine Motivation theory has an important theoretical advantage. DM theory gives us a unitary theory of all evaluative properties, divine as well as human, whereas DC theory does not. DC theory is most naturally interpreted as an ethics of law, a divine deontological theory, wherein the content of the law is promulgated by divine commands. God's own goodness and the rightness of God's own acts, however, are not connected to divine commands. In contrast, DM theory makes the features of the divine nature in virtue of which God is morally good the foundation for the moral goodness of those same features in creatures. Both divine and human goodness are explained in terms of good motives, and the goodness of human motives is derived from the goodness of the divine motives. DM theory, then, is a virtue theory that applies to both divine and human moral properties.

We have already seen another feature of DM theory that gives it an advantage over DC theory, and that is that DM theory shows the importance of Christology for ethics, whereas DC theory does not. DC theory ignores the doctrines of the Trinity and the Incarnation, focusing on the will of the Creator-God as the source of moral value. It is, in effect, an Old Testament theory. The features of Christian ethics that derive from the life of Christ do not appear in the theory, at least not in any straightforward way. The fact that DM theory integrates these features into the theory makes it theologically preferable as well as easier to apply.

Elsewhere I have argued that DM theory, like DC theory, has the resources to solve some important puzzles in natural theology: the paradoxes of perfect goodness and the logical problem of evil.[23] I will not review these arguments here, but if they work, they point to an advantage that both DM and DC theory have over other theories. If DM theory also has the advantages over DC theory I have mentioned here, that suggests that a strong case could be made for DM theory. I will undertake a full defense of the theory in a longer project.[24]

Notes

1 Bernard Williams argues in *Ethics and the Limits of Philosophy* (Cambridge, Mass: Harvard University Press, 1985) that we ought to jettison moral theorizing because it takes away the knowledge needed in ordinary moral practice. Ethical theorizing has been rejected for a number of other reasons as well. See S. G. Clarke and E. Simpson, eds, *Anti-Theory in Ethics and Moral Conservatism* (Albany, NY: SUNY Press, 1989).

2 But Julia Annas argues that in ancient ethics there is no such thing as a substantial notion of the natural which is not dependent upon holding certain moral theses to be true. See *The Morality of Happiness* (Oxford University Press, 1993), p. 441.

3 See, for example, the recent book, *Is There a Human Nature?*, ed. Leroy S. Rouner (University of Notre Dame Press, 1997).

4 See Julia Annas, (*The Morality of Happiness*). A good collection of essays on happiness in ethics is *Aristotle, Kant, and the Stoics*, ed. by Stephen Engstrom and Jennifer Whiting (Cambridge: Cambridge University Press, 1996).

5 Some of these questions are usually considered meta-ethical. I reject the independence of meta-ethics from normative ethics and believe that a complete ethical theory, whether or not it is a virtue theory, should include answers to these questions.

6 *Virtues of the Mind: An Inquiry into the Nature of Virtue and the Ethical Foundations of Knowledge* (Cambridge University Press, 1996), Part II. A more detailed presentation of the theory appears in the first of my Jellema Lectures, "Making Motivation Ethically Primary," delivered at Calvin College March 1995.

7 Cf. Dietrich von Hildebrand's claim that "Moral values necessarily presuppose a person" in *Christian Ethics* (NY: David McKay Company, 1953), p. 169.

8 Compare Robert Roberts' definition of an emotion as a "concern-based construal" in "What an Emotion Is: A Sketch," *Philosophical Review* 97, 2 (April 1988), 183–209. I agree with Roberts that some aspect of the world is construed to be such-and-such in an emotional state. I add the suggestion that the such-and-such is a concept of the type listed above. These concepts are or include what Bernard Williams calls thick ethical concepts, but I will not discuss this part of my theory of emotion here. I pursue that question in "Emotion and Moral Judgment," in progress.

9 Kant's so-called pure motive of duty might be an exception to my thesis that all morally significant motives are emotions. I doubt that it is an exception, but will not discuss it here.

10 One of the problems in discussing motives is that our vocabulary about emotions and virtues is rather limited. Often we have no word for an emotion that is a component of a particular virtue or vice when we have a word for the virtue or vice itself. This is probably the case with courage and cowardice, fairness and unfairness. On the other hand, sometimes the word for the virtue or vice is borrowed from the word for the component emotion. This is probably the case with benevolence, compassion, cruelty, kindness, and many others.

11 I am using a modification of the Lewis definition of "might" in terms of "would" that appears in *Counterfactuals* (Cambridge, Harvard University Press, 1973). Lewis's definition applies to "would" and "might" as they appear in counterfactual conditionals; mine does not.

12 This distinction roughly corresponds to the distinction between perfect and imperfect duties.

13 A bad state of affairs can also be defined as one that a good motive would attempt to prevent or to eliminate, and a good state of affairs can be defined as one that a bad motive would attempt to prevent or to eliminate.

14 "Undesirable" is probably too weak a word to apply to what we think is truly repulsive, but I know of no more appropriate word.

15 A natural question to raise at this point is whether we could define the undesirable in terms of what despicable persons desire, and if so, whether the definition would parallel the definition of "desirable". I have not thought about this sufficiently to have an answer.

16 This raises questions about what counts as perfect success. Is it the highest possible number of successes? That, of course, leads to paradoxes. I will leave the analysis of perfect success for another project, but I think we can at least say that it is impossible for God to try and fail. God's perfect compassion means at least that whenever he attempts to act compassionately, he succeeds in his aim.

17 See Norman Kretzmann, *The Metaphysics of Theism: Aquinas's Natural Theology in* Summa contra gentiles I (Oxford: Clarendon Press, 1997) for the most detailed commentary on Aquinas's natural theology in recent decades. The translation to which I refer appears in Chapter Eight.

18 I thank Norman Kretzmann for suggesting this line of reply to the objection that nothing is good for God.

19 Translation by Norman Kretzmann, quoted in Kretzmann, *The Metaphysics of Theism*, p. 251.

20 See Menachem Kellner, "Jewish Ethics," *A Companion to Ethics,* ed. Peter Singer (Blackwell, 1991), p. 84.

21 Adams, "Divine Command Metaethics Modified Again," *Journal of Religious Ethics 7* (1979), 66–79.

22 Eleonore Stump and Norman Kretzmann, "Absolute Simplicity," *Faith and Philosophy* 2 (1985), 353–82. Stump and Kretzmann present the same view in "Being and Goodness," *Divine and Human Action,* ed. Thomas V. Morris (Ithaca: Cornell University Press, 1988).

23 "An Agent-Based Approach to the Problem of Evil," *International Journal for the Philosophy of Religion*, 39 (June 1996) 127–39; "Perfect Goodness and Divine Motivation Theory," *Midwest Studies*, vol. 20 (Philosophy of Religion), 1997.

24 *Divine Motivation Theory* (Cambridge University Press, 2004).

C

Natural Law

1

Selections from *Treatise on Law*

Thomas Aquinas

Thomas Aquinas (1225–74) was a Dominican friar and arguably the most influential Christian philosopher and theologian of all time. In this reading he distinguishes four kinds of law – eternal, natural, human, and divine. The eternal law is, roughly, God's provident governance of the world and is the most fundamental of the four laws. The eternal law is, in part, "imprinted on" created things so that they are inclined towards their proper ends; this is the natural law. The human law refers to laws that result from humans' use of reason to derive specific rules from the natural law imprinted on them. Finally, the divine law refers to the part of the eternal law that is revealed to us by God; divine law is needed because of the limitations of human understanding.

First Article: Whether there is an Eternal Law?

We proceed thus to the First Article:

Objection 1. It would seem that there is no eternal law. Because every law is imposed on someone. But there was not someone from eternity on whom a law could be imposed: since God alone was from eternity. Therefore no law is eternal.

Obj. 2. Further, promulgation is essential to law. But promulgation could not be from eternity: because there was no one to whom it could be promulgated from eternity. Therefore no law can be eternal.

Obj. 3. Further, a law implies order to an end. But nothing ordained to an end is eternal: for the last end alone is eternal. Therefore no law is eternal.

On the contrary, Augustine says (*De Lib. Arb.* i. 6): *That Law which is the Supreme Reason cannot be understood to be otherwise than unchangeable and eternal.*

I answer that, As stated above (Q. XC., A. 1 *ad* 2; AA. 3, 4), a law is nothing else but a dictate

Thomas Aquinas, *Treatise on Law* from *Summa Theologica*, trans. Fathers of the English Dominican Province (Benziger Bros, 1947), pp. 12–22.

of practical reason emanating from the ruler who governs a perfect community. Now it is evident, granted that the world is ruled by Divine Providence, as was stated in the First Part (Q. XXII., AA. 1, 2), that the whole community of the universe is governed by Divine Reason. Wherefore the very Idea of the government of things in God the Ruler of the universe, has the nature of a law. And since the Divine Reason's conception of things is not subject to time but is eternal, according to Prov. viii. 23, therefore it is that this kind of law must be called eternal.

Reply Obj. 1. Those things that are not in themselves, exist with God, inasmuch as they are foreknown and pre-ordained by Him, according to Rom. iv. 17: *Who calls those things that are not, as those that are.* Accordingly the eternal concept of the Divine law bears the character of an eternal law, in so far as it is ordained by God to the government of things foreknown by Him.

Reply Obj. 2. Promulgation is made by word of mouth or in writing; and in both ways the eternal law is promulgated: because both the Divine Word and the writing of the Book of Life are eternal. But the promulgation cannot be from eternity on the part of the creature that hears or reads.

Reply Obj. 3. The law implies order to the end actively, in so far as it directs certain things to the end; but not passively, – that is to say, the law itself is not ordained to the end, – except accidentally, in a governor whose end is extrinsic to him, and to which end his law must needs be ordained. But the end of the Divine government is God Himself, and His law is not distinct from Himself. Wherefore the eternal law is not ordained to another end.

Second Article: Whether there is a Natural Law?

We proceed thus to the Second Article:

Objection 1. It would seem that there is no natural law in us. Because man is governed sufficiently by the eternal law: for Augustine says (*De Lib. Arb.* i) that *the eternal law is that by which it is right that all things should be most orderly.* But nature does not abound in superfluities as neither does she fail in necessaries. Therefore no law is natural to man.

Obj. 2. Further, by the law man is directed, in his acts, to the end, as stated above (Q. XC., A. 2). But the directing of human acts to their end is not a function of nature, as is the case in irrational creatures, which act for an end solely by their natural appetite; whereas man acts for an end by his reason and will. Therefore no law is natural to man.

Obj. 3. Further, the more a man is free, the less is he under the law. But man is freer than all the animals, on account of his free-will, with which he is endowed above all other animals. Since therefore other animals are not subject to a natural law, neither is man subject to a natural law.

On the contrary, A gloss on Rom. ii. 14: *When the Gentiles, who have not the law, do by nature those things that are of the law,* comments as follows: *Although they have no written law, yet they have the natural law, whereby each one knows, and is conscious of, what is good and what is evil.*

I answer that, As stated above (Q. XC., A. 1 *ad* 1), law, being a rule and measure, can be in a person in two ways: in one way, as in him that rules and measures; in another way, as in that which is ruled and measured, since a thing is ruled and measured, in so far as it partakes of the rule or measure. Wherefore, since all things subject to Divine providence are ruled and measured by the eternal law, as was stated above (A. 1); it is evident that all things partake somewhat of the eternal law, in so far as, namely, from its being imprinted on them, they derive their respective inclinations to their proper acts and ends. Now among all others, the rational creature is subject to Divine providence in the most excellent way, in so far as it partakes of a share of providence, by being provident both for itself and for others. Wherefore it has a share of the Eternal Reason, whereby it has a natural inclination to its proper act and end: and this participation of the eternal law in the rational creature is called the natural law. Hence the Psalmist after saying (Ps. iv. 6): *Offer up the sacrifice of justice,* as though someone asked what the works of justice are, adds: *Many say, Who showeth us good things?* in answer to which question he says: *The light of Thy countenance, O Lord, is signed upon us:* thus implying that the light of natural reason, whereby we discern what is good and what is evil, which is the function of the natural law, is nothing else than an imprint on us of the Divine light. It is therefore evident that the natural law is nothing else than the rational creature's participation of the eternal law.

Reply Obj. 1. This argument would hold, if the natural law were something different from the eternal law: whereas it is nothing but a participation thereof, as stated above.

Reply Obj. 2. Every act of reason and will in us is based on that which is according to nature, as stated above (Q. X., A. 1): for every act of reasoning is based on principles that are known naturally, and every act of appetite in respect of the means is derived from the natural appetite in respect of the last end. Accordingly the first direction of our acts to their end must needs be in virtue of the natural law.

Reply Obj. 3. Even irrational animals partake in their own way of the Eternal Reason, just as the rational creature does. But because the rational creature partakes thereof in an intellectual and rational manner, therefore the participation of the eternal law in the rational creature is properly called a law, since a law is something pertaining to reason, as stated above (Q. XC., A. 1). Irrational creatures, however, do not partake thereof in a rational manner, wherefore there is no participation of the eternal law in them, except by way of similitude.

Third Article: Whether there is a Human Law?

We proceed thus to the Third Article:

Objection 1. It would seem that there is not a human law. For the natural law is a participation of the eternal law, as stated above (A. 2). Now through the eternal law *all things are most orderly*, as Augustine states (*De Lib. Arb.* i. 6). Therefore the natural law suffices for the ordering of all human affairs. Consequently there is no need for a human law.

Obj. 2. Further, a law bears the character of a measure, as stated above (Q. XC., A. 1). But human reason is not a measure of things, but vice versa, as stated in *Metaph.* x., text 5. Therefore no law can emanate from human reason.

Obj. 3. Further a measure should be most certain, as stated in *Metaph.* x., text. 3. But the dictates of human reason in matters of conduct are uncertain, according to Wis. ix. 14: *The thoughts of mortal men are fearful, and our counsels uncertain.* Therefore no law can emanate from human reason.

On the contrary, Augustine (*De Lib. Arb.* i. 6), distinguishes two kinds of law, the one eternal, the other temporal, which he calls human.

I answer that, As stated above (Q. XC., A. 1 *ad* 2), a law is a dictate of the practical reason. Now it is to be observed that the same procedure takes place in the practical and in the speculative reason: for each proceeds from principles to conclusions, as stated above (*ibid.*). Accordingly we conclude that just as, in the speculative reason, from naturally known indemonstrable principles, we draw the conclusions of the various sciences, the knowledge of which is not imparted to us by nature, but acquired by the efforts of reason, so too it is from the precepts of the natural law, as from general and indemonstrable principles, that the human reason needs to proceed to the more particular determination of certain matters. These particular determinations, devised by human reason, are called human laws, provided the other essential conditions of law be observed, as stated above (Q. XC., AA. 2, 3, 4). Wherefore Tully says in his *Rhetoric* (*De Invent. Rhet.* ii.) that *justice has its source in nature; thence certain things came into custom by reason of their utility; afterwards these things which emanated from nature and were approved by custom, were sanctioned by fear and reverence for the law.*

Reply Obj. 1. The human reason cannot have a full participation of the dictate of the Divine Reason, but according to its own mode, and imperfectly. Consequently, as on the part of the speculative reason, by a natural participation of Divine Wisdom, there is in us the knowledge of certain general principles, but not proper knowledge of each single truth, such as that contained in the Divine Wisdom; so too, on the part of the practical reason, man has a natural participation of the eternal law, according to certain general principles, but not as regards the particular determinations of individual cases, which are, however, contained in the eternal law. Hence the need for human reason to proceed further to sanction them by law.

Reply Obj. 2. Human reason is not, of itself, the rule of things: but the principles impressed on it by nature, are general rules and measures of all things relating to human conduct, whereof the natural reason is the rule and measure, although it is not the measure of things that are from nature.

Reply Obj. 3. The practical reason is concerned with practical matters, which are singular and contingent: but not with necessary things, with which the speculative reason is concerned. Wherefore human laws cannot have that inerrancy that belongs to the demonstrated conclusions of sciences. Nor is it necessary for every measure to be altogether unerring and certain, but according as it is possible in its own particular genus.

Fourth Article: Whether there was any Need for a Divine Law?

We proceed thus to the Fourth Article:

Objection 1. It would seem that there was no need for a Divine law. Because, as stated above (A. 2), the natural law is a participation in us of the eternal law. But the eternal law is a Divine law, as stated above (A. 1). Therefore there is no need for a Divine law in addition to the natural law, and human laws derived therefrom.

Obj. 2. Further, it is written (Ecclus. xv. 14) that *God left man in the hand of his own counsel.* Now counsel is an act of reason, as stated above (Q. XIV., A. 1). Therefore man was left to the direction of his reason. But a dictate of human reason is a human law, as stated above (A. 3). Therefore there is no need for man to be governed also by a Divine law.

Obj. 3. Further, human nature is more self-sufficing than irrational creatures. But irrational creatures have no Divine law besides the natural inclination impressed on them. Much less, therefore, should the rational creature have a Divine law in addition to the natural law.

On the contrary, David prayed God to set His law before him, saying (Ps. cxviii. 33): *Set before me for a law the way of Thy justifications, O Lord.*

I answer that, Besides the natural and the human law it was necessary for the directing of human conduct to have a Divine law. And this for four reasons. First, because it is by law that man is directed how to perform his proper acts in view of his last end. And indeed if man were ordained to no other end than that which is proportionate to his natural faculty, there would be no need for man to have any further direction on the part of his reason, besides the natural law and human law which is derived from it. But since man is ordained to an end of eternal happiness which is inproportionate to man's natural faculty, as stated above (Q. V., A. 5), therefore it was necessary that, besides the natural and the human law, man should be directed to his end by a law given by God.

Secondly, because, on account of the uncertainty of human judgment, especially on contingent and particular matters, different people form different judgments on human acts; whence also different and contrary laws result. In order, therefore, that man may know without any doubt what he ought to do and what he ought to avoid, it was necessary for man to be directed in his proper acts by a law given by God, for it is certain that such a law cannot err.

Thirdly, because man can make laws in those matters of which he is competent to judge. But man is not competent to judge of interior movements, that are hidden, but only of exterior acts which appear: and yet for the perfection of virtue it is necessary for man to conduct himself aright in both kinds of acts. Consequently human law could not sufficiently curb and direct interior acts; and it was necessary for this purpose that a Divine law should supervene.

Fourthly, because, as Augustine says (*De Lib. Arb.* i. 5, 6), human law cannot punish or forbid all evil deeds: since while aiming at doing away with all evils, it would do away with many good things, and would hinder the advance of the common good, which is necessary for human intercourse. In order therefore, that no evil might remain unforbidden and unpunished, it was necessary for the Divine law to supervene, whereby all sins are forbidden.

And these four causes are touched upon in Ps. cxviii. 8, where it is said: *The law of the Lord is unspotted, i.e.,* allowing no foulness of sin; *converting souls,* because it directs not only exterior, but also interior acts; *the testimony of the Lord is faithful,* because of the certainty of what is true and right; *giving wisdom to little ones,* by directing man to an end supernatural and Divine.

Reply Obj. 1. By the natural law the eternal law is participated proportionately to the capacity of human nature. But to his supernatural end man needs to be directed in a *yet* higher way. Hence the additional law given by God, whereby man shares more perfectly in the eternal law.

Reply Obj. 2. Counsel is a kind of inquiry: hence it must proceed from some principles. Nor is it enough for it to proceed from principles imparted by nature, which are the precepts of the natural law, for the reasons given above: but there is need for certain additional principles, namely, the precepts of the Divine law.

Reply Obj. 3. Irrational creatures are not ordained to an end higher than that which is proportionate to their natural powers: consequently the comparison fails.

VII

THE PROBLEM OF EVIL

Introduction

Plato says in the *Republic*, our first reading in the section, that God is good, and therefore cannot be the cause of evil. But if God is also omnipotent, why is there evil in the world? In the second reading, Lactantius, one of the early Church Fathers, quotes Epicurus as asking, "God either wishes to take away evils, and is unable; or he is able, and is unwilling; or he is neither willing nor able, or he is both willing and able . . . If he is both willing and able, which alone is suitable to God, from what source then are evils? or why does he not remove them?" This is the logical problem of evil. The basic structure of the problem has remained unchanged up to the contemporary period, but the variation known as the evidential problem of evil currently receives more attention (see the selection from Rowe). According to this version of the problem, the existence of evil seems to be *evidence* against the existence of an omnipotent and perfectly good God. Proponents of the problem interpreted this way acknowledge the logical possibility that an omnipotent and perfectly good being would have a morally sufficient reason to permit evil. The difficulty is that there is no evidence that there *is* such a reason for many evils that actually occur.

St Augustine maintained that good and evil are not ontologically on a par. Evil is a lack of being; corruptible things have lesser degrees of being than the perfect being which is God, and so they necessarily lack what is good. Evil choice is a turning away of the will from God. This is the core idea of the Free Will Defense, which is still often considered the strongest response to the problem of evil among theists.

In the eighteenth century Leibniz proposed that God would create the best of all possible worlds. In his formal summary of the *Theodicy*, Leibniz contrives to demonstrate that since a being perfect in power, knowledge, and goodness would create the best world, this world must be the best. The original imperfection of the creatures of the world brings it about that even the best plan of the universe cannot admit more good or be exempted from the evils of the world. In his Myth of the Goddess Pallas, Leibniz presents his view in the form of the story of Theodorus, who travels to Athens and visits the temple of the goddess Pallas, the daughter of Jupiter. Theodorus falls asleep and Pallas speaks to him, showing him the representations of not only everything that happens, but also everything that is possible. She tells him that her father, Jupiter, surveyed all the possibilities at the beginning and chose the best world to create, a world in which crimes and suffering serve a role.

There are many developments and emendations to the classic free will defense. We have included the well-known treatment by Alvin Plantinga, who responds to Mackie's objection that even if a world with free will and evil is better than a world with no free will and no evil, even better would be a world with free will and no evil. Plantinga argues that even if there are possible worlds with free will and no evil, it is possible that none of those worlds can be strongly actualized by God, given that if God creates a world with free creatures, he only creates part of a world – matter, laws of nature, and the free creatures. Even an omnipotent God cannot control the fact that the world that *would* result from any one of his creative choices is a certain world, and it is possible that every such world contains evil.

John Hick's soul-making theodicy is another well-known addition to the free will defense. Hick argues that a complete soul in the image of God cannot be made all at once. To be like God requires choice. God cannot create a fully mature soul that exists in communion with him, so he creates an immature soul with the capacity to become a freely loving creature. Sin and suffering are part of the "soul-making" process. In Hick's theodicy, freedom is not itself the good that outweighs the evils that it brings with it, but it is a necessary accompaniment to the great good of souls freely loving and accepting a relationship with God.

Marilyn Adams argues that the problem of evil is not solved unless God guarantees to each person a life that is a great good on the whole. This requires that there be an afterlife of a special kind, one in which the evils of each life are defeated through participation in the divine life. The infinite good that God *is* engulfs the evils that humans suffer, and is the only thing good enough to defeat horrendous evils. Intimacy with God conveys meaning and value even to horrible suffering. Clearly, this is a solution that requires that death is not the end of the existence of a human person, the topic of the next section.

Some of the readings from section VI can also be usefully discussed in conjunction with the problem of evil examined in this section. This problem is almost always formulated in a way that assumes that a good agent aims to prevent outcomes independently identified as evil. What makes something evil is independent of what anybody feels, desires, or wills. But there are theistic theories of morality that understand good and evil as projections of the divine will, commands, motives, or preferences. Some forms of Divine Command Theory and Zagzebski's Divine Motivation Theory are in this category.

1

God is Not the Author of Evil

Plato

In the following brief selection from Plato's *Republic*, Socrates and Plato's brother, Adimantus, discuss the standards to which poets would be held in an ideal state, particularly concerning the way they represent the gods in relation to good and evil.

Adimantus, we are not poets, you and I at present, but founders of a state. And to founders it pertains to know the patterns on which poets must compose their fables and from which their poems must not be allowed to deviate, but the founders are not required themselves to compose fables.

Right, he said, but this very thing – the patterns or norms of right speech about the gods – what would they be?

Something like this, I said. The true quality of God we must always surely attribute to him whether we compose in epic, melic, or tragic verse.

We must.

And is not God of course good in reality and always to be spoken of as such?

Certainly.

But further, no good thing is harmful, is it?

I think not.

Can what is not harmful harm?

By no means.

Can that which does not harm do any evil?

Not that either.

But that which does no evil would not be cause of any evil either?

How could it?

Once more, is the good beneficent?

Yes.

It is the cause, then, of welfare?

Yes.

Then the good is not the cause of all things, but of things that are well it is the cause – of things that are ill it is blameless.

Entirely so, he said.

Neither, then, could God, said I, since he is good, be, as the multitude say, the cause of all things, but for mankind he is the cause of few things, but of many things not the cause. For good things are far fewer with us than evil, and for the good we must assume no other cause than God, but the cause of evil we must look for in other things and not in God.

What you say seems to me most true, he replied.

Then, said I, we must not accept from Homer or any other poet the folly of such error as this about the gods, when he says,

> Two urns stand on the floor of the palace of Zeus and are filled with Dooms he allots, one of blessings, the other of gifts that are evil.[1]

And to whomsoever Zeus gives of both commingled

> Now upon evil he chances and now again good is his portion.

But the man for whom he does not blend the lots, but to whom he gives unmixed evil –

> Hunger devouring drives him, a wanderer over the wide world.

Nor will we tolerate the saying that

> Zeus is dispenser alike of good and of evil to mortals.

But as to the violation of the oaths and the truce by Pandarus, if anyone affirms it to have been brought about by the action of Athena and Zeus, we will not approve, nor that the strife and contention of the gods were the doing of Themis and Zeus, nor again must we permit our youth to hear what Aeschylus says.

> A god implants the guilty cause in men
> When he would utterly destroy a house.

But if any poets compose a 'Sorrows of Niobe,' the poem that contains these iambics, or a tale of the Pelopidae or of Troy, or anything else of the kind, we must either forbid them to say that these woes are the work of God, or they must devise some such interpretation as we now require, and must declare that what God did was righteous and good, and they were benefited by their chastisement. But that they were miserable who paid the penalty, and that the doer of this was God, is a thing that the poet must not be suffered to say. If on the other hand he should say that for needing chastisement the wicked were miserable and that in paying the penalty they were benefited by God, that we must allow. But as to saying that God, who is good, becomes the cause of evil to anyone, we must contend in every way that neither should anyone assert this in his own city if it is to be well governed nor anyone hear it, neither younger nor older, neither telling a story in meter or without meter, for neither would the saying of such things, if they are said, be holy, nor would they be profitable to us or concordant with themselves.

I cast my vote with yours for this law, he said, and am well pleased with it.

This, then, said I, will be one of the laws and patterns concerning the gods to which speakers and poets will be required to conform, that God is not the cause of all things, but only of the good.

Note

1 *Iliad* 24.527 sq.

2

On the Anger of God

Lactantius

One of the most elegant and concise statements of the problem of evil has been attributed to Epicurus (341–270 BC), although it has not survived in his own writings. The following reading from the early Christian apologist, Lactantius (*c.* 250–*c.* 325), is of interest for two reasons. First, it contains the oldest known testimony of Epicurus' argument, and second, Lactantius responds to that argument by offering an early version of what is commonly referred to as a "greater goods defense." Lactantius argues that wisdom is not possible apart from evil; thus, God does not desire to eliminate evil because it is necessary for the sake of the greater good of wisdom.

But the Academics, arguing against the Stoics, are accustomed to ask why, if God made all things for the sake of men, many things are found even opposed, and hostile, and injurious to us, as well in the sea as on the land. And the Stoics, without any regard to the truth, most foolishly repelled this. For they say that there are many things among natural productions,[1] and reckoned among animals, the utility of which hitherto[2] escapes notice, but that this is discovered in process of the times, as necessity and use have already discovered many things which were unknown in former ages. What utility, then, can be discovered in mice, in beetles, in serpents, which are troublesome and pernicious to man? Is it that some medicine lies concealed in them? If there is any, it will at some time be found out, namely, as a remedy against evils, whereas they complain that it is altogether evil. They say that the viper, when burnt and reduced to ashes, is a remedy for the bite of the same beast. How much better had it been that it should not exist at all, than that a remedy should be required against it drawn from itself?

They might then have answered with more conciseness and truth after this manner. When

Lactantius, *On the Anger of God* from *Works of Lactantius*, vol. 2, ed. Alexander Roberts and James Donaldson. Ante-Nicene Christian Library 22 (Edinburgh: T. & T. Clark, 1871), pp. 26–8.

God had formed man as it were His own image, that which was the completion of His workmanship, He breathed wisdom into him alone, so that he might bring all things into subjection to his own authority and government, and make use of all the advantages of the world. And yet He set before him both good and evil things, inasmuch as He gave to him wisdom, the whole nature of which is employed in discerning things evil and good: for no one can choose better things, and know what is good, unless he at the same time knows to reject and avoid the things which are evil. They are both mutually connected with each other, so that, the one being taken away, the other must also be taken away. Therefore, good and evil things being set before it, then at length wisdom discharges its office, and desires the good for usefulness, but rejects the evil for safety. Therefore, as innumerable good things have been given which it might enjoy, so also have evils, against which it might guard. For if there is no evil, no danger – nothing, in short, which can injure man – all the material of wisdom is taken away, and will be unnecessary for man. For if only good things are placed in sight, what need is there of reflection, of understanding, of knowledge, of reason? since, wherever he shall extend his hand, that is befitting and adapted to nature: so that if any one should wish to place a most exquisite dinner before infants, who as yet have no taste, it is plain that each will desire that to which either impulse, or hunger, or even accident, shall attract them; and whatever they shall take, it will be useful and salutary to them. What injury will it therefore be for them always to remain as they are, and always to be infants and unacquainted with affairs? But if you add a mixture either of bitter things, or things useless, or even poisonous, they are plainly deceived through their ignorance of good and evil, unless wisdom is added to them, by which they may have the rejection of evil things and the choice of good things.

You see, therefore, that we have greater need of wisdom on account of evils; and unless these things had been proposed to us, we should not be a rational animal. But if this account is true, which the Stoics were in no manner able to see, that argument also of Epicurus is done away. God, he says, either wishes to take away evils, and is unable; or He is able, and is unwilling; or He is neither willing nor able, or He is both willing and able. If He is willing and is unable, He is feeble, which is not in accordance with the character of God; if He is able and unwilling, He is envious, which is equally at variance with God; if He is neither willing nor able, He is both envious and feeble, and therefore not God; if He is both willing and able, which alone is suitable to God, from what source then are evils? or why does He not remove them? I know that many of the philosophers, who defend providence, are accustomed to be disturbed by this argument, and are almost driven against their will to admit that God takes no interest in anything, which Epicurus especially aims at; but having examined the matter, we easily do away with this formidable argument. For God is able to do whatever He wishes, and there is no weakness or envy in God. He is able, therefore, to take away evils; but He does not wish to do so, and yet He is not on that account envious. For on this account He does not take them away, because He at the same time gives wisdom, as I have shown; and there is more of goodness and pleasure in wisdom than of annoyance in evils. For wisdom causes us even to know God, and by that knowledge to attain to immortality, which is the chief good. Therefore, unless we first know evil, we shall be unable to know good. But Epicurus did not see this, nor did any other, that if evils are taken away, wisdom is in like manner taken away; and that no traces of virtue remain in man, the nature of which consists in enduring and overcoming the bitterness of evils. And thus, for the sake of a slight gain[3] in the taking away of evils, we should be deprived of a good, which is very great, and true, and peculiar to us. It is plain, therefore, that all things are proposed for the sake of man, as well evils as also goods.

Notes

1 "Gignentium."
2 "Adhuc," omitted in many manuscripts.
3 "Propter exiguum compendium sublatorum malorum."

3

That Which Is, Is Good

Augustine

Aurelius Augustinus (354–430), or St Augustine of Hippo, converted to Christianity at the age of thirty-two and went on to become Bishop of Hippo Regius, a city in North Africa. His writings had (and continue to have) a profound influence on philosophers and theologians, and he was perhaps the single individual most responsible for uniting Christianity and Greek philosophy into a single intellectual tradition. The following passages are from book VII of the *Confessions*, Augustine's spiritual and intellectual autobiography. In them, Augustine wrestles with the nature of good and evil, arguing that everything that exists is good, and that evil is not itself a thing, but rather a corruption of that which is good.

11

And I considered the other things which are below you, and I saw that, in a complete sense, they neither are nor are not in existence. They are, since they are from you; they are not, since they are not what you are. For that which truly is, is that which remains unchangeably. *It is good then for me to hold fast unto God*; because if I do not remain in Him, I shall not be able to remain in myself. But He, remaining in Himself, renews all things. And *Thou art my Lord, since Thou standest not in need of my goodness.*

12

And it became clear to me that things which are subject to corruption are good. They would not be subject to corruption if they were either supremely good or not good at all; for, if they were supremely good, they would be incorruptible,

Augustine, Book VII: Chapters 11, 12, 16 from *The Confessions of St Augustine*, trans. Rex Warner (New York: New American Library, 1963), extracts from pp. 150–1, 153.

and, if there was nothing good in them, there would be nothing which could be corrupted. For corruption does harm, and, unless what is good in a thing is diminished, no harm could be done. Therefore, either corruption does no harm (which is impossible), or (which is quite certain) all things which suffer corruption are deprived of something good in them. Supposing them to be deprived of all good, they will cease to exist altogether. For, if they continue to exist and can no longer be corrupted, they will be better than before, because they will be permanently beyond the reach of corruption. What indeed could be more monstrous than to assert that things could become better by losing all their goodness? So if they are deprived of all good, they will cease to exist altogether. Therefore, so long as they exist, they are good. Therefore, all things that are, are good, and as to that evil, the origin of which I was seeking for, it is not a substance, since, if it were a substance, it would be good. For it would either have to be an incorruptible substance (which is the highest form of goodness) or else a corruptible substance (which, unless it had good in it, could not be corruptible). So I saw plainly and clearly that you have made all things good, nor are there any substances at all which you have not made. And because you did not make all things equal, therefore they each and all have their existence; because they are good individually, and at the same time they are altogether very good, because our God *made all things very good.*

[. . .]

16

I knew from my own experience that there is nothing strange in the fact that a sick person will find uneatable the same bread which a healthy person enjoys, or that good eyes love the light and bad eyes hate it. Your justice too displeases the wicked, and even more displeasing are vipers and reptiles, though you created them good and well fitted to the lower parts of your creation, and to these lower parts of creation the wicked themselves are well fitted and become the better fitted the more they are unlike you, although in becoming more like you they will become better fitted to the higher parts of your creation. And I asked: "What is wickedness?" and found that it is not a substance but a perversity of the will turning away from you, God, the supreme substance, toward lower things – casting away, as it were, its own insides, and swelling with desire for what is outside it.

4

On the Free Choice of the Will

Augustine

For biographical information about Augustine, see the introduction to the last reading selection. The following reading is taken from Augustine's dialogue *On Free Choice of the Will.* In the dialogue, Augustine's friend Evodius questions him concerning God's responsibility for evil and Augustine presents an important early version of a free will theodicy.

Book II

i, 1. *Evodius* – Now explain to me, if it can be done, why God has given man free choice in willing, for if he had not received that freedom he would not have been able to sin. [. . .]

3. *Aug.* – [. . .] If man is good, and if he would not be able to act rightly except by willing to do so, he ought to have free will because without it he would not be able to act rightly. Because he also sins through having free will, we are not to believe that God gave it to him for that purpose. It is, therefore, a sufficient reason why he ought to have been given it, that without it man could not live aright. That it was given for this purpose can be understood from this fact. If anyone uses his free will in order to sin, God punishes him. That would be unjust unless the will was free not only to live aright but also to sin. How could he be justly punished who uses his will for the purpose for which it was given? Now when God punishes a sinner what else do you suppose he will say to him than "Why did you not use your free will for the purpose for which I gave it to you, that is, in order to do right?" Justice is praised as a good thing because it condemns sins and honours righteous actions. How could that be done if man had not free will? An action would be neither sinful nor righteous unless it were done voluntarily. For the same reason both punishment and reward would be unjust, if man did not have free will. But in punishing and in rewarding there must have been justice since justice is one of the good things

Augustine, Books II and III from *Augustine: Earlier Writings*, LCC vol. VI, ed. John H. S. Burleigh (John Knox Press, 1953; SCM Press, 1958), pp. 396–9.

which come from God. God, therefore, must have given and ought to have given man free will.

ii, 4. *Ev.* – I admit now that God has given us free will. But don't you think, pray, that, if it was given for the purpose of well-doing, it ought not to have been possible to convert it to sinful uses? Justice itself was given to man so that he might live rightly, and it is not possible for anyone to live an evil life by means of justice. So no one ought to be able to sin voluntarily if free will was given that we might live aright. *Aug.* – God will, I hope, give me ability to answer you, or rather will give you the ability to answer your own question. Truth, which is the best master of all, will inwardly teach us both alike. But I wish you would tell me this: I asked you whether you know with perfect certainty that God has given us free will and you replied that you did. Now if we allow that God gave it, ought we to say that he ought not to have given it? If it is uncertain whether he gave it, we rightly ask whether it was good that it was given. If then we find that it was good, we find also that it was given by him who bestows all good things on men. If, however, we find that it was not a good thing we know that it was not given by him whom it is impious to accuse. If it is certain that he has given it, we ought to confess that, however it was given, it was rightly given. We may not say that it ought not to have been given or that it ought to have been given in some other way. If he has given it his action cannot in any way be rightly blamed.

5. *Ev.* – I believe all that unshakably. Nevertheless, because I do not know it, let us inquire as if it were all uncertain. I see that because it is uncertain whether free will was given that men might do right since by it we can also sin, another uncertainty arises, namely whether free will ought to have been given to us. If it is uncertain that it was given that we should act righteously, it is also uncertain that it ought to have been given at all. [. . .]

Book III

45. *Aug.* – God owes nothing to any man, for he gives everything gratuitously. If anyone says God owes him something for his merits, God did not even owe him existence. Nothing could be owing to one who did not yet exist. And what merit is there in turning to him from whom you derive existence, that you may be made better by him from whom you derive existence? Why do you ask him for anything as if you were demanding repayment of a debt? If you were unwilling to turn to him, the loss would not be his but yours. For without him you would be nothing, and from him you derive such existence as you have; but on condition that, unless you turn to him, you must pay him back the existence you have from him, and become, not indeed nothing, but miserable. All things owe him, first, their existence so far as they are natural things, and secondly, that they can become better if they wish, receiving additional gifts if they wish them and being what they ought to be. No man is guilty because he has not received this or that power. But because he does not do as he ought he is justly held guilty. Obligation arises if he has received free will and sufficient power.

46. No blame attaches to the Creator if any of his creatures does not do what he ought. Indeed, that the wrong-doer suffers as he ought redounds to the praise of the Creator. In the very act of blaming anyone for not doing as he ought, he is praised to whom the debt is owed. If you are praised for seeing what you ought to do, and you only see it in him who is unchangeable truth, how much more is he to be praised who has taught you what you ought to wish, has given you the power to do it, and has not allowed you to refuse to do it with impunity? If "oughtness" depends upon what has been given, and man has been so made that he sins by necessity, then he ought to sin. So when he sins he does what he ought. But it is wicked to speak like that. No man's nature compels him to sin, nor does any other nature. No man sins when he suffers what he does not wish. If he has to suffer justly he does not sin in suffering unwillingly. He sinned in that he did something voluntarily which involved him in suffering justly what he did not wish. If he suffers unjustly, where is the sin? There is no sin in suffering something unjustly but in doing something unjustly. So, if no one is compelled to sin either by his own nature or by another, it remains that he sins by his own will. If you want to attribute his sin to the Creator you will make the sinner guiltless because he has simply obeyed the laws of the Creator. If the sinner can be rightly defended he is not a sinner, and there is no sin to attribute to the Creator. Let us then praise the Creator whether or not the sinner can be defended. If he is justly defended he is no sinner and we can therefore praise the Creator. If he cannot be defended, he is a sinner so far as he turns away from the Creator. Therefore praise the Creator. I find, therefore, no way at all, and I assert that there is none to be found, by which our sins can be ascribed to the Creator, our God. I find that he is to be praised even for sins, not only because he punishes them, but also because sin arises only when a man departs from his truth.

Evodius – I most gladly approve all you have said, and assent with all my heart to the truth that there is no way at all of rightly ascribing our sins to our Creator.

xvii, 47. But I should like to know, if possible, why those beings do not sin whom God knew beforehand would not sin, and why those others do sin whom he foresaw would sin. I do not now think that God's foreknowledge compels the one to sin and the other not to sin. But if there were no cause rational creatures would not be divided into classes as they are: those who never sin, those who continually sin, and the intermediary class of those who sometimes sin and sometimes are turned towards well-doing. What is the reason for this division? I do not want you to reply that it is the will that does it. What I want to know is what cause lies behind willing. There must be some reason why one class never wills to sin, another never lacks the will to sin, and another sometimes wills to sin and at other times does not so will. For they are all alike in nature. I seem to see that there must be some cause for this threefold classification of rational beings according to their wills, but what it is I do not know.

48. *Augustine* – Since will is the cause of sin, you now ask what is the cause of will. If I could find one, are you not going to ask for the cause of the cause I have found? What limit will there be to your quest, what end to inquiry and explanation? You ought not to push your inquiry deeper, for you must beware of imagining that anything can be more truly said than that which is written: "Avarice is the root of all evils" (I Tim. 6:10), that is, wanting more than is sufficient. That is sufficient which is demanded by the need of preserving any particular creature. Avarice, in Greek *philarguria*, derives its name from *argentum* [silver], because among the ancients coins were made of silver or more frequently with an admixture of silver. But avarice must be understood as connected not only with silver and money but with everything which is immoderately desired, in every case where a man wants more than is sufficient. Such avarice is cupidity, and cupidity is an evil will. An evil will therefore, is the cause of all evils. If it were according to nature it would preserve nature and not be hostile to it, and so it would not be evil. The inference is that the root of all evils is not according to nature. That is sufficient answer to all who want to accuse nature. But you ask what is the cause of this root. How then will it be the root of all evils? If it has a cause, that cause will be the root of evil. And if you find a cause, as I said, you will ask for a cause of that cause, and there will be no limit to your inquiry.

49. But what cause of willing can there be which is prior to willing? Either it is a will, in which case we have not got beyond the root of evil will. Or it is not a will, and in that case there is no sin in it. Either, then, will is itself the first cause of sin, or the first cause is without sin. Now sin is rightly imputed only to that which sins, nor is it rightly imputed unless it sins voluntarily. I do not know why you should want to inquire further, but here is a further point. If there is a cause of willing it is either just or unjust. If it is just, he who obeys it will not sin, if unjust he who does not obey it will not sin either.

5

Formal Summary of the Theodicy

Gottfried Leibniz

Gottfried Leibniz (1646–1716) is one of the most impressive figures of the seventeenth and eighteenth centuries. In addition to important philosophical work, he also made substantial contributions to mathematics (including the development of calculus), the sciences, history, and political theory. The following selection is taken from an appendix to his *Theodicy*, a systematic treatment of the problem of evil. In the appendix Leibniz offers a concise, formal summary of his argument.

Some persons of discernment have wished me to make this addition. I have the more readily deferred to their opinion, because of the opportunity thereby gained for meeting certain difficulties, and for making observations on certain matters which were not treated in sufficient detail in the work itself.

Objection I

Whoever does not choose the best course is lacking either in power, or knowledge, or goodness.

God did not choose the best course in creating this world.

Therefore God was lacking in power, or knowledge, or goodness.

Answer

I deny the minor, that is to say, the second premiss of this syllogism, and the opponent proves it by this.

Prosyllogism

Whoever makes things in which there is evil, and which could have been made without any evil, or

G. W. Leibniz, "Summary of the Controversy Reduced to Formal Arguments" from *Theodicy: Essays on the Goodness of God, the Freedom of Man and the Origin of Evil*, ed. Austin Farrer (La Salle, IL: Open Court, 1985), pp. 377–88.

need not have been made at all, does not choose the best course.

God made a world wherein there is evil; a world, I say, which could have been made without any evil or which need not have been made at all.

Therefore God did not choose the best course.

Answer

I admit the minor of this prosyllogism: for one must confess that there is evil in this world which God has made, and that it would have been possible to make a world without evil or even not to create any world, since its creation depended upon the free will of God. But I deny the major, that is, the first of the two premisses of the prosyllogism, and I might content myself with asking for its proof. In order, however, to give a clearer exposition of the matter, I would justify this denial by pointing out that the best course is not always that one which tends towards avoiding evil, since it is possible that the evil may be accompanied by a greater good. For example, the general of an army will prefer a great victory with a slight wound to a state of affairs without wound and without victory. I have proved this in further detail in this work by pointing out, through instances taken from mathematics and elsewhere, that an imperfection in the part may be required for a greater perfection in the whole. I have followed therein the opinion of St Augustine, who said a hundred times that God permitted evil in order to derive from it a good, that is to say, a greater good; and Thomas Aquinas says (in libr. 2, *Sent. Dist.* 32, qu. 1, art. 1) that the permission of evil tends towards the good of the universe. I have shown that among older writers the fall of Adam was termed *felix culpa*, a fortunate sin, because it had been expiated with immense benefit by the incarnation of the Son of God: for he gave to the universe something more noble than anything there would otherwise have been amongst created beings. For the better understanding of the matter I added, following the example of many good authors, that it was consistent with order and the general good for God to grant to certain of his creatures the opportunity to exercise their freedom, even when he foresaw that they would turn to evil: for God could easily correct the evil, and it was not fitting that in order to prevent sin he should always act in an extraordinary way. It will therefore sufficiently refute the objection to show that a world with evil may be better than a world without evil. But I have gone still further in the work, and have even shown that this universe must be indeed better than every other possible universe.

Objection II

If there is more evil than good in intelligent creatures, there is more evil than good in all God's work.

Now there is more evil than good in intelligent creatures.

Therefore there is more evil than good in all God's work.

Answer

I deny the major and the minor of this conditional syllogism. As for the major, I do not admit it because this supposed inference from the part to the whole, from intelligent creatures to all creatures, assumes tacitly and without proof that creatures devoid of reason cannot be compared or taken into account with those that have reason. But why might not the surplus of good in the non-intelligent creatures that fill the world compensate for and even exceed incomparably the surplus of evil in rational creatures? It is true that the value of the latter is greater; but by way of compensation the others are incomparably greater in number; and it may be that the proportion of number and quantity surpasses that of value and quality.

The minor also I cannot admit, namely, that there is more evil than good in intelligent creatures. One need not even agree that there is more evil than good in the human kind. For it is possible, and even a very reasonable thing, that the glory and the perfection of the blessed may be incomparably greater than the misery and imperfection of the damned, and that here the excellence of the total good in the smaller number may exceed the total evil which is in the greater number. The blessed draw near to divinity through a divine Mediator, so far as can belong to these created beings, and make such progress in good as is impossible for the damned to make in evil, even though they should approach as nearly as may be the nature of demons. God is infinite, and the Devil is finite; good can and does go on *ad infinitum*, whereas evil has its bounds. It may be therefore, and it is probable, that there happens in the comparison between the blessed and the damned the opposite of what I said could happen in the comparison between the happy and the unhappy, namely that in the latter the proportion of degrees surpasses that of numbers, while in the comparison between intelligent and non-intelligent the proportion of numbers is greater than that of values. One is justified in assuming that a thing may be so as long as one does not prove that it is impossible, and indeed what is here put forward goes beyond assumption.

But secondly, even should one admit that there is more evil than good in the human kind, one still has every reason for not admitting that there is more evil than good in all intelligent creatures. For there is an inconceivable number of Spirits, and perhaps of other rational creatures besides: and an opponent cannot prove that in the whole City of God, composed as much of Spirits as of rational animals without number and of endless different kinds, the evil exceeds the good. Although one need not, in order to answer an objection, prove that a thing is, when its mere possibility suffices, I have nevertheless shown in this present work that it is a result of the supreme perfection of the Sovereign of the Universe that the kingdom of God should be the most perfect of all states or governments possible, and that in consequence what little evil there is should be required to provide the full measure of the vast good existing there.

Objection III

If it is always impossible not to sin, it is always unjust to punish.

Now it is always impossible not to sin, or rather all sin is necessary.

Therefore it is always unjust to punish.

The minor of this is proved as follows.

First prosyllogism

Everything predetermined is necessary.

Every event is predetermined.

Therefore every event (and consequently sin also) is necessary.

Again this second minor is proved thus.

Second prosyllogism

That which is future, that which is foreseen, that which is involved in causes is predetermined.

Every event is of this kind.

Therefore every event is predetermined.

Answer

I admit in a certain sense the conclusion of the second prosyllogism, which is the minor of the first; but I shall deny the major of the first prosyllogism, namely that everything predetermined is necessary; taking 'necessity', say the necessity to sin, or the impossibility of not sinning, or of not doing some action, in the sense relevant to the argument, that is, as a necessity essential and absolute, which destroys the morality of action and the justice of punishment. If anyone meant a different necessity or impossibility (that is, a necessity only moral or hypothetical, which will be explained presently) it is plain that we would deny him the major stated in the objection. We might content ourselves with this answer, and demand the proof of the proposition denied: but I am well pleased to justify my manner of procedure in the present work, in order to make the matter clear and to throw more light on this whole subject, by explaining the necessity that must be rejected and the determination that must be allowed. The truth is that the necessity contrary to morality, which must be avoided and which would render punishment unjust, is an insuperable necessity, which would render all opposition unavailing, even though one should wish with all one's heart to avoid the necessary action, and though one should make all possible efforts to that end. Now it is plain that this is not applicable to voluntary actions, since one would not do them if one did not so desire. Thus their prevision and predetermination is not absolute, but it presupposes will: if it is certain that one will do them, it is no less certain that one will will to do them. These voluntary actions and their results will not happen whatever one may do and whether one will them or not; but they will happen because one will do, and because one will will to do, that which leads to them. That is involved in prevision and predetermination, and forms the reason thereof. The necessity of such events is called conditional or hypothetical, or again necessity of consequence, because it presupposes the will and the other requisites. But the necessity which destroys morality, and renders punishment unjust and reward unavailing, is found in the things that will be whatever one may do and whatever one may will to do: in a word, it exists in that which is essential. This it is which is called an absolute necessity. Thus it avails nothing with regard to what is necessary absolutely to ordain interdicts or commandments, to propose penalties or prizes, to blame or to praise; it will come to pass no more and no less. In voluntary actions, on the contrary, and in what depends upon them, precepts, armed with power to punish and to reward, very often serve, and are included in the order of causes that make action exist. Thus it comes about that not only pains and effort but also prayers are effective, God having had even these prayers in mind before he ordered things, and having made due allowance for them. That is why the precept *Ora et labora* (Pray and work) remains intact. Thus not only those who (under the empty pretext of the necessity of events) maintain that one can spare oneself the pains demanded by affairs, but also those who argue against prayers, fall into that which the ancients even in their time called 'the Lazy Sophism'. So the predetermination of events by their causes is precisely what contributes to morality instead of destroying it, and the causes incline the will without necessitating it. For this reason the determination we are concerned with is not a necessitation. It is certain (to him who knows all) that the effect will follow this inclination; but this effect does not follow thence by a consequence which is necessary, that is, whose contrary implies contradiction; and it is also by such an inward inclination that the will is determined, without the presence of necessity. Suppose that one has the greatest possible passion (for example, a great thirst), you will admit that the soul can find some reason for resisting it, even if it were only that of displaying its power. Thus though one may never have complete indifference of equipoise, and there is always a predominance of inclination for the course adopted, that predominance does not render absolutely necessary the resolution taken.

Objection IV

Whoever can prevent the sin of others and does not so, but rather contributes to it, although he be fully apprised of it, is accessary thereto.

God can prevent the sin of intelligent creatures; but he does not so, and he rather contributes to it by his co-operation and by the opportunities he causes, although he is fully cognizant of it.

Therefore, etc.

Answer

I deny the major of this syllogism. It may be that one can prevent the sin, but that one ought not to do so, because one could not do so without committing a sin oneself, or (when God is concerned) without acting unreasonably. I have given instances of that, and have applied them to God himself. It may be also that one contributes to the evil, and that one even opens the way to it sometimes, in doing things one is bound to do. And when one does one's duty, or (speaking of God) when, after full consideration, one does that which reason demands, one is not responsible for events, even when one foresees them. One does not will these evils; but one is willing to permit them for a greater good, which one cannot in reason help preferring to other considerations. This is a *consequent* will, resulting from acts of *antecedent* will, in which one wills the good. I know that some persons, in speaking of the antecedent and consequent will of God, have meant by the antecedent that which wills that all men be saved, and by the consequent that which wills, in consequence of persistent sin, that there be some damned, damnation being a result of sin. But these are only examples of a more general notion, and one may say with the same reason, that God wills by his antecedent will that men sin not, and that by his consequent or final and decretory will (which is always followed by its effect) he wills to permit that they sin, this permission being a result of superior reasons. One has indeed justification for saying, in general, that the antecedent will of God tends towards the production of good and the prevention of evil, each taken in itself, and as it were detached (*particulariter et secundum quid*: Thorn., I, qu. 19, art. 6) according to the measure of the degree of each good or of each evil. Likewise one may say that the consequent, or final and total, divine will tends towards the production of as many goods as can be put together, whose combination thereby becomes determined, and involves also the permission of some evils and the exclusion of some goods, as the best possible plan of the universe demands. Arminius, in his *Antiperkinsus*, explained very well that the will of God can be called consequent not only in relation to the action of the creature considered beforehand in the divine understanding, but also in relation to other anterior acts of divine will. But it is enough to consider the passage cited from Thomas Aquinas, and that from Scotus (I, dist. 46, qu. 11), to see that they make this distinction as I have made it here. Nevertheless if anyone will not suffer this use of the terms, let him put 'previous' in place of 'antecedent' will, and 'final' or 'decretory' in place of 'consequent' will. For I do not wish to wrangle about words.

Objection V

Whoever produces all that is real in a thing is its cause.

God produces all that is real in sin.

Therefore God is the cause of sin.

Answer

I might content myself with denying the major or the minor, because the term 'real' admits of interpretations capable of rendering these propositions false. But in order to give a better explanation I will make a distinction. 'Real' either signifies that which is positive only, or else it includes also privative beings: in the first case, I deny the major and I admit the minor; in the second case, I do the opposite. I might have confined myself to that; but I was willing to go further, in order to account for this distinction. I have therefore been well pleased to point out that every purely positive or absolute reality is a perfection, and that every imperfection comes from limitation, that is, from the privative: for to limit is to withhold extension, or the more beyond. Now God is the cause of all perfections, and consequently of all realities, when they are regarded as purely positive. But limitations or privations result from the original imperfection of creatures which restricts their receptivity. It is as with a laden boat, which the river carries along more slowly or less slowly in proportion to the weight that it bears: thus the speed comes from the river, but the retardation which restricts this speed comes from the load. Also I have shown in the present work how the creature, in causing sin, is a deficient cause; how errors and evil inclinations spring from privation; and how privation is efficacious accidentally. And I have justified the opinion of St Augustine (lib. I, *Ad. Simpl.*, qu. 2) who explains (for example) how God hardens the soul, not in giving it something evil, but because the effect of the good he imprints is restricted by the resistance of the soul, and by the circumstances contributing to this resistance, so that he does not give it all the good that would overcome its evil. 'Nec (*inquit*) ab illo erogatur aliquid quo homo fit deterior, sed tantum quo fit melior non erogatur.' But if God had willed to do more here he must needs have produced either fresh natures in his creatures or fresh miracles to change their natures, and this the best plan did not allow. It is just as if the current of the river must needs be more rapid than its slope permits or the boats themselves be less laden, if they had to be impelled at a greater speed. So the limitation or original imperfection of creatures brings it about that even the best plan of the universe cannot admit more good, and cannot be exempted from certain evils, these, however, being only of such a kind as may tend towards a greater good. There are some disorders in the parts which wonderfully enhance the beauty of the whole, just as certain dissonances, appropriately used, render harmony more beautiful. But that depends upon the answer which I have already given to the first objection.

Objection VI

Whoever punishes those who have done as well as it was in their power to do is unjust.

God does so.

Therefore, etc.

Answer

I deny the minor of this argument. And I believe that God always gives sufficient aid and grace to those who have good will, that is to say, who do not reject this grace by a fresh sin. Thus I do not admit the damnation of children dying unbaptized or outside the Church, or the damnation of adult persons who have acted according to the light that God has given them. And I believe that, *if anyone has followed the light he had*, he will undoubtedly receive thereof in greater measure as he has need, even as the late Herr Hulsemann, who was celebrated as a profound theologian at Leipzig, has somewhere observed; and if such a man had failed to receive light during his life, he would receive it at least in the hour of death.

Objection VII

Whoever gives only to some, and not to all, the means of producing effectively in them good will and final saving faith has not enough goodness.

God does so.

Therefore, etc.

Answer

I deny the major. It is true that God could overcome the greatest resistance of the human heart, and indeed he sometimes does so, whether by an inward grace or by the outward circumstances that can greatly influence souls; but he does not always do so. Whence comes this distinction, someone will say, and wherefore does his goodness appear to be restricted? The truth is that it would not have been in order always to act in an extraordinary way and to derange the connexion of things, as I have observed already in answering the first objection. The reasons for this connexion, whereby the one is placed in more favourable circumstances than the other, are hidden in the depths of God's wisdom: they depend upon the universal harmony. The best plan of the universe, which God could not fail to choose, required this. One concludes thus from the event itself; since God made the universe, it was not possible to do better. Such management, far from being contrary to goodness, has rather been prompted by supreme goodness itself. This objection with its solution might have been inferred from what was said with regard to the first objection; but it seemed advisable to touch upon it separately.

Objection VIII

Whoever cannot fail to choose the best is not free.

God cannot fail to choose the best.

Therefore God is not free.

Answer

I deny the major of this argument. Rather is it true freedom, and the most perfect, to be able to make the best use of one's free will, and always to exercise this power, without being turned aside either by outward force or by inward passions, whereof the one enslaves our bodies and the other our souls. There is nothing less servile and more befitting the highest degree of freedom than to be always led towards the good, and always by one's own inclination, without any constraint and without any displeasure. And to object that God therefore had need of external things is only a sophism. He creates them freely: but when he had set before him an end, that of exercising his goodness, his wisdom determined him to choose the means most appropriate for obtaining this end. To call that a *need* is to take the term in a sense not usual, which clears it of all imperfection, somewhat as one does when speaking of the wrath of God.

Seneca says somewhere, that God commanded only once, but that he obeys always, because he obeys the laws that he willed to ordain for himself: *semel jussit, semper paret.* But he had better have said, that God always commands and that he is always obeyed: for in willing he always follows the tendency of his own nature, and all other things always follow his will. And as this will is always the same one cannot say that he obeys that will only which he formerly had. Nevertheless, although his will is always indefectible and always tends towards the best, the evil or the lesser good which he rejects will still be possible in itself. Otherwise the necessity of good would be geometrical (so to speak) or metaphysical, and altogether absolute; the contingency of things would be destroyed, and there would be no choice. But necessity of this kind, which does not destroy the possibility of the contrary, has the name by analogy only: it becomes effective not through the mere essence of things, but through that which is outside them and above them, that is, through the will of God. This necessity is called moral, because for the wise what is necessary and what is owing are equivalent things; and when it is always followed by its effect, as it indeed is in the perfectly wise, that is, in God, one can say that it is a happy necessity. The more nearly creatures approach this, the closer do they come to perfect felicity. Moreover, necessity of this kind is not the necessity one endeavours to avoid, and which destroys morality, reward and commendation. For that which it brings to pass does not happen whatever one may do and whatever one may will, but because one desires it. A will to which it is natural to choose well deserves most to be commended; and it carries with it its own reward, which is supreme happiness. And as this constitution of the divine nature gives an entire satisfaction to him who possesses it, it is also the best and the most desirable from the point of view of the creatures who are all dependent upon God. If the will of God had not as its rule the principle of the best, it would tend towards evil, which would be worst of all; or else it would be indifferent somehow to good and to evil, and guided by chance. But a will that would always drift along at random would scarcely be any better for the government of the universe than the fortuitous concourse of corpuscles, without the existence of divinity. And even though God should abandon himself to chance only in some cases, and in a certain way (as he would if he did not always tend entirely towards the best, and if he were capable of preferring a lesser good to a greater good, that is, an evil to a good, since that which prevents a greater good is an evil) he would be no less imperfect than the object of his choice. Then he would not deserve absolute trust; he would act without reason in such a case, and the government of the universe would be like certain games equally divided between reason and luck. This all proves that this objection which is made against the choice of the best perverts the notions of free and necessary, and represents the best to us actually as evil: but that is either malicious or absurd.

6

Myth of the Goddess Pallas

Gottfried Leibniz

Near the end of his *Theodicy*, Leibniz offers an informal, mythical presentation of his views. He begins by discussing a mythological dialogue concerning freedom and foreknowledge written by a fifteenth-century Italian philosopher named Laurentius Valla. The dialogue involves Sextus Tarquinius, the son of Rome's last king, whose rape of Lucretia led to the end of his father's reign. In Valla's dialogue, Apollo foretells Sextus' future. When Sextus complains about the future Apollo declares for him, Apollo answers that he has not chosen this future for Sextus, but is simply foretelling what will happen – things will happen as Jupiter has providently decreed. Sextus acknowledges that Apollo is not responsible because of his foreknowledge, but objects that Jupiter is responsible since he has decreed what Sextus will do. Our reading begins where Leibniz adds on to the dialogue, imagining that Sextus goes on to question Jupiter. When Theodorus, the high priest who is present for Sextus and Jupiter's brief discussion, asks Jupiter for further clarification, Jupiter sends him to his daughter Pallas.

Sextus, quitting Apollo and Delphi, seeks out Jupiter at Dodona. He makes sacrifices and then he exhibits his complaints. Why have you condemned me, O great God, to be wicked and unhappy? Change my lot and my heart, or acknowledge your error. Jupiter answers him: If you will renounce Rome, the Parcae shall spin for you different fates, you shall become wise, you shall be happy. SEXTUS – Why must I renounce the hope of a crown? Can I not come to be a good king? JUPITER – No, Sextus; I know better what is needful for you. If you go to Rome, you are lost. Sextus, not being able to resolve upon so great a sacrifice, went forth from the temple, and

G. W. Leibniz, "Essays on the Justice of God and Freedom of Man in the Origin of Evil" from *Theodicy: Essays on the Goodness of God, the Freedom of Man and the Origin of Evil*, ed. Austin Farrer (La Salle, IL: Open Court, 1985), pp. 369–73.

abandoned himself to his fate. Theodorus, the High Priest, who had been present at the dialogue between God and Sextus, addressed these words to Jupiter: Your wisdom is to be revered, O great Ruler of the Gods. You have convinced this man of his error; he must henceforth impute his unhappiness to his evil will; he has not a word to say. But your faithful worshippers are astonished; they would fain wonder at your goodness as well as at your greatness: it rested with you to give him a different will. JUPITER – Go to my daughter Pallas, she will inform you what I was bound to do.

414. Theodorus journeyed to Athens: he was bidden to lie down to sleep in the temple of the Goddess. Dreaming, he found himself transported into an unknown country. There stood a palace of unimaginable splendour and prodigious size. The Goddess Pallas appeared at the gate, surrounded by rays of dazzling majesty.

Qualisque videri
Coelicolis et quanta solet.

She touched the face of Theodorus with an olive-branch, which she was holding in her hand. And lo! he had become able to confront the divine radiancy of the daughter of Jupiter, and of all that she should show him. Jupiter who loves you (she said to him) has commended you to me to be instructed. You see here the palace of the fates, where I keep watch and ward. Here are representations not only of that which happens but also of all that which is possible. Jupiter, having surveyed them before the beginning of the existing world, classified the possibilities into worlds, and chose the best of all. He comes sometimes to visit these places, to enjoy the pleasure of recapitulating things and of renewing his own choice, which cannot fail to please him. I have only to speak, and we shall see a whole world that my father might have produced, wherein will be represented anything that can be asked of him; and in this way one may know also what would happen if any particular possibility should attain unto existence. And whenever the conditions are not determinate enough, there will be as many such worlds differing from one another as one shall wish, which will answer differently the same question, in as many ways as possible. You learnt geometry in your youth, like all well-instructed Greeks. You know therefore that when the conditions of a required point do not sufficiently determine it, and there is an infinite number of them, they all fall into what the geometricians call a locus, and this locus at least (which is often a line) will be determinate. Thus you can picture to yourself an ordered succession of worlds, which shall contain each and every one the case that is in question, and shall vary its circumstances and its consequences. But if you put a case that differs from the actual world only in one single definite thing and in its results, a certain one of those determinate worlds will answer you. These worlds are all here, that is, in ideas. I will show you some, wherein shall be found, not absolutely the same Sextus as you have seen (that is not possible, he carries with him always that which he shall be) but several Sextuses resembling him, possessing all that you know already of the true Sextus, but not all that is already in him imperceptibly, nor in consequence all that shall yet happen to him. You will find in one world a very happy and noble Sextus, in another a Sextus content with a mediocre state, a Sextus, indeed, of every kind and endless diversity of forms.

415. Thereupon the Goddess led Theodorus into one of the halls of the palace: when he was within, it was no longer a hall, it was a world,

Solemque suum, sua sidera norat.

At the command of Pallas there came within view Dodona with the temple of Jupiter, and Sextus issuing thence; he could be heard saying that he would obey the God. And lo! he goes to a city lying between two seas, resembling Corinth. He buys there a small garden; cultivating it, he finds a treasure; he becomes a rich man, enjoying affection and esteem; he dies at a great age, beloved of the whole city. Theodorus saw the whole life of Sextus as at one glance, and as in a stage presentation. There was a great volume of writings in this hall: Theodorus could not refrain from asking what that meant. It is the history of this world which we are now visiting, the Goddess told him; it is the book of its fates. You have seen a number on the forehead of Sextus. Look in this book for the place which it indicates. Theodorus looked for it, and found there the history of Sextus in a form more ample than the outline he had seen. Put your finger on any line you please, Pallas said to him, and you will see represented actually in all its detail that which the line broadly indicates. He obeyed, and he saw coming into view all the characteristics of a portion of the life of that Sextus. They passed into another hall, and lo! another world, another Sextus, who, issuing from the temple, and having resolved to obey Jupiter, goes to Thrace. There he marries the daughter of the king, who had no other children; he succeeds him, and he is adored by his subjects. They went into other rooms, and always they saw new scenes.

416. The halls rose in a pyramid, becoming even more beautiful as one mounted towards the apex, and representing more beautiful worlds. Finally they reached the highest one which completed the pyramid, and which was the most beautiful of all: for the pyramid had a beginning, but one could not see its end; it had an apex, but no base; it went on increasing to infinity. That is (as the Goddess explained) because amongst an endless number of possible worlds there is the best of all, else would God not have determined to create any; but there is not any one which has not also less perfect worlds below it: that is why the pyramid goes on descending to infinity. Theodorus, entering this highest hall, became entranced in ecstasy; he had to receive succour from the Goddess, a drop of a divine liquid placed on his tongue restored him; he was beside himself for joy. We are in the real true world (said the Goddess) and you are at the source of happiness. Behold what Jupiter makes ready for you, if you continue to serve him faithfully. Here is Sextus as he is, and as he will be in reality. He issues from the temple in a rage, he scorns the counsel of the Gods. You see him going to Rome, bringing confusion everywhere, violating the wife of his friend. There he is driven out with his father, beaten, unhappy. If Jupiter had placed here a Sextus happy at Corinth or King in Thrace, it would be no longer this world. And nevertheless he could not have failed to choose this world, which surpasses in perfection all the others, and which forms the apex of the pyramid. Else would Jupiter have renounced his wisdom, he would have banished me, me his daughter. You see that my father did not make Sextus wicked; he was so from all eternity, he was so always and freely. My father only granted him the existence which his wisdom could not refuse to the world where he is included: he made him pass from the region of the possible to that of the actual beings. The crime of Sextus serves for great things: it renders Rome free; thence will arise a great empire, which will show noble examples to mankind. But that is nothing in comparison with the worth of this whole world, at whose beauty you will marvel, when, after a happy passage from this mortal state to another and better one, the Gods shall have fitted you to know it.

417. At this moment Theodorus wakes up, he gives thanks to the Goddess, he owns the justice of Jupiter. His spirit pervaded by what he has seen and heard, he carries on the office of High Priest, with all the zeal of a true servant of his God, and with all the joy whereof a mortal is capable. It seems to me that this continuation of the tale may elucidate the difficulty which Valla did not wish to treat. If Apollo has represented aright God's knowledge of vision (that which concerns beings in existence), I hope that Pallas will have not discreditably filled the rôle of what is called knowledge of simple intelligence (that which embraces all that is possible), wherein at last the source of things must be sought.

7

Evil and Omnipotence

J. L. Mackie

The following essay by J. L. Mackie (1917–81) was first published in 1955 and sparked renewed interest in the problem of evil among philosophers. Mackie argues that theism is irrational because a logical contradiction can be derived from ordinary theistic beliefs. He begins the essay with a brief statement of the argument against theism; then, in the remainder of the essay he examines a number of attempted theistic solutions and argues that none of them succeeds. Mackie's contention that an omnipotent God could have created free creatures that never choose to do evil was a particularly important and controversial contribution to the contemporary debate.

The traditional arguments for the existence of God have been fairly thoroughly criticised by philosophers. But the theologian can, if he wishes, accept this criticism. He can admit that no rational proof of God's existence is possible. And he can still retain all that is essential to his position, by holding that God's existence is known in some other, non-rational way. I think, however, that a more telling criticism can be made by way of the traditional problem of evil. Here it can be shown, not that religious beliefs lack rational support, but that they are positively irrational, that the several parts of the essential theological doctrine are inconsistent with one another, so that the theologian can maintain his position as a whole only by a much more extreme rejection of reason than in the former case. He must now be prepared to believe, not merely what cannot be proved, but what can be *disproved* from other beliefs that he also holds.

The problem of evil, in the sense in which I shall be using the phrase, is a problem only for someone who believes that there is a God who is both omnipotent and wholly good. And it is a logical problem, the problem of clarifying and reconciling a number of beliefs: it is not a scientific problem that might be solved by further observations, or a practical problem that might be

J. L. Mackie, "Evil and Omnipotence". *Mind* 64 (1955): 200–12.

solved by a decision or an action. These points are obvious; I mention them only because they are sometimes ignored by theologians, who sometimes parry a statement of the problem with such remarks as 'Well, can you solve the problem yourself?' or 'This is a mystery which may be revealed to us later' or 'Evil is something to be faced and overcome, not to be merely discussed'.

In its simplest form the problem is this: God is omnipotent; God is wholly good; and yet evil exists. There seems to be some contradiction between these three propositions, so that if any two of them were true the third would be false. But at the same time all three are essential parts of most theological positions: the theologian, it seems, at once *must* adhere and *cannot consistently* adhere to all three. (The problem does not arise only for theists, but I shall discuss it in the form in which it presents itself for ordinary theism.)

However, the contradiction does not arise immediately; to show it we need some additional premises, or perhaps some quasi-logical rules connecting the terms 'good', 'evil', and 'omnipotent'. These additional principles are that good is opposed to evil, in such a way that a good thing always eliminates evil as far as it can, and that there are no limits to what an omnipotent thing can do. From these it follows that a good omnipotent thing eliminates evil completely, and then the propositions that a good omnipotent thing exists, and that evil exists, are incompatible.

A. Adequate Solutions

Now once the problem is fully stated it is clear that it can be solved, in the sense that the problem will not arise if one gives up at least one of the propositions that constitute it. If you are prepared to say that God is not wholly good, or not quite omnipotent, or that evil does not exist, or that good is not opposed to the kind of evil that exists, or that there are limits to what an omnipotent thing can do, then the problem of evil will not arise for you.

There are, then, quite a number of adequate solutions of the problem of evil, and some of these have been adopted, or almost adopted, by various thinkers. For example, a few have been prepared to deny God's omnipotence, and rather more have been prepared to keep the term 'omnipotence' but severely to restrict its meaning, recording quite a number of things that an omnipotent being cannot do. Some have said that evil is an illusion, perhaps because they held that the whole world of temporal, changing things is an illusion, and that what we call evil belongs only to this world, or perhaps because they held that although temporal things *are* much as we see them, those that we call evil are not really evil. Some have said that what we call evil is merely the privation of good, that evil in a positive sense, evil that would really be opposed to good, does not exist. Many have agreed with Pope that disorder is harmony not understood, and that partial evil is universal good. Whether any of these views is *true* is, of course, another question. But each of them gives an adequate solution of the problem of evil in the sense that if you accept it this problem does not arise for you, though you may, of course, have *other* problems to face.

But often enough these adequate solutions are only *almost* adopted. The thinkers who restrict God's power, but keep the term 'omnipotence', may reasonably be suspected of thinking, in other contexts, that his power is really unlimited. Those who say that evil is an illusion may also be thinking, inconsistently, that this illusion is itself an evil. Those who say that 'evil' is merely privation of good may also be thinking, inconsistently, that privation of good is an evil. (The fallacy here is akin to some forms of the 'naturalistic fallacy' in ethics, where some think, for example, that 'good' is just what contributes to evolutionary progress, and that evolutionary progress is itself good.) If Pope meant what he said in the first line of his couplet, that 'disorder' is only harmony not understood, the 'partial evil' of the second line must, for consistency, mean 'that which, taken in isolation, falsely appears to be evil', but it would more naturally mean 'that which, in isolation, really is evil'. The second line, in fact, hesitates between two views, that 'partial evil' isn't really evil, since only the universal quality is real, and that 'partial evil' is really an evil, but only a little one.

In addition, therefore, to adequate solutions, we must recognise unsatisfactory inconsistent solutions, in which there is only a half-hearted or temporary rejection of one of the propositions which together constitute the problem. In these, one of the constituent propositions is explicitly rejected, but it is covertly re-asserted or assumed elsewhere in the system.

B. Fallacious Solutions

Besides these half-hearted solutions, which explicitly reject but implicitly assert one of the constituent propositions, there are definitely fallacious solutions which explicitly maintain all the constituent propositions, but implicitly reject at least one of them in the course of the argument that explains away the problem of evil.

There are, in fact, many so-called solutions which purport to remove the contradiction without abandoning any of its constituent propositions. These must be fallacious, as we can see from the very statement of the problem, but it is not so easy to see in each case precisely where the fallacy lies. I suggest that in all cases the fallacy has the general form suggested above: in order to solve the problem one (or perhaps more) of its constituent propositions is given up, but in such a way that it appears to have been retained, and can therefore be asserted without qualification in other contexts. Sometimes there is a further complication: the supposed solution moves to and fro between, say, two of the constituent propositions, at one point asserting the first of these but covertly abandoning the second, at another point asserting the second but covertly abandoning the first. These fallacious solutions often turn upon some equivocation with the words 'good' and 'evil', or upon some vagueness about the way in which good and evil are opposed to one another, or about how much is meant by 'omnipotence'. I propose to examine some of these so-called solutions, and to exhibit their fallacies in detail. Incidentally, I shall also be considering whether an adequate solution could be reached by a minor modification of one or more of the constituent propositions, which would, however, still satisfy all the essential requirements of ordinary theism.

1. 'Good cannot exist without evil' or 'Evil is necessary as a counterpart to good.'

It is sometimes suggested that evil is necessary as a counterpart to good, that if there were no evil there could be no good either, and that this solves the problem of evil. It is true that it points to an answer to the question 'Why should there be evil?' But it does so only by qualifying some of the propositions that constitute the problem.

First, it sets a limit to what God can do, saying that God *cannot* create good without simultaneously creating evil, and this means either that God is not omnipotent or that there are *some* limits to what an omnipotent thing can do. It may be replied that these limits are always presupposed, that omnipotence has never meant the power to do what is logically impossible, and on the present view the existence of good without evil would be a logical impossibility. This interpretation of omnipotence may, indeed, be accepted as a modification of our original account which does not reject anything that is essential to theism, and I shall in general assume it in the subsequent discussion. It is, perhaps, the most common theistic view, but I think that some theists at least have maintained that God can do what is logically impossible. Many theists, at any rate, have held that logic itself is created or laid down by God, that logic is the way in which God arbitrarily chooses to think. (This is, of course, parallel to the ethical view that morally right actions are those which God arbitrarily chooses to command, and the two views encounter similar difficulties.) And *this* account of logic is clearly inconsistent with the view that God is bound by logical necessities – unless it is possible for an omnipotent being to bind himself, an issue which we shall consider later, when we come to the Paradox of Omnipotence. This solution of the problem of evil cannot, therefore, be consistently adopted along with the view that logic is self created by God.

But, secondly, this solution denies that evil is opposed to good in our original sense. If good and evil are counterparts, a good thing will not 'eliminate evil as far as it can'. Indeed, this view suggests that good and evil are not strictly qualities of things at all. Perhaps the suggestion is that good and evil are related in much the same way as great and small. Certainly, when the term 'great' is used relatively as a condensation of 'greater than so-and-so', and 'small' is used correspondingly, greatness and smallness are counterparts and cannot exist without each other. But in this sense greatness is not a quality, not an intrinsic feature of anything; and it would be absurd to think of a movement in favour of greatness and against smallness in this sense. Such a movement would be self-defeating, since relative greatness can be promoted only by a simultaneous promotion of relative smallness. I feel sure that no theists would be content to regard God's goodness as analogous to this – as if what he supports were not the *good* but the *better*, and as if he had the paradoxical aim that all things should be better than other things.

This point is obscured by the fact that 'great' and 'small' seem to have an absolute as well as a relative sense. I cannot discuss here whether there is absolute magnitude or not, but if there is, there could be an absolute sense for 'great', it could mean of at least a certain size, and it would make sense to speak of all things getting bigger, of a universe that was expanding all over, and therefore it would make sense to speak of promoting greatness. But in *this* sense great and small are not logically necessary counterparts: either quality could exist without the other. There would be no logical impossibility in everything's being small or in everything's being great.

Neither in the absolute nor in the relative sense, then, of 'great' and 'small' do these terms provide an analogy of the sort that would be needed to support this solution of the problem of evil. In neither case are greatness and smallness *both* necessary counterparts *and* mutually opposed forces or possible objects for support and attack.

It may be replied that good and evil are necessary counterparts in the same way as any quality and its logical opposite: redness can occur, it is suggested, only if non-redness also occurs. But unless evil is merely the privation of good, they are not logical opposites, and some further argument would be needed to show that they are counterparts in the same way as genuine logical opposites. Let us assume that this could be given. There is still doubt of the correctness of the metaphysical principle that a quality must have a real opposite: I suggest that it is not really impossible that everything should be, say, red, that the truth is merely that if everything were red we should not notice redness, and so we should have no word 'red'; we observe and give names to qualities only if they have real opposites. If so, the principle that a term must have an opposite would belong only to our language or to our thought, and would not be an ontological principle, and, correspondingly, the rule that good cannot exist without evil would not state a logical necessity of a sort that God would just have to put up with. God might have made everything good, though *we* should not have noticed it if he had.

But, finally, even if we concede that this *is* an ontological principle, it will provide a solution for the problem of evil only if one is prepared to say, 'Evil exists, but only just enough evil to serve as the counterpart of good.' I doubt whether any theist will accept this. After all, the *ontological* requirement that non-redness should occur would be satisfied even if all the universe, except for a minute speck, were red, and, if there were a corresponding requirement for evil as a counterpart to good, a minute dose of evil would presumably do. But theists are not usually willing to say, in all contexts, that all the evil that occurs is a minute and necessary dose.

2. 'Evil is necessary as a means to good.'

It is sometimes suggested that evil is necessary for good not as a counterpart but as a means. In its simple form this has little plausibility as a solution of the problem of evil, since it obviously implies a severe restriction of God's power. It would be a *causal* law that you cannot have a certain end without a certain means, so that if God has to introduce evil as a means to good, he must be subject to at least some causal laws. This certainly conflicts with what a theist normally means by omnipotence. This view of God as limited by causal laws also conflicts with the view that causal laws are themselves made by God, which is more widely held than the corresponding view about the laws of logic. This conflict would, indeed, be resolved if it were possible for an omnipotent being to bind himself, and this possibility has still to be considered. Unless a favourable answer can be given to this question, the suggestion that evil is necessary as a means to good solves the problem of evil only by denying one of its constituent propositions, either that God is omnipotent or that 'omnipotent' means what it says.

3. 'The universe is better with some evil in it than it could be if there were no evil.'

Much more important is a solution which at first seems to be a mere variant of the previous one, that evil may contribute to the goodness of a whole in which it is found, so that the universe as a whole is better as it is, with some evil in it, than it would be if there were no evil. This solution may be developed in either of two ways. It may be supported by an aesthetic analogy, by the fact that contrasts heighten beauty, that in a musical work, for example, there may occur discords which somehow add to the beauty of the work as a whole. Alternatively, it may be worked out in connexion with the notion of progress, that the best possible organisations of the universe will not be static, but progressive, that the gradual overcoming of evil by good is really a finer thing than would be the eternal unchallenged supremacy of good.

In either case, this solution usually starts from the assumption that the evil whose existence gives rise to the problem of evil is primarily what is called physical evil, that is to say, pain. In Hume's rather half-hearted presentation of the problem of evil, the evils that he stresses are pain and disease, and those who reply to him argue that the existence of pain and disease makes possible the existence of sympathy, benevolence, heroism, and the gradually successful struggle of doctors and reformers to overcome these evils. In fact, theists often seize the opportunity to accuse those who stress the problem of evil of taking a low, materialistic view of good and evil, equating these with pleasure and pain, and of ignoring the more spiritual goods which can arise in the struggle against evils.

But let us see exactly what is being done here. Let us call pain and misery 'first order evil' or 'evil (1)'. What contrasts with this, namely, pleasure and happiness, will be called 'first order good' or 'good (1)'. Distinct from this is 'second order good' or 'good (2)' which somehow emerges in a complex situation in which evil (1) is a necessary component – logically, not merely causally, necessary. (Exactly *how* it emerges does not matter: in the crudest version of this solution good (2) is simply the heightening of happiness by the contrast with misery, in other versions it includes sympathy with suffering, heroism in facing danger, and the gradual decrease of first order evil and increase of first order good.) It is also being assumed that second order good is more important than first order good or evil, in particular that it more than outweighs the first order evil it involves.

Now this is a particularly subtle attempt to solve the problem of evil. It defends God's goodness and omnipotence on the ground that (on a sufficiently long view) this is the best of all logically possible worlds, because it includes the important second order goods, and yet it admits that real evils, namely first order evils, exist. But does it still hold that good and evil are opposed? Not, clearly, in the sense that we set out originally: good does not tend to eliminate evil in general. Instead, we have a modified, a more complex pattern. First order good (*e.g.* happiness) *contrasts with* first order evil (*e.g.* misery): these two are opposed in a fairly mechanical way; some second order goods (*e.g.* benevolence) try to maximise first order good and minimise first order evil; but God's goodness is not this, it is rather the will to maximise *second* order good. We might, therefore, call God's goodness an example of a third order goodness, or good (3). While this account is different from our original one, it might well be held to be an improvement on it, to give a more accurate description of the way in which good is opposed to evil, and to be consistent with the essential theist position.

There might, however, be several objections to this solution.

First, some might argue that such qualities as benevolence – and *a fortiori* the third order goodness which promotes benevolence – have a merely derivative value, that they are not higher sorts of good, but merely means to good (1), that is, to happiness, so that it would be absurd for God to keep misery in existence in order to make possible the virtues of benevolence, heroism, etc. The theist who adopts the present solution must, of course, deny this, but he can do so with some plausibility, so I should not press this objection.

Secondly, it follows from this solution that God is not in our sense benevolent or sympathetic: he is not concerned to minimise evil (1), but only to promote good (2); and this might be a disturbing conclusion for some theists.

But, thirdly, the fatal objection is this. Our analysis shows clearly the possibility of the existence of a *second* order evil, an evil (2) contrasting with good (2) as evil (1) contrasts with good (1).

This would include malevolence, cruelty, callousness, cowardice, and states in which good (1) is decreasing and evil (1) increasing. And just as good (2) is held to be the important kind of good, the kind that God is concerned to promote, so evil (2) will, by analogy, be the important kind of evil, the kind which God, if he were wholly good and omnipotent, would eliminate. And yet evil (2) plainly exists, and indeed most theists (in other contexts) stress its existence more than that of evil (1). We should, therefore, state the problem of evil in terms of second order evil, and against this form of the problem the present solution is useless.

An attempt might be made to use this solution again, at a higher level, to explain the occurrence of evil (2): indeed the next main solution that we shall examine does just this, with the help of some new notions. Without any fresh notions, such a solution would have little plausibility: for example, we could hardly say that the really important good was a good (3), such as the increase of benevolence in proportion to cruelty, which logically required for its occurrence the occurrence of some second order evil. But even if evil (2) could be explained in this way, it is fairly clear that there would be third order evils contrasting with this third order good: and we should be well on the way to an infinite regress, where the solution of a problem of evil, stated in terms of evil (n), indicated the existence of an evil ($n + 1$), and a further problem to be solved.

4. 'Evil is due to human freewill.'

Perhaps the most important proposed solution of the problem of evil is that evil is not to be ascribed to God at all, but to the independent actions of human beings, supposed to have been endowed by God with freedom of the will. This solution may be combined with the preceding one: first order evil (*e.g.* pain) may be justified as a logically necessary component in second order good (*e.g.* sympathy) while second order evil (*e.g.* cruelty) is not *justified*, but is so ascribed to human beings that God cannot be held responsible for it. This combination evades my third criticism of the preceding solution.

The freewill solution also involves the preceding solution at a higher level. To explain why a wholly good God gave men freewill although it would lead to some important evils, it must be argued that it is better on the whole that men should act freely, and sometimes err, than that they should be innocent automata, acting rightly in a wholly determined way. Freedom, that is to say, is now treated as a third order good, and as being more valuable than second order goods (such as sympathy and heroism) would be if they were deterministically produced, and it is being assumed that second order evils, such as cruelty, are logically necessary accompaniments of freedom, just as pain is a logically necessary pre-condition of sympathy.

I think that this solution is unsatisfactory primarily because of the incoherence of the notion of freedom of the will: but I cannot discuss this topic adequately here, although some of my criticisms will touch upon it.

First I should query the assumption that second order evils are logically necessary accompaniments of freedom. I should ask this: if God has made men such that in their free choices they sometimes prefer what is good and sometimes what is evil, why could he not have made men such that they always freely choose the good? If there is no logical impossibility in a man's freely choosing the good on one, or on several, occasions, there cannot be a logical impossibility in his freely choosing the good on every occasion. God was not, then, faced with a choice between making innocent automata and making beings who, in acting freely, would sometimes go wrong: there was open to him the obviously better possibility of making beings who would act freely but always go right. Clearly, his failure to avail himself of this possibility is inconsistent with his being both omnipotent and wholly good.

If it is replied that this objection is absurd, that the making of some wrong choices is logically necessary for freedom, it would seem that 'freedom' must here mean complete randomness or indeterminacy, including randomness with regard to the alternatives good and evil, in other words that men's choices and consequent actions can be 'free' only if they are not determined by their characters. Only on this assumption can God escape the responsibility for men's actions; for if he made them as they are, but did not determine their wrong choices, this can only be because the wrong choices are not determined by men as they are. But then if freedom is randomness, how can it be a characteristic of *will*? And, still more, how can it be the most important good? What value or merit would there be in free choices if these were random actions which were not determined by the nature of the agent?

I conclude that to make this solution plausible two different senses of 'freedom' must be confused, one sense which will justify the view that freedom is a third order good, more valuable than other goods would be without it, and another sense, sheer randomness, to prevent us from ascribing to God a decision to make men such that they sometimes go wrong when he might have made them such that they would always freely go right.

This criticism is sufficient to dispose of this solution. But besides this there is a fundamental difficulty in the notion of an omnipotent God creating men with free will, for if men's wills are really free this must mean that even God cannot control them, that is, that God is no longer omnipotent. It may be objected that God's gift of freedom to men does not mean that he *cannot* control their wills, but that he always *refrains* from controlling their wills. But why, we may ask, should God refrain from controlling evil wills? Why should he not leave men free to will rightly, but intervene when he sees them beginning to will wrongly? If God could do this, but does not, and if he is wholly good, the only explanation could be that even a wrong free act of will is not really evil, that its freedom is a value which outweighs its wrongness, so that there would be a loss of value if God took away the wrongness and the freedom together. But this is utterly opposed to what theists say about sin in other contexts. The present solution of the problem of evil, then, can be maintained only in the form that God has made men so free that he *cannot* control their wills.

This leads us to what I call the Paradox of Omnipotence: can an omnipotent being make things which he cannot subsequently control? Or, what is practically equivalent to this, can an omnipotent being make rules which then bind himself? (These are practically equivalent because any such rules could be regarded as setting certain things beyond his control, and *vice versa*.) The second of these formulations is relevant to the suggestions that we have already met, that an omnipotent God creates the rules of logic or causal laws, and is then bound by them.

It is clear that this is a paradox: the questions cannot be answered satisfactorily either in the affirmative or in the negative. If we answer 'Yes', it follows that if God actually makes things which he cannot control, or makes rules which bind himself, he is not omnipotent once he has made them: there are *then* things which he cannot do. But if we answer 'No', we are immediately asserting that there are things which he cannot do, that is to say that he is already not omnipotent.

It cannot be replied that the question which sets this paradox is not a proper question. It would make perfectly good sense to say that a human mechanic has made a machine which he cannot control: if there is any difficulty about the question it lies in the notion of omnipotence itself.

This, incidentally, shows that although we have approached this paradox from the free will theory, it is equally a problem for a theological determinist. No one thinks that machines have free will, yet they may well be beyond the control of their makers. The determinist might reply that anyone who makes anything determines its ways of acting, and so determines its subsequent behaviour: even the human mechanic does this by his *choice* of materials and structure for his machine, though he does not know all about either of these: the mechanic thus determines, though he may not foresee, his machine's actions. And since God is omniscient, and since his creation of things is total, he both determines and foresees the ways in which his creatures will act. We may grant this, but it is beside the point. The question is not whether God *originally* determined the future actions of his creatures, but whether he can *subsequently* control their actions, or whether he was able in his original creation to put things beyond his subsequent control. Even on determinist principles the answers 'Yes' and 'No' are equally irreconcilable with God's omnipotence.

Before suggesting a solution of this paradox, I would point out that there is a parallel Paradox of Sovereignty. Can a legal sovereign make a law restricting its own future legislative power? For example, could the British parliament make a law forbidding any future parliament to socialise banking, and also forbidding the future repeal of this law itself? Or could the British parliament, which was legally sovereign in Australia in, say,

1899, pass a valid law, or series of laws, which made it no longer sovereign in 1933? Again, neither the affirmative nor the negative answer is really satisfactory. If we were to answer 'Yes', we should be admitting the validity of a law which, if it were actually made, would mean that parliament was no longer sovereign. If we were to answer 'No', we should be admitting that there is a law, not logically absurd, which parliament cannot validly make, that is, that parliament is not now a legal sovereign. This paradox can be solved in the following way. We should distinguish between first order laws, that is laws governing the actions of individuals and bodies other than the legislature, and second order laws, that is laws about laws, laws governing the actions of the legislature itself. Correspondingly, we should distinguish two orders of sovereignty, first order sovereignty (sovereignty (1)) which is unlimited authority to make first order laws, and second order sovereignty (sovereignty (2)) which is unlimited authority to make second order laws. If we say that parliament is sovereign we might mean that any parliament at any time has sovereignty (1), or we might mean that parliament has both sovereignty (1) and sovereignty (2) at present, but we cannot without contradiction mean both that the present parliament has sovereignty (2) and that every parliament at every time has sovereignty (1), for if the present parliament has sovereignty (2) it may use it to take away the sovereignty (1) of later parliaments. What the paradox shows is that we cannot ascribe to any continuing institution legal sovereignty in an inclusive sense.

The analogy between omnipotence and sovereignty shows that the paradox of omnipotence can be solved in a similar way. We must distinguish between first order omnipotence (omnipotence (1)), that is unlimited power to act, and second order omnipotence (omnipotence (2)), that is unlimited power to determine what powers to act things shall have. Then we could consistently say that God all the time has omnipotence (1), but if so no beings at any time have powers to act independently of God. Or we could say that God at one time had omnipotence (2), and used it to assign independent powers to act to certain things, so that God thereafter did not have omnipotence (1). But what the paradox shows is that we cannot consistently ascribe to any continuing being omnipotence in an inclusive sense.

An alternative solution of this paradox would be simply to deny that God is a continuing being, that any times can be assigned to his actions at all. But on this assumption (which also has difficulties of its own) no meaning can be given to the assertion that God made men with wills so free that he could not control them. The paradox of omnipotence can be avoided by putting God outside time, but the freewill solution of the problem of evil cannot be saved in this way, and equally it remains impossible to hold that an omnipotent God *binds himself* by causal or logical laws.

Conclusion

Of the proposed solutions of the problem of evil which we have examined, none has stood up to criticism. There may be other solutions which require examination, but this study strongly suggests that there is no valid solution of the problem which does not modify at least one of the constituent propositions in a way which would seriously affect the essential core of the theistic position.

Quite apart from the problem of evil, the paradox of omnipotence has shown that God's omnipotence must in any case be restricted in one way or another, that unqualified omnipotence cannot be ascribed to any being that continues through time. And if God and his actions are not in time, can omnipotence, or power of any sort, be meaningfully ascribed to him?

8

The Free Will Defense

Alvin Plantinga

Alvin Plantinga (b. 1932) is John A. O'Brien Professor of Philosophy at the University of Notre Dame and one of the leading contributors to contemporary philosophy of religion. The following selection from his book *God, Freedom, and Evil* (1974) is a highly influential critique of Mackie's essay (see previous reading). Plantinga argues that Mackie fails to reveal any contradiction within theistic beliefs because two principles to which Mackie appeals are false. Plantinga goes on to offer a sophisticated free will defense, claiming that it can be used to demonstrate that theistic belief is logically consistent.

2. Does the Theist Contradict Himself?

In a widely discussed piece entitled "Evil and Omnipotence" John Mackie repeats this claim:

> I think, however, that a more telling criticism can be made by way of the traditional problem of evil. Here it can be shown, not that religious beliefs lack rational support, but that they are positively irrational, that the several parts of the essential theological doctrine are *inconsistent* with one another....[1]

Is Mackie right? Does the theist contradict himself? But we must ask a prior question: just what is being claimed here? That theistic belief contains an inconsistency or contradiction, of course. But what, exactly, is an inconsistency or contradiction? There are several kinds. An *explicit* contradiction is a *proposition* of a certain sort – a conjunctive proposition, one conjunct of which is the denial or negation of the other conjunct. For example:

> Paul is a good tennis player, and it's false that Paul is a good tennis player.

(People seldom assert explicit contradictions.) Is Mackie charging the theist with accepting such a contradiction? Presumably not; what he says is:

Alvin Plantinga, "The Free Will Defense" from *God, Freedom, and Evil* (Grand Rapids, MI: William B. Eerdmans, 1977), pp. 12–49.

> In its simplest form the problem is this: God is omnipotent; God is wholly good; yet evil exists. There seems to be some contradiction between these three propositions, so that if any two of them were true the third would be false. But at the same time all three are essential parts of most theological positions; the theologian, it seems, at once *must* adhere and *cannot consistently* adhere to all three.[2]

According to Mackie, then, the theist accepts a group or set of three propositions; this set is inconsistent. Its members, of course, are

(1) God is omnipotent
(2) God is wholly good

and

(3) Evil exists.

Call this set A; the claim is that A is an inconsistent set. But what is it for a *set* to be inconsistent or contradictory? Following our definition of an explicit contradiction, we might say that a set of propositions is explicitly contradictory if one of the members is the denial or negation of another member. But then, of course, it is evident that the set we are discussing is not explicitly contradictory; the denials of (1), (2), and (3), respectively are

(1′) God is not omnipotent (or it's false that God is omnipotent)
(2′) God is not wholly good

and

(3′) There is no evil

none of which are in set A.

Of course many sets are pretty clearly contradictory, in an important way, but not *explicitly* contradictory. For example, set B:

(4) If all men are mortal, then Socrates is mortal
(5) All men are mortal
(6) Socrates is not mortal.

This set is not explicitly contradictory; yet surely *some* significant sense of that term applies to it. What is important here is that by using only the rules of ordinary logic – the laws of propositional logic and quantification theory found in any introductory text on the subject – we can deduce an explicit contradiction from the set. Or to put it differently, we can use the laws of logic to deduce a proposition from the set, which proposition, when added to the set, yields a new set that is explicitly contradictory. For by using the law *modus ponens* (if *p*, then *q*; *p*; therefore *q*) we can deduce

(7) Socrates is mortal

from (4) and (5). The result of adding (7) to B is the set {(4), (5), (6), (7)}. This set, of course, is explicitly contradictory in that (6) is the denial of (7). We might say that any set which shares this characteristic with set B is *formally* contradictory. So a formally contradictory set is one from whose members an explicit contradiction can be deduced by the laws of logic. Is Mackie claiming that set A is formally contradictory?

If he is, he's wrong. No laws of logic permit us to deduce the denial of one of the propositions in A from the other members. Set A isn't formally contradictory either.

But there is still another way in which a set of propositions can be contradictory or inconsistent. Consider set C, whose members are

(8) George is older than Paul
(9) Paul is older than Nick

and

(10) George is not older than Nick.

This set is neither explicitly nor formally contradictory; we can't, just by using the laws of logic, deduce the denial of any of these propositions from the others. And yet there is a good sense in which it is inconsistent or contradictory. For clearly it is *not possible* that its three members all be true. It is *necessarily true* that

(11) If George is older than Paul, and Paul is older than Nick, then George is older than Nick.

And if we add (11) to set C, we get a set that is formally contradictory; (8), (9), and (11) yield, by the laws of ordinary logic, the denial of (10).

I said that (11) is *necessarily true*; but what does *that* mean? Of course we might say that a proposition is necessarily true if it is impossible that it be false, or if its negation is not possibly true. This would be to explain necessity in terms of possibility. Chances are, however, that anyone who does not know what necessity is, will be equally at a loss about possibility; the explanation is not likely to be very successful. Perhaps all we can do by way of explanation is give some examples and hope for the best. In the first place many propositions can be established by the laws of logic alone – for example

(12) If all men are mortal and Socrates is a man, then Socrates is mortal.

Such propositions are truths of logic; and all of them are necessary in the sense of question. But truths of arithmetic and mathematics generally are also necessarily true. Still further, there is a host of propositions that are neither truths of logic nor truths of mathematics but are nonetheless necessarily true; (11) would be an example, as well as

(13) Nobody is taller than himself
(14) Red is a color
(15) No numbers are persons
(16) No prime number is a prime minister

and

(17) Bachelors are unmarried.

So here we have an important kind of necessity – let's call it "broadly logical necessity." Of course there is a correlative kind of *possibility*: a proposition p is possibly true (in the broadly logical sense) just in case its negation or denial is not necessarily true (in that same broadly logical sense). This sense of necessity and possibility must be distinguished from another that we may call *causal* or *natural* necessity and possibility. Consider

(18) Henry Kissinger has swum the Atlantic.

Although this proposition has an implausible ring, it is not necessarily false in the broadly logical sense (and its denial is not necessarily true in that sense). But there is a good sense in which it is impossible: it is *causally* or *naturally* impossible. Human beings, unlike dolphins, just don't have the physical equipment demanded for this feat. Unlike Superman, furthermore, the rest of us are incapable of leaping tall buildings at a single bound or (without auxiliary power of some kind) traveling faster than a speeding bullet. These things are *impossible* for us – but not *logically* impossible, even in the broad sense.

So there are several senses of necessity and possibility here. There are a number of propositions, furthermore, of which it's difficult to say whether they are or aren't possible in the broadly logical sense; some of these are subjects of philosophical controversy. Is it possible, for example, for a person never to be conscious during his entire existence? Is it possible for a (human) person to exist *disembodied*? If that's possible, is it possible that there be a person who *at no time at all* during his entire existence has a body? Is it possible to see without eyes? These are propositions about whose possibility in that broadly logical sense there is disagreement and dispute.

Now return to set C (p. 351). What is characteristic of it is the fact that the conjunction of its members – the proposition expressed by the result of putting "and's" between (8), (9), and (10) – is necessarily false. Or we might put it like this: what characterizes set C is the fact that we can get a formally contradictory set by adding a necessarily true proposition – namely (11). Suppose we say that a set is *implicitly contradictory* if it resembles C in this respect. That is, a set S of propositions is implicitly contradictory if there is a necessary proposition p such that the result of adding p to S is a formally contradictory set. Another way to put it: S is implicitly contradictory if there is some necessarily true proposition p such that by using just the laws of ordinary logic, we can deduce an explicit contradiction from p together with the members of S. And when Mackie says that set A is contradictory, we may properly take him, I think, as holding that it is implicitly contradictory in the explained sense. As he puts it:

> However, the contradiction does not arise immediately; to show it we need some additional premises, or perhaps some quasi-logical rules connecting the terms "good" and "evil" and "omnipotent." These additional principles are that good is opposed to evil, in such a way that a good thing always eliminates evil as far as it can, and that there are no limits to what an omnipotent thing can do. From these it follows that a good omnipotent thing eliminates evil completely, and then the propositions that a good omnipotent thing exists, and that evil exists, are incompatible.[3]

Here Mackie refers to "additional premises"; he also calls them "additional principles" and "quasi-logical rules"; he says we need them to show the contradiction. What he means, I think, is that to get a formally contradictory set we must add some more propositions to set A; and if we aim to show that set A is implicitly contradictory, these propositions must be necessary truths – "quasi-logical rules" as Mackie calls them. The two additional principles he suggests are

(19) A good thing always eliminates evil as far as it can

and

(20) There are no limits to what an omnipotent being can do.

And, of course, if Mackie means to show that set A is implicitly contradictory, then he must hold that (19) and (20) are not merely *true* but *necessarily true.*

But, are they? What about (20) first? What does it mean to say that a being is omnipotent? That he is *all-powerful*, or *almighty*, presumably. But are there no limits *at all* to the power of such a being? Could he create square circles, for example, or married bachelors? Most theologians and theistic philosophers who hold that God is omnipotent, do not hold that He can create round squares or bring it about that He both exists and does not exist. These theologians and philosophers may hold that there are no *nonlogical* limits to what an omnipotent being can do, but they concede that not even an omnipotent being can bring about logically impossible states of affairs or cause necessarily false propositions to be true. Some theists, on the other hand – Martin Luther and Descartes, perhaps – have apparently thought that God's power is unlimited even by the laws of logic. For these theists the question whether set A is contradictory will not be of much interest. As theists they believe (1) and (2), and they also, presumably, believe (3). But they remain undisturbed by the claim that (1), (2), and (3) are jointly inconsistent – because, as they say, God can do what is logically impossible. Hence He can bring it about that the members of set A are all true, even if that set is contradictory (concentrating very intensely upon this suggestion is likely to make you dizzy). So the theist who thinks that the power of God isn't limited *at all*, not even by the laws of logic, will be unimpressed by Mackie's argument and won't find any difficulty in the contradiction set A is alleged to contain. This view is not very popular, however, and for good reason; it is quite incoherent. What the theist typically means when he says that God is omnipotent is not that there are *no* limits to God's power, but at most that there are no nonlogical limits to what He can do; and given this qualification, it is perhaps initially plausible to suppose that (20) is necessarily true.

But what about (19), the proposition that every good thing eliminates every evil state of affairs that it can eliminate? Is that necessarily true? Is it true at all? Suppose, first of all, that your friend Paul unwisely goes for a drive on a wintry day and runs out of gas on a deserted road. The temperature dips to −10°, and a miserably cold wind comes up. You are sitting comfortably at home (twenty-five miles from Paul) roasting chestnuts in a roaring blaze. Your car is in the garage; in the trunk there is the full five-gallon can of gasoline you always keep for emergencies. Paul's discomfort and danger are certainly an evil, and one which you could eliminate. You don't do so. But presumably you don't thereby forfeit your claim to being a "good thing" – you simply didn't know of Paul's plight. And so (19) does not appear to be necessary. It says that every good thing has a certain property – the property of eliminating every evil that it can. And if the case I described is possible – a good person's failing through ignorance to eliminate a certain evil he can eliminate – then (19) is by no means necessarily true.

But perhaps Mackie could sensibly claim that if you *didn't know* about Paul's plight, then in fact you were *not*, at the time in question, able to eliminate the evil in question; and perhaps he'd be right. In any event he could revise (19) to take into account the kind of case I mentioned:

(19a) Every good thing always eliminates every evil that *it knows about* and can eliminate.

{(1), (2), (3), (20), (19a)}, you'll notice, is not a formally contradictory set – to get a formal contradiction we must add a proposition specifying that God *knows about* every evil state of affairs. But most theists do believe that God is omniscient or all-knowing; so if this new set – the set that results when we add to set A the proposition that God is omniscient – is implicitly contradictory then Mackie should be satisfied and the theist confounded. (And, henceforth, set A will be the old set A together with the proposition that God is omniscient.)

But is (19a) necessary? Hardly. Suppose you know that Paul is marooned as in the previous example, and you also know another friend is similarly marooned fifty miles in the opposite direction. Suppose, furthermore, that while you can rescue one or the other, you simply can't rescue both. Then each of the two evils is such that it is within your power to eliminate it; and you know about them both. But you can't eliminate *both*; and you don't forfeit your claim to being a good person by eliminating only one – it wasn't within your power to do more. So the fact that you don't doesn't mean that you are not a good person. Therefore (19a) is false; it is not a necessary truth or even a truth that every good thing eliminates every evil it knows about and can eliminate.

We can see the same thing another way. You've been rock climbing. Still something of a novice, you've acquired a few cuts and bruises by inelegantly using your knees rather than your feet. One of these bruises is fairly painful. You mention it to a physician friend, who predicts the pain will leave of its own accord in a day or two. Meanwhile, he says, there's nothing he can do, short of amputating your leg above the knee, to remove the pain. Now the pain in your knee is an evil state of affairs. All else being equal, it would be better if you had no such pain. And it is within the power of your friend to eliminate this evil state of affairs. Does his failure to do so mean that he is not a good person? Of course not; for he could eliminate this evil state of affairs only by bringing about another, much worse evil. And so it is once again evident that (19a) is false. It is entirely possible that a good person fail to eliminate an evil state of affairs that he knows about and can eliminate. This would take place, if, as in the present example, he couldn't eliminate the evil without bringing about a *greater* evil.

A slightly different kind of case shows the same thing. A really impressive good state of affairs *G* will *outweigh* a trivial evil *E* – that is, the conjunctive state of affairs *G and E* is itself a good state of affairs. And surely a good person would not be obligated to eliminate a given evil if he could do so only by eliminating a good that outweighed it. Therefore (19a) is not necessarily true; it can't be used to show that set A is implicitly contradictory.

These difficulties might suggest another revision of (19); we might try

(19b) A good being eliminates every evil *E* that it knows about and that it can eliminate without either bringing about a greater evil or eliminating a good state of affairs that outweighs *E*.

Is this necessarily true? It takes care of the second of the two difficulties afflicting (19a) but leaves the first untouched. We can see this as follows. First, suppose we say that a being *properly eliminates* an evil state of affairs if it eliminates that evil without either eliminating an outweighing good or bringing about a greater evil. It is then obviously possible that a person find himself in a situation where he could properly eliminate an evil *E* and could also properly eliminate another evil *E′*, but couldn't properly eliminate them *both*. You're rock climbing again, this time on the dreaded north face of the Grand Teton. You and your party come upon Curt and Bob, two mountaineers stranded 125 feet apart on the face. They untied to reach their cigarettes and then carelessly dropped the rope while lighting up. A violent, dangerous thunderstorm is approaching. You have time to rescue one of the stranded climbers and retreat before the storm hits; if you rescue both, however, you and your party and the two climbers will be caught on the face during the thunderstorm, which will very likely destroy your entire party. In this case you can eliminate one evil (Curt's being stranded on the face) without causing more evil or eliminating a greater good; and you are also able to properly eliminate the other evil (Bob's being thus stranded). But you can't properly eliminate them *both*. And so the fact that you don't rescue Curt, say, even though you could have, doesn't show that you aren't a good person. Here, then, each of the evils is such that you can properly eliminate it; but you can't properly eliminate them both, and hence can't be blamed for failing to eliminate one of them.

So neither (19a) nor (19b) is necessarily true. You may be tempted to reply that the sort of counterexamples offered – examples where someone is able to eliminate an evil *A* and also able to eliminate a different evil *B*, but unable to eliminate them both – are irrelevant to the case of a being who, like God, is both omnipotent and omniscient. That is, you may think that if an omnipotent and omniscient being is able to eliminate *each* of two evils, it follows that he can eliminate them *both*. Perhaps this is so; but it is not strictly to the point. The fact is the counterexamples show that (19a) and (19b) are not necessarily true and hence can't be used to show that set A is implicitly inconsistent. What the reply does suggest is that perhaps the atheologian will have more success if he works the properties of omniscience and omnipotence into (19). Perhaps he could say something like

(19c) An omnipotent and omniscient good being eliminates every evil that it can properly eliminate.

And suppose, for purposes of argument, we concede the necessary truth of (19c). Will it serve Mackie's purposes? Not obviously. For we don't get a set that is formally contradictory by adding (20) and (19c) to set A. This set (call it A′) contains the following six members:

(1) God is omnipotent
(2) God is wholly good
(2′) God is omniscient
(3) Evil exists
(19c) An omnipotent and omniscient good being eliminates every evil that it can properly eliminate

and

(20) There are no nonlogical limits to what an omnipotent being can do.

Now if A′ were formally contradictory, then from any five of its members we could deduce the denial of the sixth by the laws of ordinary logic. That is, any five would *formally entail* the denial of the sixth. So if A′ were formally inconsistent, the denial of (3) would be formally entailed by the remaining five. That is, (1), (2), (2′), (19c), and (20) would formally entail

(3′) There is no evil.

But they don't; what they formally entail is not that there is no evil *at all* but only that

(3″) There is no evil that God can properly eliminate.

So (19c) doesn't really help either – not because it is not necessarily true but because its addition [with (20)] to set A does not yield a formally contradictory set.

Obviously, what the atheologian must add to get a formally contradictory set is

(21) If God is omniscient and omnipotent, then he can properly eliminate every evil state of affairs.

Suppose we agree that the set consisting in A plus (19c), (20), and (21) is formally contradictory. So if (19c), (20), and (21) are all necessarily true, then set A is implicitly contradictory. We've already conceded that (19c) and (20) are indeed necessary. So we must take a look at (21). Is this proposition necessarily true?

No. To see this let us ask the following question. Under what conditions would an omnipotent being be unable to eliminate a certain evil *E* without eliminating an outweighing good? Well, suppose that *E* is *included in* some good state of affairs that outweighs it. That is, suppose there is some good state of affairs *G* so related to *E* that it is impossible that *G* obtain or be actual and *E* fail to obtain. (Another way to put this: a state of affairs *S* includes *S′* if the conjunctive state of affairs *S but not S′* is impossible, or if it is necessary that *S′* obtains if *S* does.) Now suppose that some good state of affairs *G* includes an evil state of affairs *E* that it outweighs. Then not even an omnipotent being could eliminate *E* without eliminating *G*. But *are* there any cases where a good state of affairs includes, in this sense, an evil that it outweighs?[4] Indeed there are such states of affairs. To take an artificial example, let's suppose that *E* is Paul's suffering from a minor abrasion and *G* is your being deliriously happy. The conjunctive state of affairs, *G and E* – the state of affairs that obtains if and only if both *G* and *E* obtain – is then a good state of affairs: it is better, all else being equal, that you be intensely happy and Paul suffer a mildly annoying abrasion than that this state of affairs not obtain. So *G and E* is a good state of affairs. And clearly *G and E* includes *E*: obviously it is necessarily true that if you are deliriously happy and Paul is suffering from an abrasion, then Paul is suffering from an abrasion.

But perhaps you think this example trivial, tricky, slippery, and irrelevant. If so, take heart; other examples abound. Certain kinds of values, certain familiar kinds of good states of affairs, can't exist apart from evil of some sort. For example, there are people who display a sort of creative moral heroism in the face of suffering and adversity – a heroism that inspires others and creates a good situation out of a bad one. In a situation like this the evil, of course, remains evil; but the total state of affairs – someone's bearing pain magnificently, for example – may be good. If it is, then the good present must outweigh the evil; otherwise the total situation would not be *good*. But, of course, it is not possible that such a good state of affairs obtain unless some evil also obtain. It is a necessary truth that if someone bears pain magnificently, then someone is in pain.

The conclusion to be drawn, therefore, is that (21) is not necessarily true. And our discussion thus far shows at the very least that it is no easy matter to find necessarily true propositions that yield a formally contradictory set when added to set A.[5] One wonders, therefore, why the many atheologians who confidently assert that this set is contradictory make no attempt whatever to *show* that it is. For the most part they are content just to *assert* that there is a contradiction here. Even Mackie, who sees that some "additional premises" or "quasi-logical rules" are needed, makes scarcely a beginning towards finding some additional premises that are necessarily true and that together with the members of set A formally entail an explicit contradiction.

3. Can We Show That There Is No Inconsistency Here?

To summarize our conclusions so far: although many atheologians claim that the theist is involved in contradiction when he asserts the members of set A, this set, obviously, is neither *explicitly* nor *formally* contradictory; the claim, presumably, must be that it is *implicitly* contradictory. To make good this claim the atheologian must find some necessarily true proposition *p* (it could be a conjunction of several propositions) such that the addition of *p* to set A yields a set that is formally contradictory. No atheologian has produced even a plausible candidate for this role, and it certainly is not easy to see what such a proposition might be. Now we might think we should simply declare set A implicitly consistent on the principle that a proposition (or set) is to be presumed consistent or possible until proven otherwise. This course, however, leads to trouble. The same principle would impel us to declare the atheologian's claim – that set A is *in*consistent – possible or consistent. But the claim that a given set of propositions is implicitly contradictory, is itself either necessarily true or necessarily false; so if such a claim is *possible*, it is not necessarily false and is, therefore, true (in fact, necessarily true). If we followed the suggested principle, therefore, we should be obliged to declare set A implicitly consistent (since it hasn't been shown to be otherwise), but we should have to say the same thing about the atheologian's claim, since we haven't shown *that* claim to be inconsistent or impossible. The atheologian's claim, furthermore, is necessarily true if it is possible. Accordingly, if we accept the above principle, we shall have to declare set A both implicitly consistent and implicitly inconsistent. So all we can say at this point is that set A has not been shown to be implicitly inconsistent.

Can we go any further? One way to go on would be to try to *show* that set A is implicitly consistent or possible in the broadly logical sense. But what is involved in showing such a thing? Although there are various ways to approach this matter, they all resemble one another in an important respect. They all amount to this: to show that a set *S* is consistent you think of a *possible state of affairs* (it needn't *actually obtain*) which is such that if it were actual, then all of the members of *S* would be true. This procedure is sometimes called *giving a model of S*. For example, you might construct an axiom set and then show that it is consistent by giving a model of it; this is how it was shown that the denial of Euclid's parallel postulate is formally consistent with the rest of his postulates.

There are various special cases of this procedure to fit special circumstances. Suppose, for example, you have a pair of propositions *p* and *q* and wish to show them consistent. And suppose we say that a proposition p_1 *entails* a proposition p_2 if it is impossible that p_1 be true and p_2 false – if the conjunctive proposition p_1 *and not* p_2 is necessarily false. Then one way to show that *p* is consistent with *q* is to find some proposition *r* whose conjunction with *p* is both possible, in the broadly logical sense, and entails *q*. A rude and unlettered behaviorist, for example, might hold that thinking is really nothing but movements of the larynx; he might go on to hold that

> *P* Jones did not move his larynx after April 30

is inconsistent (in the broadly logical sense) with

> *Q* Jones did some thinking during May.

By way of rebuttal, we might point out that *P* appears to be consistent with

> *R* While convalescing from an April 30 laryngotomy, Jones whiled away the idle hours by writing (in May) a splendid paper on Kant's *Critique of Pure Reason*.

So the conjunction of *P* and *R* appears to be consistent; but obviously it also entails *Q* (you can't write even a passable paper on Kant's *Critique of Pure Reason* without doing some thinking); so *P* and *Q* are consistent.

We can see that this is a special case of the procedure I mentioned above as follows. This proposition *R* is consistent with *P*; so the proposition *P and R* is possible, describes a possible state of affairs. But *P and R* entails *Q*; hence if *P and R* were true, *Q* would also be true, and hence both *P* and *Q* would be true. So this is really a case of producing a possible state of affairs such that, if it were actual, all the members of the set in question (in this case the pair set of *P* and *Q*) would be true.

How does this apply to the case before us? As follows. Let us conjoin propositions (1), (2), and (2′) and henceforth call the result (1):

> (1) God is omniscient, omnipotent, and wholly good

The problem, then, is to show that (1) and (3) (evil exists) are consistent. This could be done, as we've seen, by finding a proposition *r* that is consistent with (1) and such that (1) and (*r*) together entail (3). One proposition that might do the trick is

> (22) God creates a world containing evil and has a good reason for doing so.

If (22) is consistent with (1), then it follows that (1) and (3) (and hence set A) are consistent. Accordingly, one thing some theists have tried is to show that (22) and (1) are consistent.

One can attempt this in at least two ways. On the one hand, we could try to apply the same method again. Conceive of a possible state of affairs such that, if it obtained, an omnipotent, omniscient, and wholly good God would have a good reason for permitting evil. On the other, someone might try to specify *what God's reason is* for permitting evil and try to show, if it is not obvious, that it is a good reason. St Augustine, for example, one of the greatest and most influential philosopher-theologians of the Christian Church, writes as follows:

> ... some people see with perfect truth that a creature is better if, while possessing free will, it remains always fixed upon God and never sins; then, reflecting on men's sins, they are grieved, not because they continue to sin, but because they were created. They say: He should have made us such that we never willed to sin, but always to enjoy the unchangeable truth.
>
> They should not lament or be angry. God has not compelled men to sin just because He created them and gave them the power to choose between sinning and not sinning. There are angels who have never sinned and never will sin.
>
> Such is the generosity of God's goodness that He has not refrained from creating even that creature which He foreknew would not only sin, but remain in the will to sin. As a runaway horse is better than a stone which does not run away because it lacks self-movement and sense perception, so the creature is more excellent which sins by free will than that which does not sin only because it has no free will.[6]

In broadest terms Augustine claims that God could create a better, more perfect universe by permitting evil than He could by refusing to do so:

> Neither the sins nor the misery are necessary to the perfection of the universe, but souls as such are necessary, which have the power to sin if they so will, and become miserable if they sin. If misery persisted after their sins had been abolished, or if there were misery before there were sins, then it might be right to say that the order and government of the universe were at fault. Again, if there were sins but no consequent misery, that order is equally dishonored by lack of equity.[7]

Augustine tries to tell us *what God's reason is* for permitting evil. At bottom, he says, it's that God can create a more perfect universe by permitting evil. A really top-notch universe requires the existence of free, rational, and moral agents; and some of the free creatures He created went wrong. But the universe with the free creatures it contains and the evil they commit is better than it would have been had it contained neither the free creatures nor this evil. Such an attempt to specify God's reason for permitting evil is what I earlier called a *theodicy*; in the words of John Milton it is an attempt to "justify the ways of God to man," to show that God is just in permitting evil. Augustine's kind of theodicy might be called a Free Will Theodicy, since the idea of rational creatures with free will plays such a prominent role in it.

A theodicist, then, attempts to tell us why God permits evil. Quite distinct from a Free Will Theodicy is what I shall call a Free Will Defense. Here the aim is not to say what God's reason *is*, but at most what God's reason *might possibly be*. We could put the difference like this. The Free Will Theodicist and Free Will Defender are both trying to show that (1) is consistent with (22), and of course if so, then set A is consistent. The Free Will Theodicist tries to do this by finding some proposition *r* which in conjunction with (1) entails (22); he claims, furthermore, that this proposition is *true*, not just consistent with (1). He tries to tell us what God's reason for permitting evil *really is*. The Free Will Defender, on the other hand, though he also tries to find a proposition *r* that is consistent with (1) and in conjunction with it entails (22), does *not* claim to know or even believe that *r* is true. And here, of course, he is perfectly within his rights. His aim is to show that (1) is consistent with (22); all he need do then is find an *r* that is consistent with (1) and such that (1) and (*r*) entail (22); whether *r* is *true* is quite beside the point.

So there is a significant difference between a Free Will Theodicy and a Free Will Defense. The latter is sufficient (if successful) to show that set A is consistent; in a way a Free Will Theodicy goes beyond what is required. On the other hand, a theodicy would be much more satisfying, if possible to achieve. No doubt the theist would rather know what God's reason *is* for permitting evil than simply that it's possible that He has a good one. But in the present context (that of investigating the consistency of set A), the latter is all that's needed. Neither a defense nor a theodicy, of course, gives any hint as to what God's reason for some *specific* evil – the death or suffering of someone close to you, for example – might be. And there is still another function – a sort of pastoral function[8] – in the neighborhood that neither serves. Confronted with evil in his own life or suddenly coming to realize more clearly than before the *extent* and *magnitude* of evil, a believer in God may undergo a crisis of faith. He may be tempted to follow the advice of Job's "friends"; he may be tempted to "curse God and die." Neither a Free Will Defense nor a Free Will Theodicy is designed to be of much help or comfort to one suffering from such a storm in the soul (although in a specific case, of course, one or the other could prove useful). Neither is to be thought of first of all as a means of pastoral counseling. Probably neither will enable someone to find peace with himself and with God in the face of the evil the world contains. But then, of course, neither is intended for that purpose.

4. The Free Will Defense

In what follows I shall focus attention upon the Free Will Defense. I shall examine it more closely, state it more exactly, and consider objections to it; and I shall argue that in the end it is successful. Earlier we saw that among good states of affairs there are some that not even God can bring about without bringing about evil: those goods, namely, that *entail* or *include* evil states of affairs. The Free Will Defense can be looked upon as an effort to show that there may be a very different kind of good that God can't bring about without permitting evil. These are good states of affairs that don't include evil; they do not entail the existence of any evil whatever; nonetheless God Himself can't bring them about without permitting evil.

So how does the Free Will Defense work? And what does the Free Will Defender mean when he says that people are or may be free? What is relevant to the Free Will Defense is the idea of *being free with respect to an action*. If a person is free with respect to a given action, then he is free to perform that action and free to refrain from performing it; no antecedent conditions and/or causal laws determine that he will perform the action, or that he won't. It is within his power, at the time in question, to take or perform the action and within his power to refrain from it. Freedom so conceived is not to be confused with unpredictability. You might be able to predict what you will do in a given situation even if you are free, in that situation, to do something else. If I know you well, I may be able to predict what action you will take in response to a certain set of conditions; it does not follow that you are not free with respect to that action. Secondly, I shall say that an action is *morally significant*, for a given person, if it would be wrong for him to perform the action but right to refrain or *vice versa*. Keeping a promise, for example, would ordinarily be morally significant for a person, as would refusing induction into the army. On the other hand, having Cheerios for breakfast (instead of Wheaties) would not normally be morally significant. Further, suppose we say that a person is *significantly free*, on a given occasion, if he is then free with respect to a morally significant action. And finally we must distinguish between *moral evil* and *natural evil*. The former is evil that results from free human activity; natural evil is any other kind of evil.[9]

Given these definitions and distinctions, we can make a preliminary statement of the Free Will Defense as follows. A world containing creatures who are significantly free (and freely perform more good than evil actions) is more valuable, all else being equal, than a world containing no free creatures at all. Now God can create free creatures, but He can't *cause* or *determine* them to do only what is right. For if He does so, then they aren't significantly free after all; they do not do what is right *freely*. To create creatures capable of *moral good*, therefore, He must create creatures capable of moral evil; and He can't give these creatures the freedom to perform evil and at the same time prevent them from doing so. As it turned out, sadly enough, some of the free creatures God created went wrong in the exercise of their freedom; this is the source of moral evil. The fact that free creatures sometimes go wrong, however, counts neither against God's omnipotence nor against His goodness; for He could have forestalled the occurrence of moral evil only by removing the possibility of moral good.

I said earlier that the Free Will Defender tries to find a proposition that is consistent with

(1) God is omniscient, omnipotent, and wholly good

and together with (1) entails that there is evil. According to the Free Will Defense, we must find this proposition somewhere in the above story. The heart of the Free Will Defense is the claim that it is *possible* that God could not have created a universe containing moral good (or as much moral good as this world contains) without creating one that also contained moral evil. And if so, then it is possible that God has a good reason for creating a world containing evil.

Now this defense has met with several kinds of objections. For example, some philosophers say that *causal determinism* and *freedom*, contrary to what we might have thought, are not really incompatible.[10] But if so, then God could have created free creatures who were free, and free to do what is wrong, but nevertheless were causally determined to do only what is right. Thus He could have created creatures who were free to do what was wrong, while nevertheless preventing them from ever performing any wrong actions – simply by seeing to it that they were causally determined to do only what is right. Of course this contradicts the Free Will Defense, according to which there is inconsistency in supposing that God determines free creatures to do only what is right. But is it really possible that all of a person's actions are causally determined while some of them are free? How could that be so? According to one version of the doctrine in question, to say that George acts freely on a given occasion is to say only this: *if George had chosen to do otherwise, he would have done otherwise.* Now George's action *A* is causally determined if some event *E* – some event beyond his control – has already occurred, where the state of affairs consisting in *E*'s occurrence conjoined with George's *refraining* from performing *A*, is a causally impossible state of affairs. Then one can consistently hold both that all of a man's actions are causally determined and that some of them are free in the above sense. For suppose that all of a man's actions are causally determined and that he *couldn't*, on any occasion, have made any choice or performed any action different from the ones he did make and perform. It could still be true that if he *had* chosen to do otherwise, he would have done otherwise. Granted, he couldn't have chosen to do otherwise; but this is consistent with saying that *if* he had, things would have gone differently.

This objection to the Free Will Defense seems utterly implausible. One might as well claim that being in jail doesn't really limit one's freedom on the grounds that if one were *not* in jail, he'd be free to come and go as he pleased. So I shall say no more about this objection here.[11]

A second objection is more formidable. In essence it goes like this. Surely it is possible to do only what is right, even if one is free to do wrong. It is *possible*, in that broadly logical sense, that there be a world containing free creatures who always do what is right. There is certainly no *contradiction* or *inconsistency* in this idea. But God is omnipotent; his power has no nonlogical limitations. So if it's possible that there be a world containing creatures who are free to do what is wrong but never in fact do so, then it follows that an omnipotent God could create such a world. If so, however, the Free Will Defense must be mistaken in its insistence upon the possibility that God is omnipotent but unable to create a world containing moral good without permitting moral evil. J. L. Mackie (above, p. 350) states this objection:

> If God has made men such that in their free choices they sometimes prefer what is good and sometimes what is evil, why could he not have made men such that they always freely choose the good? If there is no logical impossibility in a man's freely choosing the good on one, or on several occasions, there cannot be a logical impossibility in his freely choosing the good on every occasion. God was not, then, faced with a choice between making innocent automata and making beings who, in acting freely, would sometimes go wrong; there was open to him the obviously better possibility of making beings who would act freely but always go right. Clearly, his failure to avail himself of this possibility is inconsistent with his being both omnipotent and wholly good.[12]

Now what, exactly, is Mackie's point here? This. According to the Free Will Defense, it is possible both that God is omnipotent and that He was unable to create a world containing moral good without creating one containing moral evil. But, replies Mackie, this limitation on His power to create is inconsistent with God's omnipotence. For surely it's *possible* that there be a world containing perfectly virtuous persons – persons who are significantly free but always do what is right. Surely there are *possible worlds* that contain moral good but no moral evil. But God, if He is omnipotent, can create any possible world He chooses. So it is *not* possible, contrary to the Free Will Defense, both that God is omnipotent and that He could create a world containing moral good only by creating one containing moral evil. If He is omnipotent, the only limitations of His power are *logical* limitations; in which case there are no possible worlds He could not have created.

This is a subtle and important point. According to the great German philosopher G. W. Leibniz, *this* world, the actual world, must be the best of all possible worlds. His reasoning goes as follows. Before God created anything at all, He was confronted with an enormous range of choices; He could create or bring into actuality any of the myriads of different possible worlds. Being perfectly good, He must have chosen to create the best world He could; being omnipotent, He was able to create any possible world He pleased. He must, therefore, have chosen the best of all possible worlds; and hence *this* world, the one He did create, must be the best possible. Now Mackie, of course, agrees with Leibniz that God, if omnipotent, could have created any world He pleased and would have created the best world he could. But while Leibniz draws the conclusion that this world, despite appearances, must be the best possible, Mackie concludes instead that there is no omnipotent, wholly good God. For, he says, it is obvious enough that this present world is not the best of all possible worlds.

The Free Will Defender disagrees with both Leibniz and Mackie: In the first place, he might say, what is the reason for supposing that *there is* such a thing as the best of all possible worlds? No matter how marvelous a world is – containing no matter how many persons enjoying unalloyed bliss – isn't it possible that there be an even better world containing even more persons enjoying even more unalloyed bliss? But what is really characteristic and central to the Free Will Defense is the claim that God, though omnipotent, could not have actualized just any possible world He pleased.

5. Was It within God's Power to Create Any Possible World He Pleased?

This is indeed the crucial question for the Free Will Defense. If we wish to discuss it with insight and authority, we shall have to look into the idea of *possible worlds*. And a sensible first question is this: what sort of thing is a possible world? The basic idea is that a possible world is a *way things could have been*; it is a *state of affairs* of some kind. Earlier we spoke of states of affairs, in particular of good and evil states of affairs. Suppose we look at this idea in more detail. What sort of thing is a state of affairs? The following would be examples:

> Nixon's having won the 1972 election
> 7 + 5's being equal to 12
> All men's being mortal

and

> Gary, Indiana's, having a really nasty pollution problem.

These are *actual* states of affairs: states of affairs that do in fact *obtain*. And corresponding to each such actual state of affairs there is a true proposition – in the above cases, the corresponding propositions would be *Nixon won the 1972 presidential election, 7 + 5 is equal to 12, all men are mortal*, and *Gary, Indiana, has a really nasty pollution problem*.

A proposition *p corresponds* to a state of affairs *s*, in this sense, if it is impossible that *p* be true and *s* fail to obtain and impossible that *s* obtain and *p* fail to be true.

But just as there are false propositions, so there are states of affairs that do *not* obtain or are *not* actual. *Kissinger's having swum the Atlantic* and *Hubert Horatio Humphrey's having run a mile in four minutes* would be examples. Some states of affairs that do not obtain are *impossible*: e.g., *Hubert's having drawn a square circle, 7 + 5's being equal to 75*, and *Agnew's having a brother who was an only child*. The propositions corresponding to these states of affairs, of course, are necessarily false. So there are states of affairs that *obtain* or *are actual* and also states of affairs that don't obtain. Among the latter some are *impossible* and others are possible. And a possible world is a possible state of affairs. Of course not every possible state of affairs is a possible world; *Hubert's having run a mile in four minutes* is a possible state of affairs but not a possible world. No doubt it is an *element* of many possible worlds, but it isn't itself inclusive enough to be one. To be a possible world, a state of affairs must be very large – so large as to be *complete* or *maximal*.

To get at this idea of completeness we need a couple of definitions. As we have already seen (above, pp. 355–6) a state of affairs *A includes* a state of affairs *B* if it is not possible that *A* obtain and *B* not obtain or if the conjunctive state of affairs *A but not B* – the state of affairs that obtains if and only if *A* obtains and *B* does not – is not possible. For example, *Jim Whittaker's being the first American to climb Mt Everest* includes *Jim Whittaker's being an American.* It also includes *Mt Everest's being climbed, something's being climbed, no American's having climbed Everest before Whittaker did*, and the like. *Inclusion* among states of affairs is like *entailment* among propositions; and where a state of affairs *A* includes a state of affairs *B*, the proposition corresponding to *A* entails the one corresponding to *B*. Accordingly, *Jim Whittaker is the first American to climb Everest* entails *Mt Everest has been climbed, something has been climbed*, and *no American climbed Everest before Whittaker did.* Now suppose we say further that a state of affairs *A precludes* a state of affairs *B* if it is not possible that *both* obtain, or if the conjunctive state of affairs *A and B* is impossible. Thus *Whittaker's being the first American to climb Mt Everest* precludes *Luther Jerstad's being the first American to climb Everest*, as well as *Whittaker's never having climbed any mountains.* If *A* precludes *B*, then *A*'s corresponding proposition entails the denial of the one corresponding to *B*. Still further, let's say that the *complement* of a state of affairs is the state of affairs that obtains just in case *A* does not obtain. [Or we might say that the complement (call it $\bar{A}$) of *A* is the state of affairs corresponding to the *denial* or *negation* of the proposition corresponding to *A*.] Given these definitions, we can say what it is for a state of affairs to be *complete:* *A* is a complete state of affairs if and only if for every state of affairs *B*, either *A includes B or A precludes B*. (We could express the same thing by saying that if *A* is a complete state of affairs, then for every state of affairs *B*, either *A* includes *B* or *A* includes $\bar{B}$, the complement of *B*.) And now we are able to say what a possible world is: a possible world is any possible state of affairs that is complete. If *A* is a possible world, then it says something about everything; every state of affairs *S* is either included in or precluded by it.

Corresponding to each possible world *W*, furthermore, there is a set of propositions that I'll call *the book on W*. A proposition is in the book on *W* just in case the state of affairs to which it corresponds is included in *W*. Or we might express it like this. Suppose we say that a proposition *P* is *true in a world W* if and only if *P would have been true if W had been actual* – if and only if, that is, it is not possible that *W* be actual and *P* be false. Then the book on *W* is the set of propositions true in *W*. Like possible worlds, books are *complete*; if *B* is a book, then for any proposition *P*, either *P* or the denial of *P* will be a member of *B*. A book is a *maximal consistent set* of propositions; it is so large that the addition of another proposition to it always yields an explicitly inconsistent set.

Of course, for each possible world there is exactly one book corresponding to it (that is, for a given world *W* there is just one book *B* such that each member of *B* is true in *W*); and for each book there is just one world to which it corresponds. So every world has its book.

It should be obvious that exactly one possible world is actual. At *least* one must be, since the set of true propositions is a maximal consistent set and hence a book. But then it corresponds to a possible world, and the possible world corresponding to this set of propositions (since it's the set of *true* propositions) will be actual. On the other hand there is at *most* one actual world. For suppose there were two: *W* and *W′*. These worlds cannot include all the very same states of affairs; if they did, they would be the very same world. So there must be at least one state of affairs *S* such that *W* includes *S* and *W′* does not. But a possible world is maximal; *W′*, therefore, includes the complement *S* of $\bar{S}$. So if both *W* and *W′* were actual, as we have supposed, then both *S* and $\bar{S}$ would be actual – which is impossible. So there can't be more than one possible world that is actual.

Leibniz pointed out that a proposition *p* is necessary if it is true in every possible world. We may add that *p* is possible if it is true in one world and impossible if true in none. Furthermore, *p entails q* if there is no possible world in which *p* is true and *q* is false; and *p is consistent with q* if there is at least one world in which both *p* and *q* are true.

A further feature of possible worlds is that people (and other things) *exist* in them. Each of us exists in the actual world, obviously; but a person also exists in many worlds distinct from the actual world. It would be a mistake, of course, to think of all of these worlds as somehow "going on" at the same time, with the same person reduplicated through these worlds and actually existing in a lot of different ways. This is not what is meant by saying that the same person exists in different possible worlds. What is meant, instead, is this: a person Paul exists in each of those possible worlds *W* which is such that, if *W had been actual*, Paul would have existed – actually existed. Suppose Paul had been an inch taller than he is, or a better tennis player. Then the world that does in fact obtain would not have been actual; some other world – *W′*, let's say – would have obtained instead. If *W′* had been actual, Paul would have existed; so Paul exists in *W′*. (Of course there are still other possible worlds in which Paul does not exist – worlds, for example, in which there are no people at all.) Accordingly, when we say that Paul exists in a world *W*, what we mean is that Paul *would have* existed had *W* been actual. Or we could put it like this: Paul exists in each world *W* that includes the state of affairs consisting in Paul's existence. We can put this still more simply by saying that Paul exists in those worlds whose books contain the proposition *Paul exists*.

But isn't there a problem here? *Many* people are named "Paul": Paul the apostle, Paul J. Zwier, John Paul Jones, and many other famous Pauls. So who goes with "Paul exists"? Which Paul? The answer has to do with the fact that books contain *propositions* – not sentences. They contain the sort of thing sentences are used to express and assert. And the same sentence – "Aristotle is wise," for example – can be used to express many different propositions. When Plato used it, he asserted a proposition predicating wisdom of his famous pupil; when Jackie Onassis uses it, she asserts a proposition predicating wisdom of her wealthy husband. These are distinct propositions (we might even think they differ in truth value); but they are expressed by the same sentence. Normally (but not always) we don't have much trouble determining which of the several propositions expressed by a given sentence is relevant in the context at hand. So in this case a given person, Paul, exists in a world *W* if and only if *W*'s book contains the proposition that says that *he* – that particular person – exists. The fact that the sentence we use to express this proposition can also be used to express *other* propositions is not relevant.

After this excursion into the nature of books and worlds we can return to our question. Could God have created just any world He chose? Before addressing the question, however, we must note that God does not, strictly speaking, *create* any possible worlds or states of affairs at all. What He creates are the heavens and the earth and all that they contain. But He has not created states of affairs. There are, for example, the state of affairs consisting in God's existence and the state of affairs consisting in His nonexistence. That is, there is such a thing as the state of affairs consisting in the existence of God, and there is also such a thing as the state of affairs consisting in the nonexistence of God, just as there are the two propositions *God exists* and *God does not exist*. The theist believes that the first state of affairs is actual and the first proposition true; the atheist believes that the second state of affairs is actual and the second proposition true. But, of course, both propositions *exist*, even though just one is true. Similarly, there are two states of affairs here, just one of which is actual. So both states of affairs *exist*, but only one *obtains*. And God has not created either one of them since there never was a time at which either did not exist. Nor has He created the state of affairs consisting in the earth's existence; there was a time when *the earth* did not exist, but none when the state of affairs consisting in the earth's existence didn't exist. Indeed, God did not bring into existence any states of affairs at all. What He did was to perform actions of a certain sort – creating the heavens and the earth, for example – which resulted in the *actuality* of certain states of affairs. God *actualizes* states of affairs. He actualizes the possible world that does in fact obtain; He does not create it. And while He has created Socrates, He did not create the state of affairs consisting in Socrates' existence.[13]

Bearing this in mind, let's finally return to our question. Is the atheologian right in holding that if God is omnipotent, then he could have actualized or created any possible world He pleased? Not obviously. First, we must ask ourselves whether God is a *necessary* or a *contingent* being. A *necessary* being is one that exists in every possible world – one that would have existed no matter which possible world had been actual; a contingent being exists only in some possible worlds. Now if God is not a necessary being (and many, perhaps most, theists think that He is not), then clearly enough there will be many possible worlds He could not have actualized – all those, for example, in which He does not exist. Clearly, God could not have created a world in which He doesn't even exist.

So, if God is a contingent being then there are many possible worlds beyond His power to create. But this is really irrelevant to our present concerns. For perhaps the atheologian can maintain his case if he revises his claim to avoid this difficulty; perhaps he will say something like this: if God is omnipotent, then He could have actualized any of those possible worlds *in which He exists*. So if He exists and is omnipotent, He could have actualized (contrary to the Free Will Defense) any of those possible worlds in which He exists and in which there exist free creatures who do no wrong. He could have actualized worlds containing moral good but no moral evil. Is this correct?

Let's begin with a trivial example. You and Paul have just returned from an Australian hunting expedition: your quarry was the elusive double-wattled cassowary. Paul captured an aardvark, mistaking it for a cassowary. The creature's disarming ways have won it a place in Paul's heart; he is deeply attached to it. Upon your return to the States you offer Paul $500 for his aardvark, only to be rudely turned down. Later you ask yourself, "What would he have done if I'd offered him $700?" Now what is it, exactly, that you are asking? What you're really asking in a way is whether, under a *specific set of conditions*, Paul would have sold it. These conditions include your having offered him $700 rather than $500 for the aardvark, everything else being as much as possible like the conditions that did in fact obtain. Let S' be this set of conditions or state of affairs. S' includes the state of affairs consisting in your offering Paul $700 (instead of the $500 you did offer him); of course it does not include his *accepting* your offer, and it does not include his *rejecting* it; for the rest, the conditions it includes are just like the ones that did obtain in the actual world. So, for example, S' includes Paul's being free to accept the offer and free to refrain; and if in fact the going rate for an aardvark was $650, then S' includes the state of affairs consisting in the going rate's being $650. So we might put your question by asking which of the following conditionals is true:

(23) If the state of affairs S' had obtained, Paul would have accepted the offer

(24) If the state of affairs S' had obtained, Paul would not have accepted the offer.

It seems clear that at least one of these conditionals is true, but naturally they can't both be; so exactly one is.

Now since S' includes neither Paul's accepting the offer nor his rejecting it, the antecedent of (23) and (24) does not entail the consequent of either. That is,

(25) S' obtains

does not entail either

(26) Paul accepts the offer

or

(27) Paul does not accept the offer.

So there are possible worlds in which both (25) and (26) are true, and other possible worlds in which both (25) and (27) are true.

We are now in a position to grasp an important fact. Either (23) or (24) is in fact true; and either way there are possible worlds God could not have actualized. Suppose, first of all, that (23) is true. Then it was beyond the power of God to create a world in which (1) Paul is free to sell his aardvark and free to refrain, and in which the other states of affairs included in S' obtain, and (2) Paul does not sell. That is, it was beyond His power to create a world in which (25) and (27) are both true. There is at least one possible world like this, but God, despite His omnipotence, could not have brought about its actuality. For let W be such a world. To actualize W, God must bring it about that Paul is free with respect to this action, and that the other states of affairs included in S' obtain. But (23), as we are supposing, is true; so if God had actualized *S′* and left Paul *free* with respect to this action, he would have sold: in which case *W* would not have been actual. If, on the other hand, God had *brought it about* that Paul didn't sell or had *caused him* to refrain from selling, then Paul would not have been free with respect to this action; then *S′* would not have been actual (since *S′* includes Paul's being free with respect to it), and *W* would not have been actual since *W* includes *S′*.

Of course if it is (24) rather than (23) that is true, then another class of worlds was beyond God's power to actualize – those, namely, in which *S′* obtains and Paul *sells* his aardvark. These are the worlds in which both (25) and (26) are true. But either (23) or (24) is true. Therefore, there are possible worlds God could not have actualized. If we consider whether or not God could have created a world in which, let's say, both (25) and (26) are true, we see that the answer depends upon a peculiar kind of fact; it depends upon what Paul would have freely chosen to do in a certain situation. So there are any number of possible worlds such that it is partly up to Paul whether God can create them.[14]

That was a past tense example. Perhaps it would be useful to consider a future tense case, since this might seem to correspond more closely to God's situation in choosing a possible world to actualize. At some time *t* in the near future Maurice will be free with respect to some insignificant action – having freeze-dried oatmeal for breakfast, let's say. That is, at time *t* Maurice will be free to have oatmeal but also free to take something else – shredded wheat, perhaps. Next, suppose we consider *S′*, a state of affairs that is included in the actual world and includes Maurice's being free with respect to taking oatmeal at time *t*. That is, *S′* includes Maurice's being free at time *t* to take oatmeal and free to reject it. *S′* does not include Maurice's taking oatmeal, however; nor does it include his rejecting it. For the rest *S′* is as much as possible like the actual world. In particular there are many conditions that do in fact hold at time *t* and are *relevant* to his choice – such conditions, for example, as the fact that he hasn't had oatmeal lately, that his wife will be annoyed if he rejects it, and the like; and *S′* includes each of these conditions. Now God no doubt knows what Maurice will do at time *t*, if *S* obtains; He knows which action Maurice would freely perform if *S* were to be actual. That is, God knows that one of the following conditionals is true:

(28) If *S′* were to obtain, Maurice will freely take the oatmeal

or

(29) If *S′* were to obtain, Maurice will freely reject it.

We may not know which of these is true, and Maurice himself may not know; but presumably God does.

So either God knows that (28) is true, or else He knows that (29) is. Let's suppose it is (28). Then there is a possible world that God, though omnipotent, cannot create. For consider a possible world *W′* that shares *S′* with the actual world (which for ease of reference I'll name "Kronos") and in which Maurice does *not* take oatmeal. (We know there *is* such a world, since *S′* does not include Maurice's taking the oatmeal.) *S′* obtains in *W′* just as it does in Kronos. Indeed, everything in *W′* is just as it is in Kronos up to time *t*. But whereas in Kronos Maurice takes oatmeal at time *t*, in *W′* he does not. Now *W′* is a perfectly possible world; but it is not within God's power to create it or bring about its actuality. For to do so He must actualize *S′*. But (28) is in fact true. So if God actualizes *S′* (as He must to create *W′*) and leaves Maurice free with respect to the action in question, then he will take the oatmeal; and then, of course, *W′* will not be actual. If, on the other hand, God causes Maurice to *refrain* from taking the oatmeal, then he is not *free* to take it. That means, once again, that *W′* is not actual; for in *W′* Maurice is free to take the oatmeal (even if he doesn't do so). So if (28) is true, then this world *W′* is one that God can't actualize; it is not within His power to actualize it even though He is omnipotent and it is a possible world.

Of course, if it is (29) that is true, we get a similar result; then too there are possible worlds that God can't actualize. These would be worlds which share *S′* with Kronos and in which Maurice *does* take oatmeal. But either (28) or (29) *is* true; so either way there is a possible world that

God can't create. If we consider a world in which S' obtains and in which Maurice freely chooses oatmeal at time t, we see that whether or not it is within God's power to actualize it depends upon what Maurice would do if he were free in a certain situation. Accordingly, there are any number of possible worlds such that it is partly up to Maurice whether or not God can actualize them. It is, of course, up to God whether or not to create Maurice and also up to God whether or not to make him free with respect to the action of taking oatmeal at time t. (God could, if He chose, cause him to succumb to the dreaded *equine obsession*, a condition shared by some people and most horses, whose victims find it *psychologically impossible* to refuse oats or oat products.) But if He creates Maurice and creates him free with respect to this action, then whether or not he actually performs the action is up to Maurice – not God.[15]

Now we can return to the Free Will Defense and the problem of evil. The Free Will Defender, you recall, insists on the possibility that it is not within God's power to create a world containing moral good without creating one containing moral evil. His atheological opponent – Mackie, for example – agrees with Leibniz in insisting that *if* (as the theist holds) God is omnipotent, then it *follows* that He could have created any possible world He pleased. We now see that this contention – call it "Leibniz' Lapse" – is a mistake. The atheologian is right in holding that there are many possible worlds containing moral good but no moral evil; his mistake lies in endorsing Leibniz' Lapse. So one of his premises – that God, if omnipotent, could have actualized just any world He pleased – is false.

6. Could God Have Created a World Containing Moral Good but No Moral Evil?

Now suppose we recapitulate the logic of the situation. The Free Will Defender claims that the following is possible:

(30) God is omnipotent, and it was not within His power to create a world containing moral good but no moral evil.

By way of retort the atheologian insists that there are possible worlds containing moral good but no moral evil. He adds that an omnipotent being could have actualized any possible world he chose. So if God is omnipotent, it follows that He could have actualized a world containing moral good but no moral evil; hence (30), contrary to the Free Will Defender's claim, is not possible. What we have seen so far is that his second premiss – Leibniz' Lapse – is false.

Of course, this does not settle the issue in the Free Will Defender's favor. Leibniz' Lapse (appropriately enough for a lapse) is false; but this doesn't show that (30) is possible. To show this latter we must demonstrate the possibility that among the worlds God could not have actualized are all the worlds containing moral good but no moral evil. How can we approach this question?

Instead of choosing oatmeal for breakfast or selling an aardvark, suppose we think about a morally significant action such as taking a bribe. Curley Smith, the mayor of Boston, is opposed to the proposed freeway route; it would require destruction of the Old North Church along with some other antiquated and structurally unsound buildings. L. B. Smedes, the director of highways, asks him whether he'd drop his opposition for \$1 million. "Of course," he replies. "Would you do it for \$2?" asks Smedes. "What do you take me for?" comes the indignant reply. "That's already established," smirks Smedes; "all that remains is to nail down your price." Smedes then offers him a bribe of \$35,000; unwilling to break with the fine old traditions of Bay State politics, Curley accepts. Smedes then spends a sleepless night wondering whether he could have bought Curley for \$20,000.

Now suppose we assume that Curley was free with respect to the action of taking the bribe – free to take it and free to refuse. And suppose, furthermore, that he would have taken it. That is, let us suppose that

(31) If Smedes had offered Curley a bribe of \$20,000, he would have accepted it.

If (31) is true, then there is a state of affairs S' that (1) includes Curley's being offered a bribe of \$20,000; (2) does not include either his accepting the bribe or his rejecting it; and (3) is otherwise as much as possible like the actual world. Just to make sure S' includes every relevant circumstance, let us suppose that it is a *maximal world segment.* That is, add to S' any state of affairs compatible with but not included in it, and the result will be an entire possible world. We could think of it roughly like this: S' is included in at least one world W in which Curley takes the bribe and in at least one world W' in which he rejects it. If S' is a maximal world segment, then S' is what remains of W when *Curley's taking the bribe* is deleted; it is also what remains of W' when *Curley's rejecting the bribe* is deleted. More exactly, if S' is a maximal world segment, then every possible state of affairs that includes S', but isn't included by S', is a possible world. So if (31) is true, then there is a maximal world segment S' that (1) includes Curley's being offered a bribe of $20,000; (2) does not include either his accepting the bribe or his rejecting it; (3) is otherwise as much as possible like the actual world – in particular, it includes Curley's being free with respect to the bribe; and (4) is such that if it were actual then Curley would have taken the bribe. That is,

(32) If S' were actual, Curley would have accepted the bribe

is true.

Now, of course, there is at least one possible world W' in which S' is actual and Curley does not take the bribe. But God could not have created W'; to do so, He would have been obliged to actualize S', leaving Curley free with respect to the action of taking the bribe. But under these conditions Curley, as (32) assures us, would have accepted the bribe, so that the world thus created would not have been S'.

Curley, as we see, is not above a bit of Watergating. But there may be worse to come. Of course, there are possible worlds in which he is significantly free (i.e., free with respect to a morally significant action) and never does what is wrong. But the sad truth about Curley may be this. Consider W', any of these worlds: in W' Curley is significantly free, so in W' there are some actions that are morally significant for him and with respect to which he is free. But at least one of these actions – call it A – has the following peculiar property. There is a maximal world segment S' that obtains in W' and is such that (1) S' includes Curley's being free *re* A but neither his performing A nor his refraining from A; (2) S' is otherwise as much as possible like W'; and (3) if S' had been actual, Curley would have gone wrong with respect to A.[16] (Notice that this third condition holds in fact, in the actual world; it does not hold in that world W'.)

This means, of course, that God could not have actualized W'. For to do so He'd have been obliged to bring it about that S' is actual; but then Curley would go wrong with respect to A. Since in W' he always does what is right, the world thus actualized would not be W'. On the other hand, if God *causes* Curley to go right with respect to A or *brings it about that* he does so, then Curley isn't free with respect to A; and so once more it isn't W' that is actual. Accordingly God cannot create W'. But W' was just any of the worlds in which Curley is significantly free but always does only what is right. It therefore follows that it was not within God's power to create a world in which Curley produces moral good but no moral evil. Every world God can actualize is such that if Curley is significantly free in it, he takes at least one wrong action.

Obviously Curley is in serious trouble. I shall call the malady from which he suffers *transworld depravity*. (I leave as homework the problem of comparing transworld depravity with what Calvinists call "total depravity.") By way of explicit definition:

(33) A person P *suffers from transworld depravity* if and only if the following holds: for every world W such that P is significantly free in W and P does only what is right in W, there is an action A and a maximal world segment S' such that

(1) S' includes A's being morally significant for P

(2) S' includes P's being free with respect to A

(3) S' is included in W and includes neither P's performing A nor P's refraining from performing A

and

(4) If S' were actual, P would go wrong with respect to A.

(In thinking about this definition, remember that (4) is to be true in fact, in the actual world – not in that world W.)

What is important about the idea of transworld depravity is that if a person suffers from it, then it wasn't within God's power to actualize any world in which that person is significantly free but does no wrong – that is, a world in which he produces moral good but no moral evil.

We have been considering a crucial contention of the Free Will Defender: the contention, namely, that

(30) God is omnipotent, and it was not within His power to create a world containing moral good but no moral evil.

How is transworld depravity relevant to this? As follows. Obviously it is possible that there be persons who suffer from transworld depravity. More generally, it is possible that *everybody* suffers from it. And if this possibility were actual, then God, though omnipotent, could not have created any of the possible worlds containing just the persons who do in fact exist, and containing moral good but no moral evil. For to do so He'd have to create persons who were significantly free (otherwise there would be no moral good) but suffered from transworld depravity. Such persons go wrong with respect to at least one action in any world God could have actualized and in which they are free with respect to morally significant actions; so the price for creating a world in which they produce moral good is creating one in which they also produce moral evil.

Notes

1 John Mackie, "Evil and Omnipotence," in *The Philosophy of Religion*, ed. Basil Mitchell (London: Oxford University Press, 1971), p. 92.

2 Ibid., pp. 92–3.

3 Ibid., p. 93.

4 More simply, the question is really just whether any good state of affairs includes an evil; a little reflection reveals that no good state of affairs can include an evil that it does *not* outweigh.

5 In Plantinga, *God and Other Minds* (Ithaca, NY: Cornell University Press, 1967), chap. 5, I explore further the project of finding such propositions.

6 *The Problem of Free Choice*, Vol. 22 of *Ancient Christian Writers* (Westminster, Md.: The Newman Press, 1955), bk. 2, pp. 14–15.

7 Ibid., bk. 3, p. 9.

8 I am indebted to Henry Schuurman (in conversation) for helpful discussion of the difference between this pastoral function and those served by a theodicy or a defense.

9 This distinction is not very precise (how, exactly, are we to construe "results from"?); but perhaps it will serve our present purposes.

10 See, for example, A. Flew, "Divine Omnipotence and Human Freedom," in *New Essays in Philosophical Theology*, eds. A. Flew and A. MacIntyre (London: SCM, 1955), pp. 150–3.

11 For further discussion of it see Plantinga, *God and Other Minds*, pp. 132–5.

12 Mackie, in *The Philosophy of Religion*, pp. 100–1.

13 Strict accuracy demands, therefore, that we speak of God as *actualizing* rather than creating possible worlds. I shall continue to use both locutions, thus sacrificing accuracy to familiarity. For more about possible worlds see my book *The Nature of Necessity* (Oxford: The Clarendon Press, 1974), chaps. 4–8.

14 For a fuller statement of this argument see Plantinga, *The Nature of Necessity*, chap. 9, secs. 4–6.

15 For a more complete and more exact statement of this argument see ibid.

16 A person goes wrong with respect to an action if he either wrongfully performs it or wrongfully fails to perform it.

9

Soul-making Theodicy

John Hick

John Hick (b. 1922) is Emeritus Professor at both the University of Birmingham in the UK and Claremont Graduate University in California and has been one of the most influential contemporary philosophers of religion. His publications cover an impressively wide range of topics, but his most important contributions have been on the problem of evil and the problem of religious pluralism (see section IX.1 below). In the following essay Hick explains why he finds traditional Augustinian free will defenses (such as Plantinga's from the previous reading) unsatisfactory, and he develops an alternative response to the problem of evil that he traces to the early church father Irenaeus. According to Hick's Irenaean theodicy, God created humanity in a state of immaturity – we are created in God's image, but only through a process of growth will we be fully transformed into God's likeness. The suffering and evil in this world are a necessary part of this transformation process.

Can a world in which sadistic cruelty often has its way, in which selfish lovelessness is so rife, in which there are debilitating diseases, crippling accidents, bodily and mental decay, insanity, and all manner of natural disasters be regarded as the expression of infinite creative goodness? Certainly all this could never by itself lead anyone to believe in the existence of a limitlessly powerful God. And yet even in a world which contains these things innumerable men and women have believed and do believe in the reality of an infinite creative goodness, which they call God. The theodicy project starts at this point, with an already operating belief in God, embodied in human living, and attempts to show that this belief is not rendered irrational by the fact of evil. It attempts to explain how it is that the universe, assumed to be created and ultimately ruled by a

John Hick, "Soul-Making Theodicy" in *Encountering Evil: Live Opinions in Theodicy*, ed. Stephen T. Davis (Atlanta, GA: Westminster, John Knox, 1981), pp. 39–52. Used by permission of Westminster John Knox Press.

limitlessly good and limitlessly powerful Being, is as it is, including all the pain and suffering and all the wickedness and folly that we find around us and within us. The theodicy project is thus an exercise in metaphysical construction, in the sense that it consists in the formation and criticism of large-scale hypotheses concerning the nature and process of the universe.

Since a theodicy both starts from and tests belief in the reality of God, it naturally takes different forms in relation to different concepts of God. In this essay I shall be discussing the project of a specifically Christian theodicy; I shall not be attempting the further and even more difficult work of comparative theodicy, leading in turn to the question of a global theodicy.

The two main demands upon a theodicy-hypothesis are (1) that it be internally coherent, and (2) that it be consistent with the data both of the religious tradition on which it is based, and of the world, in respect both of the latter's general character as revealed by scientific enquiry and of the specific facts of moral and natural evil. These two criteria demand, respectively, possibility and plausibility.

Traditionally, Christian theology has centered upon the concept of God as both limitlessly powerful and limitlessly good and loving; and it is this concept of deity that gives rise to the problem of evil as a threat to theistic faith. The threat was definitively expressed in Stendhal's bombshell, "The only excuse for God is that he does not exist!" The theodicy project is the attempt to offer a different view of the universe which is both possible and plausible and which does not ignite Stendhal's bombshell.

Christian thought has always included a certain range of variety, and in the area of theodicy it offers two broad types of approach. The Augustinian approach, representing until fairly recently the majority report of the Christian mind, hinges upon the idea of the fall, which has in turn brought about the disharmony of nature. This type of theodicy is developed today as "the free-will defense." The Irenaean approach, representing in the past a minority report, hinges upon the creation of humankind through the evolutionary process as an immature creature living in a challenging and therefore person-making world. I shall indicate very briefly why I do not find the first type of theodicy satisfactory, and then spend the remainder of this essay in exploring the second type.

In recent years the philosophical discussion of the problem of evil has been dominated by the free-will defense. A major effort has been made by Alvin Plantinga and a number of other Christian philosophers to show that it is logically possible that a limitlessly powerful and limitlessly good God is responsible for the existence of this world. For all evil may ultimately be due to misuses of creaturely freedom. But it may nevertheless be better for God to have created free than unfree beings; and it is logically possible that any and all free beings whom God might create would, as a matter of contingent fact, misuse their freedom by falling into sin. In that case it would be logically impossible for God to have created a world containing free beings and yet not containing sin and the suffering which sin brings with it. Thus it is logically possible, despite the fact of evil, that the existing universe is the work of a limitlessly good creator.

These writers are in effect arguing that the traditional Augustinian type of theodicy, based upon the fall from grace of free finite creatures – first angels and then human beings – and a consequent going wrong of the physical world, is not logically impossible. I am in fact doubtful whether their argument is sound, and will return to the question later. But even if it should be sound, I suggest that their argument wins only a Pyrrhic victory, since the logical possibility that it would establish is one which, for very many people today, is fatally lacking in plausibility. For most educated inhabitants of the modern world regard the biblical story of Adam and Eve, and their temptation by the devil, as myth rather than as history; and they believe that so far from having been created finitely perfect and then falling, humanity evolved out of lower forms of life, emerging in a morally, spiritually, and culturally primitive state. Further, they reject as incredible the idea that earthquake and flood, disease, decay, and death are consequences either of a human fall, or of a prior fall of angelic beings who are now exerting an evil influence upon the earth. They see all this as part of a pre-scientific world view, along with the stories of the world having been created in six days and of the sun standing still for twenty-four hours at Joshua's command. One cannot, strictly speaking, disprove any of these ancient biblical myths and sagas, or refute their confident elaboration in the medieval Christian picture of the universe. But those of us for whom the resulting theodicy, even if logically possible, is radically implausible, must look elsewhere for light on the problem of evil.

I believe that we find the light that we need in the main alternative strand of Christian thinking, which goes back to important constructive suggestions by the early Hellenistic Fathers of the Church, particularly St Irenaeus (AD 120–202). Irenaeus himself did not develop a theodicy, but he did – together with other Greek-speaking Christian writers of that period, such as Clement of Alexandria – build a framework of thought within which a theodicy became possible which does not depend upon the idea of the fall, and which is consonant with modern knowledge concerning the origins of the human race. This theodicy cannot, as such, be attributed to Irenaeus. We should rather speak of a type of theodicy, presented in varying ways by different subsequent thinkers (the greatest of whom has been Friedrich Schleiermacher), of which Irenaeus can properly be regarded as the patron saint.

The central theme out of which this Irenaean type of theodicy has arisen is the two-stage conception of the creation of humankind, first in the "image" and then in the "likeness" of God. Re-expressing this in modern terms, the first stage was the gradual production of *Homo sapiens*, through the long evolutionary process, as intelligent ethical and religious animals. The human being is an animal, one of the varied forms of earthly life and continuous as such with the whole realm of animal existence. But the human being is uniquely intelligent, having evolved a large and immensely complex brain. Further, the human being is ethical – that is, a gregarious as well as an intelligent animal, able to realize and respond to the complex demands of social life. And the human being is a religious animal, with an innate tendency to experience the world in terms of the presence and activity of supernatural beings and powers. This then is early *Homo sapiens*, the intelligent social animal capable of awareness of the divine. But early *Homo sapiens* is not the Adam and Eve of Augustinian theology, living in perfect harmony with self, with nature, and with God. On the contrary, the life of this being must have been a constant struggle against a hostile environment, and capable of savage violence against one's fellow human beings, particularly outside one's own immediate group; and this being's concepts of the divine were primitive and often bloodthirsty. Thus existence "in the image of God" was a potentiality for knowledge of and relationship with one's Maker rather than such knowledge and relationship as a fully realized state. In other words, people were created as spiritually and morally immature creatures, at the beginning of a long process of further growth and development, which constitutes the second stage of God's creative work. In this second stage, of which we are a part, the intelligent, ethical, and religious animal is being brought through one's own free responses into what Irenaeus called the divine "likeness." The human animal is being created into a child of God. Irenaeus' own terminology (*eikon, homoiosis; imago, similitudo*) has no particular merit, based as it is on a misunderstanding of the Hebrew parallelism in Genesis 1:26; but his conception of a two-stage creation of the human, with perfection lying in the future rather than in the past, is of fundamental importance. The notion of the fall was not basic to this picture, although it was to become basic to the great drama of salvation depicted by St Augustine and accepted within western Christendom, including the churches stemming from the Reformation, until well into the nineteenth century. Irenaeus himself however could not, in the historical knowledge of his time, question the fact of the fall; though he treated it as a relatively minor lapse, a youthful error, rather than as the infinite crime and cosmic disaster which has ruined the whole creation. But today we can acknowledge that there is no evidence at all of a period in the distant past when humankind was in the ideal state of a fully realized "child of God." We can accept that, so far as actual events in time are concerned, there never was a fall from an original righteousness and grace. If we want to continue to use the term fall, because of its hallowed place in the Christian tradition, we must use it to refer to the immense gap between what we actually are and what in the divine intention is eventually to be. But we must not blur our awareness that the ideal state is not something already enjoyed and lost, but is a future and as yet unrealized goal. The reality is not a perfect creation which has gone tragically wrong, but a still continuing creative process whose completion lies in the eschaton.

Let us now try to formulate a contemporary version of the Irenaean type of theodicy, based on this suggestion of the initial creation of humankind, not as a finitely perfect, but as an immature creature at the beginning of a long process of further growth and development. We may begin by asking why one should have been created as an imperfect and developing creature rather than as the perfect being whom God is presumably intending to create? The answer, I think, consists in two considerations which converge in their practical implications, one concerned with the human's relationship to God and the other with the relationship to other human beings. As to the first, we could have the picture of God creating finite beings, whether angels or persons, directly in his own presence, so that in being conscious of that which is other than one's self the creature is automatically conscious of God, the limitless divine reality and power, goodness and love, knowledge and wisdom, towering above one's self. In such a situation the disproportion between Creator and creatures would be so great that the latter would have no freedom in relation to God; they would indeed not exist as independent autonomous persons. For what freedom could finite beings have in an immediate consciousness of the presence of the one who has created them, who knows them through and through, who is limitlessly powerful as well as limitlessly loving and good, and who claims their total obedience? In order to be a person, exercising some measure of genuine freedom, the creature must be brought into existence, not in the immediate divine presence, but at a "distance" from God. This "distance" cannot of course be spatial; for God is omnipresent. It must be an epistemic distance, a distance in the cognitive dimension. And the Irenaean hypothesis is that this "distance" consists, in the case of humans, in their existence within and as part of a world which functions as an autonomous system and from within which God is not overwhelmingly evident. It is a world, in Bonhoeffer's phrase, *etsi deus non daretur*, as if there were no God. Or rather, it is religiously ambiguous, capable both of being seen as a purely natural phenomenon and of being seen as God's creation and experienced as mediating his presence. In such a world one can exist as a person over against the Creator. One has space to exist as a finite being, a space created by the epistemic distance from God and protected by one's basic cognitive freedom, one's freedom to open or close oneself to the dawning awareness of God which is experienced naturally by a religious animal. This Irenaean picture corresponds, I suggest, to our actual human situation. Emerging within the evolutionary process as part of the continuum of animal life, in a universe which functions in accordance with its own laws and whose workings can be investigated and described without reference to a creator, the human being has a genuine, even awesome, freedom in relation to one's Maker. The human being is free to acknowledge and worship God; and is free – particularly since the emergence of human individuality and the beginnings of critical consciousness during the first millennium BC – to doubt the reality of God.

Within such a situation there is the possibility of the human being coming freely to know and love one's Maker. Indeed, if the end-state which God is seeking to bring about is one in which finite persons have come in their own freedom to know and love him, this requires creating them initially in a state which is not that of their already knowing and loving him. For it is logically impossible to create beings already in a state of having come into that state by their own free choices.

The other consideration, which converges with this in pointing to something like the human situation as we experience it, concerns our human moral nature. We can approach it by asking why humans should not have been created at this epistemic distance from God, and yet at the same time as morally perfect beings? That persons could have been created morally perfect and yet free, so that they would always in fact choose rightly, has been argued by such critics of the free-will defense in theodicy as Antony Flew and J. L. Mackie, and argued against by Alvin Plantinga and other upholders of that form of theodicy. On the specific issue defined in the debate between them, it appears to me that the criticism of the free-will defense stands. It appears to me that a perfectly good being, although formally free to sin, would in fact never do so. If we imagine such a being in a morally frictionless environment, involving no stresses or temptation, then we must assume that one would exemplify the ethical equivalent of Newton's first law of motion, which states that a moving body will continue in uniform motion until interfered with by some outside force. By analogy, a perfectly good being would continue in the same moral course forever, there being nothing in the environment to throw one off it. But even if we suppose the morally perfect being to exist in an imperfect world, in which one is subject to temptations, it still follows that, in virtue of moral perfection, one will always overcome those temptations – as in the case, according to orthodox Christian belief, of Jesus Christ. It is, to be sure, logically possible, as Plantinga and others argue, that a free being, simply as such, may at any time contingently decide to sin. However, a responsible free being does not act randomly, but on the basis of moral nature. And a free being whose nature is wholly and unqualifiedly good will accordingly never in fact sin.

But if God could, without logical contradiction, have created humans as wholly good free beings, why did he not do so? Why was humanity not initially created in possession of all the virtues, instead of having to acquire them through the long hard struggle of life as we know it? The answer, I suggest, appeals to the principle that virtues which have been formed within the agent as a hard won deposit of his own right decisions in situations of challenge and temptation, are intrinsically more valuable than virtues created within him ready made and without any effort on his own part. This principle expresses a basic value-judgment, which cannot be established by argument but which one can only present, in the hope that it will be as morally plausible, and indeed compelling, to others as to oneself. It is, to repeat, the judgment that a moral goodness which exists as the agent's initial given nature, without ever having been chosen by him in the face of temptations to the contrary, is intrinsically less valuable than a moral goodness which has been built up through the agent's own responsible choices through time in the face of alternative possibilities.

If, then, God's purpose was to create finite persons embodying the most valuable kind of moral goodness, he would have to create them, not as already perfect beings but rather as imperfect creatures who can then attain to the more valuable kind of goodness through their own free choices as in the course of their personal and social history new responses prompt new insights, opening up new moral possibilities, and providing a milieu in which the most valuable kind of moral nature can be developed.

We have thus far, then, the hypothesis that one is created at an epistemic distance from God in order to come freely to know and love the Maker; and that one is at the same time created as a morally immature and imperfect being in order to attain through freedom the most valuable quality of goodness. The end sought, according to this hypothesis, is the full realization of the human potentialities in a unitary spiritual and moral perfection in the divine kingdom. And the question we have to ask is whether humans as we know them, and the world as we know it, are compatible with this hypothesis.

Clearly we cannot expect to be able to deduce our actual world in its concrete character, and our actual human nature as part of it, from the general concept of spiritually and morally immature creatures developing ethically in an appropriate environment. No doubt there is an immense range of possible worlds, any one of which, if actualized, would exemplify this concept. All that we can hope to do is to show that our actual world is one of these. And when we look at our human situation as part of the evolving life of this planet we can, I think, see that it fits this specification. As animal organisms, integral to the whole ecology of life, we are programmed for survival. In pursuit of survival, primitives not only killed other animals for food but fought other human beings when their vital interests conflicted. The life of prehistoric persons must indeed have been a constant struggle to stay alive, prolonging an existence which was, in Hobbes' phrase, "poor, nasty, brutish and short." And in his basic animal self-regardingness humankind was, and is, morally imperfect. In saying this I am assuming that the essence of moral evil is selfishness, the sacrificing of others to one's own interests. It consists, in Kantian terminology, in treating others, not as ends in themselves, but as means to one's own ends. This is what the survival instinct demands. And yet we are also capable of love, of self-giving in a common cause, of a conscience which responds to others in their needs and dangers. And with the development of civilization we see the growth of moral insight, the glimpsing and gradual assimilation of higher ideals, and tension between our animality and our ethical values. But that the human being has a lower as well as a higher nature, that one is an animal as well as a potential child of God, and that one's moral goodness is won from a struggle with one's own innate selfishness, is inevitable given one's continuity with the other forms of animal life. Further, the human animal is not responsible for having come into existence as an animal. The ultimate responsibility for humankind's existence, as a morally imperfect creature, can only rest with the Creator. The human does not, in one's own degree of freedom and responsibility, choose one's origin, but rather one's destiny.

This then, in brief outline, is the answer of the Irenaean type of theodicy to the question of the origin of moral evil: the general fact of humankind's basic self-regarding animality is an aspect of creation as part of the realm of organic life; and this basic self-regardingness has been expressed over the centuries both in sins of individual selfishness and in the much more massive sins of corporate selfishness, institutionalized in slavery and exploitation and all the many and complex forms of social injustice.

But nevertheless our sinful nature in a sinful world is the matrix within which God is gradually creating children for himself out of human animals. For it is as men and women freely respond to the claim of God upon their lives, transmuting their animality into the structure of divine worship, that the creation of humanity is taking place. And in its concrete character this response consists in every form of moral goodness, from unselfish love in individual personal relationships to the dedicated and selfless striving to end exploitation and to create justice within and between societies.

But one cannot discuss moral evil without at the same time discussing the non-moral evil of pain and suffering. (I propose to mean by "pain" physical pain, including the pains of hunger and thirst; and by "suffering" the mental and emotional pain of loneliness, anxiety, remorse, lack of love, fear, grief, envy, etc.). For what constitutes moral evil as evil is the fact that it causes pain and suffering. It is impossible to conceive of an instance of moral evil, or sin, which is not productive of pain or suffering to anyone at any time. But in addition to moral evil there is another source of pain and suffering in the structure of the physical world, which produces storms, earthquakes, and floods and which afflicts the human body with diseases – cholera, epilepsy, cancer, malaria, arthritis, rickets, meningitis, etc. – as well as with broken bones and other outcomes of physical accident. It is true that a great deal both of pain and of suffering is humanly caused, not only by the inhumanity of man to man but also by the stresses of our individual and corporate life-styles, causing many disorders – not only lung cancer and cirrhosis of the liver but many cases of heart disease, stomach and other ulcers, strokes, etc. – as well as accidents. But there remain nevertheless, in the natural world itself, permanent causes of human pain and suffering. And we have to ask why an unlimitedly good and unlimitedly powerful God should have created so dangerous a world, both as regards its purely natural hazards of earthquake and flood etc., and as regards the liability of the human body to so many ills, both psychosomatic and purely somatic.

The answer offered by the Irenaean type of theodicy follows from and is indeed integrally bound up with its account of the origin of moral evil. We have the hypothesis of humankind being brought into being within the evolutionary process as a spiritually and morally immature creature, and then growing and developing through the exercise of freedom in this religiously ambiguous world. We can now ask what sort of a world would constitute an appropriate environment for this second stage of creation? The development of human personality – moral, spiritual, and intellectual – is a product of challenge and response. It does not occur in a static situation demanding no exertion and no choices. So far as intellectual development is concerned, this is a well-established principle which underlies the whole modern educational process, from pre-school nurseries designed to provide a rich and stimulating environment, to all forms of higher education designed to challenge the intellect. At a basic level the essential part played in learning by the learner's own active response to environment was strikingly demonstrated by the Held and Heim experiment with kittens.[1] Of two litter-mate kittens in the same artificial environment one was free to exercise its own freedom and intelligence in exploring the environment, whilst the other was suspended in a kind of "gondola" which moved whenever and wherever the free kitten moved. Thus the second kitten had a similar succession of visual experiences as the first, but did not exert itself or make any choices in obtaining them. And whereas the first kitten learned in the normal way to conduct itself safely within its environment, the second did not. With no interaction with a challenging environment there was no development in its behavioral patterns. And I think we can safely say that the intellectual development of humanity has been due to interaction with an objective environment functioning in accordance with its own laws, an environment which we have had actively to explore and to co-operate with in order to escape its perils and exploit its benefits. In a world devoid both of dangers to be avoided and rewards to be won we may assume that there would have been virtually no development of the human intellect and imagination, and hence of either the sciences or the arts, and hence of human civilization or culture.

The fact of an objective world within which one has to learn to live, on penalty of pain or death, is also basic to the development of one's moral nature. For it is because the world is one in which men and women can suffer harm – by violence, disease, accident, starvation, etc. – that our actions affecting one another have moral significance. A morally wrong act is, basically, one which harms some part of the human community; whilst a morally right action is, on the contrary, one which prevents or neutralizes harm or which preserves or increases human well being. Now we can imagine a paradise in which no one can ever come to any harm. It could be a world which, instead of having its own fixed structure, would be plastic to human wishes. Or it could be a world with a fixed structure, and hence the possibility of damage and pain, but whose structure is suspended or adjusted by special divine action whenever necessary to avoid human pain. Thus, for example, in such a miraculously pain-free world one who falls accidentally off a high building would presumably float unharmed to the ground; bullets would become insubstantial when fired at a human body; poisons would cease to poison; water to drown, and so on. We can at least begin to imagine such a world. And a good deal of the older discussion of the problem of evil – for example in Part XI of Hume's *Dialogues Concerning Natural Religion* – assumed that it must be the intention of a limitlessly good and powerful Creator to make for human creatures a pain-free environment; so that the very existence of pain is evidence against the existence of God. But such an assumption overlooks the fact that a world in which there can be no pain or suffering would also be one in which there can be no moral choices and hence no possibility of moral growth and development. For in a situation in which no one can ever suffer injury or be liable to pain or suffering there would be no distinction between right and wrong action. No action would be morally wrong, because no action could have harmful consequences; and likewise no action would be morally right in contrast to wrong. Whatever the values of such a world, it clearly could not serve a purpose of the development of its inhabitants from self-regarding animality to self-giving love.

Thus the hypothesis of a divine purpose in which finite persons are created at an epistemic distance from God, in order that they may gradually become children of God through their own moral and spiritual choices, requires that their environment, instead of being a pain-free and stress-free paradise, be broadly the kind of world of which we find ourselves to be a part. It requires that it be such as to provoke the theological problem of evil. For it requires that it be an environment which offers challenges to be met, problems to be solved, dangers to be faced, and which accordingly involves real possibilities of hardship, disaster, failure, defeat, and misery as well as of delight and happiness, success, triumph and achievement. For it is by grappling with the real problems of a real environment, in which a person is one form of life among many, and which is not designed to minister exclusively to one's well-being, that one can develop in intelligence and in such qualities as courage and determination. And it is in the relationships of human beings with one another, in the context of this struggle to survive and flourish, that they can develop the higher values of mutual love and care, of self-sacrifice for others, and of commitment to a common good.

To summarize thus far:

(1) The divine intention in relation to humankind, according to our hypothesis, is to create perfect finite personal beings in filial relationship with their Maker.
(2) It is logically impossible for humans to be created already in this perfect state, because in its spiritual aspect it involves coming freely to an uncoerced consciousness of God from a situation of epistemic distance, and in its moral aspect, freely choosing the good in preference to evil.
(3) Accordingly the human being was initially created through the evolutionary process, as a spiritually and morally immature creature, and as part of a world which is both religiously ambiguous and ethically demanding.
(4) Thus that one is morally imperfect (i.e., that there is moral evil), and that the world is a challenging and even dangerous environment (i.e., that there is natural evil), are necessary aspects of the present stage of the process through which God is gradually creating perfected finite persons.

In terms of this hypothesis, as we have developed it thus far, then, both the basic moral evil in the human heart and the natural evils of the world are compatible with the existence of a Creator who is unlimited in both goodness and power. But is the hypothesis plausible as well as possible? The principal threat to its plausibility comes, I think, from the sheer amount and intensity of both moral and natural evil. One can accept the principle that in order to arrive at a freely chosen goodness one must start out in a state of moral immaturity and imperfection. But is it necessary that there should be the depths of demonic malice and cruelty which each generation has experienced, and which we have seen above all in recent history in the Nazi attempt to exterminate the Jewish population of Europe? Can any future fulfillment be worth such horrors? This was Dostoevski's haunting question: "Imagine that you are creating a fabric of human destiny with the object of making men happy in the end, giving them peace and rest at last, but that it was essential and inevitable to torture to death only one tiny creature – that baby beating its breast with its fist, for instance – and to found that edifice on its unavenged tears, would you consent to be the architect on those conditions?"[2] The theistic answer is one which may be true but which takes so large a view that it baffles the imagination. Intellectually one may be able to see, but emotionally one cannot be expected to feel, its truth; and in that sense it cannot satisfy us. For the theistic answer is that if we take with full seriousness the value of human freedom and responsibility, as essential to the eventual creation of perfected children of God, then we cannot consistently want God to revoke that freedom when its wrong exercise becomes intolerable to us. From our vantage point within the historical process we may indeed cry out to God to revoke his gift of freedom, or to overrule it by some secret or open intervention. Such a cry must have come from millions caught in the Jewish Holocaust, or in the yet more recent laying waste of Korea and Vietnam, or from the victims of racism in many parts of the world. And the thought that humankind's moral freedom is indivisible, and can lead eventually to a consummation of limitless value which could never be attained without that freedom, and which is worth any finite suffering in the course of its creation, can be of no comfort to those who are now in the midst of that suffering. But whilst fully acknowledging this, I nevertheless want to insist that this eschatological answer may well be true. Expressed in religious language it tells us to trust in God even in the midst of deep suffering, for in the end we shall participate in his glorious kingdom.

Again, we may grant that a world which is to be a person-making environment cannot be a pain-free paradise but must contain challenges and dangers, with real possibilities of many kinds of accident and disaster, and the pain and suffering which they bring. But need it contain the worst forms of disease and catastrophe? And need misfortune fall upon us with such heartbreaking indiscriminateness? Once again there are answers, which may well be true, and yet once again the truth in this area may offer little in the way of pastoral balm. Concerning the intensity of natural evil, the truth is probably that our judgments of intensity are relative. We might identify some form of natural evil as the worst that there is – say the agony that can be caused by death from cancer – and claim that a loving God would not have allowed this to exist. But in a world in which there was no cancer, something else would then rank as the worst form of natural evil. If we then eliminate this, something else; and so on. And the process would continue until the world was free of all natural evil. For whatever form of evil for the time being remained would be intolerable to the inhabitants of that world. But in removing all occasions of pain and suffering, and hence all challenge and all need for mutual care, we should have converted the world from a person-making into a static environment, which could not elicit moral growth. In short, having accepted that a person-making world must have its dangers and therefore also its tragedies, we must accept that whatever form these take will be intolerable to the inhabitants of that world. There could not be a person-making world devoid of what we call evil; and evils are never tolerable – except for the sake of greater goods which may come out of them.

But accepting that a person-making environment must contain causes of pain and suffering, and that no pain or suffering is going to be acceptable, one of the most daunting and even terrifying features of the world is that calamity strikes indiscriminately. There is no justice in the incidence of disease, accident, disaster and tragedy. The righteous as well as the unrighteous are struck down by illness and afflicted by misfortune. There is no security in goodness, but the good are as likely as the wicked to suffer "the slings and arrows of outrageous fortune." From the time of Job this fact has set a glaring question mark against the goodness of God. But let us suppose that things were otherwise. Let us suppose that misfortune came upon humankind, not haphazardly and therefore unjustly, but justly and therefore not haphazardly. Let us suppose that instead of coming without regard to moral considerations, it was proportioned to desert, so that the sinner was punished and the virtuous rewarded. Would such a dispensation serve a person-making purpose? Surely not. For it would be evident that wrong deeds bring disaster upon the agent whilst good deeds bring health and prosperity; and in such a world truly moral action, action done because it is right, would be impossible. The fact that natural evil is not morally directed, but is a hazard which comes by chance, is thus an intrinsic feature of a person-making world.

In other words, the very mystery of natural evil, the very fact that disasters afflict human beings in contingent, undirected and haphazard ways, is itself a necessary feature of a world that calls forth mutual aid and builds up mutual caring and love. Thus on the one hand it would be completely wrong to say that God sends misfortune upon individuals, so that their death, maiming, starvation or ruin is God's will for them. But on the other hand God has set us in a world containing unpredictable contingencies and dangers, in which unexpected and undeserved calamities may occur to anyone; because only in such a world can mutual caring and love be elicited. As an abstract philosophical hypothesis this may offer little comfort. But translated into religious language it tells us that God's good purpose enfolds the entire process of this world, with all its good and bad contingencies, and that even amidst tragic calamity and suffering we are still within the sphere of his love and are moving towards his kingdom.

But there is one further all-important aspect of the Irenaean type of theodicy, without which all the foregoing would lose its plausibility. This is the eschatological aspect. Our hypothesis depicts persons as still in course of creation towards an end-state of perfected personal community in the divine kingdom. This end-state is conceived of as one in which individual egoity has been transcended in communal unity before God. And in the present phase of that creative process the naturally self-centered human animal has the opportunity freely to respond to God's non-coercive self-disclosures, through the work of prophets and saints, through the resulting religious traditions, and through the individual's religious experience. Such response always has an ethical aspect; for the growing awareness of God is at the same time a growing awareness of the moral claim which God's presence makes upon the way in which we live.

But it is very evident that this person-making process, leading eventually to perfect human community, is not completed on this earth. It is not completed in the life of the individual – or at best only in the few who have attained to sanctification, or moksha, or nirvana on this earth. Clearly the enormous majority of men and women die without having attained to this. As Eric Fromm has said, "The tragedy in the life of most of us is that we die before we are fully born."[3] And therefore if we are ever to reach the full realization of the potentialities of our human nature, this can only be in a continuation of our lives in another sphere of existence after bodily death. And it is equally evident that the perfect all-embracing human community, in which self-regarding concern has been transcended in mutual love, not only has not been realized in this world, but never can be, since hundreds of generations of human beings have already lived and died and accordingly could not be part of any ideal community established at some future moment of earthly history. Thus if the unity of humankind in God's presence is ever to be realized it will have to be in some sphere of existence other than our earth. In short, the fulfillment of the divine purpose, as it is postulated in the Irenaean type of theodicy, presupposes each person's survival, in some form of bodily death, and further living and growing towards that end-state. Without such an eschatological fulfillment, this theodicy would collapse.

A theodicy which presupposes and requires an eschatology will thereby be rendered implausible in the minds of many today. I nevertheless do not see how any coherent theodicy can avoid dependence upon an eschatology. Indeed I would go further and say that the belief in the reality of a limitlessly loving and powerful deity must incorporate some kind of eschatology according to which God holds in being the creatures whom he has made for fellowship with himself, beyond bodily death, and brings them into the eternal fellowship which he has intended for them, I have tried elsewhere to argue that such an eschatology is a necessary corollary of ethical monotheism; to argue for the realistic possibility of an after-life or lives, despite the philosophical and empirical arguments against this; and even to spell out some of the general features which human life after death may possibly have.[4] Since all this is a very large task, which would far exceed the bounds of this essay, I shall not attempt to repeat it here but must refer the reader to my existing discussion of it. It is that extended discussion that constitutes my answer to the question whether an Irenaean theodicy, with its eschatology, may not be as implausible as an Augustinian theodicy, with its human or angelic fall. (If it is, then the latter is doubly implausible; for it also involves an eschatology!)

There is however one particular aspect of eschatology which must receive some treatment here, however brief and inadequate. This is the issue of "universal salvation" versus "heaven and hell" (or perhaps annihilation instead of hell). If the justification of evil within the creative process lies in the limitless and eternal good of the end-state to which it leads, then the completeness of the justification must depend upon the completeness, or universality, of the salvation achieved. Only if it includes the entire human race can it justify the sins and sufferings of the entire human race throughout all history. But, having given human beings cognitive freedom, which in turn makes possible moral freedom, can the Creator bring it about that in the end all his human creatures freely turn to him in love and trust? The issue is a very difficult one; but I believe that it is in fact possible to reconcile a full affirmation of human freedom with a belief in the ultimate universal success of God's creative work. We have to accept that creaturely freedom always occurs within the limits of a basic nature that we did not ourselves choose; for this is entailed by the fact of having been created. If then a real though limited freedom does not preclude our being endowed with a certain nature, it does not preclude our being endowed with a basic Godward bias, so that, quoting from another side of St Augustine's thought, "our hearts are restless until they find their rest in Thee."[5] If this is so, it can be predicted that sooner or later, in our own time and in our own way, we shall all freely come to God; and universal salvation can be affirmed, not as a logical necessity but as the contingent but predictable outcome of the process of the universe, interpreted theistically. Once again, I have tried to present this argument more fully elsewhere, and to consider various objections to it.[6]

On this view the human, endowed with a real though limited freedom, is basically formed for relationship with God and destined ultimately to find the fulfillment of his or her nature in that relationship. This does not seem to me excessively paradoxical. On the contrary, given the theistic postulate, it seems to me to offer a very probable account of our human situation. If so, it is a situation in which we can rejoice; for it gives meaning to our temporal existence as the long process through which we are being created, by our own free responses to life's mixture of good and evil, into "children of God" who "inherit eternal life."

Notes

1 R. Held and A. Heim, "Movement-produced stimulation in the development of visually guided behaviour," *Journal of Comparative and Physiological Psychology* 56 (1963): 872–6.
2 Fyodor Dostoyevsky, *The Brothers Karamozov*, trans. Constance Garnett (New York: Modern Library, n.d.), Bk. V, ch. 4, p. 254.
3 Erich Fromm, "Values, Psychology, and Human Existence," in *New Knowledge of Human Values*, ed. A. Maslow (New York: Harper & Row, 1959), p. 156.
4 John Hick, *Death and Eternal Life* (New York: Harper & Row; and London: Collins, 1976; revised, London: Macmillan, 1987).
5 *The Confessions of St. Augustine*, trans. F. J. Sheed (New York: Sheed and Ward, 1942), Bk. 1, ch. 1, p. 3.
6 Hick, *Death and Eternal Life*, ch. 13.

10

Friendly Atheism, Skeptical Theism, and the Problem of Evil

William L. Rowe

William L. Rowe (b. 1931) is Professor Emeritus at Purdue University. His essay, "The Problem of Evil and Some Varieties of Atheism" (1979), initiated a fundamental shift in discussions of the problem of evil. Rowe conceded that theistic beliefs are not implicitly self-contradictory – that is, he conceded that the *logical* problem of evil defended by Mackie (and others) fails for the sorts of reasons Plantinga (and others) identified. Nevertheless, Rowe argued that the kinds and quantity of evil in the world provide powerful evidence against God's existence. A good God might have just reasons for allowing some evil, but would not allow pointless or gratuitous evil. Since it seems likely that our world contains pointless evil, Rowe concluded that it is likely that God does not exist. One of the most persistent criticisms of Rowe's new *evidential* problem of evil has come from Stephen Wykstra and other so-called "skeptical theists" who argue that we simply are not in an appropriate epistemic position to determine whether there are any pointless evils. In this recent essay, Rowe offers a concise summary of over twenty years of exchanges between himself and the skeptical theists.

In 1979, a quarter of a century ago, I published a paper entitled "The Problem of Evil and Some Varieties of Atheism."[1] It received a good deal of attention in the professional journals, and was frequently included in anthologies for use in the classroom. Indeed, nothing I've written before or since has received anything near the attention that was given to that paper. So, in that respect, my career as a philosopher has been downhill ever since. In that paper I focused on a particular example of evil: a fawn being horribly burned in a fire caused by lightning, and suffering terribly

William L. Rowe, "Friendly Atheism, Skeptical Theism, and the Problem of Evil". *International Journal for Philosophy of Religion* 59 (2006): 79–92.

for 5 days before death ended its life. Unlike humans, fawns are not credited with free will, and so the fawn's suffering cannot be attributed to a misuse of free will. Why then would God permit it when, if he exists, he could have so easily prevented it? It is generally admitted that we are simply unable to imagine any greater good whose realization can reasonably be thought to require God to permit that fawn's terrible suffering. And it hardly seems reasonable to suppose there is some greater evil that God would have been unable to prevent had he not permitted that fawn's terrible suffering. Suppose that by a "pointless evil" we mean an evil that God (if he exists) could have prevented without thereby losing an outweighing good or having to permit an evil equally bad or worse. Is the fawn's suffering a pointless evil? Clearly, it certainly *seems to us* to be pointless. On that point there appears to be near universal agreement. For given God's omniscience and absolute power it would be child's play for him to have prevented either the fire or the fawn's being caught in the fire. Moreover, as we've noted it is extraordinarily difficult to think of, or even imagine, a greater good whose realization can sensibly be thought to require God to permit that fawn's terrible suffering.[2] And, it is just as difficult to imagine an equal or even worse evil that God would be required to permit were he to have prevented the fawn's suffering. It therefore seems altogether reasonable for us to think that the fawn's suffering is likely to be a pointless evil, an evil that God (if he exists) could have prevented without thereby losing some outweighing good or having to permit some other evil just as bad or worse.

In light of such examples of horrendous evils, evils that occur all too frequently in our world, I proposed an argument similar to this:

1. Probably, there are pointless evils. (e.g., the fawn's suffering).
2. If God exists, there are no pointless evils, therefore,
3. Probably, God does not exist.

How can a theist respond to this argument? Since the conclusion logically follows from its two premises, and since the second premise is generally admitted to be not only true but necessarily true, theists are limited, I believe, to basically three different responses. The first is the response that I, rather naively, thought is the most reasonable response for the theist to give. It consists in simply accepting the argument as showing that we have *a reason* to think it unlikely that God exists. For given that no good we can imagine can be reasonably thought to justify God in permitting that fawn's terrible suffering, it does *seem unlikely* that there is a good that in fact does justify God in permitting that suffering. After all, we can think of many goods, even the greatest good of all – life eternal in the loving presence of God. And none of the goods we can think of appears to require the fawn's terrible suffering as a condition of its realization.[3] Of course, it remains possible that some good that is unknowable by us justifies God in permitting the fawn's suffering and death. So, even though the argument may make it somewhat unlikely that God exists, if, as some theists will surely claim, we have stronger reasons to think he does exist – for example, a personal experience of an all powerful, all-knowing, perfectly good creator – we will be justified in believing that some good unknown to us does justify God in permitting the fawn's 5 days of terrible suffering. On the other hand, if someone has no outweighing reason to believe that God exists, the fawn's suffering, along with numerous other instances of seemingly pointless evils, may well justify such a person in thinking that it is unlikely that there is any such being as God.

In a relatively short time, however, I came to see that I was mistaken in thinking that philosophers, whether theists or nontheists, would agree with me in accepting the first premise of the argument, the premise that says it is likely that pointless evils occur. Indeed, I came to see this as early as 1982, just 3 years later, when I conducted an NEH Summer Seminar for College Teachers. I had a group of young, able philosophers who held teaching positions in various colleges. We covered several topics during the 6 weeks they were at Purdue, and toward the end we spent a week on the problem of evil. Among the group was a chap named Stephen Wykstra who had accepted a teaching position in philosophy at Calvin college. Wykstra talked only occasionally in the seminar, but when he became excited about some point or argument he would talk a good deal, sometimes having difficulty stopping talking, even after having fully made his point. At such times he would finally become aware that he had gone on too long, stop for moment, and then say, "Shut up Wykstra!" And when he said that, to our surprise he would stop talking. When the 6 weeks were up, many of those in the seminar departed. But Wykstra remained at Purdue for about two additional weeks, coming in to see me and discussing further the problem of evil. I have only dim recollections of those discussions, but I rightly sensed that Wykstra was very focused on providing a philosophical critique of my argument from evil. I also correctly sensed he would not rest until he had done so. A year later, he presented an important paper on the problem of evil at the Pacific Division of the American Philosophical Association, to which I was invited to respond. I recall that meeting of the Pacific Division very well. For it took place on board the Queen Mary, and each person's private room on the vessel was about the size of a rather spacious coat closet. I don't recall much at all of what went on at the session with Wykstra. I do recall, however, what was then referred to as 'the smoker', an evening session at all APA meetings in which the main activity is sipping wine and talking with one's friends in the profession. My recollection is that I felt it altogether proper and good to be on the Queen Mary, drinking wine while talking with other philosophers. And it did not seem to matter that the Queen Mary was going nowhere at all, being permanently in dock.

In 1984 Wykstra's paper was published in the *International Journal for Philosophy of Religion*, along with my reply.[4] The publication of his paper significantly advanced a position in philosophy that has come to be known as 'skeptical theism.' For Wykstra presented a *skeptical argument* against the justification I gave for the crucial premise at work in my argument from evil, the premise stating that probably there are pointless evils. Why did I believe that the fawn's suffering is likely to be pointless? It was because we cannot think of or even imagine a good that would both outweigh the fawn's suffering and be such that an all-powerful, all-knowing being could not find some way of bringing about that good, or some equal or better good, without having to permit the fawn's suffering. For think for a moment of the fawn's suffering. It is not only terribly burned, but it lies for 5 days on the forest floor in agony, before death finally ends its life. Is there some great good that an all-powerful, all-knowing being could bring about *only* by allowing that fawn to suffer for *five full days*, rather than say, four, three, two, one, or even not at all – say, by bringing it about that its death is instantaneous? It baffles the human mind to think that an all-powerful, all-knowing being would find itself in such a predicament. But the skeptical theist's response is that, for all we know, the reason why the human mind is baffled by this state of affairs is simply because it doesn't know enough. For if we were to know what God knows then our human minds would know that God really had no choice at all. For, according to the skeptical theist, God knew that if he prevented that fawn's being terribly burned, or prevented even 1 day of the fawn's 5 days of terrible suffering, he either would have to permit some other evil equally bad or worse or forfeit some great good, without which the world as a whole would be worse than it is by virtue of his permitting that fawn to suffer intensely for five full days. And the fact that we have no idea of what that good might be is not at all surprising, given the disparity between the goods knowable by our minds and the goods knowable by a perfectly good and all-knowing creator of the world. So, according to the skeptical theist, we simply are in no position to *reasonably judge* that God, if he exists, could have prevented the fawn's 5 days of terrible suffering without losing some outweighing good or having to permit some equally bad or worse evil. For our limited minds are simply unable to think of the goods that the mind of God would know. And since we are simply unable to know many of the goods God would know, the fact that no good *we know of* can reasonably be thought to justify an infinitely good, all-powerful being in permitting the fawn's terrible suffering is not really surprising. In fact, given the enormous gulf between God's knowledge and our knowledge, that no good we know of appears to in any way justify God in permitting the fawn's terrible suffering is perhaps just what we should expect if such a being as God actually exists.

In developing his view Wykstra argued that to reasonably believe that the fawn's suffering is likely to have been pointless, we must have a *positive reason* to think that if some good should justify God's permitting the fawn's suffering it is likely that we would know of that good. He then claimed that goods knowable to God are quite likely not going to be knowable to us. To support his claim Wykstra pointed out that upon looking in his garage and seeing no dog, we would be entitled to conclude that there is no dog in the garage. But upon looking in his garage and seeing no fleas, we would not be entitled to conclude that there are no fleas in his garage. For we have reason to think that if there were any fleas in his garage, it would not be likely that we would see them. And similarly, he argued, our not being able to think of a good that might justify God in permitting the fawn's suffering is no reason to think there isn't such a good. For, on Wykstra's view, were there such a God-purposed good for permitting the fawn's suffering it is altogether likely that we would not know of it. So, the fact that we cannot even imagine what such a good would be, far from being a reason to think it unlikely that God exists, is just what we should expect to be true if God does exist.

Toward the end of his paper Wykstra notes that I am right in holding that a wholly good God would allow suffering, such as the fawn's terrible suffering, only if "there is an outweighing good served by so doing." He also agrees with me "that such goods are, in many cases, nowhere within our ken." But he then says:

> The linchpin of my critique has been that if theism is true, this is just what one would expect: for if we think carefully about the sort of being theism proposes for our belief, it is entirely expectable – given what we know of our cognitive limits – that the goods by virtue of which this Being allows known suffering should very often be beyond our ken. Since this state of affairs is just what one should expect if theism were true, how can its obtaining be evidence *against* theism? (p. 91)

II

Wykstra's elegant and carefully argued paper forced me to make some distinctions that are all too easily overlooked in responses to objections to the claim that the theistic God exists.[5] In making these distinctions, I let the capital letter 'O' abbreviate 'an omnipotent, omniscient, wholly good being'. I then suggested that *standard theism* is "any view which holds that O exists." Thus, traditional Christianity, Islam, and Judaism are all examples of standard theism. However, within standard theism we can distinguish *restricted* standard theism and *expanded* standard theism. Expanded theism is the view that O exists, conjoined with certain other significant religious claims, claims that are not *entailed* by the proposition that there exists an omnipotent, omniscient, wholly good being who has created the world. For that proposition is common to traditional Christianity, Islam, and Judaism. What are some of the independent religious ideas that have been added to standard theism so as to produce the version of expanded theism that we now know as Christianity? There is, of course, the idea that God is a trinity: God the Father, God the Son, and God the Holy Ghost, an idea that took several centuries to be worked out, and is held only in Christianity. It was first established at the Council of Nicea in 325 AD when Athanasius, accused of heresy and exiled several times in his lifetime, won out over Arius who denied that Jesus of Nazareth was a divine being. In addition, of course, there are claims about original sin, Adam and Eve in the garden, redemption, a future life, a last judgment, and the like. Orthodox Christian theism is a version of expanded theism, for the doctrine that God took on human form and died for our sins is essential to orthodox Christianity, but not deducible merely from the claim that the theistic God exists. Since some might be led to think that if the theistic God exists, then certain other *logically independent* religious claims must also be true – claims about sin, redemption, heaven, the divinity of the son of Mary and Joseph, etc. – in my reply to Wykstra I insisted on using the expression 'O exists' rather than the expression 'God exists'. I did this to assist the reader in recognizing that from the assumption that there exists an omnipotent, omniscient, wholly good being who created the world nothing can be *logically deduced* concerning whether certain other religious claims held by Judaism, Islam or Christianity are true or false.[6] And this means, of course, that from the fact that O exists we cannot logically deduce that there is a life beyond our three score years and ten, that there is a heaven or a hell, that Jesus of Nazareth is the Son of God, or that the Bible is divinely inspired. With this in mind I noted that in answer to my claim that it appears that the fawn's suffering is pointless, Wykstra's principle response is that we have *no reason* at all to think that were O to exist things would strike us any differently. And we can formulate his argument for this point as follows:

4. O's mind grasps goods beyond our ken.
5. It is likely that the goods in relation to which O permits many sufferings are beyond our ken.

therefore,

6. It is likely that many of the sufferings in our world do not appear to have a point – we can't see what goods justify O in permitting them.

I then pointed out that the fact that O's mind grasps goods beyond our ken does not entail that it is likely that the goods in relation to which O permits many sufferings are *beyond our ken*. For once such goods occur we have reason to think that we would know them, given that they are goods involving those who have suffered. Moreover, the mere fact that O exists gives us no reason to think that the goods for the sake of which O permits horrendous human and animal suffering are goods that occur only in some far distant future, perhaps in some other form of existence altogether unknown and perhaps unknowable by us. But what about expanded theism? Reading the writings attributed to Saint Paul, one may conclude that the goods for the sake of which O permits vast amounts of human and animal suffering will be realized only at the end of the world, or in some state of existence quite unknown to us. If we conjoin this claim with the horrendous suffering that occurs in our world, we do seem to have some reason to think just what Wykstra claims: that it is likely that the goods in question would be beyond our ken. But as we've noted, the mere fact that O exists gives us no reason to think that what we find in the Bible or the Koran is anything more than what it probably is, the writings of various human beings scattered over time who, for whatever reasons (if any) came to believe that a divine being exists and is the creator of everything else, and that this being has a plan for his creatures (at least, human beings) and will provide them with some sort of existence after bodily death, etc.

In his paper Wykstra claimed that the theistic hypothesis "contains" the claim that the goods for the sake of which O permits the sufferings in the world are, to a large extent, quite beyond our ken. He speaks of it as a "logical extension of theism." He says this claim is not an "additional postulate" but instead was "implicit" in theism all along. In my reply I said that Wykstra is mistaken about this. What is implicit in theism is that O's mind grasps goods that are beyond our ken. That does seem to be a "logical extension" implicit in theism. For O is omniscient, and we quite clearly are not. However, the claim that these goods are realizable *only* in a world beyond the world of our earthly existence is not a part of the hypothesis that O exists. It is an additional postulate that produces a form of *expanded theism*, a version that is not rendered unlikely by the facts about suffering that I claim to render restricted standard theism unlikely. Indeed, I now rather suspect that Wykstra was supposing that the Bible, or at least much of the New Testament, is somehow guaranteed to be true by virtue of the assumption that O exists. And that is a supposition that I, along with a number of biblical scholars, am unwilling to concede.

Wykstra noted in his essay that among believers, as well as nonbelievers, there is a "persistent intuition that the inscrutable suffering in our world in some sense disconfirms theism." This observation by Wykstra strikes me as exactly right. It is not just unbelievers who tend to see the inscrutable suffering in our world as in some sense discontinuing theism; it is a near universal, natural phenomenon. Believers too, as Wykstra notes, have a strong, natural tendency to see inscrutable suffering, especially as it affects those they dearly love, as an intellectual difficulty or obstacle to belief, something that in the absence of a sensible explanation tends to count against theism. He, nevertheless, thinks that this persistent intuition of believers and nonbelievers is a mistake. For given our cognitive limitations and O's omniscience and omnipotence, Wykstra believes that it should be expected that much of the suffering in our world will be inscrutable to us. So, he concludes that believers and nonbelievers simply fail to see what is really contained in the theistic hypothesis. But if I am right, what Wykstra has unwittingly done is change the question. He has supplemented the theistic hypothesis that O (an omnipotent, omniscient, wholly good, perfectly loving being) exists with other propositions such that the supplemented result is not disconfirmed by the facts that are claimed to count against the hypothesis that O exists. I ended my response, however, by pointing out that Wykstra would likely disagree with me about whether he has really supplemented the hypothesis that O exists. For Wykstra seems to think that what I hold to be supplements to the hypothesis that O exists are in some way already *logically contained* in that very hypothesis. But clearly, they are not.

An analogy to which theists often appeal in defending the reasonableness of supposing that the goods justifying the horrendous evils in our world are unknowable by us is the good-parent analogy. The idea is that God is to us humans as good parents are to their children whom they love. And just as their children often cannot comprehend the goods for which their loving parents permit things to happen to them, so too we humans cannot comprehend the goods for which God permits us, his created children, to endure the evils that happen to us. My own judgment is that this analogy, very much favored by theists, is actually unfavorable to theism. It is true that good, loving parents may have to permit their ailing child to be separated from them, confined to a hospital, forced to swallow evil tasting medicines, and put in the care of strangers in order to cure the child of some illness. The very young child, of course, may not understand why his parents have removed him from his home and put him in the care of strangers. So too, the theist may say, our sin, or something else, may have separated us from God. But the analogy is a dismal failure. When children are ill and confined to a hospital, the loving parents by any means possible seek to comfort their child, giving special assurances of their love while he is separated from them and suffering for a reason he does not understand. No loving parents use their child's stay in the hospital as an occasion to take a holiday, saying to themselves that the doctors and nurses will surely look after little Johnny while they are away. But many human beings have endured horrendous suffering without any awareness of God's assurances of his love and concern during their period of suffering. If you are in doubt of this, try reading the literature concerning the holocaust victims. Unlike the good parents, God has been on holiday for centuries. Indeed, even in the 11th century, during the age of faith, the great Christian saint, St Anselm of Canterbury, lamented:

> I have never seen thee, O Lord my God; . . . What O most high Lord, shall this man do, an exile far from thee? He longs to come to thee, and thy dwelling place is inaccessible. . . . I was created to see thee and not yet have I done that for which I was made.[7]

In an age of faith, before the growth of the scientific knowledge that produced alternative, credible explanations of the emergence of human life, Anselm's lament, quite reasonably, would not lead to disbelief. But the age of faith has been replaced by an age of reason and science. And in this age of reason and science, for many human beings the idea of God no longer plays an *essential, rational* role in explaining the world and human existence. The idea that human suffering may be divine punishment for human sin and wickedness is no longer a credible explanation for many educated human beings. My own inclination is to think that given the horrendous evils in our world, the absence of the God who supposedly walked with Adam and Eve in the garden is evidence that there is no God. For surely, if there were a God he would wish to provide us with strong reasons to think that he exists, given that the horrendous evils in our world, both natural and moral, seem to provide us with reason to doubt his existence. Of course, one can come up with elaborate stories in which God's hiddenness, even given all the horrendous evils that occur in our world, is not altogether implausible. John Hick and Richard Swinburne, for example, have endeavored to provide such stories. They are called theodicies. Agnostics and atheists tend to view these efforts at explaining God's permission of evil as rather unconvincing. And skeptical theists, following Alvin Plantinga, tend to dismiss theodicies as unnecessary, weak, and unpersuasive. My own judgment is that the theodicies provided by Swinburne and Hick do go some way toward reconciling theism with the horrendous evils that afflict us. But given the enormity of evil in our world, both natural and moral, coupled with the inexplicable absence of the God of traditional theism, I continue to think that the horrendous evils in our world provide evidence against the existence of God.

III

Of course, believing, as I and many others do, that the horrendous evils in our world count against the existence of the theistic God is not the same as being *rationally justified* in holding that belief. And I must confess that my earlier confidence in the inference from

> no good *we know of* justifies God in permitting many of the evils in our world to the conclusion
>
> probably no good justifies God in permitting those evils

has been somewhat diminished by the objections raised by skeptical theists.[8] The crucial objection is this: In order to have confidence in the inference, it seems that I must suppose that the goods we know of are representative of the goods there are.[9] But given that God, if he exists, would likely know of goods beyond our wildest dreams, why should we think that the goods we know of are a representative sample of the goods there are? Of course, we do know of some very great goods, even the greatest good of all – life eternal in the loving presence of God. But that isn't the same as being justified in thinking that the goods we know of are representative of the goods there are. In response to this serious objection posed by skeptical theists I have tried to do two things. First, I have supplemented my original argument in an effort to blunt the challenge raised by the objection that the goods we know of are not known to be representative of the goods there are. And second, I have sought to show that the skeptical theist's objection, if correct, leads into a black hole for those theists who endeavor to support and defend some of their religious beliefs by philosophical arguments. The supplement I have added to my original argument is the good parent analogy that I relied on in responding to Wykstra's challenging objection to my original argument. So, I can be now be very brief in showing how it lends support to my original argument. God, if he exists, is all-powerful, all-knowing, perfectly good and a supremely loving being. He is to us as loving parents are to their children. It is not for nothing that the common prayer begins with the words: "Our *father* which art in heaven." Morever, he is our loving father. What do loving parents do when their children are suffering for reasons they cannot comprehend? Loving parents do their best to relieve the suffering of their children. And if the suffering should be the result of necessary discipline of the child, the loving parents endeavor as best they can to help the child understand what the discipline is for; and they strive to enable the child to be aware of the constancy of their love. And should their children suffer from injury or illness, the loving parents make special efforts to be consciously present to them, showing their love and concern. Moreover, they do their best to help the child understand the illness and what needs to be done to cure it. But in a world supposedly created by their loving heavenly father, countless people suffer horrendously without any sense of his comforting presence or his helping them to understand why he permits them to endure such suffering. The point is this: love *entails* doing the best one can to be consciously present to those one loves when they are suffering, and particularly so when they are suffering for reasons they do not or cannot comprehend. And given the absence of any loving, heavenly father, the evil and suffering in our world only increases the likelihood that God does not exist.

Emphasizing these implications of God's love for his human creatures, however, does not refute the line of reasoning advanced by skeptical theists. For since we are unable to prove that the goods we know of are representative of the goods known by God, there remains the logical possibility that some outweighing good would be lost were God to yield to his perfect love and be consciously present to his human creatures, comforting them while permitting them to suffer for reasons they are unable to comprehend.

IV

The skeptical theist's emphasis on our inability to be confident that the goods we know of are representative of the goods there are does raise important questions about the inference in the argument from evil. But when we apply their skeptical thesis to the religious beliefs that they and other believers hold, the position of the skeptical theist is seen to lead to conclusions that are very unfriendly to traditional theism. Christian theists, for example, believe that there is a glorious life after death, at least for those who accept Christ as their savior and endeavor to live in accordance with his teachings. What rational grounds do Christians have for these beliefs? They believe, not unreasonably, that God's ultimate purpose for their lives is seldom, if ever, fulfilled in this earthly life; and that, being perfectly good and loving, God will surely grant them the greatest good conceivable to mankind: everlasting life in the presence of God himself. In addition, they also find some support for these beliefs in the Bible. On the basis of these two sources – the recognition that God's purpose for their lives is not fulfilled on earth, and the teachings of the Bible – they not unreasonably conclude that they have *rational grounds* for their belief that there is life after death, a glorious everlasting life in the presence of God himself.

As forceful as this line of reasoning may seem to the faithful, the position of the "skeptical theists" shows it to be utterly inadequate. For given their skeptical theses, we human beings are simply *in the dark about how likely it is* that God will bring it about that faithful believers will have a glorious, everlasting life in his presence. We humans are in the dark about this important matter because, as the skeptical theists tell us, we simply are *in the dark* about the goods that God will know, and the conditions of their realization. For we have no sufficient reason to suppose that the goods we know are representative of the goods there are. And for all we know there is some good far greater than the good of eternal life for the faithful on earth, a good the realization of which precludes God's granting eternal life to the faithful on earth. For example, consider the Christian belief that there are fallen angels: Satan and his cohorts. They are judged to be higher beings than mere humans on earth. And, if we follow the skeptical theists we must conclude that *for all we know*, the good of the fallen angels being redeemed by God far exceeds the good of faithful human beings being granted eternal life. And *for all we know* the cost of God's redeeming the fallen angels precludes God from granting eternal life to any humans. For remember, according to the skeptical theists we are simply in the dark not only about the goods there are but also the conditions of their realization. And it clearly follows from this skeptical view that our being unable to think of any possible good that would justify God in *not* permitting faithful Christians to experience an afterlife *provides* no adequate reason to conclude that probably there is no good that justifies God in precluding faithful Christians from experiencing an afterlife. Moreover, as we've seen, *for all we know*, a condition of the realization of the salvation of Satan and the fallen angels may require God to permit the faithful on earth to perish along with atheists, agnostics, and those who have lived without even forming an idea of such a being as God.

Skeptical theists choose to ride the trolley car of skepticism concerning the goods that God would know so as to undercut the evidential argument from evil. But once on that trolley car it may not be easy to prevent that skepticism from also undercutting any reasons they may suppose they have for thinking that God will provide them and the worshipful faithful with life everlasting in his presence. Of course, they may still appeal to some *special* divine revelation in which God himself supposedly informs them that he will provide faithful, Christian believers with life everlasting in his presence. But to the rest of us, particularly philosophers who find ourselves without the benefit of such special revelations, such a carefully crafted philosophical skepticism will surely appear to be something less than genuine skepticism about whether the goods we know of are representative of the goods there are. Morever, while philosophers may respect religious appeals to special divine revelations, such appeals can hardly provide a *philosophical response* to the skeptical implications of the philosophical claims of skeptical theism.

Notes

1 "The Problem of Evil and Some Varieties of Atheism." *American Philosophical Quarterly* 16 (1979): 335–41.
2 Skeptical theists will say that we are in no position to assert this. For they claim that several of the goods we can think of may, *for all we know*, be goods, any one of which in fact may be the good that does justify God, if he exists, in permitting the fawn's terrible suffering. They would prefer that the sentence in question be revised as follows: "Moreover, it is extraordinarily difficult to think of, or even imagine, a greater good whose realization *we know* would require God to permit that fawn's terrible suffering."
3 If some good G outweighs an evil e, then the good state of affairs G&e outweighs e and cannot be obtained without permitting e. I take it as given that if G can exist without e, a perfectly good being (other things being equal) would prevent e.
4 "The Humean Obstacle to Evidential Arguments from Suffering: On Avoiding the Evils of "Appearance," *International Journal for the Philosophy of Religion*, 16 (1984): 73–93. "Evil and the Theistic Hypothesis: A Response to Wykstra," *International Journal for the Philosophy of Religion*, 16 (1984): 95–100.
5 Since there is a natural tendency to associate the word 'God' with various *religious* beliefs about *when* the goods for the sake of which God permits horrendous evils will be realized, beliefs that are not themselves logically derivable from the concept of God, I used the letter 'O' to free the mind from the tendency to think that those religious beliefs are logically entailed by the mere concept of an omnipotent, omniscient, creator of the world.
6 Of course, since these three religious systems contradict one another, we can be sure not all these religious claims can be true.
7 Proslogium, Ch. 1, pp. 3–7 in *Anselm: Basic Writings*, trans. S. N. Deane. (LaSalle, IL: Open Court, 2n. ed., 1966).
8 Two objections have been raised. The first is that the premise is too strong. Instead, it should read as follows: "no good we know of (is known by us to justify) God in permitting many of the evils in our world." The second, more crucial objection is as I go on to state.
9 The best presentation of Skeptical Theism I am aware of is by my colleague, Michael Bergmann. See his important paper, "Skeptical Theism and Rowe's New Evidential Argument from Evil," *Nous* 35 (2001): 278–96.

11

Horrendous Evils and the Goodness of God

Marilyn Adams

Marilyn McCord Adams (b. 1943) is Regius Professor of Divinity at the University of Oxford. In the following essay she argues that recent discussions of the problem of evil have been carried out at too abstract a level. Atheologians must pay closer attention to the theological richness of the theistic conception of God's nature, and theists must face squarely the actual kinds and quantity of evil present in our world. Adams focuses on what she calls "horrendous evils," arguing that standard theistic responses to the problem of evil fail to address such evils. She then suggests that Christian theology has the resources to develop a more adequate account of how God will ultimately defeat horrendous evils.

1. Introduction

Over the past thirty years, analytic philosophers of religion have defined 'the problem of evil' in terms of the prima-facie difficulty in consistently maintaining

(1) God exists, and is omnipotent, omniscient, and perfectly good

and

(2) Evil exists.

In a crisp and classic article, 'Evil and Omnipotence',[1] J. L. Mackie emphasized that the problem is not that (1) and (2) are logically inconsistent by themselves, but that they together with quasi-logical rules formulating attribute-analyses – such as

(P1) A perfectly good being would always eliminate evil so far as it could,

Marilyn Adams, "Horrendous Evils and the Goodness of God", *Proceedings of the Aristotelian Society*, supp. vol. 63 (1989): 297–310. © 1989 by The Aristotelian Society. Reprinted by courtesy of the Editor of the Aristotelian Society. (Revised version in Marilyn McCord Adams and Robert Merrihew Adams (eds.) *The Problem of Evil*. Oxford University Press, 1990, pp. 209–21.)

and

(P2) There are *no limits* to what an omnipotent being can do – constitute an inconsistent premiss-set. He added, of course, that the inconsistency might be removed by substituting alternative and perhaps more subtle analyses, but cautioned that such replacements of (P1) and (P2) would save 'ordinary theism' from his charge of positive irrationality, only if true to its 'essential requirements'.[2]

In an earlier paper, 'Problems of Evil: More Advice to Christian Philosophers',[3] I underscored Mackie's point and took it a step further. In debates about whether the argument from evil can establish the irrationality of religious belief, care must be taken, both by the atheologians who deploy it and by the believers who defend against it, to ensure that the operative attribute-analyses accurately reflect that religion's understanding of divine power and goodness. It does the atheologian no good to argue for the falsity of Christianity on the ground that the existence of an omnipotent, omniscient, pleasure-maximizer is incompossible with a world such as ours, because Christians never believed God was a pleasure-maximizer anyway. But equally, the truth of Christianity would be inadequately defended by the observation that an omnipotent, omniscient egoist could have created a world with suffering creatures, because Christians insist that God loves other (created) persons than Himself. The extension of 'evil' in (2) is likewise important. Since Mackie and his successors are out to show that 'the several parts of the *essential* theological doctrine are inconsistent with *one another*',[4] they can accomplish their aim only if they circumscribe the extension of 'evil' as their religious opponents do. By the same token, it is not enough for Christian philosophers to explain how the power, knowledge, and goodness of God could coexist with some evils or other; a full account must exhibit the compossibility of divine perfection with evils in the amounts and of the kinds found in the actual world (and evaluated as such by Christian standards).

The moral of my earlier story might be summarized thus: where the internal coherence of a system of religious beliefs is at stake, successful arguments for its inconsistency must draw on premisses (explicitly or implicitly) internal to that system or obviously acceptable to its adherents; likewise for successful rebuttals or explanations of consistency. The thrust of my argument is to push both sides of the debate towards more detailed attention to and subtle understanding of the religious system in question.

As a Christian philosopher, I want to focus in this paper on the problem for the truth of Christianity raised by what I shall call 'horrendous' evils. Although our world is riddled with them, the biblical record punctuated by them, and one of them – namely, the passion of Christ; according to Christian belief, the judicial murder of God by the people of God – is memorialized by the Church on its most solemn holiday (Good Friday) and in its central sacrament (the Eucharist), the problem of horrendous evils is largely skirted by standard treatments for the good reason that they are intractable by them. After showing why, I will draw on other Christian materials to sketch ways of meeting this, the deepest of religious problems.

2. Defining the Category

For present purposes, I define 'horrendous evils' as 'evils the participation in (the doing or suffering of) which gives one reason prima facie to doubt whether one's life could (given their inclusion in it) be a great good to one on the whole'.[5] Such reasonable doubt arises because it is so difficult humanly to conceive how such evils could be overcome. Borrowing Chisholm's contrast between *balancing off* (which occurs when the opposing values of *mutually exclusive* parts of a whole partially or totally cancel each other out) and *defeat* (which cannot occur by the mere addition to the whole of a new part of opposing value, but involves some 'organic unity' among the values of parts and wholes, as when the positive aesthetic value of a whole painting defeats the ugliness of a small colour patch),[6] horrendous evils seem prima facie, not only to balance off but to engulf the positive value of a participant's life. Nevertheless, that very horrendous proportion, by which they threaten to rob a person's life of positive meaning, cries out not only to be engulfed, but to be made meaningful through positive and decisive defeat.

I understand this criterion to be objective, but relative to individuals. The example of habitual complainers, who know how to make the worst of a good situation, shows individuals not to be incorrigible experts on what ills would defeat the positive value of their lives. Nevertheless, nature and experience endow people with different strengths; one bears easily what crushes another. And a major consideration in determining whether an individual's life is/has been a great good to him/her on the whole, is invariably and appropriately how it has seemed to him/her.[7]

I offer the following list of paradigmatic horrors: the rape of a woman and axing off of her arms, psychophysical torture whose ultimate goal is the disintegration of personality, betrayal of one's deepest loyalties, cannibalizing one's own offspring, child abuse of the sort described by Ivan Karamazov, child pornography, parental incest, slow death by starvation, participation in the Nazi death camps, the explosion of nuclear bombs over populated areas, having to choose which of one's children shall live and which be executed by terrorists, being the accidental and/or unwitting agent of the disfigurement or death of those one loves best. I regard these as *paradigmatic*, because I believe most people would find in the doing or suffering of them prima-facie reason to doubt the positive meaning of their lives.[8] Christian belief counts the crucifixion of Christ another: on the one hand, death by crucifixion seemed to defeat Jesus' Messianic vocation; for according to Jewish law, death by hanging from a tree made its victim ritually accursed, definitively excluded from the compass of God's people, *a fortiori* disqualified from being the Messiah. On the other hand, it represented the defeat of its perpetrators' leadership vocations, as those who were to prepare the people of God for the Messiah's coming, killed and ritually accursed the true Messiah, according to later theological understanding, God Himself.

3. The Impotence of Standard Solutions

For better and worse, the by now standard strategies for 'solving' the problem of evil are powerless in the face of horrendous evils.

3.1. Seeking the reason-why

In his model article 'Hume on Evil',[9] Pike takes up Mackie's challenge, arguing that (P1) fails to reflect ordinary moral intuitions (more to the point, I would add, Christian beliefs), and traces the abiding sense of trouble to the hunch that an omnipotent, omniscient being could have no reason compatible with perfect goodness for permitting (bringing about) evils, because all legitimate excuses arise from ignorance or weakness. Solutions to the problem of evil have thus been sought in the form of counter-examples to this latter claim, i.e. logically possible reasons-why that would excuse even an omnipotent, omniscient God! The putative logically possible reasons offered have tended to be *generic* and *global*: generic in so far as some *general* reason is sought to cover all sorts of evils; global in so far as they seize upon some feature of the world as a whole. For example, philosophers have alleged that the desire to make a world with one of the following properties – 'the best of all possible worlds',[10] 'a world a more perfect than which is impossible', 'a world exhibiting a perfect balance of retributive justice',[11] 'a world with as favorable a balance of (created) moral good over moral evil as God can weakly actualize'[12] – would constitute a reason compatible with perfect goodness for God's creating a world with evils in the amounts and of the kinds found in the actual world. Moreover, such general reasons are presented as so powerful as to do away with any need to catalogue types of evils one by one, and examine God's reason for permitting each in particular. Plantinga explicitly hopes that the problem of horrendous evils can thus be solved without being squarely confronted.[13]

3.2. The insufficiency of global defeat

A pair of distinctions is in order here: (i) between two dimensions of divine goodness in relation to creation – namely, 'producer of global goods' and 'goodness to' or 'love of individual created persons'; and (ii) between the overbalance/defeat of evil by good on the global scale, and the overbalance/defeat of evil by good within the context of an individual person's life.[14] Correspondingly, we may separate two problems of evil parallel to the two sorts of goodness mentioned in (i).

In effect, generic and global approaches are directed to the first problem: they defend divine goodness along the first (global) dimension by suggesting logically possible strategies for the global defeat of evils. But establishing God's excellence as a producer of global goods does not automatically solve the second problem, especially in a world containing horrendous evils. For God cannot be said to be good or loving to any created persons the positive meaning of whose lives He allows to be engulfed in and/or defeated by evils – that is, individuals within whose lives horrendous evils remain undefeated. Yet, the only way unsupplemented global and generic approaches could have to explain the latter, would be by applying their general reasons-why to particular cases of horrendous suffering.

Unfortunately, such an exercise fails to give satisfaction. Suppose for the sake of argument that horrendous evil could be included in maximally perfect world orders; its being partially constitutive of such an order would assign it that generic and global positive meaning. But would knowledge of such a fact defeat for a mother the prima-facie reason provided by her cannibalism of her own infant to wish that she had never been born? Again, the aim of perfect retributive balance confers meaning on evils imposed. But would knowledge that the torturer was being tortured give the victim who broke down and turned traitor under pressure any more reason to think his/her life worth while? Would it not merely multiply reasons for the torturer to doubt that his/her life could turn out to be a good to him/her on the whole? Could the truck-driver who accidentally runs over his beloved child find consolation in the idea that this middle-known[15] but unintended side-effect was part of the price God accepted for a world with the best balance of moral good over moral evil he could get?

Not only does the application to horrors of such generic and global reasons for divine permission of evils fail to solve the second problem of evil; it makes it worse by adding *generic prima-facie* reasons to doubt whether human life would be a great good to individual human beings in possible worlds where such divine motives were operative. For, taken in isolation and made to bear the weight of the whole explanation, such reasons-why draw a picture of divine indifference or even hostility to the human plight. Would the fact that God permitted horrors because they were constitutive means to His end of global perfection, or that He tolerated them because He could obtain that global end anyway, make the participant's life more tolerable, more worth living for him/her? Given radical human vulnerability to horrendous evils, the ease with which humans participate in them, whether as victim or perpetrator, would not the thought that God visits horrors on anyone who caused them, simply because he/she deserves it, provide one more reason to expect human life to be a nightmare?

Those willing to split the two problems of evil apart might adopt a divide-and-conquer strategy, by simply denying divine goodness along the second dimension. For example, many Christians do not believe that God will ensure an overwhelmingly good life to each and every person He creates. Some say the decisive defeat of evil with good is promised only within the lives of the obedient, who enter by the narrow gate. Some speculate that the elect may be few. Many recognize that the sufferings of this present life are as nothing compared to the hell of eternal torment, designed to defeat goodness with horrors within the lives of the damned.

Such a road can be consistently travelled only at the heavy toll of admitting that human life in worlds such as ours is a bad bet. Imagine (adapting Rawls's device) persons in a pre-original position, considering possible worlds containing managers of differing power, wisdom, and character, and subjects of varying fates. The question they are to answer about each world is whether they would willingly enter it as a human being, from behind a veil of ignorance as to which position they would occupy. Reason would, I submit, dictate a negative verdict for worlds whose omniscient and omnipotent manager permits ante-mortem horrors that remain undefeated within the context of the human participant's life; *a fortiori*, for worlds in which some or most humans suffer eternal torment.

3.3. *Inaccessible reasons*

So far, I have argued that generic and global solutions are at best incomplete: however well their account of divine motivating reasons deals with the first problem of evil, the attempt to extend it to the second fails by making it worse. This verdict might seem prima facie tolerable to standard generic and global approaches and indicative of only a minor modification in their strategy: let the above-mentioned generic and global reasons cover divine permission of non-horrendous evils, and find other *reasons* compatible with perfect goodness *why* even an omnipotent, omniscient God would permit horrors.

In my judgement, such an approach is hopeless. As Plantinga[16] points out, where horrendous evils are concerned, not only do we not know God's *actual* reason for permitting them; we cannot even *conceive* of any plausible candidate sort of reason consistent with worthwhile lives for human participants in them.

4. The How of God's Victory

Up to now, my discussion has given the reader cause to wonder whose side I am on anyway. For I have insisted, with rebels like Ivan Karamazov and John Stuart Mill, on spotlighting the problem horrendous evils pose. Yet, I have signalled my preference for a version of Christianity that insists on both dimensions of divine goodness, and maintains not only (*a*) that God will be good enough to created persons to make human life a good bet, but also (*b*) that each created person will have a life that is a great good to him/her on the whole. My critique of standard approaches to the problem of evil thus seems to reinforce atheologian Mackie's verdict of 'positive irrationality' for such a religious position.

4.1. *Whys versus hows*

The inaccessibility of reasons-why seems especially decisive. For surely an all-wise and all-powerful God, who loved each created person enough (*a*) to defeat any experienced horrors within the context of the participant's life, and (*b*) to give each created person a life that is a great good to him/her on the whole, would not permit such persons to suffer horrors for no reason.[17] Does not our inability even to conceive of plausible candidate reasons suffice to make belief in such a God positively irrational in a world containing horrors? In my judgement, it does not.

To be sure, motivating reasons come in several varieties relative to our conceptual grasp: There are (i) reasons of the sort we can readily understand when we are informed of them (e.g. the mother who permits her child to undergo painful heart surgery because it is the only humanly possible way to save its life). Moreover, there are (ii) reasons we would be cognitively, emotionally, and spiritually equipped to grasp if only we had a larger memory or wider attention span (analogy: I may be able to memorize small town street plans; memorizing the road networks of the entire country is a task requiring more of the same, in the way that proving Gödel's theorem is not). Some generic and global approaches insinuate that divine permission of evils has motivating reasons of this sort. Finally, there are (iii) reasons that we are cognitively, emotionally, and/or spiritually too immature to fathom (the way a two-year-old child is incapable of understanding its mother's reasons for permitting the surgery). I agree with Plantinga that our ignorance of divine reasons for permitting horrendous evils is not of types (i) or (ii), but of type (iii).

Nevertheless, if there are varieties of ignorance, there are also varieties of reassurance.[18] The two-year-old heart patient is convinced of its mother's love, not by her cognitively inaccessible reasons, but by her intimate care and presence through its painful experience. The story of Job suggests something similar is true with human participation in horrendous suffering: God does not give Job His reasons-why, and implies that Job isn't smart enough to grasp them; rather Job is lectured on the extent of divine power, and sees God's goodness face to face! Likewise, I suggest, to exhibit the logical compossibility of both dimensions of divine goodness with horrendous suffering, it is not necessary to find logically possible reasons *why* God might permit them. It is enough to show *how* God can be good enough to created persons despite their participation in horrors – by defeating them within the context of the individual's life and by giving that individual a life that is a great good to him/her on the whole.

4.2. *What sort of valuables?*

In my opinion, the reasonableness of Christianity can be maintained in the face of horrendous evils only by drawing on resources of religious value theory. For one way for God to be *good to* created persons is by relating them appropriately to relevant and great goods. But philosophical and religious theories differ importantly on what valuables they admit into their ontology. Some maintain that 'what you see is what you get', but nevertheless admit a wide range of valuables, from sensory pleasures, the beauty of nature and cultural artefacts, the joys of creativity, to loving personal intimacy. Others posit a transcendent good (e.g. the Form of the Good in Platonism, or God, the Supremely Valuable Object, in Christianity). In the spirit of Ivan Karamazov, I am convinced that the depth of horrific evil cannot be accurately estimated without recognizing it to be incommensurate with any package of merely non-transcendent goods and so unable to be balanced off, much less defeated, thereby.

Where the *internal* coherence of Christianity is the issue, however, it is fair to appeal to its own store of valuables. From a Christian point of view, God is a being a greater than which cannot, be conceived, a good incommensurate with both created goods and temporal evils. Likewise, the good of beatific, face-to-face intimacy with God is simply incommensurate with any merely non-transcendent goods or ills a person might experience. Thus, the good of beatific face-to-face intimacy with God would *engulf* (in a sense analogous to Chisholmian balancing off) even the horrendous evils humans experience in this present life here below, and overcome any prima-facie reasons the individual had to doubt whether his/her life would or could be worth living.

4.3. *Personal meaning, horrors defeated*

Engulfing personal horrors within the context of the participant's life would vouchsafe to that individual a life that was a great good to him/her on the whole. I am still inclined to think it would guarantee that immeasurable divine goodness to any person thus benefited. But there is good theological reason for Christians to believe that God would go further, beyond engulfment to defeat. For it is the nature of persons to look for meaning, both in their lives and in the world. Divine respect for and commitment to created personhood would drive God to make all those sufferings which threaten to destroy the positive meaning of a person's life meaningful through positive defeat.[19]

How could God do it? So far as I can see, only by integrating participation in horrendous evils into a person's relationship with God. Possible dimensions of integration are charted by Christian soteriology. I pause here to sketch three:[20] (i) First, because God in Christ participated in horrendous evil through His passion and death, human experience of horrors can be a means of *identifying* with Christ, either through *sympathetic* identification (in which each person suffers his/her own pains, but their similarity enables each to know what it is like for the other) or through *mystical* identification (in which the created person is supposed literally to experience a share of Christ's pain).[21] (ii) Julian of Norwich's description of heavenly welcome suggests the possible defeat of horrendous evil through divine gratitude. According to Julian, before the elect have a chance to thank God for all He has done for them, God will say, 'Thank you for all your suffering, the suffering of your youth.' She says that the creature's experience of divine gratitude will bring such full and unending joy as could not be merited by the whole sea of human pain and suffering throughout the ages.[22] (iii) A third idea identifies temporal suffering itself with a vision into the inner life of God, and can be developed several ways. Perhaps, contrary to medieval theology, God is not impassible, but rather has matched capacities for joy and for suffering. Perhaps, as the Heidelberg catechism suggests, God responds to human sin and the sufferings of Christ with an agony beyond human conception.[23] Alternatively, the inner life of God may be, strictly speaking and in and of itself, beyond both joy and sorrow. But, just as (according to Rudolf Otto) humans experience divine presence now as *tremendum* (with deep dread and anxiety), now as *fascinans* (with ineffable attraction), so perhaps our deepest suffering as much as our highest joys may themselves be direct visions into the inner life of God, imperfect but somehow less obscure in proportion to their intensity. And if a face-to-face vision of God is a good for humans incommensurate with any non-transcendent goods or ills, so any vision of God (including horrendous suffering) would have a good aspect in so far as it is a vision of God (even if it has an evil aspect in so far as it is horrendous suffering). For the most part, horrors are not recognized as experiences of God (any more than the city slicker recognizes his visual image of a brown patch as a vision of Beulah the cow in the distance). But, Christian mysticism might claim, at least from the post-mortem perspective of the beatific vision, such sufferings will be seen for what they were, and retrospectively no one will wish away any intimate encounters with God from his/her life-history in this world. The created person's experience of the beatific vision together with his/her knowledge that intimate divine presence stretched back over his/her ante-mortem life and reached down into the depths of his/her worst suffering, would provide retrospective comfort independent of comprehension of the reasons-why akin to the two-year-old's assurance of its mother's love. Taking this third approach, Christians would not need to commit themselves about what in any event we do not know: namely, whether we will (like the two-year-old) ever grow up enough to understand the reasons why God permits our participation in horrendous evils. For by contrast with the best of earthly mothers, such divine intimacy is an incommensurate good and would cancel out for the creature any need to know why.

5. Conclusion

The worst evils demand to be defeated by the best goods. Horrendous evils can be overcome only by the goodness of God. Relative to human nature, participation in horrendous evils and loving intimacy with God are alike disproportionate: for the former threatens to engulf the good in an individual human life with evil, while the latter guarantees the reverse engulfment of evil by good. Relative to one another, there is also disproportion, because the good that God *is*, and intimate relationship with Him, is incommensurate with created goods and evils alike. Because intimacy with God so outscales relations (good or bad) with any creatures, integration into the human person's relationship with God confers significant meaning and positive value even on horrendous suffering. This result coheres with basic Christian intuition: that the powers of darkness are stronger than humans, but they are no match for God!

Standard generic and global solutions have for the most part tried to operate within the territory common to believer and unbeliever, within the confines of religion-neutral value theory. Many discussions reflect the hope that substitute attribute-analyses, candidate reasons-why, and/or defeaters could issue out of values shared by believers and unbelievers alike. And some virtually make this a requirement on an adequate solution. Mackie knew better how to distinguish the many charges that may be levelled against religion. Just as philosophers may or may not find the existence of God plausible, so they may be variously attracted or repelled by Christian values of grace and redemptive sacrifice. But agreement on truth-value is not necessary to consensus on internal consistency. My contention has been that it is not only legitimate, but, given horrendous evils, necessary for Christians to dip into their richer store of valuables to exhibit the consistency of (1) and (2).[24] I would go one step further: assuming the pragmatic and/or moral (I would prefer to say, broadly speaking, religious) importance of believing that (one's own) human life is worth living, the ability of Christianity to exhibit how this could be so despite human vulnerability to horrendous evil, constitutes a pragmatic/moral/religious consideration in its favour, relative to value schemes that do not.

To me, the most troublesome weakness in what I have said lies in the area of conceptual under-development. The contention that God suffered in Christ or that one person can experience another's pain requires detailed analysis and articulation in metaphysics and philosophy of mind. I have shouldered some of this burden elsewhere,[25] but its full discharge is well beyond the scope of this paper.

Notes

1 J. L. Mackie, 'Evil and Omnipotence', *Mind*, 64 (1955) [repr. in Marilyn McCord Adams and Robert Merrihew Adams (eds.) *The Problem of Evil* (Oxford: Oxford University Press, 1990), Chapter 1) and] repr. in Nelson Pike (ed.), *God and Evil* (Englewood Cliffs, NJ: Prentice-Hall, 1964), 46–60.

2 Ibid. 47.

3 Marilyn McCord Adams, 'Problems of Evil: More Advice to Christian Philosophers', *Faith and Philosophy* (Apr. 1988), 121–43.

4 Mackie, 'Evil and Omnipotence', pp. 46–7 (emphasis mine).

5 Stewart Sutherland (in his comment 'Horrendous Evils and the Goodness of God – II', *Proceedings of the Aristotelian Society*, suppl. vol. 63 (1989), 311–23; esp. 311) takes my criterion to be somehow 'first-person'. This was not my intention. My definition may be made more explicit as follows: an evil *e* is horrendous if and only if participation in *e* by person *p* gives everyone prima-facie reason to doubt whether *p*'s life can, given *p*'s participation in *e*, be a great good to *p* on the whole.

6 Roderick Chisholm, 'The Defeat of Good and Evil' [Chapter III in Adams and Adams, *The Problem of Evil*].

7 Cf. Malcolm's astonishment at Wittgenstein's dying exclamation that he had had a wonderful life, *Ludwig Wittgenstein: A Memoir* (London: Oxford University Press, 1962), 100.

8 Once again, more explicitly, most people would agree that a person *p*'s doing or suffering of them constitutes prima-facie reason to doubt whether *p*'s life can be, given such participation, a great good to *p* on the whole.

9 'Hume on Evil', *Philosophical Review*, 72 (1963), 180–97 [Chapter II in Adams and Adams, *The Problem of Evil*]; reprinted in Pike (ed.), *God and Evil*, p. 88.

10 Following Leibniz, Pike draws on this feature as part of what I have called his Epistemic Defence ('Problems of Evil: More Advice to Christian Philosophers', pp. 124–5).

11 Augustine, *On Free Choice of Will*, iii. 93–102, implies that there is a maximum value for created worlds, and a plurality of worlds that meet it. All of these contain rational free creatures; evils are foreseen but unintended side-effects of their creation. No matter what they choose, however, God can order their choices into a maximally perfect universe by establishing an order of retributive justice.

12 Plantinga takes this line in numerous discussions, in the course of answering Mackie's objection to the Free Will Defence, that God should have made sinless free creatures. Plantinga insists that, given incompatibilist freedom in creatures, God cannot strongly actualize any world He wants. It is logically possible that a world with evils in the amounts and of the kinds found in this world is the best that He could do, Plantinga argues, given His aim of getting some moral goodness in the world.

13 Alvin Plantinga, 'Self-Profile', in James E. Tomberlin and Peter van Inwagen (eds.), *Profiles: Alvin Plantinga* (Dordrecht; Boston, Mass., and Lancaster, Pa.: Reidel, 1985), 38.

14 I owe the second of these distinctions to a remark by Keith De Rose in our Fall 1987 seminar on the problem of evil at UCLA.

15 Middle knowledge, or knowledge of what is 'in between' the actual and the possible, is the sort of knowledge of what a free creature *would do* in every situation in which that creature could possibly find himself. Following Luis de Molina and Francisco Suarez, Alvin Plantinga ascribes such knowledge to God, prior in the order of explanation to God's decision about which free creatures to actualize (in *The Nature of Necessity* (Oxford: Clarendon Press, 1974), pp. 164–93 [Chapter V in this collection]). Robert Merrihew Adams challenges this idea in his article 'Middle Knowledge and the Problem of Evil', *American Philosophical Quarterly*, 14 (1977) [Chapter VI in this collection]; repr. in *The Virtue of Faith* (New York: Oxford University Press, 1987), 77–93.

16 Alvin Plantinga, 'Self-Profile', pp. 34–5.

17 This point was made by William Fitzpatrick in our Fall 1987 seminar on the problem of evil at UCLA.

18 Contrary to what Sutherland suggests ('Horrendous Evils', pp. 314–15), so far as the compossibility problem is concerned, I intend no illicit shift from reason to emotion. My point is that intimacy with a loving other is a good, participation in which can defeat evils, and so provide everyone with reason to think a person's life can be a great good to him/her on the whole, despite his/her participation in evils.

19 Note, once again, contrary to what Sutherland suggests ('Horrendous Evils', pp. 321–3) 'horrendous evil *e* is defeated' entails *none* of the following propositions: '*e* was not horrendous', '*e* was not unjust', '*e* was not so bad after all'. Nor does my suggestion that even horrendous evils can be defeated by a great enough (because incommensurate and uncreated) good, in any way impugn the reliability of our moral intuitions about injustice, cold-bloodedness, or horror. The judgement that participation in *e* constitutes prima-facie reason to believe that *p*'s life is ruined, stands and remains a daunting measure of *e*'s horror.

20 In my paper 'Redemptive Suffering: A Christian Solution to the Problem of Evil', in Robert Audi and William J. Wainwright (eds.), *Rationality, Religious Belief, and Moral Commitment: New Essays in Philosophy of Religion* (Cornell University Press, 1986), 248–67, I sketch how horrendous suffering can be meaningful by being made a vehicle of divine redemption for victim, perpetrator, and onlooker, and thus an occasion of the victim's collaboration with God. In 'Separation and Reversal in Luke–Acts', in Thomas Morris (ed.), *Philosophy and the Christian Faith* (Notre Dame, Ind.: Notre Dame University Press, 1988), 92–117, I attempted to chart the redemptive plot-line

whereby horrendous sufferings are made meaningful by being woven into the divine redemptive plot. My considered opinion is that such collaboration would be too strenuous for the human condition were it not to be supplemented by a more explicit and beatific divine intimacy.

21 For example, Julian of Norwich tells us that she prayed for and received the latter (*Revelations of Divine Love*, ch. 17). Mother Theresa of Calcutta seems to construe Matthew 25: 31–46 to mean that the poorest and the least *are* Christ, and that their sufferings *are* Christ's (Malcolm Muggeridge, *Something Beautiful for God* (New York: Harper & Row, 1960), 72–5).

22 *Revelations of Divine Love*, ch. 14. I am grateful to Houston Smit for recognizing this scenario of Julian's as a case of Chisholmian defeat.

23 Cf. Plantinga, 'Self-Profile', p. 36.

24 I develop this point at some length in 'Problems of Evil: More Advice to Christian Philosophers', pp. 127–35.

25 For example in 'The Metaphysics of the Incarnation in Some Fourteenth Century Franciscans', in William A. Frank and Girard J. Etzkorn (eds.), *Essays Honoring Allan B. Wolter* (St. Bonaventure, NY: The Franciscan Institute, 1985), 21–57.

In the development of these ideas, I am indebted to the members of our Fall 1987 seminar on the problem of evil at UCLA – especially to Robert Merrihew Adams (its co-leader) and to Keith De Rose, William Fitzpatrick, and Houston Smit. I am also grateful to the Very Revd. Jon Hart Olson for many conversations in mystical theology.

VIII
DEATH AND IMMORTALITY

Introduction

It is natural for humans to think that life is good and death is bad, at least, in general. We might say that death is not bad if it is a transition to another life, but that usually presupposes that the afterlife is a good life. If the afterlife is an eternity in hell, we might prefer annihilation.

In the first reading Epicurus argues that we should get used to the idea that death is annihilation, and annihilation is not a bad thing for the one who is annihilated because the only bad thing is a bad experience, and we cannot experience death. Nor should we fear something that will not be bad for us when it happens. The contemporary philosopher, Thomas Nagel, accepts Epicurus' assumption that death is annihilation, and argues that the ending of a good thing is a bad thing, even though that has the peculiar implication that something can be bad for a person at the time that person does not exist.

Plato thought that it could be demonstrated by philosophical argument that there is life after death, the topic of his dialogue, *Phaedo*. Aquinas took the more modest position that reason supports but does not demonstrate our postmortem existence. Contemporary philosophers are even less optimistic about philosophical arguments for an afterlife. They generally address only the question whether life after death is metaphysically possible. Of course, if they conclude that it is impossible, then from their perspective the investigation is over, but if they conclude it is possible, the investigation must continue, but it is doubtful whether philosophy can be helpful at that stage of the discussion. Traditional believers looked to revelation at that point, whereas contemporary people are more inclined to look at empirical evidence of near-death experiences. In the readings in this section, the selection by the medieval Islamic philosopher Averroes (Ibn Rushd), exhibits a combination of natural philosophy and reference to sacred texts, whereas the entry by Paul Badham evaluates the empirical evidence.

The issue of whether a person can survive the death of her body is clearly connected to the issue of what makes a person at one time the same person as at a later time. If a person is identical with a soul, the death of a body might not affect the continued existence of the person, but that depends upon what it takes for a soul to persist. Plato argued that a soul is the kind of thing that cannot be dissolved, but those philosophers who maintain that a human body and a human soul are distinct substances (dualists) do not necessarily also think that the person is identical with the soul alone and that the soul cannot cease to exist. Nonetheless, life after death is usually thought to be more plausible on a dualist theory than on a physicalist theory, the theory that a person is identical with a body or some part of the body.

Another historically important position on personal identity is that of John Locke, who argued that a person is not identical to a substance, whether physical or non-physical, but is a stream of conscious states held together by memory. If after death you wake up with the same memories you had before you died, then you are the same person, whether or not the substance of which you are composed is the same as the one you had at death. However, other philosophers claim that continuity of consciousness depends upon the continued existence of the brain, which makes life after death very unlikely (see the reading from Bertrand Russell).

One other historically important position on personal identity is the Thomistic view that a person is a combination of matter and form, a position Aquinas adapted from Aristotle. On this position, you will not exist after death unless your form can revivify a body that counts as your body, whatever that might require. To truly exist in the afterlife as the same person you are now, your body must be resurrected. Since Aquinas maintains that the resurrection of the body is a doctrine of faith that cannot be demonstrated by reason, he does not attempt philosophical arguments supporting the resurrection, and we have not included an entry on the resurrection.

The last reading of section VII, the section on the problem of evil, is a paper by Marilyn Adams who argues that the problem of evil is solved only if evils are defeated by union with God in the afterlife. That problem therefore provides one of the motives for belief in an afterlife – in fact, an afterlife of a certain kind. But certain religious teachings on the afterlife lead to other philosophical problems, in particular, the problem of the diversity of religions. One form of this problem is the issue of whether the afterlife taught by a given religion is reserved only for those who practice that religion. We will address this problem in section IX.

A

Is Death Bad?

1

Death is Nothing to Us

Epicurus

Epicurus (341–270 BC) grew up on the Greek island of Samos; he later moved to Athens and founded a philosophical school known as the Garden. His thought remained influential after his death and Epicureanism became one of the leading philosophical schools. He defended an egoistic form of hedonism: one's personal happiness is the only thing that has intrinsic value, and happiness is understood in terms of pleasure and freedom from pain and disturbance. Epicurus believed that the fear of death and divine punishment in the afterlife are some of the primary causes of human anxiety, and he sought to undermine their power by arguing that they are irrational. According to Epicurus, the gods are unconcerned with human affairs, there is no afterlife, and, as he argues in the following selection, death itself is nothing to be feared. Death is annihilation and annihilation is not a bad thing for the one who is annihilated, since the only bad thing is a bad experience and no one experiences death.

Letter to Menoeceus

Greeting.

Let no one be slow to seek wisdom when he is young nor weary in the search thereof when he is grown old. For no age is too early or too late for the health of the soul. And to say that the season for studying philosophy has not yet come, or that it is past and gone, is like saying that the season for happiness is not yet or that it is now no more. Therefore, both old and young ought to seek wisdom, the former in order that, as age comes over him, he may be young in good things because of the grace of what has been, and the latter in order that, while he is young, he may at the same time be old, because he has no fear of the things which are to come. So we

Epicurus, "Letter to Menoeceus" trans. Robert Drew Hicks. http://classics.mit.edu/Epicurus/menoec.html

must exercise ourselves in the things which bring happiness, since, if that be present, we have everything, and, if that be absent, all our actions are directed toward attaining it.

[. . .]

Accustom yourself to believe that death is nothing to us, for good and evil imply awareness, and death is the privation of all awareness; therefore a right understanding that death is nothing to us makes the mortality of life enjoyable, not by adding to life an unlimited time, but by taking away the yearning after immortality. For life has no terror; for those who thoroughly apprehend that there are no terrors for them in ceasing to live. Foolish, therefore, is the person who says that he fears death, not because it will pain when it comes, but because it pains in the prospect. Whatever causes no annoyance when it is present, causes only a groundless pain in the expectation. Death, therefore, the most awful of evils, is nothing to us, seeing that, when we are, death is not come, and, when death is come, we are not. It is nothing, then, either to the living or to the dead, for with the living it is not and the dead exist no longer. But in the world, at one time people shun death as the greatest of all evils, and at another time choose it as a respite from the evils in life. The wise person does not deprecate life nor does he fear the cessation of life. The thought of life is no offense to him, nor is the cessation of life regarded as an evil. And even as people choose of food not merely and simply the larger portion, but the more pleasant, so the wise seek to enjoy the time which is most pleasant and not merely that which is longest. And he who admonishes the young to live well and the old to make a good end speaks foolishly, not merely because of the desirability of life, but because the same exercise at once teaches to live well and to die well. Much worse is he who says that it were good not to be born, but when once one is born to pass with all speed through the gates of Hades. For if he truly believes this, why does he not depart from life? It were easy for him to do so, if once he were firmly convinced. If he speaks only in mockery, his words are foolishness, for those who hear believe him not.

[. . .]

Exercise yourself in these and kindred precepts day and night, both by yourself and with him who is like to you; then never, either in waking or in dream, will you be disturbed, but will live as a god among people. For people lose all appearance of mortality by living in the midst of immortal blessings.

2

Death

Thomas Nagel

Thomas Nagel (b. 1937) is University Professor, Professor of Law, and Professor of Philosophy at New York University. His writings, including *The View from Nowhere* (1986) and *The Last Word* (1997), cover most of the central questions of philosophy. In this reading, Nagel addresses the topic of death and seeks to reply to Epicurus' claim that death is not a bad thing for the one who dies.

If death is the unequivocal and permanent end of our existence, the question arises whether it is a bad thing to die.

There is conspicuous disagreement about the matter: some people think death is dreadful; others have no objection to death per se, though they hope their own will be neither premature nor painful. Those in the former category tend to think those in the latter are blind to the obvious, while the latter suppose the former to be prey to some sort of confusion. On the one hand it can be said that life is all we have and the loss of it is the greatest loss we can sustain. On the other hand it may be objected that death deprives this supposed loss of its subject, and that if we realize that death is not an unimaginable condition of the persisting person, but a mere blank, we will see that it can have no value whatever, positive or negative.

Since I want to leave aside the question whether we are, or might be, immortal in some form, I shall simply use the word *death* and its cognates in this discussion to mean *permanent* death, unsupplemented by any form of conscious survival. I want to ask whether death is in itself an evil, and how great an evil, and of what kind, it might be. The question should be of interest even to those who believe in some form of immortality, for one's attitude toward immortality must depend in part on one's attitude toward death.

If death is an evil at all, it cannot be because of its positive features, but only because of what it deprives us of. I shall try to deal with the

Thomas Nagel, "Death" from *Mortal Questions* (Cambridge: Cambridge University Press, 1979), pp. 1–10.

difficulties surrounding the natural view that death is an evil because it brings to an end all the goods that life contains. We need not give an account of these goods here, except to observe that some of them, like perception, desire, activity, and thought, are so general as to be constitutive of human life. They are widely regarded as formidable benefits in themselves, despite the fact that they are conditions of misery as well as of happiness, and that a sufficient quantity of more particular evils can perhaps outweigh them. That is what is meant, I think, by the allegation that it is good simply to be alive, even if one is undergoing terrible experiences. The situation is roughly this: There are elements that, if added to one's experience, make life better; there are other elements that, if added to one's experience, make life worse. But what remains when these are set aside is not merely *neutral*: it is emphatically positive. Therefore life is worth living even when the bad elements of experience are plentiful and the good ones too meager to outweigh the bad ones on their own. The additional positive weight is supplied by experience itself, rather than by any of its contents.

I shall not discuss the value that one person's life or death may have for others, or its objective value, but only the value it has for the person who is its subject. That seems to me the primary case, and the case that presents the greatest difficulties. Let me add only two observations. First, the value of life and its contents does not attach to mere organic survival: almost everyone would be indifferent (other things equal) between immediate death and immediate coma followed by death twenty years later without reawakening. And second, like most goods, this can be multiplied by time: more is better than less. The added quantities need not be temporally continuous (though continuity has its social advantages). People are attracted to the possibility of long-term suspended animation or freezing, followed by the resumption of conscious life, because they can regard it from within simply as a *continuation* of their present life. If these techniques are ever perfected, what from outside appeared as a dormant interval of three hundred years could be experienced by the subject as nothing more than a sharp discontinuity in the character of his experiences. I do not deny, of course, that this has its own disadvantages. Family and friends may have died in the meantime; the language may have changed; the comforts of social, geographical, and cultural familiarity would be lacking. Nevertheless, these inconveniences would not obliterate the basic advantage of continued, though discontinuous, existence.

If we turn from what is good about life to what is bad about death, the case is completely different. Essentially, though there may be problems about their specification, what we find desirable in life are certain states, conditions, or types of activity. It is *being* alive, *doing* certain things, having certain experiences, that we consider good. But if death is an evil, it is the *loss of life*, rather than the state of being dead, or nonexistent, or unconscious, that is objectionable.[1] This asymmetry is important. If it is good to be alive, that advantage can be attributed to a person at each point of his life. It is a good of which Bach had more than Schubert, simply because he lived longer. Death, however, is not an evil of which Shakespeare has so far received a larger portion than Proust. If death is a disadvantage, it is not easy to say when a man suffers it.

There are two other indications that we do not object to death merely because it involves long periods of nonexistence. First, as has been mentioned, most of us would not regard the *temporary* suspension of life, even for substantial intervals, as in itself a misfortune. If it ever happens that people can be frozen without reduction of the conscious lifespan, it will be inappropriate to pity those who are temporarily out of circulation. Second, none of us existed before we were born (or conceived), but few regard that as a misfortune. I shall have more to say about this later.

The point that death is not regarded as an unfortunate *state* enables us to refute a curious but very common suggestion about the origin of the fear of death. It is often said that those who object to death have made the mistake of trying to imagine what it is like to *be* dead. It is alleged that the failure to realize that this task is logically impossible (for the banal reason that there is nothing to imagine) leads to the conviction that death is a mysterious and therefore terrifying prospective *state*. But this diagnosis is evidently false, for it is just as impossible to imagine being totally unconscious as to imagine being dead (though it is easy enough to imagine oneself, from the outside, in either of those conditions). Yet people who are averse to death are not usually averse to unconsciousness (so long as it does not entail a substantial cut in the total duration of waking life).

If we are to make sense of the view that to die is bad, it must be on the grounds that life is a good and death is the corresponding deprivation or loss, bad not because of any positive features but because of the desirability of what it removes. We must now turn to the serious difficulties that this hypothesis raises, difficulties about loss and privation in general, and about death in particular.

Essentially, there are three types of problems. First, doubt may be raised whether *anything* can be bad for a man without being positively unpleasant to him: specifically, it may be doubted that there are any evils that consist merely in the deprivation or absence of possible goods, and that do not depend on someone's *minding* that deprivation. Second, there are special difficulties, in the case of death, about how the supposed misfortune is to be assigned to a subject at all. There is doubt both as to *who* its subject is and as to *when* he undergoes it. So long as a person exists, he has not yet died, and once he has died, he no longer exists; so there seems to be no time when death, if it is a misfortune, can be ascribed to its unfortunate subject. The third type of difficulty concerns the asymmetry, mentioned above, between our attitudes to posthumous and prenatal nonexistence. How can the former be bad if the latter is not?

It should be recognized that, if these are valid objections to counting death as an evil, they will apply to many other supposed evils as well. The first type of objection is expressed in general form by the common remark that what you don't know can't hurt you. It means that even if a man is betrayed by his friends, ridiculed behind his back, and despised by people who treat him politely to his face, none of it can be counted as a misfortune for him so long as he does not suffer as a result. It means that a man is not injured if his wishes are ignored by the executor of his will, or if, after his death, the belief becomes current that all the literary works on which his fame rests were really written by his brother, who died in Mexico at the age of 28. It seems to me worth asking what assumptions about good and evil lead to these drastic restrictions.

All the questions have something to do with time. There certainly are goods and evils of a simple kind (including some pleasures and pains) that a person possesses at a given time simply in virtue of his condition at that time. But this is not true of all the things we regard as good or bad for a man. Often we need to know his history to tell whether something is a misfortune or not; this applies to ills like deterioration, deprivation, and damage. Sometimes his experiential *state* is relatively unimportant – as in the case of a man who wastes his life in the cheerful pursuit of a method of communicating with asparagus plants. Someone who holds that all goods and evils must be temporally assignable states of the person may of course try to bring difficult cases into line by pointing to the pleasure or pain that more complicated goods and evils cause. Loss, betrayal, deception, and ridicule are on this view bad because people suffer when they learn of them. But it should be asked how our ideas of human value would have to be constituted to accommodate these cases directly instead. One advantage of such an account might be that it would enable us to explain *why* the discovery of these misfortunes causes suffering – in a way that makes it reasonable. For the natural view is that the discovery of betrayal makes us unhappy because it is bad to be betrayed – not that betrayal is bad because its discovery makes us unhappy.

It therefore seems to me worth exploring the position that most good and ill fortune has as its subject a person identified by his history and his possibilities, rather than merely by his categorical state of the moment – and that while this subject can be exactly located in a sequence of places and times, the same is not necessarily true of the goods and ills that befall him.[2]

These ideas can be illustrated by an example of deprivation whose severity approaches that of death. Suppose an intelligent person receives a brain injury that reduces him to the mental condition of a contented infant, and that such desires as remain to him can be satisfied by a custodian, so that he is free from care. Such a development would be widely regarded as a severe misfortune, not only for his friends and relations, or for society, but also, and primarily, for the person himself. This does not mean that a contented infant is unfortunate. The intelligent adult who has been *reduced* to this condition is the subject of the misfortune. He is the one we pity, though of course he does not mind his condition – there is some doubt, in fact, whether he can be said to exist any longer.

The view that such a man has suffered a misfortune is open to the same objections that have been raised in regard to death. He does not mind his condition. It is in fact the same condition he was in at the age of three months, except that he is bigger. If we did not pity him then, why pity him now; in any case, who is there to pity? The intelligent adult has disappeared, and for a creature like the one before us, happiness consists in a full stomach and a dry diaper.

If these objections are invalid, it must be because they rest on a mistaken assumption about the temporal relation between the subject of a misfortune and the circumstances that constitute it. If, instead of concentrating exclusively on the oversized baby before us, we consider the person he was, and the person he *could* be now, then his reduction to this state and the cancellation of his natural adult development constitute a perfectly intelligible catastrophe.

This case should convince us that it is arbitrary to restrict the goods and evils that can befall a man to nonrelational properties ascribable to him at particular times. As it stands, that restriction excludes not only such cases of gross degeneration but also a good deal of what is important about success and failure, and other features of a life that have the character of processes. I believe we can go further, however. There are goods and evils that are irreducibly relational; they are features of the relations between a person, with spatial and temporal boundaries of the usual sort, and circumstances that may not coincide with him either in space or in time. A man's life includes much that does not take place within the boundaries of his body and his mind, and what happens to him can include much that does not take place within the boundaries of his life. These boundaries are commonly crossed by the misfortunes of being deceived, or despised, or betrayed. (If this is correct, there is a simple account of what is wrong with breaking a deathbed promise. It is an injury to the dead man. For certain purposes it is possible to regard time as just another type of distance.) The case of mental degeneration shows us an evil that depends on a contrast between the reality and the possible alternatives. A man is the subject of good and evil as much because he has hopes that may or may not be fulfilled, or possibilities that may or may not be realized, as because of his capacity to suffer and enjoy. If death is an evil, it must be accounted for in these terms, and the impossibility of locating it within life should not trouble us.

When a man dies we are left with his corpse, and while a corpse can suffer the kind of mishap that may occur to an article of furniture, it is not a suitable object for pity. The man, however, is. He has lost his life, and if he had not died, he would have continued to live it, and to possess whatever good there is in living. If we apply to death the account suggested for the case of dementia, we shall say that although the spatial and temporal locations of the individual who suffered the loss are clear enough, the misfortune itself cannot be so easily located. One must be content just to state that his life is over and there will never be any more of it. That *fact*, rather than his past or present condition, constitutes his misfortune, if it is one. Nevertheless if there is a loss, someone must suffer it, and *he* must have existence and specific spatial and temporal location even if the loss itself does not. The fact that Beethoven had no children may have been a cause of regret to him, or a sad thing for the world, but it cannot be described as a misfortune for the children that he never had. All of us, I believe, are fortunate to have been born. But unless good and ill can be assigned to an embryo, or even to an unconnected pair of gametes, it cannot be said that not to be born is a misfortune. (That is a factor to be considered in deciding whether abortion and contraception are akin to murder.)

This approach also provides a solution to the problem of temporal asymmetry, pointed but by Lucretius. He observed that no one finds it disturbing to contemplate the eternity preceding his own birth, and he took this to show that it must be irrational to fear death, since death is simply the mirror image of the prior abyss. That is not true, however, and the difference between the two explains why it is reasonable to regard them differently. It is true that both the time before a man's birth and the time after his death are times when he does not exist. But the time after his death is time of which his death deprives him. It is time in which, had he not died then, he would be alive. Therefore any death entails the loss of *some* life that its victim would have led had he not died at that or any earlier point. We know perfectly well what it would be for him to have had it instead of losing it, and there is no difficulty in identifying the loser.

But we cannot say that the time prior to a man's birth is time in which he would have lived had he been born not then but earlier. For aside from the brief margin permitted by premature labor, he *could* not have been born earlier: anyone born substantially earlier than he was would have been someone else. Therefore the time prior to his birth is not time in which his subsequent birth prevents him from living. His birth, when it occurs, does not entail the loss to him of any life whatever.

The direction of time is crucial in assigning possibilities to people or other individuals. Distinct possible lives of a single person can diverge from a common beginning, but they cannot converge to a common conclusion from diverse beginnings. (The latter would represent not a set of different possible lives of one individual, but a set of distinct possible individuals, whose lives have identical conclusions.) Given an identifiable individual, countless possibilities for his continued existence are imaginable, and we can clearly conceive of what it would be for him to go on existing indefinitely. However inevitable it is that this will not come about, its possibility is still that of the continuation of a good for him, if life is the good we take it to be.[3]

We are left, therefore, with the questions whether the nonrealization of this possibility is in every case a misfortune, or whether it depends on what can naturally be hoped for. This seems to me the most serious difficulty with the view that death is always an evil. Even if we can dispose of the objections against admitting misfortune that is not experienced, or cannot be assigned to a definite time in the person's life, we still have to set some limits on *how* possible a possibility must be for its nonrealization to be a misfortune (or good fortune, should the possibility be a bad one). The death of Keats at 24 is generally regarded as tragic; that of Tolstoy at 82 is not. Although they will both be dead forever, Keats's death deprived him of many years of life that were allowed to Tolstoy; so in a clear sense Keats's loss was greater (though not in the sense standardly employed in mathematical comparison between infinite quantities). However, this does not prove that Tolstoy's loss was insignificant. Perhaps we record an objection only to evils that are gratuitously added to the inevitable; the fact that it is worse to die at 24 than at 82 does not imply that it is not a terrible thing to die at 82, or even at 806. The question is whether we can regard as a misfortune any limitation, like mortality, that is normal to the species. Blindness or near-blindness is not a misfortune for a mole, nor would it be for a man, if that were the natural condition of the human race.

The trouble is that life familiarizes us with the goods of which death deprives us. We are already able to appreciate them, as a mole is not able to appreciate vision. If we put aside doubts about their status as goods and grant that their quantity is in part a function of their duration, the question remains whether death, no matter when it occurs, can be said to deprive its victim of what is in the relevant sense a possible continuation of life.

The situation is an ambiguous one. Observed from without, human beings obviously have a natural lifespan and cannot live much longer than a hundred years. A man's sense of his own experience, on the other hand, does not embody this idea of a natural limit. His existence defines for him an essentially open-ended possible future, containing the usual mixture of goods and evils that he has found so tolerable in the past. Having been gratuitously introduced to the world by a collection of natural, historical, and social accidents, he finds himself the subject of a *life*, with an indeterminate and not essentially limited future. Viewed in this way, death, no matter how inevitable, is an abrupt cancellation of indefinitely extensive possible goods. Normality seems to have nothing to do with it, for the fact that we will all inevitably die in a few score years cannot by itself imply that it would not be good to live longer. Suppose that we were all inevitably going to die in *agony* – physical agony lasting six months. Would inevitability make *that* prospect any less unpleasant? And why should it be different for a deprivation? If the normal lifespan were a thousand years, death at 80 would be a tragedy. As things are, it may just be a more widespread tragedy. If there is no limit to the amount of life that it would be good to have, then it may be that a bad end is in store for us all.

Notes

1 It is sometimes suggested that what we really mind is the process of *dying*. But I should not really object to dying if it were not followed by death.

2 It is certainly not true in general of the things that can be said of him. For example, Abraham Lincoln was taller than Louis XIV. But when?

3 I confess to being troubled by the above argument, on the grounds that it is too sophisticated to explain the simple difference between our attitudes to prenatal and posthumous nonexistence. For this reason I suspect that something essential is omitted from the account of the badness of death by an analysis that treats it as a deprivation of possibilities. My suspicion is supported by the following suggestion of Robert Nozick. We could imagine discovering that people developed from individual spores that had existed indefinitely far in advance of their birth. In this fantasy, birth never occurs naturally more than a hundred years before the permanent end of the spore's existence. But then we discover a way to trigger the premature hatching of these spores, and people are born who have thousands of years of active life before them. Given such a situation, it would be possible to imagine *oneself* having come into existence thousands of years previously. If we put aside the question whether this would really be the same person, even given the identity of the spore, then the consequence appears to be that a person's birth at a given time *could* deprive him of many earlier years of possible life. Now while it would be cause for regret that one had been deprived of all those possible years of life by being born too late, the feeling would differ from that which many people have about death. I conclude that something about the future *prospect* of permanent nothingness is not captured by the analysis in terms of denied possibilities. If so, then Lucretius's argument still awaits an answer. I suspect that it requires a general treatment of the difference between past and future in our attitudes toward our own lives. Our attitudes toward past and future pain are very different, for example. Derek Parfit's writings on this topic have revealed its difficulty to me.

B

Life after Death

1

The Separation of the Soul from the Body

Plato

The following reading is from Plato's *Phaedo*, a dialogue set against the background of Socrates' last day in prison before his death. In this selection Socrates and Simmias discuss the nature of death. According to Socrates, the body and its desires prevent the soul from attaining pure knowledge during life. At death the soul is freed from the body, a state that is not to be feared, says Socrates, since it is what all true philosophers strive for.

All these considerations, said Socrates, must surely prompt serious philosophers to review the position in some such way as this. It looks as though this were a bypath leading to the right track. So long as we keep to the body and our soul is contaminated with this imperfection, there is no chance of our ever attaining satisfactorily to our object, which we assert to be truth. In the first place, the body provides us with innumerable distractions in the pursuit of our necessary sustenance, and any diseases which attack us hinder our quest for reality. Besides, the body fills us with loves and desires and fears and all sorts of fancies and a great deal of nonsense, with the result that we literally never get an opportunity to think at all about anything. Wars and revolutions and battles are due simply and solely to the body and its desires. All wars are undertaken for the acquisition of wealth, and the reason why we have to acquire wealth is the body, because we are slaves in its service. That is why, on all these accounts, we have so little time for philosophy. Worst of all, if we do obtain any leisure from the body's claims and turn to some line of inquiry, the body intrudes once more into our investigations, interrupting, disturbing, distracting, and preventing us from getting a glimpse of the truth. We are in fact convinced that if we are ever to have pure knowledge of anything, we must get rid of the body and

Plato, "Phaedo" trans. Hugh Tredennick from *The Collected Dialogues of Plato: Including the Letters*, ed. Edith Hamilton and Huntington Cairns (Princeton, NJ: Princeton University Press, 1961), pp. 49–50.

contemplate things by themselves with the soul by itself. It seems, to judge from the argument, that the wisdom which we desire and upon which we profess to have set our hearts will be attainable only when we are dead, and not in our lifetime. If no pure knowledge is possible in the company of the body, then either it is totally impossible to acquire knowledge, or it is only possible after death, because it is only then that the soul will be separate and independent of the body. It seems that so long as we are alive, we shall continue closest to knowledge if we avoid as much as we can all contact and association with the body, except when they are absolutely necessary, and instead of allowing ourselves to become infected with its nature, purify ourselves from it until God himself gives us deliverance. In this way, by keeping ourselves uncontaminated by the follies of the body, we shall probably reach the company of others like ourselves and gain direct knowledge of all that is pure and uncontaminated – that is, presumably, of truth. For one who is not pure himself to attain to the realm of purity would no doubt be a breach of universal justice.

Something to this effect, Simmias, is what I imagine all real lovers of learning must think themselves and say to one another. Don't you agree with me?

Most emphatically, Socrates.

Very well, then, said Socrates, if this is true, there is good reason for anyone who reaches the end of this journey which lies before me to hope that there, if anywhere, he will attain the object to which all our efforts have been directed during my past life. So this journey which is now ordained for me carries a happy prospect for any other man also who believes that his mind has been prepared by purification.

It does indeed, said Simmias.

And purification, as we saw some time ago in our discussion, consists in separating the soul as much as possible from the body, and accustoming it to withdraw from all contact with the body and concentrate itself by itself, and to have its dwelling, so far as it can, both now and in the future, alone by itself, freed from the shackles of the body. Does not that follow?

Yes, it does, said Simmias.

Is not what we call death a freeing and separation of soul from body?

Certainly, he said.

And the desire to free the soul is found chiefly, or rather only, in the true philosopher. In fact the philosopher's occupation consists precisely in the freeing and separation of soul from body. Isn't that so?

Apparently.

Well then, as I said at the beginning, if a man has trained himself throughout his life to live in a state as close as possible to death, would it not be ridiculous for him to be distressed when death comes to him?

It would, of course.

Then it is a fact, Simmias, that true philosophers make dying their profession, and that to them of all men death is least alarming. Look at it in this way. If they are thoroughly dissatisfied with the body, and long to have their souls independent of it, when this happens would it not be entirely unreasonable to be frightened and distressed? Would they not naturally be glad to set out for the place where there is a prospect of attaining the object of their lifelong desire – which is wisdom – and of escaping from an unwelcome association? Surely there are many who have chosen of their own free will to follow dead lovers and wives and sons to the next world, in the hope of seeing and meeting there the persons whom they loved. If this is so, will a true lover of wisdom who has firmly grasped this same conviction – that he will never attain to wisdom worthy of the name elsewhere than in the next world – will he be grieved at dying? Will he not be glad to make that journey? We must suppose so, my dear boy, that is, if he is a real philosopher, because then he will be of the firm belief that he will never find wisdom in all its purity in any other place. If this is so, would it not be quite unreasonable, as I said just now, for such a man to be afraid of death?

2

The Future Life

Averroes (Ibn Rushd)

Ibn Rushd (1126–98), better known in the Western world as Averroes, was the most important of the Spanish Islamic philosophers. He held positions on certain tenets of the Muslim faith that were trenchantly critiqued by al-Ghazāli in *The Incoherence of the Philosophers*. Nevertheless, the works of Averroes and other Islamic philosophers provided an important link between the philosophy of ancient Greece and the medieval Christian philosophy in the Western world. In the following reading, Averroes discusses three different conceptions of the afterlife popular in Islamic thought: (1) that it is just like existence in this life, except that it is unending; (2) that it is a purely spiritual existence; and (3) that it is a corporeal existence, but one that differs in kind from our present corporeal existence.

All religions, as we have said, agree on the fact that souls experience states of happiness or misery after death, but they disagree in the manner of symbolizing these states and explaining their existence to men.[1] And it seems that the [kind of] symbolization which is found in this religion of ours is the most perfect means of explanation to the majority of men, and provides the greatest stimulus to their souls to [pursue the goals of] the life beyond; and the primary concern of religions is with the majority. Spiritual symbolization, on the other hand, seems to provide less stimulus to the souls of the masses towards [the goals of] the life beyond, and the masses have less desire and fear of it than they do of corporeal symbolization. Therefore it seems that corporeal symbolization provides a stronger stimulus to [the goals of] the life beyond than spiritual; the spiritual [kind] is more acceptable to the class of debating theologians, but they are the minority.

Averroes (Ibn Rushd), "The Future Life" from *Averroes on the Harmony of Religion and Philosophy*, trans. George F. Hourani (London: Luzac, 1961), pp. 76–8.

[. . .]

For this reason we find the people of Islam divided into three sects with regard to the understanding of the symbolization which is used in [the texts of] our religion referring to the states of the future life. One sect holds that that existence is identical with this existence here with respect to bliss and pleasure, i.e. they hold that it is of the same sort and that the two existences differ only in respect of permanence and limit of duration, i.e. the former is permanent and the latter of limited duration. Another group holds that there is a difference in the kind of existence. This [group] is divided into two subdivisions. One [sub-] group holds that the existence symbolized by these sensible images is spiritual, and that it has been symbolized thus only for the purpose of exposition; these people are supported by many well-known arguments from Scripture, but there would be no point in enumerating them. Another [sub-] group thinks that it is corporeal, but believes that that corporeality existing in the life beyond differs from the corporeality of this life in that the latter is perishable while the former is immortal. They too are supported by arguments from Scripture, and it seems that Ibn 'Abbās was one of those who held this opinion, for he is reported to have said, 'There is nothing in this lower world like the next world except the names.'

It seems that this opinion is more suitable for the élite; for the admissibility of this opinion is founded on facts which are not discussed in front of everyone. One is that the soul is immortal. The second is that the return of the soul to other bodies does not involve the same absurdity as ⟨its⟩ return ⟨to⟩ those same [earthly] bodies. This is because it is apparent that the materials of the bodies that exist here are successively transferred from one body to another: i.e. one and the same material exists in many persons at different times. Bodies like these cannot possibly all exist actually [at the same time], because their material is one: for instance, a man dies, his body is transformed into dust, that dust is transformed into a plant, another man feeds on that plant; then semen proceeds from him, from which another man is born. But if other bodies are supposed, this state of affairs does not follow as a consequence.

The truth in this question is that every man's duty is [to believe] whatever his study of it leads him to [conclude], provided that it is not such a study as would cause him to reject the principle altogether, by denying the existence [of the future life] altogether; for this manner of belief obliges us to call its holder an unbeliever, because the existence of this [future] state for man is made known to people through their Scriptures and their intellects.

[. . .]

The whole of this [argument] is founded on the immortality of the soul.[2] If it is asked 'Does Scripture contain an indication of the immortality of the soul or [at least] a hint of it?', we reply: This is found in the precious Book in the words of the Exalted, 'God receives the souls at the time of their death, and those which have not died He receives in their sleep', [and so on to the end of] the verse. The significant aspect of this verse is that in it He has equated sleep and death with respect to the annihilation of the soul's activity. Thus if the cessation of the soul's activity in death were due to the soul's dissolution, not to a change in the soul's organ, the cessation of its activity in sleep [too] would have to be due to the dissolution of its essential being; but if that were the case, it would not return on waking to its normal condition. So since it does return to it, we know that this cessation does not happen to it through anything which attaches to it in its substantial nature, but is only something which attaches to it owing to a cessation of its organ; and [we know] that it does not follow that if the organ ceases the soul must cease. Death *is* a cessation; it must therefore be of the organ, as is the case in sleep. As the Philosopher says, 'If the old man were to find an eye like the young man's eye, he would see as the young man sees'.[3]

This is as much as we see fit to affirm in our investigation of the beliefs of this religion of ours, the religion of Islam.

Notes

1 Summary: For the doctrine of this section, the superiority of corporeal symbols for the masses,

cf. *Tahāfut*, (M. J. Müller, *Philosophie and Theologie von Averroes* (Munich, 1859)) p. 585. Aristotle, *Metaphysics*, *a*, 3, 995a 4–6: "The force of habit is shown by the laws, in which the legendary and childish elements prevail over our knowledge about them, owing to habit"; and Ibn Rushd's comments, *Tafsīr*, (Müller, *Philosophie*), pp. 42–3: The laws have been laid down for imparting virtue to the people, not for acquainting them with the truth, so it has fashioned parables for them. [. . .]

2 Summary. The argument of the following section is stated more simply in *Tahāfut* (Müller, *Philosophie*), p. 557: "And the comparison of death with sleep in this question is an evident proof that the soul survives, since the activity of the soul ceases in sleep through the inactivity of its organ, but the existence of the soul does not cease, and therefore it is necessary that its condition in death should be like its condition in sleep, for the parts follow the same rule" (Eng. tr. S. Van den Bergh). [. . .]

3 "As the Philosopher . . . 'sees' ": Aristotle, *De animā*, i, 4, 408b 21. I.e. the condition of the organ makes all the difference to the function, while the substance (soul) remains unchanged.

3

The Possibility of Immortality

René Descartes

A prolific scientist, mathematician, and philosopher, René Descartes (1596–1650) is often credited as the father of modern philosophy. Prior to publishing his most important work, *Meditations on First Philosophy*, Descartes sent copies to other scholars seeking their comments and criticisms. Their objections, along with Descartes's answers, were appended to the text under the title "Objections and Replies." The selections below begin with Descartes's famous "Meditation VI" argument that his soul or mind is a substance distinct from his material body, and as such could exist without his body. That is followed by two brief excerpts from the "Objections and Replies" – first, Mersenne's objection that Descartes never demonstrates that the soul is immortal, and second, Descartes's explanation of why he does not attempt to prove this.

And first of all, because I know that all things which I apprehend clearly and distinctly can be created by God as I apprehend them, it suffices that I am able to apprehend one thing apart from another clearly and distinctly in order to be certain that the one is different from the other, since they may be made to exist in separation at least by the omnipotence of God; and it does not signify by what power this separation is made in order to compel me to judge them to be different: and, therefore, just because I know certainly that I exist, and that meanwhile I do not remark that any other thing necessarily pertains to my nature or essence, excepting that I am a thinking thing, I rightly conclude that my essence consists solely in the fact that I am a thinking thing [or a substance whose whole essence or nature is to think]. And although possibly (or rather certainly, as I shall say in a moment) I possess a body with which I am very intimately conjoined, yet

René Descartes, "The Possibility of Immortality" from *The Philosophical Works of Descartes*, trans. Elizabeth S. Haldane and G. R. T. Ross, vol. 1 (Cambridge: Cambridge University Press, 1968), p. 190; vol. 2 (Cambridge: Cambridge University Press, 1967), pp. 29, 47.

because, on the one side, I have a clear and distinct idea of myself inasmuch as I am only a thinking and unextended thing, and as, on the other, I possess a distinct idea of body, inasmuch as it is only an extended and unthinking thing, it is certain that this I [that is to say, my soul by which I am what I am], is entirely and absolutely distinct from my body, and can exist without it.

[. . .]

Mersenne's Objection

Seventhly, *you say not one word [in your Meditations] about the immortality of the human soul, which nevertheless you should above all things have proved and demonstrated as against those men – themselves unworthy of immortality – who completely deny it and perchance have an enmity against it. But over and above this you do not seem to have sufficiently proved the distinctness of the soul from every species of body, as we have already said in our first criticism; to which we now add that it does not seem to follow from the distinction you draw between it and the body that it is incorruptible or immortal. What if its nature be limited by the duration of the life of the body, and God has granted it only such a supply of force and has so measured out its existence that, in the cessation of the corporeal life, it must come to an end?*

[. . .]

Seventhly, in the synopsis of my Meditations[1] I stated the reason why I have said nothing about the immortality of the soul. That I have sufficiently proved its distinctness from any body, I have shown above. But I admit that I cannot refute your further contention, viz. that *the immortality of the soul does not follow from its distinctness from the body, because that does not prevent its being said that God in creating it has given the soul a nature such that its period of existence must terminate simultaneously with that of the corporeal life.*[2] For I do not presume so far as to attempt to settle by the power of human reason any of the questions that depend upon the free-will of God. Natural knowledge shows that the mind is different from the body, and that it is likewise a substance; but that the human body, in so far as it differs from other bodies, is constituted entirely by the configuration of its parts and other similar accidents, and finally that the death of the body depends wholly on some division or change of figure. But we know no argument or example such as to convince us that the death or the annihilation of a substance such as the mind is, should follow from so light a cause as is a change in figure, which is no more than a mode, and indeed not a mode of mind, but of body that is really distinct from mind. Nor indeed is there any argument or example calculated to convince us that any substance can perish. But this is sufficient to let us conclude that the mind, so far as it can be known by aid of a natural philosophy, is immortal.

But if the question, which asks whether human souls cease to exist at the same time as the bodies which God has united to them are destroyed, is one affecting the Divine power, it is for God alone to reply. And since He has revealed to us that this will not happen, there should be not even the slightest doubt remaining.

Notes

1 Cf. *The Philosophical Works of Descartes*, Vol. I p. 141, ll. 9 sqq.

2 Cf. *The Philosophical Works of Descartes*, Obj. II. p. 29.

4

Personal Identity and Consciousness

John Locke

John Locke (1632–1704) was a British philosopher and medical doctor who, as a result of his friendship with the Earl of Shaftesbury, also had an active public political life. His vast treatise, *An Essay Concerning Human Understanding*, is one of the premier works of empiricism and, indeed, of the modern period as a whole. In the following selection from this work, Locke argues that the continued identity of a person depends not upon the sameness of any material or immaterial substance (i.e. body or soul) but upon sameness of consciousness. Since Locke holds that the same consciousness can be transferred from one substance to another, his view implies that personal immortality does not require the continued existence of any particular substance.

Book II

Chapter XXVII

[. . .]

8. It is not [. . .] unity of substance that comprehends all sorts of identity, or will determine it in every case; but to conceive and judge of it aright, we must consider what idea the word it is applied to stands for: it being one thing to be the same *substance*, another the same *man*, and a third the same *person*, if *person, man*, and *substance*, are three names standing for three different ideas; – for such as is the idea belonging to that name, such must be the identity; which, if it had been a little more carefully attended to, would possibly have prevented a great deal of that confusion which often occurs about this matter, with no small seeming difficulties, especially concerning *personal* identity, which therefore we shall in the next place a little consider.

9. An animal is a living organized body; and consequently the same animal, as we have

John Locke, *An Essay Concerning Human Understanding*, ed. Alexander Campbell Fraser, vol. 1 (New York: Dover, 1959), pp. 445–6, 448–52, 454–64.

observed, is the same continued *life* communicated to different particles of matter, as they happen successively to be united to that organized living body. And whatever is talked of other definitions, ingenious observation puts it past doubt, that the idea in our minds, of which the sound man in our mouths is the sign, is nothing else but of an animal of such a certain form. Since I think I may be confident, that, whoever should see a creature of his own shape or make, though it had no more reason all its life than a cat or a parrot, would call him still a *man*; or whoever should hear a cat or a parrot discourse, reason, and philosophize, would call or think it nothing but a *cat* or a *parrot*; and say, the one was a dull irrational man, and the other a very intelligent rational parrot.

[...]

For I presume it is not the idea of a thinking or rational being alone that makes the *idea of a man* in most people's sense: but of a body, so and so shaped, joined to it; and if that be the idea of a man, the same successive body not shifted all at once, must, as well as the same immaterial spirit, go to the making of the same man.

This being premised, to find wherein personal identity consists, we must consider what *person* stands for; – which, I think, is a thinking intelligent being, that has reason and reflection, and can consider itself as itself, the same thinking thing, in different times and places; which it does only by that consciousness which is inseparable from thinking, and, as it seems to me, essential to it: it being impossible for any one to perceive without *perceiving* that he does perceive. When we see, hear, smell, taste, feel, meditate, or will anything, we know that we do so. Thus it is always as to our present sensations and perceptions: and by this every one is to himself that which he calls *self*: – it not being considered, in this case, whether the same self be continued in the same or divers substances. For, since consciousness always accompanies thinking, and it is that which makes every one to be what he calls self, and thereby distinguishes himself from all other thinking things, in this alone consists personal identity, i.e. the sameness of a rational being: and as far as this consciousness can be extended backwards to any past action or thought, so far reaches the identity of that person; it is the same self now it was then; and it is by the same self with this present one that now reflects on it, that that action was done.

10. But it is further inquired, whether it be the same identical substance. This few would think they had reason to doubt of, if these perceptions, with their consciousness, always remained present in the mind, whereby the same thinking thing would be always consciously present, and, as would be thought, evidently the same to itself. But that which seems to make the difficulty is this, that this consciousness being interrupted always by forgetfulness, there being no moment of our lives wherein we have the whole train of all our past actions before our eyes in one view, but even the best memories losing the sight of one part whilst they are viewing another; and we sometimes, and that the greatest part of our lives, not reflecting on our past selves, being intent on our present thoughts, and in sound sleep having no thoughts at all, or at least none with that consciousness which remarks our waking thoughts, – I say, in all these cases, our consciousness being interrupted, and we losing the sight of our past selves, doubts are raised whether we are the same thinking thing, i.e. the same *substance* or no. Which, however reasonable or unreasonable, concerns not *personal* identity at all. The question being what makes the same person; and not whether it be the same identical substance, which always thinks in the same person, which, in this case, matters not at all: different substances, by the same consciousness (where they do partake in it) being united into one person, as well as different bodies by the same life are united into one animal, whose identity is preserved in that change of substances by the unity of one continued life. For, it being the same consciousness that makes a man be himself to himself, personal identity depends on that only, whether it be annexed solely to one individual substance, or can be continued in a succession of several substances. For as far as any intelligent being *can* repeat the idea of any past action with the same consciousness it had of it at first, and with the same consciousness it has of any present action; so far it is the same personal self. For it is by the consciousness it has of its present thoughts and actions, that it is *self to itself* now, and so will be the same self, as far as

the same consciousness can extend to actions past or to come; and would be by distance of time, or change of substance, no more two persons, than a man be two men by wearing other clothes to-day than he did yesterday, with a long or a short sleep between: the same consciousness uniting those distant actions into the same person, whatever substances contributed to their production.

11. That this is so, we have some kind of evidence in our very bodies, all whose particles, whilst vitally united to this same thinking conscious self, so that *we feel* when they are touched, and are affected by, and conscious of good or harm that happens to them, are a part of ourselves; i.e. of our thinking conscious self. Thus, the limbs of his body are to every one a part of himself; he sympathizes and is concerned for them. Cut off a hand, and thereby separate it from that consciousness he had of its heat, cold, and other affections, and it is then no longer a part of that which is himself, any more than the remotest part of matter. Thus, we see the *substance* whereof personal self consisted at one time may be varied at another, without the change of personal identity; there being no question about the same person, though the limbs which but now were a part of it, be cut off.

12. But the question is, Whether if the same substance which thinks be changed, it can be the same person; or, remaining the same, it can be different persons?

[. . .]

[I]t must be allowed, that, if the same consciousness (which, as has been shown, is quite a different thing from the same numerical figure or motion in body) can be transferred from one thinking substance to another, it will be possible that two thinking substances may make but one person. For the same consciousness being preserved, whether in the same or different substances, the personal identity is preserved.

14. As to the second part of the question, Whether the same immaterial substance remaining, there may be two distinct persons; which question seems to me to be built on this, – Whether the same immaterial being, being conscious of the action of its past duration, may be wholly stripped of all the consciousness of its past existence, and lose it beyond the power of ever retrieving it again: and so as it were beginning a new account from a new period, have a consciousness that *cannot* reach beyond this new state. All those who hold pre-existence are evidently of this mind; since they allow the soul to have no remaining consciousness of what it did in that pre-existent state, either wholly separate from body, or informing any other body; and if they should not, it is plain experience would be against them. So that 'personal identity, reaching no further than consciousness reaches, a pre-existent spirit not having continued so many ages in a state of silence, must needs make different persons. Suppose a Christian Platonist or a Pythagorean should, upon God's having ended all his works of creation the seventh day, think his soul hath existed ever since; and should imagine it has revolved in several human bodies; as I once met with one, who was persuaded his had been the *soul* of Socrates (how reasonably I will not dispute; this I know, that in the post he filled, which was no inconsiderable one, he passed for a very rational man, and the press has shown that he wanted not parts or learning); – would any one say, that he, being not conscious of any of Socrates's actions or thoughts, could be the same *person* with Socrates? Let any one reflect upon himself, and conclude that he has in himself an immaterial spirit, which is that which thinks in him, and, in the constant change of his body keeps him the same: and is that which he calls *himself*: let him also suppose it to be the same soul that was in Nestor or Thersites, at the siege of Troy, (for souls being, as far as we know anything of them, in their nature indifferent to any parcel of matter, the supposition has no apparent absurdity in it), which it may have been, as well as it is now the soul of any other man: but he now having no consciousness of any of the actions either of Nestor or Thersites, does or can he conceive himself the same person with either of them? Can he be concerned in either of their actions? attribute them to himself, or think them his own, more than the actions of any other men that ever existed? So that this consciousness, not reaching to any of the actions of either of those men, he is no more one *self* with either of them than if the soul or immaterial spirit that now informs him had been created, and began to exist, when it began to inform his present body; though it were never so true, that the same *spirit*

that informed Nestor's or Thersites' body were numerically the same that now informs his. For this would no more make him the same person with Nestor, than if some of the particles of matter that were once a part of Nestor were now a part of this man; the same immaterial substance, without the same consciousness, no more making the same person, by being united to any body, than the same particle of matter, without consciousness, united to any body, makes the same person. But let him once find himself conscious of any of the actions of Nestor, he then finds himself the same person with Nestor.

15. And thus may we be able, without any difficulty, to conceive the same person at the resurrection, though in a body not exactly in make or parts the same which he had here, – the same consciousness going along with the soul that inhabits it. But yet the soul alone, in the change of bodies, would scarce to any one but to him that makes the soul the man, be enough to make the same man. For should the soul of a prince, carrying with it the consciousness of the prince's past life, enter and inform the body of a cobbler, as soon as deserted by his own soul, every one sees he would be the same *person* with the prince, accountable only for the prince's actions: but who would say it was the same *man*? The body too goes to the making the man, and would, I guess, to everybody determine the man in this case, wherein the soul, with all its princely thoughts about it, would not make another man: but he would be the same cobbler to every one besides himself. I know that, in the ordinary way of speaking, the same person, and the same man, stand for one and the same thing. And indeed every one will always have a liberty to speak as he pleases, and to apply what articulate sounds to what ideas he thinks fit, and change them as often as he pleases. But yet, when we will inquire what makes the same *spirit*, *man*, or *person*, we must fix the ideas of spirit, man, or person in our minds; and having resolved with ourselves what we mean by them, it will not be hard to determine, in either of them, or the like, when it is the same, and when not.

16. But though the same immaterial substance or soul does not alone, wherever it be, and in whatsoever state, make the same *man*; yet it is plain, consciousness, as far as ever it can be extended – should it be to ages past – unites existences and actions very remote in time into the same *person*, as well as it does the existences and actions of the immediately preceding moment: so that whatever has the consciousness of present and past actions, is the same person to whom they both belong. Had I the same consciousness that I saw the ark and Noah's flood, as that I saw an overflowing of the Thames last winter, or as that I write now, I could no more doubt that I who write this now, that saw the Thames overflowed last winter, and that viewed the flood at the general deluge, was the same *self*, – place that self in what *substance* you please – than that I who write this am the same *myself* now whilst I write (whether I consist of all the same substance, material or immaterial, or no) that I was yesterday. For as to this point of being the same self, it matters not whether this present self be made up of the same or other substances – I being as much concerned, and as justly accountable for any action that was done a thousand years since, appropriated to me now by this self-consciousness, as I am for what I did the last moment.

17. *Self* is that conscious thinking thing, – whatever substance made up of, (whether spiritual or material, simple or compounded, it matters not) – which is sensible or conscious of pleasure and pain, capable of happiness or misery, and so is concerned for itself, as far as that consciousness extends. Thus every one finds that, whilst comprehended under that consciousness, the little finger is as much a part of himself as what is most so. Upon separation of this little finger, should this consciousness go along with the little finger, and leave the rest of the body, it is evident the little finger would be the person, the same person; and self then would have nothing to do with the rest of the body. As in this case it is the consciousness that goes along with the substance, when one part is separate from another, which makes the same person, and constitutes this inseparable self: so it is in reference to substances remote in time. That with which the consciousness of this present thinking thing *can* join itself, makes the same person, and is one self with it, and with nothing else; and so attributes to itself, and owns all the actions of that thing, as its own, as far as that consciousness reaches, and no further; as every one who reflects will perceive.

18. In this personal identity is founded all the right and justice of reward and punishment; happiness and misery being that for which every one is concerned for *himself*, and not mattering what becomes of any *substance*, not joined to, or affected with that consciousness. For, as it is evident in the instance I gave but now, if the consciousness went along with the little finger when it was cut off, that would be the same self which was concerned for the whole body yesterday, as making part of itself, whose actions then it cannot but admit as its own now. Though, if the same body should still live, and immediately from the separation of the little finger have its own peculiar consciousness, whereof the little finger knew nothing, it would not at all be concerned for it, as a part of itself, or could own any of its actions, or have any of them imputed to him.

19. This may show us wherein personal identity consists: not in the identity of substance, but, as I have said, in the identity of consciousness, wherein if Socrates and the present mayor of Queinborough agree, they are the same person: if the same Socrates waking and sleeping do not partake of the same consciousness, Socrates waking and sleeping is not the same person. And to punish Socrates waking for what sleeping Socrates thought, and waking Socrates was never conscious of, would be no more of right, than to punish one twin for what his brother-twin did, whereof he knew nothing, because their outsides were so like, that they could not be distinguished; for such twins have been seen.

20. But yet possibly it will still be objected, – Suppose I wholly lose the memory of some parts of my life, beyond a possibility of retrieving them, so that perhaps I shall never be conscious of them again; yet am I not the same person that did those actions, had those thoughts that I once was conscious of, though I have now forgot them? To which I answer, that we must here take notice what the word *I* is applied to; which, in this case, is the *man* only. And the same man being presumed to be the same person, I is easily here supposed to stand also for the same person. But if it be possible for the same man to have distinct incommunicable consciousness at different times, it is past doubt the same man would at different times make different persons; which, we see, is the sense of mankind in the solemnest declaration of their opinions, human laws not punishing the mad man for the sober man's actions, nor the sober man for what the mad man did, – thereby making them two persons: which is somewhat explained by our way of speaking in English when we say such an one is 'not himself,' or is 'beside himself'; in which phrases it is insinuated, as if those who now, or at least first used them, thought that self was changed; the selfsame person was no longer in that man.

[. . .]

22. But is not a man drunk and sober the same person? why else is he punished for the fact he commits when drunk, though he be never afterwards conscious of it? Just as much the same person as a man that walks, and does other things in his sleep, is the same person, and is answerable for any mischief he shall do in it. Human laws punish both, with a justice suitable to *their* way of knowledge; – because, in these cases, they cannot distinguish certainly what is real, what counterfeit: and so the ignorance in drunkenness or sleep is not admitted as a plea. [For, though punishment be annexed to personality, and personality to consciousness, and the drunkard perhaps be not conscious of what he did, yet human judicatures justly punish him; because the fact is proved against him, but want of consciousness cannot be proved for him.] But in the Great Day, wherein the secrets of all hearts shall be laid open, it may be reasonable to think, no one shall be made to answer for what he knows nothing of; but shall receive his doom, his conscience accusing or excusing him.

23. Nothing but consciousness can unite remote existences into the same person: the identity of substance will not do it; for whatever substance there is, however framed, without consciousness there is no person.

5

Do We Survive Death?

Bertrand Russell

Bertrand Russell (1872–1970) was one of the most important philosophers and logicians of the twentieth century. In the following essay he defends a Lockean psychological continuity approach to personal identity, and he argues that it is highly unlikely that psychological continuity survives the death of the body. He goes on to argue that belief in immortality is born not from reason but from emotions such as the fear of death and admiration of human excellence.

Before we can profitably discuss whether we shall continue to exist after death, it is well to be clear as to the sense in which a man is the same person as he was yesterday. Philosophers used to think that there were definite substances, the soul and the body, that each lasted on from day to day, that a soul, once created, continued to exist throughout all future time, whereas a body ceased temporarily from death till the resurrection of the body.

The part of this doctrine which concerns the present life is pretty certainly false. The matter of the body is continually changing by processes of nutriment and wastage. Even if it were not, atoms in physics are no longer supposed to have continuous existence; there is no sense in saying: this is the same atom as the one that existed a few minutes ago. The continuity of a human body is a matter of appearance and behavior, not of substance.

The same thing applies to the mind. We think and feel and act, but there is not, in addition to thoughts and feelings and actions, a bare entity, the mind or the soul, which does or suffers these occurrences. The mental continuity of a person is a continuity of habit and memory: there was yesterday one person whose feelings I can remember, and that person I regard as myself of yesterday; but, in fact, myself of yesterday was only certain mental occurrences which are now remembered and are regarded as part of the person who now recollects them. All that

Bertrand Russell, "Do We Survive Death?" from *Why I am Not a Christian*, ed. Paul Edwards (Simon & Schuster, 1957), pp. 88–93.

constitutes a person is a series of experiences connected by memory and by certain similarities of the sort we call habit.

If, therefore, we are to believe that a person survives death, we must believe that the memories and habits which constitute the person will continue to be exhibited in a new set of occurrences.

No one can prove that this will not happen. But it is easy to see that it is very unlikely. Our memories and habits are bound up with the structure of the brain, in much the same way in which a river is connected with the riverbed. The water in the river is always changing, but it keeps to the same course because previous rains have worn a channel. In like manner, previous events have worn a channel in the brain, and our thoughts flow along this channel. This is the cause of memory and mental habits. But the brain, as a structure, is dissolved at death, and memory therefore may be expected to be also dissolved. There is no more reason to think otherwise than to expect a river to persist in its old course after an earthquake has raised a mountain where a valley used to be.

All memory, and therefore (one may say) all minds, depend upon a property which is very noticeable in certain kinds of material structures but exists little if at all in other kinds. This is the property of forming habits as a result of frequent similar occurrences. For example: a bright light makes the pupils of the eyes contract; and if you repeatedly flash a light in a man's eyes and beat a gong at the same time, the gong alone will, in the end, cause his pupils to contract. This is a fact about the brain and nervous system – that is to say, about a certain material structure. It will be found that exactly similar facts explain our response to language and our use of it, our memories and the emotions they arouse, our moral or immoral habits of behavior, and indeed everything that constitutes our mental personality, except the part determined by heredity. The part determined by heredity is handed on to our posterity but cannot, in the individual, survive the disintegration of the body. Thus both the hereditary and the acquired parts of a personality are, so far as our experience goes, bound up with the characteristics of certain bodily structures. We all know that memory may be obliterated by an injury to the brain, that a virtuous person may be rendered vicious by encephalitis lethargica, and that a clever child can be turned into an idiot by lack of iodine. In view of such familiar facts, it seems scarcely probable that the mind survives the total destruction of brain structure which occurs at death.

It is not rational arguments but emotions that cause belief in a future life.

The most important of these emotions is fear of death, which is instinctive and biologically useful. If we genuinely and wholeheartedly believed in the future life, we should cease completely to fear death. The effects would be curious, and probably such as most of us would deplore. But our human and subhuman ancestors have fought and exterminated their enemies throughout many geological ages and have profited by courage; it is therefore an advantage to the victors in the struggle for life to be able, on occasion, to overcome the natural fear of death. Among animals and savages, instinctive pugnacity suffices for this purpose; but at a certain stage of development, as the Mohammedans first proved, belief in Paradise has considerable military value as reinforcing natural pugnacity. We should therefore admit that militarists are wise in encouraging the belief in immortality, always supposing that this belief does not become so profound as to produce indifference to the affairs of the world.

Another emotion which encourages the belief in survival is admiration of the excellence of man. As the Bishop of Birmingham says, "His mind is a far finer instrument than anything that had appeared earlier – he knows right and wrong. He can build Westminster Abbey. He can make an airplane. He can calculate the distance of the sun. . . . Shall, then, man at death perish utterly? Does that incomparable instrument, his mind, vanish when life ceases?"

The Bishop proceeds to argue that "the universe has been shaped and is governed by an intelligent purpose," and that it would have been unintelligent, having made man, to let him perish.

To this argument there are many answers. In the first place, it has been found, in the scientific investigation of nature, that the intrusion of moral or aesthetic values has always been an obstacle to discovery. It used to be thought that the heavenly bodies must move in circles because the circle is the most perfect curve, that species must be immutable because God would only create what was perfect and what therefore stood in no need of improvement, that it was useless to combat epidemics except by repentance because they were sent as a punishment for sin, and so on. It has been found, however, that, so far as we can discover, nature is indifferent to our values and can only be understood by ignoring our notions of good and bad. The Universe may have a purpose, but nothing that we know suggests that, if so, this purpose has any similarity to ours.

Nor is there in this anything surprising. Dr Barnes tells us that man "knows right and wrong." But, in fact, as anthropology shows, men's views of right and wrong have varied to such an extent that no single item has been permanent. We cannot say, therefore, that man knows right and wrong, but only that some men do. Which men? Nietzsche argued in favor of an ethic profoundly different from Christ's, and some powerful governments have accepted his teaching. If knowledge of right and wrong is to be an argument for immortality, we must first settle whether to believe Christ or Nietzsche, and then argue that Christians are immortal, but Hitler and Mussolini are not, or vice versa. The decision will obviously be made on the battlefield, not in the study. Those who have the best poison gas will have the ethic of the future and will therefore be the immortal ones.

Our feelings and beliefs on the subject of good and evil are, like everything else about us, natural facts, developed in the struggle for existence and not having any divine or supernatural origin. In one of Aesop's fables, a lion is shown pictures of huntsmen catching lions and remarks that, if he had painted them, they would have shown lions catching huntsmen. Man, says Dr Barnes, is a fine fellow because he can make airplanes. A little while ago there was a popular song about the cleverness of flies in walking upside down on the ceiling, with the chorus: "Could Lloyd George do it? Could Mr. Baldwin do it? Could Ramsay Mac do it? Why, no." On this basis a very telling argument could be constructed by a theologically-minded fly, which no doubt the other flies would find most convincing.

Moreover, it is only when we think abstractly that we have such a high opinion of man. Of men in the concrete, most of us think the vast majority very bad. Civilized states spend more than half their revenue on killing each other's citizens. Consider the long history of the activities inspired by moral fervor: human sacrifices, persecutions of heretics, witch-hunts, pogroms leading up to wholesale extermination by poison gases, which one at least of Dr Barnes's episcopal colleagues must be supposed to favor, since he holds pacifism to be un-Christian. Are these abominations, and the ethical doctrines by which they are prompted, really evidence of an intelligent Creator? And can we really wish that the men who practiced them should live forever? The world in which we live can be understood as a result of muddle and accident; but if it is the outcome of deliberate purpose, the purpose must have been that of a fiend. For my part, I find accident a less painful and more plausible hypothesis.

6

Religious and Near-death Experience in Relation to Belief in a Future Life

Paul Badham

Paul Badham (b. 1942) is Professor of Theology and Religious Studies at the University of Wales, Lampeter and a director of the Alister Hardy Religious Experience Research Centre. In the following essay he argues that religious experiences, and especially near-death experiences, provide experiential support for belief in an afterlife. Although reports of near-death experiences are difficult to assess, Badham urges that further research has the potential to determine the objectivity of such experiences.

The Primacy of Experience in Religious Believing

Claims to personal experience seem to be at the heart of religion. For although some come to belief by inheritance, some by acceptance of a revelation-tradition and some by rational argument, the belief remains at 'second-hand' until it has been appropriated through some kind of personal awareness. Only when faith is thought to have a real basis in the experience of the individual can it be said to be existentially real to the believer. In contemporary philosophy of religion, such experience is given a key role, in that in a religiously ambiguous world which can be interpreted theistically or atheistically, it is the additional evidence of personal religious experience which for the believer tips the balance in favour of theism (Hick, 1989; Mitchell, 1973; Swinburne, 1979).

In this context beliefs about a future life might seem to be an exception, for apart from Christian claims concerning Jesus Christ, no-one who has died has returned to give assurance of a future hope, and it might seem therefore that of necessity this must be one belief that is forever without an experiential foundation. The purpose of this paper is to argue that this is not

Paul Badham, "Religious and Near-death Experience in Relation to Belief in a Future Life". *Mortality* 2:1 (1997): 7–21.

the case. Though there is no direct evidence of a future life there are features both in religious experience, and increasingly today in near-death experience, which do provide an experiential foundation for a future hope.

Experience and the Finality of Death

Normal everyday human experience has always pointed to the view that death is the end of any meaningful personal existence. This is very forcefully expressed in the Old Testament: 'We must all die. We are like water spilt on the ground which cannot be gathered again'; 'Human beings perish for ever like their own dung'. They are 'of dust and will return to dust'. In the grave they will rot away 'with maggots beneath and worms on top'; 'In that same hour all thinking ends' (2 Samuel 14:14; Job 20:7; Genesis 2:7; Isaiah 14:11; Psalm 146:4). It is true, of course, that for a generation or two the dead will live on in some kind of shadowy half-life in the memories of those who knew them. John Bowker argues that such memory traces explain why so many ancient cultures had a notion of the dead having some kind of thin, insubstantial, shadowy existence underground (the Hebrew *Sheol* or Greek *Hades*). But in neither Ancient Greece, Mesopotamia, India, China nor Israel was there any notion that life in this 'underworld' had any real significance or substance. There was 'nothing after death to which one could look forward . . . For our ancestors, there was definitely no future in dying' (Bowker, 1991, p. 30). In the face of this universal human experience of death as the ending of personal life how is it that notions of a 'real' life after death ever got off the ground at all? To answer this question I think we need to look at those features of human experience which, as a matter of historical fact, did lead to the emergence of such beliefs.

The Experiential Basis for Belief in a Future Life in the Judaeo-Christian Tradition

Ancient Israel is a dramatic example of how beliefs can change in the light of new experiences. As we have already seen, the classic position in ancient Israel was that death must mean extinction because human beings are irreducibly physical entities who are totally at one with nature. They 'have no advantage over the beasts' and are 'like the grass that withers and the flowers that fade' (Ecclesiastes 3:19; Psalm 90:5). However, in spite of this, a firm belief in a future life gradually evolved as religious experience came to be understood in personal terms. What appears to have happened is that conviction of a future hope grew out of the experience of individuals who came to believe that they were experiencing a personal relationship with God. This was not the original form of early Judaism, which at first thought only of a relationship between God and the whole nation of Israel. But from the time of the exile in Babylon onwards (from 597 BCE) the idea of a covenant between God and humanity was increasingly seen in individualistic terms. As that conviction developed so the thought of Israel moved along a path which led to the flowering of the future hope in the intertestamental period. As Wheeler Robinson puts it: 'The faith of the Old Testament logically points towards a life beyond death, because it is so sure of an inviolable fellowship with God' (Robinson, 1962, p. 103). The foundation for the faith ultimately arrived at was the conviction that if human persons can really enjoy a personal relationship with God which God values, and if the believer really matters as a unique individual to the all-powerful and all-loving God then God will not allow that individual and that relationship to be destroyed by death. Throughout the subsequent history of monotheism this conviction has remained dominant. As Edward Schillebeeckx argued: 'The breeding ground of belief in life after death . . . was always seen in a communion of life between God and man . . . Living communion with God, attested as the meaning, the foundation, and the inspiring content of human existence, is the only climate in which the believer's trust in life after death comes, and evidently can come to historical fruition' (Schillebeeckx, 1980, p. 797). We shall see later that this is not wholly correct in that belief in a future destiny has also come into being in some Buddhist cultures. But within the Jewish, Christian and Islamic cultures Schillebeeckx is undoubtedly right that the experience of a direct encounter between God and the individual soul has been the prime foundation for assurance that death can never triumph over that divine love.

The Claim to have Experience of 'the Risen Christ'

Within the Christian tradition the belief, held in common with Judaism and Islam, of knowing God has been supplemented by a conviction that the death and resurrection of Jesus provide further ground for confidence in a future hope. For many Christians faith in the resurrection of Jesus is a faith based on historical considerations, namely that the disciples' experience of seeing the risen Christ was the fount and origin of Christianity. But from the time of St Athanasius onwards other Christians have asserted a more direct experiential base (Athanasius, 1963, pp. 60–1). They believe that Jesus rose from the dead because they claim to have come to know him directly as their personal saviour. For such Christians the primary experiential knowledge of the defeat of death is derived from this evangelical claim to know the risen Christ in their own lives.

Religious Experience Today

However, there is a problem for Christianity in contemporary Europe in that religious experiencing in its classic form does not appear to be anything like as prevalent as it once was. Many students of Religious Studies find difficulty with Otto's classic book *The idea of the holy* (Otto, 1923) because the sense of the numinous which Otto argued is the basis of religion seems to be something of which some have little experience. Otto assumed that a profound sense of awe and wonder at a fascinating and tremendous mystery identified as the presence of the divine was normative within Christian worship. But it does not appear any longer to be characteristic of contemporary Church life in modern Europe. Similarly, the classic hymns of personal devotion display an intensity of religious feeling which goes beyond the more communal and social emphasis of much modern hymnody. And there is no longer the same expectation as there was in the past that ordinands would necessarily have felt a direct 'call' in the way Church tradition presupposes. This may be illustrated by the fact that in current controversies over the ordination of women to the Christian priesthood the argument from women's sense of being called by God to this ministry has not been given much weight.

It is of course true that a succession of empirical studies has shown that religious experience of a kind is far more widespread than often supposed. For example, in David Hay's *Religious experience today* it is claimed that as many as 65% of postgraduate students of education in England had a religious experience which mattered to them (Hay, 1990, p. 59). But in most of these cases the experience seemed very diffuse and hard to clarify. The main impression left from studying them is how non-specific and vague they really were, and how different from the intense life-transforming experiences characteristic of classic conversion experience. Very few modern accounts describe the kind of personal relationship with God which historically formed a foundation for belief in a communion of love which not even death could end.

Near-death Experiences

In this context the recent upsurge in reports of near-death experience seems particularly important. This is often a profound and life-changing experience which people never forget. It shares many of the characteristics of the deepest religious experiences known to humanity, and yet through the spread of modern resuscitation techniques it has become available to hundreds of thousands of ordinary people. Twenty-five thousand such cases have now been collected from all over the world (Kübler-Ross, 1991, p. 47; Becker, 1993, p. 77) and, as medical technology advances, so every year does the number of people who have been resuscitated from apparent death, and of these a significant proportion (somewhere between 10 and 35%) have a series of vivid experiences. The experiences include reports of 'leaving the body'; 'looking down on the resuscitation attempts'; 'feeling a sense of life-review'; 'meeting deceased relatives and friends' and enjoying a series of religious experiences of a mystical type including 'encounters' with a bright light sometimes perceived in personal terms and identified with a figure from the percipients' own religious traditions. The pattern of experiencing appears to be common across religious traditions, cultures and world-views, though naturally the terminology used in the religious descriptions is culture-specific.

Earlier Accounts of Similar Experiences

These experiences are not new. They go back to the dawn of human history and it seems likely that in many cultures they gave rise to a belief in the possibility of a future life. Mircea Eliade suggests that some ideas about life after death may have originated in Shamanistic trances which characteristically include a notion of the Shaman leaving his body (Eliade, 1977, p. 17). Daniel Van Egmond argues that 'it is highly probable that some types of (religious) experience suggested to man that he is able to exist independently of his physical body. For instance, the so-called near-death experiences, out-of-the-body experiences and shamanistic trances are easily interpreted this way. Indeed, the occurrence of altered states of consciousness is such a common feature in most cultures that it is very probable that such experiences were interpreted as perceptions of so-called "higher worlds" ' (Van Egmond, 1993, p. 15). Dean Shiels's research into out-of-the body experiences in primitive cultures showed that 64 of the 67 cultures investigated believe in the reality of such states. He tested the conventional explanations given for such phenomena by western scholars and found that they did not apply in these cultures. His conclusion was that: 'When different cultures at different times and in different places arrive at the same or a very similar out-of-the-body-belief we begin to wonder if this results from a common experience of this happening' (Shiels, 1978).

Most claims to out-of-the-body experience occur near the point of death. It seems likely, therefore, that it is the fact of such reported experiences which have given rise to the traditional description of death as 'the moment when the soul leaves the body'. The experience of simply watching a person die leads to a much simpler picture of death as 'the moment when the person breathed-out (expired) for the last time'. The fact that this description has been felt to need supplementation suggests that other facts of human experiencing have been given weight as well as what is most immediately apparent.

However, in the past the distinctive near-death experience happened only to a tiny handful of people who had spontaneously recovered from apparent death or who had, after much prayer, meditation, fast and vigil, seen comparable otherworldly visions. When such an unusual experience happened to someone it was deemed to give that person very special authority on religious matters.

St Paul's 'Out of the Body' Experience and Heavenly Visions

Consider, for example, the situation of St Paul. On what did his faith in the end ultimately depend? One's immediate response might be to cite 1 Corinthians 15 and his rehearsal there of the faith handed on to him. Yet it is intriguing that when the Corinthians challenged St Paul's authority and asked him on what authority he spoke and acted, he did not appeal to the tradition he had received from others but instead felt impelled to describe his own foundational experience:

> It may do no good but I must go on with my boasting; I come now to visions and revelations granted by the Lord. I know a Christian man who fourteen years ago (whether in the body or out of the body I don't know – God knows) was caught up as far as the third heaven. And I know that this same man, (whether in the body or apart from the body I don't know – God knows) was caught up into paradise, and heard words so secret that human lips may not repeat them. About such a man I am ready to boast (2 Corinthians 12:1–5).

Few commentators doubt that St Paul was speaking autobiographically here, especially as a few verses later he laments that 'to keep me from being unduly elated by the magnificence of such revelations I was given a thorn in the flesh . . . to keep me from being too elated' (2 Corinthians 12:7). What is intriguing for our present purpose is that St Paul's experience included out-of-the-body experiences and visions of paradise, both of which are key features of the near-death experience.

Commenting on these verses in 2 Corinthians 12, St John of the Cross, the great 16th-century mystic, remarked that such experiences normally only occur when the soul 'goes forth from the flesh and departs this mortal life'. But in St Paul's case he was allowed these visions by special grace. Such visions, however, occur 'very rarely and to very few for God works such things only in those who are very strong in the spirit and in the law of God' (St John of the Cross, 1957, p. 84). St John of the Cross almost certainly had a comparable experience himself, as evidenced by his poems where he speaks of 'living without inhabiting himself', 'dying yet I do not die' and as 'soaring to the heavens' (St John of the Cross, 1960, p. 51; see also pp. 47–57). (That secular love poems of that time use the phrase 'dying that I do not die' as a sexual metaphor does not prevent us from supposing that St John was using the expression in its primary sense.)

What is intriguing is that St Paul regarded his experience as giving him unique insight and authority, and St John of the Cross speaks of the experience as coming very rarely and to very few. What I suggest is that modern medical technology has, as it were, 'democratized' and made available to thousands an experience which has from the beginning lain at the heart of much of the world's religious perceiving and formed an important experiential basis for the future hope.

Near-death Experience and the *Tibetan Book of the Dead*

One of the most striking features of near-death experiences is that they are not confined to theistic traditions but appear to be common across all human cultures. In particular they appear to have played a key role in both Tibetan and Japanese forms of Buddhism. In both these Mahayana traditions we can see very close parallels between contemporary near-death experience and that which seems to be reflected in their foundational scriptures. This has been widely noted in connection with the *Bardo Thodol* (the *Tibetan Book of the Dead*). The descriptions of what happens after death in this work correspond very closely to what contemporary near-death experiencers report (Evans-Wentz, 1957, pp. 98, 101). Consider, for example, how contemporary near-death experiences report looking down on their bodies, observing the distress of their relatives, and the activities of the medical staff. So too in the *Tibetan Book of the Dead* we read that when the person's 'consciousness-principle gets outside its body' he sees his relatives and friends gathered round weeping and watches as they remove the clothes from the body or take away the bed.

Seventy-two per-cent of contemporary near-death experiencers report seeing a radiant light which they often describe as a loving presence and sometimes name in accordance with a religious figure from their own traditions. A few experience a review of their past life and many experience a range of mental images which have led many commentators to suggest that the next stage of existence could be a mind-dependent world. Once again this is precisely what the *Tibetan Book* says, for it speaks of the dying person seeing the radiant, pure and immutable light of Amida Buddha before passing into what is explicitly described as a world of mental-images, in which whatever is desired is fulfilled, and in which everything that is seen is in form an hallucination reflecting the karma of the percipient.

Concerning the Being of Light which contemporary experiencers see and name in accordance with their own tradition, this also is in accord with the *Tibetan Book of the Dead* where we read: 'The Dharmakaya (The Divine Being) of clear light will appear in what ever shape will benefit all beings'. Commenting on this verse for his English translation, Lama Kazi Dawa-Samdup says: 'To appeal to a Shaivite devotee, the form of Shiva is assumed; to a Buddhist the form of the Buddha Shakya Muni; to a Christian, the form of Jesus, to a Muslim the form of the Prophet; and so for other religious devotees; and for all manner and conditions of mankind a form appropriate to the occasion' (Evans-Wentz, 1957, p. 94). A similar consideration applies when thinking of the vivid imagery which abounds in the *Tibetan Book.* These mental images are not thought of as universalizable. Rather as Lama Anagarika Govinda points out in his introduction: 'The illusory Bardo visions vary, in keeping with the religious or cultural tradition in which the percipient has grown up' (Evans-Wentz, 1957, p. xii).

When we examine contemporary near-death accounts this is precisely what we find. What is seen appears to be cross-cultural, but how it is named depends on the religious or non-religious background of the believer. Thus it is only to be expected that a Christian evangelist in the Anglican 'Church Army' would say that he had seen Jesus (BBC, 1982), whereas the notable atheist philosopher A. J. Ayer would say 'I was aware that this light was responsible for the government of the Universe' (Ayer, 1992). What matters is that both contemporary observers seem to have had an experience which had much in common.

Near-death Experiences in Pure-Land Buddhism

The place where contemporary experience and foundational religious beliefs come closest together is in the Scriptures, and even the contemporary architecture of Pure-Land Buddhism, particularly in that of the True Pureland Sect (Jodo Shinshu Buddhism). Looking first at the Scriptures three features spring to mind. The first is that the Buddha's Pure Land seems to have many features in common with the idea of a mind-dependent world, reflecting the karma of the individual. 'All the wishes those beings may think of, they will be fulfilled, as long as they are rightful' (Conze, 1959, p. 233). This idea spelt out with many examples in the *Sukhavativyuha* (The Pure Land Sutra) corresponds exactly with some contemporary descriptions by resuscitated people.

The second striking feature is the experience of so many resuscitated people of seeing and being welcomed into the world beyond by a wonderful and gracious 'Being of light'. They sense that this Being knows them completely and has limitless compassion to them in welcoming them into the life beyond. We have already noted the tendency of those who see this vision to identify this Being with a religious figure from their own tradition such as Jesus or Rama. But it is interesting that the descriptions given of the role of this being do not accord with traditional expectations in the Christian or Hindu traditions but do accord with the Pure-Land vision of Amida Buddha as 'The Buddha of Infinite Light and Boundless Life' who has vowed to appear at the moment of death. 'When they come to the end of life they will be met by Amida Buddha and the Bodhisatvas of Compassion and Wisdom and will be led by them into Buddha's Land' (Bukyo Dendo Kyokai, 1980, p. 218). This combination of radiant light, wisdom and compassion corresponds precisely to the descriptions given by the resuscitated of their experience of this encounter.

A third common feature is that the imagery in which the Pure Land is described is remarkably similar to the descriptions of the land beyond given by the resuscitated. I am thinking here of the imagery in the *Smaller Sukavativyuhasutra* (The Smaller Pure Land Sutra) of a wonderful garden with flowers of intense vividness of colour, of bright jewels and of 'the air vibrant with celestial harmonies' (Kyokai, 1980, p. 220). This corresponds almost verbatim to a description given on BBC television by a young resuscitated child concerning what she saw, and I was particularly struck by the way she too stressed the intensity of the colouring of the various flowers and jewels (BBC, 1982). Yet the rest of the description is also very interesting, for the imagery of a beautiful garden to describe heaven is common to all religious traditions, as is the notion of celestial music, and indeed the word 'paradise' was originally the word used for a Royal garden or park on earth.

The link between contemporary near-death experience and the Pure-Land religious tradition seems exemplified in the recent building of a Great Buddha Statue by the Tokyo Honganji. The statue itself was completed in 1991 and the Tokyo Honganji claim it to be the largest statue in the world. It is situated in the heart of the traditional burial grounds of the Pure-Land Sect. These burial grounds are being surrounded by beautiful gardens. One is permitted to enter the Buddha statue and ascend to eye level. As one enters the lift the lights go out and one experiences the sensation of rising rapidly upwards through a tunnel of darkness till one reaches the top. Then as one leaves the lift one sees a pillar of radiant white light reaching upwards and one looks out at the world through the eyes of Buddha and what one sees is designed to evoke images of Buddha's Pure Land, and the paradise described by past and present near-death experiencers.

What Contemporary Experiencers Report

So far I have discussed the NDE [near-death experience] in general terms and suggested that knowledge of contemporary experiences throws considerable light on key experiences of St Paul and of St John of the Cross in the Christian tradition, and on what appears in foundational Tibetan and Japanese texts in the Buddhist tradition. I propose now to look in more detail at the largest and most detailed survey of contemporary experiences to see what these tend to have in common and what the impact on the experiencer usually is.

Since the pioneering works of Raymond Moody and J. C. Hampe published independently of each other in the USA and Germany in the early 1970s (Hampe, 1979; Moody, 1973) there has been a flood of individual accounts, scientific surveys and television documentaries (Ring, 1980; Becker, 1993; Blackmore, 1993; Fenwick & Fenwick, 1995). Most of these are based on relatively small samples of between 50 and 100 cases, but recently Peter and Elizabeth Fenwick have published a comprehensive survey based on 344 British experiencers, all of whom filled in a detailed questionnaire as well as writing a long personal account (Fenwick & Fenwick, 1995 [summarized in Badham & Ballard, 1996, from which the following details derive]). This survey probably gives us the fullest account available yet of what are the characteristic features of a near-death experience.

According to the Fenwicks' report 72% of near-death experiencers speak of seeing the light. Asked to clarify the colour 56% described it as brilliant white, 21% as golden, 6% as yellow, 3% as orange, 2% red and 7% said it had no colour. Only 5% thought of it at the cold end of the spectrum as green (2%) or blue (3%). Seventy-six per cent talked of seeing a landscape which was invariably described in terms of a beautiful garden or an idyllic pastoral scene. Nineteen per cent heard wonderful music.

The near-death experience carries with it very strong positive emotions. Of those who underwent it, 82% felt calmness and peace, 40% felt joy and 38% felt love. Individuals write in glowing terms of their feelings, some speaking of utter peace and complete happiness: 'no person could experience such joy'; 'I was filled with elation'. Many felt that they were at peace because they understood everything: 'I was peaceful, utterly content, I knew the light held all the answers'.

For many people the experience of the transforming light was the most profound emotional experience they have ever had. Their feeling was of being overwhelmed with universal love, of being accepted by some loving being. This led a high proportion of the percipients (72%) to feel that they had been changed by the experience: 42% felt that they had become more spiritual as a result, 22% talked of becoming 'better persons' and 40% described themselves as more socially conscious.

The most common change was that 82% said they now had less fear of death. This does not necessarily mean that these all came to a firm belief in a life after death, for 48% said that they did not believe in personal survival. However, it is unclear how we should interpret this, given that some who said this also thought that some important part of them, their consciousness or soul, might yet continue. What this lack of clarity suggests to me is that an NDE can very strongly encourage belief in a future life but cannot override strongly-held philosophical beliefs about what it means to be a person. We shall see a further illustration of this below when we examine the complexity of A. J. Ayer's response. On the other hand, the finding that 82% had less fear of death remains significant, as does the fact that for at least some the experience was interpreted as guaranteeing a future hope.

The near-death experience does not, however, simply change people's attitude to death, but also gives them a much more affirmative attitude to this life. Many speak of every day as a new gift, and feel that they should live life more fully and purposefully. One intriguing fact is that 47% of those who had near-death experiences felt themselves to be more psychically sensitive. By this is meant feelings of being able to predict the future, or to possess powers of healing the sick. Clearly it would be useful to check such claims to see if there is any empirical evidence to support them. But it is at least worth noting that such beliefs often follow other deeply-felt religious experiences which suggests that, for many, the NDE falls into this kind of category.

Another feature which NDEs have in common with other kinds of religious experience is that they are not always positive experiences. Almost 1% talked of a hellish experience, 15% felt a sense of fear, and 9% a sense of loss. These figures are in line with other contemporary surveys, but out of line with reports from earlier cultures where hellish experiences were much more commonly reported (Bede, 1962 [first published 731]; Zaleski, 1987). Once again this is a feature which NDEs share with contemporary religious experience which tends to focus on a sense of the love of God while earlier generations talked of a sense of 'fear'. In both cases, however, there has always been a spectrum of positive and negative experiences which might justify the speculation that beliefs about both heaven and hell may have a basis in such experiences.

On matters of religious belief most of the Fenwicks' respondents felt that their religious outlook had been broadened rather than simply confirmed. In the responses they received there was a tendency to speak of feeling in the presence of a higher Being, rather than talking of God, and in this British sample Jesus or Mary were only rarely named. The dominant characteristic was a sense of spiritual awakening which sometimes feels uneasy at any continuing acceptance of narrow doctrinal system. There was a sense that the Reality glimpsed was of more universal significance than simply to one's inherited tradition. Again this is a characteristic of experientially-based beliefs in that mystics of all traditions tend to feel closer to one another than do those who base their belief-system more strongly on an inherited tradition.

Near-death Experiences, Heaven and Hell

These findings of Peter and Elizabeth Fenwick are very much in line with the findings of other researchers in other countries. Carl Becker, Professor of Comparative Thought at Kyoto University, remarks how reminiscent modern NDEs are to accounts in Chinese and Japanese literature concerning 'those who have been to heaven and back' (Becker, 1993, pp. 90–1), and he notes also that surveys in India and America among Christians, Jews and Hindus all present closely similar reports. J. C. Hampe in Germany comes to the same conclusion (Hampe, 1979). The experience seems to cut across all cultural and religious boundaries and yet to present the archetypal imagery of a paradisal heaven of flowery gardens, suffused in warm light and radiant with peace and joy and in the loving presence of a Being of light, of love and of compassion. However, the few negative experiences also echo archetypal imageries of hell. It seems overwhelmingly likely that reports from past near-death experiences are what have shaped our traditions and provided the content of our religious imagery concerning the future life.

These considerations are why I suggest that the experiential foundation for belief in a future life derives both from religious experience of a relationship with God, and from the reports of people who near the frontier of death believe they have caught a glimpse of a life beyond.

The Problem of Analysing Near-death and Religious Experiences

If one tries to see any pattern in this data it does seem that to classify NDEs under the heading 'contemporary religious experience' makes good sense. It shares the ambiguity of all religious experience in that the boundaries are fuzzy and what is true of the majority of cases is not true of all. Like all religious experiences, what convinces the percipient does not necessarily influence the thinking of one who is merely told of another's experience. And while the Fenwicks' survey throws useful light on the subjective feelings of people who have NDEs, this does not solve the question of what, if any, may be the explanation we give to such phenomena.

For me one of the most impressive features of the NDE is the profound effect it has on the majority of those who experience it. Long ago William James argued that religious experiences are real because they have real effects. In the case of the NDE this is particularly noticeable. As we saw in the survey quoted above, 72% felt their lives transformed. Comparable findings have been confirmed by others. Bruce Greyson, Editor of the *Journal of Near-Death Studies* and a Professor of Psychiatry, sums up the data thus: 'It is the most profound experience I know of, . . . nothing affects people as strongly as this' (Brown, 1993). This is further endorsed by Professor Kenneth Ring in his book *Life at death* which shows that the most impressive feature of the near-death experience is the impact it has on the beliefs and attitudes of those who have it (Ring, 1980, pp. 81, 169, 240). Of course, as with all such experiences, the impact is not epistemically coercive, so that it remains possible for a person to be unpersuaded by it. This is both illustrated and illuminated by the impact his NDE experience had on A. J. Ayer. His first response was to think that 'on the face of it, these experiences are rather strong evidence that death does not put an end to consciousness'. However, after rehearsing some of the philosophical problems associated with life after death his conclusion was more modest, namely that 'my recent experiences have slightly weakened my conviction that my genuine death, which is due fairly soon, will be the end of me, though I continue to hope it will'. Later he retracted even this, but from a person with his long and carefully-thought-out position his testimony to the power of the initial experience remains striking (Ayer, 1992).

An Important Research Project

From a scientific perspective one feature which is a permanent difficulty in the way of investigating topics like religious or near-death experiences is that the most one can normally do is to collect and analyse subjective reports. But at least we can now do this on a massive scale. Carl Becker has pointed out that the availability of modern computerized storage and comparison enables thousands of such cases to be collected from all over the world and analysed together. There is certainly value in such a project, for if it can be totally established that tens of thousands of people from totally disparate cultures, worldviews and backgrounds have all reported a common set of experiences near the point of death this does at least provide some grounds for supposing that this might actually be what happens at that point. As Richard Swinburne suggests: 'in the absence of special considerations, how things seem to be is good grounds for a belief about how things are' (Swinburne, 1979, p. 254).

But there is a problem in applying this to the claim that near-death experiences show that at death the soul goes out of the body and moves on to a new mode of existence, as so many NDE experiencers believe. The problem is precisely the existence of such 'special considerations', namely the mass of evidence that human consciousness cannot possibly subsist except within a functioning physical brain. But if it could ever be established that this 'limiting principle' did not apply then this barrier against taking NDEs as evidential of survival would not apply.

One intriguing fact about the NDE is that many who report 'going out of the body' at the time of apparent death not only enjoy mystical experiences such as we have already described but also claim to 'look down from above' on the resuscitation attempts, and are incredibly accurate in the observations they subsequently report which turn out to be correct in terms of what a person would have seen if he or she really had been viewing from the ceiling. These facts are accepted even by that most resolutely sceptical of the NDE inquirers, Susan Blackmore. She accepts that 'there is no doubt that people describe reasonably accurately events that have occurred around them during their NDE'. However, she suggests that a combination of 'prior knowledge, fantasy, and lucky guesses and the remaining operating senses of hearing and touch' may provide the information for the images seen which are viewed autoscopically from above because that is the perspective from which we see ourselves in memory (Blackmore, 1993, pp. 114–15). People who actually have the experience always see such explanations as alien 'hetero-interpretations' which fail to account for the way it actually seems to them. And the very large number of correct observations which do not fit into any of Blackmore's explanatory categories (other than the catch-all category of 'lucky guesses'), suggest that the data cannot easily be accommodated in so narrow a Procrustean bed.

However, this issue could actually be resolved if a large enough prospective survey could be done in hospital contexts where it could be established on a non-anecdotal basis whether or not correct observation actually took place of a kind that could not be accounted for by any 'natural' means. For this to happen requires the collaboration of medical staff and hospital administrators in the placing of objects in cardiac wards and casualty units which could only be seen and described by an agent actually looking down from the ceiling. Such a project would be fully scientific in that it offers a proposal that is in Popperian terms falsifiable. On average 10% of people admitted to a cardiac ward can be expected to have a near-death experience and well over half of these will report an autoscopic experience. If out of a hundred such patients none mention seeing the objects one could safely conclude that 'seeing' from out-of-the-body does not occur and that NDEs are only subjectively real in this regard. But if a single case of correct 'seeing' could be proven beyond dispute the principle that consciousness can exist outside the body will have been established and one roadblock across the path of belief in immortality will have been removed.

Such a project is not impossible to establish since Peter Fenwick and I did successfully negotiate a pilot study in two hospitals during a 2-year period. However, the handful of cases that occurred in this time did nothing but confirm the sad fact that most people resuscitated from a close encounter with death actually die without ever regaining sufficient strength to be interviewed about what, if anything, they experienced. However, if such a prospective study could be undertaken over a large enough number of hospitals for a sufficiently long time to build up a worthwhile database, the truth or falsity of the claim that near-death experiences provide evidence that consciousness can exist apart from the body could be established. Whatever the result of the experiment, it would be good to know the answer!

Conclusion

The question of whether or not there is a life after death is potentially the most important issue that could be raised. What I have sought to show in this paper is that, like most of the things we believe about the nature of reality, our answers to this question depend in part on our experiencing. A person who believes that they have truly encountered a personal and loving God, perhaps identified as the Risen Christ, is likely to believe that they have an eternal destiny. Likewise a person who has had a profound near-death experience may also come to such a belief. In neither case is the experience epistemically coercive and many will conclude that, like so much else about our world, the data are ambiguous and capable of a range of alternative explanations. However, in the case of the near-death experience there is the tantalizing prospect that future research could tip the balance of probability one way or the other. Let us hope that this challenge will be taken up so that we may know whether mortality or immortality is to be our ultimate end!

References

Athanasius (1963) *On the incarnation.* London: Mowbray. (First published AD 318.)

Ayer, A. J. (1992) What I saw when I was dead. In P. Edwards, *Immortality.* New York: Macmillan.

Badham, P. & Ballard, P. (1996) *Facing death.* Cardiff: University of Wales Press.

BBC (1982, March). *At the hour of death* [Television programme]. London: BBC.

Becker, C. (1993) *Paranormal experience and survival of death.* New York: SUNY.

Bede (1962) *A history of the English church and people* (Book 5, pp. 284–89). Harmondsworth: Penguin. (Originally published in AD 731.)

Blackmore, S. (1993) *Dying to live.* London: Grafton.

Bowker, J. (1991) *The meaning of death.* Cambridge: CUP.

Brown, M. (1993) Life after death. *Daily Telegraph,* March 27, Magazine section, p. 21.

Bukyo Dendo Kyokai (1980) *The teaching of Buddha.* Tokyo: Buddhist Promoting Foundation. (Quoting from *Amitayurdhyana-sutra.*)

Conze, E. (1959) *Buddhist Scriptures.* Harmondsworth: Penguin. (Part of a series of extracts from the *Sukhavativyuha,* pp. 15–19, 21–2, 24, 26–7.)

Eliade, M. (1977) Mythologies of death. In F. E. Reynolds & E. H. Waugh (eds.), *Religious encounters with death.* Pennsylvania: Pennsylvania University Press.

Evans-Wentz, W. Y. (1957) *The Tibetan Book of the Dead or the after-death experiences on the Bardo plane, according to Lama Kazi Dawa-Sumdup's English rendering* (3rd ed.). Oxford: OUP. (Originally published 1927.)

Fenwick, P. & Fenwick, E. (1995) *The truth in the light.* London: Headline.

Hampe, J. C. (1979) *To die is gain.* London: Darton, Longman & Todd. (Original [German] work published 1975.)

Hay, D. (1990) *Religious experience today.* London: Mowbrays.

Hick, J. (1989) *An interpretation of religion.* Oxford: OUP.

John of the Cross (1957) *The dark night of the soul* (Book 2, ch. 24.) (K. Reinhardt, trans.). London: Constable. (First written AD 1579.)

John of the Cross (1960) *Poems* (R. Campbell, trans.). Harmondsworth: Penguin.

Kübler-Ross, E. (1991) *On life after death.* Berkeley: Celestial.

Mitchell, B. (1973) *The justification of religious belief.* London: Macmillan.

Moody, R. A. (1973) *Life after life.* Atlanta: Mockingbird.

Otto, R. (1923) *The idea of the holy.* Oxford: OUP.

Ring, K. (1980) *Life at death: a scientific account of the near-death experience.* New York: Coward, McCann & Geohagen.

Robinson, W. (1962) *Inspiration and revelation in the Old Testament.* Oxford: Oxford University Press.

Schillebeeckx, E. (1980) *Christ, the Christian experience in the modern world.* London: SCM.

Shiels, D. (1978). A cross-cultural study of beliefs in out-of-the-body experiences. *Journal of the Society for Psychical Research* 49 (775), 699.

Smith, T. (1980) Called back from the dead. *Pulse,* July 19.

Swinburne, R. (1979) *The existence of God.* Oxford: OUP.

Van Egmond, D. (1993) *Body, subject and self: the possibilities of survival after death.* Utrecht: Utrecht University Press.

Zaleski, C. (1987) *Otherworldly journeys.* Oxford: Oxford University Press.

IX

THE DIVERSITY OF RELIGIONS

Introduction

The topic of this section is the only one in the book without a long history. Polytheistic religions generally did not compete for the allegiance of a particular person. The pantheon of gods of one group of people were worshiped by the people of a certain place, but those people typically would not deny the existence of the gods of other peoples. Before the religions of other peoples can pose a problem for the belief of a given person, then, it must be clear that other religions teach something that contradicts her own beliefs, for example, that her own gods do not exist. In addition, it must be possible for her to adopt the beliefs of the other religion. Many religions are so closely tied to the way of life of a given cultural group that it is no more possible to adopt the beliefs of another religion than it is for a Hopi to become a Navajo. So the diversity of religions is only a problem when religions have genuinely conflicting beliefs that compete for the allegiance of a given person. For the most part, these conditions did not obtain before the modern period.

Medieval Christian theologians were obviously aware of the existence of Jews, Muslims, and non-theists, but they did not think that the existence of non-Christian religions was a problem for the rationality of their own beliefs. Instead, the problem they examined was whether unbaptized persons could be saved. This problem applied not only to those who lived in non-Christian countries or in non-Christian communities in Christian countries, but it also applied to righteous persons who lived before the Christian era. Aquinas proposed that babies who died unbaptized and righteous Jews who died before the time of Christ went to Limbo, a pleasant place that was neither heaven nor hell, and which included neither reward nor punishment. The fate of non-Christians after the coming of Christ and after the ordinary age of baptism was a different matter. Throughout the Christian era the ultimate fate of non-Christians has been a difficult and debated issue. Exclusivists about salvation maintain that the only path to salvation is through the practice of their own religion, whereas inclusivists about salvation argue that salvation is open to people of other faiths. In traditional Christian theology, salvation is closely associated with baptism, but Aquinas argued that the sacramental practice of baptism by water is not the only way in which a person can be baptized. Righteous non-Christian martyrs have "baptism by blood" and righteous persons who follow the innate desire for a God they do not understand have "baptism by desire." In this way exclusivism about salvation begins to look a lot closer to inclusivism about salvation. In this volume the Jesuit theologian, Karl Rahner, defends a form of inclusivism according to which righteous persons of non-Christian faiths can be saved through the death of Christ. He calls these people "anonymous Christians." The Dalai Lama seems to say that non-Buddhists can eventually reach nirvana, although only Buddhists can reach it in this life. A more radically inclusivist position is John Hick's pluralism, according to which all the major religions are salvific, and we can see that because they all have something analogous to Christian saints who model a path to transforming a person's consciousness from self-centeredness to reality-centeredness.

In addition to the religious debate over exclusivism vs. inclusivism about salvation, there is a philosophical debate about exclusivism vs. inclusivism about truth. If two religions have teachings that genuinely conflict, then they cannot both be true. The options then seem to be as follows: (a) when the teachings of two different religions appear to conflict, they do not really conflict, or (b) at most one religion teaches the truth about that particular issue. Those who take option (b) are exclusivists about truth. Hick attempts an ingenious approach to option (a), arguing that on one level the world's great religions have conflicting teachings, but on another level they are all talking about the same ultimate reality. All the world's religions are true in a sense and false in a sense. So Hick is generous in his application of truth to diverse religions, but also generous in his application of falsehood to those religions.

A third problem posed by the diversity of religions is the issue of exclusivism vs. inclusivism about rationality. Given a set of important but conflicting beliefs of the major religions, are they all rational, or is rationality limited to only one? Most exclusivists about truth take the inclusivist position about rationality, maintaining that given some set of conflicting beliefs, each of which is taught by a different religion, at most one is true, but it is quite possible for all of them to be rational. To say otherwise is to take the rather unpalatable position that not only are all religions but one teaching falsehoods, but what they are teaching is irrational.

Unfortunately, this position is unstable because it drives a wedge between rationality and truth, thereby devaluing rationality and the connection between being rational and trying to get the truth. If we think all of the beliefs in a set of conflicting beliefs of the world's religions are rational, but at most one is true, we must not think there is a very close connection between being rational and being true. If we hold one of the beliefs in the set ourselves, it is little comfort to tell ourselves that we are rational if we also think that being rational is a property of the beliefs of the other conflicting beliefs in the set, a property that gives a belief no very high probability of being true.

In Zagzebski's essay in this collection the plight of the individual believer is investigated – one who trusts himself, his faculties, and the beliefs he has acquired in his lifetime, but who also trusts others, including others who have conflicting beliefs, but whose manner of believing and style of living is admirable. What should we do when we trust ourselves but recognize that there is no reason to think that we have won the epistemic lottery, that we are the ones who won the truth and others whom we admire and trust did not?

1

Religious Pluralism and Salvation

John Hick

John Hick (b. 1922) is Emeritus Professor at both the University of Birmingham in the UK and Claremont Graduate University in California and has been one of the most influential contemporary philosophers of religion. In many of his articles and books, especially *An Interpretation of Religion* (1989), he has defended religious pluralism. In the following essay, Hick argues for religious pluralism by considering the salvific claims of the major world religions. Each religion offers a path of transformation from self-centeredness to Reality-centeredness, and as far as we can tell, such transformation occurs equally within all the religions. The best explanation of these facts, Hick argues, is the hypothesis that there is a single ultimate Reality that lies beyond the limits of human concepts; each of the world religions represents a genuine but culturally and conceptually colored response to this Real.

Let us approach the problems of religious pluralism through the claims of the different traditions to offer salvation – generically, the transformation of human existence from self-centeredness to Reality-centeredness. This approach leads to a recognition of the great world faiths as spheres of salvation; and so far as we can tell, more or less equally so. Their different truth-claims express (a) their differing perceptions, through different religio-cultural 'lenses,' of the one ultimate divine Reality; (b) their different answers to the boundary questions of origin and destiny, true answers to which are however not necessary for salvation, and (c) their different historical memories.

John Hick, "Religious Pluralism and Salvation". *Faith and Philosophy* 5:4 (1988): 365–77.

I

The fact that there is a plurality of religious traditions, each with its own distinctive beliefs, spiritual practices, ethical outlook, art forms and cultural ethos, creates an obvious problem for those of us who see them, not simply as human phenomena, but as responses to the Divine. For each presents itself, implicitly or explicitly, as in some important sense absolute and unsurpassable and as rightly claiming a total allegiance. The problem of the relationship between these different streams of religious life has often been posed in terms of their divergent belief-systems. For whilst there are various overlaps between their teachings there are also radical differences: is the divine reality (let us refer to it as the Real) personal or non-personal; if personal, is it unitary or triune; is the universe created, or emanated, or itself eternal; do we live only once on this earth or are we repeatedly reborn? and so on and so on. When the problem of understanding religious plurality is approached through these rival truth-claims it appears particularly intractable.

I want to suggest, however, that it may more profitably be approached from a different direction, in terms of the claims of the various traditions to provide, or to be effective contexts of, salvation. 'Salvation' is primarily a Christian term, though I shall use it here to include its functional analogues in the other major world traditions. In this broader sense we can say that both Christianity and these other faiths are paths of salvation. For whereas pre-axial religion was (and is) centrally concerned to keep life going on an even keel, the post-axial traditions, originating or rooted in the 'axial age' of the first millenium BCE – principally Hinduism, Judaism, Buddhism, Christianity, Islam – are centrally concerned with a radical transformation of the human situation.

It is of course possible, in an alternative approach, to define salvation in such a way that it becomes a necessary truth that only one particular tradition can provide it. If, for example, from within Christianity we define salvation as being forgiven by God because of Jesus' atoning death, and so becoming part of God's redeemed community, the church, then salvation is by definition Christian salvation. If on the other hand, from within Mahayana Buddhism, we define it as the attainment of *satori* or awakening, and so becoming an ego-free manifestation of the eternal Dharmakaya, then salvation is by definition Buddhist liberation. And so on. But if we stand back from these different conceptions to compare them we can, I think, very naturally and properly see them as different forms of the more fundamental conception of a radical change from a profoundly unsatisfactory state to one that is limitlessly better because rightly related to the Real. Each tradition conceptualizes in its own way the wrongness of ordinary human existence – as a state of fallenness from paradisal virtue and happiness, or as a condition of moral weakness and alienation from God, or as the fragmentation of the infinite One into false individualities, or as a self-centeredness which pervasively poisons our involvement in the world process, making it to us an experience of anxious, unhappy unfulfillment. But each at the same time proclaims a limitlessly better possibility, again conceptualized in different ways – as the joy of conforming one's life to God's law; as giving oneself to God in Christ, so that 'it is no longer I who live, but Christ who lives in me' (Galatians 2:20), leading to eternal life in God's presence; as a complete surrender (*islam*) to God, and hence peace with God, leading to the bliss of paradise; as transcending the ego and realizing oneness with the limitless being-consciousness-bliss (*satchitananda*) of Brahman; as overcoming the ego point of view and entering into the serene selflessness of nirvana. I suggest that these different conceptions of salvation are specifications of what, in a generic formula, is the transformation of human existence from self-centeredness to a new orientation, centered in the divine Reality. And in each case the good news that is proclaimed is that this limitlessly better possibility is actually available and can be entered upon, or begin to be entered upon, here and now. Each tradition sets forth the way to attain this great good: faithfulness to the Torah, discipleship to Jesus, obedient living out of the Qur'anic way of life, the Eightfold Path of the Buddhist dharma, or the three great Hindu *margas* of mystical insight, activity in the world, and self-giving devotion to God.

II

The great world religions, then, are ways of salvation. Each claims to constitute an effective context within which the transformation of human existence can and does take place from self-centeredness to Reality-centeredness. How are we to judge such claims? We cannot directly observe the inner spiritual quality of a human relationship to the Real; but we can observe how that relationship, as one's deepest and most pervasive orientation, affects the moral and spiritual quality of a human personality and of a man's or woman's relationship to others. It would seem, then, that we can only assess these salvation-projects insofar as we are able to observe their fruits in human life. The inquiry has to be, in a broad sense, empirical. For the issue is one of fact, even though hard to define and difficult to measure fact, rather than being settleable by *a priori* stipulation.

The word 'spiritual' which occurs above is notoriously vague; but I am using it to refer to a quality or, better, an orientation which we can discern in those individuals whom we call saints – a Christian term which I use here to cover such analogues as arahat, bodhisattva, jivanmukti, mahatma. In these cases the human self is variously described as becoming part of the life of God, being 'to the Eternal Goodness what his own hand is to a man'; or being permeated from within by the infinite reality of Brahman; or becoming one with the eternal Buddha nature. There is a change in their deepest orientation from centeredness in the ego to a new centering in the Real as manifested in their own tradition. One is conscious in the presence of such a person that he or she is, to a startling extent, open to the transcendent, so as to be largely free from self-centered concerns and anxieties and empowered to live as an instrument of God/Truth/Reality.

It is to be noted that there are two main patterns of such a transformation. There are saints who withdraw from the world into prayer or meditation and saints who seek to change the world – in the medieval period a contemplative Julian of Norwich and a political Joan of Arc, or in our own century a mystical Sri Aurobindo and a political Mahatma Gandhi. In our present age of sociological consciousness, when we are aware that our inherited political and economic structures can be analyzed and purposefully changed, saintliness is more likely than in earlier times to take social and political forms. But, of whichever type, the saints are not a different species from the rest of us; they are simply much more advanced in the salvific transformation.

The ethical aspect of this salvific transformation consists in observable modes of behavior. But how do we identify the kind of behavior which, to the degree that it characterizes a life, reflects a corresponding degree of reorientation to the divine Reality? Should we use Christian ethical criteria, or Buddhist, or Muslim . . . ? The answer, I suggest, is that at the level of their most basic moral insights the great traditions use a common criterion. For they agree in giving a central and normative role to the unselfish regard for others that we call love or compassion. This is commonly expressed in the principle of valuing others as we value ourselves, and treating them accordingly. Thus in the ancient Hindu *Mahabharata* we read that 'One should never do to another that which one would regard as injurious to oneself. This, in brief, is the rule of Righteousness' (*Anushana parva*, 113:7). Again, 'He who . . . benefits persons of all orders, who is always devoted to the good of all beings, who does not feel aversion to anybody . . . succeeds in ascending to Heaven' (*Anushana parva*, 145:24). In the Buddhist *Sutta Nipata* we read, 'As a mother cares for her son, all her days, so towards all living things a man's mind should be all-embracing' (149). In the Jain scriptures we are told that one should go about 'treating all creatures in the world as he himself would be treated' (*Kitanga Sutra*, I.ii.33). Confucius, expounding humaneness (*jen*), said, 'Do not do to others what you would not like yourself' (*Analects*, xxi, 2). In a Taoist scripture we read that the good man will 'regard [others'] gains as if they were his own, and their losses in the same way' (*Thai Shang*, 3). The Zoroastrian scriptures declare, 'That nature only is good when it shall not do unto another whatever is not good for its own self' (*Dadistan-i-dinik*, 94:5). We are all familiar with Jesus' teaching, 'As ye would that men should do to you, do ye also to them likewise' (Luke 6:31). In the Jewish Talmud we read 'What is hateful to yourself do not do to your fellow man. That is the whole of the Torah' (*Babylonian Talmud*, Shabbath 31a). And in the Hadith of Islam we read Muhammad's words, 'No man is a true believer unless he desires for his brother that which he desires for himself' (*Ibn Madja*, Intro. 9). Clearly, if everyone acted on this basic principle, taught by all the major faiths, there would be no injustice, no avoidable suffering, and the human family would everywhere live in peace.

When we turn from this general principle of love/compassion to the actual behavior of people within the different traditions, wondering to what extent they live in this way, we realize how little research has been done on so important a question. We do not have much more to go on than general impressions, supplemented by travellers tales and anecdotal reports. We observe among our neighbors within our own community a great deal of practical loving-kindness; and we are told, for example, that a remarkable degree of self-giving love is to be found among the Hindu fishing families in the mud huts along the Madras shore; and we hear various other similar accounts from other lands. We read biographies, social histories and novels of Muslim village life in Africa, Buddhist life in Thailand, Hindu life in India, Jewish life in New York, as well as Christian life around the world, both in the past and today, and we get the impression that the personal virtues (as well as vices) are basically much the same within these very different religio-cultural settings and that in all of them unselfish concern for others occurs and is highly valued. And, needless to say, as well as love and compassion we also see all-too-abundantly, and apparently spread more or less equally in every society, cruelty, greed, hatred, selfishness and malice.

All this constitutes a haphazard and impressionistic body of data. Indeed I want to stress, not how easy it is, but on the contrary how difficult it is, to make responsible judgments in this area. For not only do we lack full information, but the fragmentary information that we have has to be interpreted in the light of the varying natural conditions of human life in different periods of history and in different economic and political circumstances. And I suggest that all that we can presently arrive at is the cautious and negative conclusion that we have no good reason to believe that any one of the great religious traditions has proved itself to be more productive of love/compassion than another.

The same is true when we turn to the large-scale social outworkings of the different salvation-projects. Here the units are not individual human lives, spanning a period of decades, but religious cultures spanning many centuries. For we can no more judge a civilization than a human life by confining our attention to a single temporal cross-section. Each of the great streams of religious life has had its times of flourishing and its times of deterioration. Each has produced its own distinctive kinds of good and its own distinctive kinds of evil. But to assess either the goods or the evils cross-culturally is difficult to say the least. How do we weigh, for example, the lack of economic progress, and consequent widespread poverty, in traditional Hindu and Buddhist cultures against the endemic violence and racism of Christian civilization, culminating in the twentieth century Holocaust? How do we weigh what the west regards as the hollowness of arranged marriages against what the east regards as the hollowness of a marriage system that leads to such a high proportion of divorces and broken families? From within each culture one can see clearly enough the defects of the others. But an objective ethical comparison of such vast and complex totalities is at present an unattainable ideal. And the result is that we are not in a position to claim an over-all moral superiority for any one of the great living religious traditions.

Let us now see where we have arrived. I have suggested that if we identify the central claim of each of the great religious traditions as the claim to provide, or to be an effective context of, salvation; and if we see salvation as an actual change in human beings from self-centeredness to a new orientation centered in the ultimate divine Reality; and if this new orientation has both a more elusive 'spiritual' character and a more readily observable moral aspect – then we arrive at the modest and largely negative conclusion that, so far as we can tell, no one of the great world religions is salvifically superior to the rest.

III

If this is so, what are we to make of the often contradictory doctrines of the different traditions?

In order to make progress at this point, we must distinguish various kinds and levels of doctrinal conflict.

There are, first, conceptions of the ultimate as Jahweh, or the Holy Trinity, or Allah, or Shiva, or Vishnu, or as Brahman, or the Dharmakaya, the Tao, and so on.

If salvation is taking place, and taking place to about the same extent, within the religious systems presided over by these various deities and absolutes, this suggests that they are different manifestations to humanity of a yet more ultimate ground of all salvific transformation. Let us then consider the possibility that an infinite transcendent divine reality is being differently conceived, and therefore differently experienced, and therefore differently responded to from within our different religio-cultural ways of being human. This hypothesis makes sense of the fact that the salvific transformation seems to have been occurring in all the great traditions. Such a conception is, further, readily open to philosophical support. For we are familiar today with the ways in which human experience is partly formed by the conceptual and linguistic frameworks within which it occurs. The basically Kantian insight that the mind is active in perception, and that we are always aware of our environment as it appears to a consciousness operating with our particular conceptual resources and habits, has been amply confirmed by work in cognitive psychology and the sociology of knowledge and can now be extended with some confidence to the analysis of religious awareness. If, then, we proceed inductively from the phenomenon of religious experience around the world, adopting a religious as distinguished from a naturalistic interpretation of it, we are likely to find ourselves making two moves. The first is to postulate an ultimate transcendent divine reality (which I have been referring to as the Real) which, being beyond the scope of our human concepts, cannot be directly experienced by us as it is in itself but only as it appears through our various human thought-forms. And the second is to identify the thought-and-experienced deities and absolutes as different manifestations of the Real within different historical forms of human consciousness. In Kantian terms, the divine noumenon, the Real *an sich*, is experienced through different human receptivities as a range of divine phenomena, in the formation of which religious concepts have played an essential part.

These different 'receptivities' consist of conceptual schemas within which various personal, communal and historical factors have produced yet further variations. The most basic concepts in terms of which the Real is humanly thought-and-experienced are those of (personal) deity and of the (non-personal) absolute. But the Real is not actually experienced either as deity in general or as the absolute in general. Each basic concept becomes (in Kantian terminology) schematized in more concrete form. It is at this point that individual and cultural factors enter the process. The religious tradition of which we are a part, with its history and ethos and its great exemplars, its scriptures feeding our thoughts and emotions, and perhaps above all its devotional or meditative practices, constitutes an uniquely shaped and coloured 'lens' through which we are concretely aware of the Real specifically as the personal Adonai, or as the Heavenly Father, or as Allah, or Vishnu, or Shiva . . . or again as the non-personal Brahman, or Dharmakaya, or the Void or the Ground . . . Thus, one who uses the forms of Christian prayer and sacrament is thereby led to experience the Real as the divine Thou, whereas one who practices advaitic yoga or Buddhist zazen is thereby brought to experience the Real as the infinite being-consciousness-bliss of Brahman, or as the limitless emptiness of *sunyata* which is at the same time the infinite fullness of immediate reality as 'wondrous being.'

Three explanatory comments at this point before turning to the next level of doctrinal disagreement. First, to suppose that the experienced deities and absolutes which are the intentional objects of worship or content of religious meditation, are appearances or manifestations of the Real, rather than each being itself the Real *an sich*, is not to suppose that they are illusions – any more than the varying ways in which a mountain may appear to a plurality of differently placed observers are illusory. That the same reality may be variously experienced and described is true even of physical objects. But in the case of the infinite, transcendent divine reality there may well be much greater scope for the use of varying human conceptual schemas producing varying modes of phenomenal experience.

Whereas the concepts in terms of which we are aware of mountains and rivers and houses are largely (though by no means entirely) standard throughout the human race, the religious concepts in terms of which we become aware of the Real have developed in widely different ways within the different cultures of the earth.

As a second comment, to say that the Real is beyond the range of our human concepts is not intended to mean that it is beyond the scope of purely formal, logically generated concepts – such as the concept of being beyond the range of (other than purely formal) concepts. We would not be able to refer at all to that which cannot be conceptualized in any way, not even by the concept of being unconceptualizable! But the other than purely formal concepts by which our experience is structured must be presumed not to apply to its noumenal ground. The characteristics mapped in thought and language are those that are constitutive of human experience. We have no warrant to apply them to the noumenal ground of the phenomenal, i.e., experienced, realm. We should therefore not think of the Real *an sich* as singular or plural, substance or process, personal or non-personal, good or bad, purposive or non-purpose. This has long been a basic theme of religious thought. For example, within Christianity, Gregory of Nyssa declared that:

> The simplicity of the True Faith assumes God to be that which He is, namely, incapable of being grasped by any term, or any idea, or any other device of our apprehension, remaining beyond the reach not only of the human but of the angelic and all supramundane intelligence, unthinkable, unutterable, above all expression in words, having but one name that can represent His proper nature, the single name being 'Above Every Name.' (*Against Eunomius*, I, 42)

Augustine, continuing this tradition, said that 'God transcends even the mind' (*True Religion*, 36:67), and Aquinas that 'by its immensity, the divine substance surpasses every form that our intellect reaches' (*Contra Gentiles*, I, 14, 3). In Islam the Qur'an affirms that God is 'beyond what they describe' (6:101). The Upanishads declare of Brahman, 'There the eye goes not, speech goes not, nor the mind' (*Kena Up.*, 1, 3), and Shankara wrote that Brahman is that 'before which words recoil, and to which no understanding has ever attained' (Otto, *Mysticism East and West*, E. T. 1932, p. 28).

But, third, we might well ask, why postulate an ineffable and unobservable divine-reality-in-itself? If we can say virtually nothing about it, why affirm its existence? The answer is that the reality or non-reality of the postulated noumenal ground of the experienced religious phenomena constitutes the difference between a religious and a naturalistic interpretation of religion. If there is no such transcendent ground, the various forms of religious experience have to be categorized as purely human projections. If on the other hand there is such a transcendent ground, then these phenomena may be joint products of the universal presence of the Real and of the varying sets of concepts and images that have crystallized within the religious traditions of the earth. To affirm the transcendent is thus to affirm that religious experience is not solely a construction of the human imagination but is a response – though always culturally conditioned – to the Real.

Those doctrinal conflicts, then, that embody different conceptions of the ultimate arise, according to the hypothesis I am presenting, from the variations between different sets of human conceptual schema and spiritual practice. And it seems that each of these varying ways of thinking-and-experiencing the Real has been able to mediate its transforming presence to human life. For the different major concepts of the ultimate do not seem – so far as we can tell – to result in one religious totality being soteriologically more effective than another.

IV

The second level of doctrinal difference consists of metaphysical beliefs which cohere with although they are not exclusively linked to a particular conception of the ultimate. These are beliefs about the relation of the material universe to the Real: creation *ex nihilo*, emanation, an eternal universe, an unknown form of dependency . . . ? And about human destiny: reincarnation or a single life, eternal identity or transcendence of the self . . . ? Again, there are questions about the existence of heavens and hells and purgatories and angels and devils and many other subsidiary states and entities. Out of this mass of disputed religious issues let me pick two major examples: is the universe created *ex nihilo*, and do human beings reincarnate?

I suggest that we would do well to apply to such questions a principle that was taught by the Buddha two and a half millennia ago. He listed a series of 'undetermined questions' (*avyakata*) – whether the universe is eternal, whether it is spatially infinite, whether (putting it in modern terms) mind and brain are identical, and what the state is of a completed project of human existence (a Tathagata) after bodily death. He refused to answer these questions, saying that we do not need to have knowledge of these things in order to attain liberation or awakening (nirvana); and indeed that to regard such information as soteriologically essential would only divert us from the single-minded quest for liberation. I think that we can at this point profitably learn from the Buddha, even extending his conception of the undetermined questions further than he did – for together with almost everyone else in his own culture he regarded one of our examples, reincarnation, as a matter of assured knowledge. Let us, then, accept that we do not *know* whether, e.g., the universe was created *ex nihilo*, nor whether human beings are reincarnated; and, further, that it is not necessary for salvation to hold a correct opinion on either matter.

I am not suggesting that such issues are unimportant. On their own level they are extremely important, being both of great interest to us and also having widely ramifying implications within our belief-systems and hence for our lives. The thought of being created out of nothing can nourish a salutary sense of absolute dependence. (But other conceptions can also nurture that sense.) The idea of reincarnation can offer the hope of future spiritual progress; though, combined with the principle of karma, it can also serve to validate the present inequalities of human circumstances. (But other eschatologies also have their problems, both theoretical and practical.) Thus these – and other – disputed issues do have a genuine importance. Further, it is possible that some of them may one day be settled by empirical evidence. It might become established, for example, that the 'big bang' of some fifteen billion years ago was an absolute beginning, thus ruling out the possibility that the universe is eternal. And again, it might become established, by an accumulation of evidence, that reincarnation does indeed occur in either some or all cases. On the other hand it is possible that we shall never achieve agreed knowledge in these areas. Certainly, at the present time, whilst we have theories, preferences, hunches, inherited convictions, we cannot honestly claim to have secure knowledge. And the same is true, I suggest, of the entire range of metaphysical issues about which the religions dispute. They are of intense interest, properly the subject of continuing research and discussion, but are not matters concerning which absolute dogmas are appropriate. Still less is it appropriate to maintain that salvation depends upon accepting some one particular opinion or dogma. We have seen that the transformation of human existence from self-centeredness to Reality-centeredness seems to be taking place within each of the great traditions despite their very different answers to these debated questions. It follows that a correct opinion concerning them is not required for salvation.

V

The third level of doctrinal disagreement concerns historical questions. Each of the great traditions includes a larger or smaller body of historical beliefs. In the case of Judaism these include at least the main features of the history described in the Hebrew scriptures; in the case of Christianity, these plus the main features of the life, death and resurrection of Jesus as described in the New Testament; in the case of Islam, the main features of the history described in the Qur'an; in the case of Vaishnavite Hinduism, the historicity of Krishna; in the case of Buddhism, the historicity of Guatama and his enlightenment at Bodh Gaya; and so on. But although each tradition thus has its own records of the past, there are rather few instances of direct disagreement between these. For the strands of history that are cherished in these different historical memories do not generally overlap; and where they do overlap they do not generally involve significant differences. The overlaps are mainly within the thread of ancient near eastern history that is common to the Jewish, Christian and Muslim scriptures; and within this I can only locate two points of direct disagreement – the Torah's statement that Abraham nearly sacrificed his son Isaac at Mount Moriah (Genesis 22) versus the Muslim interpretation of the Qur'anic version (in Sura 37) that it was his other son Ishmael; and the New Testament witness that Jesus died on the cross versus the Qur'anic teaching that 'they did not slay him, neither crucified him, only a likeness of that was shown them' (Sura 4:156). (This latter however would seem to be a conflict between an historical report, in the New Testament, and a theological inference – that God would not allow so great a prophet to be killed – in the Qur'an.)

All that one can say in general about such disagreements, whether between two traditions or between any one of them and the secular historians, is that they could only properly be settled by the weight of historical evidence. However, the events in question are usually so remote in time, and the evidence so slight or so uncertain, that the question cannot be definitively settled. We have to be content with different communal memories, enriched as they are by the mythic halo that surrounds all long-lived human memories of events of transcendent significance. Once again, then, I suggest that differences of historical judgment, although having their own proper importance, do not prevent the different traditions from being effective, and so far as we can tell equally effective, contexts of salvation. It is evidently not necessary for salvation to have correct historical information. (It is likewise not necessary for salvation, we may add, to have correct scientific information.)

VI

Putting all this together, the picture that I am suggesting can be outlined as follows: our human religious experience, variously shaped as it is by our sets of religious concepts, is a cognitive response to the universal presence of the ultimate divine Reality that, in itself, exceeds human conceptuality. This Reality is however manifested to us in ways formed by a variety of human concepts, as the range of divine personae and metaphysical impersonae witnessed to in the history of religions. Each major tradition, built around its own distinctive way of thinking-and-experiencing the Real, has developed its own answers to the perennial questions of our origin and destiny, constituting more or less comprehensive and coherent cosmologies and eschatologies. These are human creations which have, by their association with living streams of religious experience, become invested with a sacred authority. However they cannot all be wholly true; quite possibly none is wholly true; perhaps all are partly true. But since the salvific process has been going on through the centuries despite this unknown distribution of truth and falsity in our cosmologies and eschatologies, it follows that it is not necessary for salvation to adopt any one of them. We would therefore do well to learn to tolerate unresolved, and at present unresolvable, differences concerning these ultimate mysteries.

One element, however, to be found in the belief-systems of most of the traditions raises a special problem, namely that which asserts the sole salvific efficacy of that tradition. I shall discuss this problem in terms of Christianity because it is particularly acute for those of us who are Christians. We are all familiar with such New Testament texts as 'There is salvation in no one else [than Jesus Christ], for there is no other name under heaven given among men by which we must be saved (Acts 4:12), and with the Catholic dogma *Extra ecclesiam nulla salus* (No salvation outside the church) and its Protestant equivalent – never formulated as an official dogma but nevertheless implicit within the 18th and 19th century Protestant missionary expansion, – no salvation outside Christianity. Such a dogma differs from other elements of Christian belief in that it is not only a statement about the potential relationship of Christians to God but at the same time about the actual relationship of non-Christians to God. It says that the latter, in virtue of being non-Christians, lack salvation. Clearly such a dogma is incompatible with the insight that the salvific transformation of human existence is going on, and so far as we can tell going on to a more or less equal extent, within all the great traditions. Insofar, then, as we accept that salvation is not confined to Christianity we must reject the old exclusivist dogma.

This has in fact now been done by most thinking Christians, though exceptions remain, mostly within the extreme Protestant fundamentalist constituencies. The *Extra ecclesiam* dogma, although not explicitly repealed, has been outflanked by the work of such influential Catholic theologians as Karl Rahner, whose new approach was in effect endorsed by Vatican II. Rahner expressed his more inclusivist outlook by suggesting that devout people of other faiths are 'anonymous Christians,' within the invisible church even without knowing it, and thus within the sphere of salvation. The present Pope [John Paul II], in his Encyclical *Redemptor Hominis* (1979) has expressed this thought even more comprehensively by saying that 'every man without exception has been redeemed by Christ' and 'with every man without any exception whatever Christ is in a way united, even when man is unaware of it' (para. 14). And a number of Protestant theologians have advocated a comparable position.

The feature that particularly commends this kind of inclusivism to many Christians today is that it recognizes the spiritual values of other religions, and the occurrence of salvation within them, and yet at the same time preserves their conviction of the ultimate superiority of their own religion over all others. For it maintains that salvation, wherever it occurs, is Christian salvation; and Christians are accordingly those who alone know and preach the source of salvation, namely in the atoning death of Christ.

This again, like the old exclusivism, is a statement not only about the ground of salvation for Christians but also for Jews, Muslims, Hindus, Buddhists and everyone else. But we have seen that it has to be acknowledged that the immediate ground of their transformation is the particular spiritual path along which they move. It is by living in accordance with the Torah or with the Qur'anic revelation that Jews and Muslims find a transforming peace with God; it is by one or other of their great *margas* that Hindus attain to *moksha*; it is by the Eightfold Path that Theravada Buddhists come to *nirvana*; it is by *zazen* that Zen Buddhists attain to *satori*; and so on. The Christian inclusivist is, then, by implication, declaring that these various spiritual paths are efficacious, and constitute authentic contexts of salvation, because Jesus died on the cross; and, by further implication, that if he had not died on the cross they would not be efficacious.

This is a novel and somewhat astonishing doctrine. How are we to make sense of the idea that the salvific power of the dharma taught five hundred years earlier by the Buddha is a consequence of the death of Jesus in approximately 30 CE? Such an apparently bizarre conception should only be affirmed for some very good reason. It was certainly not taught by Jesus or his apostles. It has emerged only in the thought of twentieth century Christians who have come to recognize that Jews are being salvifically transformed through the spirituality of Judaism, Muslims through that of Islam, Hindus and Buddhists through the paths mapped out by their respective traditions, and so on, but who nevertheless wish to retain their inherited sense of the unique superiority of Christianity. The only outlet left for this sense, when one has acknowledged the salvific efficacy of the various great spiritual ways, is the arbitrary and contrived notion of their metaphysical dependency upon the death of Christ. But the theologian who undertakes to spell out this invisible causality is not to be envied. The problem is not one of logical possibility – it only requires logical agility to cope with that – but one of religious or spiritual plausibility. It would be a better use of theological time and energy, in my opinion, to develop forms of trinitarian, christological and soteriological doctrine which are compatible with our awareness of the independent salvific authenticity of the other great world faiths. Such forms are already available in principle in conceptions of the Trinity, not as ontologically three but as three ways in which the one God is humanly thought and experienced; conceptions of Christ as a man so fully open to and inspired by God as to be, in the ancient Hebrew metaphor, a 'son of God'; and conceptions of salvation as an actual human transformation which has been powerfully elicited and shaped, among his disciples, by the influence of Jesus.

There may indeed well be a variety of ways in which Christian thought can develop in response to our acute late twentieth century awareness of the other world religions, as there were of responding to the nineteenth century awareness of the evolution of the forms of life and the historical character of the holy scriptures. And likewise there will no doubt be a variety of ways in which each of the other great traditions can rethink its inherited assumption of its own unique superiority. But it is not for us to tell people of other traditions how to do their own business. Rather, we should attend to our own.

Note

This paper was originally delivered as the second Kegley Lecture at California State University, Bakersfield, on February 10th, 1988. For a fuller account of its proposals the reader is invited to see my *An Interpretation of Religion* (New Haven: Yale University Press and London: Macmillan, 1988).

2

The Bodhgaya Interview (1981)

The Dalai Lama

The fourteenth Dalai Lama (b. 1935) is a Buddhist monk and the spiritual and political leader of Tibet, although since 1959 he has been living in exile in India. In 1989 he was awarded the Nobel Peace Prize in recognition of his non-violent struggle for the liberation of Tibet. He is one of the world's most highly respected religious leaders and is regarded by his followers as a Bodhisattva – that is, an individual who has achieved the ideal of enlightenment, but has chosen to forgo nirvana and be reincarnated in order to serve others and help them achieve enlightenment. In the following interview, the Dalai Lama discusses his views on the relationship between Buddhism and other religions.

His Holiness: Welcome, I am very glad to meet with you all here. I am open to your questions. Besides that, I have nothing to say.

Question: Do you see any possibility of an integration of Christianity and Buddhism in the West? An overall religion for Western society?

His Holiness: It depends upon what you mean by integration. If you mean by this the possibility of the integration of Buddhism and Christianity within a society, where they co-exist side by side, then I would answer affirmatively. If, however, your view of integration envisions all of society following some sort of composite religion which is neither pure Buddhism nor pure Christianity, then I would have to consider this form of integration implausible.

It is, of course, quite possible for a country to be predominantly Christian, and yet that some of the people of that country choose to follow Buddhism. I think it is quite possible that a person who is basically a Christian, who accepts the idea of a God, who believes in God, could

The Dalai Lama, excerpts from "The 1981 Interview" from *The Bodhgaya Interviews: His Holiness the Dalai Lama*, edited by José I. Cabezón (Ithaca, NY: Snow Lion Publications, 1988), extracts from pp. 11–14, 21–4.

at the same time incorporate certain Buddhist ideas and techniques into his/her practice. The teachings of love, compassion, and kindness are present in Christianity and also in Buddhism. Particularly in the Bodhisattva vehicle there are many techniques which focus on developing compassion, kindness, etc. These are things which can be practiced at the same time by Christians and by Buddhists. While remaining committed to Christianity it is quite conceivable that a person may choose to undergo training in meditation, concentration, and one-pointedness of mind, that, while remaining a Christian, one may choose to practice Buddhist ideas. This is another possible and very viable kind of integration.

Question: Is there any conflict between the Buddhist teachings and the idea of a creator God who exists independently from us?

His Holiness: If we view the world's religions from the widest possible viewpoint, and examine their ultimate goal, we find that all of the major world religions, whether Christianity or Islam, Hinduism or Buddhism, are directed to the achievement of permanent human happiness. They are all directed toward that goal. All religions emphasize the fact that the true follower must be honest and gentle, in other words, that a truly religious person must always strive to be a better human being. To this end, the different world's religions teach different doctrines which will help transform the person. In this regard, all religions are the same, there is no conflict. This is something we must emphasize. We must consider the question of religious diversity from *this* viewpoint. And when we do, we find no conflict.

Now from the philosophical point of view, the theory that God is the creator, is almighty and permanent, is in contradiction to the Buddhist teachings. From this point of view there is disagreement. For Buddhists, the universe has no first cause and hence no creator, nor can there be such a thing as a permanent, primordially pure being. So, of course, doctrinally, there is conflict. The views are opposite to one another. But if we consider the purpose of these different philosophies, then we see that they are the same. This is my belief.

Different kinds of food have different tastes: one may be very hot, one may be very sour, and one very sweet. They are opposite tastes, they conflict. But whether a dish is concocted to taste sweet, sour or hot, it is nonetheless made in this way so as to taste good. Some people prefer very spicy hot foods with a lot of chili peppers. Many Indians and Tibetans have a liking for such dishes. Others are very fond of bland tasting foods. It is a wonderful thing to have variety. It is an expression of individuality; it is a personal thing.

Likewise, the variety of the different world religious philosophies is a very useful and beautiful thing. For certain people, the idea of God as creator and of everything depending on his will is beneficial and soothing, and so for that person such a doctrine is worthwhile. For someone else, the idea that there is no creator, that ultimately, one is oneself the creator – in that everything depends upon oneself – is more appropriate. For certain people, it may be a more effective method of spiritual growth, it may be more beneficial. For such persons, this idea is better and for the other type of person, the other idea is more suitable. You see, there is no conflict, no problem. This is my belief.

Now conflicting doctrines are something which is not unknown even within Buddhism itself. The Mādhyamikas and Cittamātrins, two Buddhist philosophical subschools, accept the theory of emptiness. The Vaibhāṣikas and Sautrāntikas, two others, accept another theory, the theory of selflessness, which, strictly speaking, is not the same as the doctrine of emptiness as posited by the two higher schools. So there exists this difference, some schools accepting the emptiness of phenomena and others not. There also exists a difference as regards the way in which the two upper schools explain the doctrine of emptiness. For the Cittamātrins, emptiness is set forth in terms of the non-duality of subject and object. The Mādhyamikas, however, repudiate the notion that emptiness is tantamount to idealism, the claim that everything is of the nature of mind. So you see, even within Buddhism, the Mādhyamika and Cittamātra schools are in conflict. The Mādhyamikas are again divided into Prāsaṅgikas and Svātantrikas, and between these two sub-schools there is also conflict. The latter accept that things exist by virtue of an inherent characteristic, while the former do not.

So you see, conflict in the philosophical field is nothing to be surprised at. It exists even within Buddhism itself.

[. . .]

Question: It is generally said that teachers of other religions, no matter how great, cannot attain liberation without turning to the Buddhist path. Now suppose there is a great teacher, say he is a Śaivite, and suppose he upholds very strict discipline and is totally dedicated to other people all of the time, always giving of himself. Is this person, simply because he follows Śiva, incapable of attaining liberation, and if so, what can be done to help him?

His Holiness: During the Buddha's own time, there were many non-Buddhist teachers whom the Buddha could not help, for whom he could do nothing. So he just let them be.

The Buddha Śākyamuni was an extraordinary being, he was the manifestation (*nirmānakāya*), the physical appearance, of an already enlightened being. But while some people recognized him as a Buddha, others regarded him as a black magician with strange and evil powers. So, you see, even the Buddha Śākyamuni himself was not accepted as an enlightened being by all of his contemporaries. Different human beings have different mental predispositions, and there are cases when even the Buddha himself could not do much to overcome these – there was a limit.

Now today, the followers of Śiva have their own religious practices and they reap some benefit from engaging in their own forms of worship. Through this, their life will gradually change. Now my own position on this question is that Śivaji's followers should practice according to their own beliefs and traditions, Christians must genuinely and sincerely follow what they believe, and so forth. That is sufficient.

Questioner: But they will not attain liberation!

His Holiness: We Buddhists ourselves will not be liberated at once. In our own case, it will take time. Gradually we will be able to reach *mokṣa* or *nirvāṇa*, but the majority of Buddhists will not achieve this within their own lifetimes. So there's no hurry. If Buddhists themselves have to wait, perhaps many lifetimes, for their goal, why should we expect that it be different for non-Buddhists? So, you see, nothing much can be done.

Suppose, for example, you try to convert someone from another religion to the Buddhist religion, and you argue with them trying to convince them of the inferiority of their position. And suppose you do not succeed, suppose they do not become Buddhist. On the one hand, you have failed in your task, and on the other hand, you may had weakened the trust they have in their own religion, so that they may come to doubt their own faith. What have you accomplished by all this? It is of no use. When we come into contact with the followers of different religions, we should not argue. Instead, we should advise them to follow their own beliefs as sincerely and as truthfully as possible. For if they do so, they will no doubt reap certain benefit. Of this there is no doubt. Even in the immediate future they will be able to achieve more happiness and more satisfaction. Do you agree?

This is the way I usually act in such matters, it is my belief. When I meet the followers of different religions, I always praise them, for it is enough, it is sufficient, that they are following the moral teachings that are emphasized in every religion. It is enough, as I mentioned earlier, that they are trying to become better human beings. This in itself is very good and worthy of praise.

Questioner: But is it only the Buddha who can be the ultimate source of refuge?

His Holiness: Here, you see, it is necessary to examine what is meant by liberation or salvation. Liberation in which "a mind that understands the sphere of reality annihilates all defilements in the sphere of reality" is a state that only Buddhists can accomplish. This kind of *mokṣa* or *nirvāṇa* is only explained in the Buddhist scriptures, and is achieved only through Buddhist practice. According to certain religions, however, salvation is a place, a beautiful paradise, like a peaceful valley. To attain such a state as this, to achieve such a state of *mokṣa*, does not require the practice of emptiness, the understanding of reality. In Buddhism itself, we believe that through the accumulation of merit one can obtain rebirth in heavenly paradises like Tuṣita.

Questioner: So, if one is a follower of Vedānta, and one reaches the state of *satcitānanda*, would this not be considered ultimate liberation?

His Holiness: Again, it depends upon how you interpret the words, "ultimate liberation." The mokṣa which is described in the Buddhist religion is achieved only through the practice of emptiness. And this kind of *nirvāṇa* or liberation, as I have defined it above, cannot be achieved even by Svātantrika Mādhyamikas, by Cittamātras, Sautrāntikas or Vaibhāṣikas. The followers of these schools, *though Buddhists*, do not understand the actual doctrine of emptiness. Because they cannot realize emptiness, or reality, they cannot accomplish the kind of liberation I defined previously.

3

Christianity and the Non-Christian Religions

Karl Rahner

Karl Rahner (1904–84) was one of the most influential Catholic theologians of the twentieth century. In the following reading, Rahner defends a form of Christian inclusivism – the view that Jesus Christ is the only true path to salvation, but that followers of other religions can attain the salvation Christ provides. He argues that God is at work in and through the non-Christian religions and that sincere followers of these religions have experienced divine grace; they are "anonymous Christians" who have not been brought to explicit self-awareness of this fact.

'Open Catholicism' involves two things. It signifies the fact that the Catholic Church is opposed by historical forces which she herself cannot disregard as if they were purely 'worldly' forces and a matter of indifference to her but which, on the contrary, although they do not stand in a positive relationship of peace and mutual recognition to the Church, do have a significance for her. 'Open Catholicism' means also the task of becoming related to these forces in order to understand their existence (since this cannot be simply acknowledged), in order to bear with and overcome the annoyance of their opposition and in order to form the Church in such a way that she will be able to overcome as much of this pluralism as should not exist, by understanding herself as the higher unity of this opposition. 'Open Catholicism' means therefore a certain attitude towards the present-day pluralism of powers with different outlooks on the world. We do not, of course, refer to pluralism merely as a fact which one simply acknowledges without explaining it. Pluralism is meant here as a fact which ought to be thought about and one which, without denying that – in part at least – it should not exist at all, should be incorporated once more from a more elevated viewpoint into the totality and unity of the Christian understanding

Karl Rahner, "Christianity and the Non-Christian Religions" in *Christianity and Other Religions*, ed. John Hick and Brian Hebblethwaite (London: Fortress Press, 1981), extracts from pp. 52–79.

of human existence. For Christianity, one of the gravest elements of this pluralism in which we live and with which we must come to terms, and indeed the element most difficult to incorporate, is the pluralism of religions.

[. . .]

But quite apart from this, this pluralism is a greater threat and a reason for greater unrest for Christianity than for any other religion. For no other religion – not even Islam – maintains so absolutely that it is *the* religion, the one and only valid revelation of the one living God, as does the Christian religion.

The fact of the pluralism of religions, which endures and still from time to time becomes virulent anew even after a history of two thousand years, must therefore be the greatest scandal and the greatest vexation for Christianity. And the threat of this vexation is also greater for the individual Christian today than ever before. For in the past, the other religion was in practice the religion of a completely different cultural environment. It belonged to a history with which the individual only communicated very much on the periphery of his own history; it was the religion of those who were even in every other respect alien to oneself. It is not surprising, therefore, that people did not wonder at the fact that these 'others' and 'strangers' had also a different religion. No wonder that in general people could not seriously consider these other religions as a challenge posed to themselves or even as a possibility for themselves. Today things have changed. The West is no longer shut up in itself; it can no longer regard itself simply as the centre of the history of this world and as the centre of culture, with a religion which even from this point of view (i.e. from a point of view which has really nothing to do with a decision of faith but which simply carries the weight of something quite self-evident) could appear as the obvious and indeed sole way of honouring God to be thought of for a European. Today everybody is the next-door neighbour and spiritual neighbour of everyone else in the world. And so everybody today is determined by the intercommunication of all those situations of life which affect the whole world. Every religion which exists in the world is – just like all cultural possibilities and actualities of other people – a question posed, and a possibility offered, to every person. And just as one experiences someone else's culture in practice as something relative to one's own and as something existentially demanding, so it is also involuntarily with alien religions. They have become part of one's own existential situation – no longer merely theoretically but in the concrete – and we experience them therefore as something which puts the absolute claim of our own Christian faith into question. Hence, the question about the understanding of and the continuing existence of religious pluralism as a factor of our immediate Christian existence is an urgent one and part of the question as to how we are to deal with today's pluralism.

This problem could be tackled from different angles. In the present context we simply wish to try to describe a few of those basic traits of a Catholic dogmatic interpretation of the non-Christian religions which may help us to come closer to a solution of the question about the Christian position in regard to the religious pluralism in the world of today.

[. . .]

1st Thesis: We must begin with the thesis which follows, because it certainly represents the basis in the Christian faith of the theological understanding of other religions. This thesis states that Christianity understands itself as the absolute religion, intended for all men, which cannot recognize any other religion beside itself as of equal right. This proposition is self-evident and basic for Christianity's understanding of itself. There is no need here to prove it or to develop its meaning. After all, Christianity does not take valid and lawful religion to mean primarily that relationship of man to God which man himself institutes on his own authority. Valid and lawful religion does not mean man's own interpretation of human existence. It is not the reflection and objectification of the experience which man has of himself and by himself.

Valid and lawful religion for Christianity is rather God's action on men, God's free self-revelation by communicating himself to man. It is God's relationship to men, freely instituted by God himself and revealed by God in this institution. *This* relationship of God to man is basically the same for all men, because it rests on the Incarnation, death and resurrection of the one Word of God become flesh. Christianity is God's own interpretation in his Word of this relationship of God to man founded in Christ by God himself. And so Christianity can recognize itself as the true and lawful religion for all men only where and when it enters with existential power and demanding force into the realm of another religion and – judging it by itself – puts it in question. Since the time of Christ's coming – ever since he came in the flesh as the Word of God in absoluteness and reconciled, i.e. united the world with God by his death and resurrection, not merely theoretically but really – Christ and his continuing historical presence in the world (which we call 'Church') is *the* religion which binds man to God.

[...]

2nd Thesis: Until the moment when the Gospel really enters into the historical situation of an individual, a non-Christian religion (even outside the Mosaic religion) does not merely contain elements of a natural knowledge of God, elements, moreover, mixed up with human depravity which is the result of original sin and later aberrations. It contains also supernatural elements arising out of the grace which is given to men as a gratuitous gift on account of Christ. For this reason a non-Christian religion can be recognized as a *lawful* religion (although only in different degrees) without thereby denying the error and depravity contained in it. This thesis requires a more extensive explanation.

We must first of all note the point up to which this evaluation of the non-Christian religions is valid. This is the point in time when the Christian religion becomes a historically real factor for those who are of this religion. Whether this point is the same, theologically speaking, as the first Pentecost, or whether it is different in chronological time for individual peoples and religions, is something which even at this point will have to be left to a certain extent an open question. We have, however, chosen our formulation in such a way that it points more in the direction of the opinion which seems to us the more correct one in the matter although the *criteria* for a more exact determination of this moment in time must again be left an open question.

The thesis itself is divided into two parts. It means first of all that it is *a priori* quite possible to suppose that there are supernatural, grace-filled elements in non-Christian religions. Let us first of all deal with this statement. It does not mean, of course, that all the elements of a polytheistic conception of the divine, and all the other religious, ethical and metaphysical aberrations contained in the non-Christian religions, are to be or may be treated as harmless either in theory or in practice. There have been constant protests against such elements throughout the history of Christianity and throughout the history of the Christian interpretation of the non-Christian religions, starting with the Epistle to the Romans and following on the Old Testament polemics against the religion of the 'heathens'. Every one of these protests is still valid in what was really meant and expressed by them. Every such protest remains a part of the message which Christianity and the Church has to give to the peoples who profess such religions. Furthermore, we are not concerned here with an *a posteriori* history of religions. Consequently, we also cannot describe empirically what should not exist and what is opposed to God's will in these non-Christian religions, nor can we represent these things in their many forms and degrees. We are here concerned with dogmatic theology and so can merely repeat the universal and unqualified verdict as to the unlawfulness of the non-Christian religions right from the moment when they came into real and historically powerful contact with Christianity (and at first only thus!). It is clear, however, that this condemnation does not mean to deny the very basic differences within the non-Christian religions especially since the pious, God-pleasing pagan was already a theme of the Old Testament, and especially since this God-pleasing pagan cannot simply be thought of as living absolutely outside the concrete socially constituted religion and constructing his own religion on his native foundations – just as St Paul in his speech on the Areopagus did not simply exclude a positive and basic view of the pagan religion.

The decisive reason for the first part of our thesis is basically a theological consideration. This consideration (prescinding from certain more precise qualifications) rests ultimately on the fact that, if we wish to be Christians, we must profess belief in the universal and serious salvific purpose of God towards all men which is true even within the post-paradisean phase of salvation dominated by original sin. We know, to be sure, that this proposition of faith does not say anything certain about the *individual* salvation of man understood as something which has in fact been reached. But God desires the salvation of everyone. And this salvation willed by God is the salvation won by Christ, the salvation of supernatural grace which divinizes man, the salvation of the beatific vision. It is a salvation really intended for all those millions upon millions of people who lived perhaps a million years before Christ – and also for those who have lived after Christ – in nations, cultures and epochs of a very wide range which were still completely shut off from the viewpoint of those living in the light of the New Testament. If, on the one hand, we conceive salvation as something specifically *Christian*, if there is no salvation apart from Christ, if according to Catholic teaching the supernatural divinization of mankind can never be replaced merely by goodwill on the part of man but is necessary as something itself given in this earthly life; and if, on the other hand, God has really, truly and seriously intended this salvation for all men – then these two aspects cannot be reconciled in any other way than by stating that every human being is really and truly exposed to the influence of divine, supernatural grace which offers an interior union with God and by means of which God communicates himself whether the individual takes up an attitude of acceptance or of refusal towards this grace. It is senseless to suppose cruelly – and without any hope of acceptance by the man of today, in view of the enormous extent of the extra-Christian history of salvation and damnation – that nearly all men living outside the official and public Christianity are so evil and stubborn that the offer of supernatural grace ought not even to be made in fact in most cases, since these individuals have already rendered themselves unworthy of such an offer by previous, subjectively grave offences against the natural moral law.

If one gives more exact theological thought to this matter, then one cannot regard nature and grace as two phases in the life of the individual which follow each other in time. It is furthermore impossible to think that this offer of supernatural, divinizing grace made to all men on account of the universal salvific purpose of God, should in general (prescinding from the relatively few exceptions) remain ineffective in most cases on account of the personal guilt of the individual. For, as far as the Gospel is concerned, we have no really conclusive reason for thinking so pessimistically of men. On the other hand, and contrary to every merely human experience, we do have every reason for thinking optimistically of God and his salvific will which is more powerful than the extremely limited stupidity and evil-mindedness of men. However little we can say with certitude about the final lot of an individual inside or outside the officially constituted Christian religion, we have every reason to think optimistically – i.e. truly hopefully and confidently in a Christian sense – of God who has certainly the last word and who has revealed to us that he has spoken his powerful word of reconciliation and forgiveness into the world.

[. . .]

We must take into consideration that whenever the religious person acts really religiously, he makes use of, or omits unthinkingly, the manifold forms of religious institutions by making a consciously critical choice among and between them. We must consider the immeasurable difference – which it seems right to suppose to exist even in the Christian sphere – between what is objectively wrong in moral life and the extent to which this is really realized with subjectively grave guilt. Once we take all this into consideration, we will not hold it to be impossible that grace is at work, and is even being accepted, in the spiritual, personal life of the individual, no matter how primitive, unenlightened, apathetic and earth-bound such a life may at first sight appear to be. We can say quite simply that, wherever, and in so far as, the individual makes a moral decision in his life [. . .] this moral decision can also be thought to measure up to the character of a supernaturally elevated, believing and thus saving act, and hence to be more in actual fact than merely 'natural morality'. Hence, if one believes seriously in the universal salvific purpose of God towards all men in Christ, it need not and cannot really be doubted that gratuitous influences of properly Christian supernatural grace are conceivable in the life of all men (provided they are first of all regarded as individuals) and that these influences can be presumed to be accepted in spite of the sinful state of men and in spite of their apparent estrangement from God.

Our second thesis goes even further than this, however, and states in its second part that, from what has been said, the actual religions of 'pre-Christian' humanity too must not be regarded as simply illegitimate from the very start, but must be seen as quite capable of having a positive significance. This statement must naturally be taken in a very different sense which we cannot examine here for the various particular religions. This means that the different religions will be able to lay claim to being lawful religions only in very different senses and to very different degrees. But precisely this variability is not at all excluded by the notion of a 'lawful religion', as we will have to show in a moment. A lawful religion means here an institutional religion whose 'use' by man at a certain period can be regarded on the whole as a positive means of gaining the right relationship to God and thus for the attaining of salvation, a means which is therefore positively included in God's plan of salvation.

That such a notion and the reality to which it refers can exist even where such a religion shows many theoretical and practical errors in its concrete form becomes clear in a theological analysis of the structure of the Old Covenant. We must first of all remember in this connection that only in the New Testament – in the Church of Christ understood as something which is eschatologically final and *hence* (and only for this reason) 'indefectible' and infallible – is there realized the notion of a Church which, because it is instituted by God in some way or other, already contains the permanent norm of differentiation between what is right (i.e. willed by God) and what is wrong in the religious sphere, and contains it both as a permanent institution and as an intrinsic element of this religion. There was nothing like this in the Old Testament, although it must undoubtedly be recognized as a lawful religion. The Old Covenant – understood as a concrete, historical and religious manifestation – contained what is right, willed by God, *and* what is false, erroneous, wrongly developed and depraved.

[...]

Hence it cannot be a part of the notion of a lawful religion in the above sense that it should be free from corruption, error and objective moral wrong in the concrete form of its appearance, or that it should contain a clear objective and permanent final court of appeal for the conscience of the individual to enable the individual to differentiate clearly and with certainty between the elements willed and instituted by God and those which are merely human and corrupt.

We must therefore rid ourselves of the prejudice that we can face a non-Christian religion with the dilemma that it must either come from God in everything it contains and thus correspond to God's will and positive providence, or be simply a purely human construction. If man is under God's grace even in these religions – and to deny this is certainly absolutely wrong – then the possession of this supernatural grace cannot but show itself, and cannot but become a formative factor of life in the concrete, even where (though not only where) this life turns the relationship to the absolute into an explicit theme, viz. in religion.

[...]

Furthermore, it must be borne in mind that the individual ought to and must have the possibility in his life of partaking in a genuine saving relationship to God, and this at all times and in all situations of the history of the human race. Otherwise there could be no question of a serious and also actually effective salvific design of God for all men, in all ages and places.

[...]

The second part of this second thesis, [...] states two things positively. It states that even religions other than the Christian and the Old Testament religions contain quite certainly elements of a supernatural influence by grace which must make itself felt even in these objectifications. And it also states that by the fact that in practice man as he really is can live his proffered relationship to God only in society, man must have had the right and indeed the duty to live this his relationship to God within the religious and social realities offered to him in his particular historical situation.

3rd Thesis: If the second thesis is correct, then Christianity does not simply confront the member of an extra-Christian religion as a mere non-Christian but as someone who can and must already be regarded in this or that respect as an anonymous Christian. It would be wrong to regard the pagan as someone who has not yet been touched in any way by God's grace and truth. If, however, he has experienced the grace of God – if, in certain circumstances, he has already accepted this grace as the ultimate, unfathomable entelechy of his existence by accepting the immeasurableness of his dying existence as opening out into infinity – then he has already been given revelation in a true sense even before he has been affected by missionary preaching from without. For this grace, understood as the *a priori* horizon of all his spiritual acts, accompanies his consciousness subjectively, even though it is not known objectively.

[...]

But if it is true that a person who becomes the object of the Church's missionary efforts is or may be already someone on the way towards his salvation, and someone who in certain circumstances finds it, without being reached by the proclamation of the Church's message – and if it is at the same time true that this salvation which reaches him in this way is Christ's salvation, since there is no other salvation – then it must be possible to be not only an anonymous theist but also an anonymous Christian. And then it is quite true that in the last analysis, the proclamation of the Gospel does not simply turn someone absolutely abandoned by God and Christ into a Christian, but turns an anonymous Christian into someone who now also knows about his Christian belief in the depths of his grace-endowed being by objective reflection and in the profession of faith which is given a social form in the Church.

[...]

4th Thesis: It is possibly too much to hope, on the one hand, that the religious pluralism which exists in the concrete situation of Christians will disappear in the foreseeable future. On the other hand, it is nevertheless absolutely permissible for the Christian himself to interpret this non-Christianity as Christianity of an anonymous kind which he does always still go out to meet as a missionary, seeing it as a world which is to be brought to the explicit consciousness of what already belongs to it as a divine offer or already pertains to it also over and above this as a divine gift of grace accepted unreflectedly and implicitly. If both these statements are true, then the Church will not so much regard herself today as the exclusive community of those who have a claim to salvation but rather as the historically tangible vanguard and the historically and socially constituted explicit expression of what the Christian hopes is present as a hidden reality even outside the visible Church.

[...]

Non-Christians may think it presumption for the Christian to judge everything which is sound or restored (by being sanctified) to be the fruit in every man of the grace of his Christ, and to interpret it as anonymous Christianity; they may think it presumption for the Christian to regard the non-Christian as a Christian who has not yet come to himself reflectively. But the Christian cannot renounce this 'presumption' which is really the source of the greatest humility both for himself and for the Church. For it is a profound admission of the fact that God is greater than man and the Church. The Church will go out to meet the non-Christian of tomorrow with the attitude expressed by St Paul when he said: What therefore you do not know and yet worship [and yet *worship*!] that I proclaim to you (Acts 17:23). On such a basis one can be tolerant, humble and yet firm towards all non-Christian religions.

4

Self-trust and the Diversity of Religions

Linda Zagzebski

Linda Zagzebski (b. 1946) is George Lynn Cross Research Professor of Philosophy at the University of Oklahoma and one of the editors of this volume. In the following essay Zagzebski argues that awareness of disagreement does not automatically raise an epistemic problem; rather, it is the awareness that epistemically admirable people disagree with us that raises a problem because admiration involves viewing someone as worth imitating. At root, the problem is a conflict within self-trust. Given that we must have a significant degree of self-trust, we must trust our emotion of admiration. Thus, the epistemic problem posed by religious diversity is one of choosing between trusting our opinions and trusting our admiration of persons who disagree with us.

I. The Problem of Religious Disagreement

The diversity of religions is widely regarded as one of the most serious problems for conscientious belief in a particular religion, both among ordinary people and among professional philosophers. The problem is not unique to religious belief because people have the same reaction to any instance of irresolvable disagreement. I think it is illuminating that this is not just a philosopher's puzzle. If the philosophically untutored think of it, that probably means there is something in ordinary beliefs and experiences that generates the problem. But since few, if any, people worried about it for millennia, those beliefs and experiences are probably modern in origin.

There are two modern sources of the perception that diversity is a threat. One is a principle about human nature that I believe we should reject, but the other is a kind of experience that we ought to take very seriously. I will argue that we should trust the experiences that generate

Linda Zagzebski, "Self-trust and the Diversity of Religions" in *Philosophic Exchange*, 36 (2005–2006): 63–76. © 2006 by the Center for Philosophic Exchange, State University of New York, College at Brockpoint, New York.

the problem because of self-trust, and I think that the way out of the problem requires us to look more deeply at what self-trust commits us to.

At some time in the distant past, people probably began to realize that some of their most cherished beliefs conflicted with the beliefs of other groups of people, but for many centuries, nobody saw this as a problem for their own beliefs. They simply responded by saying, "We are right, and they disagree with us, so they are wrong, and that's the end of that." And some people still take that line. (And there are people who wouldn't dream of taking that line about religion who don't hesitate to take that line about other things, such as politics).

However, we are past the time when we can take this line in good faith. Ever since the much-maligned Enlightenment, the perception of the world in the West has changed irreversibly. People gave up the idea that each of us can treat our own point of view as epistemically privileged just because it is our own. The story of why we did that is interesting because I think it combines both an important advance in human sensibilities with at least one philosophical mistake.

An important assumption governing much of Enlightenment philosophy is intellectual egalitarianism, a position endorsed by John Locke.[1] The idea is that all normal human beings are roughly equal in the capacity to get knowledge. Aside from the fact that some have acquired greater expertise or have greater access to information in some fields, there are no epistemic elites. Given this assumption, I am not being epistemically honest if I treat my own viewpoint as privileged. Locke combined his egalitarianism with optimism about the human ability to get knowledge, but there is a pessimistic interpretation that also comes from the Enlightenment. We could think of subjective points of view as equally bad ways to get the truth. All of them are limited and distorted, so it does no good to replace your own perspective with someone else's, equally limited and distorted. Notoriously, the Enlightenment enshrined the perspective of the impartial observer, a being without culture or history or personal preferences. But we also know that there are many disagreements in belief that cannot be resolved from such a perspective. If a conflict in belief can be resolved neither from the impartial perspective nor from the point of view of the disputants, and if I accept epistemic egalitarianism, I have to admit that my belief is no more likely to be true than the belief of my opponent. A conscientious believer finds this bothersome. Let me call this the Enlightenment worry: *Irresolvable disagreement over a belief threatens the conscientiousness of the belief.*

The Enlightenment worry is unstable for at least two reasons. One is that conscientiousness in belief has two aspects, only one of which is expressed in the worry over irresolvable disagreement. If we think disagreement threatens the conscientiousness of our beliefs, it is because we think that disagreement makes our own beliefs less likely to be true, and we might think we can escape the perceived threat to the truth of our belief if we withhold belief – neither believe nor disbelieve. But if we do that, we violate another demand of conscientiousness. A conscientious believer not only desires that the beliefs she has are true, she also desires to acquire beliefs in the domains she cares about as conscientiously as she can. To deny ourselves beliefs in important domains denies us important elements of a desirable life. People who do not have beliefs in important domains, who turn away from ultimate questions, tend to be shallow people. So one source of the instability of the Enlightenment worry is that it reflects one of the demands of conscientious belief but not the other.

There is another problem with the Enlightenment worry. The truth is, most of us are not epistemic egalitarians, and we would be hard pressed to defend egalitarianism if we wanted to. In particular, I don't think many of us worry about disagreements with people whom we do not admire. If you believe acts of terrorism or genocide are wrong (by whatever definition you want), I doubt that you think the conscientiousness of your belief is threatened when you find out there are people who disagree, even though you are not likely to resolve the conflict by talking it over with them. If you think that it is a bad idea to devote your life primarily to acquiring money and fame, I doubt that it will bother you to find out that there are people who think the contrary. Nor should it. What really bothers us, I think, is that we recognize admirable people among those who believe differently than we do about certain things and we observe that the beliefs of different exemplars conflict with each other. The exemplars I have in mind are people who have a sense of the importance of certain domains of life and the beliefs needed to sustain those domains, and who are epistemically admirable in the way they believe as well as in the way they act.[2]

This version of the disagreement worry is also modern because sympathetic contact between people of different cultures only occurred on a large scale in the last few hundred years. That experience, I think, is much more important than the Enlightenment principles that allegedly threaten the conscientiousness of our beliefs. When we have direct and sympathetic contact with people of another culture, it is almost impossible not to notice that many of them are as admirable as the most admirable people in our own culture. So my position is that it is not irresolvable disagreement *per se* that causes a problem. What really worries us is irresolvable disagreement among people whom we admire and between people we admire and ourselves.

This form of the problem would not be threatening unless we ought to trust our emotion of admiration, and I think that we not only ought to, but have no choice but to do so. But to explain that, let me turn to some observations about self-trust.

II. Self-trust

Richard Foley argues in his book, *Intellectual Trust in Oneself and Others* (Cambridge University Press, 2001), that any normal, non-skeptical life will have to include a significant degree of self-trust in our intellectual faculties, procedures, and opinions (99). The reason is that any defense of our most fundamental faculties and opinions will make use of those same faculties and opinions, so there are no non-question-begging guarantees of our own reliability. For example, we test our memory by perception, we test one perception by another perception, we test much of what we believe by consulting other people, so we use beliefs about them to test other beliefs, and so on. There is no way to get out of the circle of our faculties and opinions to test the reliability of the opinions and faculties in the circle.

Foley prefaces his observation about the need for self-trust with the claim that there is no answer to the radical skeptic and the project of classical foundationalism has failed. The proper reaction to that, he says, is to accept it and to acknowledge the consequence that intellectual inquiry always involves a substantial element of trust in our own faculties and the opinions they generate. But I think we need not accept Foley's contention that there is no answer to the radical skeptic in order to agree with his view on the need for self-trust. There are many kinds and degrees of skepticism, and no matter what you think of global skepticism, we are still left with concerns about the reliability of our faculties and the trustworthiness of our beliefs, and Foley's point about the lack of non-circular tests for our reliability seems to me to be justified independent of his views on global skepticism.

Foley gives an interesting argument that self-trust logically commits us to trust in others. He begins by defining three positions with respect to epistemic trust, each of which has an ethical analogue (85–9).[3] The first is *epistemic universalism*. According to the epistemic universalist, *the fact that someone else has a belief gives me some reason to believe it.* That reason may be outweighed by other reasons; nonetheless, the fact that another person has a certain belief is a mark in favor of its credibility. The ethical analogue is the position that the interests and goals of other persons always count morally for me. Again, they can be outweighed by some other value, but they should always count in my deliberations.

What Foley calls egoists and egotists reject univeralism. The *epistemic egoist* maintains that *the fact that someone else has a belief can be a reason for me to believe it, but only if I have evidence that the person is reliable, that is, I have evidence that her beliefs will further my desire for the truth.* So I may believe what another person believes on her say-so, but only because I have information that her beliefs are reliably calibrated with truth in the domain in which she is making the claim.

This view also has an ethical analogue. The ethical egoist says I may care about the interests of others, but only when I adopt their interests as my own interests. The egoist insists that I am under no obligation to care about somebody else's interests, and I am not irrational if I do not. But sometimes I take an interest in their interests. Similarly, the epistemic egoist says that I am not irrational if I pay no attention to what another person believes, but sometimes I see for myself that what she believes serves my interest in getting the truth because I see for myself that she is reliable. So notice that for both kinds of egoist I have no reason to pay attention to what somebody else says or to their interests unless I see that what they say serves my interests; I see (or decide) that their interests are my interests.

The most extreme position identified by Foley is *epistemic egotism* (86). Epistemic egotists maintain that *it is never rational to grant credibility to the opinions of others simply because it is their opinion*. The only legitimate way for someone else to influence my beliefs is through Socratic demonstration. Anyone who wants to convince me of her belief must demonstrate to me that, given what I already believe, her opinion is one I ought to adopt, but it is never reasonable for me to believe what she believes on her say-so.

This is the analogue of ethical egotism, the view that I should not adopt the interests of others as my interests just because they are their interests. If I act in the interest of others, that is because my interests and theirs happen to coincide, but the mere fact that something is in their interests ought to play no part in my deliberations. Similarly, the epistemic egotist says that I might believe what somebody else believes, but the fact that she believes it ought to play no part in my reasons for believing it.

Now Foley argues that self-trust makes both epistemic egoism and epistemic egotism incoherent. Because of the social construction of belief, if we have basic trust in our own opinions and intellectual faculties, we cannot coherently withhold trust from others because in so far as the opinions of others have shaped our own opinions, we would not be reliable unless they are. And this trust is not limited to people who preceded us historically. If our contemporaries were shaped by many of the same conditions that shaped us, then on pain of inconsistency, if I trust myself, I should trust them.

But Foley does not stop there. He argues that even though we tend to be fascinated with differences between people and we like to exaggerate them, there are many more commonalities than differences in human faculties and environment. In fact, the similarities extend to people all over the world at all times. So the fact that some person somewhere at some time has a certain belief gives me *some* reason to believe it myself, given that I have trust in myself and I am relevantly similar to them. Self-trust therefore commits me to universalism (103), but notice that Foley assumes epistemic egalitarianism to get the conclusion. Self-trust, together with epistemic egalitarianism, requires me to accept epistemic universalism. The conclusion is that given that I have reason to believe that someone else believes p, I have at least a weak reason to believe p myself. I do not need to know anything special about the reliability of the person (105). Self-trust commits me to trust others unless I have reason to think they are unreliable. I need special reason not to trust them. I do not need special reason to trust them.

Now suppose that I have a belief that conflicts with the belief of another. Foley argues that my belief defeats the belief of the other person because by my lights the other person has been unreliable (108). Since it is trust in myself that creates in me a presumption of trust in another, then unless I have evidence that the other person is more reliable than I am (e.g., the other person is a medical specialist and I am not), my trust in that other is defeated by my trust in myself. Notice first that the fact that someone else has a belief that conflicts with one of mine is not evidence that the other person is unreliable. After all, it is only a single case. But more importantly, notice that Foley's treatment of the conflict case makes him an epistemic egoist in such cases, although he does not say that in his book. In order to trust the other person, I need evidence that he is more reliable than I am, but I do not need evidence that I am more reliable than he is in order to trust myself. That is epistemic egoism. Yet according to his own argument, I would not be reliable unless the other is.[4]

Foley says nothing about religion in his book, but we can easily apply his points to religious belief. The *religious epistemic egotist* would be a person who accepts no religious belief on the word of another. He expects a demonstration of the existence of God that uses premises he accepts himself, and he will accept the beliefs of a particular religion only if the same conditions can be satisfied for each doctrine of the religion. It is very unlikely that these conditions can be satisfied by any religion. Theism might satisfy these conditions for some people and atheism for others, whereas still others will be convinced neither by arguments for atheism nor by arguments for theism and will become agnostic. Religious epistemic egotism puts the agnostic in the position of either caring very much about a domain about which he does not have conscientiously acquired beliefs, thereby violating one of the demands of conscientiousness I mentioned earlier, or perhaps more likely, it leads him to cease to care. I suspect that many contemporary atheists and agnostics satisfy this definition of a religious epistemic egotist.

The less extreme *religious epistemic egoist* will accept religious beliefs on the word of another provided that there is good evidence of the reliability of the source. John Locke is an epistemic egoist about belief in Christianity. Locke defines Revelation as a communication from God, and faith as the acceptance of beliefs on the word of God.[5] Locke says we have good evidence that the Gospels are a communication from God, given the miracles performed by Jesus. We have reason to believe the miracles occurred in the same way we have reason to believe testimony about other historical occurrences. Miracles are evidence that the source of the teachings of Jesus is divine, and hence, is reliable.

For the egoist, belief in particular Christian teachings does not require demonstration of the content of the revelation, as it does for the egotist. But reason judges whether something *is* a revelation, that is, whether it is reliable. And Locke allows that it can be rational to believe a revelation even when the content is improbable. He says that is to be expected since revelation is about matters above the limit of our faculties to attain on our own, such as the revelation that the angels rebelled against God.

I think Foley is correct that epistemic egotism and epistemic egoism are not coherent positions, given that we have self-trust, and his argument applies to religious epistemic egotism and egoism. I think this is an interesting consequence because both positions are so common. But given Foley's egalitarianism, the only option left is universalism, so the position to which we are committed by self-trust, according to Foley's argument, is religious epistemic universalism. The *religious epistemic universalist* would grant *prima facie* credence to the religious beliefs of all other persons.

I find Foley's approach to self-trust generally helpful, but unfortunately, I don't think it is helpful in giving the conscientious believer guidance in cases of conflict. For people who already have religious beliefs (or anti-religious beliefs), self-trust means that my own belief trumps the belief of others, assuming I am being careful. I assume they are unreliable because they disagree with me, and as I've said, this view reduces to epistemic egoism. Furthermore, I think it is too much like the "I'm right so they must be wrong" view that I've said we can no longer support.

What about cases in which a person is agnostic in religious matters? In that case Foley's position also is not very helpful because the agnostic can't choose between conflicting religious beliefs without evidence of the relative reliability of one group over another – atheists, deists, Christians, Buddhists, etc. – in order to adjudicate the conflict, and it's not likely that she is going to get that. So Foley's approach is not helpful whether or not a person already has religious beliefs. Still, I think a closer look at self-trust reveals something interesting both about the source of the worry over religious diversity and the way a person who trusts herself ought to proceed.

III. Emotional Self-trust and Conflict

In my judgment Foley is right that any non-skeptical intellectual life must include a substantial amount of self-trust in whatever aspects of ourselves produce or support our beliefs. What those aspects are depends upon the nature of the self and what you think that is is one of the things you need to trust. Foley limits the aspects of the self that are relevant to epistemic self-trust to cognitive and perceptual faculties and a set of beliefs one already has, but I think they must include more than that. Foley does not mention emotions, but I think we must trust our emotions for the same reason we must trust our perceptual faculties, memory, and beliefs. Emotion dispositions can be reliable or unreliable and particular emotions may fit or not fit their objects. But we can't tell whether our emotion dispositions are reliable without using those same dispositions in conjunction with our other faculties. How can we tell whether our disposition to pity is reliably directed at the pitiful, whether our disposition to disgust is reliably directed towards the disgusting, whether we reliably fear the fearsome, or admire the admirable without appealing to further emotions? We trust what we think we see when we take a hard look in good environmental conditions, and if others agree, we take that as confirmation. Similarly, we trust what we feel when we feel admiration or pity or revulsion and we take the agreement of others as confirmation. So the grounds for trusting our emotions are parallel to the grounds for trusting our perceptions and memory.

Emotions are the ground of many beliefs that lead to action, so trust in those beliefs depends upon trusting an emotion. Fear of a situation grounds the belief that I ought to escape. Compassion for a person grounds the belief that we ought to give her aid. Respect for a person grounds the belief that we may not treat her in certain ways, and so on. So the self-trust we need in order to act requires trust in beliefs that depend upon trust in emotions. If epistemic self-trust includes trust in the beliefs that ground action, then epistemic self-trust requires emotional self-trust. It follows that to live a normal, non-skeptical life we need to trust our emotions as well as our faculties, procedures, and beliefs. Our emotions are therefore within the set of faculties, procedures, and beliefs whose reliability we need to depend upon but whose reliability we cannot test in a non-circular way.

Foley says that we need to trust the beliefs we have that we acquired at some time in the distant past that we can't remember. And he concludes from that that we must trust the people from whom we acquired those beliefs. But more follows from that observation as well. Many beliefs are not just passed along from one person to the next like a virus. Beliefs are imbedded in traditions from which we both acquire and learn how to interpret the beliefs, so trusting those beliefs commits me to trusting the traditions from which I acquired them. If I am a little slice of history, trusting myself commits me to trusting the longer span of history of which I am a part. So one modification I want to make to Foley's line of reasoning about self-trust is to extend it in two ways. In addition to trusting our faculties, procedures, and beliefs, we also need emotional self-trust, and we need trust in traditions and historical institutions from which we acquire our beliefs and learn how to interpret our experience.

To trust an emotion means to have confidence that the emotion is appropriate for the circumstances. In my theory of emotion an emotion is an affective state whose intentional object is seen as falling under a distinctive thick affective concept, so pity is feeling pity for someone seen as pitiful, love is loving someone seen as lovable, contempt is feeling contempt for someone seen as contemptible, reverence is revering what is seen as sacred, admiration is admiring someone seen as admirable.[6] The admirable cannot be understood apart from the feeling that is a component of the emotion of admiration, but we can say something about the admirable. I think it is something like the imitably attractive. We feel a positive emotion towards the person we admire that would lead to imitating the person given the right practical conditions. To trust the emotion of admiration, then, means to have confidence that it is appropriate to feel the kind of attraction and desire to imitate that is intrinsic to admiration.

Notice, however, that even though self-trust is a crucial part of any non-skeptical life, we do not trust ourselves equally all the time, and this applies both to our beliefs and to our emotions. Suppose that I give up in adulthood a belief I had as a child. I think the later belief is better than the earlier one. Similarly, if I have a different emotion in a certain situation in adulthood than I had as a child, I think the later emotion is more appropriate. I believe that my older self is more trustworthy than my younger self, and I believe *that* primarily because I trust my older self more than my younger self. There are defenses for this attitude, but the defenses also require self-trust. For example, we might think that other things being equal, greater experience is more trustworthy than less experience, but that also is not something for which we have a non-circular defense.

I also trust some of my current beliefs more than others. I trust the beliefs I have when carefully reflecting, considering open-mindedly contrary views, treating opponents fairly, and not indulging in strong emotional reactions which tend to distort beliefs into extremes. So I trust beliefs arising from my intellectual virtues and not those arising from vices. It is probably true that I have a better track record of getting the truth when my beliefs are formed in the virtuous ways I've mentioned rather than in vicious ways, but there is still no non-circular way for me to tell that the virtuously formed beliefs are the reliable ones. That is because my final decision about what the truth is in some case is determined by what I believe when I'm being as virtuous as I can.[7]

I trust some of my emotions more than others for the same reason I trust some of my beliefs more than others. I trust the ones that are stable, do not change upon reflection, and which do not arise from vices. Again, there is no non-circular way to tell that the virtuously formed and stable emotions are the trustworthy ones since I need emotions to tell whether a previous emotion was trustworthy.

But if there are no non-circular grounds for trusting some of my beliefs and emotions more than others, why is it that I trust myself more in some circumstances than in others? The answer, I think, is that I admire myself more when I am behaving in an intellectually virtuous way than when I am not. Self-admiration is not an emotion we are comfortable with and I hesitate to use the term because of its connotations of vanity and conceit,[8] but I think it is fairly obvious that if we are capable of admiring and not admiring others, we are capable of admiring and not admiring ourselves. We trust ourselves more in some of our beliefs than in others because we admire the way we came to believe some of our beliefs more than others. Again I want to make it clear that I do not treat my intellectual virtues as evidence that I am admirable and have grounds for trusting myself. Being trustworthy is not something I infer about myself in a non-circular way, nor is being admirable.

Now if I am consistent, I admire the way some people form some of their beliefs more than I admire the way I form some of my beliefs, and so consistency requires me to trust the beliefs of others formed in these ways more than my own when my own are not admirable. So self-trust commits me to trusting more than myself those who are more admirable than myself, who have the traits I trust in myself in a greater degree than I have myself.

This means we must reject intellectual egalitarianism. We know that there are people who are generally more virtuous than others in epistemic behavior. So my trust is not universal, and its non-universality is based on the way I treat trust in myself. And this explains why I do not trust those who are not admirable. I do not trust the beliefs of terrorists about terrorism, not because I have evidence of their unreliability, but because I don't admire them. The difference between those we trust intellectually and those we do not cannot be explained by the fact that we have evidence of the reliability of the admirable and the unreliability of the non-admirable. So the position I am endorsing is not a form of epistemic egoism.

I think, then, that Foley is right that epistemic egotism and egoism are incompatible with self-trust, but epistemic egalitarianism, which Foley uses to support epistemic universalism, must be rejected. So I differ from Foley's position in two further respects: (1) I think that self-trust leads to trusting the people I admire more than the people I do not admire and the difference does not rest upon the fact that I have evidence of the greater reliability of the former. (2) I maintain that self-trust commits me to trusting some other people more than myself. I am forced to these conclusions by trusting my own emotion of admiration.

Now let us return to conflict in beliefs. Suppose that I trust my emotion of admiration of some person more than I trust a given belief I have. Maybe I do not admire the way I formed my own belief as much as I admire the way the other person formed hers. And suppose the other person's belief conflicts with mine, and I am not aware of another person I admire just as much whose belief agrees with mine. Self-trust would lead me to trust the admired person's belief more than my own. If I am able to imitate the admired person by adopting her belief without changing anything else about myself that I trust even more than I trust my admiration for her, then self-trust should lead me to change my belief. For example, suppose that I hastily form a belief about a recently published book without reading it, and then become aware of a contrary opinion about the book by an acquaintance whose intellectual judgment I admire and who has clearly made a more careful study of the book than I have. If I am not aware of anyone else I admire just as much whose opinion agrees with mine, and if I can change my belief without changing anything else about myself I trust more than I trust the judgment of my acquaintance, then I probably should change my belief.

This seems to me the right thing to do for beliefs that are not deeply embedded in the self. I think, then, that Foley is mistaken in saying that self-trust will always lead me to decide a conflict between my belief and the belief of another in favor of my own.

But even if I trust my admiration for another person more than I trust my belief, it does not always follow that I should change it. Whether I should change a belief is not simply determined by how much I trust the belief itself, but how much I trust the other aspects of myself that I would have to change if I changed the belief. Foley emphasizes the social construction of belief, but as I've pointed out, that commits me to trusting much more than the individual persons from whom I learned the belief. To trust myself commits me to trusting the traditions that shape me and the institutions on which I depend. Religious beliefs are usually connected with an entire network of other beliefs as well as religious emotions, experiences, communal loyalties, and connections with many other admirable people, all of which I trust. Admiration is an emotion that leads me to imitate the admirable person in suitable circumstances, but often the circumstances are not suitable. So I can admire the belief system of a Hindu without the inclination to adopt that system for myself.

Suppose, however, that I trust my admiration for the Hindu more than I trust the aspects of myself I would have to change if I imitated the Hindu by adopting her religion. I still might not imitate her because it might not be possible. Just as I can admire an Olympic swimmer without the slightest inclination to imitate her, I can admire a devout Hindu without the inclination to imitate, and the reason is the same in both cases: I can't do it. But some people can. It *is* possible to convert to another religion, and I would not accept any position on religious diversity that rules out conversion for the conscientious believer.

If I convert to Hinduism, there is a sense in which I can imitate the devout Hindu and a sense in which I cannot because what one converts to is never what one sees when one admires an exemplar from a radically different culture. When I see an admirable person with a very different belief system, I see an alternate self. I don't mean that *that* person is an alternate self. Rather, I mean that I know that if I had met that person at an early age, I might have imitated her because then I might have trusted her more than I trusted my conflicting beliefs. If so, I would be a very different person today. And even now becoming an alternate self is still an option through conversion. So respect for admirable others in other religions includes recognition of an alternate self. This forever changes the way I relate to them. But I only get one life. I might respect the self I could have been, but it does not follow that I should now try to become that self. I *might* trust my alternate Hindu self more than my present self, in which case I should convert, but given the nature of self-trust, we would expect conversion on that scale to be rare, and I am arguing that that is perfectly compatible with conscientiousness.

In a situation in which a choice whether to convert is made, some element of self-trust becomes the bottom line – that to which we refer in adjudicating between those elements of ourselves that pull us one way and those that pull in another direction. Lee Yearley gives a brief but moving account of this process in himself while contemplating an enormous Buddha and imagining what it would be like to become a Buddhist. Yearley writes: – "I could imagine attempting to incarnate the excellences I saw in the Sokkurum Buddha that morning in Korea. I admired them, they tempted me, and I believe I could have chosen them and remained myself. But I did not want to choose them, and I hoped that those about whom I most care would not choose them" (247).[9]

Notice Yearley does not say he didn't want to become a Buddhist because he thinks his Christian beliefs are true and Buddhist beliefs are false. Presumably, he *did* think that, but that is not sufficient to explain why he would not become a Buddhist. As long as it was possible for him to change his beliefs, given his admiration for another religion, imitation of that religion was possible. And Yearley might have been conscientious if he did become a Buddhist on that morning in Korea. If his admiration for Buddhism had been strong enough and he had trusted it more than the other aspects of himself he would have had to change if he became a Buddhist, I think he would have been a conscientious believer. But he didn't change, and his reason seems to me not only to show a high degree of self-knowledge, but it gives us a hint about how self-trust often operates. He genuinely admires Buddhism, but he does not like the self he would become if he converted to Buddhism, nor does he want those he loves the most to adopt such a self. He does not try to find some *reason* to reject Buddhism either in its doctrines or its way of life. I am assuming that he has already thought through the reasons and still admires Buddhism. The bottom line is that he doesn't *like* himself as a Buddhist. He trusts that emotion, and I not only think that he can be conscientious in doing so, but I've tried to show that he has few other options. Whatever he does, there will be some element of the self to which he defers in a situation of this kind.

The problem of this paper is therefore a conflict that arises within self-trust. I trust my admiration of others and my other emotions, and I trust the aspects of myself from which I gain my beliefs and the traditions that support them. I think this conflict produces a genuine problem of religious diversity. In contrast, the problem that arises from an assumption of intellectual egalitarianism seems to me to be much less threatening because I have less reason to trust egalitarianism than to trust my emotions. So I am not much taken with the well-known argument that says, "Other people are as well placed to get the truth as we are. There is an irresolvable conflict between their beliefs and ours. Hence, we have no more reason to think our beliefs are true than that their beliefs are true." This is what I called the Enlightenment Worry. What I do take seriously is the admiration I have for alternate ways of life and the beliefs that go with them. I may have full confidence in my beliefs, emotions, and their sources in the traditions that shape me, and I am conscientious in doing so. But as long as I trust my emotion of admiration and admiration includes the urge to imitate, conversion is also compatible with conscientiousness, and the diversity of religions will put some people in the position of making a choice, a position that puts those aspects of herself she trusts the most in the forefront of her consciousness.

Admiration may not require me to change my beliefs, but it adds something to the dialogue between people with conflicting religious beliefs that did not exist in the pre-modern era. What it adds, I think, is the feeling that I *would* imitate them if I had grown up with a different social construction of the self. That prevents me from taking the line, "We're right, so they're wrong, and that's the end of that." Of course, we think we're right, but there's more to be said. Respect for others comes from trusting that we *are* right in the admiration we have for many people who have very different beliefs, and *that* logically requires us to think of them as like the self I could have been if I had been raised in a different way.

Admiration is a tricky emotion. On the one hand, it is of central importance to the moral life because most of what we learn is by imitation and admiration is the emotion we use to distinguish those who are worthy of imitation from those who are not. But admiration raises the problem of the boundaries of the self. We would not want to imitate every admirable person in every way they are admirable, even if it were possible, which it isn't. There is a domain of the self that does not respond by imitation even when the admiration is genuine. Many of our central beliefs are in that domain. The problem of conflict between our own beliefs and the beliefs of those we admire reflects the complexity of admiration. We *are* inclined to imitate the admirable beliefs of others, but we are also right to know the difference between being as admirable as *we* can be and trying to become another person.

Notes

1 John Locke, *An Essay Concerning Human Understanding*. See Nicholas Wolterstorff, *John Locke and the Ethics of Belief* (Cambridge University Press, 1996) for a recent interpretation of Locke's epistemology.

2 I have argued elsewhere that the ability to sense the important affects the ethics of belief and blurs the lines between moral and intellectual exemplars. See "Epistemic Value and the Primacy of What We Care About," in *Immoral Believing* (special issue of *Philosophical Papers*, edited by Ward Jones, 2005.

3 The ethical analogues play no role in either Foley's argument or mine, but I mention them because they are interesting.

4 Foley has said in conversation that he has changed his mind about the conflict situation.

5 *Essay Concerning Human Understanding*, Book IV, Chap. 19, "Faith and reason." See also Locke's *Discourse of Miracles.*

6 For a fuller account of this theory of emotion, see "Emotion and Moral Judgment," *Philosophy and Phenomenological Research*, January 2003, pp. 104–24, and *Divine Motivation Theory* (Cambridge University Press, 2004), chap. 2

7 I am not suggesting that truth is *defined* as what I believe when I am being as careful as I can.

8 An alternate is "self-approval," but that term does not capture the aspect of a tendency to imitate, which I think is included in admiration. We want to imitate our better selves as well as admirable others.

9 Yearley, L., "Conflicts among ideals of human flourishing," in Outka, G. & Reeder, J., Jr. (eds.) *Prospects for a Common Morality* (Princeton University Press, 1993), pp. 231–53.

X

FAITH, REASON, AND THE ETHICS OF BELIEF

Introduction

In philosophy we explore ultimate questions about the nature of the universe, human beings, and our destiny. It is commonly said that the method used is reason, but that may not be very illuminating because the nature of reason is not obvious. It seems to preclude believing on trust, but that cannot be right either since it is reasonable for us to believe many things on trust. Reason is also contrasted with authority, so a person who accepts a belief on the authority of Scripture or the Church believes on faith, whereas a person who uses reason is one who figures out the truth as best she can by using her own experience and natural faculties. In theory, these sources of belief can conflict, and from the earliest years of the Christian era that conflict was discussed.

The second century church Father, Justin Martyr, came to Christian faith through philosophy, described in his dialogue with the distinguished Jew, Trypho, but many Christians were suspicious of Greek culture and particularly Greek philosophy. Tertullian's outburst against philosophy is frequently quoted: "What has Jerusalem to do with Athens, the Church with the Academy, the Christian with the heretic?" But Tertullian's contemporary, Clement of Alexandria, became a Christian in part through reading Plato, and many Christian and Islamic philosophers of the medieval period defended philosophy even when it apparently conflicted with revelation. In the twelfth century the important Islamic philosopher Averroes (Ibn Rushd), argued that Aristotle can be reconciled with Islam, and his commentaries on Aristotle influenced Aquinas, who attempted to demonstrate a century later that Aristotle can be reconciled with Christianity.

Like Averroes, Aquinas thought that reason and revelation cannot conflict because truth cannot conflict with truth. His position was that there are religious truths discoverable by reason, and these he called "Preambles to the Faith," but there are also truths that go beyond reason and can only be learned through revelation. It takes faith to accept these truths, and everyone needs faith. The central truths of the Christian faith such as the Trinity, Incarnation, and Redemption are in this category. Revelation is not just for the unlearned; it is essential to grasping the Christian faith.

The alleged conflict between faith and reason cannot be resolved without a clarification of both faith and reason. John Locke claimed that faith is belief upon the word of God, but whether something is the revealed word of God is determined by reason. Arguably, Locke thereby makes faith an application of reason. In general, the task of clarifying faith is the job of religion, not philosophy, but philosophy has much to say on the forms of reason. Some contemporary disputes about the nature of reason focus on whether it is ever reasonable to believe something without evidence. This position, called evidentialism, is supported in the classic essay by W. K. Clifford and criticized in the essay by the Calvinist philosopher Kelly James Clark. A non-evidentialist form of reason that has an intriguing history in philosophical discussion is pragmatic reasoning. Pascal's famous Wager on the existence of God is intended to show that it is rational to believe that God exists, but the rationality of belief is based on a practical computation of the expected outcome of belief and non-belief. A different sort of defense of belief on non-evidential grounds is given by William James in his essay, "The Will to Believe." James argues that there are propositions which would be significant, if true, but which cannot be decided on evidential grounds or on any intellectual grounds. The agent must therefore decide on passional grounds. The passion to get truth governs our belief-forming activity in a different way than the passion to avoid falsehood. The evidentialist principle is an expression of the latter passion, but it can be just as rational for a person to be governed by the former.

A

Faith and Reason

1

How Justin Found Philosophy

Justin Martyr

St Justin Martyr (*c.* 100–*c.* 165) converted to Christianity when he was approximately thirty years old and went on to become an apologist for the Christian faith. In his *Dialogue with Trypho*, from which this selection is taken, he recounts his studies with Stoic, Peripatetic (Aristotelian), Pythagorean, and Platonist philosophers. He then portrays his conversion to Christianity, not as a rejection of philosophy, but as a conversion from an unsatisfactory to a satisfactory philosophy.

Chapter 2

"I will tell you," I replied, "my personal views on this subject. Philosophy is indeed one's greatest possession, and is most precious in the sight of God, to whom it alone leads us and to whom it unites us, and in truth they who have applied themselves to philosophy are holy men. But, many have failed to discover the nature of philosophy, and the reason why it was sent down to men; otherwise, there would not be Platonists, or Stoics, or Peripatetics, or Theoretics,[1] or Pythagoreans, since this science is always one and the same.

2. "Now, let me tell you why it has at length become so diversified. They who first turned to philosophy, and, as a result, were deemed illustrious men were succeeded by men who gave no time to the investigation of truth, but, amazed at the courage and self-control of their teachers as well as with the novelty of their teachings, held that to be the truth which each had learned from his own teacher. And they in turn transmitted to their successors such opinions, and others like them, and so they became known by the name of him who was considered the father of the doctrine. When I first desired to contact one of these philosophers, [3.] I placed myself under the tutelage of a certain Stoic.[2] After spending some time with him and learning nothing new about God (for my instructor had no knowledge of God, nor did he consider

St Justin Martyr, Chapters 2–8, "How Justin Found Philosophy" from *Selections from the Fathers of the Church*, vol. 3; *St Justin Martyr Dialogue with Trypho*, trans. Thomas B. Falls, rev. Thomas P. Halton, ed. Michael Slusser (Washington, DC: The Catholic University of America Press, 2003), extracts from pp. 5–15.

such knowledge necessary), I left him and turned to a Peripatetic who considered himself an astute teacher. After a few days with him, he demanded that we settle the matter of my tuition fee in such a way that our association would not be unprofitable to him. Accordingly, I left him, because I did not consider him a real philosopher.

4. "Since my spirit still yearned to hear the specific and excellent meaning of philosophy, I approached a very famous Pythagorean, who took great pride in his own wisdom. In my interview with him, when I expressed a desire to become his pupil, he asked me, 'What? Do you know music, astronomy, and geometry? How do you expect to comprehend any of those things that are conducive to happiness, if you are not first well acquainted with those studies which draw your mind away from objects of the senses and render it fit for the intellectual, in order that it may contemplate what is good and beautiful?'

5. "He continued to speak at great length in praise of those sciences, and of the necessity of knowing them, until I admitted that I knew nothing about them; then he dismissed me. As was to be expected, I was downcast to see my hopes shattered, especially since I respected him as a man of considerable knowledge. But, when I reflected on the length of time that I would have to spend on those sciences, I could not make up my mind to wait such a long time.

6. "At my wit's end,[3] it occurred to me to consult the Platonists,[4] whose reputation was great. Thus it happened that I spent as much time as possible in the company of a wise man who was highly esteemed by the Platonists and who had but recently arrived in our city.[5] Under him I forged ahead in philosophy and day by day I improved. The perception of incorporeal things quite overwhelmed me and the Platonic theory of ideas added wings to my mind,[6] so that in a short time I imagined myself a wise man. So great was my folly that I fully expected immediately to gaze upon God, for this is the goal of Plato's philosophy.

Chapter 3

"As I was in this frame of mind and desired absolute solitude devoid of human distractions, I used to take myself to a certain spot not far from the sea. One day, as I approached that place with the intention of being alone, a respectable old man,[7] of meek and venerable appearance, followed me at a short distance. I stopped, turned quickly, and stared sharply at him.

2. " 'Do you know me?' he asked.

" 'I do not,' I replied.

" 'Why, therefore,' he continued, 'do you stare at me so?'

" 'Because,' I answered, 'I am surprised to find you here. I didn't expect to see anyone here.'

" 'I am worried,' he said, 'about some missing members of my household, and I am therefore looking around in the hope that they may show up somewhere in the vicinity. But what brings you here?'

" 'I take great delight,' I answered, 'in such walks, where I can converse with myself without hindrance because there is nothing to distract my attention. Places like this are most suitable for philology.'[8]

3. " 'Are you, then,' he asked, 'a lover of words,[9] rather than a lover of deeds and of truth? Do you not strive to be a practical man rather than a sophist?'

" 'But what greater deed,' I replied, 'could one perform than to prove that reason[10] rules all, and that one who rules reason and is sustained by it can look down upon the errors and undertakings of others, and see that they do nothing reasonable or pleasing to God. Man cannot have prudence without philosophy and straight thinking. Thus, every man should be devoted to philosophy and should consider it the greatest and most noble pursuit; all other pursuits are only of second- or third-rate value, unless they are connected with philosophy. Then they are of some value and should be approved; if they are devoid of philosophy and are not connected with it in any way, they then become base and coarse pursuits to those who practice them.'

4. "Interrupting, he asked, 'Does philosophy therefore produce happiness?'

" 'Absolutely,' I replied, 'and it alone.'

" 'Tell me,' he asked, 'what is philosophy and what is the happiness it engenders, if there is nothing which prevents your speaking?'

" 'Philosophy,' I answered, 'is the knowledge of that which exists, and a clear understanding of the truth; and happiness is the reward of such knowledge and understanding.'

5. "'But how do you define God?' he asked.

"'God is the Being who always has the same nature in the same manner, and is the cause of existence to all else,' I replied.

"Pleased with my words, he once again asked, 'Is not *knowledge* a word applied commonly to different matters? For, whoever is skilled in any of the arts, for example, in the art of military strategy, or of navigation, or of medicine, is called skillful. But this is not true in divine and human matters. Is there a science which furnishes us with an understanding of human and divine things, and, besides, a higher science of the divinity and virtue in them?'

"'Certainly,' I replied.

6. "'Well now,' he asked, 'is the knowledge of man and God similar to that of music, arithmetic, astronomy, and the like?'

"'Not at all,' I answered.

"'Your answer has not been correct, then,' he continued, 'for we acquire the knowledge of some things by study or practice, and of other things by sight. Now, if anyone were to say to you that in India there exists an animal different from all others, of such and such a species, assuming many shapes and colors, you would have no definite knowledge of it unless you saw it, nor could you attempt to give any description of it, unless you had heard of it from one who had seen it.'

"'Absolutely not,' I agreed.

7. "'Then, how,' he reasoned, 'can the philosophers speculate correctly or speak truly of God, when they have no knowledge of him, since they have never seen nor heard him?'

"'But the Deity, father,' I rejoined, 'cannot be seen by the same eyes as other living beings are. He is to be perceived by the mind alone, as Plato affirms, and I agree with him.'[11]

Chapter 4

"'Does our mind, then,' he inquired, 'possess such and so great a power? Or does it not perceive that which exists through the senses? Or will the human mind be capable of seeing God, if not aided by the Holy Spirit?'

"'Plato truly states,' I retorted, 'that the eye of the mind[12] has this special power, which has been given to us in order that we may see with it, when it is pure, the very Being who is the cause of everything the mind perceives, who has neither color, nor form, nor size, nor anything the eye can see, but who is beyond all essence, who is ineffable and indescribable, who alone is beautiful and good, and who comes at once into those souls which are well disposed because of their affinity to and desire of seeing him.'

2. "'What affinity, then,' he asked, 'have we with God? Is the soul also divine and immortal and a part of the Supreme Mind itself? And as this Supreme Mind sees God, are we, in like manner, able to perceive the Deity in our mind, and thus be happy even now?'

"'Absolutely,' I replied.

"'Do all the souls,' he asked, 'of all the animals perceive him? Or is man's soul different from that of a horse or an ass?'

"'No,' I answered, 'the souls of all creatures are the same.'

3. "'Then,' he continued, 'shall horses and asses see God, or have they ever seen God at any time?'

"'No,' I replied, 'for not even most men see him; only those who are honest in their life, and who have been purified through their justice and every other virtue.'

"'Then you would say,' he persisted, 'that man does not see God because of his affinity with him, nor because he possesses an intellect, but because he is temperate and just?'

"'Certainly,' I answered, 'and also because he has the faculty of thinking of God.'

"'Would you say,' he asked, 'that goats or sheep do an injustice to anyone?'

"'They do not in any way do an injustice to anyone,' I replied.

4. "'So, according to your reasoning,' he said, 'these animals will see God?'

"'No, they won't,' I answered, 'because they are hindered from doing so by the form of their bodies.'

"'If these animals had the power of speech,' he retorted, 'you can be sure that they would have more right to revile our bodies. But, for the present let us ignore this topic and I'll concede that what you say is true. Tell me this: Does the soul see God while it is in the body, or after it has been released from it?'

5. "'Even while it is in the human body,' I replied, 'it can see God by means of the intellect,

but especially after it has been released from the body, and exists of itself, does it perceive God whom it always loved.'

"'Does it remember,' he asked, 'this vision of God when it is again united to a human body?'

"'I don't think so,' I answered.

"'What, then,' he continued, 'is the advantage of having seen God? What advantage has he who has seen God over him who has not, unless he at least remembers the fact that he has seen him?'

6. "'That I cannot answer,' I admitted.

"'And what,' asked he, 'will be the punishment for those deemed unworthy to see God?'

"'As a punishment,' I answered, 'they will be imprisoned in the bodies of certain wild beasts.'[13]

"'Will they be conscious that for this reason they are imprisoned in such bodies and that they have committed some sin?'

"'I don't think so.'

7. "'Then, it would seem that they benefit in no way from such punishment; in fact, I would say that they suffer no punishment at all, unless they are conscious that it is a punishment.'

"'No, indeed,' I conceded.

"'Therefore,' he concluded, 'souls do not see God, nor do they transmigrate into other bodies, for they would know that they were being thus punished, and they would be afraid thereafter to commit even the slightest sin. But I do concede that souls can perceive that there is a God, and that justice and piety are admirable.'

"'You speak the truth,' I agreed.

Chapter 5

"'Those philosophers, then, know nothing,' he went on, 'about such matters, for they can't even explain the nature of the soul.'

"'It seems not,' I concurred.

"'Nor should we call the soul immortal, for, if it were, we would certainly have to call it unbegotten.'

"'Some Platonists,' I answered, 'consider the soul both unbegotten and immortal.'

"'Do you affirm,' he asked, 'that the universe also is unbegotten?'

"'There are some who hold that opinion,' I replied, 'but I don't agree with them.'

2. "'Right you are,' he continued. 'Why would one think that a body that is so solid, firm, composite, and mutable, a body that deteriorates and is renewed each day, has not originated from some first cause? Now, if the universe has been begotten, souls, too, of necessity, are begotten. Perhaps there is a time when they do not exist, for they were created for the sake of men and other living creatures, even if you claim that they have been begotten separately by themselves, and not together with their own bodies.'

"'I think you are right.'

"'Souls, then, are not immortal.'[14]

"'No,' I said, 'since it appears that the world itself was generated.'

3. "'On the other hand,' he continued, 'I do not claim that any soul ever perishes, for this would certainly be a benefit to sinners. What happens to them? The souls of the devout dwell in a better place, whereas the souls of the unjust and the evil abide in a worse place, and there they await the judgment day. Those, therefore, who are deemed worthy to see God will never perish, but the others will be subjected to punishment as long as God allows them to exist and as long as he wants them to be punished.'[15]

4. "'Does not your assertion agree with what Plato taught in his *Timaeus*[16] concerning the world, namely, that it can be destroyed, since it is a created thing, but that it will not be destroyed or be destined for destruction since such is the will of God? Don't you think that the same thing could be said of the soul and, in short, of all other creatures? For, whatever exists or shall exist after God has a nature subject to corruption, and therefore capable of complete annihilation, for only God is unbegotten and incorruptible. For this reason he is God, and all other things after him are created and corruptible.

5. "'This is also the reason why souls die and are punished, for, if they were unbegotten, they would not have sinned, nor have become so foolish; they would not have been so timid at one time, and so daring at another; nor would they, of their own account, ever have entered into swine, serpents, and dogs. Furthermore, if they were unbegotten, it would not be right to coerce them, for one who is unbegotten is similar and equal to another unbegotten, nor can

he be preferred to the other either in power or in honor.

6. "'We must conclude, therefore, that there are not many beings that are unbegotten, for, if there were some difference between them, you could not, no matter how you searched, find the cause of such difference; but, after sending your thought always to infinity, you would finally become tired and have to stop before the one Unbegotten and declare that he is the cause of all things. Do you think,' I said, 'that these things escaped the notice of Plato and Pythagoras, those wise men who became, so to say, a wall and bulwark of our philosophy?'

Chapter 6

"'I don't care,' he answered, 'if Plato or Pythagoras or anyone else held such views.[17] What I say is the truth and here is how you may learn it. The soul itself either is life or it possesses life. If it is life, it would cause something else to exist, not itself, just as motion causes something other than itself to move. Now, no one would deny that the soul lives; and if it lives, it does not live as life itself, but as a partaker of life. But, that which partakes of anything is different from that of which it partakes. Now, the soul partakes of life because God wishes it to live.

2. "'It will no longer partake of life whenever God doesn't wish it to live. For the power to live is not an attribute of the soul as it is of God. As man does not live forever, and his body is not forever united to his soul, since, whenever this union must be discontinued, the soul leaves the body and man no longer exists, so also, whenever the soul must cease to live, the spirit of life is taken from it and it is no more, but it likewise returns to the place of its origin.'

Chapter 7

"'If these philosophers,' I asked, 'do not know the truth, what teacher or method shall one follow?'

"'A long time ago,' he replied, 'long before the time of those so-called philosophers, there lived blessed men who were just and loved by God, men who spoke through the inspiration of the Holy Spirit and predicted events that would take place in the future, which events are now taking place. We call these men the prophets. They alone knew the truth and communicated it to men, whom they neither deferred to nor feared. With no desire for personal glory, they reiterated only what they heard and saw when inspired by a holy spirit.

2. "'Their writings are still extant, and whoever reads them with the proper faith will profit greatly in his knowledge of the origin and end of things, and of any other matter that a philosopher should know. In their writings they gave no proof at that time of their statements, for, as reliable witnesses of the truth, they were beyond proof; but the happenings that have taken place and are now taking place force you to believe their words.

3. "'They also are worthy of belief because of the miracles which they performed, for they exalted God, the Father and Creator of all things, and made known Christ, his Son, who was sent by him. This the false prophets, who are filled with an erring and unclean spirit, have never done, nor even do now, but they undertake to perform certain wonders to astound men, and they glorify the demons[18] and spirits of error. Above all, beseech God to open to you the gates of light,[19] for no one can perceive or understand these truths unless he has been enlightened by God and his Christ.'

Chapter 8

"When he had said these and many other things, which it is not convenient to recount right now, he went his way, after admonishing me to meditate on what he had told me, and I never saw him again. But my spirit was immediately set on fire, and an affection for the prophets, and for those who are friends of Christ, took hold of me; while pondering on his words, I discovered that his was the only sure and useful philosophy.

2. "Thus it is that I am now a philosopher."

Notes

1 No satisfactory explanation as yet of the identity of the Theoretic group; see J. C. M. van Winden, *An Early Christian Philosopher: Justin Martyr's Dialogue with Trypho, Chapters One to Nine*

(Leiden: Brill, 1971), 47; N. Hyldahl, "Tryphon und Tarphon," *Studia Theologica* 10 (1956): 77–88, 113.

2 On Stoicism in the *Apologies* see P. Montini, "Elementi di filosofia stoica in S. Giustino," *Aquinas* (Roma) 28 (1985): 457–76.

3 Van Winden's felicitous translation of ἐν ἀμηχανίᾳ δέ μου ὄντος.

4 On Platonism see Thomas B. Halton's new Introduction in St Justin Martyr Dialogue with Trypho, n. 5 [see bibliographic information for this chapter].

5 Probably Ephesus. Others think it might be Flavia Neapolis (Nablus), the city of his birth, or even the city of Alexandria. For Nablus see Jerome Murphy-O'Connor, *The Holy Land*, 4th ed. (Oxford: Oxford University Press, 1998), 372–3.

6 A Platonic expression. See *Phaedrus* 249D.

7 On the old man's identity see van Winden, 53–4, 117–18. Skarsaune, 246, suggests "the fascinating possibility that the Old Man may have been a Palestinian or a Syrian Christian." G. I. Gargano, "L'anziano incontrato di Giustino. Un amico del Logos? O il Logos stesso?" in *Geist und Erkenntnis: zu spirituellen Grundlagen Europas. Festschrift zum 65. Geburtstag von Prof. ThDr. Tomáš Špidlík SJ*, ed. K. Mácha (Munchen: Minerva Publication, 1985), 41–65 and A. Hofer ("The Old Man as Christ in Justin's *Dialogue with Trypho*," *VigChr* 57.1 [2003]: 1–21) raise the intriguing possibility that Trypho is Christ himself.

8 Justin used the word "philology" in the sense of an exercise of the reasoning faculty. See van Winden, 53–5.

9 The old man, however, employs the term "philology" to denote skill in the use of words.

10 Reason, i.e., in the philosophical sense. "Logos" is the term in common.

11 See Thomas B. Halton's new Introduction in St Justin Martyr Dialogue with Trypho, n. 5.

12 On the "eye of the mind," see van Winden, 69–71, quoting Plato, *Republic* 7.533d and *Sophist* 254a10.

13 On the transmigration of souls see *EECh*, s.v. "metempsychosis"; M. Maritano, "Giustino Martire: di fronte al problema della metempsicosi (*Dial.* 4, 4–7, e 5, 5)," *Salesianum* 54 (1992): 231–81.

14 St Justin teaches that the soul is not immortal in the sense that it cannot be destroyed, but that it is immortal in the sense that, by the grace of God, it will live forever. See van Winden, 86–7.

15 These words merely show that God could, if he desired, reduce all souls to nothingness. See M. Young, "Justin Martyr and The Death of Souls," *SP* 16.2 (TU 129; 1985), 209–15.

16 See Plato, *Timaeus* 41AB; van Winden, 92–4.

17 See R. M. Grant, "Aristotle and the Conversion of Justin," *JThS*, n.s., 7 (1956): 246–8; van Winden, 100.

18 See Hyldahl, "Tryphon und Tarphon," 229. On demons see D. C. Trakatellis, *The Pre-Existence of Christ in the Writings of Justin Martyr* (Missoula, Mont.: Scholars Press, 1976), 96–102.

19 On the gates of light see A. Cacciari, "In margine a Giustino, *dial.* vii, 3, le porte della luce," in *In Verbis verum amare* (Florence: La Nuova Italia, 1980), 101–34.

2

Prescriptions against the Heretics

Tertullian

Tertullian (*c.* 145–*c.* 220) was a presbyter in the church of Carthage and is famous for his "anti-intellectualism." In the following selection from his *Prescriptions against the Heretics* Tertullian fiercely condemns philosophy as the culmination of worldly (i.e. non-spiritual) wisdom and the source of heresy. It is worth noting, however, that many scholars think this oft-quoted selection paints an unbalanced picture of Tertullian's thought. They point out that Tertullian elsewhere makes use of philosophical arguments, and they contend that his target in the following passage is not philosophy *per se*, but rather particular philosophical views.

6. [. . .] it is the same Paul who elsewhere, when writing to the Galatians, classes heresy among the sins of the flesh, and who counsels Titus to shun a heretic after the first reproof because such a man is perverted and sinful, standing self-condemned. Besides, he censures heresy in almost every letter when he presses the duty of avoiding false doctrine, which is in fact the product of heresy. This is a Greek word meaning choice, the choice which anyone exercises when he teaches heresy or adopts it. That is why he calls a heretic self-condemned; he chooses for himself the cause of his condemnation. We Christians are forbidden to introduce anything on our own authority or to choose what someone else introduces on his own authority. Our authorities are the Lord's apostles, and they in turn chose to introduce nothing on their own authority. They faithfully passed on to the nations the teaching which they had received from Christ. So we should anathematize even an angel from heaven if he were to preach a different gospel. The Holy Ghost had already at that time foreseen that an angel of deceit would come in a virgin called

Tertullian, *The Prescriptions against the Heretics* in S. L. Greenslade (ed.), *Early Latin Theology*, Library of Christian Classics vol. V (London: SCM Press, 1956), extracts from pp. 34–5.

Philumene, transforming himself into an angel of light, by whose miracles and tricks Apelles was deceived into introducing a new heresy.

7. These are human and demonic doctrines, engendered for itching ears by the ingenuity of that worldly wisdom which the Lord called foolishness, choosing the foolish things of the world to put philosophy to shame. For worldly wisdom culminates in philosophy with its rash interpretation of God's nature and purpose. It is philosophy that supplies the heresies with their equipment. From philosophy come the aeons and those infinite forms – whatever they are – and Valentinus's human trinity. He had been a Platonist. From philosophy came Marcion's God, the better for his inactivity. He had come from the Stoics. The idea of a mortal soul was picked up from the Epicureans, and the denial of the restitution of the flesh was taken over from the common tradition of the philosophical schools. Zeno taught them to equate God and matter, and Heracleitus comes on the scene when anything is being laid down about a god of fire. Heretics and philosophers perpend the same themes and are caught up in the same discussions. What is the origin of evil, and why? The origin of man, and how? And – Valentinus's latest subject – what is the origin of God? No doubt in Desire and Abortion! A plague on Aristotle, who taught them dialectic, the art which destroys as much as it builds, which changes its opinions like a coat, forces its conjectures, is stubborn in argument, works hard at being contentious and is a burden even to itself. For it reconsiders every point to make sure it never finishes a discussion.

From philosophy come those fables and endless genealogies and fruitless questionings, those 'words that creep like as doth a canker.' To hold us back from such things, the Apostle testifies expressly in his letter to the Colossians that we should beware of philosophy. 'Take heed lest any man circumvent you through philosophy or vain deceit, after the tradition of men,' against the providence of the Holy Ghost. He had been at Athens where he had come to grips with the human wisdom which attacks and perverts truth, being itself divided up into its own swarm of heresies by the variety of its mutually antagonistic sects. What has Jerusalem to do with Athens, the Church with the Academy, the Christian with the heretic? Our principles come from the Porch of Solomon, who had himself taught that the Lord is to be sought in simplicity of heart. I have no use for a Stoic or a Platonic or a dialectic Christianity. After Jesus Christ we have no need of speculation, after the Gospel no need of research. When we come to believe, we have no desire to believe anything else; for we begin by believing that there is nothing else which we have to believe.

8. I come then to the point which members of the Church adduce to justify speculation and which heretics press in order to import scruple and hesitation. It is written, they say: 'Seek, and ye shall find.' But we must not forget *when* the Lord said these words. It was surely at the very beginning of his teaching when everyone was still doubtful whether he was the Christ. Peter had not yet pronounced him to be the Son of God, and even John had lost his conviction about him. It was right to say: 'Seek, and ye shall find,' at the time when, being still unrecognized, he had still to be sought. Besides, it applied only to the Jews. Every word in that criticism was pointed at those who had the means of seeking Christ. 'They have Moses and Elijah,' it says; that is, the law and the prophets which preach Christ. Similarly he says elsewhere, and plainly: 'Search the Scriptures, in which ye hope for salvation, for they speak of me.' That will be what he meant by 'Seek, and ye shall find.'

The following words, 'Knock, and it shall be opened unto you,' obviously apply to the Jews. At one time inside the house of God, the Jews found themselves outside when they were thrown out because of their sins. The Gentiles, however, were never in God's house. They were but a drop from the bucket, dust from the threshing-floor, always outside. How can anyone who has always been outside knock where he has never been? How can he recognize the door if he has never been taken in or thrown out by it? Surely it is the man who knows that he was once inside and was turned out, who recognizes the door and knocks? Again, the words, 'Ask, and ye shall receive,' fit those who know whom to ask and by whom something has been promised, namely the God of Abraham, of Isaac, and of Jacob, of whose person and promises the Gentiles were equally ignorant. Accordingly he said to Israel: 'I am not sent but unto the lost sheep of the house of Israel.' He had not yet begun to cast the children's bread to the dogs nor yet told the apostles to go into the way of the Gentiles. If at the end he ordered them to go and teach and baptize the Gentiles, it was only because they were soon to receive the Holy Spirit, the Paraclete, who would guide them into all truth. This also supports our conclusion. If the apostles, the appointed teachers of the Gentiles, were themselves to receive the Paraclete as their teacher, then the words, 'Seek, and ye shall find,' were much less applicable to us than to the Jews. For we were to be taught by the apostles without any effort of our own, as they were taught by the Holy Spirit. All the Lord's sayings, I admit, were set down for all men. They have come through the ears of the Jews to us Christians. Still, many were aimed at particular people and constitute for us an example rather than a command immediately applicable to ourselves.

9. However, I shall now make you a present of that point. Suppose that 'Seek, and ye shall find' was said to us all. Even then it would be wrong to determine the sense without reference to the guiding principles of exegesis. No word of God is so unqualified or so unrestricted in application that the mere words can be pleaded without respect to their underlying meaning.

My first principle is this. Christ laid down one definite system of truth which the world must believe without qualification, and which we must seek precisely in order to believe it when we find it. Now you cannot search indefinitely for a single definite truth. You must seek until you find, and when you find, you must believe. Then you have simply to keep what you have come to believe, since you also believe that there is nothing else to believe, and therefore nothing else to seek, once you have found and believed what he taught who bids you seek nothing beyond what he taught. If you feel any doubt as to what this truth is, I undertake to establish that Christ's teaching is to be found with us. For the moment, my confidence in my proof allow me to anticipate it, and I warn certain people not to seek for anything beyond what they came to believe, for that was all they needed to seek for. They must not interpret, 'Seek, and ye shall find,' without regard to reasonable methods of exegesis.

10. The reasonable exegesis of this saying turns on three points: matter, time, and limitation. As to matter, you are to consider what is to be sought; as to time, when; and as to limitation, how far. What you must seek is what Christ taught, and precisely as long as you are not finding it, precisely until you do find it. And you did find it when you came to believe. You would not have believed if you had not found, just as you would not have sought except in order to find. Since finding was the object of your search and belief of your finding, your acceptance of the faith debars any prolongation of seeking and finding. The very success of your seeking has set up this limitation for you. Your boundary has been marked out by him who would not have you believe, and so would not have you seek, outside the limits of his teaching.

But if we are bound to go on seeking as long as there is any possibility of finding, simply because so much has been taught by others as well, we shall be always seeking and never believing. What end will there be to seeking? What point of rest for belief? Where the fruition of finding? With Marcion? But Valentinus also propounds: 'Seek, and ye shall find.' With Valentinus? But Apelles also will knock at my door with the same pronouncement, and Ebion and Simon and the whole row of them can find no other way to ingratiate themselves with me and bring me over to their side. There will be no end, as long as I meet everywhere with, 'Seek and ye shall find,' and I shall wish I had never begun to seek, if I never grasp what Christ taught, what should be sought, what must be believed.

3

In What Respect Philosophy Contributes to the Comprehension of Divine Truth

Clement of Alexandria

Clement of Alexandria (*c.* 150–*c.* 215) was a Greek convert and an early Christian theologian in Alexandria. He was one of the first to make a concentrated effort to harmonize Christianity and philosophy in a way that would both appeal to non-Christians and avoid theological compromise. In the following passage from his *Miscellanies* Clement defends philosophy as a method for comprehending truth; however, to prevent the misunderstanding that he intends to undermine the need for revelation, he is careful to add that philosophy is only a "concurrent and cooperating cause of true apprehension" and is neither necessary, nor by itself sufficient for a full understanding of the truth.

As many men drawing down the ship, cannot be called many causes, but one cause consisting of many; – for each individual by himself is not the cause of the ship being drawn, but along with the rest; – so also philosophy, being the search for truth, contributes to the comprehension of truth; not as being the cause of comprehension, but a cause along with other things, and co-operator; perhaps also a joint cause. And as the several virtues are causes of the happiness of one individual; and as both the sun, and the fire, and the bath, and clothing are of one getting warm: so while truth is one, many things contribute to its investigation. But its discovery is by the Son. If then we consider, virtue is, in power, one. But it is the case, that when exhibited in some things, it is called prudence, in others temperance, and in others manliness or righteousness. By the same analogy, while truth is one, in geometry there is the truth of geometry; in music, that of music; and in the right philosophy, there will be Hellenic truth. But that is the only authentic truth, unassailable, in which we are instructed by the Son of God. In the same way we say, that the drachma being one and the same, when given to the shipmaster, is called the fare; to the tax-gatherer, tax; to the

Clement, "In What Respect Philosophy Contributes to the Comprehension of Divine Truth" from Ante-Nicene Christian Library: *Translations of the Writings of the Fathers*, ed. Rev. Alexander Roberts and James Donaldson, vol. 4, *Clement of Alexandria*, vol. 1 (Edinburgh: T. and T. Clark, 1867), chapter XX, pp. 418–20.

landlord, rent; to the teacher, fees; to the seller, an earnest. And each, whether it be virtue or truth, called by the same name, is the cause of its own peculiar effect alone; and from the blending of them arises a happy life. For we are not made happy by names alone, when we say that a good life is happiness, and that the man who is adorned in his soul with virtue is happy. But if philosophy contributes remotely to the discovery of truth, by reaching, by diverse essays, after the knowledge which touches close on the truth, the knowledge possessed by us, it aids him who aims at grasping it, in accordance with the Word, to apprehend knowledge. But the Hellenic truth is distinct from that held by us (although it has got the same name), both in respect of extent of knowledge, certainty of demonstration, divine power, and the like. For we are taught of God, being instructed in the truly "sacred letters"[1] by the Son of God. Whence those, to whom we refer, influence souls not in the way we do, but by different teaching. And if, for the sake of those who are fond of fault-finding, we must draw a distinction, by saying that philosophy is a concurrent and co-operating cause of true apprehension, being the search for truth, then we shall avow it to be a preparatory training for the enlightened man (*τοῦ γνωστικοῦ*); not assigning as the cause that which is but the joint-cause; nor as the upholding cause, what is merely co-operative; nor giving to philosophy the place of a *sine quâ non*. Since almost all of us, without training in arts and sciences, and the Hellenic philosophy, and some even without learning at all, through the influence of a philosophy divine and barbarous, and by power, have through faith received the word concerning God, trained by self-operating wisdom. But that which acts in conjunction with something else, being of itself incapable of operating by itself, we describe as co-operating and concausing, and say that it becomes a cause only in virtue of its being a joint-cause, and receives the name of cause only in respect of its concurring with something else, but that it cannot by itself produce the right effect.

Although at one time philosophy justified the Greeks, not conducting then to that entire righteousness to which it is ascertained to co-operate, as the first and second flight of steps help you in your ascent to the upper room, and the grammarian helps the philosopher. Not as if by its abstraction, the perfect Word would be rendered incomplete, or truth perish; since also sight, and hearing, and the voice contribute to truth, but it is the mind which is the appropriate faculty for knowing it. But of those things which co-operate, some contribute a greater amount of power; some, a less. Perspicuity accordingly aids in the communication of truth, and logic in preventing us from falling under the heresies by which we are assailed. But the teaching, which is according to the Saviour, is complete in itself and without defect, being "the power and wisdom of God";[2] and the Hellenic philosophy does not, by its approach, make the truth more powerful; but rendering powerless the assault of sophistry against it, and frustrating the treacherous plots laid against the truth, is said to be the proper "fence and wall of the vineyard." And the truth which is according to faith is as necessary for life as bread; while the preparatory discipline is like sauce and sweetmeats. "At the end of the dinner, the dessert is pleasant," according to the Theban Pindar. And the Scripture has expressly said, "The innocent will become wiser by understanding, and the wise will receive knowledge."[3] "And he that speaketh of himself," saith the Lord, "seeketh his own glory; but He that seeketh His glory that sent Him is true, and there is no unrighteousness in Him."[4] On the other hand, therefore, he who appropriates what belongs to the barbarians, and vaunts it is his own, does wrong, increasing his own glory, and falsifying the truth. It is such an one that is by Scripture called a "thief." It is therefore said, "Son, be not a liar; for falsehood leads to theft." Nevertheless the thief possesses really, what he has possessed himself of dishonestly, whether it be gold, or silver, or speech, or dogma. The ideas, then, which they have stolen, and which are partially true, they know by conjecture and necessary logical deduction: on becoming disciples, therefore, they will know them with intelligent apprehension.

Notes

1 *ἱερὰ γράμματα* (2 Tim. iii. 15), translated in A. V. "sacred scriptures"; also in contradistinction to the so-called sacred letters of the Egyptians, Chaldeans, etc.

2 1 Cor. i. 24.

3 Prov. xxi. 11.

4 John vii. 18.

4

The Decisive Treatise, Determining the Nature of the Connection between Religion and Philosophy

Averroes (Ibn Rushd)

Ibn Rushd (1126–98), better known in the Western world as Averroes, was the most distinguished of the Spanish Islamic philosophers. His literary exchange with al-Ghazāli in his *Decisive Treatise* clearly delineates the role that philosophical strategies have to play in interpreting revelation. In this reading, Averroes argues (1) that the Law (i.e. scripture) requires the study of philosophy, (2) that philosophy and scripture cannot conflict, and (3) that when they appear to conflict scripture should be interpreted allegorically.

Thus spoke the lawyer, *imām*, judge, and unique scholar, Abul Walīd Muḥammad Ibn Aḥmad Ibn Rushd:

Praise be to God with all due praise, and a prayer for Muḥammad His chosen servant and apostle. The purpose of this treatise is to examine, from the standpoint of the study of the Law, whether the study of philosophy and logic is allowed by the Law, or prohibited, or commanded – either by way of recommendation or as obligatory.

[Chapter One]

[The Law Makes Philosophic Studies Obligatory]

[. . .]

We say: If the activity of 'philosophy' is nothing more than study of existing beings and reflection on them as indications of the Artisan,[1] i.e. inasmuch as they are products of art (for beings only indicate the Artisan through our knowledge

Averroes (Ibn Rushd), *The Decisive Treatise, Determining the Nature of the Connection between Religion and Philosophy* from *Averroes on the Harmony of Religion and Philosophy*, trans. of Ibn Rushd's *Kitab fasl al-maqal*, with its app. (Damima) and an extract from *Kitab al-kashf 'an manahiju al-adilla*, by George F. Hourani (London: Luzac & Co., 1961), extracts from pp. 44–5, 50–3.

of the art in them, and the more perfect this knowledge is, the more perfect the knowledge of the Artisan becomes),[2] and if the Law has encouraged and urged reflection on beings, then it is clear that what this name signifies is either obligatory or recommended by the Law.

[. . .]

That the Law summons to reflection on beings, and the pursuit of knowledge about them, by the intellect is clear from several verses of the Book of God, Blessed and Exalted, such as the saying of the Exalted, 'Reflect, you have vision': this is textual authority for the obligation to use intellectual reasoning, or a combination of intellectual and legal reasoning. Another example is His saying, 'Have they not studied the kingdom of the heavens and the earth, and whatever things God has created?': this is a text urging the study of the totality of beings. Again, God the Exalted has taught that one of those whom He singularly honoured by this knowledge was Abraham, peace on him, for the Exalted said, 'So we made Abraham see the kingdom of the heavens and the earth, that he might be' [and so on to the end of the verse]. The Exalted also said, 'Do they not observe the camels, how they have been created, and the sky, how it has been raised up?', and He said, 'and they give thought to the creation of the heavens and the earth', and so on in countless other verses.

[. . .]

Since it has now been established that the Law has rendered obligatory the study of beings by the intellect, and reflection on them, and since reflection is nothing more than inference and drawing out of the unknown from the known, and since this is reasoning or at any rate done by reasoning, therefore we are under an obligation to carry on our study of beings by intellectual reasoning. It is further evident that this manner of study, to which the Law summons and urges, is the most perfect kind of study using the most perfect kind of reasoning; and this is the kind called 'demonstration'.

[. . .]

[Chapter Two]

[Philosophy Contains Nothing Opposed to Islam]

[. . .]

Now since this religion is true and summons to the study which leads to knowledge of the Truth, we the Muslim community know definitely that demonstrative study does not lead to [conclusions] conflicting with what Scripture has given us; for truth does not oppose truth but accords with it and bears witness to it.

[. . .]

This being so, whenever demonstrative study leads to any manner of knowledge about any being, that being is inevitably either unmentioned or mentioned in Scripture. If it is unmentioned there is no contradiction, and it is in the same case as an act whose category is unmentioned, so that the lawyer has to infer it by reasoning from Scripture. If Scripture speaks about it, the apparent meaning of the words inevitably either accords or conflicts with the conclusions of demonstration about it. If this [apparent meaning] accords there is no argument. If it conflicts there is a call for allegorical interpretation of it. The meaning of 'allegorical interpretation' is: extension of the significance of an expression from real to metaphorical significance, without forsaking therein the standard metaphorical practices of Arabic, such as calling a thing by the name of something resembling it or a cause or consequence or accompaniment of it, or other things such as are enumerated in accounts of the kinds of metaphorical speech.

[. . .]

Now if the lawyer does this in many decisions of religious law, with how much more right is it done by the possessor of demonstrative knowledge! For the lawyer has at his disposition only reasoning based on opinion, while he who would know [God] ⟨has at his disposition⟩ reasoning based on certainty. So we affirm definitely that whenever the conclusion of a demonstration is in conflict with the apparent meaning of Scripture, that apparent meaning admits of allegorical interpretation according to the rules for such interpretation in Arabic. This proposition is questioned by no Muslim and doubted by no believer. But its certainty is immensely increased for those who have had close dealings with this idea and put it to the test, and made it their aim to reconcile the assertions of intellect and tradition. Indeed we may say that whenever a statement in Scripture conflicts in its apparent meaning with a conclusion of demonstration, if Scripture is considered carefully, and the rest of its contents searched page by page, there will invariably be found among the expressions of Scripture something which in its apparent meaning bears witness to that allegorical interpretation or comes close to bearing witness.

[. . .]

In the light of this idea the Muslims are unanimous in holding that it is not obligatory either to take all the expressions of Scripture in their apparent meaning or to extend them all from their apparent meaning by allegorical interpretation. They disagree [only] over which of them should and which should not be so interpreted: the Ash'arites for instance give an allegorical interpretation to the verse about God's directing Himself[3] and the Tradition about His descent,[4] while the Hanbalites take them in their apparent meaning.

[. . .]

The reason why we have received a Scripture with both an apparent and an inner meaning lies in the diversity of people's natural capacities and the difference of their innate dispositions with regard to assent. The reason why we have received in Scripture texts whose apparent meanings contradict each other is in order to draw the attention of those who are well grounded in science to the interpretation which reconciles them. This is the idea referred to in the words received from the Exalted, 'He it is who has sent down to you the Book, containing certain verses clear and definite' [and so on] down to the words 'those who are well grounded in science'.

[. . .]

It may be objected: 'There are some things in Scripture which the Muslims have unanimously agreed to take in their apparent meaning, others [which they have agreed] to interpret allegorically, and others about which they have disagreed; is it permissible, then, that demonstration should lead to interpreting allegorically what they have agreed to take in its apparent meaning, or to taking in its apparent meaning what they have agreed to interpret allegorically?' We reply: If unanimous agreement is established by a method which is certain, such [a result] is not sound; but if [the existence of] agreement on those things is a matter of opinion, then it may be sound. This is why Abū Ḥāmid, Abul-Ma'ālī, and other leaders of thought said that no one should be definitely called an unbeliever for violating unanimity on a point of interpretation in matters like these.

That unanimity on theoretical matters is never determined with certainty, as it can be on practical matters, may be shown to you by the fact that it is not possible for unanimity to be determined on any question at any period unless that period is strictly limited by us, and all the scholars existing in that period are known to us (i.e. known as individuals and in their total number), and the doctrine of each of them on the question has been handed down to us on unassailable authority, and, in addition to all this, unless we are sure that the scholars existing at the time were in agreement that there is not both an apparent and an inner meaning in Scripture, that knowledge of any question ought not to be kept secret from anyone, and that there is only one way for people to understand Scripture. But it is recorded in Tradition that many of the first believers used to hold that Scripture has both an apparent and an inner meaning, and that the inner meaning ought not to be learned by anyone who is not a man of learning in this field and who is incapable of understanding it. Thus, for example, Bukhārī reports a saying of 'Alī Ibn Abī Ṭālib, may God be pleased with him, 'Speak to people about what they know. Do you want God and His Prophet to be accused of lying?' Other examples of the same kind are reported about a group of early believers. So how can it possibly be conceived that a unanimous agreement can have been handed down to us about a single theoretical question, when we know definitely that not a single period has been without scholars who held that there are things in Scripture whose true meaning should not be learned by all people?

The situation is different in practical matters: everyone holds that the truth about these should be disclosed to all people alike, and to establish the occurrence of unanimity about them we consider it sufficient that the question [at issue] should have been widely discussed and that no report of controversy about it should have been handed down to us. This is enough to establish the occurrence of unanimity on matters of practice, but on matters of doctrine the case is different.

Notes

1 [. . .] "Artisan" (Gr.) conveys a hint of Ibn Rushd's conception of God as a *dēmiourgos* (Pl. *Timaeus*), not as a Creator *ex nihilo*.

2 "knowledge of the Artisan": Ibn Rushd attached great value to teleological arguments for the existence and nature of God. *Manāhij* (M. J. Müller, *Philosophie und Theologie von Averroes* (Munich, 1859)), pp. 43–6, 79: the *Qur'ān* proves the existence of God from indications of providence for man and of form and design in the world. These proofs are for all classes of men, but the learned understand the art and the Artisan more deeply. [. . .]

3 "the verse about God's directing Himself": *āyat alistiwā'*. *Qur'ān*, ii, 29: "He it is who has created for you all that is on earth; then He directed Himself towards the heaven and made them [sic] seven heavens. He is the knower of all things." [. . .] The Ash'arites objected to the physical implications of a literal "direction" taken by God.

4 "the Tradition about His descent": *ḥadīth an-nuzūl*. "God descends to the heaven of the lower world", i.e. of our sublunary sphere. [. . .]

5

Faith and Reason

Thomas Aquinas

Thomas Aquinas (1225–74) was a Dominican friar and arguably the most influential Christian philosopher and theologian of all time. In this selection from his *Summa Contra Gentiles* Aquinas distinguishes between those truths about God that can be discovered using only reason and those that are above reason and must be made known by God. Aquinas defends the propriety of belief in both kinds of truth and argues that the truth discovered through reason and the truth revealed by God cannot conflict with one another. It must be possible to answer any argument brought against the revealed truths of the Christian faith.

Chapter 4

That the Truth about God to which the Natural Reason Reaches is Fittingly Proposed to Men for Belief

[1] Since, therefore, there exists a twofold truth concerning the divine being, one to which the inquiry of the reason can reach, the other which surpasses the whole ability of the human reason, it is fitting that both of these truths be proposed to man divinely for belief. This point must first be shown concerning the truth that is open to the inquiry of the reason; otherwise, it might perhaps seem to someone that, since such a truth can be known by the reason, it was uselessly given to men through a supernatural inspiration as an object of belief.

[2] Yet, if this truth were left solely as a matter of inquiry for the human reason, three awkward consequences would follow.

[3] The first is that few men would possess the knowledge of God. For there are three reasons why most men are cut off from the fruit of diligent inquiry which is the discovery of truth. Some do

St Thomas Aquinas, Chapters 4–7 from *On the Truth of the Catholic Faith: Summa Contra Gentiles*, Book One: *God*, trans., with intro. and notes, by Anton C. Pegis (Garden City, NY: Image Books, 1955), pp. 66–75.

not have the physical disposition for such work. As a result, there are many who are naturally not fitted to pursue knowledge; and so, however much they tried, they would be unable to reach the highest level of human knowledge which consists in knowing God. Others are cut off from pursuing this truth by the necessities imposed upon them by their daily lives. For some men must devote themselves to taking care of temporal matters. Such men would not be able to give so much time to the leisure of contemplative inquiry as to reach the highest peak at which human investigation can arrive, namely, the knowledge of God. Finally, there are some who are cut off by indolence. In order to know the things that the reason can investigate concerning God, a knowledge of many things must already be possessed. For almost all of philosophy is directed towards the knowledge of God, and that is why metaphysics, which deals with divine things, is the last part of philosophy to be learned. This means that we are able to arrive at the inquiry concerning the aforementioned truth only on the basis of a great deal of labor spent in study. Now, those who wish to undergo such a labor for the mere love of knowledge are few, even though God has inserted into the minds of men a natural appetite for knowledge.

[4] The second awkward effect is that those who would come to discover the abovementioned truth would barely reach it after a great deal of time. The reasons are several. There is the profundity of this truth, which the human intellect is made capable of grasping by natural inquiry only after a long training. Then, there are many things that must be presupposed, as we have said. There is also the fact that, in youth, when the soul is swayed by the various movements of the passions, it is not in a suitable state for the knowledge of such lofty truth. On the contrary, "one becomes wise and knowing in repose," as it is said in the *Physics*,[1] The result is this. If the only way open to us for the knowledge of God were solely that of the reason, the human race would remain in the blackest shadows of ignorance. For then the knowledge of God, which especially renders men perfect and good, would come to be possessed only by a few, and these few would require a great deal of time in order to reach it.

[5] The third awkward effect is this. The investigation of the human reason for the most part has falsity present within it, and this is due partly to the weakness of our intellect in judgment, and partly to the admixture of images. The result is that many, remaining ignorant of the power of demonstration, would hold in doubt those things that have been most truly demonstrated. This would be particularly the case since they see that, among those who are reputed to be wise men, each one teaches his own brand of doctrine. Furthermore, with the many truths that are demonstrated, there sometimes is mingled something that is false, which is not demonstrated but rather asserted on the basis of some probable or sophistical argument, which yet has the credit of being a demonstration. That is why it was necessary that the unshakeable certitude and pure truth concerning divine things should be presented to men by way of faith.[2]

[6] Beneficially, therefore, did the divine Mercy provide that it should instruct us to hold by faith even those truths that the human reason is able to investigate. In this way, all men would easily be able to have a share in the knowledge of God, and this without uncertainty and error.

[7] Hence it is written: "Henceforward you walk not as also the Gentiles walk in the vanity of their mind, having their understanding darkened" (Eph. 4:17–18). And again: "All thy children shall be taught of the Lord" (Isa. 54:13).

Chapter 5
That the Truths the Human Reason is Not Able to Investigate are Fittingly Proposed to Men for Belief

[1] Now, perhaps some will think that men should not be asked to believe what the reason is not adequate to investigate, since the divine Wisdom provides in the case of each thing according to the mode of its nature. We must therefore prove that it is necessary for man to receive from God as objects of belief even those truths that are above the human reason.

[2] No one tends with desire and zeal towards something that is not already known to him.

But, as we shall examine later on in this work, men are ordained by the divine Providence towards a higher good than human fragility can experience in the present life.[3] That is why it was necessary for the human mind to be called to something higher than the human reason here and now can reach, so that it would thus learn to desire something and with zeal tend towards something that surpasses the whole state of the present life. This belongs especially to the Christian religion, which in a unique way promises spiritual and eternal goods. And so there are many things proposed to men in it that transcend human sense. The Old Law, on the other hand, whose promises were of a temporal character, contained very few proposals that transcended the inquiry of the human reason. Following this same direction, the philosophers themselves, in order that they might lead men from the pleasure of sensible things to virtue, were concerned to show that there were in existence other goods of a higher nature than these things of sense, and that those who gave themselves to the active or contemplative virtues would find much sweeter enjoyment in the taste of these higher goods.

[3] It is also necessary that such truth be proposed to men for belief so that they may have a truer knowledge of God. For then only do we know God truly when we believe Him to be above everything that it is possible for man to think about Him; for, as we have shown,[4] the divine substance surpasses the natural knowledge of which man is capable. Hence, by the fact that some things about God are proposed to man that surpass his reason, there is strengthened in man the view that God is something above what he can think.

[4] Another benefit that comes from the revelation to men of truths that exceed the reason is the curbing of presumption, which is the mother of error. For there are some who have such a presumptuous opinion of their own ability that they deem themselves able to measure the nature of everything; I mean to say that, in their estimation, everything is true that seems to them so, and everything is false that does not. So that the human mind, therefore, might be freed from this presumption and come to a humble inquiry after truth, it was necessary that some things should be proposed to man by God that would completely surpass his intellect.

[5] A still further benefit may also be seen in what Aristotle says in the *Ethics*.[5] There was a certain Simonides who exhorted people to put aside the knowledge of divine things and to apply their talents to human occupations. He said that "he who is a man should know human things, and he who is mortal, things that are mortal." Against Simonides Aristotle says that "man should draw himself towards what is immortal and divine as much as he can." And so he says in the *De animalibus* that, although what we know of the higher substances is very little, yet that little is loved and desired more than all the knowledge that we have about less noble substances.[6] He also says in the *De caelo et mundo* that when questions about the heavenly bodies can be given even a modest and merely plausible solution, he who hears this experiences intense joy.[7] From all these considerations it is clear that even the most imperfect knowledge about the most noble realities brings the greatest perfection to the soul. Therefore, although the human reason cannot grasp fully the truths that are above it, yet, if it somehow holds these truths at least by faith, it acquires great perfection for itself.

[6] Therefore it is written: "For many things are shown to thee above the understanding of men" (Ecclus. 3:25). Again: "So the things that are of God no man knoweth but the Spirit of God. But to us God hath revealed them by His Spirit" (I Cor. 2:11, 10).

Chapter 6
That to Give Assent to the Truths of Faith is not Foolishness even though They are above Reason

[1] Those who place their faith in this truth, however, "for which the human reason offers no experimental evidence,"[8] do not believe foolishly, as though "following artificial fables" (II Peter 1:16). For these "secrets of divine Wisdom" (Job 11:6) the divine Wisdom itself, which knows all things to the full, has deigned to reveal to men. It reveals its own presence, as well as the truth of its teaching and inspiration, by fitting arguments; and in order to confirm those truths that exceed natural knowledge, it gives visible manifestation to works that surpass the ability of all nature. Thus, there are the wonderful cures of

illnesses, there is the raising of the dead, and the wonderful immutation in the heavenly bodies; and what is more wonderful, there is the inspiration given to human minds, so that simple and untutored persons, filled with the gift of the Holy Spirit, come to possess instantaneously the highest wisdom and the readiest eloquence. When these arguments were examined, through the efficacy of the abovementioned proof, and not the violent assault of arms or the promise of pleasures, and (what is most wonderful of all) in the midst of the tyranny of the persecutors, an innumerable throng of people, both simple and most learned, flocked to the Christian faith. In this faith there are truths preached that surpass every human intellect; the pleasures of the flesh are curbed; it is taught that the things of the world should be spurned. Now, for the minds of mortal men to assent to these things is the greatest of miracles, just as it is a manifest work of divine inspiration that, spurning visible things, men should seek only what is invisible. Now, that this has happened neither without preparation nor by chance, but as a result of the disposition of God, is clear from the fact that through many pronouncements of the ancient prophets God had foretold that He would do this. The books of these prophets are held in veneration among us Christians, since they give witness to our faith.

[2] The manner of this confirmation is touched on by St Paul: "Which," that is, human salvation, "having begun to be declared by the Lord, was confirmed unto us by them that hear Him: God also bearing them witness of signs, and wonders, and divers miracles, and distributions of the Holy Ghost" (Heb. 2:3–4).

[3] This wonderful conversion of the world to the Christian faith is the clearest witness of the signs given in the past; so that it is not necessary that they should be further repeated, since they appear most clearly in their effect. For it would be truly more wonderful than all signs if the world had been led by simple and humble men to believe such lofty truths, to accomplish such difficult actions, and to have such high hopes. Yet it is also a fact that, even in our own time, God does not cease to work miracles through His saints for the confirmation of the faith.

[. . .]

Chapter 7

That the Truth of Reason is not Opposed to the Truth of the Christian Faith

[1] Now, although the truth of the Christian faith which we have discussed surpasses the capacity of the reason, nevertheless that truth that the human reason is naturally endowed to know cannot be opposed to the truth of the Christian faith. For that with which the human reason is naturally endowed is clearly most true; so much so, that it is impossible for us to think of such truths as false. Nor is it permissible to believe as false that which we hold by faith, since this is confirmed in a way that is so clearly divine. Since, therefore, only the false is opposed to the true, as is clearly evident from an examination of their definitions, it is impossible that the truth of faith should be opposed to those principles that the human reason knows naturally.

[2] Furthermore, that which is introduced into the soul of the student by the teacher is contained in the knowledge of the teacher – unless his teaching is fictitious, which it is improper to say of God. Now, the knowledge of the principles that are known to us naturally has been implanted in us by God; for God is the Author of our nature. These principles, therefore, are also contained by the divine Wisdom. Hence, whatever is opposed to them is opposed to the divine Wisdom, and, therefore, cannot come from God. That which we hold by faith as divinely revealed, therefore, cannot be contrary to our natural knowledge.

[3] Again. In the presence of contrary arguments our intellect is chained, so that it cannot proceed to the knowledge of the truth. If, therefore, contrary knowledges were implanted in us by God, our intellect would be hindered from knowing truth by this very fact. Now, such an effect cannot come from God.

[4] And again. What is natural cannot change as long as nature does not. Now, it is impossible that contrary opinions should exist in the same knowing subject at the same time. No opinion or belief, therefore, is implanted in man by God which is contrary to man's natural knowledge.

[5] Therefore, the Apostle says: "The word is nigh thee, even in thy mouth and in thy heart. This is the word of faith, which we preach" (Rom. 10:8). But because it overcomes reason, there are some who think that it is opposed to it: which is impossible.

[6] The authority of St Augustine also agrees with this. He writes as follows: "That which truth will reveal cannot in any way be opposed to the sacred books of the Old and the New Testament."[9]

[7] From this we evidently gather the following conclusion: whatever arguments are brought forward against the doctrines of faith are conclusions incorrectly derived from the first and self-evident principles imbedded in nature. Such conclusions do not have the force of demonstration; they are arguments that are either probable or sophistical. And so, there exists the possibility to answer them.

Notes

1 Aristotle, *Physics*, VII, 3 (247b 9).

2 Although St Thomas does not name Maimonides or his *Guide for the Perplexed* (*Dux neutrorum*), there are evident points of contact between the Catholic and the Jewish theologian. On the reasons for revelation given here, on our knowledge of God, on creation and the eternity of the world, and on Aristotelianism in general, St Thomas has Maimonides in mind both to agree and to disagree with him. By way of background for *SCG*, I, the reader can usefully consult the references to Maimonides in E. Gilson, *History of Christian Philosophy in the Middle Ages* (New York, 1955), pp. 649–51.

3 *SCG*, III, ch. 48.

4 See *Summa Contra Gentiles*, Book 1, ch. 3.

5 Aristotle, *Nicomachean Ethics*, X, 7 (1177b 31).

6 Aristotle, *De partibus animalium*, I, 5 (644b 32).

7 Aristotle, *De caelo et mundo*, II, 12 (291b 26).

8 St Gregory, *Homiliae in evangelia*, II, hom. 26, i (*PL*, 76, col. 1197).

9 St Augustine, *De genesi ad litteram*, II, c. 18 (*PL*, 34, col. 280).

6

Belief in God is Natural

John Calvin

John Calvin (1509–64) was one of the leaders of the Protestant Reformation and its greatest theologian. In the following selection from his *Institutes of the Christian Religion* Calvin argues that God has implanted within the human mind a natural instinctual knowledge of himself.

The *Sensus Divinitatis*

There is within the human mind, and indeed by natural instinct, an awareness of divinity. This we take to be beyond controversy. To prevent anyone from taking refuge in the pretence of ignorance, God himself has implanted in all men a certain understanding of his divine majesty. Ever renewing its memory, he repeatedly sheds fresh drops. Since, therefore, men one and all perceive that there is a God and that he is their Maker, they are condemned by their own testimony because they have failed to honour him and to consecrate their lives to his will. If ignorance of God is to be looked for anywhere, surely one is most likely to find an example of it among the more backward folk and those more remote from civilization. Yet there is, as the eminent pagan says, no nation so barbarous, no people so savage, that they have not a deep-seated conviction that there is a God. And they who in other aspects of life seem least to differ from brutes still continue to retain some seed of religion. So deeply does the common conception occupy the minds of all, so tenaciously does it inhere in the hearts of all. Therefore, since from the beginning of the world there has been no region, no city, in short, no household, that could do without religion, there lies in this a tacit confession of a sense of deity inscribed in the hearts of all.

Indeed, even idolatry is ample proof of this conception. We know how man does not willingly

John Calvin, *Institutes of the Christian Religion*, Library of Christian Classics vol. XX, I.iii. 1–3, trans. Ford Lewis Battles, ed. John T McNeill (London: SCM Press, 1961), pp. 43–5. This reading taken from Paul Helm (ed.), *Faith and Reason*. Oxford and New York: Oxford University Press, 1999, pp. 142–5.

humble himself so as to place other creatures over himself. Since, then, he prefers to worship wood and stone rather than to be thought of as having no God, clearly this is a most vivid impression of a divine being. So impossible is it to blot this from man's mind that natural disposition would be more easily altered, as altered indeed it is when man voluntarily sinks from his natural haughtiness to the very depths in order to honour God!

Therefore it is utterly vain for some men to say that religion was invented by the subtlety and craft of a few to hold the simple folk in thrall by this device and that those very persons who originated the worship of God for others did not in the least believe that any God existed. I confess, indeed, that in order to hold men's minds in greater subjection, clever men have devised very many things in religion by which to inspire the common folk with reverence and to strike them with terror. But they would never have achieved this if men's minds had not already been imbued with a firm conviction about God, from which the inclination toward religion springs as from a seed. And indeed it is not credible that those who craftily imposed upon the ruder folk under pretence of religion were entirely devoid of the knowledge of God. If, indeed, there were some in the past, and today not a few appear, who deny that God exists, yet willy-nilly they from time to time feel an inkling of what they desire not to believe. One reads of no one who burst forth into bolder or more unbridled contempt of deity than Gaius Caligula; yet no one trembled more miserably when any sign of God's wrath manifested itself; thus – albeit unwillingly – he shuddered at the God whom he professedly sought to despise. You may see now and again how this also happens to those like him; how he who is the boldest despiser of God is of all men the most startled at the rustle of a falling leaf [cf. Lev. 26: 36]. Whence does this arise but from the vengeance of divine majesty, which strikes their consciences all the more violently the more they try to flee from it? Indeed, they seek out every subterfuge to hide themselves from the Lord's presence, and to efface it again from their minds. But in spite of themselves they are always entrapped. Although it may sometimes seem to vanish for a moment, it returns at once and rushes in with new force. If for these there is any respite from anxiety of conscience, it is not much different from the sleep of drunken or frenzied persons, who do not rest peacefully even while sleeping because they are continually troubled with dire and dreadful dreams. The impious themselves therefore exemplify the fact that some conception of God is ever alive in all men's minds.

Men of sound judgment will always be sure that a sense of divinity which can never be effaced is engraved upon men's minds. Indeed, the perversity of the impious, who though they struggle furiously are unable to extricate themselves from the fear of God, is abundant testimony that this conviction, namely, that there is some God, is naturally inborn in all, and is fixed deep within, as it were in the very marrow. Although Diagoras and his like may jest at whatever has been believed in every age concerning religion, and Dionysius may mock the heavenly judgment, this is sardonic laughter, for the worm of conscience, sharper than any cauterizing iron, gnaws away within. I do not say, as Cicero did, that errors disappear with the lapse of time, and that religion grows and becomes better each day. For the world (something will have to be said of this a little later) tries as far as it is able to cast away all knowledge of God, and by every means to corrupt the worship of him. I only say that though the stupid hardness in their minds, which the impious eagerly conjure up to reject God, wastes away, yet the sense of divinity, which they greatly wished to have extinguished, thrives and presently burgeons. From this we conclude that it is not a doctrine that must first be learned in school, but one of which each of us is master from his mother's womb and which nature itself permits no one to forget, although many strive with every nerve to this end.

Besides, if all men are born and live to the end that they may know God, and yet if knowledge of God is unstable and fleeting unless it progresses to this degree, it is clear that all those who do not direct every thought and action in their lives to this goal degenerate from the law of their creation. This was not unknown to the philosophers. Plato meant nothing but this when he often taught that the highest good of the soul is likeness to God, where, when the soul has grasped the knowledge of God, it is wholly transformed into his likeness. In the same manner also Gryllus, in the writings of Plutarch, reasons very skillfully, affirming that, if once religion is absent from their life, men are in no wise superior to brute beasts, but are in many respects far more miserable. Subject, then, to so many forms of wickedness, they drag out their lives in ceaseless tumult and disquiet. Therefore, it is worship of God alone that renders men higher than the brutes, and through it alone they aspire to immortality.

7

Faith, Reason, and Enthusiasm

John Locke

John Locke (1632–1704) was a British philosopher and medical doctor who, as a result of his friendship with the Earl of Shaftesbury, also had an active public political life. His vast treatise, *An Essay Concerning Human Understanding*, is one of the premier works of empiricism and, indeed, of the modern period as a whole. In the following selection from this work, Locke defends an evidentialist position on the relationship between faith and reason. He says that "faith is nothing but a firm assent of the mind" and that "if it be regulated, as is our duty, cannot be afforded to anything but upon good reason; and so cannot be opposite to it." Belief based upon divine revelation is permissible if (and only if) there is adequate evidence that God really is the source of the revelation.

Book IV, Chapter XVI
Of the Degrees of Assent

[. . .]

14. Besides those we have hitherto mentioned, there is one sort of propositions that challenge the highest degree of our assent, upon bare testimony, whether the thing proposed agree or disagree with common experience, and the ordinary course of things, or no. The reason whereof is, because the testimony is of such an one as cannot deceive nor be deceived: and that is of God himself. This carries with it an assurance beyond doubt, evidence beyond exception. This is called by a peculiar name, *revelation*, and our assent to it, *faith*, which [as absolutely determines our minds, and as perfectly excludes all wavering,] as our knowledge itself; and we may as well doubt of our own being, as we can whether any revelation from God be true. So that faith is a settled and sure principle of assent and assurance, and

John Locke, "Faith, Reason, and Enthusiasm" from *An Essay Concerning Human Understanding*, ed. Alexander Campbell Fraser, vol. 2 (New York: Dover, 1959), pp. 383–4, 412–41.

leaves no manner of room for doubt or hesitation. *Only we must be sure that it be a divine revelation, and that we understand it right*: else we shall expose ourselves to all the extravagancy of enthusiasm, and all the error of wrong principles, if we have faith and assurance in what is not *divine* revelation. And therefore, in those cases, our assent can be rationally no higher than the evidence of its being a revelation, and that this is the meaning of the expressions it is delivered in. If the evidence of its being a revelation, or that this is its true sense, be only on probable proofs, our assent can reach no higher than an assurance or diffidence, arising from the more or less apparent probability of the proofs. But of *faith*, and the precedency it ought to have before other arguments of persuasion, I shall speak more hereafter; where I treat of it as it is ordinarily placed, in contradistinction to reason; though in truth it be nothing else but *an assent founded on the highest reason*.

[...]

Chapter XVII
Of Reason

[...]

23. By what has been before said of reason, we may be able to make some guess at the distinction of things, into those that are according to, above, and contrary to reason. 1. *According to reason* are such propositions whose truth we can discover by examining and tracing those ideas we have from sensation and reflection; and by natural deduction find to be true or probable. 2. *Above reason* are such propositions whose truth or probability we cannot by reason derive from those principles. 3. *Contrary to reason* are such propositions as are inconsistent with or irreconcilable to our clear and distinct ideas. Thus the existence of one God is according to reason; the existence of more than one God, contrary to reason; the resurrection of the dead, above reason. *Above reason* also may be taken in a double sense, viz. either as signifying above probability, or above certainty: and in that large sense also, *contrary to reason*, is, I suppose, sometimes taken.

24. There is another use of the word *reason*, wherein it is *opposed to faith*: which, though it be in itself a very improper way of speaking, yet common use has so authorized it, that it would be folly either to oppose or hope to remedy it. Only I think it may not be amiss to take notice, that, however faith be opposed to reason, faith is nothing but a firm assent of the mind: which, if it be regulated, as is our duty, cannot be afforded to anything but upon good reason; and so cannot be opposite to it. He that believes without having any reason for believing, may be in love with his own fancies; but neither seeks truth as he ought, nor pays the obedience due to his Maker, who would have him use those discerning faculties he has given him, to keep him out of mistake and error. He that does not this to the best of his power, however he sometimes lights on truth, is in the right but by chance; and I know not whether the luckiness of the accident will excuse the irregularity of his proceeding. This at least is certain, that he must be accountable for whatever mistakes he runs into: whereas he that makes use of the light and faculties God has given him, and seeks sincerely to discover truth by those helps and abilities he has, may have this satisfaction in doing his duty as a rational creature, that, though he should miss truth, he will not miss the reward of it. For he governs his assent right, and places it as he should, who, in any case or matter whatsoever, believes or disbelieves according as reason directs him. He that doth otherwise, transgresses against his own light, and misuses those faculties which were given him to no other end, but to search and follow the clearer evidence and greater probability. But since reason and faith are by some men opposed, we will so consider them in the following chapter.

Chapter XVIII
Of Faith and Reason, and their Distinct Provinces

1. It has been above shown, 1. That we are of necessity ignorant, and want knowledge of all sorts, where we want ideas. 2. That we are ignorant, and want rational knowledge, where we want proofs. 3. That we want certain knowledge and certainty, as far as we want clear and determined specific ideas. 4. That we want probability to direct our assent in matters where

we have neither knowledge of our own nor testimony of other men to bottom our reason upon.

From these things thus premised, I think we may come to lay down *the measures and boundaries between faith and reason*: the want whereof may possibly have been the cause, if not of great disorders, yet at least of great disputes, and perhaps mistakes in the world. For till it be resolved how far we are to be guided by reason, and how far by faith, we shall in vain dispute, and endeavour to convince one another in matters of religion.

2. I find every sect, as far as reason will help them, make use of it gladly: and where it fails them, they cry out, It is matter of faith, and above reason. And I do not see how they can argue with any one, or ever convince a gainsayer who makes use of the same plea, without setting down strict boundaries between faith and reason; which ought to be the first point established in all questions where faith has anything to do.

Reason, therefore, here, as contradistinguished to *faith*, I take to be the discovery of the certainty or probability of such propositions or truths, which the mind arrives at by deduction made from such ideas, which it has got by the use of its natural faculties; viz. by sensation or reflection.

Faith, on the other side, is the assent to any proposition, not thus made out by the deductions of reason, but upon the credit of the proposer, as coming from God, in some extraordinary way of communication. This way of discovering truths to men, we call *revelation*.

3. *First*, Then I say, that *no man inspired by God can by any revelation communicate to others any new simple ideas which they had not before from sensation or reflection*. For, whatsoever impressions he himself may have from the immediate hand of God, this revelation, if it be of new simple ideas, cannot be conveyed to another, either by words or any other signs. Because words, by their immediate operation on us, cause no other ideas but of their natural sounds: and it is by the custom of using them for signs, that they excite and revive in our minds latent ideas; but yet only such ideas as were there before. For words, seen or heard, recall to our thoughts those ideas only which to us they have been wont to be signs of, but cannot introduce any perfectly new, and formerly unknown simple ideas. The same holds in all other signs; which cannot signify to us things of which we have before never had any idea at all.

Thus whatever things were discovered to St Paul, when he was rapt up into the third heaven; whatever new ideas his mind there received, all the description he can make to others of that place, is only this, That there are such things, 'as eye hath not seen, nor ear heard, nor hath it entered into the heart of man to conceive.' And supposing God should discover to any one, supernaturally, a species of creatures inhabiting, for example, Jupiter or Saturn, (for that it is possible there may be such, nobody can deny,) which had six senses; and imprint on his mind the ideas conveyed to theirs by that sixth sense: he could no more, by words, produce in the minds of other men those ideas imprinted by that sixth sense, than one of us could convey the idea of any colour, by the sound of words, into a man who, having the other four senses perfect, had always totally wanted the fifth, of seeing. For our simple ideas, then, which are the foundation, and sole matter of all our notions and knowledge, we must depend wholly on our reason, I mean our natural faculties; and can by no means receive them, or any of them, from traditional revelation. I say, *traditional revelation*, in distinction to *original revelation*. By the one, I mean that first impression which is made immediately by God on the mind of any man, to which we cannot set any bounds; and by the other, those impressions delivered over to others in words, and the ordinary ways of conveying our conceptions one to another.

4. *Secondly*, I say that *the same truths may be discovered, and conveyed down from revelation, which are discoverable to us by reason, and by those ideas we naturally may have*. So God might, by revelation, discover the truth of any proposition in Euclid; as well as men, by the natural use of their faculties, come to make the discovery themselves. In all things of this kind there is little need or use of revelation, God having furnished us with natural and surer means to arrive at the knowledge of them. For whatsoever truth we come to the clear discovery of, from the knowledge and contemplation of our own ideas, will always be certainer to us than those which are conveyed to us by *traditional revelation*. For the knowledge we have that this revelation came at first from God, can never be so sure as the knowledge we have from the clear and distinct

perception of the agreement or disagreement of our own ideas: v. g. if it were revealed some ages since, that the three angles of a triangle were equal to two right ones, I might assent to the truth of that proposition, upon the credit of the tradition, that it was revealed: but that would never amount to so great a certainty as the knowledge of it, upon the comparing and measuring my own ideas of two right angles, and the three angles of a triangle. The like holds in matter of fact knowable by our senses; v. g. the history of the deluge is conveyed to us by writings which had their original from revelation: and yet nobody, I think, will say he has as certain and clear a knowledge of the flood as Noah, that saw it; or that he himself would have had, had he then been alive and seen it. For he has no greater an assurance than that of his senses, that it is writ in the book supposed writ by Moses inspired: but he has not so great an assurance that Moses wrote that book as if he had seen Moses write it. So that the assurance of its being a revelation is less still than the assurance of his senses.

5. In propositions, then, whose certainty is built upon the clear perception of the agreement or disagreement of our ideas, attained either by immediate intuition, as in self-evident propositions, or by evident deductions of reason in demonstrations we need not the assistance of revelation, as necessary to gain our assent, and introduce them into our minds. Because the natural ways of knowledge could settle them there, or had done it already; which is the greatest assurance we can possibly have of anything, unless where God immediately reveals it to us: and there too our assurance can be no greater than our knowledge is, that it *is* a revelation from God. But yet nothing, I think, can, under that title, shake or overrule plain knowledge; or rationally prevail with any man to admit it for true, in a direct contradiction to the clear evidence of his own understanding. For, since no evidence of our faculties, by which we receive such revelations, can exceed, if equal, the certainty of our intuitive knowledge, we can never receive for a truth anything that is directly contrary to our clear and distinct knowledge; v. g. the ideas of one body and one place do so clearly agree, and the mind has so evident a perception of their agreement, that we can never assent to a proposition that affirms the same body to be in two distant places at once, however it should pretend to the authority of a divine revelation: since the evidence, first, that we deceive not ourselves, in ascribing it to God; secondly, that we understand it right; can never be so great as the evidence of our own intuitive knowledge, whereby we discern it impossible for the same body to be in two places at once. And therefore *no proposition can be received for divine revelation, or obtain the assent due to all such, if it be contradictory to our clear intuitive knowledge.* Because this would be to subvert the principles and foundations of all knowledge, evidence, and assent whatsoever: and there would be left no difference between truth and falsehood, no measures of credible and incredible in the world, if doubtful propositions shall take place before self-evident; and what we certainly know give way to what we may possibly be mistaken in. In propositions therefore contrary to the clear perception of the agreement or disagreement of any of our ideas, it will be in vain to urge them as matters of faith. They cannot move our assent under that or any other title whatsoever. For faith can never convince us of anything that contradicts our knowledge. Because, though faith be founded on the testimony of God (who cannot lie) revealing any proposition to us: yet we cannot have an assurance of the truth of its being a divine revelation greater than our own knowledge. Since the whole strength of the certainty depends upon our knowledge that God revealed it; which, in this case, where the proposition supposed revealed contradicts our knowledge or reason, will always have this objection hanging to it, viz. that we cannot tell how to conceive that to come from God, the bountiful Author of our being, which, if received for true, must overturn all the principles and foundations of knowledge he has given us; render all our faculties useless; wholly destroy the most excellent part of his workmanship, our understandings; and put a man in a condition wherein he will have less light, less conduct than the beast that perisheth. For if the mind of man can never have a clearer (and perhaps not so clear) evidence of anything to be a divine revelation, as it has of the principles of its own reason, it can never have a ground to quit the clear evidence of its reason, to give a place to a proposition, whose revelation has not a greater evidence than those principles have.

6. Thus far a man has use of reason, and ought to hearken to it, even in immediate and original revelation, where it is supposed to be made to himself. But to all those who pretend not to immediate revelation, but are required to pay obedience, and to receive the truths revealed to others, which, by the tradition of writings, or word of mouth, are conveyed down to them, reason has a great deal more to do, and is that only which can induce us to receive them. For matter of faith being only divine revelation, and nothing else, faith, as we use the word, (called commonly *divine faith*), has to do with no propositions, but those which are supposed to be divinely revealed. So that I do not see how those who make revelation alone the sole object of faith can say, That it is a matter of faith, and not of reason, to believe that such or such a proposition, to be found in such or such a book, is of divine inspiration; unless it be revealed that that proposition, or all in that book, was communicated by divine inspiration. Without such a revelation, the believing, or not believing, that proposition, or book, to be of divine authority, can never be matter of faith, but matter of reason; and such as I must come to an assent to only by the use of my reason, which can never require or enable me to believe that which is contrary to itself: it being impossible for reason ever to procure any assent to that which to itself appears unreasonable.

In all things, therefore, where we have clear evidence from our ideas, and those principles of knowledge I have above mentioned, reason is the proper judge; and revelation, though it may, in consenting with it, confirm its dictates, yet cannot in such cases invalidate its decrees: nor can we be obliged, where we have the clear and evident sentence of reason, to quit it for the contrary opinion, under a pretence that it is matter of faith: [which can have no authority against the plain and clear dictates of reason][1].

7. But, *Thirdly*, There being many things wherein we have very imperfect notions, or none at all; and other things, of whose past, present, or future existence, by the natural use of our faculties, we can have no knowledge at all; these, as being beyond the discovery of our natural faculties, and *above reason*, are, when revealed, *the proper matter of faith*. Thus, that part of the angels rebelled against God, and thereby lost their first happy state: and that [the dead shall rise, and live again]: these and the like, being beyond the discovery of reason, are purely matters of faith, with which reason has directly nothing to do.

8. But since God, in giving us the light of reason, has not thereby tied up his own hands from affording us, when he thinks fit, the light of revelation in any of those matters wherein our natural faculties are able to give a probable determination; *revelation*, where God has been pleased to give it, *must carry it against the probable conjectures of reason*. Because the mind not being certain of the truth of that it does not evidently know, but only yielding to the probability that appears in it, is bound to give up its assent to such a testimony which, it is satisfied, comes from one who cannot err, and will not deceive. But yet, it still belongs to reason to judge of the truth of its being a revelation, and of the signification of the words wherein it is delivered. Indeed, if anything shall be thought revelation which is contrary to the plain principles of reason, and the evident knowledge the mind has of its own clear and distinct ideas; there reason must be hearkened to, as to a matter within its province. Since a man can never have so certain a knowledge, that a proposition which contradicts the clear principles and evidence of his own knowledge was divinely revealed, or that he understands the words rightly wherein it is delivered, as he has that the contrary is true, and so is bound to consider and judge of it as a matter of reason, and not swallow it, without examination, as a matter of faith.

9. First, Whatever proposition is revealed, of whose truth our mind, by its natural faculties and notions, cannot judge, that is purely matter of faith, and above reason.

Secondly, All propositions whereof the mind, by the use of its natural faculties, can come to determine and judge, from naturally acquired ideas, are matter of reason; with this difference still, that, in those concerning which it has but an uncertain evidence, and so is persuaded of their truth only upon probable grounds, which still admit a possibility of the contrary to be true, without doing violence to the certain evidence of its own knowledge, and overturning the principles of all reason; in such probable propositions,

I say, an evident revelation ought to determine our assent, even against probability. For where the principles of reason have not evidenced a proposition to be certainly true or false, there clear revelation, as another principle of truth and ground of assent, may determine; and so it may be matter of faith, and be also above reason. Because reason, in that particular matter, being able to reach no higher than probability, faith gave the determination where reason came short; and revelation discovered on which side the truth lay.

10. Thus far the dominion of faith reaches, and that without any violence or hindrance to reason; which is not injured or disturbed, but assisted and improved by new discoveries of truth, coming from the eternal fountain of all knowledge. Whatever God hath revealed is certainly true: no doubt can be made of it. This is the proper object of faith: but whether it be a *divine* revelation or no, reason must judge; which can never permit the mind to reject a greater evidence to embrace what is less evident, nor allow it to entertain probability in opposition to knowledge and certainty. There can be no evidence that any traditional revelation is of divine original, in the words we receive it, and in the sense we understand it, so clear and so certain as that of the principles of reason: and therefore *Nothing that is contrary to, and inconsistent with, the clear and self-evident dictates of reason, has a right to be urged or assented to as a matter of faith, wherein reason hath nothing to do.* Whatsoever is divine revelation, ought to overrule all our opinions, prejudices, and interest, and hath a right to be received with full assent. Such a submission as this, of our reason to faith, takes not away the landmarks of knowledge: this shakes not the foundations of reason, but leaves us that use of our faculties for which they were given us.

11. If the provinces of faith and reason are not kept distinct by these boundaries, there will, in matters of religion, be no room for reason at all; and those extravagant opinions and ceremonies that are to be found in the several religions of the world will not deserve to be blamed. For, to this crying up of faith in *opposition* to reason, we may, I think, in good measure ascribe those absurdities that fill almost all the religions which possess and divide mankind. For men having been principled with an opinion, that they must not consult reason in the things of religion, however apparently contradictory to common sense and the very principles of all their knowledge, have let loose their fancies and natural superstition; and have been by them led into so strange opinions, and extravagant practices in religion, that a considerate man cannot but stand amazed at their follies, and judge them so far from being acceptable to the great and wise God, that he cannot avoid thinking them ridiculous and offensive to a sober good man. So that, in effect, religion, which should most distinguish us from beasts, and ought most peculiarly to elevate us, as rational creatures, above brutes, is that wherein men often appear most irrational, and more senseless than beasts themselves. *Credo, quia impossible est*: I believe, because it is impossible, might, in a good man, pass for a sally of zeal; but would prove a very ill rule for men to choose their opinions or religion by.

Chapter XIX
[Of Enthusiasm][2]

[1. He that would seriously set upon the search of truth, ought in the first place to prepare his mind with a love of it. For he that loves it not, will not take much pains to get it; nor be much concerned when he misses it. There is nobody in the commonwealth of learning who does not profess himself a lover of truth: and there is not a rational creature that would not take it amiss to be thought otherwise of. And yet, for all this, one may truly say, that there are very few lovers of truth, for truth's sake, even amongst those who persuade themselves that they are so. How a man may know whether he be so in earnest, is worth inquiry: and I think there is one unerring mark of it, viz. The not entertaining any proposition with greater assurance than the proofs it is built upon will warrant. Whoever goes beyond this measure of assent, it is plain receives not the truth in the love of it; loves not truth for truth's sake, but for some other bye-end. For the evidence that any proposition is true (except such as are self-evident) lying only in the proofs a man has of it, whatsoever degrees of assent he affords it beyond the degrees of that evidence, it is plain that all the surplusage of assurance is owing to some other affection, and not to the love of truth: it being as impossible that the love of truth should carry my assent above the evidence there is to me, that it is true, as that the love of truth should make me assent to any proposition for the sake of that evidence which it has not, that it is true: which is in effect to love it as a truth, because it is possible or probable that it may not be true. In any truth that gets not possession of our minds by the irresistible light of self-evidence, or by the force of demonstration, the arguments that gain it assent are the vouchers and gage of its probability to us; and we can receive it for no other than such as they deliver it to our understandings. Whatsoever credit or authority we give to any proposition more than it receives from the principles and proofs it supports itself upon, is owing to our inclinations that way, and is so far a derogation from the love of truth as such: which, as it can receive no evidence from our passions or interests, so it should receive no tincture from them.

2. The assuming an authority of dictating to others, and a forwardness to prescribe to their opinions, is a constant concomitant of this bias and corruption of our judgments. For how almost can it be otherwise, but that he should be ready to impose on another's belief, who has already imposed on his own? Who can reasonably expect arguments and conviction from him in dealing with others, whose understanding is not accustomed to them in his dealing with himself? Who does violence to his own faculties, tyrannizes over his own mind, and usurps the prerogative that belongs to truth alone, which is to command assent by only its own authority, i.e. by and in proportion to that evidence which it carries with it.

3. Upon this occasion I shall take the liberty to consider *a third ground of assent*, which with some men has the same authority, and is as confidently relied on as either faith or reason; I mean *enthusiasm*: which, laying by reason, would set up revelation without it. Whereby in effect it takes away both reason and revelation, and substitutes in the room of them the ungrounded fancies of a man's own brain, and assumes them for a foundation both of opinion and conduct.

4. *Reason* is *natural revelation*, whereby the eternal Father of light and fountain of all knowledge, communicates to mankind that portion of truth which he has laid within the reach of their natural faculties: *revelation* is *natural reason enlarged* by a new set of discoveries communicated by God immediately; which reason vouches the truth of, by the testimony and proofs it gives that they come from God. So that he that takes away reason to make way for revelation, puts out the light of both, and does muchwhat the same as if he would persuade a man to put out his eyes, the better to receive the remote light of an invisible star by a telescope.

5. Immediate revelation being a much easier way for men to establish their opinions and regulate their conduct, than the tedious and not always successful labour of strict reasoning, it is no wonder that some have been very apt to pretend to revelation, and to persuade themselves that they are under the peculiar guidance of heaven in their actions and opinions, especially in those of them which they cannot account for by the ordinary methods of knowledge and principles of reason. Hence we see, that, in all ages, men in whom melancholy has mixed with devotion, or whose conceit of themselves has raised them into an opinion of a greater familiarity with God, and a nearer admittance to his favour than is afforded to others, have often flattered themselves with a persuasion of an immediate intercourse with the Deity, and frequent communications from the Divine Spirit. God, I own, cannot be denied to be able to enlighten the understanding by a ray darted into the mind immediately from the fountain of light: this they understand he has promised to do, and who then has so good a title to expect it as those who are his peculiar people, chosen by him, and depending on him?

6. Their minds being thus prepared, whatever groundless opinion comes to settle itself strongly upon their fancies, is an illumination from the Spirit of God, and presently of divine authority: and whatsoever odd action they find in themselves a strong inclination to do, that impulse is concluded to be a call or direction from heaven, and must be obeyed: it is a commission from above, and they cannot err in executing it.

7. This I take to be properly *enthusiasm*, which, though founded neither on reason nor divine revelation, but rising from the conceits of a warmed or overweening brain, works yet, where it once gets footing, more powerfully on

the persuasions and actions of men than either of those two, or both together: men being most forwardly obedient to the impulses they receive from themselves; and the whole man is sure to act more vigorously where the whole man is carried by a natural motion. For strong conceit, like a new principle, carries all easily with it, when got above common sense, and freed from all restraint of reason and check of reflection, it is heightened into a divine authority, in concurrence with our own temper and inclination.

8. Though the odd opinions and extravagant actions enthusiasm has run men into were enough to warn them against this wrong principle, so apt to misguide them both in their belief and conduct: yet the love of something extraordinary, the ease and glory it is to be inspired, and be above the common and natural ways of knowledge, so flatters many men's laziness, ignorance, and vanity, that, when once they are got into this way of immediate revelation, of illumination without search, and of certainty without proof and without examination, it is a hard matter to get them out of it. Reason is lost upon them, they are above it: they see the light infused into their understandings, and cannot be mistaken; it is clear and visible there, like the light of bright sunshine; shows itself, and needs no other proof but its own evidence: they feel the hand of God moving them within, and the impulses of the Spirit, and cannot be mistaken in what they feel. Thus they support themselves, and are sure reasoning hath nothing to do with what they see and feel in themselves: what they have a sensible experience of admits no doubt, needs no probation. Would he not be ridiculous, who should require to have it proved to him that the light shines, and that he sees it? It is its own proof, and can have no other. When the Spirit brings light into our minds, it dispels darkness. We see it as we do that of the sun at noon, and need not the twilight of reason to show it us. This light from heaven is strong, clear, and pure; carries its own demonstration with it: and we may as naturally take a glow-worm to assist us to discover the sun, as to examine the celestial ray by our dim candle, reason.

9. This is the way of talking of these men: they are sure, because they are sure: and their persuasions are right, because they are strong in them. For, when what they say is stripped of the metaphor of seeing and feeling, this is all it amounts to: and yet these similes so impose on them, that they serve them for certainty in themselves, and demonstration to others.

10. But to examine a little soberly this internal light, and this feeling on which they build so much. These men have, they say, clear light, and they see; they have awakened sense, and they feel: this cannot, they are sure, be disputed them. For when a man says he sees or feels, nobody can deny him that he does so. But here let me ask: This seeing, is it the perception of the truth of the proposition, or of this, that it is a revelation from God? This feeling, is it a perception of an inclination or fancy to do something, or of the Spirit of God moving that inclination? These are two very different perceptions, and must be carefully distinguished, if we would not impose upon ourselves. I may perceive the truth of a proposition, and yet not perceive that it is an immediate revelation from God. I may perceive the truth of a proposition in Euclid, without its being, or my perceiving it to be, a revelation: nay, I may perceive I came not by this knowledge in a natural way, and so may conclude it revealed, without perceiving that it is a revelation of God. Because there be spirits which, without being divinely commissioned, may excite those ideas in me, and lay them in such order before my mind, that I may perceive their connexion. So that the knowledge of any proposition coming into my mind, I know not how, is not a perception that it is from God. Much less is a strong persuasion that it is true, a perception that it is from God, or so much as true. But however it be called light and seeing, I suppose it is at most but belief and assurance: and the proposition taken for a revelation, is not such as they *know* to be true, but *take* to be true. For where a proposition is known to be true, revelation is needless: and it is hard to conceive how there can be a revelation to any one of what he knows already. If therefore it be a proposition which they are persuaded, but do not know, to be true, whatever they may call it, it is not seeing, but believing. For these are two ways whereby truth comes into the mind, wholly distinct, so that one is not the other. What I see, I know to be so, by the evidence of the thing itself: what I believe, I take to be so upon the testimony of another. But this testimony I must know to be given, or else what ground have I of

believing? I must see that it is God that reveals this to me, or else I see nothing. The question then here is: How do I know that God is the revealer of this to me; that this impression is made upon my mind by his Holy Spirit; and that therefore I ought to obey it? If I know not this, how great soever the assurance is that I am possessed with, it is groundless; whatever light I pretend to, it is but *enthusiasm*. For, whether the proposition supposed to be revealed be in itself evidently true, or visibly probable, or, by the natural ways of knowledge, uncertain, the proposition that must be well grounded and manifested to be true, is this, That God is the revealer of it, and that what I take to be a revelation is certainly put into my mind by Him, and is not an illusion dropped in by some other spirit, or raised by my own fancy. For, if I mistake not, these men receive it for true, because they presume God revealed it. Does it not, then, stand them upon to examine upon what grounds they presume it to be a revelation from God? Or else all their confidence is mere presumption: and this light they are so dazzled with is nothing but an *ignis fatuus*, that leads them constantly round in this circle; *It is a revelation, because they firmly believe it*; and *they believe it, because it is a revelation.*

11. In all that is of divine revelation, there is need of no other proof but that it is an inspiration from God: for he can neither deceive nor be deceived. But how shall it be known that any proposition in our minds is a truth infused by God; a truth that is revealed to us by him, which he declares to us, and therefore we ought to believe? Here it is that enthusiasm fails of the evidence it pretends to. For men thus possessed, boast of a light whereby they say they are enlightened, and brought into the knowledge of this or that truth. But if they know it to be a truth, they must know it to be so, either by its own self-evidence to natural reason, or by the rational proofs that make it out to be so. If they see and know it to be a truth, either of these two ways they in vain suppose it to be a revelation. For they know it to be true the same way that any other man naturally may know that it is so, without the help of revelation. For thus, all the truths, of what kind soever, that men uninspired are enlightened with, came into their minds, and are established there. If they say they know it to be true, because it is a revelation from God, the reason is good: but then it will be demanded how they know it to be a revelation from God. If they say, by the light it brings with it, which shines bright in their minds, and they cannot resist: I beseech them to consider whether this be any more than what we have taken notice of already, viz. that it is a revelation, because they strongly believe it to be true. For all the light they speak of is but a strong, though ungrounded persuasion of their own minds, that it is a truth. For rational grounds from proofs that it is a truth, they must acknowledge to have none; for then it is not received as a revelation, but upon the ordinary grounds that other truths are received: and if they believe it to be true because it is a revelation, and have no other reason for its being a revelation, but because they are fully persuaded, without any other reason, that it is true, then they believe it to be a revelation only because they strongly believe it to be a revelation; which is a very unsafe ground to proceed on, either in our tenets or actions. And what readier way can there be to run ourselves into the most extravagant errors and miscarriages, than thus to set up fancy for our supreme and sole guide, and to believe any proposition to be true, any action to be right, only because we believe it to be so? The strength of our persuasions is no evidence at all of their own rectitude: crooked things may be as stiff and inflexible as straight: and men may be as positive and peremptory in error as in truth. How come else the untractable zealots in different and opposite parties? For if the light, which every one thinks he has in his mind, which in this case is nothing but the strength of his own persuasion, be an evidence that it is from God, contrary opinions have the same title to be inspirations; and God will be not only the Father of lights, but of opposite and contradictory lights, leading men contrary ways; and contradictory propositions will be divine truths, if an ungrounded strength of assurance be an evidence that any proposition is a Divine Revelation.

12. This cannot be otherwise, whilst firmness of persuasion is made the cause of believing, and confidence of being in the right is made an argument of truth. St Paul himself believed he did well, and that he had a call to it, when he persecuted the Christians, whom he confidently thought in the wrong: but yet it was he, and not

they, who were mistaken. Good men are men still liable to mistakes, and are sometimes warmly engaged in errors, which they take for divine truths, shining in their minds with the clearest light.

13. Light, true light, in the mind is, or can be, nothing else but the evidence of the truth of any proposition; and if it be not a self-evident proposition, all the light it has, or can have, is from the clearness and validity of those proofs upon which it is received. To talk of any other light in the understanding is to put ourselves in the dark, or in the power of the Prince of Darkness, and, by our own consent, to give ourselves up to delusion to believe a lie. For, if strength of persuasion be the light which must guide us; I ask how shall any one distinguish between the delusions of Satan, and the inspirations of the Holy Ghost? He can transform himself into an angel of light. And they who are led by this Son of the Morning are as fully satisfied of the illumination, i. e. are as strongly persuaded that they are enlightened by the Spirit of God as any one who is so: they acquiesce and rejoice in it, are actuated by it: and nobody can be more sure, nor more in the right (if their own strong belief may be judge) than they.

14. He, therefore, that will not give himself up to all the extravagances of delusion and error must bring this guide of his *light within* to the trial. God when he makes the prophet does not unmake the man. He leaves all his faculties in the natural state, to enable him to judge of his inspirations, whether they be of *divine* original or no. When he illuminates the mind with supernatural light, he does not extinguish that which is natural. If he would have us assent to the truth of any proposition, he either evidences that truth by the usual methods of natural reason, or else makes it known to be a truth which he would have us assent to by his authority, and convinces us that it is from him, by some marks which reason cannot be mistaken in. *Reason must be our last judge and guide in everything.* I do not mean that we must consult reason, and examine whether a proposition revealed from God can be made out by natural principles, and if it cannot, that then we may reject it: but consult it we must, and by it examine whether it be a revelation from God or no: and if reason finds it to be revealed from God, reason then declares for it as much as for any other truth, and makes it one of her dictates. Every conceit that thoroughly warms our fancies must pass for an inspiration, if there be nothing but the strength of our persuasions, whereby to judge of our persuasions: if reason must not examine their truth by something extrinsical to the persuasions themselves, inspirations and delusions, truth and falsehood, will have the same measure, and will not be possible to be distinguished.

15. If this internal light, or any proposition which under that title we take for inspired, be conformable to the principles of reason, or to the word of God, which is attested revelation, reason warrants it, and we may safely receive it for true, and be guided by it in our belief and actions: if it receive no testimony nor evidence from either of these rules, we cannot take it for a revelation, or so much as for true, till we have some other mark that it is a revelation, besides our believing that it is so. Thus we see the holy men of old, who had revelations from God, had something else besides that internal light of assurance in their own minds, to testify to them that it was from God. They were not left to their own persuasions alone, that those persuasions were from God, but had *outward signs* to convince them of the Author of those revelations. And when they were to convince others, they had a power given them to justify the truth of their commission from heaven, and by visible signs to assert the divine authority of a message they were sent with. Moses saw the bush burn without being consumed, and heard a voice out of it: this was something besides finding an impulse upon his mind to go to Pharaoh, that he might bring his brethren out of Egypt: and yet he thought not this enough to authorize him to go with that message, till God, by another miracle of his rod turned into a serpent, had assured him of a power to testify his mission, by the same miracle repeated before them whom he was sent to. Gideon was sent by an angel to deliver Israel from the Midianites, and yet he desired a sign to convince him that this commission was from God. These, and several the like instances to be found among the prophets of old, are enough to show that they thought not an inward seeing or persuasion of their own minds, without any other proof, a sufficient evidence that it was from God; though the

Scripture does not everywhere mention their demanding or having such proofs.

16. In what I have said I am far from denying, that God can, or doth sometimes enlighten men's minds in the apprehending of certain truths or excite them to good actions, by the immediate influence and assistance of the Holy Spirit, *without any extraordinary signs accompanying it.* But in such cases too we have reason and Scripture; unerring rules to know whether it be from God or no. Where the truth embraced is consonant to the revelation in the written word of God, or the action conformable to the dictates of right reason or holy writ, we may be assured that we run no risk in entertaining it as such: because, though perhaps it be not an immediate revelation from God, extraordinarily operating on our minds, yet we are sure it is warranted by that revelation which he has given us of truth. But it is not the strength of our private persuasion within ourselves, that can warrant it to be a light or motion from heaven: nothing can do that but the written Word of God without us, or that standard of reason which is common to us with all men. Where reason or Scripture is express for any opinion or action, we may receive it as of divine authority: but it is not the strength of our own, persuasions which can by itself give it that stamp. The bent of our own minds may favour it as much as we please: that may show it to be a fondling of our own, but will by no means prove it to be an offspring of heaven, and of divine original.]

Notes

1 Added in second edition.
2 This chapter was added in the fourth edition.

8

Return to Reason: The Irrationality of Evidentialism

Kelly James Clark

In the 1970s and 1980s Alvin Plantinga, Nicholas Wolterstorff, and several other philosophers raised criticisms of the evidentialist approach to faith and reason and promoted an alternative approach known as "Reformed Epistemology." Our next reading is an overview and defense of this important movement from Kelly James Clark's book *Return to Reason* (1990). Kelly James Clark (b. 1956) is Professor of Philosophy at Calvin College in Michigan.

1. Introduction

As we have seen in [chapter 3 of *Return to Reason* (see bibliographical information for this chapter)], a new approach to faith and reason is being pursued by Alvin Plantinga. His most developed essay is "Reason and Belief in God" (hereafter *R&BG*).[1] Rejecting the Enlightenment assumptions, he gleans insights from recent developments in philosophy, from John Calvin, and from the recently rediscovered Scottish philosopher Thomas Reid. Plantinga contends that one may be perfectly rational in believing in God without the evidential support of an argument. In this chapter I will outline Plantinga's claim that rational belief in God does not require the evidential support of an argument, I will locate it within a Reidian theory of rationality, and I will consider criticisms of this claim.

2. The Structure of Believings

Let us begin by investigating the structure of beliefs. The discussion will prove most illuminating if we consider the framework of our believings prior to any critical analysis. The question before us, then, is this: How do we in fact acquire and

Kelly James Clark, "Return to Reason: The Irrationality of Evidentialism" from *Return to Reason: A Critique of Enlightenment Evidentialism and a Defense of Reason and Belief in God* (Grand Rapids, MI: William B. Eerdmans Pub. Co., 1990), pp. 125–58.

maintain beliefs? To maximize understanding, we need to consider the plethora of our believings and their relations to one another.

Plantinga calls *the system of one's beliefs, with their relations to one another*, one's **noetic structure** (*R&BG*, 48). Consider your own noetic structure. Notice that some of your beliefs are acquired immediately – that is, *without the support of other beliefs*. These are called **basic beliefs**: *beliefs that one holds but not on the basis of other beliefs that one holds*, that is, not inferentially. I believe, for example, that 2 + 2 = 4 without the evidential support of any other beliefs; the belief that 2 + 2 = 4 is basic for me. A belief is called "basic" because it is in the *foundations* of one's noetic structure; while it is not based on other beliefs that one holds, it may provide the basis or foundation for other beliefs that one holds.

Some of my beliefs, therefore, are mediate: that is, I hold some beliefs because of other beliefs that I hold; these are called **nonbasic beliefs**: *beliefs that are held inferentially, on the evidential support of other beliefs that one holds.* The beliefs upon which my nonbasic beliefs are held constitute evidence or arguments for those beliefs. For example, although the belief that 2 + 2 = 4 is basic for me, the belief that 572 + 382 = 954 is not. I believe the latter because I believe that 2 + 2 = 4 and 8 + 7 = 15 and 5 + 3 = 8 (among other beliefs that are involved).

Consider the many different kinds of beliefs in your noetic structure. For example, consider *perceptual beliefs*, such as that the sky is blue, the dogwood tree is blooming, the walls are gray, and the mountains look purple. Perceptual beliefs are usually acquired immediately, that is, without the evidential support of other beliefs. For example, one simply *finds oneself believing* that the sky is blue when one is in the *appropriate circumstances*: one is outside, one looks at the sky, and the sky is blue. Or if one is far enough away from a mountain and the day is clear with the sun glinting off the mountain at just the right angle, then one will immediately acquire the belief that the mountain looks purple.

This raises the interesting issue of the veridicality of one's perceptual judgments. If one is in the mountains at sunset and the valley is covered in shadow with the mountains yet bathed in the rays of the sun, the mountains will display a glorious golden hue; this is called alpen glow. At this time the mountains will look golden. The point so far is not which belief is true – whether the mountain is purple or gold – but how one's beliefs are acquired and maintained. One's perceptual beliefs are typically acquired immediately in the appropriate circumstances, without consideration of other beliefs that one holds. The belief that the mountain is not really purple or golden is a belief that one must reason to, and is, therefore, a nonbasic belief. Hence, the appearance-belief that the mountain looks golden is nonbasic in the described circumstances, and the belief that the mountain is not really golden is an inferred belief in the described circumstances and is, therefore, a nonbasic belief.

One also has *memory beliefs*, such as that I had oatmeal for breakfast this morning, that I went for a bike ride yesterday, and that my mother washed my brother's mouth out with soap when I was a child. Are these beliefs basic or nonbasic? These seem typically to be basic beliefs: one simply finds oneself believing them in certain circumstances, and one does not believe them on the basis of other beliefs that one holds. Consider *beliefs about the past*, such as that many people died on D-Day, that Greece was the cradle of democracy, that Luther was tried at Worms and Augsburg, and that the earth is more than five minutes old. Again, these beliefs are typically basic. One acquires these beliefs immediately upon reading them in a history book or hearing of them from an instructor – if one does not immediately forget them, as is wont to happen with historical beliefs. Beliefs about the past raise another form of belief: we typically find ourselves believing things simply because someone tells us, or on the basis of *testimony*. For example, one believes that it is 2:00 pm when one is told what time it is; one believes that Luther was tried at Worms simply because one's instructor or an author said so; and one believes that China is the most populous country in the world in the same way. One does not typically reason to these beliefs on the basis of other beliefs one holds – unless one is a scholar in the relevant field. Beliefs accepted on the basis of testimony are, therefore, basic.

An interesting immediate belief that has already proven of significance for our discussion of the rationality of religious belief is the *belief in other minds*. No philosopher has ever constructed a good argument for the existence of other minds, and it is difficult to see how this task might be accomplished.[2] If you are not a philosopher, you might think that one who asks such questions is weird; and perhaps you would be right. You are not tempted by the possibility that while other people may act *as if* they had minds they are nonetheless no more than sophisticated and subtle automata programmed to respond in ways that deceptively imply that they are persons. You are not moved by the thought that although people may look *as if* they feel pain – by grimacing, crying, or holding their finger – they no more feel pain than a computer feels pain when its hardware begins to rust. The same may hold for all of the mental life of these alleged other persons: they may behave as if they were experiencing pain, were swept up by love, were pensively reflecting, etc., and yet in reality they have none of our familiar mental life at all. The belief that there are other minds is tantamount to the belief that there are persons other than oneself.

Now this belief that there are other minds or persons is one that is basic. Not only has no one developed a good argument for that belief; none of us, in fact, believes in other minds on the basis of other beliefs we hold. Belief in other minds is a basic belief.

A whole host of other kinds of beliefs are also typically basic. There are, for example, elementary *truths of logic* such as the beliefs that every proposition is either true or false; if a statement P implies a statement Q, and P is true, then Q is also true; and if equals are added to equals the results are equals. There is the *principle of induction* that the future will be like the past. There are certain *mathematical beliefs*. And there are certain framework or fundamental beliefs such as *belief in an external world, belief in the self*, etc. These are foundational beliefs that we typically reason from and not to; hence, such beliefs are typically basic.

Of course, not all of our beliefs are basic. Some beliefs are acquired and maintained because of other beliefs we hold. As already noted some higher-level mathematical truths and some factual beliefs, such as the belief that the mountain is not purple, are nonbasic beliefs. Typically, *beliefs in scientific hypotheses* – say, the belief that there are electrons or that $E = mc^2$ – are nonbasic and are acquired upon performing certain experiments in a laboratory or examining the evidence. This is true at least for the physicist; most of the rest of us can barely understand the evidence. We accept the belief simply because someone told us that there are electrons and that $E = mc^2$. It is unfitting for a physicist to accept noninferentially a scientific hypothesis: he must carefully attend to the evidence and to the counter-evidence and not assent to a scientific hypothesis without the support of the evidence. We would not look kindly upon a scientist who committed himself to a scientific hypothesis because it just occurred to him on a whim or because it just seemed to be true.

After hearing testimony at a trial one might form the nonbasic, inferential belief that the defendant is guilty. After weighing the evidence one may believe that giving up eggs or chocolate will reduce one's cholesterol count.[3] Upon reading the medical reports one may conclude that secondary smoke is dangerous to one's health or that one ought to reduce one's exposure to the sun because of the declining ozone layer. Upon considering the mathematical formulas relating the orbits of the planets one may acquire the belief in the universal law of gravitation. All of the beliefs that one *reasons to*, beliefs produced by *reasoning*, are nonbasic, inferential beliefs.

A set of beliefs whose status is not altogether clear is the set of one's *moral beliefs*. I would argue that fundamental moral beliefs, more often than not, are basic beliefs for most persons. They are typically beliefs one finds oneself with and they are not the sorts of beliefs for which one generally has good arguments or evidence. One does not typically believe that murder is wrong on the basis of other beliefs one has, unless this belief is based on a more basic belief that it is wrong to harm another person. In this case, the belief that murder is wrong is mediate and is based on the belief that it is wrong to harm another person. But then the belief that it is wrong to harm another person is itself a basic belief; it is not accepted on the basis of other beliefs one holds. Somewhere in one's moral reasoning one reaches a set of beliefs that are bearers of intrinsic value; they are not valued as a means to some other end or for some extrinsic reason. At this level one reaches one's basic moral beliefs. So perhaps it is best to say that some of one's moral beliefs, those that are valued for some reason, are nonbasic and some of one's moral beliefs, the fundamental bearers of intrinsic value, are basic.

Finally consider, if you are a theist, *religious belief*, or belief in God. Think back to the origin of this belief, not your subsequent attempts to understand that belief through reasoning. Have you believed since childhood, because you were brought up in a believing family? Did you come to belief on a retreat, in the mountains, or while gazing at a starry sky? Were you converted as a result of the persistence of close friends, a pastor, or a priest? Did you study the great proofs of Anselm and Aquinas and find your intellect moved to belief in God? Were you destitute and sought God as your only hope? Did you feel moved to pray or attend church and gradually find yourself embracing what people who pray and worship believe? Were you made aware of God's providential action in the world by a series of apparently chance events through which you came to see the benevolent hand of God? Did you feel increasingly guilty, as if you were responsible to someone greater than human persons, and find in God the open arms of forgiveness? Were you moved by the world-views powerfully portrayed in the fiction of, say, C. S. Lewis or G. K. Chesterton? Were you impressed by the joyful and centered lives of Christian friends or Christians in literature? Were you moved to despair by the absurdity of life without God through reading Sartre and Kierkegaard and took a leap of faith into the abyss of the divine? Did you make a pact with God that if he existed and saved you from some peril you would reorient your life around him? Did you, like Pascal, make a wager where you calculated the benefits and costs of belief and disbelief and decided to believe to avoid the potential terrible suffering of hell and to gain the potential infinite benefits of eternal bliss? Did you simply find yourself taken with belief in God upon hearing a clear presentation of the gospel of Jesus Christ? Believers have recounted in countless ways their journeys to God – or perhaps more fittingly put, God's journey to them.

We have very briefly described the actual structure of our believings. Some of our beliefs are basic, beliefs not believed on the basis of other beliefs we hold, and some beliefs are non-basic, beliefs that are acquired and maintained by the evidential support of other beliefs. Let us make one more observation about our actual noetic structures: the overwhelming majority of our beliefs are in fact basic, not acquired or maintained on the basis of others of our beliefs. Given that most of our beliefs are perceptual beliefs, memory beliefs, or beliefs acquired because someone told us that such and such is the case, this should not be surprising. If one carefully attends to the structure of one's believings, one will note that the number of beliefs that one reasons to – that is, the number of inferential, non-basic beliefs – is slim indeed.

So far our discussion has simply described the actual structure of our believings. We made no normative judgments and we avoided calling some beliefs rational or irrational, right or wrong, true or false. We simply recited the list of one's typical beliefs with their attendant relations to other beliefs that one holds. Having considered how one's believings are in fact structured, we have said nothing about how one's believings ought to be structured. The crucial question then is, Which of one's beliefs are *properly* basic? **Properly basic beliefs** are *basic beliefs that are justified*. One may not be rationally permitted to hold some beliefs as basic. I have already suggested that a physicist would not be justified in holding $E = mc^2$ as a basic belief; thus, for the physicist the belief that $E = mc^2$ is not properly basic.

Furthermore, which of one's beliefs are properly nonbasic? **Properly nonbasic beliefs** are *beliefs that one justifiably holds on the basis of other beliefs*. Surely some of the beliefs in one's noetic structure are irrational. It is our purpose next to discuss the Enlightenment strategy for separating the rational from the irrational in one's believings, and to assess the Enlightenment criteria for guiding our judgments about the proper holdings of our beliefs. In particular we will consider how this view of rationality affects belief in God.

3. Faith and Foundationalism

The Enlightenment challenge to theistic belief – the charge that belief in God requires propositional evidence or arguments to be rational – typically presupposes a classical foundationalist theory of rationality (*R&BG*, 17–59). On the **foundationalist** conception of rationality, *the system of one's beliefs and their logical relations to one another – that is, one's noetic structure – must be properly structured*. Nicholas Wolterstorff, in Reformed epistemology's first recent foray into these matters, characterizes foundationalism as an attempt "to form a body of theories from which all prejudice, bias, and unjustified conjecture have been eliminated. To attain this, we must begin with a firm foundation of certitude and build the house of theory on it by methods of whose reliability we are equally certain."[4] The metaphor of the proper construction and support of a house is appropriate given that the primary intuition of foundationalism is that some beliefs are properly or justifiably held without the evidential support of other beliefs. This is best illustrated by imagining the structure of one's believings as a pyramid. The bottom layer represents the foundations of one's believings, which are one's properly basic beliefs. If the foundations are solid, then one may continue to build higher-level beliefs upon it, using the proper tools (rules of inference). Each successive level must be properly built upon the preceding layers. Thus, in a rational noetic structure, to complete the metaphor, the rock-solid foundations are properly basic beliefs, each additional layer consists in properly nonbasic, or inferential, beliefs, and the mortar consists in proper rules of inference. The intention is to specify the foundational beliefs in such a way as to secure their absolutely certain truth and to use truth-preserving rules of inference to transfer the absolute certain truth up to the higher levels (see Figure X.A.8a, below).

The structure is ultimately supported, of course, by the foundational layer. The crucial issue then is this: Which beliefs may one properly include among the foundations of a rational noetic structure – that is, which beliefs are properly basic? Granting that one may have many basic beliefs which are not justified, classical foundationalism offers a criterion for critically scrutinizing beliefs. One must determine which basic beliefs are, indeed, justified – that is, are properly basic beliefs. If belief in God is a properly basic belief, then one would not need an argument to justify one's belief. Hence, the project for the classical foundationalist is to specify what kinds of beliefs are properly basic. These beliefs, for the classical foundationalist, are propositions which are

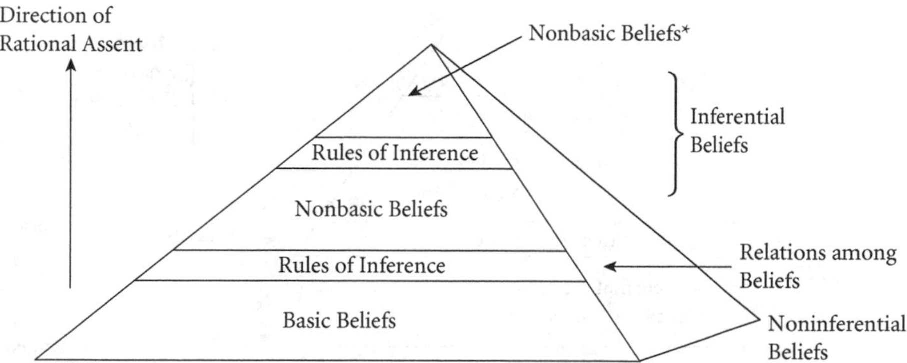

Figure X.A.8a. Foundationalism. Foundationalism is a theory about the structure of rational beliefs. There is a certain set of beliefs that is justified without the support of other beliefs; this set of beliefs, basic beliefs, provides the foundations upon which all other beliefs are ultimately supported. Rational assent moves only from the bottom to the higher levels as warrant for beliefs is transferred from the lower levels to the higher levels by rules of inference.

*Higher-level nonbasic beliefs. I have included only three, but it is possible there are many more higher levels that derive their evidential support, and hence rational warrant, from lower levels.

either evident to the senses, self-evident, or what philosophers call incorrigible. Beliefs that are **evident to the senses** are *reports of immediate experience* – such as that there is a piece of paper before me, there is a tree before me, and the wall that I am looking at is yellow. Beliefs that are **self-evident** are those which *upon understanding them one sees them to be true* – such as that 2 + 2 = 4, all bachelors are unmarried males, and the whole is equal to the sum of its parts. And, finally, beliefs that are **incorrigible** are *propositions about which one cannot be wrong*. These are usually reports of one's own immediate subjective states – much like the appearance beliefs discussed earlier – such as the beliefs that it seems to me that the wall in front of me is yellow, it appears to me that there is a tree before me, and the mountains appear purple.

The unifying characteristic of foundational propositions is that a person may be rational in believing them without evidential support from other beliefs; they are, to use our terminology, properly basic. Justified basic beliefs constitute the foundations of a rational system of beliefs. One's nonbasic beliefs must be believed *on the basis of* one's basic beliefs to be rational. In order for nonbasic beliefs to be rational they must be inferred from one's basic beliefs by either inductive or deductive logic (see Figure X.A.8b).

The evidentialist objection to theistic belief consists in two claims:

1. To be rational the theist must have sufficient evidence for the existence of God.
2. There is not sufficient evidence for the existence of God.

In the first chapter we discussed the second claim. Let us now examine the first claim.

The evidentialist objection is typically rooted in classical foundationalism. Belief in God is neither self-evident, evident to the senses, nor incorrigible. So, according to classical foundationalism, it is not a justified basic belief; it is not properly basic. If one accepts belief in God without the support of a good argument, then one would be holding it improperly. Such a person would be at best foolish and at worst deserving of censure. Belief in God therefore stands, says the classical foundationalist, in need of argument or evidence to be held rationally.

Is it a requirement of rationality that one must have sufficient evidence to believe rationally in God? The evidentialist contention that the theist

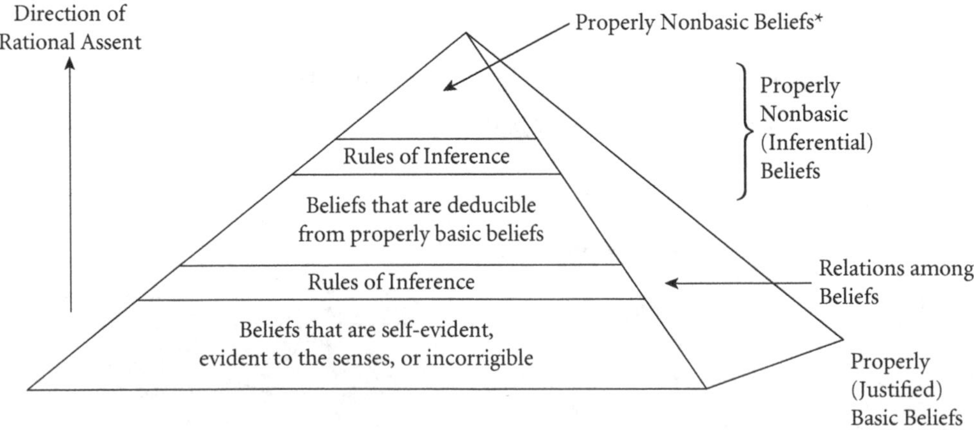

Figure X.A.8b Classical foundationalism. Since the foundations are certain the laws of logic are truth-preserving (and truth-transferring) the properly nonbasic beliefs are also certain and true. Any belief that is not properly basic (that is, not self-evident, evident to the senses, or incorrigible) must be supported by argument from lower-level beliefs. Hence, belief in God requires the evidential support of an argument.

*Higher-level, justified nonbasic beliefs.

must have adequate evidence for rational belief in God is grounded in the classical foundationalist conception that belief in God is not properly basic and hence requires an argument or evidence in order for the belief to be rational.[5] But why accept classical foundationalism?

4. Foundationalism Founders

Rather than capitulate to the evidentialist's charge of irrationality, perhaps we should examine its shortcomings. Let us call **classical foundationalism (CF)** the position that holds that a belief P is rational if and only if P is

1. Self-evident, evident to the senses, or incorrigible or
2. Inferable from a set of beliefs that are self-evident, evident to the senses, or incorrigible.

Wolterstorff says that there is very little positive that can be said of CF: "On all fronts foundationalism is in bad shape. It seems to me that there is nothing to do but give it up for mortally ill and learn to live in its absence."[6] What has spelled the death of classical foundationalism? Wolterstorff points to the austerity of such a theory.[7] After all, he contends, there are precious few beliefs which can properly take their place among the foundations.[8] If there are few such foundational beliefs, then there is a precious thin evidential base to support the rest of one's beliefs.

Plantinga attacks CF more directly. Given CF, he asks, is it rational to accept CF? First, is CF a properly basic belief? Surely CF is not evident to the senses since it is clearly not a report of one's immediate experiences. Also, it is not incorrigible: surely one can be mistaken about the truth of CF. And lastly, upon understanding CF one does not thereby see it to be self-evidently true (I understand it and think it false). Thus, CF does not satisfy its own first condition for rationality.

Does CF fare any better with respect to the second condition for rationality? On the classical foundationalist conception of rationality, one may be justified in holding to a nonbasic or inferential belief only if one can infer that proposition from the set of one's properly basic beliefs. The problem for CF itself is that no one has yet produced a good argument for CF from a set of beliefs warranted by the classical foundationalist criterion. In fact, it is difficult to see how one could possibly infer CF from a set of beliefs such as that I am appeared to greenly, that there is a tree before me, and that the whole is equal to the sum of its parts. Thus, CF cannot be justified by its own criterion. CF is, therefore, *self-referentially inconsistent* (*R&BG*, 60–1). Hence, either CF is false or one can embrace it only on the pain of irrationality. Thus, it clearly follows that no one ought to accept CF.

Classical foundationalism has a further telling defect: it excludes cases of clearly justified beliefs. Surely one is perfectly rational in believing that one had breakfast this morning, that there is an external world, and that one's wife is a person. These beliefs, however, are not self-evident, evident to the senses, or incorrigible. Therefore, classical foundationalism requires that they be supported by an argument from properly basic beliefs. But no one has ever produced a good argument for these beliefs. Plantinga argues:

> One crucial lesson to be learned from the development of modern philosophy – Descartes through Hume, roughly – is just this: relative to propositions that are self-evident and incorrigible, most of the beliefs that form the stock in trade of ordinary everyday life are not probable – at any rate there is no reason to think they are probable. Consider all those propositions that entail, say, that there are enduring physical objects, or that there are persons distinct from myself, or that the world has existed for more than five minutes: none of these propositions, I think, is more probable than not with respect to what is self-evident or incorrigible for me; at any rate no one has given good reason to think any of them is. (*R&BG*, 59–60)

Any philosophical principle that excludes cases of obviously rational beliefs ought to be rejected.

Thus, classical foundationalism founders. It is self-referentially inconsistent and it excludes obvious cases of justified belief. If one would be irrational in believing CF, then surely one ought not to believe it and use it as an argument against the rationality of belief in God. In conclusion:

> Accordingly, I ought not to accept [CF] in the absence of argument from premises that meet the condition it lays down. The same goes for the foundationalist: if he cannot find such an argument for [CF], he ought to give it up. Furthermore, he ought not to urge and I ought not to accept any objection to theistic belief that crucially depends upon a proposition that is true only if I ought not believe it. . . . It is evident, however, that classical foundationalism is bankrupt, and insofar as the evidentialist objection is rooted in classical foundationalism, it is poorly rooted indeed. (*R&BG*, 61–2)

5. Belief in God as Properly Basic

Why was belief in God excluded from the foundations of a rational noetic structure? For the evidentialist objector this was done because of his arbitrary assumption of classical foundationalism. However, Plantinga and Wolterstorff have offered conclusive reasons for rejecting classical foundationalism and hence its characterization of properly basic beliefs. Given the collapse of classical foundationalism, what sorts of statements may one properly include among the foundations of one's noetic structure? Surely one would be perfectly rational in including beliefs that are self-evident, evident to the senses, or incorrigible; Plantinga and Wolterstorff do not dispute this. They are, however, bothered by the arbitrary commitment that one may include *only* these beliefs. The question is, What other beliefs may one properly include? Can belief in God be added to this set? Plantinga, in the Calvinian tradition, contends that it can:

> In the passages I quoted earlier, Calvin claims the believer does not need argument – does not need it, among other things, for epistemic respectability. We may understand him as holding, I think, that a rational noetic structure may very well contain belief in God among its foundations. Indeed, he means to go further, and in two separate directions. In the first place he thinks a Christian *ought* not believe in God on the basis of other propositions; a proper and well-formed Christian noetic structure will *in fact* have belief in God among its foundations. And in the second place Calvin claims that one who takes belief in God as basic can *know* that God exists. Calvin holds that one can *rationally accept* belief in God as basic; he also claims that one can *know* that God exists even if he has no argument, even if he does not believe on the basis of other propositions. (*R&BG*, 73)

And as he writes in an earlier work:

> It is worth noting, by way of conclusion, that the mature believer, the mature theist, does not typically accept belief in God tentatively, or hypothetically, or until something better comes along. Nor, I think, does he accept it as a conclusion from other things he believes; he accepts it as basic, as part of the foundations of his noetic structure. The mature theist commits himself to belief in God; this means that he accepts belief in God as basic. Our present inquiry suggests that there is nothing contrary to reason or irrational in so doing.[9]

Wolterstorff affirms the proper basicality of Christian belief, contending that it is a fundamental commitment in the structure of the theist's believings; it ought to function as a *control belief* – a belief according to which or on the basis of which other beliefs ought to be rejected, suggested, and developed. As he states: "The Christian scholar ought to allow the belief-content of his authentic Christian commitment to function as control within his devising and weighing of theories."[10]

On Plantinga's conception of rationality, a rational belief system will display the characteristic foundationalist structure: there is still a foundation that is noninferentially justified and the relation of rational supports proceeds upward through the higher levels (*R&BG*, 47–55).[11] Where his foundationalism departs from classical foundationalism is in his specification of properly basic beliefs. The classical foundationalist has a rather sparse set of properly basic beliefs. Plantinga's foundationalism is much less parsimonious in its specification of properly basic beliefs. He also includes memory beliefs, beliefs about the external world, acceptance of testimony, and belief in God, among others.

Plantinga has rejected the classical foundationalist conception of rationality. Does that make just any belief rational? Surely not. Although Plantinga does not offer an alternative account of rationality in *R&BG*, we will consider his endorsement of the epistemology of Thomas Reid. While not offering a criterion of proper basicality, Plantinga suggests a Reidian procedure for assessing such criteria (*R&BG*, 74–8). The proper method is *inductive*; the epistemologist ought to assemble beliefs he considers properly basic and proceed to frame a principle of rationality on the basis of this set of beliefs. One may proceed, on the other hand, by *beginning* with a principle or theory and then judge beliefs by the principle. This was the approach of classical foundationalism. Should one start from a theory or from a set of beliefs?

One may observe the differences between these two approaches from an example in the history of science. Medieval astronomers started with an astronomical theory: they believed that the heavens were perfect and without blemish and that everything in the heavens partook of perfect, circular motion. They then took this commitment to their astronomical work as a methodological principle and performed the difficult task of fitting all their astronomical observations into uniform, circular motion. Copernicans, on the other hand, started from the complex set of astronomical observations and proceeded to abstract the motion of the planets from this set. Eventually, Kepler argued that the abstracted principle of planetary motion is elliptical. Thus, one may either start with a theory, as did the medievals, and fit one's observations with that principle, or one may start with a set of observations, as did the Copernicans, and abstract a law or principle from the observations.

Let us consider another example, this one from biblical theology. In Greek thought a perfect being is necessarily unchanging, that is, immutable. Influenced by Greek thought, the medievals believed that if God is perfect, then he could not change. Armed with this interpretive principle, one interprets the biblical passages which suggest that God does indeed change – where he changes his mind, repents, seems to forget, etc. – as anthropomorphism. The methodological principle that perfection implies immutability guides the evaluation of particular biblical passages. One might proceed, however, in a rather different fashion. One might attempt to form a conception of the divine nature from the particular texts rather than from a preconceived method. Hence, one might start with the particular biblical texts and derive one's theology from these. Some narrative passages indicate that God changes, and a few epistolary passages suggest that God does not change. It is from these passages that the acceptance or rejection of divine immutability is to be derived. With the latter approach, the doctrine of divine immutability is not inevitable.

Starting with a theory, as noted in the scientific example, may prove detrimental to the pursuit of knowledge. Thus, the approach to rationality which starts with a theory is less preferable than starting with a set of beliefs and deriving a theory from them. The theist may take belief in God as one of the set of paradigm basic beliefs and frame his principles of rationality according to that set of beliefs. On this theory a great many beliefs will be excluded. Thus, this method will refute the charge that the rejection of classical foundationalism entails that "anything goes."

Plantinga suggests addressing the issue of rationality not in terms of the beliefs themselves but from the perspective of cognitive faculties or belief-producing mechanisms. It is precisely this approach which is suggested but not developed in *R&BG* and which finds its best expression in the writings of the 19th-century Scottish philosopher Thomas Reid.

6. Reid and Rationality

In Plantinga's published writings on faith and rationality, he has offered little more than a promissory note on developing a criterion of rationality. This lacuna, as one might imagine, has engendered vigorous criticism.[12] However, Plantinga has suggested an intellectual debt to the epistemology of Thomas Reid[13] and his religious epistemology makes most sense when located within the context of Reid's philosophy.[14] Let us, then, briefly examine Reid's thought.

Reid's project was, in part, a critique of the classical tradition that began with Descartes and culminated in Humean skepticism. He developed as well a more constructive approach to rationality. Reid embraces the contention that classical foundationalism excludes obvious cases of justified belief:

> Descartes, Malebranche, and Locke, have all employed their genius and skill to prove the existence of a material world; and with very bad success. Poor untaught mortals believe undoubtedly that there is a sun, moon, stars, an earth, which we inhabit; country, friends, and relations, which we enjoy; land, houses, and moveables, which we possess. But philosophers, pitying the credulity of the vulgar, resolve to have no faith but what is founded on reason[ing]. (Reid, 5; emphasis mine)

In the final sentence Reid signals a shift from a Cartesian reliance upon **reasoning** as the sole, reliable *cognitive faculty which produces belief by urging assent to a proposition upon reflecting on other propositions.* In Reid's estimation precious little was proved by these philosophers, and what ought to be rejected are not our ordinary beliefs, but the philosophers' sole reliance upon reasoning.

Reid is determined not to let a philosophical theory take precedence over the facts:

> That we have clear and distinct conceptions of extension, figure, and motion, and other attributes of body, which are neither sensations, nor like any sensation, is a fact of which we may be as certain as that we have sensations. And that all mankind have a fixed belief of an external material world – a belief which is neither got by reasoning nor education, and a belief which we cannot shake off, even when we seem to have strong arguments against it and not a shadow of argument for it – is likewise a fact, for which we have all the evidence that the nature of the thing admits. *These facts are phaenomena of human nature, from which we may justly argue against any hypothesis, however generally received. But to argue from a hypothesis against facts, is contrary to the rules of true philosophy.* (Reid, 61; emphasis mine)

In Reid's own earthy style, we have been led astray:

> A traveller of good judgment may mistake his way, and be unawares led into a wrong track; and, while the road is fair before him, he may go on without suspicion and be followed by others; but, when it ends in a coal-pit it requires no great judgment to know that he hath gone wrong, nor perhaps to find out what misled him. (Reid, 11)

This sole reliance upon reasoning, assumed by classical foundationalism, has led us astray. Reid wholeheartedly endorses reasoning as *a* legitimate belief-producing faculty, yet he rejects the idea that it is *the* legitimate belief-producing faculty. He notes that many cognitive faculties produce beliefs. He calls these faculties, taken together, "Common Sense." We have, for example, a disposition, in certain circumstances, to believe what we sense and remember:

> There is a smell, is the immediate testimony of sense; there was a smell, is the immediate testimony of memory. If you ask me, why I believe that the smell exists, I can give no other reason, nor shall ever be able to give any other, than that I smell it. If you ask why I believe that it existed yesterday, I can give no other reason but that I remember it. Sensation and memory, therefore, are simple, original, and perfectly distinct operations of the mind, and both of them are original principles of belief. (Reid, 15)

The belief-producing mechanisms of sense and memory are as much a part of the human constitution as reasoning and there is no reason to exalt reasoning over sense and memory. They are all "equally grounded on our constitution: none of them depends upon, or can be resolved into another. To reason against any of these kinds of evidence, is absurd; nay to reason for them is absurd" (Reid, 18–19).

Hume rightly recognizes that no one has offered a proof that we have minds, although we have a strong tendency to believe that we do (it might not always be quite so strong in the case of certain others). Either this belief is folly or it is wisdom. Hume argues for the former, Reid contends the latter:

> What shall we say, then? Either those inferences which we draw from our sensations – namely, the existence of a mind, and of powers or faculties belonging to it – are prejudices of philosophy or education, mere fictions of the mind, which a wise man should throw off as he does the belief of fairies; or they are judgments of nature – judgments not got by comparing ideas, and perceiving agreements and disagreements, but *immediately* inspired by our constitution. (Reid, 23; my emphasis)

Reid believes that we are under some necessity in our noetic constitution to believe that we have minds and that to reject this belief is "not to act the philosopher, but the fool or the madman" (Reid, 23).

So, Reid recognizes, we have a tendency to believe, in the appropriate circumstances, that there is an external world, that we have a mind, that there are other persons; and we tend to believe inductively supported statements, what other people tell us, what we remember, what we sense, etc. What is significant about these noetic faculties is that, with the exception of the reasoning faculty, they produce their effects *immediately*, without the evidential support of other beliefs. For example, belief in an enduring mind and belief in sensate knowledge, Reid says, are "immediately inspired by our constitution" (Reid, 23). And, as with senses and memory, these noetic faculties do not need to be justified by reasoning.

Reid recognizes – a psychological point of some philosophical significance – that the vast majority of our beliefs are produced in us by innate tendencies or dispositions to believe in an immediate, noninferential manner. That is, *most* of our beliefs are basic and are justified.

Reid contends that the classical foundationalists employ a *guilty-until-proven-innocent* principle of rationality. The paradigm instance of this principle is the Cartesian method of doubt: reject any belief that can possibly be doubted and accept only what is indubitable or what can be established by absolutely certain evidence. Indeed, this principle is the guiding philosophy of modern epistemology at least since the time of Descartes.

Reid, on the other hand, suggests an *innocent-until-proven-guilty* principle of rationality. We ought to trust, he contends, the deliverances of our noetic faculties, unless reason provides us with substantial grounds for questioning that belief. With respect to our noetic faculties, Reid states: "I have found her in all other matters an agreeable companion, a faithful counsellor, a friend to common sense, and to the happiness of mankind. This justly entitles her to my correspondence and confidence, *till I find infallible proofs of her infidelity*" (Reid, 12; emphasis mine). Under the presumption of innocence, a belief ought to be accepted as reliable until it is shown to be specious.

Wolterstorff affirms Reid's intuitions and develops them into a criteria of rationality. Wolterstorff contends that

> A person is rationally justified in believing a certain proposition which he does believe unless he has adequate reason to cease from believing it. Our beliefs are rational unless we have reason for refraining; they are not nonrational unless we have reason *for* believing. They are innocent until proved guilty, not guilty until proved innocent.[15]

Thus reason plays a different role in securing rationality than is assumed by classical foundationalism; rationality is in terms of both belief dispositions and adequate reasons against beliefs produced by one's cognitive faculties.

Why does Reid think that our noetic faculties typically produce justified beliefs? One reason is his belief that our cognitive equipment has been given to us by our Creator. That we are endowed by God with our noetic faculties is a sufficient reason for trusting them. Because of the divine power and goodness, there is no good reason to prefer reasoning to common sense:

> Common Sense and Reason[ing] have both one author; that Almighty Author in all whose other works we observe a consistency, uniformity, and beauty which charm and delight the understanding: there must, therefore, be some order and consistency in the human faculties, as well as in other parts of his workmanship. (Reid, 53)

Reid believes that reasoning is impotent unless Common Sense supplies it with materials for thought. He rightly notes that if we, in a Cartesian and Humean vein, admit only what can be established by reasoning, we will admit nothing. Without the principles of common sense, we will believe nothing:

> All reasoning must be from first principles; and for first principles no other reason can be given but this, that, by the constitution of our nature, we are under a necessity of assenting to them. Such principles are parts of our constitution, no less than the power of thinking: reason can neither make nor destroy them; nor can it do anything without them: it is like a telescope,

> which may help a man see farther, who hath not eyes; but, without eyes, a telescope shews nothing at all. A mathematician cannot prove the truth of his axioms, nor can he prove anything, unless he takes them for granted. We cannot prove the existence of our minds, nor even of our thoughts and sensations. A historian, or a witness, can prove nothing, unless it is taken for granted that the memory and senses may be trusted. A natural philosopher can prove nothing, unless it is taken for granted that the course of nature is steady and uniform. (Reid, 57–8)

Without the beliefs produced by our manifold cognitive faculties, reasoning wouldn't lead us to embrace much of anything.

Now it would be thoroughly consonant with this Reidian epistemology not only to believe that God has endowed us with the noetic faculties mentioned above which produce their effects immediately, but also to believe that he has endowed us with a disposition to believe in himself in the appropriate circumstances. It also seems that God, intending that his creatures come to knowledge of himself, would provide means perfectly adequate to this intention. Thus, a theist would believe that God has created us not only with noetic faculties that produce belief in an external world, memory, other persons, and the like, but also with a noetic faculty that produces belief in him. This belief may be produced in us immediately as we contemplate a starry sky and are taken with the belief that God has created all of this. Or when in the midst of heartfelt guilt we come to believe that we are forgiven. Or when in the appropriate circumstances we feel an urge to pray to God or praise him.

Calvin's view is likewise that God has implanted in us a **sense of the divine**: *a tendency or disposition to believe in him in the appropriate circumstances*:

> 'There is within the human mind, and indeed by natural instinct, an awareness of divinity.' This we take to be beyond controversy. To prevent anyone from taking refuge in the pretense of ignorance, God himself has implanted in all men a certain understanding of his divine majesty. Ever renewing its memory, he repeatedly sheds fresh drops. Since, therefore, men one and all perceive that there is a God and that he is their Maker, they are condemned by their own testimony because they have failed to honor him and to consecrate their lives to his will. If ignorance of God is to be looked for anywhere, surely one is most likely to find an example of it among the more backward folk and those more remote from civilization. Yet there is, as the eminent pagan says, no nation so barbarous, no people so savage, that they have not a deep-seated conviction that there is a God. So deeply does the common conception occupy the minds of all, so tenaciously does it inhere in the hearts of all! Therefore, since from the beginning of the world there has been no region, no city, in short, no household, that could do without religion, there lies in this a tacit confession of a sense of deity inscribed in the hearts of all.
>
> Indeed, the perversity of the impious, who though they struggle furiously are unable to extricate themselves from the fear of God, is abundant testimony that this conviction, namely, that *there is some God*, is naturally inborn in all, and is fixed deep within, as it were in the very marrow. . . . From this we conclude *that it is not a doctrine that must first be learned in school*, but one of which each of us is master from his mother's womb and which nature itself permits no one to forget. (Calvin as quoted in *R&BG*, 65–6)

Calvin also contends that this disposition to believe is often suppressed or overlaid by *the noetic effects of sin*. This would explain unbelief; everyone has this sense of the divine, but belief in God is often repressed because of the cognitive effects (better, defects) of sin.

While there is surely much more to be said on the topic of rationality, this discussion of Reid points in a direction the Christian might take in developing a theory of justification. This theory considers one's noetic equipment as designed by a Creator and as typically producing its effects immediately in the appropriate circumstances. Furthermore, the theist might contend that one of those noetic faculties which produces its effects immediately is Calvin's sense of the divine. Thus, the theist will develop a conception of the structure of believings which will legitimately capture his intuition that belief in God is properly basic (see Figure X.A.8c, p. 527).

Some might think it inappropriate for the theist to consider God in his philosophizing.

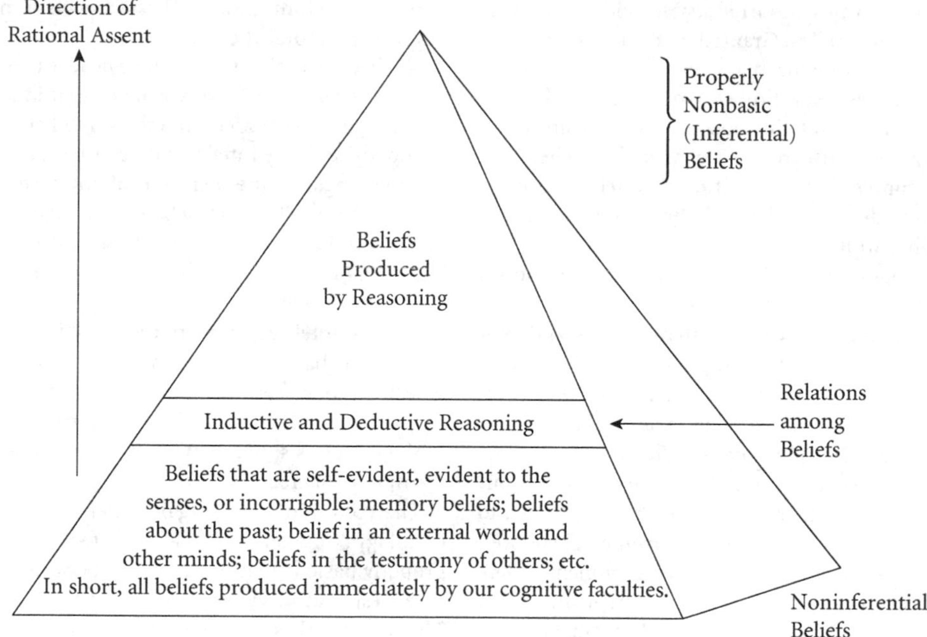

Figure X.A.8c Reidian foundationalism. For Reid, the set of properly basic beliefs includes all the beliefs which are produced by our cognitive faculties in the appropriate circumstances. Note that Reid's set of properly basic beliefs is huge compared to the sparse set of properly basic beliefs as specified by classical foundationalism. In fact, the entire set of justified beliefs is substantially larger. Reformed epistemology would include belief in God in the set of properly basic beliefs.

But why should the theist ignore his deepest commitments about reality when constructing a theory of knowledge? It is clearly relevant to rationality whether or not one's cognitive equipment is of divine manufacture.

7. A Defense of Belief in God as Properly Basic

Let us now consider some criticisms of belief in God as properly basic. Gary Gutting argues that the theist may not include belief in God in his set of properly basic beliefs because there is widespread disagreement about the claim.[16] Gutting contends that when there is widespread disagreement about a truth among one's intellectual peers (people who are roughly equivalent in intelligence and education), then that claim needs to be justified by an argument. Given disagreement among intellectual peers about the existence of God, Gutting claims, the theist needs to justify the claim that there is a God; the theist cannot take belief in God as basic.

Let us consider an example. Suppose a person, say Theodore, is alone on a mountain and acquires the belief that he has seen a timber wolf. Surely he is initially justified in the belief that there is a timber wolf before him. Suppose further that when he descends and tells his intellectual peers that he saw a timber wolf, they disagree with his claim and roundly denounce his credulity (perhaps, since the wolves are nowhere to be found, they even design facetious bumper stickers that say "Free Ted's Timber Wolves"). Does the mere fact of disagreement constitute a reason against his belief that he saw a timber wolf? Presumably it would be difficult for him to produce a good argument for his belief. Furthermore, timber wolves aren't the sorts of things that sit around waiting to provide irrefragable evidence to convince one's peers. Granted, the reasons for which Theodore's intellectual peers disagree – suppose they know that timber wolves are extinct or that they don't live above a certain altitude – *may* constitute reasons against his belief. But the simple disagreement of his intellectual peers is not detrimental to his belief that he saw a timber wolf.

Suppose, instead, that on a mountaintop on a starry night Theodore is overcome with the conviction that God created all this and that when he descends to the flatland he is met by disagreement from his intellectual peers. It seems that initially Theodore is justified in his belief in God. The question is, Why would the fact of disagreement contradict that justification? Why would other people's not being inclined to accept belief in God undermine Theodore's right to believe without a good argument? There is no reason to believe that he accepts this belief arbitrarily; he did not just pick it out of a hat. Surely the existence of disagreement by his intellectual peers does not discredit his belief. Theodore will probably believe that his intellectual peers disagree because they were not in the same situation; they did not have the same experience. Of course, if his intellectual peers present him with arguments against his belief (say, the problem of evil), they *may* constitute good reasons against his belief. But then again, they may not, as we discussed in the second chapter. But the mere fact of disagreement does not carry sufficient evidential weight for him not to take belief in God as basic.

The irrelevance of widespread disagreement for the evaluation of properly basic beliefs can be seen in the moral sphere. I may approach the construction of a moral theory in either of two ways: I may start with those moral beliefs that seem to me to be intuitively correct, or I may start with a moral theory. Let us call the beliefs considered in the first approach my *morally basic beliefs*. Presumably my list of morally basic beliefs will include some beliefs which are almost universally held: it is wrong to hurt innocent people for fun, human beings have some sort of dignity, and human life is valuable. But my list will also include basic beliefs that are not universally maintained: perhaps I believe that sex outside of marriage, infanticide, or cannibalism is wrong. From this set of morally basic beliefs I may abstract my moral theory.

Surely the fact that some people believe that sex outside of marriage is not wrong or that infanticide is right does not count against my beliefs in the opposite. If my intellectual peers have a good argument against the inclusion of any beliefs in my set of morally basic beliefs, then that argument would constitute a good reason against the inclusion of such a belief; but mere disagreement does not. I may include moral beliefs, about which my intellectual peers disagree, in my set of morally basic beliefs, simply because upon reflection they seem true to me. The mere fact of disagreement does not count against a belief in the religious sphere any more than it does in the moral sphere.

The common charge against Reformed epistemology's contention that belief in God is properly basic is that it can't be so because there is widespread disagreement about the claim. That charge, these examples imply, is not accurate. People disagree about nearly every belief of fundamental human concern – and this fact is scarcely relevant to the assessment of one's rationality with respect to belief, including belief in God.[17]

8. Fideism?

Plantinga's conception of belief in God has been accused of being fideistic by many critics.[18] A fideist is one who accepts or maintains religious belief in defiance of or contrary to reason. Fideism comes from the Latin *fide*, which means "faith." A fideist, therefore, affirms that one comes to belief in God as a matter of faith alone. Why is fideism considered odious and worth avoiding? In its antipathy for reason, it neglects or downplays a critical aspect of our nature.

One could be a fideist in one of three ways. First, one could maintain that reason is worthless in leading one to faith. Theologian Karl Barth, for example, sees philosophy and logic as proper in their own right, but as irrelevant to theology. Reason, he believes, is fallen and is incapable of eliciting belief in God. Emil Brunner, who was influenced by Barth, also holds this position, contending that "Christ conquers reason and in so doing makes it free to serve."

Second, one might believe that reason leads in the wrong direction and that it is contrary to faith. This clash between faith and reason is resolved by the courageous and defiant acceptance of belief in God. Kierkegaard held this position with respect to belief in the Christian God. Belief in Jesus as God in the flesh entails accepting such contradictions as that the infinite is finite, the eternal is temporal, and the omnipotent is a babe. If one simply follows reason, one would be led to reject belief in God. But, this position maintains, reason must give way to faith. The Russian theologian Shestof held a position that is fideistic in this respect: "he held that one can attain religious truth only by rejecting the proposition that 2 + 2 = 4 and accepting instead 2 + 2 = 5" (*R&BG*, 87).

Finally, one may contend that while reason is sufficient for some beliefs – say, that God exists and is omnipotent – it is not sufficient for other beliefs, such as belief in the Trinity or that God revealed himself in Christ. The latter beliefs must be accepted as a matter of faith alone. This, indeed, is a rather weak version of fideism. It surely does not denigrate the use of reason; rather, it merely ascribes some realistic limits to the realm of reason. It would be folly to believe that one could acquire belief in the Trinity or that God was in Christ reconciling the world to himself through reason alone, unaided by revelation. Aquinas and Augustine, among a great many others, held this commonsensical view. This seems to be the position which is closest to Plantinga's. It scarcely merits the ascription of fideism.

William Abraham accuses Plantinga of fideism:

> Others besides myself feel it natural to read Plantinga's recent work as a version of fideism. First, his central claim is that belief in God does not require reasons to be rational. That is surely what most fideists have fundamentally believed. Secondly, Plantinga can very easily use language which clearly echoes prominent fideistic themes. . . . Thirdly, Plantinga happily associates himself with a version of the Calvinistic tradition which has able exponents of fideism in its ranks. Certainly Plantinga is not hostile to Bavinck or Barth or Calvin when he is in a fideistic mood. . . . On our account of the fideist tradition he is a moderate fideist, indeed a moderate of moderates, but he is a fideist nonetheless. Perhaps he is one of the best philosophical fideists to appear of late.[19]

Is Plantinga a fideist? On Abraham's account Plantinga becomes a fideist by definition. Abraham believes that a fideist is one who does not require reasons for belief in God. Plantinga defends belief in God, but believes that it need not be based on arguments or evidence. Surely, however, he does not denigrate or downplay the crucial role of reason in the formation and sustenance of faith. Indeed, belief in God is among the deliverances of reason. Is fideism applicable in any sense to Plantinga? Plantinga does not contend that one *cannot* believe in God on the basis of evidence or arguments; rather, he argues only that one *need* not believe in God on the basis of evidence or arguments (see *R&BG*, 29–30). He has, furthermore, made a major contribution to the development and defense of the ontological argument for the existence of God.[20] And in his 1987 Gifford lectures, Plantinga offered more than two dozen theistic arguments. He is no fideist in the first two senses mentioned above. Plantinga clearly does not contend that reason is either irrelevant to or in opposition to belief in God. In attributing fideism to a position, it is fitting to proceed with caution; "Fideism is a nonce-word," states the *Oxford English Dictionary*, and it is surely a term that has been all too freely bandied about. Fideism is clearly inappropriate when applied to Plantinga's conception of reason and belief in God.

Far from denigrating reason, Plantinga argues that belief in God is one of the deliverances of reason. Faith is wholly in harmony with and is supported by or an outcome of right *reason*, although it is not typically a product of the faculty of reason*ing*. As Plantinga puts the issue:

> A former professor of mine for whom I had and have enormous respect once said that theists and nontheists have different conceptions of reason. At the time I did not know what he meant, but now I think I do. On the Reformed view I have been urging, the deliverances of reason include the existence of God just as much as perceptual truths, self-evident truths, memory truths, and the like. It is not that theist and nontheist agree as to what reason delivers, the theist then going on to accept the existence

of God by faith; there is, instead, disagreement in the first place as to what are the deliverances of reason. But then the Reformed epistemologist is no more a fideist with respect to belief in God than is, for example, Thomas Aquinas. Like the latter, he will no doubt hold that there are other truths of Christianity that are not to be found among the deliverances of reason – such truths, for example, as that God was in Christ, reconciling the world to himself. But he is not a fideist by virtue of his views on our knowledge of God. (*R&BG*, 90)

9. Conclusion: The Rationality of My Grandmother

Before making your final estimation of the significance of evidentialism, consider the rationality of my grandmother. My grandmother has never heard of the cosmological and ontological arguments or the argument from design; even if she had, it is not clear that she would immediately resonate to them or scintillate to their sophisticated criticisms. Now my grandmother is not all that untypical: she is an ordinary woman of faith (although she is an extraordinary grandmother!).

If evidentialism is true, then my grandmother has a noetic defect – she believes in God without sufficient propositional evidence. I prefer to look at the matter in my grandmother's favor. My grandmother does not have a noetic defect – hence evidentialism is false. It is difficult for me to imagine that God has put her in a cognitive situation which makes her belief in God positively irrational. I am constrained by the goodness of God to believe that he has created her with the noetic faculties that produce belief in him in the appropriate circumstances.

Why consider the experience of my grandmother? I believe that evidentialism, motivated by a quest for mathematical certainty in all believings, has offered an inappropriate paradigm of rationality. The Enlightenment conception of rationality, as we have demonstrated, is foreign to our believing experience. This reduces rationality to the model of a calculating machine: a mere algorithm for calculating the deductive consequences of beliefs that are independently verified. The more closely one's mental life resembles the workings of a computer, the more likely one is to be rational. If the arguments of the preceding chapters are persuasive, then it should be clear that human cognition is vastly different from computer calculation. Rationality is not simply a relation that obtains between one's beliefs. Rather, it is the complex relation between one's cognitive equipment – divinely designed – one's experiences, and the world.

If one attempts to preserve the considered beliefs of ordinary believers, then one's theory of rationality will more closely resemble the theories of the Reidian and Reformed epistemologists. Theistic epistemology preserves the rationality of my grandmother.

Classical Enlightenment epistemology, with its overly stringent conception of rationality and its unduly negative assessment of the rationality of religious belief, has been found wanting. The evidentialist objection to belief in God, poorly rooted in classical foundationalism, has been seriously challenged. A theistic epistemology along the lines developed by Reid and Plantinga would seem to more accurately capture our intuitions concerning the structure of rational believings. The pretensions of reasoning have been found out, signaling a return to reason and belief in God.

Notes

1 Plantinga is the most prominent proponent of this position, which is being developed by Nicholas Wolterstorff of Yale University, George Mavrodes of the University of Michigan, and William Alston of Syracuse University, among others. Plantinga's most developed essay (and the one to which our discussion will refer) on the topic is "Reason and Belief in God," in *Faith and Rationality*, ed. Plantinga and Wolterstorff (Notre Dame: University of Notre Dame Press, 1983), 16–93. There are very fine essays in this volume by Wolterstorff ("Can Belief in God Be Rational If It Has No Foundations?"), Alston ("Christian Experience and Christian Belief"), and Mavrodes ("Jerusalem and Athens Revisited"). See also by Plantinga, *God and Other Minds* (Ithaca: Cornell University Press, 1967); *God, Freedom, and Evil* (Grand Rapids: Eerdmans, 1974); "Is Belief in God Rational?" in *Rationality and Religious Belief*, ed. C. F. Delaney (Notre Dame: University of Notre Dame Press, 1979), 7–27; and "The Reformed Objection to Natural Theology,"

Proceedings of the American Catholic Philosophical Association (1980): 49–63.

2 See Alvin Plantinga, *God and Other Minds*, 187–244.

3 I am not advocating giving up either. Indeed, it seems to me that one ought not give up this belief without a great deal of evidence; this principle would not hold with the same tenacity with the belief that one ought to give up beets or canned peas. One may wrongly believe that chocolate raises one's cholesterol level. For our purposes it is significant only that one acquire the belief on the basis of other beliefs that he holds.

4 Nicholas Wolterstorff *Reason Within the Bounds of Religion* (Grand Rapids: Eerdmans, 1976), 24; hereafter, *RWBR*.

5 Let me remind the reader that by evidence is meant propositional evidence in the form of an argument; nonpropositional or experiential evidence of God is typically discounted by contemporary evidentialist objectors. As Mackie claimed in the Introduction, belief in God can be established only on the basis of deductive or inductive arguments or inference to best explanation.

6 *RWBR*, 52.

7 *RWBR*, 24.

8 See *RWBR*, 42–51.

9 Alvin Plantinga, "Is Belief in God Rational?" in C. F. Delaney, ed., *Rationality and Religious Belief* (Notre Dame: University of Notre Dame Press, 1979), 27.

10 *RWBR*, 72. For the entire discussion of the role of Christian belief in one's believings see 59–71.

11 Plantinga and Wolterstorff reject the coherence theory of justification, which states that a proposition is justified if and only if it coheres or is logically consistent with the set of one's beliefs. On this account, coherence is both a necessary and a sufficient condition for rational justification.

12 For example, see Philip Quinn, "In Search of the Foundations of Theism," *Faith and Philosophy* 2, 4 (October 1985): 469–86. Plantinga is working on a book on these matters entitled *Warrant*, which may answer some of the issues raised by his critics. Now published as *Warrant: The Current Debate* (Oxford: Oxford University Press, 1993).

13 Reid, "An Inquiry Into the Human Mind on the Principles of Common Sense," in Ronald Beanblossom and Keith Lehrer, *Inquiry and Essays* (Indianapolis: Hackett, 1983).

14 Nicholas Wolterstorff, in his "Can Belief in God Be Rational If It Has No Foundations?" (in *Faith and Rationality*) and in "Thomas Reid on Rationality" (*Rationality in the Calvinian Tradition*, edited by Hendrik Hark, Johan van der Hoven, and Nicholas Wolterstorff [Lanham, MD: University Press of America], 43–69), addresses these issues. I would highly commend these articles to the curious.

15 Nicholas Wolterstorff, "Can Belief in God Be Rational If It Has No Foundations?" in *Faith and Rationality*, 163.

16 Gary Gutting, *Religious Belief and Religious Skepticism* (Notre Dame: University of Notre Dame, 1982), 79–80.

17 I don't intend my account of this debate to suggest that these matters have been settled to everyone's satisfaction. Indeed, significant debate rages on. One of the more trenchant criticisms of Reformed epistemology is Stephen Wykstra's "Toward a Sensible Evidentialism: On the Notion of 'Needing Evidence,'" in William Rowe and William Wain wright, eds., *Philosophy of Religion* (New York: Harcourt Brace Jovanovich, 1989), 426–37. See also Phil Quinn, "In Search of the Foundations of Theism," *Faith and Philosophy* 2, 4 (October 1985): 469–86; Richard Swinburne, *Faith and Reason* (Oxford: Oxford University Press, 1981), 33–71; and Anthony Kenny, *Reason and Faith* (New York: Columbia University Press, 1984).

18 Terence Penelhum, *God and Skepticism* (Boston: D. Reidel, 1983), 146.

19 William Abraham, *An Introduction to the Philosophy of Religion* (Englewood Cliffs, NJ: Prentice-Hall, 1985), 92–3.

20 See Alvin Plantinga, *God, Freedom, and Evil* (Grand Rapids: Eerdmans, 1977).

B

Pragmatism and the Ethics of Belief

1

The Wager

Blaise Pascal

Blaise Pascal (1623–62) was a French scientist and mathematician who made important contributions to the development of probability theory. After a religious experience in 1654 he abandoned science and mathematics and devoted his attention entirely to religious matters. Towards the end of his life Pascal began working on a defense of the Christian faith, but he died before he had the chance to complete it. After his death, his sketchy notes for the work were edited and published as *Pensées* (*Thoughts*). In the following selection from this work, Pascal argues that even though the evidence concerning God's existence is inconclusive, the rational wager is to bet that God exists.

343. *Infinite. Nothing*. Our soul is tossed into the body where it finds number, time, dimensions. It argues about them, calls them nature or necessity, and cannot believe in anything else.

Unity joined to infinity does not add anything to it, any more than a foot to a measure which is infinite. The finite is annihilated in the presence of the infinite, and becomes pure nothingness. Thus it is with our mind in the presence of God; thus our justice in face of divine justice.

There is not such a great disproportion between our justice and God's as between unity and infinity.

The justice of God must be immense like his mercy. Now justice shown to the damned is less overwhelming and must be less shocking, than mercy towards the saved.

We know that there is an infinite, but are ignorant of its nature. Since we know that it is untrue that numbers are finite, it follows that there is infinity in number. But we do not know what it is: it is untrue to say that it is even, untrue to say that it is odd; for the addition of unity does not alter its nature; yet it is a number and every number is odd or even (it is true that this applies to all finite numbers). Thus we may be sure that there is a God without knowing what he is.

Is there not one substantial truth, since there are so many true things which are not truth itself?

Blaise Pascal, *Pascal's Pensées*, trans. and intro. by Martin Turnell (New York: Harper & Brothers, 1962), extracts from pp. 200–5, 206–7.

We therefore know the existence and nature of the finite because we are finite and like it consist of extension in space. We know the existence of the infinite and do not know its nature because it possesses extension like ourselves, but not limits like us. But we do not know either the existence or the nature of God because he has neither extension nor limits.

But through faith we know that he exists; through glory we shall come to know his nature. Now, I have already shown that we can perfectly well know the existence of something without knowing its nature.

Let us now speak according to our natural lights.

If there is a God, he is infinitely incomprehensible because having neither dimensions nor limits, he has no relation to us. We are therefore incapable of knowing either what he is, or whether he exists. That being so, who will be bold enough to attempt the solution of the problem? Not we who have no communication with him.

Who then will blame Christians for not being able to give reasons for their beliefs since they profess belief in a religion which they cannot explain? They declare, when they expound it to the world, that it is foolishness, *stultitiam*; and then you complain because they do not prove it! If they proved it, they would not keep their word; it is through their lack of proofs that they show they are not lacking in sense.

'Yes, but even if it excuses those who present it in such a way, and if it excuses them for presenting it without giving reasons, it does not excuse those who accept it.'

Let us consider the point and say: 'Either God exists, or he does not exist.' But which of the alternatives shall we choose? Reason can determine nothing: there is an infinite chaos which divides us. A coin is being spun at the extreme point of this infinite distance which will turn up heads or tails. What is your bet? If you rely on reason you cannot settle for either, or defend either position.

Do not therefore accuse those who have made their choice of falseness because you know nothing about it.

'No, I do not blame them for their choice, but for making a choice at all because he who calls heads and he who calls tails are guilty of the same mistake, they are both wrong: the right course is not to wager.' 'Yes, but we have to wager. You are not a free agent; you are committed. Which will you have then? Come on. Since you are obliged to choose, let us see which interests you least. You may lose two things: the true and the good; and there are two things that you stake: your reason and your will, your knowledge and your beatitude; and your nature has two things from which to escape: error and unhappiness. Your reason is not more deeply wounded by choosing one rather than the other because it is bound to choose. That disposes of one point. But what about your beatitude? Let us measure the gain and the loss by saying: "Heads God exists." Let us compare the two cases; if you win, you win everything; if you lose, you lose nothing. Don't hesitate then. Take a bet that he exists.'

'That's fine. Yes, I must take a bet; but perhaps I am staking too much.'

'Come. Since there is an equal chance of gain and loss, if you were only to win two lives for one, you could still wager; but if there were three to be won, you would have to gamble (since you are bound to gamble), and it would be imprudent, when you are obliged to gamble, not to risk your life in order to win three lives at a game in which there is such a chance of loss and gain. But there is an eternity of life and happiness at stake. And since it is so, if there were an infinite number of chances of which only one was for you, you would still be right to risk one to win two; and you would be taking the wrong road if, being forced to gamble, you refuse to stake one life against three in a game in which, out of an infinite number of chances, one is for you, if the prize were an infinity of life which was infinitely happy. But in this game you can win eternal life which is eternally happy; you have one chance of winning against a finite number of chances of losing, and what you are staking is finite. That settles it: wherever there is infinity, and where there is not an infinity of chances of losing against the chance of winning, there is no room for hesitation: you must stake everything. And so, since you are forced to gamble, you must abandon reason in order to save your life, rather than risk it for the infinite gain which is just as likely to turn up as the loss of nothing.'

For it is useless to say that it is doubtful whether we shall win, that it is certain that we are running a risk, and that the infinite distance which lies between the *certainty* of what we stake and the *uncertainty* of what we shall win, is equal to the finite good which we certainly stake against the uncertain infinite. It is not like that; every gambler risks something that is certain in the hope of winning something which is uncertain; and nevertheless he risks a finite certainty in order to win a finite uncertainty without committing a sin against reason. There is not an infinite distance between the certainty of the risk and the uncertainty of a win; that is untrue. There is, to be sure, an infinite distance between the certainty of winning and the certainty of losing. But the uncertainty of winning is proportionate to the certainty of what we risk, depending on the proportion between the chances of gain and loss. Thus if there are as many chances on one side as on the other, the odds are equal; and then the certainty of the stake is equal to the uncertainty of the prize: it is far from being true that the distance between them is infinite. And so our argument is of overwhelming force, when the finite must be staked in a game in which the chances of gain and loss are equal, and the infinite is the prize. That can be demonstrated; and if men are capable of grasping any truth, that is one.

'I confess, I admit it. But is there still no means of seeing the reverse side of the cards?' 'Yes, Scripture and the rest, etc.'

'Yes, but my hands are tied and my lips sealed; I am forced to gamble and am not free; they will not let go of me. And I am made in such a way that I cannot believe. What do you expect me to do?'

'That's true. But at any rate, you must realise that since your reason inclines you to believe and yet you cannot believe, your inability to believe comes from your passions. Try then, not to convince yourself by multiplying the proofs of the existence of God, but by diminishing your passions. You want to find faith but you do not know the way; you want to cure yourself of unbelief, and you ask for the remedies: learn from the examples of those who like yourself were in bondage and who now stake their whole fortune: they are people who know the path that you would like to follow, and who have been cured of an ill of which you wish to be cured. Follow the method by which they began: it is by behaving as though they did believe, by taking holy water, by having masses said, etc. That will naturally make you inclined to believe and will calm you.'

'But that's just what I'm afraid of.' 'But why? What have you got to lose?'

'But in order to prove to you that it works, it will diminish the passions which for you are the great stumbling-block.'

End of the address. 'Now, what harm will you come to if you adopt this course? You will be faithful, honest, humble, grateful, beneficent, a true friend, genuine. In truth, you will no longer find yourself submerged in poisonous pleasures, such as lust and desire for fame: but will you have no others? I tell you that you will gain in this life; and that with every step you take along this path, you will see such certainty of gain and so much of the worthlessness of what you risk, that you will have gambled on something that is certain, infinite and has cost you nothing.'

'Oh, these words delight and ravish me, etc.'

If the argument appeals to you and appears well founded, you must know that it was composed by a man who went down on his knees, before and after it, to pray to the Infinite Indivisible Being to whom he submitted the whole of his being that God might grant the submission of the whole of your being for your own good and for his glory, and that in this way strength might be given to lowliness.

[...]

349. *Objection.* Those who hope for salvation are happy in that respect, but it is counterbalanced by the fear of hell.

Reply. Who has the greater reason to fear hell, the man who does not know whether there is a hell and who is certain of damnation if there is one; or the man who is to a certain extent convinced that there is a hell, and hopes to be saved if there is?

[...]

Fear, not the fear which comes from the fact that we believe in God, but the fear which comes from doubting whether he exists or not. The right kind of fear comes from faith: the wrong kind from doubt. The right kind linked to hope because it is born of faith, and because we hope in the God in whom we believe: wrong kind linked to despair because we fear the God in whom we do not believe. Some fear to lose him, – others fear to find him.

2

Pascalian Wagering

Thomas V. Morris

Thomas V. Morris (b. 1952) was Professor of Philosophy at the University of Notre Dame where he taught for fifteen years. More recently, he has founded the Morris Institute for Human Values, become a well-known speaker on business leadership, and published numerous books aimed at making philosophy accessible and applicable to a wide audience – e.g. *If Aristotle Ran General Motors* (1997) and *Philosophy for Dummies* (1999). In this essay Morris defends Pascal's famous wager, arguing that many of the most common criticisms of it are misguided.

> "Either God is or he is not." But to which view shall we be inclined? Reason cannot decide this question. Infinite chaos separates us. At the far end of this infinite distance, a coin is being spun which will come down heads or tails. How will you wager? Reason cannot make you choose either, reason cannot prove either wrong.

In this vivid and memorable passage, Blaise Pascal began to develop the famous argument which has come to be known as 'Pascal's Wager'.[1] The Wager is widely regarded as an argument for the rationality of belief in God which completely circumvents all considerations of proof or evidence that there is a God. Viewed as such, it has both excited and aggravated philosophers for years. Some have applauded it as a simple, down-to-earth, practical, and decisive line of reasoning which avoids altogether the esoteric, mind-boggling intricacies and apparently inevitable indecisiveness of the traditional theistic arguments that year after year continue to be revised and re-evaluated. They seem to share the view of Pascal himself who once wrote that

> The metaphysical proofs for the existence of God are so remote from human reasoning and so involved that they make little impact, and, even

Thomas V. Morris, "Pascalian Wagering" from *Anselmian Explorations: Essays in Philosophical Theology* (Notre Dame, IN: University of Notre Dame Press, 1987), pp. 194–202, 210–12.

> if they did help some people, it would only be for the moment during which they watched the demonstration, because an hour later they would be afraid they had made a mistake.[2]

Others have been exceedingly offended by the very idea of wagering on God in hopes of obtaining infinite gain, and shocked by the suggestion that rational belief can be established by wholly non-evidential, or non-epistemic means. Such philosophers have succeeded in raising an impressive number of objections to Pascal's case, objections which in the eyes of many render the argument of the Wager a failure. In this essay, I propose to examine this common view of the Wager as intended to secure the rationality of religious belief without any regard to purely epistemic matters. I want to suggest that such a view involves a misunderstanding of the Wager based on a neglect to take seriously an important feature of its original context, manifested by those initial remarks which Pascal used to launch his argument, and from which this paper began. A proper understanding of the epistemic context within which the Wager was intended to be used can provide us with a way of answering a number of the most standard and imposing objections to this interesting argument.

I

In attempting to show on prudential grounds that everyone ought to be a theist, Wager enthusiasts often seek to maximize the rhetorical force of their argument by conceding almost everything to the epistemically reasonable atheist and then producing from his own premises their desired conclusion. The rhetoric of their presentation often develops like this. First, it is pointed out that rational gamblers seeking to maximize their gains over the long run bet in accordance with the highest mathematical expectation, where expectation is established with the formula

(E): (Probability × Payoff) – Cost = Expectation

and is ranked for all possible bets in the contest or game situation. Then the confident Pascalian announces that in this life we are all in a forced betting situation in which the possible wagers are that there is a God and that there is no God. The situation is said to be forced in the sense that not acting as if there is a God – not praying, not seeking God's will for one's life, not being thankful to God – is considered to be equivalent to acting as if there is no God, practically speaking.[3] So one either acts as if there is a God, thereby betting on God, or one does not so act, thereby betting there is no God. Which bet should a rational person make? To answer this question, we must make assignments to the expectation formula and compare outcomes for the bets of theism and atheism. And this is where the rhetorical flourishes come into play whose assumptions result in disaster for the argument.

Let atheism be assigned an extremely high probability, and theism accordingly a very low one, the modern-day Pascalian suggests. It will not matter, so long as neither value is 0 or 1. And so long as theism is even a possibility, it is claimed, its probability is greater than 0, however small, and atheism's is less than 1. Now consider the question of cost. What does it cost to be an atheist? The Pascalian is typically ready to concede that it costs nothing. For, remember, in betting situations the cost is figured under the presumption that the outcome is unknown. So atheism cannot be said here to cost the loss of eternal bliss. And further, any values of the religious life whose descriptions do not entail the existence of God, such as the aesthetic pleasures of liturgy, and the social fulfillment of religious community, are in principle available to atheists as well as theists, if they are sufficiently shrewd. Even the comfort of believing in an after-life need not be the exclusive possession of theists. So even in this life atheism can be conceded to bear no cost. But religious belief, on the contrary, can be acknowledged to exact quite a cost from the believer. An adherent to typical theistic religions finds himself under all sorts of prohibitions and rules not recognized by the nonbeliever. So, the Pascalian is often quick to agree, the cost of betting on God is great.

Unlike standard betting situations, we have not to this point had determinate, precise assignments of probability and cost, but rather have contented ourselves with very general, comparative indications. According to the view of the

Wager under consideration, this does not matter, however, since the values we must assign to the payoff variable will work in the formula for expectation in such a way as to render any precision with respect to the other variables irrelevant. Theism promises infinite, eternal reward. Atheism at best carries with it a promise of finite rewards – whatever pleasure in this life would have been prohibited to the theist. So the Pascalian claims.

Respective expectations of atheism and theism are then figured and ranked as follows. In the case of atheism, multiplying a very high probability by a great finite payoff, and subtracting no cost at all will yield at best a very large finite value. For theism, on the other hand, the product of an infinite payoff and any positive finite probability, however small, will yield an infinite expectation, regardless of how great a finite cost is subtracted. So theism has an infinitely higher expectation than atheism. Thus, the rational person seeking to maximize his gains in this betting situation ought to bet on God.

II

Many objections have been raised against Pascal's Wager. I want to focus for a moment on those which I think to be particularly problematic for the sort of presentation of the Wager just elucidated. Let us refer to that development of the argument as the epistemically unconcerned version of the Wager, a version in which it does not matter what the precise epistemic status of theism or of atheism is, as long as neither is certainly true. Such a version is vulnerable to a number of objections.

First of all, many people who accept (E) as a formula appropriate for use in normal betting situations may hesitate or refuse to use it in this situation. For the conditions under which it is appropriately used may not obtain with respect to this quite unusual bet. In normal situations, for which the formula was constructed, possible payoffs are always finite in value. The insertion of an infinite value here so over-rides considerations of probability and cost as to render them nearly irrelevant. Can (E) be expected to serve its ordinary function with such an extraordinary assignment to one of its variables?

Likewise, in normal betting situations there is usually a controlled range of divergence between probability values when the cost of some bet is high. And, again, it is in such situations that (E) has its appropriate application. Often, this feature of a betting situation is not perceived as being so important. And it need not be, so long as there is, as there usually is, a direct correlation and otherwise proper sort of relation between magnitude of cost and magnitude of probability. But in this version of the Wager, there is an inverse correlation between these factors. Under such conditions, degree of divergence between probabilities becomes a concern. The epistemically unconcerned version of the Wager purports to work regardless of the disparity between the probabilities of theism and atheism, even if, for example, there is only a one in a trillion chance, or less, of theism's being true. It can be rational to distrust the formula's application under such conditions. Further, there is some serious question about the use of probability assignments at all by this version of the Wager. It seems clear that the only interpretation of probability relevant and useable here is the subjective one; yet, how are even subjective probability assignments supposed to arise out of the mere insistence that theism is not demonstrably impossible? Its mere possibility need not be taken to endow it with any positive probability at all.

Thirdly, (E) clearly functions to aid a rational gambler in maximizing his gains over the long-run. And this it does, since long-run success is compatible with the losing of many individual bets along the way. Now, despite the fact that one often hears Pascalians insist on the formula's appropriateness in this case since "there is no longer run than eternity," it is clear that in the bet concerning God we do not have a situation of repetitive wagering, in which ultimate maximization of gain is compatible with numerous losses along the way. And so again it could be argued that conditions do not obtain in which the rational bettor is best guided by (E). But of course, if (E) is not used, this form of the Wager does not work.

A fourth objection to the Wager we must consider, one raised and developed by numerous critics in recent years, is the Many Claimants Objection, one which is often characterized as resulting from a partitioning problem. The Wager, it is said, partitions the variously possible bets on the issue of God inadequately, presenting us with only two options, theism and atheism, when in reality there are many, perhaps innumerably many. And this is much more than an easily correctable oversight. First of all, there are numerous different versions of theism extant, all vying for our credence. For any which promises eternal bliss, and many do, (E) will yield an infinite expectation, as long as there is the slightest positive probability that it is true. And if mere possibility yields some positive probability, as the epistemically unconcerned version of the Wager alleges, matters are even worse. For if it is even logically possible that there exists a being who promises infinite eternal reward to all and only those who deny the existence of all other claimants to worship, including the Christian God, (E) yields a dilemma equivalent to a practical contradiction: a rational person both ought and ought not bet on, say, the Christian God. Further, as if this were not enough, not even will it be the case that some theism or other will be preferable to all forms of atheism. For consider the apparent logical possibility that there is no God and that by some weird law of nature there will be an infinite, eternally blissful after-life for all and only those who in this life live as convinced atheists. On the basic assumptions of the epistemically unconcerned version of the Wager, the expectation associated with this form of atheism will also be infinite. Clearly, we have here a serious problem.[4]

Most recent commentators have seen one or more of these objections as decisive against the Wager, sufficient to show it to have no rational force. And this is, I think, a correct judgment with respect to the epistemically unconcerned version of the Wager. But it is neither the only version of a Wager-style argument nor, I believe, the sort of version we should attribute to Pascal. When the formula (E) is allowed to work on very low probability values, even those so low as to be approaching 0, and the positive probability of a bet is thought to be provided by the mere logical possibility of its outcome, a context is created in which the production of absurd results is unavoidable. But this is not the context of the original Wager.

It is almost anyone's guess as to what Pascal's planned defense of the Christian faith would have looked like in detail had he lived to complete it. One thing that is clear though is that it was not an epistemically unconcerned project. In fact, even a fairly casual reading of the *Pensées* will show that Pascal felt it important to try to defeat *prima facie* evidential considerations which could be held to count seriously against the truth of Christian beliefs, considerations such as, for example, the hidden-ness of God, and the rejection by most of his Jewish contemporaries of the Christian claim that Jesus was the long awaited Messiah sent from God. Furthermore, although he engages in no natural theology at all, Pascal does marshal together quite a few considerations in favor of the reliability of the Bible and the trustworthiness of Christian claims. We have no reason to think that he intended his Wager argument to operate in complete isolation from any purely epistemic considerations. In fact quite the contrary is indicated even by the remarks with which he launched the argument. Recall the claim in the quote from which we began this essay that "Reason cannot decide this question." If epistemic conditions were such that Christian theism could properly receive a very low assignment of subjective probability by any well-informed rational person, and its denial a correspondingly high value, it would not be the case that "reason cannot decide this question." I think we have here sufficient textual indication that the Wager argument was intended to work only for people who judge the theism Pascal had in mind and its denial to be in rough epistemic parity.

If reason cannot decide whether the Christian God exists or not, there cannot be a clear preponderance of purely epistemic considerations either way. Thus there cannot be a great disparity between the assigned probability values of theism and atheism. If it can be rational for a person to judge these positions to be in rough epistemic parity, it can be rational to dismiss altogether one objection to the Wager we considered, the one in which hesitation is expressed concerning the application of (E) to situations with greatly disparate probability values. The objection in this context becomes irrelevant.

Likewise, the hesitation to employ (E) with an infinite value for one of its variables is groundless unless there is reason to believe that allowing such a value assignment will have obviously absurd or unacceptable consequences. A moment's consideration will show that the only problematic and absurd consequences of applying (E) with an infinite payoff value are displayed in the famous Many Claimants problem, a problem which as we have seen results only from the additional assumptions as well that (1) apparent logical possibility should be translated into some positive non-zero probability value, and (2) the Wager formula can and should be employed regardless of the probability disparity between possible bets. But if both these assumptions are rejected, the Many Claimants problem does not arise, and the importation of an infinite value into (E) has no clearly problematic results.

So holding the Wager to be appropriate only under conditions of rough epistemic parity between Christian theism and its denial avoids altogether three otherwise interesting and worrisome objections. What about the fourth we considered? We do not have here a repetitive wagering situation in which short term loss is compatible with long term gain. There is only one bet; it is either won or lost. But if (E) is thought not to be relevant, how is a decision between theism and atheism to be made? If theism and atheism are in rough epistemic parity, no decision between them can be made on purely epistemic grounds. Some form of agnosticism would be the appropriate doxastic stance if no considerations other than purely epistemic ones could or should enter into such decisions. But, according to Pascal, this is betting against God. One's doxastic stance is a form of, and a function of, behavior which amounts, in the context, to the placing of a bet. And surely there are values other than purely epistemic values which are relevant in the placing of a bet. What sorts of values? Just the ones which function in (E). So even though the wager concerning God is not only one episode in a repetitive wagering situation, there seems to be no good alternative to (E) to employ here when choosing one's bet. So given our restriction of the Wager argument to conditions of rough epistemic parity, this objection is neutralized as well.

This view of the wager is an improvement over the epistemically unconcerned version then in two respects. It seems to be more in line with Pascal's original intentions, and it is immune to certain difficult objections which plague the more contemporary version. But this version of the wager can have use for a rational person only if it can be reasonable to judge Christian theism and its denial to be in rough epistemic parity. Pascal seems to have thought this was possible. But others have offered reasons to think otherwise.

[. . .]

IV

It seems to have been Pascal's conviction that a person's epistemic condition with respect to theism and atheism is a function of his attitudes, desires, and other commitments, and that in turn these are a function of the sorts of patterns of behavior he liked to call 'habit'. It is a dangerous illusion to think of our epistemic capacities as existing and operating independently of the other features of our lives. The person who loves God, according to Pascal, is able to see that everything is created by him (781). The person with contrary passions is bereft of this perspicacity. It was Pascal's view that there exists evidence for the truth of Christian theism which exceeds, or at least equals, evidence to the contrary (835). But he was convinced that it is a person's passional state which will determine how he sees the evidence, and what he does on the basis of it.

The enjoinder to wager on God is the recommendation, on prudential grounds, to adopt a Christian form of life to the extent that one is able. Pascal thought that an entry into that sort of life pattern would have a long-term and cumulative effect on a person's attitudes, desires, and epistemic state. As contrary passions were bridled and finally put aside, he was convinced that anyone who formerly was incapable of seeing or knowing God would attain this capacity, and only with the onset of such a capacity could true faith come.

It is not an assumption of the Wager that God will reward a person for a deliberate, calculated charade of belief undertaken and maintained on grounds of the grossest self-interest. So the famous objection of William James, who was offended by such an assumption, misses the point. There is no doubt that the argument as constructed by Pascal appeals to self-interest.

But its intent and goal is to induce a wager whose outcome will yield true faith, an attitudinal state in which self-interest takes its rightful and surbordinate place as a behavior motivation. Furthermore, the Wager need not be formulated as an appeal to self-interest at all. It can be presented as an appeal to altruism. One then bets on God so that one will be in a proper position non-hypocritically to urge others to do so, thereby potentially providing them with the greatest amount of good one possibly could.

Likewise, other moral objections to the Wager are easily defeated. James found it morally offensive that God would reward those who want reward. Terence Penelhum apparently has found it repugnant that God would punish anyone who did not otherwise believe for failing to follow such a course of attempted aggrandizement.[5] Both James and Penelhum impose a conception of the eternal economy on the argument which it in no way requires and then object to their own creations. In particular, they have what we may call an inappropriately externalist conception of after-life. One reads Pascal's original wager passage in vain for the language of rewards and punishment. He does not there portray God at all as either granting or withholding benefits in accordance with how people bet. It seems on the contrary that a more internalist conception of eternal beatitude can both accord with Pascal's own Wager presentation and serve to neutralize the James and Penelhum type of objection. One's state after bodily death is then viewed as being in proper moral and spiritual continuity with one's earthly existence. Those who have hungered and thirsted after righteousness are satisfied. Those who have not, are not. Now, it might appear odd to characterize all those who align themselves with the Christian God as those who hunger and thirst after righteousness. In particular this may seem an inappropriate description of those who are, on Pascalian grounds, wagering on God. However, as indicated already, this is the sort of mind-set meant to eventuate from the particular wagering behavior recommended. Further, the infinite "payoff" as characterized in the Christian tradition, if delineated carefully enough, just may not appeal to a person with no taste for moral and spiritual good. For the heaven of Pascal is not the heaven of, say, popular Islam. It is not an infinite expansion of sensual delights. In fact it is the sort of infinite bliss which will be attractive only to those with at least a latent capacity to exemplify the attitude characterized biblically as a hunger and thirst for righteousness. And only such as these are, in the theology of Christian theism, able to commune with God at all.

It is not my intent here to defend Pascal's Wager against all extant criticism, although I think it eminently more defensible than most recent commentators have allowed. My primary aim has been merely to suggest that when we attend carefully to some important clues in Pascal's text, we can see that the sort of argument he intended is immune to numerous potent objections which have been raised against contemporary versions of the argument differing in important respects from his own. When these objections have been cleared away, it becomes possible to consider more seriously other philosophical and religious questions raised by the whole idea of Pascalian Wagering.

Notes

1 Blaise Pascal, *Pensées*, trans. A. J. Krailsheimer (New York: Penguin Books, 1966), 150.
2 Pascal, pensée 190, page 86. Hereafter citations from the *Pensées* will all be from the edition cited above, and will be given by the pensée numbering therein adopted.
3 Such a claim has been made or implied by many theists in different contexts. Recently, for example, Peter Geach has written: "Now for those who believe in an Almighty God, a man's every act is an act either of obeying or of ignoring or of defying that God . . .", "The Moral Law and the Law of God," in Paul Helm, ed. *Divine Commands and Morality* (Oxford: Oxford University Press, 1980), 173. It is easy to see how ignoring and defying God could be categorized together as acting as if there is no God.
4 One of the best recent explications of this sort of problem is Michael Martin's essay "Pascal's Wager as an Argument for Not Believing in God," *Religious Studies* 19 (1983), 57–64.
5 Terence Penelhum, *Religion and Rationality* (New York: Random House, 1971), 211–19.

3

The Ethics of Belief

W. K. Clifford

W. K. Clifford (1845–79) was an English mathematician and philosopher who taught at University College London. The following essay is a classic critique of pragmatic reasoning and defense of evidentialism. Much like Locke (see selection X.A.7), Clifford urges that one must always proportion one's belief to the evidence; however, Clifford's evidentialism has a stronger moral tone than Locke's. He regards believing without sufficient evidence as wrong, unlawful, and even sinful.

I. The Duty of Inquiry

A shipowner was about to send to sea an emigrant-ship. He knew that she was old, and not over-well built at the first; that she had seen many seas and climes, and often had needed repairs. Doubts had been suggested to him that possibly she was not seaworthy. These doubts preyed upon his mind and made him unhappy; he thought that perhaps he ought to have her thoroughly overhauled and refitted, even though this should put him to great expense. Before the ship sailed, however, he succeeded in overcoming these melancholy reflections. He said to himself that she had gone safely through so many voyages and weathered so many storms that it was idle to suppose she would not come safely home from this trip also. He would put his trust in Providence, which could hardly fail to protect all these unhappy families that were leaving their fatherland to seek for better times elsewhere. He would dismiss from his mind all ungenerous suspicions about the honesty of builders and contractors. In such ways he acquired a sincere and comfortable conviction that his vessel was thoroughly safe and seaworthy; he watched her departure with a light heart, and benevolent wishes for the success of the exiles in their

W. K. Clifford, "The Ethics of Belief" from *Lectures and Essays*, ed. Leslie Stephen and Sir Frederick Pollock, vol. 2 (London: Macmillan and Co., 1901), pp. 163–76.

strange new home that was to be; and he got his insurance-money when she went down in mid-ocean and told no tales.

What shall we say of him? Surely this, that he was verily guilty of the death of those men. It is admitted that he did sincerely believe in the soundness of his ship; but the sincerity of his conviction can in no wise help him, because *he had no right to believe on such evidence as was before him.* He had acquired his belief not by honestly earning it in patient investigation, but by stifling his doubts. And although in the end he may have felt so sure about it that he could not think otherwise, yet inasmuch as he had knowingly and willingly worked himself into that frame of mind, he must be held responsible for it.

Let us alter the case a little, and suppose that the ship was not unsound after all; that she made her voyage safely, and many others after it. Will that diminish the guilt of her owner? Not one jot. When an action is once done, it is right or wrong for ever; no accidental failure of its good or evil fruits can possibly alter that. The man would not have been innocent, he would only have been not found out. The question of right or wrong has to do with the origin of his belief, not the matter of it; not what it was, but how he got it; not whether it turned out to be true or false, but whether he had a right to believe on such evidence as was before him.

There was once an island in which some of the inhabitants professed a religion teaching neither the doctrine of original sin nor that of eternal punishment. A suspicion got abroad that the professors of this religion had made use of unfair means to get their doctrines taught to children. They were accused of wresting the laws of their country in such a way as to remove children from the care of their natural and legal guardians; and even of stealing them away and keeping them concealed from their friends and relations. A certain number of men formed themselves into a society for the purpose of agitating the public about this matter. They published grave accusations against individual citizens of the highest position and character, and did all in their power to injure these citizens in the exercise of their professions. So great was the noise they made, that a Commission was appointed to investigate the facts; but after the Commission had carefully inquired into all the evidence that could be got, it appeared that the accused were innocent. Not only had they been accused on insufficient evidence, but the evidence of their innocence was such as the agitators might easily have obtained, if they had attempted a fair inquiry. After these disclosures the inhabitants of that country looked upon the members of the agitating society, not only as persons whose judgment was to be distrusted, but also as no longer to be counted honourable men. For although they had sincerely and conscientiously believed in the charges they had made, *yet they had no right to believe on such evidence as was before them.* Their sincere convictions, instead of being honestly earned by patient inquiring, were stolen by listening to the voice of prejudice and passion.

Let us vary this case also, and suppose, other things remaining as before, that a still more accurate investigation proved the accused to have been really guilty. Would this make any difference in the guilt of the accusers? Clearly not; the question is not whether their belief was true or false, but whether they entertained it on wrong grounds. They would no doubt say, "Now you see that we were right after all; next time perhaps you will believe us." And they might be believed, but they would not thereby become honourable men. They would not be innocent, they would only be not found out. Every one of them, if he chose to examine himself *in foro conscientiæ*, would know that he had acquired and nourished a belief, when he had no right to believe on such evidence as was before him; and therein he would know that he had done a wrong thing.

It may be said, however, that in both of these supposed cases it is not the belief which is judged to be wrong, but the action following upon it. The shipowner might say, "I am perfectly certain that my ship is sound, but still I feel it my duty to have her examined, before trusting the lives of so many people to her." And it might be said to the agitator, "However convinced you were of the justice of your cause and the truth of your convictions, you ought not to have made a public attack upon any man's character until you had examined the evidence on both sides with the utmost patience and care."

In the first place, let us admit that, so far as it goes, this view of the case is right and necessary;

right, because even when a man's belief is so fixed that he cannot think otherwise, he still has a choice in regard to the action suggested by it, and so cannot escape the duty of investigating on the ground of the strength of his convictions; and necessary, because those who are not yet capable of controlling their feelings and thoughts must have a plain rule dealing with overt acts.

But this being premised as necessary, it becomes clear that it is not sufficient, and that our previous judgment is required to supplement it. For it is not possible so to sever the belief from the action it suggests as to condemn the one without condemning the other. No man holding a strong belief on one side of a question, or even wishing to hold a belief on one side, can investigate it with such fairness and completeness as if he were really in doubt and unbiassed; so that the existence of a belief not founded on fair inquiry unfits a man for the performance of this necessary duty.

Nor is that truly a belief at all which has not some influence upon the actions of him who holds it. He who truly believes that which prompts him to an action has looked upon the action to lust after it, he has committed it already in his heart. If a belief is not realised immediately in open deeds, it is stored up for the guidance of the future. It goes to make a part of that aggregate of beliefs which is the link between sensation and action at every moment of all our lives, and which is so organised and compacted together that no part of it can be isolated from the rest, but every new addition modifies the structure of the whole. No real belief, however trifling and fragmentary it may seem, is ever truly insignificant; it prepares us to receive more of its like, confirms those which resembled it before, and weakens others; and so gradually it lays a stealthy train in our inmost thoughts, which may some day explode into overt action, and leave its stamp upon our character for ever.

And no one man's belief is in any case a private matter which concerns himself alone. Our lives are guided by that general conception of the course of things which has been created by society for social purposes. Our words, our phrases, our forms and processes and modes of thought, are common property, fashioned and perfected from age to age; an heirloom which every succeeding generation inherits as a precious deposit and a sacred trust to be handed on to the next one, not unchanged but enlarged and purified, with some clear marks of its proper handiwork. Into this, for good or ill, is woven every belief of every man who has speech of his fellows. An awful privilege, and an awful responsibility, that we should help to create the world in which posterity will live.

In the two supposed cases which have been considered, it has been judged wrong to believe on insufficient evidence, or to nourish belief by suppressing doubts and avoiding investigation. The reason of this judgment is not far to seek: it is that in both these cases the belief held by one man was of great importance to other men. But forasmuch as no belief held by one man, however seemingly trivial the belief, and however obscure the believer, is ever actually insignificant or without its effect on the fate of mankind, we have no choice but to extend our judgment to all cases of belief whatever. Belief, that sacred faculty which prompts the decisions of our will, and knits into harmonious working all the compacted energies of our being, is ours not for ourselves, but for humanity. It is rightly used on truths which have been established by long experience and waiting toil, and which have stood in the fierce light of free and fearless questioning. Then it helps to bind men together, and to strengthen and direct their common action. It is desecrated when given to unproved and unquestioned statements, for the solace and private pleasure of the believer; to add a tinsel splendour to the plain straight road of our life and display a bright mirage beyond it; or even to drown the common sorrows of our kind by a self-deception which allows them not only to cast down, but also to degrade us. Whoso would deserve well of his fellows in this matter will guard the purity of his belief with a very fanaticism of jealous care, lest at any time it should rest on an unworthy object, and catch a stain which can never be wiped away.

It is not only the leader of men, statesman, philosopher, or poet, that owes this bounden duty to mankind. Every rustic who delivers in the village alehouse his slow, infrequent sentences, may help to kill or keep alive the fatal superstitions which clog his race. Every hard-worked wife of an artisan may transmit to her children beliefs which shall knit society together, or rend it in pieces. No simplicity of mind, no obscurity of station, can escape the universal duty of questioning all that we believe.

It is true that this duty is a hard one, and the doubt which comes out of it is often a very bitter thing. It leaves us bare and powerless where we thought that we were safe and strong. To know all about anything is to know how to deal with it under all circumstances. We feel much happier and more secure when we think we know precisely what to do, no matter what happens, than when we have lost our way and do not know where to turn. And if we have supposed ourselves to know all about anything, and to be capable of doing what is fit in regard to it, we naturally do not like to find that we are really ignorant and powerless, that we have to begin again at the beginning, and try to learn what the thing is and how it is to be dealt with – if indeed anything can be learnt about it. It is the sense of power attached to a sense of knowledge that makes men desirous of believing, and afraid of doubting.

This sense of power is the highest and best of pleasures when the belief on which it is founded is a true belief, and has been fairly earned by investigation. For then we may justly feel that it is common property, and holds good for others as well as for ourselves. Then we may be glad, not that *I* have learned secrets by which I am safer and stronger, but that *we men* have got mastery over more of the world; and we shall be strong, not for ourselves, but in the name of Man and in his strength. But if the belief has been accepted on insufficient evidence, the pleasure is a stolen one. Not only does it deceive ourselves by giving us a sense of power which we do not really possess, but it is sinful, because it is stolen in defiance of our duty to mankind. That duty is to guard ourselves from such beliefs as from a pestilence, which may shortly master our own body and then spread to the rest of the town. What would be thought of one who, for the sake of a sweet fruit, should deliberately run the risk of bringing a plague upon his family and his neighbours?

And, as in other such cases, it is not the risk only which has to be considered; for a bad action is always bad at the time when it is done, no matter what happens afterwards. Every time we let ourselves believe for unworthy reasons, we weaken our powers of self-control, of doubting, of judicially and fairly weighing evidence. We all suffer severely enough from the maintenance and support of false beliefs and the fatally wrong actions which they lead to, and the evil born when one such belief is entertained is great and wide. But a greater and wider evil arises when the credulous character is maintained and supported, when a habit of believing for unworthy reasons is fostered and made permanent. If I steal money from any person, there may be no harm done by the mere transfer of possession; he may not feel the loss, or it may prevent him from using the money badly. But I cannot help doing this great wrong towards Man, that I make myself dishonest. What hurts society is not that it should lose its property, but that it should become a den of thieves; for then it must cease to be society. This is why we ought not to do evil that good may come; for at any rate this great evil has come, that we have done evil and are made wicked thereby. In like manner, if I let myself believe anything on insufficient evidence, there may be no great harm done by the mere belief; it may be true after all, or I may never have occasion to exhibit it in outward acts. But I cannot help doing this great wrong towards Man, that I make myself credulous. The danger to society is not merely that it should believe wrong things, though that is great enough; but that it should become credulous, and lose the habit of testing things and inquiring into them; for then it must sink back into savagery.

The harm which is done by credulity in a man is not confined to the fostering of a credulous character in others, and consequent support of false beliefs. Habitual want of care about what I believe leads to habitual want of care in others about the truth of what is told to me. Men speak the truth to one another when each reveres the truth in his own mind and in the other's mind; but how shall my friend revere the truth in my mind when I myself am careless about it, when I believe things because I want to believe them, and because they are comforting and pleasant? Will he not learn to cry, "Peace," to me, when there is no peace? By such a course I shall surround myself with a thick atmosphere of falsehood and fraud, and in that I must live. It may matter little to me, in my cloud-castle of sweet illusions and darling lies; but it matters much to Man that

I have made my neighbours ready to deceive. The credulous man is father to the liar and the cheat; he lives in the bosom of this his family, and it is no marvel if he should become even as they are. So closely are our duties knit together, that whoso shall keep the whole law, and yet offend in one point, he is guilty of all.

To sum up: it is wrong always, everywhere, and for any one, to believe anything upon insufficient evidence.

If a man, holding a belief which he was taught in childhood or persuaded of afterwards, keeps down and pushes away any doubts which arise about it in his mind, purposely avoids the reading of books and the company of men that call in question or discuss it, and regards as impious those questions which cannot easily be asked without disturbing it – the life of that man is one long sin against mankind.

If this judgment seems harsh when applied to those simple souls who have never known better, who have been brought up from the cradle with a horror of doubt, and taught that their eternal welfare depends on *what* they believe, then it leads to the very serious question, *Who hath made Israel to sin?*

It may be permitted me to fortify this judgment with the sentence of Milton[1] –

"A man may be a heretic in the truth; and if he believe things only because his pastor says so, or the assembly so determine, without knowing other reason, though his belief be true, yet the very truth he holds becomes his heresy."

And with this famous aphorism of Coleridge[2] –

"He who begins by loving Christianity better than Truth, will proceed by loving his own sect or Church better than Christianity, and end in loving himself better than all."

Inquiry into the evidence of a doctrine is not to be made once for all, and then taken as finally settled. It is never lawful to stifle a doubt; for either it can be honestly answered by means of the inquiry already made, or else it proves that the inquiry was not complete.

"But," says one, "I am a busy man; I have no time for the long course of study which would be necessary to make me in any degree a competent judge of certain questions, or even able to understand the nature of the arguments." Then he should have no time to believe.

Notes

[Originally published in] *Contemporary Review*, January 1877.

1 *Areopagitica.*

2 *Aids to Reflection.*

4

The Will to Believe

William James

William James (1842–1910) was a professor of psychology and philosophy at Harvard, and the most influential of the American pragmatist philosophers. Some of his famous works include *The Principles of Psychology* (1890), *The Varieties of Religious Experience* (1902), and *The Will to Believe and Other Essays in Popular Philosophy* (1897), which was named after our next essay. In it, James argues that although Clifford's evidentialism is a good rule to follow in most circumstances, there are occasions in which we are within our rights to believe something even if we are not rationally compelled to believe it by the evidence.

In the recently published Life by Leslie Stephen of his brother, Fitz-James, there is an account of a school to which the latter went when he was a boy. The teacher, a certain Mr Guest, used to converse with his pupils in this wise: "Gurney, what is the difference between justification and sanctification? – Stephen, prove the omnipotence of God!" etc. In the midst of our Harvard freethinking and indifference we are prone to imagine that here at your good old orthodox College conversation continues to be somewhat upon this order; and to show you that we at Harvard have not lost all interest in these vital subjects, I have brought with me tonight something like a sermon on justification by faith to read to you – I mean an essay in justification *of* faith, a defence of our right to adopt a believing attitude in religious matters, in spite of the fact that our merely logical intellect may not have been coerced. "The Will to Believe," accordingly, is the title of my paper.

I have long defended to my own students the lawfulness of voluntarily adopted faith; but as soon as they have got well imbued with the

William James, "The Will to Believe" in *Philosophy in the Twentieth Century: An Anthology*, vol. 1, ed. and with intros by William Barrett and Henry D. Aiken (New York: Random House, 1962), extracts from pp. 241–7, 250–8. Originally published in *Essays in Pragmatism*, William James, edited by Alburey Castell, pp. 88–109. Hafner Publishing Company, Inc., New York, 1948.

logical spirit, they have as a rule refused to admit my contention to be lawful philosophically, even though in point of fact they were personally all the time chock-full of some faith or other themselves. I am all the while, however, so profoundly convinced that my own position is correct, that your invitation has seemed to me a good occasion to make my statements more clear. Perhaps your minds will be more open than those with which I have hitherto had to deal. I will be as little technical as I can, though I must begin by setting up some technical distinctions that will help us in the end.

1

Let us give the name of *hypothesis* to anything that may be proposed to our belief; and just as the electricians speak of live and dead wires, let us speak of any hypothesis as either *live* or *dead*. A live hypothesis is one which appeals as a real possibility to him to whom it is proposed. If I ask you to believe in the Mahdi, the notion makes no electric connection with your nature – it refuses to scintillate with any credibility at all. As an hypothesis it is completely dead. To an Arab, however (even if he be not one of the Mahdi's followers), the hypothesis is among the mind's possibilities: it is alive. This shows that deadness and liveness in an hypothesis are not intrinsic properties, but relations to the individual thinker. They are measured by his willingness to act. The maximum of liveness in an hypothesis means willingness to act irrevocably. Practically, that means belief; but there is some believing tendency wherever there is willingness to act at all.

Next, let us call the decision between two hypotheses an *option*. Options may be of several kinds. They may be – first, *living* or *dead*; secondly, *forced* or *avoidable*; thirdly, *momentous* or *trivial*; and for our purposes we may call an option a *genuine* option when it is of the forced, living, and momentous kind.

1. A living option is one in which both hypotheses are live ones. If I say to you: "Be a theosophist or be a Mohammedan," it is probably a dead option, because for you neither hypothesis is likely to be alive. But if I say: "Be an agnostic or be a Christian," it is otherwise: trained as you are, each hypothesis makes some appeal, however small, to your belief.

2. Next, if I say to you: "Choose between going out with your umbrella or without it," I do not offer you a genuine option, for it is not forced. You can easily avoid it by not going out at all. Similarly, if I say, "Either love me or hate me," "Either call my theory true or call it false," your option is avoidable. You may remain indifferent to me, neither loving nor hating, and you may decline to offer any judgment as to my theory. But if I say, "Either accept this truth or go without it," I put on you a forced option, for there is no standing place outside of the alternative. Every dilemma based on a complete logical disjunction, with no possibility of not choosing, is an option of this forced kind.

3. Finally, if I were Dr Nansen and proposed to you to join my North Pole expedition, your option would be momentous; for this would probably be your only similar opportunity, and your choice now would either exclude you from the North Pole sort of immortality altogether or put at least the chance of it into your hands. He who refuses to embrace a unique opportunity loses the prize as surely as if he tried and failed. *Per contra*, the option is trivial when the opportunity is not unique, when the stake is insignificant, or when the decision is reversible if it later prove unwise. Such trivial options abound in the scientific life. A chemist finds an hypothesis live enough to spend a year in its verification: he believes in it to that extent. But if his experiments prove inconclusive either way, he is quit for his loss of time, no vital harm being done.

It will facilitate our discussion if we keep all these distinctions well in mind.

2

The next matter to consider is the actual psychology of human opinion. When we look at certain facts, it seems as if our passional and volitional nature lay at the root of all our convictions. When we look at others, it seems as if they could do nothing when the intellect had once said its say. Let us take the latter facts up first.

Does it not seem preposterous on the very face of it to talk of our opinions being modifiable at will? Can our will either help or hinder our intellect in its perceptions of truth? Can we, by just willing it, believe that Abraham Lincoln's existence is a myth, and that the portraits of him in *McClure's Magazine* are all of some one else? Can we, by any effort of our will, or by any strength of wish that it were true, believe ourselves well and about when we are roaring with rheumatism in bed, or feel certain that the sum of the two one-dollar bills in our pocket must be a hundred dollars? We can *say* any of these things, but we are absolutely impotent to believe them; and of just such things is the whole fabric of the truths that we do believe in made up – matters of fact, immediate or remote, as Hume said, and relations between ideas, which are either there or not there for us if we see them so, and which if not there cannot be put there by any action of our own.

In Pascal's *Thoughts* there is a celebrated passage known in literature as Pascal's wager. In it he tries to force us into Christianity by reasoning as if our concern with truth resembled our concern with the stakes in a game of chance. Translated freely his words are these: You must either believe or not believe that God is – which will you do? Your human reason cannot say. A game is going on between you and the nature of things which at the day of judgment will bring out either heads or tails. Weigh what your gains and your losses would be if you should stake all you have on heads, or God's existence: if you win in such case, you gain eternal beatitude; if you lose, you lose nothing at all. If there were an infinity of chances, and only one for God in this wager, still you ought to stake your all on God; for though you surely risk a finite loss by this procedure, any finite loss is reasonable, even a certain one is reasonable, if there is but the possibility of infinite gain. Go, then, and take holy water, and have masses said; belief will come and stupefy your scruples – *Cela vous fera croire et vous abêtira*. Why should you not? At bottom, what have you to lose?

You probably feel that when religious faith expresses itself thus, in the language of the gaming-table, it is put to its last trumps. Surely Pascal's own personal belief in masses and holy water had far other springs; and this celebrated page of his is but an argument for others, a last desperate snatch at a weapon against the hardness of the unbelieving heart. We feel that a faith in masses and holy water adopted wilfully after such a mechanical calculation would lack the inner soul of faith's reality; and if we were ourselves in the place of the Deity, we should probably take particular pleasure in cutting off believers of this pattern from their infinite reward. It is evident that unless there be some pre-existing tendency to believe in masses and holy water, the option offered to the will by Pascal is not a living option. Certainly no Turk ever took to masses and holy water on its account; and even to us Protestants these means of salvation seem such foregone impossibilities that Pascal's logic, invoked for them specifically, leaves us unmoved. As well might the Mahdi write to us, saying, "I am the Expected One whom God has created in his effulgence. You shall be infinitely happy if you confess me; otherwise you shall be cut off from the light of the sun. Weigh, then, your infinite gain if I am genuine against your finite sacrifice if I am not!" His logic would be that of Pascal; but he would vainly use it on us, for the hypothesis he offers us is dead. No tendency to act on it exists in us to any degree.

The talk of believing by our volition seems, then, from one point of view, simply silly. From another point of view it is worse than silly, it is vile. When one turns to the magnificent edifice of the physical sciences, and sees how it was reared; what thousands of disinterested moral lives of men lie buried in its mere foundations; what patience and postponement, what choking down of preference, what submission to the icy laws of outer fact are wrought into its very stones and mortar; how absolutely impersonal it stands in its vast augustness – then how besotted and contemptible seems every little sentimentalist who comes blowing his voluntary smoke-wreaths, and pretending to decide things from out of his private dream! Can we wonder if those bred in the rugged and manly school of science should feel like spewing such subjectivism out of their mouths? The whole system of loyalties which grow up in the schools of science go dead against its toleration; so that it is only natural that those who have caught the scientific fever should pass over to the opposite extreme, and write sometimes as if the incorruptibly truthful intellect ought positively to prefer bitterness and unacceptableness to the heart in its cup.

It fortifies my soul to know
That though I perish, Truth is so –

sings Clough, while Huxley exclaims: "My only consolation lies in the reflection that, however bad our posterity may become, so far as they hold by the plain rule of not pretending to believe what they have no reason to believe, because it may be to their advantage so to pretend [the word 'pretend' is surely here redundant], they will not have reached the lowest depth of immorality." And that delicious *enfant terrible* Clifford writes: "Belief is desecrated when given to unproved and unquestioned statements for the solace and private pleasure of the believer. . . . Whoso would deserve well of his fellows in this matter will guard the purity of his belief with a very fanaticism of jealous care, lest at any time it should rest on an unworthy object, and catch a stain which can never be wiped away. . . . If [a] belief has been accepted on insufficient evidence [even though the belief be true, as Clifford on the same page explains] the pleasure is a stolen one. . . . It is sinful because it is stolen in defiance of our duty to mankind. That duty is to guard ourselves from such beliefs as from a pestilence which may shortly master our own body and then spread to the rest of the town. . . . It is wrong always, everywhere, and for every one, to believe anything upon insufficient evidence."

3

All this strikes one as healthy, even when expressed, as by Clifford, with somewhat too much of robustious pathos in the voice. Free will and simple wishing do seem, in the matter of our credences, to be only fifth wheels to the coach. Yet if any one should thereupon assume that intellectual insight is what remains after wish and will and sentimental preference have taken wing, or that pure reason is what then settles our opinions, he would fly quite as directly in the teeth of the facts.

It is only our already dead hypotheses that our willing nature is unable to bring to life again. But what has made them dead for us is for the most part a previous action of our willing nature of an antagonistic kind. When I say "willing nature," I do not mean only such deliberate volitions as may have set up habits of belief that we cannot now escape from – I mean all such factors of belief as fear and hope, prejudice and passion, imitation and partisanship, the circumpressure of our caste and set. As a matter of fact we find ourselves believing, we hardly know how or why. Mr Balfour gives the name of "authority" to all those influences, born of the intellectual climate, that make hypotheses possible or impossible for us, alive or dead. Here in this room, we all of us believe in molecules and the conservation of energy, in democracy and necessary progress, in Protestant Christianity and the duty of fighting for "the doctrine of the immortal Monroe," all for no reasons worthy of the name. We see into these matters with no more inner clearness, and probably with much less, than any disbeliever in them might possess. His unconventionality would probably have some grounds to show for its conclusions; but for us, not insight, but the *prestige* of the opinions, is what makes the spark shoot from them and light up our sleeping magazines of faith. Our reason is quite satisfied, in nine hundred and ninety-nine cases out of every thousand of us, if it can find a few arguments that will do to recite in case our credulity is criticized by some one else. Our faith is faith in some one else's faith, and in the greatest matters this is most the case. Our belief in truth itself, for instance, that there is a truth, and that our minds and it are made for each other – what is it but a passionate affirmation of desire, in which our social system backs us up? We want to have a truth; we want to believe that our experiments and studies and discussions must put us in a continually better and better position towards it; and on this line we agree to fight out our thinking lives. But if a Pyrrhonistic sceptic asks us *how we know* all this, can our logic find a reply? No! certainly it cannot. It is just one volition against another – we willing to go in for life upon a trust or assumption which he, for his part, does not care to make.[1]

As a rule we disbelieve all facts and theories for which we have no use. Clifford's cosmic emotions find no use for Christian feelings. Huxley belabors the bishops because there is no use for sacerdotalism in his scheme of life. Newman, on the contrary, goes over to Romanism, and finds all sorts of reasons good for staying there, because a priestly system is for him an organic need and delight. Why do so few "scientists" even look at the evidence for telepathy, so called? Because they think, as a leading biologist, now dead, once said to me, that even if such a thing were true, scientists ought to band together to keep it suppressed and concealed. It would undo the uniformity of Nature and all sorts of other things without which scientists cannot carry on their pursuits. But if this very man had been shown something which as a scientist he might *do* with telepathy, he might not only have examined the evidence, but even have found it good enough. This very law which the logicians would impose upon us – if I may give the name of logicians to those who would rule out our willing nature here – is based on nothing but their own natural wish to exclude all elements for which they, in their professional quality of logicians, can find no use.

Evidently, then, our non-intellectual nature does influence our convictions. There are passional tendencies and volitions which run before and others which come after belief, and it is only the latter that are too late for the fair; and they are not too late when the previous passional work has been already in their own direction. Pascal's argument, instead of being powerless, then seems a regular clincher, and is the last stroke needed to make our faith in masses and holy water complete. The state of things is evidently far from simple; and pure insight and logic, whatever they might do ideally, are not the only things that really do produce our creeds.

4

Our next duty, having recognized this mixed-up state of affairs, is to ask whether it be simply reprehensible and pathological, or whether, on the contrary, we must treat it as a normal element in making up our minds. The thesis I defend is, briefly stated, this: *Our passional nature not only lawfully may, but must, decide an option between propositions, whenever it is a genuine option that cannot by its nature be decided on intellectual grounds; for to say, under such circumstances, "Do not decide, but leave the question open," is itself a passional decision – just like deciding yes or no – and is attended with the same risk of losing the truth.* The thesis thus abstractly expressed will, I trust, soon become quite clear. But I must first indulge in a bit more of preliminary work.

[...]

7

One more point, small but important, and our preliminaries are done. There are two ways of looking at our duty in the matter of opinion – ways entirely different, and yet ways about whose difference the theory of knowledge seems hitherto to have shown very little concern. *We must know the truth*; and *we must avoid error* – these are our first and great commandments as would-be knowers; but they are not two ways of stating an identical commandment, they are two separable laws. Although it may indeed happen that when we believe the truth *A*, we escape as an incidental consequence from believing the falsehood *B*, it hardly ever happens that by merely disbelieving *B* we necessarily believe *A*. We may in escaping *B* fall into believing other falsehoods, *C* or *D*, just as bad as *B*; or we may escape *B* by not believing anything at all, not even *A*.

Believe truth! Shun error! – these, we see, are two materially different laws; and by choosing between them we may end by coloring differently our whole intellectual life. We may regard the chase for truth as paramount, and the avoidance of error as secondary; or we may, on the other hand, treat the avoidance of error as more imperative, and let truth take its chance. Clifford, in the instructive passage which I have quoted, exhorts us to the latter course. Believe nothing, he tells us, keep your mind in suspense forever, rather than by closing it on insufficient evidence incur the awful risk of believing lies. You, on the other hand, may think that the risk of being in error is a very small matter when compared with the blessings of real knowledge, and be ready to be duped many times in your investigation rather than postpone indefinitely the chance of guessing true. I myself find it impossible to go with Clifford. We must remember that these feelings of our duty about either truth or error are in any case only expressions of our passional life. Biologically considered, our minds are as ready to grind out falsehood as veracity, and he who says, "Better go without belief forever than believe a lie!" merely shows his own preponderant private horror of becoming a dupe. He may be critical of many of his desires and fears, but this fear he slavishly obeys. He cannot imagine any one questioning its binding force. For my own part, I have also a horror of being duped; but I can believe that worse things than being duped may happen to a man in this world: so Clifford's exhortation has to my ears a thoroughly fantastic sound. It is like a general informing his soldiers that it is better to keep out of battle forever than to risk a single wound. Not so are victories either over enemies or over nature gained. Our errors are surely not such awfully solemn things. In a world where we are so certain to incur them in spite of all our caution, a certain lightness of heart seems healthier than this excessive nervousness on their behalf. At any rate, it seems the fittest thing for the empiricist philosopher.

8

And now, after all this introduction, let us go straight at our question. I have said, and now repeat it, that not only as a matter of fact do we find our passional nature influencing us in our opinions, but that there are some options between opinions in which this influence must be regarded both as an inevitable and as a lawful determinant of our choice.

I fear here that some of you my hearers will begin to scent danger, and lend an inhospitable ear. Two first steps of passion you have indeed had to admit as necessary – we must think so as to avoid dupery, and we must think so as to gain truth; but the surest path to those ideal consummations, you will probably consider, if from now onwards to take no further passional step.

Well, of course, I agree as far as the facts will allow. Wherever the option between losing truth and gaining it is not momentous, we can throw the chance of *gaining truth* away, and at any rate save ourselves from any chance of *believing falsehood*, by not making up our minds at all till objective evidence has come. In scientific questions, this is almost always the case; and even in human affairs in general, the need of acting is seldom so urgent that a false belief to act on is better than no belief at all. Law courts, indeed, have to decide on the best evidence attainable for the moment, because a judge's duty is to make law as well as to ascertain it, and (as a learned judge once said to me) few cases are worth spending much time over: the great thing is to have them decided on *any* acceptable principle, and got out of the way. But in our dealings with objective nature we obviously are recorders, not makers, of the truth; and decisions for the mere sake of deciding promptly and getting on to the next business would be wholly out of place. Throughout the breadth of physical nature facts are what they are quite independently of us, and seldom is there any such hurry about them that the risks of being duped by believing a premature theory need be faced. The questions here are always trivial options, the hypotheses are hardly living (at any rate not living for us spectators) the choice between believing truth or falsehood is seldom forced. The attitude of sceptical balance is therefore the absolutely wise one if we would escape mistakes. What difference, indeed, does it make to most of us whether we have or have not a theory of the Röntgen rays, whether we believe or not in mind-stuff, or have a conviction about the causality of conscious states? It makes no difference. Such options are not forced on us. On every account it is better not to make them, but still keep weighing reasons *pro et contra* with an indifferent hand.

I speak, of course, here of the purely judging mind. For purposes of discovery such indifference is to be less highly recommended, and science would be far less advanced than she is if the passionate desires of individuals to get their own faiths confirmed had been kept out of the game. See for example the sagacity which Spencer and Weismann now display. On the other hand, if you want an absolute duffer in an investigation, you must, after all, take the man who has no interest whatever in its results: he is the warranted incapable, the positive fool. The most useful investigator, because the most sensitive observer, is always he whose eager interest in one side of the question is balanced by an equally keen nervousness lest he become deceived.[2] Science has organized this nervousness into a regular *technique*, her so-called method of verification; and she has fallen so deeply in love with the method that one may even say she has ceased to care for truth by itself at all. It is only truth as technically verified that interests her. The truth of truths might come in merely affirmative form, and she would decline to touch it. Such truth as that, she might repeat with Clifford, would be stolen in defiance of her duty to mankind. Human passions, however, are stronger than technical rules. "*Le cœur a ses raisons*," as Pascal says, "*que la raison ne connaît pas*"; and however indifferent to all but the bare rules of the game the umpire, the abstract intellect, may be, the concrete players who furnish him the materials to judge of are usually, each one of them, in love with some pet "live hypothesis" of his own. Let us agree, however, that wherever there is no forced option, the dispassionately judicial intellect with no pet hypothesis, saving us, as it does, from dupery at any rate, ought to be our ideal.

The question next arises: Are there not somewhere forced options in our speculative questions, and can we (as men who may be interested at least as much in positively gaining truth as in merely escaping dupery) always wait with impunity till the coercive evidence shall have arrived? It seems *a priori* improbable that the truth should be so nicely adjusted to our needs and powers as that. In the great boarding-house of nature, the cakes and the butter and the syrup seldom come out so even and leave the plates so clean. Indeed, we should view them with scientific suspicion if they did.

9

Moral questions immediately present themselves as questions whose solution cannot wait for sensible proof. A moral question is a question not of what sensibly exists, but of what is good, or would be good if it did exist. Science can tell us what exists; but to compare the *worths*, both of what exists and of what does not exist, we must consult not science, but what Pascal calls our heart. Science herself consults her heart when she lays it down that the infinite ascertainment of fact and correction of false belief are the supreme goods for man. Challenge the statement, and science can only repeat it oracularly, or else prove it by showing that such ascertainment and correction bring man all sorts of other goods which man's heart in turn declares. The question of having moral beliefs at all or not having them is decided by our will. Are our moral preferences true or false, or are they only odd biological phenomena, making things good or bad for *us*, but in themselves indifferent? How can your pure intellect decide? If your heart does not *want* a world of moral reality, your head will assuredly never make you believe in one.

[. . .]

Moral scepticism can no more be refuted or proved by logic than intellectual scepticism can. When we stick to it that there *is* truth (be it of either kind), we do so with our whole nature, and resolve to stand or fall by the results. The sceptic with his whole nature adopts the doubting attitude; but which of us is the wiser, Omniscience only knows.

Turn now from these wide questions of good to a certain class of questions of fact, questions concerning personal relations, states of mind between one man and another. *Do you like me or not?* – for example. Whether you do or not depends, in countless instances, on whether I meet you half-way, am willing to assume that you must like me, and show you trust and expectation. The previous faith on my part in your liking's existence is in such cases what makes your liking come. But if I stand aloof, and refuse to budge an inch until I have objective evidence, until you shall have done something apt, as the absolutists say, *ad extorquendum assensum meum*, ten to one your liking never comes. How many women's hearts are vanquished by the mere sanguine insistence of some man that they *must* love him! He will not consent to the hypothesis that they cannot. The desire for a certain kind of truth here brings about that special truth's existence; and so it is in innumerable cases of other sorts. Who gains promotions, boons, appointments, but the man in whose life they are seen to play the part of live hypotheses, who discounts them, sacrifices other things for their sake before they have come, and takes risks for them in advance? His faith acts on the powers above him as a claim, and creates its own verification.

A social organism of any sort whatever, large or small, is what it is because each member proceeds to his own duty with a trust that the other members will simultaneously do theirs. Wherever a desired result is achieved by the co-operation of many independent persons, its existence as a fact is a pure consequence of the precursive faith in one another of those immediately concerned. A government, an army, a commercial system, a ship, a college, an athletic team, all exist on this condition, without which not only is nothing achieved, but nothing is even attempted. A whole train of passengers (individually brave enough) will be looted by a few highwaymen, simply because the latter can count on one another, while each passenger fears that if he makes a movement of resistance, he will be shot before any one else backs him up. If we believed that the whole car-full would rise at once with us, we should each severally rise, and train-robbing would never even be attempted. There are, then, cases where a fact cannot come at all unless a preliminary faith exists in its coming. *And where faith in a fact can help create the fact*, that would be an insane logic which should say that faith running ahead of scientific evidence is the "lowest kind of immorality" into which a thinking being can fall. Yet such is the logic by which our scientific absolutists pretend to regulate our lives!

10

In truths dependent on our personal action, then, faith based on desire is certainly a lawful and possibly an indispensable thing.

But now, it will be said, these are all childish human cases, and have nothing to do with great cosmical matters, like the question of religious faith. Let us then pass on to that. Religions differ so much in their accidents that in discussing the religious question we must make it very generic and broad. What then do we now mean by the religious hypothesis? Science says things are; morality says some things are better than other things; and religion says essentially two things.

First, she says that the best things are the more eternal things, the overlapping things, the things in the universe that throw the last stone, so to speak, and say the final word. "Perfection is eternal" – this phrase of Charles Secrétan seems a good way of putting this first affirmation of religion, an affirmation which obviously cannot yet be verified scientifically at all.

The second affirmation of religion is that we are better off even now if we believe her first affirmation to be true.

Now, let us consider what the logical elements of this situation are *in case the religious hypothesis in both its branches be really true.* (Of course, we must admit that possibility at the outset. If we are to discuss the question at all, it must involve a living option. If for any of you religion be a hypothesis that cannot, by any living possibility, be true, then you need go no farther. I speak to the "saving remnant" alone.) So proceeding, we see, first, that religion offers itself as a *momentous* option. We are supposed to gain, even now, by our belief, and to lose by our non-belief, a certain vital good. Secondly, religion is a *forced* option, so far as that good goes. We cannot escape the issue by remaining sceptical and waiting for more light, because, although we do avoid error in that way *if religion be untrue*, we lose the good, *if it be true*, just as certainly as if we positively chose to disbelieve. It is as if a man should hesitate indefinitely to ask a certain woman to marry him because he was not perfectly sure that she would prove an angel after he brought her home. Would he not cut himself off from that particular angel-possibility as decisively as if he went and married some one else? Scepticism, then, is not avoidance of option; it is option of a certain particular kind of risk. *Better risk loss of truth than chance of error* – that is your faith-vetoer's exact position. He is actively playing his stake as much as the believer is; he is backing the field against the religious hypothesis, just as the believer is backing the religious hypothesis against the field. To preach scepticism to us as a duty until "sufficient evidence" for religion be found, is tantamount therefore to telling us, when in presence of the religious hypothesis, that to yield to our fear of its being error is wiser and better than to yield to our hope that it may be true. It is not intellect against all passions, then; it is only intellect with one passion laying down its law. And by what, forsooth, is the supreme wisdom of this passion warranted? Dupery for dupery, what proof is there that dupery through hope is so much worse than dupery through fear? I, for one, can see no proof; and I simply refuse obedience to the scientist's command to imitate his kind of option, in a case where my own stake is important enough to give me the right to choose my own form of risk. If religion be true and the evidence for it be still insufficient, I do not wish, by putting your extinguisher upon my nature (which feels to me as if it had after all some business in this matter), to forfeit my sole chance in life of getting upon the winning side – that chance depending, of course, on my willingness to run the risk of acting as if my passional need of taking the world religiously might be prophetic and right.

All this is on the supposition that it really may be prophetic and right, and that, even to us who are discussing the matter, religion is a live hypothesis which may be true. Now, to most of us religion comes in a still further way that makes a veto on our active faith even more illogical. The more perfect and more eternal aspect of the universe is represented in our religions as having personal form. The universe is no longer a mere *It* to us, but a *Thou*, if we are religious; and any relation that may be possible from person to person might be possible here. For instance, although in one sense we are passive portions of the universe, in another we show a curious autonomy, as if we were small active centres on our own account. We feel, too, as if the appeal of religion to us were made to our own active good-will, as if evidence might be forever withheld from us unless we met the hypothesis half-way. To take a trivial illustration: just as a man who in a company of gentlemen made no advances, asked a warrant for every concession, and believed no one's word without proof, would cut himself off by such churlishness from all the social rewards that a more trusting spirit would earn – so here, one who should shut himself up in snarling logicality and try to make the gods extort his recognition willy-nilly, or not get it at all, might cut himself off forever from his only opportunity of making the gods' acquaintance. This feeling, forced on us we know not whence, that by obstinately believing that there are gods (although not to do so would be so easy both for our logic and our life) we are doing the universe the deepest service we can, seems part of the living essence of the religious hypothesis. If the hypothesis *were* true in all its parts, including this one, then pure intellectualism, with its veto on our making willing advances, would be an absurdity; and some participation of our sympathetic nature would be logically required. I, therefore, for one, cannot see my way to accepting the agnostic rules for truth-seeking, or willfully agree to keep my willing nature out of the game. I cannot do so for this plain reason, that *a rule of thinking which would absolutely prevent me from acknowledging certain kinds of truth if those kinds of truth were really there, would be an irrational rule.* That for me is the long and short of the formal logic of the situation, no matter what the kinds of truth might materially be.

I confess I do not see how this logic can be escaped. But sad experience makes me fear that some of you may still shrink from radically saying with me, in *abstracto*, that we have the right to believe at our own risk any hypothesis that is live enough to tempt our will. I suspect, however, that if this is so, it is because you have got away from the abstract logical point of view altogether, and are thinking (perhaps without realizing it) of some particular religious hypothesis which for you is dead. The freedom to "believe what we will" you apply to the case of some patent superstition; and the faith you think of is the faith defined by the schoolboy when he said, "Faith is when you believe something that you know ain't true." I can only repeat that this is misapprehension. *In concreto*, the freedom to believe can only cover living options which the intellect of the individual cannot by itself resolve; and living options never seem absurdities to him who has them to consider. When I look at the religious question as it really puts itself to concrete men, and when I think of all the possibilities which both practically and theoretically it involves, then this command that we shall put a stopper on our heart, instincts, and courage, and *wait* – acting of course meanwhile more or less as if religion were *not* true[3] – till doomsday, or till such time as our intellect and senses working together may have raked in evidence enough – this command, I say, seems to me the queerest idol ever manufactured in the philosophic cave. Were we scholastic absolutists, there might be more excuse. If we had an infallible intellect with its objective certitudes, we might feel ourselves disloyal to such a perfect organ of knowledge in not trusting to it exclusively, in not waiting for its releasing word. But if we are empiricists, if we believe that no bell in us tolls to let us know for certain when truth is in our grasp, then it seems a piece of idle fantasticality to preach so solemnly our duty of waiting for the bell. Indeed we *may* wait if we will – I hope you do not think that I am denying that – but if we do so, we do so at our peril as much as if we believed. In either case we *act*, taking our life in our hands. No one of us ought to issue vetoes to the other, nor should we bandy words of abuse. We ought, on the contrary, delicately and profoundly to respect one another's mental freedom: then only shall we bring about the intellectual republic; then only shall we have that spirit of inner tolerance without which all our outer tolerance is soulless, and which is empiricism's glory; then only shall we live and let live, in speculative as well as in practical things.

I began by a reference to Fitz-James Stephen; let me end by a quotation from him. "What do you think of yourself? What do you think of the world? . . . These are questions with which all must deal as it seems good to them. They are riddles of the Sphinx, and in some way or other we must deal with them. . . . In all important transactions of life we have to take a leap in the dark. . . . If we decide to leave the riddles unanswered, that is a choice; if we waver in our answer, that, too, is a choice: but whatever choice we make, we make it at our peril. If a man chooses to turn his back altogether on God and the future, no one can prevent him; no one can show beyond reasonable doubt that he is mistaken. If a man thinks otherwise and acts as he thinks, I do not see that any one can prove that *he* is mistaken. Each must act as he thinks best; and if he is wrong, so much the worse for him. We stand on a mountain pass in the midst of whirling snow and blinding mist, through which we get glimpses now and then of paths which may be deceptive. If we stand still we shall be frozen to death. If we take the wrong road we shall be dashed to pieces. We do not certainly know whether there is any right one. What must we do? 'Be strong and of a good courage.' Act for the best, hope for the best, and take what comes. . . . If death ends all, we cannot meet death better."[4]

Notes

1 Compare the admirable page 310 in S. H. Hodgson's *Time and Space*, London, 1865.

2 Compare Wilfrid Ward's Essay, "The Wish to Believe," in his *Witnesses to the Unseen*, Macmillan & Co., 1893.

3 Since belief is measured by action, he who forbids us to believe religion to be true, necessarily also forbids us to act as we should if we did believe it to be true. The whole defence of religious faith hinges upon action. If the action required or inspired by the religious hypothesis is in no way different from that dictated by the naturalistic hypothesis, then religious faith is a pure superfluity, better pruned away, and controversy about its legitimacy is a piece of idle trifling, unworthy of serious minds. I myself believe, of course, that the religious hypothesis gives to the world an expression which specifically determines our reactions, and makes them in a large part unlike what they might be on a purely naturalistic scheme of belief.

4 *Liberty, Equality, Fraternity*, p. 353, 2nd edition. London, 1874.

XI

SCIENCE, RELIGION, AND NATURALISM

Introduction

The medieval philosophers worried about a conflict between religion and philosophy. The modern worry is more apt to be about a conflict between religion and science. Even if religion and science never conflict, apparent conflict is sufficient to produce a challenge for belief, and there are a number of questions we can ask about what it is reasonable to believe. One such question is this: Is it ever reasonable to believe something that conflicts with the best science of the day? A second and quite different question is this: Is it ever reasonable to believe anything that science cannot explain? The issue of whether it is ever reasonable to believe a miracle occurred can be associated with either one of these questions. If a miracle is an incident in which a law of nature appears to be violated, we might think that it is something that science cannot explain, or instead we might think that it is something that science maintains cannot happen. Aquinas says that a miracle is an event wrought by God that is above nature, but it is not contrary to nature. That is because God is related to everything that happens as the artist is related to a work of art. Nothing brought about by the prime agent is contrary to nature. Nonetheless, miracles are violations of the usual established order of events and no natural explanation will suffice.

Like Aquinas, Locke defines a miracle as an event that is against the established order of nature and which is divine in origin. He argues that it is reasonable to think that miracles have occurred based on testimony, and miracles are confirmation that the worker of miracles (e.g. Moses or Jesus) comes from God and that their word is divinely revealed. In the selection from Locke's *Essay Concerning Human Understanding* in section X, Locke argues that faith is belief based on revelation, but reason determines whether something *is* a revelation – that is, that it comes from God. That reading is a good companion piece to Locke's essay on miracles in this section because of the way Locke links miracles, revelation, and faith.

Hume's famous argument that it is never rational to believe a miracle has occurred is based on the idea that the probability that the testimony of a miracle is false is always greater than the probability that the miracle occurred, even when the source of the testimony is otherwise reliable. Many philosophers have offered responses to Hume. In this collection we have chosen an essay by George Mavrodes, who argues that our ordinary cognitive life provides numerous counterexamples to Hume's principles of evidence and probability.

Another question we can ask about the relation between science and religion is this: When is a question scientific, and when is it metaphysical or religious? The Galileo affair was partly a dispute about the authority to interpret Scripture, but one of the outcomes of that crisis was the independence of science in the area of discoveries about the natural world. In one of his two arguments for the compatibility of evolution and divine Providence, theologian John Haught argues that both evolutionary materialism and Intelligent Design Theory do not clearly distinguish between metaphysics and science. In contrast, Intelligent Design Theorists such as William Dembski argue that Darwinism is materialist atheism in disguise and ought to be rejected by theists.

In contemporary philosophy the words "materialism" and "naturalism" have many different meanings. One of the senses of naturalism is the metaphysical thesis that nothing exists except the physical universe, the world studied by science. Alvin Plantinga argues that on the hypothesis of naturalism the probability that a belief in naturalism is true is either low or inscrutable. That is, the hypothesis of naturalism has the consequence that the hypothesis itself is unlikely to be true. If naturalism is true, you should not believe it. If naturalism is false, you should not believe it. Therefore, you should not believe it. In reply, Timothy O'Connor, a fellow theist, argues that naturalism has nothing to fear from Plantinga's argument.

The final readings in this book highlight a contemporary debate over the limits of the practices of science, religion, and philosophy. This book is not about science, but hopefully, it includes enough work from the history of philosophy of religion to enable readers to understand the contours of the practice of philosophy as applied to the practice of religion.

A

Miracles

1

Miracles

Thomas Aquinas

Thomas Aquinas (1225–74) was a Dominican friar and arguably the most influential Christian philosopher and theologian of all time. In this selection from his *Summa Contra Gentiles* Aquinas discusses the nature of miracles and distinguishes several kinds or ranks of miracles. Aquinas held that created things are incapable of producing any effects by themselves; created beings continually depend upon God for their continued existence, and in order to produce any effects they require divine concurrence or cooperation. Since God's involvement in nature is so ubiquitous Aquinas argues that nothing God does can properly be described as *contrary to* nature, although it may be *beyond* or *different from* the usual order of nature.

That the things which God does beyond the Order of Nature are not Contrary to Nature

Since God is prime agent, all things inferior to Him are as His instruments. But instruments are made to serve the end of the prime agent, according as they are moved by Him: therefore it is not contrary to, but very much in accordance with, the nature of the instrument, for it to be moved by the prime agent. Neither is it contrary to nature for created things to be moved in any way whatsoever (*qualitercunque*) by God: for they were made to serve Him.

4. The first measure of every being and of every nature is God, seeing that He is the first being and canse of being to all. And since everything must be judged by its measure, that must be called 'natural' to a thing whereby it is conformed to its measure, or standard. That then will be natural to a thing, which has been put into it by God. Therefore, though something further be impressed upon a thing, making it otherwise than as it was before, that is not against nature.

St Thomas Aquinas, *Of God and His Creatures*, trans. of the *Summa Contra Gentiles of Saint Thomas Aquinas* by Joseph Rickaby (London: Burns and Oates, 1905), chs 100–2.

5. All creatures stand to God as the products of art to the artist (B. II, Chap. XXIV). Hence all nature may be called an artistic product of divine workmanship (*artificiatum divinae artis*). But it is not contrary to the notion of workmanship for the artist to work something to a different effect in his work, even after he has given it the first form. Neither then is it contrary to nature if God works something in natural things to a different effect from that which the ordinary course of nature involves.

Hence Augustine says: 'God, the Creator and Founder of all natures, does nothing contrary to nature, because to every creature that is natural which He makes so, of whom is all measure, number and order of nature.'

Of Miracles

Things that are done occasionally by divine power outside of the usual established order of events are commonly called miracles (wonders). We wonder when we see an effect and do not know the cause. And because one and the same cause is sometimes known to some and unknown to others, it happens that of the witnesses of the effect some wonder and some do not wonder: thus an astronomer does not wonder at seeing an eclipse of the sun, at which a person that is ignorant of astronomy cannot help wondering. An event is wonderful relatively to one man and not to another. The absolutely wonderful is that which has a cause absolutely hidden. This then is the meaning of the word 'miracle,' an event of itself full of wonder, not to this man or that man only. Now the cause absolutely hidden to every man is God, inasmuch as no man in this life can mentally grasp the essence of God (Chap. XLVII). Those events then are properly to be styled miracles, which happen by divine power beyond the order commonly observed in nature.

Of these miracles there are several ranks and orders. Miracles of the highest rank are those in which something is done by God that nature can never do. Miracles of the second rank are those in which God does something that nature can do, but not in that sequence and connexion. Thus it is a work of nature that an animal should live, see and walk: but that it should live after death, see after blindness, walk after lameness, these things nature is powerless to effect, but God sometimes brings them about miraculously. A miracle of the third rank is something done by God, which is usually done by the operation of nature, but is done in this case without the working of natural principles, as when one is cured by divine power of a fever, in itself naturally curable, or when it rains without any working of the elements.

That God Alone Works Miracles

What is entirely subject to established order cannot work beyond that order. But every creature is subject to the order which God has established in nature. No creature therefore can work beyond this order, which working beyond the order of nature is the meaning of working miracles.

2. When any finite power works the proper effect to which it is determined, that is no miracle, though it may surprise one who does not understand the operation. But the power of every creature is limited to some definite effect, or effects. Whatever therefore is done by the power of any creature cannot properly be called a miracle. But what is done by the power of God, infinite and incomprehensible, is properly a miracle.

3. Every creature in its action requires some subject to act upon: for it belongs to God alone to make a thing out of nothing (B. II, Chap. XXI). But nothing that requires a subject for its action can act except to the production of those effects to which that subject is in potentiality: for the work of action upon a subject is to educe that subject from potentiality to actuality. As then a creature can never create, so it can never act upon a thing except to the production of that which is in the potentiality of that thing. But in many miracles done by divine power a thing is done, which is not in the potentiality of that upon which it is done, as in the raising of the dead.

Hence it is said of God: *Who doth great wonderful works alone (Ps. cxxxv, 4).*

2

A Discourse of Miracles

John Locke

John Locke (1632–1704) was a British philosopher and medical doctor who, as a result of his friendship with the Earl of Shaftesbury, also had an active public political life. Our next reading is his *A Discourse of Miracles* in which Locke discusses the definition and purpose of miracles. At the end of his essay Locke informs his readers that it was "occasioned by my reading Mr. Fleetwood's *Essay on Miracles*, and the letter writ to him on that subject. The one of them defining a miracle to be an extraordinary operation performable by God alone: and the other writing of miracles without any definition of a miracle at all." Locke considers Fleetwood's definition useless since we have only a limited understanding of the laws of nature, and hence of what is "performable by God alone"; he proposes instead that miracles must be defined in terms of what *seems to a spectator* to be contrary to natural laws. Locke then discusses the role of miracles in attesting to the authenticity of divine revelations.

To discourse of miracles without defining what one means by the word miracle, is to make a shew, but in effect to talk of nothing.

A miracle then I take to be a sensible operation, which, being above the comprehension of the spectator, and in his opinion contrary to the established course of nature, is taken by him to be divine.

He that is present at the fact, is a spectator. He that believes the history of the facts, puts himself in the place of a spectator.

This definition, 'tis probable, will not escape these two exceptions.

1. That hereby what is a miracle is made very uncertain; for it depending on the opinion of the spectator, that will be a miracle to one which will not be so to another.

John Locke, "A Discourse of Miracles" from *The Reasonableness of Christianity*, ed. I. T. Ramsey (Stanford, CA: Stanford University Press, 1958), pp. 79–87.

In answer to which, it is enough to say, that this objection is of no force, but in the mouth of one who can produce a definition of a miracle not liable to the same exception, which I think not easy to do; for it being agreed, that a miracle must be that which surpasses the force of nature in the established, steady laws of causes and effects, nothing can be taken to be a miracle but what is judged to exceed those laws. Now every one being able to judge of those laws only by his own acquaintance with Nature; and notions of its force (which are different in different men) it is unavoidable that that should be a miracle to one, which is not so to another.

2. Another objection to this definition, will be, that the notion of a miracle thus enlarged, may come sometimes to take in operations that have nothing extraordinary or supernatural in them, and thereby invalidate the use of miracles for the attesting of divine revelation.

To which I answer, not at all, if the testimony which divine revelation receives from miracles be rightly considered.

To know that any revelation is from God, it is necessary to know that the messenger that delivers it is sent from God, and that cannot be known but by some credential given him by God himself. Let us see then whether miracles, in my sense, be not such credentials, and will not infallibly direct us right in the search of divine revelation.

It is to be considered, that divine revelation receives testimony from no other miracles, but such as are wrought to witness his mission from God who delivers the revelation. All other miracles that are done in the world, how many or great soever, revelation is not concerned in. Cases wherein there has been, or can be need of miracles for the confirmation of revelation, are fewer than perhaps is imagined. The heathen world, amidst an infinite and uncertain jumble of deities, fables and worships, had no room for a divine attestation of any one against the rest. Those owners of many gods were at liberty in their worship; and no one of their divinities pretending to be the one only true God, no one of them could be supposed in the pagan scheme to make use of miracles to establish his worship alone, or to abolish that of the other; much less was there any use of miracles to confirm any articles of faith, since no one of them had any such to propose as necessary to be believed by their votaries. And therefore I do not remember any miracles recorded in the Greek or Roman writers, as done to confirm any one's mission or doctrine. Conformable hereunto we find St Paul, 1 Cor. i. 22, takes notice that the Jews ('tis true) required miracles, but as for the Greeks they looked after something else; they knew no need or use there was of miracles to recommend any religion to them. And indeed it is an astonishing mark how far the God of this world had blinded men's minds, if we consider that the Gentile world received and stuck to a religion, which, not being derived from reason, had no sure foundation in revelation. They knew not its original, nor the authors of it, nor seemed concerned to know from whence it came, or by whose authority delivered; and so had no mention or use of miracles for its confirmation. For though there were here and there some pretences to revelation, yet there were not so much as pretences to miracles that attested it.

If we will direct our thoughts by what has been, we must conclude that miracles, as the credentials of a messenger delivering a divine religion, have no place but upon a supposition of one only true God; and that it is so in the nature of the thing, and cannot be otherwise, I think will be made appear in the sequel of this discourse. Of such who have come in the name of the one only true God, professing to bring a law from him, we have in history a clear account but of three, viz. Moses, Jesus and Mahomet. For what the Persees say of their Zoroaster, or the Indians of their Brama (not to mention all the wild stories of the religions farther east) is so obscure, or so manifestly fabulous, that no account can be made of it. Now of the three before-mentioned, Mahomet having none to produce, pretends to no miracles for the vouching of his mission; so that the only revelations that come attested by miracles, being only those of Moses and Christ, and they confirming each other, the business of miracles, as it stands really in matter of fact, has no manner of difficulty in it; and I think the most scrupulous or sceptical cannot from miracles raise the least doubt against the divine revelation of the gospel.

But since the speculative and learned will be putting of cases which never were, and it may be presumed never will be; since scholars and disputants will be raising of questions where there are none, and enter upon debates whereof there is no need; I crave leave to say, that he who comes with a message from God to be delivered to the world, cannot be refused belief if he vouches his mission by a miracle, because his credentials have a right to it. For every rational thinking man must conclude as Nicodemus did, "We know that thou art a teacher come from God, for no man can do these signs which thou doest, except God be with him."

For example, Jesus of Nazareth professes himself sent from God: He with a word calms a tempest at sea. This one looks on as a miracle, and consequently cannot but receive his doctrine. Another thinks this might be the effect of chance, or skill in the weather and no miracle, and so stands out; but afterwards seeing him walk on the sea, owns that for a miracle and believes; which yet upon another has not that force, who suspects it may possibly be done by the assistance of a spirit. But yet the same person, seeing afterwards Our Saviour cure an inveterate palsy by a word, admits that for a miracle, and becomes a convert. Another overlooking it in this instance, afterwards finds a miracle in his giving sight to one born blind, or in raising the dead, or his raising himself from the dead, and so receives his doctrine as a revelation coming from God. By all which it is plain, that where the miracle is admitted, the doctrine cannot be rejected; it comes with the assurance of a divine attestation to him that allows the miracle, and he cannot question its truth.

The next thing then is, what shall be a sufficient inducement to take any extraordinary operation to be a miracle, i.e. wrought by God himself for the attestation of a revelation from him?

And to this I answer, the carrying with it the marks of a greater power than appears in opposition to it. For:

1. First, this removes the main difficulty where it presses hardest, and clears the matter from doubt, when extraordinary and supernatural operations are brought to support opposite missions, about which methinks more dust has been raised by men of leisure than so plain a matter needed. For since God's power is paramount to all, and no opposition can be made against him with an equal force to his; and since his honour and goodness can never be supposed to suffer his messenger and his truth to be born down by the appearance of a greater power on the side of an impostor, and in favour of a lie; wherever there is an opposition, and two pretending to be sent from heaven clash, the signs, which carry with them the evident marks of a greater power, will always be a certain and unquestionable evidence, that the truth and divine mission are on that side on which they appear. For though the discovery, how the lying wonders are or can be produced, be beyond the capacity of the ignorant, and often beyond the conception of the most knowing spectator, who is therefore forced to allow them in his apprehension to be above the force of natural causes and effects; yet he cannot but know they are not seals set by God to his truth for the attesting of it, since they are opposed by miracles that carry the evident marks of a greater and superior power, and therefore they cannot at all shake the authority of one so supported. God can never be thought to suffer that a lie, set up in opposition to a truth coming from him, should be backed with a greater power than he will shew for the confirmation and propagation of a doctrine which he has revealed, to the end it might be believed. The producing of serpents, blood and frogs, by the Egyptian sorcerers and by Moses, could not to the spectators but appear equally miraculous, which of the pretenders then had their mission from God: and the truth on their side could not have been determined if the matter had rested there. But when Moses's serpent ate up theirs, when he produced lice which they could not, the decision was easy. 'Twas plain Jannes and Jambres acted by an inferior power, and their operations, how marvellous and extraordinary soever, could not in the least bring in question Moses's mission; that stood the firmer for this opposition, and remained the more unquestionable after this, than if no such signs had been brought against it.

So likewise the number, variety and greatness of the miracles, wrought for the confirmation of the doctrine delivered by Jesus Christ, carry with them such strong marks of an extraordinary divine power, that the truth of his mission will stand firm and unquestionable, till any one rising up in opposition to him shall do greater miracles than he and his apostles did. For any thing less will not be of weight to turn the scales in the opinion of any one, whether of an inferior or more exalted understanding. This is one of those palpable truths and trials, of which all mankind are judges; and there needs no assistance of learning, no deep thought to come to a certainty in it. Such care has God taken that no pretended revelation should stand in competition with what is truly divine, that we need but open our eyes to see and be sure which came from him. The marks of his over-ruling power accompany it; and therefore to this day we find, that wherever the gospel comes, it prevails to the beating down the strongholds of Satan, and the dislodging the Prince of the Power of Darkness, driving him away with all his living wonders; which is a standing miracle, carrying with it the testimony of superiority.

What is the uttermost power of natural agents or created beings, men of the greatest reach cannot discover; but that it is not equal to God's omnipotency is obvious to everyone's understanding; so that the superior power is an easy, as well as sure guide to divine revelation, attested by miracles where they are brought as credentials to an embassy from God.

And thus upon the same grounds of superiority of power, uncontested revelation will stand too.

For the explaining of which, it may be necessary to premise:

1. That no mission can be looked on to be divine, that delivers any thing derogating from the honour of the one, only, true, invisible God, or inconsistent with natural religion and the rules of morality: because God having discovered to men the unity and majesty of his eternal Godhead, and the truths of natural religion and morality by the light of reason, he cannot be supposed to back the contrary by revelation; for that would be to destroy the evidence and the use of reason, without which men cannot be able to distinguish divine revelation from diabolical imposture.

2. That it cannot be expected that God should send any one into the world on purpose to inform men of things indifferent, and of small moment, or that are knowable by the use of their natural faculties. This would be to lessen the dignity of his majesty in favour of our sloth, and in prejudice to our reason.

3. The only case then wherein a mission of any one from heaven can be reconciled to the high and awful thoughts men ought to have of the deity, must be the revelation of some supernatural truths relating to the glory of God, and some great concern of men. Supernatural operations attesting such a revelation may, with reason, be taken to be miracles, as carrying the marks of a superior and over-ruling power, as long as no revelation accompanied with marks of a greater power appears against it. Such supernatural signs may justly stand good, and be received for divine, i.e. wrought by a power superior to all, 'till a mission attested by operations of a greater force shall disprove them: because it cannot be supposed, God should suffer his prerogative to be so far usurped by any inferior being, as to permit any creature, depending on him, to set his seals, the marks of his divine authority, to a mission coming from him. For these supernatural signs being the only means God is conceived to have to satisfy men as rational creatures of the certainty of any thing he would reveal, as coming from himself, can never consent that it should be wrested out of his hands, to serve the ends and establish the authority of an inferior agent that rivals him. His power being known to have no equal, always will, and always may be safely depended on, to shew its superiority in vindicating his authority, and maintaining every truth that he hath revealed. So that the marks of a superior power accompanying it, always have been, and always will be a visible and sure guide to divine revelation; by which men may conduct themselves in their examining of revealed religions, and be satisfied which they ought to receive as coming from God; though they have by no means ability precisely to determine what it is, or is not above the force of any created being; or what operations can be performed by none but a divine power, and require the immediate hand of the Almighty. And therefore we see 'tis by that Our Saviour measures the great unbelief of the Jews, John xv. 24, saying, "If I had not done among them the works which no other man did, they had not had sin, but now have they both seen and hated both me and my Father"; declaring, that they could not but see the power and presence of God in those many miracles he did, which were greater than ever any other man had done. When God sent Moses to the children of Israel with a message, that now according to his promise he would redeem them by his hand out of Egypt, and

furnished him with signs and credentials of his mission; it is very remarkable what God himself says of those signs, Exod. iv. 8, "And it shall come to pass, if they will not believe thee, nor hearken to the voice of the first sign" (which was turning his rod into a serpent) "that they will believe, and the voice of the latter sign" (which was the making his hand leprous by putting it in his bosom); God further adds, ver. 9, "And it shall come to pass, if they will not believe also these two signs, neither hearken unto thy voice, that thou shalt take of the water of the river and pour upon the dry land: And the water which thou takest out of the river shall become blood upon the dry land." Which of those operations was or was not above the force of all created beings, will, I suppose, be hard for any man, too hard for a poor brick-maker to determine; and therefore the credit and certain reception of the mission, was annexed to neither of them, but the prevailing of their attestation was heightened by the increase of their number; two supernatural operations shewing more power than one, and three more than two. God allowed that it was natural, that the marks of greater power should have a greater impression on the minds and belief of the spectators. Accordingly the Jews, by this estimate judged of the miracles of Our Saviour, John vii. 31, where we have this account, "and many of the people believed on him, and said when Christ cometh will he do more miracles than these which this man hath done?" This perhaps, as it is the plainest, so it is also the surest way to preserve the testimony of miracles in its due force to all sorts and degrees of people. For miracles being the basis on which divine mission is always established, and consequently that foundation on which the believers of any divine revelation must ultimately bottom their faith, this use of them would be lost, if not to all mankind, yet at least to the simple and illiterate (which is the far greatest part) if miracles be defined to be none but such divine operations as are in themselves beyond the power of all created beings, or at least operations contrary to the fixed and established laws of Nature. For as to the latter of those, what are the fixed and established laws of Nature, philosophers alone, if at least they can pretend to determine. And if they are to be operations performable only by divine power, I doubt whether any man learned or unlearned, can in most cases be able to say of any particular operation, that can fall under his senses, that it is certainly a miracle. Before he can come to that certainty, he must know that no created being has a power to perform it. We know good and bad angels have abilities and excellencies exceedingly beyond all our poor performances or narrow comprehensions. But to define what is the utmost extent of power that any of them has, is a bold undertaking of a man in the dark, that pronounces without seeing, and sets bounds to his narrow cell to things at an infinite distance from his model and comprehension.

Such definitions therefore of miracles, however specious in discourse and theory, fail us when we come to use, and an application of them in particular cases.

These thoughts concerning miracles, were occasioned by my reading Mr Fleetwood's *Essay on Miracles*, and the letter writ to him on that subject. The one of them defining a miracle to be an extraordinary operation performable by God alone: and the other writing of miracles without any definition of a miracle at all.

3

Of Miracles

David Hume

The skeptical Scottish empiricist David Hume (1711–76) is widely regarded as the greatest philosopher of the English language. Hume's "Of Miracles," which is a chapter from his *Enquiry Concerning Human Understanding* (1748), is the most famous and influential critique of miracles ever offered – one that is still widely discussed and debated today. Hume does not argue that miracles could not occur or even that they do not occur; rather, he defends the more cautious thesis that we cannot rationally believe one has occurred on the basis of testimony. Anytime we hear testimony, we must assess it by comparing two probabilities: the probability of what the testifier asserts and the probability that the testifier is either lying or mistaken. Since miracles are, by definition, exceedingly improbable, it will always be equally or more probable that the testifier is lying or mistaken than that the reported miracle actually occurred.

Section X. *Of Miracles*

Part I

There is, in Dr Tillotson's writings, an argument against the *real presence*, which is as concise, and elegant, and strong as any argument can possibly be supposed against a doctrine, so little worthy of a serious refutation. It is acknowledged on all hands, says that learned prelate, that the authority, either of the scripture or of tradition, is founded merely in the testimony of the apostles, who were eye-witnesses to those miracles of our Saviour, by which he proved his divine mission. Our evidence, then, for the truth of the *Christian* religion is less than the evidence for the truth of our senses; because, even in the first authors of our religion, it was no greater; and it is evident it must diminish in passing from them to their disciples; nor can any one rest such confidence

David Hume, "Of Miracles" from *Essays: Moral, Political, and Literary*, ed. T. H. Green and T. H. Grose, vol. 2 (London: Longmans, Green, and Co., 1912), pp. 88–108.

in their testimony, as in the immediate object of his senses. But a weaker evidence can never destroy a stronger; and therefore, were the doctrine of the real presence ever so clearly revealed in scripture, it were directly contrary to the rules of just reasoning to give our assent to it. It contradicts sense, though both the scripture and tradition, on which it is supposed to be built, carry not such evidence with them as sense; when they are considered merely as external evidences, and are not brought home to every one's breast, by the immediate operation of the Holy Spirit.

Nothing is so convenient as a decisive argument of this kind, which must at least *silence* the most arrogant bigotry and superstition, and free us from their impertinent solicitations. I flatter myself, that I have discovered an argument of a like nature, which, if just, will, with the wise and learned, be an everlasting check to all kinds of superstitious delusion, and consequently, will be useful as long as the world endures. For so long, I presume, will the accounts of miracles and prodigies be found in all history, sacred and profane.

Though experience be our only guide in reasoning concerning matters of fact; it must be acknowledged, that this guide is not altogether infallible, but in some cases is apt to lead us into errors. One, who in our climate, should expect better weather in any week of JUNE than in one of DECEMBER, would reason justly, and conformably to experience; but it is certain, that he may happen, in the event, to find himself mistaken. However, we may observe, that, in such a case, he would have no cause to complain of experience; because it commonly informs us beforehand of the uncertainty, by that contrariety of events, which we may learn from a diligent observation. All effects follow not with like certainty from their supposed causes. Some events are found, in all countries and all ages, to have been constantly conjoined together: Others are found to have been more variable, and sometimes to disappoint our expectations; so that, in our reasonings concerning matter of fact, there are all imaginable degrees of assurance, from the highest certainty to the lowest species of moral evidence.

A wise man, therefore, proportions his belief to the evidence. In such conclusions as are founded on an infallible experience, he expects the event with the last degree of assurance, and regards his past experience as a full *proof* of the future existence of that event. In other cases, he proceeds with more caution: He weighs the opposite experiments: He considers which side is supported by the greater number of experiments: To that side he inclines, with doubt and hesitation; and when at last he fixes his judgment, the evidence exceeds not what we properly call *probability*. All probability, then, supposes an opposition of experiments and observations, where the one side is found to overbalance the other, and to produce a degree of evidence, proportioned to the superiority. A hundred instances or experiments on one side, and fifty on another, afford a doubtful expectation of any event; though a hundred uniform experiments, with only one that is contradictory, reasonably beget a pretty strong degree of assurance. In all eases, we must balance the opposite experiments, where they are opposite, and deduct the smaller number from the greater, in order to know the exact force of the superior evidence.

To apply these principles to a particular instance; we may observe, that there is no species of reasoning more common, more useful, and even necessary to human life, than that which is derived from the testimony of men, and the reports of eye-witnesses and spectators. This species of reasoning, perhaps, one may deny to be founded on the relation of cause and effect. I shall not dispute about a word. It will be sufficient to observe, that our assurance in any argument of this kind is derived from no other principle than our observation of the veracity of human testimony, and of the usual conformity of facts to the reports of witnesses. It being a general maxim, that no objects have any discoverable connexion together, and that all the inferences, which we can draw from one to another, are founded merely on our experience of their constant and regular conjunction; it is evident, that we ought not to make an exception to this maxim in favour of human testimony, whose connexion with any event seems, in itself, as little necessary as any other. Were not the memory tenacious to a certain degree; had not men commonly an inclination to truth and a principle of probity; were they not sensible to shame, when detected in a falsehood:

Were not these, I say, discovered by *experience* to be qualities, inherent in human nature, we should never repose the least confidence in human testimony. A man delirious, or noted for falsehood and villany, has no manner of authority with us.

And as the evidence, derived from witnesses and human testimony, is founded on past experience, so it varies with the experience, and is regarded either as a *proof* or a *probability*, according as the conjunction between any particular kind of report and any kind of object has been found to be constant or variable. There are a number of circumstances to be taken into consideration in all judgments of this kind; and the ultimate standard, by which we determine all disputes, that may arise concerning them, is always derived from experience and observation. Where this experience is not entirely uniform on any side, it is attended with an unavoidable contrariety in our judgments, and with the same opposition and mutual destruction of argument as in every other kind of evidence. We frequently hesitate concerning the reports of others. We balance the opposite circumstances, which cause any doubt or uncertainty; and when we discover a superiority on any side, we incline to it; but still with a diminution of assurance, in proportion to the force of its antagonist.

This contrariety of evidence, in the present case, may be derived from several different causes; from the opposition of contrary testimony; from the character or number of the witnesses; from the manner of their delivering their testimony; or from the union of all these circumstances. We entertain a suspicion concerning any matter of fact, when the witnesses contradict each other; when they are but few, or of a doubtful character; when they have an interest in what they affirm; when they deliver their testimony with hesitation, or on the contrary, with too violent asseverations. There are many other particulars of the same kind, which may diminish or destroy the force of any argument, derived from human testimony.

Suppose, for instance, that the fact, which the testimony endeavours to establish, partakes of the extraordinary and the marvellous; in that case, the evidence, resulting from the testimony, admits of a diminution, greater or less, in proportion as the fact is more or less unusual. The reason, why we place any credit in witnesses and historians, is not derived from any *connexion*, which we perceive *à priori*, between testimony and reality, but because we are accustomed to find a conformity between them. But when the fact attested is such a one as has seldom fallen under our observation, here is a contest of two opposite experiences; of which the one destroys the other, as far as its force goes, and the superior can only operate on the mind by the force, which remains. The very same principle of experience, which gives us a certain degree of assurance in the testimony of witnesses, gives us also, in this case, another degree of assurance against the fact, which they endeavour to establish; from which contradiction there necessarily arises a counterpoise, and mutual destruction of belief and authority.

I should not believe such a story were it told me by CATO; was a proverbial saying in ROME, even during the lifetime of that philosophical patriot.[1] The incredibility of a fact, it was allowed, might invalidate so great an authority.

The INDIAN prince, who refused to believe the first relations concerning the effects of frost, reasoned justly; and it naturally required very strong testimony to engage his assent to facts, that arose from a state of nature, with which he was unacquainted, and which bore so little analogy to those events, of which he had had constant and uniform experience. Though they were not contrary to his experience, they were not conformable to it.[2]

But in order to encrease the probability against the testimony of witnesses, let us suppose, that the fact, which they affirm, instead of being only marvellous, is really miraculous; and suppose also, that the testimony, considered apart and in itself, amounts to an entire proof; in that case, there is proof against proof, of which the strongest must prevail, but still with a diminution of its force, in proportion to that of its antagonist.

A miracle is a violation of the laws of nature; and as a firm and unalterable experience has established these laws, the proof against a miracle, from the very nature of the fact, is as entire as any argument from experience can possibly be imagined. Why is it more than probable, that all men must die; that lead cannot, of itself, remain suspended in the air; that fire consumes wood, and is extinguished by water; unless it be, that these events are found agreeable to the laws of nature, and there is required a violation of these laws, or in other words, a miracle to prevent them? Nothing is esteemed a miracle, if it ever happen in the common course of nature. It is no miracle that a man, seemingly in good health, should die on a sudden: because such a kind of death, though more unusual than any other, has yet been frequently observed to happen. But it is a miracle, that a dead man should come to life; because that has never been observed, in any age or country. There must, therefore, be a uniform experience against every miraculous event, otherwise the event would not merit that appellation. And as an uniform experience amounts to a proof, there is here a direct and full *proof*, from the nature of the fact, against the existence of any miracle; nor can such a proof be destroyed, or the miracle rendered credible, but by an opposite proof, which is superior.[3]

The plain consequence is (and it is a general maxim worthy of our attention), 'That no testimony is sufficient to establish a miracle, unless the testimony be of such a kind, that its falsehood would be more miraculous, than the fact, which it endeavours to establish: And even in that case there is a mutual destruction of arguments, and the superior only gives us an assurance suitable to that degree of force, which remains, after deducting the inferior.' When any one tells me, that he saw a dead man restored to life, I immediately consider with myself, whether it be more probable, that this person should either deceive or be deceived, or that the fact, which he relates, should really have happened. I weigh the one miracle against the other; and according to the superiority, which I discover, I pronounce my decision, and always reject the greater miracle. If the falsehood of his testimony would be more miraculous, than the event which he relates; then, and not till then, can he pretend to command my belief or opinion.

Part II

In the foregoing reasoning we have supposed, that the testimony, upon which a miracle is founded, may possibly amount to an entire proof, and that the falsehood of that testimony would be a real prodigy: But it is easy to shew, that we have been a great deal too liberal in our concession, and that there never was a miraculous event established on so full an evidence.

For *first*, there is not to be found in all history, any miracle attested by a sufficient number of men, of such unquestioned good-sense, education, and learning, as to secure us against all delusion in themselves; of such undoubted integrity, as to place them beyond all suspicion of any design to deceive others; of such credit and reputation in the eyes of mankind, as to have a great deal to lose in case of their being detected in any falsehood; and at the same time, attesting facts, performed in such a public manner, and in so celebrated a part of the world, as to render the detection unavoidable: All which circumstances are requisite to give us a full assurance in the testimony of men.

Secondly. We may observe in human nature a principle, which, if strictly examined, will be found to diminish extremely the assurance, which we might, from human testimony, have, in any kind of prodigy. The maxim, by which we commonly conduct ourselves in our reasonings, is, that the objects, of which we have no experience, resemble those, of which we have; that what we have found to be most usual is always most probable; and that where there is an opposition of arguments, we ought to give the preference to such as are founded on the greatest number of past observations. But though, in proceeding by this rule, we readily reject any fact which is unusual and incredible in an ordinary degree; yet in advancing farther, the mind observes not always the same rule; but when anything is affirmed utterly absurd and miraculous, it rather the more readily admits of such a fact, upon account of that very circumstance, which ought to destroy all its authority. The passion of *surprize* and *wonder*, arising from miracles, being an agreeable emotion, gives a sensible tendency towards the belief of those events, from which it is derived. And this goes so far, that even those who cannot enjoy this pleasure immediately, nor can believe those miraculous events, of which they are informed, yet love to partake of the satisfaction at second-hand or by rebound, and place a pride and delight in exciting the admiration of others.

With what greediness are the miraculous accounts of travellers received, their descriptions of sea and land monsters, their relations of wonderful adventures, strange men, and uncouth manners? But if the spirit of religion join itself to the love of wonder, there is an end of common sense; and human testimony, in these circumstances, loses all pretensions to authority. A religionist may be an enthusiast, and imagine he sees what has no reality: He may know his narrative to be false, and yet persevere in it, with the best intentions in the world, for the sake of promoting so holy a cause: Or even where this delusion has not place, vanity, excited by so strong a temptation, operates on him more powerfully than on the rest of mankind in any other circumstances; and self-interest with equal force. His auditors may not have, and commonly have not, sufficient judgment to canvass his evidence: What judgment they have, they renounce by principle, in these sublime and mysterious subjects: Or if they were ever so willing to employ it, passion and a heated imagination disturb the regularity of its operations. Their credulity encreases his impudence: And his impudence overpowers their credulity.

Eloquence, when at its highest pitch, leaves little room for reason or reflection; but addressing itself entirely to the fancy or the affections, captivates the willing hearers, and subdues their understanding. Happily, this pitch it seldom attains. But what a TULLY or a DEMOSTHENES could scarcely effect over a ROMAN or ATHENIAN audience, every *Capuchin*, every itinerant or stationary teacher can perform over the generality of mankind, and in a higher degree, by touching such gross and vulgar passions.

The many instances of forged miracles, and prophecies, and supernatural events, which, in all ages, have either been detected by contrary evidence, or which detect themselves by their absurdity, prove sufficiently the strong propensity of mankind to the extraordinary and the marvellous, and ought reasonably to beget a suspicion against all relations of this kind. This is our natural way of thinking, even with regard to the most common and most credible events. For instance: There is no kind of report, which rises so easily, and spreads so quickly, especially in country places and provincial towns, as those concerning marriages; insomuch that two young persons of equal condition never see each other twice, but the whole neighbourhood immediately join them together. The pleasure of telling a piece of news so interesting, of propagating it, and of being the first reporters of it, spreads the intelligence. And this is so well known, that no man of sense gives attention to these reports, till he find them confirmed by some greater evidence. Do not the same passions, and others still stronger, incline the generality of mankind to believe and report, with the greatest vehemence and assurance, all religious miracles?

Thirdly. It forms a strong presumption against all supernatural and miraculous relations, that they are observed chiefly to abound among ignorant and barbarous nations; or if a civilized people has ever given admission to any of them, that people will be found to have received them from ignorant and barbarous ancestors, who transmitted them with that inviolable sanction and authority, which always attend received opinions. When we peruse the first histories of all nations, we are apt to imagine ourselves transported into some new world; where the whole frame of nature is disjointed, and every element performs its operations in a different manner, from what it does at present. Battles, revolutions, pestilence, famine, and death, are never the effect of those natural causes, which we experience. Prodigies, omens, oracles, judgments, quite obscure the few natural events, that are intermingled with them. But as the former grow thinner every page, in proportion as we advance nearer the enlightened ages, we soon learn, that there is nothing mysterious or supernatural in the case, but that all proceeds from the usual propensity of mankind towards the marvellous, and that, though this inclination may at intervals receive a check from sense and learning, it can never be thoroughly extirpated from human nature.

It is strange, a judicious reader is apt to say, upon the perusal of these wonderful historians, *that such prodigious events never happen in our days*. But it is nothing strange, I hope, that men should lie in all ages. You must surely have seen instances enow of that frailty. You have yourself heard many such marvellous relations started, which, being treated with scorn by all the wise and judicious, have at last been abandoned even by the vulgar. Be assured, that those renowned lies, which have spread and flourished to such a monstrous height, arose from like beginnings; but being sown in a more proper soil, shot up at last into prodigies almost equal to those which they relate.

It was a wise policy in that false prophet, ALEXANDER, who, though now forgotten, was once so famous, to lay the first scene of his impostures in PAPHLAGONIA, where, as LUCIAN tells us, the people were extremely ignorant and stupid, and ready to swallow even the grossest delusion. People at a distance, who are weak enough to think the matter at all worth enquiry, have no opportunity of receiving better information. The stories come magnified to them by a hundred circumstances. Fools are industrious in propagating the imposture; while the wise and learned are contented, in general, to deride its absurdity, without informing themselves of the particular facts, by which it may be distinctly refuted. And thus the impostor above-mentioned was enabled to proceed, from his ignorant PAPHLAGONIANS, to the enlisting of votaries, even among the GRECIAN philosophers, and men of the most eminent rank and distinction in ROME: Nay, could engage the attention of the sage emperor MARCUS AURELIUS; so far as to make him trust the success of a military expedition to his delusive prophecies.

The advantages are so great, of starting an imposture among an ignorant people, that, even though the delusion should be too gross to impose on the generality of them (*which, though seldom, is sometimes the case*) it has a much better chance for succeeding in remote countries, than if the first scene has been laid in a city renowned for arts and knowledge. The most ignorant and barbarous of these barbarians carry the report abroad. None of their countrymen have a large correspondence, or sufficient credit and authority to contradict and beat down the delusion. Men's inclination to the marvellous has full opportunity to display itself. And thus a story, which is universally exploded in the place where it was first started, shall pass for certain at a thousand miles distance. But had ALEXANDER fixed his residence at ATHENS, the philosophers of that renowned mart of learning had immediately spread, throughout the whole ROMAN empire, their sense of the matter; which, being supported by so great authority, and displayed by all the force of reason and eloquence, had entirely opened the eyes of mankind. It is true; LUCIAN, passing by chance through PAPHLAGONIA, had an opportunity of performing this good office. But, though much to be wished, it does not always happen, that every ALEXANDER meets with a LUCIAN, ready to expose and detect his impostures.

I may add as a *fourth* reason, which diminishes the authority of prodigies, that there is no testimony for any, even those which have not been expressly detected, that is not opposed by an infinite number of witnesses; so that not only the miracle destroys the credit of testimony, but the testimony destroys itself. To make this the better understood, let us consider, that, in matters of religion, whatever is different is contrary; and that it is impossible the religions of ancient ROME, of TURKEY, of SIAM, and of CHINA should, all of them, be established on any solid foundation. Every miracle, therefore, pretended to have been wrought in any of these religions (and all of them abound in miracles), as its direct scope is to establish the particular system to which it is attributed; so has it the same force, though more indirectly, to overthrow every other system. In destroying a rival system, it likewise destroys the credit of those miracles, on which that system was established; so that all the prodigies of different religions are to be regarded as contrary facts, and the evidences of these prodigies, whether weak or strong, as opposite to each other. According to this method of reasoning, when we believe any miracle of MAHOMET or his successors, we have for our warrant the testimony of a few barbarous ARABIANS: And on the other hand, we are to regard the authority of TITUS LIVIUS, PLUTARCH, TACITUS, and, in short, of all the authors and witnesses, GRECIAN, CHINESE, and ROMAN CATHOLIC, who have related any miracle in their particular religion; I say, we are to regard their testimony in the same light as if they had mentioned that MAHOMETAN miracle, and had in express terms contradicted it, with the same certainty as they have for the miracle they relate. This argument may appear over subtile and refined; but is not in reality different from the reasoning of a judge, who supposes, that the credit of two witnesses, maintaining a crime against any one, is destroyed by the testimony of two others, who affirm him to have been two hundred leagues distant, at the same instant when the crime is said to have been committed.

One of the best attested miracles in all profane history, is that which TACITUS reports of

VESPASIAN, who cured a blind man in ALEXANDRIA, by means of his spittle, and a lame man by the mere touch of his foot; in obedience to a vision of the god SERAPIS, who had enjoined them to have recourse to the Emperor, for these miraculous cures. The story may be seen in that fine historian;[4] where every circumstance seems to add weight to the testimony, and might be displayed at large with all the force of argument and eloquence, if any one were now concerned to enforce the evidence of that exploded and idolatrous superstition. The gravity, solidity, age, and probity of so great an emperor, who, through the whole course of his life, conversed in a familiar manner with his friends and courtiers, and never affected those extraordinary airs of divinity assumed by ALEXANDER and DEMETRIUS. The historian, a cotemporary writer, noted for candour and veracity, and withal, the greatest and most penetrating genius, perhaps, of all antiquity; and so free from any tendency to credulity, that he even lies under the contrary imputation, of atheism and profaneness: The persons, from whose authority he related the miracle, of established character for judgment and veracity, as we may well presume; eye-witnesses of the fact, and confirming their testimony, after the FLAVIAN family was despoiled of the empire, and could no longer give any reward, as the price of a lie. *Utrumque, qui interfuere, nunc quoque memorant, post quam nullum mendacio pretium.* To which if we add the public nature of the facts, as related, it will appear, that no evidence can well be supposed stronger for so gross and so palpable a falsehood.

There is also a memorable story related by Cardinal DE RETZ, which may well deserve our consideration. When that intriguing politician fled into SPAIN, to avoid the persecution of his enemies, he passed through SARAGOSSA, the capital of ARRAGON, where he was shewn, in the cathedral, a man, who had served seven years as a door-keeper, and was well known to every body in town, that had ever paid his devotions at that church. He had been seen, for so long a time, wanting a leg; but recovered that limb by the rubbing of holy oil upon the stump; and the cardinal assures us that he saw him with two legs. This miracle was vouched by all the canons of the church; and the whole company in town were appealed to for a confirmation of the fact; whom the cardinal found, by their zealous devotion, to be thorough believers of the miracle. Here the relater was also cotemporary to the supposed prodigy, of an incredulous and libertine character, as well as of great genius; the miracle of so *singular* a nature as could scarcely admit of a counterfeit, and the witnesses very numerous, and all of them, in a manner, spectators of the fact, to which they gave their testimony. And what adds mightily to the force of the evidence, and may double our surprize on this occasion, is, that the cardinal himself, who relates the story, seems not to give any credit to it, and consequently cannot be suspected of any concurrence in the holy fraud. He considered justly, that it was not requisite, in order to reject a fact of this nature, to be able accurately to disprove the testimony, and to trace its falsehood, through all the circumstances of knavery and credulity which produced it. He knew, that, as this was commonly altogether impossible at any small distance of time and place; so was it extremely difficult, even where one was immediately present, by reason of the bigotry, ignorance, cunning, and roguery of a great part of mankind. He therefore concluded, like a just reasoner, that such an evidence carried falsehood upon the very face of it, and that a miracle supported by any human testimony, was more properly a subject of derision than of argument.

There surely never was a greater number of miracles ascribed to one person, than those, which were lately said to have been wrought in FRANCE upon the tomb of Abbé PARIS, the famous JANSENIST, with whose sanctity the people were so long deluded. The curing of the sick, giving hearing to the deaf, and sight to the blind, were every where talked of as the usual effects of that holy sepulchre. But what is more extraordinary; many of the miracles were immediately proved upon the spot, before judges of unquestioned integrity, attested by witnesses of credit and distinction, in a learned age, and on the most eminent theatre that is now in the world. Nor is this all: A relation of them was published and dispersed every where; nor were the *Jesuits*, though a learned body, supported by the civil magistrate, and determined enemies to those opinions, in whose favour the miracles were said to have been wrought, ever able distinctly to refute or detect them. Where shall we find such a number of circumstances, agreeing to the corroboration of one fact? And what have we to oppose to such a cloud of witnesses, but the absolute impossibility or miraculous nature of the events, which they relate? And this surely, in the eyes of all reasonable people, will alone be regarded as a sufficient refutation.

Is the consequence just, because some human testimony has the utmost force and authority in some cases, when it relates the battle of PHILIPPI or PHARSALIA for instance; that therefore all kinds of testimony must, in all cases, have equal force and authority? Suppose that the CÆSAREAN and POMPEIAN factions had, each of them, claimed the victory in these battles, and that the historians of each party had uniformly ascribed the advantage to their own side; how could mankind, at this distance, have been able to determine between them? The contrariety is equally strong between the miracles related by HERODOTUS or PLUTARCH, and those delivered by MARIANA, BEDE, or any monkish historian.

The wise lend a very academic faith to every report which favours the passion of the reporter; whether it magnifies his country, his family, or himself, or in any other way strikes in with his natural inclinations and propensities. But what greater temptation than to appear a missionary, a prophet, an ambassador from heaven? Who would not encounter many dangers and difficulties, in order to attain so sublime a character? Or if, by the help of vanity and a heated imagination, a man has first made a convert of himself, and entered seriously into the delusion; who ever scruples to make use of pious frauds, in support of so holy and meritorious a cause?

The smallest spark may here kindle into the greatest flame; because the materials are always prepared for it. The *avidum genus auricularum*,[5] the gazing populace, receive greedily, without examination, whatever sooths superstition, and promotes wonder.

How many stories of this nature, have, in all ages, been detected and exploded in their infancy? How many more have been celebrated for a time, and have afterwards sunk into neglect and oblivion? Where such reports, therefore, fly about, the solution of the phænomenon is obvious; and we judge in conformity to regular experience and observation, when we account for it by the known and natural principles of credulity and delusion. And shall we, rather than have a recourse to so natural a solution, allow of a miraculous violation of the most established laws of nature?

I need not mention the difficulty of detecting a falsehood in any private or even public history, at the place, where it is said to happen; much more when the scene is removed to ever so small a distance. Even a court of judicature, with all the authority, accuracy, and judgment, which they can employ, find themselves often at a loss to distinguish between truth and falsehood in the most recent actions. But the matter never comes to any issue, if trusted to the common method of altercation and debate and flying rumours; especially when men's passions have taken part on either side.

In the infancy of new religions, the wise and learned commonly esteem the matter too inconsiderable to deserve their attention or regard. And when afterwards they would willingly detect the cheat, in order to undeceive the deluded multitude, the season is now past, and the records and witnesses, which might clear up the matter, have perished beyond recovery.

No means of detection remain, but those which must be drawn from the very testimony itself of the reporters: And these, though always sufficient with the judicious and knowing, are commonly too fine to fall under the comprehension of the vulgar.

Upon the whole, then, it appears, that no testimony for any kind of miracle has ever amounted to a probability, much less to a proof; and that, even supposing it amounted to a proof, it would be opposed by another proof; derived from the very nature of the fact, which it would endeavour to establish. It is experience only, which gives authority to human testimony; and it is the same experience, which assures us of the laws of nature. When, therefore, these two kinds of experience are contrary, we have nothing to do but substract the one from the other, and embrace an opinion, either on one side or the other, with that assurance which arises from the remainder. But according to the principle here explained, this substraction, with regard to all popular religions, amounts to an entire annihilation; and therefore we may establish it as a maxim, that no human testimony can have such force as to prove a miracle, and make it a just foundation for any such system of religion.

I beg the limitations here made may be remarked, when I say, that a miracle can never be proved, so as to be the foundation of a system of religion. For I own, that otherwise, there may possibly be miracles, or violations of the usual course of nature, of such a kind as to admit of proof from human testimony; though, perhaps, it will be impossible to find any such in all the records of history. Thus, suppose, all authors, in all languages, agree, that, from the first of January 1600, there was a total darkness over the whole earth for eight days: Suppose that the tradition of this extraordinary event is still strong and lively among the people: That all travellers, who return from foreign countries, bring us accounts of the same tradition, without the least variation or contradiction: It is evident, that our present philosophers, instead of doubting the fact, ought to receive it as certain, and ought to search for the causes whence it might be derived. The decay, corruption, and dissolution of nature, is an event rendered probable by so many analogies, that any phænomenon, which seems to have a tendency towards that catastrophe, comes within the reach of human testimony, if that testimony be very extensive and uniform.

But suppose, that all the historians who treat of England, should agree, that, on the first of January 1600, Queen Elizabeth died; that both before and after her death she was seen by her physicians and the whole court, as is usual with persons of her rank; that her successor was acknowledged and proclaimed by the parliament; and that, after being interred a month, she again appeared, resumed the throne, and governed England for three years: I must confess that I should be surprized at the occurrence of so many odd circumstances, but should not have the least inclination to believe so miraculous an event. I should not doubt of her pretended death, and of those other public circumstances that followed it: I should only assert it to have been pretended, and that it neither was, nor possibly could be real. You would in vain object to me the difficulty, and almost impossibility of deceiving the world in an affair of such consequence; the wisdom and solid judgment of that renowned queen; with the little or no advantage which she could reap from so poor an artifice: All this might astonish me; but I would still reply, that the knavery and folly of men are such common phænomena, that I should rather believe the most extraordinary events to arise from their concurrence, than admit of so signal a violation of the laws of nature.

But should this miracle be ascribed to any new system of religion; men, in all ages, have been so much imposed on by ridiculous stories of that kind, that this very circumstance would be a full proof of a cheat, and sufficient, with all men of sense, not only to make them reject the fact, but reject it without farther examination. Though the Being to whom the miracle is ascribed, be, in this case, Almighty, it does not, upon that account, become a whit more probable; since it is impossible for us to know the attributes or actions of such a Being, otherwise than from the experience which we have of his productions, in the usual course of nature. This still reduces us to past observation, and obliges us to compare the instances of the violation of truth in the testimony of men, with those of the violation of the laws of nature by miracles, in order to judge which of them is most likely and probable. As the violations of truth are more common in the testimony concerning religious miracles, than in that concerning any other matter of fact; this must diminish very much the authority of the former testimony, and make us form a general resolution, never to lend any attention to it, with whatever specious pretence it may be covered.

Lord Bacon seems to have embraced the same principles of reasoning. 'We ought,' says he, 'to make a collection or particular history of all monsters and prodigious births or productions, and in a word of every thing new, rare, and extraordinary in nature. But this must be done with the most severe scrutiny, lest we depart from truth. Above all, every relation must be considered as suspicious, which depends in any degree upon religion, as the prodigies of Livy: And no less so, every thing that is to be found in the writers of natural magic or alchimy, or such authors, who seem, all of them, to have an unconquerable appetite for falsehood and fable.'[6]

I am the better pleased with the method of reasoning here delivered, as I think it may serve to confound those dangerous friends or disguised enemies to the *Christian Religion*, who have undertaken to defend it by the principles of human reason. Our most holy religion is founded on *Faith*, not on reason; and it is a sure method of exposing it to put it to such a trial as it is, by no means, fitted to endure. To make this more evident, let us examine those miracles, related in scripture; and not to lose ourselves in too wide a field, let us confine ourselves to such as we find in the *Pentateuch*, which we shall examine, according to the principles of those pretended Christians, not as the word or testimony of God himself, but as the production of a mere human writer and historian. Here then we are first to consider a book, presented to us by a barbarous and ignorant people, written in an age when they were still more barbarous, and in all probability long after the facts which it relates, corroborated by no concurring testimony, and resembling those fabulous accounts, which every nation gives of its origin. Upon reading this book, we find it full of prodigies and miracles. It gives an account of a state of the world and of human nature entirely different from the present: Of our fall from that state: Of the age of man, extended to near a thousand years: Of the destruction of the world by a deluge: Of the arbitrary choice of one people, as the favourites of heaven; and that people the countrymen of the author: Of their deliverance from bondage by prodigies the most astonishing imaginable: I desire any one to lay his hand upon his heart, and after a serious consideration declare, whether he thinks that the falsehood of such a book, supported by such a testimony, would be more extraordinary and miraculous than all the miracles it relates; which is, however, necessary to make it be received, according to the measures of probability above established.

What we have said of miracles may be applied, without any variation, to prophecies; and indeed, all prophecies are real miracles, and as such only, can be admitted as proofs of any revelation. If it did not exceed the capacity of human nature to foretel future events, it would be absurd to employ any prophecy as an argument for a divine mission or authority from heaven. So that, upon the whole, we may conclude, that the *Christian Religion* not only was at first attended with miracles, but even at this day cannot be believed by any reasonable person without one. Mere reason is insufficient to convince us of its veracity: And whoever is moved by *Faith* to assent to it, is conscious of a continued miracle in his own person, which subverts all the principles of his understanding, and gives him a determination to believe what is most contrary to custom and experience.

Notes

1 Plutarch, in vita Catonis Min. 19.

2 No Indian, it is evident, could have experience that water did not freeze in cold climates. This is placing nature in a situation quite unknown to him; and it is impossible for him to tell *à priori* what will result from it. It is making a new experiment, the consequence of which is always uncertain. One may sometimes conjecture from analogy what will follow; but still this is but conjecture. And it must be confessed, that, in the present case of freezing, the event follows contrary to the rules of analogy, and is such as a rational Indian would not look for. The operations of cold upon water are not gradual, according to the degrees of cold; but whenever it comes to the freezing point, the water passes in a moment, form the utmost liquidity to perfect hardness. Such an event, therefore, may be denominated *extraordinary*, and requires a pretty strong testimony, to render it credible to people in a warm climate: But still it is not *miraculous*, nor contrary to uniform experience of the course of nature in cases where all the circumstances are the same. The inhabitants of Sumatra have always seen water fluid in their own climate, and the freezing of their rivers ought to be deemed a prodigy: But they never saw water in Muscovy during the winter; and therefore they cannot reasonably be positive what would there be the consequence. (This note first appears in the last page of Edition F, with the preface: The distance of the Author from the Press is the Cause, why the following Passage arriv'd not in time to be inserted in its proper Place.)

3 Sometimes an event may not, *in itself, seem* to be contrary to the laws of nature, and yet, if it were real, it might, by reason of some circumstances, be denominated a miracle; because, in *fact*, it is contrary to these laws. Thus if a person, claiming a divine authority, should command a sick person to be well, a healthful man to fall down dead, the clouds to pour rain, the winds to blow, in short, should order many natural events, which immediately follow upon his command; these might justly be esteemed miracles, because they are really, in this

case, contrary to the laws of nature. For if any suspicion remain, that the event and command concurred by accident, there is no miracle and no transgression of the laws of nature. If this suspicion be removed, there is evidently a miracle, and a transgression of these laws; because nothing can be more contrary to nature than that the voice or command of a man should have such an influence. A miracle may be accurately defined, *a transgression of a law of nature by a particular volition of the Deity, or by the interposition of some invisible agent.* A miracle may either be discoverable by men or not. This alters not its nature and essence. The raising of a house or ship into the air is a visible miracle. The raising of a feather, when the wind wants ever so little of a force requisite for that purpose, is as real a miracle, though not so sensible with regard to us.

4 Hist. lib. v. cap. 8. SUETONIUS gives nearly the same account *in vita* VESP. 7.

5 LUCRET. iv. 594.

6 Nov. Org. lib. ii. aph. 29.

4

David Hume and the Probability of Miracles

George I. Mavrodes

George Mavrodes (b. 1926) is Professor Emeritus of Philosophy at the University of Michigan. In this essay, Mavrodes offers a critique of Hume's argument against belief in miracles. He argues that although Hume's epistemic principles concerning testimony may sound intuitively plausible, they are at odds with the way we actually treat testimonial evidence in everyday life. Upon closer examination, Hume's argument fails to demonstrate that it is never rational to believe in miracles on the basis of testimony.

Section X of David Hume's *An Enquiry Concerning Human Understanding* is probably the most celebrated and most influential discussion of miracles in Western philosophical literature. That essay is unusually provocative and suggestive, not least because it is full of claims and arguments whose mutual coherence is immediately suspect.[1] In addition, it is suggestive as much for what it does not say as for what it does say. Hume's openly expressed conclusions are remarkable modest, at least when compared with the inferences which some later enthusiasts have drawn from the essay. In particular, it is noteworthy that the essay itself is explicity restricted to the way in which *testimony* bears on the credibility of miracles. The maxim which Hume claims to have established is that "no human testimony can have such force as to prove a miracle, and make it a just foundation for any such system of religion."[2] Hume says nothing at all about whether people who were themselves *witnesses* of a miracle might thereby have a satisfactory ground for believing in that miracle, and perhaps even for making it the foundation of their religion. But if there were no witnesses of miracles, or at least no people who claimed to be witnesses, there would presumably be no miracle testimonies. We should not, therefore, hastily assume that testimonial evidence is the whole evidential story about miracles. In this paper, however, I will not further explore this particular avenue. Like Hume's essay, this paper is restricted to the bearing of testimonial evidence on the credibility of miracles.

George I. Mavrodes, "David Hume and the Probability of Miracles" in *International Journal for Philosophy of Religion*, 43(3) (1998): 167–82.

The avenues which I do explore here are suggested to me by at least two factors. One is the fact that I believe that there have been some miracles in the history of the world, and that there are credible testimonies to some of these miracles. No doubt some of the readers of this essay will share this factor with me. Others, of course, will not. But the second factor may be more widely shared.

Hume's essay, it seems to me, gives rise to a profound cognitive dissonance entirely apart from its religious implications. On the one hand, the principles and premisses to which Hume appeals in his argument strike one as plausible and reasonable or so, at least, they seem to me. Hume says that they lead to the conclusion quoted above. But the Humean principles (unlike his conclusions here) do not seem to have anything *special* in them about miracles or any other distinctively religious matters. They are general principles about evidence, reasonable credibility, probability, and the like. It looks as though they should be applicable outside the special field of religious belief. And indeed Hume himself puts them forward as general principles. Do we then conduct our own intellectual lives in accordance with these plausible principles, employed in the Humean way, in the ordinary course of affairs? Outside of religion, do we treat testimonial evidence in the way in which Hume's essay seems to suggest is the proper way? It seems to me clear that we do not.

I do not mean merely that we sometimes fall a little short of what we might think of as a Humean ideal. No, the fact is that our ordinary cognitive life is filled with *massive* counterexamples to what appears to be the Humean proposal. Think, for example, of reading an account of one of the games played in a bridge tournament, the sort of account which one may readily find in a newspaper. Such an account will often have a diagram showing just what cards were dealt to the four hands for that game. And now think of what is the antecedent probability which we would estimate for exactly that distribution of cards, making the estimate prior to having this testimony. There are a vast number of ways – millions I suppose – in which four bridge hands can be dealt from a shuffled deck, and this is just one particular way out of that enormous range of possibilities. When I think of being invited to bet, *beforehand*, that exactly this hand would be dealt, then the probability seems vanishingly small, so close to zero that I can hardly tell the difference. But when I have the newspaper article before me, then I judge it to be very likely – not absolutely certain, of course, but fairly probable – that exactly this set of hands was indeed dealt in that tournament. A single testimony, often by a reporter completely unknown to us, seems sufficient to convert a staggering improbability into something considerably more likely than not.

Our cognitive lives are filled with similar examples. Auto accidents happen every day, and are reported every day. But almost every one of those accidents is antecedently enormously improbable. Think of being invited to bet that exactly those drivers, accompanied by just those passengers, in those cars, would collide in that particular intersection, on that particular day – betting, that is, antecedently to having the report in hand.[3] Here again a single testimony seems to make an enormous difference to our estimate of the relevant probability.

That such dramatic reversals could occur on the basis of a single testimony, and that such reversals could be epistemically respectable, is not something which would be suggested by a reading of Hume's essay. And yet almost all of us, at least when we are not thinking about religion, take these enormous reversals as a matter of course, and we have no doubt that they comport very well indeed with the canons of rationality. That dissonance – the initial plausibility of Hume's principles, and their apparently dismal record in everyday life – is the second source of the reflections I pursue here.

I organize this paper around a single element, a crucial element, in Hume's argument – or rather in Hume's proposal for the rational conduct of our cognitive lives. Hume proposes a strategy for a rational thinker to use in considering miracle testimonies. He treats the credibility of miracles – at least insofar as that credibility involves some important appeal to testimony – as depending upon a comparison of probabilities. He wants to compare the probability of miracles with the probability of error and deception in human testimony. The desired outcome of this comparison – desired by Hume, that is – is that the probability of the miracle is always lower than the probability that the testimony is mistaken or lying.[4] Applying the principle which he puts forward early in the essay[5] – "A wise man, therefore, proportions his belief to the evidence" – he reaches the conclusion that the course of wisdom would be that of rejecting the testimony rather than accepting the miracle. And in order for this line of argument to be successful, it is necessary that the probability assigned to the miraculous should always be very low.

Of course, in order to make such a comparison we must somehow "have" the relevant probabilities. That is, we must make some estimate of the probabilities. I suppose that our probability judgments need not be precise, carried out to four decimal places. They can be rough estimates. But they must have enough substance in them to allow us, at least, to say something like "This is more likely than that." If we don't have probability judgments which can sustain that minimum level of comparison, then there is no hope of carrying out the Humean strategy.

So we need two probabilities, one about miracles and one about testimony. Both of these generate interesting and important questions. In this paper I will focus on the probability of miracles, bringing in considerations about the other probability only peripherally. And I will be considering two questions, more or less concurrently. The first question asks for a clearer specification of just what it is for which we are trying to estimate a probability. So far I have tried to speak rather vaguely on this point – "the probability of miracles" and the like. But there are several distinct probabilities, not just one, associated with miracles, and some of these may be vastly different from the others. Which probability is relevant to the Humean project?

The second question concerns the way in which a reasonable judgment about that probability might be grounded. And here I will concentrate on Hume's suggestion that probability judgments are properly grounded, in the end, upon experience. I will be asking whether it is plausible to suppose that Hume had any experience which was relevant to an appropriate probability judgment, and also whether we ourselves have any such experience.

We can begin the exploration by considering a hypothetical case which Hume himself puts forward:

> When any one tells me, that he saw a dead man restored to life, I immediately consider with myself, whether it be more probable, that this person should either deceive or be deceived, or that the fact, which he relates, should really have happened. I weigh the one miracle against the other; and according to the superiority, which I discover, I pronounce my decision, and always reject the greater miracle. If the falsehood of his testimony would be more miraculous, than the event which he relates; then, and not till then, can he pretend to command my belief or opinion.[6]

The terminology of this passage is unfortunate, I think, in Hume's use here of the terms "miracle" and "miraculous." It seems obvious, from other things that Hume says in this essay, that he does not think that there is anything at all miraculous about the falsehood of human testimony. He does not, for example, think a mistaken or lying testimony is a transgression of a law of nature. It seems to me, therefore, that the only plausible way to make sense of this passage is to take the words "miracle" and "miraculous," when they refer to the possibility that the testimony is true, not in the sense which Hume defined, nor in the perhaps vaguer sense which they have in ordinary religious speech and writing, but merely as rhetorical surrogates there for "improbable."[7]

On the other hand, it seems probable that Hume really did think that "a dead man restored to life" would be a miracle in his defined sense, a transgression of a law of nature.[8] In fact, it seems probable that Hume's hypothetical case was intended to mirror the fact that many Christians believe that the resurrection of Jesus is the miracle *par excellence* in the Christian faith.

Reading the passage in this way gives us, I think, a pretty good idea of the core of the Humean strategy on this topic. That strategy consists, as I said, of comparing the probability of miracles with the probability of error and deception in human testimony.

Well, OK. That procedure seems to have at least some *prima facie* plausibility about it. We may not be ready to swallow the Wise Man's Principle just as it stands. Hume himself, we may notice, does not give any argument or reason in support of it. Even if we take evidence to be relevant to the rational propriety of belief we may not be ready to commit ourselves to the claim that it is the *only* relevant factor.[9] At least, I am not ready for that commitment.

But that is a line of criticism which I will not pursue here. I will go along, for the time being, with the initial plausibility of this Humean strategy.

So, let us try to get some feel for what this strategy involves by actually trying it on Hume's hypothetical example. We can begin by formulating a proposition asserting that a miraculous event, a resurrection, has occurred:

> M: Henry was restored to life a few days after his death.

And we can also imagine the sort of testimony which might impel us to consider the possibility that the resurrection did indeed take place:

> T: I saw Henry, alive and well, a few days after his death, we have had breakfast together a couple of times since then, I've gone fishing with him once, . . .[10]

And then we can think of assigning a probability to M – that is, the probability that M is true, that the event "should really have happened." We can also assign a probability to T – the probability that the testifier really did have the experiences, etc., which he or she reports.[11]

When we have these values in hand then we can easily calculate probability values for the negations of both M and T. A standard rule for consistent probabilities stipulates that the probability of ~M is simply 1 – P(M).[12] And the probability of ~T (i.e., that the testifier "should either deceive or be deceived") is 1 – P(T). So altogether we can get four probabilities, and then we can compare them by pairs.

Hume himself suggests that he compares the probability of M with that of ~T. And he says that he will always "reject the greater miracle." Presumably that means that he will reject whichever of this pair has the lower probability. And when he refers to something which would "command my belief or opinion," perhaps he is also suggesting that he will accept whichever of this pair has the higher probability.

However, that project is complicated (and compromised!) by the fact that M and T are not logically independent propositions. That fact is not idiosyncratic to this example. Miracle assertions and the corresponding miracle testimonies are characteristically not logically independent. The content of a miracle testimony usually entails either the corresponding miracle assertion, or some closely related proposition. But the entailment often does not run in the opposite direction. So, in our example here, T entails M, and M does not entail T.

The entailment from T to M has an important probability consequence. M imposes a "probability cap" on T. In a consistent set of probability assignments. T cannot have a probability higher than M. That is, if Henry did not rise from the dead then the testifier did not have the reported experiences. So the probability that the experiences really transpired – breakfast with Henry a few days after his death, etc. – cannot be higher than the probability that Henry really was restored to life. Looked at from the other side, T puts a "probability floor" under M. M cannot have a probability lower than that of T. So we can say that, in a consistent system.

$$P(T) \leq P(M)$$
$$P(M) \geq P(T)$$

Suppose then that Hume begins by assigning a low probability to M. (I suspect, indeed, that he did begin in that way.) That requires, if his probabilities are to be consistent, that the probability of T also be that low or lower. So if the assigned probability of M is less than 0.5, then the probability of T is also less than 0.5. But then the probability of ~T must be greater than 0.5. Hume says that he compares the probability of M with that of ~T, and he rejects whichever has the lower probability. But of course the probability of M (less than 0.5) turns out to be lower than that of ~T (greater than 0.5). So Hume, proceeding in this way, would of course reject the miracle, and would presumably believe that the testifier was either deceived or deceiving.

I say, "proceeding in this way." In fact, I suspect that Hume did proceed in this way. However, there is something misleading in saying that this procedure involves a genuine comparison of probabilities. For the first probability which is assigned generates arithmetically *all* the other values, including the one with which the first one will be compared. Thus, the result of the putative comparison is guaranteed by the assignment of that single probability. Surely there is something fishy in that.

Perhaps that fishy odor becomes a little stronger when we notice that we could just as easily have worked in the opposite direction, beginning instead with the assignment of a probability to T. Maybe, e.g. we have had a long experience with this testifier, and have found him to be moderately reliable. Suppose we estimate, on the basis of our past experience with him, that his reliability is about 0.7. So we assign that probability to T. Consistency then requires an assignment at least that high to M, so we give M also the value of 0.7. Arithmetic tells us that the probability of ~T is 0.3. If we now make the Humean comparison, M against ~T, we find that it is ~T which has much the lower probability and is to be rejected. And so we accept M, and presumably T along with it.

The initial proposal had at least the appearance of plausibility and evenhandedness about it. We were to compare the probability of two propositions (or, perhaps, two possible states of affairs, etc.), and then we were to prefer, as a candidate for our belief, the one which had the higher probability. But it turns out that we can, to a large extent, manipulate the result of this putative comparison merely by a careful choice of which of the probabilities to assign first. And that seems to be epistemically (rationally, etc.) unsatisfactory.

It might be suggested, therefore, that the initial assignments of probability to both M and T really should be made independently of each other, with no concern over whether these assignments are mutually consistent. Concerns with consistency should be postponed to a later stage of the investigation, when we may have a (relatively) final set of probability assignments, with values perhaps radically revised from the initial estimates. The initial assignments would be, in some sense, "antecedent" probabilities, and the later assignments would be their "consequent" descendants.

If this suggestion is adopted, then it is important to remember that the Humean comparison must be made on the basis of the initial antecedent probabilities, even if these values are mutually incompatible. For Hume wants the comparison of probabilities to serve as a guide to the rational use of the testimonial evidence. If we are to be Humeans here, then we don't know what to do with the testimonial evidence until *after* we have made this comparison. In the remainder of this paper I will assume that this is the project which we are attempting. And I will focus on just one half of that project, that of assigning a probability to the miracle side of the comparison *independently of making any judgment about the testimony*.

On what basis should we assign the miracle probability? Not on the basis of testimony, of course. We must, therefore, have a miracle probability which is "antecedent" to testimonial evidence. But perhaps it need not be antecedent to everything; perhaps the probability judgment can have *some* basis. Several times in this essay Hume suggests that we have to acquire the relevant probabilities from *experience*. It is a general maxim, Hume says, "that no objects have any discoverable connexion together, and that all the inferences, which we can draw from one to another, are founded merely on our experience of their constant and regular conjunction."[13] And he explicitly applies this to our reliance on human testimony, which has no basis, he claims, other than our experience of the usual conjunction of testimony and truth.[14] And it is in the same way, by appeal to experience, that we judge that all men must die, that fire consumes wood, and so on.[15]

Well, what experience might Hume have had which would be relevant to assigning a low probability to the miraculous? Or, for that matter, what experience do *we* have which would be relevant to our assignment of such a probability? Hume makes some claims about human experience in general, and I will come to them shortly. But he does not, I think, say anything about his own experience specifically. Human experience in general, however, must be somehow a function of the experience of particular human beings. To begin, therefore, I want to speculate a little about what may have been Hume's own experience with regard to miracles. This exercise is somewhat conjectural, but that need not trouble us much. For if we can recall and recognize some experience of our own which seems more relevant than the experience which I attribute to Hume, then we can shift to consideration of that experience of our own. I must confess, however, that I do not recall any experience of my own which would be more relevant to Hume's purpose than the experience which I here attribute to him. And what if it turns out that neither Hume's experience nor ours is relevant? Well, that might be a significant result.

If we are to speculate about Hume's experience relative to some miracle, however, what miracle (or alleged miracle) shall we think about? I have no problem with supposing that Hume really did have some experience which would support his assigning a very low probability to the claim that a particular friend of his had been restored to life within a week of his death. And, for that matter, I think that I have some experience which would justify me in a similar assignment of probabilities with respect to some of my own acquaintances. But these cases are not of much interest, because nobody (so far as I know) has made them "the foundation of his religion." But there is a case which does generate just that sort of interest, and Hume no doubt had it in mind when he introduced the subject of resurrection into this essay. That case, of course, is the alleged resurrection of Jesus of Nazareth a few days after his execution. That putative miracle does play an important role in an actual religion, many of the followers of that religion count believing in that resurrection as one of their important religious beliefs, and it may in some sense be a "foundation" of that religion. I propose, therefore, to replace the hypothetical Henry of our previous example with Jesus. We thus get a miracle claim which is an element in an actual religion, one which is believed and professed by many people, and about which there apparently were actual testimonies.

> J: Jesus of Nazareth was restored to life a few days after his execution.

What is the probability of that proposition? And on what basis might that probability be assigned?

I suppose that different people will give very different answers to the first of those questions. I, for example, assign a very high probability to it – maybe about as close to 1 as makes no difference. But in saying that, I suppose that I am not really being as "antecedent" as the Humean project requires. I might try to abstract, imaginatively, from my interaction with the biblical texts, the creeds, the church, etc., and to estimate what probability I would assign to it if I were to get back to some "bare bones" state. But in speculating about that I would not be much better off than in speculating about Hume.

I suspect that Hume thought that the probability of J is very low, maybe so close to O as to make no difference. But as a matter of fact, Hume (so far as I know) says nothing at all about assigning a probability directly to this proposition, or to any similar proposition. And, given his professed stance of relying on experience, that reticence is understandable. For the resurrection of Jesus, if it happened at all, happened more than 1,500 years prior to Hume's birth. And, if it happened, it happened somewhere in the vicinity of Jerusalem, far distant from Edinburgh. It is not hard to imagine that some first century resident of Judea might have had some ordinary experience which was directly relevant to the probability of J. Someone, for example, might have seen Jesus (or somebody who looked just like Jesus, etc.) walking about, eating, conversing, etc., a few days after the crucifixion. Or, for that matter, someone may have seen Jesus' corpse (or a corpse which looked just like Jesus, etc.) decaying over a period of three or four weeks. But it is hard to imagine that Hume might have had either of those experiences, or anything in the same ballpark. He just lived in the wrong place and time for that. And, of course, we are no better off than Hume in this respect. Neither Hume nor we seem to be in a good position to assign a probability *directly* to J on the basis of our own experience.

It does not follow immediately, however, that the Humean project must be a failure. For there may be an *indirect* way of basing such a judgment on experience. And that is where some generalization about resurrections may become relevant. For consider the following generalization:

> R: There are some resurrections (i.e., at least one) in the history of the world.

And also its contradictory

> NR: There are no resurrections in the history of the world.

J entails R (thought not *vice versa*). And is logically incompatible with NR. And so, in a consistent system of probabilities, R imposes a probability cap on J. Therefore, if Hume's experience (or ours) could directly justify assigning a low probability of R, then it would also indirectly justify at least that low a probability for J. And a high probability for J would imply a high probability for R. (The entailments do not run in the opposite direction. E.g., a high probability for R does not entail a high probability for J.) Of course, a low probability for R is equivalent to a high probability for NR. So we get corresponding relations between the probabilities for J and NR.

Generalizations about miracles, resurrections, etc., are attractive for the Humean project because of the interaction of two factors. First, Hume (and we also) really do have experiences which can plausibly ground probability judgments about some such generalizations. And second, some such generalizations really do have a bearing on the probability of relevant singular claims, such as J. We must remember, however, that apart from their bearing on some important singular claim, generalizations about miracles, resurrections, etc., would seem to be of little importance to Christianity.[16] And so it would be, I suppose, with most religions.

What then would be the relevant feature of Hume's experience? I think it is the fact that in his own experience he had never come across a miraculous event. Or, at any rate, he had never come across an event in his own experience which he took to be miraculous. More specifically, with reference to this particular case, the relevant feature of Hume's experience would be that he had never himself personally witnessed a resurrection. Various of his friends and acquaintances had, I suppose, died by the time he wrote this essay. But he had not seen a single one of them restored to life. Leaving aside, for the moment, the general experience of the human race, this would be the feature of Hume's own personal experience which might seem relevant to assessing the probability of miracles, or at least to assessing the probability of this particular miracle, a resurrection from the dead.

I focus on this conjecture for the time being for three reasons. First, I have no reason to doubt that Hume's experience really did have this negative feature. Second, I share that negative experience with Hume. Like him, I have never witnessed a case of a dead person restored to life. And I think that many of you who read or hear this paper will say the same about yourself. And third, I think that this negative experience, on Hume's part and on our own, is indeed relevant to probability judgments about miracles.

But just how is it relevant? Perhaps this is the most important question we can ask about Hume's strategy here. Hume, we have supposed, never observed a resurrection. I have not observed one, and perhaps you have not either. How do facts like that bear on the probability of a resurrection – on the probability, that is, of R? Here I can put forward what is perhaps the central thesis of this paper.

> *These negative experiences, Hume's and yours and mine, are (for all practical purposes) completely irrelevant to the probabilities of R and NR.*

And the reason is simple and straightforward. Hume's sample is just too small to support, to any significant degree, any probability judgment at all about propositions R and NR. And so is your sample and mine.

There have been, I suppose, at least several billion human deaths in the history of the world. R and NR are propositions whose truth value might be determined by the presence or absence of a *single* quick resurrection within that vast panoply of cases. Now, suppose for the moment that there was, in fact, one resurrection in the history of the world. In that case R would be true and NR would be false. But what is the likelihood that Hume's sample of deaths and their immediate aftermath – 20 cases, 40, even 100 – would have caught that one anomalous event? In the absence of any reason to suppose that Hume was in a specially advantageous position to observe that event, if it happened, it seems to me that the probability of his catching it is almost infinitesimally small. The experience which I have here attributed to Hume is, of course, just what we should have expected it to be if NR is true, i.e., if there are no resurrections at all. But it is also just what we should have expected it to be if R is true, and the number of resurrections is very small – maybe one, or two, or half a dozen. Because these two different assumptions make only a tiny, practically infinitesimal, difference to the likelihood of Hume's observing a resurrection, his failure to observe one makes no significant difference to the probability of one rather than the other. But they are contradictories. So Hume's negative experience is irrelevant to their probability.[17] And so, of course, is your negative experience and mine, and for the same reason.

I said above, however, that these negative experiences really are relevant to some generalizations about resurrections, and about miracles more generally. Think, for example, of the following claim:

> CR: Speedy resurrections are very common in the history of the world (more than half of all human deaths are followed by a restoration to life within a week, etc.).

And the contrasting claim:

> RR: Speedy resurrections, if they occur at all, are extremely rare in the history of the world.

Hume's negative experience, it seems to me, really is relevant to assigning probabilities to these propositions. (And so also is our experience.) And the reason is the mirror image of the reason for the earlier irrelevance. If resurrections were really common occurrences, then it is quite likely that Hume would have come across one or more of them in his own experience. I too would probably have noticed one, and so would you. But in fact Hume did not observe any resurrection, I have not, etc. So it is unlikely that resurrections are common occurrences. That is, the probability of CR is very low. And the probability of RR is high.

But what does that have to do with any actual religion? Well, for Christianity at least, very little. No Christian that I know of asserts CR, or anything remotely resembling CR. None of them would be disturbed by the claim that CR is very improbable. (They might, I suppose, wonder who it was who thought that CR was probable.) And what if someone claimed that RR was probable? Well, RR might well strike the Christians as what they have always believed. No surprises there, no problem for them.

It is, of course, crucial to recognize (and to remember) that RR is not the same proposition as NR. NR is incompatible with J, and so a high probability for NR entails a low probability for J. But RR is not incompatible with J, and so a high probability for RR need not impose a low probability on J. The world is chock-full of things which are rare, but which nevertheless really do happen. Take quintuplets, for example. The birth of quintuplets is very rare among humans, averaging only one out of many thousands of pregnancies. A lot of my friends have children, but none of them have quints. So far as I know, none of my friends are themselves part of a set of quints. For quintuplet births, the analogue of RR has an extremely high probability. We have very good experiential evidence that quintuplet births are very rare. But the analogue of J also has a very high probability. For we also have good evidence – for a few of us experiential, and for the rest of us testimonial – that there really are some quintuplet births. And that is by no means an uncommon pattern in the world. The world is full of unlikely events.

This point sometimes gets obscured by an unfortunate way of speaking. Sometimes a person will say something like

> QU: Quintuplets are unlikely.

And this is the analogue of

> RU: Resurrections are unlikely.

I suppose that people who say QU probably do not mean to say that it is unlikely that there are any quints in the history of the world. Probably they believe, like most of the rest of us, that there have been some actual quintuplet births. But what then do they mean by QU? Sometimes, I think, QU is used just as a stylistic variant of the statement that quintuplets are rare. And sometimes it really does express a probability judgment, a judgment which is based on that rarity. If you think, for example, of picking out a pregnancy pretty much at random – the first woman to give birth in Ann Arbor's St Joseph Mercy Hospital in 2001, say – and you think of betting that the upshot will be a quintuplet birth, then you probably will think that such a bet is very unlikely to win. And you would, I suppose, be right. QU is sometimes used, I think, to express a probability judgment like that one.

RU has the same form as QU. And it can be used to say the analogous sorts of things. It can, I think, mean merely that resurrections are rare, which is just what RR says. Or it can mean that a randomly selected death is unlikely to be followed by a speedy resurrection. And that would not be disputed by many Christians. But RU is that it might also be taken to mean something quite different, i.e., that it is unlikely that there are any resurrections. It might be taken, that is, as expressing the judgment that the probability of R is very low. There is nothing wrong with expressing that judgment. But it is unfortunate and misleading when the plausibility of RU *in its other senses* gets transferred, perhaps without our noticing it, to this last sense.

We really do have to be on guard against this transference. If someone says to me, "But doesn't your own experience suggest that resurrections are unlikely?", then I feel right away like saying, "Yes, of course it does." What I'm doing in that response is taking his question in one (or both) of the first senses above – a question about rarity, or about the probability for a random case. If the interlocutor goes on to say, "But isn't that just what Hume is saying?", then I have to say, "No. Or at least, it's not what he needs to say. What Hume needs is the claim that it is unlikely that there are any resurrections in the world, not just that resurrections are rare. And that's not what I'm saying."

Well, where are we now? What we've come to is that neither Hume's experience nor ours gives us any good direct ground for assigning a low probability to J. (Of course, it doesn't give us any ground for a high probability there either.) On the other hand, Hume's experience (and ours) does give us grounds for probability judgments about some generalizations concerning resurrections. But those generalizations do not support a low probability for J. There is a generalization which would have that consequence, but our experience does not give us a ground for thinking that generalization to be probable. So far Hume's project looks unpromising.

It might be suggested, of course, that we have been looking too narrowly, just at Hume's personal experience and ours. But might we not expand the sample by adding to our own experience the experiences of other people? Of course. And indeed in this essay Hume appears to make just that attempt. He makes repeated references to human experience in general.

This attempt, however, generates at least two related problems. I will mention the first here, but I will not say very much about it. A person who attempts to estimate the probability of some proposition may know what his or her own experience has been, and may then try to assess the relevance of that experience to the task at hand. But if one wants to cast a wider net, and to include the experience of others, then how can one get in touch with those experiences which are not one's own? It would seem that the normal way – perhaps the only way available to human beings – is by way of the testimony of those other people. But Hume's strategy here seems to require us to decide upon whether to accept a testimony by *first* comparing the probability of its falsehood with the probability of the event which the testimony reports. That would seem to require us first to estimate the probability of the event on, at best, the evidence of our own limited experience, and then, if that probability is low, we would be required to reject contrary testimony. It is hard to see how Hume, if he were consistent, could ever take seriously the wider body of experience which would give him a sounder basis for a reasonable probability estimate.

The second (and related) problem, about which I will say a little more, is this. If we do try to expand the sample beyond Hume's own personal experience (or mine or yours), then what do we find? What do we find, that is, not by armchair theorizing but by actually examining that expanded sample? Well, Hume seems eager to tell us what the result of that trial is. He says that "it is a miracle that a dead man should come to life; because that has never been observed in any age or country. There must therefore be a uniform experience against every miraculous event . . ."[18] So Hume's picture of things seems to go like this. His own personal experience has the negative feature of not including any observation of a resurrection. And when he expands the sample to include the experience of the whole human race he gets the same negative result. The miraculous event, Hume tells us, "has never been observed in any age or country."

But why should we believe Hume on this point? Why, that is, should we believe that the universal experience of the human race has uniformly been devoid of any experience of the miraculous? I have no problem with accepting pretty much whatever negative feature Hume may want to claim for his own experience. But I am not at all inclined to believe him when he assigns that same negative feature to the experience of the whole human race. He says not merely that he has never observed a resurrection, but that a resurrection has never been observed in any age or country. But he suggests absolutely no evidence at all for this latter claim. Of course, the claim might possible be true. But why should we suppose that it is? The clearest fact in this whole area would seem to be that *the testimony about resurrections, and other apparently miraculous happenings, is not uniform.* Some people, like Hume, profess not to have observed any such things. Well and good. Perhaps they have not. But the fact is that some other people profess that they have personally observed just such events. When it comes to resurrections, for example, there have apparently been some people who claimed to have seen Jesus a few days after his execution, alive and well, talking with them, eating with them, and so on.

Where does that leave us? We can, if we want, choose to rely entirely on our own personal experience. A consequence will be that, in many important cases, that body of experience which belongs to us personally will be too small to provide a reasonable basis for the kind of probability judgments which we want to make. Or we can try to expand the base by adding to our own experience the experiences of a large number of other people. But our only way of carrying out that expansion is by appealing to the testimony of those other people. In that case, at least if we are to proceed empirically, we have to take the testimonies as we actually find them. We cannot just make up testimonies to suit ourselves. *Nor can we properly leave out testimonies just to suit ourselves.* In the case of miracles, the fact that there are these other troubling minority testimonies, the testimonies of those who claim to have experienced miracles themselves, becomes part of the data with which we must deal.[19]

It might, of course, turn out that the whole Humean project is flawed at some deeper level than I have examined here. Maybe, for example, Hume's attraction to a radical empiricism is at fault, leading him to ignore some other essential features of a viable intellectual life, features which have more of an a *priori*, or innatist, flavor about them. Maybe, for example, there are some probability judgments which are important to our cognitive life, but which are not based on experience. Here I have said nothing for or against this conjecture, or any other alternative to Hume's own professed project. In any case, however, the project to which he seems to commit himself in this essay provides no sound basis for assigning a low probability to the general thesis that there are some miracles in the history of the world. Nor does it provide a sound basis for assigning a low antecedent probability to singular miracle claims, such as that of Jesus' resurrection. Consequently, probability comparisons which involve any of those probabilities as one of the terms need not be expected to be always unfavorable to the miracle claims.

Acknowledgement

An earlier version of this paper was presented at the March 1997 meeting of the Society for Philosophy of Religion.

Notes

1 Compare, for example, what Hume says about the quality of miracle testimonies in the first part of Part II, pp. 78–80, with what he says about the reports of miracles associated with the tomb of Abbè Paris (pp. 83–5). The quotations in this paper, along with the page citations and footnote citations, are taken from the edition of the *Enquiry* edited by Eric Steinberg (Indianapolis: Hackett Publishing Company, 1977). The *Enquiry* was first published in 1758.

2 Part II, p. 88.

3 Almost any driver, I would suppose, who judged that there was even a 50–50 chance that they would have a serious accident if they were to drive on a given day, would almost surely refrain from driving on that day. I would, anyway.

4 If the probability of the miracle were not always lower than the probability that the testimony is false, then Hume's strategy would sometimes yield a belief in a miracle.

5 Part I, p. 73.

6 Part I, p. 77.

7 But elsewhere in the essay Hume really does seem to use "miracle" in more or less the sense which he defines – "a transgression of a law of nature by a particular volition of the Deity, or by the interposition of some invisible agent." Part I, p. 77.

8 Or that it at least satisfies the first clause of that definition. Perhaps Hume here, like many later interlocutors, simply ignores the second clause of the definition. Or maybe he thinks that the second clause is really redundant, implied by the first.

9 William James is, of course, famous for an additional suggestion in "The Will to Believe."

10 I express both of these propositions without using the word "miracle," and that is deliberate. I take it that a person might give a miracle testimony without using that word, and indeed without having any concept of a miracle. Or he might have that concept and believe that the event he was reporting did not satisfy that concept and hence was not a miracle. But if the event as described does in fact satisfy that concept, then the testifier is testifying to the occurrence of a miracle, regardless of whether he recognizes that significance in his testimony. Whatever his own evaluation of his report may be, that report might give *us* reason to believe that a miracle had occurred.

11 This is not, of course, the probability that the testifier *thinks* that he or she had these experiences. We are not assessing the sincerity of the testifier, but rather the reliability of the testimony. Cf. Hume's concern that the testifier may be either deceiving or deceived.

12 Where P(M) is the probability of M, etc. We need not have numerical values for these probabilities in order to make the relevant "calculations." If we judge that the probability of M is simply *very low*, then we will also judge that the probability of ~M is *very high*.

13 Part I, p. 74.

14 Ibid. Hume's Scottish contemporary, Thomas Reid, put forth an alternative view, that there is an innate human disposition to accept testimony, and that human intellectual life could not get under way without this disposition. Was Hume aware of this dissenting voice?

15 Part I, p. 76.

16 In the SPR discussion, this point was strongly urged by Professor Paul Draper. My thanks to him for stressing it.

17 This is, of course, the line of reasoning which is formalized in Bayes' Theorem.

18 Part I, p. 77.

19 It might be suggested that the wider experience of the human race provides us with something stronger than merely a collection of testimonies – it provides us with well-grounded laws of nature. And so perhaps "no resurrections" is a law of nature, or a consequence of some more general and fundamental laws of nature. And maybe it is (I'm inclined to think so myself). But that cannot help with this project.

Either a law of nature logically allows for a few exceptions (i.e., Humean "transgressions") in the actual course of events, or else it does not. If it allow for a few actual exceptions, then establishing "When you're dead, you stay dead" as a law of nature will have no bearing on the probability of R and of NR, and hence no bearing on the probability of J.

Some philosophers – e.g. Alastair McKinnon, "'Miracle' and 'Paradox'," in *American Philosophical Quarterly*, vol. IV (1967), pp. 308–14 – have argued that the idea of a violation of a law of nature is logically incoherent. A law of nature cannot (logically) have any exceptions; the law just is whatever actually happens. That seems to me implausible, but I will not argue it here. (But cf. the discussion by Richard Swinburne in *The Concept of Miracle* (London: MacMillan, 1970), Chap. 3.) In any case, this way of construing a law of nature will leave us with roughly the same difficulty, though perhaps in a different place. We cannot use the "no resurrections" thesis to rule out R (and thus to rule out J) until we know whether it is indeed a (McKinnon-type) law of nature. But we cannot know that it is a law of nature of that sort until we have a way of ruling out the minority testimonies, the testimonies to a resurrection.

B

Science, Religion, and Naturalism

1

Letter to Castelli

Galileo Galilei

Galileo (1564–1642) was a prominent Italian scientist most famous for having defended the new, and still controversial, Copernican heliocentric model of the solar system. In a letter written to a monk and Copernican named Castelli, Galileo outlined his response to religious critics who regarded the Copernican system as inconsistent with scripture. Although Galileo affirms that scripture does not contain errors, he also insists that a rigidly literal interpretation of many passages does lead to errors. Galileo's intent was to reconcile Copernican science and scripture, but when a copy of the letter fell into the hands of Father Lorini, an opponent of Copernicanism, it only served to fuel the debate. Lorini altered the text to make Galileo's opinions sound more controversial and sent a corrupted copy to the Roman Inquisition. Our reading is Galileo's original letter; Lorini's corruptions are mentioned in the endnotes.

To the Very Reverend Father and Most Worthy Gentleman:

Yesterday I met Sig. Niccolò Arrighetti, who gave me a report about you from which I derived the infinite pleasure of learning what I have never doubted; namely, the great satisfaction which you have given to the whole University, to its administrators as much as to its teachers and to every group of students. This applause has not increased the number of your competitors, as usually happens among men of similar accomplishments, but has restricted them to only a very few. Even these few will become quiet if they wish that this competition, which still usually merits the title of being a virtue at times, will not degenerate and change in character into a blameful affection which ultimately is more dangerous to those who clothe themselves in it than to anyone else. But what was most to my liking was to hear the account of the discussions which, thanks to the great kindness of the Grand Duchess, you had occasion to bring up at table and to continue later in the private chambers of the Grand Duchess, in the presence of the Grand Duke and the Archduchess, and the most illustrious and renowned Don Antonio and Don Paolo Giordano, and some well-known philosophers. What greater good fortune could one have than to see the Grand Duchess herself taking satisfaction from having this discussion with you, from raising doubts, from listening to solutions, and from remaining satisfied with your replies?

The particulars which you brought up, as reported by Sig. Arrighetti, have given me an occasion to return to some general considerations about natural conclusions, and in particular about the passage in Joshua which was mentioned by the Grand Duchess, with a few rejoinders from the Archduchess, as contradictory to the mobility of the earth and the stability of the sun.

In regard to the Grand Duchess' first general question,[1] I agree, as you most prudently proposed, conceded, and established, that it is not possible for Sacred Scripture ever to deceive or to err; rather its decrees have absolute and inviolable truth. Only I would have added that, although Scripture itself cannot err, nevertheless some of its interpreters and expositors can sometimes err, and in various ways.[2] The most serious and most frequent of these errors occurs when they wish to maintain always the direct meaning of the words, because from this there results not only various contradictions but even grave and blasphemous heresies. Accordingly it would be necessary to attribute to God feet and hands and eyes and even human and bodily feelings like anger, regret, hatred, and even occasional forgetfulness of the past and ignorance of the future. Many propositions are found in the Scriptures which, in respect to the bare meaning of the words, give an impression which is different from the truth, but they are stated in this way in order to be accommodated to the incapacities of the common man.[3] As a result, for those few who deserve to be distinguished from the common people, it is necessary that wise expositors provide the true meanings and indicate the particular reasons why the Scriptures are expressed in such words.

Granting then that in many passages the Scriptures not only can be, but necessarily must be, interpreted differently from the apparent meaning of the words, it seems to me that in cases of natural disputes Scripture ought to be put off to the last place. For both Sacred Scripture and nature are derived from the Divine Word, the former as dictated by the Holy Spirit and the latter as most carefully discovered in the laws of God. Moreover it is agreed that, to accommodate itself to the understanding of everyone, Scripture says many things which are different from absolute truth in the impression it gives and in the meaning of its words. On the other hand nature is inexorable and immutable and cares not whether its hidden causes and modes of operation are or are not open to the capacities of humans, and hence it never violates the terms of its established laws. As a result it seems that natural effects, which either sense experience places before our eyes or necessary demonstrations reveal, should never be placed in doubt by passages of Scripture whose words give a different impression; and further not everything said in the Scriptures ought to be associated strictly with some effect in nature. Because of this characteristic alone, i.e., that Scripture accommodates itself to the capacity of uncouth and uneducated people, Scripture does not refrain from faintly sketching its most important dogmas, thus attributing to God himself conditions which are very far from, and contrary to, his essence.[4] So who would wish to maintain with certainty that Scripture abandons this characteristic when it speaks incidentally of the earth or the sun or other creatures, and has chosen to restrain itself completely within the limited and narrow meaning of the words? – and especially when it speaks about those created things which are very far from the primary purpose of the Scriptures? – or even when it speaks of things which, when stated and presented as bare and unadorned truths, would quickly damage its primary intention by making the common man more stubbornly resistant to be persuaded of the articles concerning his salvation?

Granting this, and also granting that it is even more obvious that two truths can never be contrary to each other, it is the task of wise expositors to try to find the true meanings of sacred passages in accordance with natural conclusions which previously have been rendered certain and secure by manifest sensation or by necessary demonstrations. Furthermore, as I have said, although Scripture has been dictated by the Holy Spirit, for the reasons mentioned above it is open in many passages to interpretations far removed from the literal meaning; and moreover we cannot determine with certitude that all the interpreters speak with divine inspiration. As a result I believe that it would be prudent to agree that no one should fix the meaning of passages of Scripture and oblige us to maintain as true any natural conclusions which later sensation or necessary and demonstrative proofs might show to be contrary to truth. Who would wish to place limits on human understanding? Who would wish to assert that everything which is knowable about the world is already known? And therefore, except for the articles concerning salvation and the foundations of the faith, against the strength of which there is no danger that any valid and forceful doctrine could ever arise, it would be perhaps the best advice not to add anything without necessity. Granting this, what greater confusion could arise than from the increase of questions from people who, besides our not knowing whether they speak with inspiration by heavenly power, we do know are totally barren of the intelligence needed not only to challenge but even to understand the demonstrations used by the most exact sciences to confirm their conclusions?

I believe that the authority of Sacred Scripture has the sole aim of persuading men of those articles and propositions which, being necessary for salvation but being beyond all human discourse, cannot come to be believed by any science or by any means other than by the mouth of the Holy Spirit himself. I do not think that it is necessary to have belief in cases in which God himself, who is the source of meaning, of discourse, and of intellect, has put the use of revelation to one side and has decided to give to us in another way the knowledge which we can obtain through science. This is especially true of those sciences of which only a very small part, and then as projected in conclusions, is to be found in the Scriptures. Such is precisely the case with astronomy, of which there is such a small part in the Scriptures that the planets are not even mentioned. However if the sacred writers had intended to teach us about the arrangements and movements of the celestial bodies, they would not have said so little, almost nothing, in comparison with the infinite, highest, and admirable conclusions contained in this science.

Let me show you, Father, if I am not mistaken, how those who immediately quote passages of Scripture in natural disputes which are not directly related to the faith, proceed in a disorderly way, and are even often harmful to their own interests. Such people really believe that they know the true meaning of a particular passage in Scripture, and consequently they firmly think that they already have in hand the absolute truth about the question they intend to dispute. Then let them tell me quite frankly whether they think that he who maintains what is true in a natural dispute has a great advantage over someone else who maintains what is false. I know that they would answer "yes," and that one who maintains the true side will have a thousand experiences and a thousand necessary demonstrations on his side, while the other can have only sophisms, fallacies, and paralogisms. But if one knows that he has such an advantage over his adversary when he stays within the limits of nature and uses only philosophical weapons, then why, when he comes later to a debate, would he quickly use dreadful and irresistible weapons, which alone would terrify any more skillful and expert defender? To tell the truth, I believe that he is the terrified one, and that, sensing his inability to stand firm against the assaults of his adversary, he will shake in his boots to find a way of not allowing himself to draw near. As I have already said, he who has truth on his side has a great advantage, indeed the greatest advantage, over an adversary. And it is impossible for two truths to conflict. As a result we should not fear the assaults which come against us, whatever they be, as long as we still have room to speak and to be heard by people who are experts and who are not excessively affected by their own interests and feelings.

To confirm this, I come now to a consideration of the particular passage from Joshua which occasioned three comments to the Grand Duchess. And I will seize upon the third, which was presented as mine, as indeed it truly is. But I will add for you some further considerations which I do not believe have been put in writing previously.

Let it be granted and conceded to an adversary for now that the sacred text should be taken in its exact literal meaning; namely, that God was asked by Joshua to make the sun stand still and to prolong the day so that he could obtain the victory. And I also ask my adversary to observe the same rule that I observe, that is, that he not bind me but free himself in regard to altering or changing the meaning of the words. I say, then, that this passage most clearly shows the falsity and impossibility of the Aristotelian and Ptolemaic world system, and is also very well accommodated to the Copernican system.

First I ask my adversary if he knows by what motions the sun is moved. If he knows, he must reply that the sun has two motions; namely, an annual motion towards the east and a daily motion towards the west.

Next I ask him whether both of these motions, which are different and contrary to each other, belong to the sun and are both proper to it. He must reply "no," for the only proper and special motion of the sun is its annual motion. The other motion is not proper to it, but belongs to the highest heaven, that is, the first sphere, which in its rotation carries along the sun and the other planets and the stellar sphere and which is ordained to give a rotation around the earth in twenty-four hours by means of a motion, as I have said, which is contrary to the sun's natural and proper motion.

I come then to the third question, and I ask him which of these two motions of the sun causes day and night; namely, its own proper and real motion, or the motion of the first sphere. He must reply that day and night are caused by the motion of the first sphere, and that the proper motion of the sun does not produce day and night but rather the various seasons and the year itself.

Now if the day depends not on the motion of the sun but on the motion of the first sphere, who does not see that, in order to lengthen the day, one needs to make the first sphere stop, and not the sun? Thus if someone understands these first elements of astronomy, does he not also recognize that if God had stopped the motion of the sun, then instead of lengthening the day, he would have shortened it and made it briefer? For since the motion of the sun is contrary to the daily rotation, then to the degree that the sun moves towards the east, to the same degree it will be slowed down in its motion towards the west. And if the motion of the sun is decreased or annulled, it will move to the west in a proportionally shorter time. This is observable if one looks at the moon, whose daily rotation is slower than that of the sun in proportion to its own proper motion being faster than that of the sun. Therefore it is absolutely impossible in the system of Ptolemy and Aristotle to stop the motion of the sun and thereby to lengthen the day, as the Scripture states to have happened. Hence either one must say that the motions are not arranged as Ptolemy said, or one must alter the meaning of the words, and say that, when the Scripture says that God stopped the sun, he really wished to say that he stopped the first sphere. But in order to accommodate himself to the capacity of those who are hardly able to understand the rising and setting of the sun, he said the contrary of what he ought to have said as he spoke to humans steeped in the senses.

Let me add that it is not credible that God would have stopped the sun without paying attention to the other spheres. For without any reason he would have changed all the laws, relations, and dispositions of the other stars in respect to the sun, and would have greatly disturbed the whole course of nature. But it is credible that he stopped the whole system of celestial spheres which, after an intervening period of rest, he returned consistently to their functions without any confusion or alteration.

But since we have already agreed not to alter the meaning of the words of the text, we must have recourse to another arrangement of the parts of the world, and then see if it agrees with the bare meaning of the words, taken straightforwardly and without hesitation, as to what actually happened.

Now I have discovered and have proven with necessity that the globe of the sun rotates on itself, making one full revolution in about one lunar month, in exactly the same way that all the other celestial rotations occur. Moreover it is quite probable and reasonable that the sun, as the instrument and highest minister of nature, as if it were the heart of the world, gives not only light, as it clearly does, but also motion to all the planets which revolve around it. Therefore, if in agreement with the position of Copernicus we attribute the daily rotation primarily to the earth, then who does not see that, in order to stop the whole system without any alteration in the remaining mutual relation of the planets but only to prolong the space and time of the daylight, it is sufficient to make the sun stop, exactly as the literal meaning of the sacred text says? Behold then that in this second way it is possible to lengthen the day on earth by stopping the sun, without introducing any confusion among the parts of the world and without altering the words of Scripture.

I have written much more than my indisposition allows. So I will end, offering my services and kissing your hands, petitioning Our Lord for a good holiday and every happiness.

Florence, 21 December 1613

Notes

1 Lorini's adulterated copy of this letter begins with this sentence. In addition to several minor modifications, there are three major changes, plus an omission of any reference to the Tuscan royal family. See *Opere*, XIX, 299–301 for all the modifications in Lorini's text.

2 In Lorini's copy, the words, "some of" and "sometimes" are omitted from this sentence.

3 In Lorini's copy this sentence is changed to read: "... which, in respect to the bare meaning of the words, are false, but they are stated ..."

4 In Lorini's copy this sentence is changed to read: "... Scripture does not refrain from perverting its most important dogmas ..."

2

Signs of Intelligence

William A. Dembski

William A. Dembski (b. 1960) is Research Professor in Philosophy at Southwestern Baptist Theological Seminary in Fort Worth, Texas and is one of the leading proponents of the Intelligent Design movement. A mathematician, philosopher, and public lecturer, Dembski is the author of *The Design Inference* (Cambridge University Press, 1998), and *Intelligent Design: The Bridge Between Science and Theology* (Intervarsity Press, 1999), as well as many other books and articles. In the following essay, he considers the distinctions between necessity, blind contingency (or chance), and directed contingency (or design). Since approximately the nineteenth century the notion of design has been largely repudiated in science, but Dembski contends that this has been a mistake. He goes on to develop and explain a criterion for detecting design.

Intelligent design examines the distinction between three modes of explanation: necessity, chance, and design. In our workaday lives we find it important to distinguish between these modes of explanation. Did she fall or was she pushed? And if she fell, was it simply bad luck or was her fall unavoidable? More generally, given an event, object, or structure, we want to know:

1. Did it have to happen?
2. Did it happen by accident?
3. Did an intelligent agent cause it to happen?

Given an event to be explained, the first thing to determine is whether it had to happen. If so, the event is necessary. By "necessary" I don't just mean logically necessary, as in true across all

William A. Dembski, "Signs of Intelligence: A Primer on the Discernment of Intelligent Design" from *Signs of Intelligence: Understanding Intelligent Design*, eds. William A. Dembski and James M. Kushiner (Grand Rapids, MI: Brazos Press, 2001), pp. 171–92.

possible worlds, but I also include physical necessity, as in a law-like relation between antecedent circumstances and consequent events. Not all events are necessary.

Events that happen but do not have to happen are said to be contingent. In our everyday lives we distinguish two types of contingency: one blind, the other directed. A blind contingency lacks a superintending intelligence and is usually characterized by probabilities. Blind contingency is another name for chance. A directed contingency, on the other hand, is the result of a superintending intelligence. Directed contingency is another name for design.

An Ancient Question

This characterization of necessity, chance, and design is pretheoretical and therefore inadequate for building a precise scientific theory of design. We therefore need to inquire whether there is a principled way to distinguish these modes of explanation. Philosophers and scientists have disagreed not only about how to distinguish these modes of explanation, but also about their very legitimacy. The Epicureans, for instance, gave pride of place to chance. The Stoics, on the other hand, emphasized necessity and design, but rejected chance. In the Middle Ages, Moses Maimonides contended with the Islamic interpreters of Aristotle who viewed the heavens as, in Maimonides's words, "the necessary result of natural laws." Where the Islamic philosophers saw necessity, Maimonides saw design.

In arguing for design in his *Guide for the Perplexed*, Maimonides looked to the irregular distribution of stars in the heavens. For him that irregularity demonstrated contingency. But was that contingency the result of chance or design? Neither Maimonides nor the Islamic interpreters of Aristotle had any use for Epicurus and his views on chance. For them chance could never be fundamental but was at best a placeholder for ignorance. Thus for Maimonides and his Islamic colleagues, the question was whether a principled distinction could be drawn between necessity and design. Maimonides, arguing from observed contingency in nature, said yes. The Islamic philosophers, intent on keeping Aristotle pure of theology, said no.

A Modern Demise

Modern science has also struggled with how to distinguish between necessity, chance, and design. Newtonian mechanics, construed as a set of deterministic physical laws, seemed only to permit necessity. Nonetheless, in the General Scholium to his *Principia*, Newton claimed that the stability of the planetary system depended not only on the regular action of the universal law of gravitation, but also on the precise initial positioning of the planets and comets in relation to the sun. As he explained: "Though these bodies may, indeed, persevere in their orbits by the mere laws of gravity, yet they could by no means have at first derived the regular position of the orbits themselves from those laws.... [Thus] this most beautiful system of the sun, planets, and comets, could only proceed from the counsel and dominion of an intelligent and powerful being." Like Maimonides, Newton saw both necessity and design as legitimate explanations, but gave short shrift to chance.

Newton published his *Principia* in the seventeenth century. By the nineteenth century, necessity was still in, chance was still out, but design had lost much of its appeal. When asked by Napoleon where God fit into his equations of celestial mechanics, astronomer and mathematician Laplace famously replied, "Sire, I have no need of that hypothesis." In place of a designing intelligence that precisely positioned the heavenly bodies, Laplace proposed his nebular hypothesis, which accounted for the origin of the solar system strictly as the result of natural gravitational forces.

Since Laplace's day, science has largely dispensed with design. Certainly Darwin played a crucial role here by eliminating design from biology. Yet at the same time science was dispensing with design, it was also dispensing with Laplace's vision of a deterministic universe (recall Laplace's famous demon who could predict the future and retrodict the past with perfect precision provided that present positions and momenta of particles were fully known). With the rise of statistical mechanics and then quantum mechanics, the role of chance in physics came to be regarded as ineliminable. Consequently, a deterministic, necessitarian universe has given way to a stochastic universe in which chance and necessity are both regarded as fundamental modes of scientific explanation, neither being reducible to the other. To sum up, contemporary science allows a principled distinction between necessity and chance, but repudiates design.

Bacon and Aristotle

But was science right to repudiate design? My aim in *The Design Inference* is to rehabilitate design. I argue that design is a legitimate and fundamental mode of scientific explanation on a par with chance and necessity. Since my aim is to rehabilitate design, it will help to review why design was removed from science in the first place. Design, in the form of Aristotle's formal and final causes, after all, had once occupied a perfectly legitimate role within natural philosophy, or what we now call science. With the rise of modern science, however, these causes fell into disrepute.

We can see how this happened by considering Francis Bacon. Bacon, a contemporary of Galileo and Kepler, though himself not a scientist, was a terrific propagandist for science. Bacon was concerned about the proper conduct of science and provided detailed canons for experimental observation, the recording of data, and drawing inferences from data. What interests us here, however, is what he did with Aristotle's four causes. For Aristotle, to understand any phenomenon properly, one had to understand its four causes, namely its material, efficient, formal, and final cause.

Two points about Aristotle's causes are relevant to this discussion. First, Aristotle gave equal weight to all four causes and would have regarded any inquiry that omitted one of his causes as fundamentally deficient. Second, Bacon adamantly opposed the inclusion of formal and final causes within science (see his *Advancement of Learning*). For Bacon, formal and final causes belonged to metaphysics and not to science. Science, according to Bacon, needed to limit itself to material and efficient causes, thereby freeing science from the sterility that inevitably results when science and metaphysics are conflated. This was Bacon's line, and he argued it forcefully.

We see Bacon's line championed in our own day. For instance, in his book *Chance and Necessity*,[1] biologist and Nobel laureate Jacques Monod argued that chance and necessity alone suffice to account for every aspect of the universe. Now whatever else we might want to say about chance and necessity, they provide at best a reductive account of Aristotle's formal causes and leave no room for Aristotle's final causes. Indeed, Monod explicitly denies any place for purpose within science.

Now I don't want to give the impression that I'm advocating a return to Aristotle's theory of causation. There are problems with Aristotle's theory, and it needed to be replaced. My concern, however, is with what replaced it. By limiting scientific inquiry to material and efficient causes, which are of course perfectly compatible with chance and necessity, Bacon championed a view of science that could only end up excluding design.

The Design Instinct

But suppose we lay aside *a priori* prohibitions against design. In that case, what is wrong with explaining something as designed by an intelligent agent? Certainly there are many everyday occurrences that we explain by appealing to design. Moreover, in our daily lives it is absolutely crucial to distinguish accident from design. We demand answers to such questions as: Did she fall or was she pushed? Did someone die accidentally or commit suicide? Was this song conceived independently or was it plagiarized? Did someone just get lucky on the stock market or was there insider trading?

Not only do we demand answers to such questions, but entire industries are also devoted to drawing the distinction between accident and design. Here we can include forensic science, intellectual property law, insurance claims investigation, cryptography, and random number generation – to name but a few. Science itself needs to draw this distinction to keep itself honest. As a January 1998 issue of *Science*[2] made clear, plagiarism and data falsification are far more common in science than we would like to admit. What keeps these abuses in check is our ability to detect them.

If design is so readily detectable outside of science, and if its detectability is one of the key factors keeping scientists honest, why should design be barred from the actual content of science? There's a worry here. The worry is that when we leave the constricted domain of human artifacts and enter the unbounded domain of scientific inquiry, the distinction between design and nondesign cannot be reliably drawn. Consider, for instance, the following remark by Darwin in the concluding chapter of his *Origin of Species*:

> Several eminent naturalists have of late published their belief that a multitude of reputed species in each genus are not real species; but that other species are real, that is, have been independently created. . . . Nevertheless they do not pretend that they can define, or even conjecture, which are the created forms of life, and which are those produced by secondary laws. They admit variation as a *vera causa* in one case, they arbitrarily reject it in another, without assigning any distinction in the two cases.[3]

It's this worry of falsely attributing something to design (here construed as creation) only to have it overturned later, that has prevented design from entering science proper.

This worry, though perhaps understandable in the past, can no longer be justified. There does in fact exist a rigorous criterion for discriminating intelligently from unintelligently caused objects. Many special sciences already use this criterion, though in a pretheoretic form (e.g., forensic science, artificial intelligence, cryptography, archeology, and the search for extraterrestrial intelligence). In *The Design Inference* I identify and make precise this criterion. I call it the *complexity-specification criterion*. When intelligent agents act, they leave behind a characteristic trademark or signature – what I call *specified complexity*. The complexity-specification criterion detects design by identifying this trademark of designed objects.

The Complexity-specification Criterion

A detailed explanation and justification of the complexity-specification criterion is technical and can be found in *The Design Inference*. Nevertheless, the basic idea is straightforward and easily illustrated. Consider how the radio astronomers in the movie *Contact* detected an extraterrestrial intelligence. This movie, based on a novel by Carl Sagan, was an enjoyable piece of propaganda for the SETI research program – the Search for Extraterrestrial Intelligence. To make the movie interesting, the SETI researchers in *Contact* actually did find an extraterrestrial intelligence (the nonfictional SETI program has yet to be so lucky).

How, then, did the SETI researchers in *Contact* convince themselves that they had found an extraterrestrial intelligence? To increase their chances of finding an extraterrestrial intelligence, SETI researchers monitor millions of radio signals from outer space. Many natural objects in space produce radio waves (e.g., pulsars). Looking for signs of design among all these naturally produced radio signals is like looking for a needle in a haystack. To sift through the haystack, SETI researchers run the signals they monitor through computers programmed with pattern-matchers. So long as a signal doesn't match one of the preset patterns, it will pass through the pattern-matching sieve (and that even if it has an intelligent source). If, on the other hand, it does match one of these patterns, then, depending on the pattern matched, the SETI researchers may have cause for celebration.

The SETI researchers in *Contact* did find a signal worthy of celebration, namely the following:

11011101111101111111011111111111011111
11111111111111111111111101111111111111
11110111111111111111111111101111111111
11111111111111111110111111111111111111
11111111111011111111111111111111111111
11111111110111111111111111111111111111
11111111111110111111111111111111111111
11111111111111111011111111111111111111
11111111111111111111111111011111111111
11111111111111111111111111111111111111
11101111111111111111111111111111111111
11111111111111111111111111011111111111
11111111111111111111111111111111111111
11111111111111111011111111111111111111
11111111111111111111111111111111111111
11111111111011111111111111111111111111

```
111111111111111111111111111111111111111
111111101111111111111111111111111111111
111111111111111111111111111111111111111
111111111101111111111111111111111111111
111111111111111111111111111111111111111
111111111111111011111111111111111111111
111111111111111111111111111111111111111
111111111111111111111111111011111111111
111111111111111111111111111111111111111
111111111111111111111111111111111111111
111111111101111111111111111111111111111
111111111111111111111111111111111111111
111111111111111111111111111111111
```

The SETI researchers in *Contact* received this signal as a sequence of 1,126 beats and pauses, where 1s correspond to beats and 0s to pauses. This sequence represents the prime numbers from 2 to 101, where a given prime number is represented by the corresponding number of beats (i.e., 1s), and the individual prime numbers are separated by pauses (i.e., 0s). The SETI researchers in *Contact* took this signal as decisive confirmation of an extraterrestrial intelligence.

What is it about this signal that implicates design? Whenever we infer design, we must establish three things: *contingency*, *complexity*, and *specification*. Contingency ensures that the object in question is not the result of an automatic and therefore unintelligent process that had no choice in its production. Complexity ensures that the object is not so simple that it can readily be explained by chance. Finally, specification ensures that the object exhibits the type of pattern characteristic of intelligence. Let us examine these three requirements more closely.

Contingency

In practice, to establish the contingency of an object, event, or structure, one must establish that it is compatible with the regularities involved in its production, but that these regularities also permit any number of alternatives to it. Typically these regularities are conceived as natural laws or algorithms. By being compatible with but not required by the regularities involved in its production, an object, event, or structure becomes irreducible to any underlying physical necessity. Michael Polanyi and Timothy Lenoir have both described this method of establishing contingency.

The method applies quite generally: the position of Scrabble pieces on a Scrabble board is irreducible to the natural laws governing the motion of Scrabble pieces; the configuration of ink on a sheet of paper is irreducible to the physics and chemistry of paper and ink; the sequencing of DNA bases is irreducible to the bonding affinities between the bases; and so on. In the case at hand, the sequence of 0s and 1s to form a sequence of prime numbers is irreducible to the laws of physics that govern the transmission of radio signals. We therefore regard the sequence as contingent.

Complexity

To see next why complexity is crucial for inferring design, consider the following sequence of bits:

110111011111

These are the first twelve bits in the previous sequence representing the prime numbers 2, 3, and 5 respectively. Now it is a sure bet that no SETI researcher, if confronted with this twelve-bit sequence, is going to contact the science editor at the *New York Times*, hold a press conference, and announce that an extraterrestrial intelligence has been discovered. No headline is going to read, "Aliens Master First Three Prime Numbers!"

The problem is that this sequence is much too short (and thus too simple) to establish that an extraterrestrial intelligence with knowledge of prime numbers produced it. A randomly beating radio source might by chance just happen to produce this sequence. A sequence of 1,126 bits representing the prime numbers from 2 to 101, however, is a different story. Here the sequence is sufficiently long (and therefore sufficiently complex) to allow that an extraterrestrial intelligence could have produced it.

Complexity as I am describing it here is a form of probability. (Later in this essay I will require a more general conception of complexity to unpack the logic of design inferences. But for now complexity as a form of probability is all we need.) To see the connection between complexity and probability, consider a combination lock. The more possible combinations of the lock, the more complex the mechanism, and, correspondingly, the more improbable that the mechanism can be opened by chance. Complexity and probability therefore vary inversely: the greater the complexity, the smaller the probability. Thus to determine whether something is sufficiently complex to warrant a design inference is to determine whether it has sufficiently small probability.

Even so, complexity (or improbability) isn't enough to eliminate chance and establish design. If I flip a coin one thousand times, I'll participate in a highly complex (i.e., highly improbable) event. Indeed, the sequence I end up flipping will be one in a trillion trillion trillion . . . , where the ellipsis indicates twenty-two more "trillions." This sequence of coin tosses won't, however, trigger a design inference. Though complex, this sequence won't exhibit a suitable pattern. Contrast this with the previous sequence representing the prime numbers from 2 to 101. Not only is this sequence complex, but it also embodies a suitable pattern. The SETI researcher who in the movie *Contact* discovered this sequence put it this way: "This isn't noise; this has structure."

Specification

What is a *suitable* pattern for inferring design? Not just any pattern will do. Some patterns can legitimately be employed to infer design whereas others cannot. The intuition underlying the distinction between patterns that alternately succeed or fail to implicate design is, however, easily motivated. Consider the case of an archer. Suppose an archer stands fifty meters from a large wall with bow and arrow in hand. The wall is sufficiently large that the archer cannot help but hit it. Now suppose each time the archer shoots an arrow at the wall, the archer paints a target around the arrow so that the arrow sits squarely in the bull's-eye. What can be concluded from this scenario? Absolutely nothing about the archer's ability as an archer. Yes, a pattern is being matched, but it is a pattern fixed only after the arrow has been shot. The pattern is thus purely *ad hoc*.

But suppose instead the archer paints a fixed target on the wall and then shoots at it. Suppose the archer shoots a hundred arrows, and each time hits a perfect bull's-eye. What can be concluded from this second scenario? Confronted with this second scenario we are obligated to infer that here is a world-class archer, one whose shots cannot legitimately be referred to luck, but rather must be referred to the archer's skill and mastery. Skill and mastery are of course instances of design.

The archer example introduces three elements that are essential for inferring design:

1. A reference class of possible events (here the arrow hitting the wall at some unspecified place);
2. A pattern that restricts the reference class of possible events (here a target on the wall); and
3. The precise event that has occurred (here the arrow hitting the wall at some precise location).

In a design inference, the reference class, the pattern, and the event are linked, with the pattern mediating between event and reference class, and helping to decide whether the event is due to chance or design. Note that in determining whether an event is sufficiently improbable or complex to implicate design, the relevant improbability is not that of the precise event that occurred, but that of the target/pattern. Indeed, the bigger the target, the easier it is to hit it by chance and thus apart from design.

The type of pattern in which an archer fixes a target first and then shoots at it is common to statistics, where it is known as setting a *rejection region* prior to an experiment. In statistics, if the outcome of an experiment falls within a rejection region, the chance hypothesis supposedly responsible for the outcome is rejected. The reason for setting a rejection region prior to an experiment is to forestall what statisticians call "data snooping" or "cherry picking." Just about any data set will contain strange and improbable patterns if we look hard enough. By forcing experimenters to set their rejection regions prior to an experiment, the statistician protects the experiment from spurious patterns that could just as well result from chance.

Now a little reflection makes clear that a pattern need not be given prior to an event to eliminate chance and implicate design. Consider the following cipher text:

nfuijolt ju jt mjlf b xfbtfm

Initially this looks like a random sequence of letters and spaces – you lack any pattern for rejecting chance and inferring design.

But suppose that someone comes along and tells you to treat this sequence as a Caesar cipher, moving each letter one notch down the alphabet. Now the sequence reads,

methinks it is like a weasel

Even though the pattern (in this case, the decrypted text) is given after the fact, it still is the right sort of pattern for eliminating chance and inferring design. In contrast to statistics, which always identifies its patterns before an experiment is performed, cryptanalysis must discover its patterns after the fact. In both instances, however, the patterns are suitable for inferring design.

Patterns thus divide into two types: those that in the presence of complexity warrant a design inference and those that, despite the presence of complexity, do not warrant a design inference. The first type of pattern I call a *specification*, the second *a fabrication*. Specifications are the non-*ad hoc* patterns that can legitimately be used to eliminate chance and warrant a design inference. In contrast, fabrications are the *ad hoc* patterns that cannot legitimately be used to warrant a design inference.

To sum up, the complexity-specification criterion detects design by establishing three things: contingency, complexity, and specification. When called to explain an event, object, or structure, we have to decide: Are we going to attribute it to *necessity*, *chance*, or *design*? According to the complexity-specification criterion, to answer this question is to answer three simpler questions: Is it contingent? Is it complex? Is it specified? Consequently, the complexity-specification criterion can be represented as a flowchart with three decision nodes. I call this flowchart the Explanatory Filter.

Independent Patterns Are Detachable

For a pattern to count as a specification, the important thing is not when it was identified, but whether in a certain well-defined sense it is *independent* of the event it describes. Drawing a target around an arrow already embedded in a wall is not independent of the arrow's trajectory. Consequently, such a target/pattern cannot be used to attribute the arrow's trajectory to design. Patterns that are specifications cannot simply be read off the events whose design is in question. Rather, to count as specifications, patterns must be suitably independent of events. I refer to this relation of independence as *detachability*, and say that a pattern is detachable only if it satisfies that relation.

Detachability can be understood as asking this question: Given an event (whose design is in question) and a pattern describing it, would we be able to construct that pattern if we had no knowledge of which event occurred? Assume an event has occurred. A pattern describing the event is given. The event is one from a range of possible events. If all we knew was the range of possible events without any specifics about which event actually occurred, could we still construct the pattern describing the event? If so, the pattern is detachable from the event.

A Trick with Coins

To see what's at stake, consider the following example. (It was this example that finally clarified for me what transforms a pattern *simpliciter* into a pattern *qua* specification.) The following event E to all appearances was obtained by flipping a fair coin one hundred times:

THTTTHHTHHTTTTTHTHTTHHHTTHT
HHHTHHTTTTTTTHTTHTTTHHTHTTT
HTHTHHTTHHHTTTHTTHHTHTHTHHH
HTTHHTHHHHTHHHHTT E

Is E the product of chance or not? A standard trick of statistics professors with an introductory statistics class is to divide the class in two and have students in one half of the class each flip a coin one hundred times and write down the sequence of heads and tails on a slip of paper; students in the other half each generate with their minds a "random-looking" string that mimics the tossing of a coin one hundred times and also write down the sequence of heads and tails on a slip of paper. When the students then hand in their

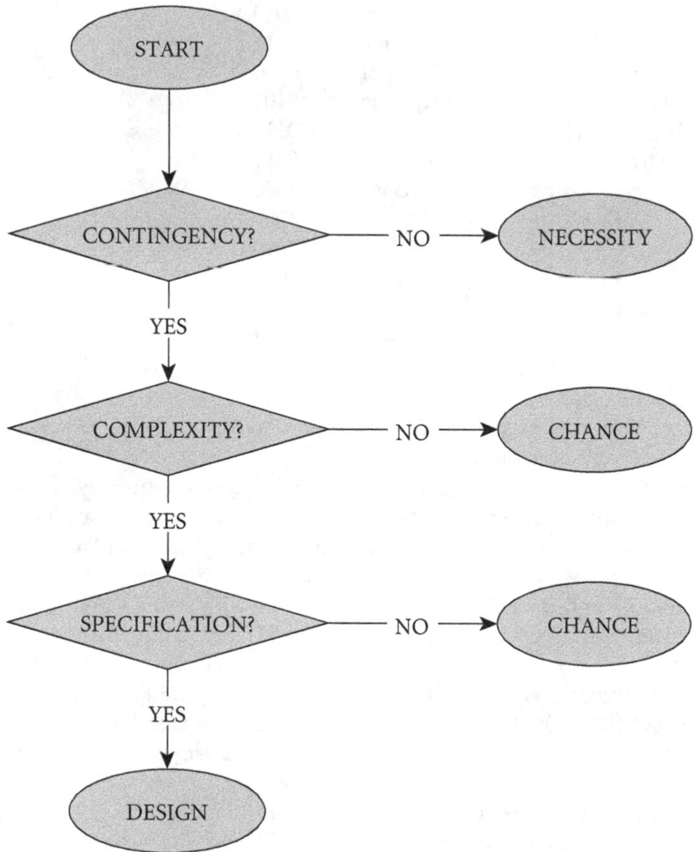

Figure XI.B.2a Explanatory filter [Complexity-specification criterion flowchart]. (Source: William A. Dembski, chart from *Mere Creation*, ed. William A. Dembski (Downers Grove, IL: InterVarsity Press, 1998), p. 99. © 1998 by Christian Leadership Ministries. Used with permission of InterVarsity Press, PO Box 1400, Downers Grove, IL 60515. ivpress.com)

slips of paper, it is the professor's job to sort the papers into two piles, those generated by flipping a fair coin, and those concocted in the students' heads. To the amazement of the students, the statistics professor is typically able to sort the papers with 100 percent accuracy.

There's no mystery here. The statistics professor simply looks for a repetition of six or seven heads or tails in a row to distinguish the truly random from the pseudo-random sequences. In a hundred coin flips, one is quite likely to see such a repetition. On the other hand, people concocting pseudo-random sequences with their minds tend to alternate between heads and tails too frequently. Whereas with a truly random sequence of coin tosses there is a 50 percent chance that one toss will differ from the next, as a matter of human psychology people expect that one toss will differ from the next around 70 percent of the time.

How, then, will our statistics professor fare when confronted with E? Will she attribute E to chance or to the musings of someone trying to mimic chance? According to the professor's crude randomness checker, E would be assigned to the pile of sequences presumed to be truly random, for E contains a repetition of seven tails in a row. Everything that at first blush would lead us to regard E as truly random checks out. There are exactly fifty alternations between heads and tails (as opposed to the seventy that would be expected from human beings trying to mimic chance). What's more, the relative frequencies of heads and tails check out: there were forty-nine heads and fifty-one tails. Thus it's not as though the coin supposedly responsible for generating E was heavily biased in favor of one side versus the other.

But Is It Really Chance?

Suppose, however, that our statistics professor suspects she is not up against a neophyte statistics student, but instead a fellow statistician who is trying to put one over on her. To help organize her problem, study it more carefully, and enter it into a computer, she will find it convenient to let strings of 0s and 1s represent the outcomes of coin flips, with 1 corresponding to heads and 0 to tails. In that case the following pattern D will correspond to the event E:

0100011011000001010011100101110111000000
01001000110100010101100111100010011010
1011110011011110111100 D

Now, the mere fact that the event E conforms to the pattern D is no reason to think that E did not occur by chance. As things stand, the pattern D has simply been read off the event E.

But D need not have been read off of E. Indeed, D could have been constructed without recourse to E. To see this, let us rewrite D as follows:

0
1
00
01
10
11
000
001
010
011
100
101
110
111
0000
0001
0010
0011
0100
0101
0110
0111
1000
1001
1010
1011
1100
1101
1110
1111
00 D

By viewing D this way, anyone with the least exposure to binary arithmetic immediately recognizes that D was constructed simply by writing binary numbers in ascending order, starting with the one-digit binary numbers (i.e., 0 and 1), proceeding then to the two-digit binary numbers (i.e., 00, 01, 10, and 11), and continuing on until one hundred digits were recorded. It's therefore intuitively clear that D does not describe a truly random event (i.e., an event gotten by tossing a fair coin), but rather a pseudo-random event, concocted by doing a little binary arithmetic.

Side Information Does the Trick

Although it's now intuitively clear why chance cannot properly explain E, we need to consider more closely why this mode of explanation fails here. We started with a putative chance event E, supposedly the result of flipping a fair coin one hundred times. Since heads and tails each have probability $^1/_2$, and since this probability gets multiplied for each flip of the coin, it follows that the probability of E is 2^{-100}, or approximately 10^{-30}.

In addition, we constructed a pattern D to which E conforms. Initially D proved insufficient to eliminate chance as the explanation of E since in its construction D was simply read off E. Rather, to eliminate chance we also had to recognize that D could have been constructed quite easily by performing some simple arithmetic operations with binary numbers. Thus to eliminate chance we needed to employ additional *side information*, which in this case consisted of our knowledge of binary arithmetic. This side information detached the pattern D from the event E and thereby rendered D a specification.

For side information to detach a pattern from an event, it must satisfy two conditions, *conditional independence* and *tractability*. First, the side information must be conditionally independent of the event E. Conditional independence, a well-defined notion from probability theory, means that the probability of E doesn't change once the side information is taken into account. Conditional independence is the standard probabilistic way of unpacking epistemic independence. Two things are epistemically independent if knowledge about one thing (in this case the side information) does not affect knowledge about the other (in this case the occurrence of E). This is certainly the case here since our knowledge of binary arithmetic does not affect the probabilities we assign to coin tosses.

The second condition, the tractability condition, requires that the side information enable us to construct the pattern D to which E conforms. This is evidently the case here as well, since our knowledge of binary arithmetic enables us to arrange binary numbers in ascending order, and thereby construct the pattern D.

But what exactly is this ability to construct a pattern on the basis of side information? Perhaps the most slippery words in philosophy are "can," "able," and "enable." Fortunately, just as there is a precise theory for characterizing the epistemic independence between an event and side information – namely, probability theory – so too there is a precise theory for characterizing the ability to construct a pattern on the basis of side information – namely, complexity theory.

Complexity Theory

Complexity theory, conceived now quite generally and not merely as a form of probability, assesses the difficulty of tasks given the resources available for accomplishing those tasks. If I may generalize computational complexity theory, it ranks tasks according to difficulty and then determines which tasks are sufficiently manageable to be doable or tractable. For instance, given current technology we find sending a person to the moon tractable, but sending a person to the nearest galaxy intractable.

In the tractability condition, the task to be accomplished is the construction of a pattern, and the resources for accomplishing that task are side information. Thus, for the tractability condition to be satisfied, side information must provide the resources necessary for constructing the pattern in question. All of this admits a precise complexity-theoretic formulation and makes definite what I called "the ability to construct a pattern on the basis of side information."

Taken jointly, the tractability and conditional independence conditions mean that side information enables us to construct the pattern to which an event conforms, yet without recourse to the actual event. This is the crucial insight. Because the side information is conditionally and therefore epistemically independent of the event, any pattern constructed from this side information is obtained without recourse to the event. In this way any pattern that is constructed from such side information avoids the charge of being *ad hoc*. These, then, are the detachable patterns. These are the specifications.

A Matter of Choice

The complexity-specification criterion is exactly the right instrument for detecting design. To see why, we need to understand what makes intelligent agents detectable in the first place. The principal characteristic of intelligent agency is choice. Even the etymology of the word "intelligent" makes this clear. "Intelligent" derives from two Latin words, the preposition *inter*, meaning between, and the verb *lego*, meaning to choose or select. Thus, according to its etymology, intelligence consists in *choosing between*. For an intelligent agent to act is therefore to choose from a range of competing possibilities.

This is true not just of humans, but of animals as well as of extraterrestrial intelligences. A rat navigating a maze must choose whether to go right or left at various points in the maze. When SETI researchers attempt to discover intelligence in the extraterrestrial radio transmissions they are monitoring, they assume an extraterrestrial intelligence could have chosen any number of possible radio transmissions, and then attempt to match the transmissions they observe with certain patterns as opposed to others. Whenever a human being utters meaningful speech, a choice is made from a range of possible sound combinations that might have been uttered. Intelligent agency always entails discrimination, choosing certain things, ruling out others.

Recognizing Intelligence

Given this characterization of intelligent agency, the crucial question is how to recognize it. Intelligent agents act by making a choice. How, then, do we recognize that an intelligent agent has made a choice? A bottle of ink spills accidentally onto a sheet of paper; someone takes a fountain pen and writes a message on a sheet of paper. In both instances ink is applied to paper. In both instances one among an almost infinite set of possibilities is realized. In both instances a contingency is actualized and others are ruled out. Yet in one instance we ascribe agency, in the other chance.

What is the relevant difference? Not only do we need to observe that a contingency was actualized, but we need also to be able to specify that contingency. The contingency must conform to an independently given pattern, and we must be able independently to construct that pattern. A random inkblot is unspecified; a message written with ink on paper is specified. The exact message recorded may not be specified, but orthographic, syntactic, and semantic constraints will nonetheless specify it.

Actualizing one among several competing possibilities, ruling out the rest, and specifying the one that was actualized encapsulates how we recognize intelligent agency, or equivalently, how we detect design. Experimental psychologists who study animal learning and behavior have known this all along. To learn a task an animal must acquire the ability to actualize behaviors suitable for the task as well as the ability to rule out behaviors unsuitable for the task. Moreover, for a psychologist to recognize that an animal has learned a task, it is necessary not only to observe the animal making the appropriate discrimination, but also to specify the discrimination.

Rats and Mazes

Thus, to recognize whether a rat has successfully learned how to traverse a maze, a psychologist must first specify which sequence of right and left turns conducts the rat out of the maze. No doubt, a rat randomly wandering a maze also discriminates a sequence of right and left turns. But by randomly wandering the maze, the rat gives no indication that it can discriminate the appropriate sequence of right and left turns for exiting the maze. Consequently, the psychologist studying the rat will have no reason to think the rat has learned how to traverse the maze.

Only if the rat executes the sequence of right and left turns specified by the psychologist will the psychologist recognize that the rat has learned how to traverse the maze. Now it is precisely the learned behaviors we regard as intelligent in animals. Hence it is no surprise that the same scheme for recognizing animal learning recurs for recognizing intelligent agency generally, to wit: actualizing one among several competing possibilities, ruling out the others, and specifying the one actualized.

Note that complexity is implicit here as well. To see this, consider again a rat traversing a maze, but now take a very simple maze in which two right turns conduct the rat out of the maze. How will a psychologist studying the rat determine whether it has learned to exit the maze? Just putting the rat in the maze will not be enough. Because the maze is so simple, the rat by chance could just happen to take two right turns and thereby exit the maze. The psychologist will therefore be uncertain whether the rat actually learned to exit this maze or just got lucky.

But contrast this with a complicated maze in which a rat must take just the right sequence of left and right turns to exit the maze. Suppose the rat must take one hundred appropriate right and left turns, and that any mistake will prevent the rat from exiting the maze. A psychologist who sees the rat take no erroneous turns and quickly exit the maze will be convinced that the rat has indeed learned how to exit the maze, and that it was not dumb luck.

This general scheme for recognizing intelligent agency is but a thinly disguised form of the complexity-specification criterion. In general, to recognize intelligent agency we must observe an actualization of one among several competing possibilities, note which possibilities were ruled out, and then be able to specify the possibility that was actualized. What's more, the competing possibilities that were ruled out must be live possibilities, and sufficiently numerous so that specifying the possibility that was actualized cannot be attributed to chance. In terms of complexity, this is just another way of saying that the range of possibilities is complex. In terms of probability, this is just another way of saying that the possibility that was actualized has small probability.

All the elements in this general scheme for recognizing intelligent agency (i.e., actualizing, ruling out, and specifying) find their counterpart in the complexity-specification criterion. It follows that this criterion formalizes what we have been doing right along when we recognize intelligent agency. The complexity-specification criterion pinpoints how we detect design.

Design, Metaphysics, and Beyond

Where is this work on design heading? Specified complexity, that key trademark of design, is, as it turns out, a form of information (though one considerably richer than Claude Shannon's purely statistical form of it). Although called by different names and developed with different degrees of rigor, specified complexity is starting to have an effect on the special sciences.

For instance, specified complexity is what Michael Behe has uncovered with his irreducibly complex biochemical machines, what Manfred Eigen regards as the great mystery of life's origin, what for cosmologists underlies the fine-tuning of the universe, what David Chalmers hopes will ground a comprehensive theory of human consciousness, what enables Maxwell's demon to outsmart a thermodynamic system tending toward thermal equilibrium, and what within the Kolmogorov–Chaitin theory of algorithmic information identifies the highly compressible, nonrandom strings of digits. How complex specified information gets from an organism's environment into an organism's genome was one of the key questions at the October 1999 Santa Fe Institute symposium, "Complexity, Information & Design: A Critical Appraisal."

Shannon's purely statistical theory of information is giving way to a richer theory of complex specified information whose possibilities are only now coming to light. A natural sequel to *The Design Inference* is therefore to develop a general theory of complex specified information.

Yet despite its far-reaching implications for science, I regard the ultimate significance of this work on design to lie in metaphysics. In my view, design died not at the hands of nineteenth-century evolutionary biology, but at the hands of the mechanical philosophy two centuries earlier – and that despite the popularity of British natural theology at the time. Though the originators of the mechanical philosophy were typically theists, the design they retained was at best an uneasy rider on top of a mechanistic view of nature. Design is neither use nor ornament within a strictly mechanistic world of particles or other mindless entities organized by equally mindless principles of association, even if these be natural laws ordained by God.

The primary challenge, once the broader implications of design for science have been worked out, is therefore to develop a relational ontology in which the problem of being resolves thus: to be is to be in communion, and to be in communion is to transmit and receive information. Such an ontology will not only safeguard science and leave adequate breathing space for design, but will also make sense of the world as sacrament.

The world is a mirror representing the divine life. The mechanical philosophy was ever blind to this fact. Intelligent design, on the other hand, readily embraces the sacramental nature of physical reality. Indeed, intelligent design is just the Logos theology of John's Gospel restated in the idiom of information theory.

Notes

1 Jacques Monod, *Chance and Necessity* (New York: Knopf, 1971).

2 Eliot Marshall, "Medline Searches Turn Up Cases of Plagiarism," *Science* 279 (January 1998): 473–4.

3 Charles Darwin, *On the Origin of Species* (Cambridge, Mass.: Harvard University Press, 1963), p. 482.

3

Atheism and Evolution

Daniel C. Dennett

Daniel Dennett (b. 1942) is University Professor and Austin B. Fletcher Professor of Philosophy at Tufts University in Massachusetts. He has made important contributions to philosophy of mind, philosophy of science, and philosophy of religion, including *Darwin's Dangerous Idea* (1995), *Freedom Evolves* (2003), and *Breaking the Spell: Religion as a Natural Phenomenon* (2006). In the following essay Dennett argues that evolutionary biology supports atheism, not by proving that God does not or cannot exist, but by showing that we lack any good positive reason for thinking God does exist. He ends by suggesting that evolutionary social science may also explain why theistic belief has been so widespread.

Descartes, in the Meditations (1641), notes that "there are only two ways of proving the existence of God, one by means of his effects, and the other by means of his nature or essence" (AT VII, 120). The latter, a priori path, represented paradigmatically by the ontological argument of St Anselm (and its offspring, including Descartes' own version), has perennial appeal to a certain sort of philosopher, but leaves most people cold. The former, represented paradigmatically by the argument from design, is surely the most compelling of all arguments against atheism, and it apparently arises spontaneously whenever people anywhere are challenged to justify their belief in God. William Paley's example of finding a watch while strolling on the heath epitomizes the theme and leads, he says, to "the inference we think is inevitable, that the watch must have had a maker – that there must have existed, at some time and at some place or other, an artificer or artificers who formed it for the purpose which we find it actually to answer, who comprehended its construction and designed its use" (Paley 1800). Until Darwin came along, this

Daniel C. Dennett, "Atheism and Evolution" from *The Cambridge Companion to Atheism*, ed. Michael Martin (Cambridge: Cambridge University Press, 2007), ch. 8, pp. 135–48.

was a respectable argument, worthy of Hume's corrosive but indecisive broadside in his *Dialogues Concerning Natural Religion* (1779). Descartes himself subscribed to a version of the argument from design, in his notorious Third Meditation argument that his idea of God was too wonderful to have been created by him. Though Descartes surely considered himself intelligent, and moreover an accomplished designer of ideas, he could not imagine that he could be the intelligent designer of his own idea of God.

The familiar idea that the marvels of the universe prove the existence of God as its creator is perhaps as old as our species, or even older. Did *Homo habilis*, the "handy" man who made the first crude tools, have some dim and inarticulate sense that it always takes a big fancy smart thing to make a less fancy thing? We never saw a pot making a potter, or a horseshoe making a blacksmith, after all. This trickle-down, mind-first vision of design seems self-evident at first. A creationist propaganda pamphlet I was once given by a student exploits this intuition with a mock questionnaire:

> TEST TWO
> Do you know of any building that didn't have a builder? [YES] [NO]
> Do you know of any painting that didn't have a painter? [YES] [NO]
> Do you know of any car that didn't have a maker? [YES] [NO]
> If you answered YES for any of the above, give details: ______________________
> ______________________________
> ______________________________

The presumed embarrassment of the test taker when faced with this tall order evokes the incredulity that many – probably most – people feel when they confront Darwin's great idea. It does seem just obvious, doesn't it, that there couldn't be any such designs without designers, any such creations without a creator! The vertigo and revulsion this prospect provokes in many was perfectly expressed in an early attack on Darwin, published anonymously in 1868:

> In the theory with which we have to deal, Absolute Ignorance is the artificer; so that we may enunciate as the fundamental principle of the whole system, that, IN ORDER TO MAKE A PERFECT AND BEAUTIFUL MACHINE, IT IS NOT REQUISITE TO KNOW HOW TO MAKE IT. This proposition will be found, on careful examination, to express, in condensed form, the essential purport of the Theory, and to express in a few words all Mr Darwin's meaning; who, by a strange inversion of reasoning, seems to think Absolute Ignorance fully qualified to take the place of Absolute Wisdom in all the achievements of creative skill. (MacKenzie 1868)

Exactly! Darwin's "strange inversion of reasoning" was in fact a new and wonderful way of thinking, completely overturning the mind-first way that even David Hume had been unable to cast aside, and replacing it with a bubble-up vision in which intelligence – the concentrated, forward-looking intelligence of an anthropomorphic agent – eventually emerges as just one of the products of mindless, mechanistic processes. These processes are fueled by untold billions of pointless, undesigned collisions, some vanishing small fraction of which fortuitously lead to tiny improvements in the lineages in which they occur. Thanks to Darwin's principle of "descent with modification," these ruthlessly tested design innovations accumulate over the eons, yielding breathtakingly brilliant designs that never had a designer – other than the purposeless, distributed process of natural selection itself.

The signatures of these unplanned innovations are everywhere to be found in a close examination of the marvels of nature, in the inside-out retina of the vertebrate eye, the half-discarded leftovers in the genes and organs of every species, the prodigious wastefulness and apparent cruelty of so many of nature's processes. These departures from wisdom, "frozen accidents," in the apt phrase of Francis Crick, confront the theist with a dilemma: if God is responsible for these designs, then his intelligence looks disturbingly like human obtuseness and callousness. Moreover, as our understanding of the mechanisms of evolution grows, we can sketch out ever more detailed accounts of the historical sequence of events by which the design innovations appeared and were incorporated into the branching tree of genomes. A voluminously predictive account of the creative process is now emerging, replete with thousands of mutually supporting details, and no contradictions at all. As the pieces of this mega–jigsaw puzzle fall into place with increasing rapidity, there can be no reasonable doubt that it is, in all its broad outlines if not yet in all its unsettled details, the true story of how all living things came to have the designs we observe.

Unreasonable doubt flourishes, however, thanks to the incessant propaganda efforts of creationists and intelligent design (ID) spokespeople, such as William Dembski and Michael Behe, who have managed to persuade a distressingly large proportion of the lay population that there are genuine scientific controversies brewing in biology about its backbone theory, evolution by natural selection. There are not. Genuine scientific controversies abound in every corner of biology, but none of them challenges evolution. The legitimate way to stir up a storm in any scientific discipline is to come up with an alternative theory that

1. makes a prediction that is crisply denied by the reigning theory but turns out to be true or
2. explains something that has been baffling defenders of the status quo or
3. unifies two distant theories, at the cost of some element of the currently accepted view

To date, the proponents of ID have not produced a single instance of anything like that. There are no experiments with results that challenge any standard neo-Darwinian understanding, no observations from the fossil record or genomics or biogeography or comparative anatomy that undermine standard evolutionary thinking, no theoretical unifications or simplifications, and no surprising predictions that have turned out to be true. In short, no science – just advertising. No ID hypothesis has even been ventured as a rival explanation of any biological phenomenon. To formulate a competing hypothesis, you have to get down in the trenches and offer some details that have testable implications, but the ID proponents conveniently sidestep that requirement, claiming that they have no specifics in mind about who or what the intelligent designer might be.

To see this shortcoming in relief, consider an imaginary hypothesis of intelligent design that could explain the emergence of human beings on this planet:

> About six million years ago, intelligent genetic engineers from another galaxy visited Earth and decided that it would be a more interesting planet if there was a language-using, religion-forming species on it, so they sequestered some primates (from among the ancestors of both humans and chimpanzees and bonobos), and genetically re-engineered them to give them the language instinct, and enlarged frontal lobes for planning and reflection. It worked.

If some version of this hypothesis were true, it could actually explain how and why human beings differ from their nearest relatives, and it would disconfirm all the competing neo-Darwinian hypotheses that are currently being pursued on this fascinating question. We'd still have the problem of how these intelligent genetic engineers came to exist on their home planet, but we could safely ignore that complication for the time being, since there is not the slightest shred of evidence in favor of this hypothesis. And – here is something the ID community is reluctant to discuss – no other intelligent-design hypothesis has anything more going for it. In fact, my farfetched – but possible – hypothesis has the distinct advantage of being testable in principle: we could look in the human and chimpanzee genome for unmistakable signs of tampering by these genetic engineers (maybe they left a "Kilroy was here" message in human DNA for us to decode!). Finding some sort of user's manual neatly embedded in the apparently functionless "junk DNA" that makes up most of the human genome would be a Nobel Prize–winning knockout coup for the ID gang, but if they are even looking, they are not telling anyone. They know better. Ironically, William Dembski's "design inference" argument is supposed to set up a sure-fire test for finding just such telltale signs of intelligent tinkering in the causal ancestry of phenomena, but instead of trying to demonstrate the test in action, Dembski (2005) settles for the observation that the ID perspective "encourages biologists to investigate whether systems that first appear functionless might in fact have a function" – and no neo-Darwinian would disagree with that strategy.

Between the richly detailed and ever-ramifying evolutionary story and the featureless mystery of God the creator of all creatures great and small, there is no contest. This is a momentous reversal for the ancient conviction that God's existence can be read off the wonders of nature. Anyone who has ever been struck by the magnificent intricacy of design and prodigious variety of the living world and wondered what – if not God – could possibly account for its existence must now confront not just a plausible alternative, but an alternative of breathtaking explanatory power supported by literally thousands of confirmed predictions and solved puzzles. Richard Dawkins has put the point crisply: "Although atheism might have been logically tenable before Darwin, Darwin made it possible to be an intellectually fulfilled atheist" (1986: 6).

Undermining the best argument anybody ever thought of for the existence of God is not, of course, proving the nonexistence of God, and many careful thinkers who have accepted evolution by natural selection as the explanation of the wonders of the living world have cast about for other supports for their continuing belief in God. The idea of treating mind as an effect rather than as a first cause is too revolutionary for some. Alfred Russel Wallace, the codiscoverer with Darwin of natural selection, could never accept the full inversion, proclaiming that "the marvelous complexity of forces which appear to control matter, if not actually to constitute it, are and must be mind-products" (quoted by Gould 1985: 397). More recently, the physicist Paul Davies, in his book, *The Mind of God* (1992: 232), opines that the reflective power of human minds can be "no trivial detail, no minor by-product of mindless purposeless forces." This is a most revealing way of expressing a familiar denial, for it betrays an ill-examined prejudice. Why, we might ask Davies, would its being a by-product of mindless, purposeless forces make it trivial? Why couldn't the most important thing of all be something that arose from unimportant things? Why should the importance or excellence of anything have to rain down on it from on high, from something more important, a gift from God? Darwin's inversion suggests that we abandon that presumption and look for sorts of excellence, of worth and purpose, that can emerge, bubbling up out of "mindless, purposeless forces."

But before we settle into the bubble-up perspective on ultimate importance, with whatever comfort we can muster, we need to deal with the residual skepticism of the traditional trickle-down perspective: once mindless, purposeless evolution gets under way, it generates magnificent design over time, but how did it get started? Don't we need God to kindle the process by miraculously and improbably assembling the first self-replicating thing? This hope – and the contrary conviction that the origin of life can be accounted for somehow by a natural series of events of low but not negligible probability – grounds the intense interest, not to say passion, surrounding contemporary research on the origin of life. The details of the process are not yet settled, but the presence of fairly complex building blocks – not just amino acids and basic "organic" molecules – in the prebiotic world is now established, and the problem confronting scientists today is less a matter of imponderable mystery than an embarrassment of riches: so many possibilities are not yet excluded. The conviction that it must have taken a miracle – a temporary violation of the standing laws of physics and chemistry – for life to get initiated has lost whatever plausibility it ever had.

But, then, those standing laws themselves require an explanation, do they not? If God the Artificer and God the Kindler have lost their jobs, what of God the Lawgiver? This suggestion has been popular since the earliest days of Darwinian thinking, and Darwin himself toyed with this attractive retreat. In a letter in 1860 to the American naturalist, Asa Gray, an early supporter, Darwin wrote, "I am inclined to look at everything as resulting from *designed* [emphasis added] laws, with the details whether good or bad, left to the working out of what we may call chance" (Darwin 1911: 105).

Automatic processes are themselves often creations of great brilliance. From today's vantage point, we can see that the inventors of the automatic transmission and the automatic door-opener were no idiots, and their genius lay in seeing how to create something that could do something "clever" without having to think about it. Indulging in some anachronism, we could say that to some observers in Darwin's day, it seemed that he had left open the possibility that God did his handiwork by designing an automatic design maker. And to some of these, the idea was not just a desperate stop-gap but a positive improvement on tradition. The first chapter of Genesis describes the successive waves of Creation and ends each with the refrain "and God saw that it was good." Darwin had discovered a way to eliminate this retail application of intelligent quality control; natural selection would take care of that without further intervention from God. (The seventeenth-century philosopher Gottfried Wilhelm Leibniz had defended a similar hands-off vision of God the Creator.) As Henry Ward Beecher put it, "Design by wholesale is grander than design by retail" (Rachels 1991: 99). Asa Gray, captivated by Darwin's new idea but trying to reconcile it with as much of his traditional religious creed as possible, came up with this marriage of convenience: God intended the "stream of variations" and foresaw just how the laws of nature he had laid down would prune this stream over the eons. As John Dewey later aptly remarked (1910: 12), invoking yet another mercantile metaphor, "Gray held to what may be called design on the installment plan."

What is the difference between order and design? As a first stab, we might say that order is mere regularity, mere pattern; design is Aristotle's "telos," an exploitation of order for a purpose, such as we see in a cleverly designed artifact. The solar system exhibits stupendous order, but does not (apparently) have a purpose – it isn't for anything. An eye, in contrast is for seeing. Before Darwin, this distinction was not always clearly marked. Indeed, it was positively blurred:

> In the thirteenth century, Aquinas offered the view that natural bodies [such as planets, raindrops, or volcanos] act as if guided toward a definite goal or end "so as to obtain the best result." This fitting of means to ends implies, argued Aquinas, an intention. But, seeing as natural bodies lack consciousness, they cannot supply that intention themselves. "Therefore some intelligent being exists by whom all natural things are directed to their end, and this being we call God." (Davies 1992: 200)

Hume's Cleanthes, following in this tradition, lumps the adapted marvels of the living world with the regularities of the heavens – it's all like a wonderful clockwork to him. But Darwin suggests a division: give me order, he says, and time, and I will give you design. Let me start with regularity – the mere purposeless, mindless, pointless regularity of physics – and I will show you a process that eventually will yield products that exhibit not just regularity but purposive design. (This was just what Karl Marx thought he saw when he declared that Darwin had dealt a deathblow to teleology: Darwin had reduced teleology to nonteleology, design to order.)

A more recent idea about the difference – and tight relation – between design and order will help to clarify the picture. This is the proposal, first popularized by the physicist Erwin Schrödinger (1967), that life can be defined in terms of the second law of thermodynamics. In physics, order or organization can be measured in terms of heat differences between regions of space-time; entropy is simply disorder, the opposite of order, and according to the second law, the entropy of any isolated system increases with time. In other words, things run down, inevitably. According to the second law, the universe is unwinding out of a more ordered state into the ultimately disordered state known as the heat death of the universe. What then are living things? They are things that defy this crumbling into dust, at least for awhile, by not being isolated – by taking in from their environment the wherewithal to keep life and limb together. The psychologist Richard Gregory summarizes the idea:

> Time's arrow given by Entropy – the loss of organization, or loss of temperature differences – is statistical and it is subject to local small-scale reversals. Most striking: life is a systematic reversal of Entropy, and intelligence creates structures and energy differences against the supposed gradual "death" through Entropy of the physical Universe. (1981: 136)

Gregory goes on to credit Darwin with the fundamental enabling idea: "It is the measure of the concept of Natural Selection that increases in the complexity and order of organisms in biological time can now be understood." Not just individual organisms, then, but the whole process of evolution that creates them, can thus be seen as fundamental physical phenomena running contrary to the larger trend of cosmic time.

A designed thing, then, is either a living thing or a part of a living thing, or the artifact of a living thing, organized in any case in aid of this battle against disorder. It is not impossible to oppose the trend of the Second Law, but it is costly. Gregory dramatizes this with an unforgettable example. A standard textbook expression of the directionality imposed by the second law of thermodynamics is the claim that you can't unscramble an egg. Well, not that you absolutely can't, but that it would be an extremely costly, sophisticated task, uphill all the way against the second law. Now consider: how expensive would it be to make a device that would take scrambled eggs as input and deliver unscrambled eggs as output? There is one ready solution: put a live hen in the box! Feed it scrambled eggs, and it will be able to make eggs for you – for a while. Hens don't normally strike us as near-miraculously sophisticated entities, but here is one thing a hen can do, thanks to the design that has organized it, that is still way beyond the reach of the devices created by human engineers.

The more design a thing exhibits, the more R&D work had to have occurred to produce it. Minds are among the most designed of entities (in part because they are the self-redesigning things). But this means that they are among the most advanced effects (to date) of the creative process, not – as in the old version – its cause or source. Their products in turn – the human artifacts that were our initial model – must count as more designed still. This may seem counterintuitive at first. A Keats ode may seem to have some claim to having a grander R&D pedigree than a nightingale – at least it might seem so to a poet ignorant of biology – but what about a paper clip? Surely, a paper clip is a trivial product of design compared with any living thing, however rudimentary. In one obvious sense, this is true, but reflect for a moment. Put yourself in Paley's shoes, but walking along the apparently deserted beach on an alien planet. Which discovery would excite you the most: a clam or a clam rake? Before the planet could make a clam rake, it would have to make a clam rake maker, and that is a more designed thing by far than a clam.

Only a theory with the logical shape of Darwin's could explain how designed things came to exist, because any other sort of explanation would be either viciously circular or an infinite regress (Dennett 1975). The old way, the mind-first way, endorsed the principle that it takes an intelligence to make an intelligence. Children chant, "It takes one to know one," but an even more persuasive slogan would seem to be "It takes a greater one to make a lesser one." Any view inspired by this slogan immediately faces an embarrassing question, however, as Hume had noted: If God created and designed all these wonderful things, who created God? Supergod? And who created Supergod? Superdupergod? Or did God create himself? Was it hard work? Did it take time? Don't ask! Well then, we may ask instead whether this bland embrace is any improvement over just denying the principle that intelligence (or design) must spring from intelligence. Darwin offered an explanatory path that actually honored Paley's insight: real work went into designing this watch, and work isn't free. Richard Dawkins summarizes the point:

> Organized complexity is the thing we are having difficulty explaining. Once we are allowed simply to postulate organized complexity, if only the organized complexity of the DNA/protein replicating engine, it is relatively easy to invoke it as a generator of yet more organized complexity. . . . But of course any God capable of intelligently designing something as complex as the DNA/protein replicating machine must have been at least as complex and organized as the machine itself. . . . To explain the origin of the DNA/protein machine by invoking a supernatural Designer is to explain precisely nothing, for it leaves unexplained the origin of the Designer. (1986: 141)

As Dawkins goes on to say, "The one thing that makes evolution such a neat theory is that it explains how organized complexity can arise out of primeval simplicity" (p. 316). But still, that primeval simplicity exhibits order, and what of the laws of nature themselves? Don't they manifest the existence of a lawgiver? The physicist and cosmologist Freeman Dyson puts the point cautiously: "I do not claim that the architecture of the universe proves the existence of God. I claim only that the architecture of the universe is consistent with the hypothesis that mind plays an essential role in its functioning" (Dyson 1979: 251). Since, as Dawkins notes, the hypothesis that (organized, complex) mind plays such a role could not possibly be explanatory, we should ask: With what other hypotheses is the architecture of the universe consistent? There are several.

As more and more has been learned about the development of the universe since the big bang, about the conditions that permitted the formation of galaxies and stars and the heavy elements from which planets can be formed, physicists and cosmologists have been more and more struck by the exquisite sensitivity of the laws of nature. The speed of light is approximately 186,000 miles per second. What if it were only 185,000 miles per second, or 187,000 miles per second? Would that change much of anything? What if the force of gravity were 1 percent more or less than it is? The fundamental constants of physics – the speed of light, the constant of gravitational attraction, the weak and strong forces of subatomic interaction, Planck's constant – have values that of course permit the actual development of the universe as we know it to have happened. But it turns out that if in imagination we change any of these values by just the tiniest amount, we thereby posit a universe in which none of this could have happened, and indeed in which apparently nothing lifelike could ever have emerged: no planets, no atmospheres, no solids at all, no elements except hydrogen and helium, or maybe not even that – just some boring plasma of hot, undifferentiated stuff, or an equally boring nothingness. So isn't it a wonderful fact that the laws are just right for us to exist? Indeed, one might want to add, we almost didn't make it!

Is this wonderful fact something that needs an explanation, and if so, what kind of explanation might it receive? According to the anthropic principle, we are entitled to infer facts about the universe and its laws from the undisputed fact that we (we anthropoi, we human beings) are here to do the inferring and observing. The anthropic principle comes in several flavors. In the "weak form" it is a sound, harmless, and on occasion useful application of elementary logic: if x is a necessary condition for the existence of y, and y exists, then x exists. Believers in any of the proposed strong versions of the anthropic principle think they can deduce something wonderful and surprising from the fact that we conscious observers are here – for instance, that in some sense the universe exists for us, or perhaps that we exist so that the universe as a whole can exist, or even that God created the universe the way he did so that we would be possible. Construed in this way, these proposals are attempts to restore Paley's argument from design, readdressing it to the design of the universe's most general laws of physics, not the particular constructions those laws make possible. Here, once again, Darwinian countermoves are available.

The boldest is that somehow there might have been some sort of differential reproduction of whole universes, with some varieties having more "offspring" than others, due to their more fecund laws of nature. Hume's mouthpiece Philo toyed with this idea, in the *Dialogues Concerning Natural Religion*, when he imagined a designer-god who was far from intelligent:

> And what surprise must we entertain, when we find him a stupid mechanic, who imitated others, and copied an art, which, through a long succession of ages, after multiplied trials, mistakes, corrections, deliberations, and controversies, had been gradually improving? Many worlds might have been botched and bungled, throughout an eternity, ere this system was struck out: Much labour lost: Many fruitless trials made: And a slow, but continued improvement carried on during infinite ages of world-making. (part V)

Hume imputes the "continued improvement" to the minimal selective bias of a "stupid mechanic," but we can replace the stupid mechanic with something even stupider without dissipating the lifting power: a purely algorithmic Darwinian process of world-trying. Hume obviously didn't think this was anything but an amusing philosophical fantasy, but the idea has recently been developed in some detail by the physicist Lee Smolin (1992). The basic idea is that the singularities known as black holes are in effect the birthplaces of offspring universes, in which the fundamental physical constants would differ slightly, in random ways, from the physical constants in the parent universe. So, according to

Smolin's hypothesis, we have differential reproduction and mutation, the two essential features of any Darwinian selection algorithm. Those universes that just happened to have physical constants that encouraged the development of black holes would ipso facto have more offspring, which would have more offspring, and so forth – that's the selection step. Note that there is no grim reaper of universes in this scenario; they all live and "die" in due course, but some merely have more offspring. According to this idea, then, it is no mere interesting coincidence that we live in a universe in which there are black holes. But neither is it an absolute logical necessity; it is rather the sort of conditional near-necessity you find in any evolutionary account. The link, Smolin claims, is carbon, which plays a role both in the collapse of gaseous clouds (or in other words, the birth of stars, a precursor to the birth of black holes) and, of course, in our molecular engineering.

Is the theory testable? Smolin offers some predictions that would, if disconfirmed, pretty well eliminate his idea: it should be the case that all the "near" variations in physical constants from the values we enjoy should yield universes in which black holes are less probable or less frequent than in our own. In short, he thinks our universe should manifest at least a local, if not global, optimum in the black hole–making competition. The trouble is that there are too few constraints, so far as I can see, on what should count as a "near" variation and why, but perhaps further elaboration on the theory will clarify this. Needless to say, it is hard to know what to make of this idea yet, but whatever the eventual verdict of scientists, the idea already serves to secure a philosophical point. Freeman Dyson, and others who think they see a wonderful pattern in the laws of physics, might be tempted to make the tactical mistake of asking the rhetorical question, "What else but God could possibly explain it?" Smolin offers a nicely deflating reply. If we follow the Darwinian down this path, God the Artificer turns first into God the Lawgiver, who then can be seen to merge with God the Lawfinder, who does not invent the laws of nature, but just eventually stumbles across them in the course of blind trial and error of universes. God's hypothesized contribution is becoming less personal – and hence more readily performable by something dogged and mindless!

But suppose, for the sake of argument, that Smolin's speculations are all flawed; suppose selection of universes doesn't work after all. There is a weaker, semi-Darwinian speculation that also answers the rhetorical question handily. Hume also toyed with this weaker idea, in part VIII of his *Dialogues*:

> Instead of supposing matter infinite, as Epicurus did, let us suppose it finite. A finite number of particles is only susceptible of finite transpositions: And it must happen, in an eternal duration, that every possible order or position must be tried an infinite number of times. . . .
>
> Suppose . . . that matter were thrown into any position, by a blind, unguided force; it is evident that this first position must in all probability be the most confused and most disorderly imaginable, without any resemblance to those works of human contrivance, which, along with a symmetry of parts, discover an adjustment of means to ends and a tendency to self-preservation. . . . [S]uppose, that the actuating force, whatever it be, still continues in matter. . . . Thus the universe goes on for many ages in a continued succession of chaos and disorder. But is it not possible that it may settle at last . . . ? May we not hope for such a position, or rather be assured of it, from the eternal revolutions of unguided matter, and may not this account for all the appearing wisdom and contrivance, which is in the universe?

This idea exploits no version of selection at all, but simply draws attention to the fact that we have eternity to play with. There is no five-billion-year deadline in this instance, the way there is for the evolution of life on Earth. Several versions of this speculation have been seriously considered by physicists and cosmologists in recent years. John Archibald Wheeler (1974), for instance, has proposed that the universe oscillates back and forth for eternity: a big bang is followed by expansion, which is followed by contraction into a big crunch, which is followed by another big bang, and so forth forever, with random variations in the constants and other crucial parameters occurring in each oscillation. Each possible setting is tried an infinity of times, and so every variation on every theme, both those that "make sense" and those that are absurd, spins itself out, not once but an infinity of times.

It is hard to believe that this idea is empirically testable in any meaningful way, but we should reserve judgment. Variations or elaborations on the theme just might have implications that could be confirmed or disconfirmed. In the meantime it is worth noting that this family of hypotheses does have the virtue of extending the principles of explanation that work so well in testable domains all the way out. Consistency and simplicity are in its favor. And that, once again, is certainly enough to blunt the appeal of the traditional alternative. Here's why: if the universe were structured in such a way that an infinity of different "laws of physics" get tried out in the fullness of time, we would be mistaken to think that there is anything special about our finding ourselves with such exquisitely well-tuned laws. It had to happen eventually, with or without help from a benign God. This is not an argument for the conclusion that the universe is, or must be, so structured, but just an argument for the more modest conclusion that no feature of the observable "laws of nature" could be invulnerable to this alternative, deflationary interpretation.

Once these ever more speculative, ever more attenuated Darwinian hypotheses are formulated, they serve – in classic Darwinian fashion – to diminish by small steps the explanatory task facing us. All that is left over in need of explanation at this point is a certain perceived elegance or wonderfulness in the observed laws of physics. If you doubt that the hypothesis of an infinity of variant universes could actually explain this elegance, you should reflect that this has at least as much claim to being a non-question-begging explanation as any traditional alternative; by the time God has been depersonalized to the point of being some abstract and timeless principle of beauty or goodness, not an artificer or a lawgiver or even a lawfinder but at best a sort of master of ceremonies, it is hard to see how the existence of God could explain anything. What would be asserted by the "explanation" that was not already given in the description of the wonderful phenomenon to be explained? The Darwinian perspective doesn't prove that God – in any of these guises – couldn't exist, but only that we have no good reason to think God does exist. Not a classical reductio ad absurdum argument, then, but nevertheless a rational challenge that reduces the believer's options to an absurdly minimalist base. As the Reverend Mackerel says, in Peter De Vries's comic novel, *The Mackerel Plaza* (1958), "It is the final proof of God's omnipotence that he need not exist in order to save us."

Evolutionary biology also supports atheism indirectly by providing an explanatory framework for what we might call the genealogy of theology. Since belief in God cannot be justified by any scientific or logical argument, but is nevertheless a nearly ubiquitous ingredient in human civilization, what explains the maintenance of this belief? This is an oft-neglected part of the atheist's burden of proof: not merely showing the fallacies and dubieties in the various arguments that have been offered for the existence of God, but explaining why such a dubious proposition would be favored by anybody in the first place. There has been no shortage of dismissive hypotheses offered over the centuries: neuroses that are the inevitable by-products of civilization, a conspiracy of ultimately selfish priests, and sheer stupidity, for instance, are perennially popular hunches. Recent works in evolutionary social science (Boyer 2001; Atran 2002; Dennett 2006) demonstrate that there are both more interesting and more plausible – and scientifically confirmable – hypotheses to pursue.

Note

Passages in this chapter are drawn, with revisions, from Dennett 1995 and 2005.

References

Atran, Scott. 2002. *In Gods We Trust: The Evolutionary Landscape of Religion*. New York: Oxford University Press.

Boyer, Pascal. 2001. *Religion Explained: The Evolutionary Origins of Religious Thought*. New York: Basic Books.

Darwin, Francis. 1911. *The Life and Letters of Charles Darwin*. 2 vols. New York: Appleton (original edition, 1887).

Davies, Paul. 1992. *The Mind of God*. London: Simon and Schuster.

Dawkins, Richard. 1986. *The Blind Watchmaker.* London: Longmans.

De Vries, Peter. 1958. *The Mackerel Plaza.* Boston: Little, Brown.

Dembski, William. 2005. "In Defense of Intelligent Design." Http://www.designinference.com, and in Philip Clayton (ed)., *Oxford Handbook of Religion and Science.* Oxford; New York: Oxford University Press, 2006.

Dennett, Daniel. 1975. "Why the Law of Effect Will Not Go Away." *Journal of the Theory of Social Behaviour* 5: 179–87.

Dennett, Daniel. 1995. *Darwin's Dangerous Idea.* New York: Simon & Schuster.

Dennett, Daniel. 2005. "Show Me the Science." *New York Times* op./ed. page, August 28, 2005.

Dennett, Daniel C. 2006. *Breaking the Spell: Religion as a Natural Phenomenon.* New York: Viking Penguin.

Descartes, Rene. 1641. *Meditations on First Philosophy.* Paris: Michel Soly.

Dewey, John. 1910. *The Influence of Darwin on Philosophy.* New York: Henry Holt; Bloomington: Indiana University Press, 1965.

Dyson, Freeman. 1979. *Disturbing the Universe.* New York: Harper and Row.

Gould, Stephen Jay. 1985. *The Flamingo's Smile.* New York: Norton.

Gregory, Richard L. 1981. *Mind in Science: A History of Explanations in Psychology and Physics.* Cambridge: Cambridge University Press.

Hume, David. 1779. *Dialogues Concerning Natural Religion.* London.

MacKenzie, Robert Beverley. 1868. *The Darwinian Theory of the Transmutation of Species Examined.* London: Nisbet &. Co. Quoted in a review, *Athenaeum*, no. 2102 (February 8): 217.

Paley, William. 1800. *Natural Theology.* Oxford: J. Vincent.

Rachels, James. 1991. *Created from Animals: The Moral Implications of Darwinism.* Oxford: Oxford University Press.

Schrödinger, Erwin. 1967. *What Is Life?* Cambridge: Cambridge University Press.

Smolin, Lee. 1992. "Did the Universe Evolve?" *Classical and* Quantum *Gravity* 9:173–91.

Wheeler, John Archibald. 1974. "Beyond the End of Time." In Martin Rees, Remo Ruffini, and John Archibald Wheeler (eds.), *Black Holes, Gravitational Waves and Cosmology: An Introduction to Current Research.* New York: Gordon and Breach.

4

Darwin, Design, and Divine Providence

John F. Haught

John F. Haught (b. 1942) is Senior Fellow, Science and Religion, at Georgetown University's Woodstock Theological Center, and formerly chaired the Theology Department at Georgetown. He has published broadly on issues concerning the relationship between science and religion, including *God after Darwin* (2000), *Deeper than Darwin* (2003), and *Is Nature Enough? Meaning and Truth in an Age of Science* (2006). In the following essay, Haught argues that evolutionary naturalists (such as Daniel Dennett) and intelligent design theorists (such as William Dembski) share a common mistaken assumption – namely, that evolution and divine providence are incompatible. Haught contends that evolutionary biology does not commit one to a materialistic, anti-supernatural metaphysic, and that it can be reconciled with divine providence.

To the theist, a central question after Darwin is whether evolution renders implausible the notion of divine Providence. Do the rough and ragged features of the new story of life place in question the idea of a personal God who cares for the world? Most theologians today would say no, but the more intimately the idea of Providence is tied to that of "intelligent design," the more difficult becomes the task of reconciling theology with evolutionary biology. I suspect that much of the energy underlying so-called Intelligent Design (ID) theory, in spite of explicit denials by some of its advocates, is an achingly religious need to protect the classical theistic belief in divine Providence from potential ruination by ideas associated with Darwinian science. It is impossible not to notice that the advocates of IDT are themselves almost always devout Christian, Muslim, and occasionally Jewish theists. It is difficult, therefore, for most scientists and theologians

John F. Haught, "Darwin, Design, and Divine Providence" from *Debating Design: From Darwin to DNA*, ed. William A. Dembski and Michael Ruse (New York: Cambridge University Press, 2004), pp. 229–45.

to accept the claim that no theological agenda is at work in the ID movement.

It is highly significant, moreover, that scientific proponents of ID, although often themselves experts in mathematics and specific areas of science, are generally hostile to evolutionary theory (Behe 1996; Dembski, 1998, 1999; Johnson, 1991, 1995). The justification they usually give for rejecting what most scientists take as central to biology is that Darwinism, or neo-Darwinism, is simply a naturalist belief system and not science at all. Evolution, they claim, is so permeated with materialist metaphysics that it does not qualify as legitimate science in the first place (Johnson 1991, 1999). This protest is indicative of a religious sensitivity that recognizes materialism to be inherently incompatible with theism.

Although, as I shall illustrate more extensively, it is clearly the case that contemporary presentations of evolution are often interlaced with a heavy dose of materialist ideology, it is not likely that a concern for science's methodological purity is the driving force behind ID's energetic protests against Darwinism. Rather, I would suggest, the flight from Darwin is rooted quite simply in an anxiety that his evolutionary ideas may be incompatible with any coherent notion of God or divine Providence. And the suspicion that Darwinism conflicts with the doctrine of Providence is ultimately rooted in the ID judgment that Darwinism, if true, would render the notion of intelligent design unbelievable. Hence the way to defend Providence – by which I mean here the "general" doctrine that God cares or "provides" for the universe – is to defend design.[1] Quite candidly, it seems to me that beneath all of the complex logical and mathematical argumentation generated by the ID movement there lies a deeply human and passionately religious concern about whether the universe resides in the bosom of a loving, caring God or is instead perched over an abyss of ultimate meaninglessness.

What may add some credibility to the ID preoccupations, rendering them less specious than they might at first seem, is the fact that many evolutionary biologists (and philosophers of biology) agree that Darwin's "dangerous idea" does indeed destroy the classical argument from design and that in so doing it exorcizes from scientifically enlightened consciousness the last remaining traces of cosmic teleology and supernaturalism. Since religion, as the renowned American philosopher W. T. Stace pointed out long ago, stands or falls with the question of cosmic purpose (Stace 1948, 54), the Darwinian debunking of design – and with it the apparent undoing of cosmic teleology as well – strikes right at the heart of the most prized religious intuitions of humans, now and always. Darwinism seems to many Darwinians – and not just to IDT advocates such as Phillip Johnson, Michael Behe, and William Dembski – to entail a materialist and even anti-theistic philosophy of nature. Michael Ruse even refers to Darwinism as "the apotheosis of a materialist theory" (Ruse 2001, 77). Consequently, it seems to many theists as well as to many scientists that we must choose *between* Darwinism and divine Providence.

A straightforward example of this either/or thinking is Gary Cziko's book *Without Miracles* (1995), a work that from beginning to end explicitly places "providential" in opposition to "selectionist" explanations for all the various features of life. For Cziko, as for many other Darwinians, there isn't enough room in the same human mind to hold both scientific and theological explanations simultaneously, so we must choose one over the other. In her discussion of sociobiology, Ullica Segerstråle (2000, 399–400) insightfully comments that Richard Dawkins likewise assumes that in accounting for living phenomena there can be only one "explanatory slot." And so, if Darwinism now completely fills that single aperture, there can be no room for any theological explanation to exist alongside it.

In my own reading of contemporary works on evolution, I have observed time and again a tacitly monocausal or univalent logic (laced with curt appeals to Occam's razor) that inevitably puts biological and providential arguments into a competitive relationship. To give just one of many possible examples, in *Darwin's Spectre*, Michael R. Rose illustrates the widespread belief that accounting for life must be the job *either* of theology *or* of Darwinism, but not of both. "Without Darwinism," he claims, "biological science would need one or more deities to explain the marvelous contrivances of life. Physics and chemistry are not enough. And so without Darwinism science would remain theistic, in whole or in part" (Rose 1998, 211). Clearly, the assumption here is that evolutionary science has now assumed occupancy of the *same* explanatory alcove that was formerly the dwelling place of the gods. And now that Darwin has expelled the deities from this niche, there is no longer any plausible explanatory place left for religion or theology.

Historically, it is true, religious ideas have often played a quasi-scientific or prescientific explanatory role, even while also providing ultimate explanations. But science has now – providentially, we may say – liberated theology from the work of satisfying the more mundane forms of inquiry. Yet even today, scriptural literalists want religious ideas to fill explanatory spaces that have been assigned more appropriately to science. Not everyone embraces the distinction that mainstream Western theology has made between scientific and theological levels of explanation. Cziko's and Rose's books, along with the better-known works of Richard Dawkins (1986, 1995, 1996), Daniel Dennett (1995), and E. O. Wilson (1998), demonstrate that today's biblical literalists are not alone in assuming that religious and theological readings of the world lie at essentially the same explanatory level as natural science.

Only this assumption could have led to the forced option between Providence, on the one hand, and natural selection, on the other. Thus, for many evolutionists there is no legitimate cognitive role left for religion or theology after Darwin, only (at best) an emotive or evaluative one. For them, as Rose's book lushly exemplifies, Darwinism goes best with materialism (Rose 1998, 211). It is not entirely surprising, then, that religiously sensitive souls would balk at evolution if they were persuaded by the words of evolutionists themselves that Darwinism is indeed inseparable from "materialism" – a philosophy that is logically irreconcilable not only with intelligent design but also with each and every religious interpretation of reality.

If the appeal by biologists to "materialism" were simply methodological, then the ID community would have no cause for complaint. By its very nature, science is obliged to leave out any appeal to the supernatural, and so its explanations will always sound naturalistic and purely physicalist. In many cases, I believe that ID advocates unnecessarily mistake methodological naturalism/materialism for metaphysical explanation. Alvin Plantinga (1997) even argues that there can be no sharp distinction between methodological and metaphysical naturalism. Practicing the latter, he thinks, is a slippery slope to the former. But even aside from Plantinga's questionable proposal, the ID intuition that Darwinians often illegitimately conflate science with materialist ideology is completely accurate. The problem is that, like their Darwinian opponents, ID theorists typically accept the assumption that only one "explanatory slot" is available and that if we fill it up completely with naturalistic explanations, there will be no room left anywhere for theological explanations.

Consequently, if the contemporary discussion of the question of Darwinism and design is ever going to penetrate beneath surface accusations, it must consider two questions. First, is Darwinian biology unintelligible apart from a philosophical commitment to materialism – a philosophy of nature that theists everywhere and of all stripes will take to be inherently atheistic? That is, does the information gathered by the various sciences tributary to evolutionary theory (geology, paleontology, comparative anatomy, radiometric dating, biogeography, genetics, etc.) remain unintelligible unless it is contextualized within a materialist philosophy of nature? And, second, would the elimination of the notion of "intelligent design" in scientific explanations of life's organized complexity logically entail the downfall of a credible doctrine of divine Providence, as both ID theorists and their evolutionary antagonists generally seem to agree would be the case? In the interest of fairness, we owe the IDT advocates a careful consideration of their suspicion that Darwinism is materialist atheism in disguise. But for the sake of giving a fair hearing to the full spectrum of theological reflection after Darwin, we should also look at the question of just how vital the notion of "intelligent design" is to a religiously robust notion of Providence. I will now consider each of these two questions in turn.

I. Is Darwinism Inherently Materialistic?

It is not without interest to our inquiry that in the intellectual world today, critics of theism are increasingly turning for support to Charles

Darwin. Many skeptics who seek to ground their suspicions about the existence of God in science no longer look as fervently to Freud, Marx, Nietzsche, Sartre, or Derrida as they do to Darwin. Especially for those already convinced that science is essentially ruinous to religion, Darwin has become more appealing than ever. His portrait of nature's apparent indifference seems to offer more compelling reasons than ever for scientific atheism. In fact, for some critics today natural selection provides much more secure grounds for atheism than do the impersonal laws of physics, which had already rendered the idea of divine action apparently superfluous several centuries ago. Even the renowned physicist Steven Weinberg considers Darwinism to be a much more potent challenge to theism than his own discipline (Weinberg 1992, 246). He singles out the ID enthusiast Phillip Johnson as the most sophisticated example of a theological alternative to Darwin and then proceeds to shred theism by destroying the arguments of one who, at least to Weinberg, speaks most eloquently for belief in God after Darwin (247–8). For many others among the scientific elite today, the ways of evolution are so coarse that even if the universe appears on the surface to be an expression of design, beneath this deceptive veneer there lurks a long and tortuous process in which an intelligent Deity could not conceivably have played any role.

It is not only the waste, struggle, suffering, and indifference of the evolutionary process that place in question the idea of a benevolent providential Deity. The three main evolutionary ingredients – randomness, the impersonal law of selection, and the immensity of cosmic time – seem to be enough to account causally for all the phenomena we associate with life, including design. The apparent completeness of the evolutionary recipe makes us wonder whether the universe requires any additional explanatory elements, including the creativity of a truly "interested" God. We may easily wonder, then, whether we can reconcile the ragged new picture of life not only with the idea of an intelligent Designer but also with any broader notion of divine Providence. Darwin himself, reflecting on the randomness, pain, and impersonality of evolution, abandoned the idea that nature could have been ordered in its particulars by a designing Deity. It is doubtful that he ever completely renounced the idea of God, since he often seems to have settled for a very distant divine law maker. But he gradually became convinced that the design in living beings could be accounted for in a purely naturalistic way. After Darwin, many others, including a number of the most prominent neo-Darwinian biologists writing today, have come close to equating Darwin's science with atheism. Sensitive to the conflation of Darwin's science with philosophical materialism that prominent biologists often make, ID proponents have drawn the conclusion that Darwinian biology, as evidenced in the publications of Darwinians themselves, is simply incapable of being reconciled with theistic belief. In order to save theism, then, Darwin must be directly refuted.

Not only scientific skeptics but also other intellectuals are now making the figurative pilgrimage to Down House in order to nourish their materialist leanings. A good example is the noted critic Frederick Crews, who recently published a titillating two-part essay, "Saving God from Darwin," in *The New York Review of Books* (October 4 and 18, 2001). Crews is best known for his constant pummelling of Sigmund Freud, whose ideas he considers blatantly unscientific. But in all of his blasting of psychoanalysis he has never challenged Freud's materialist metaphysics. Crews clearly shares with Freud the unshakable belief that beneath life, consciousness, and culture there lies *ultimately* only mindless and meaningless material stuff.

In Crews's opinion, Darwin has uncovered the ultimate truth to which all intelligent and courageous humans must now resign themselves. Referring to Daniel Dennett's radically materialist interpretation of Darwin, Crews is convinced that Dennett has "trenchantly shown" that Darwin's ideas lead logically to "a satisfyingly materialistic reduction of mind and soul" and that evolutionary theory entails a "naturalistic account of life's beginning" (Crews, October 4, p. 24). Even though the materialism and naturalism he is referring to are really examples of metaphysics and not pure science, for Crews they have become part and parcel of biology itself. Crews, of course, is not a biologist, but he could easily point to many ideological associates in the scientific community who share his view that the ultimate "truth" of Darwinism is a materialist and Godless cosmos.

This, of course, is exactly the same not-so-subtle message that proponents of ID have detected in contemporary evolutionary thought. Crews upbraids the ID literature for sneaking theology into an explanatory slot that science alone should inhabit. But interestingly, his own comprehension of Darwinism – a conflation of science with materialist metaphysics – is identical to that of his ID opponents. In both instances, the idea of evolution is understood to be inseparable from the nonscientific *belief* that matter is all there is and that the universe is inherently pointless – an assumption that is inherently antithetical to theism of any kind. For Crews, as well as for numerous biologists and philosophers today, evolution and materialism come as a package deal (see also Dennett 1995). And so the only difference between them and ID disciples is that the latter throw the package away, whereas the former hold onto it tightly. Both evolutionary materialists and ID advocates discern at the bottom of Darwinism a fundamentally pointless universe.

We may have good reason to wonder, then, whether the evolutionist alloy of scientific information and philosophically materialist belief is any closer to pure science than the conflation of biology with Intelligent Design that is now the object of so much scientific scorn. If ID is advised to keep theological explanation (under the guise of an abstract notion of "Intelligent Design") from intruding into biology, are not Darwinians also obliged to keep whatever philosophical biases they may have from invading their public presentations of evolutionary science?

Strictly speaking, after all, it is no more appropriate to say that Darwinism is a materialist theory than it is to say that the theory of relativity is. All science *must* be methodologically materialist – in the sense that it is not permissible when doing science to invoke nonphysical causes. It is one thing to hold that evolutionary science provides a picture of nature that supports a purely materialist philosophy of life, if you happen to have one. But it is quite another to claim – as Rose, Cziko, Dawkins, Dennett, and many others do – that the facts of evolution *do not make sense* outside of a materialist philosophical landscape. How would we ever know for sure that this is the case? Such a claim is based as much on belief as on research, and it is one that will forever remain logically unsupportable by scientific evidence as such. Moreover, there is always the possibility that alternative metaphysical frameworks may turn out to be no less illuminating settings for interpreting evolutionary information (Haught 2000).

For now, however, it is sufficient to note that, strictly speaking, neither Darwinians nor their ID adversaries can logically claim that evolutionary biology is an expression of materialism. Like all other applications of scientific method, evolutionary biology remains methodologically naturalistic. *As such*, it makes no formal appeal to the idea of God, purpose, or intelligence in its own self-restricting mode of explanation. But likewise, any inferences that a scientist might make from doing the work of pure science to materialist conclusions about that work is not itself an exercise intrinsic to science. The energizing force behind scientism and materialism is never the purely scientific desire to know, but something quite extrinsic to science. The slippage from methodological naturalism into metaphysical materialism is not justifiable by scientific method itself. Logically speaking, therefore, we must conclude that it is not at all evident that evolution necessarily entails philosophical materialism.

II. Is Design Essential to the Idea of Providence?

The more intimately the idea of God or "Providence" is associated with "Intelligent Design," as is implicit in the theological assumptions underlying most of the ID movement, the more it seems that the most efficient way to oppose materialist "Darwinism" is to shore up arguments from design. But just how closely do we have to connect Providence with Intelligent Design in the first place? I shall propose here that the two ideas are quite distinct and that evolutionary biology may cohere quite nicely with a theologically grounded notion of Providence, even if it does not fit a simplistic understanding of divine design. If such a case can be made, then there should be no reason for theists to oppose evolutionary biology, even if they must oppose Darwinian materialism.

There is no denying, however, that to many scientists and philosophers, as well as to devotees of ID, Darwinian biology connotes a universe empty of any conceivable divine governance, compassion, or care. In view of the obvious challenges that so many sincere skeptics and religiously devout people perceive to be inherent in evolution, can the idea of Providence now have any plausibility at all? Responses to this question fall roughly into three distinct classes. Evolutionary materialism and ID fall together as one, since they both view Darwinian accounts of evolution as incompatible with Providence. But there are two distinct kinds of theological response that have no difficulty embracing both conventional biological science and, at the same time, a biblically grounded notion of divine Providence. Let us consider each of these in turn.

A. *Theological Response I*

Evolutionary science, though perhaps disturbing to a superficial theism, is no more threatening to theistic faith than is any other development in modern science. Science and religion, after all, are radically distinct ways of understanding, and they should be kept completely apart from each other.[2] Science answers one set of questions, religion an entirely different one. Science asks about physical causes, while religion looks for ultimate explanations and meanings. If we keep science and religion separate, there can be no conflict. The ugly disputes between Galileo and the Roman Catholic Church, and later between Darwin and Christianity, could have been avoided if theologians had never intruded into the world of science and if certain highly visible evolutionists had refrained from making sweeping metaphysical claims about evolution as though they were scientific statements.

Thus Darwin's ideas – which may be quite accurate, scientifically speaking – carry not even the slightest threat to theism. The apparent contradiction arises not from the scientific theory of evolution itself, but from the confusion of the biblical accounts of creation with "science" in the case of biblical literalists, the confusion of Providence with intelligent design in the case of ID theorists, and the equally misbegotten confusion of evolutionary data with metaphysical materialism in the case of some evolutionary scientists and philosophers. There is no squabble here with the purely *scientific* aspects of evolution. What is objectionable is the uncritical mixing of evolutionary science with nonscientific beliefs, whatever these beliefs may be. The "danger" of Darwinism to theism, then, is not so much Darwin's own ideas but the way in which they get captured by materialist ideologies that are indeed incompatible with theism but that have nothing inherently to do with *scientific* truth.

At some point, of course, if we dig toward the deepest roots of life's designs, we will have to yield to metaphysical explanations. But both evolutionary materialism and ID move prematurely into metaphysical discourse. They reach for ultimate explanations at a point when there is still plenty of room left for more subtle scientific inquiry into the proximate causes of the complex patterns evident in living phenomena. Darwinian materialists, therefore, cannot credibly object that ID theorists turn prematurely to metaphysics, since materialism – as a worldview and not just as a method – permeates their own inquiry from the outset – even tacitly helping them to decide what are and are not worthwhile research projects. Their materialist metaphysics consists of the controlling belief that mindless "matter" is the ultimately real stuff underlying everything – even if contemporary physics has shown this "stuff" to be much more subtle than was previously thought. (One may use the term "physicalist" here if the term "materialist" seems too harsh.) In any case, many evolutionists commit themselves to a physicalist or materialist creed, and not just to methodological naturalism, long before they ever embark on their "purely scientific" explorations of life. So the fact that ID would want to propose a metaphysical framework of its own as the setting for explaining living design does not, *as such*, make it any more objectionable than evolutionary materialism.

The real problem, however, is that *both* ID and evolutionary materialism take flight into ultimate metaphysical explanations too early in their explanations of life. One of the lessons that a more seasoned theology has learned from modern science is that we must all postpone metaphysical gratification. To introduce ideas about God or intelligence as the direct "cause" of design would be theologically as well as scientifically ruinous. A mature theology allows natural science to carry its own methods and explanations as far as they can possibly go. This reserve does not entail, however, that theology is irrelevant at every level of a rich explanation of life. Theology is now freed from moonlighting in the explanatory domain that science now occupies, so that it may now gravitate toward its more natural setting – at levels of depth to which science cannot reach. Theology can now devote its full attention to the truly big questions that constitute its proper domain. Theology, after all, assumes that there is more than one level of explanation for everything. It endorses the idea of a plurality of explanations, perhaps hierarchically arranged, such that no discipline can give an exhaustive account of anything whatsoever. Any particular explanation, including the Darwinian explanation, is inevitably an abstraction and needs to be complemented by a luxuriant explanatory pluralism. When it comes to living beings, for example, there is more than one explanatory slot available, though it is entirely appropriate to push scientific explanations (physical, chemical, biological) as far as they can possibly go at their own proper levels within die many explanatory layers. The main problem with ID is that, ironically, it shares with evolutionary materialism the unfounded belief that only one authoritative kind of explanation is available to us today – namely, the scientific – and so feels compelled to push impatiently a metaphysically and theologically loaded notion of "intelligent design" into a logical space that is entirely too small for it.

If there is anything like a providential significance to the historical arrival of the scientific method, it may lie in the fact that science has now distanced the divine from any immediate grasp or human cognitional control. Darwin's science, in particular, has removed easy religious access to an *ultimate* explanation of design that formerly seemed to lurk just beneath the surface of living complexity. By allowing for purely scientific inquiries into living design, theology can now function at a deeper level of explanation, addressing questions such as why there is any order at all, rather than just chaos; or why there is anything at all, rather than nothing; or why the universe is intelligible; or why we should bother to do science at all. Today, as a result of science, the long path from surface design down to nature's ultimate depths turns out to be much less direct than ID theorists seem to crave.

Postponing metaphysics, however, calls for an asceticism that neither ID nor evolutionary materialism is disciplined enough to practice. They both try to arrive at the ultimate foundations of design too soon, pretending to have reached the basement level before even commencing the long journey down the stairs. One way of manifesting this metaphysical impatience is to fasten the phenomenon of living complexity directly onto the cozy idea of divine intelligent design without first looking into nature's own self-organizing, emergent spontaneity. But no less impatient, and prematurely metaphysical, are assertions that design is "nothing but" the outcome of blind natural selection of inheritable variation. ID is a "science stopper," since it appeals to a God-of-the-gaps explanation at a point in inquiry when there is still plenty of room for further scientific elucidation. But invoking the idea of "natural selection" as though it were an incomparably *deep* explanation of life's design could be called a "depth suppressor." Evolutionist materialism, not unlike ID, capitulates to the craving for ultimate explanations of life at a point when the journey into the depth of design may have just barely started.

It seems to me that "dreams of a final theory" are as conspicuous among Darwinians today as they are among physicist-philosophers. The fantasies of categorical finality among some evolutionary thinkers exhibit a dogmatism as rigid as that of any creationist. Science can have a future, however, only if its devotees retain a tacit sense of the unfathomable depth beneath nature's surface. And this is why any premature appeal to either theological or naturalistic metaphysics blunts our native intuition of nature's endless depths, supposing as it does that human inquiry has already arrived at the bottom of it all. The deadening thud of metaphysical finality is audible on both sides of the ID versus evolution debate. An appropriate theology of divine Providence and its relation to nature, on the other hand, abhors such premature metaphysical gratification. It sets forth a vision of the world in which science has an interminable future, since nature has an inexhaustible depth. Accordingly, the unwillingness of either ID or evolutionary materialism to dig very deep into the explanatory roots of life's organized complexity is an insult to the human mind's need for an endless horizon of intelligibility.

If there are still any doubts about the conflation of materialist ideology with biological science, then the following words of Stephen Jay Gould, one of the most eloquent interpreters of Darwin, should dispel them:

> I believe that the stumbling block to [the acceptance of Darwin's theory] does not lie in any scientific difficulty, but rather in the *philosophical content* of Darwin's message – in its challenge to a set of entrenched Western attitudes that we are not yet ready to abandon. First, Darwin argues that evolution has no purpose. Individuals struggle to increase the representation of their genes in future generations, and that is all. . . . Second, Darwin maintained that evolution has no direction; it does not lead inevitably to higher things. Organisms become better adapted to their local environments, and that is all. The "degeneracy" of a parasite is as perfect as the gait of a gazelle. Third, Darwin applied a consistent philosophy of materialism to his interpretation of nature. Matter is the ground of all existence; mind, spirit and God as well, are just words that express the wondrous results of neuronal complexity. (Gould 1977, 12–13, emphasis added)

Gould would argue that Darwin himself had already begun the process of mixing materialism and evolution and that the current materialism among biologists is not a departure from a trend initiated by the master himself. In any case, today what is so threatening to ID about Darwinism is not just the scientific information it gathers, but even more the ideology of materialism that has taken hold of this data, twisting it into a tangle of science and faith assumptions – all in the name of science. The only solution to the ID versus Darwinism debate, therefore, is for everyone to distinguish science from all belief systems, whether religious or materialist. This would mean that the idea of divine Providence after Darwin remains pretty much the same as it was before. Evolutionary science cannot tell us anything significant about God that we did not already know from revelation, nor can our experience of God add much to our understanding of evolution. Evolution is a purely scientific theory that should be taken hostage neither by theism nor by materialism.

Of course, the inevitable objection will arise, from both ID and evolutionary materialism, that evolution cannot really be separated from the materialist beliefs that have dogged it ever since Darwin. For example, don't the elements of chance, suffering, and impersonal natural selection, operative over the course of a wasteful immensity of time, entail a materialist and therefore Godless universe? Aren't Dennett, Dawkins, Rose, Cziko, Crews, and the rest fully justified in reading evolution as the direct refutation of any plausible notion of divine Providence?

Such a conclusion is not at all necessary. For example, what appears to the scientist to be contingent, random, or accidental in natural history or genetic processes may have these apparent attributes because of our general human ignorance. After all, any purely human angle of vision, as the great religions have always taught, is always limited and narrow. As for complaints about the struggle, cruelty, waste, and pain inherent in evolution – realities that seem at first to place the universe beyond the pale of any conceivable Providence – these are already familiar issues to religion and theology. Darwin has contributed nothing qualitatively new to the perennial problem of suffering and evil, the harsh realities to which religions have always been sensitive. Robust religious faith has never cleared up these mysteries, but mystery is a stimulus and not a defeat for the endless religious adventure. Faith, after all, means unflagging trust *in spite of* the cruelties of life. Too much certitude actually renders faith impossible. So our new knowledge of evolution's indifference is no more an impediment to trust in divine Providence than suffering and evil have always been.

B. *Theological Response II*

The response just summarized, Theological Response I, is one that scientifically educated believers have often made in defense of the notion of Providence in the post-Darwinian period. A good number of scientists and theologians have reacted to Darwin's allegedly "dangerous" ideas at least roughly along the lines of this response. However, let us now consider another approach, one that goes far beyond just affirming the logical compatibility of evolutionary biology and theism. The following proposal argues that theology can fruitfully and enthusiastically embrace the Darwinian portrayal of life once the latter has been purged of its excess philosophical baggage.[3]

Although the sharp distinctions made by Theological Response I are essential, it is too willing to let science and religion go their separate ways. It is true that science and religion are distinct, but they both flow forth from a single human quest for truth. They are oriented toward reality in different ways, but the unity of truth demands that we not keep such scientific facts as evolution separate from our reflections on the notion of Providence. Once we accept evolutionary science in an intellectually serious way, we cannot have exactly the same thoughts about Providence as we had before Darwin. And so another kind of theological response than the one just given is necessary.

Like the first approach, this second one is critical of the implicitly theological maneuvers of ID as well as of the usually unacknowledged ideological agenda of evolutionary materialism. However, it candidly admits that contemporary evolutionary biology demands a deepening of the theological sense of what divine care or Providence could possibly mean in the light of the disturbing picture of life that Darwin's science has now set before us.

Unfortunately, most contemporary theology has still not undergone the transformation that evolution demands. This delay is not entirely surprising, since the Darwinian shock is still ringing, and religions often take centuries to react to such an earthquake. The sobering fact, however, is that the world's religions have still barely begun to respond to evolutionary biology. A few religious thinkers have made evolution the backbone of their understanding of God and the world, but they are the exception rather than the rule. Modern Western theology began to lose interest in the natural world soon after the historical emergence of science, and this is one reason why the topic of evolution still remains outside the general concerns of theology. Such a slighting of evolution, however, is a lost opportunity for theological growth and renewal. A serious encounter with Darwinism might not only deepen the theology of Providence but also help to expose both the theological and the scientific evasiveness of ID.

In fact, it is now conceivable that theology's understanding of divine Providence can be restated in evolutionary terms without any loss in its power to provide a basis for religious hope. How, though, can the idea of divine providential wisdom be rendered compatible with the obvious randomness or contingency in life's evolution? This is a question that both ID proponents and Darwinian materialists will inevitably ask. The first theological response, summarized earlier, would respond that we humans resort to words like "randomness," "accident," and "chance" simply because of our abysmal human ignorance of the larger divine plan for the universe. In other words, randomness and contingency are illusions beneath which the properly initiated may be able to discern God's deeper designs. There is admittedly something deeply religious about trusting in a vision wider than meager human awareness can command, but it is entirely unnecessary – and indeed wrong theologically – to deny that chance is a real aspect of the world. Contingency, to use the general philosophical term, must be accepted as a fact of nature – as Stephen Jay Gould, among others, has rightly emphasized. But instead of logically refuting Providence or rendering the universe absurd, the fact of contingency in natural history and in genetic processes allows us to correlate the facts of nature more intimately than ever with actual religious experience and belief.

The real issue here is not whether evolution rules out a divine designer, but whether the Darwinian picture of life refutes the notion that divine Providence is essentially self-giving love. The approach of evolutionists such as Dawkins and Dennett is first to reduce the idea of God to that of a designer, then to argue that Darwinism explains design adequately, and finally to conclude that Darwinism has thus made God superfluous. It does not help things theologically, of course, that ID also – at least in its formal argumentation – implicitly reduces ultimate explanation to that of intelligent design. However, in any serious discussion of evolution and theism, there is little point in abstract references to emaciated philosophical ideas of deity, especially those that picture this ultimate reality as essentially an engineer, mechanic, or designer. Instead, scientists and scientifically educated philosophers must converse with thoughts about God that arise from *actual* religious symbols and teachings. This advice will make the conversations regarding evolution and theology more complex, but also more pertinent, than they are when the only idea being debated is that of design or a designer. Most theists, after all, are not willing to spend every ounce of their theological energy defending such simplistic philosophical abstractions as "divine design." Many of them will be much more concerned with the question of whether and how Darwinism fits the vision of God as humble, self-giving love.

To be more specific, if there is anything to the religious intuition that the universe is the consequence of selfless divine love (a belief held by countless theists), then the fact of contingency in the created universe and life's evolution may easily be understood as a manifestation rather than a refutation of that love. An infinite love, if we think about it seriously, would manifest itself in the creation of a universe free of any rigid determinism (either natural or divine) that would keep it from arriving at its own independence, autonomy, and self-coherence. Contingency, it is true, can lead life down circuitous pathways, but that is precisely the risk that love takes when it allows genuine otherness to emerge as the object of that love. In any wholesome human experience of being loved, we already intuitively know that true concern or care for the other does not resort to control or compulsion, but rather in some way "lets the other be." Can we expect less than this respect for the otherness and eventual freedom of created reality on the part of what religious faith confesses to be an infinite love?

Love, at the very minimum, allows others sufficient scope to become themselves. So if there is any substance at all to the belief that God really loves and *cares* for the integrity of the created universe as something truly other than God, then this universe must possess a degree of autonomy. Relative independence must be inherent in the universe from the outset. If the universe were not percolating with contingency, it would be nothing more than an extension of God's being, an appendage of the Deity, rather than something genuinely other than God. A central tenet of theism, as distinct from pantheism, is that the world is not God. But if the world is distinct from and *other* than God, then its existence is not necessary (as is God's existence), nor are its specific characteristics. In other words, the world is contingent, and wherever there is contingency, there has to be room for the undirected events we call accidental or random. Chance is an inevitable part of any universe held to be both distinct from and simultaneously loved by God (Johnson, 1996). Even the medieval philosopher and theologian Saint Thomas Aquinas observed that the idea of a universe devoid of accidents would be theologically incoherent (Mooney 1996, 162).

Moreover, once we allow that God's creative and providential activity is essentially a liberation of the world to "be itself," then it comes as no surprise to the informed theist that the creation would have its own autonomously operative "laws" (such as natural selection), and that the universe would probably not be finished in one magical moment but would instead unfold stepwise – perhaps consuming billions and trillions of human years. The point is, there could be no genuine self-giving of God to any universe that is not first allowed to become something radically distinct from God. This means that in some sense the created world must be self-actualizing, and even self-creative, though within the limits of relevant possibilities held out to it by its Creator. Theologically speaking, therefore, the vastness of evolutionary duration, the spontaneity of random variations or mutations, and even the automatic machinations of natural selection could be thought of as essential ingredients in the emergence of cosmic independence. Perhaps only in some such matrix as this could life, mind, and eventually human freedom come into being. Maybe the entirety of evolution, including all the suffering and contingency that seem to render it absurd, are quite consistent, after all, with the idea of a Providence that cares for the internal growth and emergent independence of the world.

To some evolutionary materialists and followers of ID, the "wasteful" multi-millennial journey of evolution counts against a plausible trust in divine Providence. For both schools of thought the idea of Providence has been implicitly reduced to design, so evolution is logically inconsistent with theism. If God were intelligent and all-powerful, both sides assume, then the creative process would not be as rough and ragged as it is. Nontheistic evolutionists and ID proponents alike insist that a competent creator would have to be an intelligent designer. But their blueprints for an acceptable deity seem, at least to a theology in touch with actual religious experience, to resemble a conjurer or a distant architect rather than the infinitely humble and suffering love that theologians such as Wolfhart Pannenberg (1991), Elizabeth Johnson (1996), and Karl Rahner (1978) have set before us. Unfortunately, these and many other highly respected interpreters of theism are seldom consulted by those involved in the so-called Darwin wars.

A theology after Darwin also argues that divine Providence influences the world in a persuasive rather than a coercive way. Since God is love and not domineering force, the world must be endowed with an inner spontaneity and self-creativity that allows it to "become itself" and thus to participate in the adventure of its own creation (Haught 1995, 2000). Any other kind of world, in fact, is theologically inconceivable. If God were a directive dictator rather than persuasive love, the universe could never arrive at the point of being able to emerge into freedom. If God were the engineering agency that ID and evolutionary materialism generally project onto the divine, evolution could not have occurred. The narrative grandeur that Darwin observed in life's evolution would have given way to a monotonously perfect design devoid of an open future.

If one still wonders why Providence would wait so long for the world to be finished, some words of theologian Jürgen Moltmann are worth hearing:

> God acts in the history of nature and human beings through his patient and silent presence, by way of which he gives those he has created space to unfold, time to develop, and power for their own movement. We look in vain for God in the history of nature or in human history if what we are looking for are special divine interventions. Is it not much more that God waits and awaits, that – as process theology rightly says – he 'experiences' the history of the world and human beings, that he is "patient and of great goodness" as Psalm 103:8 puts it? . . . "Waiting" is never disinterested passivity, but the highest form of interest in the other. Waiting means expecting, expecting means inviting, inviting means attracting, alluring and enticing. By doing this, the waiting and awaiting keeps an open space for the other, gives the other time, and creates possibilities of life for the other. (Moltmann 2001, 149)

In the well-known words of Saint Paul, such a picture of God's hiddenness, patience, and vulnerability sounds like "foolishness" (1 Cor 1:25) when compared to our typical preference for Providence in the form of a designing divine magician. But a magician could never provide what a self-effacing love can provide – namely, the space within which something truly unpredictable, and therefore truly other than God, might emerge into being. Ever since Darwin, the most profound theologies have had no difficulty reconciling evolution with a God who does not compel but rather awaits the world so as not to detract from its independence and integrity. Today, of course, many will still find Darwinian evolution too troubling a notion to be allied so closely with theology. But the notion of a God whose essence is self-giving love, a God who opens up an endlessly new future for the world, actually anticipates the idea of evolution. Thus it should not be difficult for theology to understand Providence in terms of a picture of life approximately like the one that Darwin and contemporary evolutionary science have given us, rather than in terms of the abstract – and rather lifeless – notion of a divine designer.

Conclusion

I hope to have demonstrated in this chapter, first, that Darwinian evolution does not inevitably entail a materialist metaphysics, and second, that the theological notion of Providence is quite distinct from the idea of Intelligent Design. I have summarized two quite different theological positions, both of which argue for the compatibility of evolution and divine Providence without conceiving of Providence as essentially design. The special strength of the first approach is that it distinguishes clearly between metaphysics and science, a point lost on both evolutionary materialism and ID theory. Sooner or later, the appeal to metaphysics is unavoidable and necessary for deep explanation. Both materialism and ID theory implicitly realize this point, but they lurch too quickly toward ultimate explanations. The advantage of the second theological approach, then, is that it both allows science full scope to do its own work and simultaneously sets forth a metaphysical alternative to evolutionary materialism that can fully contextualize Darwinian discovery without jeopardizing either scientific explanation or the religious doctrine of Providence. In doing so, it also responds compassionately to the religious anxiety that turns ID theorists away from good biology and shows how unnecessary it is to import theological ideas into the work of science.

Notes

1 Theologians often distinguish between general Providence, God's care for the universe as a whole, and particular Providence, God's involvement in a specific event or in an individual's life. Here the focus will be on general Providence.
2 Ian Barbour (1990) refers to this theological way of relating science to religion as the "independence" model, and I refer to it (1995) as the "contrast" approach.
3 I have developed this approach more fully in *God after Darwin* (Haught 2000).

References

Barbour, Ian G. 1990. *Religion in an Age of Science.* San Francisco: Harper and Row.

Behe, Michael J. 1996. *Darwin's Black Box: The Biochemical Challenge to Evolution.* New York: The Free Press.

Crews, Frederick. 2001. Saving us from Darwin. *The New York Review of Books* 48 (October 4 and 18).

Cziko, Gary. 1995. *Without Miracles: Universal Selection Theory and the Second Darwinian Revolution.* Cambridge, MA: MIT Press.

Dawkins, Richard. 1986. *The Blind Watchmaker.* New York: Norton.

1995. *River Out of Eden.* New York: Basic Books.

1996. *Climbing Mount Improbable.* New York: Norton.

Dembski, William A. 1999. *Intelligent Design: The Bridge between Science and Theology.* Downers Grove, IL: InterVarsity Press.

Dembski, William A. (ed.) 1998. *Mere Creation: Science, Faith and Intelligent Design.* Downers Grove, IL: InterVarsity Press.

Dennett, Daniel C. 1995. *Darwin's Dangerous Idea: Evolution and the Meaning of Life.* New York: Simon and Schuster.

Gould, Stephen Jay. 1977. *Ever since Darwin.* New York: Norton.

Haught, John F. 1995. *Science and Religion: From Conflict to Conversation.* Mahwah, NJ: Paulist Press.

2000. *God after Darwin: A Theology of Evolution.* Boulder, CO: Westview Press.

Johnson, Elizabeth. 1996. Does God play dice? Divine Providence and chance. *Theological Studies* 57 (March): 3–18.

Johnson, Phillip E. 1991. *Darwin on Trial.* Washington, DC: Regnery Gateway.

1999. *The Wedge of Truth: Splitting the Foundations of Naturalism.* Downers Grove, IL: InterVarsity Press.

Moltmann, Jürgen. 2001. God's kenosis in the creation and consummation of the world. In *The Work of Love: Creation as Kenosis*, ed. John Polkinghorne. Grand Rapids, MI: Eerdmans.

Mooney, Christopher, S. J. 1996. *Theology and Scientific Knowledge.* Notre Dame and London: University of Notre Dame Press.

Pannenberg, Wolfhart. 1991. *Systematic Theology*, Vol. I, trans. Geoffrey W. Bromiley. Grand Rapids, MI: Eerdmans.

Plantinga, Alvin. 1997. Methodological naturalism. *Perspectives on Science and Christian Faith* 49: 143–54.

Rahner, Karl. 1978. *Foundations of Christian Faith: An Introduction to the Idea of Christianity*, trans. William V. Dych. New York: Seabury Press.

Rose, Michael R. 1998. *Darwin's Spectre: Evolutionary Biology in the Modern World.* Princeton: Princeton University Press.

Ruse, Michael. 2001. *Can a Darwinian Be a Christian?* Cambridge: Cambridge University Press.

Segerstråle, Ullica. 2000. *Defenders of the Truth: The Battle for Science in the Sociology Debate and Beyond.* New York: Oxford University Press.

Stace, W. T. 1948. Man against darkness. *The Atlantic Monthly* 182 (September 1948).

Weinberg, Steven. 1992. *Dreams of a Final Theory.* New York: Pantheon Books.

Wilson, E. O. 1998. *Consilience: The Unity of Knowledge.* New York: Knopf.

5

How Naturalism Implies Skepticism

Alvin Plantinga

Alvin Plantinga (b. 1932) is John A. O'Brien Professor of Philosophy at the University of Notre Dame and one of the leading contributors to contemporary philosophy of religion. In the following essay he presents a somewhat simplified version of an influential argument he first offered in *Warrant and Proper Function* (1993). Plantinga argues that atheistic naturalism implies a thoroughgoing form of skepticism; thus, atheistic naturalism is a theory such that if it were true, one ought not believe it.

My topic is naturalism, skepticism, and the connection there between. I propose to argue that there is a connection between the two, and that indeed the former commits one to the latter. But first a word about each.

Varieties of Skepticism

The term 'naturalism', of course, is used in a wide variety of senses. For example, there is the naturalism in ethics with which G. E. Moore did battle; there is naturalism in art and literature; there is naturalism as the pursuit of one who studies nature. I use the term as follows: a naturalist is someone who thinks there is no such person as God or anything much like God. Naturalism thus entails atheism. The converse, however, doesn't hold; it is possible to be an atheist but not rise to the heights (or perhaps sink to the depths) of naturalism. Thus a Hegelian might well be an atheist; she will not be a naturalist, however, because Hegel's absolute is too much like God. The same goes for a serious follower of Plato, with his Idea of the Good, and similarly for Aristotle with his First Mover who thinks just about himself. Naturalism, as I'm thinking of it, includes the views of people like John Dewey, Bertrand Russell, Daniel Dennett, Richard Dawkins, Steven Pinker, and the like. We

Alvin Plantinga, "How Naturalism Implies Skepticism" from *Analytic Philosophy without Naturalism*, ed. Antonella Corradini, Sergio Galvan, and E. Jonathan Lowe (London: Routledge, 2006), ch. 2, pp. 29–44.

might call it 'Atheism Plus' or perhaps 'High Octane Atheism'. According to Oxford philosopher John Lucas, naturalism is the orthodoxy of the western academy. That may be a bit strong; there are also those myriads of postmodern anti-realists with respect to truth. But naturalism is at the least very popular these days. And I propose, as I say, to argue that naturalism commits one to skepticism.

Second, skepticism. Unlike 'naturalism', 'skepticism' doesn't have a host of different senses. Still, there are several brands of skepticism. Consider, for example, contextualism in epistemology, and in particular the contextualist response to skepticism. According to Keith DeRose, an eminent authority on contextualism, 'contextualist theories of knowledge attributions have almost invariably been developed with an eye toward providing some kind of answer to philosophical skepticism' (DeRose 1999: 185). The basic idea of the contextualist response to the skeptic is as follows. The terms 'know', 'knowledge' and their like are in fact multiply ambiguous, in that in different contexts, different standards apply for their correct application. We are in an epistemology seminar; the topic is Descartes's evil genius who creates us only to deceive us. In this context, the standard for the application of the term 'know' is very high; one, or one's belief, must be in an exceptionally good epistemic position to warrant application of the term 'know'. It may well turn out, therefore, that in that high-standard sense of the term, I don't know that I'm not being deceived by such a Cartesian demon. In that same sense I don't know that I'm not a brain in a vat, holding mainly false beliefs; and if I don't know that, then presumably I don't know any proposition that entails that I am not thus envatted. In other more ordinary and everyday contexts, however, the standards for the correct application of the term aren't nearly as stringent. If you ask me whether I know my mother's phone number, I will reply, quite correctly, that I do. Also I know my name and where I live. In those contexts, the term 'knowledge' may properly apply to a given belief, even if it is not in an epistemic position good enough to warrant the term in its high-standard seminar sense.

'According to contextualists', says DeRose, 'the skeptic, in presenting her argument, manipulates the semantic standards of knowledge, thereby creating a context in which she can *truthfully* say that we know nothing or very little' (1999: 185). The skeptic, by raising her skeptical doubts, creates a context in which the standards for the proper use of the term 'know' go way up; hence she can correctly say that no one has knowledge. More exactly, her use of the sentence 'No one has knowledge' expresses a truth in that context. But of course this is compatible with its being the case that when, in an ordinary context, I say, 'I know that Tom was at the party; I saw him there' that sentence also expresses a truth.

Well, suppose the skeptic succeeds in confusing me; I apply the wrong standards in an everyday context, and form the belief that no one knows much of anything. What I am then committed to is the thought that our beliefs don't meet the high standards (for justification, warrant, rationality, whatever) required for the proper application of the term 'knowledge' in the seminar context. That is, there are some high standards of epistemic justification or warrant – those required by the application of the term 'knowledge' in the seminar context – that hardly anyone's beliefs ever meet. Of course that is entirely compatible with thinking I've got very good reason for many of my beliefs.

Now this is not the kind of skepticism that has traditionally been urged, or lamented, by the Humes and Sextus Empiricists of our tradition. It is also not the sort of skepticism to which I claim the naturalist is committed. We can see why by considering the Hume of the conclusion of Book I of the *Treatise* (Hume 1951: 263ff.). Here he isn't coolly announcing, as an interesting fact about us, that few if any of our beliefs meet those very high standards of justification or warrant to which the contextualist refers. Instead, he finds himself in a crisis which is both epistemic and existential; he simply doesn't know what to believe. When he follows out what seem to be the promptings and leading of reason, he winds up time after time in a black coal pit, not knowing which way to turn:

> Where am I, or what? From what causes do I derive my existence, and to what condition shall I return? Whose favour shall I court, and whose anger must I dread? What beings surround me? and on whom have I any influence, or who have

> any influence on me? I am confounded with all these questions, and begin to fancy myself in the most deplorable condition imaginable, inviron'd with the deepest darkness, and utterly depriv'd of the use of every member and faculty. (Hume 1951: 269)

Of course, this is Hume in his study, some time before he emerges for that famous game of backgammon. Nature herself, fortunately, dispels these clouds of despair:

> [she] cures me of this philosophical melancholy and delirium, either by relaxing this bent of mind, or by some avocation, and lively impression of my senses, which obliterate all these chimeras. I dine, I play a game of back-gammon, I converse, and am merry with my friends. (ibid.)

Still, the enlightened person, Hume thinks, holds the consolations of nature at arm's length. She knows she can't help acquiescing in the common illusion, but she maintains her skepticism of 'the general maxims of the world' and adopts a certain ironic distance, a wary double-mind-edness: 'I may, nay, I must yield to the current of nature, in submitting to my senses and understanding; and in this blind submission I shew most perfectly my sceptical disposition and principles' (ibid.: 269). This is the irony of the human condition: those who are enlightened can see that nature inevitably leads us to believe what is probably false, or arbitrary, or at best extremely dubious; they also see, however, that even the best of us simply don't have it in them to successfully resist her blandishments. We can't help believing those 'general maxims', or if we can, it is only for brief periods of time and in artificial situations. No one can think Humean thoughts about, say, induction, when under attack by a shark, or when clinging precariously to a rock face high above the valley floor. (You won't find yourself saying, 'Well, I do of course believe that if this handhold breaks out, I'll hurtle down to the ground and get killed, but of course (fleeting sardonic, self-deprecatory smile) I also know that this thought is just a deliverance of my nature and is therefore not really to be taken seriously'.) Still, in other circumstances one can take a sort of condescending and dismissive stance with respect to these promptings of nature; in reflective moments in my study, for example, I see through them. As a rational creature I can rise above them, recognizing that they have little or nothing to be said for them. Indeed, I see more: this skepticism is itself a *reflexive* skepticism; it arises even with respect to this very thought; this very doubt, this feeling of superiority, this seeing through what our natures impose on us, is itself a deliverance of my nature and is thus as suspect as any other. The true skeptic, says Hume, 'will be diffident of his philosophical doubts, as well as of his philosophical conviction' (ibid.: 273).[1] The true skeptic, we might say, has a defeater for each of his beliefs, including those that lead to skepticism; and it is this kind of skepticism to which the naturalist is committed.

Reduction and Supervenience

Most naturalists accept *materialism* with respect to human beings: the claim that human beings are material objects, and material objects with no immaterial parts – no immaterial soul, or mind, or self, for example. From this perspective it is not the case that a human person is an immaterial substance or thing that is connected with or joined to a material body; nor is it the case that a human being *has* an immaterial soul or mind. Instead, so the materialist thinks, a person *just is* her body, or perhaps some part of her body, or perhaps some other material object constituted by her body. I *am* my body (or perhaps my brain, or some part of it, or some other part of my body).

Now what sort of thing will a *belief* be, from this materialist perspective? Suppose you are a materialist, and also think, as we ordinarily do, that there are such things as beliefs. For example, you believe that Proust is more subtle than Louis L'Amour. What kind of a thing is this belief? Well, from a materialist perspective, it looks as if it would have to be something like a long-standing event or structure in your brain or nervous system. Presumably this event will involve many neurons connected to each other in various ways. There are plenty of neurons to go around: a normal human brain contains some 100 billion neurons. These neurons, furthermore, are connected with other neurons at synapses; a single neuron can be involved in many synapses. The total number of possible brain states, then, is absolutely enormous, much greater than the number of electrons in the universe. Under certain conditions, a neuron fires, i.e., produces an electrical impulse; by virtue of its connection with other neurons, this impulse can be transmitted (with appropriate modification) down the cables of neurons that constitute effector nerves to muscles or glands, causing, e.g., muscular contraction and thus behavior.

So (from the materialist's point of view) a belief will be a neuronal event or structure of this sort, with input from other parts of the nervous system and output to still other parts. But if this is the sort of thing beliefs are, they will have two quite different sorts of properties. On the one hand there will be *electro-chemical* or *neurophysiological* properties (NP properties, for short). Among these would be such properties as that of involving n neurons and n* connections between neurons, properties that specify which neurons are connected with which others, what the rates of fire in the various parts of the event are, how these rates of fire change in response to changes in input, and so on. But if the event in question is really a *belief*, then, in addition to those NP properties, it will have another property as well: it will have to have a *content*.[2] It will have to be the belief that *p*, for some proposition *p*. If it's the belief that Proust is a more subtle writer than Louis L'Amour, then its content is the proposition *Proust is more subtle than Louis L'Amour*. If it is instead the belief that Cleveland is a beautiful city, then its content is the proposition *Cleveland is a beautiful city*. My belief that naturalism is all the rage these days has as content the proposition *Naturalism is all the rage these days*. (That same proposition is the content of the German speaker's belief that naturalism is all the rage these days, even though he expresses this belief by uttering the German sentence 'Der Naturalismus ist diese Tage ganz groß in Mode'; beliefs, unlike sentences, do not come in different languages.) It is in virtue of having a content, of course, that a belief is true or false: it is true if the proposition which is its content is true, and false otherwise. My belief that all men are mortal is true because the proposition which constitutes its content is true, but Hitler's belief that the Third Reich would last a thousand years was false, because the proposition that constituted its content is (was) false.

Given materialism, therefore, beliefs would be long-standing neural events. As such, they would have content, but also neurophysiological properties (NP properties). Now how is it that we human beings have come to have beliefs, and how is it that those beliefs come to have the content they do in fact have? Naturalists (and of course others as well) ordinarily believe that human beings have come to be by way of evolution; they have evolved according to the mechanisms specified in contemporary evolutionary theory. (The prime candidates are natural selection operating on some source of genetic variability such as random genetic mutation.) We have something of an idea as to the history of those neurophysiological properties: structures with these properties have come to exist by small increments, each increment (ignoring spandrels and pliotropy) such that it has proved to be useful in the struggle for survival. But what about the *content* of belief? If a belief is a neuronal event, where does its content come from? How does it get to be associated in that way with a given proposition?

Materialists offer two main theories here. According to the first, content *supervenes upon* NP properties; according to the second content *is reducible to* NP properties.[3] Suppose we think about the second theory first. Consider the property of having as content the proposition *Naturalism is all the rage these days*, and call this property 'C'. On the present suggestion, C *just is* a certain combination of NP properties. It might be a disjunction of such properties: where P_1 to P_n are NP properties, C, the property of having the content in question, might be something like (where 'v' represents 'or')

$$P_1vP_3vP_8v\ldots P_n.$$

More likely, it would be something more complicated: perhaps a disjunction of conjunctions, something like (where '&' represents 'and')

$$(P_1\&P_7\&P_{28}\ldots)\ v\ (P_3\&P_{34}\&P_{17}\&\ldots)\ v\ (P_8\&P_{83}\&P_{107}\&\ldots)\ v.\ldots$$

We could put this by saying that any content property is a Boolean combination of NP properties, that is, a combination constructed from NP properties by disjunction, conjunction and negation. And to say that content properties are reducible to NP properties is just to say that every content property is some Boolean combination of NP properties. In fact, if we think that any Boolean combination of NP properties is itself an NP property, we could say that content properties just are NP properties – a special sort of NP property, to be sure, but still NP properties. So, on this theory, content properties – e.g., the property of having *Naturalism is all the rage these days* as content – are or are reducible to NP properties.

That's one of the two materialistic proposals; the other is that a content property isn't a NP property, or a Boolean combination of NP properties, but rather *supervenes on* NP properties. What does that mean; what is this 'supervention'? The basic idea is that a set of properties S supervenes on a set of properties S* just if any pair of objects which agree on the S* properties must also agree on the S properties. For example, beauty (of a picture, a face) supervenes on molecular constitution; any two pictures (or faces) with the same molecular constitution will be beautiful to the same degree. Content properties supervene on NP properties, then, if and only if any two objects or structures with the same NP properties must have the same content properties. You couldn't have a pair of structures – neuronal events, say – that had the same NP properties but different contents.[4] Content is a *function* of NP properties.

We can put this officially as follows:

(S) Necessarily, any structures that have the same NP properties have the same content.

This is a *weak* form of supervenience; a stronger one could be put as:

(S+) For any possible worlds W and W* and any structures S and S*, if S has the same NP properties in W as S* has in W*, then S has the same content in W as S* has in W*.

Those who think that content properties supervene on NP properties for the most part think, I believe, that the former supervene on the latter in the stronger sense (S+) (and hence also, of course, in the weaker sense (S)). For present purposes, however, it doesn't matter which sense we employ. But what about that 'necessarily'? Here this supervention suggestion divides into two branches. On the first branch, the necessity in question is broadly logical necessity. According to the other branch of the supervenience theory, the necessity in question isn't broadly logical necessity, but something more obscure – something we could call 'causal' or 'natural' or 'nomic' necessity.

Naturalism and Reliability

Return now to the question that led us into reduction and supervenience: how does it happen that those neural structures, the ones that constitute belief, have *content*? Where does it come from and how do they get it? The basic idea is something like this. As we go up the evolutionary scale, we find neural structures with greater and greater complexity. Near one end of the scale, for example, we find C. *elegans*, a small but charismatic worm with a nervous system composed of only a few neurons. (The nervous system of C. *elegans* has been completely mapped.) We human beings are at the other end of the scale; our brains contain many billions of neurons connected in complex and multifarious ways. And now the idea is that as you rise in the evolutionary scale, as you progress through more and more complex neural structures, at a certain point content shows up. At a certain level of complexity, these neural structures start to display content. Perhaps this starts gradually and early on (possibly C. *elegans* displays just the merest glimmer of consciousness and the merest glimmer of content), or perhaps later and more abruptly; that doesn't matter. What does matter is that at a certain level of complexity of neural structures, content appears. This is true whether content properties are reducible to NP properties or supervene on them.

So (given materialism), some neural structures at a certain level of complexity acquire content; they thus become beliefs. And the question I want to ask is this: what is the likelihood, given naturalism, that the content that thus arises is in fact *true*? In particular, what is the likelihood, given N, that the content associated with *our* neural structures is true? More generally, what is the likelihood, given naturalism, that our cognitive faculties are reliable, thereby producing mostly true beliefs?

We commonsensically assume that our cognitive faculties are for the most part reliable, at least over a large area of their functioning. I remember where I was last night and that my elder son's name is not Archibald; I can see that the light is on in my study, that the flower garden is overgrown with weeds, and that my neighbor put on weight over the winter. I know a few truths of mathematics and logic, mostly pretty simple, no doubt, but still . . . The natural thing to assume, and what we all do assume (at least before we are corrupted by philosophy (or neuroscience)) is that when our cognitive faculties aren't subject to malfunction, then, for the most part and over a wide area of everyday life, the beliefs they produce in us are true. We assume that our cognitive faculties are reliable. But what I want to argue is that the naturalist has a powerful reason against this initial presumption and should give it up.

By way of entering this argument, suppose we conduct a thought experiment. Consider a hypothetical species that is cognitively a lot like us: members of this species hold beliefs, make inferences, change beliefs, and the like. And let us suppose naturalism holds for them; they exist in a world in which there is no such person as God or anything like God. Our question, then, is this: what is the probability that their cognitive faculties are reliable? Consider any particular belief on the part of one of these hypothetical creatures. That belief, of course, is a neural structure of a given sort, and one sufficiently complex to generate content. We may add, if we like, that this structure occurs or takes place in response to something in the environment; perhaps it is a certain pattern of firing of neurons in the optical portion of the brain, and perhaps this pattern arises in response to the appearance of a predator in the middle distance. And a certain proposition has somehow come to be associated with this structure, so that the structure acquires belief content and is a belief.

Now what is the probability (given naturalism) that this proposition is *true?* Well, what we know about the belief in question is that it is a neurological structure that has certain NP properties, properties, the possession of which is logically or causally sufficient for the possession of that particular content. We are assuming also that this structure arises in response to the presence of that predator, and we can also assume, if we like, that this structure is a reliable indicator of that kind of predator. This structure, we may suppose, arises when and only when there is a predator in the middle distance. But even so, of course, the content generated by this structure, on this occasion, need have nothing to do with that predator, or with anything else in the environment. Indication is one thing; belief content is something else altogether, and we know of no reason why the one should be related to the other. By way of something like a necessary accident, content simply arises upon the appearance of neural structures of sufficient complexity. But we can see no reason why that content need be related to what the structures indicate, if anything. The proposition constituting that content need not be so much as *about* that predator.

So what, then, is the likelihood that this proposition, this content, is true? Given this much, shouldn't we suppose that the proposition in question is as likely to be false as true? Shouldn't we suppose that the proposition in question has a probability of roughly one-half of being true? Shouldn't we estimate its probability, on the condition in question, as in the neighborhood of 0.5? That would be the sensible course. Neither seems more probable than the other; hence we estimate the probability of its being true as 0.5.

But am I not relying upon the notorious Principle of Indifference? We are trying to estimate the probability that the content in question is true, given that it is generated by adaptive neural structures; I say that given this condition, for all we can see, it is as likely to be false as to be true; so we should judge that probability to be around 0.5; isn't that to endorse some version of the Principle of Indifference? And hasn't that principle been discredited?[5] Not really. The Bertrand paradoxes show that certain incautious statements of PI come to grief – just as Goodman's grue/bleen paradoxes show that incautious statements of a principle governing the projection of predicates or properties come to grief. But of course the fact is we project properties all the time, and do so perfectly sensibly. In the same way, I think, we often employ a principle of indifference in ordinary reasoning, and do so quite properly. We also use it in science, for example, in statistical mechanics.[6] Of course, problems arise where there are equally natural or plausible ways of selecting the relevant possibilities and where these different ways carry incompatible probability assignments with them.

But aren't we forgetting something important? These hypothetical creatures have arisen, presumably, by way of evolution. They have come to be by way of something like natural selection working on some process of genetic variation – perhaps random genetic mutation. Presumably, then, it has proven adaptively useful for creatures of that sort to display that neural structure in the circumstances in which this creature finds itself. This structure's arising in those circumstances has (or had) survival value; it contributes to the reproductive fitness of the creature in question, perhaps by helping cause the right sort of behavior (fleeing, or wary watchfulness, maybe). Whatever exactly the appropriate action is, the neuronal event in question is useful because it is a cause (part cause) of that behavior. And doesn't that mean that it's likely that the content associated with this structure is in fact a true proposition?

It is crucially important to see that the answer to this question is NO. This neuronal event or structure has NP properties such as sending electrical signals to other parts of the nervous system as well as to muscles and/or glands. By virtue of these NP properties, it causes adaptive behavior such as fleeing. This neuronal structure also displays NP properties that are sufficient, causally or logically, for the presence of content. As a result of having that neuronal event with that particular constellation of NP properties, the creature in which this event is to be found also believes a certain proposition. But what reason is there to think that proposition *true*? Granted, the structure in question helps cause adaptive behavior. But that doesn't so much as slyly suggest that the content that gets associated with the structure – by way of a logical accident, so to say – is *true*. As far as its causing the right kind of behavior is concerned, it simply doesn't matter whether the content, that associated proposition, is true or false. At this point, as far as the truth or falsehood of the content that arises, natural selection just has to take pot luck. (Not that it minds – it's interested, so to speak, just in adaptive behavior, not in true belief.) Natural selection selects for structures that have adaptive NP properties; as it happens, these structures are of sufficient complexity to generate content; but there isn't even the faintest reason to think that content true. Given naturalism, it would be sheer coincidence, an enormous cosmic serendipity, if the content that is associated with adaptively useful neurophysiological properties should also turn out to be all or mostly true content. Naturalists who think content supervenes on neurophysiological properties (and that would be most naturalists) tend to assume automatically (at least when it comes to us human beings) that the content in question *would be* true; but why think that? This assumption is at best a piece of charming but ingenuous piety. Given naturalism, the belief in question is as likely to be false as to be true.

So, with respect to the relevant facts about the origin and provenance of this particular belief on the part of this hypothetical creature, the probability of its being true – i.e., the probability that the content of the neural structure in question should be a true proposition – would have to be estimated as about 0.5. The associated content in question could, of course, be true; but it could also, and with equal likelihood, be false. What, then, is the probability that the cognitive faculties of these creatures will be *reliable*? A reliable belief-producing faculty will produce a considerable preponderance of true belief over false belief. We ordinarily think our cognitive faculties are more reliable in some circumstances than in others; we are good at such things as remembering what we had for breakfast or perceiving whether there are any trees in the backyard; we are less good at determining (without artificial aids) whether a mountain goat we see at 500 yards has horns. We are also less reliable when working at the limits of our faculties, as in trying to determine what happened in the first 10^{-33} seconds after the Big Bang. (Given all the disagreements, perhaps we are also less reliable when it comes to philosophy.) But any reasonable degree of reliability, as we ordinarily think of it, requires producing a substantial preponderance of true beliefs. A thermometer that didn't produce many more true than false readings (in normal circumstances and within the appropriate limits of error) would not be reliable.

And the same sort of thing goes for the reliability of cognitive faculties; they too are reliable, and reliable in a certain area, only if they produce a preponderance of true beliefs over false. Going back to those hypothetical creatures, what we've seen is that the probability, on the relevant condition, that any given belief of theirs should be true is in the neighborhood of 1/2. This means that the probability that their faculties produce the preponderance of true beliefs over false required by reliability is very small indeed. If I have 1000 independent[7] beliefs, for example, the probability (under these conditions) that three-quarters or more of these beliefs are true (certainly a modest enough requirement for reliability) will be less than 10^{-58}.[8] And even if I am running a modest epistemic establishment of only 100 beliefs, the probability that 3/4 of them are true, given that the probability of any one's being true is 1/2, is very low, something like 0.000001. So the chances that this creature's true beliefs substantially outnumber its false beliefs (even in a particular area) are small. The conclusion to be drawn is that it is very unlikely that the cognitive faculties of those creatures are reliable.

So far what we've seen is that, given naturalism and the supervenience of content upon neurophysiological properties, it is unlikely that the cognitive faculties of these creatures are reliable; this is true even if we add that the content of their beliefs is generated by structures with NP properties that are fitness-enhancing, adaptively useful.

That's how things stand if content *supervenes* upon NP properties. But what about the other option, reductionism? What if content properties (for example, the property of having as content the proposition *Naturalism is all the rage these days*) just *are* NP properties, or complex clusters of NP properties? In this case we get the very same results. To see why, consider, again, a given belief on the part of a given member of that hypothetical group of creatures. That belief, of course, is a neuronal event, a congeries of neurons connected in complex ways and firing away in the fashion neurons are wont to do. This neuronal event displays a lot of NP properties. Again, we may suppose that it is adaptively useful for a creature of the kind in question to harbor neuronal structures of the sort in question in the circumstances in question. The event's having the NP properties it does have is fitness-enhancing in that by virtue of having these properties, the organism is caused to perform adaptively useful action – fleeing, for example. But some subset of these NP properties together constitute its having a certain content, constitute its being associated, in that way, with some proposition. What is the probability that this content is true? What is the probability that the associated proposition is a true proposition? The answer is the same as in the case we've already considered. The content doesn't have to be true, of course, for the neuronal structure to cause the appropriate kind of behavior. It just happens that this particular arrangement of adaptive NP properties also constitutes having this particular content. But again: it would be a piece of enormous serendipity if this content, this proposition, were *true*; it could just as well be false. So the probability that this content is true would have to be rated at about 1/2, just as in the case of supervenience. If this is true for each of the independent beliefs of the organism in question, the probability (on naturalism) that the cognitive faculties of these creatures are reliable would have to be rated as low. The conclusion to be drawn so far, then, is that given naturalism, it is unlikely that these creatures have reliable cognitive faculties.

Now the next step in the argument is to note that of course what goes for these hypothetical creatures also goes for us. Suppose naturalism (construed as including materialism) is in fact true with respect to us human beings: there is no such person as God or anything like God. Then the probability that our cognitive faculties are reliable is low, just as in the case of those hypothetical creatures. For us, too, the main possibilities would have to be supervenience (logical or causal) and reduction or identity. In our case, too, if we focus on any particular belief – say, the belief that naturalism is all the rage these days – on the part of a particular believer, we see that this belief (given materialism) will have to be a neuronal event of some kind. This event will be of sufficient complexity to generate content (by supervenience or reduction); somehow a proposition gets associated with it as its content. We may suppose, if we wish, that it is adaptively useful for creatures like us to harbor structures of that kind in the circumstances in which the believer finds herself. It would be the merest coincidence, however, if the content generated by the structure in question should be *true* content, if the proposition which is the content of the belief in question should turn out to be a *true* proposition. That means that the probability of this belief's being true would have to be judged to be in the neighborhood of 1/2, not much more likely to be true than to be false. But then it will be exceedingly improbable that the whole set of this believer's beliefs should display the preponderance of true belief over false required by the reliability of her cognitive faculties. So our case is like that of those hypothetical creatures; in our case too the probability that our cognitive faculties are reliable, 'P(R/N)', is low.

Naturalism and Defeat

But now let's take one more step: a person who accepts naturalism and recognizes that P(R/N) is low, thereby acquires a *defeater* for R. A defeater[9] for a belief B I hold – at any rate this kind of defeater – is another belief B* I come to hold which is such that given that I hold B*, I can no longer rationally hold B. For example, I look into a field and see what I take to be a sheep. You come along, identify yourself as the owner of the field, and tell me that there aren't any sheep in that field and that what I see is really a dog that at this distance is indistinguishable from a sheep. Then I give up the belief that what I see is a sheep. Another example: on the basis of what the guidebook says I form the belief that the University of Aberdeen was established in 1695. You, the university's public relations director, tell me the embarrassing truth: this guidebook is notorious for giving the wrong date for the foundation of the university. (It was actually established in 1595.) My new belief that the university was established in 1595 is a defeater for my old belief. In the same way, if I accept naturalism and see that P(R/N) is low, then I have a defeater for R; I can no longer rationally believe that my cognitive faculties are reliable.

The problem isn't that I don't have enough *evidence* for R, to believe it rationally. The fact is I don't *need* evidence for R. That's a good thing, because it doesn't seem possible to acquire evidence for it, at least if I have any doubts about it. For suppose I think up some argument for R, and on the basis of this argument come to believe that R is indeed true. Clearly this is not a sensible procedure; to become convinced of R on the basis of that argument, I must of course believe the premises of the argument, and also believe that if those premises are true, then so is the conclusion. But if I do that, I am already assuming R to be true, at least for the faculties or belief-producing processes that produce in me belief in the premises of the argument and belief that if the premises are true, so is the conclusion. As the great Scottish philosopher Thomas Reid says,

> If a man's honesty were called into question, it would be ridiculous to refer to the man's own word, whether he be honest or not. The same absurdity there is in attempting to prove, by any kind of reasoning, probable or demonstrative, that our reason is not fallacious, since the very point in question is, whether reasoning may be trusted.[10]

My accepting any argument for R, or any evidence for it, would clearly presuppose my believing R; any such procedure would therefore be viciously circular.

More important, however, is the following. We all naturally assume R, and assume it from our earliest days as cognitive agents. Now rationality is best explained in terms of proper function: a belief is rational, in a given set of circumstances, just if a rational person, one whose cognitive faculties are functioning properly, could hold that belief in those circumstances.[11] But then clearly, it is perfectly rational to assume, without evidence, that your cognitive faculties are functioning reliably. We rational agents do this all the time, and do not thereby display cognitive malfunction. You might wind up in a care facility for believing that you are *Napoleon*, but not for believing that your cognitive faculties are functioning reliably. It is therefore perfectly rational to believe R, and to believe it in the basic way, i.e., not on the basis of prepositional evidence.

But that doesn't mean that it is not possible to acquire a defeater for R; even if a belief is properly basic it is still possible to acquire a defeater for it. In the above example about the sheep in the field, my original belief, we may suppose, was basic, and properly so; I still acquired a defeater for it. Here is another famous example to show the same thing. You and I are driving through southern Wisconsin; I see what looks like a fine barn and form the belief *Now that's a fine barn!* Furthermore, I hold that belief in the basic way; I don't accept it on the basis of evidence from other propositions I believe. You then tell me that the whole area is full of barn facades (indistinguishable, from the highway, from real barns) erected by the local inhabitants in an effort to make themselves look more prosperous than they really are. If I believe you, I then have a defeater for my belief that what I saw was a fine barn, even though I was rational in holding the defeated belief in the basic way. It is therefore perfectly possible to acquire a defeater for a belief B even when it is rational to hold B in the basic way. This is what happens when I believe naturalism, and come to see that P(R/N) is low: I acquire a defeater for R. I can then no longer rationally accept R; I must be agnostic about it, or believe its denial.

Perhaps we can see more clearly here by considering an analogy. Imagine a drug – call it XX – that destroys your cognitive reliability. Some 95 percent of those who ingest XX become cognitively unreliable within two hours of ingesting it; they then believe mostly false propositions. Suppose further that I now believe both that I've ingested XX a couple of hours ago and that

P(R/I've ingested XX a couple of hours ago)

is low; taken together, these two beliefs give me a defeater for my initial belief that my cognitive faculties are reliable. Furthermore, I can't appeal to any of my other beliefs to show or argue that my cognitive faculties are still reliable. For example, I can't appeal to my belief that my cognitive faculties have always been reliable in the past or seem to me to be reliable now; any such other belief is now just as suspect or compromised as R is. Any such other belief B is a product of my cognitive faculties: but then in recognizing this and having a defeater for R, I also have a defeater for B.

Two final matters. First, perhaps you believe the thing to think about P(R/N) is not that it is low, but that it is *inscrutable*. How, you ask, can we possibly tell what that probability would be? Return to the question of the probability that a belief is true, conditional on N and its supervening on or being reducible to adaptive NP properties. There I said that this probability should be thought of as in the neighborhood of 1/2 (in which case it would be unlikely *in excelsis* that the creature's true beliefs should exceed its false with a preponderance sufficient for its cognitive faculties being reliable). But maybe the right answer is that we just can't tell what that probability is: it's inscrutable.

There may be something to this objection. But all the argument as stated really requires is that the probability in question not be very high; that it isn't very high seems clear enough. Suppose, however, that this probability really is completely inscrutable: we haven't the faintest idea what it is. As far as we can tell, it could be as high as 1; it could also be zero; and it could be anything in between. We still get the same result. If this probability is inscrutable, then so will be P(R/N); but *N&P(R/N) is inscrutable* is a defeater for R, just as is *N&P(R/N) is low*. Consider an analogy. You learn that your cousin Sam, whose cognitive faculties you have always assumed to be reliable, has ingested XX. You know that *some* proportion of those who ingest XX become wholly unreliable; but you don't know what that proportion is; as far as you are concerned, P(Sam's faculties are reliable/Sam has ingested XX) is inscrutable. It could be as low as zero; it could be as high as 1; and it could be anything in between. Under these conditions you have a defeater for your assumption that Sam's cognitive faculties are reliable. You would also have a defeater for R if you believed you had ingested XX and that P (R/I've ingested XX) is inscrutable. So what the argument really requires is only that P(R/N) be low or inscrutable.[12]

Finally, there is one more wrinkle, or perhaps fly in the ointment.[13] Consider someone who is cognitively normal, and who comes to believe that she has ingested XX, that reliability-destroying drug mentioned above. This person may very well continue to assume that her cognitive faculties are functioning properly. She may very well carry on her cognitive life in the usual way, even if she becomes convinced she's contracted mad cow disease, a disease, as she believes, that renders its victims cognitively unreliable. And of course the same goes (in spades) if she believes N and sees that P(R/N) is low. But (and this is the crucial point) in so doing, might she not be functioning perfectly properly, without so much as a hint of dysfunction or malfunction? The answer certainly seems to be Yes. If so however, then given my account of defeat (in terms of proper function) she doesn't have a defeater for R in the belief that she has ingested XX or has contracted mad cow disease, and my argument fails.

Here I can only gesture at the response.[14] The first thing to see is that one who really rejects R is in a state of cognitive disaster. And some modules of our cognitive design plan are aimed, not at the production of true beliefs, but at the production of other worthwhile conditions, including, presumably, avoidance of cognitive disaster. For example, if you fall victim to a usually fatal disease, you may somehow think your chances are much better than is indicated by the statistics you know; this is the so-called 'optimistic overrider'. Your faculties may be functioning perfectly properly in producing this belief; this particular bit of the cognitive design plan is aimed, not at producing true beliefs about the possible course of your disease, but beliefs that will maximize your chances of recovery. Still, in some sense those statistics really do give you a defeater for your belief that in all likelihood you will recover. What they give you is a *Humean Defeater*. You have a Humean defeater for a belief B in a given situation if: (1) the production of B is governed by a bit of the design plan that is aimed, not at the production of true belief, but at some other state of affairs (such as recovery from disease or the avoidance of cognitive disaster); and (2) if only truth-aimed processes were at work in this situation, you would have an ordinary rationality defeater for B. One who believes she's taken XX has a Humean defeater for R, as does someone who thinks she has mad cow disease. My claim is that the naturalist who sees that P(R/N) is low has a Humean defeater for R.

I therefore have a defeater for R. But if I consider R and do not believe it, then I have a defeater for any belief I take to be a product of my cognitive faculties. Naturally enough, that would be *all* of my beliefs; all of my beliefs are products of my cognitive faculties. The result so far, then, is that if I believe N (construed as including materialism) and I also see that the probability of R with respect to N is low, then I have a defeater for each of my beliefs. Therefore, if you believe N and see that P(R/N) is low, you will be enmeshed in that virulent, bottomless, self-reflexive sort of Humean skepticism mentioned above. No doubt you can't really reject R in the heat and press of day-to-day activities, when you are playing poker with your friends, or building a house, or climbing a cliff. But in the calm and reflective atmosphere of your study, you see that you do in fact have a defeater for R. Of course, you also see that the very reflections that lead you to this position are also no more acceptable than their denials; you have a universal defeater for whatever it is you find yourself believing. This is that really crushing skepticism, and it is this skepticism to which the naturalist is committed.

Notes

1 And this leads to the scandal of skepticism: if I *argue* to skepticism, then of course I rely upon the very cognitive faculties whose unreliability is the conclusion of my skeptical argument.

2 It is of course extremely difficult to see how a material structure or event could have content in the way a belief does.

3 Note that if content properties are reducible to NP properties in the sense of 'reducible' suggested below, then they also supervene upon them. Note also that for present purposes I ignore so-called 'wide content'. If we were to take wide content into account, we'd say that content supervenes, not just on NP properties, but on NP properties together with certain properties of the environment. The same would go, *mutatis mutandis*, for the suggestion that content is reducible to or identical with NP properties. In the interest of simplicity, I ignore wide content; nothing in my argument below hinges on this omission.

4 So the second possibility is really a special case of the first: if content properties are reducible to NP properties, then clearly structures with the same NP properties will have the same content properties.

5 See, e.g., van Fraassen (1989: 293ff).

6 According to Weatherford: 'an astonishing number of extremely complex problems in probability

theory have been solved, and usefully so, by calculation based entirely on the assumption of equiprobable alternatives' (1983: 35). See also Collins (1998).

7 'Independent': it could be that a pair of neural structures with content were such that if either occurred, so would the other; then the beliefs in question would not be independent. Similarly when the content of one neural structure entails the content of another: there too the beliefs in question won't be independent.

8 My thanks to Paul Zwier, who performed the calculation.

9 Of course there are several kinds of defeaters; here it isn't necessary to canvass these kinds. The kind of defeater presently relevant would be a *rationality* defeater, and an *undercutting* rationality defeater. In addition to rationality defeaters, there are also *warrant* defeaters; these too come in several kinds. For more on defeaters, see Bergmann (2000, 1997), and see Plantinga (2002: 205–11).

10 Reid (1983: 276).

11 See Plantinga (1993a: 133–7).

12 The first clause of (D) should thus be amended to '(1) S sees that P(A/B) is low or inscrutable'.

13 As William Talbott pointed out to me.

14 For a fuller version of the response, see Plantinga (2002: 205–11).

References

Bergmann, M. (2000) 'Deontology and Defeat', *Philosophy and Phenomenological Research*, 60: 87–102.

Collins, R. (1998) 'A Defense of the Probabilistic Principle of Indifference', lecture to History and Philosophy of Science Colloquium, University of Notre Dame, Oct. 8. Unpublished.

DeRose, K. (1999) 'Solving the Skeptical Problem', in K. DeRose and T. Warfield (eds.) *Skepticism: A Contemporary Reader*, New York: Oxford University Press, pp. 183–219.

Hume, D. (1951) *Treatise of Human Nature*, ed. L. A. Selby-Bigge, Oxford: Clarendon Press.

Plantinga, A. (1993) *Warrant: The Current Debate*, Oxford: Oxford University Press

(2002) 'Reply to Beilby's Cohorts', in J. Beilby (ed.) *Naturalism Defeated? Essays on Plantinga's Evolutionary Argument Against Naturalism*, Ithaca, NY: Cornell University Press, pp. 205–25.

Reid, T. (1983) *Essays on the Intellectual Powers of Man* in *Thomas Reid's Inquiry and Essays*, ed. R. Beanblossom and K. Lehrer, Indianapolis, IN: Hackett Publishing Co.

Van Fraassen, B. (1989) *Laws and Symmetry*, Oxford: Clarendon Press.

Weatherford, R. (1983) *Philosophical Foundations of Probability Theory*, London: Routledge and Kegan Paul.

6

A House Divided Against Itself Cannot Stand: Plantinga on the Self-defeat of Evolutionary Naturalism

Timothy O'Connor

Timothy O'Connor (b. 1965) is Professor of Philosophy at Indiana University. His research examines central questions in metaphysics, philosophy of mind, and philosophy of religion and his publications include *Persons and Causes* (2000) and *Theism and Ultimate Explanation* (2008). In this essay he offers a critique of Plantinga's argument against naturalism by drawing an analogy between theists' responses to the problem of evil and naturalists' responses to Plantinga's argument. O'Connor argues that a naturalist who, in spite of Plantinga's argument, continues to believe in the reliability of her faculties is in a position similar to a theist who, in spite of the problematic evidence of evil, continues to believe in God's existence.

Alvin Plantinga argues that belief in evolutionary naturalism is self-defeating. Let R denote the thesis that our basic cognitive faculties are mostly reliable, and EN the thesis that human beings and their cognitive faculties arose by means of entirely natural processes of the kind posited by current evolutionary biology, processes unguided and undesigned by God or any other supernatural being. The probability of R on EN, Plantinga plausibly maintains, is inscrutable by us. Since EN is relevant to the truth of R, the inscrutability of R on EN gives the adherent of EN a reason to withhold belief in R: EN is *evidence*, for the naturalist, that calls into question his belief in R. Withholding belief in R clearly would have disastrous implications for one's beliefs, as R's truth underpins the warrant for all our other beliefs. Worse still, Plantinga contends, there is no reasonable means of escaping this predicament once one is mired in it. Since the argument provides a defeater for all the naturalist's beliefs, he is left with nothing that might enable him to

Timothy O'Connor, "A House Divided Against Itself Cannot Stand: Plantinga on the Self-defeat of Evolutionary Naturalism" from *Naturalism Defeated? Essays on Plantinga's Evolutionary Argument against Naturalism*, ed. James Beilby (Ithaca, NY: Cornell University Press, 2002), pp. 129–34. © 2002 by Cornell University. Used by permission of the publisher, Cornell University Press.

defeat the defeater. Hume's game of backgammon beckons.

Since R has a foundational status in our system of beliefs, we can evaluate the force of Plantinga's reasoning only in the context of a general account of epistemic justification or warrant. For the purposes of this essay, I will adopt Plantinga's own 'proper functionalism', on which "a belief has warrant, for a person, if it is produced by her cognitive faculties functioning properly in a congenial epistemic environment according to a design plan successfully aimed at [truth]."[1] As with other externalist theories, this account allows that cognitively basic beliefs such as R may be fully warranted despite the fact that a person cannot give a non-question-begging argument on its behalf. It simply need be *true* that our faculties function properly (and aim at truth) in giving rise to this belief – one needn't be in a position to argue that this is (or is likely to be) so.

This, at any rate, is how things initially stand for R, on Plantinga's account. His critique of belief in naturalism presupposes that as we begin to reflect on our beliefs concerning the origins of our cognitive faculties and their probabilistic connections to R, we should begin modifying our confidence in R. In the language of probabilistic reasoning, it is appropriate to 'start off' assigning a very high probability to R, independent of any opinion we may have concerning the absolute a priori probability of R. Subsequently, however, we should *conditionalize* the value we assign to R on factors that are relevant to the probability that R is true. If we believe such factors to obtain and judge the probability of R on them to be inscrutable, we should declare all bets off regarding the truth of R and suspend belief. We should do so because this is precisely how we should proceed in analogous circumstances with more mundane beliefs. Suppose I am driving through the countryside and come to believe there is a sheep in the field. But then I am told by a humorless and reliable friend that this is yet another locale in which the residents like to play tricks on strangers by carefully dressing up dogs to look like sheep. Since I don't know the proportion of sheep to look-alikes in this vicinity, the reasonable course is to refrain from believing that what I see is a real sheep.

Are matters as straightforward as this with respect to R? Consider two examples that Plantinga himself discusses in other contexts. The first is the Case of the Purloined Letter. You are presented with powerful evidence that you have stolen an important letter. You had motive, means, and opportunity. Sadly, it is known that you are not above such shameful activities as filching letters. Finally, there is very strong evidence that you were the only person who could have stolen the letter and it was later recovered from your bureau drawer. Now, before hearing the prosecutor's case, you believed that you had not stolen the letter. And with good reason: you had no reason to doubt your memory in this regard (which was in fact functioning normally), and you distinctly recalled seeing the letter and resisting the temptation to take it. Should you change your belief in the face of the powerful evidence to the contrary? Presumably not. You have countervailing evidence in the form of a distinct memory of not having taken the letter.

Second case. A Christian theist reflects on the dismal facts of pain and suffering in human history. He knows of no convincing account of adequate reasons God might have for permitting these things to occur. He then considers the probability that God exists on this evidence. Suppose that, impressed by our finitude, he judges it unlikely that we could figure out what God's reasons would be for creating a world with such features, were He to exist and have created a world just like ours. He concludes that the conditional probability that God exists on facts about the magnitude and distribution of human suffering is inscrutable. Should he become agnostic? As Plantinga himself emphasizes, if his proper functionalist account of warrant is basically correct, we cannot divorce this question from others concerning God's existence and His intentions concerning the functioning of human cognitive capacities. It is a plausible to suppose that if traditional Christian teaching is essentially correct, then God does not intend for human beings to cease believing in Him under such circumstances. On such teaching, a Christian who confidently persists in belief despite not knowing what to say about the evidential bearing of the facts of evil on God's existence is, other things being equal, regulating his beliefs in accordance with God's design plan. It is the tendency toward doubt or disbelief that reflects noetic malfunction.[2]

These examples highlight the fact that simple conditionalization on new evidence need not always be required within a proper functionalist epistemology. Some beliefs will have a special status, depending on certain facts about the *design plan* of the cognizer in question. An evolutionary naturalist will naturally begin his reflections on Plantinga's challenge by considering the implications EN itself might have for thinking about proper function, just as the theist does in considering the challenge to theism from evil. An astute naturalist will note first of all that the argument doesn't, as a psychological matter, tend to push people to cognitive despair, as Plantinga claims it ought to do. Our belief in R is quite tenacious. Given EN, this is not surprising. There is no plausible evolutionary story one might tell about why our cognitive faculties should be designed to *regulate* this belief strictly in accordance with our evidence for it. Doing so would obviously be disastrous for our coming to true beliefs about other matters. But it would equally undercut our ability to come to a true belief about R itself. It is plausible, given EN, that the naturalist's unshaken confidence in R reflects our cognitive design plan, stemming from a module aimed at truth. We're designed to start off accepting R without evidence and to continue on that way. In view of our cognitive limitations – we're not able to pull off any version of Descartes's project – it is proper that we adopt R and related beliefs as unquestioned framework principles, against which we can sensibly adjudicate our beliefs about less foundational matters.

I think we can say something even stronger. Strictly speaking, there *couldn't* be a defeater for R, for any creatures in any possible world. That would require a *design plan* which reliably aimed at truth in some circumstances, a part of which was that we ought to give up belief in R when we take note of certain of our beliefs about the world and about related conditional probabilities. But as that potential upshot would lead one to abandon the attempt to form true beliefs, it surely could not be part of a design plan with that very end. Or if the concept of a design plan is to be quite broad, then only egregiously flawed instances would contain in this way internal obstacles to their own success.

At this point, Plantinga might protest that our argument has proven too much. Are we not claiming that R is necessarily immune from evidence? And isn't this plainly wrong – couldn't one have, for instance, good reason to think one was or was in the process of becoming insane?

But we are not claiming that R is indefeasible. One could *rationally* conclude that R is false (in relation to oneself) by having powerful, direct evidence that there *is no design plan successfully aimed at truth*. This would seem reasonable if one's cognitive output were persistently and massively inconsistent – which, I take it, might well capture the circumstances under which one might rationally take oneself to be insane.[3] Of course, once one draws this conclusion, it will undercut one's confidence in the very evidence that led to it, thereby giving rise to Hume's loop of reason against itself, at least until one retires to more soothing pursuits such as backgammon. But note that we shouldn't say that one would be *warranted* in drawing this fateful conclusion, for that term of art is tied to the notion of a design plan aimed at truth, and there is no purchase on the idea of such a plan that generates persistent, massive inconsistency. (What then is the operative notion of 'rational' here? It's hard to say precisely – perhaps a basic kind of theoretical rationality which requires a minimal degree of evidential consistency.)

Plantinga, however, argues that massive internal inconsistency is not the only way one might reasonably be led to abandon R. For suppose I come to believe that I am the victim of Descartes's evil demon, who is bent on my being deceived about my true situation. Don't I then have good reason to abandon R?[4] To evaluate this analogy properly, we must first tighten it up a bit. As the evil demon hypothesis is usually presented, we know that if it's true, then R is false. (By hypothesis, all of my beliefs about the material world are false.) But in the challenge posed to the naturalist, we are urged to say only that the probability of R on evolutionary naturalism is inscrutable. So let us modify the evil demon story accordingly. We will now say that I believe that there is an evil demon who has created my cognitive faculties, but I judge the probability of R on this origin to be inscrutable. (Perhaps I believe that this demon has created numerous races on various planets, and in at least one case has chosen to massively deceive them, and in at least one other case has chosen to give them reliable faculties. But I have no idea whether either case was an isolated act of whimsy or reflected a decided tendency on his part.)

Once we make this change in our hypothesis, however, it isn't plausible that we are rationally required to abandon R. There isn't massive inconsistency of the sort noted just above, a sort that would make it unreasonable to continue believing there is any coherent design plan underlying one's belief formations. And whether R would have or lack warrant under those circumstances depends on the demon's design plan: has he so designed the cognitive system in question that a properly functioning specimen would abandon R under such circumstances? Well, if the agent is like most naturalists who encounter Plantinga's argument, he is not *inclined* to do so. So the only evidence the agent has in this matter – his own tenacious belief – suggests that he is functioning properly in continuing to believe R. Nothing in the structure of Plantinga's argument as applied to this case would give him reason to think otherwise.

Let me bring the issue into sharper focus by yoking the cases of the Christian theist's response to the evidential bearing of evil on theism and the naturalist's response to the evidential bearing of evolutionary naturalism on R, and then posing a dilemma. Plantinga would say that the probability of theism given the facts of pain and suffering as we know them – P(T/E) – is (at best) inscrutable for the theist. Must the theist, if he is to adjust his beliefs properly, conditionalize on his ignorance, so to speak? There are four possibilities here:

(1) He must conditionalize on his ignorance and thereby come to regard the probability of theism itself as inscrutable for him in the circumstances. If one accepts this, one is also likely to accept Plantinga's own verdict on the case of naturalism. But the larger upshot will be that *every* reflective person should come to withhold belief in R!

(2) He must conditionalize on his ignorance, but he need not come to judge the probability of theism as inscrutable. For he has an independent source of warrant that neutralizes the potential defeater of his belief before it takes hold: the internal testimony of the Holy Spirit that sustains the Christian's confident trust in the existence and character of God. This is a kind of evidence, in a broad sense of the term, that counteracts the potential impact of the inscrutability of P(T/E) for him.[5] But if the theist should say this, why should not the naturalist say the same concerning the 'evidence' coming from his own tenacious belief that R?

(3) He need not conditionalize on his ignorance or modify his beliefs in any other way. Theism continues to have warrant for him. (But then by parity of reasoning the same should hold for the naturalist.)

(4) He need not conditionalize on his ignorance, but he should adjust his belief concerning P(T/E). If theism is true, it is part of my design plan that I should believe T despite my inability to discern a priori P(T/E). But since it is also part of my design plan that I adjust my beliefs, as best I can, in the direction of greater probabilistic consistency, I should *conclude* that P(T/E) is high. Put differently, I should see on reflection that T's having a good deal of warrant for me commits me to believing tacitly that the probability of T on all the relevant evidence I possess is high. And because of the special status T has in my God-given design plan, it should trump any beliefs I may hazard concerning conditional probabilities governing T, i.e., my belief in T has more warrant than do any of my beliefs concerning the conditional probability of T on any particular proposition. Although Bayesian accounts of theory confirmation have a difficult time handling this fact, we clearly can rationally revise our estimates of conditional probabilities. (Consider a scientist who comes better to understand the implications of a complex theory and so revises his estimates of the probability of that theory on various bits of potential evidence.) But again, if this is so for the theist, what reason have we to assume it is different for the naturalist? If one is to challenge the propriety of the naturalist's doing this, it cannot depend on assuming facts about the design plan inconsistent with naturalism.

Of these four options, (1) will be implausible to all nonskeptics, and (2) strikes me as stretching the notion of evidence beyond useful limits, so that it becomes little more than a terminological variant on (4). Whichever way we go on (3) or (4) – a verdict that will reflect one's judgment on whether it is appropriate to extend the machinery of probability theory to belief kinematics quite generally – since parallel moves are ready to hand, the naturalist has nothing to fear from Plantinga's argument.

Notes

I thank Al Plantinga for helpful correspondence on the subject of this chapter in response to an earlier paper of mine ("An Evolutionary Argument against Naturalism?" *Canadian Journal of Philosophy* 24 [1994]: 527–40). During that time, many a breakfast of mine was given over to reflections such as those below – so much so, that for some time afterward, eating muesli regularly triggered thoughts concerning the machinations of evil demons. I have written the present essay partly in the hope that I may again eat my breakfast in peace.

1 *Warrant and Proper Function* (New York: Oxford University Press, 1993) 237.
2 More needs to be said about the instantiation of a proper functionalist epistemology within a Christian theistic metaphysics to make these claims convincing, of course. There is no better place to begin exploring this matter than Plantinga's own *Warranted Christian Belief* (New York: Oxford University Press, 2000).
3 Perhaps a second way is this: rather than believing merely that the general probability of R on a certain broad *type* of origin for our cognitive faculties is low or inscrutable, we come to believe confidently that the specific circumstances of the actual past, together with the evolutionary processes at work, were such that R is improbable on them. But how could we know that, apart from the kind of direct evidence (pervasively inconsistent outputs and the like) discussed in the text?
4 "Naturalism Defeated" (unpublished), 51–2.
5 A brief remark by Plantinga in correspondence several years ago suggested this interpretation to me. But he appears to reject this view of the matter in *Warranted Christian Belief*, 478ff.

CPSIA information can be obtained
at www.ICGtesting.com
Printed in the USA
BVHW051448140122
626033BV00019B/279

9 781405 180917